THE OXFORD COMPANION TO
WORLD EXPLORATION

THE OXFORD COMPANION

TO

WORLD EXPLORATION

David Buisseret

Editor in Chief

PUBLISHED IN ASSOCIATION WITH
THE NEWBERRY LIBRARY

VOLUME 1

A—L

OXFORD
UNIVERSITY PRESS
2007

OXFORD
UNIVERSITY PRESS

Oxford University Press, Inc., publishes works that further
Oxford University's objective of excellence
in research, scholarship, and education.

Oxford   New York
Auckland   Cape Town   Dar es Salaam   Hong Kong   Karachi
Kuala Lumpur   Madrid   Melbourne   Mexico City   Nairobi
New Delhi   Shanghai   Taipei   Toronto

With offices in
Argentina   Austria   Brazil   Chile   Czech Republic   France   Greece
Guatemala   Hungary   Italy   Japan   Poland   Portugal   Singapore
South Korea   Switzerland   Thailand   Turkey   Ukraine   Vietnam

Copyright © 2007 by Oxford University Press, Inc.

Published by Oxford University Press, Inc.
198 Madison Avenue, New York, New York, 10016
http://www.oup-usa.org

Library of Congress Cataloging-in-Publication Data

The Oxford companion to world exploration / [edited by] David Buisseret.
    p. cm.
Includes bibliographical references and index.
ISBN-13: 978-0-19-514922-7 (hardcover : alk. paper)
ISBN-10: 0-19-514922-X (hardcover : alk. paper)
1. Discoveries in geography. I. Buisseret, David.
G80.O95 2007
910.92′2—dc22
                    2006027968

Printing number: 9 8 7 6 5 4 3 2 1
Printed in the United States of America
on acid-free paper

EDITORIAL AND PRODUCTION STAFF

CONTENTS

THE OXFORD COMPANION TO
WORLD EXPLORATION

LIST OF ENTRIES

LIST OF COLOR PLATES

Volume I

Following page 194:

INTRODUCTION

It is hard to know what a *Companion* is meant to be. Perhaps it is what its name implies, a sort of friendly handbook, ready with ideas that invite further reading and reflection. As a recent reviewer in the *Times Literary Supplement* explained, it "implies something more intimate and less predictable . . . I have come to imagine [a *Companion*] as a person, perhaps a woman of a certain age and reassuring heft . . . She is informed but not infallible, quirky, opinionated, worldly yet parochial. You need to be companionable yourself to do her justice."

This present *Companion*, hard to define like all of them, also takes on a theme that defies sharp definition. "Discovery" is often the easily defined consequence of "exploration." But exploration may take many legitimate forms—a baby may explore his toes, just as a surgeon may explore a wound. Etymology is for once no help, since the word seems to go back to the cry uttered by a huntsman upon sighting the prey— from the Latin *plorare*, "to cry out." Eschewing subtlety, we have defined it as the process by which one or more people leave their society and venture to another part of the world (or, now, heavens), then return in order to explain what they have seen. In this sense, one can of course explore lands perfectly well known to other peoples.

We have had constantly, and often vainly, to struggle against the European connotations of the word. We have not gone so far, in spite of temptation, as to cover the novelist V. S. Naipaul's exploration of English or Indian society. But we have tried to give a fair shake to extra-European explorers, even if we have scarcely succeeded. Most of the literature easily available is written from a European perspective, and this writing has provided us with a large pool of experts, hardly found outside the European and North American sphere. It is, moreover, worth noting again that the history of our modern world can in large part be explained by the effects of the progressive expansion of European influence.

On the matter of the actual selection of topics, it seemed best to think in terms of different professions. Among the botanists, for instance, Henry Walter Bates on the Amazon clearly was an explorer, while Carolus Linnaeus, in spite of one or two ventures into Lapland, does not qualify. The Hudson River artists cannot be described as explorers, whereas the Dutch artist Frans Post in Brazil can. In spite of his remarkable administrative and climbing skills, Sir Edmund Hillary was not in our sense an explorer, whereas Sven Hedin clearly was, with his many reports on his travels into remote lands. Of course, this is a boundary that is hard to establish.

The editor has to admit to a certain prejudice in favor of women, partly because their role has often been overlooked, but also because they often seem to have had a distinctive "take" on societies. This was very well expressed in a review of Janet Wallach's *Desert Queen* (New York, 1996), which dealt with the life of the writer Gertrude Bell. "Women," the reviewer wrote, "perhaps make the best travelers, for when they have the true wanderer's spirit they are more enduring and, strange to say, more indifferent to hardship and discomfort than men. They are unquestionably more observant of details and quicker to receive impressions. Their sympathies are more acute, and they get in touch with strangers more readily."

Readers will thus understand why we have included the naturalist and flower-painter Marianne North, even though her travels rarely carried her far from some governor's hospitable verandah. Among travel writers, we have included Freya Stark, even though Patrick Leigh-Fermor, and perhaps even Evelyn Waugh, might seem to have had equally valid claims. The writers Isabella Bird and Amelia Edwards have also forced their way in, perhaps as much out of admiration for their imagery as out of respect for their powers as explorers.

The modern, specially drawn maps were a great problem. A book about exploration needs such maps to make sense of many of the entries, but to construct fresh maps would be a major enterprise in itself. As Eric Newby put it in *A Book of Travellers' Tales* (New York, 1986), "the problem of adequate maps for a book such as this is an insoluble problem." We have tried to overcome it to some degree by providing maps that combine information from maps in *The Oxford Atlas of Exploration* (New York, 1997), *The Oxford Atlas of World History* (Oxford, 2002) and the atlas volume of the *New Cambridge Modern History* (Cambridge, U.K., 1978). Our maps will give the reader an idea of where an explorer went, but for fuller information it will be necessary to consult these specialized atlases.

On the other hand, we have been able to offer the reader many historical maps, chosen to elucidate the accompanying text. We have also made use of many other images, from the time of the Egyptian explorers onward. On the whole, we have not made use of portraits, believing that images from explorers' accounts are generally more informative. We have, of course, tried to bring out the way in which both text and image are subject to the whims of both their creators and their readers and also to the nature of existing techniques.

We hope that our readers will be varied and numerous. We have tried to slough off the discouragement felt when we read in Sara Wheeler's *Cherry: A Life of Apsley Cherry-Garrard* (New York, 2002) of Apsley's dealings with his neighbor, George Bernard Shaw. Apsley had in 1950 bought from Shaw the latter's copy of *The Oxford Companion to English Literature* (1937 edition), and took it back to the celebrated author for an inscription. Shaw, admittedly past his best, wrote in a shaky hand on the flyleaf: "I never opened this book, and am astonished to find that I ever possessed it. Companions are no use to me. But it is a pleasant surprise to find that it has passed on to so valued a friend as Apsley Cherry-Garrard."

We hope that those who come by this book will not follow Shaw's bad example, but that having begun in one place, they will be drawn on to find out what other treasures it may contain. May their exploration be fruitful!

ACKNOWLEDGMENTS

This *Companion* was planned from the start to make the most of a collaboration between Oxford University Press and The Newberry Library in Chicago, and it has from its inception enjoyed the support of Casper Grathwohl of the Press, and of James Grossman, director of Research and Education at the Library. Work was based at the Library in the Hermon Dunlap Smith Center for the History of Cartography, whose director is Jim Akerman, and I was able to call on the advice of the Library's staff, as well as on the photographic expertise of Catherine Gass.

Although it may not be obvious at the time, a *Companion*'s successful emergence depends largely on the four or five scholars who agree at the start to recruit contributors for areas in which they are expert. Here this *Companion* was remarkably fortunate, for Professors Sanford Bederman, Carla Rahn Phillips, Richard Talbert, and Glyn Williams have been able to offer sustained support over five years, finding replacements for contributors who had to drop out and themselves writing a number of articles. Professor Marina Tolmacheva also began in this way, until she left Washington State University to become president of the American University in Kuwait.

These area editors were in turn sustained by those who agreed to be advisors. All of them offered useful criticisms of the original proposal, and some were able to help with areas in which they were particularly competent: Professor Roy Bridges for African themes, Professor Patricia Gilmartin for the story of women explorers, Professor Laura Hostetler for Chinese cartography, Dr. Steven Dick for the history of space exploration, and Professor Carol Urness for the Russian explorers. Professor Norman Thrower offered general advice out of his great experience; alas, our cartographic expert, Professor David Woodward, died as the volume was in preparation.

As may be imagined, once an enterprise like this is under way, it becomes clear that some themes lack obvious authors, or indeed that the obvious authors cannot undertake the work. We have been most fortunate, then, to be able to call upon the expertise of members of the Society for the History of Discoveries. Their enthusiasm has been a great encouragement and has allowed the *Companion* to cover a greater range than would otherwise have been possible. The editors have also been encouraged by the zeal of the representatives of Oxford University Press. In the early phases, Joe Clements worked diligently on acquiring articles; the project has greatly benefited in its final stages from the hard work of Georgia Maas, managing editor, and of Eric Stannard, who was in charge of imagery. My former employer, the University of Texas at Arlington, generously allowed me to take the fall semester off during five years in order to work on this *Companion*.

Samuel Johnson once summarized the nature of the work upon which we all have been engaged: "There are two things which I am confident I can do very well; one is an introduction to any literary work, stating what it is to contain, and how it should be executed in the most perfect manner. The other is a conclusion, showing from various causes why the execution has not been equal to what the author promised to himself and to the publick." We could of course provide such a conclusion, but hope that we have done enough to lead our readers into a newly relevant and fascinating field of study, opening up themes we hope that they will explore further.

SEPTEMBER 1, 2006   DAVID BUISSERET

THE OXFORD COMPANION TO
WORLD EXPLORATION

A

Abbadie, Antoine d' (1810–1897), Irish-born surveyor and linguist. Antoine Thompson d'Abbadie was born in Dublin, a product of Franco-Irish-Basque parentage. He was educated in Dublin, Toulouse, and Paris. A linguist who was early attracted to the idea of exploration and prepared himself for it, Abbadie balanced his literary and scientific studies with an intense immersion in physical culture. For Abbadie, travel and scientific research were integral parts of a single activity; he explored in the physical world around him, in the heavens, and in the world of intellect and thought.

Abbadie's first voyage (1837) took him to Brazil to make magnetic observations. His second voyage (1837–1839) was an extended reconnaissance to Ethiopia where, after a return to Europe to obtain supplies and financial, political, and missionary support, he and his brother Arnauld spent ten years (1839–1849). In order to survey some 120 square miles (300 square kilometers), Abbadie invented a rapid survey method and critically reviewed his instruments. His later development of a simplified theodolite, the aba, and his continual stress on simplicity and lightness in instrument design derived from his experience in Ethiopia.

Following his return to France, Abbadie spent years preparing ten maps of Ethiopia and writing up the geographical, ethnographic, and linguistic materials that he had accumulated. If his maps, like the *Géodésie d'Ethiopie* (Paris, 1860–1873), prepared in collaboration with his paid assistant Rudolph Radau (1833–1911), and the *Géographie de l'Ethiopie* laid the foundations of the modern cartography of the region, Abbadie's *Dictionnaire de la langue Amarina* (Paris, 1859) and the 234 manuscripts (see *Catalogue raisonné des manuscrits éthiopiens*, Paris, 1859) he collected were equally important in linguistic studies.

Although Abbadie continued to travel extensively after his marriage to Virginie de Saint Bonnet in 1859, his voyages were shorter and had more specific objectives, usually to make magnetic or astronomical observations, particularly those of eclipses or

transits. Wealthy, Abbadie built a neo-Gothic home and observatory designed by Viollet-le-Duc, and he subsidized prizes and expeditions organized by the Académie des Sciences and the Société de Géographie, both bodies of which he became president. One of the few members of the latter body to have practical experience in exploration, Abbadie had considerable influence. He sided with the more progressive members and helped orient the society toward exploring Africa. A committed and active proponent of total decimalization, he carried out extensive basic research on gravity, verticality, and microseismology. He died in Paris on March 19, 1897.

[*See also* Africa, *subentry on* Scientific Exploration; Ethiopia; *and* Geographical Society of Paris.]

BIBLIOGRAPHY

Davant, Jean-Louis. *Antoine d'Abbadie 1897–1997: Congrès International.* Hendaye, Spain: Académie de la Langue Basque, 1997.

Poirier, Jean-Paul, and Anthony Turner. *Antoine d'Abbadie. Mémoire de la Science* 2. Paris: Académie des Sciences, 2002.

ANTHONY TURNER

Abi-Serour, Mordecai (c. 1831–1886), an obscure rabbi from Akka, Morocco, who journeyed to Timbuctoo in 1859 and played a small but important role in opening the dry interior of west Africa to trade and settlement by non-Muslims. Abi-Serour resided in Timbuctoo for a decade, during which time ten more Jews joined him. Upon his return to Morocco in 1869, he was befriended by the French consul, Auguste Beaumier, for whom he wrote a positive account of how he had broken the Arab monopoly on Sudanese trade with Morocco. This account was a timely catalyst for the already active French mercantile, political, and military interests in the Sahara. Rabbi Mordecai provided specific information on caravan routes across the desert to Timbuctoo, and he presented detailed data regarding which goods were most commonly traded. He even mentioned a direct trade communication with Cairo.

In 1874 and 1875, Abi-Serour made two expeditions into little-known parts of southern Morocco to collect intelligence and harvest rare plants for Beaumier and the French botanist Ernest Cosson. These journeys were recorded by Henri Duveyrier in the Bulletin of the Geographical Society of Paris. At age fifty-two, Abi-Serour accompanied Charles de Foucauld on his extremely dangerous eleven-month exploration of Morocco (1883–1884), during which the Frenchman, speaking little Arabic, disguised himself as a Russian rabbi. On occasion, Abi-Serour told the Jews in the *mellah* where he and Foucauld were lodged that Foucauld was a medical doctor who was a specialist in eye diseases. In the town of Taza, Abi-Serour swore that the astronomical instruments being assembled were a preventative against cholera. Rabbi Mordecai unquestionably helped Foucauld survive this Moroccan journey, but Foucauld nonetheless later characterized him as being an unhelpful, if not worthless, companion. Abi-Serour's last years were spent in Algiers, where he dabbled in alchemy and died on April 6, 1886.

[*See also* Foucauld, Charles de, *and* Timbuctoo.]

BIBLIOGRAPHY
Bederman, Sanford H. *God's Will: The Travels of Rabbi Mordochai Abi-Serour*. Atlanta: Georgia State University, Department of Geography, 1980.

SANFORD H. BEDERMAN

Abruzzi, Luigi

Abruzzi, Luigi (1873–1933), Spanish-born Italian mountaineer, Arctic explorer, and naval commander. Luigi Amedeo di Savoia-Aosta, Duke of the Abruzzi—commonly known as Abruzzi—was born on January 29, 1873, in Madrid, where his father was briefly the ruling king of Spain. Abruzzi also was a grandson of King Vittorio Emanuele II of Italy. Leading a highly skilled party of mountaineers, Abruzzi became the first person to ascend Mount Saint Elias (18,008 feet [5,489 meters]) in Alaska in 1897. In 1906, with one of the most efficient expeditions ever assembled, Abruzzi climbed Margherita Peak (16,767 feet [5,111 meters]) in the Ruwenzori Range in central Africa. His party of scientists also conducted considerable surveying and mapping, and it brought back superb pictures of these so-called Mountains of the Moon, taken by the famed photographer Vittorio Sella. His third famous mountain adventure took place in 1909, when his expedition thoroughly mapped the region surrounding the God-

win Austen glaciers in the Himalayas. Before being forced to turn back, Abruzzi ascended to over 24,000 feet (7,315 meters) on K2, a peak he called the "third pole."

In 1899–1900, Abruzzi commanded an Italian expedition to the Arctic, where an attempt was made to reach the North Pole from Franz Josef Land. One member of his party, Umberto Cagni, came within 209 miles (336 kilometers) of their destination. This expedition was the first Arctic success by a southern European nation. Promoted to admiral, Abruzzi served as commander in chief of the Italian navy from 1913 to 1917. After World War I and the rise of fascism in Italy, Abruzzi moved to Somaliland, where he died near Mogadishu on March 18, 1933.

[*See also* Africa, *subentry on* Scientific Exploration, *and* North Pole.]

BIBLIOGRAPHY
Tenderini, Mirella, and Michael Shandrick. *The Duke of the Abruzzi: An Explorer's Life*. London: Bâton Wicks, 1997.

SANFORD H. BEDERMAN

Acosta, José de

Acosta, José de (1540–1600), Jesuit missionary, philosopher, and theologian. Acosta was born at Medina del Campo, Spain, into a wealthy merchant family of Jewish ancestry. In 1552 he entered the Jesuits. After studying humanities, he was sent to Alcalá (1559–1567) for philosophy and theology, and here he was strongly influenced by the Dominican scholastic theologians Francisco de Vitoria and Domingo de Soto.

He taught theology in Spain from 1567 to 1571, before being sent to Lima, Peru, in 1572, where he taught theology and then served as rector at the Jesuit college. He was Jesuit provincial superior of Peru from 1576 to 1581. The important Third Provincial Council of Lima (1582–1583) entrusted him with drawing up its decrees and writing a catechism for use among Indians.

Acosta spent 1586 and early 1587 in Mexico, where he met the Jesuit Alonso Sánchez, who was advocating that Spain invade China. Acosta wrote a tract against this misguided scheme. He returned to Spain in 1587; two years later the Jesuit General Claudio Acquaviva appointed him visitor of the provinces of Aragon and Andalusia to suggest reforms among the Spanish Jesuits, partly to head off the threat that Philip II might commission a non-Jesuit visitor. He served as superior at Valladolid (1592–1595) and at Salamanca (1597–1600). During the in-

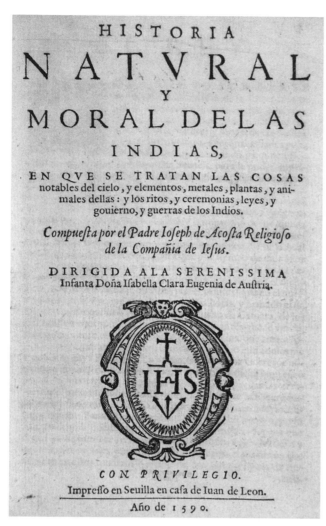

Historia natural y moral de las Indias. Title pages contain a great wealth of information; here we learn that Acosta was a Jesuit (note the Jesuit emblem), that he aimed at an all-compassing history, and that this first edition was published at Seville. COURTESY THE NEWBERRY LIBRARY, CHICAGO

terval he prepared three volumes of his sermons for publication.

Acosta's relations with Acquaviva were stormy. He told Clement VIII that Acquaviva was a tyrant. In Rome in 1594 Acosta attended the Fifth General Congregation of the Jesuits and strongly opposed its ban on men of Islamic or Jewish ancestry becoming Jesuits.

Acosta wrote two works of lasting influence. *On Procuring the Salvation of the Indians* was written in Mexico and published in Salamanca in 1588. Its six books reflect on the best ways to Christianize Native Americans. Acosta criticized Spanish treatment of Indians and questioned whether Spanish conquests were just wars. He argued that Spanish greed and cruelty hindered conversions. The last book of *Procuring* explores the problems that missionaries faced.

Acosta's second major work, *Natural and Moral History of the Indies,* contains a total of seven books and was published in Seville in 1590; Italian, French, German, Dutch, and English translations followed. Four books present a traditional view of the cosmos and earth, then discuss climate, geography, flora, fauna, and minerals in the Americas. Two books describe and evaluate Indian customs and religious practices, some positively, some negatively. The seventh book examines Mexican history before the Spanish conquest.

[*See also* Jesuits.]

BIBLIOGRAPHY

Acosta, José de. *Natural and Moral History of the Indies.* Edited by Jane Mangan. Translated by Frances López-Morillas. Durham, N.C.: Duke University Press, 2002.
Burgaleta Claudio M. *José de Acosta, S.J. (1540–1600): His Life and Thought.* Chicago: Jesuit Way, 1999.

JOHN PATRICK DONNELLY, S.J.

Aerial Survey. Aerial (or air) survey and the related topics of photogrammetry and remote sensing of the environment have a comparatively short history. Although dating essentially from the beginning of controlled flight in the early twentieth century, there are antecedents. From time immemorial humans have envied, and at times tried to emulate, the flight of birds—as the classical Greek myth of Icarus attests. However, before the end of the eighteenth century the best available "platforms" for viewing the Earth from above were mountains and hills, trees, or towers. Prior to the invention of viable photography, however, an aerial platform from which to take photographs was available in the form of the hot air balloon of the Montgolfier brothers, Jacques-Etienne (1745–1799) and Joseph-Michel (1740–1810), of France. At first the passengers were animals and birds, but soon humans were lofted, and shortly the hydrogen-filled balloon was developed. Anchored observational balloons were used by Napoleon Bonaparte (1769–1821), and also by both sides during the American Civil War (1861–1865) when sketch maps were made from aerial observations.

Age of Flight. Apparently, the first aerial photograph was taken in 1858 by the Frenchman Gaspard-Félix Tournachon (1820–1910), who preferred the name

Nadar. Nadar made a simple (black-and-white) positive on glass from a tethered balloon 262 feet (80 meters) up, to be followed two years later by one of Boston from an elevation of 1,200 feet (366 meters) by the Americans Samuel A. King (1828–1914) and his assistant James Wallace Black. Meanwhile, great improvements were being made in optical equipment, especially in Germany, including the binocular stereoscope. What was now needed was a more controlled means of flight, made possible by the heavier-than-air craft (airplane) pioneered in the first decade of the twentieth century by the Wright brothers, Orville (1871–1948) and Wilbur (1867–1912), and others. Photographs, usually ad hoc obliques, were taken from reconnaissance planes during World War I (1914–1918), but soon cameras were actually mounted on aircraft and overlapping vertical photos taken at regular intervals. As a result of this development and of the increased altitude soon attained, a new branch of surveying known as photogrammetry was developed in the late 1920s and 1930s. Only rarely had artists drawn landscapes (as opposed to maps) from a purely vertical view, a notable exception being the "Topography of Niagara" in 1827 by the American painter George Catlin (1796–1872).

Most topographic maps of large scale are now based on aerial surveys, undertaken by national governments. Understandably, they differ greatly in symbolism, coverage, and in quality but are fundamentally photogrammetrical. Photogrammetry is the science of obtaining reliable measurements by means of photography and, by extension, mapping from air photos. Although it is possible to "rectify" oblique aerial photographs geometrically and optically, the preferred source materials for aerial surveys are vertical photographs with a 60 percent overlap along the line of flight of the aircraft taking pictures (endlap) and a 25 percent overlap with adjacent flight lines (sidelap). The endlap and sidelap ensure that only the most accurate part of any particular photo—the center—need be used, and, more significant, make possible stereoscopic analysis. This is accomplished with the aid of the stereoscope and much more elaborate and refined optical instruments (such as the Multiplex) based on the same principle, enabling a viewer to observe a miniature, three-dimensional model of a given area.

Such models, made by visually fusing photographic images of the area taken from different places (stations), are used for contouring as well as for planimetric mapping. Because by this method the stereoscopic model, with all its rich detail, is in the photogrammetrist's view, it is obvious why aerial surveys,

especially in areas of high relief, are generally superior to field surveys, in which one must interpolate between a finite number of points of known value. Of course, some horizontal and vertical control points to which the aerial photo coverage is tied must be determined in the field; first-, second-, and third-order points (the numbers refer to the degree of accuracy of these control points, which varies in different surveys) used for this purpose are indicated on the ground by metal tablets. After a map is compiled by photogrammetric means and before it is finally rendered, field checking is most desirable, but in the case of areas difficult of access, this is not always undertaken or absolutely necessary. The use of aerial photography for surveying was a prelude to the more spectacular imaging made possible by space flight. However, the two methods and technologies are complementary, rather than competitive.

In its broadest sense the term "remote sensing of the environment" can be used for any method of viewing objects when the viewer is not in direct, physical contact with the object. But this term has come into specialized use in the space age, particularly in relation to more exotic sensors, and hyper-altitude imaging. The latter has been made possible by rockets and missiles, of greater and greater range and complexity. Rocketry and the associated propellant of gunpowder (explosives) appeared in China and the Islamic world before they were "invented" in the West. After artillery became available in the late Middle Ages in Europe, workers on that continent studied ballistic science. However, it was some time before there was power enough to propel a missile skyward any considerable distance and much longer before rockets were used as platforms for imaging Earth. Apparently this occurred when a camera was fitted to a rocket by German artillery in 1910 (applying theoretical ideas of Swedish industrialist and philanthropist Alfred Nobel); it marked the beginning of controlled, unmanned remote sensing.

Imaging from Space. There were some advances in this field during the following years, but phenomenal progress was made through the German experience with V-2 rocketry during World War II. When, in about 1945, German rocket scientists joined the incipient U.S. space program, advanced by Robert Goddard (1882–1945) in Massachusetts and Theodor von Karman (1881–1963) in California, as well as that of the then USSR, extraterrestrial flight became possible. From 1960 on, TIROS (a series of unmanned satellites) was launched in the United States and demonstrated a great potential for meteorology—the first science to be improved by the new technology. Meanwhile, the Soviets launched Sputnik in 1957, imaged the far side of the Moon in 1959, and put a human in space in 1961. The next year marked the first manned space flight by the United States, which soon began a series of missions imaging the Earth from space—Gemini (1965–1966) and Apollo (1968–1969)—with the use of hand-held cameras loaded with color and, later, color infrared (CIR) film, which had been perfected during World War II. The Apollo 11 mission of July 1969 landed two men on the Moon, and many images were taken of this body and of Earth.

The next development was continuous, extensive surveillance of the surface of the planet, first accomplished by the Earth Resources Technology Satellite (ERTS) in 1972. Another similar unmanned satellite was launched in 1975, and the program was renamed Landsat. Since that time, the surface of the Earth (except the polar regions, which the system does not cover) has been scanned by Landsat as frequently as every nine days (depending, of course, on cloud cover). By international agreement, Landsat imagery, which is telemetered to the Earth in at least four multispectral bands, is available to users in any part of the world. One of the problems with Landsat has been its low spatial resolution—that is, the ability of the system to render a sharply defined image—but this has not prevented its use in monitoring the Earth's resources, as intended, or in the creation of mosaics such as the National Geographic Society's "Space Portrait U.S.A."

Consortia such as the European Space Agency and individual countries including France and, most recently, China have been involved in space programs, but Russia and the United States have taken the leading roles in this activity. The National Aeronautics and Space Administration (NASA) came into being in the United States in 1958, and since that time one of the most successful applications of its missions has been with respect to the atmosphere. Over the years a number of geostationary and other satellites with various acronyms—ESSA, ATS, GOES, NOAA—have been launched. In aggregate, these high-altitude satellites have been fitted with a variety of sensors—television, infrared, vidicon, radar—which have given scientists an immense data source with which to better understand the mechanics of the atmosphere, to appreciate climate, and to forecast weather conditions.

However, many other distributions have been surveyed and monitored aerially by satellite imagery, including forest cover, field crops, urbanization, and so on. But space imaging has not taken the place of more conventional survey methods. Such topics as land ownership (cadastral) survey and population and public health surveys depend heavily on more traditional means of data gathering, including the census. Modern topographic mapping, likewise, is dependent on conventional aerial photography, in part because space imagery has limited ability to provide the stereoscopic information needed for constructing detailed relief maps.

Nevertheless, in total, progress in aerial surveying of all kinds has advanced remarkably in the past century owing to the conquest of air and space and new imaging systems. Methods developed to better understand the Earth are now being applied to extraterrestrial bodies such as the Moon, the planets of the solar system, and beyond.

[*See also* Space Program.]

BIBLIOGRAPHY

Colwell, Robert N., ed. *Manual of Photographic Interpretation.* Washington, D.C.: American Society of Photogrammetry, 1960.

Colwell, Robert N., ed. *Manual of Remote Sensing.* Falls Church, Va.: American Society of Photogrammetry, 1983

Denègre, J., ed. *Thematic Mapping from Satellite Imagery: a Guidebook.* Oxford and New York: Elsevier Science / International Cartographic Association, 1994.

Jensen, John R. *Introductory Digital Image Processing: A Remote Sensing Perspective.* Englewood Cliffs, N.J.: Prentice-Hall, 1986.

Sabins, Floyd B. *Remote Sensing: Principles and Interpretation.* 2nd ed. New York: W.H. Freeman, 1987.

Short, Nicholas M. *The Landsat Tutorial Workbook: Basics of Remote Sensing.* Washington D.C.: National Aeronautics and Space Administration, 1982. Includes a good bibliography.

Thrower, Norman J. W. *Satellite Photography as a Geographic Tool for Land Use Mapping.* Washington D.C.: United States Geological Survey, 1970.

Wasowski, Ronald J. "Some Ethical Aspects of International Remote Sensing." *Photogrammetric Engineering and Remote Sensing* 57 (1991): 41–48.

NORMAN J. W. THROWER

Africa

This entry contains seven subentries:

Early Exploration of East Africa

The human species evolved in Africa and at successive times during the last two million years left the continent and settled in Europe and Asia. The last migration event involving modern humans took place between 100,000 and 60,000 years ago. The story of the exploration of Africa undertaken largely by non-Africans is a sensitive issue because indigenous African communities knew about their own landscape for millennia. Discovery and exploration by non-Africans was really a prelude for exploitation of the continent's raw materials and human resources (especially slaves), which ultimately led to the colonization of the continent by European powers in the nineteenth century.

Early Exploration. It was trade that certainly motivated the ancient Egyptians to plan significant expeditions into sub-Saharan Africa, which they identified as the lands of Yam and Punt. Early expeditions followed the Nile southward. Harkhuf (c. 2300 B.C.E.), whose tomb is just below the First Cataract on the Nile in Aswan, records four expeditions into the Sudan during the Sixth Dynasty; he returned on the last expedition with a "dancing dwarf of the gods from the land of the spirits." Punt was reached by the Red Sea, and expeditions set out from Sinai and Quseir in the Old, Middle, and New Kingdoms, beginning during the Fifth Dynasty (c. 2450 B.C.E.). Extensive reliefs of one of these expeditions in c. 1492 B.C.E., under the instigation of Queen Hatshepsut, are preserved on the walls of the Deir al-Bahri temple complex at Thebes. These show the boats used, the indigenous peoples encountered, and the products obtained, which included gold, ebony, ivory, and live wild animals, as well as the animals' skins and incense. New evidence of these voyages has come from an archaeological survey of Marsa Gawasis on the Red Sea, where remains of rigging and ships timbers, as well as containers naming Punt with the cartouche of Amenemhat III (c. 1800 B.C.E.), have been found in man-made caves. No definitive archaeological evidence for the location of Punt has yet been obtained, although current opinion favors the African coast at the southern end of the Red Sea, rather than the lands beyond the Bab el-Mandeb. The trade goods, however, seem to have come from a wide area of eastern Africa. These voyages to Punt were major state-sponsored expeditions that involved the portage of ships across the desert and their reassembly on the Red Sea, and they apparently ceased in the Twentieth Dynasty.

Greek interest in African exploration developed through the Greeks' control of Egypt from 323 B.C.E A primary motivation was a reliable supply of war elephants, and Ptolemy II Philadelphus (281–246 B.C.E) established a series of elephant-hunting stations along the African coast of the Red Sea, extending as far south as Adulis. These stations developed as trading posts, enabling the connection of the maritime trade of the Indian Ocean with the Red Sea. Early voyages into the Indian Ocean include that of Eudoxus of Cyzicus (c. 146 B.C.E.), whose account is preserved by Strabo. On his return from India, Eudoxus was cast onto the east African coast, where he discovered a ship's prow shaped like a horse's head, which he carried home and believed was similar to those used off the coast of Spain—thus, to him, proving that Africa could be circumnavigated. Significantly, prows of the east African *mtepe* sewn boats are shaped as animal heads, and these may be part of a very ancient design. Eudoxus set out to prove his theory of circumnavigation, sailing to Cádiz and then southward, but he never returned.

More problematic are two voyages recorded in Greek literature that, it is claimed, reached East Africa, but the voyages are largely fictional in their content, recalling the utopian tradition of Plato's Atlantis. The voyage of Euhemerus (fl. 316 B.C.E, quoted by Eusebius in his *Praeparatio*) reached an island called Paanchea, while the voyage of Iambulus (second century B.C.E, quoted by Diodorus Siculus in his *Bibliotheke*) reached the "Islands of the Sun," which numbered seven and lay off the African coast. Neither account contains details that are convincing, but the accounts may indicate that eastern Africa was being drawn into maritime trade networks, as has been suggested by recent archaeological finds on Zanzibar and Mafia islands, including finds of Egyptian marlwares. On the west coast of Africa, another Greek, the historian Polybius, set out to repeat the voyage of Hanno (c. 143 B.C.E), and Polybius's account is partly preserved by Pliny.

Roman Advances. The Romans saw Egypt's potential as a gateway into Africa, following the Nile, as well as a gateway into the Indian Ocean. A military expedition under Petronius (23–21 B.C.E) reached as far as Zapata (Gable Barkel), and the most southerly frontier of the Roman Empire was briefly established at Qasr Ibrim; excavations have produced evidence of the Roman garrison and marching camps. Thereafter, a peace treaty was signed, and the frontier moved north. Pliny recorded an expedition sent by Nero in 61 C.E. that reached Meroe, the Nubian capital, and this was probably the farthest into continental East Africa that the Romans traveled.

The sea route to East Africa was an easier proposition, since the Red Sea coast had become the terminus of regular trade with India. However, while ships could sail to India in a single monsoon, the voyage to East Africa required two monsoons, and most of the trade seems to have been under the control of Arabian seaman. The *Periplus of the Erythraean Sea* (c. 40 C.E.) contains a very detailed account of the coastline and its ports as far south as "Rhapta," a market that exported ivory and tortoise shell. Rhapta has not been located, although Roman beads have been found close to the Rufiji River in Tanzania. Claudius Ptolemy (c. 150 C.E.) was interested in the dimensions of East Africa, as part of his calculating the dimensions of the known earth. Ptolemy relied upon two accounts recorded by Marinus of Tyre (fl. 120 C.E.), that of Diogenes, who was driven southward for twenty-five days, reaching the "lake from which the Nile flows," and that of Theophilus, who took twenty days to sail from Rhapta to Cape Guardafui. Elsewhere Ptolemy gives precise coordinates of the east African ports, which broadly follow those in the *Periplus*. Ptolemy also records the location of the Mountains of the Moon "from which the lakes of the Nile receive their snow water," and he is aware that they can be reached from the east coast. This mountain range is probably the snow-covered Ruwenzori mountains in Uganda, and it was this information of Ptolemy's that was used to guide the Victorian explorers to the source of the Nile.

Islamic and Chinese Geography. Byzantine interest in Africa was directed toward obtaining gold and ivory and toward supporting the Aksum to develop its trade with the East. Aksum had developed as a major trading center in highland Ethiopia, and the ruling family had been converted to Christianity by the mid-fourth century C.E. through the activities of two Coptic missionaries, Fumentius and Edesius. The fullest account of Aksum and its trade, complete with illustrations, is found in an account of a merchant-turned-monk, Kosmas Indicopleustes, whose *Christian Topography* (c. 550 C.E.) set out the notion that the world was flat and that the heavens were a dome overhead. He had visited Aksum as well as ports along the Red Sea, but he did not venture south of Cape Guardafui. Archaeological evidence suggests that regular trade did take place as far south as Zanzibar from the sixth century, although mostly with the Sasanian rather than with Byzantine or Aksumite merchants.

With the spread of Islam across the Indian Ocean and into northern Africa, geographical knowledge of Africa rapidly increased. Trade routes crossed the desert, reaching the urban communities of the Sahel and inland Niger delta, while monsoon trade connected the Swahili communities of East Africa. Numerous accounts, often fantastical, were collected of these places from returning merchants, but actual eyewitness accounts are rare. Most noteworthy are the descriptions of al-Mas'udi, who states that he visited East Africa in 916; of Ibn Battuta, who traveled between Mogadishu and Kilwa in 1332 and to western Sudan in 1352–1353; and of Leo Africanus, whose *Description of Africa* was first published in 1550. The Islamic geographers relied heavily on the classical authors for material beyond the trading centers, including the idea that the African continent stretched to the east to join Asia. There was little or no travel by outsiders to the indigenous states in the interior, such as Great Zimbabwe, the interlacaustrine region, or the Congo.

Chinese sources for this period are surprisingly accurate and fuller in ethnographic details than many of the Islamic accounts. The Chinese gathered much of their information at home from merchants, and even on one occasion in the tenth century from visiting Africans. Eyewitness explorations by the Chinese are rare, but Du Huan did reach the coast of Somalia or Eritrea in the mid-eighth century, and his description survives. A contemporary of Ibn Battuta was Wang Dayuan, who may also have visited East Africa. A Chinese map drawn by Zhu Siben, dated 1311–1320, clearly shows the southern coastline of Africa, in a way quite different from that of prevailing Arabic knowledge, suggesting some first-hand knowledge. The most significant Chinese exploration was by the naval expeditions of Zheng He, which first reached East Africa on the fifth voyage (1417–1419), returning on the sixth (1421–1422) and seventh voyages (1431–1432). Many of the records of this massive undertaking have been lost, but Zheng He's fleet visited many of the Swahili ports, including Malindi and Mogadishu, and may have ventured a short distance into the Atlantic, as is suggested by a note on the Fra Mauro map of 1453. There have been recent claims of the discovery of a Chinese shipwreck on the Pasali rocks off Pate Island, near Lamu, as well as long-recorded traditions that the people of the nearby town of Shanga, which was abandoned in the early fifteenth century, were descended in part from shipwrecked Chinese sailors.

[*See also* Arabo-Islamic Geography; Chinese Exploration; Herodotus; Ibn Battuta; Leo Africanus; Pliny the Elder; Ptolemy; *and* Zheng He.]

BIBLIOGRAPHY

Brown Robert, ed. *A History and Description of Africa and of the Notable Things Therein Contained . . . but Better Known as Leo Africanus: Done into English in the Year 1600 by John Pory.* 3 vols. London: Hakluyt Society, 1896. Reprint. New York: B. Franklin, 1963.

Casson, Lionel, trans. *The Periplus Maris Erythraei.* Princeton, N.J.: Princeton University Press, 1989.

Chami, Felix. "The Graeco-Romans and Paanchea/Azania: Sailing in the Erythraean Sea." *Society of Arabia Studies* (2002).

Chami, Felix. "People and Contacts in the Ancient Western Indian Ocean Seaboard or Azania." *Man and the Environment* 27, no. 1 (2002): 33–44.

Chami, Felix. "Roman Beads from the Rufiji Delta, Tanzania." *Current Anthropology* 40, no. 2 (1999): 237–241.

Freeman-Grenville, G. S. P. *The East African Coast: Select Documents from the First to the Earlier Nineteenth Century.* London: Oxford University Press, 1962.

Horton, Mark. "Africa in Egypt: New Evidence from Qasr Ibrim." In *Egypt and Africa: Nubia from Prehistory to Islam,* edited by W. V. Davies, 264–277. London: British Museum, 1991.

Horton, Mark. *Shanga: The Archaeology of a Muslim Trading Community on the Coast of East Africa.* London: British Institute in Eastern Africa, 1996.

Horton, Mark, and John Middleton. *The Swahili: The Social Landscape of Mercantile Society.* Oxford and Malden, Mass.: Blackwell, 2000.

Kitchen, Kenneth. "The Land of Punt." In *The Archaeology of Africa: Food, Metals, and Towns,* edited by Thurston Shaw et al., 587–609. London and New York: Routledge, 1993.

Levtzion, N., and J. F. Hopkins, eds. *Corpus of Early Arabic Sources for West African History.* Cambridge, U.K., and New York: Cambridge University Press, 1981.

McCrindle, J. W., trans. *The Christian Topography of Cosmas, an Egyptian Monk.* London: Hakluyt Society, 1897.

Snow, Philip. *The Star Raft: China's Encounter with Africa.* Ithaca, N.Y.: Cornell University Press, 1988.

MARK HORTON

Exploration

The hominids who developed into *Homo sapiens* must have explored areas around their East African Rift Valley homes as they spread out from there, but such ventures can be only inferred; no records have survived. Exploration implies communication to others in tangible form about what has been discovered. Hence the true exploration of Africa is a phenomenon of only the last 2,500 years. For almost all of that period a distinction has to be made between the accumulation of knowledge about the coasts and about the interior, which was difficult of access and often had a separate history. Not until well into the nineteenth century were those barriers properly overcome by explorers.

Ancient Civilizations, c. 2500 B.C.E.–500 C.E. During the period of Africa's ancient civilizations, outsiders explored the continent by land and by sea, but the data accumulated were transmitted to later ages in a fragmentary and often confusing form.

Ventures by Land. From the north of the continent, some ingress by land to the interior of Africa was possible and the rulers of ancient Egypt sent expeditions southward up the Nile valley. Inscriptions record three trading ventures by one Herkhof, the first-ever known explorer recorded by name, into the Sudan in about 2200 B.C.E. He brought back ivory, ebony, incense, and a Pygmy. Yet such expeditions did not bring much information; even by the time of the Alexandrian geographer Ptolemy in the second century C.E., Egypt's knowledge of the Nile Valley did not reliably extend much beyond the latitude of present-day Khartoum and only touched the borders of Ethiopia. Farther west, caravan routes were established across the Sahara despite its steadily becoming more desiccated in this period. Successive rulers of North Africa (that is, Egypt) the Greeks, then the Romans, among others, learned something of the peoples south of the desert, but there are few first-hand records of particular expeditions.

Herodotus (484–425 B.C.E.), a traveler and historian who reached Aswan, collected much information. He rejected myths about the Nile but did mention five young men from Syrtis (modern Libya) who had traveled southwest to reach a great river that he assumed was the Upper Nile but which must have been the Niger. This confusion was to bedevil scholarship until 1830 C.E. Information on later travelers is scant partly because some rulers like the Carthaginians tended to keep details of their trade secret, although it is clear they had contacts with Negro peoples and used a system of "dumb barter" that had first been reported by Herodotus. When Rome conquered Carthage, Balbus was sent to extend Roman rule south over the Garamantes in Fezzan. Later, Septimius Flaccus penetrated even beyond there and Julius Maternus reached Agisymba (Tibesti). By 100 B.C.E. camels were in use for desert expeditions but no other Roman activities are precisely recorded.

Ventures by Sea: The Phoenician Circumnavigation. There is slightly better evidence about ventures by sea from North Africa during this long period but details remain lacking or confused. As early as 2480 B.C.E., Sahure took an Egyptian expedition to obtain frankincense and myrrh from "Punt," meaning probably southern Arabia or the Somali coast. A similar voyage was made by Hennu in 2007 B.C.E. Despite the continuous need for myrrh for em-

"A View of a Bridge over the Ba-Fing or Black River." From Mungo Park's *Travels in the Interior Districts of Africa* (London, 1799). The images of early exploration in Africa are singularly lacking in the attractive elegance of those showing Pacific islands. Here Park, apparently seated at the right, watches a party crossing what looks like a most improbable bridge. The British Library/HIP/Art Resource, NY

balming purposes, not until 1485 B.C.E. is another such venture recorded—in a mortuary temple frieze for Queen Hatshepsut. Nehsi was sent with a large fleet to explore the Red Sea coasts. In fact, the Egyptians never became great mariners and employed the Phoenicians instead. So, too, did King Solomon in about 950 B.C.E. in order to obtain gold from Ophir, which was presumably somewhere in eastern Africa. Much better attested, although disbelieved even by him, is the account Herodotus gave of the Egyptian use of a Phoenician fleet to sail around Africa in about 600 B.C.E. King Necho sent them south through the Red Sea and instructed them to return via the Pillars of Hercules (Strait of Gibraltar). The venture took three years because the sailors landed from time to time to grow crops for their food supplies. Although no details of places visited were

noted, credibility is given to their story by their report that the sun was on their right-hand side, as it must have been when they were south of the Equator. The significance was, as Herodotus pointed out, that men came to know that Africa was "washed on all sides by the sea, except where it is attached to Asia."

Currents and winds would have favored the circumnavigation clockwise but going the other way was more difficult. One Sataspes perhaps reached West Africa by sea but better attested is another Phoenician venture at the bidding of Hanno, king of Carthage, which, in about 450 B.C.E. sailed southward along the coast of Morocco founding trading settlements. It seems fairly certain that the Senegal River was reached and just possibly the Gulf of Guinea. Yet the expedition was never followed up

"The City of Timbuktoo." From René Caillié's *Journal d'un Voyage à Tembouctou et à Jenne* (Paris, 1842). This image of Timbuktoo compares interestingly with the version offered a little later by Heinrich Barth. Caillé's suggests a less well-organized city, but it looks as if they are describing the same reality: one or two large structures with tall central towers, many smaller square buildings, and rounded huts on the outskirts. THE BRITISH LIBRARY/HIP/ART RESOURCE, NY

from the Mediterranean for another eighteen hundred years.

It was easier to navigate Africa's east coast because of the alternating northeast and southwest monsoon winds, and Greek traders became familiar with the "Erythraean Sea," that is, the northwest part of the Indian Ocean. One mariner, whose name we do no know, recorded a *periplus* or guide in perhaps about 100–130 C.E. Various places on the East African coast, which was known as Azania, are mentioned. The most important was Rhapta, where tortoiseshell was obtained. No one can say where Rhapta was but it could be Zanzibar or the Rufiji delta. It is to the period of Greek dominance that one may attribute the probably mythical expedition of Diogenes who allegedly went inland to some lakes.

By 500 C.E., then, records existed of the northern littoral regions of Africa, caravan routes across the Sahara, and there was vague awareness of coastal areas farther south on both coasts. A potentially important legacy of classical learning was the knowledge that Africa was probably surrounded by sea. Unfortunately, the author of the most important version of the legacy, Claudius Ptolemy, seems not to have believed this latter characteristic so there was conflicting evidence. Ptolemy's *Geographike Syntaxis*, compiled in Alexandria in about 150 C.E., is mostly a long list of places with supposedly astronomically fixed latitudes and longitudes. None of Ptolemy's own maps survived, and it is uncertain whether any of the medieval versions are true copies or merely guesses. Ptolemy gave an accurate version of North Africa, but the "Fisheaters" of West Africa and the "Mountains of the Moon" and two lakes at the head of the Nile are myth or garbled information. Nevertheless, Ptolemy's data were a source of information and speculation for medieval Arab and European geographers and for many later ones as well.

Arab Civilization's Contribution, c. 500 C.E.–1400 C.E. The learning of the ancient civilizations about

Africa was carried forward and extended by Islamic scholars. The rapid territorial expansion of Islam from the seventh to the ninth centuries meant discovery as a result of conquests and military ventures into North Africa, the West Sudan where there was gold, and along the East African coast. The names of pioneers are rarely known, but the results of their work were incorporated into Arab geographies and cosmologies, especially in the tenth and eleventh centuries. The travelers whose exploits are known, including the greatest of all, Ibn Battuta, were not primary discoverers but commentators on the Islamic world as they found it.

From at least the tenth century people from the Middle East were sailing their ships along the East African coast establishing colonies that included Arabs and Persians. There is an account of one Ismailawaih reaching Sofala to trade in 922 C.E., although the story includes unbelievable details. It is more certain that al-Mas'udi (d. 956) visited and described Pemba in about 915 although the geography is poor and incidental detail again more like the *Arabian Nights*. Ibn Hawqal is another tenth-century traveler who claimed to know East Africa but more certainly did visit the kingdom of Ghana in the Western Sudan. Information from such travelers informed the geographies of El Bekri of c.1050, the great Sicily-based writer Al Idrisi (1100–1166), and Abu al-Fida (1273–1331).

The fourteenth century is dominated by Ibn Battuta (1304–1369), who made two major ventures that provided information on Africa. His first took him along the north coast from his home in Tangier to Egypt and ultimately Mecca; performing the hajj was for him, like numerous other Muslim travelers, a prime reason for setting out. After a stay in Arabia, he sailed south along the Somali coast, visiting Zeila and Mogadishu. In 1331 he went on to the flourishing East African trading cities of Mombasa and Kilwa, where he learned about Sofala farther south whence came the gold Kilwa sent to the Persian Gulf. After equally remarkable journeys in Asia, Ibn Battuta returned to the Mahgreb, from which he made his last major journey in 1351–1352 when he crossed the Sahara to the Niger, describing the empires of Mali and Songhay and staying in Timbuctoo before recrossing the desert from Gao to Fez. Not long before Ibn Battuta's visit to the Western Sudan, Islam inspired an African ruler, the great Mansa Musa of Mali, to make the pilgrimage from Timbuctoo to Egypt and Mecca. Legends about the gold he and his party distributed abound, but unfortunately no detailed itinerary exists.

By about 1400, then, the Islamic world and its scholars were reasonably well informed on the North African coastal region, on the Islamic societies of the Western Sudan in the region of the Upper Niger, and on the cities of the East African coast as far south as Kilwa. But of the inland areas of the continent south of the Tropic of Cancer almost nothing was known.

Chinese Knowledge to c. 1500. The other great and much older Asiatic civilization was the Chinese empire. Despite the advantages it possessed in the shape of astronomical knowledge and the compass, it was much less interested in parts of the world distant from its center. As early as 138 B.C.E. Zhang Qian knew something of Egypt, and there continued to be perhaps a few direct and certainly indirect contacts with East Africa via the Indian Ocean. A fourteenth-century map by Zhu Siben appears to show Africa reasonably correctly while there was knowledge of its wildlife. Then in the period 1405–1433 the Chinese Muslim and eunuch Admiral Zheng He made seven long voyages, on one of which a visit was made to the East African coast. Ming pottery certainly became known in Kilwa. But Cheng Ho's navy was broken up and such knowledge as he acquired was never followed up. No widely available major geographical data on Africa resulted from Chinese visits.

Beginnings of European Interest. It is no accident that the Maghreb, the home of Ibn Battuta, should also be the original focus of European interest in Africa, for a considerable amount of information had passed from Islamic sources to Europe. Real geography tended to be mixed up with myth, supposition, or misinformation. Hence some commentators assumed that Paradise had been built in Africa with the Nile assumed to be the River Gihon mentioned in Genesis 2. Alternatively, this was perhaps the kingdom of Prester John, a mighty potentate and potential ally against the Muslims. Real information on Ethiopia gave him more credibility. Such mixtures of fact and fancy can be found in the Catalan Map of 1375, which shows genuine knowledge of Mali in the Western Sudan with an exaggeration of the power of its ruler and his riches in gold. A pass in the Atlas Mountains is labeled "through here pass the merchants who come to trade with the negroes in Guinea." In fact, European merchants were in constant touch with the Arabs and Jewish merchants of North Africa, who knew the Saharan routes, which Europeans themselves were rarely allowed to travel. Nevertheless, the Toulouse merchant Anselm d'Isalguier some time before 1413 claimed to have visited the Western Sudanic kingdoms and brought back a Negro wife as proof. His gold was of even greater interest. At this time Europe had a great need of gold to pay for its growing dependence on spices and other goods from Asia. Would it be possible to meet this need by reaching the sources of African gold? And if the Muslims of North Africa would not allow access to the Saharan routes, could sea routes be the way to the mysterious Guinea from which gold came? It was to be the Portuguese who attempted to answer this question. Yet another question was implicit in the series of exploratory voyages they were about to undertake. Was it really possible to sail around Africa to Asia as the evidence of the Phoenician voyage suggested? Hence there was an inherent disjunction of aims: to explore Africa for gold and Prester John or to find a way around it.

The Portuguese Initiative: Prince Henry the Navigator, 1394–1460. With its old nobility broken by feuding, Portugal entered the fifteenth century with a more commercially minded nobility and a royal family anxious to increase its power and prestige. Although on the margin of Mediterranean-centered Europe, it was well placed to develop new kinds of oceanic enterprises. Two- or three-masted shallow-draft caravels were ideal for maritime exploration. The use of the compass enabled portolan charts to be made while latitudes could be determined with the astrolabe. His crusading spirit encouraged Prince Henry to attack Ceuta (opposite Gibraltar) in 1415. Victory and dawning knowledge of the Maghreb's gold trade with the Western Sudan spurred him to send out a series of expeditions to see if supplies could be obtained by sea. Although Henry was curious, energetic, determined, and did encourage the development of navigational techniques at Sagres, it is misleading to see him as a Renaissance figure.

No actual map recording the early voyages survived the Lisbon earthquake of 1755 but it seems that Henry's first concern was to secure the Azores, Madeira, and the Canary Islands. Much was learned about Atlantic currents and winds. Serious examination of the African coast began when Gil Eanes rounded Cape Juby in 1434 (although it is often assumed he reached Cape Bojador farther south). In 1435, Eanes did reach Bojador and then, with Alfonso Baldaya, Rio de Oro. These voyages dispelled the scare stories about a "sea of darkness" and Nuno Tristão and Antão Gonçalves got beyond the Tropic of Cancer to Cape Blanco where they captured and enslaved twelve men. Dinis Dias rounded Cape Verde

in 1444. Tristão set up a trading post at Arguim from which Lançarote later obtained two hundred slaves before going on to meet his death a little way into the Gambia Valley in 1446. After a hiatus caused by domestic politics, Henry sent more expeditions in 1455–1456 when a Venetian in his service, Alvise de Cadamosto (1432–1480), reached what is now Guinea Bissau and the Cape Verde Islands. Pedro de Sintra reached Sierra Leone in 1456, but by his return Henry was dead.

Enough gold to encourage further efforts had been obtained and Henry's work showed that progress along the African coast was possible; all this was the essential prelude to the great age of discovery that was to follow. There was, however, a negative aspect: Henry's navigators had shown that slaves could be obtained from the West African coast and could be sold profitably in Europe.

The Great Age of Discoveries and Africa, 1460–1600. The period between1460 and 1600 saw Europeans making important discoveries throughout the whole world, including Africa. However, maritime discoveries around the coasts of Africa were not followed up to the extent that comparable discoveries were in Asia and the Americas; the major part of the African interior was to remain unknown.

Portuguese Expeditions: The Route to India. In the century and a half after Prince Henry's death, maritime enterprise continued apace. King Afonso made a contract in 1469 with Fernão Gomes for the exploration of 2,000 miles (3,200 kilometers) of coast over five years. In 1471, Sueiro da Costa reached Axim and Pero de Escolar with João de Santarem reached Elmina on the Gold Coast, thereby paving the way for the fort of São Jorge da Minha of 1482. In 1472, Fernando Po reached the island in the Gulf of Guinea that long bore his name, and three years later, Rui de Sequeira crossed the Equator to reach the vicinity of the Ogowe. Even more extraordinary discoveries were inaugurated by King João II after 1481. Diogo Cão reached as far south as about 22° S at Walvis Bay. He also sailed into the Congo River, possibly seeking a way to Prester John's empire but actually opening up a relationship with the kingdom of Congo from 1482.

Cão's discoveries tend to be overshadowed by the following voyages of Bartholomew Dias. These carried him around the "Cape of Storms," which King João renamed "Good Hope," in 1487–1488 and on as far as the Great Fish River. The king had also sent Pero de Covilhã (c. 1450–1545) to find Prester John's kingdom by traveling south from Egypt along the

Red Sea. In fact, de Covilhã reached India before returning to enter Ethiopia where he was to remain for the rest of his life. His letters home almost certainly encouraged the sending of Vasco da Gama to sail around Africa into the Indian Ocean. The fleet of four ships set off in July 1497. By Christmas, the Cape had been rounded and a landfall made near what is now Durban. Gama sailed on, calling at Quelimane and then Mozambique, where Arab traders proved hostile as they did at Mombasa. But Malindi's ruler furnished a pilot to take the Portuguese on to India. The return voyage in 1499 included visits to Mogadishu and Zanzibar. Further expeditions, essentially ones of conquest, especially Francisco de Almeida's of 1505–1509, soon came and culminated in the building of Fort Jesus at Mombasa in 1593 to seal Portugal's dominance of the East African coast.

Later Portuguese Activity: Contacts with the Interior.
The Portuguese fort at Elmina was soon accompanied by other trading forts in western Africa. Luanda and, later, Benguela were the major centers south of the Congo and there was considerable interaction with neighboring African polities, especially the kingdom of Congo. Yet little was learned about the farther interior perhaps because Africans brought goods to the coast readily enough and there were always ample supplies of slaves for Brazil. On the eastern side of the continent the story was slightly different. Although most of the captured cities were essentially on the western margin of the Indian Ocean rather than integral parts of Africa, there was a major exception—Sofala, which was in contact with gold-producing areas on the interior plateau under the control of the Rozwi group of the Karanga Bantu and their ruler, the "Monomotapa." As early as 1511 Antonio Fernandes was sent inland to establish contacts and get direct access to the gold; he probably reached as far as present-day Mashonaland. Much exaggerated accounts of the Monomotapa's wealth began to circulate although his empire was in decline and gold production low. Intermittent contacts continued and attempts were made to carry Christianity inland, notably by the Jesuit Gonçalo da Silveira in 1560–1561. His martyrdom led to the dispatch of Francisco Barreto's military expedition, which came to an inglorious end in 1573. In fact, the Portuguese were never powerful enough to exert control so far into the interior even if some of the rulers became nominal Christians. Sena and Tete on the Zambesi did hold on and enough knowledge was garnered for João dos Santos to write a full account of the region but one whose geographical details were rather imprecise. South of the Zambesi the only information accruing came from the accounts of shipwrecked sailors who learned something of the Natal coast but no systematic descriptions emerged.

Ethiopia.
Pero de Covilhã was still alive in 1520 when a new Portuguese mission led by Rodrigo da Lima and Francisco Alvares arrived in Ethiopia in response to calls for help to repel encroaching Muslims. Little geographical work resulted although Alvares wrote an entertaining book about Prester John. A major military expedition under Christoph da Gama followed in 1541. He penetrated south from Massawa but was killed in battle. Nevertheless, Portuguese contact with Ethiopia was maintained into the next century.

Leo Africanus 1494–1552.
Despite the dominance achieved by Portugal during the great age of discoveries, its instinct to maintain secrecy meant that the knowledge of Africa that it had accumulated was not always widely dispersed. Oddly, therefore, the most comprehensive account of Africa to emerge in the sixteenth century was written by a Moor drawing on his own experiences and Arab sources. Born in Granada, educated in Fez, and captured by Christian pirates in 1518, Leo Africanus was freed by Pope Leo X, who encouraged him to write his *Description of Africa*. He had crossed the Sahara to reach the Niger and visit Songhai, Gao, the Hausa kingdoms, and Bornu and had gained a great knowledge of Arab geographical learning. Appearing in Italian in 1526 and translated into English in 1600, the *Description* remained a key source of information until about 1800. Unfortunately and inexplicably, it left a legacy of confusion about one key issue: Leo Africanus repeated Ibn Battuta's idea that the Niger flowed westward.

The Legacy of the Age of Discoveries.
By 1600, Portugal's near monopoly of European contact with Africa was coming to an end. French, English, Dutch, and Brandenburg traders competed for slaves in West Africa. In East Africa, Portugal had never entirely overcome Arabian and Asian competitors, and other Europeans would soon become new rivals in the Indian Ocean. Portugal, a military and ecclesiastical power not yet embracing active capitalism, could not compete in a mercantilist world. Yet the rival forces made no significant contributions to discovery in Africa. One of the paradoxical results of the great age of discoveries was that once Dias had rounded the Cape of Good Hope, the chief focus of European interest became Asia; Africa was more a barrier than a destination. Meanwhile, the opening up of the Americas was not only another rival focus but also a

reason for the burgeoning slave trade. Europeans need go no farther than their coastal forts to get slaves. For all these reasons, there was as yet little reason to break through the barriers between coast and interior and learn about the heart of the continent.

Seventeenth and Early Eighteenth Centuries. The comparative neglect of Africa by Europeans continued well into the eighteenth century, even if a great many books and maps were published. *Paradise Lost* displays John Milton's enormous knowledge of African geography as it was then known from his "less maritime kings" of East Africa to the supposed site of Paradise. Maps like those of Ortelius showed Ptolemaic knowledge modified only to some small degree by Portuguese information.

Western Africa. As the slave trade proceeded, knowledge of the coastal areas of western Africa was refined. Richard Jobson's *Golden Trade* (1623) and Jean Barbot's extensive writings, first published in English in 1732, are examples of notable works on West Africa proper. Farther south, the Portuguese hold on the Congo and Angola coast remained tenuous as embroilment in African war and politics proved often a losing game, while, for a time, the Dutch took over Luanda and Benguela. The one significant Portuguese attempt to penetrate the interior came in 1608 when Rebelo de Aragão reached about 400 miles (644 kilometers) inland.

South Africa. The Portuguese had always neglected South Africa, but in 1652 the Dutch East India Company established a post at the Cape of Good Hope as a refreshment stop for India-bound ships. Settlers, especially the *trekboers* (wandering cattle farmers), did begin to penetrate inland, but these half-Africanized pastoralists were neither literate nor knowledgeable enough to make any significant contribution to formal geographical knowledge.

Eastern Africa. On the East African coast, Portuguese power weakened, especially after Arabs from Oman captured Fort Jesus in 1699. A hold was maintained south of Cape Delgado but attempts to control the Monomotapas or convert their peoples had completely failed by the 1690s. The handful of settlers, or *prazeros*, along the Zambesi became Africanized and paid little attention to Portuguese orders. Only two journeys of significance are recorded. In 1616, Gaspar Bocarro traveled from Tete on the Zambesi overland to Kilwa passing "a lake which looks like the sea." Whether this was actually Lake Malawi has been disputed but a lake in roughly the right position did begin to appear on maps. In 1643,

Sisnado Dias Bayao pushed into what is now Matabeleland but information on this expedition is even less available than for Bocarro's.

Ethiopia was the other area of significant penetration. The Jesuit presence was reinforced by the learned, prudent, and adventurous Pedro Paez (1564–1622) who reached the capital, Gondar, in 1604 and established that Lake Tana was the source of the Blue Nile in 1618. This was confirmed by Jeronimo Lobo in 1628. Yet the most remarkable journey was that of Antonio Fernandes in 1613 when he traveled south along the Great Rift Valley to Lake Ziwa at about 12° N. However, the Jesuits were expelled in 1633 and there were few other visitors until 1770. The main publication on Ethiopia, that by Jacob Ludolf, of 1681, was more a compilation of earlier knowledge than of new. Even the discovery of the Blue Nile source was not widely known in Europe. [See color plates 1 and 2 in this volume.]

Age of Scientific Exploration, c. 1770–1840. A new era in the exploration of Africa began toward the end of the eighteenth century as a result of changes in Europe's material and intellectual attitudes. Intellectually, there came to be a desire for precise and accurate knowledge to replace the myths and vague reports, especially the ones about the heart of the continent; it was recognized that even classical knowledge might be superseded. Places must be given latitudes and longitudes, rivers' courses traced from source to mouth, flora and fauna classified, and the true political and social condition of inhabitants described. Maps most clearly demonstrate the changes as cartographers, led by J. B. d'Anville (1697–1782), began to use mathematical techniques and to rid their African maps of poorly authenticated data so leaving a space entirely blank except for the words "tout à fait inconnue." To be sure, the desire for scientific knowledge was not entirely disinterested. Although the increased economic prosperity of Europe made it possible to satisfy curiosity, it also created the need for an expansion of markets. Another factor was a growing feeling among many groups that a new type of "legitimate" trade must develop to replace the purely extractive and immoral slave trade. Political imperatives also had their impact: international rivalries, most notably a succession of wars between Britain and France, could lead to explorers competing for primacy in Africa.

African developments began to have more significance as more European visitors arrived. The Islamic jihads in the Western Sudan, the "Great Trek" of the Boers and the "scattering" of the Nguni peoples in South Africa, and the penetration of East Africa by Arab and Swahili coast men are only the most obvious examples of African changes that were to affect the process of exploration.

The downside of the new situation was that Europe came to know or think it knew Africa and Africans better than Africans themselves. In some respects this was true, but it had the unfortunate effect of reinforcing ideas of superiority—technical, social, and moral. Some explorers undoubtedly helped to create the gulf.

Maritime Activity: Captain Owen. Although from 1750 the emphasis switched to landward exploration in Africa; increased European attention meant more shipping and a need for better coastal charts. The British Admiralty sent Captain W. F. Owen to carry out a long and detailed survey of the coasts in 1822–1826. Although the officers made some limited forays inland, the essential results were good hydrographical charts.

West Africa: The Western Sudanic Kingdoms and the Problem of the Niger, 1788–1841. The new era in exploration was most clearly signaled by the founding in 1788 of the African Association, dominated by Joseph Banks and with James Rennell as its leading geographer. The focus for the African Association was the Western Sudan. Their first two expeditions were sent from the north but one traveler died in Cairo and another in Fezzan. Perhaps it would be better to avoid the desert with its jealous and suspicious traders and approach from the coast at Senegal or the Gambia. Daniel Houghton was sent to use this means of reaching Timbuctoo and the Hausa kingdoms. He died when he was 400 miles (644 kilometers) inland, but his example encouraged the dispatch of the African Association's most famous explorer, Mungo Park. Very much an Enlightenment figure, Park did much more to illumine Africa than simply show in 1796 that the Niger did flow eastward, although he is chiefly remembered for this. He confirmed that there were well-organized societies in the interior with which it was worth establishing contact. Meanwhile, W. G. Browne had visited Darfur in 1793–1796 and Friedrich Hornemann got himself from Cairo to Murzuk and on to Bornu in the years 1798–1801. Although he died and his records were lost, he, Park, and Browne had made it clear that expeditions to the interior could succeed. The British government, persuaded that important markets might be found and that possible French activity must be forestalled, now took over the organization of exploration and sent Park back to the Niger in 1805–1806 to find his way down to wherever its end was—a matter that had become

one of intense speculation and debate. Park died at Bussa in 1806 but his fate was a mystery for twenty-five years.

Strategic and economic factors ensured continued British support for exploration in West Africa while the ending of the British slave trade in 1807 gave reasons for finding opportunities for legitimate trade. Scholarly and more general interest aroused by the Niger problem and Park's fate further encouraged initiatives. Meanwhile, in West Africa itself, the jihad of Uthman dan Fodio and his son Mohammed Bello created a new and confident Islamic power, the "Fulani Empire" centered on Sokoto, but also tensions with other states, notably Bornu. In 1826, Alexander Gordon Laing (1793–1826) reached the almost fabled city of Timbuctoo only to be murdered, and it was a French explorer, René Caillié, who two years later got there from Freetown and went on northward over the desert to return to Paris and collect a ten-thousand-franc prize. More important was the British expedition sent from Tripoli in 1822. In the next four years, Walter Oudney, Dixon Denham, and Hugh Clapperton explored Lake Chad, Bornu, and Bello's new Fulani sultanate. Almost immediately after reaching home, Clapperton agreed to return to Sokoto but on this occasion penetrated from the Guinea coast at Badagry. He learned of Park's fate at Bussa and continued across the Niger to Sokoto. Here, however, his dispute with Bornu made Bello more suspicious and unhelpful than before, and Clapperton left a disappointed man and died shortly afterward. His servant Richard Lander, returned home with Clapperton's reports. He himself was soon sent back to confirm in 1830 what had now become obvious—that the Niger flowed into the Gulf of Guinea. However, the discovery of an apparent water route to the interior was misleading: Lander was to die in one attempted follow-up while even more sailors and missionaries were to succumb to malaria and other diseases on the ambitious British Niger expedition of 1841. European explorers had penetrated to the heart of West Africa but the desert barriers in the north and the disease barriers to the south were still in place.

The Congo and Portuguese-Influenced Africa, c. 1770–1840. When it was still thought that the Niger might connect with the Congo, J. H. Tuckey was sent in 1816 to repeat Cão's attempt of 334 years before but with the aid of a steamboat now used in Africa for the very first time. It was a complete failure. Tuckey and many of his men died.

Farther south, Portuguese settlements remained on both coasts of the continent and were for the most part moribund and unhealthily dependent on the slave trade. Nevertheless, the Enlightenment did have some impact, most importantly on Dr. Francisco de Lacerda (1753–1798), a skilled observer who led an expedition from Sena on the Zambesi aiming to cross the continent and so forge a linkup with his compatriots on the west coast, which would frustrate any British push north from Capetown. Lacerda died in October 1798 having reached the Cazembe's kingdom near Lake Mweru. The wish for an east-west link prompted a bit later the sending of two half-African traders, Pedro Batista and Amaro José, from Cassange in Angola to Tete on the Zambesi in the years 1806–1812. Then in 1831–1832 Majors José Monteiro and António Gamitto repeated Lacerda's journey but could get no farther. Among these travelers, only Lacerda was capable of scientific description, although the 1830 journey produced valuable information. Unfortunately, these travels remained largely unknown outside Portugal.

Southern Africa, c. 1770–1849. Lacerda's fear of rivals pressing northward from Capetown was well-founded. The desire for scientific exploration was easier to gratify in the nonmalarial south than in tropical Africa. Botanical exploration inspired by Linnaeus was especially evident. Karl Thunberg (1742–1828) spent 1772–1775 botanizing in South Africa and in 1776 Anders Sparrman reached almost as far north as the Orange River in his search for plants new to science. Robert Gordon and William Paterson were also plant collectors who reached the Orange and followed it to its mouth in 1779. By 1795, when the British captured Capetown from the Dutch East India Company, the whole area south of the Orange River was reasonably well known. Britain gave up the Cape in 1803 but took over permanently again in 1806. New influences made better knowledge imperative. The restlessness of the Boer pastoralists, their dislike of British moves to ameliorate conditions for slaves and then in 1833 free them, wars with the Bantu to the east and the rise of Zulu power in the 1820s, and the desire of the London Missionary Society (LMS) pastors to evangelize to the north were among factors that meant trouble or disorder beyond the colony's boundaries. William Burchell continued the tradition of scholarly scientific study with his travels of 1811–1815 across the Orange River into what is now Botswana. LMS missionaries wished to move beyond the areas of Boer activity and John Campbell went farther than Burchell to reach the sources of the Limpopo in 1820. Robert Moffat of the LMS established a base among the Tswana at Kuruman from which he made various forays from

1820 to the 1860s, one as far north as what is now Zimbabwe in the 1850s. The way was being prepared for Moffat's illustrious son-in-law, David Livingstone.

East Africa, Ethiopia, and Northeast Africa, c. 1770–1845. Along the largely Omani-controlled coast north of Cape Delgado, Arabs, backed by Indian financiers, increased their demands for ivory and slaves. By the 1820s European and American as well as Asian traders frequented Zanzibar and Arab traders began to go inland instead of relying on Africans to come to the coast. But their information was little known and, as yet, there were no journeys of scientific exploration, with one attempt by Lieutenant Maizan of the French navy resulting in his murder in 1845.

Ethiopia, almost completely closed to visitors after 1633, was visited and made famous, or notorious, by the colorful James Bruce. Despite his bombast, he was a scientific explorer as well as a fascinating recorder of a turbulent period of Ethiopia's history. His visiting the source of the Blue Nile and following it down to its confluence with the White Nile in 1772 was a major achievement. Ethiopia and the northeast generally now became a focus of strategic interest to both Britain and France. But Napoleon's great expedition to Egypt in 1798 was scientific and archaeological as well as military. Henry Salt, secretary to Lord Valentia's mission and British consul in Egypt, sent more travelers into Ethiopia and wrote much on the region in 1805. The African Association staged a revival in the 1820s and began to take up the question Bruce had left unanswered—where was the source of the White Nile? Linant de Bellefonds reached beyond the confluence of the two rivers in 1828 but was forced to turn back; a major problem remained to be tackled. Meanwhile, important geographical investigations in Ethiopia were undertaken in the 1830s and 1840s by the formidably scientific Antoine d'Abbadie and the argumentative Charles Beke, while both Roman Catholic and Protestant missionaries became active in the country. Among the latter, Johann Ludwig Krapf (who was later to move south to Mombasa) was notable for his geographical interests. The Bombay presidency sent W. C. Harris on an official mission in 1844 and his book helped to generate interest in Shoa and areas even farther south of Ethiopia proper.

Second Great Age of African Discovery, c. 1840–1876. During the middle decades of the nineteenth century, the central areas of Africa were at last to be traversed and described in considerable detail.

Within little more than twenty-five years, a group of outstanding travelers achieved more than had been managed in the previous five hundred. They succeeded because they were backed directly or indirectly by an increasingly powerful set of European governments and geographical societies keen to obtain scientific information. One may argue about the extent to which economic interest or political imperative lay behind the science but one new and obvious feature was the way the explorers attracted popular attention by their exploits. This was partly because of the adventure element in the travel literature involving, it seemed, wild animals, "savage tribes," and formidable physical obstacles. But more serious questions of public policy were raised by the explorers. Could the lakes they found be navigated by steamboats carrying trade goods; what was to be done about the slave trade; could Africans be taught the Gospel of Christianity; what, indeed, was to be the relationship of Africa to the outside world? Such questions became acute after 1876 but were implicit as the explorers sought the truth about the interior.

West and Northwest Africa. Although West Africa was not the focus of such intense interest as it had been during the era of the Niger controversy, much remained to be done. The region of the upper and middle Niger valley remained the prize but so did doubt about which of the desert routes, the Senegal Valley, or the coast ports near the Niger estuary were the best means of ingress. A British government expedition of 1849–1855, consisting of James Richardson and the two Germans Heinrich Barth and Adolf Overweg, was sent from Tripoli to explore, promote legitimate trade, and frustrate French ambitions in the Niger, Benue, and Lake Chad region. Richardson and Overweg both died but Barth emerged as one of the century's greatest scholar-travelers. Having showed that the Benue drainage was distinct from Lake Chad, he moved west to Timbuctoo, making treaties and amassing detailed data on the Islamic societies of this vast region. Gerhard Rohlfs made several journeys in the Sahara from 1862 and then in 1865–1867 crossed from Tripoli to the coast near Lagos. In 1869, a third distinguished German explorer, Gustav Nachtigal, traveled from Tripoli to Bornu and then went eastward through Darfur to the Nile and Egypt. Hence, by the end of this period, West Africa from the Mediterranean to the Guinea coast was reasonably well known.

The Central Belt of Africa. During this period of discovery, the most intense interest was focused on the interior of Africa in the equatorial latitudes as its lakes and rivers were revealed. Broadly speaking,

successive explorers attempted to reach the central areas from the west coast, from South Africa, from the east coast, or by going up the Nile.

In the west, travelers from the Portuguese settlements made some notable forays into the interior. Ladislaus Magyar and Silva Porto both reached the upper Zambesi in the 1850s before Livingstone, but both had their efforts overshadowed (and unfairly ignored) by Livingstone. Paul du Chaillu in 1855–1859 and 1863–1865 made journeys in the Ogowe River region but he mixed fact and fantasy to such an extent that many of his stories were disbelieved. Yet he did see gorillas and did meet Pygmy peoples. In terms of their ultimate political importance, the most significant ventures were made by Pierre Savorgnan de Brazza and Alfred Marche as they tried to use the Ogowe Valley as a possible route to the far interior in 1875.

The story of expeditions into the central area from the south is dominated by the work of David Livingstone. His discovery of Lake Ngami in 1849 and then gaining the Zambesi Valley was the prelude to his great transcontinental journey of 1852–1856, which took him first to the west coast and then, via the Victoria Falls, eastward to the mouth of the Zambesi. This has been regarded as one of the two or three major exploratory feats of the nineteenth century. The river, Livingstone suggested, could become the highway into the interior, and the British government agreed, despite unhappy Niger experiences, to fund the ambitious Zambezi Expedition of 1858–1864. Whatever its other failures, the expedition did put the Shire Valley and Lake Malawi accurately on the map.

At the same time as Livingstone's exploits along the Zambesi Valley were being accomplished, very significant discoveries were being made rather farther north as a result of expeditions from the east coast. Taking advantage of African-developed routes now used by Arab "caravans" and of British domination of Zanzibar, travelers began to go inland. The missionaries Krapf and Johannes Rebmann had started the process in 1848–1849 with sightings of the snow-covered mountains, Kilimanjaro and Kenya, and some confused hearsay about waters farther into the interior which one of their companions, Erhardt, reported as one monster slug-shaped lake. The Royal Geographical Society (RGS) sent a series of missions to the East African lakes. Richard Burton and John Hanning Speke reached Lake Tanganyika in 1857 and, in the following year, Speke alone reached the southern end of the lake he named Victoria. Then Speke, now accompanied by James Augustus Grant, examined more of the lake and reached the kingdom of Buganda before Speke alone visited the spot where the Nile flows out of the lake at the Ripon Falls. The date was July 28, 1862. Some said Speke had not proved the stream was the Nile and when, coming from the north up the Nile, Samuel Baker found Lake Albert, others now said there must be sources more remote than Speke's Ripon Falls. Controversy continued for some twelve years or more. Meanwhile, in 1861–1865, Baron Karl Claus von der Decken visited Kilimanjaro, proved there was snow, which some commentators had refused to believe, and then went on to explore the Juba River Valley. He was murdered at Bardera.

Livingstone now began what was to prove his final journey. Lasting from 1866 to 1873, it became an obsessional attempt to solve the question of the Nile's source. In fact, he was working on the upper waters of the Congo when exploring around Lakes Mweru and Bangweulu. In 1873 Cameron, sent by the RGS on the last of several expeditions seeking news of Livingstone, met only his corpse being carried to the coast by his remaining porters. Cameron went on to explore Lake Tanganyika more thoroughly than anyone had done before and then continued across the continent. This remarkable achievement had a great impact on the thinking of King Leopold II. Two years before Cameron, Henry Stanley had made a reputation and a journalistic "scoop" by meeting Livingstone at Ujiji in October 1871. He now became an explorer in his own right, extremely competent but also ruthless. His great journey of 1874–1877 ranks with Livingstone's of twenty years before. First he proved that Speke was right about Lake Victoria and its outlet. He solved various other puzzles, the most notable of which was the precise course of the Congo from its upper waters to the sea.

By the time of Stanley's journey, attempts were being made to reach the lakes region from the north via the Nile itself under the aegis of the khedive of Egypt who hoped thus to remedy the indebtedness of his domain. After his 1864 journey, Baker seemed the obvious man to establish Egyptian authority; he led an expedition from 1869 to 1873, made himself a fortune, but exaggerated his actual achievements. Charles Gordon was the next to be appointed "Governor of Equatoria" followed by Emin Pasha. They and their lieutenants accomplished a considerable amount of more detailed exploration in the Upper Nile region with Chaillé Long, for example, visiting Lake Kyoga and proving that Speke's Nile really did link up with the stream north from Lake Albert.

Meanwhile, two Russo-German explorers separately accomplished remarkable scientific journeys in the areas west of the Upper Nile. Georg Schweinfurth between 1868 and 1871 reached the Welle River and encountered Pygmy peoples. Wilhelm Junker was in the same region from 1879 to 1886 exploring Bahr-el Ghazel and the Nile-Congo watershed area before entering the Lake Albert area, where he met Emin Pasha with consequences that were important less for scientific exploration than for European imperial moves.

From the Brussels Geographical Conference to Imperialism and Colonial Rule. The Brussels Geographical Conference of 1876 marks a watershed in the story of the exploration of Africa. Although some basic exploration remained to be done, henceforward there was to be much greater emphasis on objects beyond the avowedly scientific. Africa was to be "redeemed" in one way or another as various groups acted on the lessons apparently learned from the explorers. Very soon, the international cooperation envisaged at Brussels was transformed via "national committees" into international rivalry to establish spheres of interest, protectorates, and colonies. Attempts were made at the Berlin Conference of 1884–1885 to halt this process and maintain a "fair field" for all in Africa but it failed and in another ten years nearly all the continent had been parceled out between European powers.

Initially, after 1876, the emphasis was on establishing viable routes to the interior lake regions. Hence Brazza further explored the Ogowe but emerged on the north bank of the Congo where he clashed with Stanley now working to establish for Leopold the Congo as a way inland for the "Congo Free State." On the other side of the continent, the RGS sent Keith Johnston and Joseph Thomson to find a good route from the coast to Lake Malawi and then on to Lake Tanganyika. Having accomplished this after the death of Johnston, Thomson was to pioneer the route from Mombasa through Maasailand to Lake Victoria in 1883–1885. Lake Turkana (Rudolf), the remaining unvisited large Rift Valley lake, was reached by Teleki and Von Höhnel in 1888.

Numerous other expeditions made for the great lakes, some organized by "national committees" responding to Leopold and not a few others by missionary societies. Alexander Mackay of the CMS who went to Buganda and Edward Hore of the LMS who worked around Lake Tangayika are examples of missionaries who carried out geographical work of some importance. One or two intrepid lady travelers now appeared. Most significant as a scientific explorer was the admirable Mary Kingsley in the Gabon region in 1893 and 1894–1895, while May French Sheldon explored parts of eastern Kenya in 1891.

The Portuguese responded to the challenge of Leopold with the expedition of Serpa Pinto in 1877–1879 from Benguela via the Victoria Falls to Natal while Lieutenants Capello and Ivens explored the upper reaches of the Cuango River. The two men then crossed Africa in a vain effort to achieve the long-desired link from Benguela to Mozambique. Serpa Pinto restored Portuguese pride but the veteran Silva Porto committed suicide in 1890 in despair at Portugal's supercession in Africa by other powers.

Besides Brazza, France had active explorers such as Giraud who reached Lake Bangweulu in 1884, but the principal efforts were in West Africa where military expeditions from Senegal sought to bring the upper Niger under French hegemony. Louis Binger reached the same goal from the south via the Volga Basin in 1887–1889. Some ten years later, Jean-Baptiste Marchand made an expedition from France's equatorial colonies to the Nile at Fashoda, which was exploratory as well as imperialistic. German and Austrian travelers became extremely active in response to the Brussels Conference. Hermann von Wissmann crossed the continent from Luanda to Zanzibar in 1881–1882 and repeated the feat in 1886. Oscar Lenz visited the Lower Ogowe and then Timbuctoo before, on his third expedition, he, too, crossed the continent from the Congo to the Zambesi in 1885–1887. Less geographically significant but politically explosive were the two expeditions of Karl Peters. In 1884, he set off the "scramble" in East Africa by treaty making in what is now Tanzania and then in 1890 provoked British antagonism by trying to annex Buganda.

The expedition in these years that was at once the most geographically significant and the most politically influential was Stanley's Emin Pasha Relief Expedition of 1886–1889. This remarkable and controversial affair was designed ostensibly to take relief to Emin Pasha who was, as Junker reported, still in the Upper Nile region and cut off from Egypt by the Mahdist revolt. Here was "Equatoria," apparently a ready-made bit of empire, which Leopold hoped Emin Pasha could be persuaded to attach to his Congo Free State while some British groups wanted it for "British East Africa." By going up the Congo and then cutting his way through the jungle to Lake Albert, Stanley accomplished a great feat of primary exploration. Arthur Jermy Mounteney Jephson, with Stanley, revealed the existence of a new set of snow mountains in the shape of Ruwenzori. Politically, Leopold got a temporary foothold on the Nile but Uganda became a British sphere in 1890 when Britain and Germany made an agreement.

Other scientific cum imperial expeditions were similarly rendered irrelevant politically by agreements made in Europe. Nevertheless, exploration did continue, if only to establish where boundaries arbitrarily drawn on maps in Europe actually were on the ground. As European administrations were established in the 1890s–1920s period, officials had to undertake what, in effect, were exploratory "tours" to learn about their territories. Meanwhile, certain prominent features were further explored as when Halford Mackinder made the first ascent of Mount Kenya in 1899 and the Duc d'Abruzzi scaled Ruwenzori's twin peaks in 1906.

By 1903 the first motor car was in Uganda and several railways linked coast and interior often along routes first pioneered by the explorers. A new age had dawned in which, for fifty years or more, Africa was dominated by Europe. The two-thousand-year period of exploration traced here was, in fact, the long, slow prelude to Africa's inclusion in a globalized world. The accelerations of exploration in the sixteenth century and the nineteenth century were the most significant episodes in the building up of a knowledge of the continent as a part of its incorporation in the wider world. The consequences of that process for Africans are still being worked out and the context in which that process happens is very much conditioned by the picture that the explorers presented of Africa and its peoples.

[*See also* African Association; Brussels Geographical Conference; Chad, Lake; East African Lakes; Expeditions, World Exploration; Fictitious and Fantastic Places; Ibn Battuta; Niger River; Nile River; Royal Geographical Society; Sahara; Timbuctoo; Zanzibar; *and biographical entries on figures mentioned in this article.*]

BIBLIOGRAPHY

Axelson, Eric. *Congo to Cape. Early Portuguese Explorers*. Edited by G. Woodcock. London: Faber, 1973.

Axelson, Eric. *The Portuguese in South-East Africa, 1600–1700*. Johannesburg: Witwatersrand University Press, 1960.

Boahen, A. Adu. *Britain, the Sahara and the Western Sudan, 1788–1861*. Oxford: Clarendon Press, 1964.

Boxer, Charles R. *The Portuguese Seaborne Empire 1415–1825*. London: Hutchinson, 1969.

Bridges, Roy. "Towards the Prelude to the Partition of East Africa." *In Imperialism, Decolonization, and Africa*, edited by Roy Bridges, 65–113. Houndmills, U.K.: Macmillan; New York: St. Martin's Press, 2000.

Bridges, Roy C. "The Historical Role of British Explorers in East Africa." *Terrae Incognitae* 14 (1982): 1–12.

Buisseret, David. *The Mapmakers' Quest: Depicting New Worlds in Renaissance Europe.* Oxford and New York: Oxford University Press, 2003.

Cary, Max, and E. H. Warmington. *The Ancient Explorers.* London: Methuen, 1929. Rev. ed. Harmondsworth, U.K.: Penguin Books, 1963.

Curtin, Philip D. *The Image of Africa: British Ideas and Action, 1780–1850.* Madison: University of Wisconsin Press; London: Macmillan, 1965.

Diffie, Bailey W., and George D. Winius. *Foundations of the Portuguese Empire 1415–1580.* Minneapolis: University of Minnesota Press, 1977.

Duyvendak, J. J. L. *China's Discovery of Africa.* London: A. Probsthain, 1949.

Filesi, Teobaldo. *China and Africa in the Middle Ages.* Translated by David L. Morison. London: Cass, 1972.

Hall, Richard. *Empires of the Monsoon: A History of the Indian Ocean and Its Invaders.* London: HarperCollins, 1996.

Hallett, Robin. *The Penetration of Africa: European Enterprise and Exploration Principally in Northern and Western Africa up to 1830.* London: Routledge and Kegan Paul; New York: Praeger, 1965.

Moorehead, Alan. *The White Nile.* London: Hamish Hamilton; New York: Harper, 1960.

Relaño, Francesc. "Paradise in Africa: The History of a Geographical Myth from its Origins in Medieval Thought to its Gradual Demise in Early Modern Europe." *Terrae Incognitae* 36 (2004): 1–11.

Relaño, Francesc. *The Shaping of Africa. Cosmographic Discourse and Cartographic Science in Late Medieval and Early Modern Europe.* Aldershot, U.K.: Ashgate, 2002.

Rotberg, Robert I., ed. *Africa and its Explorers: Motives, Methods and Impact.* Cambridge, Mass.: Harvard University Press, 1970.

Stone, Jeffrey C. *A Short History of the Cartography of Africa.* Lewiston, N.Y.: Edward Mellen, 1995.

Strandes, Justus. *The Portuguese Period in East Africa.* Translated by Jean Wallwork. Edited with notes by J. S. Kirkman. Nairobi: East African Literature Bureau, 1961.

Thomson, J. Oliver. *History of Ancient Geography.* Cambridge, U.K.: Cambridge University Press, 1948.

Ure, John. *Prince Henry the Navigator.* London: Constable, 1977.

Vogt, John. *Portuguese Rule on the Gold Coast 1469–1682.* Athens: University of Georgia Press, 1979.

ROY BRIDGES

Geographical Barriers to Exploration

It has often been asserted that various geographical factors explain the difficulties that outsiders seem to have had in penetrating the continent of Africa. Certainly it was not until almost the end of the nineteenth century that even the most basic features of many parts of the interior of Africa could be put on maps. Still, to ask why it was that explorers, traders, missionaries, and road or rail builders could not get into Africa may be to pose the question wrongly; in fact, they did get into Africa when they really wanted to. Moreover, as the slave trade testified, Africans could move or be moved out of the continent in large numbers. Perhaps the real question is why it was that outsiders with technological skills—including skill in mapmaking—superior to those of most of the indigenous peoples found it difficult to deploy their technology effectively, especially at any distance from the coasts.

Position, Size, Shape, and Wind Regimes. Africa juts out from the Eurasian landmass and is readily accessible from other landmasses only along its northern coast. As some societies developed long-distance sea transport, eastern Africa became open to traffic from Arabia and India, but the wind regimes to the west of the continent are less favorable to sailing ships than the Indian Ocean trade winds, and European mariners found difficulty in sailing south of the Equator along the coast, or back northward if they had reached that far. Africa became a barrier, with ships more readily reaching the Cape of Good Hope from far out in the Atlantic and then proceeding to Asia by going east of Madagascar. More important than position, however, are size and shape. The area of Africa including Madagascar is reckoned to be about 11.7 million square miles. Yet the coastline is only some 16,000 miles long: this means there are few major inlets and indentations to furnish natural harbors, but the principal consequence is that a very high proportion of the continent is a long way from any access to the sea; the contrast with Europe, which has an area of 3.75 million square miles but a coastline of about 20,000 miles, can hardly be more apparent.

Geomorphology, Relief, and Drainage. Most of Africa's interior is an ancient erosion surface dating from the period when Africa was not a separate continent but rather part of Gondwanaland. This surface breaks sharply to a series of younger, lower, and narrower surfaces near the coast. Drainage on the slightly warped main plateau tends to be indeterminate or broken by the Great Rift Valley—hence many of the difficulties that explorers had in determining river courses. More significantly, rivers that reach the coast are marked by waterfalls and rapids at the discontinuities between the erosion surfaces. Only the Nile is navigable for any distance inland, although the Niger and the Zaire can be navigated for long stretches of their middle and upper courses. In any case, very few large rivers actually reach the sea; there are only five major river basins, and more than half of Africa's drainage does not reach the sea at all. Thus, by and large, the opportunities offered by African river valleys as routes inland are few, and the routes themselves difficult.

Climate, Vegetation, and Disease. Access to Africa from the sea is further inhibited by the fact that large stretches of coastline border deserts. Europeans long assumed that nearly all of the interior of the continent was "burning deserts." The Sahara, however, was traversable, if not easily, and afforded the only means of reaching tropical Africa from the north until the fifteenth century, and a fair amount of geographical information was brought back. During the nineteenth century, "burning deserts" were replaced by "impenetrable jungles" in European mythology. Parts of the Zaire Basin may indeed be dense equatorial forest, but most of Africa from the Tropic of Capricorn south is savannah. The idea of "fever-ridden swamps" near the coast being a barrier has slightly more validity than the ideas of deserts or jungle, but the implication that the problem is the climate is false. The real point is that certain kinds of insects that carry parasites causing diseases in men and animals tend to flourish in Africa. Malaria, blackwater fever, and sleeping sickness affect humans, while draft animals, including camels, bullocks, and horses, are also subject to a form of sleeping sickness. Indigenous zebras or elephants have never been successfully domesticated. Until the advent of modern medicines and prophylactics, these diseases were a real barrier to the penetration of Africa by outsiders who had no built-in immunity.

The People. It used to be alleged that African peoples rejected and repulsed outsiders. Historically speaking, this generalization simply cannot be maintained; African societies regularly interacted and traded with outsiders, naturally insisting on doing so on their own terms. Equally incorrect is the still prevalent idea that conditions in Africa were unsettled by constant "tribal wars." What perhaps can be said is that, if one examines the migrations, conquests, and state building of African peoples, it does appear that development tended to be along interior lines and was rarely oriented toward the sea. This in itself, of course, may be attributed to some of the inhibiting geographical factors already mentioned. If, indeed, access to the sea was of little importance, it follows that ingress by outsiders was not made possible by established lines of communication. Arguably, this basic situation did not change until the

growth of the Atlantic and Indian Ocean systems of trade had begun, by 1800, to create the need for contacts with the coast. Even then, the situation changed only slowly, and it was not until another hundred years had passed that even the most basic facts about Africa's interior had become known to European geographical science.

[*See also* Sahara.]

BIBLIOGRAPHY
Aryeetey-Attoh, Samuel. *Geography of Sub-Saharan Africa.* 2nd ed. New York: Prentice Hall, 2003.

ROY BRIDGES

Indigenous Porters and Guides

Travelers who came from the outside world to explore Africa were successful in achieving their objectives, it can be argued, to the extent that they were able to recruit reliable guides and porters. In fact, indigenous guides and porters played a vital part in exploration but they are usually known by no more than name, if even that. Those that emerge in the historical record almost always do so through unreliable testimonies that are very rarely their own. The example of those men who were with David Livingstone at his death shows that Chuma and Susi were applauded by Europeans because they could be described as embodying the virtues of faithful and uncomplaining service to their saintly leader. Jacob Wainwright, on the other hand, who could read and write and showed considerable initiative and independence of mind, did not conform to the stereotype and was discredited and treated with disdain (although he had not been treated thus by Livingstone himself).

Travelers often found their followers troublesome and would have preferred to do without porters and guides. Yet explorers who lacked local help were rarely successful. Walking alone made one no better than a beggar, as Mungo Park discovered. To some extent, trek wagons in South Africa could insulate the traveler from depending on those around him but one still needed drivers and guides, as one did with the caravan of camels across the Sahara. Even in the era of steamboats, when theoretically one should have been able to penetrate along waterways untroubled by the need for guides or carriers, stops had to be made for fuel and food. In most cases, in fact, neither animals nor boats could obviate the need for human porters. The "caravan" of people could be several hundred strong for a major expedition. It must include servants to cook and care for the explorer himself, bearers to carry his tents, medicines, scientific instruments, and other paraphernalia and yet others to carry the trade goods that would pay for food or provide presents for those controlling territory through which the traveler wished to pass. However, more than carrying power was required: the simple problem of the existence of a variety of languages meant interpreters were needed. The interpreter or some other figure must also explain local custom or judge to whom it was desirable to give presents.

How were these varying needs met? Some travelers tried to take fellow outsiders to manage the porters and the diplomacy but this was rarely efficacious; local knowledge and local contacts were essential. In 1869, for example, Nachtigal found his Piedmontese assistant more a hindrance than a help and came to rely on one Bui Mohammed who knew the peoples of the Western Sudan. Guides like Bui Mohammed tended to be those who had traveled in the course of trading activities. Arabs from North Africa who had been across the Sahara, or Omanis resident in Zanzibar who had been into the interior of East Africa were frequently employed by European travelers. In fact, the major European exploratory expeditions into East Africa in the nineteenth century were modeled for their organization on the Zanzibar Arab expeditions into the interior for ivory and slaves. In West Africa, the "landlord and stranger" system could be adapted to the needs of the traveler; the landlord made himself responsible for providing guides and porters. Local Africans who had traveling experience might become caravan leaders and guides. Krapf relied on the Akamba chief and ivory trader Kivoi, whose death effectively ended the missionary's secondary career as an explorer. Livingstone's great cross-continental journey of 1853–1856, it has been argued, was so dependent upon the Makololo as guides, negotiators, and carriers that it was their expedition rather than his.

Ordinary porters were difficult to recruit from agricultural societies, especially in the growing season, but people like the Banyamwezi or the Yao of Tanzania lived in a marginal areas where hunting and traveling to sell ivory had become customary and they easily adapted themselves to professional porterage. Some other porters might be slaves hired out to an explorer by their owner while freed slaves also provided a pool of labor.

Besides the actual carriers within an explorer's caravan, there were many other people. Women brought or acquired during the expedition to cook and care for the men would be present. An armed guard was a feature of many expeditions. Its function was to keep order in the caravan and protect it from any hostile local inhabitants. Yet to keep order in the guard itself could be difficult while using armed men to force a way through an area was almost always to court disaster. Until the era of the Maxim machine gun, armed expeditions could not assume they had superior force. Henry Stanley was an explorer well supplied with guns and ruthless enough to use them frequently but even he, like most other explorers, had to rely in the end on diplomacy.

The expedition, the caravan, often had a life of its own with complex hierarchies and rivalries and sometimes its own ways of dealing with those encountered. The traveler himself might be only dimly aware of such complications. Nevertheless, the traveler's own relationship with his followers was crucial. Force, cajolery, bribery with extra payments might all be tried in various measure but in the end, the porters had the last word for if they all deserted, the explorer could not go on. If the explorer was fortunate, or, like Joseph Thomson, a good manager of men, he could develop harmonious relationships with prominent members of the porters and try to work through them to achieve his ends. The former slave "Bombay," served John Henning Speke, Stanley, and Verney Lovett Cameron, and was awarded a special Royal Geographical Society (RGS) medal for his work. Another of Speke's 1859 party, Baraka, was an excellent diplomat, but his independence of spirit led to a severing of ties and Speke dubbed him one of his "unfaithfuls." Another of this group, Uledi, seems to have become a minor warlord. Porterage could provide at least some former slaves with the opportunity to carve out new careers for themselves.

Despite the colorful characters among them as well as their importance to explorers, porters and guides have attracted relatively little attention from scholars. However, François Bontinck's studies in a series of articles in *Zaire* and Donald Simpson's *Dark Companions* (if too inclined to accept explorers' character judgments) have shown that useful information on such individuals can be assembled.

[*See also* Cameron, Verney Lovett; Livingstone, David; Park, Mungo; Speke, John Hanning; *and* Stanley, Henry.]

BIBLIOGRAPHY

Bridges, Roy C. "John Hanning Speke: Negotiating a Way to the Source of the Nile." In *Africa and its Explorers*, edited by Robert Rotberg, 95–137. Cambridge, Mass.: Harvard University Press, 1970.

Fisher, Allan G. B., and Humphrey J. Fisher. "Nachtigal's Companions." *Paideuma* 33 (1987): 231–262.

Simpson, Donald. *Dark Companions. The African Contribution to the European Exploration of East Africa.* London: Elek, 1975.

ROY BRIDGES

Maps

From the late eighteenth century, penetration of the interior of Africa by Europeans resulted in change—but not always improvement—to the maps of the continent. Exploration was intermittent and not every European traveler could be relied upon to observe and record accurately and truthfully, while compilers of maps continued to consult earlier sources such as Ptolemy, al-Idrisi, and de Barros.

The subject matter of the maps of Africa that resulted from European exploration reflected the objectives of the explorers themselves. The driving forces, at least up until the late nineteenth century, were science, commerce, and Christianity, as well as imperialistic ideals—but not ideals motivated by colonial intentions. For example, Mungo Park's travels up the Gambia River to the Niger River from 1795 to 1797 were sponsored by the Association for Promoting the Discovery of the Interior Parts of Africa, formed in 1788 to increase scientific knowledge of the continent. Park's cartography was compiled not by the explorer himself, but by James Rennell, a military officer and scholar, who checked and reconciled the explorer's observations of the latitudes, distances, and bearings of physical features, selected for mapping in preference to the more transitory sites of human habitation. Scientific interest in Africa was particularly concerned with hydrology. The course of the Niger was also observed by Walter Oudney, Hugh Clapperton, and Dixon Denham in 1822, while the lower course of the river was finally followed by Richard and John Lander in 1830. The route maps that accompanied the published accounts of all these travels fed through successively to the depiction of the Niger on contemporary small-scale maps.

The Royal Geographical Society of London was one of several national geographical societies in Europe that systematically planned and funded journeys of exploration into Africa. A range of motivations for exploration was to be found within their membership: not only pure science, but also perceived economic opportunity, the preaching of the Gospel, or, more generally, the application of European technological and organizational skills in what

was seen as a civilizing role. In this context, it was appropriate for explorers to compile maps of the highest scientific caliber and for the sponsoring societies to train and equip the explorers for the task.

The best-known African explorer to be supported by the Royal Geographical Society was David Livingstone, the missionary doctor who became drawn into the controversy over the source of the Nile, having earlier investigated the navigability of major rivers as routes to the interior. Commerce as a civilizing influence, the elimination of slavery, the Gospel, and scientific discovery were entirely compatible for Livingstone, whose meticulous instrumental observations were compiled into maps by Aaron Arrowsmith in London. Earlier, two German missionaries, Johannes Rebmann and Ludwig Krapf, had led the way into the interior of East Africa; they were followed by Richard F. Burton and John Hanning Speke, who were less concerned with saving souls than with hydrology. Indeed, Speke wrote at one point of "applying myself solely to mapping." Both parties measured and observed to the best of their ability and training, their cartographic impact differing in the extent and duration of their travels. But perhaps the most remarkable example of the cartography of exploration in Africa are the maps that accompanied Henry Stanley's report of his trans-Africa journey, a journey that began in 1874 and resolved most of the outstanding hydrographic problems of equatorial Africa. Stanley's detailed transects are notable, not so much for their descriptive detail as for their precision in locating named sites, often authenticated by actual measurements of distance and altitude. The lectures, papers, maps, and journals that Stanley and other explorers customarily published on their return to Europe were factored into the evolving map of Africa.

The cartographic evolution of Africa during the classic period of exploration—up to about 1870—was not driven only by explorers in the field, as geographical societies also encouraged debate at home about the sometimes inconclusive evidence of these explorers. Such armchair geographers weighed the evidence against earlier sources and propounded their own theories without leaving Europe; for example, William Desborough Cooley's work on East Africa influenced map compilers in the 1850s. Then there were military expeditions, which, despite being few in number and limited in their coverage, resulted in surveys on the ground in southern Africa and most notably in the Nile Valley, where Napoleon's invasion of Egypt in 1798 gave rise to large-scale topographic cover as far south as Aswan.

In the second half of the nineteenth century, there was a shift of emphasis in the motivation of travelers to the interior of Africa. Increasingly, self-funded exploration was incidental to specific purposes such as hunting, trading, prospecting, or missionary work. For example, Frederick Courteney Selous, in the course of hunting trips, broke much new ground in the Kalahari and Zambezi basin. He compiled only rough sketch maps sufficient for finding routes, without the meticulous instrumental observations that characterized the scientific work of earlier sponsored explorers. Few pioneer missionaries intent on saving souls possessed Livingstone's motivation or skills in mensuration. In these circumstances, the quality of new data for map compilation was not always of a high standard.

By the first decade of the twentieth century, exploration was taking place contemporaneously with the imposition of colonial rule. While parts of Africa were selectively and rapidly surveyed in delimiting boundaries, building roads and railways, or laying out townships, there was no need, over the large parts of colonial Africa seen by Europeans for the first time, for a high order of accuracy in the route maps that needed only to suffice to locate the peoples then being administered. The quality of new data for map compilation became variable.

The impact of explorers' maps on the nineteenth-century cartography of Africa is evident in atlases published throughout the century. At the beginning of the nineteenth century, maps of the continent showed only very few physical features in the interior, some of these deriving from Arabic or earlier Portuguese sources, and the maps had extensive areas either blank or with text of an ethnographic nature. Through the first half of the nineteenth century, there was an increasing tendency to leave large areas blank or labeled "unexplored," while including recent discoveries so that major rivers often appear fragmented. As the century progressed, the hydrology shown on the maps became less disjointed, though cartographers still used pecked lines to indicate tentative alignments. Ethnological descriptions were finally removed and a new category of information in the form of European territorial claims made its appearance.

[*See also* Maps, Mapmaking, and Mapmakers; Niger River; Nile River; *and biographical entries on figures mentioned in this article*.]

BIBLIOGRAPHY

Fernández-Armesto, Felipe. *The Times Atlas of World Exploration*. London: Times Books, 1991.

Norwich, Oscar I. *Norwich's Maps of Africa: An Illustrated and Annotated Carto-bibliography*. 2nd ed. Norwich, Vt.: Terra Nova Press, 1997.

Skelton, R. A. *Explorers' Maps: Chapters in the Cartographic Record of Geographical Discovery*. New York: Spring Books, 1970.

Stone, Jeffrey C. *A Short History of the Cartography of Africa*. Lewiston, N.Y.: Edwin Mellen Press, 1995.

JEFFREY STONE

Patrons, Sponsors, and Supporters

The motives of those who sought knowledge of Africa by exploration include economic, political, strategic, religious, scientific, and intellectual concerns. These were promoted by organizations ranging from governments through scientific societies to missionary bodies. Some individuals became so powerful or influential within such organizations as to become akin to individual patrons. Five names stand out in the relatively modern period: Prince Henry of Portugal, Joseph Banks, John Barrow, Roderick Murchison, and Clements Markham. Such individuals were part of government or had the ability to call on government support. Indeed, investigating Africa either along its coasts by sea or over land into the interior was so difficult and therefore costly that, usually, only governments could mobilize the necessary resources and power.

The Phoenicians, who may have circumnavigated Africa in about 600 B.C.E., were presumably interested in trade but they were actually sent, it seems, by King Necho of Egypt. The name or names of those who sponsored the Greek traders who produced an account of East Africa in the *Periplus of the Erythraean Sea* is unknown. The Carthaginian travelers who may have reached West Africa were sent by a monarch, Hanno. Similarly, the Roman centurions who attempted to ascend the Nile valley were supposed to have been sent by Emperor Nero partly to gain knowledge and partly to investigate possibilities for conquest. However, in general one can say very little about the sponsorship of the expeditions by which the classical world learned something of Africa.

The European Middle Ages saw little accession of direct knowledge by Europe but this was the great age for Islamic scholar-travelers, not least, for example, Ibn Battuta who in the earlier fourteenth century went overland to the Western Sudan and by sea to East Africa. How he was financed, especially on his initial journey to make the hajj, is not apparent but other scholars, holy men, and rulers seemed to be ready to give hospitality to such a well-traveled man who could tell so much about the farther reaches of the Islamic world. The situation was similar for other Arab travelers.

European religious enthusiasm, which was essentially anti-Islam, explains in part the series of exploratory voyages along the African seacoast organized and patronized by Prince Henry of Portugal, "the Navigator," in the fifteenth century. The aim was to outflank Islam and link up with Prester John, a powerful Christian king rumored to reside on the African continent. "Gold and glory" were soon added as motives: one must get around Africa to obtain the riches of the East but there was literally gold to be had in Africa itself, too. Prince Henry (1394–1460) could draw on the power of the Portuguese state and so inaugurated one hundred years or more of Portuguese investigations around and into Africa, which were essentially seeking fields for domination or plunder and evangelization; sponsorship of exploration in this era was for the purposes of state mercantilist success. The Dominican missionaries, who were often also explorers, were expected to and generally did fit into this mercantilist pattern.

During the seventeenth and eighteenth centuries, European involvement in Africa greatly increased especially because of the slave trade. Yet for the most part, slave traders remained at the coast, not seeking to find the sources of their wealth inland. This was true of the Dutch East India Company at the Cape of Good Hope, too. Yet the desire to find ways into Africa as well as around its coasts became stronger, principally, it would seem, on the part of learned and scientific academies and societies. Botanical exploration was particularly important, with Sir Joseph Banks using his position as head of Kew Gardens in London as a means of sponsoring explorers in various parts of Africa. Banks was also the effective head of the African Association formed in 1788 to sponsor expeditions to West Africa. Later, the Second Secretary at the Admiralty, John Barrow, used his position to act as a sort of quasi-patron of West African travelers. Later still, Sir Roderick Murchison, head of the Geological Survey Department but also president of the Royal Geographical Society (RGS), could use his position to exercise patronage of travelers. Banks's African Association had merged with the newly formed Royal Geographical Society in 1831. The RGS, like the Paris Geographical Society and to a lesser extent the Berlin Geographical Society, consisted of members who were connected with government or indeed worked for it. Hence the societies

and academies, much as they might be devoted to science and disinterested enquiry, in fact received much state help directly in the form of finance or indirectly by such means as the secondment of personnel. The three RGS explorers—Richard Burton, John Hanning Speke, and James Augustus Grant—for example, were all Indian Army officers. Governments saw the need for accurate information about Africa so that they could more effectively pursue their strategic, political, or economic objects. In the first half of the nineteenth century, both the British and French governments sent their own expeditions to West Africa. Geographical prizes like Timbuctoo or the course of the Niger were easily meshed with a strategy of engaging politically and economically with the developing new Islamic societies of the Western Sudan or combating the slave trade. Meanwhile, the Bombay government in India was sending naval and other expeditions to East Africa.

By the 1870s, several avowedly commercial geographical societies had emerged in Europe but, on the whole, practical traders, chambers of commerce, and investors did not support exploration; they waited for more certain dividends than an expedition to the source of the Nile could provide. Yet certain individuals with the power of government did send expeditions during this period that were at least half scientific exploration and half economic. The two major examples were the Khedive Ismā'īl of Egypt and King Leopold of the Belgians.

A new element from about 1800 was the Protestant evangelical revival in northern Europe. This led to the foundation of missionary societies keen to seek converts in Africa and so to some notable missionary explorations, the most famous being those of David Livingstone. Missionary societies could get some financial support from their churches but found the costs of pure exploration burdensome. However, their usually anti-slave-trade positions usually coincided with government, especially British government, policy and they might be in concert with officialdom. "Christianity, Commerce and Civilization" for Africa was seen as consonant with a Palmerstonian type foreign policy that led most notably to the Niger Expedition of 1841 and the Zambezi Expedition of 1858.

As exploration became a popular interest, some new types of sponsorship emerged with public subscriptions for travelers. But more significant was the popular element channeled through newspaper sponsorship, especially in the case of the *New York Herald Tribune* and the *Daily Telegraph* financing of Henry Stanley.

By the 1880s and 1890s, international rivalry and territorial acquisition had begun in Africa; neither religion and philanthropy nor pure science, however much they were invoked, was the real reason for expeditions. Imperialist pressure groups sought and usually obtained state endorsement, perhaps sometimes because there was popular public support. The greatest exploratory feat in this era was Stanley's Emin Pasha Relief Expedition, which was essentially funded by King Leopold II though with some private British commercial and missionary backing.

Throughout two thousand years of African exploration, merchants, scholars, divines, and politicians may have formed associations of one kind and another to sponsor expeditions but their success nearly always depended upon the extent to which governments were involved.

[*See also* African Association; Royal Geographical Society; *and biographical entries on figures mentioned in this article.*]

BIBLIOGRAPHY
Cary, M., and E. H. Warmington. *The Ancient Explorers*. Rev. ed. Harmondsworth, U.K.: Penguin, 1963.
Diffie, Bailey W., and George D. Winius. *The Foundations of the Portuguese Empire 1415–1580*. Minneapolis: Minnesota University Press, 1977.
Hallett, Robin, ed. *The Records of the African Association, 1788–1831*. London: T. Nelson 1964.
Markham, Clements R. *The Fifty Years' Work of the Royal Geographical Society*. London: J. Murray, 1881.

ROY BRIDGES

Scientific Exploration

The motivations for geographical exploration in Africa ranged from individual desire for adventure, through missionary zeal, through big-game hunting, and through the search for political hegemony. But from roughly the middle of the eighteenth century, all travelers were expected to conduct scientific inquiries, and some of the travelers became notable for their contributions, especially to geographical science and natural history. Increasingly, geographical data were required on relief and drainage patterns, and it came to be expected that the "scientific explorer" would know how to use at least a sextant so that his positions could be accurately plotted on maps. A strong strand in scientific exploration was botanical inquiry; Sir Joseph Banks established the practice of sending out botanical collectors to obtain specimens for Kew Gardens in London, and this sci-

entific approach affected the African Association, which Banks set up in 1788 to encourage the exploration of Africa.

For more than one hundred and fifty years, Africa has been looked upon as a vast natural laboratory for scientific inquiry. Questions regarding the location of the sources of well-known rivers were particularly common. The sources of the Nile River occupied much of the interest of geographers and cartographers between the 1770s and the 1850s, and the Niger River generated similar interest. Was the Niger a tributary of the Nile, did it flow into an unknown interior lake in central Africa, or did it debouch into the Gulf of Benin? This geographical mystery was resolved in 1832, when Richard and John Lander sailed down the river into the Gulf of Benin.

Explorers came to Africa not only to resolve specific geographical problems: many came to learn about Africa's natural history. Anders Sparrman (1748–1820), Carl Peter Thunberg (1743–1828), William Burchell (1782–1863), and Georg Schweinfurth (1836–1925) were superb botanists; Mary Kingsley (1862–1900) performed meritorious ichthyological work in Gabon; and Karl Johan Andersson (1827–1867) studied South African bird life. Although they were primarily big-game hunters, William Cornwallis Harris (1807–1848) and Frederick Selous (1851–1917) were major contributors of unknown African animals to natural history museums in Britain. Selous was also responsible for helping mapmakers determine the southern limits of the tsetse fly, which in turn helped European pastoralists decide where to herd their cattle. Wilhelm Junker (1840–1892) resided in the upper Nile region for eleven years (1875–1886), where he collected plant and animal specimens for museums in Berlin and Saint Petersburg and wrote an ethnological account of a tribe of cannibals he knew well. Beginning in 1856, the American Paul du Chaillu (1831–1903) added to the store of knowledge of African natural history—he was the first to describe the unusual otter-shrew and the bald chimpanzee, and he confirmed the existence of Pygmies. But his major achievement was the description of the elusive lowland forest gorilla in Gabon. He claimed to be "the only white man who could speak of the gorilla from personal knowledge."

Perhaps no explorers of Africa produced more material of scientific interest than did Heinrich Barth (1821–1865), David Livingstone (1813–1873), and Joseph Thomson (1858–1895). The five volumes that Barth wrote after he returned from central Africa in 1855 are loaded with ethnological and geographical data, as well as information regarding plants and animals, and certainly architecture. Barth's eyewitness account of Timbuctoo was the first since René Caillié had visited the city in 1828, and it was valuable for corroborating Caillié's account, which had aroused skepticism. Thomson, a Scottish geologist and naturalist, made five journeys to Africa between 1879 and 1890. Among his accomplishments were carefully explaining the geography and physical properties of the lands and lake systems in East Africa. Because of his scientific knowledge of Africa, Thomson was hired by Cecil Rhodes to negotiate mining agreements in what is now Zambia. Although David Livingstone was a medical missionary, all of his journeys were of a scientific nature, and during his last expedition, which began in 1867, he expended considerable effort attempting to determine the watershed of interior southern Africa.

Other, lesser-known nineteenth-century scientific explorers of interest include Karl von der Decken (1833–1865), Leopold Janikowski (1855–1942), and James Grant (1827–1892). By almost ascending Mount Kilimanjaro in 1861–1862, Decken, a talented naturalist, proved to skeptical armchair geographers in Europe that ice and snow indeed were found on high tropical mountains. Janikowski, a member of the Polish expedition to the Cameroons in 1883–1885, was an outstanding linguist who produced important ethnological studies in that region. Grant is best known for being John Speke's companion when the Nile question was solved, but he was trained in botany and natural history and produced considerable scientific data while exploring in Africa.

French scientific explorers were quite active in Africa in the latter half of the nineteenth century. Henri Duveyrier (1840–1892) did much to explain the ethnology of Saharan tribes, whereas in tropical Africa, the Marquis de Compiègne (1846–1877) and Alfred Marche (1844–1898) conducted ethnographical and zoological studies in the Ogowe River region in the 1870s. Marche also made important contributions to the Paris Museum of Natural History.

In the twentieth century, the ornithologist Boyd Alexander (1873–1910) made Europeans aware of the myriad bird life in Fernando Póo, the Cape Verde Islands, São Thomé, the Cameroons, and the Lake Chad region during his many journeys—journeys that ceased only with his murder while traveling in eastern Chad in 1910. During his expedition that began in 1904, southern Lake Chad was carefully mapped for the first time. The Italian mountaineer Luigi Abruzzi (1873–1933) led an expedition to the Ruwenzori Mountains in 1906 that resulted in considerable mapping and surveying; most important,

however, the expedition gave the world superb photographs of the "Mountains of the Moon."

Carl Akeley (1864–1926), along with his first wife, Delia (1875–1970), spent months in Africa in 1905 collecting animals to display at the Field Museum of Natural History in Chicago. Later, after World War I, on a commission from the Brooklyn Museum of Arts and Sciences, Delia Akeley collected animals in Kenya and Somalia. Mary Akeley (1878–1966), Carl's second wife, conducted a study of gorillas in the Congo, and she helped her husband develop the Great African Hall at the American Museum of Natural History in New York.

Among the most important scientists working in Africa in the twentieth century were Louis Leakey (1903–1972), his wife Mary (1913–1996), and their son Richard (b. 1944). When Mary Leakey discovered the *Zinjanthropus* cranium at the Olduvai Gorge in 1959, the modern science of paleoanthropology was launched. A contemporary of the Leakeys, the primatologist Jane Goodall (b. 1934), performed pioneer research while living with mountain chimpanzees in East Africa. Her research significantly aided the movement to preserve the species from extinction.

The distinguished French archaeologist Henri Lhote (1903–1991) traveled extensively in the Sahara region before and after World War II, and his greatest achievement was discovering the mural paintings at Tassili n'Ajjer, Algeria, which depict Saharan life as far back as 10,000 B.C.E. Émile Félix Gautier (1864–1940), who was the world's expert on the camel, and Theodore Monod (1903–2000) also conducted important scientific research during their travels in North Africa in the twentieth century.

[*See also* African Association; Chad, Lake; Niger River; Nile River; *and biographical entries on figures mentioned in this article.*]

BIBLIOGRAPHY

Desmond, Ray. *Kew: The History of the Royal Botanic Gardens.* London: Harvill Press, with the Royal Botanic Gardens, Kew, 1995.

Lhote, Henri. In *Search of the Tassili Frescoes.* 2nd ed. London: Hutchinson Press, 1973.

Livingstone, David. *The Life and African Explorations of Dr. David Livingstone: Comprising All His Extensive Travels and Discoveries as Detailed in His Diary, Reports, and Letters, Including His Famous Last Journals: with Maps and Numerous Illustrations.* With an introduction by Christopher Hibbert. New York: Cooper Square Press, 2002.

Rotberg, Robert. *Joseph Thomson and the Exploration of Africa.* New York: Oxford University Press, 1971.

Schweinfurth, Georg August. *The Heart of Africa: Three Years' Travels and Adventures of the Unexplored Regions of Central*

Africa from 1868 to 1871. Chicago: Afro-Am Books, 1969. First published in 1873.

SANFORD H. BEDERMAN

African Association. On June 9, 1788, a group of nine aristocrats in the habit of meeting to eat at the Saint Alban's Tavern in London resolved to turn their dining club into an association "for promoting the discovery of the interior parts of Africa," the map of which, they said, was "still but a wide-extended blank." They were anxious, they added, to improve geography and remove the "reproach upon the present age" of the stigma of ignorance. It was further added that discoveries in Africa would prove practical and useful. Indeed, this first modern geographical society could be argued to be an unconscious product of interests aroused by the rise of Britain as a powerful economic entity with an ever-expanding need for markets around the world.

The African Association, always exclusive, had fewer than three hundred members in its whole existence and was dominated by Sir Joseph Banks. It sent a succession of travelers to West Africa, most notably Daniel Houghton from 1790 to 1791, Mungo Park from 1795 to 1796, and Friedrich Hornemann from 1797 to 1801. The object was to learn about the West Sudanic polities and the course of the Niger River that ran through them. As the British government took over the sponsorship of expeditions, the association's importance diminished; however, it had some hand in the expeditions of James H. Tuckey, Johann Ludwig Burckhardt, and Henry Salt, as well as Louis-Maurice-Adolphe Linant de Bellefonds the elder's attempt to ascend the Nile in the late 1820s. Proceedings were issued to the members irregularly from 1788 to 1810, and a comprehensive version was published in 1810. A key figure attached to the African Association was James Rennell, who produced "geographical elucidations," especially of Mungo Park's work.

In 1831, the African Association decided to merge with the newly founded Royal Geographical Society, which the Association's example had done so much to inspire.

[*See also* Royal Geographical Society *and biographical entries on figures mentioned in this article.*]

BIBLIOGRAPHY
Hallett, Robin. *The Penetration of Africa: European Enterprise and Exploration Principally in Northern and Western Africa up to 1830.* London: Routledge and Kegan Paul; New York: Praeger, 1965.
Hallett, Robin, ed. *Records of the African Association, 1788–1831.* London and New York: T. Nelson, 1964.
Proceedings of the Association for Promoting the Discovery of the Interior Parts of Africa. 2 vols. London: W. Bulmer and Co., 1810.
Sattin, Anthony. *The Gates of Africa: Death, Discovery and the Search for Timbuktu.* London: HarperCollins, 2003.

ROY BRIDGES

Agnese, Battista (1514–1564), Genoa-born Venetian who produced many maps and atlases between 1535 and 1564. At this time chart production in the western Mediterranean was mostly in the hands of great dynasties: the Freducci family of Ancona, the Maggiolo family of Genoa, and the Oliva family, split between Majorca and Marseille. But Agnese did not belong to any similar dynasty; by himself, he (and his workshop) produced about sixty certainly attributable atlases, as well as many others whose origin lies more or less in doubt.

Agnese's work was always elegant, and stylistically it represents a turning point between the portolan charts of the Middle Ages and the modern charts that replaced them. Color plate 3 in this volume shows that while he retained medieval features like the system of compass roses and the set of wind cherubs, he carefully marked in the latest geographical information; indeed, he was the first to show the peninsula of California. Agnese also followed a generally coherent system of coloration.

These elegant atlases were designed for princes and wealthy merchants rather than for seamen, and Agnese took care to insert such major feats of discovery as the circumnavigation begun by Ferdinand Magellan. From the start, Agnese's atlases were highly prized, which is, no doubt, both why so many of them survive and why so many of them have been forged.

[*See also* Europe and the Mediterranean, *subentry on* Medieval West Mapmaking, *and* Maps, Mapmaking, and Mapmakers.]

BIBLIOGRAPHY
Howse, Derek, and Michael Sanderson. *The Sea Chart: An Historical Survey Based on the Collections in the National Maritime Museum.* New York: McGraw-Hill, 1973.
Mollat Du Jourdin, Michel, and Monique de La Roncière. *Sea Charts of the Early Explorers, 13th to 17th Century.* Translated by L. Le R. Dethan. New York: Thames and Hudson, 1984.
Wagner, Henry R. *Manuscript Atlases of Battista Agnese.* Chicago: University of Chicago Press, 1931.

DAVID BUISSERET

Akeley, Delia (1875–1970), American explorer of Africa. Journeying from the mouth of the Tana River on Africa's east coast to the mouth of the Congo on the west coast, Delia Denning Akeley was the first white woman to head an expedition that crossed the African continent from east to west. The trip, sponsored in 1924 by the Brooklyn Museum of Arts and Sciences in New York, was intended to collect wild animal specimens for the museum's exhibits. Akeley was also interested in learning more about the Pygmy of the Belgian Congo and ended up living with them for several months, recording their lives in thousand of photographs. Through her efforts, the museum acquired more than thirty specimens of wild animals, and the Newark Museum in New Jersey received almost two hundred cultural artifacts from her trip.

Akeley was born on a Wisconsin farm on December 5, 1875, to Patrick and Margaret Denning. The youngest of nine children, she ran away from home at the age of thirteen and never saw her parents again. In 1902 she married Carl Akeley, the famous sculptor and taxidermist whose innovative methods of taxidermy revolutionized the field. She traveled with him several times to Africa to collect big game for museum exhibits and became an expert markswoman. The Akeleys were divorced in 1923, in part because of her unnatural devotion to a pet monkey that she brought back from Africa.

Delia Akeley's accomplishments have been overshadowed by those of her famous husband and even, to some extent, by his second wife, Mary Jobe Akeley. However, Akeley made valuable contributions to our knowledge of Africa and its people, first as Carl Akeley's assistant and later as head of her own expedition. She died on May 22, 1970, at her home in Daytona, Florida, at the age of ninety-five.

[*See also* Women Explorers.]

BIBLIOGRAPHY
Olds, Elizabeth Fagg. *Women of the Four Winds.* Boston: Houghton Mifflin, 1985, pp. 71–153.

PATRICIA GILMARTIN

Alaska and the Yukon Gold Rush.

Alaska and the Yukon Gold Rush. The first maps of Alaska were drawn by native people who had crossed the Bering Land Bridge from Siberia thousands of years ago. Native maps are still poorly understood because they require a different mind-set—one that can consider maps as embracing time itself. This mind-set is specific to the Tlingit Indians of southeastern Alaska, but its basic ideas are found in many other aboriginal cultures. The maps of this kind are mental, based on territorial geographic place-names handed down for countless generations. They are landscapes of the mind that reach back to when animals and people could talk to each other. The names are not only site-specific, but clan-specific as well, and thus apply to clan descendents. Children memorize these names in order of direction so that, even if they never see the places themselves, they have a clear mental map—a map of the area that in turn is a map of their own being, as much part of them as their lungs or kidneys. At the same time, the maps are also spatiotemporal. Detailed linear maps, including fish camps, trails, or the bay that a giant beaver destroyed, can be easily drawn. Early Europeans were completely dependent on native guides and their maps.

The first Europeans known to come through the Bering Strait were Semen Deshnev and his companions in 1648, who were searching for walrus tusks. These men were some of the first *promyshlenniki* (lower-class or low-ranking fur traders). Four of their initial six *koches* (round-bottomed ice boats) wound up on the shores of Anadyr Bay, Siberia. These explorers had seen nothing but fog and the Siberian shore on their epic voyage, but—unknowingly—they had made history.

The next European to visit the strait was Mikhail Gvozdev in 1732. A geodesist, he constructed a chart after meeting hostile Inupiat Eskimos (one of the four native groups of Alaska) around the Seward Peninsula, but he did not go ashore. Vitus Bering made his first foray to the north in 1725, but the notorious fogs of the strait later named for him kept him from seeing the Alaskan coast. Shortly after, mostly illiterate *promyshlenniki* rushed to the Aleutians for "soft gold"—sea otter and fur-seal pelts. There were at least ninety-two voyages in the early years. Because of the sweeping storms and strong currents at deeply indented shores of the Aleutian Islands, the gateway to the Bering Sea, it was almost impossible to chart the area accurately with only a sextant. Andreian Tolstykh discovered the central islands in 1749, and Stepan Glotov found new islands, including Kodiak Island, between 1763 and 1765.

The reports of the new discoveries and the rich furs led to royal interest. The secret Levashov-Krenitsyn expedition from 1764 to 1771 found fifteen of the Aleutian Islands and the north shore of the Alaska Peninsula. The charts remained unpublished in order to keep the findings secret.

Lieutenant Ivan (Johann) Sindt and the Englishman Joseph Billings were sent by the Russian government in 1764 and 1785, respectively, to chart the Bering Sea. Both are remembered in history as bumblers who accomplished little, but this assessment is unfair. The Von Staehlen Map, a highly erroneous document which was attributed to Sindt, was in fact prepared in 1754 by two Cossacks, Lazarev and Vasyutinsky, under Tolstykh; it was later carried by James Cook. Actually, Sindt's chart of the Diomedes and part of the Seward Peninsula is perfectly adequate. Billings submitted his journal of the expedition, which has never been published, unlike the book of his secretary Martin Sauer. Sauer loathed Billings, and his well-known account made Billings's seven years of voyage seem like a series of failures. On the other hand, examination of the accounts of Gavril Sarichev, Billings's co-captain, and of Heinrich Merck, the expedition's naturalist, paints a totally different picture.

Gradually the chaos of the individual entrepreneur was replaced by the organization of the corporation. The Russian American Company (RAC) was granted the royal franchise in 1799, shortly after Gregory Shelikov, its primary founder, died. While Shelikov overstated the grandeur of the company and its accomplishments, he did hire the legendary Alexandr Baranov. Baranov's tenure until 1818 consolidated the company's power in Alaska, produced handsome profits, and made Baranov famous as "Lord of Alaska" throughout the Pacific. Meanwhile, Vasilii Ivanov, Gerasim Ismailov, Dmitrii Bocharov, and Petr Korsakovskii all explored southwestern Alaska overland in 1792, and from 1818 to 1819, Adolf Etholen and Vasilii Khromchenko explored by sea. Andrei Glazunov made three lengthy explorations in western Alaska between 1833 and 1839, one of which lasted 104 days and covered nearly 1,400 miles (2,333 kilometers).

Southeastern Alaska was first surveyed by the Spanish and English. Juan Bodega y Quadra and Antonio Mourelle sailed as far as Icy Strait in 1775. In all, six voyages were made by the Spanish, the most famous being that of Alejandro Malaspina, who led the last great Spanish around-the-world voyage in 1791. Although they reached Unalaska, the Spanish left nothing except some place-names.

Captain Cook searched for the Northwest Passage in 1778 and was stopped by ice at 72° N, but he charted the first outline of Alaska's coast to that point. After his death the ships returned, but failed again. George Vancouver charted southeastern Alaska and Cook Inlet from 1793 to 1794, proving that no passage existed there. Representing France, Jean-François de Galaup de La Pérouse discovered Lituya Bay in 1786, but suffered serious losses.

By 1847, not only was the coast of Alaska mostly charted, but the great rivers (the Yukon, Kusko-kwim, Nushagak, and Copper) were well known. *Odinochkas*, or trading posts, were quickly established along them. Finding beaver pelts was the objective, and the Russians traveled vast distances to obtain them from the natives. Semen Lukin from Kolmakovskii was warned in 1839 not to make his annual thousand-mile (1,667-kilometer) trek to the Copper River because the people there blamed the Russians for the smallpox epidemic. The exploration of the Yukon-Kuskokwim Delta from 1842 to 1844 by Lieutenant Lavrenti Zagoskin resulted in a valuable account as well as map.

Experience had shown that the cheapest and most efficient supply route to Alaska lay in around-the-world voyages. Associated with these were Yuri Lisianskii and I. F. Kruzenstern (on the first such Russian voyage), V. M. Golovnin, Aleksandr Avinov, Gleb Shismarev, M. D. Teben'kov (author of the great 1852 marine atlas), and Otto von Kotzebue. Besides surveying for the RAC, Kotzebue explored what would be named Kotzebue Sound on a privately financed expedition from 1815 to 1818. Baron Ferdinand von Wrangell—explorer, geographer, ethnographer, manager, and diplomat—also sent subordinates in quest of information. Cook had named the main coastal features, but the Russians filled in the details, including the stormy and heavily indented Aleutian Islands.

F. W. Beechey was sent to Kotzebue Sound from 1826 to 1827 to wait for Sir John Franklin and survey as far as east of Point Barrow. Franklin never arrived, but valuable charts resulted nevertheless. Edward Belcher was with Beechey, and in 1837 he examined Prince William Sound. More charting was done by the Franklin Relief Expedition of 1849 to 1854. In 1855 a United States survey was made by the Ringgold-Rodgers expedition, which took advantage of the Crimean War to examine the Aleutians in aid of the whalers in the Bering Sea. It is said that some of those charts were used as late as World War II.

Robert Kennicott and other United States scientists of the Western Union Telegraph Expedition surveyed the Seward Peninsula and Norton Sound from 1865 to 1866. The successful laying of the Atlantic telegraph cable ended the effort, but William Healey Dall, "dean of Alaska experts," stayed on two more years at his own expense and later surveyed in the Aleutians. His 1870 *Alaska and Its Resources* was the first book about Alaska published in English. Kennicott died in the Yukon in 1866 at age 30.

The first explorer to ascend the mighty Yukon River was Ivan Lukin, in 1861. He was Creole, the child of a Russian father and native Alaskan mother. The Creoles are mainly forgotten today, but they did much of the Russian mapping and were charged with keeping journals detailing geology, flora, fauna, natives, and everything else that was encountered. The Kashevarov family alone contributed ten important members over four generations. From 1838 to 1839, Petr Malakhov established the northernmost RAC post, at Nulato on the middle Yukon River, and discovered the Koyukuk River. Ruf Serebrennikov lost his life exploring the Copper River in 1848 and, among other adventures, Afanasii Klimovskii distributed 636 doses of smallpox vaccine from Kodiak to Saint Michael at the mouth of the Yukon River in an overland trip in 1837.

The sale of Alaska in 1867 meant that the United States now had control of the region. Several seasons by the United States Coast and Geodetic Survey (USC&GS) in southeastern Alaska built on the old charts. The cities of Juneau (founded in 1880) and Sitka were considered valuable but, other than the Pribilof Islands and its fur-seal herds, little else was.

Gold changed this situation. In response to the discovery of gold, prospectors needed maps and the United States Geological Survey (USGS) was sent to gather information. Captain William Abercrombie failed to ascend the Copper River in 1884, but in 1898 he divided his twenty men into two groups: one examined Prince William Sound, and the other traversed from Valdez to the Yukon River. Lieutenant Henry Allen and party made in 1885 a remarkable journey of 1,500 miles (2,500 kilometers) up the Copper River to the Yukon and down to Saint Michael. Geologist Alfred Hulse Brooks made twenty-four trips to Alaska and surveyed the Seward Peninsula and Tanana and Kuskokwim river basins. Another explorer on the Copper River, as well as on the Susitna and the Tanana Rivers, was Captain Edwin Glenn from 1898 to 1899. Joseph Herron, under Glenn, went from Cook Inlet across the Alaska Range to the Kuskokwim drainage and the Yukon. Many other USGS personnel examined this giant land and conducted coast surveys, many of which continue today.

After the gold rush, interest in Alaska faded; generally only mountaineers and geologists still cared to explore it. Archdeacon Hudson Stuck, who traveled extensively in the interior, had Walter Harper, a Creole, climb the final few feet during the first ascent of Mount McKinley in 1913. Luigi Abruzzi's Italian party ascended to the summit of Mount Saint Elias in 1898, and I. C. Russell combined geology and mountaineering from 1890 to 1891 when he mapped a thousand square miles (2,600 square kilometers)

around Saint Elias. Bradford Washburn, whose wife, Barbara, became the first woman to climb Mount McKinley, began a long career among the mountains in 1934.

Occasionally other explorers appeared in the region. In 1931, the forester Robert Marshall named the "Gates of the Arctic" in the Brooks Range, and Ernest Leffingwell spent 1909 to 1912 and 1913 to 1914 around Flaxman Island, mostly at his own expense, mapping and learning Inupiat Eskimo nomenclature. The revenue steamer *Bear*, with "Hellroaring Mike" Healy as its most famous captain, patrolled Alaska during thirty-four summers between 1885 and 1926. Lieutenant David Jarvis and three companions drove a reindeer herd from Teller to Barrow in 1899 to relieve icebound whalers.

Yukon Territory, Canada, was under the purview of the Hudson's Bay Company (HBC), although from 1825 to 1827 Sir John Franklin charted the coast from the Mackenzie River to within a hundred miles (167 kilometers) of Beechey's survey before being stopped by ice. That last 100 miles, to longitude 154°25' W, was completed in 1837 by Peter Dease and Thomas Simpson of the HBC, mostly overland.

In 1847, Alexander Murray deliberately established Fort Yukon on the river about 150 miles (250 kilometers) inside the Alaska boundary, but the HBC feigned ignorance, as it was their most lucrative post in the district. Russia resented this action, but lacked the force to remove the post; it was, however, able to block the HBC from using the river. Captain Charles Raymond proved that Fort Yukon was within Alaska in 1869, and the fort was moved. Veteran Robert Campbell established Fort Selkirk in 1848, but it was destroyed in 1852.

Canadian government geologists George Dawson, R. C. McConnell, and William Ogilvie surveyed and mapped (based on Indian guides and maps) the territory in the 1880s. There were also various prospectors present after the Cassiar gold discovery of 1872. Jack McQuesten, Al Mayo, Arthur Harper (father of Walter), and later, Joseph Ladue, all traded and prospected along the Fortymile River.

From 1889 to 1891, a United States boundary survey was completed along the 141st meridian by John Turner and John McGrath of the USC&GS. Lieutenant Frederick Schwatka later wrote popular accounts of his travels in the area.

In 1898, the Klondike gold discovery burst suddenly upon a world undergoing financial turmoil and thousands flocked to the Yukon, most to have a grand adventure and a few prospectors to become rich—but it was the shipowners and merchants from Seattle, Edmonton, Juneau, and Skagway who won the most. Whaling, on the other hand, was the bonanza of the north coast. Joe Tuckfield and several Inupiat traveled 500 miles (833 kilometers) from Barrow to Herschel Island from 1888 to 1889 and found many bowheads, making the island the headquarters in the Beaufort Sea for years. Roald Amundsen stopped there on his famous transit of the Northwest Passage. In 1905, Amundsen mushed over 500 miles round-trip to Eagle, Alaska, to telegraph his victory.

[*See also* Hudson's Bay Company; Russian American Company; *and biographical entries on figures mentioned in this article.*]

BIBLIOGRAPHY

Beaglehole, J. C., ed. *Journals of Captain James Cook on His Voyages of Discovery*. 7 vols. London: Hakluyt Society, 1955–1974.

Coates, Ken S., and William R. Morrison. *Land of the Midnight Sun: A History of the Yukon*. Edmonton, Alberta: Hurtig, 1988.

Cook, Warren L. *Flood Tide of Empire: Spain and the Pacific Northwest, 1543–1819*. New Haven, Conn.: Yale University Press, 1973.

Gibson, James R. *Imperial Russia in Frontier America: The Changing Geography of Supply of Russian America, 1784–1867*. New York: Oxford University Press, 1976.

Golder, F. A. *Russian Expansion of the Pacific, 1641–1850* (1914). Reprint. New York: Paragon Books, 1971.

Jones, Ed and Star. *All that Glitters: The Life and Times of Joe Ladue*. Whitehorse, Yukon, Canada: Wolf Creek Press, 2005.

Michael, Henry, N., ed. *Lieutenant Zagoskin's Travels in Russian America, 1842–1844*. Toronto: Arctic Institute of North America–University of Toronto Press, 1967.

Sauer, Martin. *An Account of a Geographical and Astronomical Expedition to the Northern Parts of Russia*. London: T. Cadell and W. Davies, 1802. Reprint. Richmond, U.K.: Richmond Publishing, 1972.

Tikhmenev, P. A. *History of the Russian American Company*. Translated and edited by Richard A. Pierce and Alton S. Donnelly. Seattle: University of Washington Press, 1978.

VanStone, James W., ed., and David H. Kraus, trans. *Russian Exploration in Southwest Alaska: The Travel Journals of Petr Korsakovskiy (1818) and Ivan Ya. Vasilev (1829)*. Fairbanks: University of Alaska Press. 1988.

VanStone, James W., ed., and David H. Kraus, trans. *V. S. Khromchenko's Coastal Explorations in Southwestern Alaska, 1822*. Fieldiana Anthropology, vol. 64. Chicago: Field Museum of Natural History, 1973.

Wright, Allen A. *Prelude to Bonanza: The Discovery and Exploration of the Yukon*. Sidney, British Columbia: Gray's Publishing, 1976.

DEE LONGENBAUGH

Alexander, Boyd

Alexander, Boyd (1873–1910), British army officer and prominent ornithologist who made two dangerous journeys to the African Sahel, and who is considered the most important early twentieth-century explorer of Africa. Boyd Alexander was born in Cranbrook, Kent, England. As a schoolboy he avidly studied and collected birds, and in 1897 he spent four months on the Cape Verde Islands. He received his commission in 1901 but obtained leave the next year to travel to Fernando Póo where he had his most successful birding experience. His first exploration of Africa began in 1904, and he traveled with companions George Goslin (co-leader), Claud Alexander (his brother), P. A. Talbot, and José Lopes, his personal assistant. The Alexander-Goslin Expedition began at the Niger Delta, and when it reached Maiduguri, Claud Alexander was fatally stricken with enteric fever. The group subsequently spent six months mapping southern Lake Chad; this mapping provided the first additional knowledge of the lake by Englishmen since Dixon Denham was there from 1823 to 1824. Talbot returned to England, but the reduced expedition continued across the Congo Free State where, on June 12, 1906, Goslin died of blackwater fever. Returning to England, Alexander quickly wrote *From the Niger to the Nile*, which was highly received by the geographical establishment, and he was awarded the Founder's Medal of the Royal Geographical Society in early 1908.

Alexander began his second journey in 1908, traveling first to Annobón and the São Thomé Islands, then to coastal Cameroon, where he resided for five months. In addition to ascending Mount Cameroon, he experienced first-hand its eruption in April 1909. His next destinations were Fort Lamy (now Ndjamena) and Abéche (also known as Abeshir; in present-day Chad), where he sought permission to cross the interior regions of Wadai and Darfur. He was murdered by dissident tribesmen near Abeshir on April 2, 1910. José Lopes rescued his body for proper burial, and French soldiers salvaged his travel diary. This valuable document was published posthumously in 1912 as *Boyd Alexander's Last Journey*.

[*See also* Africa, *subentry on* Scientific Exploration, *and* Chad, Lake.]

BIBLIOGRAPHY

Alexander, Boyd. *From the Niger to the Nile*. 2 vols. London: Edward Arnold, 1907.

Alexander, Herberted, ed. *Boyd Alexander's Last Journey*. London: Edward Arnold, 1912.

SANFORD H. BEDERMAN

Alexander the Great

This entry contains two subentries:

Fact
Fiction

Fact

Alexander was born in Macedonia, in northern Greece, in the summer of 356 B.C.E. Word came to Philip II, king of Macedonia, that his queen, Olympias, had given birth to a son at the same time that word came that his horses had won the premier chariot race at the Olympics. It would not be the last time that such omens attended Alexander. When Alexander was thirteen, his father brought the philosopher Aristotle to Macedonia to tutor Alexander, and from him Alexander developed an interest in geography, an interest that complemented his drive for adventure and fame. Philip was in the process of creating a truly national state in Macedonia: pushing frontiers north and west, draining swamps for farmland, founding cites, incorporating new peoples into Macedonia. These were all things Alexander would do as well.

When Alexander was sixteen, Philip left him as regent in Macedonia, and soon Alexander conducted his first campaign against a hill tribe; the campaign culminated in the founding of his first city, Alexandropolis. By eighteen, Alexander commanded the elite Companion Cavalry at the Battle of Chaeronea, which gave Philip control of Greece and at which the army itself named Alexander hero of the battle. By twenty, with Philip's death, Alexander was king. He inherited a state that was the largest and most advanced in the Aegean, a modern army, and a war with Persia. By the time he died only thirteen years later, in June of 323 B.C.E., he had conquered a vast territory that stretched from the eastern Mediterranean coast in the west to the central Asian republics, Afghanistan, and Pakistan in the east. In a life lived on so large a scale, it is hard to separate the romantic legend from the fact.

There is no doubt about Alexander's charisma; he was able to get his men to do things even when they doubted that they could, and he was able to lead them to places that were only legend. He does seem to have had an ambition to make himself the equal of heroes and gods such as Hercules and Dionysus, who had seen the limits of the world. The sources refer to this longing in Alexander as a *pothos* (un-

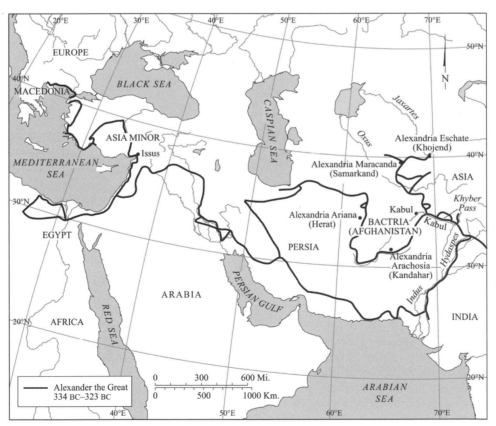

Alexander the Great. Alexander's expeditions covered more than 20,000 miles (32,000 kilometers). MAP BY BILL NELSON

deniable urge). In 335, it led him while campaigning in the northern Balkans to cross the Danube. In the campaigns in eastern Iran, it led him across the Oxus (Amu Darya) and Jaxartes (Syr Darya) rivers into central Asia. In the 320s, it was part of his drive to the Himalayas and the Hindu Kush. His track through the Khyber Pass and into Pakistan, and then across the Punjab, was sparked in part by his desire to see the "Ocean" that defined the limits of the world. Even in his march down the Indus River, the idea of exploration tinted what he saw—he thought that he had found the source of the Nile.

But all of these travels, which Alexander did in fact accomplish, were done as part of his military campaigns, and not as a drive for exploration. Further, though unknown or unseen by the average Greek, these places lay along well-established trade routes, and were not "discoveries" as such. Trade into the upper Balkans goes back to the Bronze Age; the Silk Road into central Asia had been enriching the Persians for centuries; the Spice Route to India had prompted Darius the Great to conquer what is now Pakistan at the end of the sixth century B.C.E. Instead of "Ocean," Alexander found the Ganges plain and the Indian subcontinent, which led his soldiers to refuse to go farther and ended the grand expedition altogether. Even the search for the headwaters of the Nile was frustrated by the time he reached the mouth of the Indus and found the Indian Ocean instead.

So in what sense is Alexander an explorer? First of all, for the Greek and, later, Roman worlds, Alexander opened up central Asia directly to trade and settlement by them. In this he is no different than the European voyagers in the age of discovery. More important, Alexander can be seen as a "frontiersman" in the classical sense: he created a European frontier in central Asia as part of his means of controlling his empire. An integral part of creating the frontier was the foundation of cities and the settlement of Greco-Macedonians into those cities alongside the native populations. Plutarch claims that Alexander founded some seventy cities, though this number is doubted by modern scholarship.

Alexandria in Egypt may be the most famous of the Alexandrias, but the majority of them were founded in the East. In some cases, Alexander's city augmented existing cities with Greek and Macedonian settlers, mostly discharged veterans and mercenaries who intermarried and settled alongside the natives. These were cities such as Alexandria Maracanda (Samarkand on the old Silk Road), Alexandria Ariana, and Alexandria Arachosia (modern Herat

and Kandahar in Afghanistan). Others, such as Alexandria Eschate—"at the end of the World" (modern Khojent) on the Jaxartes (Syr Darya)—were new foundations, placed strategically but made up of the same veteran and native elements. These may have included the city remains at the modern Ai Khanum, on the Oxus River. Traditional scholarship thought this had been Alexandria Oxiana, but in fact none of the remains are older than the third century B.C.E. Recent scholarship looks to a foundation by the Greek kings of Bactria (Afghanistan). What cannot be disputed is that these settlements begun by Alexander formed the basis of a Greek society in central Asia that flourished for three hundred more years. Through two dynasties, the Greek kings of Bactria left an indelible imprint on the remains and art of the region, and maintained their independence until at least the first century B.C.E. and possibly into the first century C.E.

The facts of Alexander as "explorer" show enough to justify a real interest in exploring, if not enough to justify the legend that he was a great explorer. His last plans speak of his preparations to explore the Caspian Sea and circumnavigate the Arabian Peninsula. But he did not live to fulfill those plans.

[*See also* Colonization, Greek and Phoenician, *and* Europe and the Mediterranean, *subentry on* Greek and Roman Geography and Worldview.]

BIBLIOGRAPHY

Bosworth, A. Brian. *Alexander and the East: The Tragedy of Triumph*. Oxford: Oxford University Press, 1996.

Bosworth, A. Brian. *Conquest and Empire: The Reign of Alexander the Great*. Cambridge, U.K.: Cambridge University Press, 1988.

Fraser, Peter Marshall. *Cities of Alexander the Great*. Oxford: Oxford University Press, 1996.

Holt, Frank Lee. *Into the Land of Bones: Alexander the Great in Afghanistan*. Berkeley: University of California Press, 2005.

WINTHROP LINDSAY ADAMS

Fiction

For more than two millennia writers have been fascinated by Alexander the Great. One set of ancient authors pored over sources and created a historical Alexander. Another—larger—set of both ancient and medieval authors embellished those historical accounts and developed a huge corpus of legends. This tradition of legends, called the "Alexander Romance," is an exotic, fantastic, and occasionally romantic exploration of the real and imaginary world of the great hero. Though neglected today by readers more interested in the historical Alexander, the Romance's popularity and influence on the literature and arts of many cultures is still vividly demonstrated by the scores of manuscripts in more than two dozen languages that preserve Alexander's fictional escapades.

The historical Alexander, King of Macedon in 336 B.C.E. at the age of twenty, traveled from his home in northern Greece into Asia Minor, through Mesopotamia as far as the Indus valley, and returned to Babylon, where he died in 323 B.C.E. Throughout this long march he and his retinue of soldiers and scholars learned much about the peoples and places they witnessed. Accounts of their travels were written and transmitted in a textual tradition that survives today through such authors as Diodorus Siculus, Plutarch, and Arrian, all of whom wrote during the Roman era, three to four centuries after Alexander. The tradition of legends also has its roots in Alexander's own day. Tales were told and retold by Alexander's soldiers, his scholars, and the peoples he conquered. Over the centuries this sort of storytelling produced an array of fabulous fictions that far outstrip the surviving historical accounts in creativity, diversity, and cultural influence.

Of the extant legendary accounts, the oldest is Greek and may date to as early as the third or second century B.C.E. Some manuscripts even attribute the work, though dubiously, to Callisthenes, the nephew and pupil of Aristotle and the scholarly companion of Alexander. Much of the Alexander Romance of pseudo-Callisthenes follows the life of the historical Alexander in a pattern retained in subsequent versions. In this earliest version, however, extraordinary alterations already appear. Alexander's father is no longer Philip but is Nektanebos, the magician and former pharaoh of Egypt, and Alexander is born like a lion—with teeth like nails, strangely colored eyes, and a golden mane of hair. When he marches east and reaches the Indus valley, fantasy takes flight and Alexander is said to march deeper into India and even beyond the reaches of the known world, witnessing such marvels as cynocephalic (dog-headed) and acephalic (headless) people, talking trees, inflammable fowl, and, in a later version, even a basilisk. When he extends his explorations into the heavens and into the depths of the sea, Alexander continues to run into extraordinary creatures, including a celestial being—bird or man—that makes him look down and remember his mortality, and a sea creature that grows with the tradition, always becoming larger and larger.

As versions of the Greek tradition become more elaborate in other languages, Alexander explores ever more fantastic places and peoples and is transmuted into an ever-changing hero. A Syrian text of the seventh or eighth century C.E. develops an erotic motif by having the daughter of the Persian king fall in love with the invading Alexander simply from seeing a painting of him; this creates a romantic hero but also supports Alexander's accession to the Persian throne. Alexander's genius for invention is, in this version, first showcased when he designs bronze cavalry that will spew flames to defeat the monstrous elephants that challenge him in India; in Europe, the elephants are joined by unicorns. In Ferdowsi's great eleventh-century Persian poem *Shahnameh*, or *Epic of Kings*, Iskandar (Alexander) is Persian as well as Macedonian, having been sired by the Persian king himself but born of the daughter of Philip. Rejected because of her bad breath, she is sent back to Macedonia where she gives birth to Alexander. Despite being born abroad, Alexander returns to Persia, his other home, to claim the throne, and he is adopted as a hero of Persian legend.

The cultural and religious views attributed to Alexander reflect those of his authors, and such views sometimes appear in even the smallest of details. Middle Eastern versions introduce a clever culinary simile, through which Alexander compares a few spicy mustard seeds to handfuls of bland sesame seeds—his Macedonian soldiers versus Darius's innumerable Persian troops. In a similarly food-filled dream before the siege of Tyre, Alexander prophetically treads upon a cheese—*turos* in Greek and a clear reference to the city of Tyre—but in other languages the cheese is translated into a bunch of grapes, whose treading more universally symbolizes the shedding of blood. On a higher plane, the Alexander who was known as a persecutor of Zoroastrianism becomes, in Ferdowsi's *Shahnameh*, its protector, pledging to the dying King Darius that he will keep alive the flame and faith of Urmuzd (Ahura Mazda); soon after this, Alexander visits the ancient Kaaba at Mecca. This pair of scenes reflects Ferdowsi's own literary and personal background as a Zoroastrian writing for a Muslim ruler. In the later Persian *Iskandarnamah*, Alexander is a Muslim conqueror who joins battle shouting "Allah Akbar." In the Ethiopian version, Alexander reads about himself in the Book of Daniel and also meets and honors the Brahmans, or famous wise men of India, who are presented as the descendants of the seven thousand faithful whom God revealed to Elijah (1 Kings 19:18). In European accounts, Alexander is a model for Christian kings who defend western lands against rulers from the East; he reigns as a philosopher-king and becomes a courtly hero of the chivalric code. The scene of his knighting in European accounts abounds with magical weapons and apparel wrought for the much-favored king by gods and fairies.

For ages these legends of Alexander's exploits charged readers' imaginations with awe, and Alexander's success as a warrior, diplomat, and wise man inspired emulation. For the modern reader who wants to wander through a kaleidoscope of texts, all these versions of the Alexander Romance are still a thrilling adventure and they open windows into the literary and imaginative worlds of three continents. Although the historical Alexander may have wanted to rival the glory of Achilles, the legendary Alexander rouses readers to join him and follow the path of Odysseus, exploring many wondrous lands and meeting the all people and creatures who dwell in them.

[*See also* Fictions of Exploration, *subentry* Ancient.]

BIBLIOGRAPHY

Bunt, Gerrit H. V. *Alexander the Great in the Literature of Medieval Britain.* Groningen, Germany: Egbert Forsten, 1994. An accessible, thorough introduction to the British versions of the tradition, with a good bibliography that also includes editions of other European texts.

Kratz, Dennis M., trans. *The Romances of Alexander.* New York: Garland, 1991. English translations of Medieval Latin versions of the Romance and related texts.

Ross, David J. A. *Alexander Historiatus: A Guide to the Medieval Illustrated Alexander Literature.* 2nd ed. Frankfurt, Germany: Athenaeum, 1988. A scholarly guide to the many European versions and derivatives of the Alexander legend.

Southgate, Minoo S., trans. *Iskandarnamah: A Persian Medieval Alexander-Romance.* New York: Columbia University Press, 1978. Includes a useful bibliography for other non-European versions, including the Syriac, Ethiopic, and Persian.

Stoneman, Richard., ed. and trans. *The Greek Alexander Romance.* London: Penguin, 1991. English translation with accessible, far-ranging introduction.

BRAD L. COOK

'Ali Celebi (c. 1500–1562), Ottoman admiral, geographer, astronomer, and poet. 'Ali Celebi, who was also known as Sidi 'Ali, was born in Constantinople (Konstantiniye), modern-day Istanbul, in the beginning of the sixteenth century. He is also known as Katibi or Katib-i Rumi. He participated in Ottoman naval expeditions that included the conquest of Rhodes (1522), the battle of Preveza (1538), the sailings of Hayr al-Din Pasha, and the conquest of Libyan Tripoli (1551); he also rose to the rank of steward (*kethuda*) of the imperial arsenal (Tersane-i Amire)

at Galata; his father (Hussein Reis) and grandfather had occupied the same post. Because he belonged to one of the most distinguished families of his time, 'Ali Celebi had taken part in most of the naval engagements of the time under such famous navigators as Hayr al-Din Pasha Barbarossa and Admiral Sinan Pasha.

Sidi 'Ali's historical importance, however, rests on his activities and events to the east of Suez. In 1552 he accompanied Sultan Süleyman (r. 1520–1566) on his eastern campaign to Aleppo. In 1553 he was appointed to the post of admiral of the Egyptian fleet, and was ordered to recover from Basra the fleet that Piri Reis, the ill-starred commander of the Ottoman Suez fleet, had left in Basra, and return it to Suez.

Sidi 'Ali reached Basra in 1554. When he prepared to leave Basra with the fleet, he met the powerful Portuguese fleet on July 2, 1554, which attacked its Turkish counterpart. The Ottoman fleet was also stricken by a severe storm that ran several of his vessels aground. His plans frustrated, Sidi 'Ali barely escaped with a few remaining Turkish ships toward India. Fearing Portuguese warships patrolling the coast, and giving up hope of returning by sea, Sidi 'Ali disembarked at the port of Surat on September 28, 1554. He was welcomed by its Muslim governor, and was asked by Ahmad III, the sultan of Gujarat, to assist him in the siege of Broach. Some two hundred men from what remained of the Ottoman fleet joined Ahmad, but Sidi 'Ali, with fifty-three companions, set out on an overland trip to what is today Turkey at the end of November 1554. Leaving his ships in charge of the ruler of the place, he traveled by land over Punjab, Afghanistan, Transoxania, Khorasan, Azerbaijan, Ahmadabad, Delhi, Lahore, Kabul, Samarkand, Buhara, Mashad, Rayy, and Kazwin, before reaching Ottoman-held Baghdad at the end of February 1557.

Sidi 'Ali then set out for Istanbul after three years, and having learned that Süleyman was at Edirne, he hurried there, arriving in May. His possible worries that a fate similar to that of Piri Reis was awaiting him proved unfounded, for the sultan received him kindly, and was the first to appreciate the seaman's story; moreover, Sidi 'Ali's journey had also been a diplomatic achievement, for he brought back eighteen letters from various rulers and kings addressed to the Ottoman sultan. While he was on his long journey he had been dismissed by his admiral of Egypt. But when he came back he first was appointed as defterdar of timars (a financial office) of Diyarbakir at 80 akcas per day (June 9, 1557), and then became chief of the Galata royal ship (January 11, 1560). After his retirement (April 21, 1560) he spent his last years mostly in Istanbul, until his death on December 28, 1562. His mansion became a center of gathering for the intellectual elite. Sidi ʿAli could speak and write in Arabic, Persian, and Caghatay as well as in Turkish.

Sidi ʿAli wrote books on geography, mathematics, and astronomy. His works, also in Turkish, are chiefly translations from Persian or Arabic and deal with mathematics, astronomy, and navigation in the Indian Ocean. Some of his works have been translated into many languages. Sidi ʿAli's works show his scientific and navigational experience and knowledge.

[*See also* Reis, Piri.]

BIBLIOGRAPHY
Soucek, Svat. "Sidi ʿAli Reis. (Seydi ʿAli Reis)". In *The Encyclopaedia of Islam*. CD-ROM edition. Leiden: Brill, 1999.
Süssheim, Karl. "ʿAli (Sidi ʿAli) b. Husain." In *Encyclopaedia of Islam: A Dictionary of the Geography, Ethnography and Biography of the Muhammadan Peoples*. Vol. 1. Leiden: Brill, 1913.

SALIM AYDUZ

Alterity. The word "alterity" comes late to English dictionaries. Absent from many English dictionaries, the word figures prominently in French lexicons, where it is glossed as "change" from its affiliation with the Low Latin *alteritas*. Pierre Bayle—an author and proto-philosophe who exerted great influence on the travel literature of Montesquieu, Diderot, and Voltaire—gave the term "alterity" a social inflection in his ethnographic masterpiece the *Dictionnaire historique et critique* (1697); there, "alterity" is the nature of being another, or the quality of "being-other." Having as its antonym "identity," "alterity" has since figured strongly in writings of exploration to indicate the character of peoples and places that have no analogue or comparative measure for the observer. Alterity can be felt as a threat or menace that needs to be tamed or overcome in the name of identity, or it serves as the beginning of anthropological inquiry. What alterities define the geographic and cultural landscapes that cause the traveler to become conscious of his or her own displacement or difference? From that question the "science of man," what the eighteenth century called *les sciences humaines*, is said to begin.

Alterity has witnessed a rich history from the sixteenth century to the present. Its effects were felt long before Montaigne described it in his *Essays* (1580–1592). In "Of Coaches," a companion piece to "Of Cannibals," Montaigne launches unremitting criticism of the Spanish mercantile ventures in the New World, and he writes—ostensibly for the first time in the history of colonial literature—from the point of view of the *other*, of the Amerindians, who face the threatening alterity of the conquering Spaniards. The natives "see arrive so unexpectedly bearded men, diverse in language, religion, in form and countenance, from a place so remote and from where they would never have imagined there would be any kind of dwelling, mounted on great unknown monsters . . ." Alterity of the conquistador becomes identity when, changing the point of view, Montaigne continues in the same sentence, " . . . against those [now the Amerindians] who had not only never seen a horse, but any kind of beast led to bear and uphold a man or any other charge." And the point of view reverses twice again: "garnished with a luminous and hard skin and with trenchant and glittering weapons, against those who, for the miracle of the reflective glimmer of a mirror or a knife, would exchange great riches in gold and pearls, and who had neither knowledge nor matter by which they could easily know how to pierce our steel." Montaigne moves back and forth from what is recognizable and selfsame to what is other. He puts the one in the place of the other, and vice versa: horses are portrayed as "unknown monsters," Spanish armor as "gleaming skin," and the civilized conquerors themselves are "bearded" beings (*barbus*), thus suggestively affiliated with barbarians.

Surely Pierre Bayle had read these pages when he coined the word "*altérité*." Soon after, Montesquieu used alterity to portray an Asian envoy's description of the strange world of the French ancien régime in his *Lettres persanes* (1721). So did Diderot when he called into question European mores in his *Supplément au voyage de Bougainville* (c. 1760). Voltaire wrote *Candide* (1759) and his *Contes philosophiques* at the same time and in the same vein. Among these writers the idea of alterity was mobilized and soon bore impact on the French Revolution.

In the nineteenth century, alterity is a key concept in the anthropology and political economy of Karl Marx. The *change* or shift of objects in their state of use-value to that of exchange-value is built on alterity perceived as difference. Marx's critique of capitalism was used to rethink the economic bases of colonization. Similar inflections are scattered in the novels of Charles Dickens and Honoré de Balzac. In the later twentieth century structural anthropology is grounded on alterity as it is inherited from Montaigne, the eighteenth-century philosophes, Marx, and, too, Sigmund Freud. Claude Lévi-Strauss, a founding father of structuralism, based his research on the ways that Freud and Marx used alterity to inquire of the processes of exchange in both traditional and industrial societies and also in both physical and mental spheres. It was Michel de Certeau who later (1983) coined the term "heterology" to shape the study of alterity in general: its role in the history of discovery and conquest, in demonic possession, in mystical thinking in early modern Europe and the New World, in historiography, and even in gender and cultural studies. "Alterity" has come to refer to the "otherness" that everyone accords and respects as what belongs to human beings and to the world at large. In recent usage it tends to emphasize respect for cultural differences.

[*See also* Central and South America, *subentry on* Conquests and Colonization.]

BIBLIOGRAPHY
Certeau, Michel de. *The Capture of Speech* and *Culture in the Plural.* Translated by Tom Conley. Minneapolis: University of Minnesota Press, 1997.
Certeau, Michel de. *Heterologies.* Translated by Brian Massumi. Minneapolis: University of Minnesota Press, 1983.
Certeau, Michel de. *The Mystic Fable.* Translated by Michael B. Smith. Chicago: University of Chicago Press, 1992.
Certeau, Michel de. *The Writing of History.* Translated by Tom Conley. New York: Columbia University Press, 1992.
Montaigne, Michel de. *Essais.* Edited by Albert Thibaudet and Maurice Rat. Paris: Gallimard/Pléiade, 1950.

TOM CONLEY

Amazon River. Explorers of the enigmatic Amazon region have bequeathed us tales of heroism, drama, misfortune, dedication, avarice, cruelty, and scientific integrity. They explored against a backdrop of massive geopolitical power struggles. On the chessboard of competition for colonial supremacy, the Amazon frequently proved a crucial pawn.

Three Spanish expeditions, seeking the Indies, discovered the mouths of the Amazon in the year before the inadvertent arrival of Pedro Alvares Cabral in 1500 upon the land that was to become Brazil. All three noticed, while well out of sight of land, a huge volume of brown, fresh water, and deduced it must indicate a major river, perhaps the Ganges. The first to do so was probably the controversial Amerigo Vespucci, despite the credit often accorded Yáñez Pinzón, who called it the river of the Freshwater Sea. All three expeditions ventured a short distance into the estuary. The Spanish authorities, reluctant to antagonize Portugal (in whose territory it lay, according to the Treaty of Tordesillas), denied permission for follow-up voyages.

In 1535, having conquered Cuzco, the Inca capital, Francisco Pizarro's conquistadores heard rumors of another city of gold, Ambaya, which lay in the forests to the east. One of Pizarro's most trusted comrades, Pedro de Candía, assembled a large, well-equipped contingent to seek and conquer Ambaya. He soon encountered conditions appalling to horsemen—steep, muddy slopes blanketed by wet tropical vegetation. Months later, the pitiful remnants of his force managed to struggle back to Cuzco.

Also chasing myths of a fabulously wealthy El Dorado, this time in the Forest of Cinnamon, was another of the Pizarro brothers, Gonzalo. In 1541 he ventured eastward from Quito into the fringe of the Amazon basin. There, he too discovered the difficulties of rain forest logistics and was bogged down. A small party, led by his subordinate Francisco de Orellana, headed downstream to seek food and assistance. Finding none, and unable to return, Orellana was obliged to continue. He eventually arrived, starving, at the river's estuary. His scribe, Carvajal, reported that they had been opposed all the way, once even attacked by a tribe of warrior women he identified as the Amazons.

Stories continued to filter to the ears of the avaricious and unruly Spaniards occupying the Andes. They told of wealthy nations along the middle reaches of the Amazon, particularly the Omagua. In 1560, Pedro de Ursúa was given command of a major expeditionary force to contact and conquer the Omagua. One among his many rebellious subordinates, Lope de Aguirre, proved fatal for Ursúa. Aguirre's gang seized control of the expedition, murdering Ursúa and a hundred others before emerging into the Atlantic. Aguirre sent a defiant letter to King Philip II, who dispatched a retaliatory force to hunt down and summarily execute the rebels.

Almost a century after Orellana's journey, another expedition left Quito for the eastern forests. They intended to establish a Franciscan mission on the river Napo. After being attacked by locals and having their leader killed, they abandoned the plan, but a few, including two lay brothers, elected to continue downstream. Their arrival in Pará at the estuary in 1637 disconcerted the Portuguese governor. He ordered the veteran Pedro de Teixeira to assemble a large expedition to explore upstream as far as Quito. Teixeira's two-year round-trip journey produced the first detailed description of the river.

Portuguese slave raiders followed, moving ever westward, disrupting the local people. A Jesuit missionary from Quito, Samuel Fritz, attempted to arouse Spanish opposition to the incursions, but was unsuccessful. However, he did produce a detailed map of much of the river. [See color plate 4 in this volume.]

The first scientist to explore the length of the Amazon improved upon Fritz's cartography. After having worked in the Andes for seven years to help determine the shape of the earth, Charles-Marie de La Condamine descended the river before returning to Paris. He summarized his findings to the French Académie in 1745. His reports on its wealth of natural history stimulated generations of European explorer-scientists to visit the region. These included Alexander von Humboldt, Johann Baptist von Spix and Karl Friedrich Phillip von Martius, Louis Agassiz, Henry Walter Bates, Richard Spruce, and Alfred Russel Wallace.

The arduous and dangerous process of mapping the myriad tributaries, mainly by native canoe, was accomplished by expeditions from many nationalities throughout the nineteenth century and well into the twentieth. However, not until the advent of airborne radar in the early 1970s could all the rivers—including one over 700 miles (1,000 kilometers) long—be added to the map of the Amazon basin.

[*See also* Amazons; Fritz, Samuel; Teixeira, Pedro de; *and* Wallace, Alfred Russel.]

BIBLIOGRAPHY
Furneaux, Robin. *The Amazon: The Story of a Great River*. London: Hamish Hamilton, 1969.
Goodman, Edward J. *The Explorers of South America*. New York: Macmillan, 1972.
Smith, Anthony. *Explorers of the Amazon*. London: Viking, 1990.

MICHAEL LAYLAND

Amazons. The Amazons were a legendary tribe of nomadic female warriors, variously located by the Greeks and Romans on the shores of the Black Sea, in the Central Asian steppes, or near the Caucasus range. Their society's inversion of normative gender roles fascinated ancient authors from Homer onward, and the heroic theme of Greco-Amazonian warfare was elaborated in many works of literature and art. Ancient historians, too, treated the Amazons as an authentic and contemporaneous people whose customs could be described ethnographically. In the Middle Ages the Amazons joined other "unclean" nations of the East, such as Gog and Magog, in the isolated realm outside the gates or wall erected by Alexander the Great.

Greek portrayals of the Amazons drew heavily on what was known in the Hellenic world of the Scythians and other Asiatic peoples: dressed in leather or skins, and often wearing Persian-style trousers and caps, they wielded axes, bows, and arrows and generally devoted themselves to horsemanship and the hunt. The absence of males in their population was usually explained (as in Diodorus Siculus 2.45.3) as the result of a selective breeding system: children were conceived during brief rendezvous with neighboring tribes, and male infants were either exposed or dispatched to their fathers. According to some authors all Amazons had the right breast amputated in childhood so that they could thereafter draw the bow unhindered (hence the tribe's name, which by a spurious etymology was taken to mean "lacking a breast"). In their physical appearance the Amazons were considered unusually tall, strong, and beautiful. Their religious rites were thought to center on Ares, who was considered the ancestor of their race, and Artemis, whose dress and customs closely paralleled their own.

A central motif of the Amazon legends popular in the Greco-Roman world is that of the Amazon queen who is conquered by a Hellenic hero both sexually and militarily, or whose prowess on the battlefield is matched by her erotic power. Thus Achilles, the greatest of Greek warriors, was thought to have fallen passionately in love with the Amazon queen Penthesilea at the very moment that he killed her in combat outside the walls of Troy. Heracles was sent by Eurystheus to obtain the girdle of the Amazon queen, a quest with obvious sexual implications; and Theseus (whose feats are often patterned on those of Heracles) abducted an Amazon ruler, known variously as Hippolyta or Antiope, to be his wife (Hippolytus, the chaste hero of the Phaedra tragedies, was their son). In later legends developed out of the history of Alexander the Great's conquests, an Amazon queen named Thalestris supposedly seduced Alexander and spent thirteen days having sex with him in hope of conceiving a child by the world's greatest conqueror. A similar idea lies behind an ethnographic legend told by Herodotus, but with gender roles reversed: here (4.110) a band of Scythian soldiers, encountering Amazons for the first time, become determined to beget children with the warrior women, and the two tribes merge to form a hybrid race, the Sauromatae. All these legends explore the tension between the warlike spirit that made the Amazon race fearsome to its foes and a female sexuality that, in Greek eyes at least, rendered it more tractable, vulnerable, or seductive.

Though their queens might thus attract the erotic interest of Greek heroes, the Amazons generally were considered a fearsome enemy by the Greeks, and in art and literature they came to stand as a symbol of the Asiatic opposition to Hellenism that had culminated in the Persian invasions. In the Trojan War the Amazons were thought to have allied themselves with Priam, but to have been routed by a force led by Bellerophon. An important Athenian legend described an invasion of Attica by an army of Amazons determined to reclaim Hippolyta or Antiope from her abductor, Theseus. This invasion was stopped in a great battle outside Athens, a scene commemorated in several prominent fifth-century temple friezes (including those on the Parthenon and the temple of Apollo at Bassae). These Amazonomachy friezes show Amazons who wear Persian dress and gear being subdued by near-naked Greeks, emblematizing the perceived triumph of Hellenic over Asiatic political values in the period of the Persian wars (490–479 B.C.E.). Because she represented the inversion of normative Greek social structures, the Amazon came to be adopted, like the semi-bestial centaur, as an embodiment of all the violent and elemental forces that were felt to be the enemies of classical Hellenism.

In the Middle Ages this Greek idea of the Amazon as barbarian foe was adapted into a Christian scheme by mapmakers and geographic writers, who placed the Amazon queen among the "unclean" nations in the northeastern corner of the world. The irruption of these nations into the central sphere of Christendom would, it was supposed, herald the End of Days.

[*See also* Alexander the Great, *subentry on* Fiction.]

BIBLIOGRAPHY

Blok, Josine H. *The Early Amazons: Modern and Ancient Perspectives on a Persistent Myth*. Leiden, Netherlands, and New York: Brill, 1995.

duBois, Page. *Centaurs and Amazons: Women and the Prehistory of the Great Chain of Being*. Ann Arbor: University of Michigan Press, 1982.

Tyrrell, William Blake. *Amazons: A Study in Athenian Mythmaking*. Baltimore: Johns Hopkins University Press, 1984.

JAMES ROMM

American West, Visual Images of.

The exploration of the American West resulted in a vast array of visual images depicting the region's physical environment and its indigenous inhabitants. As part of the record of western exploration, those images revealed much about the land and even more about the explorers' perceptions and the motives of their supporters. The process of exploring the American West before 1800 involved numerous European powers who implicitly understood that claiming a region required not only words but also images, such as maps, that proved those claims.

From about 1500 to 1800, the western portion of North America was part of Spain's northern frontier, but at times the French claimed portions of it in present-day Texas and the British in the Pacific Northwest. During this period, explorers' visual imagery of the region consisted largely of maps; Spain had the best maps, but was reluctant to publish them. Although the coastal areas were explored early, the interior remained terra incognita until the very early nineteenth century. Occasionally, a Spanish explorer would also record what was encountered by drawing or sketching it (for example, Gomara's sketch of a bison from 1554), but these too were rarely published. The visual imagery of the West is indebted to pioneering Spanish natural history expeditions, including those by Alejandro Malaspina (1789–1794), who explored the West Coast, and Alexander von Humboldt (1799–1804), who helped conceptualize the geography of the region in maps.

Following the 1803 Louisiana Purchase and Lewis and Clark's Corps of Discovery from 1804 to 1806, the West became associated with American expansion. This association coincided with technological developments in publishing that both fueled and were a result of increasing public literacy. Part of this literacy involved a growing "graphicacy"—that is, the knowledge of how to "read," and hence understand, visual imagery. By the time Lewis and Clark explored the West, expeditions usually included surveyors, mapmakers, scientists, and artists, all of whom left an elaborate visual record. As was typical of exploration during the early modern period, the explorers had invariably prepared maps, but now other images, such as landscape depictions and natural history illustrations, began to flourish. These not only helped explorers to better understand the character of the region they traversed, but they also helped the public to better visualize the huge area that would by 1848 become the western United States. These images—maps, sketches, and scientific illustrations—are commonly thought of as different from each other, but they are closely related. Studied simultaneously, they reveal the increasingly detailed, and increasingly accurate, understanding that resulted from scientific inquiry.

Maps were arguably the most important images produced by an expedition. They enabled explorers' supporters to determine where explored lands were located, and an accurate map ensured that others could find those places again. Because maps generally convey a sense of authority, mapping helps endorse a claim to an area. At first, maps tended to be fairly simple, as only the broadest outlines of hydrology and topography were indicated. With increased exploration, however, maps became more detailed.

Maps of the interior North American West reveal this process of elaboration. Winterbotham's 1795 map shows most of the region as a blank space, although a huge lake with streams running into it is probably the Great Salt Lake. By about 1810, Zebulon Pike's map of New Spain, which appears to be based on Alexander von Humboldt's map, shows portions of the West in greater detail. Dr. John Robinson's 1819 map presents an increasingly detailed, but in places quite erroneous, picture of the West's interior. Robinson's map depicts several rivers, such as the Buenaventura, running across the interior to the Pacific Coast, when no river actually does so. By 1844, the explorer John Charles Frémont's expedition had confirmed that a large portion of the West was an area of interior drainage. The expedition's map by Charles Preuss represented a visual watershed in the exploration of the intermountain West.

Preuss not only was a cartographer, but also was adept at drawing landscapes. Although Frémont unsuccessfully attempted to use new photographic techniques, namely the daguerreotype, to record what his expedition experienced, the line drawing dominated for much of the nineteenth century because reports still relied on lithography rather than on photography. As was typical of the period of the explorer-scientists (as historian William Goetzmann calls them), the Frémont expedition's report featured sketches of locations such as Pyramid Lake in present-day Nevada. Even the name "Pyramid Lake," coined by Frémont for the geographic feature's similarity to the Pyramid of Cheops, suggests how important the human imagination is in visualizing places. The publication of Frémont's report was greeted by a public eager for information—and images—of the region that would soon become part of the United States. By the later nineteenth century, color lithography helped reveal the intense coloration of western landscapes and natural history subjects.

In addition to landscape imagery, government reports also featured drawings of the flora and fauna. Because of the establishment of a binomial system of identifying plants and animals in the 1700s, and the rise of the science of geology in the early 1800s, virtually everything found by explorers could now be categorized by visual means. This included rocks and minerals (which were classified according to physical parameters) and plants and animals (which were now placed into genus and species). Of intense interest were the indigenous peoples encountered on these expeditions, and they, too, were frequently recorded. Among the most revealing of such cultural images are the watercolors of the Plains Indians by George Catlin.

The West experienced a remarkable series of reconnaissances from about 1835 to the 1880s. These included railway surveys seeking the five best routes from the eastern United States to the Pacific Ocean, border surveys, and geological surveys. By the 1850s, the explorations were quite comprehensive and their visual imagery very rich. Consider, for example, William Emory's 1857 survey of the United States–Mexico borderlands, which is widely regarded as one of the most visually stunning records of a western region. Through maps, line drawings, and color lithography, the survey revealed the geographic and cultural features of the region. Emory's survey eclipsed an earlier doomed survey by Bartlett, as scientific accuracy became the watchword. Emory's survey report features not only fairly accurate maps, but also images of landscapes, flora, fauna, and even fossils.

The exploration of the American West after the Civil War coincided with the rising stature of the U.S. Geological Survey, whose reports not only documented a wide range of natural history features and included sketches of geological features, but also used another visual technique: the geological cross section. These slices of earth revealed the form of geological structure underground. As with virtually all western exploration, these images revealed that the driving force behind exploration was ultimately both intellectual (or scientific) and commercial. Through the use of images, the West could be better marketed as public land that was available for settlement, mining, and logging. In turn, those beautifully illustrated reports stimulated the public's interest in personally experiencing some of the West's unique features, such as Yellowstone and the Grand Canyon, that were ultimately preserved as national parks. Consider the case of Ferdinand Vandeveer Hayden's beautifully illustrated geological survey of the Yellowstone country of western Wyoming that resulted from his 1870–1871 reconnaissance. The visual images in that publication also helped put that previously remote area into the public consciousness. Through its wide publication, this report helped lead to the creation of America's first national park in 1872. By the 1880s, exploration of the West was tapering off, as much of the region was no longer terra incognita. However, although the age of geographic exploration ended about 1900, scientific exploration of the West continues to the present, and visual images of the region (such as detailed satellite images) continue to inspire the public. [See color plate 5 in this volume.]

[*See also* Frémont, John Charles, *and* Maps, Mapmaking, and Mapmakers.]

BIBLIOGRAPHY

Allen John Logan, ed. *North American Exploration.* 3 vols. Lincoln: University of Nebraska Press, 1997.

Cohen Michael. *Mapping the West.* New York: Rizzoli International, 2003.

Francaviglia, Richard. *Mapping and Imagination in the Great Basin: A Cartographic History.* Reno: University of Nevada Press, 2005.

Goetzmann William H. *Exploration and Empire: The Explorer and the Scientist in the Winning of the American West.* New York: Knopf, 1966.

Reinhartz, Dennis, and Gerald, Saxon, eds. *The Mapping of the Entradas into the Greater Southwest.* Norman: University of Oklahoma Press, 1998.

Wheat Carl. *Mapping the Trans-Mississippi West, 1540–1861.* 6 vols. San Francisco: The Institute of Historical Cartography, 1957–1963.

RICHARD FRANCAVIGLIA

Amundsen, Roald (1872–1928), Norwegian polar explorer. During the years 1903 to 1906, Roald Amundsen became the first person to navigate the whole length of the Northwest Passage. Amundsen was accompanied by six well-paid men aboard the Norwegian herring boat *Gjøa*, which weighed a mere forty-seven tons and was the same age as the explorer.

Amundsen was born on July 16, 1872, into a family of shipowners and shipmasters on a farm in the parish of Borge, south of Oslo, at a time when Norway was joined to Sweden under a Swedish monarch. Amundsen's father was Jens Engebreth Amundsen and his mother was Hanna (née Sahlquist). The tragic story of the British explorer Sir John Franklin, who died in 1847 during his voyage in search of the Northwest Passage, had captured Amundsen's imagination in boyhood. He was thrilled, too, by Fridtjof Nansen's first crossing of the Greenland ice sheet and by that great Norwegian's remarkable voyage in the *Fram* into the ice of the Arctic Ocean in 1893 to 1896. Amundsen served his own apprenticeship in the pack ice, partly by sealing in the Arctic and, more important, by serving as second officer during the Antarctic voyage of the *Belgica*, led by Adrien de Gerlache from 1897 to 1899. Amundsen's plans were then made to reach the North Magnetic Pole (while secretly intending to navigate the Northwest Passage from the Atlantic Ocean to the Pacific Ocean). Amundsen's plans matured with the help of Professor Georg Neumayer, director of the Deutsche See-

Fixing the propeller. This photograph comes from *My Polar Flight* (London, 1925), the book Amundsen wrote when he had become convinced that the future of Arctic exploration was by air; three years later he would perish in the course of an aerial expedition. COURTESY THE NEWBERRY LIBRARY, CHICAGO

warte in Hamburg, the German marine observatory, of Dr. F. A. Cook, and of Nansen himself. The magnetic pole had been first attained in 1831 by James Clark Ross, a British naval officer. Its position is of particular importance to navigation. Unlike the geographic poles, the magnetic poles migrate over the centuries owing to the changing relationship between the metallic core of the earth and its outer mantle—so that seventy years after Ross's achievement, the North Magnetic Pole needed to be located again. It cannot be said that Amundsen was fascinated or even truly interested in polar science, whose problems puzzled and intrigued the British Antarctic explorer Captain Robert F. Scott. However, he did realize that involvement in a venture with a scientific objective could arouse not only the approval of men such as Nansen, but funding for the enterprise. In the introduction to his narrative *The North West Passage* (1908), Amundsen remarked on the discovery by Franklin's overland expeditions of a strip of saltwater washing the north coast of America, and the knowledge obtained subsequently (through the Franklin Search expeditions) of "a sea passage round Northern America." However, "we did not know," he continued, "whether this passage was practicable for ships and no one had yet navigated it throughout." By May 1903, the *Gjøa*, equipped with a small petrol (gasoline) engine (to whose excellence Amundsen largely attributed their successful navigation), was ready to attempt the Northwest Passage. Equipped with scientific instruments, food for five years, and six sled dogs, but with his financial difficulties not entirely solved, Amundsen departed from Christiania (Oslo) in June 1903, "following in the track of our predecessors." [See color plate 6 in this volume.]

The *Gjøa* sailed up the west coast of Greenland as far as Wolstenholme Sound. It then entered Lancaster Sound and traversed Barrow Strait. It was able to navigate Peel Sound, Franklin Strait, and James Ross Strait, passing east of King William Island and so avoiding the heavy multiyear ice from the Central Polar Basin, which had trapped Franklin's ships in Victoria Strait. On the south coast of King William Island, a safe harbor was found, which Amundsen named Gjøahavn. From there the second in command, the Danish naval officer Godfred Hansen, mapped the east coast of Victoria Island, one of the few then yet uncharted coastlines of the Arctic Archipelago, while Amundsen journeyed toward the region of the North Magnetic Pole. Unfortunately, his observations were in error and he is said by Roland Huntford to have reproached himself in that respect for the rest of his life. The Netsilik Eskimo (Inuit) of

---

---

the area proved of great interest during the months in Gjøahavn; they demonstrated the art of survival in those desolate lands. Amundsen learned from them and collected their artifacts.

Continuing westward on leaving Gjøahavn in August 1905, the navigation became nerve-racking, leading Amundsen to express his great admiration for Captain Richard Collinson, who had taken HMS *Enterprise*, a large vessel, into these hazardous waters half a century earlier in search of Franklin. The *Gjøa* was stopped by ice off the mainland coast and was forced to winter again, this time at King Point. Meanwhile, Amundsen left his party for five months to travel northward overland to the nearest telegraph office, to break the news of his success to the world. After his return, the little engine enabled the *Gjøa* to progress through the sea ice and around Cape Barrow (Alaska) before sailing through Bering Strait on August 30, 1906; thence it went south to San Francisco, where the vessel remained until 1972, when it was shipped to Oslo. In the maritime museum outside the Norwegian capital, the *Gjøa* can be seen next to the *Fram*, both memorials to the extraordinary determination, daring, and imagination of Nansen and his younger countryman Roald Amundsen, who is also celebrated as the first person to reach the South Pole.

After an unsuccessful and costly voyage in the *Maud* along the north coast of Siberia during 1918–1920, Amundsen decided that the future of Arctic expedition lay with the airship and airplane. He disappeared during a flight to rescue the lost crew of the airship *Italia* in 1928, a fitting death for this hardy Viking.

[*See also* Antarctica; North Pole; Northwest Passage; Polar Flights; *and biographical entries on figures mentioned in this article.*]

BIBLIOGRAPHY

Amundsen, Roald. *The North West Passage*. 2 vols. London: Constable, 1908.

Huntford, Roland. *Scott and Amundsen*. London: Hodder and Stoughton, 1979.

Huntford, Roland, ed. *The Amundsen Photographs*. London: Hodder and Stoughton, 1987; New York: Atlantic Monthly Press, 1987.

Savours, Ann. *The Search for the North West Passage*. London: Chatham, 1999; New York, St. Martin's Press, 1999.

ANN SAVOURS

Andersson, Karl Johan (1827–1867), Swedish hunter, naturalist, and explorer of southwest Africa. Andersson was born in Vänersborg, Sweden, in 1827. After a year at the University of Lund in 1847, and a short stint as a professional hunter, he went to England where he met Francis Galton, who was seeking a companion to accompany him on an expedition to southern Africa. Arriving at Walvis Bay in late 1850, they set out for the interior searching for Lake Ngami, a place discovered earlier by David Livingstone. They journeyed through previously unexplored Owamboland, but only got slightly farther than Etosha Pan. In August 1851, they trekked to the western edge of the Kalahari. After Galton returned to England, Andersson explored alone in the Kalahari, and this time he made it to Lake Ngami in 1853.

In 1859 Andersson traveled in northern present-day Namibia where he reached the Cunene River, and later he became the first European to see and describe the Okovango River. Andersson married Sarah Jane Aitchison in July 1860, and during the next few years they resided with the Herero tribe in Damaraland. Andersson authored many books, the best known of which are *Lake Ngami* (1855) and *The Okovango River* (1861). A book published after his death, *Lion and the Elephant* (1873), reveals him to be an avid, but indiscriminate, big game hunter. In just one evening in Bechuanaland (now Botswana),

"A Well-stocked Hunting-ground." Illustration from Karl Johan Andersson's *The Okovango River* (London, 1861). This image shows only too well the way in which Andersson thought of Africa as full of creatures ready for his gun. The title is particularly revealing. COURTESY THE NEWBERRY LIBRARY, CHICAGO

Andersson killed eight rhinos, an action later condemned by Frederick Selous, Africa's most famous white hunter. While again exploring in Owamboland, Andersson died at the village of Ondangua on July 5, 1867.

[*See also* Galton, Francis; Livingstone, David; *and* Selous, Frederick.]

BIBLIOGRAPHY

Andersson, Charles John. *Lake Ngami, or Explorations and Discovery During Four Years' Wandering in the Wilds of South Western Africa.* Cape Town: C. Struik,1967.

Andersson, Charles John. *The Okavango River: A Narrative of Travel, Exploration, and Adventure.* Cape Town: C. Struik, 1968.

SANFORD H. BEDERMAN

Anglo-Dutch Maritime Wars. In twenty-three years (1652–1674), commercial competition spawned three Anglo-Dutch wars, which were overwhelmingly maritime with naval battles and assaults scattered from Europe to Asia. While naval strength favored England in the North Sea, the Dutch had the advantage elsewhere. Neither country decisively won any war, but overseas engagements emphasized the growing importance of global-scale geographical and navigational expertise.

Events in the 1640s that advantaged Dutch commerce precipitated the First Anglo-Dutch War (1652–1654). In 1648, after an eighty-year war, Spain recognized Dutch independence and legalized Dutch trade in Spanish territory. During the Venetian-Turkish War (1645–1649) the Dutch supplanted Venice as the dominant European commercial power in the Levant. Civil war in England (1642–1648) disrupted English navigation, and the reliance of English American colonists on Dutch merchants for shipping and financial services increased.

This rapid Dutch penetration of markets in Europe, the Levant, and the Americas complemented their commercial power in West Africa and Asia and gave them global-scale commercial dominance over European competitors. England, in turn, experienced precipitous declines in numerous markets, whether for Baltic timber, Spanish wool, Canary Islands wine, or goods from the Levant.

After privateering attacks on Dutch shipping and diplomatic pressure to forge an Anglo-Dutch alliance failed to tame the Dutch, the English Parliament passed the first Navigation Act in 1651 and declared war in 1652. England inflicted serious losses on the Dutch in the North Sea, seizing over one thousand ships. The Dutch, meanwhile, blocked English access to the Baltic, intercepted England's convoys from the Levant, and attacked English ships in Asian waters. The war ended in 1654 with neither side gaining anything significant for their great losses.

Hostilities in West Africa and North America preceded the Second Anglo-Dutch War (1665–1667). In 1663, the English captured all the Dutch forts on the Slave Coast, except Elmina and Fort Nassau, which the Dutch soon retook. In 1664, an English naval fleet took New Netherland, and privateers from Jamaica attacked Dutch vessels in the Caribbean. When the English declared war, they anticipated a quick victory through a major naval confrontation in European waters, and expected European support in checking Dutch commercial dominance. But other Europeans were wary of England's political ambitions and supported the Dutch. In the Caribbean, the English took Saint Eustatius, Saba, Pomeroon, and Essequibo. The Dutch, with Danish support, closed the Baltic to English ships. In Asia, the Dutch East India Company disrupted English trade, and in the Mediterranean English shipping virtually ceased. The Dutch retook Essequibo and Pomeroon, and occupied English Surinam. In the treaty signed at Breda in 1667, England retained New Netherland (renamed New York), but ceded Surinam, returned Saint Eustatius and Saba, relinquished claims to Pola Run in Southeast Asia, and conceded the principle of "free ship, free goods."

Unresolved problems in Surinam contributed to the Third Anglo-Dutch War (1672–1674), which began one day after Louis XIV declared war on the Dutch and invaded the United Provinces. Fearing French ambitions to control the United Provinces' global trade networks, Spain and Austria declared war against France. The Dutch exploited their advantage on the high seas by capturing English commercial vessels. After losing upward of seven hundred ships, and with nothing to gain from war, the English got out in 1674.

BIBLIOGRAPHY

Israel, Jonathan I. *Dutch Primacy in World Trade, 1585–1740.* Oxford and New York: Clarendon Press, 1989.

Jones, J. R. *The Anglo-Dutch Wars of the Seventeenth Century.* London and New York: Longman, 1996.

ELIZABETH MANCKE

Anson, George (1697–1762), British naval officer who led a voyage around the world. Born into a minor county family, the Ansons of Shugborough, Staffordshire, England, George Anson entered the Royal Navy in 1712 at the age of fourteen. Twelve years later

"A View of the Commodore's Tent at the Island of Juan Fernandes." Illustration from Richard Walter's *Anson's Voyage Around the World* (London, 1749). Here is a fine example of the way in which eighteenth-century artists imposed a sort of parklike elegance on remote landscapes. The commodore and his officers seem to be busy chatting and exercising their little dogs. COURTESY THE NEWBERRY LIBRARY, CHICAGO

he was promoted to captain, but his subsequent career in the peacetime navy was relatively undistinguished. When war with Spain broke out in 1739, Anson was informed that he was to command an expedition to the South Sea. Patronage probably explains the choice of Anson, for he was on good terms with Admiral of the Fleet Sir John Norris and also with the lord chancellor, Lord Hardwicke, whose daughter he married in 1748. After several changes of direction by the admiralty and many dockyard delays, Anson finally sailed in August 1740 as commodore of a squadron of six warships, ranging in size from the 1,000-ton *Centurion* to the small *Tryal* sloop. His orders were to raid Spanish settlements in the South Sea, encourage rebellion in Peru against Spanish rule, and capture the silver-laden Acapulco galleon on its annual voyage to Manila.

Almost from the beginning the expedition ran into trouble. Because of his late start, Anson approached Cape Horn in the southern hemisphere autumn, when the equinoctial gales were at their fiercest. With crews ravaged by scurvy, the squadron was battered by relentless storms as it tried to round Cape Horn. Two ships turned back, while a third, the *Wager*, was wrecked off the coast of Chile. When Anson and his three remaining ships reached the old buccaneer haven of Juan Fernández, only 335 men were left alive out of the ships' original complement of 961—not enough to man even the *Centurion* at normal levels. In September 1741, Anson set sail to carry out what he could of his instructions. He took the little town of Paita and captured a few prizes, but off Acapulco he missed the galleon by three weeks. After a distressing voyage across the North Pacific—during which only a spell on the island of Tinian kept the remnants of the crew alive—Anson reached Macao in November 1742 with one vessel left, the *Centurion*. The symbolic turning point of the voyage finally came the following summer, when Anson captured the westbound galleon from Acapulco, the *Nuestra Señora de Covadonga*, off the Philippines. In its hold were 1,313,843 pieces of eight (the famous Spanish silver dollar) and 35,682 ounces of virgin silver. When Anson reached England in June 1744, he received a hero's welcome despite his losses—which included no fewer than 1,400 men dead out of the original 1,900 who had left England in 1740. Anson's personal fortune was made, and so was his career. He was appointed to the Board of Admiralty almost immediately, raised to the peerage in 1748, and remained First Lord of the Admiralty (with one brief interlude) from 1751 until his death on June 6, 1762.

Anson's circumnavigation accomplished little in terms of primary exploration, although his visits to Macao and Canton threw a harsher light on Chinese government and society than was customary at this time. Anson may have made few new discoveries, but there is no doubt that the best-selling account of the voyage, published in 1748, aroused new interest in the South Sea. The book, written under Anson's close supervision, argued in favor of the expansion of British commerce and power in the Pacific. Compared with the slipshod literary efforts of most of Anson's privateering predecessors, the book was a careful, unsensational work, and the number of charts and views in it—forty-two in all—showed Anson's concern to guide future voyagers in a largely unknown region. For his successors, Anson's voyage, with its heavily armed ships, sickly crews, and unrealistic objectives, was an object lesson in how not to do things, but the interest in the Pacific that it helped to engender bore a different fruit twenty years later in the voyages of Cook and his successors.

[*See also* Cook, James; Pacific, *subentry on* European Trade Routes; *and* South Sea Company.]

BIBLIOGRAPHY

Williams, Glyndwr. *The Prize of All the Oceans: The Triumph and Tragedy of Anson's Voyage Round the World*. London: HarperCollins, 1999; New York, Viking, 2000.

Williams, Glyndwr, ed. *A Voyage Round the World by George Anson*. London: Oxford University Press, 1974.

GLYNDWR WILLIAMS

Antarctica. Ferdinand Magellan in 1520 found a strait across America and named the land to the south "Tierra del Fuego," presumed to be a peninsula of the vast polar land called "Terra Australis Incognita" by early cartographers. The exploration for a southern continent in essence began with Captain James Cook's second (1772–1776) of three British circumnavigations of 1768–1780. Much of the voyage of *Resolution* and *Adventure* was south of 60° S. On January 17, 1773, Cook made the first crossing of the Antarctic Circle. He saw evidence that a landmass had to be close by to the south. His reports of fur seal abundance brought economic impetus to explore waters of the far south. Who was first to see Cook's conjectured southern landmass? [See color plate 7 in this volume.]

Discovery and Early Exploration. Antarctica is the only continent that had not been peopled prior to first European visits, and so crediting true discovery might be expected to be easy. However, loss of ships' logs and questions over what was actually seen raise controversy. Moreover, sealing companies tended to keep secret any lucrative new grounds discovered.

Discovery of the continent is generally credited to one of three 1820 sightings. The Russian captain Fabian von Bellingshausen, of the *Vostok*, saw the front of an ice shelf (Princess Martha Coast) on January 16. On January 30, the British captain William Smith and Edward Bransfield (in the brig *Williams*) saw Trinity Island and a northern part of the Antarctic Peninsula, while on November 16, the New England fur sealer captain Nathanial Palmer (in the sloop *Hero*) visited Trinity Island and saw the peninsula. By this chronology, Bellingshausen is generally accredited as Antarctica's discoverer, even though his ice shelf likely was much farther from the continent and may also have been floating at the time. He saw no continental bedrock, but such ice must be derived from a landmass.

The question of "discovery," however, mirrors that of Christopher Columbus's October 12, 1492, landfall on a Bahamian islet, for which he generally is credited with the "discovery" of America—excluding eleventh-century Vikings and prehistoric Asians crossing the Bering land bridge. The Bahamas are "continental islands" and part of the North American continent as demarked by the continental shelf, which justifies the Columbus claim.

In 1819 contrary winds blew the brig *Williams* of the English captain William Smith, on a Valparaiso-bound trading voyage from Buenos Aires, far south of normal routes close to Cape Horn. On February 19 he encountered an unknown land and called it "New South Britain" (now Livingston Island, South Shetland Islands). The South Shetlands are continental islands that lie on the outer continental shelf of this part of the Antarctic Peninsula, as clearly shown on Tau Rho Alpha's 1989 physiographic map of Antarctica. Smith's logs were destroyed, but substantial evidence remains for this discovery.

Crediting discovery to Smith's 1819 accidental sighting, as here justified, would mean that in 1820 Bellingshausen was first to sight "East Antarctica" (the largest part of the continent in mostly east longitudes), and Smith and Bransfield were first to sight the Antarctic Peninsula. Smith's reports of rich sealing grounds quickly brought others by 1820. Eleven men from the British sealer *Lord Melville*, wrecked in 1821 on King George Island (South Shetland Islands), were Antarctica's first overwinterers.

Searches for sealing grounds continued, leading to extensive explorations around Antarctica. One standout was James Weddell, of the English brig

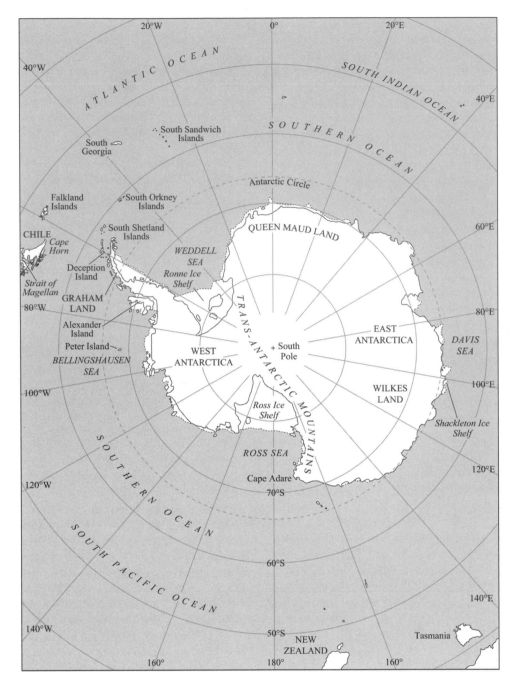

Antarctica. Map by Bill Nelson

Jane. After two South Shetland seasons' sealing, his searches in 1823 led him into the great sea at the southern end of the Atlantic Ocean, which he named "King George IV Sea" (later renamed after its discoverer). Weddell made a new southing record on 74°15′ S on February 20, 1823. The first clear sightings of the coast of East Antarctica were made February 24, 1831, in the region named Enderby Land,

by Captain John Biscoe, of the British sealing firm Enderby Brothers. Though sealing declined as herds were decimated, explorations continued for other purposes.

Three nations sent major national naval explorations. J. S. C. Dumont d'Urville led a brief 1838 French exploration in the ships *Astrolobe* and *Zélée* as part of a third circumnavigation, in which he discovered an area he claimed for France and named "Adelie Land" after his wife. The Briton James Clark Ross, after discovering the North Magnetic Pole, was sent to find its southern counterpart, which he sought in 1839–1843 in the ships *Erebus* and *Terror*. It could not be reached, but the Ross Sea, Ross Ice Shelf, and Victoria Land were among Ross's major discoveries. The American naval lieutenant Charles Wilkes led a circumnavigation by the United States Exploring Expedition in 1838–1842, which in part charted extensive coasts of East Antarctica (now Wilkes Land). Reports by Ross of right whales in the Weddell and Ross seas revived exploration interest in the 1890s. Whaling, concentrated at South Georgia and South Shetland Islands, continued into the 1930s, when populations declined.

Travels into the Interior. The heroic age of the early twentieth century brought inland explorations to reach the South Pole. Explorations were led by Robert Falcon Scott in 1901–1904 in the ship *Discovery*; by Ernest Shackleton in 1907–1909 in *Nimrod*; by Scott in 1910–1912 in *Terra Nova*; by Roald Amundsen in 1910–1912 in *Fram*; and by Shackleton in 1914–1916 in *Endurance*. The pole was first reached by the Norwegian Amundsen on December 14, 1911; Amundsen's party was soon followed by Scott's British party, who reached the pole on January 17, 1912, and whose return sledge trek ended in tragedy. Shackleton's attempt to cross the continent failed when pack ice crushed *Endurance*. Wilhelm Filchner's *Deutschland* on an earlier German attempted crossing also failed (1911–1912), though the Luitpold Coast and a major ice shelf were discovered. A Japanese expedition attempted to reach the South Pole in 1910–1912 in the ship *Kainan-maru*, under Nobu Shiraze.

An aircraft age began with the Australian outbacker George Hubert Wilkins's first Antarctic flight on December 20, 1928, over the Antarctic Peninsula, from where the American Lincoln Ellsworth took off on the first aircraft crossing of Antarctica (1935–1936), with discovery of Antarctica's highest mountains (Ellsworth Mountains). In 1929–1930 the Norwegian pilot Hjalmar Riiser-Larsen discovered Queen Maud Land. However, it was the American naval aviator Richard Evelyn Byrd who incorporated aircraft for wide-scale explorations from his Ross Ice Shelf base called Little America. After his 1926 first flight over the North Pole (though whether he was actually first remains controversial), Byrd also first flew over the South Pole, on November 28, 1929. Byrd's second expedition (1933–1935) included four aircraft for

surveys. Large regions near the Ross Sea were also explored by geologists on dogsleds. World War II terminated Byrd's third expedition, the government-sponsored U.S. Antarctic Service (1939–1941). Many discoveries were made in the southern Antarctic Peninsula by the British Graham Land Expedition (1934–1937) under John Rymill, and by the American Finn Ronne's Antarctic Research Expedition (1948–1949).

The early explorers made scientific as well as geographic discoveries. The American James Eights first discovered fossils in Antarctica in 1830 on the South Shetland Islands. The Norwegian Carl Anton Larsen, founder of Antarctica's whaling industry, in 1892 found abundant fossils (Mesozoic ammonites) and sedimentary rocks that demonstrated the continental character of the peninsula, which enticed the geologist Otto Nordenskjold to go for further study, as he did with the Swedish Antarctic Expedition of 1901–1904. William Bruce (Scottish National Antarctic Expedition, 1902–1904) discovered the mostly submarine ridge connecting South America with Antarctica, naming the intervening sea "Scotia" after his ship, and he also discovered Caird Coast east of Weddell Sea. The geologist Edgeworth David and his student Douglas Mawson, of Shackleton's *Nimrod* expedition, discovered the South Magnetic Pole on January 16, 1909, and Scott's *Terra Nova* party discovered and brought back coal and the first plant fossils (Paleozoic age) from the continental interior.

IGY Brings Science Discoveries. Though scientific discoveries made on early expeditions were significant, modern Antarctic science required major investment by governments. The International Geophysical Year (IGY, 1957–1958) was organized in large part to find out more about the polar regions, especially Antarctica. Before that, little of Antarctica's interior had been visited, and Antarctica was thought possibly to consist of two smaller landmasses tied by ice sheets. Twelve nations carried out scientific studies from forty-eight stations. Wide-ranging over-ice seismic surveying traverses discovered and began mapping the true surface of the continent under ice sheets that sometimes exceeded two miles thick. Unseen mountains like the large Gamburtsev Subglacial Mountains were discovered by seismic soundings (Soviet Union IGY traverse). During the IGY, Vivian Fuchs led the first British crossing of Antarctica.

By World War II, seven nations had territorial claims in Antarctica, as did Nazi Germany from a secret expedition (New Schwabenland, 1938–1939).

Rivalries arose from overlapping claims, particularly among Argentina, Chile, and Great Britain. One of the IGY's greatest discoveries was not scientific or geographic but political: namely, how rival cold war nations could cooperate peacefully on explorations of a continent. The twelve IGY nations signed the Antarctic Treaty on December 1, 1959, a remarkable document that preserves an entire continent for peaceful uses only. Although traces of minerals—for instance, gold and copper—were found, deposits of economic significance have not been. Today's economic activity is centered on a growing tourism industry.

Further explorations were primarily for government-funded scientific research. As geographic discoveries dwindled, scientific ones rapidly expanded, in many directions—beneath the ice and seas, and into and beyond the atmosphere. In 1972–1973 the Deep Sea Drilling Project ship *Glomar Challenger* in the Ross Sea made the first of three voyages drilling into Antarctica's surrounding seafloor. Atmospheric studies led to the discovery of how polar ozone holes form. Douglas Mawson found Antarctica's first meteorite in 1912, while now some twenty thousand meteorite pieces have been recovered, some identified from the moon and some from Mars. A 1969 Japanese discovery showed how meteorites concentrate on ice sheets. Deep ice coring at the American South Pole and Russian Vostok stations have yielded ice samples preserving information on how climates change. Antarctica, the least-disturbed land, provides a natural laboratory to aid understanding the entire earth.

[*See also* International Geophysical Year; *Terra Australis Incognita*; Whaling; *and biographical entries on figures mentioned in this article*.]

BIBLIOGRAPHY

Alpha, Tau Rho, and Arthur B. Ford. *Oblique Maps of Antarctica*. U.S. Geological Survey Map I-1992. Washington, D.C.: U.S. Government Printing Office, 1989.

Bertrand, Kenneth J. *Americans in Antarctica, 1775–1948*. New York: American Geographical Society, 1971.

Gurney, Alan. *Below the Convergence: Voyages toward Antarctica, 1699–1839*. New York: Norton, 1997.

Jones, A. G. E. *Antarctica Observed: Who Discovered the Antarctic Continent?* Whitby, U.K.: Caedmon, 1982.

Mills, William James. *Exploring Polar Frontiers: A Historical Encyclopedia*. 2 vols. Santa Barbara, Calif.: ABC–CLIO, 2003.

ARTHUR B. FORD

Antichthon and Antipodes. The Greeks were aware at an early stage that the Atlantic coast of Europe was not the limit of the inhabited, or habitable, world. Homer and Hesiod, perhaps with knowledge of the Canary Islands, located the Islands of the Blessed in the far west, and Herodotus discussed the possibility that the Cassiterides or Tin Islands (part of the British Isles?) were the source of metals traded in the Aegean. Plato, however, was the first author we know of to speculate about huge landmasses, as large as or larger than that formed by Europe, Asia, and Africa, lying beyond great expanses of "Ocean in the West." His tale of Atlantis in the *Timaeus* (25a) includes mention of a "true continent" lying beyond the island empire of Atlantis and in part ruled by it (an idea that implies inhabitation). After the subsidence of Atlantis left the western seas shallow and muddy, Plato imagines, this continent had become inaccessible to sea travel. Probably contemporary with Plato is a report preserved in the pseudo-Aristotelian *On Marvelous Things Heard* regarding a fruitful but uninhabited western island, distant by "many days" from the Strait of Gibraltar, which had been discovered by Carthaginian sailors but then hushed up to prevent mass emigration.

In the Hellenistic era speculation about other worlds focused on the south rather than the west, driven by the zone theory of global climatic structure. Since the known world was thought not to extend as far south as the Equator, it could be easily supposed—given the overall pattern of north-south symmetry that had influenced Greek geographic thinking since the pre-Socratics—that there was a second world lying beyond that line, occupying a second temperate zone in the Southern Hemisphere. Aristotle hypothesized along these lines in the *Meteorologica*, and in the following century Eratosthenes visualized the whole scheme in a poem that describes the earth as seen by the god Hermes from a great distance above: "Two zones there were, opposite one another, between the heat and the showers of ice; both were temperate regions, growing with grain . . . and in them dwelt men counter-footed to each other." The idea that the inhabitants of the two temperate zones would be *antipodes*, "counter-footed" in the sense of forming mirror images across the equatorial line, soon gave a colorful new name to the hypothetical southern continent and to the inhabitants it was assumed to have. (An alternate name for this continent, *antichthon* or "counter-world," was less frequently used.)

Plato's intuition regarding a new world in the west, and the climate-based scheme of Eratosthenes that assumed one in the south, were merged by Crates of Mallos in the second century B.C.E. to create a quadripartite earth containing four inhabited worlds. North-south travel between them was thought impossible on account of the extreme heat of the Equator, while sheer distance prevented any communication from passing between eastern and western *oikoumenē*. This four-world scheme attained canonical authority in Europe after Cicero used it in the *Dream of Scipio* segment of the lost dialogue *Republic* and Macrobius subsequently annotated that text as a guide to geography in the fifth century C.E. Thus medieval world maps that show one hemisphere of the globe divided into two landmasses, the *orbis terrarum* in the north and the *Terra Antipodum* or *Terra Incognita* in the south, are today referred to as "Macrobian" though they derive in fact from Crates.

The notion that the antipodal continent was inhabited, generally assumed by ancient geographers, caused difficulties for the early church fathers, not (as is sometimes supposed) because it implied a spherical earth but because it posited a race of humans not descended from Adam and not within reach of Christian redemption. Lactantius mocked the idea of the antipodes by imagining an upside-down world where people walked with feet in the air; other Christian writers asked how antipodal humans could avoid falling off the "bottom" of the globe. Augustine, in *The City of God* (16.9), addressed the controversy in a less fantastical way, asserting simply that, without any empirical data to back it up, the theory of the inhabited antipodes must give way before the authority of the Bible, which clearly asserts the essential unity of the human race and (especially in Psalm 19) the penetration of the Word of God to all parts of the globe. Augustine's argument against antipodal humans became church dogma in the Middle Ages and continued to be echoed by European geographical writers down to the time of Columbus.

[*See also* Eratosthenes *and* Oikoumenē *and* Orbis Terrarum.]

BIBLIOGRAPHY

Rainaud, Armand. *Le continent austral: Hypothèses et découvertes*. Paris: A Colin, 1893. Reprint, Amsterdam: Meridian, 1965.

Romm, James. *The Edges of the Earth in Ancient Thought: Geography, Exploration, and Fiction*. Princeton, N.J.: Princeton University Press, 1992. See chap. 4.

JAMES ROMM

Antilia. Along with real islands, medieval cartographers included many imaginary and mythical islands on their maps of the Atlantic Ocean. Antilia is one of these imaginary islands, located beyond the Azores. The name Antilia means "island opposite," and here the opposing shore was that of Portugal. On the nautical chart of Zuane Pizzigano (1424), Antilia appears as a rectangular island almost the size of Ireland.

The island is tied to the story of the Islamic conquest of the Iberian Peninsula. According to the story, around 734 C.E. the archbishop of Oporto, Portugal, six other bishops, and their adherents fled to Antilia and created seven cities. In 1414 a Spanish ship was reported to have visited the island, as did Portuguese sailors. Later, Columbus believed in Antilia, and he hoped to use it as a staging area for the voyage to the west.

The name "Antilia" persists in what some believed was Columbus's discovery of Antilia and its neighboring islands. This is why the Portuguese called the West Indies the "Antillas" and the French called them "Les Antilles." The story of the seven cities of Antilia reappeared in the sixteenth century as the fabled Seven Cities of Cíbola in the United States and in the name of an extinct volcano crater, now called Septe Citade, on São Miguel in the Azores. The Portuguese historian Armando Cortesao, an authority on Antilia, insisted that the Portuguese crossed the Atlantic before Columbus did, and that they discovered Hispañola and Cuba. This discovery was kept secret at home, thus creating the mystery and legend connected to Antilia.

[*See also* Columbus, Christopher; Fictitious and Fantastic Places; *and* Maps, Mapmaking, and Mapmakers.]

BIBLIOGRAPHY

Johnson, Donald S. *Phantom Islands of the Atlantic: The Legends of Seven Lands That Never Were*. London: Souvenir Press, 1997.

RUSSELL M. MAGNAGHI

Antipodes. *See* **Antichthon and Antipodes.**

Anville, Jean-Baptiste d' (1697–1782), French cartographer. Jean-Baptiste Bourguignon d'Anville was born in Paris, and was a student at the Collège des Quatre-Nations with his brother Hubert Gravelot, who became a celebrated engraver. D'Anville was a skillful drawer, and his interest in modern

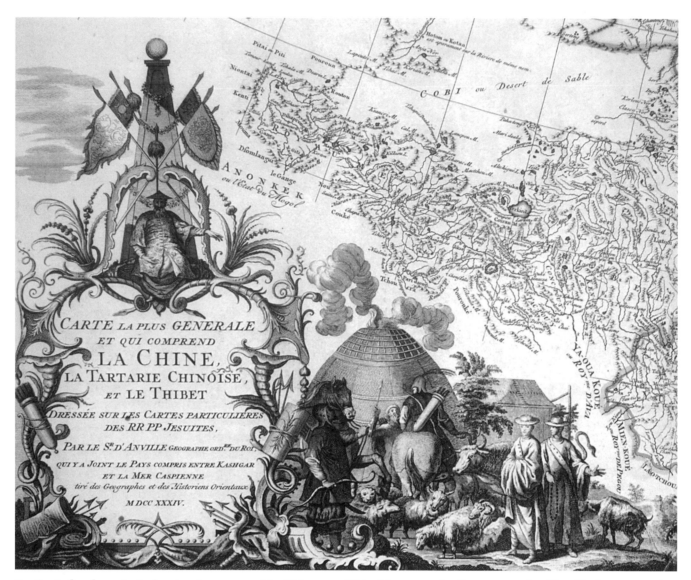

La Carte la plus générale et qui comprend la Chine. . . . This title cartouche from a map by d'Anville (Paris, 1734) is full of information; note particularly the two inquisitive-looking Jesuits on the right and the emperor on his impressive throne. COURTESY THE NEWBERRY LIBRARY, CHICAGO

geography enabled him to draw up his historic maps. These two geographical approaches to cartography—an artist's approach and a geographer's approach—are found in the maps d'Anville drew for the *Histoire de l'Isle Espagnole ou S. Domingue* (2 vols.; Paris, 1730–1731), the work of the Jesuit father François-Xavier de Charlevoix (1682–1761). D'Anville's growing reputation induced another Jesuit, Father Jean-Baptiste Du Halde (1674–1743), to ask him to codify the maps of China drawn between 1708 and 1718 by nine Jesuits acting on the instructions of the emperor K'ang-hsi (published at Peking

in 1720), as well as the map of Korea and accompanying town plans. In this way, d'Anville collaborated in Du Halde's *Description géographique, historique, chronologique, et physique de l'Empire de la Chine et de la Tartarie chinoise* (4 vols.; Paris, 1735); this was both a testament to Chinese culture and a work of Jesuit propaganda. The maps and plans of China, the Tartar kingdom, Korea, and Tibet were reprinted without authorization at The Hague in 1736 for the *Nouvel atlas de la Chine, de la Tartarie chinoise, et du Thibet*. D'Anville was also appreciated for his maps of the continents and of the world; these were regularly updated between 1746 and 1780, and since they accounted for the latest information, they were of great interest to navigators.

[*See also* Maps, Mapmaking, and Mapmakers.]

BIBLIOGRAPHY

Archier, Edwige. "Anville, Jean-Baptiste Bourguignon d'." In *Lexikon zur Geschichte der Kartographie*, edited by Ingrid Kretschmer, Johannes Dörflinger, and Franz Wawrik, vol. I, pp. 119–121. Vienna: F. Deuticke, 1986.

Landry-Deron, Isabelle. *La preuve par la Chine: La "Description" de J.-B. Du Halde, jésuite, 1735*. Civilisations et sociétés 110. Paris: Éd. De l'École des hautes études en sciences sociales, 2002.

MONIQUE PELLETIER
Translated from the French by David Buisseret

Anza, Juan Bautista de

Anza, Juan Bautista de (1736–1788), soldier in New Spain who led the first overland expedition from Arizona to Alta California. Anza was born in Sonora, near the northern frontier of New Spain. He joined the military as a young man, rapidly rising through the ranks. In 1773, while captain of the presidio at Tubac in southern Arizona, his proposal to explore an overland connection to Alta California was approved by the viceroy, Antonio María Bucareli y Ursúa. Anza's party set out on January 8, 1774. Beyond the junction of the Gila and Colorado rivers, the expedition covered unknown territory. Anza therefore enlisted a Baja California Indian, Sebastian Taraval, as guide. On March 22, Anza's party arrived at Mission San Gabriel, near present-day Los Angeles. After an excursion to Monterey, they left San Gabriel on May 5, and returned to Tubac three weeks later on May 28.

An overland route to Alta California served both practical and political objectives. It would secure reliable and timely supply lines to existing outposts, as well as create a stronger Spanish presence in the region, offsetting the inroads made by England and Russia. Anza was promoted to lieutenant colonel and was ordered to lead a colonizing expedition to the northern reaches of California, in order to establish a presidio by the San Francisco Bay.

On October 23, 1775, Anza left Tubac with some 240 colonists and soldiers. They reached Mission San Gabriel on January 4, 1776, and arrived at Monterey on March 10. As planned, the colonists later established a presidio and mission by San Francisco Bay. Anza left Monterey on April 14, 1776, and arrived at San Miguel de Horcasitas, Sonora, on June 1.

King Carlos III of Spain appointed Anza governor of New Mexico in 1777. During his term, Anza led explorations along the northern frontier, and secured several treaties with the Indian nations of the region. In 1786, Anza resigned from the governorship. He later returned to Arizpe, Sonora, where he died on December 19, 1788.

[*See also* Expeditions, World Exploration, *subentry on* Spain.]

BIBLIOGRAPHY

Bowman, J. N., and Robert F. Heizer. *Anza and the Northwest Frontier of New Spain*. Los Angeles: Southwest Museum, 1967.

Chapman, Charles Edward. *The Founding of Spanish California: The Northwest Expansion of New Spain, 1687–1783*. New York: Macmillan, 1916.

FELIPE J. GOROSTIZA ARROYO

Apollo/Saturn Launch Vehicle

***Apollo/Saturn* Launch Vehicle.** International politics drove the evolution of the *Saturn* launch vehicles. For its major contribution to activities relating to the International Geophysical Year of 1958, the United States announced its intention of rocketing the world's first artificial satellite into orbit. When the Soviet Union beat America into space on October 4, 1957, tensions of the cold war era became the principal impetus to put American astronauts on the moon ahead of the Soviets. In 1961, President John F. Kennedy gave NASA its urgent charge for manned lunar missions "before this decade is out." The venture became known as Project Apollo, in which the manned components evolved as the *Apollo* spacecraft and the rocket stages as the *Saturn* launch vehicle. Planners quickly utilized existing technology and key assets from the nation's ballistic missile programs. Among the assets transferred to NASA were elements of the Army Ballistic Missile Agency, including the "von Braun rocket team," a veteran cadre with invaluable experience dating back to Wernher von Braun's work in Germany during the 1930s.

The Saturn rockets were visible to observers and television audiences for fleeting moments during a dramatic launch. But they were the result of relentless research, development, and testing that covered years of effort by dozens of industry specialists, university personnel, and myriad businesses from coast to coast. The unprecedented size of propellant tanks and the unprecedented power required of the engines created unique challenges in engineering, fabrication, logistics, and facilities, including a new, dedicated launch site. Planners settled on Cape Canaveral on Florida's east coast to take advantage of existing military operations, to facilitate delivery of oversized components by sea-borne transportation, and to capture the additional momentum gained from launches near the Equator. Construction of the Vehicle Assembly Building, launch pads, and tracked crawlers to transport the *Saturn* launch vehicles all represented unique engineering achievements.

In order to test space hardware and to verify the reliability of clustered rockets to power the *Saturn* launch vehicle, NASA and its contractors developed the *Saturn I* and *Saturn IB*, each with two stages. The lower stages proved that several rocket engines (often temperamental beasts) could be clustered together for requisite power. The upper stages verified that volatile, liquid hydrogen (at -423° F [-253° C]) fuel could be safely used with liquid oxygen (at -297° F [-183° C]) oxidizer for propellants in the upper stages. These cryogenic propellants required new techniques for their mass production, transport, and handling. In the meantime, design and fabrication of the three-stage *Saturn V* launch vehicle proceeded with five prime contractors. The first stage, built by Boeing Company, relied on a kerosene-type fuel to power a cluster of five oversized rocket engines for lift off from the launch center at Cape Kennedy. North American Rockwell delivered the second stage, which used liquid hydrogen and a cluster of five engines to drive the launch vehicle into an Earth orbit. The third stage, manufactured by McDonnell Douglas, had one liquid hydrogen engine to thrust the Apollo Command and Space Module out of Earth orbit and into a trajectory bound for the moon. Another major contractor, Rocketdyne, supplied engines for all three stages. A separate component, the Instrument Unit, was developed by IBM. Altogether, hundreds of subcontractor firms and tens of thousands of personnel built *Saturn V* components—a reflection of the sprawling and intricate industrial matrix required for the manufacture, test, and transport of oversized components to be assembled and launched from Kennedy Space Center. The two lower stages, with a circumference of thirty-three feet (ten meters), traveled separately by barges via the Intracoastal Waterway. The third stage and instrument unit, with a twenty-two-foot (6.7 meters) circumference, usually arrived by air in a "Super Guppy," a radically modified transport plane.

NASA press releases tried to give the public some idea of the awesome size of the moon rocket by comparing its length of 363 feet (110.6 meters) to the 360 feet (109.7 meters) of a football playing field. Others noted that its height on the launch pad compared to a thirty-six-story building and explained that it weighed more (6.1 million pounds

[2,770 metric tons] at liftoff) than a standard U.S. Navy destroyer. At liftoff, the first stage engines consumed three tons of propellants per second, requiring pumps that generated the power of thirty diesel locomotives.

NASA received fifteen *Saturn V* rockets for Project Apollo; there were no failures in twelve launches. Its outstanding record owed much to innovative management procedures. Of the remaining rockets, one was used to launch the Skylab space station in 1973; the last two became museum exhibits.

[*See also* Braun, Wernher von, *and* Space Program, *subentry* American.]

ROGER E. BILSTEIN

Arabia. The Arabian Peninsula represents about a million square miles (1.6 million square kilometers)—more than a quarter of the size of the United States—and is some 2,200 miles (3,540 kilometers) in length and 1,200 miles (1,931 kilometers) in width at its extreme points. Today the peninsula comprises the countries of Saudi Arabia, Yemen, Oman, the United Arab Emirates, Qatar, and Bahrain. The population is mainly isolated along the coastal areas of the Hejaz near the Red Sea, in Yemen adjacent to the Indian Ocean, and along the eastern coasts adjacent to the Persian Gulf. In 1950, the estimated population of Arabia was 10 million, but today it exceeds 40 million. In this interval, Riyadh, Saudi Arabia, has grown from a large town of 50,000 to a major city of almost 4 million, but there are no rivals of such proportion elsewhere on the peninsula. The other areas with relatively large populations are Jeddah and Mecca on the Red Sea coast, and Jubail and Dhahran on the Persian Gulf. Most of northern, central, and eastern Arabia is desert, with no rivers or lakes to speak of and as few bays and harbors as any shoreline in the world. The northern border between the head of the Gulf of Aqaba to the head of the Persian Gulf is a stony steppe. The mountainous Hejaz (Barrier) along the western coasts is a long stretch of Precambrian exposures that is the eastern part of the Arabian-Nubian shield, extending from Aqaba in Jordan to the Bab al-Mandab Strait in Yemen. But east of the Hejaz is the vast central desert of the Najd (Upland) that stretches all the way to the Persian Gulf with soaring temperatures of 122° F (50° C) or more in the summer and less than 6 inches (150 millimeters) of rainfall a year. To the north is the Great Nafud—some 44,000 square miles (70,000 square kilometers) of sand dunes in northcentral Arabia that

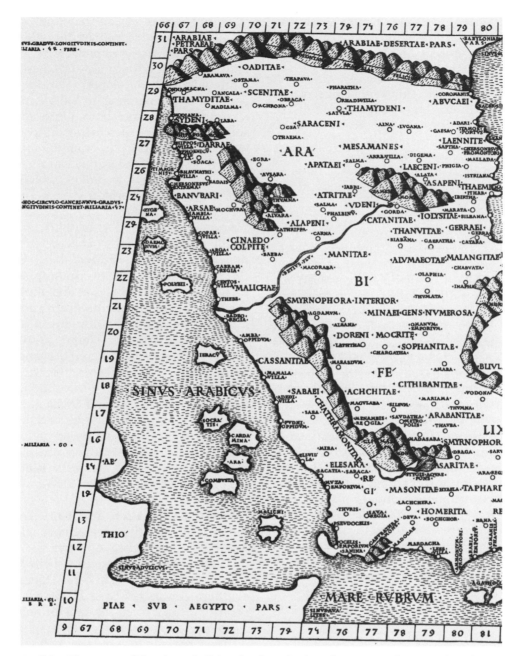

Arabia. This map of "Arabi Felix" (Araby the Blest) is the version from Ptolemy's *Geography* (Rome edition, 1490). The Red Sea ("Sinus Arabicus") is on the left; on the top right may be seen part of the Persian Gulf. Ptolemy has converted what is largely desert into an apparently well-settled region. COURTESY THE NEWBERRY LIBRARY, CHICAGO

stretch about 155 miles (250 kilometers) north from the oasis of Jauf in the Wadi Sirhan to Hail in the south, with a width of more than 185 miles (300 kilometers) from east to west. To the west is the Hisma Desert, with its scenic sandstone mountains, that extends from Ras en-Naqb in southern Jordan to Tabuk in the northern Hejaz. But the largest of the deserts is the Rub' al-Khali or "Empty Quarter"—311,000 square miles (500,000 square kilometers) of sand dunes rising as high as 200 feet (60 meters)—the very last part of the Arabian desert to be explored by westerners and the largest body of sand in the world. A sandy stretch called the Dahna connects the Nafud to the Rub' al-Khali, leaving only about one-fifth of the whole peninsula inhabitable. [See color plate 10 in this volume.]

Exploration in Antiquity. Our knowledge of the vast, forbidding, and challenging landscape of the Arabian Peninsula has come not by steady accumulative growth, but rather in sporadic bursts. In antiquity, Greek geographers designated the whole Peninsula "Arabia Felix" (Araby the Blest), but during the Augustan era the term was restricted for present-day Yemen, the source of incense and spices for the Mediterranean world. The beginning of recorded exploration of Arabia is associated with Alexander the Great's imperialistic ambition to conquer Arabia. Exploratory missions were sent out in advance c. 324–323 B.C.E., with the general Nearchus going to the Persian Gulf and the navarch Anaxicrates going from Aila (modern Aqaba) to the Red Sea. Anaxicrates probably reached as far as Qana' in Aden. The exploration continued with Alexander's successor Ptolemy II (r. 282–246 B.C.E.) in Egypt, who sent an expedition along the Arabian side of the Red Sea led by Ariston, but no traces of the official report have survived, though details from it may be subsumed in works like the third century B.C.E. *Geography* of Eratosthenes, the late second century B.C.E. *On the Erythraean Sea* of Agatharchides of Cnidus, and the Augustan era *Geography* of Strabo. The next document of importance for Arabia is the mid-first century C.E. Roman shipping manual called the *Periplus Maris Erythraei* (Voyage in the Red Sea), which provides detailed information about the commercial ports on the western and southern shores of the peninsula. But the real advance came with the Alexandrian scholar Claudius Ptolemy's *Geography* in the second century C.E., which incorporated not only the evidence from the earlier Greek geographers and from the explorations of Marinus of Tyre (c. 100 C.E.), but also the reports from the campaign to southern Arabia led by the Augustan legate Aelius Gallus in 25 B.C.E. Thus Ptolemy was able to list 114 towns and villages in the Arabian Peninsula, in contrast to just 29 that he lists for Arabia Petraea, which was within the Roman province of Arabia. The later work of Marcian of Heraclea Pontus—the *Periplus of the Outer Sea* (c. 400 C.E.)—listed 164 towns and 44 villages in the Arabian Peninsula, but the work does not survive. Stephen of Byzantium compiled a list of toponyms in about 550 C.E., but much of the earlier information appears to have been lost.

Islamic Geographers. The reemergence of any detailed information about the Arabian Peninsula appears only centuries later in works by Islamic scholars. In the ninth century, the Abbasid caliph at Baghdad was patron of a circle of scholars and scientists who produced maps of Islamic lands. By the tenth century, a developed scientific geography began that was dependent on Indian and Iranian models and on the translation into Arabic of Greek sources like those of Marinus of Tyre and Ptolemy, with amendments by the Islamic scholars. Emerging from this study of geography was the "Atlas of Islam" school of Abu Zayd al-Balkhi, which had Mecca as the center of the world; a succession of such geographies were produced in the tenth century by Al-Hamdani of Yemen, Al-Istakhri and Ibn Khurradadhbih of Iran, Ibn Hawqal from Nisibis in Mesopotamia, and Al-Muqaddasi from Palestine. But most of these works were compilations and commentaries of toponyms that appeared in the Qur'an, the Hadith, or pre-Islamic Arabic poetry; they were not based entirely on exploration of Arabia. Even the celebrated geographer Yaqut al-Rumi of Aleppo (1179–1229) merely gathered documentary evidence on Arabia for his great work, the *Mu'djam al-Buldān* (Dictionary of Toponyms), even though he did travel widely between Egypt and Syria. No Arabic scholar produced a comprehensive and accurate description of the Arabian Peninsula based on travel and investigation. Vast regions of the peninsula remained virtually unknown even within the Islamic world until the early modern era.

Western Exploration and Knowledge. From the Western perspective, scientific exploration of the Arabian Peninsula began only in the eighteenth century, stimulated by the work of the German Orientalist J. D. Michaelis (1717–1791), whose interests in southern Arabia led King Frederick of Denmark to sponsor a small scientific expedition to the region in 1761–1763, conducted by a team of six specialists: a doctor, a botanist, a zoologist, a philologist, a painter, and an engineer. The expedition to Yemen has become known for its sole survivor, Carsten Niebuhr, whose records of the enterprise were published in German (1772), French (1774), and English (1792). The importance of the pioneering venture was not immediately recognized, and there was a hiatus before further exploration. Later travelers to the region discovered pre-Islamic inscriptions, which spurred new interest. In 1810, Ulrich Jasper von Seetzen of Vienna recorded inscriptions at Zafar, and more inscriptions were copied by a British team associated with the East India Company during a survey of the coasts of southern Arabia in the 1830s. In 1843, the

Frenchman Thomas Arnaud discovered the Sabaean capital at Mar'ib—reputedly the land of the queen of Sheba—where he found fifty-six more inscriptions. These finds led to the expedition in 1869–1870 directed by the Semiticist Joseph Halévy to hunt for materials for the *Corpus inscriptionum Semiticarum* to be published by the Académie des Inscriptions et Belles-Lettres in Paris. Not only did he find more inscriptions at Mar'ib and at other Sabaean sites, but he also visited Qarnāwu, the capital of the Minaean kingdom. His efforts yielded 685 inscriptions, but this accomplishment pales in comparison to the more than 2,000 inscriptions collected during the four expeditions by the Austrian Eduard Glaser between 1882 and 1894. Today, more than 10,000 pre-Islamic Arabian inscriptions have been published.

Exploration of Southern Arabia. With these discoveries, other regions of the Arabian peninsula became of interest. The earliest exploration of Oman in the southeast of the peninsula is connected with James Raymond Wallsted in 1835 and 1836, who surveyed the coastal areas and recorded perhaps the first Himyarite inscriptions. In the southwest, Aden was explored by the British officer S. B. Miles in 1870–1886, followed by Wyman Bury in the 1890s and R. A. B. Hamilton in the 1930s. The area of Hadramawt, northeast of Aden, began to be investigated by the Germans Adolf von Wrede in 1843 and Leo Hirsch in 1893. During World War I, David Hogarth of the British Arab Bureau in Cairo had a handbook on the Hejaz prepared, covering the topography, society, and resources of the region; T. E. Lawrence played a major role in the preparation of the handbook. What remained was the vast Empty Quarter, the last area of Arabia to be investigated. Bertram Thomas in 1924 is credited with first crossing this desolate landscape of sand dunes, and he was followed by the more dramatic and intensive journey across this barren terrain by Wilfred Thesiger, whose travel is preserved in his gripping account called *Arabian Sands* (1959).

Archaeological excavations in Yemen began only after World War I. The first excavations were of a Sabaean temple and were conducted by the Germans Carl Rathjens and Hermann von Wissmann in 1928, and they continued their explorations of Yemen until 1932. In 1934, the German Hans Helfritz visited Shabwa, the capital of the kingdom of Hadramawt, stimulating the excavations later in 1938 by R. A. B. Hamilton and by Gertrude Caton Thompson; Thompson told of her excavations in her classic *The Tombs and Moon-Temple of Hureidha (Hadhramaut)* (1944). By this time, Syrian and Egyptian scholars also be-

gan combing the region for antiquities and conducted several small excavations in Hadramawt. After World War II, there was a similar burst of archaeological activity in Yemen. In 1950 and 1951, the American Foundation for the Study of Man, directed by Wendell Phillips, launched an expedition to Yemen. The expedition began at Wadi Beihan (ancient Timna), the capital of the ancient kingdom of Qataban, then went to Mahram Bilqis—the state temple of the Sabaean kingdom near Mar'ib in Yemen—and then in 1953 went to Dhofar in Oman, an outpost of the ancient kingdom of Hadramawt. A systematic inventory of the ruins of Yemen was compiled in 1959 by G. Lankester Harding and published later as *Archaeology in the Aden Protectorates* (1964); this compilation became the basis for Brian Doe's *Southern Arabia* (1971) and *Monuments of South Arabia* (1983).

International interest now began to grow. In 1970, the British were followed by a team of German scholars led by W. W. Müller and W. Diem that surveyed northern Yemen; in 1971, Giovanni Garbini and Paolo Costa of Italy began conducting a reconnaissance mission also in northern Yemen; and in 1975, a French team led by Jacqueline Pirenne began excavating at Shabwa and conducting surveys of the regions, discovering new sites and numerous temples. By the 1980s, there were more than fifteen excavations in Yemen involving French, German, Italian, American, and Russian teams. In 1998, the American Foundation for the Study of Man revived their excavations at Mahram Bilqis, directed now by Wendell Phillips's sister Merilyn Phillips Hodgson; this time their main goal was to clarify the architectural plan of the temple, but they discovered in the process more than three hundred new monumental Sabaean dedicatory inscriptions.

Exploration of Northern and Central Arabia. Western knowledge of northern and central Arabia proceeded much more slowly than it did with southern Arabia. A series of adventurers, romantics, soldiers, missionaries, pilgrims, scholars, and even slaves of various western countries visited the Arabian Peninsula at various times beginning in the sixteenth century, but the fascination was initially with the holy places of Mecca and Medina in the Hejaz and later with the tribal politics of Hail and Riyadh in Nejd, the centers of the sheikdoms of Ibn Rashid and Ibn Saud, respectively. Ludovico de Varthema in 1503, Joseph Pitts in 1685, Ali Bey el-Abbassi in 1807, and Johann Ludwig Burckhardt in 1814 all visited and described Mecca. In 1819, the British officer George Forster Sadleir, on a political mission, crossed the Arabian Peninsula from Qatif in the east to Yanbu in the west, a trajectory never mentioned previously by any westerner. More scientific was the visit to Hail in 1845 by the Finnish scholar Georg August Wallin, who recorded inscriptions, as well as the topography, flora, and fauna, during his journey. Later, another British officer, Richard Francis Burton, supported by the Royal Geographical Society, set out in 1852 with the objective of recording the eastern and central areas of Arabia—still terra incognita—but was forced to satisfy himself with visits to Mecca and Medina, although he returned later, in 1877, to investigate the legendary gold mines of the land of Midian in the northern Hejaz.

The pivotal year in the exploration of northern Arabia may be considered to be 1876, when Charles Montagu Doughty visited Mecca, observing along the way the important antiquities at Tayma, Meda'in Salih, and Khaybar in the northern Hejaz, all of which are memorialized in his classic *Travels in Arabia Deserta* (1888). In 1878, the Alsatian Charles Huber visited the Hejaz and returned in 1883 with the German archaeologist Julius Euting to record inscriptions. These efforts kindled interest in Arabia. Under the reforms of the Ottoman sultan Abdülhamīd II (r. 1876–1908), Sabri Pasha in 1889 provided a compendium of the anthropology of Arabia from pre-Islamic times to the modern era—with topographical information of the various tribes, routes, towns, and cities of Arabia. These efforts were followed by the Czech scholar Alois Musil's pioneering explorations of Najd and northern Hejaz in 1908–1914; the accounts of his explorations were later published in English by the American Geographical Society—*The Northern Hegaz* (1926), *Arabia Deserta* (1927), *Northern Negd* (1928), and his classic, *The Manners and Customs of the Rwala Bedouins* (1928), which remains the best ethnographical study of any Bedouin tribe. Around the same time, the French Dominican scholars A. J. Jaussen and R. Savignac's exhaustive *Mission archeologique en Arabie* (published in 1910 and 1914) provided a detailed description of their "archaeological mission in Arabia" during 1907–1910—primarily of the ruins and inscriptions along the Hejaz railway between Tabuk and the area of Mada'in Salih and Al-Ula. After World War I, Harry St. John Philby (1885–1960) became the explorer of Arabia par excellence, spending more than forty years exploring the Peninsula. The titles of his books tell the story: *Heart of Arabia* (1922), *Arabia of the Wahhabis* (1928), *Empty Quarter* (1933), *Sheba's Daughters* (1939), *Arabian Highlands* (1952), *Sau'di Arabia* (1955), and *Land of Midian* (1957).

After World War II, in 1951, an important enterprise took place with Philby now accompanied by the Belgian scholars Gonzague Ryckmans and Jacques Ryckmans and by Philippe Lippens. This team combed central and southwest Saudi Arabia, recording 8,000 pre-Islamic inscriptions and investigating the recently discovered pre-Islamic caravan trading post of Qaryat al-Fau. The post soon became the focus of major excavations by A. R. Al-Ansary, chair of the department of archaeology at King Saud University, beginning in 1972 and continuing today; the excavations have revealed the palace, markets, and temples, producing valuable evidence of the international trade during the late Hellenistic and early Roman eras. At the same time, northern Arabia began to be explored by leading archaeologists. In 1962, F. V. Winnett and W. L. Reed of the American Schools of Oriental Research led an expedition to northern Arabia, proceeding from the Wadi Sirhan to Tabuk, Tayma', Mada'in Salih, and Al-Ula, recording several hundred North Arabic and Nabataean inscriptions. Another important expedition to northwest Arabia was led in 1968 by P. J. Parr of the University College, London, with a team that included G. L. Harding and J. E. Dayton. These efforts were followed by a comprehensive archaeological survey across the entire vast peninsula of the Kingdom of Saudi Arabia organized by Abdullah Masry, the director of Antiquities and Museums in Saudi Arabia. The survey was conducted by teams of archaeologists and scientific specialists from the international archaeological community. Since 1976 they have recorded thousands of sites and published the results in *ATLAL: The Journal of Saudi Arabian Archaeology* (1977–). Today, more than a dozen archaeologists in the department of archaeology at King Saud University are engaged in the exploration of the peninsula, with several other ongoing projects led by European scholars.

[*See also* Arabo-Islamic Geography *and biographies of figures mentioned in this article.*]

BIBLIOGRAPHY
Bidwell, Robin. *Travellers in Arabia*. London: Hamlyn, 1976. Reprint, Berkshire, U.K.: Garnet, 1994.
Bowersock, G. W. *Roman Arabia*. Cambridge, Mass.: Harvard University Press, 1983.
Freeth, Zahra, and H. V. F. Winstone. *Explorers of Arabia from the Renaissance to the End of the Victorian Era*. New York: Holmes and Meier, 1978.
Hogarth, David George. *Hejaz before World War I*. Rev. ed. Cambridge, U.K.: Oleander, 1978.

Hogarth, David George. *The Penetration of Arabia*. London: Alston Rivers, 1905. Reprint. Beirut, Lebanon: Khayats, 1966.

Phillips, Wendell. *Qataban and Sheba: Exploring the Ancient Kingdoms on the Biblical Spice Routes of Arabia*. New York: Harcourt and Brace, 1955.

Winnett, F. V., and W. L. Reed. *Ancient Records from North Arabia*. Toronto: University of Toronto Press, 1970.

DAVID F. GRAF

Arabo-Islamic Geography. Both the Greek term "geography" and the literary and scientific discipline to which it refers were known to medieval Muslims. As early as the late seventh century, when Muslim armies spread beyond the borders of the Arabian Peninsula, issues relating to "geography" came to be of direct relevance to Muslims in three ways. First, the Muslim conquest of the Near East in the seventh and eighth centuries depended on the conquerors' ability to communicate efficiently over vast distances, for which purpose routes were created and their itineraries recorded. These itineraries would provide the basis for the earliest specimens of Arabic-language geographies, and it is no coincidence that some of the most important authors of geographies were employees of the caliphate's official postal system (*barid*). Similarly, the regions conquered yielded important tax revenues for the Muslim rulers, and a survey of the various lands that made up the Islamic Empire (or "caliphate") was un-

World Map of the Twelfth Century. Al-Idrisi was the leading Islamic cartographer of his day, and remarkably prolific. This south-oriented map of the world as he knew it (Africa in the upper part of the image) is reminiscent of the contemporary western European *mappae mundi;* they are not remarkable for what we would think of as precision but serve as a reminder of the rough outline of the known world, surrounded by the ocean sea. NATIONAL LIBRARY, CAIRO/ERICH LESSING/ART RESOURCE, NY

dertaken and summarized in administrative documents that contributed data to early Arabic geographical treatises.

Second, the centrality of Mecca to Islamic ritual meant that Muslims throughout the conquered lands were required to face this town during prayers, and to make a pilgrimage to it, health and finances permitting. For these reasons, early geographies tended to provide descriptions of the direction of prayer (*qibla*) and the pilgrimage routes for inhabitants of the Islamic world's various regions. Descriptions of the pilgrimage routes were often very detailed and included pivotal information on the availability of water, food, and lodgings along notoriously inhospitable routes.

Third, the Muslim conquests brought the conquerors into close contact with the pre-Islamic cultures of the Near East, and the Romano-Byzantine and Indo-Iranian literary and administrative heritages were gradually incorporated into the nascent Islamic civilization. But although an early eighth-century governor (al-Hajjaj ibn Yusuf, d. 714) is said to have commissioned a map of the Daylam region of northern Iran in the context of his expansion eastward, it would not be until the early ninth century that Arabic geographical works were commissioned and composed.

The Emergence of a Genre. The genre of Arabic geographical works emerged during this period for two reasons: paper and patronage. The introduction of paper-making techniques to the central Islamic lands in the late eighth century meant that this relatively cheap (and accessible) writing material came to replace the more expensive (and exclusive) papyrus and parchment on which most written works—mostly administrative documents and religious texts—were composed. Thereafter, literacy rates increased sharply and books came to be written on subjects that would interest the general population, rather than being limited to topics of interest to the religious and bureaucratic elites. Such nonessential subjects included travelogues (of both actual and imagined journeys), as well as accounts of the marvels of the world (usually focusing on India and China), and other topics that were in some way or other related to geography. Concurrently, though for unrelated reasons, caliphs such as al-Ma'mun (r. 813–833) actively encouraged scientific inquiry and the translation of (predominantly Greek) scientific texts into Arabic. Among these texts was Ptolemy's *Geography*, which was translated by al-Khwarazmi (d. 847), al-Battani (d. 961), and others, and which exerted considerable and lasting influence on Arabic geographical writings.

In addition to the Arabic translations of Greek geographical treatises, the ninth century witnessed the development of administrative geography, this being a genre that focused on the political entities of the known world (or of the Islamic world) and the routes that linked them. Administrative geography of this sort was pioneered by Ibn Khurradadhbih (d. 912), a postal chief and court official in ninth-century Iraq whose *Kitab al-Masalik wa al-Mamalik* (Book of Roads and Kingdoms) inspired and informed subsequent geographers for centuries to come. This work reflects the embryonic stage of Arabic geography in this period in that the author combines data derived from bureaucratic pamphlets (detailing the tax revenues levied in the caliphate's regions, and the postal routes and stations of the Islamic world) with pre-Islamic Iranian notions of the world's divisions. All this was presented within a transparently Ptolemaic layout: the work begins with a description of the world's size, shape, and habitable regions, and ends with a list of the sources of fresh water, as Ptolemy's work does. Specimens of administrative geography, often bearing the same title as Ibn Khurradadhbih's work, survive from such diverse periods of Islamic history as those of the Abbasids (750–1258), Fatimids (969–1171), Samanids (874–999), Buyids (945–1055), and Mamluks (1258–1517), making it the most enduring category of geographical writing in Islamic history.

Approaches to Geography. From the tenth to twelfth centuries a number of important geographical works were authored, many of which bore the same title (Book of Roads and Kingdoms) and covered similar topics. A superficial overview of the contents of these books might therefore suggest that repetition (and even plagiarism) was rife in this field. But a nuanced analysis of the distinct scientific approaches that characterized the geographical works produced during this period reveals that their authors were reflecting important cultural tensions of the time. Some authors, for instance, treated the entire known world, whereas others chose to focus on the lands of "Islam" (by which "the Abbasid caliphate" is usually meant). Ibn Khurradadhbih covers India, China, Africa, Byzantium, the Middle East, central Asia, and other regions, but to al-Muqaddasi (d. 1000), non-Muslim lands were not worthy of attention, while Qudama ibn Ja' far (d. 948) explains that he reluctantly describes Byzantium in order to provide the caliphs with information concerning their fiercest enemy. Other controversies hinged on whether the political center of the world (Iraq, centered on Baghdad) should take precedence over its spiritual center (Arabia, centered on Mecca) in descriptions of the caliphate, or vice versa, and on the role of Qur'anic pronouncements on cosmography in shaping geographical knowledge.

Perhaps the most significant dispute was between those authors whose geographical information was derived from theoretical sources, such as the Greek division of the world into climes or into Iranian *kishwars*, and those who insisted on relying on information gathered either personally (through travel to the lands described) or from eyewitnesses whose testimony was deemed trustworthy. Many scholars—particularly those who wrote administrative geographies—adopted the pre-Islamic divisions of the world, both because of the prestige associated with Ptolemy's work in the contemporary Islamic world, and because Muslims could appropriate the theory of the earth's climatic bands without having to adjust it to their situation. Inhabitants of the Muslim world shared the most favorable of the seven climes with the ancient Greeks. Detractors of this armchair geography preferred to record in their works only their own—or their informants'—personal experience. Adherents to this approach included al-Muqaddasi, al-Ya'qubi (d. 897), al-Mas'udi (d. 956), Ibn Hawqal (fl. 977), and others.

What the many competing approaches to the writing of geography indicate is that geography was a flourishing and evolving subject of inquiry during this period, and that it was considered to be a suitable medium through which the scholarly controversies could be expressed. Moreover, geography remained malleable, despite the pervasive influence of certain models such as Ptolemaic or administrative. Hence the celebrated litterateur al-Jahiz (d. 869) is said to have composed literary geographical treatises (that are no longer extant), while jurists such as Ibn al-Faqih (c. 903) and al-Muqaddasi customized their works to the needs of religious scholars by including chapters on information of direct relevance to them and by quoting statements attributed to the prophet Muhammad throughout their works.

The variety of approaches to and styles of Arabic geographical texts also indicates that there was no such thing as a typical author of such texts. In fact, it could be argued that although there were Arabic Islamic geographies, strictly speaking there were no Arabic Islamic geographers. Thus, although the famed bibliographer Ibn al-Nadim (d. 998) included numerous geographical works in his survey of the historians, scientists, courtiers, philosophers, poets, and others who produced the books available in his day, he did not set aside a separate chapter for geographers. Instead, the authors who are known to posterity for their geographical treatises are shown by Ibn al-Nadim to have been better known at the time for their contributions to other fields. Bearing this in mind, we should not be surprised that al-Mas'udi, despite having composed a voluminous geographical work himself, considered geography to be little more than a subbranch of history.

During the early medieval period, Islamic geographical writing gradually became specialized. Henceforth, the various branches of geography that had been combined within a single work in the formative period of geographical writing were often disentagled from each other, and separate works were dedicated to the description of marvels (*'aja'ib*), pilgrimage routes (*ziyarat*), imperial roads, scientific geography, travelogues, regional taxation revenues, and—in some cases—particular regions. Al-Biruni (d. 1050) wrote an incisive description of India and its people, Ibn Fadlan (c. 922) colorfully described the peoples of the Volga region, al-Hamdani (d. 945) wrote a detailed account of the Arabian Peninsula based on Ptolemaic principles, and a number of quasi-fictional accounts of the Indian Ocean region were also produced. In the early thirteenth century, Yaqut al-Hamawi (d. 1229) compiled a magesterial dictionary of place-names (*Mu'jam al-Buldan*, Dictionary of Countries) in which he collected all available information on the cities and towns of the Islamic world. A number of celebrated travelogues—such as those of Ibn Jubayr (d. 1217) and Ibn Battuta (c. 1357)—also date from this period, though traditional geographical works continued to be produced across the politically fragmented Islamic world.

The breakup of the Abbasid caliphate during the tenth to thirteenth centuries had two perceptible effects on geographical writing. First, the need for universal geographies that situated the sprawling realms of the Abbasid caliphs within their broader geographical context dissipated. Second, the emergence of independent courts that patronized scholars throughout the provinces of the Islamic world encouraged the development of regional geographies, most of which reflected the unique cultural and political circumstances that conditioned their composition. It was under the Iranian dynasty of the Samanids, for instance, that the first Persian-language geography was written c. 982 (the *Hudud al-'Alam*, Limits of the World, by an anonymous author). Turkish-language geographical works were produced as early as the fourteenth century, though Ottoman geography really flourished only after the sixteenth century, by which time it was influenced considerably by contemporary European works and was less identifiable as an heir to the Arabic Islamic tradition of geographical writing than contemporary Persian geography was.

For nearly five centuries, the somewhat amorphous field of Arabic Islamic geography produced works that were generally unrivaled in their accuracy, sophistication, and detailed information on Africa and Eurasia. Owing to its impressive size and its fortuitous location at the crossroads of Europe, Africa, central Asia, and the Indian Ocean region, the Islamic world was well placed to gather and analyze information on the various regions of the known world and their peoples. Furthermore, the spread and cultural prestige of the Arabic language meant that both the Greco-Roman and the Indo-Iranian scientific traditions were merged within a single framework for the first time, and the existence of a common language of scholarship allowed authors of many regions and periods to learn from and build upon the works of their predecessors. It is particularly telling that when the Norman king Roger II (d. 1154) decided to commission an annotated world map, he entrusted the task to a Muslim scholar, al-Idrisi (d. 1166), and that it was an Arab navigator—Ahmad ibn Majid—who is said to have shown Vasco de Gama the route from the east coast of Africa to India in 1498.

[*See also* Arabia; Hamdani, al-; Ibn Battuta; Muqaddasi, al-, Shams al-Din; *and* Ptolemy.]

BIBLIOGRAPHY

Ahmad, S. Maqbul. "Djughrafiya." In *The Encyclopaedia of Islam*, edited by H. A. R. Gibb et al. New ed. Leiden: Brill, 1960– . Vol. 2, pp. 575–587.

Ahmad, S. Maqbul. *A History of Arab-Islamic Geography: 9th–16th Century A.D.* Mafraq, Jordan: Al al-Bayt University, 1995.

Collins, Basil Anthony. *Al-Muqaddasi: The Man and His Work.* Ann Arbor: Department of Geography, University of Michigan, 1974.

Kramers, Johannes Hendrik. "Geography and Commerce." In *The Legacy of Islam*, edited by Thomas Arnold and Alfred Guillaume, 79–107. Oxford: Clarendon Press, 1931.

Lewis, Bernard. *The Muslim Discovery of Europe.* London: Phoenix Press, 1994. See especially pp. 59–69.

Miquel, André. *La géographie humaine du monde Musulman jusqu'au milieu du 11e siècle.* Paris: Éditions de l'École des Hautes Études en Sciences Sóciales, 1967–1988.

Sezgin, Fuat. *The Contribution of the Arabic-Islamic Geographers to the Formation of the World Map.* Frankfurt, Germany: Institut für Geschichte der Arabisch-Islamischen Wissenschaften an der Johann Goethe-Universität, 1987.

Shboul, Ahmad M. H. *Al-Mas'udi and His World.* London: Ithaca Press, 1979.

Tolmacheva, Marina. "Geography." In *Medieval Islamic Civilization: An Encyclopedia*, edited by Josef W. Meri et al. New York: Routledge, 2006. Vol. 1, pp. 284–288.

ADAM SILVERSTEIN

Archaeology and "Discoveries" Sites.

Archaeologists who seek to contribute to our understanding of the "Discoveries" tend to focus on two major classes of remains: ships and the settlements established by the expeditions. For the great era of European exploration, contemporary documentation is crucial as a complement to the archaeological data in making cases for identification or attribution.

Ships. Shipwreck archaeology came of age in the 1960s as a result of new technologies that permitted precise and sustained fieldwork in challenging underwater environments. Since then, researchers have developed astonishing abilities in submarine prospecting and salvaging technology. The Mediterranean has become a laboratory for the perfection of approaches and techniques, a sea where ships and boats dating to medieval, classical, and even prehistoric times have been discovered, excavated with great precision, and, occasionally, raised and reconstructed. Deep-sea robotic submersible craft are now capable of exploring ships at tremendous depths in the open oceans. Announcements that such ships as the *Titanic*, the *Lusitania*, and the *Bismarck* have been found never cease to thrill the public. Despite the availability of these new and powerful tools and techniques, however, the contribution of nautical archaeology to our understanding of the "Discoveries" is, for various reasons, not as great as might be first thought.

Archaeological analysis of a particular known ship depends upon (1) sufficient preservation of the vessel (in waters or silt deep enough to evade and/or dissuade salvors and sport divers, and in a micro-environment unaffected by organisms and earth processes that might destroy it); (2) in situ indicia of its identity, such as readable labels on armament, insignia, cargo, or other artifacts; and (3) the survival and judicious use of available and reliable historical documentation that might provide clues about the final resting place of the vessel. By no means are all celebrated ships to be sought in deep graves, nor do many enjoy the renown we might today wish on them. In 2004 a team of researchers announced the discovery of Charles Darwin's HMS *Beagle* underneath sixteen feet (five meters) of silt in an Essex marsh—an ignominious end, to be sure, to a ship that had made its own significant contribution to discovery in the 1830s, only to be sold for scrap some forty years later.

Identification of specific ships is rarely an easy matter. A controversy erupted in 2003 over the planned (and aborted) auction of the ship's bell said to be from Christopher Columbus's *Santa Maria*, dug out of silt by a diver on the Portuguese coast from the remains of a later ship to which it had been allegedly retrofitted. Scholars immediately disputed the attribution of this artifact to Columbus's flagship on a number of grounds; but for our purposes the episode illustrates the strong pull—more romantic than scholarly—of such artifacts on the popular imagination, artifacts that are invested by the public with much more value as relics than as points of scientific data.

Occasionally, however, spectacular and indisputable discoveries are made. In 1995 La Salle's ship *La Belle* was discovered in shallow water off the Texas coast. A cofferdam was built around the wreck, and it was excavated as if it were a terrestrial site. Together with ample surviving testimonia and the excavation of a nearby installation identified as Fort Saint Louis, the ship (which contained the skeleton of a crew member who had drowned belowdecks) is a vivid and poignant reminder of the desperate final months of La Salle's expedition to find the Mississippi and sail upriver in 1686. [See color plate 8 in this volume.]

Settlements. No comprehensive treatment of "Discoveries"-era settlements can be provided here; rather, several examples of types of archaeological projects will be mentioned, all of them recent and all in the New World.

There is a small Viking settlement—very possibly that of Leifr Eiríksson—at L'Anse aux Meadows in Newfoundland. But this compound, which has been securely dated by several methods to c. 1000 C.E., seems not to have been a conscious Norse effort to colonize the North American continent: its exposed coastal location and layout suggest a temporary and perhaps seasonal occupation. In what appears to have been a more purposeful and permanent colonizing endeavor: Christopher Columbus and his crew in 1493 established a more substantial settlement on the north coast of Hispaniola, which its discoverers have characterized as the first European town in the Western Hemisphere. Surviving letters, journals, and other testimonia yielded topographical details that suggested the location of the site, and subsequent meticulous excavation confirmed its identity. De-

spite persistent prospecting by several researchers who believe that some of Columbus's ships are to be found there, no convincing archaeological evidence for them has emerged.

A different sort of archaeological gloss on the topic of the "Discoveries" is provided by the expedition of Hernando de Soto. Researchers have long sought to trace the route of the Spanish conquistador through the southeastern region of North America in the years 1539–1543. In this case, the challenge has consisted largely of attempting to link disparate and often contradictory early descriptions of towns and villages in the native American chiefdoms with particular settlements known from archaeological reconnaissance and excavation.

One thing is certain: much remains to be discovered about the "Discoveries," and the methods and tools of archaeologists (in concert with historians and ethnographers) will remain central to this endeavor.

[*See also biographies of figures mentioned in this article.*]

BIBLIOGRAPHY

Deagan, Kathleen, and José María Cruxent. *Columbus's Outpost among the Taínos: Spain and America at La Isabela, 1493–1498.* New Haven, Conn.: Yale University Press, 2002.

Gould, Richard A. *Archaeology and the Social History of Ships.* Cambridge, U.K., and New York: Cambridge University Press, 2000.

Hudson, Charles M. *Knights of Spain, Warriors of the Sun: Hernando De Soto and the South's Ancient Chiefdoms.* Athens: University of Georgia Press, 1997.

Weddle, Robert S. *The Wreck of the Belle, the Ruin of La Salle.* College Station: Texas A&M University Press, 2001.

KARL M. PETRUSO

Arctic

This entry contains three subentries:

Early Knowledge
Nineteenth-Century Images
Russian Arctic

Early Knowledge

Astronomers in ancient Greece discovered that at about 66.5° northern latitude, a line parallel to the Equator went through the star Arktos in the Great Bear constellation. Defining Arctic conditions has less to do with mathematics than with physical realities, however. In the American, Greenlandic, and

Eurasian Arctic, sheltered areas nourish green valleys and forests, and the northern tundra explodes with life above the permafrost in summer. A rich terrestrial and marine animal life also adapted to the circumpolar regions, and for thousands of years human inhabitants of the Arctic have sustained life and accumulated surplus goods for trade by exploiting the natural resources.

Although relatively short distances between land areas in the Arctic made early intercontinental migrations possible in the farthest north, Arctic peoples remained isolated from the rest of the world, and Greek mathematicians of the sixth century B.C.E. could only theorize about those distant latitudes. When word finally trickled south that humanlike creatures lived along the northern fringes of the Eurasian world—all the world that was known to the scholars of antiquity—the creatures were frequently regarded as not only alien, but dangerously antisocial and physically grotesque.

Conjectures about cold Hyperborean and Scythian habitats were eventually colored by travelers' tales. Unfortunately, only echoes remain from the expedition that Pytheas, a Greek merchant from Marseilles, made early in the fourth century B.C.E. to find the sources of amber and tin, but he appears to have continued north after circumnavigating Britain. Pytheas reported the existence of an island named "Thule" where the sun is visible all night long at midsummer, but he was an able mathematician and may merely have calculated the position of the sun in Thule at the height of the Arctic summer. Pytheas possibly observed Iceland or some part of Norway before entering the Baltic Sea, which was believed to be the physical feature separating continental Europe from the Arctic.

Eratosthenes (c. 275–194 B.C.E.) calculated Thule Ultima's position to be 66° N on the Alexandrian meridian, but Strabo (c. 60 B.C.E.–25 C.E.) doubted Thule's existence altogether because Ireland was reportedly so wretched that people could not possibly exist even farther north. However, Ptolemy of Alexandria (about 90–168 C.E.) firmly placed Thule at 63° N. Evidently, the concept of Thule had been accepted even if the island's location remained as vague as the rest of the frigid north.

Baltic amber had begun to reach Mycenaean Greece about 160 B.C.E., and by the first century C.E., when the Roman Empire was in the ascendant, trade in Arctic furs was also well established in the Mediterranean region. However, so many middlemen were involved that little information from north of the Baltic reached the Greeks and Romans. In the sixth century C.E., the Germanic historian Jordanes still referred to the Baltic as the sea beyond which the Arctic lay, in which one would find Scandza (Scandinavia), the source of the lustrous blue fox furs so highly valued by the Romans. Bordering Scandza's north was a vast, unnavigable ocean with Thule in its extreme west. Jordanes nevertheless bridged Mediterranean speculations and Arctic reality by noting, among other things, that Scandza was home to the Screrefennae (Finns, Lapps, or Saami), who subsisted on wild beasts and birds' eggs.

Late in the ninth century C.E., the Norwegian chieftain Ohthere provided a further glimpse of activities in the White Sea region. During an English sojourn, he told King Alfred's court that he had voyaged around the North Cape to trade with and collect taxes from the Saami and, quite likely, from their near neighbors the Karelians. Ohthere's story survived only because Alfred wrote it down; countless other such voyages never entered the written record. This makes it hard to reconstruct the period when Norse and Russian traders and tax collectors first exploited the Kola Peninsula and White Sea region, marketing furs and walrus ivory in the Baltic, as well as in areas farther west and east.

Both before and after 1000 C.E., a major Baltic junction for this export trade was the Russian city of Novgorod, long accustomed to exacting tribute from the Finno-Ugric inhabitants of a huge hinterland. German merchants were also active in Baltic trade from the late eleventh century and had established a Hanseatic headquarters in Novgorod by 1270. Subsequent Hansa dominance over trade in the whole region streamlined the marketing of Arctic goods, but not of information. Early in the fourteenth century, King Magnús Eiríksson of Norway and Sweden exploited the traditional reputation of White Sea denizens when he asked the pope for a loan to help him fight these heathen savages that were supposedly threatening his kingdoms in the north.

In Norway, any foreign threat would surely have involved an insatiable lust for codfish. Since the early eleventh century, church and crown had encouraged the Arctic production of stockfish (unsalted, wind-dried cod) from the Lofoten Islands north. A fortress was erected at Vardø in the extreme northeast of Norway and inaugurated in 1307, together with a church that also appears on the 1507/08 world map by Johannes Ruysch. Occasionally, from the fourteenth century on, European mapmakers had indicated fish, whales, white bears, mountains, and whirlpools in the North Atlantic area, but they lacked cartographic models because the medieval Norse were uninterested in mapping. Greenland finally appeared about 1427 on a map which the Dane Claudius Clavus had based entirely on written lore, incorporating geographical theories more than two centuries old and equally old allusions to Karelian invasions.

Little information about either the Greenlandic or the American Arctic was absorbed on the European continent, despite increasing Norse familiarity with those regions after 1000 C.E. Adam of Bremen's brief accounts (c. 1075) of Norse activities in Iceland, Greenland, and Vínland (Wine Land) constituted an exception, and they have remained the earliest extant literary source concerned with Norse voyages to North America. Adam's concept of the northernmost regions also included two islands named Thule—one renamed Iceland, the other located in the frozen seas beyond Vínland—and he explained that Greenland (whose piratical inhabitants were green from seawater) also lay far out in the ocean, opposite to the Swedish mountains and a mountain chain east of Sweden that prevented knowledge of the areas beyond. These daunting peaks, called the Rhiphaean Mountains, were entirely imaginary.

About a century later, the *Historia Norvegiæ* (History of Norway) described Greenland as connected to the northwestern part of Eurasia by a land bridge and edged by frigid seas. Between Greenland and Biarmaland (the White Sea region) were islands with giants and maidens who became pregnant from drinking water. Reality nevertheless intruded with the observation that north of the Norse settlements in Greenland lived small men called Skrælingar (puny sorts), who used walrus ivory and stone instead of iron. The Norwegian author of *The King's Mirror* (c. 1250) located Greenland at the northern edge of the habitable world, where it met the globe-spanning ocean; he furthermore described the monsters, mermaids, and mermen living in the Greenland seas and noted that men seldom went there. The Icelander Snorri Sturluson (1179–1241) likewise blended myth with reality when he described an eddying void (Ginnungagap) at the northern extreme of the Arctic seas. This supposedly represented pre-Christian Norse ideas about waters whose actual dangers Norse sailors knew long before 1000 C.E. Such myths were still doing well as late as 1605 when the Icelandic bishop Guðbrandur Thorláksson drew a map showing the Ginnungagap and a whirlpool in a strait that separated southern Greenland from a nonexistent Estoteland inspired by Nicolò Zeno's spurious 1558 map.

Roiling seas, a magnetic mountain, and Pygmies (Arctic natives) appear in the scant information salvaged from the *Inventio Fortunata*, which was purportedly written about 1360 by an English Minorite after his voyage to Greenland and beyond. Like Bishop Guðbrandur's map, these literary fragments owed their survival to post-Columbian interest in Greenland's imagined land connection to the New World and added to the burgeoning of European literary and cartographic myths about the Arctic that occurred after 1500.

The 1514 publication in Paris of Saxo Grammaticus's *Danish Chronicle* contributed to this development of myths about the Arctic. A mostly mythical account of Denmark's heroic past, the *Danish Chronicle* had spent three centuries of virtual oblivion in a Danish monastery before the Danish-born archbishop Erik Valkendorf of Norway and others arranged to have it printed. At that time, Valkendorf was planning a voyage to reconnect with the Greenland Norse as a first step toward claiming ancient Nordic rights over part of North America, and, while his voyage came to nothing, he generated information and speculation about the Arctic regions beyond Iceland. A 1534 Basel edition of Saxo's work brought it wider continental recognition and inspired Valkendorf's younger friend Olaus Magnus to emulate it for his own description of "Goths" or Swedes. Whether one's focus was reindeer herders in northern Sweden or pirates with their unique navigational device on the mythical island of Hvitsark, Olaus's 1539 *Carta marina* and his 1555 compendium on the Nordic peoples (*Historia de gentibus septentrionalibus*) exercised an enduring influence on European perceptions of the Arctic and its people. [See color plate 11 in this volume.]

[*See also* Greenland; Magnus, Olaus; *and* Thule.]

BIBLIOGRAPHY

Cunliffe, Barry W. *The Extraordinary Voyage of Pytheas the Greek.* London: Allen Lane, 2001. Cunliffe's archaeological expertise is joined to extensive reading and much common sense.

Fernández-Armesto, Felipe. *The Times Atlas of World Exploration.* London: Times Books, 1991. A well-illustrated overview of the globe.

Foote, Peter G., ed. *Olaus Magnus: A Description of the Northern Peoples, 1555.* 3 vols. London: Hakluyt Society, 1996–1998.

Holland, Clive. *Arctic Exploration and Development c. 500 B.C. to 1915: An Encyclopedia.* New York: Garland, 1994.

Pálsson, Hermann, and Paul Edwards, trans. and eds. *The Book of Settlements: Landnámabók.* University of Manitoba Icelandic Studies 1. Winnipeg: University of Manitoba Press, 1972. An unbeatable source concerning North Atlantic colonization of more than a millennium ago.

Pulsiano, Phillip, and Kirsten Wolf, eds. *Medieval Scandinavia: An Encyclopedia*. New York: Garland, 1993. High editorial standard with a mostly literary focus, and with contributions from a number of well-known scholars.

KIRSTEN A. SEAVER

Nineteenth-Century Images

The revival of Arctic exploration after the Napoleonic Wars, signaled by the British naval North Pole and Baffin Bay expeditions of 1818, coincided with improved levels of literacy, new and developing technologies for the mass production of images, and expanding transport systems. Consequently more people could acquire information about the region. The public usually accessed this information through what the art historian Bernard Smith has called "imaginings." These were representations created outside the Arctic by people who often had no direct contact with the region, yet it was these, rather than primary images, that had the greater effect on the popular imagination.

Travel Narratives. The travel narrative was already popular before the nineteenth century, and the reworking of an expedition's papers and journal into an illustrated narrative that would sell was an essential task for the leader on his return. A summary of the scientific observations was usually incorporated. The narratives of expeditions during the first half of the nineteenth century were popular, and the books of John Ross, John Franklin, and William Parry could be found in many private collections as well as in subscription libraries. The number of expeditions in the 1850s searching for Franklin's lost ships resulted in a boom in travel narratives, but with a few exceptions—most notably Leopold McClintock's *The Voyage of the "Fox" in the Arctic Seas* (1859), which described the solution to the Franklin mystery—their popularity was not as great. The problem, stemming from a satiated market, was compounded by competition from the well-illustrated accounts published in magazines and in the press.

The late-nineteenth-century reader had access to travel narratives that reflected the increasing international interest in the Arctic. Exciting accounts of Nils Adolf Erik Nordenskiöld's navigation of the Northeast Passage (1878–1880), of the disaster of George W. de Long's *Jeanette* expedition of 1879–1881, of the disaster of the expedition led by Adolphus W. Greely in 1881–1884, of Gustav Holm's encounter with the Inuit of the Angmagssalik region of eastern Greenland in 1883–1885, of Fridtjof Nansen's crossing of Greenland in 1888–1889 and his voyage in the *Fram* in 1893–1896, and of Robert Peary's exploration of northern Greenland in 1891–1892 and 1893–1895 were all extensively reported in the press and made available as narratives in various languages. Many were also profusely illustrated, increasingly with photographs. In Britain, the development of the empire and an emerging interest in Antarctica meant that travel narratives of expeditions to these regions became more popular than the few Arctic ones published at that time.

Adventure Stories. Adventure stories for boys, in both juvenile magazines, such as *Boy's Own Paper*, and books were popular in the second half of the nineteenth century. Writers capitalized on the contemporary fascination with the Arctic. Some stories were entirely imaginary, such as W. H. G. Kingston's *Peter the Whaler* (1851) and R. M. Ballantyne's *The World of Ice* (1860), while others used real locations in time and space to give their stories an apparent authenticity. Nansen's crossing of the Greenland icecap formed the basis of W. Gordon Stables's *To Greenland and the Pole* (1895), and the quest for the North Pole informed Jules Verne's *The Adventures of Captain Hatteras* (1875–1876). The stories by Stables and Ballantyne benefited from their Arctic experiences, Stables as a whaler, and Ballantyne as an employee of the Hudson's Bay Company.

Many of these books placed the landscape and the native people at the center of the story. In *The World of Ice*, Ballantyne described the scenery in great detail and incorporated scenes where the skills of the Inuit were vital to the success of the white adventurers, as explorers such as John Rae of the Hudson's Bay Company had discovered. However, Stables, under the influence of social Darwinism, contributed to the stereotype of the Inuit as primitive and subhuman. Novels with a distinct moralistic purpose were written under the auspices of missionary societies. Miss Brightwell's undated *Romance of the Modern Missions* is set in the improving environment of a missionary-run settlement.

Other authors such as G. Hartwig (1892) and G. Firth Scott (1899) retold stories of real Arctic exploration for a younger audience. These were often illustrated with the same engravings that appeared in the original narratives, whereas the illustrations to the fictional adventures often undermined the quality of the narrative. Fanciful icebergs, a wintry landscape even in high summer, and stereotypical depictions of native peoples were common and were

Return of the North Pole expedition: HMS *Alert* homeward bound. This image, from the *Illustrated London News* of Saturday, November 4, 1876, is one of those that powerfully affected the British public's enthusiasm for Arctic travel. The effect of the ice-bound ship and the crashing bow-wave comes out powerfully without the need for color. COURTESY THE NEWBERRY LIBRARY, CHICAGO

clearly the result of publishers engaging artists and engravers who had no knowledge or understanding of the Arctic.

However, in the later nineteenth century, the Arctic could not rival Africa and India as the location for boys' adventure stories. Stories that encouraged boys to aspire to be part of the imperial adventure became more sought after as school prizes and as presents than accounts set in the Arctic were.

Illustrations. The scientific aspirations of most expeditions meant that cartography and meteorology were seen as prime concerns, so it was desirable to have at least one artist, usually an amateur, aboard to record views and interesting phenomena. At the start of the century the paintings of explorer-artists, such as John Ross and George Back, could be reproduced only as engravings. The process of engraving sometimes resulted in considerable alterations to the

Skating rink at the winter quarters of HMS *Discovery*. The November 4, 1876, supplement to the *Illustrated London News* contained "News of the Arctic expedition." In showing the skating rink set up alongside HMS *Discovery*, it brings out the importance of sport and exercise for ship-bound sailors and explorers. COURTESY THE NEWBERRY LIBRARY, CHICAGO

original painting, either accidentally, through the ignorance of the engraver who would not have had any familiarity with the scenes he was engraving, or intentionally, in order to satisfy the reader's expectations of the exoticism of distant places.

From 1842 the *Illustrated London News* published large numbers of engravings of Arctic scenes. This weekly paper created an appetite for illustrated articles on both sides of the Atlantic, and its competitors and some daily newspapers quickly followed suit, with the result that there were considerably more engravings in the public domain. Many of these were reused in information books or, in a colored version, as magic-lantern slides shown at both private parties and public gatherings.

William Bradford's expedition to western Greenland in 1869 realized the potential of photography for recording the landscape and the world of the explorer, and to a lesser extent of the indigenous people. Peary, working with native Greenlanders, undertook some ethnographic photography, but this

was rare. Toward the end of the century, photographers were employed alongside artists on many expeditions. However, the mass reproduction of photographs was not possible until the 1880s, so the early photographs were usually reproduced as engravings. Photographs were also used to illustrate the lectures given to geographical societies and the wider public in Europe and North America by explorers such as Peary and Nansen. [See color plate 10 in this volume.]

Exhibitions. During the first half of the century, native people were brought from their Arctic homelands by whalers, missionaries, or entrepreneurs and exhibited in *tableaux vivants*. The paying audience watched them perform traditional activities, wearing their native costume and surrounded by artifacts, while a lecturer gave a commentary. These *tableaux vivants*, however, provided only a sanitized reconstruction of a few stereotypical aspects of Arctic people's lives.

Panoramas were vast canvases depicting Arctic life and exploration covering the walls of purpose-built rotundas. Early panoramic canvases were static, but as technology developed it was possible to move the images and thus tell a story. Panoramas were often created by artists who had no knowledge of the Arctic, and though the panoramas were seen as both entertainment and education, it is clear that entertainment often took precedence, as in the 1834 panorama of *Captain Ross's Expedition to the North Pole*.

Later in the century, international exhibitions became popular worldwide. From 1859 some of these included *tableaux vivants* updated to include a "street" of native villages. At the Paris Exposition Universelle in 1889, a street included Eskimo and Lapp structures, and at the World Columbian Exhibition in Chicago in 1893 there was an Eskimo encampment from Alaska. As with the *tableaux vivants*, native peoples performed traditional activities, and organizers were able to imply a social Darwinian view of racial hierarchy. In the national pavilions, such as the Canadian pavilion at the Colonial and Indian Exhibition in London in 1886, the Arctic was promoted as a region suitable for recreation and hunting rather than as one ripe for settlement, agriculture, industry, and commerce. Arctic art was sometimes displayed at these exhibitions. Reworked paintings by Arctic explorers, such as Sir Edward Inglefield, were shown at the Royal Naval Exhibition in London in 1891. Other, better-known artists, such as J. J. Millais and Edwin Landseer, neither of whom had ever visited the Arctic, capitalized on popular interest in the region by painting large canvases that were initially exhibited at venues such as the Royal Academy.

Museums approached the display of native artifacts in a variety of ways. American museums favored the "life group," in which artifacts were contextualized with the help of mannequins and associated scenery. In the United Kingdom, museums at Hull and Exeter adopted a geographical organization; the Pitt Rivers Museum in Oxford adopted the "succession of ideas" method, where artifacts that performed similar functions from cultures across the world were displayed together; and the Horniman Museum in south London adopted the unsystematic method of the "cabinet of curiosities." In the later nineteenth century the artifacts of exploration, especially relics from Franklin's lost expedition, became increasingly popular. Museums often exhibited stuffed Arctic fauna such as whales, seals, and musk oxen, while polar bears were one of the most popular exhibits in the zoological gardens.

[*See also* Inuit; Travel Literature, European; *and biographical entries on figures mentioned in this article.*]

BIBLIOGRAPHY

David, Robert G. *The Arctic in the British Imagination 1818–1914.* Manchester, U.K.: Manchester University Press, 2000.

Houston, C. Stuart, ed. *Arctic Artist: The Journal and Paintings of George Back, Midshipman with Franklin, 1819–1822.* Montreal and Buffalo, N.Y.: McGill-Queen's University Press, 1994.

King, J. C. H., and Henrietta Lidchi, eds. *Imaging the Arctic.* London: British Museum Press, 1998.

Riffenburgh, Beau. *The Myth of the Explorer: The Press, Sensationalism, and Geographical Discovery.* London and New York: Belhaven Press, 1993.

Smith, Bernard. *Imagining the Pacific: In the Wake of the Cook Voyages.* London and New Haven, Conn.: Yale University Press, 1992.

Spufford, Francis. *I May Be Some Time: Ice and the English Imagination.* London: Faber, 1996.

ROBERT G. DAVID

Russian Arctic

Because of Novgorod's fur trade, Russians had some knowledge of Arctic regions as early as the eleventh to fifteenth centuries, but their explorations of the Arctic began in earnest only when Moscow conquered Novgorod in 1478. Ivan III (r. 1462–1505) sent several expeditions to the Ob River; he and his successors wanted control of the fur trade. The sixteenth-century interest in discovering the North-

east Passage to China led the Dutch and English to send ships to explore the Russian Arctic, which in turn spurred more exploration by Russians. Early in the seventeenth century, Tsar Mikhail Fedorovich (r. 1613–1645) forbade foreigners to navigate any waters east of Arkhangel'sk on the White Sea. Although Russians moved from one river to another along the Arctic coast in the summer, travel by means of the great rivers of Siberia was easier than sailing along the coast, so most explorations were along rivers. The wooden vessels used were of the *koch* type, with one mast. They carried about thirty men and a cargo of 30 tons. The nobleman Kondratiy Kurochkin made an important coastal voyage in 1610 from the mouth of the Yenisey eastward to the mouth of the Pyasina. A decade later, Russians were exploring the Lena River, and by the 1630s they had secured its delta. Eastward movement continued to the mouths of the Indigirka and Kolyma rivers in the 1640s.

Russians reached the Sea of Okhotsk, with access to the Pacific, via a river and land route in 1639. Although river travel was most common, the voyage of Fedot A. Popov and Semen Deshnev in 1648 is a notable exception. They sailed east along the Arctic coast from the Kolyma River and passed through the strait that separates Asia from America. Russians also explored and conquered the Kamchatka Peninsula.

When Peter the Great became ruler in 1689, he placed a high priority on mapping and describing his empire, particularly Siberia. The expeditions he inaugurated continued after his death in 1725, including the first (1726–1730) and second (1731–1742) Kamchatka expeditions, led by Vitus J. Bering and Alexei I. Chirikov, and the voyages in 1732 to the Bering Strait and North America by Mikhail Spiridonovich Gvozdev and I. Fyodorov. The Arctic mapping done by the second Kamchatka expedition was phenomenal. The coast was divided into four sections: (1) from Arkhangel'sk to the mouth of the Ob River; (2) from the Ob to the mouth of the Yenisey River; (3) from the Yenisey to the Lena River; and (4) from the Lena all the way to the Kamchatka River. Lieutenants Stepan Voinovich Murav'ev and Mikhail Pavlov began the first section in 1734 and reached the tip of the Yamal Peninsula, the northernmost part of their section, before autumn. However, they were forced to return to their winter camp on the Pechora River until the following year. Because of ice in the Kara Sea, they were unable to return to the place where they had stopped mapping. They blamed each other for their failure, and the Admiralty reduced them to the rank of seaman. Lieutenants Malygin and Skuratov, along with the geodesist Selifontov, replaced Murav'ev and Pavlov in spring 1736 and successfully completed mapping the section.

The young naval officer Dmitry Leont'evich Ovtsyn was assigned to map the second section. Beginning in 1734 from the mouth of the Ob River, Ovtsyn attempted to reach the Yenisey River in a single summer, but ice conditions in the Kara Sea forced his return. He spent the winter at the Ob; in summer he faced so many setbacks that little was done. In 1737, in a new vessel, the *Postman of the Ob*, Ovtsyn succeeded in sailing to the Yenisey and beyond. When Ovtsyn reported to Saint Petersburg the following spring, he was arrested because of his friendship with Prince Dolgorukov, an exile in Siberia. Ovtsyn was reduced to the rank of seaman, but he was later released and sailed with Bering's expedition to America in 1741.

The third section of the mapping—from the Yenisey to the Lena—was difficult because it involved sailing around the Taymyr Peninsula. The Admiralty ordered two groups to carry out the task. Fedor Minin, in the *Postman of the Ob*, was to map eastward from the Yenisey toward the Lena, while Vasily Pronchishchev, with his wife, Mariya (the first European woman explorer of the Arctic), set out westward from the Lena toward the Yenisey. Minin and his assistant Dmitri Sterlegov set out for the Kara Sea, but in 1738 ice and thick fog prevented them from continuing. Neither group reached the Taymyr Peninsula. In winter 1739, Minin mapped the mouth of the Yenisey, and in the following winter Sterlegov explored east of it. The next summer they progressed only two hundred miles (333 kilometers) farther than they had the first summer, to the Pyasina River. In autumn 1740 the Admiralty relieved Minin of his duty.

Pronchishchev and his wife, accompanied by Semen Chelyuskin, succeeded in reaching the Olenek River in the summer of 1735, and they wintered there because their ship, the *Yakutsk*, sprang a leak. The following spring, after investigating the copper deposits of the Anabar River, they continued north toward the Taymyr Peninsula. In August, nearing the northernmost tip of Asia at latitude 77°, ice stopped them. Unable to find a suitable wintering place, they returned to the Olenek River. Pronchishchev and his wife died there, and Chelyuskin returned to Yakutsk to report on the expedition. Hariton Laptev was ordered to continue the mission. In spring 1739, he sailed westward from the Lena delta in the *Yakutsk*. With winter coming, Laptev remained at the mouth of a small river that flowed into the gulf of Khatanga. In October he sent Zakhar Medvedev to the Pyasina River to map east of it. Laptev sent other crews out as well; twelve of his men died. Laptev determined to map the coast by land, using three detachments. Two of the three succeeded; one group, under N. Chekin, failed, and the northeastern corner of the Taymyr Peninsula was not mapped. The mission was finally completed seven years after Pronchishchev had begun it.

The fourth and final section of the mapping, from the Lena eastward, was the most difficult. In the spring of 1735, Pytor Lasinius and Pronchishchev ran into ice and made camp. Scurvy broke out and by the spring of 1736, thirty-seven of the forty-eight men wintering in the camp had died. The ship *Yakutsk* was not seaworthy, and mapping ended. Laptev reported on the status of the expedition to Bering; he also traveled to Saint Petersburg, where he announced that the mission was impossible because of the ice. The Admiralty ordered him to continue the mapping either by sea or by land.

In 1738, Laptev was successful in reaching the Indigirka River, then continued eastward to the Kolyma, where he set up a winter camp. The following summer was difficult. Unable to continue along the coast, he set off with a hundred men straight for Anadyr, to map the coast from there to the west. Laptev explored again in the summer of 1741, but he failed to map the Chukchi Peninsula—a feat that was not, in fact, accomplished until early in the nineteenth century by Ferdinand von Wrangell and his men, who traveled by land.

Catherine II (r. 1762–1796) also initiated exploring expeditions; for example, she sent Lieutenant Ivan Sindt to the Aleutian Islands in 1764. In 1768–1769, Pytor Krenitsyn and Mikhail Levashev explored Unalaska and Umnak in the Aleutian Islands, as well as the southern shores of Alaska. Vasily Yakovlevich Chichagov made two failed attempts to sail straight across the North Pole from Arkhangel'sk to the Pacific. In 1785–1793, Lieutenant Joseph Billings and Gavriil Sarychev explored the Chukchi Peninsula both by land and by sea. Thus by the early nineteenth century Russia had accurate maps and descriptions of its Arctic regions.

[*See also* Expeditions, World Exploration, *subentry on* Russia; Fur Trade; Northeast Passage; North Pole; Russian American Company; Siberia; *and biographical entries on figures mentioned in this article.*]

BIBLIOGRAPHY
Armstrong, Terence. *The Russians in the Arctic: Aspects of Soviet Exploration and Exploitation of the Far North, 1937–57.* London: Methuen, 1958.

Belov, M. I. *Russians in the Bering Strait, 1648–1791*. Translated by Katerina Solovjova. Edited with an introduction by J. L. Smith. Anchorage, Alaska: White Stone Press, 2000.

Imbert, Bertrand. *North Pole, South Pole: Journeys to the Ends of the Earth*. Translated by Alexandra Campbell. New York: Abrams, 1992.

Lainema, Matti. *Ultima Thule: Arctic Explorations*. Helsinki, Finland: John Nurminen Foundation, 2001.

Postnikov, Alexei V. *Mapping of Russian America: A History of Russian-American Contacts in Cartography*. American Geographical Society Collection special publication no. 4. Milwaukee: American Geographical Society Collection of the Golda Meir Library, University of Wisconsin-Milwaukee, 1995.

Postnikov, Alexei V. "Outline of the History of Russian Cartography." In *Regions: A Prism to View the Slavic-Eurasian World, Towards a Discipline of "Regionology,"* edited by Kimitaka Matsuzato. Sapporo, Japan: Slavic Research Center, Hokkaido University, 2000.

ALEXEY POSTNIKOV

Argonauts and the Golden Fleece.

A Greek legend already described as "a concern to all" in Homer's time told of Jason's journey to Aea aboard the ship *Argo* in search of the Golden Fleece, and his successful return to Iolcus with his prize and his foreign bride, Medea. The many perils and wonders he encountered along the way are best known from the Hellenistic epic *Argonautica* by Apollonius of Rhodes, the most complete extant version of the legend (some elements were dealt with earlier by Pindar in the *Fourth Pythian*). In its essence Jason's story is a coming-of-age myth, in which a young prince must prove his fearlessness and strength in order to regain the throne of which he has been dispossessed, combined with an *Odyssey*-type tale of a strange voyage on an unknown sea—in this case the Black Sea, where the kingdom of Aea was thought to be located.

Though originally situated vaguely in the mythicized East, on the borders of Ocean, Aea came to be identified early on with the land of Colchis at the eastern end of the Black Sea (modern-day Armenia). Archaic Greek interest in the *Argo* story doubtless reflects the increase in Greek trade with this eastern region and the colonization of its coastline by Greeks starting in the sixth century B.C.E. The golden fleece can thus be regarded as an emblem of the perceived (though doubtless exaggerated) mineral wealth of this newly accessible marketplace, while Jason's marriage to Medea, daughter of the local king Aeetes, reflects an experience common to many Greek colonists who were forced to find brides from among indigenous populations. Thus the events of Jason's journey parallel at many points the fabulous wanderings of Odysseus in the *Odyssey*, a set of legends

similarly derived from the voyages of actual Greek traders and colonists (although into the West rather than the East). Jason, like Odysseus, encounters navigational perils (the Symplegades or Clashing Rocks), endures assaults by winged monsters (the Harpies), and escapes from the sexual allure of females who would detain him (the Lemnian women). Perhaps most strikingly, both heroes obtain their homecoming with the help of witch-women who descend from the god Helios: Medea in Jason's case, Circe—by most accounts Medea's aunt—in that of Odysseus.

As portrayed in the *Argonautica*, the royal house of Aea represents an exaggerated version of an Asian hereditary monarchy, headed by a patriarch of enormous wealth and power. Aeetes is a terrifyingly potent figure who performs daily feats of strength by yoking a pair of fire-breathing bulls, plowing a field from which armed men spring to life, and then single-handedly defeating those warriors in combat. Jason and his crew possess more limited powers, especially after Heracles, the most powerful man aboard the *Argo*, leaves the expedition in mid-journey to search for a lost comrade. Forced to perform the feats of Aeetes in order to obtain the Golden Fleece, Jason finds himself at a loss until Medea, overcome with love for the handsome stranger, gives him a magic ointment that confers superhuman strength. Having earned Jason's gratitude, and because her position in Aea is now untenable, Medea accompanies Jason on the *Argo*'s return voyage and, ultimately, marries him (later to murder their children in the episode dramatized by Euripides).

The *Argo*'s return to Greece from foreign waters, with a Colchian vessel in pursuit, was variously described by ancient authors; some had the ship simply retrace its outward voyage, while others found ways to give the tale more variety. In Apollonius's *Argonautica* geography is subjected to poetic license to allow the *Argo* to sail by way of the Danube, Po, and Rhone rivers into the western Mediterranean, thence to Corfu and North Africa, with a stop in Crete before the final reentry into Thessaly. This improbable route was most likely devised by Apollonius as a way to incorporate into his poem a wide array of geographic facts and theories concerning the "new world" in western Europe. More perils and adventures beset the return voyage, and the pursuing Colchians were diverted only when Medea killed and dismembered her brother Apsyrtus and scattered the pieces of his corpse in the sea, forcing his shipmates to stop and collect them.

The *Argo* was thought to be the first oceangoing ship ever built, designed by the goddess Athena and constructed out of wood that possessed the power of speech. Her trip across the Black Sea was the first intercontinental voyage sailors had ever undertaken. Greek and Roman philosophers meditated on the meaning of this voyage, which had opened the era of commerce and trade that would totally transform ancient societies. The Roman Stoic Seneca, for example, brooded on the navigational theme in his tragedy *Medea*, where the launching of *Argo* is depicted as the end of humanity's golden age.

[*See also* Fictions of Exploration, *subentry* Ancient, *and* Travel Writing in Antiquity.]

BIBLIOGRAPHY

Hunter, R. L. *The Argonautica of Apollonius: Literary Studies.* Cambridge, U.K., and New York: Cambridge University Press, 1993.

Hunter, Richard L. *Jason and the Golden Fleece* (The Argonautica). Oxford: Clarendon Press, 1993.

JAMES ROMM

Armstrong, Neil (b. 1930), American astronaut. Neil Alden Armstrong became the first man to set foot on the Moon on July 20, 1969. Armstrong, a veteran test pilot, engineer, and astronaut, commanded the *Apollo 11* mission that fulfilled the late President John F. Kennedy's admonition to land a man on the Moon and return him safely to Earth by the end of the 1960s.

Armstrong was born August 5, 1930, in Wapakoneta, Ohio. As a boy he was drawn to aviation, earning his private pilot's license before he could drive an automobile. Armstrong entered Purdue University to study engineering. He entered the United States Navy in 1949, ultimately becoming a naval aviator and flying seventy-eight combat missions during the Korean War. Upon his return from Korea, Armstrong reentered Purdue and earned a bachelor's degree in aeronautical engineering.

Armstrong became a research test pilot for the National Advisory Committee for Aeronautics (NACA), the predecessor to the National Aeronautics and Space Administration (NASA). His test pilot career began at NACA's Lewis research laboratory in Cleveland, Ohio, but he was soon transferred to the NACA High Speed Flight Station at Edwards Air Force Base in California.

While at Edwards, Armstrong piloted the X-15 experimental rocket plane. In 1962, Armstrong was one of the nine-person second astronaut class selected by NASA. His first mission as an astronaut was as Command Pilot of *Gemini 8*, with Pilot David R.

Scott. *Gemini 8* achieved the first docking in space, as Armstrong guided his spacecraft into a coupling with an Agena Target Vehicle. The triumph was short-lived, however, as the spacecraft began to tumble off course due to a faulty attitude thruster. Armstrong brought the spacecraft under control, but the mission had to be terminated.

Armstrong was officially named commander of *Apollo 11*, along with Lunar Module Pilot "Buzz" Aldrin and Command Module Pilot Michael Collins, in March of 1969. *Apollo 11* was the third mission to the Moon, and the first to attempt a landing. Armstrong guided the Lunar Module *Eagle* to a landing in the Sea of Tranquility on July 20, 1969. Four hours later, Armstrong descended the landing craft's ladder and became the first man to step on the Moon's surface. "That's one small step for a man, one giant leap for mankind," Armstrong said at the time, a quote that has become familiar around the world.

Armstrong never flew another space mission, and left NASA in 1971 to teach engineering at the University of Cincinnati. A reluctant icon, Armstrong is self-effacing and quiet, a serious engineer who travels the world giving speeches to business, academic, and engineering organizations, but otherwise shuns the spotlight. He has noted that he was not chosen to be the first man on the Moon; rather, he was chosen to command an *Apollo* crew that fell in line to become the first to attempt a lunar landing.

[*See also* Moon *and* Space Program, *subentry* American.]

BIBLIOGRAPHY

Chaikin, Andrew. *A Man on the Moon: The Voyages of the Apollo Astronauts.* New York: Viking, 1994.

Hansen, James R. *First Man: The Life of Neil A. Armstrong.* New York: Simon and Schuster, 2005.

TOD A. BRYANT

Arrowsmith, Aaron (1750–1823), British geographer and cartographer. Aaron Arrowsmith published many fine maps and atlases based on the best available sources. His maps are of value to the student of exploration, most notably the student of exploration of North America. The maps are regarded as authoritative references concerning the progress of exploration and discovery.

Arrowsmith was born in Winston, in County Durham, England. Strangely, he had no formal education. He became a surveyor by experience rather than by training. He moved to London in 1770, and there—at the center of geographical study for the world—he developed a firm later operated by his

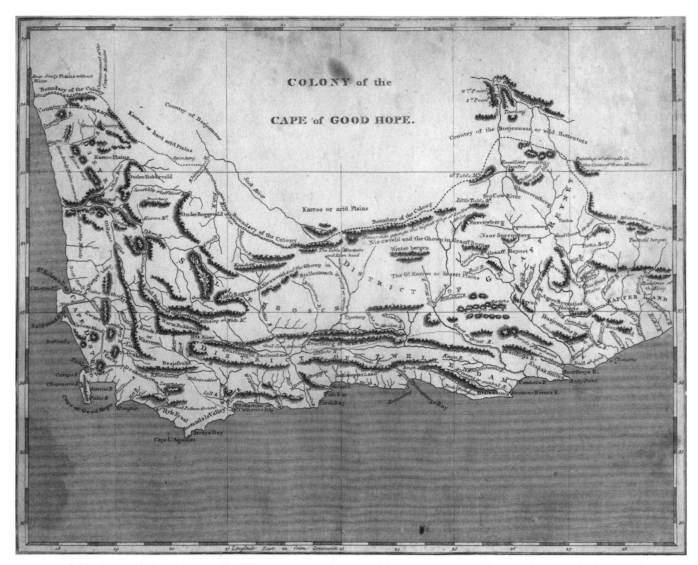

Colony of the Cape of Good Hope. The blank areas on Arrowsmith's maps are as telling as the inscribed ones. This map (London, 1804) shows Cape Colony and the blank area to the north inhabited by "Bosjesmans or wild Hottentots." The Boers would establish the Orange Free State here in thirty years or so. COURTESY THE NEWBERRY LIBRARY, CHICAGO

sons Aaron and Samuel; this same enterprise was later run by his nephew John Arrowsmith, a founder of the Royal Geographical Society, London. In short, the elder Arrowsmith began a family concern that stood at the heart of cartography and geographical science.

Arrowsmith's *Map of the World* was published 1790. His *Map of North America* appeared in 1796, followed by his *Chart of the Pacific Ocean* in 1798. Arrowsmith also produced maps of Australia, Africa, and India. Many were printed in *A New and Elegant General Atlas: Comprising All the New Discoveries to the Present Time, Containing Sixty-three Maps Drawn by Arrowsmith and [Samuel] Lewis,* published in Boston in 1812.

Arrowsmith's *Map of North America* is of particular importance to North American exploration history, based as it is on fur traders' and explorers' accounts. Arrowsmith was aggressive in his search for data, which with his concern for authenticity made for a powerful combination. He had connections to the Hudson's Bay Company (HBC) and other trading interests in North America. Arrowsmith's *Map of North America* incorporated details from another, more specialized map produced the year before, *A Map Exhibiting All the New Discoveries in the Interior*

Parts of North America (1795). In this map, Arrowsmith depicted the principal trade routes to the Rocky Mountains from Hudson Bay, the Hayes River to Lake Winnipeg, the North Saskatchewan River, and the river that Alexander Mackenzie followed to the high Arctic in 1789. The map showed scant detail from the Rockies to the Pacific Coast. Subsequent editions in 1796, 1802, and 1811 incorporated new information, mainly from the HBC's surveyor Peter Fidler, but the maps were weak on the Missouri. Meanwhile, Antoine Soulard had produced maps of upper Louisiana, including his 1802 topographical sketch (unpublished) of the Missouri and Mississippi rivers with Indian tribes and other rivers shown; this and other maps, including Arrowsmith's latest and David Thompson's unpublished upper Mississippi map, were with Lewis and Clark when they began their journey in 1804. The printed American map by Nicholas King incorporated much of Arrowsmith's information.

The 1802 edition of Arrowsmith's *Map of North America* incorporated Mackenzie's published findings and George Vancouver's surveys on the Northwest Coast. When David Thompson began his "Map of the North-West Territory" in 1812, he had many printed maps to work from but none better than Arrowsmith's, especially for northern latitudes.

[*See also* Hudson's Bay Company, *subentry on* North American Exploration; Maps, Mapmaking, and Mapmakers; *and biographical entries on figures mentioned in this article.*]

BIBLIOGRAPHY
D'Arcy, Jenish. *Epic Wanderer: David Thomson and the Mapping of the Canadian West.* Toronto: Doubleday Canada, 2003.
Wood, W. Raymond. *Prologue to Lewis and Clark: The Mackay and Evans Expedition.* Norman: University of Oklahoma Press, 2003.

BARRY M. GOUGH

Asia. *See* **Buddhist Cosmological Maps; Carpini, Giovanni; Chinese Empirical Maps; Chinese Exploration; Cipangu; Expeditions, World Exploration; Fictions of Exploration; Fu Sang; Gobi Desert; Imperialism and Exploration; Indian Ocean; Java le Grande; Manila-Acapulco Trade; Ocean Currents and Winds; Pacific; Polo, Marco; William of Rubrouck;** *and* **Zheng He.**

Astrolabe, Mariner's. *See* **Navigational Techniques.**

Atlantis. Plato introduced the story of Atlantis in his dialogue *Timaeus*, attributing the tale to a college of Egyptian priests interviewed by the Athenian statesman Solon. According to the oral traditions supposedly known to those priests, the vast island called Atlantis, situated west of the Strait of Gibraltar, had in the distant past been home to a highly advanced semidivine people who attained naval supremacy over the Atlantic and western Mediterranean. After losing a war against the Athenians, the inhabitants of Atlantis were destroyed by an earthquake and flood that overwhelmed their island and reduced it to the muddy shoals found, according to Plato, in the seas off Iberia. In a follow-up dialogue preserved only in unfinished form, the *Critias*, Plato elaborated on the tale of Atlantis by describing the genesis of the island's population from the god Poseidon, the makeup of their constitution, the physical geography of the island, and many other particulars. But it has always been the much briefer account in the *Timaeus* that has captured the popular imagination, in large part because of the details it contains about the location of Atlantis.

Atlantis as conceived by Plato was hardly a utopian society; indeed, its destruction is explained in the *Critias* as divine punishment for its fall from virtue. Nonetheless, the legend of a powerful and sophisticated Western race, able to control most of the known world through its mastery of the seas, has been burnished and idealized over the centuries. A particularly grotesque adaptation by Ignatius Donnelly in nineteenth-century America tried to make Atlantis into a colonizing power that had planted the seeds of all "higher" civilizations across the globe.

Plato's description of Atlantis hardly suggests a real locale, especially when one considers the size of the island, which reportedly exceeded that of Asia and Africa taken together. Yet as early as 300 B.C.E there were evidently some readers prepared to believe the tale told in *Timaeus* and *Critias*. Medieval and Renaissance cartographers often depicted Atlantis as a real place (sometimes assimilating it to other Atlantic islands, such as the Fortunate Isles, Antilia, or the places visited by Saint Brendan) and after Columbus, they sometimes identified the Americas as Atlantis, ignoring entirely Plato's report of the sinking of the island. In the sixteenth century, Abraham Ortelius, commenting on this identification in his *Thesaurus Geographicus*, speculated that the earthquake recounted by Plato had not sunk Atlantis but had torn it away from the Europe and Africa, noting that the coastlines of those two continents seemed to fit those of the Americas—the first rudimentary glimmers of a continental drift theory.

Modern Atlantis-hunters have tried to correlate the Bronze Age eruption of a volcano on Thera (present-day Santorini), which undoubtedly did spawn destructive tsunamis, with the cataclysm described in the *Timaeus*, or have used underwater geological surveys to identify likely locales for the island. Thus far such efforts have not produced convincing results, except to show that Plato could have known about ancient natural disasters and sunken cities and thus found inspiration for his fabulous tale.

[*See also* Antitichton and Antipodes *and* Europe and the Mediterranean, *subentry on* Greek and Roman Mapmaking.]

BIBLIOGRAPHY
De Camp, L. Sprague. *Lost Continents: The Atlantis Theme in History, Science and Literature.* New York: Dover, 1970.
Donnelly, Ignatius. *Atlantis: The Antediluvian World.* 1882. Reprint. New York: Dover, 1976.
Plato. *Timaeus and Critias.* Translated by Desmond Lee. New York: Penguin Classics, 1972.

JAMES ROMM

Atlasov, Vladimir

Atlasov, Vladimir (c. 1663–1711), eastern Russian fur trader. Born in Siberia, Atlasov served in the Yakutsk garrison, where his duties included guarding the transports carrying furs to Moscow, as well as participating in journeys to the east of Yakutsk in order to collect *yasak* (fur tax) from the native peoples. There had been some penetration of the Kamchatka region before his time, but his expedition of 1696 with a party of Cossacks marked a new drive to bring the area under Russian control. In spite of resistance by the Koryaks, Atlasov eventually succeeded in establishing two settlements along the Kamchatka River, settlements that became trading posts for Russian fur traders.

In 1697 he registered the eruption of the Klyuchevskaya volcano, and in 1700 returned in triumph from Kamchatka, greatly enriched by his tax-collecting activities. He was called to Moscow, where Peter the Great appointed him regent of the newly penetrated region. Atlasov tried to establish Moscow's power by extracting animal furs from the native Itelmen and Koryak peoples, using torture and burning villages. His cruelty was such that in the end his own men mutinied and killed him.

[*See also* Fur Trade *and* Siberia.]

BIBLIOGRAPHY
Lantzeff, George V., and Richard A. Pierce. *Eastward to Empire: Exploration and Conquest on the Russian Open Frontier, to 1750.* Montreal: McGill-Queen's University Press, 1973.

ALEXEY POSTNIKOV

Audubon, John James

Audubon, John James (1785–1851), Haitian-born American ornithologist and artist. Audubon was the illegitimate son of Jean Audubon, a sugar planter of Saint Domingue, and the French chambermaid Jeanne Rabin. He left the tumultuous Caribbean colony, soon to become Haiti, in 1791, and was then raised in France at Nantes until 1803, when he was sent to America to avoid Napoleon's program of conscription. Audubon was relatively tall for the day, and he was remarkably lean and athletic, qualities that he would need in his constant traveling and ornithological work; he always concealed the circumstances of his birth.

From childhood, Audubon had been interested in the delineation of creatures, and the story of how this interest eventually led to the compilation of the more than four hundred huge plates of his *Birds of America* (1840) is well known. Operating on the frontier of European settlement, largely in the valley of the Mississippi River, Audubon made an incomparable record of the birds that he encountered, drawing them in their habitat with amazing accuracy and liveliness. What is not so well known is the way that prescient observers like Audubon could, almost as soon as the American landscape had become known to Europeans, foresee the landscape's degradation. As his journal for 1827 put it,

> Neither this little stream, this swamp, this grand sheet of flowing water, nor these mountains will be seen in a century hence as I see them now. Nature will have been robbed of her brilliant charms. The currents will be tormented and turned away from their primitive courses . . . Oh Walter Scott, come, come to America! Set thee hence, look upon her, and see her grandeur. Nature still nurses her, cherishes her. But a tear flows in her eye. Her cheek has already changed from the peach blossom to sallow hue [and] her frame inclines to emaciation.

Audubon took an equally realistic view of the plight of the Indian peoples, whose fate was indeed bound up with the destruction of their environment. Audubon died in 1851, sadly senile, but the name of this great explorer lives on in the name of the thriving society that tries to protect those creatures whose destruction he so much deplored.

[*See also* Catesby, Mark.]

BIBLIOGRAPHY

Blaugrund, Annette, and Theodore E. Stebbins, eds. *John James Audubon: The Watercolors for "The Birds of America."* New York: The New-York Historical Society, 1993.

Rhodes, Richard. *John James Audubon: The Making of an American*. New York: Knopf, 2004.

DAVID BUISSERET

Australia, Exploration of. Aboriginal people had lived in Australia for at least forty thousand years prior to the arrival of Europeans in the early seventeenth century. There has been much speculation about the earliest contacts between Asian and European seafarers and Aboriginal people. Although it is highly probable that Malay and Papuan seafarers had earlier contact, the first authenticated account is that of the Dutchman Willem Jansz (or Janszoon) in about March 1606. The subsequent story of European exploration falls roughly into three periods. The reconnaissance era ended in the 1820s, after the Blue Mountains had been crossed and the name "Australia" appeared on a map for the first time. The heroic age of long arduous journeys across the continent and into the unknown interior ended in the 1890s. The scientific age of exploration continues today.

The Reconnaissance Era. For the first two centuries of European contact with Australia, explorers

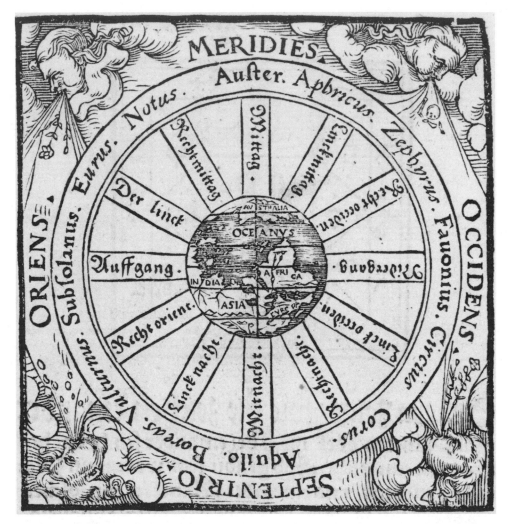

"Sphere of the Four Winds." From Cyriaco Jacob zum Barth, *Astronomia-Teutsch astronomei* (Frankfurt-am-Main, 1545). This sixteenth-century work on astronomy shows (in the central world map) a southern hemisphere landmass called "Australia." Did Flinders know of this work when he compiled his map of 1814? NATIONAL LIBRARY OF AUSTRALIA

"Carte générale de la Nouvelle Hollande." This map from Louis de Freycinet's *Voyage de découvertes aux terres australes* (1811) is the first map completely delineating the coastline of Australia; many years would pass, before the inhospitable interior became well known. NATIONAL LIBRARY OF AUSTRALIA

sought to establish the geographical extent of the continent, find commercial opportunities, and, following establishment of the Sydney Cove settlement in 1788, assess the continent's natural resources.

Willem Jansz sailed down the eastern shore of the Gulf of Carpentaria in March 1606. Later that year the Spaniard Luis Vaez de Torres sailed through the strait separating Australia from New Guinea, but it is not known whether he saw the Australian coast. Subsequently, Dutch navigators encountered parts of the north, west, and south coasts, sometimes deliberately but often accidentally. In 1642–1643 and 1644, Abel Janszoon Tasman circumnavigated the area enclosing the north and west coasts, Van Diemen's Land (called Tasmania from 1853), New Zealand, Tonga, Fiji, and the north coast of New Guinea to establish the maximum geographic limits of "New Holland." [See color plate 14 in this volume.]

British contact with Australia began with the wreck of *Tryal* on the northwest coast in 1622. Wil-

liam Dampier's *A New Voyage round the World*, published in 1697 and based on his 1688 visit, and *A Voyage to New Holland*, published in 1703 and based on his 1699 visit, painted a gloomy picture of the west coast, confirming the established Dutch assessments. From April to August 1770, James Cook, in *Endeavour*, sailed along the east coast, taking possession of "the whole east coast" for Britain on August 22. The general outline of the continent was now established. Work on filling in the details following the establishment of the British settlement at Port Jackson in January 1788.

In 1789–1790, Matthew Flinders and George Bass showed that Van Diemen's Land was separated from the mainland. George Vancouver examined the southwest coast, including King George Sound, in September 1791. From 1801 to 1803, Flinders circumnavigated the continent, showing that New Holland and New South Wales were part of the same landmass. His 1814 *General Chart of Terra Australis or Australia* contained the first cartographic use of the name "Australia."

French mapping of the Australian coastline began with Joseph-Antoine de Bruni d'Entrecasteaux's charting of the Van Diemen's Land and the southwest coast of the mainland in 1792–1793. From May 1801 to July 1803, Nicolas Baudin examined the western and southern coastlines and parts of Van Diemen's Land, meeting Flinders at Encounter Bay on April 8, 1802, in the process. Louis de Freycinet's *Carte générale de la Nouvelle Hollande*, recording their findings, was published in 1811 as the first ever complete map of Australia.

The Englishmen Phillip Parker King, in 1818–1822, and John Clements Wickham and John Lort Stokes, in 1837–1843, completed the outline map of Australia's coastline. (The detail of harbors, reefs, and so on continues to be slowly added by hydrographic surveys today.) Land exploration began immediately and a settlement was established at Sydney Cove to investigate the food resources, the rivers, and the people already living there. Governor Arthur Phillip in 1789 and 1791, Watkin Tench in 1789 and 1791, and William Dawes in 1791 explored as far as the foothills of the Blue Mountains. Knowledge of the country south of Sydney was extended to the Shoalhaven and Southern Highlands districts by John Wilson in 1798, by James Meehan in 1798 and 1818, and by Charles Throsby in 1818 and 1821. Several unsuccessful attempts were made to find a way west through the Blue Mountains before Gregory Blaxland, William Charles Wentworth, and William Lawson succeeded in mid-1813 by following the ridges rather than the rivers. In 1815, George Evans surveyed, and William Cox constructed, a road over the mountains to the site of today's Bathurst. By the 1820s the general outline of Australia had been defined and a way to the interior opened. "Australia" was on the map.

The Heroic Era. British settlements were established at today's Sydney in 1788, at Hobart in 1804, at Brisbane in 1826–1827, at Perth in 1829, at Melbourne in 1835, and at Adelaide in 1836. Explorers set out from these bases to solve geographical questions like the configuration of the inland river system; to search for overland routes between the infant settlements and across the continent; or to assess settlement opportunities. These explorers' efforts were characterized by long arduous journeys, magnificent feats of human endurance, and acts of foolhardiness. Some expeditions were followed by the tide of settlement, but others had little obvious impact.

Hamilton Hume and William Hovell pioneered a track from Sydney to the south coast of today's Victoria in 1824. In 1828, Allan Cunningham found a way through the Great Dividing Range, thus linking Brisbane to the rich pastoral country on the Darling Downs. Charles Sturt and Thomas Mitchell did much to solve the mysteries of the inland drainage system of New South Wales by investigating large sections of the Lachlan, Murrumbidgee, Darling, and Murray rivers in the 1820s and 1830s.

Angus McMillan in 1839–1840 and Paul Edmund de Strezelecki in 1840 found a way through the Australian Alps to Gippsland and created the settlement at Port Phillip. Strezelecki became the first European to climb Mount Kosciusko, mainland Australia's highest peak. In transcontinental crossings, Ludwig Leichhardt, Robert O'Hara Burke, and John McDouall Stuart traveled from the southern coast to the north in the 1840s and early 1860s. Edward Eyre traveled west around the Great Australian Bight from Fowlers Bay to King George Sound in 1841. Some thirty years later, in 1873, Peter Warburton made the first west-to-east crossing of the continent. A year earlier he had crossed the Great Sandy Desert in the northwest of western Australia. In 1875, Ernest Giles crossed from Adelaide to Perth. He also explored the Gibson Desert in 1873–1874 and 1876. William Christie Gosse became in 1873 the first European to sight Uluru (formerly Ayers Rock).

In northern Australia, Frank and Alexander Jardine pioneered a stock route into Cape York in 1864–1865. William Hann (in 1872) and Robert Logan Jack (in 1879–1880) later investigated the pastoral and mineral potential of the cape. Between 1859 and 1873, George Elphinstone Dalrymple found rich pastoral country in the Burdekin Valley, along the Herbert River and at Rockingham Bay. William Oswald Hodgkinson examined the country between the Diamantina River and the western boundary of Queensland in 1875–1876. Ernest Favenc investigated the pastoral potential of country along the Gulf of Carpentaria plain and the northern Barkly Tableland on two expeditions, in 1882–1883 and in 1883. The latter party included a pregnant Caroline Creaghe, who kept a detailed account of their journey. Between 1878 and 1881, Herbert Vere Barclay and Christopher Winnecke examined the country northeast of Alice Springs. Two years later, in 1883, David Lindsay led a government expedition into Arnhem Land. [See color plate 15 in this volume.]

In the south, Thomas Laycock led the first party across Van Diemen's Land, from north to south. James Hobbs in 1824, Jorgen Jorgensen in 1826,

Henry Hellyer in 1826–1828, and George Frankland in 1829 and 1835 led exploration parties into the unknown parts of Van Diemen's Land, locating remote harbors and finding opportunities for pastoral settlement. From 1830 to 1834, George Robinson walked around the island attempting to befriend the Aboriginals and naming many geographical features.

In the west, Surveyor-General John Septimus Roe made numerous explorations into the hinterland of Perth between 1830 and 1836. Other important expeditions were led by Robert Dale in 1829, George Grey in 1838–1839, the brothers Augustus Charles Gregory and Francis Thomas Gregory in 1846, 1848, 1858, and 1861, and the Forrest brothers through the 1870s. Augustus Gregory led the North Australia Expedition east from the Victoria River to the Gulf of Carpentaria in 1855–1856.

Albert Frederick Calvert led three expeditions into central and western Australia in 1890–1892, finding gold southeast of today's Marble Bar. The Elder Scientific Exploring Expedition led by David Lindsay and Lawrence Wells mapped a large part of central Australia in 1891–1892, but its scientific findings were disappointing. Expeditions led by Wells (in 1896) and by David Carnegie (in 1896–1897) into the Great Sandy Desert area succeeded only in demonstrating the region's aridity. By the 1890s many of the blank spaces on the map of Australia had been filled in, and a foundation had been laid for the scientific investigation of the continent that was to follow.

The Scientific Era. From the mid-1890s, serious exploration was focused on filling in the gaps of scientific knowledge. Expeditions including surveyors, geologists, botanists, anthropologists, archaeologists, and other scientists were mounted to study all aspects of the land and all the things living in it.

In 1894, Charles Winnecke led the first truly scientific expedition into central Australia. Walter Baldwin Spencer and Francis James Gillen began their study of Aboriginal life in central Australia two years later, making further expeditions in 1901–1902 and 1903. Scientific investigation of the land and people of Arnhem Land was begun in earnest by George Hubert Wilkins in 1923–1925 and continued later with major expeditions by Herbert Basedow in 1928 and Charles Mountford in 1948.

One of the major changes in exploration in the age of science was the increasing use of modern technology. Gerald Harnett Halligan was the first to use aircraft, which he did in his survey of Lake Eyre in 1922. In 1929, Cecil Thomas Madigan made an aerial survey of South Australia, naming the Simpson Desert. Donald Mackay financed aerial explorations of

central Australia in 1930, of west and northwest of the Peterman Ranges in 1933, and of the Nullabor Plain in 1935–1937. In 1937, Donald Thompson flew over Arnhem Land, helping to clarify the region's confusing river system.

Australians have played an important part in the exploration of Antarctica, with David Edgeworth, Alistair Forbes Mackay, and Douglas Mawson being the first to reach the South Magnetic Pole. Mawson returned as leader of the Australasian Antarctic Expedition (1911–1913) and again as leader of the British, Australian, and New Zealand Antarctic Research Expedition (1929–1931). As a result, about 2.3 million square miles (6 million square kilometers) of territory were ceded to Australia in 1933. Since 1947, regular expeditions to the Australian Antarctic Territory have been made by the Australian National Antarctic Research Expedition (ANARE).

Governments, both state and national, have mapped the topographic, hydrographic, and geophysical features of Australia. The Royal Australian Survey Corps and National Mapping (under various names) have been responsible for the medium- and small-scale surveying and mapping of topographical features at the national level. State agencies have carried out the large-scale mapping for local purposes. Responsibility for hydrographic mapping has rested with the Royal Australian Navy since 1920. From the 1960s, emphasis has been on detailed surveying of sea routes to provide for the deep-drafted vessels now using Australian ports. In 1980–1981, HMAS *Flinders* surveyed the first safe passage—Hydrographers Passage—through the Great Barrier Reef, saving millions of dollars for shipping using central Queensland ports. Geoscience Australia (under different names) has been responsible for the national exploration of Australia's geological resources since 1946.

The latest frontier of exploration is the 6.2 million square miles (16 million square kilometers) of ocean floor lying between the coastal shallows and the deep sea. Marine scientists are exploring and mapping the topography, geology, biology, vegetation, and limits of the huge area.

Despite a long history of exploration beginning with the Dutch in 1606, there is still much to learn about the Australian continent. Parts of Tasmania, large tracts of the arid interior, and parts of the coastline have yet to be examined in detail. Exploration of Australia continues today.

[*See also* Imperialism and Exploration; Pacific; *Terra Australis Incognita; and biographical entries on figures mentioned in this article.*]

BIBLIOGRAPHY

Estensen, Miriam. *Discovery: The Quest for the Great South Land*. Sydney: Allen and Unwin, 1998.

Favenc, Ernest. *The History of Australian Exploration from 1788 to 1888*. Sydney: Turner and Henderson, 1888. Reprint. Amsterdam: Meridian, 1967.

Heeres, J. E. *The Part Borne by the Dutch in the Discovery of Australia 1606–1756*. London: Luzac, 1899.

Lines, John D. *Australia on Paper: The Story of Australian Mapping*. Melbourne: Fortune, 1992.

McLaren, Glen. *Beyond Leichhardt: Bushcraft and the Exploration of Australia*. Fremantle, Australia: Fremantle Arts Centre Press, 1996. Reprint, 2000.

Millar, Ann. *"I See No End to Travelling": Journals of Australian Explorers 1813–76*. Sydney: Bay Books, 1986.

Radok, Rainer. *Capes and Captains: A Comprehensive Study of the Australian Coast*. Sydney: S. Beatty, 1990.

Tiley, Robert. *Australian Navigators: Picking Up Shells and Catching Butterflies in an Age of Revolution*. Sydney: Kangaroo Press, 2002.

Wilkinson, Rick. *Rocks to Riches: The Story of Australia's National Geological Survey*. Sydney: Allen and Unwin, 1996.

DENIS SHEPHARD

Ayllón, Lucas Vázquez de (c. 1480–1526), Spanish sponsor of exploration of the east coast of America. Lucas Vázquez de Ayllón was a Spanish judge of the Audiencia de Santo Domingo who sponsored explorations of the coasts of what became Virginia, the Carolinas, and Georgia (1521, 1525) and who attempted settlement on that coast, most likely near Sapelo Sound, Georgia (1526). A member of a prominent Mozarabic family of Toledo, Ayllón may have taken a law degree at the University of Salamanca. He served as district judge (*alcalde mayor*) for northern Hispaniola from 1504 to 1509, and was appointed to the Audiencia when it was formed in 1511. A slaving voyage in 1521 to the South Santee—the Winyah Bay area of modern South Carolina (the "Jordan River") —led to his claim that his men had found a new Andalusia. Awarded a contract in 1523 to settle this discovery with two towns, Ayllón sponsored another voyage in 1525 that explored the coast from northern Florida to Cape Henlopen, Delaware. His attempt at settlement followed in 1526, but collapsed following his death on October 18. Of some six hundred persons who set out on the venture, only 150 were reported to have survived.

The story of Ayllón's new Andalusia and the location for his attempted colony entered European geographic lore through Peter Martyr's *Decades* (1530) and, more importantly, Francisco López de Gomara's *General History of the Indies* (1552). Ayllón's explorations also contributed geographic information to Alonso de Chaves's manuscript *Espejo de Nav-* *egantes* (c. 1539), Juan Vespucci's manuscript map of 1526, and some later Spanish maps. In addition, this story of a new Andalusia influenced the French explorer Jean Ribault's decision to leave the Charlesfort garrison at Parris Island, South Carolina (1562–1563) and, less clearly, influenced Sir Walter Ralegh's planning for the Roanoke Island colonies and the Virginia Company's expectations. Charlesfort led to the Spanish colony of Santa Elena (1566–1587).

[*See also* Ralegh, Walter.]

BIBLIOGRAPHY

Hoffman, Paul E. *A New Andalucia and a Way to the Orient: The American Southeast During the Sixteenth Century*. Baton Rouge: Louisiana State University Press, 1990.

PAUL E. HOFFMAN

Azores. The Azores are a group of nine islands located in the Atlantic Ocean over seven hundred miles (1,167 kilometers) to the west of Portugal. The nine islands are Santa Maria, São Miguel, São Jorge, Pico, Terceira, Fayal, Graciosa, Flores, and Corvo. While it is possible that the Carthaginians had visited the Azores in antiquity, medieval Europeans did not know of their existence until the mid-fourteenth century when Genoese seafarers under the command of Lanzarote Pessagno visited the islands while in the service of Portugal. Although there is considerable debate among historians, the Azores are depicted with greater or lesser accuracy on the Medici Atlas of 1351, the Catalan Atlas of 1375, and other late medieval maps.

Nothing was done with the discovery of the Azores until 1427, when Diogo de Silves of Portugal revisited the islands, although whether his visit was intentional or by chance is unclear. Prince Henry the Navigator had domestic animals placed on the islands in 1431 or 1432 to provide supplies of fresh meat for future seafarers who might stop there. In 1439, his brother Pedro, the regent of Portugal, gave Prince Henry the right to colonize the Azores. The initial plan was to grow sugarcane on the fertile and well-watered islands but the climate turned out to be too cool for that crop. As a result, the settlers had to shift to the far less profitable farming of wheat, sheep, and cattle to make their living. The Azores would function as a rest stop for the resupply of ships returning from oceanic voyages to West Africa, the Canary Islands, or other places. Both Christopher Columbus and Vasco da Gama stopped at the Azores during their historic first voyages. The islands' situation as a way station and their distance from Portugal made the Azores relatively unattractive for settlers. A goodly portion of the first Portuguese inhabitants were convicts. By 1450 Portugal also began to allow and even to encourage foreigners, mostly Flemings, to settle on the islands.

The Azores also served as a starting point for further explorations of the high Atlantic. In 1452 Diogo de Tieve discovered Flores and Corvo, which lay some distance to the west of the rest of the Azores. Adverse winds and currents made sailing west and northwest from the Azores very difficult but many voyages went out regardless. The Flemish settlers participated in these expeditions. Jacob de Brugge, the pioneer of the Flemish settlers, died on a voyage of exploration in 1474. Another Flemish family, the Hurteres, married with the Cortereal family, some of whose members, Miguel and Garpar Gaspar, would gain fame and suffer death exploring Newfoundland. Ferdinand van Olmen was the most famous Flemish Azoran explorer; considered by some to be a stillborn Columbus, he died at sea in 1487 while exploring the Atlantic between Ireland and Newfoundland. The voyages of Columbus, Gama, John Cabot, and their successors soon revealed better routes across the Atlantic or to Asia and undercut the Azores' role in Atlantic exploration. By the early sixteenth century the islands had settled into their more prosaic role as rest stop for Atlantic voyagers.

[*See also* Columbus, Christopher; Corte-Real, Gaspar; Gama, Vasco da; *and* Henry the Navigator.]

BIBLIOGRAPHY

Bento, Carlos Melo. *History of the Azores*. Translated by Pilar Vaz Rego Pereira. Ponta Delgada, Azores: Empresa Gráfica Açoreana, 1994. This rare book can also be accessed via FirstSearch under WorldCat.

Fernández-Armesto, Felipe. *Before Columbus: Exploration and Colonisation from the Mediterranean to the Atlantic, 1229–1492*. Basingstoke, U.K.: Macmillan, 1987.

RONALD H. FRITZE

Aztec Empire. The Aztec empire arose from the overthrow of the Tepanecs in 1428, who had previously dominated the Valley of Mexico. From its emergence up until the Spanish conquest, which began in 1519 and militarily ended in 1521, there were only six Aztec emperors. With one exception, each of these rulers successfully expanded the empire until it controlled areas up to 150 miles (250 kilometers) north of present-day Mexico City and south into western Guatemala, encompassing millions of tributaries. Without draft animals or wheeled vehicles, regional integration of any sort was severely con-

strained, and the empire the Aztecs created, although widespread, was discontinuous, loosely constructed, and dominated hegemonically. To rule tributaries directly would have been extremely costly in surrogate administration and garrisoned troops; moreover, this diversion of forces would have severely hobbled further imperial expansion. So instead, the Aztecs left local kingdoms intact to rule themselves, and imposed no changes on their social practices, economic customs, gods, or religious rituals. Constabulary concerns remained local, and the Aztecs demanded only that tributaries pay their according tributes, admit their merchants, and supply the imperial armies with food on the march. This system also gave the Aztecs a significant advantage over other cities by creating extensive march zones through which their armies could pass and be supplied, permitting them to dominate over far greater distances than other states and largely cordoning off their capital city of Tenochtitlan from external attack. Without direct administrative or martial costs and dependent only on the threat of reconquest to maintain order, the empire was relatively inexpensive. But the empire was not ideologically integrated, leaving it vulnerable to rebellions should the Aztecs appear unable to enforce their will in cases of military defeat or the replacement of a deceased king with a dubious successor. Thus, if defeated, Aztec armies rapidly reembarked on campaigns and spread word of those successes, and when kings died, their untried successors quickly conducted wars, nominally to sacrifice victims for their coronations, but, more important, to demonstrate their prowess.

Tribute was generally paid in native goods, but was nevertheless a notable drain on local economies, and payment might be excused in times of crisis such as famine. Moreover, being part of the empire had other advantages, such as inclusion in its trade network, which supplied goods otherwise unavailable—particularly luxuries sought by the nobles. The tribute also served a political purpose, as it was paid four times a year in Tenochtitlan and allowed the Aztecs to watch their subordinates. Rebellion meant reconquest, but it could also lead to the replacement of the local ruler, and since imposing Aztec governors largely failed, replacement meant the selection of a more amenable local noble. Although commoner soldiers undoubtedly bore the largest burden in the expansion, as a collective if not per capita, and while nobles enjoyed the largest benefits, imperial expansion had popular support because its material gains flowed to everyone, as well as to the various gods' temples. As a consequence, the Aztec capital of Tenochtitlan, grown to over hundred thousand inhabitants, became the largest and wealthiest in the New World.

[*See also* Central and South America, *subentry on* Conquests and Colonization.]

BIBLIOGRAPHY

Carrasco, Pedro. *The Tenochca Empire of Ancient Mexico: The Triple Alliance of Tenochtitlan, Tetzcoco, and Tlacopan*. Norman: University of Oklahoma Press, 1999.

Hassig, Ross. *Aztec Warfare: Imperial Expansion and Political Control*. Norman: University of Oklahoma Press, 1985.

Ross Hassig

B

Back, George (1796–1878), British Arctic explorer who served with John Franklin. Born in Stockport, Lancashire, on November 6, 1796, George Back entered the Royal Navy as a first-class volunteer aboard HMS *Arethusa* on September 15, 1808. He first went north as midshipman aboard HMS *Trent*, commanded by Lieutenant John Franklin in 1818. Along with HMS *Dorothea* (commanded by Lieutenant David Buchan), Franklin's orders were to attempt to sail across the Arctic Ocean, from Svalbard to Bering Strait. The ships were halted by impassable ice at 80°34′ N; badly damaged by ice during a gale, they were forced to retreat.

In 1819 Franklin selected Back as a member of his first overland expedition. From winter quarters at Fort Enterprise on Winter Lake, in 1820 the expedition descended the Coppermine River by canoe, then coasted eastward. The party turned back at Point Turnagain on Kent Peninsula, then headed back overland to Fort Enterprise from Bathurst Inlet. With members of the party starting to die of starvation and exposure, Back went ahead, located a band of Yellowknife Indians, and brought help to the starving survivors at Fort Enterprise.

In 1825 Back again joined Franklin on his second overland expedition. From a base at Fort Franklin on Great Bear Lake, in 1826 Franklin and Back explored the coast by boat, westward from the Mackenzie Delta to Return Reef, just west of Prudhoe Bay.

In 1833 the Admiralty dispatched Lieutenant Back to mount a search via the Great Fish River (now the Back River) for Sir John Ross's expedition, which had disappeared into the Arctic in 1829. After wintering at Fort Reliance at the head of the East Arm of Great Slave Lake, in 1834 Back and his men descended the rapids-strewn Back River and explored Chantrey Inlet as far north as Point Ogle.

Having been promoted captain, in 1836 Back returned to the Arctic, in command of HMS *Terror*, to explore the substantial gap westward from the mouth of the Back River to Point Turnagain. Beset in the ice off the east coast of Southampton Island, *Terror* drifted southward through Foxe Channel, then eastward through Hudson Strait, before being released, badly damaged. Later that year Back was awarded the Founder's Medal and the Gold Medal of the Royal Geographical Society, and in 1839 he was knighted by Queen Victoria and received the Gold Medal of the Société de Géographie (Geographical Society of Paris). He attained the rank of admiral in 1857 and died in London on June 23, 1878.

[*See also* Franklin, John, *and* Ross, John.]

BIBLIOGRAPHY

Back, George. *Narrative of the Arctic Land Expedition to the Mouth of the Great Fish River, and along the Shores of the Arctic Ocean, in the Years 1833, 1834 and 1835.* London: John Murray, 1836.

Back, George. *Narrative of an Expedition in HMS Terror, Undertaken with a View to Geographical Discovery on the Arctic Shores, in the Years 1836–7.* London: John Murray, 1838.

Beechey, F. W. *A voyage of Discovery towards the north Pole, performed in His Majesty's Ships Dorothea and Trent under the Command of Captain David Buchan, R.N.* London: Richard Bentley, 1843.

Houston, C. Stuart, ed. *Arctic Artist: the Journal and Paintings of George Back, Midshipman with Franklin, 1819–1822.* Montreal and Buffalo: McGill–Queen's University Press, 1994.

Steele, Peter. *The Man Who Mapped the Arctic: The Intrepid Life of George Back, Franklin's Lieutenant.* Vancouver, BC: Raincoast Books, 2003.

WILLIAM BARR

Backstaff. *See* **Navigational Techniques.**

Baegert, Christoph Johannes Jakob (1717–1772), Jesuit missionary and observer of lower California. Born at Schlettstadt, in Alsace, Baegert joined the Jesuits in 1736, and in 1751 he was sent to the mission of San Luis Gonzaga in Lower California. There he intensively studied the native societies of the region. Thus when the Jesuits were forced to leave Mexico in 1767, he was able to summarize his observations in a work first published in 1772, and published in English in 1863–1864 as *Observations in Lower California*. Baegert had no illusions about the economic potential of the area, so instead of focusing on this potential, he gave an admiring description of the way that native societies made the most of unfavorable, as he saw them, circumstances. Considering what was going on in North America at the same time, his attitudes now seem to us astonishingly sympathetic toward a way of life that was doomed.

[*See also* Jesuits.]

BIBLIOGRAPHY
Baegert, Jakob. *An Account of the Aboriginal Inhabitants of the Californian Peninsula*. Washington, 1865.

DAVID BUISSERET

Baffin, William (1584?–1622),

British navigator who searched for the Northwest Passage. Reports from the survivors of Henry Hudson's voyage of their navigation of Hudson Strait and the sighting of open water beyond it led to a determination in English mercantile circles to exploit the new discovery. In July 1612 a company was established with the optimistic name of "The Governor and Company of the Merchants of London, Discoverers of the North-West Passage." Encouraged by royal patronage in the person of Henry, Prince of Wales, almost four hundred investors financed a series of expeditions to find and exploit the supposed passage to Asia. The most important of these were two voyages commanded by Robert Bylot, who had been on Hudson's last voyage and was now accompanied as pilot and mate by William Baffin. Because of his navigational skills and because his journals have survived, Baffin emerges as the key figure in these ventures, and the prominence of his name on the map of the eastern Arctic reflects this.

Little is known about Baffin's early years, but it seems unlikely that he had much formal education, for Samuel Purchas, the publisher of travel accounts, described him as "that learned-unlearned Mariner and Mathematician." From 1612 onward he served as pilot on expeditions to the west coast of Greenland and to Spitsbergen. In 1615 he and Bylot sailed for Hudson Bay, where Thomas Button in 1612–1613 had already searched in vain for a passage along the west coast of the bay. However, in the northwest corner of Hudson Bay, at latitude 65° N, Button had sailed into an opening he named Roe's Welcome. He was there turned back by ice, so the question of whether the Welcome was a bay or a

strait remained undecided, and Bylot and Baffin approached it in 1615 to find out. As their ship, the long-serving *Discovery*, sailed through Hudson Strait, Baffin made meticulous observations, calculating longitude by means of lunar observations (an unheard-of accomplishment in this period) and constructing the first reasonably accurate chart of the strait. [See color plate 9 in this volume.] Rather than following Button's track, Baffin attempted to reach the northern part of Roe's Welcome by taking the *Discovery* along the northeast coast of Southampton Island. There, ice in the channel (later named the Frozen Strait) blocked the way; on the question of whether there was a passage through Hudson Bay, Baffin pronounced himself "doubtfull, supposinge the contrarye."

Davis Strait he considered to be more promising, and in 1616 he and Bylot once more took the Discovery north. The ship pushed through heavy ice in Davis Strait, keeping to its eastern shore until they reached open water, the " North Water" of the whalers who later sailed to Baffin Bay. At latitude 78° N (the farthest north reached by ships until the nineteenth century), the voyagers sighted Smith Sound stretching even farther north, and Baffin recorded an "almost incredible" variation of the compass. As the ship turned back, going south along the west coast of Baffin Bay, another great sound came in sight, Lancaster Sound. In the nineteenth century it proved to be the entrance of the Northwest Passage, but Baffin simply noted that its approach was blocked by a ledge of ice, and sailed on. Soon Baffin and Bylot were on that part of the coast already explored by Frobisher and Davis, and Baffin concluded that "there is no passage nor hope of passage in the north of Davis Streights."

Baffin's verdict was accepted, and for another two centuries the only visits by outsiders to the region were made by whalers during the short summer season, following Baffin's report that he had seen many whales on his voyage. Unfortunately for Baffin's reputation, although his journal was published in Purchas's collection of travels in 1625, his chart and hydrographical observations were not, and they disappeared from view. As a result, in time, doubt was cast on Baffin's explorations of 1616 and on the very existence of Baffin Bay. It was not until 1818 that John Ross's voyage confirmed the reality of Baffin Bay, and the next year Edward Parry sailed through Baffin's Lancaster Sound to bring fresh hope that the Northwest Passage might yet be found.

After his Arctic ventures, Baffin found employment with the English East Company, but he was killed in an engagement with Persian forces near Hormuz in the Persian Gulf.

[*See also* Arctic, *subentry on* Early Knowledge; Hudson, Henry; *and* Northwest Passage.]

BIBLIOGRAPHY
Dodge, Ernest S. "William Baffin." *Dictionary of Canadian Biography.* Vol. 1, pp. 74–75. Toronto: University of Toronto Press, 1966.
Markham, Clements R., ed. *The Voyages of William Baffin, 1612–1622.* London: The Hakluyt Society, 1881.
Savours, Ann. *The Search for the North West Passage.* London: Chatham, 1999.

GLYNDWR WILLIAMS

Bailey, Frederick Marshman (1882–1967), explorer, military officer, and naturalist, who traveled extensively in central Asia. Bailey was born in Lahore, India. He entered Sandhurst military academy in England in 1899, but was soon ordered back to India. He was posted to Gangtok, Sikkim, on the Tibetan border, and his company was ordered to march into Tibet with Francis Younghusband, on a supposedly peaceful mission to Lhasa; a treaty was signed in 1904 after numerous engagements and loss of life—primarily Tibetan. Bailey then joined an expedition to western Tibet, a journey of three months through new territory at a very high altitude. His next appointments were at Gyangtse, then at Chumbi on the Bhutan border. In 1907 he left Peking en route for Tibet, Assam, and Burma. His main objective lay in tracing the course of the Tsangpo, arising in Tibet and flowing into any one of seven rivers in Assam and Burma. On a punitive expedition to Burma in 1913, Bailey and Captain Henry Treise Morshead left the main party and traversed several hundred miles through Tibet, eastern Bhutan, and into Assam, with formidable passes before the Tsangpo gorges. The river entered the mountains at 9,000 feet (2,743 meters) and emerged on the Assam plains at 500 feet (152 meters). They traced the Tsangpo over 380 miles (612 kilometers) and established that, while the river included extensive rapids, there were no major falls, and that the Tsangpo and Brahmaputra were regions of the same river. Bailey was awarded the Royal Geographical Society gold medal for this expedition.

During World War I Bailey was wounded at both Ypres and Gallipoli. His time after the war, though not primarily exploratory, was quite remarkable. In 1918 he was ordered into Russian Turkistan via the Pamir to assess the Bolshevik threat after the revolution. Bailey even joined the Cheka in order to enter Bokhara, where he had contacts. Eventually he escaped to Persia. In 1921, as political officer in Sikkim, he traced a new route from Gyantse to Bhutan, and in 1937 he became envoy extraordinary to Nepal. Bailey was the only British officer who could speak fluent Tibetan, so he alone was able to talk with the Dalai Lama.

Bailey was a superb naturalist—he collected butterflies, many new to science, on all his journeys, including the journey into Russian Turkistan, and he also collected birds, mammals, and plants. Oddly, considering his many geographical discoveries, Bailey is best remembered for his discovery of the Himalayan blue poppy *Meconopsis betonicifolia baileyi.*

[*See also* Royal Geographical Society.]

BIBLIOGRAPHY
Swinson, Arthur. *Beyond the Frontiers: The Biography of Colonel F. M. Bailey, Explorer and Secret Agent.* London: Hutchinson, 1971.

DAVID SPENCER SMITH

Baines, Thomas (1820–1875), English artist who traveled with David Livingstone's Zambezi expedition. John Thomas Baines was born on November 27, 1820, in King's Lynn, Norfolk, England. His father, a master mariner and amateur artist, married the daughter of a painter and decorator. His younger sister Emma studied art in London, while Thomas was encouraged as a boy in drawing, painting, and sculpture by his maternal grandfather. He was apprenticed for five years to an ornamental painter after which, in 1842, he traveled steerage to Cape Town where he began to practice his art commercially. In 1848, he joined an ox trek north to the Orange River and gained his first experience of travel into the interior, sketching and painting. In 1851 he enlisted as an artist with the British army in the Kaffir War (Cape Frontier War) of 1850–1853, before returning to England.

In 1854, his contacts in the Royal Geographical Society (RGS) led to his joining an expedition to Northern Australia as artist and storekeeper. [See color plate 13 in this volume.] On his return, Baines was officially commended for devotion to duty, elected Fellow of the RGS, and in 1858 was appointed artist-storekeeper to David Livingstone's forthcoming Zambezi expedition. Baines contributed significantly to the mapping of the lower Zambezi, despite malaria, but was dismissed by Livingstone on a dubious pretext of misappropriation. Such was Livingstone's reputation that Baines was now permanently discredited within the establishment.

In 1861, Baines joined James Chapman, recently returned from a trans-Africa journey and about to attempt to recross the continent eastward from Walvis Bay to the Victoria Falls and beyond. Baines was the seventh European to see the falls, the subject of his best-known paintings and lithographs.

Following a brief sojourn in England, Baines returned once again to the Cape in 1868, this time as "exploring superintendent and geographer" for the South African Goldfields Exploration Company, with prospecting sights on Matabeleland. The company provided inadequate support for Baines, who increasingly met costs from his own pocket. Baines was left with little to show for his travels except his sketches and maps. For the latter he was awarded a gold watch by the Royal Geographical Society. He died of dysentery in Durban in 1875.

No major discovery can be attributed to Baines. His meticulous route surveys contributed significantly to the cartography of Africa, providing detail and corroborative evidence of the findings of others. As an artist, he was phenomenally prolific, with a legacy of some four thousand works.

[*See also* Livingstone, David.]

BIBLIOGRAPHY
Stevenson, Michael. *Thomas Baines: An Artist in the Service of Science in Southern Africa.* London: Christie's International Media Division, 1999.
Wallis, J. P. R. *Thomas Baines: His Life and Explorations in South Africa, Rhodesia, and Australia, 1820–1875.* Cape Town: Balkema, 1976.

JEFFREY STONE

Baker, Samuel (1821–1893), British explorer of the Nile. Born on June 8, 1821, Samuel White Baker was the eldest son of Samuel Baker, a wealthy merchant who had invested his Jamaican fortune in railways, ships, and banks, and in sugar plantations in Mauritius. The younger Baker was educated by private tutors and briefly in Frankfurt, Germany. In 1842 the family moved to the estate of Lypiatt Park, Gloucestershire, and on August 3, Baker married Henrietta Martin, daughter of the Reverend Charles Martin of Maisemore. The following year he elected to go out to manage his father's sugar plantations on the island of Mauritius in the Indian Ocean. He soon tired of the sedentary planter life and visited Ceylon in 1845 for sport and decided to remain and establish an agricultural colony in the highlands. After initial difficulties the plantations prospered and, as they required little supervision, the Baker family returned in 1855 to England, where Henrietta tragically died of typhus on December 29. Leaving his four daughters, Edith, Agnes, Constance, and Ethel, in the care of his sister, Mary "Minnie" or "Min" Baker, Samuel assuaged his grief by aimlessly wandering and sport shooting in Europe. In January 1859 he and the Maharajah Duleep Singh arrived at Vidin, an Ottoman border town on the Danube, where he was smitten by a beautiful seventeen-year-old Hungarian woman being auctioned for sale whom he promptly abducted and fled with to Bucharest. Barbara Maria Száz had been born in Transylvania in the early 1840s, and after the failure of the Hungarian Revolution in August 1849 and the destruction of her maternal home at Nagy-Enyed she was taken to the Hungarian refugee camp at Vidin and later was abandoned, reared, educated, and became known as Florenz (Florence) in the harem of the wife of a prominent Turkish official.

Baker had avidly followed the explorations of Richard Francis Burton and John Hanning Speke to find the source of the Nile, and in 1860 when Speke, accompanied by James Augustus Grant, was sent back to Africa by the Royal Geographical Society to confirm his earlier assertion that Lake Victoria was the source of the Nile, Baker was determined to seek the source by advancing up the Nile rather than from East Africa. In 1861 he and his now devoted companion, Florence, explored at his own expense the Ethiopian Nile tributaries of the Atbara and Sobat rivers before proceeding through the Sudd, the great swamps of the Nile, to Gondokoro, where, on February 15, 1863, Speke and Grant arrived to inform them that Lake Victoria was the source of the Nile and that another lake, the Luta N'zigé, to the west might be an important feeder. Leaving Gondokoro on March 27, 1863, the Bakers overcame formidable obstacles and difficulties, particularly from the slave traders and Kamurasi, king of Bunyoro (d. 1869), to reach the Luta N'zigé a year later on March 14, 1864; they renamed it Lake Albert. They returned to England on October 14, 1865, after nearly five years in Africa, to a tumultuous reception. Three weeks later Samuel Baker legally married Florence Barbara Maria Finnian in a private ceremony. The Royal Geographical Society presented him with its gold medal, and Queen Victoria knighted him but refused to receive Florence because of her questionable origins. His books on their adventures, *The Albert Nyanza, Great Basin of the Nile and Explorations of the Nile Sources* (1866) and *The Nile Tributaries of Abyssinia and the Sword Hunters of the Hamran Arabs* (1867), were bestsellers. In February 1869 he accompanied his close friend, the Prince of Wales, to Egypt.

In Cairo the Ottoman khedive of Egypt, Ismāīl Pasha (1830–1895) appointed him governor-general of Equatoria to eradicate the slave trade and extend his empire to the equatorial lakes. During the next four years Baker Pasha, accompanied by Florence and a large Egyptian expeditionary force, struggled with the Sudd, slave traders, and the Bunyoro army led by Kamurasi's successor, Kabarega (1850–1923). When his contract expired on April 1, 1873, he had cleared a passage through the Sudd, and disrupted the slave trade, but had failed to establish Egyptian authority over Bunyoro. Returning to England he wrote another bestseller, *Ismailia: A Narrative of the Expedition to Central Africa for the Suppression of the Slave Trade* (1874), and retired with Florence to Sandford Orleigh, their estate in Devon, where he lived quietly, heaped with honors and surrounded by his children and grandchildren, until his death on December 30, 1893.

[*See also* Burton, Richard F.; Grant, James Augustus; *and* Speke, John Hanning.]

BIBLIOGRAPHY

Collins, Robert O. "Samuel White Baker: Prospero in Purgatory." In *Africa and Its Explorers: Motives, Methods, and Impact*, edited by Robert I. Rotberg. Cambridge, Mass: Harvard University Press, 1970.

Hall, Richard. *Lovers on the Nile: The Incredible African Journeys of Sam and Florence Baker*. New York: Random House, 1980.

Middleton, Dorothy. *Baker of the Nile*. London: Flacon, 1949.

Shipman, Pat. *To the Heart of the Nile: Lady Florence Baker and the Exploration of Central Africa*. New York: Morrow, 2004.

Thompson, Brian. *Imperial Vanities: The Adventures of the Baker Brothers and Gordon of Khartoum*. New York: HarperCollins, 2002.

ROBERT O. COLLINS

Balboa, Vasco Núñez de

Balboa, Vasco Núñez de (c. 1475–1517), Spanish explorer. Vasco Núñez de Balboa was born around 1475 in Jeréz de los Caballeros in the province of Extremadura, in Spain. His father, Nuño Arias de Balboa, was a member of the petty nobility, descendents of high nobility from the province of Galicia, and his mother is unknown but reputed to have been a high-born lady of Badajoz. As a youth, Balboa became a page in the household of the Lord of Moguer, where he learned important social lessons. Because Moguer was the point of departure for Columbus's voyages and—for the next decade or so—all major expeditions to the New World, Balboa became interested in traveling, too. In 1500, Balboa shipped out with Rodrigo de Bastidas on a voyage of exploration of the north coast of South America. This region became the focus of Balboa's own efforts.

In 1509, Balboa joined the expedition of Diego de Nicuesa and Alonso de Hojeda, sailing in a supply convoy under Martín Fernández de Enciso. This expedition discovered and explored the Gulf of Urabá, the point—in the Caribbean—where the Isthmus of Panama meets the continent of South America. Balboa was instrumental in the settlement and pacification of the region known as Darién, on the west coast of the Gulf of Urabá, from 1511 onward; there he founded the town of Santa María la Antigua del Darién. As part of his efforts in the pacification and settlement of the region, he launched a series of expeditions. The culminating moment of these occurred in September 1513, when he caught sight of and eventually confirmed the nearness of the Pacific Ocean. During the next two years he explored the region thoroughly and eventually sent two small brigantines into the Pacific, to as far as the Pearl Islands. Francisco Pizarro, the conqueror of Peru, was a member of these expeditions in Panama.

Although named governor of the province, Balboa faced opposition on many fronts. The most important was to come from Pedro Arias de Avila, known as Pedrarias Dávila, who in 1514 was appointed by the king as captain general of Tierra Firme. The governments of Dávila and Balboa overlapped and in fact conflicted with each other. Dávila was a ruthless governor and an implacable opponent. He sought to maximize his income from the region, as well as consolidate his power, through many mechanisms, including by taking Balboa as son-in-law. Balboa's claims on the governorship were a threat to Dávila, so Dávila set out to eliminate the competition. Many other colonists and agents at courts, including Fernández de Enciso, were opposed to Balboa for many slights, real and imagined. Dávila put Balboa on trial for treason and rebellion. The outcome was a forgone conclusion; so, in 1517, less than ten years after having taken over the government of the territory, Balboa was beheaded.

[*See also* Expeditions, World Exploration, *subentry on* Spain.]

BIBLIOGRAPHY

Alvarez Rubiano, Pablo. *Pedrarias Dávila: contribución al estudio de la figuro del "Gran justador," gobernador de Castilla de Oro y Nicaragua*. Madrid, Spain: Consejo superior de investigaciones científicas, Instituto Gonzalo Fernández de Oviedo, 1944.

Romoli, Kathleen. *Balboa of Darién: Discoverer of the Pacific*. Garden City, N.Y.: Doubleday, 1953.

Rubio, Angel. *La ruta de Balboa y el descubrimiento del Océano Pacífico*. México: Instituto Panamericano de Geografía e Historia, 1965.

JOHN F. SCHWALLER

Balkhi, al- (fl. 1100), the unknown author of the Persian geographical account *Fars-nama*. *Fars-nama* (The Book of the Fars Province) was composed in the late eleventh or early twelfth century C.E. Only a few details are known about Ibn al-Balkhi, all through his own account. His name is conventional and is related to Balkh in eastern Khorāsān, the city of his ancestors. During the sultanate of the Seljuq Barki-yaruq (1094–1105), his grandfather was chief accountant of the local governor of Fars, Atabeg Rukn al-dawla or Najm al-dawla Khumartigin. The author had often accompanied his grandfather in the latter's provincial travels.

The sultan Ghiyath al-Din Muhammad (d. 1118) appreciated Ibn al-Balkhi's thorough knowledge of Fars, and he acted as patron of the *Fars-nama*, which was completed before 1116. The account consists of two sections. The first deals primarily with the pre-Islamic kings of Iran, especially the Sasanians, with the rise of Islam, and with the subsequent conquest of Fars up to Ali's caliphate. The other section refers to a geographical and historical description of several districts of Fars under Islamic rule, mainly during the Buyid period. The account closes with a note about the last Buyids and the ascent of the Seljuqs in Fars.

Ibn al-Balkhi's local history of Fars had an impact on later local histories. The merit of the *Fars-nama* as a vital primary source for Iranian history derives from its valuable information on pre-Islamic Iran, material that often is not attested in other Arabic or Persian sources.

[*See also* Arabia.]

BIBLIOGRAPHY
Bosworth, Clifford Edmund. "Ebn al-Balkhi." In *Encyclopaedia Iranica*, edited by E. Yarshater. 2nd ed. New York: Eisenbrauns, 1998. Vol. 8, p. 4. Includes full bibliography.
Ibn al-Balkhi. *Fars-nama*. Edited by Guy LeStrange and R. A. Nicholson. London: Cambridge University Press for the Gibb Memorial; London: Luzac, 1998. First published in 1962.

EVANGELOS VENETIS

Ballard, Robert (b. 1942), undersea explorer who discovered the *Titanic* in 1985. Ballard was born in Wichita, Kansas, on June 30, 1942, one of three children of Chester and Harriet Ballard. Young Robert's interest in the sea began after the Ballard family moved to San Diego, California. As a young boy, Robert observed the marine life in the tidal pools near his home and dreamed of undersea exploration while reading and rereading Jules Verne's *20,000 Leagues under the Sea*. Ballard's interest in the ocean led him to study marine geology. As a doctoral student, Ballard participated in underwater exploration projects at Woods Hole Oceanographic Institute in Massachusetts.

Although Ballard is best known for coleading the team that located the RMS *Titanic* seventy-three years after its demise, his prior research as a marine geologist helped to revolutionize the understanding of the forces that created the earth. This research, conducted in manned submersibles along the Atlantic's Mid-Ocean Ridge, confirmed that the earth's crustal plates were diverging. This finding cemented the then fledgling theory of plate tectonics as the dominant paradigm for interpreting the earth's geologic history.

In 1977, while exploring the ocean floor near the Galápagos Islands, Ballard and his crew discovered geothermal vents bilging hot, mineral-rich water into the frigid ocean depths. The crew also discovered chemosynthetic, or chemical-based, habitats clustered around these vents. This discovery of animals thriving in inhospitable chemical conditions on the ocean floor without depending on photosynthesis for survival was revolutionary.

In the late 1970s, Ballard also began to develop complex deep-sea remote sensing equipment. Supported by the United States Navy, Ballard developed *Argo*, an unmanned submersible able to drag the depths with photographic and sonar equipment. Under Ballard's direction, *Argo* surveyed the wrecks of nuclear submarines in 1984 and 1985 for the Navy. However, it was no secret that Ballard had developed *Argo* with one project in mind: locating the wreck of the *Titanic*.

On September 1, 1985, after five weeks of trolling the ocean floor in the North Atlantic near where the *Carpathia* had encountered the *Titanic*'s lifeboats on April 15, 1912, *Argo* photographed the debris field left by the *Titanic* during its rapid descent to the ocean floor. Ballard and his crew followed the increasing debris trail—consisting of shoes, dishes, wine bottles, and boiler parts—straight to the hull of the *Titanic*. This expedition demonstrated that the ocean held a veritable history museum of humanity's relationship with the sea, and that that history was now within reach of manned and unmanned submersible technology.

After his success on the *Titanic* expedition, Ballard conducted research explorations of the wrecks of the German battleship *Bismarck*; a Roman merchant vessel, *Isis*; the RMS *Lusitania*; the *Andrea Doria*; the aircraft carrier *Yorktown*; the *Titanic*'s sister ship, HMHS *Britannic*; the Japanese battleship *Kirishima*; and President John F. Kennedy's World War II vessel, *PT-109*. Ballard continues to conduct undersea expeditions in conjunction with his educational endeavors for children, and he has become an outspoken ally for the cause of historic preservation of underwater archaeology.

[*See also* National Geographic Society.]

BIBLIOGRAPHY

Ballard, Robert D., and Malcolm McConnell. *Explorations: My Quest for Adventure and Discovery under the Sea.* New York: Hyperion, 1995.

Hill, Christine M. *Robert Ballard: Oceanographer Who Discovered the Titanic.* Berkeley Heights, N.J.: Enslow, 1999.

RYAN M. SEIDEMANN

Bancroft, Ann

Bancroft, Ann (b. 1955), contemporary American Arctic traveler, first woman to reach both the North Pole and the South Pole. Ann Bancroft was born on September 29, 1955, in Mendota Heights, Minnesota. As a child, Bancroft often went camping and canoeing with her father and organized backyard camping expeditions for her cousins.

Bancroft is the only woman to have reached both the North and South Poles. If asked what it is about the Arctic that attracts her so strongly, she will relate how as a child she read the story of Sir Ernest Shackleton's disastrous 1915 attempt to reach the South Pole and was inspired to try it herself someday. In 1986 she journeyed to the North Pole by dogsled, as a member of the Stegner International Polar Expedition. Subsequently, she organized two expeditions to Antarctica. On the first effort in 1993, she led a team of four women in an attempt to traverse the Antarctic continent by foot, skis, and sail-ski. A variety of problems prevented them from crossing the entire continent, but they did reach the South Pole, covering about 660 miles (about 1,062 kilometers) in sixty-seven days. In 2001 she and one other woman, Liv Arnesen, returned to Antarctica in a second attempt to cross the continent. This time they were successful in completing the 1,700-mile (2,736-kilometer) trip, in spite of having to pull 250-pound supply sledges and cope with temperatures that dropped to minus 35 degrees Fahrenheit.

A unique aspect of Bancroft's expeditions to the South Pole has been the emphasis on and incorporation of educational goals. She stated as one of her main goals in planning her expeditions the development of a curriculum for schoolteachers. (Bancroft and Arnesen are, themselves, former schoolteachers.) Using contemporary technology such as the Internet and satellite phones, the team sent back from Antarctica regular journal entries, progress reports, photographs, location data, and audio messages aimed at classroom use.

[*See also* Shackleton, Ernest, *and* Women Explorers.]

BIBLIOGRAPHY

Arnesen, Liv, Ann Bancroft, and Cheryl Dahle. *No Horizon Is So Far: Two Women and their Extraordinary Journey across Antarctica.* Cambridge, Mass.: Da Capo Press, 2003.

PATRICIA GILMARTIN

Banks, Joseph

Banks, Joseph (1743–1820), voyager, scientific administrator, and promoter of British exploration of the Pacific and interior Africa. Joseph Banks's importance for the history of exploration lies not so much in his own voyaging as in his ability to galvanize government interest in the cartographic and scientific mapping of the world. His ability to influence government grew out of his social position as a broad-acred member of the gentry for, when Banks was born in 1743, it was into the economic and social security of the governing classes—a security that rested ultimately on his family's substantial landholdings located chiefly around the family seat of Revesby Abbey in Lincolnshire.

As a member of the governing elite Banks was educated in the bastions of the establishment, receiving his schooling at Harrow (1752–1756) and Eton (1756–1760) before going up to Christ Church, Oxford (1760–1763). The classical education that was the standard fare at these institutions was not altogether to his taste and Banks devoted his time largely to the pursuit of natural history.

Having left Oxford, Banks based himself in London. The British Museum provided a circle of like-minded naturalists while the range of London learned societies—which embraced such bodies as the Royal Society, the Society of Antiquaries, and the Society of Dilettanti—provided the setting for pursuing both his scientific and antiquarian interests. London's extensive network of clubs, in which Banks remained a central figure all his life, also enabled him to consolidate his ties with members of the oligarchy.

Even in this early stage of his life Banks displayed his enduring ability to use his connections to advance the cause of scientific exploration. Thanks to his old Etonian school friend, Constantine John Phipps (later Lord Mulgrave), Banks was permitted to accompany the expedition of the *Niger* to Newfoundland and Labrador in 1766. The expedition acted as Banks's scientific apprenticeship, bringing with it membership of the Royal Society. The possibilities it opened up for the study of natural history and the ethnology of an area of the globe hitherto little exposed to European scrutiny convinced Banks of the great benefits to be obtained by combining British naval capability with scientific enquiry. It was a tradition that Banks was to promote throughout his lifetime laying the foundation for such great nineteenth-century voyages of scientific exploration as those of the *Beagle* and the *Challenger*.

After his experiences on board the *Niger* Banks used his considerable resources—financial, social, and scientific—to ensure his presence on board James Cook's *Endeavour* (1768–1771). The voyage was prompted chiefly by the Royal Society's determination to be involved in the international collaborative study of the second transit of Venus in 1769, but it also had the secret object of investigating the hitherto little-known landmasses in the Southern Hemisphere. For Banks this largely astronomically inspired voyage provided a rare and valuable opportunity to study whole new vistas of natural history including the human societies of the Pacific. His entourage included the Swedish scientist Daniel Solander, whose botanical skills and mastery of Linnaean classification helped to bring order and system to the vast array of new species that the Pacific would yield. [See color plate 16 in this volume.]

The adulation that Banks received on his return from the *Endeavour* voyage—which overshadowed that accorded to the humbly born Cook—led Banks to demand a much greater voice in the planning for Cook's second great Pacific voyage, that of the *Resolution* from 1772 to 1775. But on this occasion Banks was to discover the limits of his influence, particularly when he attempted to overrule the Admiralty. Thus humiliated Banks withdrew and in place of another epic Pacific voyage took the scientific party that he had recruited on a voyage to Iceland.

Thereafter Banks's traveling days were over but he was to use his considerable influence to advance the exploration of others—particularly if such exploration could advance the cause of science or the interests of the British Empire. From the time that he became president of the Royal Society in 1779,

---

Plant Collecting

Banks, a towering figure in English botany for more than fifty years, was emphatically a hands-on patron. Sailing with Captain Cook on his first voyage, in 1768–1771, Banks indefatigably investigated each land to which the expedition came, usually with his accompanying botanist, Dr. Solander. Not being able himself to return to the Pacific, Banks set up the breadfruit expedition commanded by Lieutenant Bligh of HMS Bounty.

Our collection of plants was now grown so immensely large that it was necessary that some extraordinary care should be taken of them, lest they should spoil in the books. I therefore devoted this day to that business and carried all the drying paper, near 200 quires of which the larger part was full, ashore and, spreading them upon a sail in the sun, kept them in this manner exposed the whole day, often turning them and sometimes turning the quires in which were plants inside out. By this means they came on board at night in very good condition.

The Endeavour *journal of Joseph Banks,* August 25, 1768–July 12, 1771

Banks was to accumulate a range of positions that, in the words of his contemporary Lord Auckland, made him more and more "His Majesty's Minister for Philosophical [Scientific] Affairs." Banks became in effect the director of the royal gardens at Kew, turning what had once been pleasure gardens into a virtual research institute. This acted as the center of a worldwide network of botanical gardens that facilitated the movement of plants (and to a lesser extent, animals) around the globe. His growing involvement in the Privy Council committees on trade and coin led to a closer engagement with the direct concerns of government, and he formed a close alliance with the first earl of Liverpool in the promotion of British trade.

Such growing connections with the processes of government form the backdrop to Banks's involvement in a series of voyages of exploration. The attempt to redress the problem of supplies for the slaves of the British West Indies in the wake of the disruption caused by the American War of Independence prompted the attempt by the *Bounty* expedition (1787–1789) to transplant breadfruit, a cheap source of nutrition, to the West Indies—a mission that Banks's client, William Bligh, finally brought to fruition, after the unpleasantness on board the *Bounty*, with the *Providence* expedition of 1791.

The American Revolution had also denied Britain its chief outlet for the transportation of convicts, and the attempt to find new sites in Africa to dispose of them led Banks to ensure the inclusion of the botanist Anton Hove on board the *Nautilus* expedition (1785). This was part of a broader pattern of Banks's promotion of exploration in Africa that was largely funneled through the African Association (or The Association for Promoting the Discovery of the Interior Parts of Africa), founded, largely at Banks's initiative, in 1788. It was this body that acted as the patron of the remarkable voyages into the interior of Africa by Mungo Park (1795–1799), Friedrich Hornemann (1797–1801), and Johann Ludwig Burckhardt (1809–1817).

The eventual decision to found a penal settlement at New South Wales owed a great deal to Banks's influence, and it was he that did most to advance the interests of this distant colony at a time when the British government was largely preoccupied with the menace of the French Revolution. Banks was able to harness British fear of French expansion to gain approval for Matthew Flinders's *Investigator* voyage of 1801 that circumnavigated the Australian continent and popularized the name of Australia in place of the older New Holland.

Banks's influence also extended to the other side of the Pacific, where he was anxious to build on the work of Cook's third voyage to ensure the consolidation of British influence on the west coast of North America, an area traditionally claimed by Spain. Banks encouraged the exploitation of such resources as sea otter skins and ensured that the Vancouver voyage of 1791–1795 included a naturalist in the person of Archibald Menzies.

By the time of his death in 1820 Banks had established the importance of state-sponsored exploration as a means of advancing British imperial interests. The pattern of exploration that he had promoted in hitherto little-known areas of the globe such as the Pacific and the interior of Africa was to help shape the subsequent map of British colonization. But along with such imperial ends Banks saw exploration as a means of achieving the advancement of science, and his influence was to do much to ensure that the wide reach of the British navy facilitated a better understanding of the natural world.

[*See also* Africa, *subentry on* Exploration; African Association; Burckhardt, Johann Ludwig; Cook, James; Hornemann, Friedrich; Imperialism and Exploration; Park, Mungo; *and* Royal Society.]

BIBLIOGRAPHY

Carter, Harold. *Sir Joseph Banks, 1743–1820.* London: British Museum (Natural History), 1988.

Gascoigne, John. *Joseph Banks and the English Enlightenment: Useful Knowledge and Polite Culture.* Cambridge, U.K., and New York: Cambridge University Press, 1994.

Gascoigne, John. *Science in the Service of Empire: Joseph Banks, the British State and the Uses of Science in the Age of Revolution.* Cambridge, U.K., and New York: Cambridge University Press, 1998.

Mackay, David. *In the Wake of Cook: Exploration, Science and Empire, 1780–1801.* London: Croom Helm, 1985.

O'Brian, Patrick. *Joseph Banks. A Life.* London: Collins Harvill, 1987. Reprint. Chicago: University of Chicago Press, 1997.

JOHN GASCOIGNE

Baranov, Alexandr Andreevich

Baranov, Alexandr Andreevich (1746–1819), Russian trader and general manager of the Russian American Company, in charge for twenty-eight years of a far-flung commercial venture. In 1790 he was appointed chief agent of the Shelikov company for North America, and the next year he led an expedition to explore the chain of Aleutian Islands in his ship *Tri Svyatitelya* until he was wrecked off Unalaska. In 1793 he turned to the Alaskan mainland, exploring Cook Island and Prince William Sound, where he established a shipyard and married the daughter of a local Kenaitze chief.

In 1795, Baranov continued east along the Alaskan coast and visited Sitka Island, where he purchased a tract of land from the local Tlingit chief and constructed the settlement of Saint Michael's (six miles north of present-day Sitka). In 1802 the Tlingit seized the fortress at the settlement, but two years later Baranov succeeded in reestablishing Russian power at the site of Sitka, which in 1808 became the administrative capital of Russian America, eventually boasting a cathedral, a colonial school, and shipyards.

From this new city Baranov, in the ensuing years, extended his power southward. In 1806–1808 Russians visited Bodega Bay, California, and Fort Ross was established near it in 1812; Fort Ross became the southernmost Russian outpost in North America, apart from a very small settlement at the Farallon Islands. Baranov also sent an expedition to the Hawaiian Islands, where he hoped to establish an agricultural settlement, but this soon failed. Meanwhile, Baranov was slowly losing influence in Russian ruling circles. In 1818 he was replaced and began the long journey back to Russia by sea; in the course of it, he died in Java.

[*See also* Expeditions, World Exploration, *subentry on* Russia, *and* Russian American Company.]

BIBLIOGRAPHY

Chevigny, Hector. *Lord of Alaska: Baranov and the Russian Adventure.* New York: Viking, 1942.

Khlebnikov, Kiril Timofeevich. *Baranov, Chief Manager of the Russian Colonies in America.* Translated by Colin Bearne and edited by Richard Pierce. Kingston, Ontario: Limestone, 1973.

ALEXEY POSTNIKOV

Barbot, Jean (1655–1712), French Huguenot slave trader who made two voyages to the Guinea Coast of tropical West Africa, one in 1678–1679 and the other in 1681–1682. Barbot fled to England in 1685 as a refugee. He never returned to France, nor did he ever go to sea again. Before departing for England, Barbot wrote in French an account of his short visits to Guinea, and this document was published in 1688. Twenty years after his death in 1712, a volume twice as long as the first was published in English. In 1992, an English translation of Barbot's 1688 book was published by the Hakluyt Society. Barbot's description of Guinea has for centuries been considered the standard source on the early Atlantic slave trade. Recent scholarship, however, has cast serious doubt on the authenticity of his supposedly firsthand account of life in Africa in the seventeenth century.

Barbot was born into a large Protestant family on May 25, 1655, on the Île de Ré, near the port city of La Rochelle. He was quite young when he went to sea; he was only in his twenties when he sailed to Guinea. The most dominant recurring topic in his books is how the slave trade was conducted. He wrote about the sources of slaves and about the role of Africans in this commerce of humans. It is now certain that Barbot did not witness everything he wrote about, but instead plagiarized the works of others, in particular the writings of Olfert Dapper. Nonetheless, to those opposed to slavery in the eighteenth and nineteenth centuries, his account provided powerful evidence of the horrors of the practice. Paul Hair and his coeditors of the Hakluyt Society translation now suggest that Barbot's statements regarding slavery have been given more attention than they deserve.

In addition to his knowledge of the practice of slavery, Barbot seemed to have an encyclopedic knowledge of virtually every subject. Among a vast number of topics, he wrote about how Africans practiced agriculture, about European coastal forts, about activities in coastal trading towns and villages, about the climate of Sierra Leone, about the pidgin language, and even about how hippos were hunted in the Gambia River. He also presented the erroneous notion that the Senegal and Gambia rivers were two branches of the Niger River. Enhancing the worth of his writings were the wonderful illustrations he drew. Being a good artist himself, he recommended that all travelers know how to draw.

Barbot spent his last years as a merchant in London and nearby Southampton. He died on September 27, 1712, in Southampton, the place where he most likely composed the English-language version of his voyages.

[*See also* Africa, *subentry on* Exploration.]

BIBLIOGRAPHY

Hair, P. E. H., Adam Jones, and Robin Law, eds. *Barbot on Guinea: The Writings of Jean Barbot on West Africa, 1678–1712.* 2 vols. Hakluyt Society 2nd series, vols. 175–176. London: Hakluyt Society, 1992.

SANFORD H. BEDERMAN

Barents, Willem (c. 1555–1597), Dutch navigator. Although his place of birth is unknown, Willem Barents or his ancestors probably came from the island of Terschelling. We know very little of Barents's life until 1594, when he took part in the first Dutch attempt to find the Northeast Passage. Barents (the spelling of the name varies) was an accomplished pilot with an extensive knowledge of navigation and contacts in the scientific community of Amsterdam, which included the cartographer Petrus Plancius. It is clear that Barents must have spent many years at sea. In 1596 he published the first printed sea atlas of the Mediterranean, based upon his own long experience. From the accounts of the polar voyages and remarks of contemporaries, Barents emerges as one of the scientific pilots of the sixteenth and early seventeenth centuries who played an important role in making charts and depicting unknown coasts, performing astronomical observations, and testing and improving nautical instruments.

The rapidly expanding Dutch trade in the late sixteenth century led merchants to search for a direct route to the rich trade with Asia, which until this point had been in Spanish and (mainly) Portuguese hands. From 1594 until 1596/97 the Dutch tried to find the Northeast Passage to the Pacific and Asia, a route not used by their rivals. The 1594 expedition was sponsored by a number of provincial and city

Willem Barents. Ships in Arctic waters from *Trois navigations admirables faictes par les Hollandois et Zelandois au Septentrion* by Gerrit de Veer (Paris, 1599). This unsophisticated image lets us imagine the extraordinary perils faced by Barents and his men as they navigated unknown Arctic waters. It must have been particularly difficult to land on ice floes from a sailing vessel, and then to reembark. COURTESY THE NEWBERRY LIBRARY, CHICAGO

authorities and was intended mainly as a reconnaissance voyage of the first part of the route. During this voyage Barents sailed the entire east coast of the island of Novaya Zemlya, charting it for the first time. The 1595 expedition was intended as a trading voyage, but the ships failed to cross the seas east of Nova Zembla because of heavy ice. Consequently all sponsors, with the exception of the city of Amsterdam, withdrew their support. In 1596, two small ships left Amsterdam, the first under the command of Jan Cornelisz Rijp and the second under Jacob van Heemskerck, with Barents as pilot. The plan was to sail from the North Cape on a course directly toward the North Pole. This track led to the discovery of Bear Island, the Spitsbergen archipelago, and the permanent polar ice. Forced to turn south, the two ships decided to part company. Rijp returned to the Netherlands, and Barents and Van Heemkerck sailed farther, to the north tip of Nova Zembla. On the eastern side of the island they became trapped by the ice and were forced to build a hut on land to survive the coming winter. In the following spring the ship remained icebound, and the men were forced to make the return voyage in the ship's boats. Barents had suffered severely during the hard winter and died seven days after leaving the winter camp. The survivors arrived back in Amsterdam in November 1597. One of them, Gerrit de Veer, published in 1598 a lively account of the voyages and the wintering at Nova Zembla, and the account became one of the classics of Dutch travel literature. It was soon translated into many languages, including English in 1609.

In 1821 an extremely popular epic Dutch poem by Hendrik Tollens revived interest in the Netherlands in Barents and his voyages, and in 1871 the remains of the party's hut were found. The Arctic conditions kept many objects, including documents, remarkably well preserved. The majority of the objects are now in the Rijksmuseum in Amsterdam. In the late nineteenth century the sea east of the North Cape and west of Nova Zembla was named Barents Sea.

[*See also* Northeast Passage.]

Arctic Travels

The voyages of Willem Barents into the Arctic regions took place at the time when there had been little or no contact between the indigenous peoples and western Europeans; the ensuing encounters have a remarkable immediacy in Barents's descriptions not only of the people but also of the animals, like the redoubtable polar bears.

[The Samoyeds] are for the most part of low stature, with broad, flat faces, small eyes, short legs, their knees standing outwards, and very nimble. They are appareled in deer-skins from head to foot, and wear long hair, which they pleat and fold, letting it hang down their backs. Their sleds stood always ready with one or two deer in them, which will carry a man or two swifter than our horses.

One of our men shot a musket towards the sea, wherewith they were in so great fear that they ran and leaped like madmen. We told them by our interpreter that we used our pieces instead of bows, and to convince them, one of our men took a flat stone and set it upon a hill a good distance from him, and with a bullet struck the stone asunder, whereat they wondered exceedingly.

—Gerrit de Veer, *The Second Voyage of William Barents into the North Seas, 1595* (London, 1705)

BIBLIOGRAPHY

Beke, Charles T., ed. *The Three Voyages of William Barents to the Arctic Regions, 1594–1595 and 1596, by Gerrit de Veer.* London: Hakluyt Society, 1876.

L'Honore Naber, S. P., ed. *De reizen van Willem Barents, Jacob van Heemskerck, Jan Cornelisz: Rijp en anderen naar het noorden (1594–1597).* 2 vols. The Hague: Martinus Nijhof, 1917.

DIEDERICK WILDEMAN

Barrow, John (1764–1848), British writer and promoter of expeditions to the Northwest Passage. Sir John Barrow was one of the great promoters of exploration in the first half of the nineteenth century. As second secretary of the Admiralty (1804–1806; 1807–1845), he was instrumental in dispatching numerous Royal Navy expeditions to explore the Arctic and Africa. He was supported in this by a naval administration who shared his enthusiasm for exploration and science. A Fellow of the Royal Society, he was also among the founders of the Royal Geographical Society.

Born in a two-room cottage in Lancashire in 1764, he learned mathematics and surveying at the local school. Tiring of bookkeeping at an ironworks in Liverpool, he signed on as a deckhand on a whaler and made his first, and only, voyage to the Arctic. He was never to lose his passion for that region. On his return, he got a job teaching the sons of naval officers at a school in Greenwich. As tutor to the son of Sir George Staunton, he learned Chinese from his precocious pupil, and when Staunton was appointed to Lord Macartney's embassy to China in 1792, Barrow accompanied him. He wrote an account of his observations of a land that was then almost unknown to Westerners (*Travels in China* [1804]). When Macartney became governor of the Cape Colony in 1797, Barrow again accompanied him, as his private secretary. Barrow crossed the Great Karoo and explored and surveyed the interior, an account of which he also published (*Travels into the Interior of Southern Africa* [1806]). Marrying a local girl and buying a farm, he planned to settle at the Cape, but when Britain handed the colony back to the Dutch in 1803, he sold his land and brought his wife home to England. Having made connections with the Dundas family, when Lord Melville was appointed first lord of the Admiralty in 1804, Barrow became second secretary.

Barrow was a prolific writer, and in addition to his personal travel narratives and several books on history and exploration, he used his contributions to the *Quarterly Review* to advance his theories of an ice-free polar sea and a navigable Northwest Passage. He argued for state sponsorship of voyages of discovery to test his theories, as well as to preempt the French, Russians, and Americans in what could become a strategically important region, to benefit science, to provide occupation for a portion of the navy in peacetime, and to be a focus for patriotic feeling in a time of postwar political and social unrest.

Barrow became a friend of Sir Joseph Banks, the president of the Royal Society, from whom he had received some botanical training at the Royal Botanic Gardens at Kew before going out to the Cape. With Banks's influence as a friend of the king and de facto chief scientific adviser to government, and Barrow's knowledge of naval resources and commitments, and his position in the naval administration with access to the Board of Admiralty between them, they persuaded the Admiralty and the government, once peace had come, to devote a part of the navy's resources to the mounting of a succession of scientific expeditions to unexplored regions. The first of these was James Hingston Tuckey's attempt to sail up the Congo in 1816, which was all but wiped out by disease. Barrow was not discouraged and promoted further African ventures in search of the Niger—notably the trans-Sahara expeditions of Captain G. F. Lyon and Joseph Ritchie (1818–1820), Hugh Clapperton (1822–1824) and Alexander Gordon Laing (who reached Timbuctoo in 1826), and the Lander brothers' (Richard and John) expedition of 1830–1831. But Barrow is best remembered as the principal instigator of the series of expeditions launched by the Royal Navy between 1818 and 1845 in search of a Northwest Passage, which began with the attempt in 1818 to exploit unusual ice-free conditions around Greenland reported to Banks by the whaling captain William Scoresby. Captain David Buchan and Lieutenant John Franklin were sent in two ships to attempt to sail to the Pacific over the North Pole, while two more ships, under Captain John Ross and Lieutenant Edward Parry, were to search northwest along the northern coast of Canada. Ross returned with the report that any passage to the west out of Baffin Bay was blocked by the Croker Mountains, but Barrow was not convinced (correctly) and sent three more seaborne expeditions commanded by Parry in succeeding years (1819–1820, 1821–1823, 1824–1825), as well as the two overland expeditions from Hudson Bay to the Arctic coast of Canada led by Franklin in 1819–1822 and 1825–1827. Barrow also had a hand in facilitating William Parry's attempt to sledge to the North Pole in 1827, and James Clark Ross's expedition to Antarctica (1839–1843). One of his last acts before retiring from the Admiralty in 1845 was to push through yet another attempt on the Northwest Passage, commanded by Sir John Franklin (1845–1847).

While they were, of course, great adventures into the unknown, these voyages were not simply about "conquering" territory or "filling in blanks on the map." They were conceived from the outset as carefully planned and meticulously conducted scientific expeditions. Planned in conjunction with Barrow's friends at the Royal Society, each expedition had a full program of scientific experiments to conduct and observations to make. Variations in the strength of gravity were measured to determine the precise shape of the Earth, the Earth's magnetic field was mapped, the extreme meteorology of the Far North diligently recorded, the temperature and salinity of the sea measured at different depths, specimens collected of the geology, botany, and zoology of the re-gion, and the languages and customs of the inhabitants studied.

Sir John is often confused with his son, John Barrow Jr. (1808–1898), who also worked at the Admiralty, as a clerk and keeper of the Records. A friend of Lady Jane Franklin and of several explorers, it was he who, after his father's death in 1848, did much to help promote and coordinate the relief missions that were sent in search of the lost expedition commanded by Franklin.

The town of Barrow, Alaska, among other places, is named after Sir John, as is the Barrow's Goldeneye duck, and there is an impressive monument to him outside his hometown of Ulverston.

[*See also* Africa, *subentry on* Exploration; Antarctica; Northwest Passage; Royal Geographical Society; Royal Society; *and biographies of figures mentioned in this article.*]

BIBLIOGRAPHY

Barrow, John. *An Auto-biographical Memoir* . . . London: John Murray, 1847.

Barrow, John. *A Chronological History of Voyages into the Arctic Regions* . . . London: John Murray, 1818.

Barrow, John. *Voyages of Discovery and Research within the Arctic Regions* . . . London: John Murray, 1846.

Fleming, Fergus. *Barrow's Boys*. London: Granta Books, 1998.

Lloyd, Christopher. *Mr Barrow of the Admiralty. A Life of Sir John Barrow, 1764–1848*. London: Collins, 1970.

Savours, Ann. *The Search for the North West Passage*. London: Chatham Publishing, 1999.

RANDOLPH COCK

Bar Sauma, Rabban, thirteenth-century traveler to Europe. Rabban Bar Sauma, a Christian Uighur monk, and his colleague Marcus traveled from Beijing, China, to western Europe in the mid-thirteenth century. Christian missionaries from the Nestorian, or Syrian, branch of the church had reached China in the seventh century, and they had succeeded in creating a small but learned Christian community in the Tang empire. When the Mongols under Genghis Khan conquered China in the thirteenth century, they found the Nestorians to be useful ambassadors, counselors, doctors, and merchants. Kublai Khan embraced all religions equally, but he found it helpful to set Christian and Muslim advisers against the predominant Confucians and Buddhists in China. When Bar Sauma and his disciple Marcus proposed a journey to Europe, Kublai gave them a travel permit guaranteeing safe passage through his vast empire.

Crossing central Eurasia was a terrifying and dangerous mission, but Bar Sauma and Marcus took shelter in a Nestorian community in Khorasan, then passed through Azerbaijan and reached Baghdad, the seat of the patriarch of the Nestorian Church. They toured famous churches and monasteries as they moved on to Jerusalem. Since they knew Chinese, Mongol, and Persian, they had excellent qualifications not only for religious service, but also for diplomatic service. In 1280, the patriarch appointed Marcus the head of the Nestorian Church of China. The Mongol governor, or *Ilkhan*, of Baghdad had grander designs for Rabban Sauma. The governor's greatest enemies were the Muslims who held Jerusalem, Egypt, and Syria, and he knew that the western European crusader kings likewise considered the Muslims enemies and shared his goals of conquering them. In 1287 he sent Bar Sauma to contact King Louis IX (who, however, had died in 1270) and have the king consider a Mongol-Christian alliance to recover Jerusalem. The governor gave Bar Sauma official orders, money, animals, and travel passes, and sent him with gifts for the king of the Franks, the king of the Greeks, and the pope. Bar Sauma passed through the Byzantine empire to Constantinople (modern Istanbul), met the king of Byzantium, and toured the great churches of the city. He went on to Rome, where he passed on his letters to the pope and the king of the Franks. He astounded the cardinals of Rome with the news that Christian communities had spread all across eastern Eurasia as far as China, and told them that many Mongols had been baptized as Christians. After touring Italy's famous churches, he moved on to Paris, where he met the French king Philippe IV, and, according to his account, he then met the king of England, Edward I, in Bordeaux.

Ultimately, the grand alliance of the Mongols and Christians against Islam never happened, because the Christian powers distrusted each other too much, and the Mongols had other wars to fight. Bar Sauma's journey explored a surprising opportunity that could have changed the course of history. Christians in Western Europe had heard mythical tales of a Christian kingdom of Prester John far off in Asia: now they had actually met a Christian from China. Everyone has heard of Bar Sauma's famous contemporary Marco Polo, who claimed to have crossed Eurasia from west to east. Fewer people know of Rabban Bar Sauma, but his story is more plausible than Marco Polo's. He traveled with official documents from the Mongol khan on a diplomatic and religious mission; a learned man, he impressed the nobles and religious elites of every country he visited. Compared to Bar Sauma, Marco Polo seems little more than a jailed, bankrupt merchant and tall-tale teller. Rabban Bar Sauma's adventures show how the Mongol conquests had united the entire continent of Eurasia and made it possible for learned men to cross huge distances and still find themselves in a common religious community.

[*See also* Polo, Marco, *and* Prester John.]

BIBLIOGRAPHY
Rossabi, Morris. *Voyager from Xanadu: Rabban Sauma and the First Journey from China to the West*. New York: Kodansha, 1992.

PETER C. PERDUE

Barth, Heinrich

Barth, Heinrich (1821–1865), German explorer of central Africa. One of the most significant explorers in the nineteenth century, who became the world's authority on central Africa, Barth was born in Hamburg, Germany, on February 16, 1821. A student of the estimable geographer Karl Ritter, Barth completed his PhD in 1844 at the University of Berlin after presenting a thesis on the commercial history of the Corinthians. He was an accomplished linguist (he spoke and wrote English, French, and Italian fluently), and he was also an authority on the desert ecosystem, as well as on Arab culture and language. Barth's expertise in archaeology, ethnology, and linguistics is vividly displayed often in all of his writings about his years in Africa. Further, he was an advocate of personal physical fitness, and this allowed him the endurance to survive severe environmental conditions where others perished.

After completing his doctorate, Barth commenced three years of travel in southern Europe, northern Africa, and southwestern Asia. He visited France, Spain, coastal North Africa, Palestine, Syria, Cyprus, Turkey, and Greece. These travels resulted in his book *Wanderungen durch die Küstenländer des Mittelmeeres* (1849). In October 1849 Karl Ritter informed Barth that the British government had commissioned James Richardson (1806–1851) to lead a mission to central Africa, and it wished for a German to be part of the expedition. Ritter recommended Barth, but also indicated that whoever took the position had to contribute £200 for his own personal traveling expenses. After some difficulties, Barth agreed to join Richardson with the condition that exploration, rather than diplomacy, would be his principal objective in Africa. In the event, another German scientist, Adolph Overweg (1822–1852), was added to the group, but both he and Richardson died early, and Eduard Vogel (1829–1856),

Heinrich Barth. "The Approaches of Timbuktoo," from *Reisen und Entdeckungen in Nord- und Central-Afrika* (5 vols., Gotha, 1857–1858). Here Barth enters Timbuctoo late in 1853, at the beginning of a stay there that would allow him to study the history and prospects of this fabled city. COURTESY THE NEWBERRY LIBRARY, CHICAGO

sent later to central Africa to help Barth, also died. Barth was, therefore, the only survivor, and he performed one of the most productive journeys of geographical exploration ever conducted. His five-volume book, *Travels and Discoveries in North and Central Africa* (1857–1858), comprising more than three thousand pages and published simultaneously in English and German, is now accepted as one of the best travel accounts ever written.

By early February 1850, Richardson, Barth, and Overweg convened in Tripoli, and on March 30, what was probably the best-equipped exploration expedition yet organized departed for central Africa. It did not take long for Barth to declare his independence from the others, and when the group reached Murzuk, he set out on his own and proceeded to get lost and almost died before he was rescued. After arriving at an oasis in the Air Mountains in January 1851, the explorers separated with instructions to rendezvous at Kukawa, the capital of Bornu, near Lake Chad.

Traveling in disguise as Abd el Kerim, Barth journeyed to Kano, and in early March, while on his way back to Lake Chad, he learned that Richardson had died. He and Overweg were reunited at Kukawa, where Overweg began his exploration of Lake Chad. Barth continued south, and by mid-June 1851, he entered Yola, from where he made his most important geographical contributions. Barth subsequently discovered the headwaters of the Benue River and confirmed its linkage to the Niger River rather than to Lake Chad. He then traveled east to the Shari River and determined it to be a tributary of Lake Chad.

Barth had intentions of leaving Africa via Zanzibar, but received orders from England that he was now the leader of the mission, and that he and Overweg should go to Timbuctoo instead. In September 1852, before they had left Lake Chad, Overweg died. In his book, Barth praised Overweg's cleverness but was unimpressed with his general knowledge of natural sciences. Alone, Barth began his trek to Timbuctoo, with an itinerary that took him to Sokoto and then to Say (on the Niger River). He entered Timbuctoo on September 23, 1853, and resided there nearly six months in anxious and precarious circumstances. Barth was ill much of this time, and as a stranger, he was in constant danger from local Fulani tribesmen (he could appreciate the problems experienced earlier by Alexander Gordon Laing and René Caillié). Nonetheless, he prepared a plan of the city, acquired news of Laing and Caillié, gathered information about the commercial prospects of the city, learned about the anomalous rise and fall of the waters of the Niger River, and—most important—he was able to translate documents that described the history of the fabled city.

Barth departed Timbuctoo on March 18, 1854, by traveling down the Niger River and over to Sokoto and Kano in northern Nigeria. Remarkably, he met, as he trekked eastward on the savannah toward Lake Chad, Eduard Vogel, a German scientist commissioned to help him. After a visit of only two hours, they agreed to meet in Kukawa after Vogel completed some astronomical work in the Zinder region. To-

gether again in Kukawa, Vogel explored Lake Chad, but was later murdered while traveling across the Sahara toward the Nile. Barth thanked Vogel in his book and lamented that he was not his companion from the beginning of the expedition. He claimed that Vogel's astronomical observations were the key to the accuracy of his maps.

Upon leaving Kukawa for home in May 1855, Barth wrote, "I turned my back with satisfaction upon those countries where I had spent five full years in incessant toil and exertion. On retracing my steps northward I was filled with the hope that the Merciful Providence would allow me to reach home in safety, in order to give full account of my labours and discoveries." Barth reached Tripoli by late August 1855, and after having been gone for more than five years and having traveled a total distance of over ten thousand miles, he returned to London on September 6, 1855, with little fanfare.

In due course he was named Companion of the Bath, and the Royal Geographical Society in 1856 awarded him its Victoria Medal. His immediate concern was to finish writing the account of his Africa sojourn, and within two years *Travels and Discoveries in North and Central Africa* was published. Disturbingly for Barth, little interest was expressed in his significant achievements. He had meticulously compiled a vast amount of scientific and geographical data for part of the world previously unknown in Europe; he had wandered through and described and mapped huge portions of the Sahara Desert, the Lake Chad–Benue River region, and segments of the Niger River; he had provided for the first time reliable ethnological and linguistic accounts of African tribes; and he was the only European to enter Timbuctoo between René Caillié in 1828 and Oskar Lenz in 1880.

Barth continued his work on the vocabularies of the central African languages that he had learned, but only two parts were ever published (in 1862 and 1863). He also continued his peripatetic wanderings. He traveled widely in Asia Minor in 1858, and he was in Spain in 1861, in European Turkey in 1862, in the Alps in 1863, in Italy in 1864, and in Turkey again in 1865. In 1863, Barth became professor of geography at the University of Berlin, where he founded the Karl Ritter Institute. In the same year, he became president of the Berlin Geographical Society. Barth died in Berlin on November 25, 1865, the victim of a stomach malaise that he had contracted while exploring in Africa. Although during his lifetime he never achieved the recognition he was due, Barth now is considered one of the most successful ex-

---

African Travels

Barth traveled widely in Africa between 1850 and 1855, crossing the Sahara Desert from Tripoli to Lake Chad. He made many sketches on the way, taking care to correct what he thought were the mistakes made by previous European explorers in their own sketches; the view of Timbuctoo is an example of his meticulous observation.

The style of the buildings [in Timbuctoo] was various. I could see clay houses of various characters, some low and unseemly, others rising with a second storey in front to greater elevation, and making even an attempt at architectural ornament; the whole being interrupted by a few round huts of matting. The sight of this spectacle afforded me sufficient of interest, although, the streets being very narrow, only little was to be seen of the intercourse carried on in them, with the exception of the small market in the northern quarter, which was exposed to view on account of its situation on the slope of the sand-hills, which in the course of time have accumulated around the mosque.

—Heinrich Barth, *Travels and Discoveries in North and Central Africa* (London, 1857–1858)

plorers in history. Further, because of his brilliant academic abilities, he heads the list in the pantheon of the smaller group of outstanding scholar-explorers that includes Johann Ludwig Burckhardt, Georg Schweinfurth, Anders Sparrman, Carl Peter Thunberg, and Wilhelm Junker.

[*See also* Africa, *subentry on* Scientific Exploration; Chad, Lake; Timbuctoo; *and biographical entries on figures mentioned in this article.*]

BIBLIOGRAPHY

Barth, Heinrich. *Travels and Discoveries in North and Central Africa: Being a Journal of an Expedition Undertaken under the Auspices of H.B.M.'s Government, in the Years 1849–1855.* 5 vols. London: Longman, Brown, Green, 1857–1858.

Barth, Heinrich. *Travels in Nigeria.* London: Oxford University Press, 1962.

Gardner, Brian. *The Quest for Timbuctoo.* New York: Harcourt, Brace & World, 1968.

Prothero, R. Mansell. "Heinrich Barth and the Western Sudan." *The Geographical Journal* 64, part 3 (September 1958): 326–339.

SANFORD H. BEDERMAN

Barton, Otis

Barton, Otis (1899–1992), underwater explorer and inventor. Frederick Otis Barton Jr. was born into an independently wealthy family in New York City on June 5, 1899. As a Groton student, he once trapped the gardener in a game pit patterned on one described in Henry M. Stanley's book *In Darkest Africa*, and he explored parts of Vineyard Sound with a homemade diving helmet. Later, on a trip around the world after graduating from Harvard, Barton interacted with Japanese pearl divers in the Philippines; later still, as a respite from postgraduate engineering work at Columbia University, he began designing a deep-sea-diving vehicle. As he wrote in *The World beneath the Sea* (1953),

> In those days I dreamed of building up a reputation as an explorer and a scientist, dividing my time between a comfortable apartment in New York City . . . and field trips to the oceanic depths in search of specimens for the collections of the Museum of Natural History. Of course, there was a girl in the dream, an Osa Johnson type who liked camping and photographed well in a sun helmet. She might even help me finance the expedition. (p. 7)

After reading an article about William Beebe's plans for a similar vehicle, Barton temporarily gave up his designs. He decided instead to emulate the treasure hunter Roy Chapman Andrews by traveling to Persia to collect fossils. By late 1928, however, Barton was again involved with the design of his submersible and attempted to contact Beebe, who initially was

"as unapproachable as an Indian potentate, and twice as wary." The two eventually met, and Barton's spherical design, combined with his offer to fund the project, gained Beebe's approval. A series of dives off Bermuda in 1930 led to a descent of 1,426 feet (435 meters); they reached 2,200 feet (671 meters) in 1932, and dove with the bathysphere to 3,028 feet (923 meters) in 1934. While Beebe seized most of the credit for these exploits, it seems clear that without Barton's engineering expertise and financial backing, the bathysphere would never have gotten into the water.

The Great Depression caused Barton to realize "that I must either make my interest in science and exploration earn me a living or else I must abandon it and go belatedly into some humdrum business." This realization, coupled with the influence of Frank Buck's documentary *Bring 'Em Back Alive* (1932), led to Barton's involvement with undersea photography and to his own movie, *Titans of the Deep* (1938). For a time, Barton took on the trappings of a young producer and man-about-town, successfully avoiding damages, for example, when his pet ocelot ran under a girl's skirt and emerged from the front of her open-necked dress. His attorney convinced the judge that the law had no name for such a "crime."

During World War II, Barton worked on a self-contained diving suit and eventually served as a combat photographer in the Pacific. The benthoscope he designed in 1938 was finally constructed after the war, and Barton, diving alone in the Santa Cruz Basin off California, reached a depth of 4,500 feet (1,372 meters) in August 1949. In later years, Barton turned his attention to exploring forest canopies, inventing a tree climber that he used in equatorial Africa and pioneering night photography in the region. He died in Manhattan at the age of ninety-two.

[*See also* Beebe, William.]

BIBLIOGRAPHY

Barton, Otis. *The World beneath the Sea.* New York: Crowell, 1953.

Beebe, William. *Half Mile Down.* New York: Harcourt, 1934.

Matsen, Bradford. *Descent: The Heroic Discovery of the Abyss.* New York: Pantheon, 2005.

SAMUEL PYEATT MENEFEE

Bartram, William

Bartram, William (1739–1824), American naturalist. William Bartram, an accomplished natural scientist and artist-author, explored the American Southeast in the years immediately preceding the American Revolutionary War. A Quaker, he was born in Philadelphia and died there. His portrait by

William Bartram. Portrait of Mico Chlucco from *Travels through North and South Carolina...* (Philadelphia, 1791). Bartram's *Travels* enjoyed a wide influence on both sides of the Atlantic. His portrait of Mico Chlucco, though, shows the great difficulty of making a convincing likeness of the peoples he described textually. COURTESY THE NEWBERRY LIBRARY, CHICAGO

Charles Willson Peale hangs in that city's Independence National Historical Park. As a youth Bartram followed in the footsteps of his father, John Bartram. John Bartram was widely recognized as a naturalist and joined with Benjamin Franklin and others in founding the American Philosophical Society. William spent his youth and most of his adult life on his family's farm, where his father developed what is often cited as the first botanical garden and herbarium in America.

William Bartram benefited from an excellent formal education and, thanks to the international renown enjoyed by his father's botanical garden, he met most of the leading scientific figures of the day, from Benjamin Franklin to Sweden's Pehr (Peter) Kalm. He was fourteen when he began accompanying his father on extended botanical field excursions that took him from Canada to Florida. They collected large quantities of seeds, bulbs, cuttings, and specimens, most of which were forwarded to London for the king and the socially well-connected collector-gardener Peter Collinson.

At the conclusion of their 1765–1766 Florida expedition, William chose to remain behind and try his hand as a rice and indigo planter in the new colony. William's poorly funded plantation venture failed, and, within the year he returned home. From 1767 to 1772 he struggled unsuccessfully to support himself. Aware of his financial problems, Peter Collinson brought him to the attention of Dr. John Fothergill, a wealthy London collector, who became deeply concerned by the talented young naturalist's distress. At William's request Dr. Fothergill undertook to sponsor him for a collecting trip to Florida.

On March 20, 1773, William Bartram began his nearly four-year-long peregrination through the Carolinas, Georgia, Alabama, and Florida and along the Gulf Coast of Mississippi and Louisiana to the Mississippi River at a time when this vast subtropical region was still largely under the control of Indian tribes. In addition to letters, reports, and descriptions, Bartram forwarded seeds, cuttings, and specimens as well as artistically rendered drawings of the noteworthy plants, birds, animals, and fish he encountered. The settlements and lifeways of Indians and white frontiersmen he encountered also figured in his descriptive accounts. In 1777 he returned to his home, and after his father's death William joined his younger brother in running the gardens and lived out the rest of his life at the family homestead near Philadelphia.

It would be difficult if not impossible to understand and appreciate William Bartram and his accomplishments without considering the two other natural historians who influenced him from his childhood onward. They were Mark Catesby (c. 1679–1749) and Pehr Kalm (1716–1779). Catesby was an Englishman, often called the father of American ornithology, who traveled through the southern colonies, the Bahamas, and Jamaica and lived in Virginia for a period. He was a diligent collector and painter of the wildlife and plants he encountered. In 1731 he began publishing his opus, *Natural History of Carolina, Florida, and the Bahama Islands, with Observations on the Soil, Air, and Water*. The book contained over one hundred plates, all made from his own drawings. In the following year Catesby was recognized and elected to London's prestigious Royal Society. In appreciation for the assistance he had received, Catesby presented a copy of *Natural History of Carolina, Florida, and the Bahamas* to John Bartram, who made it available to his son William as he matured. It had an enormous influence on William's work as did the book by the Swede Pehr Kalm, *Travels into North America*. Kalm was a student of the internationally renowned taxonomist Carolus Linnaeus. When Linnaeus arranged for his disciple Kalm totravel and collect in America, John Bartram became his mentor and chief informant. Kalm was a frequent visitor at the Bartram home and became friendly with young William. Experts are in agreement that both Catesby and Kalm greatly influenced William Bartram. His artwork, however, far outstripped that of Catesby while his literary competence went far beyond that of Kalm.

World recognition came to Bartram through the publication of his book *Travels through North and South Carolina, Georgia, East and West Florida . . .* in 1791. Almost immediately *Travels* caught the imagination of a wide range of readers on both sides of the Atlantic. The book contained vivid and engaging descriptions of the Southeast's flora, fauna, and human denizens, guaranteed to capture the attention of generations of natural scientists and philosophers, many of whom set out to retrace his steps. Bartram would be surprised, however, to discover the impact his words were to have on the history of literature, since he never considered himself a writer. *Travels* appeared at an auspicious moment, just as the Romantic movement was gaining momentum. Samuel Taylor Coleridge and William Wordsworth paid close attention to Bartram's work. Here in stunning prose they found a beneficent vision of nature that they seized upon. Scholars have recognized countless images, ideas, and "echoes" of Bartram's writings in both Wordsworth's and Coleridge's major published works. Several translations of *Travels* were published in Europe, where literary scholars are still exploring the full extent of Bartram's influence on writers, especially in France and Germany.

[*See also* Catesby, Mark, *and* Florida.]

BIBLIOGRAPHY

Cashin, Edward J. *William Bartram and the American Revolution on the Southern Frontier.* Columbia: University of South Carolina Press, 2000.

Harper, Francis, ed. *The Travels of William Bartram.* Athens: University of Georgia Press, 1998.

Sanders, Brad. *Guide to William Bartram's Travels: Following the Trail of America's First Great Naturalist.* Athens, Ga.: Fevertree Press, 2002.

Waselkov, Gregory A., and Kathryn E. Holland Braun, eds. *William Bartram on the Southeastern Indians.* Lincoln, Nebr. and London: University of Nebraska Press, 1995.

LOUIS DE VORSEY

Travels in North and South Carolina

Bartram devoted some remarkable pages of his hugely popular Travels *to his adventures among the alligators. He would have run greater danger from them, he thought, had a great mass of them not been busy sating themselves on schools of fish that had to pass through a narrow channel in the Florida wetlands.*

But what is yet more surprising to a stranger, is the incredibly loud and terrifying roar which [the alligators] are capable of making, especially in the spring season, their breeding time. It most resembles very heavy distant thunder, not only shaking the air and waters, but causing the earth to tremble; and when hundreds and thousands are roaring at the same time, you can scarcely be persuaded but that the whole globe is violently and dangerously agitated.

—William Bartram, *Travels through North and South Carolina, Georgia, East and West Florida* (Philadelphia, 1791)

Bass, George (1771–1803?), English naval surgeon and explorer of the strait between Australia and Tasmania. George Bass was born on January 30, 1771, at Aswarby in Lincolnshire, England, son of the tenant farmer George Bass. He was accepted into the London Corporation of Surgeons in April 1789 and two months later was certified as a surgeon's first mate in the Royal Navy. Bass arrived in New South Wales as a naval surgeon on HMS *Reliance* in September 1795; Matthew Flinders was master's mate on the same ship.

In two small rowing boats, both known as *Tom Thumb*, Bass, Flinders, and William Martin explored Georges River in October 1795 and Lake Illawarra and Port Hacking in March 1796. On a third trip, in August 1797, Bass found coal at Coalcliff. His fourth expedition, from December 3, 1797, to February 25, 1798, in a whaleboat crewed by six volunteer sailors, traveled 1,200 miles (1,950 kilometers) south and west along the coast observing the Shoalhaven River,

Twofold Bay, Wilson's Promontory, and Western Port. He returned convinced that there was a strait between the mainland and Van Diemen's Land.

On October 7, 1798, the sloop *Norfolk*, under command of Flinders and with Bass on board, sailed south from Sydney, passed through Bass Strait to circumnavigate Van Diemen's Land, and returned to Port Jackson on January 12, 1799. By confirming the existence of the strait, they reduced the duration of a voyage from England to New South Wales by a week. They also found suitable sites for European settlement in the Tamar and Derwent estuaries.

Bass sent a large collection of botanical specimens to Joseph Banks in England, published three works on Australian fauna, and was elected to the Linnaean Society in London. He disappeared while sailing toward South America in 1803.

[*See also* Australia, Exploration of, *and* Flinders, Matthew.]

BIBLIOGRAPHY

Bowden, K. M. *George Bass 1771–1803: His Discoveries, Romantic Life, and Tragic Disappearance*. Melbourne, Australia: Oxford University Press, 1952.

Estensen, Miriam. *The Life of George Bass: Surgeon and Sailor of the Enlightenment*. Sydney, Australia: Allen and Unwin, 2005.

Favenc, Ernest. *The History of Australian Exploration from 1788 to 1888*. Sydney, Australia: Turner and Henderson, 1888. Reprint. Amsterdam: Meridian, 1967.

DENIS SHEPHARD

Bates, Henry Walter (1825–1892), British explorer of the Amazon and official of the Royal Geographical Society. Few individuals in the nineteenth century played a more important role in the development of both natural science and geographical discovery than H. W. Bates. His entomological work in Amazonia led to very significant findings, adding evidence that Charles Darwin's theory of natural selection was correct. Additionally, during the twenty-eight years he served as the assistant secretary of the Royal Geographical Society (RGS), he helped scores of explorers prepare for their journeys, and saw to the publication of their reports when they returned.

Bates was born in Leicester, England, on February 8, 1825. At age thirteen he left school and was apprenticed to a hosier, but in his free time he collected insects in nearby Charnwood Forest. At age eighteen (in 1843) his article about local beetles was published in the first volume of *Zoologist* magazine. He met and befriended Alfred Russel Wallace, another eager amateur entomologist, and, inspired by Darwin's voyage on the *Beagle*, the two self-taught naturalists set out for South America to collect insects, arriving in Pará (at the mouth of the Amazon River) on May 27, 1848. Wallace traveled and collected specimens in tropical Brazil for forty-eight months, but Bates remained for eleven years, traveling widely on the upper tributaries of the Amazon River. When he returned to England in June 1859, he carried a collection that included over 14,700 species, of which 14,000 were insects and 8,000 were new to science.

Bates is best noted for his discovery of the principle of "Batesian mimicry." As an example, he showed that in order to protect themselves from predatory birds, some delectable butterflies disguised themselves as unpalatable and disagreeable species. After his return to England, he published *The Naturalist on the River Amazons* (1864), which Darwin praised as the best work of natural history travels ever published in England. For his lifetime achievement in natural science, Bates was elected a Fellow of the Royal Society in 1881.

Another career commenced in 1864 when Bates was appointed assistant secretary of the Royal Geographical Society. For almost three decades, he handled virtually all of the society's correspondence, and he edited its publications, including the *Proceedings of the Royal Geographical Society*. During his years at the RGS, the society maintained an especially strong interest in Africa, and doled out over £20,000 specifically for its exploration. It was the rare explorer interested in Africa (or anywhere else for that matter) who sought support from the RGS and did not correspond with Bates, the society's only permanent officer. Bates helped every explorer commissioned by the RGS, many of whom were unknown. When they often returned famous, Bates was there to welcome them home. During his tenure, Bates supported almost all of the great explorers of Africa—David Livingstone, Henry Stanley, and Joseph Thomson to name only a few. Never enjoying robust health, he died of influenza in London on February 16, 1892. Bates's enduring widespread interests distinguished him from those whom Charles Darwin called the "mob of naturalists without souls."

[*See also* Amazon River; Livingstone, David; Royal Geographical Society; Stanley, Henry; Thomson, Joseph; *and* Wallace, Alfred Russel.]

BIBLIOGRAPHY

Bates, Henry Walter. *The Naturalist on the River Amazons* (1864). New York: Penguin Books, 1989.

Henry Bates. "Adventure with Curl-crested Toucans" from *The Naturalist on the River Amazons* (London, 1863). This illustration from Bates's major work has a slightly farcical quality, as if some hapless London clerk had strayed into the jungle and now found himself beset by exotic birds. COURTESY THE NEWBERRY LIBRARY, CHICAGO

Travels along the Amazon

The self-taught entomologist Bates made a huge collection of zoological specimens during his stay on the Amazon River from 1848 to 1859. Our plate shows him hunting toucans, and the accompanying prose has a remarkable freshness and innocence. It was long before the time when all such investigators would be professionals, trained in universities.

One day as I was entomologizing alone and unarmed, in a dry Ygapo, where the trees were rather wide apart and the ground coated to the depth of eight or ten inches with dead leaves, I was near coming into collision with a boa constrictor. I had just entered a little thicket to capture an insect, and whilst pinning it was rather startled by a rushing noise in the vicinity. I looked up to the sky, thinking a squall was coming on, but not a breath of wind stirred in the tree-tops. On stepping out of the bushes I met face to face a huge serpent coming down a slope, and making the dry twigs crackle and fly with his weight as he passed over them. I had frequently met with a smaller boa, the Cutim-boa, in a similar way, and knew from the habits of the family that there was no danger, so stood my ground.

—Henry Bates, *The Naturalist on the River Amazons* (London, 1864)

Woodcock, George. *Henry Walter Bates: Naturalist of the Amazon*. New York: Barnes and Noble, 1969.

SANFORD H. BEDERMAN

Baudin, Nicolas (1754–1803), French naval officer who led the geographic survey of Tasmania and Australia. Nicolas-Thomas Baudin was born in Brittany on February 17, 1754. He first served on French merchant ships, joining the navy in 1774 as an officer from the middle classes, known as a "blue." Lacking an aristocratic background, he made but slow progress and decided to enter the service of Joseph II of Austria. He was sent on several scientific expeditions, including an expedition to the Indian Ocean and the Far East to collect botanical specimens for the gardens of Schönbrunn Palace. The outbreak of the French Revolution opened up new prospects and he returned to France in 1795, again going on scientific expeditions.

He had drawn plans for a voyage of exploration to the Pacific, with emphasis on the waters around Australia, where much still remained to be done. The final proposal, approved by Napoleon, had a minor political aspect, the price Baudin had to pay for official support, but the main purpose was geographic and scientific, and a number of savants were included in the complements of the two ships he was given. Their names, the *Géographe* and the *Naturaliste*, enshrined the essential aims of the project.

The ships sailed from Le Havre on October 19, 1800, making for Tenerife and Mauritius. This part of the voyage proved unusually slow, taking up a full five months, depleting the stores and causing strain on board the two ships. Baudin's rather authoritarian character, accentuated by his failing health, added to tensions among the participants and caused problems throughout the voyage. Making for southwestern Australia, the two ships reached Cape Leeuwin in May 17, 1801, veering north to Rottnest Island, where they became separated during a storm. However, after extensive, though separate, survey work along the coast, they reunited at Timor in September. In mid-November, Baudin sailed south and east to Tasmania, which he sighted on January 13, 1802. He hoped to survey the entire east and north coasts of the island, but this proved too great a task, and once again the two ships became separated. Working separately, however, they carried out a great deal of work. The *Géographe* went on to explore much of the south coast of Australia, while the *Naturaliste* made for Port Jackson, where the two ships were reunited in June.

Baudin sent the slow and cumbersome *Naturaliste* back to France and obtained a smaller ship, the *Casuarina*, as replacement. Baudin then sailed back to Tasmania for further explorations, causing some anxiety among the British authorities, who began to suspect that his work was at least partly motivated by political aims, including the possible annexation of the island. Extensive surveys were then carried out along the southeastern coast of the Australian continent, the *Géographe* and the *Casuarina* eventually making their way in a wide arc to Timor. Baudin then began work along the little-known and island-strewn northern coast as far as the Bathurst and Melville islands. However, by July 1803, the crews and Baudin himself were too exhausted to continue their work of exploration, and they turned toward Mauritius, where they arrived on August 7. Baudin died there on September 16.

In spite of shipboard dissensions, caused by the clash of personalities and political disagreements, and frequent setbacks, including the French being forestalled along part of the south coast of Australia by the Englishman Matthew Flinders, Baudin's expedition achieved a great deal, both in geography and in natural history, bringing back to France a truly astonishing cargo of zoological and botanical specimens. It also made valuable contributions to European knowledge of the Aborigine culture, following the advice of the young anthropologist Joseph-Marie Dégérando, who later assisted François Péron, who was writing his account of the expedition. Unhappily, Baudin's death meant that his rivals were able to take some of the credit that was due to him, and it is only in recent years that his drive and achievements have received the recognition they deserve.

[*See also* Flinders, Matthew.]

BIBLIOGRAPHY
Bouvier, René, and Édouard Maynial. *Une Aventure dans les mers australes: L'Expédition du Commandant Baudin (1800–1803)*. Paris: Mercure de France, 1947.
Cornell, Christine. *The Journal of Post-Captain Nicolas Baudin, Commander-in-Chief of the Corvettes Géographe and Naturaliste*. Adelaide: Libraries Board of South Australia, 1974. Reprint, 2004.
Dunmore, John. *French Explorers in the Pacific*. Vol. 2. Oxford: Clarendon Press, 1969.
Horner, Frank. *The French Reconnaissance: Baudin in Australia 1801–1803*. Melbourne, Australia: Melbourne University Press, 1987.
Péron, François. *Voyage de découvertes aux Terres australes*. 3 vols. Paris: A. Bertrand, 1807–1816.
Plomley, Norman James Brian. *The Baudin Expedition and the Tasmanian Aborigines, 1802*. Hobart, Tasmania: Blubber Head Press, 1983.

JOHN DUNMORE

Beaufort, Francis (1774–1857), surveyor, scientific explorer, and inventor of the Beaufort Scale. Francis Beaufort was born on May 27, 1774, the son of the cartographer Daniel Augustus Beaufort, rector of Navan in County Meath, Ireland. The Beauforts were a scientific and literary family, and Francis studied astronomy at Trinity College, Dublin. At the age of fourteen he sailed to Canton in an East Indiaman; a year later he began his career in the Royal Navy.

Although no stranger to naval warfare—he was at the Battle of the Glorious First of June in 1794, and was wounded several times over the years—his specialty was always surveying. In 1810 he was given command of the *Fredericksteen* and spent two years charting the southern coast of Asia Minor. His career at sea was abruptly terminated when he was injured during a local uprising, but between 1829 and 1855 he served as the hydrographer of the Navy and was responsible for organizing numerous naval surveys, some of regions previously virtually unexplored.

Best known as the inventor of the Beaufort Scale of wind strength, in fact he merely adapted and popularized an existing scale. His real significance was as a major figure in scientific exploration. A founder of the Royal Geographical Society, Beaufort encouraged the spirit of exploration among his surveyors and worked in league with organizations such as the British Association for the Advancement of Science and the Royal Society to persuade government to fund scientific expeditions. He was knighted in 1848, retired from the Admiralty in 1855, and died two years later at his home in London.

[*See also* Royal Geographical Society.]

BIBLIOGRAPHY
Beaufort, Francis. *Karamania; or, A Brief Description of the South Coast of Asia-Minor and of the Remains of Antiquity*. London: Hunter, 1817.
Courtney, Nicholas. *Gale Force 10: The Life and Legacy of Admiral Beaufort, 1774–1857*. London: Review, 2002.
Friendly, Alfred. *Beaufort of the Admiralty: The Life of Sir Francis Beaufort 1774–1857*. London: Hutchinson, 1977.

RANDOLPH COCK

Beebe, William (1877–1962), American naturalist, explorer, and bathysphere pioneer. Beebe was born in Brooklyn, New York. Although his father, Charles, was a paper dealer, the family shared an interest in nature. Beebe spent time at the American Museum of Natural History and developed a friendship with Henry Fairfield Osborn, the museum's president. From 1896 to 1898, Beebe attended Columbia under Osborn as a special student, although he did not—as was later claimed—receive a degree from that institution. When Osborn became president of the New York Zoological Society in 1899, he named Beebe assistant curator of the bird house that was under construction in the society's Zoological Park (now the Bronx Zoo).

Beebe's numerous research trips with his wife Mary, including visits to Mexico, South America, and a five-year (1910–1914) odyssey to study the pheasants of the world, were privately funded. While the two collaborated on a series of travel books, the degree to which their various travails were accurately described is less clear; in her 1913 divorce court testimony, Mary claimed that Beebe had threatened suicide in a number of spectacular ways, including "throwing himself in the river, shooting himself through the roof of the mouth with a revolver, and by cutting his throat with a razor." Beebe was certainly guilty of embellishing the facts; for instance, his initial description of a raid at Sin-Ma-How, Burma, in *Harper's Magazine* fails to mention the killing of the Karen attacker he later reported in *Pheasant Jungles*.

After World War I, Beebe's interests turned toward the oceans. A Zoological Society cruise aboard the *Arcturus* in 1925 combined his return to the Galápagos with researches in the Sargasso Sea and helmet diving. By the fall of 1926, perhaps inspired by apocryphal accounts of Alexander the Great's undersea exploits, Beebe was designing a metal cylinder with which to explore the ocean depths. In his 1934 book *Half Mile Down*, he credits Theodore Roosevelt with the concept of using a sphere and notes a similar 1902 proposal by I. H. Hazard, but makes no mention of Ernest Bazin's 1865 spherical salvage chamber or the observation ball that Charles Williamson used to film undersea movies.

In December 1928 Beebe was approached by the wealthy engineer Otis Barton, who had designed—and was willing to fund construction of—a bathysphere. Barton and Beebe met in Bermuda in 1930, and after a series of tests, they descended to a depth of 800 feet (244 meters), the greatest depth then reached by human exploration. Fifteen dives that season brought the deepest descent to 1,426 feet (435 meters), while in 1932 a dive by the pair reached 2,200 feet (671 meters). On August 15, 1934, during an expedition cosponsored by the Zoological Society and *National Geographic*, Beebe and Barton reached their greatest depth: 3,028 feet (923 meters), or more than half a mile underwater.

Beebe, who seems to have stolen the limelight from Barton with his book, was himself professionally criticized for sloppy scientific insights. Beebe's subsequent work in the Pacific was not deep-ocean in nature. His vision of scores of bathyspheres exploring the ocean depths never came to pass, although the Picards reached 10,395 feet (3.2 kilometers) in a bathyscaphe off Ponza, Italy, in 1953, and others achieved a depth of 13,287 feet (4 kilometers) off Dakar, Senegal, the following year. Beebe and Barton's bathysphere currently resides above sea level in the American Museum of Natural History.

[*See also* Barton, Otis.]

BIBLIOGRAPHY
Beebe, William. *Half Mile Down*. New York: Harcourt, Brace, 1934.
Gould, Carol Grant. *The Remarkable Life of William Beebe: Explorer and Naturalist*. Washington, D.C.: Shearwater Books, 2004.
Welker, Robert Henry. *Natural Man: The Life of William Beebe*. Bloomington: Indiana University Press, 1975.

SAMUEL PYEATT MENEFEE

Beechey, Frederick William (1796–1856),

British explorer of the North Pacific, the Arctic, and Africa. The son of the artist Sir William Beechey, Frederick William Beechey entered the British Royal Navy as a first class volunteer in 1806 at the age of ten, and he served aboard the *Vengeur* during the action at New Orleans. He was appointed lieutenant in HMS *Trent*, commanded by Lieutenant John Franklin, in an attempt to reach the North Pole in company with the *Dorothea*, under Captain David Buchan, in 1818. Like Captain Constantine John Phipps in 1773 on a similar mission, the ships were unable to navigate much beyond 80° N latitude, at the edge of the heavy multiyear ice, thus finding no proof of the existence of a supposed open polar sea. Captain Buchan wrote no narrative, and it fell to Beechey to do so years later. His *Voyage of Discovery towards the North Pole, Performed in HMS "Dorothea" and "Trent," in 1818* was published in 1843. As first lieutenant of HMS *Hecla*, Beechey took part in the remarkably successful Northwest Passage voyage of 1819–1820, commanded by Lieutenant W. E. Parry, wintering at Melville Island, where he was manager of the "Royal Arctic Theatre." In 1821–1822, Beechey made an overland survey with his brother Henry of the north African coast eastward from Tripoli in cooperation with HMS *Adventure*, under Captain W. H. Smyth.

In 1825–1828, Beechey commanded HMS *Blossom* during a voyage to the North Pacific, which was intended by the Admiralty to meet Parry and Franklin at the end of their Arctic expeditions. Neither Parry nor Franklin was able to penetrate that far west, but Beechey succeeded in exploring the coast of what is now Alaska (then Russian America) beyond Captain Cook's farthest point, Icy Cape. A boat in charge of the master of the *Blossom*, Thomas Elson, reached Point Barrow, an important landmark in Arctic navigation.

On his return to England in 1828, Beechey published his *Proceedings of the Expedition to Explore the North Coast of Africa from Tripoli Eastward*. His *Narrative of a Voyage to Behring's Strait to Co-operate with the Polar Expeditions in HMS "Blossom"* appeared in 1831. The scientific and survey results of this expedition were considerable. Beechey died in 1856, a Fellow of the Royal Society, a retired rear admiral, and president of the Royal Geographical Society.

Frederick William Beechey. "The Expedition Driven into the Ice" from Beechey's *Voyage of Discovery towards the North Pole* (London, 1843). This terrifying scene, representing the Arctic voyage of 1818, wonderfully captures the perils of sailing ships among ice floes as the crew attempts to see if there might be clear water beyond them. COURTESY THE NEWBERRY LIBRARY, CHICAGO

There is a portrait of him by his brother George Duncan Beechey in the National Maritime Museum, Greenwich.

[*See also* Franklin, John; North Pole; *and* Parry, William Edward.]

BIBLIOGRAPHY

Markham, Clements R. *The Arctic Navy List; or, A Century of Arctic and Antarctic Officers, 1773–1873.* London: Griffin, 1875. Reprint. London: Vintage Naval Library, 1992.

Peard, George. *To the Pacific and Arctic with Beechey: The Journal of Lieutenant George Peard of HMS "Blossom," 1825–1828.* Edited by Barry M. Gough. Cambridge, U.K.: Cambridge University Press for the Hakluyt Society, 1973.

ANN SAVOURS

Behaim, Martin (1459–1507), medieval German geographer. Martin Behaim was born in Nuremberg into a flourishing merchant family; it would seem that among his teachers was the celebrated mathematician and astronomer Regiomontanus. About 1482 he went to Portugal, no doubt on family business, and was then concerned with one or two expeditions down the west coast of Africa. His interest in exploration was shown by his appointment to King João's *junta dos mathematicos*, or council for mathematics and navigation.

In 1490, Behaim returned to Nuremberg, where the town council proposed that he make a globe setting out the present state of world geographical knowledge. Such globes were by no means unknown to the medieval world, but Behaim's, completed in 1492, is the oldest to survive. For many years it stood in a reception room at the town hall, but then, just when it might have been discarded as battered and out of date, it was claimed and taken away by a member of the Behaim family. The globe remained in the custody of the family until 1907, when it was given to the Germanisches Nationalmuseum, the German museum in Nuremberg, where it remains as of the early twenty-first century.

On one of the inscriptions on the globe, Behaim tells us that its information was based on Ptolemy's geography, on the tales of Marco Polo and Sir John

Mandeville, and on the explorations that had been conducted under the orders of King João of Portugal. Of course, the globe contains many inaccurate and apparently fantastic entries. But its great interest to the process of exploration is that it shows how western Europeans—including Christopher Columbus—thought of the world in about 1490. "Cipangu" (Japan) floats only about 80 degrees west of the Canaries, and "Cathay" (China) about 35 degrees farther westward. Looking at this globe, it is easy to see why Columbus set out so confidently on the journey that surely would have ended in disaster had he not accidentally encountered America.

Behaim seems to have retained his interest in exploration and in Portugal, for he returned there from about 1495. He died at the German Hospice of Saint Bartholomew in Lisbon on July 29, 1507.

[*See also* Globes.]

BIBLIOGRAPHY
Ravenstein, E. G. *Martin Behaim, His Life and His Globe*. London: G. Philip and Son, 1908. Reprint. *Translations and Commentary on Martin Behaim's "Erdapfel."* London: Greaves and Thomas, 1993.

DAVID BUISSERET

Bell, Gertrude (1868–1926), British official who traveled and wrote about her adventures in Syria and Arabia. The Arabs called Gertrude Bell a "daughter of the desert," a fitting title for a woman who spent almost a decade traveling throughout Arabia, Syria, Turkey, and Asia Minor, from 1905 until 1914. During this time she conducted archaeological investigations, mapped the sites of wells in the deserts, and, perhaps most importantly, established ties with many of the highest-ranking leaders of the Arab world. She became quite knowledgeable about the languages, history, culture, and political milieu of the Persian and Mesopotamian worlds—knowledge that turned out to be critical during World War I, when Arabia was one of the theaters of action. As she traveled, she made photographs, kept detailed notes and a diary, and wrote long letters to family back home. This material formed the basis of a number of books and articles that she published during her lifetime.

Because of her personal connections in Arabia, the British government asked Gertrude Bell to serve during the war in its Arab intelligence agency in Cairo. There she gathered information that Thomas Edward Lawrence, later known as Lawrence of Arabia, used in his exploits. Following her post in Cairo, Bell continued to serve the British government in Basra and Baghdad. She was invited by Winston Churchill to participate in the 1921 Cairo Conference where the future of Mesopotamia would be resolved. She lobbied hard in favor of Prince Faisal to lead the new nation of Iraq, and after he was named to that post, she became a close personal and political adviser to him. She composed laws designed to protect Iraq's many antiquities and founded the country's archaeological museum.

Gertrude Bell was born on July 14, 1868, in Durham, England, where her father, Sir Hugh Bell, was a leading industrialist. She grew up in a privileged environment and was one of the first women admitted to Oxford University, where she earned high honors for her history studies. As a young woman she became an accomplished mountain climber and traveled extensively. At the age of thirty-seven she organized an extended expedition to Syria and surrounding areas, and ended up spending most of the rest of her life in the Arab world. In spite of all her professional successes, her many contacts among rich and powerful people, and the energy and determination that had enabled her to reach many of her goals, at the end she felt lonely and depressed. On July, 12, 1926, at the age of fifty-eight, Bell committed suicide by taking an overdose of sleeping pills. She received a full military funeral from the British government and was buried in Baghdad, the city she loved and lived in until the last.

[*See also* Lawrence, T. E., *and* Women Explorers.]

BIBLIOGRAPHY
Bell, Gertrude. *Syria: The Desert and the Sown*. London: Heinemann, 1907. Reprint. *The Desert and the Sown: The Syrian Adventures of the Female Lawrence of Arabia*. New York: Cooper Square Press, 2001.
Wallach, Janet. *Desert Queen*. New York: Doubleday, 1996.
Winstone, H. V. F. *Gertrude Bell*. London: Jonathan Cape, 1978.

PATRICIA GILMARTIN

Bellingshausen, Fabian (1778–1852), commander of the first Russian Antarctic expedition. Born on Ezel Island (now Saaremaa in Estonia), Fabian Gottlieb von Bellingshausen graduated from the Kronshtadt Naval Cadet Corps and first served on the Baltic Sea. From 1803 to 1806 he served on the *Nadezhda* under Captain Ivan Krusenstern during the first Russian round-the-world voyage, making hydrographic surveys and astronomical observations to establish geographical coordinates. During the next thirteen years Bellingshausen commanded warships on the Baltic and Black seas.

From 1819 to 1821, Bellingshausen was captain of the sloop *Vostok* and commander of the first Russian Antarctic expedition, which amplified many of Cook's findings. Having charted South Georgia and the South Sandwich Islands, Bellingshausen edged eastward along the pack ice, twice crossing the Antarctic Circle; he was eventually forced by ice cliffs to change course to Australia. In October of 1820 the expedition again sailed to Antarctica, rounding it from the Pacific Ocean side and establishing the location of a number of islands; on the return trip Bellingshausen explored Fiji and the Society Islands. He returned to Kronstadt in August 1821, having sailed about 52,325 miles (92,256 kilometers)—through which the Antarctic was circumnavigated, the polar circle was crossed six times, and twenty-nine new islands were discovered. Bellingshausen wrote a book about his expedition, and from 1839 until his death he was chief commander of Kronstadt port and military governor of the region.

[*See also* Antarctica *and* Cook, James.]

BIBLIOGRAPHY

Barratt, Glynn. *Bellingshausen: A Visit to New Zealand, 1820.* Palmerston North, New Zealand: Dunmore Press, 1979.

Gurney, Alan. *Below the Convergence: Voyages toward Antarctica, 1699–1839.* New York: Norton, 1997.

ALEXEY POSTNIKOV

Benjamin of Tudela (fl. 1165–1171), medieval

Jewish traveler. Benjamin ben Jonah of the city of Tudela in northern Spain journeyed through Europe, as well as parts of Asia and Africa, between 1165 and 1171, and he left an account written in Hebrew of his itinerary. Five manuscripts of his work survive, including a near-contemporary one in the British Library. In the sixteenth and seventeenth centuries his book appeared in several printed editions in Hebrew, Latin, French, and English. Up to that time, his work was little known among Christians.

Benjamin went first to Rome, then across Greece to Constantinople, down the eastern coast of the Mediterranean, overland to Baghdad and Persia, and down the Persian Gulf to the Malabar Coast. He describes the island of Ceylon and tells of the length of the voyage to China, but apparently did not make that voyage himself. He returned by making his way up the Nile to Cairo and Alexandria and across the Mediterranean to Sicily. One of the most important aspects of his work is his account of the Jewish community in each city he visited, estimating its population, naming its leaders, and describing its political situation, whether privileged or oppressed. This information is particularly valuable since the Jewish people are virtually invisible to other medieval travelers.

In Baghdad, Benjamin found a community of forty thousand Jews enjoying a privileged status under the enlightened caliph, with ten different religious academies and a titular leader known as the "Head of the Exile." In Yemen there were several independent Jewish kingdoms, inhabited by fierce and aggressive warriors, and in Cochin on the Malabar Coast was a long-established community of several thousand Jews. We do not know the purpose of Benjamin's journey; it certainly included a pilgrimage to sites in the Holy Land and elsewhere in Asia, but he went far beyond that. One suggestion is that he was reporting on places where Jews might seek refuge with their coreligionists, given the currently unstable situation in Spain.

Included in his travelogue are several marvelous tales, including that staple of the Middle East, the giant bird who could carry an ox, in this case rescuing becalmed sailors who had themselves sewn into oxhides. Most of Benjamin's book is more factual, such as his succinct explanation of the cause of the flooding of the Nile, and this quality has led some scholars to assume that he was a merchant.

[*See also* Constantinople *and* Rome.]

BIBLIOGRAPHY

Adler, Elkan N. *Jewish Travellers: A Treasury of Travelogues from Nine Centuries*. 2nd ed. New York: Hermon Press, 1966.

Signer, Michael A., Marcus Nathan Adler, and A. Asher. *The Itinerary of Benjamin of Tudela*. Malibu, Calif.: Joseph Simon, 1983.

EVELYN EDSON

Benzoni, Girolamo (b. c. 1520), Milanese adventurer who spent fourteen years (1541–1555) in the New World. Details of Benzoni's life are scanty, as is knowledge of his motives for traveling to America. His travels after his arrival in Venezuela are also hard to track; he spent time in the Antilles, Colombia, Panama, Guatemala, and Nicaragua, as well as in Peru from 1547 to 1550. There is nothing known about his life after his return from the New World or when he died.

Benzoni's fame rests chiefly on his memoirs of his years in the New World, *La Historia del Mondo Nuovo*. It is a chatty pastiche of history, natural history, and personal impressions. Its major impact came from Benzoni's vivid descriptions of Spanish cruelty to the native populations, which contributed to the dissemination of "La Leyenda Negra" (the Black Legend). As much as the Protestants admired his book, the Spanish reviled it as propaganda. Eleven editions were published between 1565 and 1727, the most famous being that of Theodor de Bry in the 1590s, in Latin and German, whose graphic woodcuts provided fuel for anti-Spanish fervor.

The veracity of Benzoni's account has been questioned; indeed, much of what he wrote does strain credulity. Still, his sympathy toward the plight of the natives seems heartfelt. Despite the philosophical and historical questions surrounding it, *La Historia del Mondo Nuovo* had a powerful impact on European attitudes toward Spain during the sixteenth and seventeenth centuries.

[*See also* Black Legend *and* Spanish and Portuguese America, Reports and Descriptions of.]

BIBLIOGRAPHY

Benzoni, Girolamo.*History of the New World, by Girolamo Benzoni. Shewing His Travels in American from A.D. 1541 to 1556, with Some Particulars of the Island of Canary*. Translated by W. H. Smyth. New York: B. Franklin, 1970.

SUSAN ROM ZURIFF

Girolamo Benzoni. "Modo di fare il pane" from *La historia del Mondo Nuovo* (Venice, 1565). The images of Amerindians in Benzoni's work, though crude, are convincing. Here three women make bread from cassava, producing what are still known as "bammy-cakes" in Jamaica. COURTESY THE NEWBERRY LIBRARY, CHICAGO

Bering, Vitus (1681–1741), Danish-born Russian navigator and explorer. Vitus Jonassen Bering was born in Horsens, Jutland. After youthful service on Danish and Dutch ships, he joined the newly formed Russian Navy of Tsar Peter I (Peter the Great) as a sublieutenant in 1704. During the Russian war against Sweden, which ended in 1721, Bering was regularly promoted, and it was as an experienced sea officer that he was chosen by Peter in 1724, shortly before Peter's death, to lead an expedition east from Kamchatka. In this period, the lands and waters of the North Pacific were among the least-known regions of the globe. When the tsar visited western Europe in 1716 and 1717, the only information he could pass on to interested geographers there was that Cossacks had pushed east of the Urals and across Siberia since the sixteenth century, and that in 1706 they had reached the southern tip of the Kamchatka peninsula. The tsar seemed to have no knowledge—or, if he did, he concealed it—of the voyage of Semen Deshnev, who in 1648 sailed around the eastern tip of Asia (today's Cape Deshneva). Thus it was when Peter ordered Bering to sail from Kamchatka to "determine where it joins with America."

After a trek of six thousand miles from Saint Petersburg across Siberia, Bering and his party reached Okhotsk, the first port established by Russia on the Pacific, in 1726. There they used the materials they had dragged across a continent to build a small vessel in which they sailed to the west coast of Kamchatka. From there they crossed overland to the peninsula's east coast, where they constructed another ship, the *Saint Gabriel*, and in the summer of 1728 headed north along the coast as far as latitude 67°18′ N. Bering had sailed through the strait that now carries his name, but haze hid the opposite (American) shore, and so Bering failed to bring back definite information about the relationship between Asia and America. Bering's chart of his momentous but inconclusive voyage soon reached western Europe, where it was published. It showed the Asian promontory that Bering had reached (Cape Deshneva) as an unnamed cape close to the right-hand margin of the printed page, and so avoided any commitment as to what lay to the east. Even so, the chart considerably reduced the possibility that a land bridge joined Asia and America, and it strengthened the hopes of those who were interested in the discovery of either a Northeast Passage (around Asia) or a Northwest Passage (around America). In 1732, four years after Bering's voyage, Mikhail Gvosdev in the *Saint Gabriel* followed a track that took him farther northeast, where he sighted land. This was the American coast, but Gvosdev referred to it merely as *bolshaya zemlya* (big land), a hint—but no more than a hint—of a continent.

Soon after his return to Saint Petersburg in 1730, Bering was entrusted with an altogether more ambitious project, the Second Kamchatka, or Great Northern, Expedition. It was, in effect, a whole series of expeditions involving overland surveys in Siberia and voyages south through the Kuril Islands toward Japan. The main expedition under Bering was ordered to build two vessels at Avacha Bay on the east coast of Kamchatka. From there he was to sail southeast to the mysterious lands rumored to have been discovered by the Dutch during the previous century, and then head to where the American mainland was thought to lie. For ten years Bering and a small army of associates, scientists, and officials labored along the route from Saint Petersburg to Okhotsk and Avacha Bay, struggling against difficulties of distance and climate, financial problems, and local opposition.

Finally, in the spring of 1741, Bering in the *Saint Peter* and Alexey Chirikov in the *Saint Paul* sailed from their new base of Petropavlosk in Avacha Bay, but found no trace of the lands reported by the Dutch, and as they turned northeast they lost company with each other. Chirikov sighted the American coast at latitude 55°21′ N (near present-day Sitka, Alaska), but soon after lost both his boats with their crews. Unable to land, Chirikov negotiated a difficult passage through the Aleutian Islands to reach Avacha Bay in October 1741. Bering held a more northerly course, and his first Alaskan landfall was at the towering peak of Mount Saint Elias. He landed at tiny Kayak Island only long enough to take on water, a limitation that brought from Georg Wilhelm Steller, his German naturalist, the biting comment that ten years of preparation had resulted in ten hours of exploration. The *Saint Peter*, with its crew weakened by scurvy, sailed back through the Shumagin and Aleutian Islands to a harbor on a small island (Bering Island) a hundred miles from the mainland of Kamchatka. The uninhabited island was a death trap where Bering was among those who died (on December 8, 1741) before the survivors reached Avacha Bay the following summer. There they reported that they had encountered many natives (Aleuts) in their kayaks, and that the waters they had passed through were rich in sea otters and fur seals. During the next twenty years, at least thirty trading ventures sailed from Kamchatka to Alaska to begin a ruthless exploitation of the new trade.

The American landfalls of Bering's second voyage represented a defining moment in the geography of the North Pacific, although doubts about the significance of the explorations lingered because of the failure of the Russian authorities to publish any proper account of the voyage until 1758. Bering's character has remained an enigma. He has been criticized for timidity on his first voyage, when he failed to reach the American coast, and for indecisiveness on his second. Since 1991, when his remains were discovered on Bering Island, the traditional image of Bering as a corpulent, indolent man has been modified. He was, in fact, well built and muscular, and apparently in good health until his last terrible weeks. Taken alongside the recognition of the hardships of the colossal treks across Siberia before his ships were launched into the waters of the North Pacific, this evidence supports a new and more favorable assessment of Bering that has now emerged.

[*See also* Chirikov, Alexey; Deshnev, Semen; Gvosdev, Mikhail; Northeast Passage; Northwest Passage; *and* Steller, Georg Wilhelm.]

BIBLIOGRAPHY

Black, Lydia T. *Russians in Alaska 1732–1867*. Fairbanks: University of Alaska Press, 2004.

Fisher, Raymond H. *Bering's Voyages: Whither and Why*. Seattle: University of Washington Press 1977.

Frost, Orcutt W. *Bering: The Russian Discovery of America*. New Haven, Conn.: Yale University Press, 2003.

Frost, Orcutt W., ed. *Bering and Chirikov: The American Voyages and Their Impact*. Anchorage: Alaska Historical Society, 1992.

Müller, Gerhard Friedrich. *Bering's Voyages: The Reports from Russia*. Translated and edited by Carol Urness. Fairbanks: University of Alaska Press, 1986.

Steller, Georg Wilhelm. *Journal of a Voyage with Bering, 1741–1742*. Edited by Orcutt W. Frost and translated by Margritt A. Engel and Orcutt W. Frost. Stanford, Calif.: Stanford University Press, 1988.

GLYNDWR WILLIAMS

Bernier, Joseph (1852–1934), Canada's greatest sailor, master mariner, and Arctic explorer. Joseph-Elzéar Bernier was born at L'Islet, Quebec, on January 1, 1852, and at age fourteen he left school for the sea. Three years later he was the captain of a timber carrier from Quebec to England. For twenty-five years he was a sailing master in global trades, commanding two hundred ships and crossing the Atlantic 269 times. He knew more about Arctic navigation than any other person of his time, and his three reports on the *Dominion Government Expeditions to the Arctic Islands and Hudson Straits* (1906–1910), published in the Sessional Papers of Canada, are classics of Arctic literature.

In 1895, during a stint as the governor of a Quebec jail, Bernier devised a plan for reaching the North Pole by sea. As international rivalry increased for attaining the pole by sea or over ice, Bernier—answering the wish of the Canadian government's Department of Marine and Fisheries that he reinforce Canada's sovereignty over the region, aid the North West Mounted Police, and provide assistance to mis-

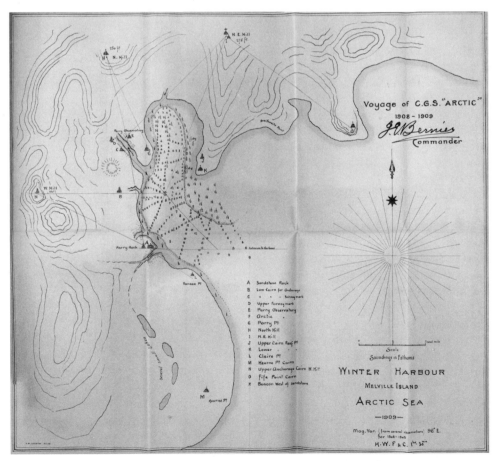

Joseph Bernier. Map of Winter Harbour from the *Report on the Dominion of Canada Government Expedition* (Ottawa, 1910). This elegant little map shows the meticulous way in which Bernier worked. COURTESY THE NEWBERRY LIBRARY, CHICAGO

sionaries in Indian and Inuit missions—sailed CGS (Canadian Government Ship) *Arctic* to the eastern Arctic. He collected dues from whalers and traders. In 1909 he unveiled a plaque on Melville Island that officially claimed the Arctic Islands for Canada. In 1911 he turned to private trading on Baffin Island. Later he commanded a convoy ship in World War I; after the war he returned to Arctic patrols and retired in 1925. He died in Levis, Quebec, on December 26, 1934, his life unheralded and his voyages of discovery scarcely known.

His specific contributions to exploration were made in three voyages. First, in 1906–1907, he took possession of Somerset, Cornwallis, Bathurst, and Byman Martin islands, and then of Melville and Ellington islands. At Beechey Island he discovered and named Moffet and Levasseur inlets. Overland parties explored Milne Inlet. After wintering at Albert Harbor, he sailed east to Baffin Island. Second, in 1908–1909, continuing previous work, he sailed as far west as McClure Strait, where he found ice conditions so good that he believed that he could have accomplished a Northwest Passage by that route if he had wished to. Searchers found relics of the Parry (1819) and Kellett (1852–1854) expeditions, and further travels in 1909 took him to Pond Inlet and Port Burwell, Hudson Strait. Third, in 1910–1911, Bernier found McClure Strait impenetrable, thus closing his authorized attempt at navigating the passage. Surveying land parties also added considerably to geographical knowledge of the Canadian Arctic islands, reinforcing Canada's claims to sovereignty. Scientific gains from all these voyages were considerable.

[*See also* Northwest Passage.]

BIBLIOGRAPHY

Cooke, Alan, and Clive Holland. *The Exploration of Northern Canada, 500 to 1920: A Chronology*. Toronto: The Arctic History Press, 1978.
Fairley, Thomas C., and Charles E. Israel. *The True North: The Story of Captain Joseph Bernier*. New York: St. Martin's, 1957.

BARRY M. GOUGH

Biedma, Manuel de (d. 1687), missionary explorer of Peru. Born in Lima, Biedma entered the Franciscan order in 1658. In 1665 he joined an expedition that followed the Huallaga River northward from Huánuco and then journeyed across the southern Pampas de Sacramento toward the Ucayali River. In 1671, near Huachón south of Huánuco, he struggled eastward across the cordillera to the Huancabamba valley. This route had been pioneered in the 1630s by fellow Franciscans seeking the Cerro de la Sal (near Villa Rica, southeast of Oxapampa), the site of an outcrop of salt where inhabitants of the *selva* (jungle) traditionally congregated. He was keen to delve farther into the jungle beyond the eastern cordillera, and his missionary zeal was intensified by tales of the rich and populous kingdom of Enim. On May 11, 1673, he initiated fresh exploration from Comas (in the province of Jauja), through Andamarca and northeastward toward Mazamari. On the right bank of the Pangoa River he founded the mission of Santa Cruz, and he used Indian labor to clear tracks and build bridges to link it with other missions. In 1674, Biedma followed the Ene River to its confluence with the Perené, and in the mid-1680s, after founding new missions, he pressed on into the Tambo River and down the upper Ucayali toward modern Bolognesi. Returning in July 1687, he was killed by natives who feared assimilation, exploitation, forced labor, and the diseases the missionaries carried. Biedma had reported on his travels to the viceroy of Peru in 1682, awakening an interest in the unknown lands, rivers, and peoples beyond the Andes.

[*See also* Central and South America *and* Franciscans.]

BIBLIOGRAPHY

Biedma, Manuel. *La conquista franciscana del Alto Ucayali*. Edited by Antonino Tibesar. Lima, Peru: Milla Batres, 1981. Includes Biedma's report of his travels and six letters.
Varese, Stefano. *Salt of the Mountain: Campa Asháninka History and Resistance in the Peruvian Jungle*. Translated by Susan Giersbach Rascón. Norman: University of Oklahoma Press, 2002.

PETER T. BRADLEY

Binger, Louis (1856–1936), French explorer and respected colonial administrator in West Africa. Born in Strasbourg on October 15, 1856, Louis-Gustave Binger became, as a young military officer in 1880, a mapmaker in the Casamance region of Senegal. He helped produce the first map of Senegal. In late 1886, the French foreign minister ordered Captain Binger to explore the region between Senegal and the Ivory Coast. His three-year, 2,400-mile (3,862-kilometer) journey began at Dakar in February 1887. He traveled through the great bend of the Niger River and, seeking the source of the Volta River, visited Ouagadougou in July 1888. He completed his trek at Grand Bassam on the Gulf of Guinea in March 1889. As part of his duties, he negotiated four treaties that established French protectorates in the Ivory Coast. Binger's book, *Du Niger au Golfe de Guinée par le pays de Kong et le Mossi* (From the Niger to the Gulf of Guinea, by the Countries of the Kong and the Mossi), proved that he was an instinctive explorer and a remarkable observer. Of considerable interest was his description of the commercial networks that connected the interior Niger River basin with the forest belt to the south.

As a colonial official, Binger was charged in 1891 with establishing the boundary of the Ivory Coast, and between 1893 and 1895 he served as governor of the new colony. In 1897 he was promoted to Director of African Affairs in the Colonial Ministry, and in 1907 he served on the Dahomey-Togo Boundary Commission. His last visit to Africa occurred in 1927. Binger died at L'Isle-Adam, France, on November 10, 1936, and was buried in Paris. His admirers described him as "infatigable et pacifique, le anti-Stanley, savant scrupuleux et curieux de tout."

[*See also* Africa, *subentry on* Exploration.]

BIBLIOGRAPHY
Binger, Louis-Gustave. *Du Niger au Golfe de Guinée par le pays de Kong et le Mossi, par le capitaine Binger (1887–1889)*. 2 vols. Paris: Hachette, 1892.

SANFORD H. BEDERMAN

Bingham, Hiram (1875–1956), American explorer best known for his descriptions of Machu Picchu, Peru, a mid-fifteenth-century Inca site he encountered in July 1911. Bingham undertook his first South American expedition (to Venezuela and Colombia) in 1906, and his continuing interest in the region propelled him to a position as lecturer at Yale University beginning in 1907. At Yale, he met influential contacts who sponsored further forays. The Yale Peruvian expeditions, undertaken between 1911 and 1915, were underwritten in part by the National Geographic Society, which devoted much of the April 1913 issue of its picture magazine to the Machu Picchu accounts. Today, Bingham is less important for what he achieved in exploration itself than for the approach to exploration that he signifies. He was a traditionalist in constructing exploration as an elite enterprise for a privileged few, yet a modernist insofar as his accounts valued images over words, a documentary form that is commonplace today. The papers of the Yale Peruvian expeditions, archived at Yale, reveal Bingham's concern for presenting himself as a scholar-adventurer, and he was the prototype for a form that lives on in the popular imagination. However, such approaches to exploration carry risks, and

> ## The Discovery of Machu Picchu
>
> *Hiram Bingham had the good fortune to stumble upon the astonishing and unknown Inca city of Machu Picchu, high in the Andes Mountains but not far from the well-known city of Cuzco. Bingham's writing style is that of an everyman dazzled by his good fortune at finding a great city, a city that today is a powerful attraction for many tourists.*
>
>
>
> It would make a dull story, full of repetition and superlatives, were I to try to describe the countless terraces, the towering cliffs, the constantly changing panorama, with the jungles in the foreground and glaciers in the lofty background. Even the so-called road got a bit monotonous, although it ran recklessly up and down rock stairways, sometimes cut out of the side of the precipice, at others running on frail bridges propped on brackets against the granite cliffs overhanging the swirling rapids. We made slow progress, but we lived in wonderland.
>
> —Hiram Bingham, "The Discovery of Machu Picchu," *Harper's Magazine*, vol. 126 (1913)

Bingham's legacy shows how concern for telling a good story, coupled with excessive faith in visual impressions, can lead to error. His hypothesis that Machu Picchu represented the ancestral home of the Incas and also the place of their last refuge after the Spanish invasion has long been disproved by scholars.

[*See also* Inca Empire.]

BIBLIOGRAPHY
Bingham, Alfred. *Portrait of an Explorer: Hiram Bingham, Discoverer of Machu Picchu*. Ames: Iowa State University Press, 1989.

ROGER BALM

Bird, Isabella (1831–1904), peripatetic British woman traveler. At the age of seventy, Isabella Bird Bishop undertook a 1,000-mile (1,609-kilometer) ride on horseback across Morocco, from Tangier to Marrakesh, a venture that was quite in character for her. In the fifty years preceding this trip, she had traveled to the far corners of the world and written nine enormously popular books about her experiences. Although less than five feet tall, she undertook daunting physical challenges, from fording flooding rivers on horseback to crossing a high Himalayan

Isabella Bird. "My House in the Rocky Mountains" from *A Lady's Life in the Rocky Mountains* (London, 1885). There is something delightfully domestic about this image, and also some curious features. Could that be a mill-wheel, protruding from the rightmost cabin? COURTESY THE NEWBERRY LIBRARY, CHICAGO

pass at night in a snowstorm, where she sank in drifts up to her shoulders and her wet clothing froze to her. Both the Scottish Geographical Society and London's Royal Geographical Society made her a Fellow of their organization, and she was much in demand as a speaker.

Isabella Bird was born on October 15, 1831, in Yorkshire, England, and died on October 7, 1904, in Edinburgh, Scotland. As her father, Edward Bird, was a clergyman, and her mother, Dora Lawson Bird, was the daughter of a clergyman, she was brought up in a strict and pious household. In 1872, after both of her parents were dead, she began to travel, on doctors' advice, for her health, which was always poor—at least when she was at home in England. Her travels took her to Australia, New Zealand, Hawaii, the United States, Canada, Japan, Malaysia, Korea, India, Kurdestan, Persia, China, and Morocco.

At the age of fifty, Isabella Bird married John Bishop, a physician of long acquaintance, and set-tled into a conventional domestic life. Her husband died after only five years, however, and she resumed her peripatetic lifestyle. Her first five books were written as "Isabella Bird" and the last four, as "Isabella Bird Bishop." She is one of the best known of women travelers today, thanks to her entertaining books, several of which have been republished with updated introductions.

Perhaps the most intriguing aspects of Isabella Bird Bishop are the contradictions that characterized her life. For example, at home in England, she suffered from severe health problems, depression, insomnia, and was even bedridden at times. Indeed, it was on doctors' orders that she took her earliest trips abroad, the doctors believing that fresh air and a change of scenery would benefit her health. Yet when she traveled, she seemed to blossom with energy, stamina, courage, and a joie de vivre. As a Victorian woman, her independence and travel-lust put her outside of society's prescribed role for women;

yet she took care of her ill relatives and established two charity hospitals in India just as a proper Victorian woman should. Although she usually traveled alone, it was not uncommon for her to join up with male travelers she met along the way and to journey with them for a time. But she took great pains to reassure her Victorian peers that she was a proper lady both at home and in the wilds.

[*See also* Women Explorers.]

BIBLIOGRAPHY

Barr, Pat. *A Curious Life for a Lady: The Story of Isabella Bird, A Remarkable Victorian Traveller*. Garden City, N.Y.: Doubleday, 1970.

Bird, Isabella. *A Lady's Life in the Rocky Mountains*. London: Murray, 1879.

PATRICIA GILMARTIN

Biscoe, John (1794–1843), British Antarctic explorer. Biscoe is best known for his Antarctic voyage of 1830–1833 in the brig *Tula* (150 tons) and the cutter *Lively* (82 tons; under the command of Captain George Avery). In these small vessels, Biscoe made the third circumnavigation of Antarctica, after James Cook and Fabian Bellingshausen, discovering icebound Enderby Land—which Biscoe named after his employers, a London whaling and sealing firm owned by the Enderbys—and Graham Land, part of the Antarctic Peninsula.

Biscoe was born at Ponders End, Middlesex, the son of Thomas and Ann Biscoe; he must have named Cape Ann, Enderby Land, after his mother. In March 1812, aged seventeen, Biscoe entered the Royal Navy as a volunteer, reaching the rank of acting-master in 1815 after service in several fighting ships. At the end of the American War, he left the navy to serve in merchant vessels, mostly as mate or master. In 1830, he was appointed by the Enderbys to command the *Tula* on a voyage toward the South Pole in search of new sealing grounds. The *Tula* and the *Lively* were separated off Enderby Land during a fierce gale in March 1831. The ships were happily reunited in Van Diemen's Land (now Tasmania). From Hobart, Biscoe sent dispatches informing the Enderbys of the important discovery of a "very considerable extent of land in a high Southern latitude," land that he believed to be a continent. The voyage continued via New Zealand. In February 1832, off the mountainous and icy west coast of the Antarctic Peninsula, Biscoe sighted both Adelaide Island and what became the Biscoe Islands. He took possession, in the name of King William IV, of what was later called Graham Land, a southern extension of Bransfield's

"Trinity Land" and of "Palmer's Land." The cutter was wrecked at the Falkland Islands on what was subsequently called Lively Island. The crews were so downhearted about the voyage—few seals and no whales having been taken—that nearly all of them deserted. Only four men and three boys sailed *Tula* home across the Atlantic to anchor in the Downs on January 31, 1833.

Accounts of this remarkable voyage were published in the *Journal of the Royal Geographical Society* and in the *Nautical Magazine*. Biscoe received the Royal Premium (later the Gold Medal) of the newly formed Royal Geographical Society. Ill health presumably caused Biscoe to withdraw from the command of another Antarctic voyage sent by the Enderbys, and he appears to have spent his remaining years sailing in warmer latitudes, settling in Hobart with his wife Emma and four children. However, in 1838–1839 he made what was said to have been a voyage of discovery to the south of Australia from Sydney in the brig *Emma*. An appeal in the newspapers of Van Diemen's Land on October 21, 1842, headed by Sir John Franklin—at that time lieutenant governor of the colony of Tasmania—requested donations to allow the incapacitated Captain John Biscoe and his family to return to England. Sadly, Biscoe died as a passenger aboard the barque *Janet Izat* on February 15, 1843, and was buried at sea during the long passage home.

[*See also* Antarctica *and* Whaling.]

BIBLIOGRAPHY

Jones, A. G. E. "John Biscoe (1794–1843)." *Mariner's Mirror 50*, no. 4 (1964): 271–281.

Savours, Ann. "John Biscoe, Master Mariner, 1794–1843." *Polar Record 21*, no. 134 (1983): 485–491.

Savours, Ann. "Three British Seafarers in the Southern Ocean: The Voyages of Captains John Biscoe (1830–33), Henry Foster (1828–31), and James Clark Ross (1839–43)." *In Science and the French and British Navies, 1700–1850*, edited by Pieter van der Merwe, 117–130. London: National Maritime Museum, 2003.

ANN SAVOURS

Bishop, Isabella. *See* **Bird, Isabella.**

Black Legend. The Black Legend ("La Leyenda Negra") portrays the Spanish people as more cruel, greedy, and ignorant than other Europeans. A Spanish journalist, Julián Juderías, coined the term in 1912, but the literature on which it is based dates to the sixteenth and early seventeenth centuries. Spain was at that time Europe's greatest power. The Revolt of the Netherlands, Spain's war with England, and the Thirty Years' War provoked a flood of anti-Spanish propaganda, while Spain's commitment to the Counter-Reformation terrified European Protestants. For more than a century, Dutch, English, and French writers produced scores of books and pamphlets that tried to arouse popular sentiment against Spain and its people. Some of these works were pure fiction, but most drew their inspiration from reports of Spanish atrocities in the Netherlands or, above all, in the conquest of America.

Ironically, much of the material on America came from Spanish sources. The conquest of America provoked a flood of controversial literature unequaled in any other colonial nation. Churchmen like Bartolomé de Las Casas and the Italian Girolamo Benzoni wrote extensively against the mistreatment of Native Americans. Their efforts persuaded the crown to intervene on behalf of the Indians, which in turn created tension between the conquerors and the officials sent by the king to assert royal authority. Official or semi-official histories therefore did nothing to whitewash Spanish behavior. Agustín de Zárate, for example, served in the *audiencia* of Blasco Nuñez Vela and hated Francisco Pizarro, whose crimes he describes with relish in his history of the conquest of Peru. Even the laudatory history of New Spain (Mexico) by Francisco López de Gómara contains stories that could be used by Spain's enemies.

Dutch and English writers discovered these works when they tried to arouse patriotic fervor in their own countries. Las Casas's *Brief Relation of the Destruction of the Indies* (1551), which portrayed the conquest as an unmitigated outrage, was widely translated, beginning with an English version by Thomas Nicholas in 1583. As recently as 1898, a rhetorically enhanced translation appeared in New York as propaganda for the Spanish American War. The writings of Zárate, Gómara, Benzoni, and others had also been translated into several European languages by the end of the sixteenth century and provided further inspiration for the pamphleteers. In Theodor de Bry's *Grand voyages* (Frankfurt, 1617), which concerns the Americas, the Spaniards were shown killing and torturing Indians in ingenious ways. The *Grands voyages* enjoyed wide dissemination.

Protestant fear of Spain inspired John Foxe to add bloodcurdling accounts of the Spanish Inquisition to the 1570 edition of his *Acts and Monuments*, otherwise known as *The Book of Martyrs*. The book went through innumerable editions, and although "the Spanish martyrs" comprised a mere fraction of the work, Foxe's treatment of the Inquisition left an indelible impression on English Protestants. In the Thirty Years' War, Cardinal Richelieu commissioned a series of anti-Spanish pamphlets in support of French intervention in Germany. In England, Oliver Cromwell recycled Elizabethan propaganda when he attacked Hispaniola in 1656. Much later, French writers of the eighteenth century attacked Spain as ignorant and backward because they thought the country as a whole was hostile to the Enlightenment.

This literature, only a small sample of which is mentioned here, encouraged widespread anti-Spanish prejudice in Europe and North America. Textbooks, popular novels, and serious histories often contained unfavorable stereotypes of Spain and the Spanish until the middle of the twentieth century. Since then, a better understanding of Spanish history, the realization that other colonizing powers also behaved badly, and a growing revulsion against ethnic stereotypes has produced a more balanced treatment of Spain and its history.

[*See also* Benzoni, Girolamo; Las Casas, Bartolomé de; *and* Pizarro, Francisco, Gonzalo Pizarro, and Hernando Pizarro.]

BIBLIOGRAPHY

Gibson, Charles. *The Black Legend; Anti-Spanish Attitudes in the Old World and the New*. New York: Knopf, 1971.

Maltby, William S. *The Black Legend in England. The Development of Anti-Spanish Sentiment, 1558–1660*. Durham, N.C.: Duke University Press, 1971.

WILLIAM S. MALTBY

Bodega y Quadra, Juan Francisco de la

(1743–1794), Peruvian-born explorer of the Pacific Northwest coast of America. Juan Francisco de la Bodega y Quadra, born a Creole in Lima, made an important contribution to the exploration of the Pacific Northwest coast. He was known to English contemporaries, and subsequently, as "Quadra." After training as a naval officer in Spain, in 1775 he was posted to San Blas on Mexico's Pacific coast. He made two voyages of exploration northward, primarily to investigate rumors of Russian incursions. On his first voyage, in a tiny, rotting, unaccompanied schooner, he reached 58° N in today's southeastern Alaska and made four Acts of Possession. Scurvy forced his return to San Blas. The viceroy commended his courage and resolution to King Carlos III of Spain. Quadra's second voyage was also intended to intercept the English explorer James Cook, who was understood to be searching for the Northwest Passage, but Quadra did not find him.

After service in Spain and promotion to the senior grade of captain, Quadra returned to San Blas in 1785. He was given responsibility for operations along what was, by then, a coast of international contention. In 1792, appointed as Spain's commissioner to implement a boundary treaty with England, Quadra sailed to the Spanish fort at Nootka to meet his counterpart, George Vancouver.

The two commissioners were unable to reconcile the differences in their instructions, and referred the matter back. Quadra was highly respected by Vancouver and his men, by independent fur traders, and by Maquinna, the local chieftain. He and Vancouver collaborated to compile a cartography of the region. Acknowledging this cooperation, Vancouver designated the island they had jointly revealed as Quadra's and Vancouver's Island. Vancouver's superiors overruled him, however, and dropped Quadra's name from published charts. Bodega y Quadra died in Mexico in 1794.

[See also Vancouver, George.]

BIBLIOGRAPHY
Cook, Warren L. *Flood Tide of Empire: Spain and the Pacific Northwest, 1543–1819*. New Haven, Conn., and London: Yale University Press, 1973.

MICHAEL LAYLAND

Boer War. The Boer, or South African, War began on October 11, 1899, when Boer commandos from the Orange Free State and the Transvaal invaded the Cape Province and Natal. They hoped to incite uprisings among Boer residents—white farmers also known as Afrikaners—in these British dominions and pressure the British into honoring the autonomy of the two Boer republics. The British, calculating a short and low-budget conflict, decided to fight. The ensuing costly and controversial war was effectively a multiethnic civil war. The Boers adopted guerilla warfare, and the British adopted a scorched earth policy, which displaced thousands of people. The British herded women and children into concentration camps, where approximately 28,000 Boers and 14,000 blacks died. Despite deploying 450,000 troops against 50,000 Boer commandos, the British only forced the Boers to surrender by constricting their movement with 8,000 blockhouses and 3,700 miles (5,955 kilometers) of wire-mesh fencing. On May 31, 1902, the British and Boers signed the Treaty of Vereeniging.

The war's causes and consequences are disputed. British-financed diamond and gold mining in Boer territory suggested a capitalist imperial war. While pressure by prominent capitalists surely influenced both sides, for the Boer republics British respect of their sovereignty was paramount. The British wanted to unite South Africa's four white settler societies in a Canadian-style confederation, and by 1910 had unified the Natal, the Cape, the Orange Republic, and the Transvaal as the Union of South Africa. Controversially, many believed the British achieved this end at the expense of the political rights of blacks and "Coloureds," people of mixed white, Asian, and African descent.

BIBLIOGRAPHY
Gooch, John, ed. *The Boer War: Direction, Experience and Image*. London and Portland, Ore.: Cass, 2000.
Smith, Iain R. *The Origins of the South African War, 1899–1902*. London and New York: Longman, 1996.

ELIZABETH MANCKE

Bombay Geographical Society. The Bombay Geographical Society (BGS) was established in April 1831 "for the purpose of encouraging and instituting geographical researches in western Asia and the countries contiguous." Its founding members were from Bombay's European elite, encompassing government officials, naval and military officers, professionals, and merchants. The BGS utilized its close relationship with the Bombay government, which provided rooms for the society and access to official records, especially those of the Bombay Marine (the Indian Navy). In 1832 it became the Bombay branch of the Royal Geographical Society, although this formal affiliation lapsed as the BGS expanded its membership and activities. From 1836, papers presented at its meetings, extracts from government records, and relevant correspondence were published in the *Transactions of the Bombay Geographical Society*, which appeared on a semi-regular basis until 1873. Of particular interest was the publication from the archive of the Bombay Marine of many important hydrographical, topographical, and meteorological surveys of, for example, East Africa, the Persian Gulf, Arabia, the Euphrates, and much of South and East Asia. The BGS also exploited the various reports and memoranda on the flora and fauna, peoples, cultures, and languages of the region. The distribution of the *Transactions* helped the BGS maintain a worldwide network of links with universities, learned institutions, and other geographical societies across India, Europe, North America, and Australasia. The BGS also offered practical assistance to expeditions leaving from India.

Despite publishing significant research and attracting the plaudits of other geographical societies, subscription arrears and attendant factors forced the BGS to merge with the Bombay branch of the Royal Asiatic Society in January 1873. During its relatively brief existence, the society made important contributions to the promotion of geography within India and to the wider understanding of the places and peoples of the subcontinent and beyond.

[*See also* Royal Geographical Society.]

BIBLIOGRAPHY
Transactions of the Bombay Geographical Society. 19 vols. Bombay, 1836–1873.

ROBERT J. BLYTH

Boone, Daniel (1734–1820), American explorer and colonizer. Daniel Boone was the son of Squire Boone, an Englishman who arrived in Pennsylvania in 1717 where he worked as a weaver and blacksmith. In 1720 he married a Welsh Quaker girl and began a large family. Daniel was the sixth of their twelve children. The Boone homestead where Daniel was born, on November 2, 1734, is open to the public under the management of the Pennsylvania Historical Society. Although literate to a degree in adulthood, it appears that as a youth Daniel received little in the way of a formal education. After difficulties with the larger Pennsylvania Quaker community, the Boone family decided to move to the North Carolina frontier when Daniel was sixteen.

As a young hunter and trapper living on the frontier Daniel Boone joined the British forces in the French and Indian War. He barely escaped capture in 1755 when General Braddock was killed and his army routed near present-day Pittsburgh. Back with his family in the following year Daniel married Rebecca Bryan, a neighbor, and went on to father ten children with her. By 1760, as one of an informal frontier group known as "long hunters" from the length of their forays into the wilderness, Daniel Boone began to penetrate and cross the Blue Ridge in pursuit of furs and deer hides. In the eyes of British officialdom this was poaching on land rightly claimed by the Cherokee and other Indian groups as their "hunting grounds." The royal government's policy of protecting the Indian hunting grounds was formalized in the autumn of 1763 when George III issued his famous Proclamation of 1763. Under the proclamation's terms, the king decreed that the watershed of the Appalachian Mountains would mark a western boundary beyond which the American colonists were forbidden to settle.

Some years earlier, however, organized land speculation companies had been forming in the seaboard colonies desirous of expanding their claims into the western lands. By 1750, the Loyal Land Company of Virginia sent a small expedition beyond Virginia's southwestern frontier to locate lands for acquisition. Indian trails and animal traces led them to Cumberland Gap. No records exist of the first "long hunts" that crossed the Gap into Kentucky but it seems certain that they began shortly after its location was reported widely. By the late 1760s Daniel Boone, already a storied "long hunter," made his first trek through Cumberland Gap on his way to Kentucky's rich hunting grounds. Boone's hunts were not particularly profitable and were marred frequently by mishaps, including capture by the Indians. But to Boone the accumulation of pelts and deer hides played a secondary role as he avidly explored the rich lands of Kentucky. In spite of its remoteness and continuing Indian threats Daniel Boone persisted in extending efforts to explore and colonize Kentucky.

In spite of the Proclamation of 1763 and subsequent royal edicts aimed at establishing an Indian boundary confining the colonists to the east of the mountains, a North Carolina group of speculators, known as the Transylvania Land Company, in 1775 purchased twenty million acres between the Cumberland and Kentucky rivers from the Cherokee Indians. It was through his service to the Transylvania Land Company that Daniel Boone was to achieve his now iconic stature as an explorer-colonizer. Boone was placed in charge of the laying out of a road from the present site of Kingsport, Tennessee, through the Cumberland Gap, and on to the Kentucky River. Upon completing the trace he established Boonesboro and returned home to lead his family and others across the mountains to the new settlement in the face of Indian hostilities. A century and a quarter later, the painter George C. Bingham immortalized this event in his heroic painting *Daniel Boone Escorting Settlers Through the Cumberland Gap.*

Earlier, Daniel Boone had been launched on his trajectory as heroic archetypal explorer-colonizer with the publication in 1784 of Kentucky booster John Filson's ghostwritten Boone autobiography, *The Adventures of Colonel Daniel Boone, Formerly A Hunter: Containing A Narrative of the Wars of Kentucky.* The tract lacked historical reliability but was enormously successful, published in numerous editions in America as well as Europe. Doubtlessly influenced as a youth by *Adventures*, James Fenimore

Cooper would pattern his own Leatherstocking frontiersman character, Natty Bumpo, on Daniel Boone. Embodying as it does a paean to the virtues of rugged individualism, Boone's life story was highlighted in Theodore Roosevelt's multivolume *The Winning of the West: From the Alleghenies to the Mississippi 1769–1774*. In the twentieth century Daniel Boone's reputation remained undimmed and was made familiar to millions through Hollywood movies and a long-running television series. In 1992 a major exhibit and companion volume appeared under the title *The Columbus of the Woods: Daniel Boone and the Typology of Manifest Destiny*.

Ever the restless frontiersman-adventurer, in 1799 Daniel Boone led his extended family to Spanish-controlled Missouri. He died in Missouri on September 26, 1820, but in 1845 his remains were reinterred in Kentucky's capital, Frankfort.

[*See also* Pioneer Trails.]

BIBLIOGRAPHY

Boone, Nathan. *My Father, Daniel Boone: The Draper Interviews with Nathan Boone*. Edited by Neal O. Hammon. Lexington: University of Kentucky Press, 1999.

Draper, Lyman C. *The Life of Daniel Boone*. Edited by Ted Franklin Belue. Mechanicsburg, Pa.: Stackpole Books, 1998.

Faragher, John Mack. *Daniel Boone: The Life and Legend of an American Pioneer*. New York: Henry Holt and Company, 1992.

Lofaro, Michael A. *Daniel Boone: An American Life*. Lexington: University of Kentucky Press, 2003.

Louis De Vorsey

Bougainville, Louis-Antoine de (1729–1811),

French explorer of the South Pacific. Bougainville was born in Paris, the son of a lawyer and local administrator with a wide circle of acquaintances among scientists and geographers. His older brother, Jean-Pierre, was particularly interested in early voyages of exploration and was the author of two books on the subject. Louis-Antoine started a military career, serving in Europe and later in French Canada. A gifted mathematician, he published a treaty on the calculus in 1755 and was elected a fellow of the Royal Society of London in the following year.

His interest in navigation and the problem of longitude developed during his crossings of the Atlantic during the Seven Year's War. After the war, he established a settlement on the then uninhabited Falkland Islands. Given the temporary rank of captain, he sailed with the *Aigle* and the *Sphinx* on September 6, 1763, taking with him a number of refugee French Canadian families. He sailed back to France in July 1764, returning to the settlement six months later, going down to the Strait of Magellan, to carry out exploration of this area and obtain supplies.

Protests by Spain, however, resulted in an amicable end to the French settlement. Bougainville sailed from France on November 15, 1766, to surrender the Falklands, and to begin a full circumnavigation in the frigate *Boudeuse*, accompanied by the storeship *Étoile*. The two ships entered the Strait of Magellan at the beginning of December 1767. After two months of arduous navigation, they emerged into the Pacific and briefly searched for land believed to have been sighted by the English buccaneer Edward Davis in 1687. After this, Bougainville discovered several small Polynesian islands and reached Tahiti on April 6, 1768. Unaware that Samuel Wallis had discovered the island a year earlier, he named it New Cythera. The French spent nine days there, greatly impressed by the reception they were given and what they imagined to be an unspoiled Eden. For the return voyage, Bougainville took on board with them a young Tahitian, Ahutoru, whose presence in Paris was to cause a sensation.

Bougainville then sailed on a largely westerly course, through the Samoas and Vanuatu, until the ships reached the outlying reefs of the Great Barrier Reef. He wisely veered north toward New Guinea, then east along a chain of islands he named the Louisiades, and north to the Solomons. The ships were sailing through unknown waters, and their passage is commemorated by the names of Choiseul Island, Bougainville Island, and Bougainville Strait. His stores now badly depleted and his ships in a parlous condition, Bougainville anchored in New Ireland in July 1768, sailed along the island's east coast and on to the Dutch East Indies and Mauritius. There the two ships separated, the *Boudeuse* leaving on December 12 and arriving in Saint Malo on March 16, 1769.

Bougainville came home to an impressive welcome. His transfer into the naval service was formalized by his being given the rank of captain retrospective to June 1763. His account of the voyage, published in 1771, was an instant success. In the second edition of 1772 he modified his views on Tahitian society, but others, including the expedition's naturalist Philibert Commerson, had already predisposed French and indeed European society to see in the island "the above of Natural Man."

Pacific Travels

Bougainville was, for the most part, full of admiration for the appearance and customs of the Tahitians, though one may notice in this passage a subtle hint or two of critical wit. He was intrigued, too, by the plants and creatures of this paradise, and was indeed responsible for introducing to the world of gardeners the lovely plant named after him, the bougainvillea.

All our transactions were carried on in as friendly a manner as possible, if we except thieving. Our people were daily walking in the isle without arms, either quite alone or in little companies. They were invited to enter the houses, where the people gave them to eat; nor did the civility of their landlords stop at a light collation. They offered them young girls; the hut was immediately filled with a curious crowd of men and women, who made a circle round the guest and the young victim of hospitality.

Louis-Antoine de Bougainville, *A Voyage round the World*, translated by John Reinhold Forster (London, 1772)

Bougainville planned other voyages of exploration, including one to the Arctic, but war intervened and his next few years were spent on various campaigns in the West Indies and off the American coast. After the war, he assisted with planning the expeditions of Jean-François de Galaup de La Pérouse and Antoine Raymond Joseph Bruni d'Entrecasteaux. He was promoted to vice admiral in 1792, and elected to the Bureau des Longitudes and the Institut de France. Napoleon appointed him a senator in 1799 and an imperial count in 1808. He died on August 20, 1811, and is buried in the Paris Pantheon.

[*See also* Carteret, Philip; Entrecasteaux, Antoine Raymond Joseph Bruni d'; La Pérouse, J. F. de Galaup de; Pacific; *and* Wallis, Samuel.]

BIBLIOGRAPHY

Dunmore, John. *Storms and Dreams: Louis de Bougainville: Soldier, Explorer, Statesman.* London: Trafalgar Square Publishing, 2005.

Dunmore, John, ed. *The Pacific Journal of Louis-Antoine de Bougainville, 1767–1768.* London: Hakluyt Society, 2002.

Kimbrough, Mary. *Louis-Antoine de Bougainville 1729–1811: A Study in French Naval History and Politics.* Lewiston, N.Y.: The Edwin Mellen Press, 1990.

Martin-Allanic, Jean Etienne. *Bougainville navigateur et les découvertes de son temps.* 2 vols. Paris: Presses Universitaires de France, 1964.

Vibart, Eric. *Tahiti: 1767–1797: naissance d'un paradis au siècle des Lumières.* Brussels: Editions Complexe, 1987.

JOHN DUNMORE

Bouvet de Lozier, Jean-Baptiste Charles

(1706–c. 1787), French explorer of the South Atlantic Ocean. Bouvet de Lozier, an officer in the French East India Company's navy, proposed in 1736 to explore the South Atlantic Ocean in search of a secure refreshment outpost for the ships of the company. Having received the support of Joseph François Dupleix, then a powerful administrator of the company in India, Bouvet de Lozier set forth from Lorient in July 1738 in command of the *Aigle* and the *Marie*, equipped with small boats for coastal survey. His instructions were to survey the Atlantic Ocean and part of the Indian Ocean from latitude 40° S between longitudes 15° W and 30° E and to effect a reconnaissance of the southern lands. He reached the area in December 1738 during the southern summer, encountering blusterous weather, with fog, icebergs, floating seaweed, Antarctic birds, penguins, and seals. Sailing farther south, he sighted on January 1, 1739, what he believed to be a projection of the continent and named it Cape Circumcision.

James Cook received instructions on his second voyage to search for this point, but his reconnaissance down to latitude 60°12′ led him to conclude "that what M. Bouvet took for Land and named Cape Circumcision was nothing but Mountains of Ice surrounded by field Ice" (Beaglehole, p. 71). Bouvet de Lozier had in fact sighted a small island, Bouvetoya, at 54°26′ S and 3°24′ E, which today belongs to Norway.

[*See also* Cook, James.]

BIBLIOGRAPHY

Beaglehole, J. C., ed. *The Journals of Captain James Cook on His Voyages of Discovery: The Voyage of the Resolution and Adventure, 1772–1775.* Cambridge, U.K.: Cambridge University Press for the Hakluyt Society, 1961.

Marchant, Leslie R. *France Australe: The French Search for the Southland.* Perth, Australia: Artlook Books, 1982.

HUGUETTE LY-TIO-FANE PINEO
MADELEINE LY-TIO-FANE

Boyd, Louise Arner (1887–1972), American

Arctic adventurer. Louise Arner Boyd was born on September 16, 1887, into a wealthy, socially prominent San Francisco family. Her father was John Franklin Boyd and her mother, Louise Cook Arner

Boyd. By the time Louise Boyd was thirty-two years old, her two brothers and both of her parents had died, leaving her the sole heir to her father's investment company and the family fortune.

Boyd's contributions to geographic knowledge center on her expeditions to Greenland, Spitsbergen, and Franz Josef Land. Her first two trips to the Arctic regions, in the late 1920s, were not for scientific purposes, however. The first one was a hunting and adventure trip with friends to Franz Josef Land, and the second one was to join the sea search for the lost explorer Roald Amundsen. By the time of this second voyage, she was hooked for life on the arctic regions but wanted to organize future trips around scientific investigations. In 1931, 1933, 1937, and 1938, she mounted expeditions to the east coast of Greenland to explore the Franz Josef–King Oscar fjord region. She and the scientists she took with her photographed, measured, surveyed, and mapped the fjords, glaciers, and topography of the area. They conducted depth soundings on which they based a profile of the floor of the Franz Josef Fjord and a bathymetric map of the Greenland Sea between Norway and East Greenland.

In 1941 Boyd was commissioned by the National Bureau of Standards to head an expedition to the waters between Greenland, Baffin Island, and the coast of Labrador. The expedition was charged with studying conditions in the ionosphere that could affect long-distance radio transmissions. These findings, along with information obtained in her earlier work in the Greenland-Spitsbergen region, proved very valuable to U.S. efforts during World War II.

In her later years, her spirit of adventure still burned, and at age sixty-eight she chartered an airplane to fly her over the North Pole, the first such flight by a woman and the first privately financed polar flight.

Boyd's expeditions to arctic regions were conducted during the summertime. During the rest of the year, she maintained a busy social and civic calendar in the San Francisco area. Always impeccably dressed, she was an important figure in the city's musical, historical, and botanical organizations. She received many honors during her lifetime, including the Cullum Medal of the American Geographical Society and election to the Society of Woman Geographers. She died on September 14, 1972, just before her eighty-fifth birthday, in a San Francisco nursing home.

[See also Amundsen, Roald, and Women Explorers.]

BIBLIOGRAPHY

Boyd, Louise Arner. *The Fiord Region of East Greenland*. New York: American Geographical Society, 1935.

Olds, Elizabeth Fagg. *Women of the Four Winds*. Boston: Houghton Mifflin, 1985. See pp. 231–296.

PATRICIA GILMARTIN

Braun, Wernher von (1912–1977), German rocket scientist. Von Braun was born in Wirsitz in East Prussia (later Wyrzysk, Poland). His father, Magnus Alexander Maximilian Freiherr (Baron) von Braun, and his mother, Emmy von Quistorp, encouraged his early interests in space. Von Braun was enthralled with the idea of exploring outer space. But at school he performed poorly in formal mathematics and in physics until he was able to start applying those subjects to propulsion for space exploration.

In 1930, while studying at the Berlin Institute of Technology, Wernher von Braun joined the spaceflight society Verein für Raumschiffahrt (VfR), assisting Hermann Oberth in liquid-fueled rocket motor development. He began secret German ordnance research on rocket weapons at Kummersdorf, and earned his doctorate in physics from Berlin University in 1934. Kummersdorf operations moved to Peenemünde in northern Germany in 1937, where development of the Vengeance Machine 2 (V-2) ballistic missile accelerated. As for his joining the Nazi party in 1940 and eventually become an SS major, von Braun later asserted that not joining would have forced him to abandon his work on rocketry and that he engaged in no political work for either the Nazi party or the SS; his ultimate motive in building army missiles, he said, was for their use in space science endeavors. These are weak justifications that fail to exonerate him for the deaths that resulted from V-2 attacks or for the slave labor used to produce the V-2s at Mittelwerk, near Nordhausen. Von Braun was aware of the conditions under which prisoners labored, and there is evidence that he recruited slave labor from two concentration camps. Neither he nor the other scientists felt any moral compunction in these matters. For von Braun and his colleagues, the means justified the ends of achieving space travel.

Rather than resign themselves to Russian troops, von Braun and members of the Peenemünde team surrendered to Americans. Through the military operation called Project Paperclip, Secretary of State Cordell Hull approved the transfer of von Braun as one of 118 scientists to the United States, though the families of these scientists remained in Landshut, Germany. Von Braun was installed at Fort Bliss in El Paso, Texas, researching the V-2 at nearby White Sands, New Mexico; in 1950 he was moved to the U.S. Army's Redstone Arsenal near Huntsville, Alabama. In 1953, the launching of the first Redstone rocket at Cape Canaveral in Florida paved the way for the 1961 Mercury capsules. A year after receiving U.S. citizenship in 1955, von Braun launched the Jupiter ballistic missile, which was the basis for the 1958 *Explorer I* satellite, and with that success, von Braun was given authorization to work on the Saturn project. Von Braun was featured on the February 17, 1958, cover of *Time* magazine. For an American society in the middle of a space race, von Braun was in popular demand, receiving high fees for appearances and speeches.

The operations of the Army Ballistic Missile Agency, part of the Redstone Arsenal in Huntsville, transferred on July 1, 1960, to the newly formed National Aeronautics and Space Administration (NASA) and to the renamed George C. Marshall Space Flight Center (MSFC). Legislative action to transfer von Braun and his team to NASA-MSFC was covered in the agenda of the 86th Congress's second session. Von Braun recognized that he relied on the United States government for financial support, just as he had relied on the German government in earlier years. Considered by NASA administrators to be an able engineer and quite conservative under fiscal constraint, von Braun always engendered teamwork and loyalty among his subordinates.

As the first director of the Marshall Space Flight Center (from 1960 to 1970), von Braun worked meticulously. The German team sought to control all aspects of their work by doing as much of it themselves as they could, rather than handing it over to contractors. However, NASA directors and the U.S. Air Force worked hard to contract out the bulk of NASA's work in order to build up the capabilities of the U.S. aerospace industry, hoping to achieve President John F. Kennedy's goal of a manned mission to the moon by the end of the 1960s. The Saturn project, from its first launch in 1961, enjoyed unprecedented favor from 1967 to 1975. After the *Apollo 17* mission, the U.S. abandoned the lunar landing program, and *Saturn V* never flew again. However, on July 22, 1969, with *Apollo 11* returning to earth, NASA authorized von Braun to work on the Apollo Applications Program, which later took the name "Skylab."

In 1970, Alexander P. Butterfield, deputy assistant to President Nixon, received an allegation of impropriety against von Braun about von Braun's past Nazi membership. Nothing came of it. Documentation of the alleged impropriety remains classified by the FBI, even though Army Intelligence declassified records on von Braun on November 27, 1985.

In the 1970s, with a tightened NASA budget, members of the so-called German team, not being American veterans, were either released from their jobs, took lesser jobs within NASA, or retired. With the space shuttle design in question, the Mars expedition and space station delayed, increasing dissatisfaction with the lack of consideration of the scientists' viewpoint in decision making, the lack of a quick and flexible challenge-and-response capability, and détente with the Soviet Union, von Braun resigned his position as Deputy Associate Administrator for Planning at NASA Headquarters in Washington on June 10, 1972. In fact, he left government service altogether for private sector work at Fairchild Industries in Germantown, Maryland. He later directed the National Space Association, which was formed in June 1974.

On July 15, 1975, von Braun returned to watch the Kennedy Space Center launching of the Apollo-Soyuz test program. It is a mark of von Braun's success that no *Saturn* booster ever exploded on the launch pad, none failed in flight, and none to complete its planned flight mission. In early 1977, President Gerald R. Ford awarded the National Medal of Science to von Braun, who, on June 16, 1977, died quietly in a hospital in Alexandria, Virginia.

[*See also Apollo/Saturn* Launch Vehicle; Skylab; *and* Space Program, *subentry* American.]

BIBLIOGRAPHY

Hunley, J. D., ed. *The Birth of NASA: The Diary of T. Keith Glennan. NASA SP-4105.* Washington, D.C.: The National Aeronautics and Space Administration, 1993.

Neufeld, Michael J. *The Rocket and the Reich: Peenemünde and the Coming of the Ballistic Missile Era.* Cambridge, Mass.: Harvard University Press, 1996.

Piszkiewicz, Dennis. *Wernher Von Braun: The Man Who Sold the Moon.* Westport, Conn.: Praeger, 1998.

ALBERT P. NOUS

Brazza, Pierre Savorgnan di (1852–1905),

explorer, colonialist, and founder of the French Congo. Brazza was born Pietro Paulo Francesco Camillo Savorgnan di Brazza on January 25, 1852, into an aristocratic family in Rome. Seeking a naval career not available in his homeland, Brazza trained at the French school for naval cadets at Brest. Brazza briefly served in the Franco-Prussian war in 1870 and afterward joined the South Atlantic fleet. While serving aboard the *Venus*, he frequently came to port at the French colony of Gabon. At this time, France's sovereignty did not effectively extend beyond the coast and estuary near Libreville. Inland, exploration of the Ogowe River—the largest Atlantic drainage between the Niger and the Congo—was in its earliest stages. The river's source, its relationship to the African Great Lakes and the Congo River, and the nature of the people inhabiting its upper course were all unknown. At age twenty-two, after encountering the Frenchmen Alfred Marche and Marquis de Compiègne freshly returned from their pioneering voyage up the Ogowe, Brazza became determined to undertake an exploratory mission up the river himself. Returning to France, he was successful in obtaining approval and a modest ten thousand French francs for the mission, as well as obtaining French citizenship.

In January 1876, on the first of what would be three Ogowe voyages, Brazza headed upriver from Lambaréné with three Frenchmen (including Marche) and ten Senegalese soldiers in nine canoes manned by natives. The expedition's small size, light armament, unhurried pace, and preference for trade and negotiation over force was unconventional for its time, but won the trust of native chiefs along the river. Brazza liberated enslaved Africans where he encountered them. The party reached the confluence of the Passa and Ogowe rivers in July 1877. At this point Brazza realized that the Ogowe was not the hoped-for riverine shortcut to larger central African watersheds. Brazza's party continued east overland to the first eastward-flowing river, the Alima, where they purchased canoes from natives. Travel down this river was interrupted by the hostile Apfourus, and in August 1878 the barefoot and nearly starving men were obliged to retrace their route back to the Gabon coast.

In 1880 the scramble for Africa was on, and Brazza returned to the Ogowe in order to make a territorial claim for France in the Stanley Pool region of the Congo River ahead of his rival Henry Morton Stanley, then in the employ of King Leopold II of Belgium. Facilitated by the good relations he had established with the natives on the previous expedition, Brazza was able to advance quickly up the Ogowe and founded the post of Franceville at the confluence with the Passa in June 1880. Again heading east on foot, but this time skirting the troublesome Apfourus, Brazza reached the north shore of

Stanley Pool and on September 10, 1880, obtained the signature of Makoko, the chief king of the Tékés, granting sovereignty of the region to France. The post established here would become Brazzaville. On his voyage to the coast via the Congo, Brazza famously met Stanley at Vivi.

To further solidify France's claim to lands north and west of the Congo's right bank, Brazza launched a third, larger expedition (1883–1885) in which he consolidated trade on the Ogowe and secured treaties in the Kouilou-Niari basin and Loango coast, north of the Congo's mouth. Brazza's efforts led to France's acquisition, at the Berlin Conference of 1884, of the territories that are now Gabon and the Republic of Congo. As commissioner general of the French Congo from 1887 until his recall in 1896, Brazza linked these territories with Oubangi-Chari and Chad, all of which would be reorganized into French Equatorial Africa in 1910. In 1905, Brazza returned to the colony from retirement to investigate charges of widespread abuse of African laborers under the French concessionary system implemented after his departure. Brazza died on the return trip to France, on September 14, 1905, in Dakar, Senegal. Accused during his lifetime of being a "negrophile" more concerned with improving Africans' well-being than the profitability of France's colony, Brazza's unique legacy as a humane and benevolent colonialist is reflected in Brazzaville's retention of his name to this day.

[*See also* Africa; Compiègne, Marquis de; Imperialism and Exploration; Marche, Alfred; *and* Stanley, Henry.]

BIBLIOGRAPHY

West, Richard. *Brazza of the Congo: European Exploration and Exploitation in French Equatorial Africa*. London: Cape, 1972.

JOHN P. SULLIVAN

Brendan, Saint (c. 486–c. 575), prominent Irish monk who, during the last seven years of his life, supposedly sailed throughout the North Atlantic and possibly visited America along the way. Known also as Saint Brendan the Navigator, his voyage made him one of the greatest, or at least the most legendary, travelers of the early Middle Ages.

The story of Saint Brendan's legendary seven-year voyage comes from the *Navigatio Sancti Brendani*. This medieval story-manuscript book was probably written by an Irish monk living in the Low Countries or the Rhineland about 870 or shortly thereafter.

Scholars do not consider the *Navigatio* to be a genuine biographical account of Saint Brendan's life. In many ways it is a religious version of the *immrama*, traditional Celtic sea-journey tales.

After hearing a tale about the utopian Land of Promise of the Saints across the western ocean, Saint Brendan decided to visit this paradise himself and invited fourteen of his monks to accompany him. The monks agreed, and a curragch (coracle) was constructed to make the journey. Saint Brendan's party sailed around the North Atlantic, visiting volcanic Iceland, the Sargasso Sea, a variety of islands—including one that turned out to be a sleeping giant fish—[see color plate 17 in this volume] and finally the vast Land of Promise of the Saints, which some commentators have identified as North America. Saint Brendan then returned to his monastery, where he died the dignified death that befitted a saintly Christian monk. No one seriously believes that Saint Brendan literally made the entire journey described in the *Navigatio*. Some scholars believe, however, that the *Navigatio* is an imaginative tale that is a composite of early medieval Irish geographical knowledge as well as speculation, myth, and legend. Separating out which component of the *Navigatio* belongs to which category is difficult and sometimes impossible.

[*See also* Fictitious and Fantastic Places *and* North America, *subentry on* Apocryphal Discoveries and Imaginary Places (pre-1500).]

BIBLIOGRAPHY
Farmer, D. H., ed. *The Age of Bede*. Harmondsworth, U.K.: Penguin, 1965. Rev. ed. 1988.
Severin, Tim. *The Brendan Voyage*. New York: McGraw-Hill, 1978.

RONALD H. FRITZE

Brieva, Domingo de, missionary explorer. A lay member of the Franciscan order, Brieva participated in hazardous expeditions of evangelization and pacification traveling northeastward from Quito (Ecuador). In 1633 and 1635 he followed the San Miguel River across the province of Sucumbíos to the Putumayo, but was twice forced back to Quito. Leaving for a third time on December 29, 1635, Brieva and his companions now explored in the region of the rivers Aguarico and Napo. On this occasion, instead of returning to Quito when attacked, Brieva and a fellow Franciscan, Andrés de Toledo, descended the Napo to its confluence with the Amazon accompanied by six soldiers, the latter enticed by stories of El Dorado rather than by missionary zeal. Setting

out in a single canoe on October 17, 1636, and reliant on the goodwill of the native population for food, they reached the Portuguese fort of Gurupá in the Amazon delta on February 5, 1637. From there they continued by canoe to Belém and then São Luís do Maranhão. Here the Portuguese governor immediately organized the expedition of Pedro de Teixeira, with Brieva as its guide, which successfully retraced his voyage upriver. In 1639, Brieva accompanied Teixeira downriver from Quito.

Brieva's voyages demonstrated the navigability of the Amazon despite its daunting environment, established a link overland and by river from the Amazon to Quito, encouraged investigation of the practicality of communication with the Andes Mountains from the Atlantic coast, and contributed to the reshaping of the region's political geography by stimulating Portuguese colonial expansion upriver.

[*See also* Amazon River; El Dorado; Franciscans; *and* Teixeira, Pedro de.]

BIBLIOGRAPHY
Smith, Anthony. *Explorers of the Amazon*. Chicago and London: University of Chicago Press, 1994.

PETER T. BRADLEY

Bristol Voyages. The question of whether ships sailing from Bristol reached America before Christopher Columbus's celebrated voyage of 1492 has long exercised historians. The evidence is indirect but intriguing. For much of the fifteenth century, ships from Bristol, as well as from other English ports, had fished and traded in the waters off Iceland and in the northwest Atlantic more generally. As Danish competition in the area increased, Bristol merchants searched for new fishing grounds farther west. By 1480 they had portolan charts that showed islands far out into the Atlantic, the largest called (confusingly) "Brasile." It is possible that such charts were obtained from Columbus, whose first long-distance voyage, to Iceland in 1477, seems to have been made in a Bristol ship.

The first voyage to search for the new island or islands of which we have definite knowledge was that of John Lloyd, who sailed from Bristol in 1480. He was at sea for nine weeks but discovered no land before storms drove him back to a port in Ireland. In 1481 two ships left Bristol "to search and find a certain isle called the Isle of Brasile," and because this reference comes from late in the year the presumption is that they returned to port safely; no other information exists as to the expedition's success or otherwise.

The next known English exploration foray into the Atlantic was that of John Cabot in 1497, who discovered land across the northern Atlantic somewhere in the region of Cape Breton, but it came five years after Columbus's voyage. However, in July 1498, Pedro de Ayala, the Spanish envoy in London, seemed to show that Cabot's voyage was part of a continuing process when he asserted that in each of the previous seven years several ships from Bristol had been sent out on Atlantic discovery. That no other evidence existed of this large-scale activity weakened the credibility of the envoy's report until the discovery in 1955 of a letter describing Cabot's 1497 voyage. Written in December 1497 or January 1498 by John Day, an English merchant living in Spain and involved in trade with Bristol, the letter was addressed to the *Almirante Major* (Grand Admiral), usually assumed to be Columbus. In it, Day located Cabot's landfall across the Atlantic as a cape 1,800 miles (2,900 kilometers) west of Dursey Head in Ireland. Then, in a sentence laden with dramatic implications, Day continued: "It is considered certain that the cape of the said land was found and discovered in the past by the men from Bristol as your Lordship well knows." Two phrases have gripped the attention of scholars. Whether "in the past" (*en otros tiempos*) refers to a discovery fairly close to the date of the letter, perhaps one associated with the voyages mentioned by Ayala, or to a discovery more distant in time, possibly the elusive voyage of 1481, is not clear. If the latter, then it would seem that "your Lordship" (Columbus) might have heard of a successful Bristol voyage before he sailed in 1492. This would put his own voyage in a different perspective, but the evidence for a pre-Columbian discovery of America by Bristol voyagers remains tantalizingly fragmentary.

[*See also* Cabot, John; Columbus, Christopher; *and* North America, *subentry on* Apocryphal Discoveries and Imaginary Places (pre-1500).]

BIBLIOGRAPHY

Quinn, David B. *England and the Discovery of America, 1481–1620*. London: Allen & Unwin, 1974.

GLYNDWR WILLIAMS

Brosses, Charles de (1709–1777), French magistrate and president of the Burgundian local assembly or *parlement*. A leading member of the Dijon Academy, Brosses was a typical representative of the Enlightenment. His interests ranged widely, from the history of Rome in the seventh century to the origin of language. His father, whose particular interest was geography, owned a large library of reference works. Brosses himself was a shareholder of the French India Company, an investment that naturally turned his thoughts toward distant and little-known regions.

Lettre sur le progrès des sciences, originally addressed to Frederick the Great of Prussia and made available as a pamphlet, was read at the Dijon Academy. It drew attention to the unexplored parts of the Southern Hemisphere, and spurred Brosses into writing a history of what had been explored so far, in the hope of stimulating French interest. Collections of voyages had already been published, but he decided to concentrate on the Pacific Ocean and to draw on original accounts, rejecting the secondhand versions found in earlier collections.

His *Histoire des navigations aux Terres Australes* was published in 1756 and became widely influential. It was translated into German and into English, although the latter translation, John Callander's *Terra Australis Cognita* (1768), was more of an adaptation, aiming to put the case for British, as against French, exploration. The originality of Brosses's work and his respect for his sources were, however, recognized by such men as Alexander Dalrymple, who became his lifelong friend.

Brosses's *Histoire* clearly shows the influence of Pierre-Louis Moreau de Maupertuis's original *Lettre* on the need for and advantages of southern exploration. The actual voyages, presented in chronological order, are encased between a lengthy essay on the benefits to be gained from discoveries and a plan for a voyage of exploration and a trading settlement. In these two discursive sections, Brosses shows himself to be a firm believer in the equilibrium theory, which required the presence of a large landmass in the Southern Hemisphere to keep the globe on an even keel, and favors New Britain, praised by Jacob Roggeveen and William Dampier, as a base for exploration. He divided the southern seas into three broad sections: Magellanica, Polynesia, and Melanesia—the latter two remaining in current use.

Brosses's influence was undeniable and lasting. Louis-Antoine de Bougainville in particular respected his work, and through Dalrymple, Brosses was indirectly influential on British attitudes and voyages of exploration.

[*See also Terra Australis Incognita and biographical entries on figures mentioned in this article.*]

BIBLIOGRAPHY

Brosses, Charles de. *Histoire des navigations aux Terres Australes.* 2 vols. Paris: Durand, 1756.

Callander, John. *Terra Australis Cognita, or Voyages to the Terra Australis or Southern Hemisphere during the Sixteenth, Seventeenth, and Eighteenth Centuries.* 5 vols. London, printed for the author, 1766–1768.

Taylor, Alan Carey. *Le président de Brosses et l'Australie.* Paris: Boivin, 1937.

JOHN DUNMORE

Bruce, James (1730–1794), British explorer of the Blue Nile and Ethiopia. In the course of a series of adventurous travels in Ethiopia, James Bruce reached the source of the Blue Nile in 1770. His reputation has nevertheless been somewhat uncertain. Although he was well received in France on his return to Europe, critics in England, led by Dr. Samuel Johnson, questioned his veracity, ridiculed his pomposity, and pointed out that his "discovery" of the source had been anticipated by the Jesuit priest Pedro Paez in 1618. Even though he was elected to the Royal Geographic Society, Bruce's considerable achievements as a scientific explorer have tended to be forgotten because of the attacks on him and because of the way he ultimately wrote up his travels. In fact, he brought back accurate astronomical and meteorological observations, data on plants and animals, as well as the more obvious wealth of information on the history of the Ethiopian Empire and its Christian church and a unique account of Ethiopian society, into which he seems to have integrated himself in a quite remarkable way.

James Bruce. "Lynx" from *Travels to Discover the Source of the Nile* (5 vols., Edinburgh, 1790). This beautifully detailed image reminds us that by the end of the eighteenth century, European artists and engravers were beginning to be able to produce striking likenesses of strange beasts. COURTESY THE NEWBERRY LIBRARY, CHICAGO

Report on the Source of the Nile

The writings of James Bruce arouse a certain skepticism, for he is quite capable of the most lurid passages. He also has a certain folksiness about his style, as in this extract, which rather accurately describes the stages leading to heatstroke and death.

I call it *hot*, when a man sweats at rest, and excessively on moderate motion. I call it *very hot*, when a man with thin or little clothing, sweats much, though at rest. I call it *excessive hot*, when a man in his shirt, at rest, sweats excessively, when all motion is painful, and the knees feel feeble, as after a fever. I call it *extreme hot*, when the strength fails, a disposition to faint comes on, a straitness is found around the temples, as if a small cord were drawn around the head, the voice impaired, the skin dry, and the head seems more than ordinary large and light. This, I apprehend, denotes death at hand.

—James Bruce, *Travels to Discover the Source of the Nile* (Edinburgh, 1790)

Born at Kinnaird in Scotland on December 14, 1730, Bruce was sent to Harrow School and attempted various careers before marriage into a wine-importing family led him to travel in Spain and Portugal, ostensibly "to inspect the vintages." Lord Halifax was impressed by some of his views on war and diplomacy in the Mediterranean and made him British Consul in Algiers, a post he held from 1763 to 1765. He soon turned to drawing historic remains with the help of Luigi Balugani, and he began to learn Arabic and Ge'ez while his journeys ranged wider and his ambition became to reach the source of the Nile. Travels in North Africa, Crete, and Syria were followed by his entering Egypt, in July 1768, where he prepared for a journey to Ethiopia. After visiting various points on the Arabian coast, he crossed to the western coast of the Red Sea, landed at Massawa in September 1769, and by November had set off for the interior making the arduous ascent to the Ethiopian plateau. It was near the ancient capital of Axum that he first saw the phenomenon of steak being cut from a living cow, which was to lead to his being called a liar on his return to Britain. By February 1770 Bruce had reached Gondar in Tigre. Already able, he claimed, to converse in the Tigre language, he became immersed in the complex and often bloody politics of Ethiopia, allying himself with Ras Michael of Tigre, whose ambition was to dominate the whole empire through the control of a puppet emperor. To maintain his position, Bruce relied on a very close relationship with the ruler's wife, the beautiful Ozoro Esther. Although he constantly had to counter the accusation made by powerful churchmen that he was a (Roman Catholic) "Frank," Bruce more generally gained prestige by his physical exploits such as shooting a bird while riding on horseback or firing a tallow candle through a wooden table, and perhaps also as a result of his sexual conquests. Yet it was probably his confident dispensing of medical advice that brought him most acceptance by both men and women. It is notable that Bruce was prepared to give proper respect to constituted authority and appears to have acted on what he claimed he believed—that men are all brethren if not all equal.

An expedition against one of Ras Michael's enemies enabled Bruce to travel south from Gondar to the eastern shores of Lake Tana and in May 1770 to reach the falls at Alata (Tisisat) near the point where the Blue Nile issues from the lake. Although this was the effective source of the Blue Nile, he accepted the Ethiopian information that a small southern feeder of the lake that rose from a fountain at Geesh could be seen to send its waters through the lake to the Nile. It took a second journey, on this occasion in company with a band of Oromo (Galla) soldiers, for Bruce to reach Geesh and the fountain on November 14, 1770, and claim that he stood on the spot "which had baffled the genius, industry and inquiry of both ancients and moderns, for the course of near three thousand years." This bombast may be balanced against the fact that Bruce succeeded in making astronomical observations to produce a latitude and even a remarkably accurate longitude for the spot. Bruce returned to Gondar traveling along the western shores of Lake Tana.

Following further battles and intrigues, Bruce left Gondar in December 1771, not by the comparatively short and easy route to the coast, but north westward to Teawa and the Blue Nile, which, in April 1772, he rejoined at Sennar. Here he was delayed for some months, but by September he had reached the junction of the Blue with the White Nile and, continuing north, avoided the loop in the Nile by making an extremely hazardous crossing of the Nubian Desert to Aswan, which he reached at the end of November 1772. Soon afterward he returned to Cairo but delayed his return to Britain until late in 1774.

Greatly upset by his reception in London, he retreated to Kinnaird in a state of great indignation, and it was only after the death of his second wife that he began serious work on the record of his travels. Five magnificent but confusing volumes appeared in 1790. These undoubtedly contain some imaginary material, and Balugani, who had died in Ethiopia, is not properly acknowledged for the excellent illustrations, but the basic story gives a true record of Bruce's extensive journeys and his insight into the manners and customs of the Ethiopians. Bruce died from a fall at Kinnaird on April 27, 1794, his reputation still in doubt. However, second and third editions of the *Travels* in 1804–1805 and 1813, skillfully edited by Alexander Murray on the basis of the traveler's own notes, did much to confirm that James Bruce had indeed made a very notable contribution to what he himself called "the noblest of all occupations, that of exploring distant parts of the Globe."

[*See also* Ethiopia *and* Nile River.]

BIBLIOGRAPHY

Beckingham, C. F., ed. *Travels to Discover the Source of the Nile by James Bruce.* Edinburgh: Edinburgh University Press, 1964.

Bredin, Miles. *The Pale Abyssinian: A Life of James Bruce, African Explorer and Adventurer.* London: HarperCollins, 2000.

Bruce, James. *Travels to Discover the Source of the Nile, in the Years 1768, 1769, 1770, 1771, 1772 and 1773.* 5 vols. Edinburgh: Ruthven; and London: G. G. J. and J. Robinson, 1790. 2nd ed., edited by A. Murray, 8 vols. Edinburgh: Constable, 1804–1805. 3rd ed., 8 vols. Edinburgh: Constable, 1813.

Head, F. B. *The Life of Bruce, the African Traveller.* London: J. Murray, 1830.

Reid, J. M. *Traveller Extraordinary: the Life of James Bruce of Kinnaird.* London: Eyre and Spottiswoode; New York: Norton, 1968.

ROY BRIDGES

Brussels Geographical Conference.

The Brussels Geographical Conference, which took place on September 12–14, 1876, was called by King Leopold II of Belgium to discuss future activity by Europeans in Africa. Many historians see the conference as the effective beginning of the "Scramble for Africa." Especially in view of the emergence of Leopold's Congo Free State, much attention has been paid to the king's possible motives. Was he using the testimony of experts on Africa he invited to Brussels as a cloak of scientific respectability for his much less worthy imperialistic ambitions? An overemphasis on issues such as these, important as they are, may serve to conceal the significance of the conference itself in the context of the exploration of Africa.

Leopold had invited explorers and leaders of geographical societies from Britain, France, Germany, Italy, and Austria-Hungary. Five other minor powers were represented but not Portugal, no doubt because it had territorial claims on much of the central belt of Africa, which was the king's main concern. Nor was any African polity, even Egypt, represented. Most significant among the delegates were those with practical experience of traveling in Africa, Lux from Austria, Henri Duveyrier and the Marquis de Compiègne from France, Gerhard Rohlfs, Gustav Nachtigal, and Georg Schweinfurth from Germany, and James Augustus Grant and Verney Lovett Cameron from Britain (with Samuel Baker invited but unable to attend). These men and the geographical society officials who had been following African developments closely constituted a source of expertise derived from supposedly disinterested scientific explorations that had taken place in the previous twenty years or so. This expertise could be tapped in order to provide recommendations for a program of future activities.

There is no doubt that Leopold and his aides directed discussions in such a way as to ensure the sort of outcome he wanted. No doubt, too, delegates found it flattering to have their expertise validated, as it were, by the king's interest. Nevertheless, the African experts did very broadly agree on a set of propositions that could be said to have emerged from their testimonies. It is worth noting in passing that the observations they recorded did not always justify the conclusions they thought they could draw from them. However that may be, in 1876, what the experts thought was apparent about Africa may perhaps be summed up as follows. Firstly, a turning point had been reached because the basic exploration to establish at least the continent's main features had been completed. Secondly, the central belt of Africa was immensely rich in natural resources. However, and this was the third point, the indigenous inhabitants were incapable of developing these resources either because of their basic incapacity or because they were oppressed by slave traders. Hence, fourthly, there was a demonstrable need for European intervention. Most of the explorers seemed to judge, fifthly, that Africans would welcome this intervention. Cameron, who was especially influential with the king, believed that Africans would flock to the European-managed scientific stations that were contemplated, seeing them as centers of order and advance.

What were the problems? Clearly Leopold's initiative was designed to prevent the danger of European rivalries. In Africa itself, the major impediment, all explorers agreed, was the difficulty of access to the interior; transport facilities would be essential. Steamboats could ply on the splendid lakes the explorers had discovered in the center of the continent, but the great task was to open up routes to these lakes along which road or rail vehicles could run. The actual work of the Brussels Geographical Conference was thus to work out where the "stations" should be established and what the most advantageous routes between them would be. A committee of the British, French, and Italians produced a scheme for an east-west route with important branches to key centers while the Austrians, Russians, and Germans suggested a more modest version with just the main route and about four stations along it. The latter idea is essentially what was agreed upon. National committees in participating countries would be set up to commission travelers to open up parts of the routes and establish the stations and man them with scientists while an international association would coordinate the efforts.

All this, as Sanford Bederman puts it, was a charade: the machinery never worked to promote cooperation. Moreover, governments, and not least the British, became suspicious of the venture fearing their geographers would lead them into difficulties over jurisdiction in Africa and over international relations. Yet one element of the machinery did work. National committees did emerge although they competed rather than cooperated. Leopold's own Belgian committee hired Henry Stanley, of the British Royal Geographical Society, although the society withdrew from the international association and set up the African Exploration Fund, which launched Joseph Thomson as an explorer; France produced Pierre Savorgnan di Brazza and the Germans a number of imperially minded travelers. The Portuguese were now stung to activity and the travels of Alejandro Serpa Pinto resulted. These new expeditions and many other initiatives by missionaries, traders, and governments resulted. Truly, Leopold's Brussels Geographical Conference had had a catalytic effect: the work of the explorers had been focused to provide the basis for a series of profound historical changes.

[*See also biographical entries on figures mentioned in this article.*]

BIBLIOGRAPHY

Bederman, Sanford. "The 1876 Brussels Geographical Conference and the Charade of European Cooperation in African Exploration." *Terrae Incognitae* 21 (1989): 63–73.

Bridges, Roy C. "The First Conference of Experts on Africa." In *Experts in Africa*, edited by J. C. Stone. Aberdeen Scotland: Aberdeen University African Studies Group, 1980.

Bridges, R. C. "The RGS and the African Exploration Fund 1876–80." *Geographical Journal* 129 (1963): 25–35

Roeykens, A. *Léopold II et la Conférence Géographique de Bruxelles 1876*. Brussels: Académie Royale des Sciences Coloniales, 1956.

ROY BRIDGES

Bry, Theodor de (1528–1598), early editor and publisher of travel accounts. Theodor de Bry was born at Liège in 1528, but having become a Protestant he found the southern Netherlands inhospitable and moved to Strasbourg in 1570. In 1586, de Bry visited England for three years, returning to live in Frankfurt until he died in 1598. He followed a number of careers—goldsmith, publisher, engraver, and bookseller—and while in England perhaps met Richard Hakluyt; de Bry certainly then agreed to publish an account of the English colony in Virginia. He was then already in his sixties, but this publication was the first of a great many others, in which he and his successors published at Frankfurt the travel accounts of many of the explorers of his day: José de Acosta, Girolamo Benzoni, John Harriott, Antonio de Herrera, René de Laudonnière, Jean de Léry, and so on. In a way, de Bry performed for travel accounts the same service that Ortelius performed for maps: he gathered the best of them together, whether they were manuscript or already printed, and produced them in a uniform format. The series went on long after de Bry's death, eventually consisting of thirteen parts, the last published in 1634. The bibliography of these volumes, which are in various languages, is complicated, but booksellers now generally distinguish between the *Grands voyages*, concerning the Americas, and the *Petits voyages*, dealing with Africa and the East Indies. De Bry became famous not only for his texts, but also for the images that accompanied them. Our plate shows one of these; the French explorer Laudonnière, arriving in Florida in 1564, is being shown by the local chief Athore the stele left

Theodor de Bry. Laudonnière and Chief Athore with the column erected by Ribaut, from the *Grands voyages* (Frankfurt, 1590–1634). This famous engraving by de Bry is one for which we have the watercolor original; a comparison of these image types shows that what de Bry gained in public accessibility, he lost in delicacy of representation. COURTESY THE NEWBERRY LIBRARY, CHICAGO

two years earlier by the French explorer Ribaut. Much of this image is entirely convincing, from the vegetables to the stele to the way in which Laudonnière is clearly punier than his well-nourished Indian host; it was probably generated from a watercolor by Jacques LeMoyne de Morgues.

De Bry's images have often inspired comment, sometimes unfavorable. Some historians have noted that de Bry spared no occasion to show the Spaniards in a bad light, thus contributing to the Black Legend. Others have analyzed his somewhat erratic portrayal of women, while some anthropologists have demonstrated that de Bry is undoubtedly inaccurate in some details. There is, moreover, no denying that his prints translate only in a rather coarse way original watercolors that were often precise and delicate. Nevertheless, de Bry's massive collection of texts and images remains one of our best sources of information concerning early European contact with the peoples of the Americas.

[*See also* Black Legend; Exploration Texts; *and* Imagery of Exploration.]

BIBLIOGRAPHY
Alexander, Michael, ed. *Discovering the New World, Based on the Works of Theodor de Bry*. New York: Harper and Row, 1976.
Bucher, Bernadette. *Icon and Conquest: A Structural Analysis of the Illustrations of de Bry's Great Voyages*. Translated by Basia Miller Gulati. Chicago: University of Chicago Press, 1981.
Hulton, Paul. *America 1585: The Complete Drawings of John White*. London: British Museum Publications, 1984.

DAVID BUISSERET

Buache, Philippe (1700–1773), French cartographer and the author of controversial geographical ideas. Buache was born in Paris and studied mathematics and architecture. After he met Guillaume Delisle (1675–1726), he gave up architecture for cartography. He came to know well Delisle's working method, which resembled that of historians. Buache was at first employed by the "Dépôt des plans, cartes et journaux de la Marine" (French Naval Cartographic Archives), which had been set up in 1720; here he came to know the earth's oceans, and to understand the need for accurate charts, particularly of the areas of French presence. Buache married Delisle's daughter in 1729, the year that he was appointed "premier géographe du roi" (first royal geographer). Then, in 1737, he left the Dépôt de la Marine and set himself up privately in Paris. At first his house was on the right bank of the Seine, but in 1745 he moved to the Ile de la Cité, in the central part of Paris; here he edited his father-in-law's work.

In 1730, the year that he was named geographer to the Académie Royale des Sciences, Buache presented the academy with a manuscript map of the Gulf of Mexico and the West Indian islands to replace the old map of the Dutchman Pieter Goos (1615–1675), and in 1740 he published this new map, incorporating material from Henry Popple's great map of 1733. In 1736, Buache corrected the longitudes provided by the same English source for the southern coasts of Newfoundland and for Ile Royale and the Grand-Banc, and five years later he published this map, carefully marking on it his corrections to Popple. To complete his documentation, Buache followed the voyages of exploration carefully. One such was the venture of Jean-Baptiste Lozier-Bouvet (1705–1786) to the South Seas; Buache drew a map of this in 1739 and called it *Carte des terres australes . . . où se voyent les nouvelles découvertes faites en 1739 au sud du Cap de Bonne Espérance* (A Map of the Southern Seas . . . to Show the New Discoveries Made in 1739 to the South of the Cape of Good Hope). In an edition of 1754, he added his own ideas about the Antarctic lands, "lands to discover," and their frozen internal sea.

Buache worked on another theme: the search for a navigable passage between the Atlantic and Pacific oceans to the north of America. This subject had already concerned Guillaume Delisle, but when his brother, Joseph-Nicolas Delisle (1688–1768), came back from Russia in 1747, he brought fresh information. In April 1750, Joseph-Nicolas Delisle presented to the Academy of Sciences a map, drawn up by Buache, of the new discoveries in the north Pacific Ocean (east of Siberia and Kamchatka, but west of New France). This map identified the Russian discoveries of Vitus Bering (1681–1741) and Alexy Chirikov (1703–1748), and included the imaginary voyage made by the Spanish admiral Bartholome de Fonte, which had been described in a letter, a forgery dated 1640.

Buache, through his knowledge of the known world, had long believed that Asia must be joined to North America by a range of mountains and by shallow seas. He devoted three years (1752–1754) to composing a treatise called *Considérations géographiques et physiques sur les nouvelles découvertes au nord de la Grande Mer* (Geographical and Physical Reflections on the New Discoveries to the North of the Great Sea); this included twelve maps showing the north Pacific and the navigable waterways that might traverse North America, California, and the islands of Hokkaido and Ryukyu. The "discoveries" of Admiral de Fonte did not convince the Academy of Sciences, though the academy still did not consider the case closed, and authorized the publication of Buache's work. [See color plate 20 in this volume.] The cartographer encountered lively opposition from his colleagues, particularly Didier Robert de Vaugondy (1723–1786). But Buache's mistakes were not immediately corrected; the third voyage of James Cook (1728–1779), from 1776 to 1779, passed too far to the north, and the expedition of Jean-François de Galaup, Comte de Lapérouse (1741–c. 1788), also failed to resolve the question. It was left to the Spanish and British voyages of the 1790s to show that the de Fonte account was fraudulent.

[*See also* Delisle, Guillaume, *and* Maps, Mapmaking, and Mapmakers.]

BIBLIOGRAPHY
Dawson, Nelson-Martin. *L'atelier Delisle: L'Amérique du Nord sur la table à dessin*. Sillery, Quebec: Septentrion, 2000.
Lagarde, Lucie. "Philippe Buache (1700–1773), cartographe ou géographe?" In *Terres à découvrir, terres à parcourir: Exploration et connaissance du monde, XIIe–XIXe siècles*, edited by Danielle Lecoq and Antoine Chambard, 146–165. Paris: L'Harmattan, 1998.
Pedley, Mary Sponberg. *Bel et utile: The Work of the Robert de Vaugondy Family of Mapmakers*. Tring, U.K.: Map Collector Publications, 1992.

MONIQUE PELLETIER
Translated from the French by David Buisseret

Buccaneers. The buccaneers were adventurers who preyed on Spanish ships and settlements in the Caribbean and along the Pacific littoral of South America during the latter half of the seventeenth century. Although some buccaneers were also pirates—seaborne outlaws—most were landsmen who embarked in ships only for conveyance in prosecuting amphibious operations. The buccaneers' antecedents were English, French, and Dutch interlopers, illicit traders who infiltrated Spain's trade with its American colonies from the beginning of the sixteenth century. The buccaneers gravitated to the islands of Hispaniola (Haiti) and Tortuga, where their practice of smoking or roasting meat on grills, in the manner of Amerindians, inspired the English word "buckaneer" (later spelled "buccaneer") from the French *boucan*, meaning "smoke," and *boucaner*, "to cure or smoke flesh."

By 1655 the buccaneers had ensconced themselves in the embryonic English colony at Port Royal, Jamaica, their most important base in the Caribbean. Successive governors of the island legitimized the activities of the buccaneers by granting privateering commissions against Spain. These operations were the island's best defense and almost its only livelihood. Despite the settlement of differences between England and Spain by the Treaty of Madrid in 1670, the buccaneers' most spectacular successes were achieved under the leadership of Henry Morgan (c. 1635–1688), himself lieutenant governor of Jamaica from 1674. His feats are recorded in Alexander O. Exquemelin's *De Americæneche Zee Roovers*, published in Amsterdam in 1678 and printed in English as *Bucaniers of America* in 1684. Morgan executed a series of preemptive strikes on Spanish towns throughout the region, culminating in an assault on Panama in 1671. On this occasion the buccaneers split booty amounting to £30,000.

In April 1680 another party of buccaneers crossed Darien to sack Panama for the second time. After failing to secure the city they burst loose into the Pacific in stolen vessels. For the next eighteen months, mainly under the leadership of Captain Bartholomew Sharpe, they scoured the coast in search of prizes. When Sharpe finally headed for home, a storm blew him south of the Strait of Magellan so that he became, perforce, the first English captain to round Cape Horn in an easterly direction. Sharpe's exploits aroused intense interest when it became known that he had seized a secret book of charts and pilot instructions—with coverage of the entire Pacific coastline from California to Cape Horn—for a prize. The value of these charts, in English hands, was inestimable.

Sharpe's narrative was first printed in Captain William Hack's *A Collection of Original Voyages* (1699). Senior members of the Royal Society, including its future president Samuel Pepys, scrutinized the voyage very closely. The drive by scientists to obtain disciplined, truthful voyage narratives had begun as early as 1666 when the society published "Directions for Sea-men, Bound for Far Voyages" in its *Philosophical Transactions*. These "directions" guided mariners in the composition of their journals so that they might be rendered "pertinent and suitable for [the society's] purpose." In his passage around Cape Horn, Sharpe had sailed farther south than any other mariner. He was able to claim that the great southern continent, *Terra Australis Incognita*, was a fiction.

In addition to Sharpe, six other crew members left narratives of the voyage. Basil Ringrose, navigator and cartographer, left a reliable account published in an expanded edition of *Bucaniers of America* (1685). William Dampier recorded the expedition, his brief coverage being incorporated in *A New Voyage round the World* (1697). The bias in Dampier's account is evidence of a meticulous editorial process designed to divorce the author from his buccaneering past. The editor, possibly Hans Sloane, later president of the Royal Society, refashioned Dampier's narrative to reflect information of scientific interest. A similar process is observable in Lionel Wafer's *A New Voyage and Description of the Isthmus of America* (1699). Wafer had abandoned the expedition in April 1681, with Dampier and about forty others, intending to return overland to the Atlantic coast. During the march Wafer sustained a knee injury that meant he was left behind at the mercy of *"wild* Indians." Wafer's spectacular narrative of life among the Kuna, alongside a natural history of Darien, was edited to emphasize contemporary scientific preoccupations and downplay his buccaneering past.

In March 1684 the *Batchelor's Delight*, commanded by Captain John Cook, joined the *Nicholas*, commanded by Captain John Eaton, off Valdivia. Together they sailed to Juan Fernández where they recovered a Moskito Indian whom Sharpe had marooned accidentally three years earlier. Dampier's description of how the castaway survived his island solitude in *New Voyage* may have informed Daniel Defoe's novel *Robinson Crusoe* (1719). After leaving Juan Fernández, Cook and Eaton sailed for the Galápagos Islands, where Cook's pilot, William Ambrose Cowley, compiled the first English map of the archipelago. Cowley's map and a narrative he kept of his voyage were also published in Hack's *Collection*.

The rash of buccaneer narratives printed after 1679 reflects the fact that travel literature became the most popular form of secular reading around the turn of the century. Mariner's journals were avidly sought by publishers and demand soon outstripped supply. The scarcity of buccaneer journals was due to two overriding factors. First, the survival of manuscripts at sea or in the tropics was often a matter of chance. Dampier's account of wading through jungle rivers with his journal rolled up in a bamboo cane illustrates the problems he encountered. Second, literacy rates among seventeenth-century seamen were generally poor, and few men were capable of recording their experiences. The scarcity of genuine narratives encouraged enterprising authors to foist counterfeits upon a credulous public. Defoe's novel *Captain Singleton* (1720) and *A New Voyage round the World* (c. 1730) are classic examples of this type.

Narratives incorporating speculative geography, particularly concerning the vast spaces of the Pacific, were highly prized by contemporary cartographers eager for the latest intelligence from abroad. One narrative carried an abiding legacy. According to Wafer, when the *Bachelor's Delight* was in the latitude of 27°20′ S, some 500 leagues south of the Galápagos, the buccaneers observed "a range of high land" that they took to be a group of islands. Hermann Moll's world map forming the frontispiece to Dampier's *New Voyage* represents "Davis Land" in its reported position. In 1721 the Dutch West India Company fitted out three ships under Jacob Roggeveen to search for it, and French and British ships were still looking at the end of the nineteenth century. "Davis Land" remains an enigma. It may represent Easter Island, but it is more likely that Davis and his men were deceived by a bank of cloud.

[*See also* Dampier, William; Exploration Texts; Roggeveen, Jacob; *and Terra Australis Incognita*.]

BIBLIOGRAPHY

Bradley, Peter T. *The Lure of Peru: Maritime Intrusion into the South Sea, 1598–1701*. London: Macmillan, 1989.
Dampier, William. *A New Voyage round the World*. Edited by Sir Albert Gray. New York: Dover, 1968.
Esquemeling, John. *The Buccaneers of America*. Edited by Henry Powell. London: Swan Sonnenschein, 1893. Reprint. Mineola, N.Y.: Dover, 2000.
Hacke, William. *A Collection of Original Voyages: A Facsimile Reproduction*. Introduction by Glyndwr Williams. New York: Scholars' Facsimiles, 1993. Includes the text of Cowley's and Sharpe's voyages.
Howse, Derek, and Norman J. W. Thrower, eds. *A Buccaneer's Atlas*. Berkeley: University of California Press, 1992.
Wafer, Lionel. *A New Voyage and Description of the Isthmus of America*. Edited and introduced by L. E. Elliott Joyce. Oxford: Hakluyt Society, 1934.
Williams, Glyndwr. *The Great South Sea: English Voyages and Encounters 1570–1750*. New Haven, Conn.: Yale University Press, 1997.
Williams, Glyndwr. "'The Inexhaustible Fountain of Gold': English Projects and Ventures in the South Seas, 1670–1750." In *Perspectives of Empire: Essays Presented to Gerald S. Graham*, edited by John E. Flint and Glyndwr Williams, 27–52. London: Longman, 1973.

JAMES KELLY

Buddhist Cosmological Maps.

An integral part of Chinese cartography is the lengthy tradition of maps based on what could be termed "Buddhist cosmology." This tradition extends to Korea, Japan, Tibet, and Southeast Asia, with the maps all displaying the same general configurations. An eighteenth-century European work includes a careful reproduction of a Tibetan world map that shows these cosmological conceptions. The characteristics of the depictions are quite intricate, and are shared with

Hindu and Jain cosmography. The Tibetan map is centered on the mountain named Meru, the center of the world, which connects the earth to the heavens. Meru is surrounded by water. Surrounding the water, in turn, we find a square-shaped group of concentric mountain ranges. Beyond, we find a vast ocean encircling those mountains. Finally, in this ocean, there are four groups of lands, or "continents," one at each side of the map. Each land includes small drawings of buildings and vegetation.

A series of Korean world maps clearly displays a similar cartographic system. The central portion appears to have been drawn in the form of a human head. China occupies the main area of this central continent, with Korea, Japan, India, and Southeast Asia nearby. The western countries are crowded at the back of the "head." The central continent is surrounded by an ocean, which contains many islands. Beyond this ocean, there is another continent; this second continent is surrounded, in turn, by water. In this final outer sea we find islands to the west and east. Most of these Korean world maps follow this basic form, with some variations. Many of the maps of this type are quite late, dating from the seventeenth and even eighteenth centuries, but they represent much earlier cartographic traditions coming from China. The Japanese scholar Hiroshi Nakamura noted that many of the place names on these maps come from the *Shanhai jing* (Classic of Mountains and Seas), a work that includes geography — fantastic and otherwise. Other toponyms are derived from other Chinese historical works, such as the *Shu jing* (Classic of History), the oldest of what are known as the five Confucian classics, and the *Mu tian zi zhuan* (Story of King Mu), an account of the Silk Road written sometime in the fifth or fourth century B.C.E.

These kinds of world maps use cartographical principles in a highly abstract form. They integrate actual knowledge about people and places into larger mythological and symbolic frameworks. Early Chinese maps include a range of representations, from empirical works with real political or topographical features, to abstract frameworks—such as the Buddhist cosmological one—that become filled with both empirical and mythical geographical elements.

This is not a uniquely Asian paradigm—in the West, we see in the medieval maps more "modern" (that is, empirical) techniques, such as attempts to represent coastlines accurately, along with the ancient symbolic and mythological map elements that are relinquished only with great reluctance. Thus,

even European maps of the period of the great discoveries include mythical islands and representations based on classical writers such as Ptolemy, from more than a thousand years earlier.

The maps influenced by traditional Buddhist cosmology, as seen in the Tibetan example, are defined by certain cartographical depictions and configurations. This type of map is usually centered on the legendary "Mount Meru" (or "Sumeru") in central Asia; this world axis is known as "Kun Lun" in Chinese, while "Meru" is the Sanskrit term. (Today the term "Kun Lun" is applied to a long mountain chain in Asia.) For the Chinese, the area around the mountain was believed to be a kind of Taoist paradise. To the west were regions unknown, and to the east was the rest of Asia, including Korea and India.

Although it is clear that the Koreans adopted the traditional Buddhist cosmological map from China, the Chinese themselves do not seem to have generated many maps of this type. However, there are Chinese maps working from religious cosmological concepts. Indian Buddhism influenced these maps in both general configuration and in their inclusion of the continent known as *Jambu-dvipa* in Sanskrit, or *Nan zhan bu zhou* in Chinese. An example of such a map is the 1613 *Si hai hua yi zong tu* (General Map of Chinese and Foreign Territory within the Four Seas) by Zhang Huang. The map has empirically based detail, but also includes mythical toponyms from the *Shanhai jing*. The configuration with Mount Meru in the center and the four continents at the cardinal points (as in the Tibetan map discussed earlier) comes from ancient Buddhist traditions. In these original traditions, the configuration was rather abstract and symmetrical, but it changed when it became combined with "real world" geography in later Chinese works. In the Buddhist cosmology, for example, *Jambu-dvipa* referred to the entire inhabited world—or simply India. With the Chinese adoption of this configuration, China occupied a central position, and *Jambu-dvipa* came to refer to the Indian subcontinent. Mount Meru came to be identified with actual mountain ranges in central Asia or Tibet.

In Japan, too, maps based on Buddhist cosmology appeared, and lasted well into the period of more modern mapmaking. Again the result was a cartographical representation that included both a traditional worldview and empirically based information. A classic example of this is the *Nansenbushu bankoku shoka no zu* (Outline Map of All the Countries of the Universe) by Zuda Rokashi, who is known by his religious name, Hotan. This map was produced in Kyoto in 1710, and it represents a fusion of Buddhist cosmology and scientific European cartography. Europe is depicted as a group of islands, and South America also appears as an island, beyond Japan—recall the "island continents" of the traditional Tibetan world. The largest part of this Japanese map shows *Jambu-dvipa*, including the sacred lake Anavatapta. Much of this traditional material was based on a Japanese version of the seventh-century C.E. Chinese work *Xi you ji* (Records of the Western Countries) written by the Tang dynasty pilgrim Xuanzang. In the upper left corner of the map, there are numerous references to both Buddhist writings and Chinese historical annals. So we see that at the core of this representation is ancient Buddhist belief, and even the new information about Europe and South America is made to fit the traditional model.

[*See also* Chinese Empirical Maps *and* Maps, Mapmaking, and Mapmakers.]

BIBLIOGRAPHY

Bagrow, Leo. *History of Cartography*. 2nd ed. Revised and enlarged with additional maps and illustrations by R. A. Skelton. Chicago: Precedent Publishers, 1985.

Giorgi, Antonio Agostino. *Alphabetum Tibetanum missionum apostolicarum commodo editum*. Rome: Typis Sacrae Congregationis de Propaganda Fide, 1762. Reprinted with an introduction. Cologne, Germany: Editiones Una Voce, 1987.

Harley, J. B., and David Woodward, eds. *The History of Cartography*. Vol. 2, book 2, *Cartography in the Traditional East and Southeast Asian Societies*. Chicago: University of Chicago Press, 1994.

McCune, Shannon. "World Maps by Korean Cartographers." *Journal of Social Sciences and Humanities* 45 (June 1977): 1–8.

Muroga, Nobuo, and Kazutaka Unno. "The Buddhist World Map in Japan and its Contact with European Maps." *Imago Mundi* 16 (1962): 49–69.

BENJAMIN B. OLSHIN

Burchell, William (1781–1863), English artist, naturalist, and explorer of South Africa. William John Burchell conducted a series of exploratory journeys in South Africa from 1811 to 1815. He was the quintessential Enlightenment traveler, supremely confident that his was a detached, rational, and scientific survey of nature, places, and people. Burchell was born in Fulham, London, on July 23, 1781, and was able to study botany and natural history at Kew Gardens before being appointed schoolmaster and botanist on the island of Saint Helena, where he remained from 1805 to 1810. Then, in 1810, he sailed to Cape Town and there fitted out ox wagons for a

trip to the northern interior. He reached as far as Kuruman and some way beyond, learning much of the Tswana peoples there before returning southeastward to the Great Kei River area.

Burchell expected to demonstrate the natural harmony of nature. His collections of sixty-three thousand plant, animal, and other specimens and his excellent drawings may have served to show harmony, but his observations of humans were less reassuring. Here was neither "primitive simplicity" nor civilized behavior by the supposedly more advanced. Burchell disapproved equally of Boer slave owners, their missionary opponents, and African petty tyrants, but he treated all with tolerant good sense, developing a notably understanding relationship with his Khoi followers.

In 1825–1829, Burchell traveled in Brazil, but little is known of his work there, and the rest of his life was something of an anticlimax. He committed suicide on March 23, 1863, at Fulham. His book on South Africa, although incomplete as a record of his travels, is attractively written and illustrated, and it forms the best memorial to this very accomplished and discerning traveler.

[*See also* Africa, *subentries on* Exploration *and* Scientific Exploration].

BIBLIOGRAPHY

Burchell, William John. *Travels in the Interior of Southern Africa*. 2 vols. London: Longman, 1822–1824. 2nd ed., with an introduction by Isaac Schapera. London: Batchworth Press, 1953.

ROY BRIDGES

Burckhardt, Johann Ludwig (1784–1817), Swiss explorer of Africa. One of history's most significant scholar-explorers, and certainly one of the most observant travelers who ever lived, Burckhardt was born in Lausanne into a distinguished Swiss family on November 24, 1784. Because his family was ruined by Bonapartists in Switzerland (this accounts for his lifelong hatred of the French), Burckhardt spent much of his early life in Germany, where he completed his studies at Leipzig and Göttingen universities. He proved to be a superb student of languages and science. Almost penniless, he migrated to England in 1806, carrying a letter of recommendation for Sir Joseph Banks from one of his professors, Johann Blumenbach. Burckhardt subsequently spent three years at Cambridge University studying Arabic culture and language, and then volunteered his services to Banks and the African Association to explore in the Niger River–Timbuctoo region. He

was readily accepted, and he left in 1809 for Syria, where he grew a beard and assumed a disguise as Sheikh Ibrahim ibn Abdullah, a Muslim merchant. Burckhardt never returned to Europe, and for the rest of his danger-filled short life, he experienced only privation and penury.

For one whose destination was Timbuctoo, Burckhardt took his time wandering around Syria and Palestine, and did not arrive at Cairo, his jumping-off point to the western Sudan, until 1812. Everywhere he traveled in the Levant, Burckhardt kept copious, but carefully concealed, notes in which he detailed the life of the peasants and also how harshly they were treated under Turkish rule. He made sketches of all the ruins he visited, and he recorded their exact names and locations. His most significant discovery was Petra (in present-day Jordan), an ancient ruin he described as "one of the most elegant remains of antiquity existing in Syria—a work of immense labour." Burckhardt was the first European to visit Petra since Roman times, but, unfortunately, he spent only hours there.

Rather than depart for the Niger River, Burckhardt began a thousand-mile trek southward into the Egyptian Sudan. At the village of Abu Simbel, on March 22, 1813, he discovered the temple of Ramses II, another archaeological site not seen by a European since ancient times and described by Alan Moorehead as "the finest spectacle on the Nile." Hindered by an eye illness, Burckhardt continued his journey by caravan across the Nubian Desert to the towns of Berber, Shendy, and Sennar. Wherever he could, Burckhardt consolidated his notes, which included almost everything he had observed. He described such things as the local architecture and languages, the annual rise and fall of the river, local wildlife, and agricultural practices.

He spent a month at Shendy, a town north of Khartoum, and while there, he prepared a superior account of life in the Egyptian Sudan. He considered Shendy to be a major crossroads along the Nile because of its location near caravan routes that led westward to the African Sahel, to Ethiopia, and to the Red Sea. Further, Shendy was a hub of the slave trade, which Burckhardt described in detail. In the summer of 1814, now disguised as an Egyptian, Burckhardt traveled to Mecca and Medina in Arabia, where again his accounts provided the most reliable information available in Europe concerning the Muslim holy cities. From Jiddah (on the Red Sea), Burckhardt informed the African Association that his Arabian detour was completed, and he was now ready to return to Cairo to embark for the Niger River and

Timbuctoo. Interestingly, he made yet another detour, this time to the Sinai Peninsula and the adjacent Gulf of Aqaba. Finally back in Cairo in 1816, Burckhardt made arrangements to join a caravan to the African interior, but his frail health forced him to remain there, where he died of dysentery on October 15, 1817. He was buried in a Muslim cemetery.

Burckhardt spent almost eight years in Syria, Palestine, Egypt, and Arabia preparing himself to explore the Niger River region and Timbuctoo. Although he had every intention of completing his mission, he never began it. Nonetheless, officials at the African Association in England could only rejoice at his accomplishments. The documents he sent back to England contained thousands of pages of precise physical and cultural geographical data, ethnological and linguistic accounts, and archaeological descriptions and renderings of almost all the ancient Nile sites. His information was laden with fact, though Burckhardt provided little analysis; still, between 1819 and 1830, the African Association published four books from Burckhardt's accounts: *Travels in Nubia*, *Travels in Syria*, *Travels in Arabia*, and *Notes on the Bedouins and Wahhabis*.

[*See also* African Association; Arabia; *and* Banks, Joseph.]

BIBLIOGRAPHY

Moorehead, Alan. *The Blue Nile.* New York: Harper & Row, 1962.
Sim, Katherine. *Desert Traveller: The Life of Jean Louis Burckhardt.* London: Phoenix Press, 2000.

SANFORD H. BEDERMAN

Burke, Robert O'Hara, and William Wills,

explorers. Robert O'Hara Burke (1821–1861), soldier, policeman, and explorer, was born in February 1821 at Saint Clerans in County Galway, Ireland, a son of the soldier and landowner James Hardiman Burke. Educated at Woolwich Academy, Burke served in the Austrian army and in the Irish Mounted Constabulary before migrating to Melbourne in 1853, where he joined the Victoria police. By 1860 he was superintendent of police at Castlemaine. William John Wills (1834–1861), surveyor and explorer, was born on January 5, 1834, at Totnes in Devon, England, a son of the surgeon William Wills. Apprenticed to his father in 1850, William migrated to Port Phillip with his brothers John and Thomas three years later. In 1860 he was working as an assistant at the Melbourne Observatory.

Burke was appointed leader of the lavishly equipped Victoria exploring expedition that was commissioned to find a safe overland route from the northern limits of occupation to the Gulf of Carpentaria. Sponsored by the Royal Society of Victoria and financed by the government and public subscription, the expedition departed Melbourne in a blaze of glory on August 20, 1860. At Menindee, George Landells was replaced as second in command by Wills, and the impatient Burke raced northward with a party of eight, leaving the balance of the expedition to follow along slowly. Having established a depot at Cooper Creek, and ignoring Augustus Gregory's earlier advice not to travel at the height of summer, Burke decided to make a dash for the Gulf of Carpentaria before the rest of the expedition arrived.

On December 16, Burke, Wills, John King (1841–1872), and Charles Grey departed Cooper Creek on foot with six camels and one horse, carrying supplies for three months. In a magnificent feat of human endurance, they traveled 1,500 miles (2,400 kilometers) in two months to reach the mangrove swamps near the mouth of the Flinders River, thus becoming the first Europeans to cross the Australian continent from south to north, by traveling from Melbourne to the Gulf of Carpentaria. Only one of the group, however, survived the return crossing. Grey died on the way back to Coopers Creek, where the three physically exhausted survivors arrived on April 21, to find that the four men who had remained behind had left the depot a few hours earlier. After resting briefly the trio headed toward Mount Hopeless station 150 miles (240 kilometers) to the west. This proved too difficult, and they settled down on Cooper Creek to wait for a rescue party. Only King lived long enough to be rescued by Alfred Howitt's party, on September 15. Burke and Wills were buried in Melbourne Cemetery on January 21, 1862.

In his last letter, dated April 22, 1861, Burke claimed to have found a "well watered and richly grassed" route to the north coast but, in reality, the route was practical only in the very best of seasons. Little of value was recorded because the party traveled so swiftly that no time was allowed for detailed observation or assessment. The real additions to geographical knowledge were made by Howitt, William Landsborough, and John McKinlay, who led parties sent out to find the lost explorers. McKinlay started from Adelaide in August 1861 on a twelve-month journey through the Cooper Creek area to the Gulf of Carpentaria, then southeast to Port Denison (Bowen). Starting from the Albert River on the north coast in November 1861, Landsborough first traveled 210 miles (340 kilometers) to the southwest before being forced to turn back by hostile Aborigines

and dry country. He then ventured east to the Flinders, then south to the Warrego, and five months after leaving the Gulf of Carpentaria, he reached Melbourne in July 1862. Both McKinlay and Landsborough had found safe stock routes across the continent.

[*See also* Australia, Exploration of, *and* Gregory, Augustus.]

BIBLIOGRAPHY

Favenc, Ernest. *The History of Australian Exploration from 1788 to 1888*. Sydney: Turner and Henderson, 1888. Reprint. Amsterdam: Meridian, 1967.
Murgatroyd, Sarah. *The Dig Tree: The Extraordinary Story of the Ill-fated Burke and Wills 1860 Expedition*. London: Bloomsbury, 2002.

DENIS SHEPHARD

Burton, Richard F. (1821–1890), British explorer of central and East Africa who searched for the source of the White Nile. A protean Victorian of enormous talent and ambition, Richard Francis Burton is best known to the history of exploration for his role in opening east-central Africa to the scrutiny of Europe. He was a great linguist who knew over twenty-five languages, a restless traveler whose journeys took him through parts of five continents, a prolific author and translator who published over fifty works, a skilled ethnographer who cofounded the Anthropological Society of London, and a fierce controversialist who outraged polite society in Britain with his unconventional views of religion, race, marriage, and sex. His career as an explorer culminated with his expedition to the lake region of east-central Africa in 1857–1859 in search of the source of the White Nile, which resulted in a highly public—and ultimately tragic—feud with his erstwhile companion, John Hanning Speke.

Richard Burton was born on March 19, 1821, in Torquay, Devonshire, the son of Joseph Burton, an Anglo-Irish lieutenant colonel in the British army, and his wife Martha Baker, the daughter of a Hertfordshire squire. His father moved the family to France shortly after Richard's birth. Richard grew up in a series of French and Italian towns and was educated for the most part by private tutor. In 1840, at the age of nineteen, he matriculated at Trinity College, Oxford, but was expelled for misbehavior before the end of the academic year. He then obtained a commission in the British East India Company Army, arriving in India in 1842 as a junior officer in the Eighteenth Native Bombay Infantry. He spent the next seven years in India, serving mainly in the newly conquered province of Sindh, where he was seconded to the Sindh Canal Survey and acquired the linguistic, ethnographic, and surveying skills he would later put to use as an explorer.

In 1849 Burton returned to Britain on a medical leave and promptly published four books about his experiences in India. When he learned in 1852 that the Royal Geographical Society was offering £200 to anyone prepared to investigate the unmapped interior of the Arabian Peninsula, Burton leaped at the opportunity, obtaining a year's leave to carry out the task. It soon became apparent, however, that his original plan to cross Arabia from Aden to Muscat was not feasible, so he decided instead to travel to Mecca and Medina disguised as a Muslim pilgrim of Pathan origin. By accomplishing this rare and risky feat in 1853, Burton established his reputation as an intrepid adventurer, and his lively and informed account of the journey, *Personal Narrative of a Pilgrimage to Al-Madinah and Meccah* (1855), added to his fame.

Burton followed up on his Arabian triumph by garnering official support for an expedition into Somalia in 1855. Although he had three British officers under his command, including Speke, who was a last-minute addition, he dispatched them on mundane assignments while reserving for himself the high-profile task of gaining entry to the highland town of Harar (in what is now Ethiopia), which was reputedly closed to outsiders. He succeeded in his objective, but Harar lacked the forbidden appeal of Mecca for the British public. Furthermore, when Burton reunited with his fellow officers at the market town of Berbera in April 1855, a surprise attack by Somali tribesmen left one of the quartet dead and both Burton and Speke seriously injured. An official investigation charged Burton with negligence in his command.

The East African Expedition. Despite his setback in Somalia, Burton made plans to launch another expedition, this time aimed at investigating unconfirmed reports of great lakes and snow-capped peaks in the interior of East Africa. Underlying these objectives was the opportunity to seek the holy grail of mid-century exploration—the source of the White Nile. Accompanied by Speke, Burton arrived in Zanzibar in late 1856 and spent the next six months gathering supplies and equipment, making initial forays along the coast, and suffering through the so-called seasoning fever that afflicted newcomers to the region. In June 1857 a party consisting of Burton and Speke, an Arab guide, a dozen Zanzibari soldiers,

---

Travels in Africa

Burton was not only a prolific author, but also a skilled one. In this passage he describes what may have been a brush with death, but he explains it with such a wealth of jocular irony that the reader is left to wonder whether the tale does not contain a good deal of exaggeration.

On the morning after my arrival at Sagharrah I felt too ill to rise, and was treated with unaffected kindness by all the establishment. The Gerard sent to Harar for millet beer, Ao Samattar went to the gardens in search of Kat, the sons Yusuf Dera and a dwarf insisted upon firing me with such ardour that no refusal could avail: and Khayrah the wife, with her daughters, two tall, dark, smiling and well-favoured girls of thirteen and fifteen, sacrificed a sheep as my Fida, or expiatory offering. Even the Galla Christians, who flocked to see the stranger, wept for the evil fate which had brought him so far from his fatherland, to die under a tree. Nothing, indeed, would have been easier than such operation; all required was the turning face to the wall, for four or five days. But to expire of an ignoble colic!—the thing was not to be thought of, and a firm resolution to live on sometimes, methinks, effects its object.

—Richard F. Burton, *First Footsteps in East Africa; or, An Exploration of Harar* (London, 1856)

---

two Goanese servants, nearly a hundred porters, and various hangers-on began a journey that would take nearly two years to complete.

This expedition was unlike anything Burton had undertaken in the past. Both in his pilgrimage to Mecca and in his journey to Harar, Burton had traveled light and in disguise, which made it impossible for him to conduct astronomical observations, collect natural specimens, or carry out any other scientific tasks. Now he ventured into East Africa at the head of a large column, exposed for all to see as an English outsider, equipped with a wide array of instruments to chart his course, and committed to the scientific protocols promoted by his sponsor, the Royal Geographical Society. He was expected to measure latitude, longitude, and altitude, record temperature, rainfall, and other climatological data, and gather geological samples, botanical specimens, and ethnographic artifacts. In short, Burton had adopted the mien of the scientific explorer, advancing the objectives of Victorian natural science.

Although Burton and Speke were entering territory unfamiliar to Europe, it was hardly isolated from the outside world. An active trade in ivory and slaves linked the lake region to the coast. The expedition followed a major caravan route and depended on the hospitality and advice of Arab and Afro-Arab merchants in the interior, most notably at Kazeh, an entrepôt in what is now western Tanzania where Burton and Speke were able to recover their strength and resupply their party both on the outward and return journeys.

The main goal of their expedition was Lake Tanganyika, where they arrived after a grueling six-month march on February 13, 1858. They spent nearly four more months investigating the lake, but were unable to reach its northern extremity to determine whether it might be the point of origin for the Nile. Concluding that they could do no more, Burton ordered the expedition to return to the coast. When they stopped at Kazeh, however, Speke persuaded Burton to let him make a quick trip to the north, where Arab traders reported the existence of another great lake. Burton, who was too ill to travel, stayed at Kazeh, conducting ethnographic and linguistic research while recovering his strength. Speke returned some seven weeks later to announce that he had discovered Lake Nyanza, which he was convinced was the source of the Nile. Burton was skeptical. If true, he had allowed one of the greatest geographical prizes of all time to escape his grasp.

The expedition returned to Zanzibar on March 4, 1859, its two British explorers physical and emotional wrecks. Speke sailed immediately for England, while Burton lingered awhile in Aden. When he arrived in London several weeks later, he found that Speke had already announced his discovery of Lake Nyanza and obtained the Royal Geographical Society's sanction to lead a return expedition to the lake in order to confirm that the Nile had its origins there. Burton was left on the sidelines, beset by criticisms of his treatment of porters in a dispute over pay and rumors circulated by Speke about his moral character. Although he initially acknowledged in his post-expedition address to the society that the Nile might flow from Lake Nyanza, his position hardened in response to Speke's animosity. He pointed out that Speke lacked the linguistic skills to be sure what his native informants may or may not have said about a river flowing from the northern end of Lake Nyanza and he hypothesized that the true source of the Nile would be traced further south to Lake Tanganyika.

The issue appeared settled in Speke's favor when he returned from his second expedition in June 1863 to announce that he had found the Nile's outlet from Lake Nyanza. Soon, however, his unpleasant personality began to antagonize leading members of the geographical fraternity, who in turn gave his geographical claims closer scrutiny, revealing flaws in some of his evidence. David Livingstone, Sir Roderick Murchison, and others came to share Burton's doubts that Lake Nyanza was the true source of the Nile. Burton was invited to debate Speke at the annual meeting of the British Association for the Advancement of Science in September 1864, an invitation that evidenced the rehabilitation of his reputation. The much-anticipated public showdown never took place, however: Speke died of a self-inflicted gunshot wound while out hunting the day before the debate. An inquest ruled the death accidental, though many people suspected suicide. Speke's claim to have discovered the source of the Nile remained in doubt until confirmation came from Henry Morton Stanley in 1875.

Burton continued to play an active role in the European exploration of other parts of the world, though he never again made a journey that carried as much weight in the British imagination as the one he took into the lake region of east-central Africa. While serving as British consul in Fernando Po, West Africa (1861–1864), he climbed Mount Cameroon in 1861, ventured into Gabon in search of gorillas and cannibals in 1862, and journeyed up the Congo River as far as its first great cataracts in 1863. He also visited Dahomey, Benin, and other independent African states in the region. When transfered to Santos, Brazil (1865–1869), he took several journeys into the interior of the continent, on one occasion traveling 1,500 miles (2,414 kilometers) down the San Francisco River and on another crossing over the Andes into Chile. During subsequent consular postings in Damascus and Trieste, he traveled through the Syrian desert and the Midian region of Arabia. He wrote books about most of these journeys, though none attracted the interest of his earlier adventures in Arabia and East Africa. His achievements were honored with a knighthood in 1886. He died of heart failure in Trieste on October 19, 1890.

[*See also* Africa; Arabia; Nile River; *and* Speke, John Hanning.]

BIBLIOGRAPHY

Burton, Richard F. *The Lake Regions of Central Africa.* 2 vols. London: Longman, Green, Longman, and Roberts, 1860.

Burton, Richard F., and James McQueen. *The Nile Basin.* London: Tinsley Brothers, 1864.

Kennedy, Dane. *The Highly Civilized Man: Richard Burton and the Victorian World.* Cambridge, Mass.: Harvard University Press, 2005.

Lovell, Mary S. *A Rage to Live: A Biography of Richard and Isabel Burton*. New York: Norton, 1998.

Speke, John Hanning. *Journal of the Discovery of the Source of the Nile*. Edinburgh and London: W. Blackwood, 1863.

DANE KENNEDY

Byrd, Richard (1888–1957), naval officer and explorer who established Little America during his first Antarctic expedition in 1928. Graduating from the U.S. Naval Academy in 1912 as a naval aviator, Richard Evelyn Byrd commanded air forces in Canada during World War I. After a flight from Spitsbergen in 1926 in the *Josephine Ford*, Byrd and his flying companion Floyd Bennett claimed to be the first to fly over the North Pole. Turning his attention to the Antarctic, Byrd organized the first American exploration since Charles Wilkes's in 1840. Byrd's base at Little America served as headquarters for the first American flight over the South Pole on November 29, 1929. [See color plate 19 in this volume.] Byrd was navigator with Bernt Balchen as pilot, Ashley McKinley as aerial photographer, and Harold June as pilot and radio operator. Promoted to admiral on his return to America in 1930, Byrd soon planned a second expedition to Antarctica in 1933, an expedition that included weekly broadcasts by the Columbia Broadcasting System from Little America. During this expedition, Byrd conducted meteorological observations from an advanced camp, almost succumbing to carbon monoxide poisoning from blocked ventilators until he was heroically rescued. Having financed his first two explorations primarily from his own private funds, Byrd received federal sponsorship from President Franklin Delano Roosevelt for his third expedition, in 1933. In this and in subsequent projects, Byrd worked on mapping the coastland of Antarctica. In his final expedition, Byrd was only a consultant and did not feel a part of the daily operations. Disappointed, he left the area for the last time in 1956. Byrd died in Boston the following year.

[*See also* Antarctica *and* Polar Flights.]

BIBLIOGRAPHY

Byrd, Richard Evelyn. *Little America*. New York and London: Putnam, 1930.

CLARENCE E. KYLANDER

Byrd, William (1674–1744), early American explorer and writer of the Piedmont frontier. A wealthy and erudite Virginia plantation owner, William Byrd earned a place in the annals of North American exploration through his eloquent accounts of journeys made into the upcountry frontier between Virginia and North Carolina at a time when most settlement was restricted to the coastal tidewater fringe. Byrd's father, known as William Byrd I, had established the family fortune as an Indian trader and slave-owning planter. At the age of seven young William was sent to England to live with relatives and receive a proper education. He attended Felsted Grammar School in Essex, spent time in Holland learning commerce, studied law at the Middle Temple, and was admitted to the bar in 1695. At age twenty-two he was elected to the Royal Society, an honor his father earlier gained through his own interest in botany and horticulture. After his admission to the bar, William II returned to Virginia for a short period during which he was elected to the House of Burgesses and took up the life of a Virginia gentleman before returning to London as the representative of the Virginia Assembly. When his father died in 1704 Byrd returned to take charge of the family holdings. William II's inheritance of 26,000 acres did little to quench his thirst for land acquisition and by the time he died he held title to 180,000 acres. At the home he built, called "Westover," Byrd assembled one of colonial America's largest libraries.

Byrd is best known for the accounts he wrote describing three expeditions into the Piedmont frontier. In 1728 he was named to lead Virginia's commission to oversee the surveying and marking of the disputed boundary with neighboring North Carolina. The survey proceeded from Currituck Inlet on the Atlantic coast and followed a straight due west course for 241 miles (388 kilometers) to the outliers of the Blue Ridge mountains where, in Byrd's words, "We determin'd to proceed no farther . . . because the way to the west grew so Mountainous." Closer to the coast, Byrd called attention to the fact that the surveyors were "the first of mankind that ventured through the Great Dismal Swamp." It was a grueling slog that Byrd and fellow commissioners avoided by skirting along the edges of the vast swamp. Byrd wrote two famous accounts of this adventure known as "The History of The Dividing Line betwixt Virginia and North Carolina, Run in the Year of Our Lord 1728," and the more candid and somewhat satirical version, "The Secret History of the Line." Both manuscripts circulated during Byrd's lifetime but were not published until the "History" appeared in 1841 and the "Secret History" in 1929. Thomas Jefferson recognized the value of the "History" and worked unsuccessfully to see it published. In 1732, a few years after the boundary survey, Byrd undertook another expedition into the interior to investigate some iron mines. He described the journey in an account he titled "A Progress to the Mines." In the following year he described his adventures in traveling to and surveying a large tract of land along the Dan River, which he had purchased after the boundary survey. Eager to attract settlers, he named his landholding "Eden" and entitled his account "A Journey to the Land of Eden."

Byrd's surveys, like others of its kind, marked an intermediate stage between primary exploration and settlement. They represented the beginning of a process of recording the main features of a region after the first wave of explorers and traders had passed through it.

BIBLIOGRAPHY

Ausband, Stephen Conrad. *Byrd's Line: A Natural History.* Charlottesville and London: University of Virginia Press, 2002.

Boyd, William K. *William Byrd's Histories of the Dividing Line Betwixt Virginia and North Carolina.* New York: Dover Publications, 1967. An unabridged republication of the work first published by the North Carolina Historical Commission in 1929, with a new introduction by Percy G. Adams.

Lockridge, Kenneth A. *The Diary and Life of William Byrd II of Virginia, 1674–1744.* Chapel Hill and London: University of North Carolina Press, 1987.

Wright, Louis B., ed. *The Prose Works of William Byrd of Westover Narratives of a Colonial Virginian.* Cambridge, Mass.: The Belknap Press of Harvard University Press, 1966.

John Byron. Hut at Tierra del Fuego from an *Account of the Voyages Undertaken by the Order of His Present Majesty for Making Discoveries in the Southern Hemisphere* (3 vols., London, 1773) ed. John Hawkesworth. The text facing this image assures us that the inhabitants of "Terra del Fuego" live "in hovels of the most rude and inartificial structure that can be imagined." But many of the artist's figures look in fact as though they have been observed on a picnic in the European countryside. COURTESY THE NEWBERRY LIBRARY, CHICAGO

Wright, Louis B., and Marion Tinling, eds. *The Great American Gentleman: William Byrd of Westover in Virginia, His Secret Diary for the Years 1709–1712.* New York: Putnam, 1963.

LOUIS DE VORSEY

Byron, John (1723–1786), British explorer of the South Pacific. John Byron, later known as "Foulweather Jack," was born at Newstead Abbey, England, the second son of William, the fourth Lord Byron. In September 1740 he sailed as a midshipman in George Anson's squadron, but Byron's ship, the *Wager*, was wrecked on the Pacific coast of Patagonia, and he had a remarkable series of adventures before eventually reaching home in February 1746.

After the Seven Years' War (1756–1763), the attention of the Admiralty turned to exploration. On July 3, 1764, under cover of an elaborate deception plan, Byron left England in command of two copper-sheathed sloops, *Dolphin* and *Tamar*. Byron's secret instructions sent him to the South Atlantic to search for the rumored Pepys Island and to forestall French and Spanish claims to the Falkland Islands, strategically positioned for controlling access to the Pacific. Having taken possession of the Falklands, Byron was instructed to search for a Northwest Passage from the Pacific coast of America. However, once through the Strait of Magellan, he set out instead across the Pacific, apparently in search of the fabled Solomon Islands. En route he discovered a number of small islands, but, fearful of the natives and wary of running out of supplies, he did not stop to explore them. The *Dolphin* returned to England on May 7, 1766, having circumnavigated the globe in a record twenty-two months.

Byron has been roundly criticized by historians for his haste and lack of significant discoveries. However, his was not intended primarily as a voyage of discovery in the Pacific, and speed was essential to preserving the health of his crew. He brought back rough charts and views of the islands he passed, as well as a fabulous story of Patagonian giants. His conviction that the mythical Great Southern Continent had lain just beyond the horizon prompted Samuel Wallis's voyage. From 1769 to 1772, Byron served as governor of Newfoundland. He saw action against the French in the American War of Independence with the rank of vice admiral.

[*See also* Solomon Islands.]

BIBLIOGRAPHY
Cock, Randolph. "Precursors of Cook: The Voyages of the Dolphin, 1764–8." *Mariner's Mirror* 85, no. 1 (Feb. 1999): 30–52.
Gallagher, Robert. E., ed. *Byron's Journal of His Circumnavigation, 1764–1766.* Hakluyt Society, series 2, no. 122. Cambridge, U.K.: Cambridge University Press, 1964.

RANDOLPH COCK

C

Cabeza de Vaca, Álvar Núñez (c. 1485–c. 1559), Spanish explorer of the Americas. Álvar Núñez Cabeza de Vaca was royal treasurer of the 1527 Pánfilo de Narváez expedition sent to settle the northern rim of the Gulf of Mexico (Spanish Florida), and he later became governor of the province of Río de la Plata (1541–1545). Two commonplaces about his life require correction: his surname comes not from a poor shepherd but from a distinguished line of Andalusian *caballeros* whose genealogy has been traced back to the early thirteenth century; and he ended his life not in poverty and obscurity but by representing his native Jerez de la Frontera at the Castilian court and ransoming a young relative who was a captive of the king of Algiers. He distinguished himself as an explorer in his long overland treks, as a servant of the Spanish king on the continents of North and South America, and as the author of a North American exploration account that greatly transcends his other accomplishments.

Cabeza de Vaca's contribution to North American exploration consisted of the overland crossing of the continent from eastern coastal Texas to the western shore of northwestern Mexico, and his communication of oral reports that stimulated further northward exploration. His contribution to exploration in the interior of South America consisted of his overland crossing from the eastern coast of Brazil to Asunción and of navigating uncharted waterways from Asunción into upper Peru.

Of greater impact than his explorations was his writing. The *Relación*, written to the emperor Charles V and published in Zamora, Spain, in 1542, was consulted by reporters of the Hernando de Soto expedition and by explorers, conquistadores, and missionaries who participated in settling the areas north of New Spain. The *Relación*'s second edition, nicknamed *Naufragios* ("shipwrecks" or "misfortunes"), was published in Valladolid in 1555 along with a favorable account of his governorship of Río de la Plata. This work influenced the reports of the Coronado expedition as well as Spanish, Spanish Creole, Latin American, Anglo-American, Latino American, and Mexican American interpreters of the Spanish experience in North America up to the present day.

For information about Cabeza de Vaca's background, North and South American explorations, and broader influence, and for a critical transcription of his original 1542 Spanish-language *Relación* as well as a new English translation of it, see Adorno and Pautz (1999). For the English translation of the account with an introduction, see Adorno and Pautz (2003).

[*See also* Soto, Hernando de.]

BIBLIOGRAPHY

Adorno, Rolena, and Patrick Charles Pautz. *Álvar Núñez Cabeza de Vaca: His Account, His Life, and the Expedition of Pánfilo de Narváez*. 3 vols. Lincoln: University of Nebraska Press, 1999.

Núñez Cabeza de Vaca, Álvar. *The Narrative of Cabeza de Vaca*. Edited and translated by Rolena Adorno and Patrick Charles Pautz. Lincoln: University of Nebraska Press, 2003.

ROLENA ADORNO

Cabot, John (c. 1450–1499), Venetian navigator and explorer for England. In contrast to his reputation as the first European navigator to visit the mainland of North America since the Norsemen, there is little incontrovertible information about the early life of John Cabot. It is likely that he was born between 1450 and 1453 in Genoa, but this is not supported by firm documentary evidence. In 1476 he received Venetian citizenship after fifteen years' residence in that city, and he continued to live there in 1484 and was recently married. He traded in the eastern Mediterranean and traveled to Mecca, where he observed the commerce in spices, believing their origin to be in Asia. It is assumed that he was the Juan Caboto Montecalunya who resided in Valencia (Spain) between 1490 and 1493, unsuccessfully proposing improvements to its harbor. He also visited Seville and Lisbon seeking support for a voyage to the Orient via a westerly route, inspired by the spice trade and possibly by news of Columbus. Thereafter, he arrived with his family in England and resided in Bristol, most probably in 1494 (or during 1495 at the latest). There his project gained the favor of King Henry VII.

Letters patent were issued on March 5, 1496, in the names of John Cabot and his three sons, Lewis, Sebastian, and Sancio. They granted him authority to equip five ships at his own expense and take possession of any lands hitherto unvisited by Christians, to be found by navigating seas to the east, west, or north, thereby excluding the discoveries of Columbus. Cabot's first voyage from Bristol in 1496 probably was begun under these provisions, but a single vessel soon returned because of poor weather and a shortage of supplies. His reputation, therefore, rests on the second venture.

He departed on or about May 20, 1497, in the *Matthew* (fifty tons) crewed by some eighteen men, the modest scale of the enterprise perhaps reflecting the skepticism with which Bristol merchants viewed his expectations. Following a good crossing of the Atlantic from the west coast of Ireland, after some thirty-five days at sea, a landfall was made on June 24. Given the lack of an official journal or any other firsthand account, it is still not possible to state categorically where Cabot landed nor along which coast he sailed. Many historians would now consider that the most plausible limits of exploration were, in the south, Cape Breton Island, and, in the north, the Strait of Belle Isle and the tip of the northern peninsula of Newfoundland near capes Bauld and Dégrat. A few scholars support an extension of these limits in the south to the coasts of Nova Scotia and Maine, and some to southern Labrador in the north, although probably no further north than Hamilton Inlet. The only landing is thought to have occurred near one of these locations, or alternatively at some point between them on the east coast of Newfoundland, for example, at Cape Bonavista or on the Avalon Peninsula. Whatever the truth, Cabot failed to encounter any local inhabitants. The return voyage is believed to have commenced about July 20 or 24, and ended in Bristol between August 6 and 8.

In London, Cabot was publicly feted and rewarded by the crown for his claim to have visited lands on the northeastern fringes of Asia. On February 3, 1498, new letters patent were issued in the anticipation that he could return to the coasts recently discovered and proceed southwestward until he reached Cathay (China) and Cipango (Japan). Now with the stronger support of merchants both in the capital and in Bristol, whose goods were carried

in five ships, Cabot sailed in early May 1498. One of the vessels reached an Irish port in a damaged state, and it is widely believed that the rest, including that captained by Cabot, were lost at sea. An alternative theory, based on cartographic evidence, argues that Cabot returned to the lands he had visited, realized that they were not Asian, and returned to live in Bristol until his death in 1499, when his pension was paid for the last time. His efforts took England into the new age of exploration and contributed to the gradual realization that a previously unsuspected landmass lay between Europe and Asia.

[*See also* Bristol Voyages *and* Cabot, Sebastian.]

BIBLIOGRAPHY

Bradley, Peter T. *British Maritime Enterprise in the New World: From the Late Fifteenth to the Mid-Eighteenth Century.* Lewiston, N.Y.: Edwin Mellen Press, 1999.

Morison, Samuel E. *The Great Explorers: The European Discovery of America.* New York and Oxford: Oxford University Press, 1986.

Pope, Peter E. *The Many Landfalls of John Cabot.* Toronto: University of Toronto Press, 1997.

PETER T. BRADLEY

Cabot, Sebastian

Cabot, Sebastian (c. 1476–1557), Venetian navigator and explorer for England. Despite claims that he was English, Sebastian Cabot was born in Venice probably no later than 1484. He died in England in 1557. It is unlikely that he accompanied his father John in 1497 on his voyage from Bristol. However, he did pursue his father's interest in a maritime route to Asia, most controversially during his expedition of 1508–1509. The objective was to find a strait beyond the territory visited by his father, by then suspected to be North America rather than Asia. The achievements of the voyage are debatable since those who mentioned it produced conflicting versions. Most significantly, they differed concerning the northernmost limit reached, two accounts implying a midpoint on the coast of Labrador (at 55° or 58° N), while another states 67.5° N (beyond the Arctic Circle). The latter has been construed to support Cabot's later claim in England that he entered a waterway leading toward Cathay (China). Turned back by ice, he explored the North American coast perhaps as far south as Cape Hatteras.

Apart from unsuccessfully proposing another northwestern voyage from England in 1521, his life from 1512 until 1548 passed in the service of Spain. Appointed pilot-major in 1518, he instructed Spanish pilots and mapmakers and oversaw the updating of the official map of discoveries in the Indies. In 1526

World Map. This extremely rare 1544 world map, probably by Sebastian Cabot, curiously combines information about the latest discoveries of European mariners with a great variety of zoological scenes, often referring to legends from the European Middle Ages. BIBLIOTHÈQUE NATIONALE DE FRANCE

he commanded a Spanish expedition seeking an alternative to the Strait of Magellan as a southwestern route to Asia. It reached no further than the Río de la Plata. Following his return to England in 1548, he was appointed governor of a company created for the discovery of Cathay. In 1553 it dispatched the expedition of Hugh Willoughby and Richard Chancellor to open a northeastern route.

Evidence of Sebastian Cabot's cartographical knowledge and character is a printed world map of 1544 (the Paris map) and its revision in 1549. The single surviving copy of the Paris map incorrectly attributes his father's discoveries in 1497 equally to himself and his father, a deception that for personal aggrandizement Sebastian never did anything to correct. No copy of the revision survives, but it supported his claim in England that in 1508–1509 he had found a northwestern strait between 61° N and 64° N, depicted trending westward and then southward, where it broadened into what he believed was the Pacific Ocean. Consequently, it has been claimed that he traversed what would become Hudson Strait and entered Hudson Bay.

[*See also* Cabot, John.]

BIBLIOGRAPHY

Bradley, Peter T. *British Maritime Enterprise in the New World: From the Late Fifteenth to the Mid-Eighteenth Century*. Lewiston, N.Y.: Edwin Mellen Press, 1999.

Pope, Peter E. *The Many Landfalls of John Cabot*. Toronto: University of Toronto Press, 1997.

Quinn, David B. *Sebastian Cabot and Bristol Exploration*. Bristol, U.K.: The Historical Association, 1968. Rev. ed., 1993.

PETER T. BRADLEY

Cabral, Pedro (1467?–1520?), explorer Brazil and India for Portugal. Pedro Álvares Cabral is credited with the accidental discovery of Brazil in 1500. Cabral came from a well-established noble family of Upper Beira, a region closely associated with Henry the Navigator earlier in the fifteenth century. In February 1500, King Manuel I chose Cabral to serve as commander in chief of the second Portuguese fleet to India. The expedition's objective was to follow up on Vasco da Gama's voyage, establish friendly relations with Calicut, and build a permanent trading station (*feitoria*) there.

Consisting of thirteen ships with some twelve hundred to fifteen hundred personnel on board, the fleet left Lisbon on May 9, 1500. It was to sail a south-westerly course, off the Cape Verde Islands, so as to cross the equator well west of the African doldrums and far enough to the south to pick up winds that would carry it safely to the Cape of Good Hope. Running much farther west than intended or necessary, however, the fleet sighted the coast of Brazil on April 22, 1500, around the latitude of 17° S. Cabral named the new land "Terra de Vera Cruz" and dispatched a vessel back to Portugal to inform King Manuel of the discovery. He then proceeded to India, arriving in Calicut on September 13. The Portuguese soon outlasted their welcome there, and Cabral moved the fleet to Cochin, one of Calicut's competitors. There he secured a valuable cargo of spices and other merchandise and returned to Portugal in 1501.

Cabral was to lead another fleet to India the following year, but the command went instead to Vasco da Gama, amid a quarrel between Cabral and the second in command, Gama's uncle Vicente Sodré. Cabral lost King Manuel's favor and was sidelined for many years. In 1518, however, he was listed as a resident of the king's household and a member of the Royal Council. He disappeared from royal records in 1520, having failed to secure an advancement comparable to that of Vasco da Gama.

[*See also* Gama, Vasco da, *and* Henry the Navigator.]

BIBLIOGRAPHY

Greenlee, William Brooks, ed. and trans. *The Voyage of Pedro Álvares Cabral to Brazil and India, from Contemporary Documents and Narratives.* London: Hakluyt Society, 1938. Reprint. St. Clair Shores, Mich.: Scholarly Press, 1972.

Martinho, Telma. *Pedro Álvares Cabral: O homem, o feito e a memória.* Vila Nova de Gaia, Portugal: Editora Ausência, 2001.

Winius, George D., ed. *Portugal, the Pathfinder: Journeys from the Medieval towards the Modern World, 1300–ca.1600.* Madison, Wis.: The Hispanic Seminary of Medieval Studies, 1995.

IVANA ELBL
MARTIN ELBL

Cabrillo, Juan Rodríguez (c. 1500–1543), explorer and discoverer of Upper California. Cabrillo was probably from Spain, though some insist he was Portuguese. Born about 1500, he left Spain as a boy and joined Pánfilo de Narváez in the conquest of Cuba. In 1520 he went to the mainland with Narváez and joined the army of Hernán Cortés. Charged with building a fleet to conquer the Aztec capital of Tenochtitlan, he is said to have used resin and human fat to make pitch for waterproofing the ships. Later he served with Francisco de Orozco and then with Pedro de Alvarado, commanding a squadron of crossbowmen. By 1532 he was in Santiago de Guatemala, with a large grant of land and Indians to do the work. He owned farms and gold mines and had ships sailing along the Pacific coast. At first he had an Indian wife and several daughters, but on a trip to Spain he married Beatríz Sánchez de Ortega, who gave him two sons. About this time Juan Rodríguez added Cabrillo to his signature, perhaps as a nickname. In 1542, with three vessels originally intended for Alvarado's use, he sailed up the California coast, intending to join Ruy López de Villalobos somewhere along the coast of Asia. His fleet sailed north to 40°, then wintered in the Channel Islands, where Cabrillo was fatally injured, dying on January 3, 1543. Bartolomé Ferrer led the fleet up the coast once more, but storms drove the ships back, and the battered survivors returned home, reaching Navidad on April 14, 1543.

[*See also* Cortés, Hernán.]

BIBLIOGRAPHY

Kelsey, Harry. *Juan Rodríguez Cabrillo.* San Marino, Calif.: Huntington Library, 1986.

HARRY KELSEY

Cadamosto, Alvise di (1432–1488), Venetian merchant, public official, and member of the well-established Mosto family, who participated in explorations along the west African coast in the 1450s and wrote an account (*relazione*) of his voyages for the senate of the Republic of Venice. His narrative was subsequently published in numerous individual editions and was incorporated in key collections of travel literature, including Giovanni Battista Ramusio's notorious *Delle navigazioni e viaggi*.

Young Alvise di Cadamosto (Ca' da Mosto), on a routine business trip to Flanders, was persuaded by representatives of Prince Henry the Navigator of Portugal to try his luck at trade and exploration in West Africa. Prince Henry, following the standard business practices of the day, outfitted Cadamosto's ship in return for a hefty share of prospective profits. Cadamosto's first expedition set sail from Lagos on March 22, 1455. It made landfalls on Porto Santo and Madeira and sailed past the Canaries before reaching the estuary of the Senegal River. Cadamosto sold most of his merchandise, largely horses, to the *damel* of Kayor, one of the component states of the Senegalese political conglomerate of Great Jolof. He spent considerable time as the *damel*'s guest, gathering valuable information on Wolof trade and society. In the company of another Italian, the Genoese Antoniotto Usodimare, he then sailed farther southeast in an unsuccessful attempt to explore the Gambia River, before turning back to Portugal.

Cadamosto returned to West Africa the following year with three ships. The expedition set out to continue the reconnaissance of the Gambia River, in search of gold. Cadamosto established friendly relations with several local rulers and traded with the *mansa* of Bati, one of the Mande states lining the river. Although the expedition did not manage to acquire gold, only slaves and civet, Cadamosto considered his voyage to the Gambia a success. The ships then sailed farther southeast, reaching the estuary of the Geba River (Rio Grande), but they were forced to turn back. On the return leg of the voyage Cadamosto discovered some of the Cape Verde Islands, a claim challenged by several other explorers.

After his return from Africa, Cadamosto retained an interest in the contemporary southbound explorations, and he compiled from eyewitness testimony a brief account of the 1460 voyage undertaken by Pedro de Sintra to Sierra Leone and the confines of Liberia. Cadamosto most likely remained in Portugal until his departure for Venice in February 1463. His travel narrative constitutes an invaluable source for the history of early Portuguese expansion in Africa, especially given his powers of observation, his objectivity, and his keen interest in both the populations and the natural phenomena he encountered.

[*See also* Africa; Expeditions, World Exploration, *subentry on* Portugal; *and* Henry the Navigator.]

BIBLIOGRAPHY

Crone, G. R., ed. and trans. *The Voyages of Cadamosto and Other Documents on Western Africa in the Second Half of the Fifteenth Century.* London: Hakluyt Society, 1937. Reprint. Nendeln, Liechtenstein: Kraus Reprint, 1967.

Russell, Peter. *Prince Henry "the Navigator": A Life.* New Haven, Conn.: Yale University Press, 2000.

IVANA ELBL
MARTIN ELBL

Caillié, René (1799–1838), French explorer, perhaps the most single-minded in history, who was the first European to reach Timbuctoo and survive to tell his story. Born on November 19, 1799, in Mauzé, France, René-Auguste Caillié was orphaned by age eleven. He claimed early on that he would be an explorer, and it was Africa that beckoned him. In April 1816, he departed Mauzé and joined an ill-fated group of settlers who were destined for Senegal.

Following many months of difficulties, the French contingent founded Saint-Louis. After working at a variety of jobs, Caillié attempted to go to Sierra Leone but detoured to Guadeloupe in the Caribbean, where, in 1818, he resided for six months. While there, his desire to go to Timbuctoo was heightened when he read Mungo Park's book about his travels in the interior of Africa. Caillié described his life from 1819 to early 1824 as uneventful; being a representative for a wine establishment in Bordeaux was one of the jobs he held during this time.

Caillié returned to Senegal in early 1824 and began seriously preparing for his attempt to reach Timbuctoo. He quickly learned the Wolof language and later became fluent in Mandingo, but he was not as facile in Arabic. He began dressing as a Muslim and spent considerable time studying the Koran and learning about African Islamic culture. On August 3, 1824, masquerading in Muslim garb, Caillié departed for the interior. He told everyone that he was a convert to Islam on his way to Mecca, and Timbuctoo was on his route. This trip proved to be nothing more than a preview for his final effort to reach the Niger River and Timbuctoo. Caillié spent eight months in the village of Brakna, but when he returned to the coast seeking financial backing, he was disappointed at every turn. By this time, however, he could pass as an Arab, even though his Arabic was imperfect. Also, Caillié's impetus for travel into the interior was strengthened when he learned that the Geographical Society of Paris had offered a Gold Medal and a 10,000-franc reward to anyone who could prove that he had been to Timbuctoo.

Before he began his journey to the Niger River, Caillié diligently taught himself how to estimate his rate of travel. Always displaying piety, he created yet another story about himself. He claimed that he had been born in Egypt of Arab parents, but was taken by a Napoleonic soldier to France when he was young. He had accompanied his master to Senegal, and the master later freed him. Now he wanted to return to Egypt to search for his family, and then to make the pilgrimage to Mecca.

Caillié moved to Kakandé, near the mouth of the Rio Nunez between Saint-Louis and Freetown, and after joining a caravan destined for Timbuctoo, he first saw the Niger River at Kouroussa early in June 1827. At Tiémé, about a quarter of the way to his destination, Caillié became very ill. Not only was he suffering from scurvy, but he also contracted malaria and one of his feet became infected. For the next five months an elderly African woman nursed him back to reasonable health. In January 1828 he continued his journey, and in March he arrived at Djenné, a bustling city in present-day Mali—200 miles (322 kilometers) upriver from Timbuctoo. He then commenced the worst segment of his trip. Caillié had now entered the dreaded Tuareg territory, and while sailing down the Niger to Kabara (Timbuctoo's port) for close to a month, he remained belowdecks suffering from fear, illness, lack of food, and debilitating heat.

On April 20, 1828, twelve years after he had left Mauzé and a year after he had started his journey at Kakandé, René Caillié entered Timbuctoo. This remarkable freelance traveler, unknown to Europe, had totally on his own made the arduous, dangerous, and illness-filled odyssey to the fabled African city that had been visited by only one other European—the ill-fated Alexander Gordon Laing in 1826. In his account of this journey, *Journal d'un voyage à Temboctou* (3 vols.), published in 1830, Caillié expressed disappointment. He said that the city did not "answer my expectations." In fact, Timbuctoo clearly was not a place of riches, but only a typical barren, monotonous, dingy desert community. Caillié claimed that Djenné was a much more active place, and that Timbuctoo seemed to be withering economically. Com-

pared to Djenné's, Timbuctoo's market was a "desert." Caillié spent two weeks there, and he found no evidence of agriculture being practiced. He discreetly sketched the local architecture (his drawing of the plan of Timbuctoo is now famous), and discovered as much as he could about Laing's stay there. Although he had no evidence, Caillié believed that the Niger flowed into the Gulf of Benin.

The final leg of the journey began when Caillié left Timbuctoo on May 4, 1828. Penniless, and soon to be suffering from dysentery, he joined a caravan headed for Morocco. After a difficult desert crossing, the caravan arrived at Tafilalt on June 23, 1828. Traveling alone, Caillié took six more grueling weeks to reach Tangier. At first, Caillié was scorned by officials in Rabat and Tangier, but finally the French consul in Tangier secreted him out of Morocco disguised as a sailor. Unlike Heinrich Barth (the third European to enter Timbuctoo), Caillié was treated quite well by the geographical establishment when he returned to France from Africa. He quickly was given his 10,000-franc reward from the Geographical Society of Paris, and he received its Gold Medal. Further, the French government awarded him a pension of 6,000 francs a year, and he was named a Chevalier of the Legion of Honor. His countrymen proudly praised him for being the "Marco Polo of Africa."

Unfortunately, Caillié's book was quite long, and to most readers, it was dull. Critics complained that his scientific notes were incomplete and that his description of Timbuctoo was superficial—for example, he said little about Laing's fate. Of course, these critics did not consider that if Caillié had delved too much into Laing's earlier visit, he would have aroused suspicion. His detractors, many of them in Britain, claimed that Caillié was a hoax and that his story was fabricated. A modern writer has demeaned Caillié's achievement by saying that all he did was "run a solo marathon."

Caillié returned to Mauzé, where he became mayor for a short time, but he soon died, on May 17, 1838, probably from a malady contracted while in Africa. Heinrich Barth later praised Caillié's accuracy in describing the fabled city, thus giving him the credit he had not received from detractors while he was alive.

[*See also* Barth, Heinrich; Laing, Alexander Gordon; Park, Mungo; *and* Timbuctoo.]

BIBLIOGRAPHY

Caillié, René. *Travels through Central Africa to Timbuctoo and across the Great Desert to Morocco, 1824–28*. London: Frank Cass, 1968. Originally published in 1830.

Gardner, Brian. *The Quest for Timbuctoo*. New York: Harcourt, Brace and World, 1968.

Travels in Africa

This passage captures the disappointment that European travelers often felt upon arriving at cities that had assumed an extraordinary importance in their imaginations. Caillié's disappointment with Timbuctoo resembles that felt by those travelers in Mesoamerica who sought the mythical cities of Cíbola, and found much less dramatic settlements. Still, as the image from the writings of Heinrich Barth shows, Timbuctoo was in fact an impressive settlement.

I had formed a totally different idea of the grandeur and wealth of Timbuctoo. The city presented, at first view, nothing but a mass of ill-looking houses, built of earth. Nothing was to be seen in all directions but immense plains of quicksand of a yellowish white colour. The sky was a pale red as far as the horizon; all nature wore a dreary aspect, and the most profound silence prevailed; not even the warbling of a bird was to be heard.

—René Caillié, *Travels through Central Africa to Timbuctoo*
(London, 1830)

The Island of California. William Berry, detail from *North America* (London, 1680). This beautifully engraved map is remarkable not only for its elegance, but also for its geographical inaccuracy, of which the delineation of California as an island is only one example. COURTESY THE NEWBERRY LIBRARY, CHICAGO

Welch, Galbraith. *The Unveiling of Timbuctoo: The Astounding Adventures of Caillié.* New York: Carroll and Graf, 1991. Originally published in 1939.

SANFORD H. BEDERMAN

California, Island of.

When Spanish explorers first reached the peninsula we now call Baja (Lower) California in 1533, they assumed that it was an island. Thus began a misconception that flourished on and off for more than two centuries.

After fighting his way across Mexico to the west coast, Hernán Cortés believed that many islands full of gold, pearls, and obliging women remained to be discovered. Belief in the ancient and medieval lore of rich islands in the great ocean (the Atlantic) had been carried westward by Columbus, and then by Balboa in 1513 to the "other ocean"—the Mar del Sur or South Sea, later known as the Pacific. Cortés hoped that Baja was one of those dream islands, as suggested by its being called "la ysla dela California." (The name is derived from a sixteenth-century sequel to a medieval Castilian romance that described the island fortress of a Muslim queen, Calafia, and her wealthy Amazons, during the Crusades.) Cortés's expectations motivated him to lead a colonizing party to Baja in 1535. The venture failed, delaying development of the region of Baja and Alta (Upper) California for almost two centuries. Several probes of the Sea of Cortés tested claims that it might be a gulf rather than a sea, but a great river (the Colorado) poured in from the north, hindering the search. The theory of Lower California's peninsularity gained ground in the following decades, but never quite displaced the notion of an island severed from the mainland by a strait, as cartographical ambiguities of the period imply (for example, on maps by Michele Tramezzino, 1554, and Jehan Cossin, 1570).

In the same period, voyagers along the outer coast sought the outlets of straits that the Spaniards feared put New Spain at risk of foreign invasion. English geographers and mariners increasingly touted the idea of a Northwest Passage across the "top" of North America whose western exit, the Strait of Anian, connected with the supposed Strait of California. When Spanish spies at the court of Queen Elizabeth I relayed rumors of Francis Drake's impending voyage in the later 1570s, this imaginary network of straits was assumed by the Spaniards to be the route of the corsairs.

The concern about straits reawakened the corollary myth of the Island of California. In 1602, Father Antonio de Ascensión sailed north from Acapulco with Sebastián Vizcaíno in quest of a northern strait and in 1608 pronounced California an island, a notion fueled by explorers on the New Mexico frontier. This second flowering was of far greater proportions, for the island now comprised not only Baja California but also the larger "Upper" territory that in the nineteenth century would become the state of California. In 1620 Ascensión's map fell into foreign hands, and renderings were soon published by the Dutch cartographer Abraham Goos, and, in England, by Henry Briggs. The latter was reprinted by Samuel Purchas in 1625, and for the rest of the century the "large island of California" concept prevailed on many European maps, such as those of Nicolas Sanson and Herman Moll.

Late in the seventeenth century, the Society of Jesus sent Father Eusebio Kino to investigate Baja California and then to establish missions in Pimería Alta (Sonora) on the opposite mainland. Through careful observation Kino inferred that a passage by land joined the two sides, and his map of 1701 depicted California as a peninsula. A desert stretching many leagues prevented Kino from conclusively demolishing the island myth, and it was another two-thirds of a century before a Franciscan missionary, Father Francisco Garcés, crossed that burning sea of sand. In 1774 he guided a party captained by Juan Bautista de Anza from the interior to the recently established mission of San Gabriel on the Pacific coast, ending at last an enduring fantasy.

[*See also* Cortés, Hernán; Drake, Francis; *and* Kino, Eusebio.]

BIBLIOGRAPHY

Leighly, John Barger. *California as an Island: An Illustrated Essay, 1622–1785*. San Francisco: Book Club of California, 1972.

McLaughlin, Glen, with Nancy H. Mayo. *The Mapping of California as an Island, an Illustrated Checklist*. Saratoga: California Map Society, 1995.

Polk, Dora Beale. *The Island of California: A History of the Myth*. Spokane, Wash.: The Arthur H. Clark Company, 1991. Reprint. Lincoln: University of Nebraska Press, 1995.

Tooley, R. V. *California as an Island, a Geographical Misconception Illustrated by 100 Examples from 1625 to 1770*. Map Collectors' Series, no. 8. London: Map Collectors' Circle, 1964.

Wagner, Henry Raup. *Spanish Voyages to the Northwest Coast of America in the Sixteenth Century*. San Francisco: California Historical Society, 1929.

DORA BEALE POLK

Cameron, Verney Lovett

Cameron, Verney Lovett (1844–1894), British scientist and the first European to cross central Africa. Verney Lovett Cameron, the first scientific traveler to cross Africa from east to west and an important influence upon King Leopold II of Belgium (r. 1865–1909), was born at Radipole in Dorset on July 1, 1844. He joined the Royal Navy and pursued a steady if unspectacular career until service in the squadron enforcing slave trade treaties off Zanzibar engendered an interest in East Africa. He tried to persuade the Royal Geographical Society (RGS) to employ him on its 1872 expedition to relieve and assist David Livingstone. Llewellyn S. Dawson was chosen instead, but Dawson's expedition disintegrated when Henry Stanley returned to the coast from his famous meeting alleging that Livingstone wanted no help from the RGS. After bitter arguments over Stanley's information died down, it became apparent that key geographical questions remained open, such as the whereabouts of Lake Tanganyika's outlet and whether the Lualaba connected to the Congo or the Nile. The RGS decided to send another expedition to help Livingstone with these problems and now chose Cameron to lead it.

Cameron was accompanied by Dr. W. E. Dillon, Lieutenant Cecil Murphy, and Livingstone's nephew, Robert Moffat, who soon died. A new anti-slave-trade treaty made recruiting porters difficult but Cameron had the aid of the very experienced leader, nicknamed "Bombay." It took from March to August 1873 to reach Tabora, where Cameron received a letter from Jacob Wainwright reporting Livingstone's death. The party carrying the body then arrived and insisted on continuing their journey to the coast. Murphy and Dillon went with them, but Dillon committed suicide.

Despite all this, Cameron decided to go on and accomplish some geographical work, spending somewhat lavishly on the credit of the RGS to the unprecedented extent of over £11,000. Arguably, the results justified the expense. During March and April 1874, Cameron surveyed the southern shores of Lake Tanganyika, calculated the lake's altitude, and identified the Lukuga as the probable outlet flowing to the Lualaba, which he reached at Nyangwe in August. Now certain that the Lualaba was the Congo, Cameron hoped to prove this by following it to the Atlantic Ocean. The Arab slave and ivory trader "Tippu Tip" (Hamed bin Muhammed) refused him aid to do so and advised him to turn southwestward. This Cameron did and traversed the vast area of the Congo's basin before finally reaching the Atlantic near Benguela in November 1875, emaciated and suffering from scurvy. Even so, Cameron was convinced the Congo Basin had enormous economic potential and tried to annex it for Britain. Although the British government was unresponsive, Léopold II was impressed and was encouraged to proceed with his schemes to develop the interior of Africa; he invited Cameron to attend the Brussels Geographical Conference of September 1876, which inaugurated a new era in the history of the continent.

Cameron himself set up a commercial geographical society, which did not attract much support, and invested in some Portuguese enterprises. To avoid the boredom of a return to service life, he visited the Gold Coast with Richard Burton, interested himself in the Indian Empire, and tried his hand at writing boys' adventure stories rather after the style of Robert Ballantyne but without Ballantyne's success. On March 26, 1894, Cameron died at Leighton Buzzard in Buckinghamshire as the result of a riding accident.

[*See also* Brussels Geographical Conference; Burton, Richard F.; Livingstone, David; *and* Stanley, Henry.]

BIBLIOGRAPHY

Cameron, Verney Lovett. *Across Africa*. 2 vols. London: Daldy, Isbister, and Co., 1877.

Casada, James A. "Verney Lovett Cameron: A Centenary Appreciation." *Geographical Journal* 141 (1975): 203–215.

Foran, William Robert. *African Odyssey: The Life of Verney Lovett-Cameron*. London: Hutchinson, 1937.

Hooker, James R. "Verney Lovett Cameron: A Sailor in Central Africa." In *Africa and Its Explorers: Motives, Methods, and Impact*, edited by Robert I. Rotberg, 255–294. Cambridge, Mass.: Harvard University Press, 1970.

ROY BRIDGES

Canada. *See* **Alaska and the Yukon Gold Rush; Arctic; Baffin, William; Cartier, Jacques; Champlain, Samuel de; Fur Trade; Geological Survey of Canada; Hearne, Samuel; Hudson's Bay Company; Inuit; James, Thomas; La Vérendrye, Sieur de; Mackenzie, Alexander; Mer de l'Ouest and Rivière de l'Ouest; Northeast Passage; North West Company; Northwest Passage; Sea Ice; Stefansson, Vilhjalmur;** *St. Roch* **and** *St. Roch II*; *and* **Whaling.**

Cannibalism. Ritual cannibalism, or the eating of human flesh and bones for religious purposes, probably had a lengthy existence in Central and South America, although very early evidence is scarce. Splintered bones found in refuse deposits in the preclassic Olmec site of San Lorenzo, Veracruz (c. 1200–900 B.C.E.), for example, suggest cannibal practices. The wide geographic spread of cannibalism is clearer. Sixteenth-century reports of the practice come from the Tarascans in Michoacan, the Lacandon Maya in Guatemala, and Álvar Núñez Cabeza de Vaca, who as governor of a Spanish colony in the Río de la Plata area of Brazil forbade natives to eat human flesh. We can identify Christopher Columbus as the source for naming the practice after the Carib Indians of the Caribbean. The Carib Indians supposedly ate their neighbors, but the evidence is not conclusive. Spanish explorers did, however, experience cannibalism first-hand. After watching the ritualistic consumption of four ship-

Cannibalism. Detail from an anonymous German woodcut, c. 1505. This early woodcut is an example of the way in which some European artists showed Amerindian peoples (often Tupinamba) as habitual gastronomic cannibals; here a human body is being casually consumed. COURTESY THE NEWBERRY LIBRARY, CHICAGO

wrecked companions, Jerónimo de Águilar (one of Hernán Cortés's eventual translators) escaped with his remaining friends from wooden cages in which they were imprisoned by their Maya captors.

Theories as to why Central and South Americans practiced cannibalism vary widely. They range from theories that cannibalism was merely a Spanish fabrication justifying conquest, to theories that cannibalism served as a correction for a dietary deficiency of protein, to theories that cannibalism provided an extreme form of political and social control. First, a large amount of material and historical evidence supports cannibalism as a long-term, widespread indigenous practice. Second, evidence is lacking for showing that cannibalism was capable of correcting protein deficiency, if one even existed. And third, cannibalistic rituals focus on far more than simply political or social issues. Although war and criminal punishment could serve as reasons for cannibalistic activities—Cabeza de Vaca outlawed it because warring tribes had gotten out of hand—cosmic sustenance and the death of one's relatives were more common reasons for cannibalism. Hence, more fruitful explanations come from those who attempt to discover the underlying religious reasons for cannibalism.

Cannibalism cannot be separated from the even more widely spread practice of sacrifice, both human and nonhuman. Some argue that all sacrifice is based on a feeding exchange among the world's diverse living beings, which could include not just hungry people and animals, but also such beings as gods, trees, streams, and mountains. In every sacrificial ritual, someone fed someone to someone else. The meal usually consisted of nothing more than perhaps an animal, or a bit of blood from one's earlobe. In some rituals, however, actual humans served as the meal. In Central America, humans often were equated with corn; for, as they ate corn to sustain their life, so too were they the corn that sustained other lives. The Hero Twins of the Quiché Maya myth the Popol Vuh, for example, sacrificed themselves so that their bones could be ground like cornmeal; this transformed them into new forms capable of controlling the forces of death and creating the current world. Similarly, the Aztec goddess Cihuacoatl fashioned people from cornlike dough made out of blood that the god Quetzalcoatl let from his member onto ground-up ancestral bones. South Americans actually ate flesh or the ashes of deceased relatives. By ingesting such tangible signs of death, they reenacted mythic destructions that had created human life in primordial times. Thus humans themselves became the sacred instruments for transformation in their fundamentally consumptive cosmos.

[*See also* Cabeza de Vaca, Álvar Núñez, *and* Spanish and Portuguese America, Reports and Descriptions of.]

BIBLIOGRAPHY

Ortiz de Montellano, Bernard R. "Aztec Cannibalism: An Ecological Necessity?" *Science* 200, no. 4342 (1978): 611–617. This is the best rebuttal of the nutritional theory for cannibalism.

Read, Kay A. *Time and Sacrifice in the Aztec Cosmos.* Bloomington: Indiana University Press, 1998. Contains a translation from Nahuatl of the tale of Quetzalcoatl retrieving the bones to make people and offers an overall logic for sacrifice, of which cannibalism is one type.

Sullivan, Lawrence E. *Icanchu's Drum: An Orientation to Meaning in South American Religions.* New York: Macmillan, 1988. Contains an extensive discussion of South American religious structures and practices, including sacrifice and cannibalism.

KAY A. READ

Cão, Diogo (1450–1486), Portuguese explorer who reached the Congo River. One of Europe's greatest explorers of the fifteenth century, mapping more than twenty degrees of south latitude during two voyages, Diogo Cão was also the first European to see the mouth of the Congo (Zaire) River. He was born in Trás-os-Montes, but little is known of his early life until 1480, when Cão is known to have been in the Gulf of Guinea. The majority of scholars argue that in the 1480s Diogo Cão made two voyages of exploration for King João II (r. 1481–1495). The first began before August 1482, most probably in the spring of that year. The voyage left Lisbon and sailed to the recently constructed fortress of São Jorge da Mina. From there Cão continued on to Cape Saint Catherine, the farthest point south discovered during the reign of King Afonso V (r. 1438–1481). It was on this voyage that Cão arrived at the mouth of the Congo River. He left a *padrão*, or dated stone column, on its south bank and sent an embassy to find the king of the Congo; then he explored the coast southward to Cape Lobo (Cabo de Santa Maria), where he left another stone pillar. Cão brought some Congolese hostages back to Portugal, arriving there at the end of March or in early April 1484. Cão also traveled and explored to the falls of Ielala, about a hundred miles up the Congo River, where he and others left their names on the nearby rocks. However, it is not clear whether this episode took place on the first or the second voyage.

Cão's second voyage began during the fall of 1485, when he returned the hostages and picked up the emissaries. He left stone columns at Lucira Grande and Cape Cross, having reached 22°10′ S. The second voyage returned to Portugal in 1486, but possibly without its leader, who is said to have died near the Serra Parda. The maps of Cristoforo Soligo (published 1485–1490) and Henricus Martellus Germanus (published c. 1489) reported Cão's discoveries to a wider world.

[*See also* Africa *and* Expeditions, World Exploration, *subentry on* Portugal.]

BIBLIOGRAPHY

Diffie, Bailey W., and George D. Winius. *Foundations of the Portuguese Empire, 1415–1580.* Minneapolis: University of Minnesota Press, 1977.

Peres, Damião. *História dos descobrimentos portugueses.* Porto, Portugal: Portucalense Editora, 1943.

FRANCIS A. DUTRA

Cape of Good Hope. In their slow exploration of the western side of Africa, the Portuguese scored a major success when, in 1488, Bartholomew Dias rounded the tip of the continent in a storm without sighting the cape and sailed along the southern coast. Anchoring in False Bay on the return journey, he observed the cape towering on the west and named it "Cape of Storms." King João II (r. 1481–1495), considering the voyage auspicious, renamed it Cape of Good Hope, his expectations being fulfilled when Vasco da Gama reached Calicut in 1498.

Although the Portuguese admiral Antonio de Saldanha climbed the "Table of the Cape" in 1503, it was Joris van Spilbergen who named Table Bay in 1601. The English claimed the bay and adjoining continent in 1620. To forestall them, the directors of the Dutch East India Company (VOC) sent out Jan van Riebeeck to establish "a fort and vegetable garden" in 1652. Under the wise administration of Simon van der Stel and his son Willem Adriaan, significant developments followed the difficult beginnings. Cattle outposts were established in outlying areas to collect the animals needed to provision the ships, and company employees were encouraged as "free burghers" to farm in the hinterland for the production of grain and other crops. Installations were made at the port to accommodate the visiting ships. In bad weather, the ships repaired north to Saldanha Bay, but more often to False Bay, where the necessary overhauls could be effected at Simonstown, a small harbor fitted with naval stores.

Cape of Good Hope. Benjamin van der Gucht, *The Cape of Good Hope* (1736). Here we recognize many of the same landforms as on John Sellers's landfall. By now, the Dutch colony on the cape was well established. THE BRITISH LIBRARY/HIP/ART RESOURCE

When Rijk Tulbagh celebrated the centenary of Kaapstad (Cape Town), the former outpost had evolved as a focal point of science and exploration. The astronomer Nicolas-Louis, Abbé de La Caille, selected "this most important station for the study of geography" to observe the austral constellations as a help to navigation, mapping some ten thousand stars. Kaapstad's botanical garden grew in fame as learned gardeners, trained at Amsterdam or at the Leiden University botanic gardens, developed its collections of native plants. Linnaeus sent his students Carl Peter Thunberg and Anders Sparrman—who was recruited by James Cook to assist his naturalists, Johann Reinhold Forster and Georg Forster—to explore and collect there.

In the late eighteenth century, the explorers of the Pacific started from the Cape of Good Hope to take advantage of the westerlies. The link between oceanic and continental exploration was reinforced by the influence of Robert Jacob Gordon, commander of the fort from 1777 to 1795, when it surrendered to the British forces. Nicolas Baudin's scientists enjoyed collecting for the Musée d'Histoire Naturelle two years before the Cape of Good Hope was returned to the English, the definitive possession being ratified by the Treaty of Paris in 1814.

[*See also biographical entries on figures mentioned in this article.*]

BIBLIOGRAPHY

Gunn, Mary, and L. E. W. Codd. *Botanical Exploration of Southern Africa: An Illustrated History of Early Botanical Literature on the Cape Flora, Biographical Accounts of the Leading Plant Collectors and Their Activities in Southern Africa from the Days of the East India Company until Modern Times.* Cape Town, South Africa: A. A. Balkema for the Botanical Research Institute, 1981.

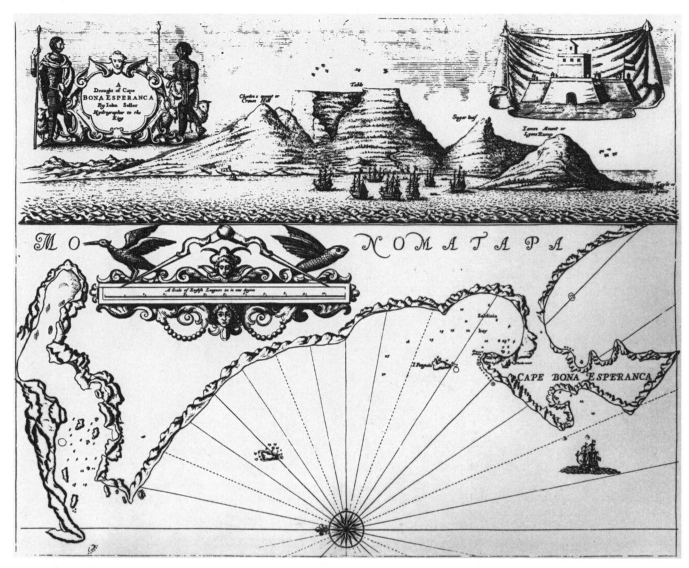

Cape of Good Hope. John Sellers, A draught of Cape Bona Esperanca from John Sellers and Charles Price, *The English Pilot, The Fifth Book* (London, 1601). This is an interesting form of map, combining a chart (below) with what was called a "landfall" (above). It dates from the time when the English and the Dutch were beginning their rivalry for the Cape. Courtesy The Newberry Library, Chicago

Rookmaaker, L. C. *The Zoological Exploration of Southern Africa, 1650–1790.* Rotterdam, Netherlands, and Brookfield, Vt.: A. Balkema, 1989.

Worden, Nigel, Elizabeth Van Heyningen, and Vivian Bickford-Smith. *Cape Town: The Making of a City—an Illustrated Social History.* Claremont, South Africa: D. Philip, 1998.

Huguette Ly-Tio-Fane Pineo
Madeleine Ly-Tio-Fane

Caravel. *See* **Vessels,** *subentry on* **Sailing Vessels.**

Caribbean Region, Exploration of. The Caribbean region includes not only the islands of the West Indies but also the mainland littoral that runs from the Yucatán Peninsula to the Guiana Coast of South America. A region defined as much by water as by land, it was explored and settled in prehistoric times by peoples whose seafaring prowess allowed them to move from mainland to island in two separate migrations, first from Mexico across the Yucatán Channel to Cuba and Hispaniola around 4000 B.C.E., and later from the mouth of the Orinoco River up through the Lesser Antilles to Puerto Rico around 2000 B.C.E. European exploration of the region is inextricably linked to Columbus, whose four Spanish-

Caribbean Region. Gonzalo Fernández de Oviedo, plate from *História general y natural de las Indias* (ed. José Amador de los Ríos, 4 vols., Madrid, 1851–1855). This nineteenth-century engraving derives in part from Oviedo's original image. It shows an Amerindian hammock and two very well-observed huts, or bohios. COURTESY THE NEWBERRY LIBRARY, CHICAGO

sponsored expeditions took him and his ships (1) through the Bahamas to Cuba and Hispaniola (1492–1493); (2) to Dominica, Guadeloupe, Puerto Rico, Hispaniola, Cuba, and Jamaica (1493–1496); (3) to Trinidad, the Paria Peninsula of Venezuela, Margarita Island, and Hispaniola (1498–1500); and (4) to Jamaica, Cuba, and Central America, whose Atlantic shores he skirted from Honduras to Panama (1502–1504). For imperial Spain, exploration and conquest went hand-in-hand. From their base of operation on Hispaniola, Spaniards mounted expeditions that saw Juan Ponce de León secure Puerto Rico, Juan de Esquivel lay claim to Jamaica, and Diego Velázquez de Cuéllar and Pánfilo de Narváez conquer Cuba. The islands of the Caribbean, however, proved to be but stepping stones for considerably more rewarding ventures, including the discovery of the Pacific by Vasco Núñez de Balboa in 1513, the conquest of Mexico by Hernán Córtes in 1519, and the conquest of Peru by Francisco Pizarro in 1532. While exploration of the Caribbean brought prosperity to Spain and, after Spanish interest in the Antilles had waned, to Britain, France, and Holland, European ambitions spelled disaster and demise for native peoples, whose island homes by the late eighteenth century were all but emptied of any autochthonous presence. [See color plate 18 in this volume.]

[*See also* Expeditions, World Exploration, *subentry on* Spain, *and biographies of figures mentioned in this article.*]

BIBLIOGRAPHY

Rouse, Irving. *The Tainos: Rise and Decline of the People Who Greeted Columbus.* New Haven, Conn.: Yale University Press, 1992.

Sauer, Carl Ortwin. *The Early Spanish Main.* Berkeley and Los Angeles: University of California Press, 1963.

W. GEORGE LOVELL

Carpini, Giovanni (1180–1252), also known as John of Plano and Giovanni di Piano Carpini, a Franciscan friar who visited the court of the Mongol khan during 1245 and 1247 and wrote the first European account of the Mongols.

Between 1237 and 1242 the hitherto unknown Mongols devastated Russia and eastern Europe, and only the death of their Great Khan Ogadai in 1241 brought the carnage to an end. Desperate for accurate information about Mongol intentions and hoping to open up diplomatic relations, Pope Innocent IV on Easter 1245 ordered the first of the Mongol missions and sent the Franciscan friar John of Plano

---

Travels in China

Carpini, a Franciscan friar who was a contemporary and friend of Saint Francis of Assisi, is an invaluable source for information on the society of the Mongols, with their round, tentlike houses, their omnivorous eating habits, and their peripatetic style of life. The Mongols thus differed greatly from their successors, the Ming dynasty.

The appearance of the Mongols or Tartars is quite different from all other nations, being much wider between the eyes and cheeks, and their cheeks very prominent with small flat noses and small eyes, having the upper lids opened up to the eyebrows, and their crowns are shaven like priests on each side, leaving some long hair in the middle, the remainder being allowed to grow long like women, which they twist into two tails or locks, and bind behind their ears.

—*A General History and Collection of Voyages and Travels,* edited by Robert Kerr (Edinburgh, 1811–1824)

Carpini as an envoy. On April 16, 1245, the sixty-five-year-old portly Carpini departed from Lyon and reached the Mongol great camp on July 22, just in time to witness the election of Guyuk as Great Khan. Much of Carpini's success in traveling came from using the Mongol post-horse system called *yams*. In two and a half years he traveled more than fifteen thousand miles, an ordeal involving hunger, thirst, cold, heat, injury, and sometimes the hostility of local people. Returning to the pope in November 1247, Carpini accomplished little diplomatically because Mongol rulers were interested only in submissive vassals, not in allies.

Carpini wrote a valuable account of his journey titled *Historia Mongolorum* (History of the Mongols), the first European description of Mongolia and China. While not as famous as his near contemporary Marco Polo, Carpini provided information about Asia that made its way into various European encyclopedic works of history and geography. After Europe lost contact with the Far East when the Ming dynasty ousted the Mongols from China in 1368, western knowledge of China remained static and increasingly obsolete. Columbus and other European explorers expected to reach the Cathay of Carpini and Marco Polo, not the China of the Mings.

[*See also* Polo, Marco.]

BIBLIOGRAPHY
Phillips, J. R. S. *The Medieval Expansion of Europe*. 2nd ed. Oxford and New York: Oxford University Press, 1998.

RONALD H. FRITZE

Carr, Jerry (b. 1932), American astronaut. Astronaut Gerald ("Jerry") Paul Carr's lasting memory of his single spaceflight is the view from the Skylab space station across the western seaboard of the United States, from northern California down to the Baja Peninsula and across the Gulf of Mexico. At a height of around 270 miles the view of earth from space was always spectacular, but below him was also the area where he had grown up and later served in the U.S. Marines. In 1973–1974, Carr commanded the longest flight in spaceflight history until that time, after his planned lunar flight was canceled. *Skylab 4* established that humans could live in weightlessness for a very long time without enduring physical problem. Carr was once told by Wernher von Braun that *Skylab 4* was his preferred mission over any other in that period, as it contributed to human destiny in space and confirmed humans' long-term ability to adapt to that environment.

Born on August 22, 1932, in Denver, Colorado, Carr was raised in Santa Ana, California, where he enjoyed woodworking, scouting, and tinkering with machinery—developing the skills that would become useful in his career as a pilot astronaut and engineering consultant. He graduated from high school in 1952, and, after earning a BS in mechanical engineering from the University of Southern California in 1954, he joined the U.S. Marine Corps and became a jet pilot. Selected to the NASA astronaut program in April 1966 (Group 5), he trained for the Apollo program with technical assignments in Lunar Module systems between 1966 and 1970.

Carr retired from NASA in 1977 to enter the private business sector, later forming his own aerospace consultancy company, CAMUS, that supported work on developing the International Space Station (ISS), and on the human exploration of the Moon and Mars. As of 2006 Carr lived in rural Arkansas with his artist-sculptor wife Pat Musick.

[*See also* International Space Station; Skylab; *and* Space Program, *subentry* American.]

BIBLIOGRAPHY
Baker, David. "Skylab: The Three Month Vigil." *Spaceflight* 16, nos. 11 and 12. British Interplanetary Society, 1974 and 1975.
Belew, Leland F., ed. *Skylab: Our First Space Station*. NASA SP-400. Washington, D.C.: Scientific Technical Information Office, National Aeronautics and Space Administration, 1977.
Compton, W. David, and Charles D. Brown. *Living and Working in Space: A History of Skylab*. NASA SP-4208. Washington, D.C.: Scientific and Technical Information Branch, National Aeronautics and Space Administration, 1983.
NASA Astronaut Biographical Data. "Gerald P. Carr." October 2003. http://www.jsc.nasa.gov/Bios/htmlbios/carr-gp.html.
NASA Oral History Transcript. "Gerald P. Carr." October 25, 2000. http://www.jsc.nasa.gov/history/oral_histories/CarrGP/GPC_10-25-00.pdf.
Shayler, David J. *Around the World in 84 Days*. Ontario: Apogee Books, 2006. Carr's authorized biography.
Shayler, David J. *Skylab America's Space Station*. London and New York: Springer-Verlag, 2001.

DAVE SHAYLER

Carteret, Philip. *See* **Wallis, Samuel, and Philip Carteret.**

Cartier, Jacques (1491–1557), navigator, explorer, European discoverer of the Saint Lawrence River. Nothing definite is known about Cartier before 1532, when he was recommended to King François I to lead an expedition to the New World in order to find a route to Asia and to discover lands where there were gold and other precious commodities. There is some evidence that he had been to Brazil and Newfoundland earlier in life.

Cartier's first expedition (1534) of two ships manned by sixty-one men sailed directly into the Strait of Belle Isle, suggesting he had been there before. As they proceeded along the north shore of the strait into the Gulf of Saint Lawrence, they saw a ship from La Rochelle and met some local Montagnais who were already familiar with Europeans. Cartier thought this stretch of Labrador to be so forbidding that he called it "the land God gave to Cain." The expedition proceeded south, along the west coast of Newfoundland, and began to circumnavigate the Gulf of Saint Lawrence. Along the north shore of Chaleur Bay it encountered several large groups of Algonquian-speaking Mi'kmaq (Micmac). Although the French were apprehensive at the sight of so many natives, they were received in a friendly manner and exchanged some trinkets for skins the Mi'kmaq wore as clothing—a transaction that Cartier considered to be of "small value." At Gaspé the expedition encountered several hundred Iroquoian-speaking peoples from Stadacona, a village at the present site of Quebec City. Gifts were given to establish friendly relations, but as Cartier's ships departed, the two teenage sons of the chief, Donnacona, were kidnapped to serve as future guides. [See color plate 22 in this volume.]

The following year the two boys guided Cartier's second expedition of three ships and 110 men up the Saint Lawrence River to their father's village. Their frequent use of the word "Canada" was interpreted by Cartier to mean the "province or territory" in which the village was located. Later specimens collected by Cartier of the local Iroquoian language show that the meaning of "Canada" is "the village." Shortly after the French arrived at Stadacona, misunderstandings between the two groups led to a deterioration of relations to the point where neither trusted the other. Unable to persuade the Stadaconans to guide him up the river, Cartier departed with fifty of his men, having ordered the rest to build a fort (Sainte-Croix) for the winter. At the village of Hochelaga, the way west was blocked by the mighty Lachine Rapids, 9 miles (14.5 kilometers) long. From the top of the mountain near the village, which he named Mount Royal, Cartier could see the Saint Lawrence leading westward beyond the rapids. Un-

---

Canadian Settlement

Unlike Columbus, Jacques Cartier had arrived in 1534 at a region (now Prince Edward Island) whose trees and other plants, and indeed animals, he could recognize from Europe. However, this early phase of French reconnaissance toward the valley of the Saint Lawrence River would eventually collapse because of the harshness of the Canadian winters.

We landed that day in four places to see the trees, which are wonderfully beautiful and very fragrant. We discovered that there were cedars, yew-trees, pines, white elms, ash trees, willows and others, any of them unknown to us and all trees without fruit. The soil where there are no trees is also very rich and is covered with pease, white and red gooseberry bushes, strawberries, raspberries and wild oats like rye, which one would say had been sowed there and tilled. It is the best-tempered region one can possibly see, and the heat is considerable. There are many turtle-doves, wood-pigeons and other birds; nothing is wanting but harbours.

—Jacques Cartier, *The Voyages of Jacques Cartier*, edited by Ramsay Cook and translated by H. P. Biggar (Toronto: University of Toronto Press, 1993)

---

able to explore farther, the French returned to their fort near Stadacona. When Cartier returned from Hochelaga, his persistent inquiries about gold and precious stones resulted in increasingly elaborate stories about a fabulously wealthy "Kingdom of Saguenay," a month's journey into the wilderness north of the Saint Lawrence River. During the winter, scurvy hit the French, and twenty-five men died before the Stadaconans could save the rest with an antiscorbutic made from boughs of a tree they called *annedda* (white cedar or hemlock). Before returning to France, Cartier kidnapped ten Stadaconans, among them Donnacona and his sons, in order to verify to King François the stories they had told him of the Kingdom of Saguenay.

With France thinking that this "Kingdom" would be like those captured by Spain in Mexico and Peru, a third expedition was organized in 1541 under the leadership of Jean-François de La Rocque de Roberval. Cartier departed first in five ships manned by fifteen hundred well-armed men, followed by Roberval in 1542 with three ships and several hundred men. Their task was to place a permanent settlement on the banks of the Saint Lawrence and conquer the Kingdom of Saguenay. Hemmed in by the rocky terrain, rapids, and dense forest along the shores of the Saint Lawrence; discouraged by an openly hostile native population and dreadful winters; and with no prospects of gold or precious stones, the would-be conquistadores returned to France, Cartier in 1542 and Roberval the following year.

With their return, Canada received the reputation of being inhabited by hostile natives, having no worthwhile resources except its offshore fishery, and being afflicted by a winter that made it difficult for Europeans to survive. Although these voyages created a negative image of Canada, Cartier's charts became the basis for the first rough maps of the Saint Lawrence River to Montreal Island, and his written accounts are the first sources on the environment of eastern Canada and its native inhabitants. His failure to establish friendly relations with the Iroquoian villagers and his unwillingness to leave the security of his ships to explore inland delayed the settlement of the shores of the Saint Lawrence until 1608, following Samuel de Champlain's surveys.

After his voyages to Canada, Cartier retired to his business ventures and the operation of his estate Limoilou near Saint-Malo, his birthplace.

[*See also* Champlain, Samuel de, *and* North America.]

BIBLIOGRAPHY
Cartier, Jacques. *The Voyages of Jacques Cartier*. Edited by Ramsay Cook and translated by H. P. Biggar. Toronto: University of Toronto Press, 1993.
Trudel, Marcel. "Cartier, Jacques." *Dictionary of Canadian Biography*. Vol. 1, pp. 1000–1017. Toronto: University of Toronto Press, 1966.

CONRAD E. HEIDENREICH

Carver, Jonathan (1710–1780), American surveyor and mapmaker who conjectured the existence of the Rocky Mountains. Born in Weymouth, Massachusetts, Jonathan Carver became a captain in the Massachusetts militia during the French wars of the 1750s. After leaving the militia, he taught himself mapmaking and surveying because he was, as he put it, determined "to explore the most unknown parts" of the "vast acquisition of territory" that Britain had gained after its conquest of New France. Among others who had inherited the French enthusiasm for western discovery was the celebrated wartime Rangers leader, Major Robert Rogers, who proposed an expedition that would cross the continent near the headwaters of the Mississippi and then proceed down the river "called by the Indians Ouragan" to the Pacific. This reincarnation of the French Rivière de l'Ouest caught Carver's imagination, and accompanied by traders and Indians he set off from Rogers's command post at Fort Michilimackinac (on the Strait of Mackinac, Michigan) in September 1766.

Carver followed the old French missionary and trading routes past Lake Michigan, Green Bay, and Fox River to the upper Mississippi, where he turned north. In November he encountered Dakota or Plains Sioux and followed the Minnesota River to the main Sioux encampment, where he claimed to have spent the winter. The Sioux informed him that there were further Indian nations to the west: the Mandan, and beyond them the Cheyenne. In the spring of 1767, Carver returned to Michilimackinac by a more northerly route by way of Lake Superior. His journey was the longest made by a trader-explorer in the period between the British conquest and the coming of the American Revolution, but in practical terms it achieved little. Carver went to England in 1769, but neither he nor Rogers was able to persuade the British government to support further western expeditions.

Carver's colorful account of his exploits, heavily rewritten, was published in 1778 as *Travels through America*. A best seller, it was translated into several European languages, but Carver died in London on January 31, 1780, in abject poverty. Despite having an element of plagiarism and the inclusion of some tall stories, the book was more than just an engaging travel narrative. Apart from containing one of the first detailed accounts of the Plains Sioux, it put forward a revised version of the old symmetrical concepts of North American geography that was influential in the last decades of the eighteenth century. Carver's was an anglicized version of the French theoretical geography that had long dominated maps of North America, but he was one of the first to commit himself in print to the existence of a great range of mountains running from north to south down the continent and forming a barrier to explorers trying to reach the Pacific from the east. The Shining Mountains, as he called them, formed a true continental divide, with rivers flowing to all points of the compass—and to the west was the "Oregon" River. Although Carver sited the range too centrally, in all except location his remarks conjured up a true image of the Rockies: "This extraordinary range of mountains is calculated to be more than three thousand miles in length, without any very considerable intervals, which I believe surpasses anything of the kind in other parts of the globe."

[*See also* Mer de l'Ouest and Rivière de l'Ouest *and* Rocky Mountains.]

BIBLIOGRAPHY
Bickham, Troy O. "Jonathan Carver." *Oxford Dictionary of National Biography*. Vol. 10, pp. 423–424. Oxford and New York: Oxford University Press, 2004.
Carver, Jonathan. *Jonathan Carver's Travels through America 1766–1768: An Eighteenth-Century Explorer's Account of Uncharted America*. Edited by Norman Gelb. New York: Wiley, 1993.
Carver, Jonathan. *The Journals of Jonathan Carver and Related Documents 1766–1770*. Edited by John Parker. Saint Paul: Minnesota Historical Society Press, 1976.

GLYNDWR WILLIAMS

Catesby, Mark (1683–1749), English naturalist. Sometimes called "the Colonial Audubon," Mark, the youngest son of John Catesby and his wife Elizabeth, was born at Castle Hedingham, his mother's home near Sudbury, England. In his will Mark's father was described as a "Gentleman of Sudbury, Suffolk," where he served in many positions in local government, including the office of mayor. Mark appears to have had a good local education, but there is no evidence that he attended university.

One of Mark Catesby's married sisters had emigrated to Williamsburg, Virginia, and this became his destination when he crossed the Atlantic in 1712.

Beasts, Fishes, Serpents, Insects and Plants . . . 2 vols. London: 1731–1743.

Frick, George F., and Raymond P. Stearns. *Mark Catesby : The Colonial Audubon.* Urbana: University of Illinois Press, 1961.

LOUIS DE VORSEY

On Depicting Natural History

As this extract shows, Catesby was modest about his achievements as a painter. Perhaps indeed he was excessively modest, for his innovation in placing bird and animal subjects alongside their appropriate trees and shrubs was very important, and clearly led the way to the extraordinary images of John Audubon.

As I was not bred a painter, I hope some faults in perspective, and other niceties, may be more readily excused; for I humbly conceive that Plants and other things, done in a Flat, tho' exact manner, may serve the Purpose of Natural History better in some measure, than a more bold and Painter-like way.

—Mark Catesby, *The Natural History of Carolina, Florida, and the Bahama Islands* (London, 1771)

In Virginia, Catesby soon met what he termed the people of quality and busied himself collecting seeds and cuttings. Through his contact with William Byrd, Catesby soon met and was deeply impressed by the American Indians and their pharmacopoeia. In his later published work Catesby made clear that he was "much indebted" to the Indians for frequently feeding and sheltering him as they guided him into the wilderness of the Appalachians and Spanish Florida. After a trip to Jamaica and Bermuda he returned to Virginia to continue his explorations and botanical collecting in the colonies. In 1725, Catesby accepted the invitation from the governor of Bahamas and explored and collected in those islands.

Mark Catesby returned to England in 1726 to devote himself to organizing and writing up his findings. In 1731 he published the first volume of his monumental *Natural History of Carolina, Florida, and the Bahama Islands: Containing the Figures of Birds, Beasts, Fishes, Serpents, Insects and Plants. . . .* In spite of its artistic limitations Catesby's *Natural History* is a rich source and regarded as the first truly American ornithology. [See color plate 21 in this volume.]

[*See also* Byrd, William.]

BIBLIOGRAPHY

Catesby, Mark, F. R. S. *Hortus Europae Americanus: Collection of 85 Curious Trees and Shrubs, the Produce of North America . . .* London: J. Millan, 1767.

Catesby, Mark, F. R. S. *The Natural History of Carolina, Florida, and the Bahama Islands: Containing the Figures of Birds,*

Catlin, George (1796–1872), American artist and portraitist known for his depictions of Indian subjects. Born in the Wyoming Valley of eastern Pennsylvania and raised on the banks of the Susquehanna River in New York, Catlin developed early an interest in Indians, canoes, hunting, and fishing. Stories of the capture of his mother, Polly, by the Iroquois in the Wyoming Massacre of 1778 fascinated him. Encouraged by his lawyer father, Putnam, to study law in Litchfield, Connecticut, Catlin began practice in Luzerne County, Pennsylvania, two years later. Doodling and sketching in the courtroom, Catlin developed an evolving passion for art that resulted in his selling his law books in 1823 and moving to Philadelphia. As a self-taught portrait painter, he attracted political figures and sketched his first Indian portraits. So successful was he that he was elected to the Pennsylvania Academy of Art in 1824.

Restless despite marriage to his sweetheart, Clara Gregory, Catlin traveled west in 1830 to begin an adventure that shaped the rest of his life. Showing his portfolio to General William Clark, superintendent of Indian Affairs at Saint Louis, Catlin gained encouragement and background information for his travels. Over the next six years he would travel by steamboat, canoe, and horseback, living with the Indians and capturing their games, their dress, and their portraits on his easel. Although his paintings have been described as uneven in quality and often seem unfinished, their realism has never been questioned. Catlin developed a strong belief that the Indians were doomed for extinction because of the westward push of civilization; he believed that he urgently needed to preserve their legacy on canvas. At one point he even espoused the need for a large national park where Indians and wildlife could roam freely and be preserved. After his travels, he assembled "Catlin's Indian Gallery" of portraits, scenes, and Indian artifacts, which became the first Wild West show and traveled to Philadelphia, Washington, Boston, New York, London, and Paris, where it was warmly received. Facing financial problems, Catlin tried unsuccessfully to have his collection purchased by the Smithsonian in 1852. His original collection was subsequently purchased by Joseph Harrison of Philadelphia and later damaged by water

George Catlin. Plate from *Life among the Indians: A Book for Youth* (London, 1861). Catlin was an indefatigable popularizer, and this book for young people is an example of the way in which he brought a popular artistic style to a wide audience. COURTESY THE NEWBERRY LIBRARY, CHICAGO

and fire. Catlin redrew many of his sketches from memory and made a last trip to South America and the Pacific coast of North America. In 1870, Catlin exhibited his re-created sketches—known as "Catlin's Cartoon Collection"—at the Smithsonian; he was granted a tower room at the Smithsonian and lived and painted there until his death in 1872.

[*See also* American West, Visual Images of.]

BIBLIOGRAPHY

Catlin, George. *Letters and Notes on the Manners, Customs, and Conditions of the North American Indians*. 2 vols. New York: Dover Publications, 1973. Unabridged republication of the work, which was first published in London in 1844.

CLARENCE E. KYLANDER

Cavendish, Thomas (1560–1592), British explorer and circumnavigator. Cavendish, a Cambridge-educated Suffolk squire whose first involvement in overseas enterprise was in the "Virginia" venture (to what is now North Carolina) of 1585, two years later led a three-ship expedition into the South Sea in an attempt to emulate Francis Drake's circumnavigation of 1577–1580. After passing through the Strait of Magellan, Cavendish sailed north along the Pacific shores of Spanish America, raiding, burning, and looting. His most spectacular success came in November 1587 when, off Cape San Lucas, he captured the *Santa Ana*, a great galleon from Manila carrying a valuable cargo of oriental goods to Acapulco. From the Californian coast Cavendish sailed in his one remaining vessel, the *Desire*, to Guam, the Philippines, and Java before returning home by way of the Cape of Good Hope. Following in the tracks of Magellan's expedition and Drake, Cavendish was the third seaman to navigate the globe, and he had done so in two years and fifty days. In England, Cavendish's return with a colossal treasure was a golden epilogue to the nation's recent victory over the Spanish Armada, and Cavendish received a warm welcome from queen and court. Although the capture of the galleon was the most dramatic evidence of Cavendish's success, there is no doubt that he saw the opening of China to English enterprise as the next step; and among the booty he brought back was a large map of China, a Portuguese pilot, and two Japanese subjects. Whereas Drake had picked up only scanty information about contacts between China and the Philippines, Cavendish identified the pivotal role of Manila in a transoceanic trade link that stretched from Canton to Acapulco. He planned another expedition that with five ships would raid the Pacific coasts of Spanish America before sailing north to open trade with Asia, but his voyage of 1591–1592 was a disaster. Harassed by storms, scurvy, and disagreements, the expedition failed to reach the Pacific. As the sole surviving ship under his command sailed for home, a disheartened Cavendish died and was buried at sea.

[See also Drake, Francis.]

BIBLIOGRAPHY
Edwards, Philip, ed. *Last Voyages—Cavendish, Hudson, Ralegh: The Original Narratives*. Oxford and New York: Oxford University Press, 1988.
Mathes, W. Michael, ed. *The Capture of the "Santa Ana"*. Los Angeles: Dawson's Book Shop, 1969.
Quinn, David B., ed. *The Last Voyage of Thomas Cavendish 1591–1592*. Chicago: University of Chicago Press, 1975.
Williams, Glyndwr. *The Great South Sea: English Voyages and Encounters 1570–1750*. New Haven, Conn., and London: Yale University Press, 1997.

GLYNDWR WILLIAMS

Çelebi Evliya (1611–1682), Turkish traveler. Çelebi Evliya's full name was Evliya bin Derviş Mehmed Zilli; his father was Mehmet Ağa (Derviş Muhammed Zilli). Çelebi Evliya was born in 1611 in Constantinople (Konstantiniye), present-day Istanbul, and educated at the Sheyhulislam Hamid Efendi Medresesi. After completing his early education he attended Enderun, a state school that educated statesmen for the empire, and he was subsequently presented to Sultan Murad IV. He learned Greek from his father's apprentice, to whom in turn he taught the Sahidi vocabulary. Çelebi Evliya died in 1682 in Egypt.

Çelebi Evliya claimed that he had a dream of the Prophet Muhammad in 1630. In his dream, instead of saying, "Intercede on my behalf. Oh envoy of God," Çelebi Evliya said, "Grant me travel. Oh envoy of God." The Prophet approved of his desire to travel, and so Çelebi Evliya's journeys commenced in 1640; he learned from and recorded the many experiences from his travels. Çelebi Evliya derived the real source of his knowledge and culture not from education but from life. He traveled in Asia, Europe, and Africa during forty years and wrote a book, *Siyahatnâme* or *Târîhi Sayyâh* (Book of Travels), which describes his travels in his own style. The work is ten volumes and runs to nearly six thousand pages, written in the spoken language. It covers the historic events of the seventeenth-century Ottoman Empire with vivid flashes of the life of that period. This book is an invaluable

source of historic and geographic knowledge and is important as a source of knowledge about Istanbul and Ottoman geography, social life, and buildings, and about peoples in Europe, Asia, and Africa. The book includes some fanciful vignettes, including the description of flights that supposedly took place at the court of Sultan Murad IV in 1630–1632. One of them was made by Hezârfen Ahmed Çelebî and the other one by Lâgarî Hasan Çelebî.

BIBLIOGRAPHY
Lybyer, A. H. "The Travels of Evliya Effendi." *Journal of American Oriental Society* 37 (1917): 224–239.
Mordtmann, J. H. "Ewliyâ Čelebî." In *The Encyclopaedia of Islam*. Leiden, Netherlands: Brill; London: Luzac, 1927. Vol. 2, pp. 33–34.

YAVUZ UNAT

Celestial Navigation. *See* **Navigational Techniques.**

Central America, Exploration of. Central America, stretching between the two isthmuses of Tehuantepec and Panama, is a land bridge between the continents of North and South America. As such it was a meeting place for peoples moving out from these landmasses. Mesoamericans, including Maya and various Nahua-speaking peoples, entered from the north and west and spread down the Pacific coast as far as Nicoya in present-day Costa Rica, with scattered pockets elsewhere. South American peoples at various disputed stages of economic and political evolution spread north and east through present-day Panama, Costa Rica, Nicaragua, and Honduras, with their deepest expansion on the Caribbean coast. Mesoamericans had created the great Maya classic states, and the area had been the scene of repeated invasions from the populous expansive empires of central Mexico.

On July 30, 1502, still searching for a water route to India and making his fourth voyage to the Caribbean, Christopher Columbus came upon the island of Guanaca in the Gulf of Honduras, and continued on thirty miles more to the Central American mainland. These ships' crews were the first recorded Europeans to land in Central America. Columbus made the decision to search for a seaway passage by sailing west and then south along the coast. (If he had sailed northwest instead he would have come upon the Maya of Yucatán, long before the Spanish slave raiders and conquistadores from Cuba found them.) As it was, Columbus's ships spent a miserable

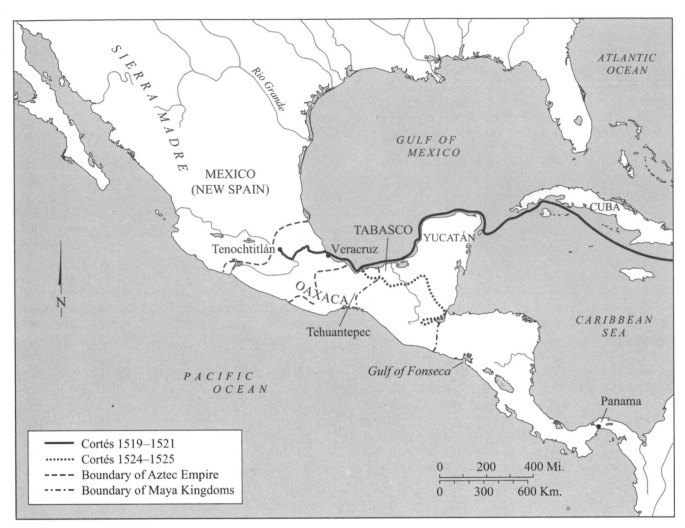

Central America and Mexico. This map shows the boundaries of the Aztec Empire and the Maya Kingdoms at the time of the voyages of Hernán Cortés. MAP BY BILL NELSON

month tacking against storms along the north coast of Honduras; then, with better sailing, they turned south and followed the Mosquito Coast all the way to Veragua and Panama. Finally, Columbus turned away from the land. It was another ten years before Vasco Núñez de Balboa's expedition sighted the Pacific Ocean there.

Apart from unofficial slave raiding to Cuba from the Yucatán and the Gulf of Honduras, Central America did not attract major Spanish interest for about twenty years after Columbus. When major invasions came, however, they repeated pre-Columbian patterns. Bands from central Mexico, originally from a Cuban base, and other invaders from Panama, originally from Hispaniola, moved toward one another in a pincerlike approach, then finally met and disputed boundaries in Honduras.

Hernán Cortés himself, in a punitive expedition against the recalcitrant Cristóbal de Olid, crossed the base of the Yucatán Peninsula through the Petén and reached the Gulf of Honduras. Francisco de Montejo in Yucatán, and the ferocious Pedro de Alvarado in Guatemala, El Salvador, and Honduras led the major Spanish *entradas* in destructive piecemeal conquests that lasted several years.

Spanish bands coming from Panama, of whom the most notable was perhaps the sanguinary Pedrarias Dávila, advanced along the Pacific coast by sea and by land, passing through Costa Rica (subsequently bypassed for many years and then reconquered) and Pacific Nicaragua. They reached the Gulf of Fonseca and Honduras, where they met and argued over rights with Alvarado and other bands from Mexico. The conquests from the Panama base were also prolonged and destructive, and for many years the major export of Nicaragua was native slaves.

These various invasions eventually colonized the highlands and the Pacific coasts. The conquest of the Petén did not happen until the late seventeenth century. Large sections of the humid Caribbean coasts were invaded even later, and some have still not been fully incorporated into the national states in the early twenty-first century.

[*See also* Central and South America; Columbus, Christopher; *and* Cortés, Hernán.]

BIBLIOGRAPHY

Alvarez Rubiano, Pablo. *Pedrarias Dávila*. Madrid, Spain: Consejo Superior de Investigaciones Científicas, 1944.

Gerhard, Peter. *The Southeast Frontier of New Spain*. Princeton, N.J.: Princeton University Press, 1979.

MURDO J. MACLEOD

Central and South America

This entry contains six subentries:

Colonies and Empires
Conquests and Colonization
Scientific Inquiry
Trade and Trade Goods
Trade Routes
Utopian Quests

Colonies and Empires

When Christopher Columbus returned from his first transatlantic voyage in 1493, Ferdinand of Aragon and Isabella of Castile quickly sought ownership of whatever lands he had reached. Pope Alexander VI acquiesced, issuing five papal bulls that vested in Castile title to already and soon to be discovered lands in return for Christianizing the natives. Although modified by Castile and Portugal in the 1494 Treaty of Tordesillas, the bulls justified Castilian conquest and settlement in the New World or "Indies." While the French and English denied papal authority to parcel out the world, some Spanish authors, including the Dominican Bartolomé de Las Casas, emphasized that Native Americans had to cede voluntarily their inherent rights to the Castilian crown for it to enjoy jurisdiction as well as property rights. Regardless of what theorists espoused, effective occupation proved the de facto basis for Spanish and Portuguese colonization.

Private capital underwrote most exploration, conquest, and settlement. It cost the Spanish crown nothing to award extensive rights and privileges over unknown lands and peoples. After receiving confirmation of rich land, valuable mineral resources, and substantial populations, however, it began to retract grants and appoint royal officials charged with providing justice—a central element of royal authority—and overseeing royal interests.

In Spain, the creation of a House of Trade in Seville in 1503 underscored the commercial objectives of empire; the establishment of a Council of the Indies in 1524 institutionalized judicial, legislative, and executive authority. Royal servants resident in the colonies included viceroys, captains-general, and presidents; judges and crown attorneys on *audiencias* (high courts that also had executive and legislative responsibilities); treasury officials; provincial administrators; and members of the ubiquitous municipal councils present in native as well as Spanish communities.

Colonial Administrators. In 1535 Antonio de Mendoza reached Mexico as the founding viceroy of the Viceroyalty of New Spain, a jurisdiction that ultimately encompassed Mexico, most of Central America and the colonized regions surrounding the Caribbean and Gulf of Mexico, and the Philippine Islands. Born into Castile's highest nobility, Viceroy Mendoza secured settlers' respect while instilling an appreciation of royal justice among the natives. He quickly demonstrated the value of his office, and in 1542 the crown created the Viceroyalty of Peru, an immense territorial unit that initially covered the whole of Spanish South America except Brazil and coastal Venezuela. Viceroy Francisco de Toledo (1569–1581) left a permanent imprint on the young Viceroyalty of Peru by establishing for the silver mines of Potosí a rotating, migrant labor system that lasted into the early nineteenth century. An effort to consolidate native villages proved less successful.

While administrative offices created in the colonies were similar to those in Spain, the distance of the empire from the metropolis slowed communication and forced the crown to allow its colonial officials greater authority and flexibility than their counterparts in Iberia. Slow communication and relative isolation also enabled royal appointees to place self-interest above royal interests. Added to the legitimate benefits of office, these conditions made holding office and having access to officeholders extremely desirable for families in local elites.

Initially the Spanish crown relied on men born and reared in Spain to serve posts in the colonies. As the population of American-born Spaniards (Creoles) increased, however, the Creoles began to obtain appointments. The number of positions they secured rose as a result of the crown's penury. The sale of municipal posts in the later sixteenth century and appointments to treasury offices beginning in 1633, provincial administrative positions in 1677, and *audiencia* posts in the 1680s brought to office ever more Americans, including native sons, men named to serve in their district of birth. Long-serving peninsulars typically enjoyed local social and economic ties as well; such "rooted" officials further compromised royal interests. These positions remained almost exclusively in the hands of peninsulars, although the crown began to sell appointments to the position of viceroy at the end of the seventeenth century.

In the first half-century of Bourbon rule after 1700, the sale of appointments to office peaked. While the crown consciously and systematically favored peninsulars in subsequent appointments, most notably for the newly created office of intendant, it could only reduce rather than eliminate local influence in office.

After initial experimentation with proprietary colonies, the Portuguese embraced royal administration in the mid-sixteenth century and relied on a combination of institutions in Portugal and officials in Brazil that, except for the notable absence of provincial officials, often resembled those in the Spanish empire.

The Spanish crown permanently carved the Viceroyalty of New Granada from Peru in 1739. Following the British seizure of Havana in 1762, the crown intensified administrative reform. It more systematically named peninsular officials, reduced reliance on tax farming, established tobacco monopolies and factories, reduced restrictions on trade, created the Viceroyalty of the Río de la Plata, established new *audiencias* in Buenos Aires, Caracas, and Cuzco, strengthened the Council of the Indies and systematically staffed it with ministers experienced in American affairs, and, between 1764 and 1790, introduced the intendant system throughout the mainland empire except for New Granada.

The central figure promoting reform efforts from 1765 to 1787 was José de Gálvez, Marqués de Sonora from 1785. Gálvez headed a successful general investigation of royal administration in New Spain from 1765 to 1771. Among other initiatives as secretary of state for the Indies from 1776 to 1787, he named visitors-general for Peru and New Granada with instructions to raise taxes and implement other

changes. Adding fuel to prior grievances, these actions provoked the Tupac Amaru rebellion in Peru and the Comunero revolt in New Granada in the early 1780s. The powerful Portuguese minister, the Marquis de Pombal, promoted both commercial and administrative reform in Brazil, but avoided inciting serious rebellion.

The longevity of the Iberian empires in the Americas testifies to administrative systems that weighed relatively lightly on colonial elites. Often able to influence the implementation of policy in self-serving ways, these elites remained loyal to their respective monarchs until the early nineteenth century.

[*See also* Columbus, Christopher; Las Casas, Bartolomé de; *and* Treaty of Tordesillas.]

BIBLIOGRAPHY

Burkholder, Mark A. "Bureaucrats." In *Cities and Society in Colonial Latin America*, edited by Louisa Schell Hoberman and Susan Migden Socolow, 77–103. Albuquerque: University of New Mexico Press, 1986.

Haring, C. H. *The Spanish Empire in America*. New York: Oxford University Press, 1947.

Pagden, Anthony. *Lords of All the World: Ideologies of Empire in Spain, Britain, and France c. 1500–c. 1800*. New Haven, Conn.: Yale University Press, 1995.

Parry, J. H. *The Spanish Seaborne Empire*. New York: Knopf, 1966.

MARK A. BURKHOLDER

Conquests and Colonization

Iberian exploration, conquest, and colonization followed Christopher Columbus's initial encounter in the Americas. Led most notably by Hernán Cortés and Francisco de Pizarro, Spanish conquistadores aided by native allies emerged victorious over the Aztec in central Mexico in 1521 and over the Inca in Peru in the 1530s. Less spectacular conquests followed. Except on the fringes of empire, by 1580 the years of conquest were over. With nearly two hundred Spanish municipalities established by 1620, the heavily urban character of Spanish colonial society was firmly in place.

Española (Hispaniola) served as the initial base for subsequent exploration, conquest, and colonization. In 1508 Juan Ponce de León led the conquest of Puerto Rico and several years later Diego Velázquez de Cuéllar brought Cuba under his control. The latter island provided Cortés with over five hundred men, sixteen horses, and supplies for his famed expedition. On the Gulf coast of Mexico, the conquistadores founded Veracruz and gained their first native allies. Bribed to leave by representatives of Montezuma II, the Aztec ruler, Cortés pushed inland instead. Bitter fighting with the Tlaxcalans, fierce enemies of the Aztec, ended with an invaluable alliance that helped to balance the Spaniards' numerical inferiority. After entering the island city of Tenochtitlan, Montezuma's capital, the Spaniards took the emperor hostage. Soon after Cortés left the capital to deal with the Pánfilo de Narváez expedition sent by Cuba's governor Velázquez to capture him, however, the Aztec besieged the conquistadores in their quarters. Although Cortés returned with reinforcements, the nocturnal effort to escape the island cost the lives of more than four hundred Spaniards and some four thousand native allies. Allowed to return to Tlaxcala, the Spaniards regrouped, gained new men and armament, and, with the Tlaxcalans' assistance, constructed a small naval fleet that cut off Tenochtitlan's freshwater and supplies. Despite losses from a smallpox epidemic unintentionally introduced by a member of the Narváez expedition, the Aztec fought valiantly and forced the invaders to tear down the capital stone by stone. In August 1521 the last Aztec warriors and Cuauhtémoc, successor to the deceased Montezuma II, surrendered. The victorious Spaniards now faced the task of conquering the rest of the Aztec empire as well as building a new capital and creating a stable colonial society.

The wealth and sophistication of the civilizations in central Mexico fired the imaginations of Spaniards encouraged by Cortés's success. None of the expeditions that soon fanned out from the Aztec heartland, however, found a comparable civilization. Although Cortés himself led an expedition to Central America in pursuit of Cristóbal de Olid, an erstwhile lieutenant who had undertaken an independent conquest, the result was misery rather than wealth or glory. It took Pedro de Alvarado, who subsequently fought a ruthless campaign, to establish Spanish control in the region and to discover that its wealth lay in natives to be enslaved rather than in accumulated treasure or rich deposits of gold or silver.

Conquest in South America. Expeditions to the northern coast of South America and Panama began in 1499, but the most spectacular conquest occurred in Peru in the 1530s. Encouraged by signs of a rich civilization found in preliminary efforts, Francisco Pizarro, an experienced Indian fighter and settler, led an expedition to Peru that resulted in the conquest of the Inca, a high civilization whose empire contained as many as 14 million people, and the acquisition of unprecedented sums of gold and silver.

After leaving a few men in Piura, the first Spanish town in Peru, in 1532 Pizarro led his small force further inland to Cajamarca. Across the adjacent valley was an Inca army of perhaps forty thousand led by Atahuallpa, victor over his half brother Huascar in a recently concluded civil war. Having lured Atahuallpa and several thousand men to Cajamarca without their weapons, the 168 Spaniards suddenly emerged from their hiding places, fell upon the natives, and captured the Inca leader. Despite Atahuallpa's capture, Inca officials and military officers obeyed his orders and dutifully brought gold and silver to Cajamarca to ransom him. Faced with rumors of an army of cannibals descending from Ecuador and the arrival of his junior partner Diego de Almagro with reinforcements, Pizarro agreed to execute Atahuallpa and to divide the ransom among his captors. Almost uniquely in the age of conquest, the "Men of Cajamarca" who shared the ransom obtained the transportable wealth that could fulfill their dreams. Freed of the need to guard Atahuallpa, the combined force of Spaniards and native allies who had backed the unsuccessful Huascar soon occupied the Inca capital of Cuzco. Despite the considerable gold and silver taken at Cuzco, Almagro and his followers felt cheated and consequently were eager to undertake a further expedition to the south. They reached Chile, but the anticipated riches did not exist. The survivors returned to Cuzco determined to seize what they considered their rightful share of the spoils of conquest from Pizarro and his supporters. An Inca rebellion complicated matters, but in 1538 Pizarro's forces proved victorious in the civil war and killed Almagro. Supporters of Almagro's son retaliated in 1541, assassinating Francisco Pizarro in his residence in the newly founded city of Lima.

The death of Pizarro did not end the strife in Peru. A provision of the "New Laws" of 1542 called for stripping participants in the civil war of their *encomiendas*, as grants of native labor and tribute were known. When a zealous viceroy prepared to implement this stricture, worried *encomenderos* and their supporters banded around Gonzalo Pizarro, a younger half brother of Francisco, and defeated the viceroy's forces in 1546. Victory was short-lived. The next royal representative, Pedro de la Gasca, won over many of Pizarro's supporters and oversaw the defeat and death of the rebellious leader in 1548.

While Spaniards in Peru were fighting among themselves, expeditions led by the lawyer Gonzalo Pérez de Quesada, the conqueror of Ecuador Sebastián de Benalcázar, and the German Nikolaus Federmann converged in the land of approximately one million Muisca, in present-day Colombia. The last high civilization to succumb to Spanish rule, the Muisca had amassed gold and emeralds soon divided among Quesada and his fewer than two hundred conquistadores, the first group on the scene.

Although the epic conquests of the Aztec, Inca, and Muisca brought the most advanced and richest New World civilizations under Spanish control, other expeditions established pockets of colonial rule in lands known today as Argentina, Paraguay, Chile, Bolivia, Venezuela, Panama, Central America, and Florida. Portuguese colonists also settled scattered locations of coastal Brazil, but the region lacked the advanced civilizations found in Spanish America. The permanent establishment of Buenos Aires in 1580 definitively ended the age of conquest.

Administering Empires. Royal administrative institutions appeared in the wake of permanent Iberian settlement and the creation of municipalities. To rule its American empires, the crowns of Spain and Portugal relied on institutions at court and royal officials and clerics in the Indies. Although their number increased in the late eighteenth century, military forces were always small.

In Spain the crown established the House of Trade (1503) to oversee commerce with the colonies and established the Council of the Indies (1524) to exercise administrative oversight as well as judicial and legislative responsibilities. Treasury officials often accompanied expeditions of conquest; the erection of a treasury office marked a region's identification as a contributor to imperial income. Starting in Santo Domingo in 1511 the crown created territorial jurisdictions called *audiencias*; each had a tribunal also called an *audiencia* that exercised legislative, executive, and judicial authority. Within a century additional tribunals were located in the *audiencia* districts of Mexico, Guadalajara, Guatemala, the Philippine Islands, Lima, Charcas, Chile, Quito, Santa Fe de Bogotá, and Panama. Depending on the title of its chief executive, these units were also termed *captaincies-general* or *presidencies*. Combinations of *audiencia* districts formed viceroyalties. The Viceroyalty of New Spain, established in 1535, ultimately included the *audiencias* of Mexico, Guadalajara, Guatemala, Santo Domingo, and the Philippines. That of Peru, created in 1542, included the remaining districts well into the eighteenth century. In 1739, the *audiencias* of Santa Fe de Bogotá and Quito were split off from Peru in the new Viceroyalty of New Granada. In 1776, Charcas was included in

a new Viceroyalty of the Río de la Plata with its capital of Buenos Aires.

Each *audiencia* district and viceroyalty, in turn, contained a number of provinces. Variously termed *corregimientos*, *alcaldías mayores*, and *gobernaciones*, these provinces typically included a number of municipalities, each with its own council and officials responsible for a variety of local services.

Royal and local officials formed one arm of the crown's authority. The church, operating under royal patronage, constituted the other. Starting with Columbus's second voyage in 1493, clerics routinely accompanied explorers, conquistadores, and settlers. Some belonged to religious orders, notably Dominicans in the early days; others were secular clergy who fell under the jurisdiction of a bishop. The crown encouraged the participation of mendicant orders in particular, and by the mid-sixteenth century, a number of Franciscans and Augustinians were at work in Spanish America; Jesuits appeared in Brazil in 1549 and a few years later in Peru and New Spain. The first bishopric in Spanish America was created in San Juan de Puerto Rico in 1511 and the first archbishopric in Lima in 1541. By 1620, the first great wave of creations had ended, and with one exception, it was over a century and a half before more bishoprics were established. By the end of the colonial period, ten archbishoprics and thirty-eight bishoprics encompassed Spanish America.

The Inquisition was another institution with empire-wide jurisdiction. While Brazil was spared a tribunal, agents of the Portuguese Inquisition could send those accused to Portugal for trial. In Spanish America, the primitive episcopal Inquisition gave way to formal Tribunals of the Holy Office in Lima in 1570 and in Mexico City in 1571; a third tribunal was created in Cartagena de Indias in 1610. Established in the Indies to deal with heretical foreigners in particular, the tribunals soon devoted much of their time to policing the morals of the non-Indian residents. In the Tribunal in Mexico, for example, between 1571 and 1700 fewer cases dealt with heresy—mostly involving Judaizers and foreigners— than with cases of sexual transgression, such as bigamy, and clerical solicitation in the confessional. Of some six thousand cases in Spanish America for the colonial period, probably fewer than one hundred persons, all nonrecanting heretics, were put to death.

In Brazil the Portuguese administered a smaller and more decentralized administrative system than existed in Spanish America. After a brief experiment in private administration (the "donatary" system), the Portuguese crown embraced royal administration and, in 1549, named a governor-general based in Salvador, Bahia, with responsibilities and restrictions similar to a viceroy in Spanish America. The first *relaçao*, a high court of appeals analogous to an *audiencia*, was created in Salvador in 1609; a second was founded in Rio de Janeiro in 1751. Although municipal councils and fiscal offices were present in Brazil, there was no counterpart to provincial administrators. The Society of Jesus dominated the colony's evangelical effort, while the secular clergy was comparatively weak.

The administrative structure established in the sixteenth century persisted with modest modifications into the eighteenth century. By the 1750s, however, efforts to strengthen royal authority were underway in Spanish America as the crown began to administer some previously farmed taxes, exerted more care in the appointment of officials, and sought to reduce corruption. Chastened by the British seizure of Havana in 1762, the crown accelerated the pace of change. An interrelated program of reform that sought better administration, an expansion of legal trade, more effective tax collection, and enlarged and improved military forces followed. Portugal also sought to expand the benefits of empire in the eighteenth century by improving Brazil's administration, expanding its trade, and strengthening its defenses.

Spanish and Portuguese exploration, conquest, and settlement in the sixteenth century established the foundation for mainland empires in the Americas that lasted three centuries. The administrative and religious institutions that the Iberians imposed contributed heavily to this imperial longevity.

[*See also* Columbus, Christopher; Cortés, Hernán; Federmann, Nikolaus; Pizarro, Francisco, Gonzalo Pizarro, and Hernando Pizarro; *and* Ponce de León, Juan.]

BIBLIOGRAPHY
Boxer, C. R. *The Portuguese Seaborne Empire, 1415–1825.* New York: Knopf, 1969.
Burkholder, Mark A., and Lyman L. Johnson. *Colonial Latin America.* 5th ed. New York: Oxford University Press, 2004.
Hassig, Ross. *Mexico and the Spanish Conquest.* London and New York: Longman, 1994.
Hemming, John. *The Conquest of the Incas.* New York: Harcourt, Brace, Jovanovich, 1970.
Hemming, John. *The Search for El Dorado.* London: Michael Joseph, 1978.
Parry, J. H. *The Spanish Seaborne Empire.* New York: Knopf, 1966.

MARK A. BURKHOLDER

Scientific Inquiry

The arrival of Europeans to the New World posed serious questions about the natural world of, and the origins of the people from, the New World. The encounter is one of the key elements in the emergence of empirical practices that shaped the new science of the sixteenth and seventeenth centuries in Europe. The encounter made possible, first, the rejection of classical authorities, who were mistaken about, or not aware of, many characteristics of the New World; and second, the validation of personal experience as a source of knowledge.

The emergence of empirical practices resulted from the relationship between entrepreneurs, artisans, and merchants, who sent reports to the crown, and crown officials, who received those reports and incorporated their methods into the bureaucratic structure of the empire. These groups needed information about the New World for commercial and imperial purposes. In the early years, no one had specific knowledge about the New World. Early sixteenth-century commercial contracts to trade in the New World refer to common commodities such as precious metals, precious stones, plants, animals, fish, birds, medicines, and "any thing of any name and quality" of value—as it appeared in the contract to the explorer Diego de Lepe in 1501. Some of these contracts referred to "monsters" and "serpents." Knowledge about natural products of the Indies was quite general in the early years of exploration.

Gathering Information. By the 1510s, the crown sought to create mechanisms to collect more and better information about the New World. It established the position of the Chief Pilot (1508) at the Casa de Contratación (House of Trade) for the purpose of collecting information for making charts (and also for the training of pilots). The crown also requested explorers to send reports about their explorations. People on the ground were sending their own reports. The letters of Christopher Columbus (1451–1506) are examples of this. Years later, the royal official Alonso de Zauzo (fl. 1515) wrote a report (1518) on natural things from Hispaniola Island (today Dominican Republic and Haiti) to Charles V. Zauzo mentions brazilwood (a red dye), guaiacum, and fragrant resins. This report contains more specific information than the rather vague list of commodities mentioned in the contracts above. By the 1520s, the letters of Hernán Cortés (1485–1547) letters brought news about the great Aztec Empire and its city-state, Tenochtitlan. In 1526, Antonio de Villasante, a merchant, brought before the Council of the Indies a report on a new medicine from Hispaniola. In the 1520s, the crown continued to request information from explorers and merchants but it also began requesting more information from its officials in the New World. In 1526, the crown ordered the royal official Luis Ponce de León to send a report describing the land of New Spain. In 1528, it ordered the judges of the *audiencia* to send reports about the land.

Up to this point, merchants and entrepreneurs sent their own reports, and the crown had also been requesting reports from explorers and merchants as well as from its own officials. In 1532, the crown added a new mechanism for collecting information. It appointed a *Cronista de Indias* (Chronicler of the Indies) to collect and organize information about the New World. The initiative came, again, from below. The humanist and natural historian Gonzalo Fernández de Oviedo (1478–1557), who had published a short natural history entitled *De la natural hystoria de las Indias* (1526), proposed an expedition to collect information from areas he had not yet visited in order to complete a larger natural history, on which he had been working for a while. The Council of the Indies supported the expedition but it seems to have been too expensive, and it decided on a different proposal. Fernández de Oviedo was to stay in Spain, and the crown sent decrees to its officials in America requesting information for him.

The royal decree sent to the governor of Fernandina Island (Cuba) asked for information "about the island, its inhabitants, and its conditions." It explained that Fernández de Oviedo was writing a general history of the Indies as well as a natural history of the lands and islands, its animals, and "its strangeness." Oviedo would have to provide, every year, a copy of his own writings to be added to the history of Spain. The governor would therefore have to send information, as promptly as possible, every time it was requested. In all cases, these reports would have to be signed by the people who provided them—a significant requirement, because it brought individual testimony into the circuit of the knowledge-gathering practice. It was also in 1532 that the crown commissioned the cosmographer Alonso de Santa Cruz (c. 1500–1572) to produce new navigational charts. He needed information about the "degrees of the lands and islands." The crown sent a royal decree to the officials of the Casa de Contratación that required shipmasters and pilots to submit to Santa Cruz all the information he needed. As a result of his

work, Fernández de Oviedo published *La historia general de las Indias* (1535; expanded edition, 1557).

Empirical Practices. During the 1530s and 1540s the crown institutionalized new mechanisms for gathering information about the New World. In the mid-1550s, just after the accession of Philip II (r. 1556–1598), Santa Cruz proposed asking specific questions of explorers and colonists, rather than asking for general information about the land and its natural characteristics. His guidelines required asking specific questions regarding the latitude and longitude of places and ports; the geographical characteristics and healthfulness of the land; descriptions of rivers, mountains, lakes, and springs; and information about mines, minerals, precious stones, pearls, animals, "monsters," trees, fruits, spices, drugs, and herbs. Finally, there were questions concerning the indigenous people—their kingdoms and provinces, borders, towns and cities, costumes, rites, types of knowledge, books, arms, trade (in general), and items that they traded.

Between 1558 and 1569, the Franciscan Bernardino de Sahagún (c. 1499–1590) crafted a questionnaire to write his *Historia general de las cosas de la Nueva España*. Sahagún sent questionnaires (reconstructed from his book) to Indian villages, asking for information about aspects of their culture, society, and land. On natural history, the questionnaire included questions about names of animals, the history of the name, physical description of the animal, its environment, its activities, its food, ways of hunting or catching it, customs of the animal, popular histories about it, and sayings related to it. Both Sahagún and Santa Cruz collected information intensely during the 1560s.

Sahagún finished his book by the mid-1570s. Santa Cruz died in 1571. The next year, the architect of the El Escorial, Juan López de Velasco (c. 1530–1598), was appointed royal cosmographer-chronicler (a joint appointment) at the Council of the Indies. The so-called Santa Cruz papers passed to him and he used them for the writing of the *Geografía y descripción universal de las Indias* (finished around 1574). The manuscript is accompanied with color maps and describes the geography and natural history of the New World. The book was a guide for the Council of the Indies and the king on matters related to the New World.

The development of empirical practices for the understanding of natural things and people in the New World culminated in the 1570s with a series of great projects, supported by the Spanish crown and implemented by physicians, architects, cosmographers, pilots, and entrepreneurs in America. First of all, the crown launched the first modern scientific expedition to the New World—the model for the expeditions sent during the Enlightenment. In 1570 Philip II sent Dr. Francisco Hernández (c. 1515–1587), his physician, to Mexico, Peru, and the Philippines to collect information about, and samples of, trees, plants, and medicinal plants. He had to collect this information in person and by interviewing indigenous and expert people in the uses of those plants and herbs. By March 1571, Hernández was already working in Mexico and he had hired a geographer and painters to help him. He was supposed to work in New Spain for a few years, move to Peru to collect information and samples there, and then move to the Philippines. In other words, his scientific expedition was designed to collect information and samples from all the Spanish Empire. He finally went back to Spain from New Spain in 1577. He never made it to the rest of the empire: he was in bad health, and felt too old to continue. His natural history, consisting of sixteen books with paintings of plants and animals, was never published (it was too large and expensive to publish). Philip II ordered the Italian physician Nardo Antonio Recchi (c. 1540–1594) to make a selection of Hernández's work for publication. Recchi's manuscript was translated into Spanish (with additions) by the Dominican Francisco Ximénez (b. c. 1560) and published under the title *Quatro libros de la naturaleza* (1615), which Ximénez describes as "very useful for all type of peoples."

Questionnaire. The second great project for gathering information about the New World was related to the Council of the Indies' statutes of 1571, in particular statute 120, ordering the newly created cosmographer-chronicler of the Indies, López de Velasco, to gather information for a natural history of the New World. The result of this statute was the elaboration of a series of questionnaires that culminated in the fifty-five-part questionnaire of 1577. This questionnaire was sent almost everywhere in the New World for gathering information on diverse aspects of the New World. The collection of answers to the questionnaire, held at the Council of the Indies, is known as the *Relaciones de Indias*. In addition to this questionnaire, López de Valasco elaborated instructions to determine the longitude of significant places in the New World based on the lunar eclipses of 1577, 1578, 1581, 1582, and 1584. As part of this overall project for determining longi-

tudes and latitudes, the crown sent yet another expedition to the New World: the expedition of the cosmographer Jaime Juan, in 1583, to map the locations of New Spain towns (he was sent before the eclipse of 1584).

By sixteenth-century standards, the Spaniards were in the forefront of natural history developments and scientific inquiry of the New World. They had institutions for collecting empirical information in the forms of questionnaires and expeditions, and they were using this information to write reports (Fernández de Oviedo's *La historia*, López de Velasco's *Geografía*, Sahagún's *Historia*, and Ximénez's summary of Hernández's work are examples) and to study the natural world in America. These activities constituted some of the most important precursors for the scientific activities developed during the seventeenth century and the Enlightenment. The early constitutive (empirical) elements of the new science of the seventeenth century and the Enlightenment are found in the Spanish scientific activities of the 1570s with their emphasis on expeditions, empirical evidence, institutions, and reporting activities.

[*See also biographies of figures mentioned in this article.*]

BIBLIOGRAPHY

The Archivo General de Indias (General Archives of the Indies) in Seville, Spain, has a wealth of primary sources about Spain's presence in Central and South America. It is available at http://www.mcu.es/archivos/visitas/indias/indias.html.

Acuña, Rene, ed. *Relaciones geográficas del siglo XVI*. 10 vols. See in particular the "Prólogo," in vol. 10. Mexico: UNAM, 1982.

Alvarez-Peláez, Raquel. *La conquista de la naturaleza Americana*. Madrid: Consejo Superior de Investigaciones Científicas, 1993.

Cline, Howard F. "The Relaciones Geográficas of the Spanish Indies, 1577–1648." In *Handbook of Middle American Indians*, edited by Howard F. Cline, vol. 12, book. Austin: University of Texas Press, 1972.

Jiménez de la Espada, Marcos, ed. *Relaciones geográficas de Indias: Perú*. 3 vols. See in particular the "Antecedentes," in vol. 1. Madrid: Atlas, 1965.

López Piñero, José M., Thomas F. Glick, Víctor Navarro Brotóns, and Eugenio Portela Marco. *Diccionario histórico de la ciencia moderna en España*. Barcelona: Ediciones Península, 1983.

Solano, Francisco de, ed. *Cuestionarios para la formación de las relaciones geográficas de Indias: Siglos XVI–XIX*. Madrid: Consejo Superior de Investigaciones Científicas, 1988.

Somolinos d'Ardois, Germán. *El Doctor Francisco Hernández y la primera expedición científica en América*. Mexico: Secretaría de Educación Pública, 1971.

Varey, Simon, ed. *The Mexican Treasury: The Writings of Dr. Francisco Hernández*. Stanford, Calif.: Stanford University Press, 2000.

Varey, Simon, Rafael Chabrán, and Dora B. Weiner, eds. *Searching for the Secrets of Nature: The Life and Works of Dr. Francisco Hernández.* Stanford, Calif.: Stanford University Press, 2000.

Vas Mingo, Milagros del. *Las capitulaciones de Indias en el siglo XVI.* Madrid: Instituto de Cooperación Iberoamericana, 1986.

ANTONIO BARRERA-OSORIO

Trade and Trade Goods

Spain and Portugal's early modern empires were born of their attempts to expand trade. Seeking a western route to Asia, Christopher Columbus's voyage reflected, in part, Spain's growing ambition to expand its commercial empire. Such efforts were paralleled by Portuguese exploration that opened up the sea route to India and led to Pedro Álvares Cabral's wayward voyage in 1500 that culminated in the encounter with Brazil. The entry of Spain and Portugal into the New World brought about significant commercial expansion.

The initial strategies of the two Iberian monarchies differed. Until 1530 Portugal pursued a policy of establishing royal factories along the coast of Brazil. These fortified outposts, similar to those set up in Africa, permitted Portuguese ships to trade with the Amerindians, exchanging European items for Brazilian products, primarily dyewood. By the end of the sixteenth century the Portuguese were extracting one hundred shiploads of dyewood per year. Spanish colonization of its dominions began with Columbus's first voyage, which resulted in the founding of a settlement on the island of Hispaniola. Early industry focused on mining in Hispaniola, Cuba, and several smaller islands, resulting in moderate exports of gold and silver, which by 1520 had totaled nearly 3.5 million pesos.

Sugar and Slavery. Rapid commercial growth followed Portugal's permanent settlement of Brazil and Spain's conquest of Amerindian civilizations in Mexico and Peru. Brazilian settlements established in 1535 at Bahia and Pernambuco resulted in the rapid expansion of sugar, especially during the boom years of 1570 to 1620. By 1600 Brazilian mills were producing 15 million pounds (6.8 million kilograms) per year, and by 1625 annual output had risen to 24 million pounds (10.9 million kilograms). Despite the growth of competition from French, British, and Dutch producers in the Caribbean especially after 1670, Brazil's production remained substantial, surpassing 32 million pounds (14.5 million kilograms)

in 1710. The Brazilian industry did, however, increasingly suffer from low sugar prices and the rising price of its costliest input, slaves. If not for the availability of African slaves, the sugar industry would not have been viable. In the early sixteenth century the Brazilian sugar plantations experimented with enslaved native Brazilian workers, but planters quickly turned to African slaves. In the sixteenth century alone, perhaps 100,000 slaves were imported to Brazil; over the three centuries of the slave trade, Brazil's total imports exceeded 3.5 million slaves.

Sugar and slavery, always in tandem, expanded rapidly in the Caribbean in the second half of the seventeenth century as plantations were established in colonies controlled by France, England, and Holland. Employing better technologies for the Brazilian plantations and enjoying direct access to their mother countries, these non-Iberian colonies eroded Brazil's world market share in sugar. By the eighteenth century Caribbean sugar output was enormous, led by the island colonies of Jamaica and Saint Domingue (Haiti). In 1791, the year that the Haitian Revolution erupted, the island produced 78,696 tons of sugar. Jamaica's output was not far behind, at 59,400 tons in 1789. These islands' labor forces were composed primarily of slaves. At the time of the slave rebellion in Saint Domingue, there were nearly half a million African slaves. Jamaica's slave population was one-quarter million. The Haitian Revolution, which emancipated the slaves and destroyed the island's plantation system, allowed for the rise of Cuba as a large-scale sugar producer. Spurred first by Great Britain's 1762 seizure of Havana and subsequent opening up of its port to free trade, Cuba emerged after the Haitian Revolution as the world's largest sugar producer. Cuban sugar production in 1774 was a mere 10,000 tons, but exceeded 43,000 tons in 1817, and on the eve of the American Civil War, Cuba produced 447,000 tons in a single year. The slave population grew accordingly from 44,300 in 1774 to 286,900 in 1827 to 367,400 in 1860. By this latter date, however, the Cuban planters had begun adapting to the inevitable end of slavery and employing other, nonslave laborers.

The Rise of Gold. In Brazil, sugar's decline led to the rise of another commodity, gold, which was discovered in large quantities in the last decade of the seventeenth century, especially in and around Minas Gerais. By 1735, Brazil's gold production had peaked at around 6,100 pounds (2,800 kilograms) per year, an elevated level that was sustained until about 1754, after which production entered into decline. By century's end gold production was less than one-third of the boom years. The search for and mining of gold was labor intensive, leading to the importation to Brazil of nearly 800,000 Africans slaves from 1700 to 1750, the boom years of the gold industry. Gold was also a lucrative industry in Spanish America. The greatest years of gold extraction in the Spanish colonies were 1551 to 1620, during which time the value of gold mined was 33.11 million silver pesos. More than two-thirds of the gold was mined in New Granada (modern-day Colombia). While important, gold mining in Spanish America never attained the significance that it enjoyed in eighteenth-century Brazil, and it never rivaled the economic importance of silver.

Brazil also produced the majority of Latin America's tobacco exports, which, until the eighteenth century, represented its second most important export after sugar. Between 1711 and 1763 Brazilian exports averaged 765,000 pounds (347,000 kilograms) per year. This marked a significant increase over sixteenth-century production sustained in Spanish America, quantities that were barely one-tenth of Brazil's later levels. Brazilian tobacco was usually sweetened with molasses and then twisted into rolls for export. Undoubtedly, Brazilian production was fueled by the demand for tobacco in Africa, one of the primary goods exchanged for human cargo.

Silver. Silver mining was the leading economic sector of Spain's colonies for the entire colonial period. In the 1540s, the Spaniards made important discoveries of silver in northern Mexico and in 1545 discovered Potosí in Peru. During the decade that followed, silver exports exceeded the total of the previous half-century of Spain's empire in America. Technological improvements in the 1570s, namely the shift from smelting of ores to the process of amalgamation, proved a major boost to Potosí's output, which rose from roughly 57,200 pounds (26,000 kilograms) to 382,000 pounds (173,000 kilograms) between 1572 and 1582. Silver production at Potosí reached a high plateau in the late 1580s, which was sustained for four decades. In 1592 output reached 444,400 pounds (202,000 kilograms) and was valued at more than 7 million pesos. In the same decade, the total of American silver imports registered at Seville reached nearly 70 million pesos, ten times greater than the total of European production in the same years. The mine at Potosí continued to lead Spanish-American production until the final third of the seventeenth century, when it was surpassed by the rapidly growing mines of Mexico. In the years 1701 to 1810, the Mexican treasury minted more than 1.4 billion silver pesos; production peaked in the 1790s when the silver mines of Mexico topped 20 million pesos in a number of years.

Other Exports. Mexico's second export after silver was cochineal, a red dye produced from the dried bodies of the cochineal insect, a parasite to the nopal cactus. Produced exclusively by the indigenous populations of southern Mexico, cochineal became the preferred red dye of European textile producers by the mid-sixteenth century. By the turn of the seventeenth century, Spain was annually importing 25,000 to 30,000 pounds (11,340 to 13,600 kilograms) of cochineal dye valued in excess of 600,000 pesos. Cochineal's zenith came in the second half of the eighteenth century, peaking in the decade of the 1770s at more than one million pounds (453,600 kilograms) per year. Its value in Mexico exceeded 3 million pesos per year during the quinquennium 1769–1774.

Hides were another significant export product and one that came from most regions of America. Cattle flourished on America's plains, free from natural predators. Throughout the sixteenth century Spanish Americans shipped annually 80,000 pieces or more to Spain. A seventeenth-century decline was followed by an export boom that was sustained throughout the eighteenth century. Between 1726 and 1770, annual exports from Brazil averaged more than 150,000 hides. Prior to the 1770s legal exports of hides from the province of Buenos Aires also averaged around 150,000 per year. The Spanish crown's 1776 formation of the Viceroyalty of Río de la Plata with its capital at Buenos Aires and the opening up of free imperial trade to the new viceregal capital in 1778 sparked a commercial boom. Between 1779 and 1795 average exports from Argentina reached 330,000 hides.

Cacao, a foodstuff indigenous to America, represented another important export sector in Spanish America. During the sixteenth century, most cacao was produced in Guatemala and sold in Mexico. Guatemala maintained its dominance of the cacao industry until the mid-seventeenth century, after which cacao from Caracas and Guayaquil began to overtake Central American production. In the 1630s, Guatemala still enjoyed one-third of the Mexico City market. In the second half of the seventeenth century, the province of Caracas emerged as the most important cacao region. In 1684, the province had half a million trees producing cacao; sixty years later, in 1744, the number of trees had increased to five million. In 1728 the Caracas Company was formed and in theory enjoyed a monopoly on cacao exports until 1780. From 1731 to 1775, the company shipped nearly 105 million pounds (47.6 million kilograms) of the commodity to Spain, valued in excess of 108 million pesos or an average export of 2.3 million pounds (1 million kilograms) per year.

Highly restrictive commercial policies and the colonial rulers' insatiable demand for precious metals ensured that international trade remained central to the fortunes of prominent colonialists. One legacy of colonial rule for the former colonies of both Spain and Portugal is that their economies were significantly integrated into the world trade system and the transatlantic world. The global orientation that began with the voyage of Columbus persisted after independence.

[*See also* Columbus, Christopher.]

BIBLIOGRAPHY
Bakewell, Peter. *A History of Latin America: c. 1450 to the Present.* 2nd ed. Malden, Mass.: Blackwell, 2004.
Bethell, Leslie. *Colonial Brazil.* Cambridge, U.K., and New York: Cambridge University Press, 1987.
Bethell, Leslie. *Colonial Spanish America.* Cambridge, U.K., and New York: Cambridge University Press, 1987.
Knight, Franklin W. *The Caribbean: The Genesis of a Fragmented Nationalism.* 2nd ed. New York: Oxford University Press, 1990.
MacLeod, Murdo J. *Spanish Central America: A Socioeconomic History, 1520–1720.* Berkeley: University of California Press, 1973. Reprinted 1984.
Schwartz, Stuart B. *Sugar Plantations in the Formation of Brazilian Society: Bahia, 1550–1835.* Cambridge, U.K., and New York: Cambridge University Press, 1985.

JEREMY BASKES

Trade Routes

The Spanish conquests of the New World were centered on Mesoamerica and the Andes, the two American regions where high civilizations had flourished for millennia before 1492. While these two Amerindian centers were economically independent of one another, the Spanish conquest initiated a process of integration that increasingly tied Mesoamerica and the Andes to one another and to the expanding global market.

The Aztec empire dominated much of Mesoamerica when Europeans arrived in the early sixteenth century. The island location of the Aztec capital, Tenochtitlan, required that this large urban center import most of its supplies, which were obtained through a mixture of market and coercive mechanisms. Local traders from neighboring communities within the central Mexican valley brought commodities to Tenochtitlan's large daily market. Other supplies were acquired via tribute exactions imposed on subject peoples within and outside of the valley. Pochteca, members of a hereditary merchant guild, engaged in long-distance trade exchanging goods manufactured by Aztec artisans for luxury items obtained as far southeast as Yucatán, Tehuantepec, and Guatemala and northwest along the Pacific coast and inland to the Chaco Canyon of present-day New Mexico.

In the Andes formal trade did not exist prior to Francisco Pizarro's conquest; instead, commodity exchange took place according to reciprocal relations between members of individual ethnic groups who took advantage of the Andes' wide variety of ecological zones that could be easily exploited within a close proximity. Andean tribes dispatched *mitmaq* (migrants) to work these microclimates, guaranteeing themselves access to goods from the coast, the sierra, and even the rainforest. The expansion of Inca rule in the fifteenth century did not radically alter these customary practices, but did allow the movement of reciprocally exchanged goods along the imperial roads that unified the 2,500-mile-long (4,000-kilometer-long) empire. Evidence suggests the involvement in maritime trade of the northern Andean peoples who supplied seashells highly coveted by the central and south Andeans. Scholars debate the extent to which this commerce brought these northerners to Central America.

The Spanish conquest altered radically existing American trade routes as the new Spanish colonies became integrated into an international system of trade. The transatlantic Carrera de Indias entailed two merchant fleets that departed from Seville in convoy with armed vessels: one, the *flota*, destined for Honduras, Havana, and especially Veracruz, and the other, "the *galeones*," for Cartagena, other Caribbean ports of South America, and especially the Isthmus of Panama. European commodities disembarked at Panama were transported across the isthmus and reshipped to Lima, administrative center of the Viceroyalty of Peru. The Atlantic fleets wintered in the Caribbean and then returned to Spain laden with colonial produce in the early spring.

In the mid-1570s Mexico City merchants entered the transpacific trade, shipping American silver from the port of Acapulco to Manila in exchange for silks, spices, and other Asian luxuries. Much of the silver exported to the Philippines and on to China in the first century originated in the Peruvian mine of Potosí. A thriving trade developed between Lima and Acapulco as Mexican merchants reexported Chinese and European wares in exchange for the Peruvian specie.

Trade within the Viceroyalty of New Spain closely followed precontact land routes. The fleet's annual arrival to Veracruz introduced tons of European merchandise, which was subsequently distributed within the colony of New Spain. From cargo warehoused in Mexico City, muleteers regularly transported goods south to Oaxaca and Guatemala, returning with indigo, cochineal, and cacao, much of which was then exported from Veracruz. Trade to the north of Mexico City became increasingly important with the development and expansion of silver production in Mexico's Bajío region in the second half of the sixteenth century.

The arrival of the galleons to Peru had a similar impact in the Andes, as the great merchants of Lima distributed these imports to their agents throughout the colony. Commerce expanded considerably with the 1545 discovery and subsequent development of the silver mine at Potosí. This remote silver mountain became an engine of growth, stimulating economic development throughout the Andes and beyond. Goods arrived along Inca roads from Quito to the north. New trade routes developed to the south of Potosí as Spanish settlers in northwestern Argentina began supplying the mines with both draft animals and foodstuffs. This southern route also developed as an outlet for contraband silver exported illegally from Potosí.

Portuguese colonization in the Americas was limited to Brazil. The introduction of sugar cultivation into Brazil in the 1530s sparked a rapid growth in exports of sugar and the equally sharp rise in the importation of African slaves. The sugar and slave trades thus opened shipping lanes among Brazil, Portugal, and the coast of Africa from Guinea to Angola. By the nineteenth century slaves arrived to Brazil from Mozambique on the east coast of Africa.

Spanish colonial centers were strategically located in Mesoamerica and the Andes, in the regions where precontact civilizations had most flourished. Spain's rigid commercial structure guaranteed that other regions of the Spanish empire developed more slowly. Until liberalization in the eighteenth century, the Spanish crown limited trade in its colonies to only a few ports of entry, principally in the colonial centers of Peru and New Spain. One result of this rigidity was contraband, which flourished in the Ca-

ribbean and, increasingly, in Río de la Plata. Havana, long an administrative center and layover for the fleet, grew rapidly after its temporary capture by Great Britain in 1762 forced the crown to liberate the island's trade. Buenos Aires remained a backwater through most of the colonial era but experienced a commercial boom in the eighteenth century, fueled first by illegal trade and then, after 1778, by Spain's opening of the port to imperial trade. Spanish shipping to Río de la Plata soared after 1778.

BIBLIOGRAPHY

Bakewell, Peter. *A History of Latin America: c. 1450 to the Present.* 2nd ed. Malden, Mass.: Blackwell Publishing, 2004.

Bethell, Leslie. *Colonial Spanish America.* Cambridge, U.K., and New York: Cambridge University Press, 1987.

Borah, Woodrow Wilson. *Early Colonial Trade and Navigation between Mexico and Peru.* Berkeley: University of California Press, 1954.

Haring, Clarence Henry. *Trade and Navigation between Spain and the Indies in the Time of the Hapsburgs.* Cambridge, Mass.: Harvard University Press, 1918.

Hassig, Ross. *Trade, Tribute, and Transportation: The Sixteenth-Century Political Economy of the Valley of Mexico.* 1st ed. Civilization of the American Indian series, vol. 171. Norman: University of Oklahoma Press, 1985.

Larson, Brooke, Olivia Harris, and Enrique Tandeter, eds. *Ethnicity, Markets, and Migration in the Andes: At the Crossroads of History and Anthropology.* Durham, N.C.: Duke University Press, 1995.

JEREMY BASKES

Utopian Quests

Myth and legend stimulated the imagination of early modern Europeans. Fabulous creatures, astonishing men and women, and remarkable geographic sites and features—the extraordinary—fed rumors and nourished credulity. The advent of printed books lent authority to stories previously spread by word of mouth. As early explorers encountered new lands, peoples, flora, and fauna in the Americas, they gathered evidence of the previously unknown and thus arguments for the existence of the extraordinary. Distance, mist, and imagination enabled men to see what they believed could exist, and this belief led them forward into lands known earlier only by native populations.

Lending credence to myths and legends was the very existence of the Americas, a "new world" of largely unknown features that had to be incorporated into both maps and minds. As long as explorers thought they were in islands or mainland attached to Southeast Asia or the Indies, legends located there attracted believers. In addition, the

Americas spawned their own legends. The combination stimulated countless Spaniards to pursue a man of gold, a city of gold, a land of gold, a fountain of youth, and other fantasies. As the marvelous yielded to the mundane, their explorations and conquests led to settlements in favored locations from Chile to Mexico.

Accompanying a surprisingly large number of the conquistadores were books of chivalry, popular reading by the literate to their unschooled companions. Garci Rodríguez de Montalvo's *Amadís of Gaul*, named after its hero, was especially beloved. Indeed Bernal Díaz del Castillo, the famous foot soldier who wrote a widely read history of the conquest of Mexico, equated the Aztec capital of Tenochtitlan at first glimpse to enchantments described in the legend of Amadís. In another chivalric romance by Montalvo, *Sergas de Esplandián* (Exploits of Esplandián), readers discovered women warriors or Amazons led by a queen from an island named California.

Gold, silver, and precious stones that Spaniards seized in the Aztec and Inca empires provided tangible and astonishing wealth while simultaneously stimulating visions of similar bounty awaiting subsequent conquistadores. Although thousands of men who succumbed to this dream of the possible perished, often in horrific ways, the lure continued. Natives understood the Spaniards' craving for gold and readily confirmed the metal's existence in locales far from their own.

In addition to the Amazons, four myths in particular influenced exploration: the Fountain of Youth, the Seven Golden Cities of Cíbola, Chicora, and El Dorado. Numerous others influenced the names that explorers, conquistadores, and settlers gave to rivers, mountains, other places, and peoples.

The allure of a fountain of youth located on the island of Bimini led Juan Ponce de León, whose experience in the Indies began with Christopher Columbus's second voyage in 1493, to obtain authorization in 1512 to explore and colonize the island. Sailing through the Bahamas, he reached the coast of Florida. There he encountered hostile natives and failed to find the mythical fountain. Nonetheless, he withdrew still believing he had reached Bimini. He returned to Florida in 1521, but was wounded and again pulled back, this time to die in Puerto Rico. The expedition of 1539–1543 led by Hernando de Soto, a companion of Francisco Pizarro in Peru, created a new legend about dense Indian populations and fertile lands in Florida, but found no rejuvenating fountain, gold mines, or rich kingdom. Before his death in what is now Louisiana, Soto's search for gold extended through what is now the southeastern United States and as far west as Texas.

Reported cities of untold wealth attracted another group of aspiring conquistadores. Upon arrival in Mexico City in 1536, Álvar Núñez Cabeza de Vaca, a Spaniard who had survived an eight-year odyssey walking from the Gulf coast of Texas to Mexico after disaster befell the ill-fated Pánfilo de Narváez expedition, related Indian claims of great civilizations to the north. Fray Marcos de Niza, a Franciscan who journeyed as far as Arizona and New Mexico in 1539, similarly reported the existence of seven rich cities—the Seven Cities of Cíbola—in the north comparable to Mexico City or Cuzco. With Fray Marcos as a guide, an expedition of some three hundred Spaniards and one thousand natives commanded by Francisco Vázquez de Coronado left Compostela, New Galicia, in February 1540 and advanced through northwestern Mexico into lands now in the southwestern United States. Told of another rich kingdom—Quivira—they continued until reaching Kansas, as Quivira is now called. While the trek revealed the Grand Canyon, the Great Plains, and some modest native villages at Zuni (Cíbola), it was a financial disaster. No opulent city existed in the north and both Coronado and Fray Marcos returned in failure to central Mexico.

For most of the sixteenth century, Spanish and later French exploration in the American Southeast north of Florida had its roots in the Chicora legend spread in 1523 by Lucas Vázquez de Ayllón of a "New Andalucia," a region rich in minerals, agricultural land, and population. A second legend associated with Giovanni da Verrazano concerned an isthmus located to the north of New Andalucia and a passage, the so-called Strait of Anian, to the Pacific Ocean. Subsequent investigation, however, revealed the fallacy of both. By 1590 the Chicora legend was dead; the Verrazano legend, however, remained attractive to some explorers into the seventeenth century, although the alleged passage's location was moved farther north.

South America. Myths about the existence of great wealth arguably had more influence in spurring expeditions in northern South America than elsewhere in the Indies. Many contemporaries shared a common belief that gold "grew" better close to the Equator. Accordingly, Diego de Ordás, an experienced conquistador who had served with Hernán Cortés in Mexico, obtained royal authorization to govern a region that he believed included the source of gold. Landing north of the Amazon River, he proceeded to an unexpected, recently founded town of Paria near the mouth of the Orinoco River. In 1531 the expedition laboriously advanced hundreds of miles inland before insurmountable rapids forced a withdrawal. Misled by captured Caribs who informed Ordás that a rich, one-eyed ruler lived in the province of Meta beyond a mountain range to the side of the river, the shrinking expedition changed course but with equally unsatisfactory financial results. Reviled by his remaining men, Ordás died en route to Spain; his legacy was unprecedented knowledge of the northern interior of South America.

The conquest of the Inca and the return of Hernando Pizarro to Spain in January 1534 with articles of gold and silver from Peru stimulated a new wave of explorers. Some sought presumed Inca wealth in Quito; others pursued the mythical source of gold located near the Equator. To these objectives were soon added El Dorado, literally a gilded man, but later synonymous with a land of gold, and the Amazons.

An expedition led from Peru by Sebastián de Benalcázar reached Quito in June 1534. He subsequently journeyed north, arriving at the region of Bogotá in 1537 before separate expeditions from the north led by Gonzalo Jiménez de Quesada and Nikolaus Federmann. Because of their prior arrival, Quesada's men benefited most from the treasure of the Muisca, the last high civilization conquered by the Spanish.

El Dorado, the gilded man, came to life in native accounts of a Muisca male assuming a position as chief in a ceremony that involved covering his body with gold dust and then immersing himself in a sacred lake while observers threw articles of gold into the water. In 1541 expeditions led by Gonzalo Pizarro, Hernán Pérez de Quesada, and Philipp von Hutten sought the gilded man and his realm. In 1543 Benalcázar joined the pursuit in a separate effort. None of the expeditions achieved its goal.

Use of the name "Amazon" was itself testimony to the power of myth. From Columbus onward, references surfaced to these women of classical legend who lived without men except when they sought impregnation. Some contracts for exploration specifically charged the expedition to look for Amazons; in at least one case, a conquistador was ennobled, among other things, for searching for Amazons. Jiménez de Quesada's men applied the name to a group of such women rumored to exist within reach of Bogotá. Gonzalo Pizarro was told early in his expedition down the world's largest river that rich Amazons lived farther down its course. Although Francisco de Orellana, one of Pizarro's lieutenants,

navigated the length of the Amazon River without reaching these reputedly wealthy inhabitants, he later claimed to have seen them, and the name Amazon was attached to the river.

Leavened with the spectacular wealth conquistadores encountered in central Mexico and Inca Peru in particular, stories of rich kingdoms, remarkable men and women, and astonishing sites were believable if usually inaccurate. The rapidity with which Spanish explorers scoured both North and South America in the sixteenth century owes much to the widespread influence of myth and legend.

[*See also* Amazons; El Dorado; Fictitious and Fantastic Places; Quivira; *and biographies of figures mentioned in this article*.]

BIBLIOGRAPHY
Hemming, John. *The Search for El Dorado*. New York: Dutton, 1978.
Hoffman, Paul E. *A New Andalucia and a Way to the Orient: The American Southeast during the Sixteenth Century*. Baton Rouge: Louisiana State University Press, 1990.
Leonard, Irving A. *Books of the Brave: Being an Account of Books and of Men in the Spanish Conquest and Settlement of the Sixteenth-Century New World*. Cambridge, Mass.: Harvard University Press, 1949.

MARK A. BURKHOLDER

Chad, Lake. Once one of the world's largest bodies of water, Lake Chad formerly approached the size of Lake Erie in North America but now claims only 550 square miles (885 square kilometers) of shallow water, virtually all of it in the south basin. Because of chronic droughts and human misuse, this body of water has been reduced to a mere shadow of its former size. In the eighteenth and nineteenth centuries, Lake Chad provided considerable concern, not for environmentalists, but for armchair geographers and explorers. On his famous 1798 map of North Africa, James Rennell carefully denoted the course of the Niger River flowing eastward into an isolated lake in the center of the continent, the lake that we now know as Lake Chad. The veracity of that map was questioned rather quickly when Mungo Park, on his second journey to West Africa, proved in 1805 that the Niger River flowed south, not east. Eighteen years later, Walter Oudney, Hugh Clapperton, and Dixon Denham became the first Europeans to see Lake Chad, and after extensive reconnaissance in 1823 and early 1824, they demonstrated that the Niger River certainly was not related to the lake.

In 1850, a British expedition comprising James Richardson, Adolph Overweg, and Heinrich Barth was dispatched to central Africa to learn about the slave trade and to develop diplomatic and economic ties with the kingdom of Bornu. Richardson perished early, but Overweg and Barth, beginning in May 1851, spent fifteen months in the Lake Chad area. Overweg explored the lake on the boat *Lord Palmerston*, which the expedition had carried across the desert. When Overweg died in September 1852, Barth continued on his storied journey to Timbuctoo. On Barth's return to Lake Chad, he encountered Eduard Vogel, with whom he subsequently worked for more than three months. After Barth returned to Europe, Vogel further explored the Lake Chad region and the headwaters of the Benue River, but shortly after he departed the lake in late 1855, he was murdered in the Darfur region.

Later travelers to Lake Chad include Gustav Nachtigal, who visited in 1870, and Gerhard Rohlfs, who visited in 1866. The French Foureau-Lamy expedition, in what turned out to be a military campaign, reached Lake Chad in 1899–1900. In spring 1904 the Frenchman Jean Tilho conducted scientific work there, and in 1905 the British Alexander-Gosling expedition spent months mapping the southern part of the lake. What is remarkable is how much the lake had changed in such a short time. Because of rainfall variation, the descriptions of Tilho and of Boyd Alexander were quite different. P. A. Talbot, a member of the Alexander-Gosling group, later published an ethnological account of the Buduma, a Nilotic-appearing tribe who inhabited the islands. Writing about Lake Chad, Boyd Alexander eloquently stated, "Every explorer looks upon the map of that part of the world which particularly calls him, and endeavors to find a spot that still affords opportunity for the special powers he may possess for finding out the secrets it hides. . . . Lake Chad was the last gem that remained uncut and wanting a proper setting. There it lay in the desert waiting."

[*See also* Africa *and biographical entries on figures mentioned in this article.*]

BIBLIOGRAPHY
Alexander, Boyd. *From the Niger to the Nile.* 2 vols. London: Edward Arnold, 1907.
Barth, Heinrich. *Travels in North and Central Africa.* London and New York: Ward, Lock, 1890.

SANFORD H. BEDERMAN

Chaillé-Long, Charles (1842–1917), American explorer of the Nile region. Chaillé-Long was a former U.S. officer in the Union army who discovered Lake Kyoga on the Victoria Nile while in Egyptian service. Of French Huguenot descent, Chaillé-Long was born at Princess Anne on Maryland's eastern shore on July 2, 1842, and served as a captain in the Union infantry during the Civil War. In 1870 he joined other American veterans in the army of Khedive Ismā'īl (1830–1895). In 1874, as chief of staff to Colonel Charles Gordon, Khedive Ismā'īl's governor of Equatorial Province, in what is present-day southern Sudan and Uganda, he led a six-month expedition 600 miles (965 kilometers) south from Gordon's headquarters at Gondokoro to the court of King Mutesa by the northern shore of Lake Victoria. On his return, Chaillé-Long reached the Victoria Nile at Urondogani, the point where hostile inhabitants had forced John Hanning Speke to leave the river. Chaillé-Long filled in the missing link on the Victorian Nile between there and Mrooli, discovering Lake Kyoga (the name "Lake Ibrahim" in honor of Khedive Ismā'īl's father lost out) along the way. Barely surviving the journey, he made it through to the southernmost Egyptian outpost at Foueira and thence back to Gondokoro. On a second expedition the following year, he established Egyptian authority southwest of Lado (whence Gordon had moved his Nile headquarters) in Azande country along the Congo-Nile divide and the headwaters of the Bahr el-Ghazel tributary of the Nile. Georg Schweinfurth had explored this region in 1870. Returning to Cairo, he presented to the khedive an Akka Pygmy woman four feet tall and addressed the newly founded Khedivial Geographical Society. British hostility aborted the H. F. McKillop expedition that Chaillé-Long accompanied to the Juba River in southern Somalia in an effort to open an east coast route to Egyptian territory on the upper Nile. Chaillé-Long then left khedivial service, but in 1882 he was back in Egypt hoping to practice law and protecting evacuees briefly in Alexandria during the Urabi revolt in the absence of the American consul general. He later practiced law in Paris and served as consul general in Korea. He died at Virginia Beach, Virginia, on March 12, 1917.

[*See also* Gordon, Charles; Khedivial Exploration; *and* Schweinfurth, Georg.]

BIBLIOGRAPHY
Chaillé-Long, Charles. *Central Africa: Naked Truths of Naked People (1876).* Farnborough, U.K.: Gregg International Publishers, 1968.

DONALD MALCOLM REID

***Challenger* Expedition.** The two leading figures in the *Challenger* Expedition of 1872–1876 were

***Challenger* Expedition.** Plate from the *Report on the Scientific Results of the Voyage of HMS* Challenger (3 vols., London, 1882–1885). Here is *Challenger*'s deck, with the engine supplementing the sails, a trawl hanging over the side, and the officers no doubt considering where next to anchor and begin the laborious task of collecting samples from the ocean. COURTESY THE NEWBERRY LIBRARY, CHICAGO

Charles Wyville Thomson (1830–1882), who persuaded the Royal Society and the British government to sponsor an exploration of the ocean depths, and John Murray (1841–1914), who was chiefly responsible for the publication of the results. Both were Scots educated at Edinburgh University. Murray claimed that the expedition represented "the greatest advance in knowledge of our planet since the celebrated discoveries of the fifteenth and sixteenth centuries" because the oceans had been unknown. Indeed, it was generally assumed that ocean floors were featureless and deep waters azoic—without life.

HMS *Challenger* was a 2,300-ton, three-masted, square-rigged corvette with its gundecks transformed into laboratories. Although basically a sailing vessel, she had an auxiliary steam engine, useful for maintaining one position while dredging and sounding. The captain was George Strong Nares (1831–1915), who tactfully reconciled the interests of the scientists and the sailors. In January 1875 he was recalled to take command of an Arctic expedition and was succeeded by Captain Frank Turle Thomson. The crew numbered over two hundred. The civilian scientists, apart from Thomson and Murray, were J. J. Wild, secretary and artist, Henry Moseley and Willemoes Suhm, naturalists, and J. Y. Buchanan, physicist and chemist.

Between December 1872 and May 1876, the *Challenger* crossed and recrossed the North Atlantic then went south to the Cape of Good Hope. From there she sailed east, becoming the first steam vessel to cross the Antarctic Circle before reaching Australia and then New Zealand. The voyage among Pacific islands and thence to Hong Kong and Japan was the prelude to reentering the Atlantic via the Strait of Magellan and returning to Britain. In all, 68,890 miles were sailed but by no means continuously: no fewer than 362 "stations" marked points where the ship stopped so that soundings of the depth could be made with a weighted hemp rope, samples of seawater and temperatures and the organisms present taken at various depths, and the bottom itself trawled for its sediments as well as its animal life. This was tedious work for all concerned as getting a dredge or trawl down to 2,500 fathoms would take three hours.

All the data amassed were utilized by the scientists on the voyage and many others so that, between 1885 and 1895, fifty large volumes on the results were produced and the science of oceanography was born. It became apparent that the ocean floor had its mountains and chasms, that its sediments included cosmic dust as well as organic and inorganic

debris from the land. Seawater was found to be constant in composition though varying in salinity and reaching near freezing in the greatest depths. Most important were the biological results. No fewer than 715 new genera were identified, which included 4,717 species of animals, many of them able to live in the enormous pressure of the greatest depths of ocean.

Following Thomson's death in 1882, it was Murray who managed the production of the fifty volumes—appropriately from the *Challenger* office in Edinburgh.

[*See also* Vessels, *subentry on* Motorized Vessels.]

BIBLIOGRAPHY

Deacon, Margaret. *Scientists and the Sea, 1650–1900: A Study of Marine Science*. Aldershot, U.K.: Ashgate, 1997.

Linklater, Eric. *The Voyage of the Challenger*. London: J. Murray, 1972.

Thomson, Charles Wyville. *The Voyage of the "Challenger."* London: Macmillan, 1877; New York: Harper and Brothers, 1878.

ROY BRIDGES

Champlain, Samuel de (c. 1570–1635), French soldier, mariner, geographer, explorer, author, cartographer, and administrator. Champlain was born in Brouage, in the province of Saintonge, France, and died on December 25, 1635, at Quebec, Canada.

Champlain was born into a seagoing family and once wrote that he had always felt an affinity to the sea. Both his father Antoine and his maternal uncle Guillaume Allène were ship's captains in the French navy. During the civil war, from 1593 to 1598, Champlain was in the quartermaster's service of Henri IV's army and, on occasion, performed "important and confidential" work for the king. After the war, from 1598 to mid-1601, he sailed on his uncle's ship the *Saint-Julien*, hired by Spain for service in the Caribbean. It is probable that he gained his knowledge of surveying and navigation through his years in the army and aboard ship. Early in 1603 he was invited by Aymar de Chaste, holder of the fur trade monopoly for Canada, to investigate the lands along the Saint Lawrence River for possible settlement and exploration westward. Based on the expeditions of Jacques Cartier, there was considerable doubt in most French circles whether Europeans could settle and profit in Canada. The long winters, deadly bouts of scurvy, and possible attacks from hostile natives made settlement doubtful, and the Lachine Rapids south of Montreal Island transformed the Saint Lawrence River into a cul-de-sac that made further navigation toward China improbable. Champlain's task

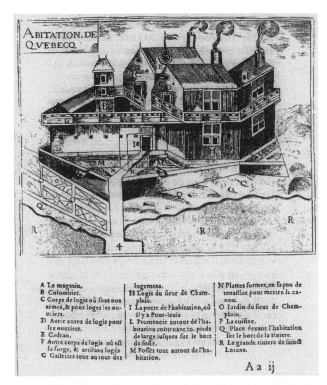

A Le magazin.
B Colombier.
C Corps de logis où font nos armes, & pour loger les ouuriers.
D Autre corps de logis pour les ouuriers.
E Cadran.
F Autre corps de logis où est la forge, & artisans logés
G Galleries tout au tour des

logemens.
H Logis du sieur de Cham-plain.
I La porte de l'habitation, où il y a Pont-leuis.
L Promenoir autour de l'ha-bitation contenant 10. pieds de large iusques fur le bort du fossé.
M Fossés tout autour de l'ha-bitation.

N Plattes formes, en façon de tenailles pour mettre le ca-non.
O Iardin du sieur de Cham-plain.
P La cuisine.
Q Place deuant l'habitation fur le bort de la riuiere.
R La grande riuiere de sainct Lorens.

A a ij

Samuel de Champlain. Plate of the Abitation de Quebec from *Des sauvages* (Paris, 1612). This is Champlain's view of his headquarters on the Saint Lawrence River at Quebec, established in 1608. COURTESY THE NEWBERRY LIBRARY, CHICAGO

was to investigate these problems and report his findings to his superior Aymar de Chaste and to King Henri IV.

When Champlain arrived at Montreal Island in July 1603, the French tested a skiff constructed specifically to navigate across the Lachine Rapids, which are 3 miles (5 kilometers) long. When it failed miserably, he became the first to recognize that European transportation technology (ships, boats, horses, even walking) was useless in the Canadian wilderness. He reasoned that exploration could be carried out only with native help, with their canoes and their ways of living off the land. This meant that the French had to develop peaceful relations with the local natives, foster strong interpersonal bonds, and help them in their wars, the latter being the one thing they demanded from the French. Champlain became convinced that without native cooperation the way to the interior of Canada was closed. On the same voyage he also discovered that the natives could draw maps and render good geographical descriptions. In fact, he learned of the existence of Hudson Bay seven

years before Henry Hudson got there, as well as the huge freshwater seas west of the Lachine Rapids, and an enormous ocean beyond them. Were these the routes to China?

Between 1604 and 1607, Champlain explored and mapped the Atlantic coast from Cape Breton Island to Nantucket Sound, honing his observational skills, gathering native geographical reports, and formulating plans for returning to the Saint Lawrence. In 1608 he had returned and, after building a settlement at Quebec, began to develop closer relations with the native populations. In 1603 the Tadoussac Montagnais had made a treaty with King Henri IV, the first of its kind in North America, permitting French settlement along the Saint Lawrence in return for military help against their ancient foes the Iroquois. With the Quebec settlement secure in 1609, it fell to Champlain to honor the commitment his king had made. With two French volunteers he joined his new native allies on a raid against the Mohawk Iroquois on Lake Champlain. This expedition ce-

---

Canadian Settlement

Like Cartier before him, Champlain was struck by the potential fruitfulness of the land to which he had come. But unlike Cartier, Champlain had a practical bent to his judgments and was also a skillful leader of people, so that he could not only see the potential of the country, but also take necessary measures, such as following the advice of indigenous people, to survive and then thrive in it.

And near this Place Royale [close to present-day Montreal] there is a small river, which leads some distance into the interior, alongside which are more than sixty arpents of land, which have been cleared and are now like meadows, where one might sow grain and do gardening . . . And there are many other fine meadows which would feed as many cattle as one would wish, and there are all the varieties of wood which we have in our forests in France, with many vines, butternuts, plums, cherries, strawberries, and other kinds of fruits which are very good to eat . . . An abundance of fish can be caught, of all the varieties we have in France, and of many other very good kinds which we do not have.

—*The Works of Samuel de Champlain*, vol. 2, *1608–1613*, edited by H. P. Biggar (Toronto: Champlain Society, 1925)

mented relations with the Montagnais and brought the Algonquin and Huron into the alliance. It was also the first time any Europeans had explored inland. To build further trust, Champlain began to exchange young men with his native allies so that they could learn each other's languages and customs. Following a report by one of these men, Nicolas de Vignau, Champlain tried to explore up the Ottawa River north to James Bay in 1613, with four men and one native paddler-guide. The Algonquin, however, nervous that these inexperienced travelers would lose their lives in their territory, refused them further passage about halfway up the river. In 1615 Champlain took the opportunity to explore westward to one of the world's great freshwater seas, or *mer douce*, Lake Huron and Georgian Bay, by agreeing to participate with a few Frenchmen on another allied expedition against the Iroquois. On this journey he became the first European to travel across southern Ontario and the eastern end of Lake Ontario to what is now New York State. To Champlain this expedition proved again that settlement, exploration, and trade depended entirely on the goodwill of his native allies and that this, unavoidably, meant helping them in their wars. In 1615 he brought Recollect missionaries to Canada to begin the conversion of the natives to Christianity. These were followed in 1632 by the Jesuits, with whom Champlain began to promote French-native intermarriage, believing that a blended French-native, Catholic community would produce a people adapted to Canadian conditions who would complete the exploration and settlement of Canada and secure it for France.

Champlain thought that his greatest accomplishments were his maps and the principles he developed for exploring the country. Not only were his maps and journals a testament to his personal achievements but they also laid the foundation for French territorial claims against the Dutch and English to parts of North America. The principles worked out by Champlain for exploration made the French effective explorers. Through their positive native relations and willingness to adapt to Canadian conditions, French explorers usually knew where they were going and what they would find well before they got to their destinations. By 1686, the year the first Dutch-English expedition reached Lake Ontario, the French had explored and roughly mapped the five Great Lakes, the river routes to James Bay, and the Mississippi River to the Gulf of Mexico. These were remarkable achievements based on the insights of a remarkable man.

[*See also* Cartier, Jacques, *and* Great Lakes, The.]

BIBLIOGRAPHY

Biggar, H. P. ed. *The Works of Samuel de Champlain*. 6 vols. Toronto: Champlain Society, 1922–1936.

Bishop, Morris. *Champlain: The Life of Fortitude*. London: Macdonald, 1949.

Heidenreich, Conrad E. "Early French Exploration in the North American Interior." In *North American Exploration*, edited by John L. Allen. 3 vols. Vol. 2, *A Continent Defined*. Lincoln: University of Nebraska Press, 1997. Pp. 65–148.

Litalien, Raymonde, and Denis Vaugeois, eds. *Champlain: The Birth of French America*. Montreal: McGill–Queen's University Press, Éditions du Septentrion, 2004.

CONRAD E. HEIDENREICH

Chancellor, Richard, and Hugh Willoughby,

English explorers who sought the Northeast Passage. In 1553, merchant adventurers in London established an enterprise to seek a northeastern passage to Cathay by dispatching a maritime expedition around the North Cape of Norway. Instead, contact with Russia was established that resulted in the creation two years later of the Muscovy Company. The commander of the expedition was Sir Hugh Willoughby (d. 1554), knighted in Scotland

---

Russian Travels

This letter is remarkable for the way in which it summarizes the natural products of northern Russia; not only corn and fish, mentioned in this extract, but also furs, hides, hemp, and wax. Chancellor describes a system of transport by sleigh that was possible only in the winter, and he also remarks on an abiding feature of Russia in modern times: its great abundance of people.

The Mosco is from Jeraslave two hundred miles. The Country betwixt them is very well replenished with small Villages, which are so well filled with people that it is wonder to see them. The ground is well stored with Corn which they carrie to the Citie of Mosco in such abundance that it is wonder to see it. You shall meet in a morning seven or eight hundred Sleds coming or going thither, that carrie Corn and some carrie fish. You shall have some that carrie Corn to the Mosco, and some that fetch Corn from thence, that at the least dwell a thousand miles off, and all their carriage is on Sleds.

—Letter from Richard Chancellor to his uncle, quoted in Richard Hakluyt, *Principal Navigations*, vol. 1 (London, 1599)

during the military campaign of 1544 and from 1549 to 1550 commander of a castle in Berwickshire. He was, therefore, a noteworthy soldier by profession but, so far as is known, without maritime expertise or experience. Richard Chancellor (d. 1556), his pilot-major and second in command, had gained practical seagoing experience during a voyage in 1550 to the Levant. He had also studied astronomy and was an acquaintance of prominent mathematicians then applying their knowledge to the advancement of the nautical sciences.

Their expedition departed from Ratcliffe on the Thames on May 10, 1553. It was composed of the *Bona Esperanza* (120 tons) commanded by Willoughby, the *Edward Bonaventure* (160 tons) captained by Chancellor, and the *Bona Confidentia* (90 tons). The ships' keels were partially covered with thin lead sheeting as protection against shipworm. There followed a lengthy delay at Harwich on discovery that some provisions were already rotten and that wine casks were leaking. Consequently, the expedition did not leave the coast of East Anglia until June 23, heading for Norway. Their first landing, on July 19, was on the Isles of Røst at the foot of the Lofoten Isles, followed by a second landing, possibly at Steenfjord, on the 27th, and then a third landing at Senja on the 30th. A few days later, as the ships prepared to round the North Cape, Chancellor's *Bonaventure* became separated from her companions amid a storm. Since such an eventuality had been anticipated, it was planned that each ship should head for Vardø on the northeastern coast in the Barents Sea and, if necessary, wait there seven days for the arrival of the others. In fact, no such reunion occurred, with the result that Willoughby was denied the services of his most experienced pilot.

The *Bona Esperanza* was driven farther north than intended as it entered the Barents Sea. Then, rejoined by the *Confidentia*, they both zigzagged eastward to make, on August 14, the most northerly landfall hitherto recorded, at 72° N on the shores of Novaya Zemlya. They then turned southeastward and then westward, recrossing the Barents Sea to the coast of Lapland. There, on September 18, Willoughby made the fatal decision to winter his men at the mouth of the Arzina River near present-day Murmansk. Their frozen bodies were discovered by fishermen the following year. What became known in England as "Willoughby's Land" is shown as an island lying north of Norway on Mercator's map of the North Pole (1595).

In marked contrast, Chancellor's voyage was one of both immediate and long-term success. After waiting as arranged at Vardø, the *Bonaventure* coasted toward the entrance to the White Sea and anchored at the mouth of the North Dvina River on August 24, 1553, not far from modern Arkhangel'sk. From there Chancellor traveled six hundred miles (965 kilometers) overland to Moscow for a meeting with the tsar that would lay the foundations of commerce between England and Russia and establish the first diplomatic links between the two countries. Chancellor returned to England in 1554. To develop both of these objectives rather than the quest for the Northeast Passage, Chancellor reached the White Sea again in 1555 to revisit Moscow, but during the return voyage to England he drowned, on November 10, 1556, when shipwrecked off Pitsligo (near Rosehearty) on the north coast of Aberdeenshire.

[*See also* Muscovy Company *and* Northeast Passage.]

BIBLIOGRAPHY
Andrews, Kenneth R. *Trade, Plunder, and Settlement: Maritime Enterprise and the Genesis of the British Empire, 1480–1630.* New York and Cambridge, U.K.: Cambridge University Press, 1984.
Mayers, Kit. *North-East Passage to Muscovy: Stephen Borough and the First Tudor Explorations.* Stroud, U.K.: Sutton, 2005.

Peter T. Bradley

Cherry-Garrard, Apsley (1886–1959), not a great explorer, but a remarkable example of the way in which things were done in Edwardian England. Born on January 2, 1886, Cherry-Garrard, after a conventional education at Winchester College and Oxford University, began a period of well-heeled but restless idleness. Like many young men of his class and time, he no doubt sought the kind of moral fulfillment that people in other times and places had found in religious orders. Cherry-Garrard eventually proved to be a writer of great subtlety.

Cherry-Garrard's calling came when he encountered Dr. "Bill" Wilson, who in effect recruited him as an assistant biologist for Robert F. Scott's second expedition to Antarctica (1910–1912). "Cherry," as he was called, proved to be an admirable member of the team, surviving a particularly arduous trip whose object was to secure an unhatched Emperor penguin egg. He did not go with the party that then made an attempt upon the South Pole, but he was entrusted with the establishment of a food depot for this party's return. Cherry-Garrard set up this depot as he had been instructed, but in the event it proved to lie eleven miles north of the farthest point that the party

On the Comforts of Reading When Near the South Pole

Apsley Cherry-Garrard was the very epitome of the amateur Edwardian explorer; he was made part of Scott's expedition more for his gentlemanly qualities than for any professional qualifications. Cherry-Garrard reflects in this passage the outlook and preoccupations of the leisured class of his day; it is hard to imagine any subsequent—or indeed previous—group of explorers taking such an interest in the fashionable literature of their time. Still, Cherry-Garrard proved to have a sterling character, one that inadvertently emerges in the remarkable book that he eventually published.

I would suggest that the literature most acceptable to us in the circumstances under which we did most of our reading, that is in Winter Quarters, was the best of the more recent novels, such as Barrie, Kipling, Merriman and Maurice Hewlett. We certainly should have taken with us as much of Shaw, Barker, Ibsen and Wells as we could lay hands on, for the train of ideas started by these works and the discussions to which they would have given rise would have been a godsend to us in our isolated circumstances. . . . I have already spoken of the importance of maps and books of reference, and these should include a good encyclopaedia and dictionaries, English, Latin and Greek. Oates was generally deep in Napier's History of the Peninsular War, and some of us found Herbert Paul's History of Modern England a great stand-by.

—Apsley Cherry-Garrard, *The Worst Journey in the World*
(London, 1922)

was capable of reaching; he seems to have felt tormented for the rest of his life by the idea that by going farther south he might have saved Scott's party.

Returning to England, Cherry-Garrard lived quietly for some years, until in 1922 his neighbor, George Bernard Shaw, suggested that he write his memoirs. The result was an epic: *The Worst Journey in the World*. Perhaps, in its subtle evocation of an apparently more innocent time, the book appealed to the generation of English people who had suffered the agonies of World War I. But in its wonderful analysis of the relationships among the members of the doomed Scott expedition, the book carried a psychological conviction that lasts to this day; it was also illustrated with extraordinarily powerful images,

many of them drawn by Dr. Wilson. [See color plate 23 in this volume.]

[*See also* Antarctica *and* Scott, Robert Falcon.]

BIBLIOGRAPHY
Cherry-Garrard, Apsley. *The Worst Journey in the World*. London: Constable, 1922.
Wheeler, Sarah. *Cherry: A Life of Apsley Cherry-Garrard*. London: Jonathan Cape, 2001.

DAVID BUISSERET

Chichagov, Vasily Yakovlevich (1726–1809),

Russian who attempted to navigate the ocean around the North Pole. A graduate of the School of Navigation, Chichagov served for a time in the British Royal Navy, and in 1742 he joined the Baltic fleet. The Russian scientist, grammarian, poet, and philosopher Mikhail Lomonosov hypothesized in 1763 that the Arctic Ocean around the North Pole was navigable, and in 1764 the Russian government decided to mount an expedition to test this hypothesis.

The expedition's leaders would be Chichagov, Nikifor Panov, and Basily Babaev, and three newly constructed ships (named after these leaders); the ships were crewed by 178 sailors, including six experienced White Sea *pomors* (coast dwellers). In May 1765 the expedition set off from the mouth of the Kola River, but at latitude 80°26′ N the ships met with impassable ice and had to return to Arkhangel'sk. Chichagov tried again the following year, but at about the same latitude he again encountered impassable ice and was forced to return, reaching Arkhangel'sk in September 1766.

So, although they failed in their main goal, Chichagov's expeditions proved without doubt that Lomonosov's theory was incorrect; such navigation became possible only in recent times, using powerful icebreakers with nuclear engines. In 1772, Chichagov commanded the Russian navy squadron in the Mediterranean, taking part in the Don River expedition of 1773. He was commander of the Baltic fleet during the Russo-Swedish war of 1779, taking part in the Russian victories off the Revel anchorage and in the Vyborg Gulf. In 1782 he became an admiral, in recognition of his many services.

[*See also* Arctic, *subentry on* Russian Arctic, *and* North Pole, *subentry* An Overview.]

ALEXEY POSTNIKOV

Chinese Empirical Maps. Chinese empirical

cartography has a long history, and includes everything from rather approximate world maps to highly accurate cartography based on grid systems. The Chinese mapmaking tradition continued for centuries until it became combined with Jesuit cartography in the sixteenth century.

One of the earliest surviving examples of Chinese empirical cartography is the twelfth-century *Hua yi tu* (Map of China and the Barbarian Countries), which is roughly one-meter square and carved of stone. Most of the map is taken up with a representation of China, with Korea and India also included, while the "barbarian countries" are discussed in notes written in the margins of the map. Another map, a version of the *Yu ji tu* (Map of the Tracks of Yu), is carved on the reverse side of the *Hua yi tu*. The *Yu ji tu* has a modern appearance because of the presence of grid lines on it; each grid space represents 100 *li*, equal to about 30 miles. The sinologist Joseph Needham remarked on the extraordinary accuracy of the Chinese coastline in this map.

This grid system also appears in a later map in an atlas by Luo Hongxian, the *Guang yu tu* (Enlarged Terrestrial Map), published in the mid-sixteenth century. This map has its origins in the early fourteenth-century *Yu tu* (Terrestrial Map) of Zhu Siben. Luo included information from other sources as well, including from the several voyages of the famous Chinese admiral Zheng He. Other maps, such the c. 1330 *Sheng jiao guang bei tu* (Map of the Vast Reach of Teaching) of Li Zemin—a work that is no longer extant—did not employ grid systems. However, a Korean map, the *Honil kangni yoktae kukto chi to* (Map of the Integrated Regions and Terrains and of Historical Countries and Capitals), created in 1402 and often referred to as the Kangnido, integrates both Li Zemin's map and the fourteenth-century *Hun yi jiang li tu* (Map of the Integrated Regions). Three versions of the Korean map survive; all are in Japan. The map shows the world centered on China, with a very large Korean peninsula and Japan directly to the south. Europe appears in a small representation just above the triangular form of Africa.

Chinese cartography preserved two traditions. The first, exemplified by the gridded maps, reflects a mapmaking process based on measurement and concern with scale. The second tradition is exemplified, in turn, by the large world maps such as the Kangnido, which were more concerned with the compilation of large amounts of general geographical information, both textual and visual.

When the Jesuits arrived in China in the late sixteenth century, a separate cartographical tradition arose, although one still steeped in Chinese carto-

graphical styles. The Jesuits introduced new knowledge in astronomy, mathematics, and surveying, while also learning about Chinese work in these fields. A key figure in this process was Father Matteo Ricci, who arrived in China in 1582 and assembled a map that combined Chinese and Western source material. His map was known as the *Yu di shan hai quan tu* (Map of the Mountains and Seas of the Earth); it was completed in 1584 but is no longer extant. A version of this map is found in the 1613 *Tu shu bian* (Compilation of Illustrations and Writings), assembled by Ricci's associate, Zhang Huang. A second Ricci map, the 1602 *Kun yu wan guo quan tu* (Complete Map of the Myriad Countries of the World), displayed greater and more accurate geographical detail. Another Jesuit, Father Ferdinand Verbiest, produced a large world map in 1674 as part of his *Kun yu tu shuo* (Illustrated Discussion of the Geography of the Earth).

Despite the magnificence of these cartographic works and the success of cross-cultural cooperation between the Chinese and the Jesuits, the cooperation did not last. In 1724, Emperor Yongzheng banned Christianity, and subsequently Chinese scholars attacked Jesuit cartography; works such as the *Huang chao wen xian tong kao* (Imperial Dynasty's Comprehensive Examination of Source Materials) claimed that Ricci's ideas were simply speculation and that they denigrated Chinese culture.

Later Chinese maps moved away from the use of mathematical frameworks, and in some sense returned to earlier models for their cartography. For example, even though Wang Qi, in his *San cai tu hui* (Illustrations of the Three Powers), was working from Ricci's maps, his rendering included no meridian lines and was placed in a more traditional circular frame. Very little information was provided concerning Europe or the Americas. Later Chinese maps go so far as to depict various mythical lands from the ancient encyclopedic work *Shanhai jing* (Classic of Mountains and Seas).

Only in the nineteenth century did the Chinese fully return to empirical mapmaking, reviving a tradition that they themselves had established centuries before. A significant work of this period was *Hai guo tu zhi* (Illustrated Gazetteer of the Maritime Countries) by Wei Yuan, a multivolume work that first appeared in 1843. It included an analysis of Western technology and a discussion of Western tactics, matters of concern to the Chinese in the face of ever-increasing British expansion. The *Hai guo tu zhi* included many maps that took from both Chinese and Western source material. Each subsequent edition of the work included increasingly up-to-date maps and geographical data.

After the middle of the nineteenth century, Chinese maps began a gradual evolution to completely empirical forms. Chinese scholars and diplomats returned from abroad bringing increasingly detailed information about the outside world, a phenomenon accelerated by international trade. There were still detours into mythical geography, but after the trauma of their losses in the Sino-Japanese War (1894–1895), and in the face of Western imperial ambitions in the East, the Chinese began to promote scientific cartography exclusively. This was continued through the New Culture movement (also known as the May Fourth movement) in the first quarter of the twentieth century, which saw a rejection of traditional Chinese thinking and a deep interest in Western science and culture. However, the Chinese can always look back at works such as the *Yu ji tu* as examples of early—and very sophisticated—Chinese empirical cartography.

[*See also* Buddhist Cosmological Maps; Jesuits; *and* Maps, Mapmaking, and Mapmakers.]

BIBLIOGRAPHY

Fuchs, Walter. "The 'Mongol Atlas' of China by Chu Ssu-pen and the Kuang-Yü-t'u." In *Monumenta Serica: Journal of Oriental Studies of the Catholic University of Peking*, monograph 8. Beijing: Fu Jen University, 1946.

Harley, J. B., and David Woodward, eds. *The History of Cartography*. Vol. 2, book 2, *Cartography in the Traditional East and Southeast Asian Societies*. Chicago: University of Chicago Press, 1994.

Ledyard, Gari. "The Kangnido: A Korean World Map, 1402." In *Art in the Age of Exploration: Circa 1492*, edited by Jay A. Levenson. New Haven, Conn.: Yale University Press, 1991.

Nakamura, Hiroshi. "Old Chinese World Maps Preserved by the Koreans." *Imago Mundi* 4 (1947): 3–22.

Smith, Richard J. *Chinese Maps: Images of "All under Heaven."* Oxford: Oxford University Press, 1996.

BENJAMIN B. OLSHIN

Chinese Exile Writers. Chinese thought traditionally divided the universe into inner and outer realms along a continuum that shaded from familiar to unfamiliar, civilized to uncivilized. These concepts applied not only in a physical or geographical context but also in the interconnected spheres of moral, cultural, political, and intellectual life. From antiquity these notions also carried over into the banishment of offenders, so that the remotest exile marked the greatest disgrace. However, even the severest banishment entailed removal only to the borders of the state and not beyond, since even offenders, in whatever category, could be put to use ad-

ministering and colonizing newly annexed territory to which others might not wish to transfer. Disgraced government officials were punished by dispatch, usually for a fixed term, to hardship posts in newly annexed frontier areas, while common criminals were sent to live on new frontiers, typically forever.

The statutory system of punishment in place, with modifications, from the seventh century, made exile a punishment second only to the death penalty, acknowledging the powerful Chinese attachment to native place. In early modern times under the Qing dynasty (1644–1912) the punishment of exile had two main tiers: at a fixed distance within China proper, and banishment to the frontier. With imperial expansion, possible exile destinations became ever more distant from the center. For the first century or so of Qing rule, those banished to the frontier went to the northeastern homelands of the Manchu rulers; after the mid-eighteenth century, they were more often sent to the vast, newly conquered territories of central Asia that came to be known as Xinjiang. Both these destinations involved very great distances and considerable estrangement from China's cultural norms. The uncertainties were terrifying; the opportunity of exploration mitigated only partially the desolation that Chinese exiles felt upon separation from home. Many drowned their sorrows in poetry and descriptive writing, a tactic that enabled them to draw upon themselves the considerable kudos of perpetuating a venerable literary tradition. It also had the effect of attaching to such exiles, after their return, a degree of prestige that surpassed the mere scarcity value of the knowledge they had acquired.

Chinese exile literature traced its origins to the third-century B.C.E. loyalist poet of antiquity, Qu Yuan. Qu's enduring reputation was attributable both to his literary skill and to his tenacious loyalty to his ruler despite his banishment, which culminated in his suicide. He set the pattern for later exile writers in two ways. Not only did he write eloquently of the desolation of the exile experience, but at the same time he showed exiles an alternative path to the immortality of which political disgrace seemed to have deprived them.

One of the best-known exile writers of the early modern period was Ji Yun (1724–1805), known for his editorship of the great imperial bibliographic project. Ji was banished to Xinjiang in 1768 following a serious breach in confidentiality. His exile writings, in which he repeatedly referred to the work of eminent predecessors, became a classic of the genre, for both their literary charm and their content, since they were among the first to provide his contemporaries with firsthand accounts of Xinjiang. Indeed, Ji's collections of notes, journals, correspondence, and belles-lettres concerning the frontier are an enormously rich source of information, both capturing the anxiety of exile and depicting vividly his life en route to and on the newly settled frontier—how Xinjiang did or did not meet his expectations, the kinds of people he saw, local customs, foods, and plants. In addition to claiming the heritage of distinguished exiled literati, Ji also took care to visit local ruins and similar sites, so that in providing factual, eyewitness information he could claim a place in the movement to "seek truth from facts," a major scholarly pursuit of the time. After Ji's return, he resumed his political career with considerable success; his exile writings also added an aura of exoticism to his reputation for erudition. His writings may have represented a veiled commentary on current affairs, with the remoteness of Xinjiang substituting for the more usual device of setting contemporary criticism in ancient times.

Other well-known Qing-period exiles included Hong Liangji (1746–1809), sometimes called "China's Malthus" for his dire predictions about China's burgeoning population. Hong was exiled in 1799 for openly criticizing the emperor for failing to deal with corruption, which in turn was blamed for causing widespread rebellion. Hong's fellow exiles held him in highest regard, and tried to console him by comparing him favorably to outstanding political and literary exiles of the past. Others urged him to take advantage of his unwanted stay in Xinjiang to gather information about this relatively unknown region. Some later exiles were specifically put to such work by the military governor of the region, which remained for the time being under special administrative arrangements. Xu Song (1781–1848), another eminent scholar banished to Xinjiang for abusing his office, was formally employed in exile to travel about collecting information. He thus both contributed to official compilations concerning Xinjiang and, along with other scholar-exiles, produced his own eyewitness account. An unanticipated advantage of that collaboration was to provide checks on potential flights of fancy, which fellow exiles would have been able to disprove. By the time Lin Zexu (1785–1850) was banished following the Opium War (1839–1842), the path to exile and the practice of writing about it were almost routine.

All the exile writings of this period, but especially those of such leading scholar-officials as those mentioned above, were enormously influential in the formation of policy toward the frontier. Upon their return, these men again circulated in the most powerful circles in Beijing, and their firsthand knowledge was recognized as invaluable. Their writings influenced proposals to use Xinjiang to relieve demographic and ecological pressure in the interior, and ultimately contributed to the decision to incorporate Xinjiang into the empire as a full-fledged province in the late nineteenth century. Thus exiled scholar-officials' writings about the frontier cast a long shadow that played a part in the formation of modern China's far-reaching footprint.

[*See also* Chinese Exploration.]

BIBLIOGRAPHY

Keenan, David L., trans. *Shadows in a Chinese Landscape: The Notes of a Confucian Scholar*. Armonk, N.Y.: M. E. Sharpe, 1999.

Waley-Cohen, Joanna. *Exile in Mid-Qing China: Banishment to Xinjiang, 1758–1820*. New Haven, Conn.: Yale University Press, 1991.

JOANNA WALEY-COHEN

Chinese Exploration. Europeans who came to China in the eighteenth and nineteenth centuries thought that the Chinese had never had any interest in the outside world. Pearl Buck perpetuated the myth of the Chinese peasant fastened to his plot of land in her novel *The Good Earth* (1931). Nothing could be further from the truth: from ancient times, Chinese people constantly explored the lands around them. Their first focus, however, was the interior of the Eurasian continent. Maritime exploration came later.

Continental Exploration. The motives of Chinese travelers were similar to the motives of other countries' travelers: power, trade, religion, and sometimes simply curiosity. The rulers and generals of powerful dynasties constantly tried to expand into central Eurasia, and they sent explorers, spies, and diplomats to learn as much as they could about the desert and grassland regions beyond the mountain passes that enclosed agrarian China. Merchants followed the military expeditions, both because the soldiers needed to buy supplies and because the prospect of new markets lured astute traders who braved the hardships of the route. Religious faith, especially in Buddhists, inspired the most dedicated travelers, who sought sacred texts and famous monks in India.

Travel across central Eurasia depended on a fragile trading infrastructure. The two-humped Bactrian camel, the hardy transport beast of the desert, was the core of the merchant's caravan, and it responded only to men who had special training. Military expedi-

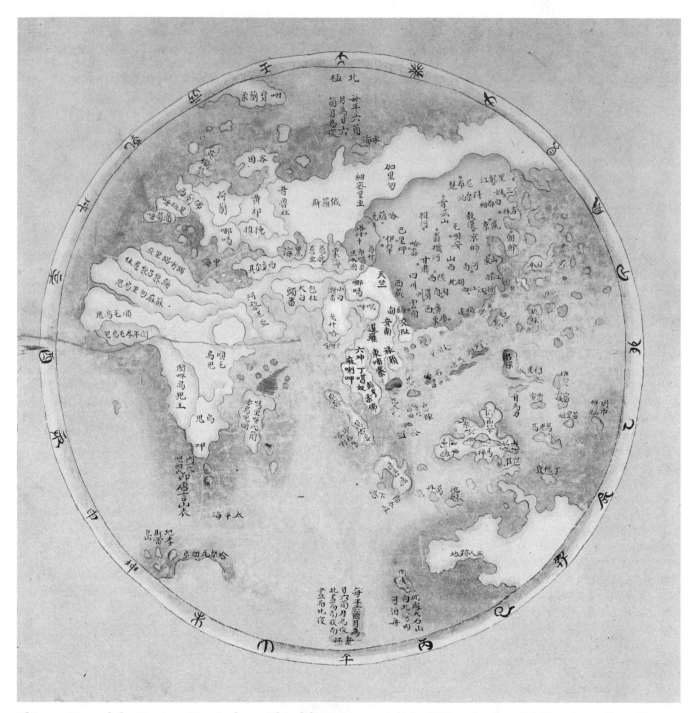

Chinese Map of the Eastern Hemisphere. This delicate map, made in 1790 under the Qing dynasty, reflects Chinese knowledge of the world at a time when China's explorers were again reaching out into the world, particularly into central Eurasia. Bildarchiv Preussischer Kulturbesitz/Art Resource, NY

tions used horses, mules, and donkeys, and brought with them huge herds of sheep and goats for food. The *caravanserai*, or inns, provided convenient stopping places for gathering goods and exchanging information. In the oases sparsely scattered across the desert lived agricultural people, who profited from the caravans passing through. In the grasslands, nomadic groups roamed with their herds, preying on or protecting the travelers. In times of peace, when China could project power into the steppe and nomads united in a large confederacy, travelers and traders could often pass through perilous lands backed by imperial seals. In times of upheaval, travel and trade became much more difficult, and most travelers could get only to trading posts on the border, or they would be held up for years in one suspicious king's land before they were allowed to proceed further. Despite constant interruptions and the vicissitudes of war, the Chinese who ventured into the heart of the continent could hope to return with riches, fame, and government favor.

According to legend, in the first millennium B.C.E. King Mu of the Zhou dynasty traveled to the "four remote corners of the world." Going deep into central Eurasia, he visited the Queen Mother of the West and held a banquet for her, then returned through forests, deserts, and plains, hunting wild game and collecting valuable furs and feathers. Whether true or not, the text describing King Mu's journey indicates the Chinese rulers' lively curiosity about the center of the continent.

Besides curiosity, Chinese rulers had one key reason to explore the continent: they needed powerful military horses. In 104 B.C.E., during the Han dynasty, the emperor sent two large expeditions to the Ferghana Valley—between modern Uzbekistan and Tajikistan—to obtain its famous "blood-sweating horses." The emperor did succeed in getting some horses, but at the cost of losing more than three-quarters of his army. The rulers of the small states of central Eurasia would not give up their valuable mounts without a fight.

Other Han emperors tried diplomacy instead of war. The greatest enemy of the Han dynasty, from the third century B.C.E. to the third century C.E., was the confederacy of nomadic warriors called the Xiongnu. Direct attacks on the Xiongnu failed, but the Han ruler had heard of another nomadic group called the Yuezhi, who were sworn enemies of the Xiongnu. He asked for volunteers to contact the Yuezhi to win them over to an alliance with the Han against the Xiongnu. Zhang Qian, an officer of the imperial household, volunteered for this perilous

mission. He had to cross Xiongnu territory to get to the Yuezhi, and the suspicious khan of the Xiongnu detained him for ten years before Zhang Qian could escape. He arrived at Dayuan, or Ferghana, a wealthy and fertile kingdom. Promised rewards from China, the Dayuan ruler sent Zhang Qian on to the Yuezhi through Sogdiana to Bactria (in modern Afghanistan). Now peacefully settled in Bactria, the Yuezhi had no interest in fighting the Xiongnu, but they allowed Zhang Qian to return home. He made a detailed report for the emperor about his travels, describing the riches of the agriculture of Ferghana, Sogdiana, and Bactria, and the different types of nomads of the steppe, which he had directly witnessed. He also passed on what he had heard about Parthia, Babylon, Syria, and India.

Zhang Qian discovered that products of Sichuan in western China had made it to Bactria by means of an Indian trade route. Zhang Qian's information greatly stimulated Chinese attempts to expand their military and commercial power in central Eurasia. When China sent more envoys to Bactria, regular trade along the silk routes opened for the first time. The silk route continued to be the main trading link between China and western Eurasia for nearly fifteen hundred years.

Religious conversion also inspired many Chinese people to travel the long road to India. Buddhism, originating along the Ganges River in northern India in the fifth century B.C.E., gradually spread northward into central Eurasia along the trade routes. Buddhist missionaries had arrived in the capital of China's Han dynasty by the second century C.E. Translating Sanskrit and Pali texts of Buddhist metaphysics into Chinese proved to be a fascinating and difficult task. The fall of the Han dynasty in the third century C.E. disrupted travel and trade greatly, but as monks arrived in China from India and central Eurasia, several Chinese monks determined to go to India to obtain personal instruction and more supplies of scriptures. The great missionary translator Kumarajiva had come to China from Parthia in the fifth century C.E., and he collected many disciples to help him produce a huge number of translations of Buddhist texts into Chinese. Fa Xian (c. 334–420), at the advanced age of sixty-five, followed the silk routes westward and southward into Afghanistan, Pakistan, and India in order to visit Buddhist centers along the Ganges. He returned by sea, stopping at Sri Lanka and Indonesia. At the age of seventy-eight, he finally returned home and wrote a detailed account of the religions, politics, economics, and customs of the lands he had seen.

Once the Tang dynasty reunited China in the seventh century, the silk routes opened up again to larger numbers of explorers. Xuanzang (c. 600–664), the most famous of these explorers, also headed for India to collect sacred texts, but he also had the advantage of a research grant from the Tang emperor, who had a special interest in Buddhism. Xuanzang returned with large numbers of texts, and he spent the rest of his life translating and commenting on them. For nearly his entire eighteen-year journey, until he crossed into India, he was still within the borders of the Tang empire.

The decline of the Tang empire in the mid-eighth century and the continued division of China during the Song, Liao, and Jin periods until the thirteenth century made it more difficult for the Chinese to explore the western regions. Travel and exploration became more domestic, but it appealed both to officials on leave from their administrative duties and to scholars who sought inspiration in distant lands. Still, the travelers found exotic landscapes within the borders of classical China, and wrote many poems about lofty mountains, misty landscapes, and exotic peoples on the southern borders.

In the thirteenth century, the Mongols briefly incorporated the core of China into a huge empire that spanned nearly the entire Eurasian continent, once again opening up the caravan routes to long-distance travel. Chingis Khan (Genghis Khan), always curious about the religions of other peoples, heard that the Daoist hermit Chang Chun knew special techniques for prolonging life, and invited him to his court in 1219 C.E. Chang Chun received a warm reception from the Khan, and stayed with him for a number of years. The Christian Rabban Sauma left Beijing in the mid-thirteenth century with an official seal of passage from the Khan that allowed him to travel all over western Europe, where a number of powerful people, both religious and political, were looking for Mongol allies against the threat of Islam.

The fall of the Mongol empire and the creation of the Ming empire in the fourteenth century once again restricted the opportunities for central Eurasian travel, but China's most famous travel writer, Xu Hongzu (or Xu Xiake; 1586–1641), spent thirty-three years of his life visiting nearly all the core provinces of China, braving dangers of storms, bandits, tigers, and illness. Unlike so many of his predecessors, he had no assigned political or religious purposes for his journey; he traveled simply to expand his mind. He took both a poetic and a scientific approach, using lyrical phrases as well as empirical description to capture his views of mountain crags or torrents.

Many of his friends read with great pleasure the excerpts from his travel diary that he passed around. Xu Xiake brings together most closely the components we associate with modern travel writing: practical information about food, lodging, and expenses, the enjoyment of scenic beauty, and the revelation of a person's feelings as expressed by his reactions to the changing scenes around him.

The Qing dynasty once again expanded the horizons of Chinese explorers, allowing them to penetrate far into the heart of central Eurasia along with the military men, merchants, and religious pilgrims. The Qing introduced another motivation for long-distance travel: the hardships of exile. Many officials convicted of crimes in office were sent to remote Xinjiang for a number of years to redeem themselves. At least a few of them actually enjoyed their experience and left moving accounts of the region. Ji Yun, a learned scholar who spent the years 1769 and 1770 in exile in Ürümchi, described with enthusiasm the bustling life of the city and the dramatic mountain winds and storms, and investigated ancient ruins in the deserts around. The Manchu Tulisen, in contrast, went as an imperially commissioned explorer to spy out the conditions in central Eurasia and Russia.

After the mid-nineteenth century, Chinese exploration became more like that in the modern Western world. Now the primary motivation of adventurous Chinese was to learn as much as possible about the powerful imperialists who had defeated China in war and demanded trade concessions. Diplomats visited Japan and Hong Kong, and by the end of the century students had gone to Japan, the United States, and Europe in large numbers. Curiosity about the interior of Eurasia declined in favor of curiosity about the lands across the Pacific. China no longer conducted its search for knowledge in isolation, but joined a global trend of travel and communication in search of wealth, power, and cultural innovation.

Maritime Exploration. Although their centers of civilization originated in the North China plain, the Chinese were still curious about what lay beyond the sea to the east. The myth of the "blessed isles" described a land of paradise off the coast. It inspired the Qin emperor, in the third century B.C.E., to gather a group of boys and girls and force them to set sail eastward in search of this blessed land. They never returned. The mythical guidebook *Guideways through Mountains and Seas*, c. 320 B.C.E.–200 C.E., describes many fantastical peoples beyond the sea and in distant mountains. Reliable accounts by travelers across the seas come from a much later period.

The Chinese also knew that the lands to their south abounded in valuable products like pearls, peacocks, elephant tusks, incense, and spices. In the third century B.C.E., the first emperor of the Qin dynasty sent an army into Vietnam to get these luxuries, and the succeeding Han dynasty ruled Vietnam in order to secure the supply of them. As long as China controlled Vietnam—that is, until the end of the Tang dynasty (907 C.E.)—Vietnam's coast provided an important bridge to Southeast Asia. Since the monsoon winds made navigation to Southeast Asia convenient, many Chinese probably set out to sea from the south coast. We do not have definite documentary evidence until the ninth century C.E., however, that historians knew about the kingdoms of Cambodia and others.

The Mongols knew of the great Angkor empire in Cambodia, and sent out ships to conquer it in 1295, but the ships never returned. The Mongols also sent the envoy Zhou Takuan in 1297 to stay there for a year, and he provided one of the most detailed accounts of Southeast Asia available from this period. He saw the great walls of Angkor and the royal city with its tower of gold. He noted differences among the Brahmins, Buddhist monks, and Hindu Shivaites. Zhou had his prejudices: to him, most Cambodians were like primitive tribes of China's southern frontier, and they all looked alike. He did admire the beautiful Cambodian women, though he considered them oversexed. He found the Cambodians interested in Chinese silver and gold articles, as well as China's classic exports of silk and porcelain. Zhou's impressions of Cambodia set the pattern for many Chinese and Western accounts of the tropics: impressions of great heat, abundant water, lazy natives, great natural wealth, and suspiciously sensuous landscapes for stern visitors from the north.

The Ming dynasty is most famous for the extensive voyages of Admiral Zheng He into the southern seas in the early fifteenth century. In this expansive venture, the Ming followed Mongol efforts to broadcast their political influence outward and to gather information from the lands to their south. Soon, however, defense against raids from the northwest took precedence over maritime exploration. But even after the Ming emperors banned overseas trade, many Chinese left the southern coast to trade and settle. The people of Fujian were particularly ambitious, and they created a widespread diaspora that linked all the major trading ports of Southeast Asia with China's southern coast.

The conquests of the Qing dynasty brought a new island into the empire: Formosa, or Taiwan. Qing officials and literati travelers were fascinated with this tropical island: some saw it as the true "blessed isles" of antiquity, while others were shocked at the heterodox sexual and family customs of its native peoples. Gradually, Han settlement on Taiwan's western coast and exploration of its mountainous interior transformed Taiwan's image from that of a remote, barren, exotic frontier to an integral part of the Qing empire. Because of the travelers of the Qing, the People's Republic of China now claims sovereignty over Taiwan, rejecting the aspirations for independence of a large fraction of its population.

Thus, many periods of Chinese history have seen military expansion, the extension of trading networks, and active exploration of new frontiers, both by land and by sea. Chinese writers have contributed to the travel literature of the world, and they have expanded the imaginative scope and the economic and political impact of the civilization that formed them.

[*See also* Africa, *subentry on* Early Exploration in East Africa; Chinese Exile Writers; Xuanzang; Zhang Qian; *and* Zheng He.]

BIBLIOGRAPHY

Mirsky, Jeanette, ed. *The Great Chinese Travelers*. Chicago: University of Chicago Press, 1974. Excerpts from accounts of Zhang Qian, Xuanzang, Chang Chun, Rabban Sauma, Zhou Takuan, and Zheng He.

Sima. *Records of the Grand Historian of China*. Translated by Burton Watson. 2 vols. New York: Columbia University Press, 1961. Contains Zhang Qian's account of his travels.

Strassberg, Richard. *Inscribed Landscapes: Travel Writing from Imperial China*. Berkeley: University of California Press, 1994.

Teng, Emma J. *Taiwan's Imagined Geography: Chinese Colonial Travel Writing and Pictures, 1683–1895*. Cambridge, Mass.: Harvard University Press, 2004.

PETER C. PERDUE

Chirikov, Alexey (1703–1748), Russian explorer who was second in command of the Kamchatka expeditions. Chirikov, a Muscovite by birth, graduated from the Saint Petersburg Naval Academy in 1721, and after serving briefly with the Baltic fleet he returned to the Naval Academy as a teacher. From 1725 to 1730 he was second in command of the *Sv. Arkhangel Gavriil* (*Saint Gabriel*) during Vitus Bering's first Kamchatka expedition and played an important part in the attempt to understand the geography of Russia's far northeastern border. In 1741 the second Kamchatka expedition set out to map the Arctic coasts, find and map routes to America and Japan, and study the newly discovered lands; this time the *Sv. Petr* (*Saint Peter*) was commanded by Bering and the *Sv. Pavel* (*Saint Paul*) by Chirikov. The two vessels became separated by fog, and consequently each continued on alone, both reaching the North American coast.

This major discovery was, however, kept secret by the Russian government. Thus distorted information about the results of the second Kamchatka expedition was brought to Europe by Joseph-Nicolas Delisle, who returned to Paris from Russia in 1747. The French astronomer brought back to France a huge collection of Russian manuscript maps and geographical descriptions (housed in the French archives), but he was only superficially acquainted with the original materials of the second Kamchatka expedition. In April 1750 Delisle read a paper at the Royal Academy of Sciences in Paris, where he gave a brief and imprecise overview of the history of Russian expeditions to the coast of America, and focused his main attention on the imaginary discoveries of an Admiral Bartholomé de Fonte. Joined by his brother-in-law Neuville, Delisle published in 1752 the *Carte générale des decouvertes de l'Admiral de Fonte et autres*, which summarized his ideas about this "entirely novel" geography.

Chirikov returned to Saint Petersburg in 1746, and in the following year he began compiling for the Admiralty College a number of papers concerning the importance of continuing Russia's expeditions into the Bering Island region, where the Kamchatka expeditions had revealed such striking opportunities. He could not himself take part in any further ventures, for his health had been damaged during the expeditions, and he died in 1748 at age forty-five.

[*See also* Arctic, *subentry on* Russian Arctic; Bering, Vitus; Expeditions, World Exploration, *subentry on* Russia, *and* Siberia.]

BIBLIOGRAPHY
Divin, Vasilii A. *The Great Russian Navigator, A. I. Chirikov*. Translated and annotated by Raymond H. Fisher. Fairbanks: University of Alaska Press, 1993.

ALEXEY POSTNIKOV

Christie, Ella (1861–1949), Scottish woman who traveled alone in Turkestan prior to World War I. Isabella (Ella) Robertson Christie was born on April 21, 1861, in Lanarkshire, Scotland. Her parents, John and Alison Christie, were quite wealthy, thanks to John's acumen in the mining industry. Ella grew up in the family home, Cowden Castle in Perthshire, and lived there the rest of her life when she was not traveling. Travel was an integral part of the Christie family's life, and even when Ella's mother was forced by health problems to forego travel, Ella continued to travel with her father. Her mother died in 1894, when Ella was thirty-four years old, and her father died eight years later. With both of her parents dead and her younger sister married and raising a family, Ella was free to expand the horizons of her travel. And travel she did for much of the second half of her life.

Christie's journeys took her to India, the United States, China, Japan, and every European country except Ireland. But she is best known for her travels to Turkestan as described in her fascinating book, *Through Khiva to Golden Samarkand* (1925). She made two trips to this region, the first one in 1910, by way of Istanbul and the Black Sea to Samarkand and via the old Silk Road into China. Her second trip, in 1912, took her from Saint Petersburg, beyond the Aral Sea, as far as Khiva. At the time of her travels, Turkestan was still very remote and difficult to reach, and her detailed accounts of the people and places she encountered added much to the world's knowledge of central Asia. She was recognized for her achievements by being among the first group of women named as Fellows of the Royal Geographical Society and was also elected a Fellow of Scotland's Society of Antiquaries. Christie died of leukemia in 1949 in Edinburgh.

[*See also* Women Explorers.]

BIBLIOGRAPHY
Christie, Ella R. *Through Khiva to Golden Samarkand: The Remarkable Story of a Woman's Adventurous Journey Alone through the Deserts of Central Asia to the Heart of Turkestan*. London: Seeley and Service, 1925.

PATRICIA GILMARTIN

Chronometer. *See* **Navigational Techniques.**

Cíbola. The place-name "Cíbola" (or "Cíbula") was used by Spanish explorers in the first half of the sixteenth century. It refers to a group of seven wealthy cities that were supposedly built and occupied by Native Americans. Like other legendary geographic features in the Americas, Cíbola is based on some truth, considerable speculation, and almost limitless gullibility. These seven communities existed, but did not meet the Spaniards' expectations.

In the late 1530s, Cíbola served as a catalyst for exploration at just the time that Spain was expanding northward into North America. The search for Cíbola began somewhat accidentally, but would not have occurred without the Spaniards' preconceived expectations of finding riches in the New World—expectations that were given some credibility by their encounter with the Aztec (1519) and Inca (1528). Many authorities suggest that the search for these seven cities resulted from Álvar Núñez Cabeza de Vaca's trek from thc Gulf coast to central Mexico (1529–1536). While in the vicinity of the Rio Grande in the mid-1530s, members of Cabeza de Vaca's group reportedly saw—well in the distance—cities that were golden in appearance. The color may have been illusory, perhaps caused by low-angle sunlight hitting the adobe or stone buildings of pueblos. Being more interested in returning to Mexico, Cabeza de Vaca did not actually visit the cities, which evidently seemed real enough to him and his bedraggled companions.

Upon returning to Mexico, Cabeza de Vaca's group related the sighting of the cities to participants in Francisco Vázquez de Coronado's expedition. One member, Fray Marcos de Niza, was especially energized by the prospect of finding what are identified in the expedition's charter as "Cíbola" or the "Seven Cities." On July 7, 1540, an advance party of Coronado's *entrada* sighted the first city of Cíbola, very likely a Zuni pueblo in present-day New Mexico. The actual location of Cíbola is vague in Coronado's diary. A 1541 map of the coast of Mar del Sur by Domingo del Castillo simply shows "La Ciudad de Cibora [sic]" as a European-style castellated town, complete with a flag, vaguely placed at the north edge of the map. That illustration, like the claim of Cíbola's wealth, was a product of fertile imagination.

Upon reaching Cíbola in 1541, Coronado searched extensively for the seven wealthy cities. His disappointment is conveyed in a letter to the king dated October 20, 1541, in which Coronado notes that "I reached the province of Cíbola (to which the Viceroy of Nueva España sent me in Your Majesty's name) and saw that there were none of the things Fray Marcos told about." Instead, Coronado found a clustering of villages that he described in some detail: "The seven ciudades are seven small towns, all consisting of the [rectangular stone] houses I describe[d earlier]." These towns, Coronado noted, "are all located within close proximity, within four leagues of each other." Of the seven, "each one has its own name, and no single one is called Cíbola."

Although members of Coronado's expedition found little wealth, they recognized Cíbola's architectural workmanship and the richness of its culture. In documenting the Coronado expedition, Castañeda de Nájera confirmed that "Cíbola comprises seven pueblos. The largest is called Mazaque." De Nájera was impressed with the size of Cíbola's buildings. He stated that "usually the buildings are three- and four-storied. At Mazaque there are buildings of four and seven stories. These people," de Nájera concluded, "are very intelligent."

Coronado's insistence that the natives of Cíbola reveal the location of the wealthy cities he sought led to the creation of yet another myth—that of Quivira. As with most such myths, the search for Cíbola resulted in increased geographical information but little actual wealth for Spain. Similarly, subsequent archaeological excavations for Cíbola, beginning at Hawiku (1917), helped lead to a better understanding both of early Native American cultural history and of the Spaniards' motives and methods in exploration.

[*See also* El Dorado; Expeditions, World Exploration, *subentry on* Spain; Fictitious and Fantastic Places; North America, *subentry on* Apocryphal Discoveries and Imaginary Places (post-1500); Quivira; *and biographical entries on figures mentioned in this article.*]

BIBLIOGRAPHY

Flint, Richard, and Shirley Cushing Flint. *Documents of the Coronado Expedition, 1539–1542.* Dallas, Tex.: Southern Methodist University Press, 2005.

RICHARD FRANCAVIGLIA

Cipangu. Also spelled Chipangu and Zipangu, Cipangu was the name for Japan used by Europeans and others from the time of Marco Polo in the thirteenth century until the early sixteenth century. "Cipangu" derives from the Chinese name "Jin-pön-kuo" for Japan, meaning "land of the rising sun." Marco Polo mentioned Cipangu in his *Travels*, although he never visited there. He described Cipangu (Yule-Cordier edition, Book 3, chap. 2) as a wealthy island,—"the quantity of gold they have is endless"—some 1,500 miles (2,414 kilometers) to the east. The palace of the ruler of Cipangu was not only roofed with gold, but paved with gold. Its inhabitants were "white, civilized, and well favored" as well as being great idolaters. Polo is the only European writer to write of Japan before the sixteenth century. Al-Idrisi (1099–1180) mentioned Japan as an island full of gold in his geography but called it Sila, while Rashid-ud Din (1247–1318) mentioned Cipangu somewhat disparagingly in his *Universal History*. Martin Behaim placed Cipangu on his globe of 1492 with notes

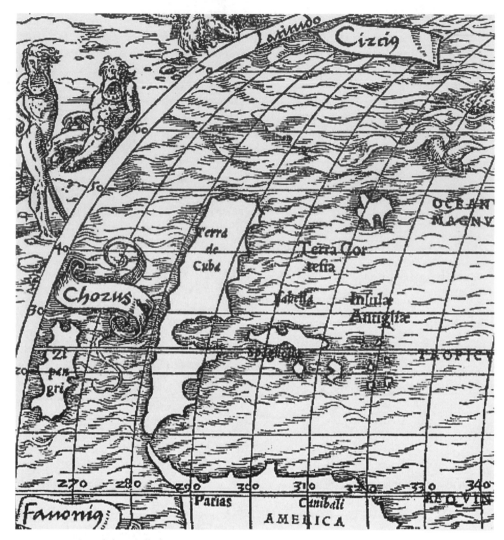

Cipangu. Detail from the world map in the Basel (1532) edition of Simon Grynaeus and Johann Huttich, *Novus orbis regionum*. Here we see a version of Central America that was already well outdated by 1532, after the conquest of Mexico by Cortés. Just beyond the coast of America to the west may be seen the island of "Zipangu"; it was some time before Europeans appreciated the immensity of the Pacific Ocean. COURTESY THE NEWBERRY LIBRARY, CHICAGO

that added spices to its considerable wealth. Cipangu inspired Paolo dal Pozzo Toscanelli, Christopher Columbus, and others to contemplate it as both a way station and a destination on western voyages in the quest for Asia. During his first voyage of 1492–1493, Columbus initially identified Cuba as Cipangu; but when he decided that Cuba was part of the Asian mainland, he decided that Hispaniola must be Cipangu, particularly because of its native name of *Cibao*. When no golden-roofed palaces appeared, that identification was also abandoned. It was not until 1542 or 1543 that some shipwrecked Portuguese

sailors became the first Europeans to visit Japan, the fabled Cipangu of Marco Polo.

[*See also* Columbus, Christopher, *and* Polo, Marco.]

BIBLIOGRAPHY

Flint, Valerie I. J. *The Imaginative Landscape of Christopher Columbus*. Princeton, N.J.: Princeton University Press, 1992.

RONALD H. FRITZE

Clapperton, Hugh (1788–1827), Scottish explorer who journeyed across the Sahara and at-

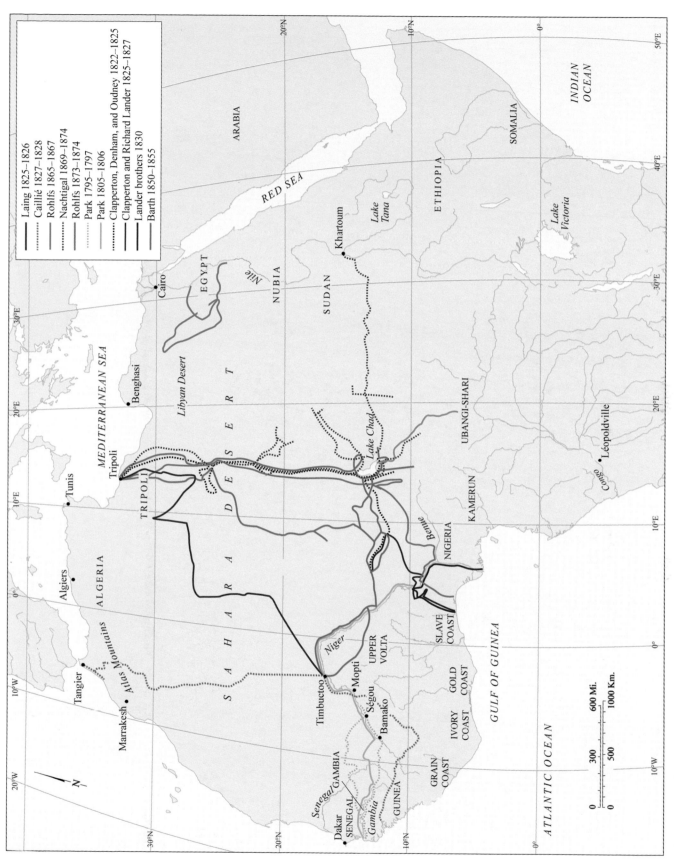

Plate 1. Northern Africa. This map shows routes of exploration in northern Africa in the nineteenth century. [See the articles on Africa; Lake Chad; East African Lakes; the Niger River; the Nile River; the Sahara; Timbuctoo; and biographical entries on individual explorers.] MAP BY BILL NELSON

Laing 1825–1826
Caillié 1827–1828
Rohlfs 1865–1867
Nachtigal 1869–1874
Rohlfs 1873–1874
Park 1795–1797
Park 1805–1806
Clapperton, Denham, and Oudney 1822–1825
Clapperton and Richard Lander 1825–1827
Lander brothers 1830
Barth 1850–1855

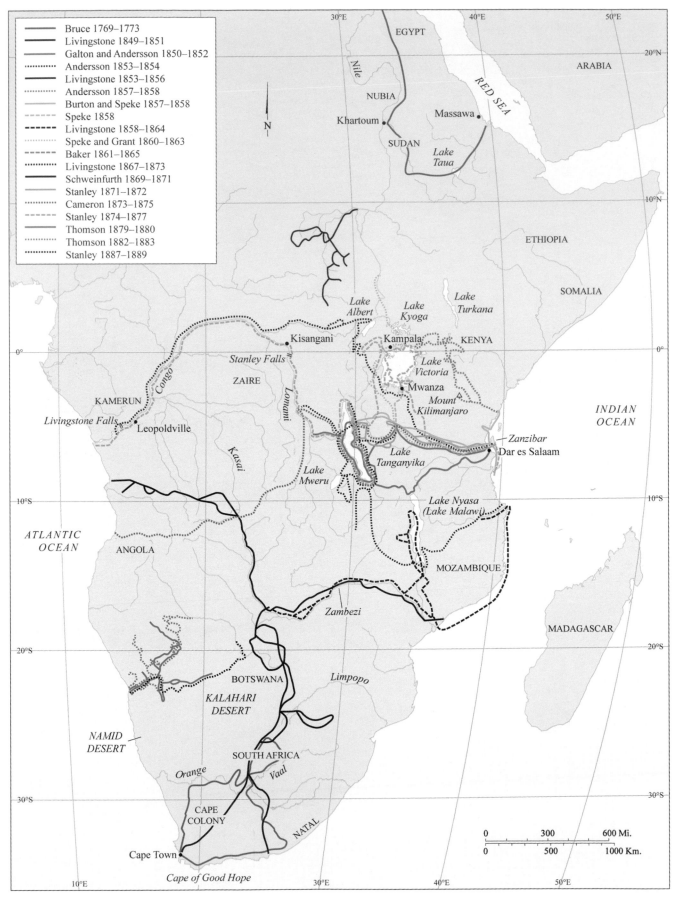

——	Bruce 1769–1773
——	Livingstone 1849–1851
——	Galton and Andersson 1850–1852
⋯⋯	Andersson 1853–1854
——	Livingstone 1853–1856
⋯⋯	Andersson 1857–1858
——	Burton and Speke 1857–1858
– – –	Speke 1858
– – –	Livingstone 1858–1864
⋯⋯	Speke and Grant 1860–1863
– – –	Baker 1861–1865
⋯⋯	Livingstone 1867–1873
——	Schweinfurth 1869–1871
——	Stanley 1871–1872
⋯⋯	Cameron 1873–1875
– – –	Stanley 1874–1877
——	Thomson 1879–1880
⋯⋯	Thomson 1882–1883
⋯⋯	Stanley 1887–1889

Plate 2. Southern Africa. This map shows routes of exploration in southern Africa in the eighteenth and nineteenth centuries. [See the articles on Africa; Cape of Good Hope; the Nile River; and biographical entries on individual explorers.] MAP BY BILL NELSON

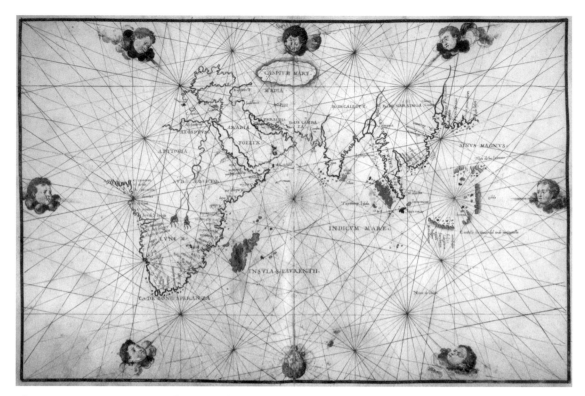

Plate 3. Battista Agnese. This map from Agnese's atlas of 1565 is a characteristic example of his elegant work, carrying the imagination of his readers out to the edges of the known world. Europeans still knew little of the coast of China and nothing of Australia. [See the articles on Battista Agnese; Australia; and Maps, Mapmakers, and Mapmaking.] COURTESY THE NEWBERRY LIBRARY CHICAGO

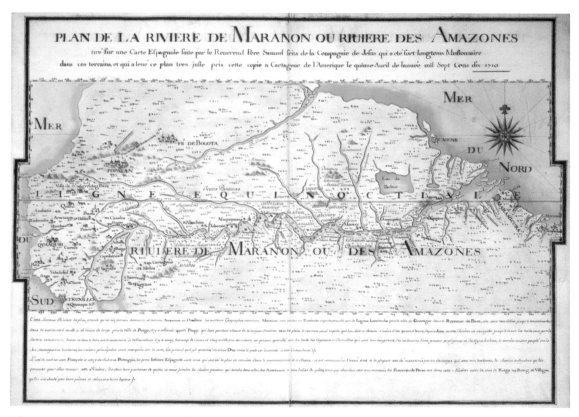

Plate 4. Amazon River. Samuel Fritz, Map of the Amazon River, c. 1690. This is a manuscript copy of the printed map eventually produced in 1707, following long explorations by the Jesuit Fritz from 1686 onward. The manuscript was among a French collection made in the 1720s; there would be nothing better for many years. [See the articles on Samuel Fritz and the Jesuits.] COURTESY THE NEWBERRY LIBRARY CHICAGO

Plate 5. American West. *The Yellowstone National Park*, a painting by Ferdinand Vandeveer Hayden (Boston: L. Pranz, 1876) is one of the very dramatic images generated at the time when the North American public was becoming acquainted with the Yellowstone region. It is far removed from the low-key style of the earlier Hudson River school. [See the article on Visual Images of the American West.] COURTESY THE NEWBERRY LIBRARY CHICAGO

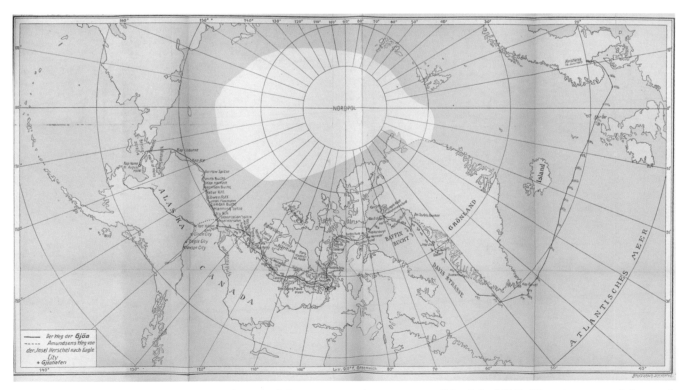

Plate 6. Roald Amundsen. "Der Weg der *Gjöa*" from *Die Nordwest-Passage* (Munich, 1908). Here is a map of the track of the *Gjöa*, from the Atlantic to the Pacific Oceans. This voyage took three years, making skillful use both of wintering-places and of Roald Amundsen's small but essential petrol (gasoline) engine. [See the article on Roald Amundsen.] COURTESY THE NEWBERRY LIBRARY CHICAGO

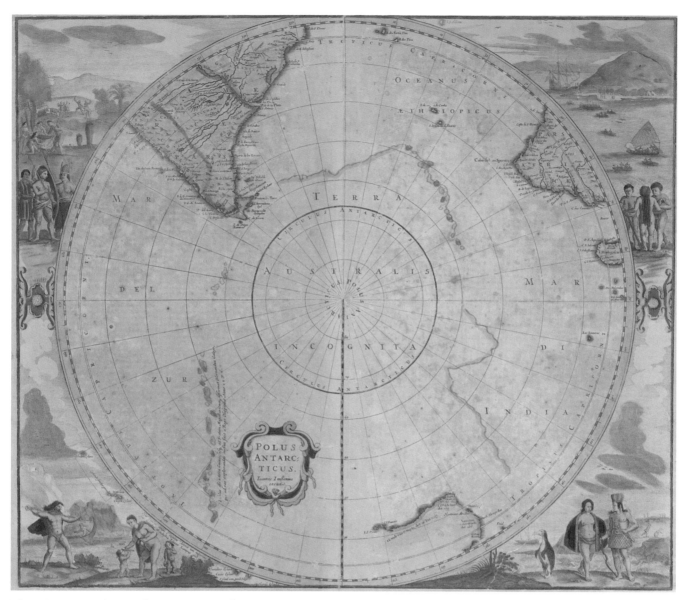

Plate 7. Antarctica. *Polus Antarcticus* by Jan Jansson (Amsterdam, c. 1650) dates from the time when Abel Janszoon Tasman had revealed the southern coast of Australia (bottom right), but before Europeans had any idea of the nature of *Terra Australis Incognita*. The images of the indigenous peoples are full of ingenuity. Note particularly the penguin at the bottom right. [See the articles on Antarctica; Abel Janszoon Tasman; and *Terra Australis Incognita*.] COURTESY THE NEWBERRY LIBRARY CHICAGO

Plate 8. Archaeology and "Discoveries" Sites. This aerial photograph shows an early stage in the excavation of La Salle's *Belle* in Matagorda Bay, Texas. The seventeenth-century wreck lies in the small dammed area, while a larger coffer dam is in process of construction around it. The area between them will be filled with sand and the central area pumped fairly dry to enable the wreck to be excavated using land techniques. [See the articles on Archaeology and "Discoveries" Sites and Cavelier de La Salle.] TEXAS DEPARTMENT OF ARCHAEOLOGY

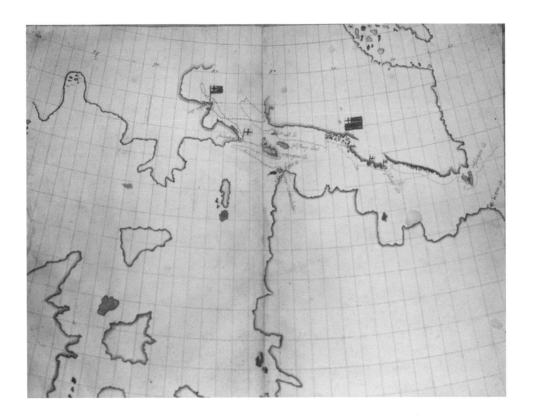

Plate 9. William Baffin. Manuscript map of Baffin's route through Hudson Strait in 1615. This remarkable document testifies to the skill with which Baffin made his observations and then plotted them onto a "reasonably accurate" chart. [See the articles on the Arctic; William Baffin; and the Northwest Passage.] THE BRITISH LIBRARY

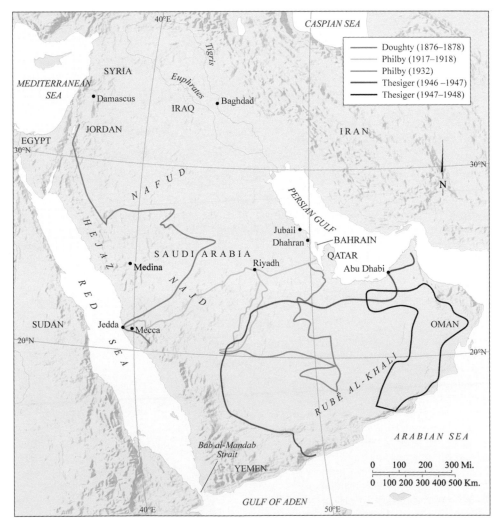

Plate 10. Arabia. This map shows the routes of three of the major explorers of the Arabian peninsula in the nineteenth and twentieth centuries. [See the article on Arabia and biographical entries on individual explorers.] MAP BY BILL NELSON

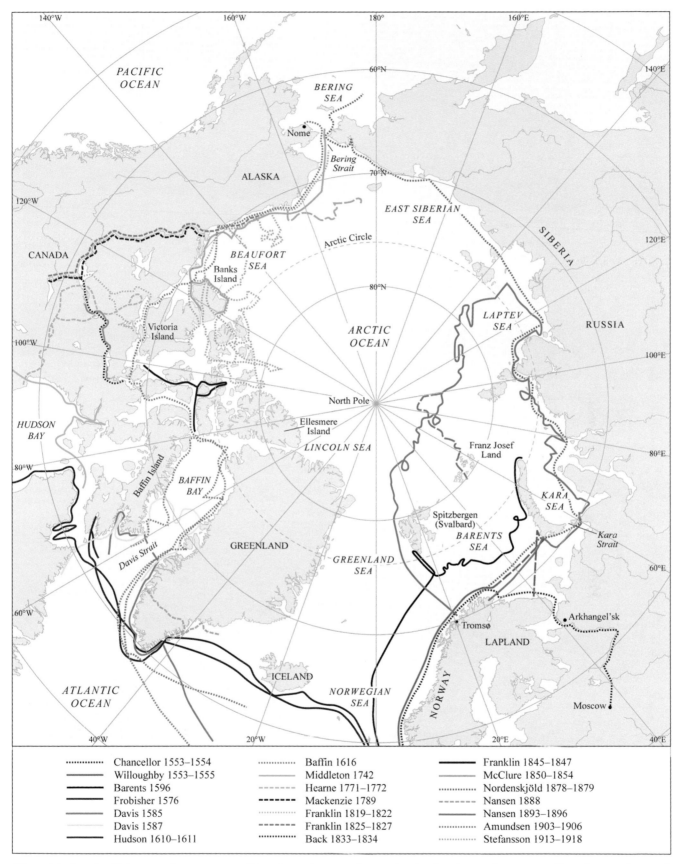

········· Chancellor 1553–1554	········· Baffin 1616	——— Franklin 1845–1847
——— Willoughby 1553–1555	——— Middleton 1742	——— McClure 1850–1854
——— Barents 1596	- - - Hearne 1771–1772	········· Nordenskjöld 1878–1879
——— Frobisher 1576	- - - Mackenzie 1789	- - - Nansen 1888
——— Davis 1585	········· Franklin 1819–1822	——— Nansen 1893–1896
——— Davis 1587	- - - Franklin 1825–1827	········· Amundsen 1903–1906
——— Hudson 1610–1611	········· Back 1833–1834	········· Stefansson 1913–1918

Plate 11. Arctic. This map shows routes of Arctic exploration beginning in the sixteenth century. [See the articles on the Arctic and biographical entries on individual explorers.] MAP BY BILL NELSON

Plate 12. The Arctic. William Henry Browne, *The Bivouac*. This tinted lithograph from *Ten Coloured Views* (London: Ackermann, 1850) testifies to the extraordinary effect that this relatively new technique could have, in delineating— and no doubt exaggerating—remote and awe-inspiring landscapes. [See the articles on the Arctic.] COURTESY THE NEWBERRY LIBRARY CHICAGO

Plate 13. Thomas Baines. *Dispersal of Hostile Tribes near Baines River*. This is a good example of Thomas Baines's spirited work from his journey to northern Australia in the mid-1850s. He was then in the service of the Royal Geographical Society, which conserves much of his work in their London library. [See the articles on Australia and Thomas Baines.] ROYAL GEOGRAPHICAL SOCIETY

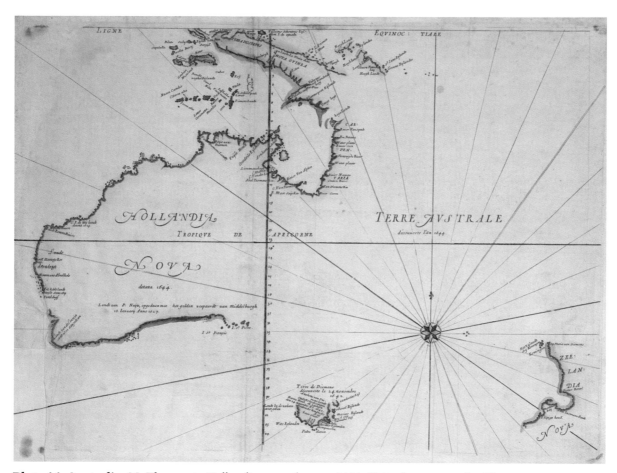

Plate 14. Australia. M. Thevenot, *Hollandia nova detecta*, 1664. This elegant map by Thevenot summarizes Dutch knowledge of Australia ("Hollandia Nova") and New Zealand ("Zeelandia") in the middle of the seventeenth century. [See the articles on Australia; New Holland; and Maps, Mapmaking, and Mapmakers.] NATIONAL LIBRARY OF AUSTRALIA

Plate 15. Australia. S. T. Gill, *Country NW of Tableland*, c. 1846. Perched on the tableland, the two men seem to be consulting a map in the hope of making some sense of the vast geographical feature spread out before them. [See the article on Australia.] NATIONAL LIBRARY OF AUSTRALIA

Plate 16. Joseph Banks. Sydney Parkinson, drawing of Xylomelum, c. 1770. Parkinson (1745–1771) sailed with James Cook and Joseph Banks on their Pacific voyage of 1768–1771 on the *Endeavour*. Banks had already employed him, and his confidence in Parkinson was amply justified by the artist's immense production of images, many of which were eventually engraved and published. Sadly, Parkinson died on the return voyage, perhaps worn out by his unremitting labors. [See the article on Joseph Banks.] NATURAL HISTORY MUSEUM, LONDON

Plate 17. Saint Brendan. In this thirteenth-century manuscript drawing, Saint Brendan's ship has landed on top of a huge fish. One sailor prepares to dive into the sea, others struggle to right the mast, and another operates a bellows to encourage a fire kindled on the back of the fish. [See the article on Saint Brendan.] THE BRITISH LIBRARY/HIP/ART RESOURCE, NY

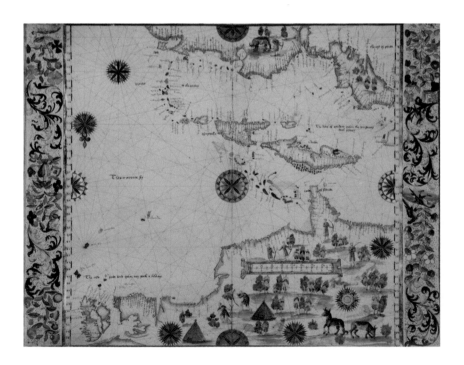

Plate 18. Caribbean Region. Chart of the Caribbean by John Rotz, from his atlas of 1541. This map is south-oriented, like most work of the Dieppe School. Rotz made the atlas for presentation to Henry VIII when he wanted to enter his service; this chart is full of imagery and also has some English legends, inserted for the benefit of the king. [See the articles on the Caribbean Region; the Dieppe School; and Maps, Mapmaking, and Mapmakers.] THE BRITISH LIBRARY

Plate 19. Richard Byrd. Francis Miller, "The Floyd Bennett Wings Its Flight over Antarctica," from *The Fight to Conquer the Ends of the Earth* (Chicago/Toronto: Winston, 1930). This image, with its grandiloquent title, coming from a book with an equally "heroic" title, takes us back to the time when exploration could still be seen as a "conquest." [See the articles on Antarctica and Richard Byrd.] Courtesy The Newberry Library Chicago

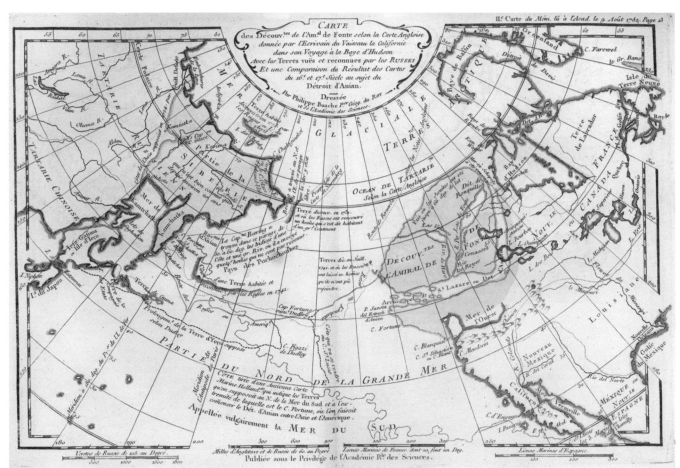

Plate 20. Philippe Buache. "Carte des découvertes de l'Amiral de Fonte" from Buache's *Considérations géographiques et physiques sur les nouvelles découvertes* (Paris, 1753). This is the Buache map that contains the imaginary discoveries of the Spanish admiral de Fonte ("Découvertes de l'Amiral de Fonte"), roughly on the present-day site of Alaska. [See the articles on Philippe Buache and Maps, Mapmaking, and Mapmakers.] Courtesy The Newberry Library Chicago

Plate 21. Mark Catesby. Watercolor of buffalo, c. 1724. It has sometimes been observed that Catesby's flora did not go very well with his fauna, and that is the case here. It is also true that his buffalo is rather ill shaped, but the mere fact of delineating the creature made Catesby a notable pioneer. [See the article on Mark Catesby.] THE ACADEMY OF NATURAL SCIENCES, EWELL SALE STEWART LIBRARY

Plate 22. Jacques Cartier. Pierre Desceliers, detail from chart of North America, c. 1536. This south-oriented image shows a group of people on the south bank of the Saint Lawrence River. On the right, a peasant is plowing; on the left, a lordly figure is handing what looks like a land title to three potential peasants. In the event, these peasants were very likely to become voyageurs rather than tillers of the soil. [See the articles on Jacques Cartier and the Dieppe School.] THE BRITISH LIBRARY/HIP/ART RESOURCE, NY

Plate 23. Apsley Cherry-Garrard. "Cape Evans in Winter," drawing from Cherry-Garrard's *The Worst Journey in the World* (London: Constable, 1922). This is one of Dr. "Bill" Wilson's images from *The Worst Journey in the World*; it captures the awe felt by people like the figure in the foreground, apparently out for a walk with two of the dogs. [See the article on Apsley Cherry-Garrard.] COURTESY THE NEWBERRY LIBRARY CHICAGO

Plate 24. Dieppe School. World map by Nicolas Desliens, c. 1566. This world map, enclosed in its rich frame, is typical of the work of the Dieppe School even if its depiction of North America is rather eccentric; it is, as is usual with this school, oriented southward. [See the article on the Dieppe School.] BIBLIOTHÈQUE NATIONALE DE FRANCE

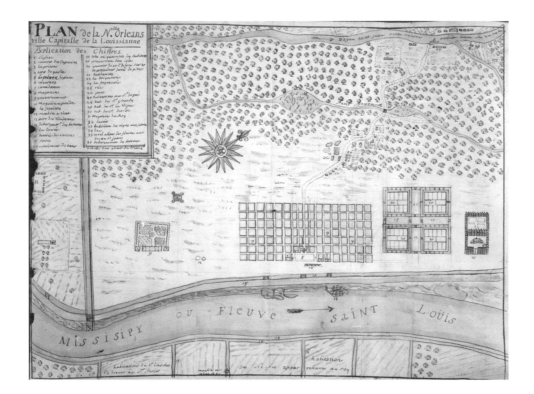

Plate 25. Dumont de Montigny. "Plan de la Nouvelle Orleans," from the Montigny manuscript, c. 1747. This charming watercolor map shows central New Orleans as it was first laid out, using a street plan that essentially survives to the present day. [See the article on Dumont de Montigny.] COURTESY THE NEWBERRY LIBRARY CHICAGO

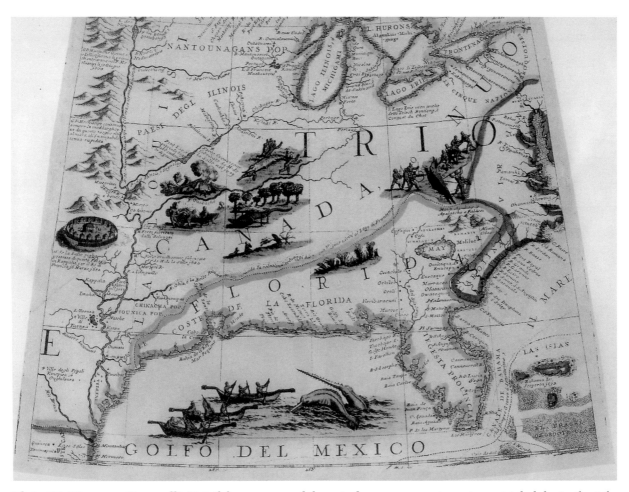

Plate 26. Vincenzo Coronelli. Detail from a gore of the set of gores composing a terrestrial globe in the *Libro dei Globi* (Venice, 1701). In this map compiled in the 1680s, Coronelli shows the Mississippi River as emerging into the Gulf of Mexico hundreds of miles to the west of its actual estuary. It was as a result of this misconception that Robert Cavelier, sieur de la Salle, disastrously led his expedition to Matagorda Bay in 1685. [See the article on Vincenzo Coronelli.] COURTESY THE NEWBERRY LIBRARY CHICAGO

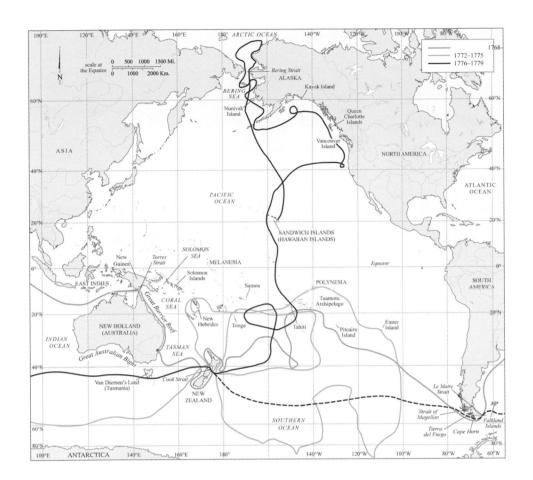

Plate 27. James Cook. This map shows the vast territory covered by Cook in his three voyages between 1768 and 1779. [See the article on James Cook.] MAP BY BILL NELSON

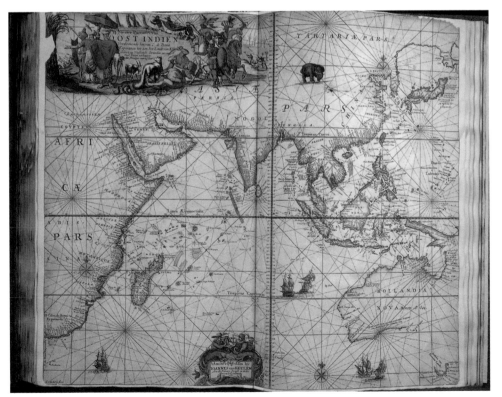

Plate 28. Dutch Expeditions of World Exploration. Johannes Van Keulen, "Nieuwe Pascaert van Oost Indien," from *El Grande Nuevo Aumentado Atlas de la Mar* (Amsterdam, 1681). This charming map from Van Keulen's great atlas typifies Dutch work of the seventeenth century. Stylistically, it retains something of the portolan chart style, with its pattern of windroses; note the emerging Australia ("Hollandia Nova"). [See the article on Expeditions, World Exploration: The Netherlands.] HARRY RANSOM CENTER FOR THE HUMANITIES, AUSTIN, TEXAS

Plate 29. Martin Frobisher. After John White, *Skirmish between Eskimos and Frobisher's Men*, 1577. This image shows Frobisher's men clashing with the Inuit during his second expedition, of 1577. It is thought that this elegant painting derives from the work of the artist John White, who may have been on the expedition. [See the articles on Martin Frobisher and John White.] THE BRITISH LIBRARY

Plate 31. Francis Drake. Image of the marriage-procedure from the *Histoire nouvelle des Indes*, ed. Verlyn Klinkenborg. This manuscript, apparently compiled by an artist accompanying Drake on his piratical voyage through the Caribbean in 1585–1586, offers a remarkable and little-known image of Amerindian life. Here a potential son-in-law demonstrates his skill as a hunter to his family-to-be. [See the article on Francis Drake.] PIERPONT MORGAN LIBRARY

Plate 30. Europe and the Mediterranean: Ancient Near East. The outer coffin of Gua, Egyptian, twelfth dynasty. The interior of this coffin is decorated with maps of the route to the Underworld, which would indeed be the final exploration. [See the articles on Europe and the Mediterranean: Ancient Near East Geography, Worldview, and Mapmaking and the Underworld.] THE BRITISH MUSEUM/HIP/ART RESOURCE, NY

tempted to reach Timbuctoo from the south. Hugh Clapperton is an explorer whose name is less well remembered than he deserves. He made two expeditions to the western Sudan region of Africa in the 1820s, encountering the new Islamic sultanates there, coming close to solving the mystery of the location of the mouth of the Niger, and learning the fate of Mungo Park.

Clapperton was born in Annan in Scotland on an unknown date in May 1788. Apprenticed in the Merchant Navy, he was press-ganged into the Royal Navy and eventually became a midshipman and then lieutenant. His incredibly adventurous naval career from 1806 to 1817 took him to the East Indies, to the capture of Mauritius from the French, and to the North American Great Lakes. Anxious for employment after the Napoleonic Wars, he welcomed the chance to join a fellow Scottish naval officer, Walter Oudney, on an exploratory and diplomatic mission from Tripoli, across the Sahara to Bornu, and then on to Kano and Sokoto. Major Dixon Denham was later added to the party with not altogether happy results, and they all set out in April 1822. Bornu was reached, but Oudney died in January 1824 and, leaving Denham, Clapperton later went on alone to Sokoto, which he reached in March 1824.

Mohammed Bello, the sultan of Sokoto and son of Uthman dan Fodio, who had initiated the great Fulani jihad by which reformed Islamic societies had been created, received his first European visitor kindly and with interest. Although Clapperton found himself unequal to Bello's theological questions, they struck up a good relationship that seemed to augur well for future trade and diplomatic relations with Britain, which the government had been anxious to promote. However, Bello would not allow Clapperton to go on to the Niger, close as it was. Perhaps he feared that Britain would, by means of the Niger, too easily be able to take over—just as they were doing in India, as Bello knew well. Clapperton returned in 1825 to Tripoli with Denham, hardly on speaking terms with him.

It was unfortunate that Clapperton's journals were edited by Sir John Barrow in such a way as to minimize his contribution to the success of the mission. Nevertheless, the colonial secretary asked Clapperton to return to Bornu and Sokoto almost immediately, and this time the approach was made from the south—Clapperton, with a servant named Richard Lander, proceeding from Badagry. On the way to Sokoto, Clapperton saw and described Oyo, the traditional center of Yoruba life and culture. He also discovered how Mungo Park had died at the Falls of Bussa in 1806, solving what had been a mystery. Having crossed the Niger and reentered Sokoto in July 1826, he found conditions changed; Bello was much less welcoming because he suspected Clapperton of favoring el-Kanemi in Bornu, with whom Bello was currently at war. Clapperton himself seems to have been less tactful than usual, possibly through the effects of the dysentery that killed him on April 13, 1827, at Chungary near Sokoto.

Lander managed to return to Britain with most of Clapperton's records, which were published in various not altogether satisfactory editions. Lander was sent back to West Africa in 1830 to demonstrate that the Niger did indeed flow into the Bight of Benin. This was implicit in Clapperton's work. He was in any case by far the greater explorer, intelligent and understanding of other cultures and with an engaging sense of humor.

[*See also* Niger River *and biographical entries on figures mentioned in this article.*]

BIBLIOGRAPHY

Bovill, E. W., ed. *Missions to the Niger*. 4 vols. Cambridge, U.K.: Cambridge University Press for the Hakluyt Society, 1964–1966.

Hallett, Robin. *The Penetration of Africa: European Enterprise and Exploration Principally in Northern and Western Africa up to 1830*. London: Routledge and Kegan Paul; New York: Praeger, 1965.

ROY BRIDGES

Clark, William. *See* **Lewis, Meriwether, and William Clark.**

Colorado River. Perhaps no major river system in the world was naturally more resistant to exploration than the Colorado and its tributaries. From the time of the arrival of Europeans in the Colorado Plateau in the mid-sixteenth century, Euro-American authorities hoped that the river might become a conduit for settlement and exploitation of the heart of what is now the southwestern United States. The complexity and height of the canyons that line the Colorado and its main tributaries for hundreds of miles, however, hindered attempts to develop even a general understanding of the river and its immediate surroundings until the nineteenth century.

Inspired by Álvar Núñez Cabeza de Vaca's fantastic reports of great cities and mineral wealth of the Kingdom of Cíbola, Francisco Vásquez de Coronado's expedition of 1540–1542 produced the first direct European knowledge of the river. Members of a scouting party led by Garcia Lopez de Cardenas briefly viewed the Colorado from the south rim of the Grand Canyon but were unable to descend to its banks. A naval expedition commanded by Hernando Ruiz de Alarcón sent to travel upriver from its mouth in the Gulf of California to a rendezvous with Coronado likewise had to turn back at the Gila River near present-day Yuma, Arizona. The governor of the new Spanish colony of New Mexico, Juan de Oñate, explored the more accessible southernmost portion of the river in 1604–1605, but with the exception of missionary activity among the Hopi and the Zuni, the Spanish were not much interested in the Colorado basin until the eighteenth century.

The perceived British and Russian threat to the Spanish empire in North America hastened Spanish exploration of the river, plateau, and canyonlands during the late eighteenth century to establish effective communication between New Mexico and the Pacific. The most notable of these expeditions, led by the Franciscans Francisco Atanasio Dominguez and Silvestre Velez de Escalante Garcia in 1776–1777, was the first to explore extensively the lands north and west of the Colorado in what is now Utah and western Colorado. Dominguez and Escalante crossed the upper Green River and traveled as far as the Sevier River in central Utah. The Sevier has no outlet to the sea, but the explorers concluded that the Green and the Sevier formed a single westerly flowing stream, the Rio San Buenaventura, which flowed all the way to the Pacific Ocean. This misconception persisted for about seventy years.

Independent Mexico initially welcomed American traders into the region during the 1820s, but it was unable to control their activities in what remained a remote frontier region. Exploiting this opening, American trappers based in Santa Fe and Saint Louis explored the upper valleys of the Green and the Grand (what is now the Colorado north of its junction with the Green) in search of profitable trapping grounds. The trapping expedition led by William H. Ashley in 1824–1825 established that the Green was indeed part of the Colorado River system. Another group of independent trappers explored the Colorado in southern Utah and northern Arizona and became the first recorded whites to descend successfully to the floor of the Grand Canyon.

The Mexican War (1848–1849), Mormon migration to Utah, and the search for the best railroad route to the Pacific Ocean prompted a series of expeditions to the Colorado Plateau in the 1840s and 1850s conducted by the U.S. Corps of Topographical Engineers. Stephen Watts Kearny's military expedi-

tion of 1846–1847 to New Mexico and California secured U.S. control of the passage from Santa Fe across southern Arizona into southern California and prompted the creation of the first reasonably accurate map of the entire Colorado drainage, by the topographical engineer William H. Emory. The Pacific railroad expeditions led by John Gunnison near the 38th parallel and Amiel W. Whipple along the 35th parallel added a great deal of topographical and scientific information, but did not explore the river itself. As tensions increased with the Mormons during the 1850s, however, control of the river and its crossings acquired new strategic importance. The 1857–1858 expedition led by Lieutenant Joseph Ives sought to determine whether the river could be navigated upstream through the canyonlands of Arizona and Utah, partly so that military posts in the area could be more easily sustained. Like Alarcón before him, Ives abandoned the attempt to navigate the river well south of the Grand Canyon and continued overland to the east along the southern rim of the canyon. Despite this setback, the scientific and topographic work of the expedition, which included the geological report by John Newberry, drawings of the canyonlands by Heinrich Baldwin Mollhausen, and the detailed topographic map of the Grand Canyon made by F. W. von Egglofstein, drew scientific and U.S. public attention to the canyonlands.

The climactic event in the exploration of the Colorado River system was undoubtedly John Wesley Powell's perilous river run through the Glen and Grand canyons in 1869. Although the expedition was poorly planned and executed, the feat, as retold by Powell in his published reports and in contemporary press accounts, stoked post–Civil War interest in the Southwest and marked a shift in American interest in the river away from the purely military, geopolitical, and economic motivations of earlier explorations to more scientific and aesthetic ones. The comprehensive but rival topographical surveys of the western United States led by George Wheeler and F. V. Hayden during the 1870s were not exclusively concerned with the Colorado Plateau. Explorations of the later nineteenth century were notable for their geological work, their reconnaissance of ancient ruins at Mesa Verde and elsewhere, and for the sublime images of the Grand Canyon drawn by the topographic artist William Henry Holmes. These helped to transform the image of the canyon (and by extension, the whole of the lower Colorado) from that of a forbidding wasteland and natural barrier (which, of course, it is) to a scenic, cultural, and scientific curiosity. Perhaps the last explorers of the Colorado were the image makers and entrepreneurs who blazed the trails and established facilities that would be exploited by twentieth-century tourists.

[*See also* American West, Visual Images of; Fur Trade; Rocky Mountains; *and biographical entries on figures mentioned this article*.]

BIBLIOGRAPHY
Bartlett, Richard A. "Scientific Exploration of the American West." In *North American Exploration*, edited by John Logan. Vol. 3, *A Continent Comprehended*. Lincoln and London: University of Nebraska Press, 1997. Pp. 461–520.
Goetzmann, William H. *Exploration and Empire*. New York: Knopf, 1966.
Lavender, David. *Colorado River Country*. Albuquerque: University of New Mexico Press, 1982.

JAMES AKERMAN

Columbia River. From its source in the mountains of British Columbia to its estuary on the Pacific Ocean, the Columbia River stretches for some 1,214 miles (1,954 kilometers). Its largest tributary, the Snake River, extends another 1,038 miles (1,670 kilometers). Together they drain a basin of about 259,000 square miles (416,820 square kilometers), including most of Idaho, over half of Oregon and Washington, large sections of British Columbia and Montana, and small parts of Wyoming and Nevada. As the Pleistocene ice age relinquished its grip sometime between thirteen and fifteen thousand years ago, massive floods—generated by the failure of ice dams impounding the waters of the glacial lake Missoula—reshaped the basin's terrain, particularly the scoured-to-bedrock "channeled scab-lands" of eastern Washington and the scenic gorge through which the Columbia breaches the Cascade Range.

Human habitation in the Columbia River basin reaches back at least ten thousand years and may extend to earlier prehistoric times. The indigenous population of the basin in the late eighteenth century, when Europeans began arriving, has been estimated at about 65,000. The Columbia and Snake rivers and their tributary streams supplied the native peoples with a rich and dependable source of food and fiber, while also providing for aboriginal trade and travel.

A Spanish naval officer, Bruno de Hezeta, was the first European known to have sighted and described the river's mouth. In the course of an exploring expedition, his ship, the frigate *Santiago*, came abreast

Columbia River. "Entrance of the Strait of Juan de Fuca" from John Meares's *Voyages Made in the Years 1788 and 1789* (London: Logographic Press, 1790). After sailing past the mouth of the Columbia River, John Meares entered the strait of Juan de Fuca, shown here. His ship's boat is accompanied by a considerable number of the local vessels, which seem frail for such waters. COURTESY THE NEWBERRY LIBRARY, CHICAGO

of the Columbia's mouth on August 17, 1775. He believed it was the mouth of a great river or strait. Many of his crewmen were down with scurvy, so Hezeta did not attempt to enter it. He did, however, sketch a map giving his discovery Spanish names: *Bahía de la Asunción* (Assumption Bay); its northern headland, *Cabo de San Roque*; and its southern point, *Cabo Frandoso* (Cape Luxuriant). The river would later appear on Spanish maps as *Entrada de Hezeta* or *Río de San Roque*.

John Meares, a British fur trader, was the next European mariner known to have encountered the river. On July 6, 1788, he came upon the latitude (46°10′ N) of Hezeta's discovery, only to conclude erroneously that it was neither a river nor a strait. Accordingly, he named it Deception Bay and named its northern headland Cape Disappointment.

Seventeen years after Hezeta's discovery, on May 11, 1792, an American fur trader, Robert Gray, captain of the Boston ship *Columbia*, arrived off the river's mouth. Hoping for increased trade with the local people, Gray ordered his ship across the river's deceptive and dangerous bar and into its estuary. Gray gave the river his ship's name, called its northern headland Cape Hancock, and called the land on its south side Adam's Point. These and other features of the river were recorded by Gray on a chart later given to the Spanish commandant at Nootka Sound, Juan Francisco de la Bodega y Quadra. This chart in turn was passed on to George Vancouver, commander of a British expedition then charting the Northwest Coast of America.

William Broughton, captain of the armed brig *Chatham*, escort of Vancouver's flag ship the *Discovery*, was ordered to follow up on Gray's information that a large river did indeed exist, as suspected by Hezeta and denied by Meares. In early October 1792, Broughton successfully steered the *Chatham* across the Columbia's bar. Considering his brig not well suited to river exploration, he explored upriver using the ship's launch and cutter. Rowing against the river's powerful currents, sometimes assisted by sails, he and his crew reached a point upriver near the western terminus of the Columbia's spectacular gorge. At a location just east of present-day Sandy River, Broughton went ashore and took formal possession of the Columbia and its vicinity in the name of the British crown. He also noted a remarkable snow-clad mountain, which he named for Admiral Sir Samuel Hood. On October 31, 1792, Broughton began descending the river. He prepared a map showing its course 100 miles (161 kilometers) inland from the Pacific.

Although an occasional fur-trading vessel traveled on it, exploration of the river ceased in the thirteen years after Broughton's departure. That changed in October 1805, when Lewis and Clark, traveling overland, reached the confluence of the Columbia and Snake rivers. From there they followed the Columbia downstream to the Pacific, mapping another 200 miles (322 kilometers) of the river's course. But some 700 miles (1,127 kilometers) remained unexplored, including the location of its headwaters.

Canadian David Thompson, geographer, surveyor, and fur trader, was a partner with the Montreal-based North West Company. In 1807 he was sent to extend the company's fur-trading operations west of the Canadian Rockies by establishing trading posts there and mapping the remaining unexplored upper reaches of the Columbia. He found that the river flows from its source (Columbia Lake) northwestward 200 miles (322 kilometers), then turns abruptly southward over 500 circuitous miles (805 kilometers) to where it is joined by the Snake River. Thompson was first to map the upper Columbia River. Finally, in the summer of 1811, he successfully descended the entire length of the river—he was the first to do so—only to find a fur-trading post, Fort Astoria, already installed there by his rival, John Jacob Astor's American-owned Pacific Fur Company.

[*See also* Fur Trade; Lewis, Meriwether, and William Clark; *and* Thompson, David.]

BIBLIOGRAPHY

Allen, John Eliot, Marjorie Burns, and Sam C. Sargent. *Cataclysms on the Columbia*. Portland: Timber, 1986.

Beals, Herbert K., ed. and trans. *For Honor and Country: The Diary of Bruno de Hezeta*. Portland: Oregon Historical Society, 1985.

Coues, Elliot, ed. *The Manuscript Journals of Alexander Henry and David Thompson, 1799–1814*. Vol. 2, *The Saskatchewan and Columbia Rivers*. Minneapolis, Minn.: Ross and Haines, 1897. Reprinted 1965.

Howay, Frederic, ed. *Voyages of the "Columbia" to the Northwest Coast, 1787–1790 and 1790–1793*. Cambridge, Mass.: Harvard University Press, 1941. Reprint. Portland, Ore.: Oregon Historical Society, 1990.

Meares, John. *Voyages Made in the Years 1788 and 1789*. London: Logographic Press, 1790.

Nisbet, Jack. *Sources of the River: Tracking David Thompson across Western North America*. Seattle, Wash.: Sasquatch, 1995.

Nokes, J. Richard. *Columbia's River: The Voyages of Robert Gray, 1787–1795*. Tacoma: Washington State Historical Society, 1991.

Swanton, John R. *Indian Tribes of Washington, Oregon, and Idaho*. Fairfield, Wash.: Ye Galleon Press, 1968.

Vancouver, George. *A Voyage of Discovery to the North Pacific Ocean and round the World, 1791–1795.* Edited by W. Kaye Lamb. London: Hakluyt Society, 1984.

HERBERT K. BEALS

Columbus, Bartolomé

Columbus, Bartolomé (c. 1461–c. 1515), Genoese explorer and brother of Christopher Columbus. The younger brother of Christopher Columbus, Bartolomé Colón (the Castilian version of his name; the name is Bartolomeo Colombo in Italian) had a life well documented from 1492 onward, but his earlier years are more obscure. According to Bartolomé de Las Casas, he made and sold maps. He joined Christopher in Lisbon sometime around 1480. In the late 1480s and early 1490s he is supposed to have traveled to England and France to seek royal support for his brother's proposed westward voyage.

When word reached him of the success of Columbus's first voyage, he secured a Castilian royal commission and traveled to La Española (Hispaniola) in the summer of 1493. He cooperated with Columbus as an administrator on the island and moved the principal seat of operations from the ill-placed La Isabela on the north coast to a more favored location in the south, where he founded the city of Santo Domingo. With Columbus, he was shipped back to Spain in chains in December 1500. He later participated in his brother's fourth voyage, distinguishing himself in actions in Central America, where local resistance checked efforts to plant a colony, and on Jamaica, where the survivors of the expedition were stranded for a year in 1503–1504. Following Christopher Columbus's death in 1506, Bartolomé worked to regain and secure the family's claims in the Americas. He traveled again to La Española in 1509 with Diego Colón, Christopher's son, and died in Santo Domingo in 1514 or 1515.

[*See also* Columbus, Christopher.]

BIBLIOGRAPHY

Colón, Fernando. *The Life of the Admiral Christopher Columbus.* Edited and translated by Benjamin Keen. 2nd ed. New Brunswick, N.J.: Rutgers University Press, 1992.

Las Casas, Bartolomé de. *Historia de las Indias.* 3 vols. México: Fondo de Cultura Económica, 1951.

WILLIAM D. PHILLIPS JR.

Columbus, Christopher

Columbus, Christopher (c. 1451–1506), Genoese navigator and explorer for Spain. Christopher Columbus made the first documented voyage across the Atlantic since the time of the Vikings. He later made three other transatlantic voyages and helped set the patterns for European activity in the Americas.

Born around 1451 in the territory of Genoa, Columbus began a career as a mariner and a merchant in the Mediterranean. In the 1470s, he settled in Portugal. On trips north to England and Ireland and south to West Africa, he gained knowledge of the Atlantic and of Portuguese economic activities in Africa. He married Felipa Moniz, a Portuguese noblewoman whose grandfather was an Italian merchant naturalized and ennobled in Portugal. Her father, Bartolomeu Perestrelo, had royal connections and was hereditary captain of the island of Porto Santo. Bartolomeu's second wife, Isabel Moniz, had ties of blood with the Portuguese and Castilian royal families.

The Enterprise of the Indies. Felipa Moniz's family's contacts at the Portuguese court allowed Columbus access to the latest news about Atlantic exploration to add to what he had learned by direct experience. Many Christian Europeans longed for a sea route to Asia that would allow them to buy Asian spices and other lucrative goods directly at their sources, bypassing Muslim control of the overland routes and maritime passages through the Red Sea or the Persian Gulf. In the 1480s, the Portuguese explored Africa's western coast while also attempting to find the southern tip of Africa and a sea passage to Asia.

Columbus became convinced that Asia could be reached by sailing westward from Europe. Columbus based his geographical ideas on previous discoveries of islands in the Atlantic, rumors of other islands still to be found, and unusual materials drifting in from the western ocean, and by wide reading of academic geography.

He relied on two incorrect propositions: that the Asian continent stretched some thirty degrees farther to the east than it really does, and that Japan lay fifteen hundred miles east of the Asian mainland. Columbus also greatly underestimated the circumference of the earth and thought that the Canary Islands lay only 2,400 nautical miles from Japan, one-quarter of the true distance. Of course, neither Columbus nor anyone else in Europe even suspected that two vast continents lay in the way of his proposed westward passage to Asia. The story that he had to confront people who believed in a flat earth is completely mythical. Well-read Europeans knew that the world was spherical.

Columbus first sought Portuguese support for his proposal for his "enterprise of the Indies," but King João II turned him down. Perhaps the Portuguese

Christopher Columbus. Woodcut from Giuliano Dati's poem of 1493, showing the three ships of Columbus. In this famous image, King Ferdinand watches as Columbus lands at the "island newly found by the King of Spain." We see the well-formed and docile inhabitants fleeing, with their well-observed huts in the background. COURTESY THE NEWBERRY LIBRARY, CHICAGO

experts disputed Columbus's geographical concepts. The Portuguese crown was already committed to seeking a route to Asia around Africa, and perhaps the Portuguese king did not want to dissipate his subjects' energies. Perhaps Columbus asked too much for himself. King João later found mariners who would attempt a westward venture without a royal subsidy or major concessions. Concurrently, members of Columbus's wife's family were involved in the political unrest that included the violent deaths of the dukes of Viseu and Braganza. As a result, Columbus probably found that his political connections had ceased to be useful.

Columbus left Portugal and transferred his efforts to Castile. Isabella and Ferdinand questioned Colum-

bus and then submitted his ideas to a group of experts who justifiably found fault with his geography. Nonetheless, the Spanish monarchs kept him on the royal payroll.

In early 1492, they agreed to help him, for two important reasons. First, a formal treaty with Portugal closed Castile's access to Africa south of the Canary Islands. If Castile were to participate in the Asian trade, it would have to be by another route that avoided Portuguese-controlled space in the Atlantic. Columbus's proposal did just that. Second, the financial costs were relatively low, allowing a modest gamble on potentially enormous riches.

The Spanish monarchs agreed to underwrite a voyage and promised Columbus, if successful, hereditary noble status and important titles. As admiral he would have the right to judge commercial disputes. As viceroy he would be the personal representative of the monarch. As governor-general he would have supreme civil and military authority. He could also participate in the funding and profits of every expedition.

The First Voyage, 1492–1493. Columbus prepared his fleet in Palos, relying on the help of Martín Alonso Pinzón and his kinsmen to outfit the *Niña*, the *Pinta*, and the *Santa María*. After reprovisioning in the Canaries, the fleet headed westward into the open ocean on September 6, 1492. As they sailed, propelled by the trade winds blowing from northeast to southwest, Columbus and the other pilots in the fleet navigated by dead reckoning, using estimates of direction by compass, time by sand clock, and speed by eye and feel to plot their course and position.

The voyage went smoothly, with fair winds and remarkably little grumbling among the crew. Before dawn on October 12, Juan Rodríguez Bermejo, the lookout on the *Pinta*, saw a light, and after dawn the fleet dropped anchor at an island in the Bahamas that local inhabitants called Guanahaní, and which Columbus renamed San Salvador. Although controversy continues over the location of the first landfall, it was probably the island formerly named Watlings Island and recently renamed San Salvador. Believing they were in the Indies, as contemporaries called Asia, they dubbed the indigenous people "Indians."

Columbus's fleet sailed through the Bahamas and visited Cuba, as he vainly sought the vast commerce and rich ports of Asia. Martín Alonso Pinzón took the *Pinta* without Columbus's permission and sailed off to explore and trade on his own. Columbus and the two remaining ships later sailed to Hispaniola and explored its northern coast. Early Christmas morning, the *Santa María* ran aground and wrecked. With only the *Niña* remaining, Columbus founded a settlement for the thirty-nine men he had to leave behind, naming it Villa de la Navidad. On January 4, 1493, Columbus in the *Niña* sailed eastward along the coast of Española (Hispaniola) on the beginning of the voyage back to Spain. Shortly afterward Pinzón rejoined him, and on January 16 the *Niña* and *Pinta* set sail for home, bringing seven captured Indians.

Columbus eventually found winds blowing from the west that would take them toward home. Fierce storms separated the two ships as they approached the Azores. Columbus on the *Niña* put in at Santa María Island on February 15 and nine days later resumed his voyage toward Spain. Another storm threatened the ship and its crew with destruction. On March 4, they found themselves along the Portuguese coast north of Lisbon, where they put in for rest and refitting. Columbus paid a courtesy call on King João II and departed for Spain on March 13,

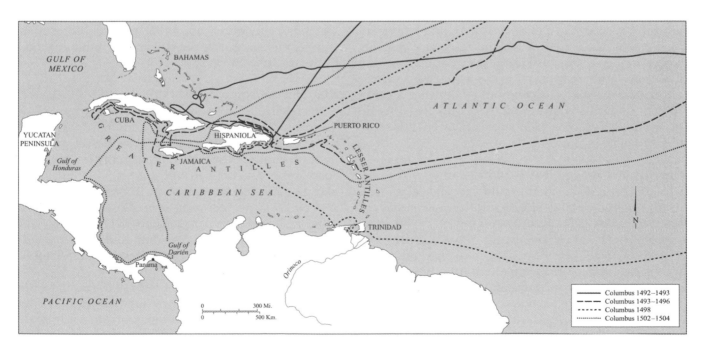

Christopher Columbus. The map shows the four voyages of Columbus to the New World. MAP BY BILL NELSON

1493, arriving in Palos two days later. Martín Alonso Pinzón brought the *Pinta* into port later that same day, having first landed at Bayona on the northwest coast of Spain.

Queen Isabella and King Ferdinand received Columbus warmly when he joined the court in Barcelona. They confirmed his privileges and quickly gave him permission for a second voyage. Columbus assured them that the rich Asian mainland lay close to the islands he had found.

Both parties seem to have assumed that he would reach Asia, tap into an existing trading network, and set up an entrepôt where the trade would be conducted as a royal monopoly with Columbus as the chief commercial agent. That was the model the Portuguese were using on the west coast of Africa and used in Asia as well. It presumably would have worked if Columbus had really reached Asia. Manila in the Philippines, which the Spaniards conquered in 1568, did eventually serve as just such an entrepôt for Spain's Asian trade. Even in the course of the first voyage, Columbus realized the differences and began to develop a replacement model: settlement, commercial farming of sugar cane and other crops, and the extraction of precious metals.

Columbus's insistence that Spanish settlers trade with the native peoples as salaried employees managed by Columbus caused problems. The Spaniards had still another model for expansion into new areas, one practiced during the reconquest of Spain from the Muslims and the conquest of the Canaries. This was the creation of municipalities, in which the inhabitants would share in government and be free in their economic activities. In the Canaries and the early Caribbean, this also implied intermarriage and other accommodations with the indigenous population. A large part of Columbus's failure as a colonial administrator came from the conflicts between the model he tried to follow and the model the colonists sought to impose.

The Second Voyage, 1493–1496. All that took some time to develop. Ferdinand and Isabella facilitated Columbus's colonizing effort, and the queen ordered that the native islanders be treated well and converted to Christianity. Departing from Cádiz on September 25, 1493, the fleet of seventeen vessels and twelve hundred men began their Atlantic crossing from the Canaries on October 12. On November 3, they landed on an island in the Caribbean that Columbus named Dominica and sailed from there through the Lesser Antilles and the Virgin Islands, and past Puerto Rico, to Hispaniola.

They found that all the men left in La Navidad the previous January were dead, most of them killed in disputes with the islanders. Increasingly wary, Columbus founded a new settlement, later abandoned. In addition to searching for gold and commercial ports, Columbus began a slave trade. If the islanders peacefully accepted takeover by the Europeans, they were protected against enslavement as subjects of the Castilian crown, but if they made war they could be seized as slaves, according to European law. By the time Columbus's second expedition arrived, some islanders were certainly at war against the Europeans, and Columbus used their resistance as a justification for their outright conquest. He and his men marched through the island, seeking gold through barter but conquering and taking captives when they met resistance.

Leaving Hispaniola under the control of his brother Diego, Columbus then took an expedition to explore the southern shores of Cuba, which he believed was part of the Asian mainland. He even made his crew members sign a document to that effect so that he could claim to his royal backers that he had truly found Asia.

The colony on Hispaniola was in chaos. Disappointed settlers returned to Spain and spread stories about the ineptitude of Columbus and his brothers as administrators. The Spanish rulers sent out an investigator, Juan Aguado, who confirmed alarmingly high deaths among the Amerindians, and the numbers of settlers reduced by disease and desertions. To defend his administration in person, Columbus sailed for Spain on March 10, 1496, leaving his brother Bartolomé in charge on Hispaniola, and reached Cádiz on June 11, 1496.

The Third Voyage, 1498–1499. By 1496, Ferdinand and Isabella had abandoned hope of short-term profits from Columbus's ventures. Only hard work and time would make the colonies pay. Despite reports about Columbus's failings as an administrator, he persuaded the monarchs to confirm his previous grants and give him permission for a third voyage, with a ship and two caravels to use for exploration plus three other caravels to carry provisions to Hispaniola, and three hundred men and three hundred women as additional colonists. Isabel prohibited the enslaving of native subjects.

Columbus took his three ships far south to the Cape Verde Islands before heading westward on July 7, and he reached the island of Trinidad on July 31. He then sailed north and west to the mainland of South America, realizing from the vast flow of water at the mouths of the Orinoco River that he had encountered an enormous landmass, which he speculated was the most easterly portion of Asia. After briefly exploring the coast of Venezuela, Columbus sailed on to Hispaniola.

There he found the situation in crisis. Some of the colonists had mutinied because they wanted greater freedom of action than Columbus's policies allowed. The Indians were increasingly hostile, and neither Bartolomé nor Diego Columbus had been able to maintain order. Ferdinand and Isabella sent out Francisco de Bobadilla to investigate, empowering him to take extraordinary measures to restore authority if necessary. He arrested the three Columbus brothers for their failure to keep order in the colony, seized their money, and sent them home in chains in December 1500.

Eventually Ferdinand and Isabella allowed Columbus to keep some of his titles and all of his property, but his titles would thereafter be empty of authority. They also delayed granting him permission for another voyage. At this time, Columbus worked on preparing two works, his *Book of Privileges*, supporting his claims to royal grants, and the *Book of Prophecies*, revealing his religious learning and speculation. Meanwhile, Ferdinand and Isabella provided their new colonies with a bureaucratic structure outside Columbus's control, appointing Nicolás de Ovando as governor of Hispaniola. Ovando sailed for the Caribbean in February 1502 with thirty ships and a large group of settlers. A month later, Ferdinand and Isabella finally granted Columbus permission for a new exploratory fleet under his command.

The Fourth Voyage, 1502–1504. Columbus's final fleet consisted of four small caravels in questionable repair, and second-rate crews. Other expeditions sponsored by the crown now claimed the best ships and men crossing the Atlantic. With Columbus and his son Hernando sailing on the flagship, the fleet left Spain on May 11, 1502. Departing the Canaries on May 25, the fleet arrived at Hispaniola on June 29, even though the monarchs had specifically forbidden Columbus to land there. Columbus knew that Governor Ovando was about to send a fleet home and saw that a hurricane was brewing. He warned Ovando of the approaching storm and asked to use the harbor to ride it out. Ovando refused to believe him and ordered the fleet to depart. Just as Columbus predicted, the hurricane struck, sinking twenty-five ships.

After Columbus left Hispaniola, he and his men explored the eastern coast of Central America. Local people fiercely resisted their efforts to found a settlement in Panama and forced them to leave, abandoning one ship when they left the area. The others were leaking badly due to shipworm and were barely seaworthy. Columbus abandoned yet another ship at sea and then was forced to ground his two remaining worn-out vessels in Jamaica and shore them up for use as strongholds. Columbus spent a miserable year on Jamaica before he was rescued and taken to Hispaniola. He arrived in Spain on November 7, 1504, never to return to the Americas.

Last Years. Columbus was no longer in the vanguard. The powerful lure of potential wealth across the ocean persuaded many other mariners to follow, most of them sponsored by the Castilian crown, but some sailing without official permission. Columbus was a wealthy man from the gold he had obtained, but he felt betrayed and slighted by his royal patrons. For their part, the Spanish sovereigns justified their withdrawal of support by Columbus's mismanagement and by his betrayal of their trust and of the agreements he had signed with them. The business of exploration and colonial settlement had quickly grown too complex for any one man to manage. Columbus refused to relinquish his claims and passed along all of them to his son Diego when he died in 1506.

[*See also* Columbus, Bartolomé; Europe and the Mediterranean, *subentry on* Medieval West Geography and Worldview; Expeditions, World Exploration, *subentries on* Portugal *and* Spain; Ovando, Nicolás de; *and* Pinzón, Vicente Yáñez, and Martín Alonso Pinzón.]

BIBLIOGRAPHY

Columbus, Christopher. *The Book of Privileges Issued to Christopher Columbus by King Fernando and Queen Isabel, 1492–1502.* Edited and translated by Helen Nader. Berkeley: University of California Press, 1996.

Columbus, Christopher. *The Book of Prophecies Edited by Christopher Columbus.* Edited by Roberto Rusconi. Translated by Blair Sullivan. Berkeley: University of California Press, 1997.

Columbus, Ferdinand. *The Life of the Admiral Christopher Columbus.* Edited and translated by Benjamin Keen. New Brunswick, N.J.: Rutgers University Press, 1959.

Henige, David P. *In Search of Columbus: The Sources for the First Voyage.* Tucson: University of Arizona Press, 1991.

Manzano Manzano, Juan. *Cristóbal Colón: Siete años decisivos de su vida, 1485–1492.* 2nd ed. Madrid: Ediciones de Cultura Hispánica, 1989.

Phillips, William D., Jr., ed. *Testimonies from the Columbian Lawsuits.* Translated by William D. Phillips Jr. and Anne Marie Wolf. Linguistic introduction by Mark D. Johnston. Turnhout, Belgium: Brepols, 2000.

Phillips, William D., Jr., and Carla Rahn Phillips. *The Worlds of Christopher Columbus*. Cambridge, U.K., and New York: Cambridge University Press, 1992.

WILLIAM D. PHILLIPS JR.

Compass. *See* **Compass, Magnetic** *and* **Navigational Techniques.**

Compass, Magnetic. A magnetic compass is an instrument used to determine the direction toward the earth's North Magnetic Pole by means of a magnetized needle that rotates. The needle may float in water (the "wet" compass) or pivot on a point (the "dry" compass). Often used to aid in navigation, the magnetic compass first appeared in Europe by the mid-twelfth century. Antecedents are found in China as early as the Later Han dynasty (25–220 C.E.). Wet compasses were in use by the Tang dynasty (618–907 C.E.) to find south, the most auspicious direction in Chinese geomancy. The dry compass was invented by the end of the Sung dynasty (960–1279 C.E.). The earliest written Chinese account of the device is found in the *Meng qi bi than* (c. 1088) by Shen Kua.

Historians have debated whether the compass developed independently in Europe or was introduced from China via Arab or Mongol intermediaries. The first known western references are found in the works of the English monk Alexander Neckam (1157–1217), who described a dry compass in his *De nominibus utensilium* (c. 1175–1183) and *De naturalis rerum* (c. 1197–1204). The French poet Guyot de Provins, a minstrel at the court of Emperor Frederick Barbarossa, described a wet compass in his *La Bible* (c. 1205). Later, the French bishop Jacques de Vitry mentioned the compass in his *Historia Orientalis seu Hierosolymitana* (c. 1218–1225). As these references predate both the earliest Arabic mention of the compass (that of Muhammad al-Awfi in 1232) and the first Mongol invasion of Europe (1223), it seems plausible that the magnetic compass had a separate European origin.

By the early thirteenth century the magnetic compass seems to have been well known in Europe. None of the early references indicated that it was a novel device. Michael Scot (c. 1195–c. 1235), a Scottish astrologer, considered the magnetic needle to be an item in everyday use in his time. Roger Bacon (c. 1213–1292) also held that it was commonly known. Around 1213, Snorri Sturluson, the Norse historian, received a compass as a gift, demonstrating that the technol-ogy had spread even to the northern regions of the continent. Such extensive knowledge of the compass by the early thirteenth century indicates that the device was probably developed during the previous century.

Increasing use of the magnetic compass led scholars to theorize about the reasons for its behavior. Various hypotheses, such as a large northern lodestone deposit, emerged to explain the apparent attraction of the magnetic needle to the north. Many thinkers, such as Vitry, the Flemish monk Thomas of Cantimpré (c. 1201–1270), and the French bishop Nicole Oresme (1323–1382), believed that the needle was attracted to Polaris (the North Star). John of Rupescissa (d. c. 1362) argued that iron was generated on earth under the influence of Polaris, thus explaining the sympathy of the magnetized needle for that star. Alternatively, the German theologian Albertus Magnus (c. 1200–1280) and the French Dominican Vincent of Beauvais (c. 1190–1264) cited pseudo-Aristotelian sources to argue that the needle was attracted to the North Pole, while Roger Bacon held that the needle could be made to point to any of the four cardinal points if properly magnetized. John of Saint Amand (fl. 1261–1298) argued that the magnetized needle actually contained elements of all four cardinal directions, but that the relative strength of the north-south component dominated.

Medieval work on the compass culminated with the *Epistola Petri Peregrini de Maricourt ad Sygerum de Foucaucourt, militem, de magnete*, written by the French mathematician Petrus Peregrinus (fl. 1261–1269) in 1269. Peregrinus introduced the idea that magnets have north and south poles and described both wet and dry compasses as well as other magnetic instruments (including a perpetual motion machine). Realizing that Polaris was not fixed, he ascribed the attraction of the needle to the celestial pole.

Use of the magnetic compass also led to the discovery of two other phenomena, known as magnetic variation and dip. Variation (or declination) occurs when the compass does not point to geographic north and represents the angle the needle makes with true north. Although known to the Chinese as early as the Tang dynasty, Europeans apparently did not discover variation until the fourteenth century. Magnetic dip (or inclination) occurs when the needle dips below the horizontal. Several descriptions of this phenomenon had appeared by the sixteenth century. In 1581, an Englishman named Robert Norman published *The New Attractive*, which both described magnetic dip and suggested that sailors keep records of magnetic variation.

An explanation for these new phenomena came from William Gilbert (1544–1603), whose *Tractatus sive physiologia nova de magnete, magneticisque corporibus, et magno magnete tellure* (1600) opened the modern field of geomagnetism. Gilbert theorized that the earth itself acted like a magnet with northern and southern magnetic poles. The attraction of the compass needle to the North Magnetic Pole, instead of to geographic north or the North Star, explained the phenomena of variation and dip.

BIBLIOGRAPHY

Mitchell, A. C. "Chapters in the History of Terrestrial Magnetism." *Terrestrial Magnetism and Atmospheric Electricity* 37 (1932): 105–146; 42 (1937): 241–280; 44 (1939): 77–80.

Smith, Julian A. "Precursors to Peregrinus: The Early History of Magnetism and the Mariner's Compass in Europe." *Journal of Medieval History* 18 (1992): 21–74.

Thorndike, Lynn, ed. *History of Magic and Experimental Science.* 8 vols. New York: Columbia University Press, 1923–1958.

CHRISTOPHER CARTER

Compiègne, Marquis de (1846–1877), aristocratic French explorer of the Ogowe River area of Africa. Born at Fuligny, Aube, France, on July 22, 1846, Louis-Alphonse-Henri-Victor Dupont, Marquis de Compiègne, first experienced wilderness travel in the Everglades of Florida before returning to France as a volunteer in the Franco-Prussian War in 1870. Compiègne fought in the battle of Sedan and was held by the Germans as a prisoner of war for seven months. After his release, he fought for the Thiers regime and was wounded in the suppression of the Commune of Paris, service for which he was nominated for the Cross of the Legion of Honor. Between 1872 and 1874, Compiègne traveled widely through coastal West Africa with the Frenchman Alfred Marche. With Marche, he ascended the Ogowe River (in present-day Gabon) farther than literate observers had before, to the confluence of the Ivindo River. Beyond this point, hostile Osyéba natives and the desertion of their native boatmen prevented further travel. Compiègne and Marche's voyage, described in Compiègne's two-volume work *L'Afrique équatoriale* (1875), influenced the French naval officer Pierre Savorgnan de Brazza to undertake an expedition up this river a year after their return. Compiègne's *Voyages, chasses, et guerres* (1876) recounts his earlier travels and war experiences. On February 28, 1877, Compiègne died from injuries sustained in a duel in Cairo while serving there as secretary of the Société Khédiviale de Géographie. A major avenue in modern Libreville, Gabon, is named for him.

[*See also* Africa, *subentry on* Exploration; Brazza, Pierre Savorgnan di; *and* Marche, Alfred.]

BIBLIOGRAPHY

Compiègne, Victor Dupont, Marquis de. *L'Afrique équatoriale: Gabonais, Pahouins, Gallois.* Paris: Plon, 1875.

Compiègne, Victor Dupont, Marquis de. *L'Afrique équatoriale: Okanda, Bangouens, Osyeba.* Paris: Plon, 1875.

Compiègne, Victor Dupont, Marquis de. *Voyages, chasses, et guerres.* Paris: Plon, 1876.

Socard, Émile. *Biographie des personnages de Troyes et du département de l'Aube.* Troyes, France: Lacroix, 1882.

JOHN P. SULLIVAN

Constantinople. Capital of the Roman Empire in the East (Byzantine Empire) until 1453 and of the Ottoman Empire until 1923, Constantinople, with its location on the Bosporus Strait, had command of the land route between Europe and Asia, as well as of the sea route between the Black Sea and the Mediterranean. This made it a regular destination for travelers of all sorts. During the Middle Ages its rich storehouse of relics attracted large numbers of Christian pilgrims, particularly those on their way to the Holy Land. During its Ottoman period, Constantinople was a favorite of European tourists.

For medieval Europeans, Constantinople was a place of legend. It was the largest and wealthiest city in the Christian world; before the thirteenth century its population exceeded that of the ten largest cities in western Europe combined. European travelers marveled at streets filled with every kind of merchandise, as well as the opulent palaces, churches, forums, and monasteries that occupied the city. No traveler failed to visit Justinian's great church, Hagia Sophia (Holy Wisdom), which before the sixteenth century was the largest building in the Christian world. The monumental walls that lined the city made it virtually impregnable before the development of gunpowder artillery.

Medieval travelers to Constantinople often wrote of their journey for those back home. The earliest surviving accounts are those of Arculf (c. 680) and Liudprand of Cremona (940–968). Marvazi, an Arab naturalist, wrote a detailed description of the city and its people in 1030. The king of Norway, Sigurd, visited Constantinople on his way to Jerusalem in 1111, which is recorded in the *Heimskringla*. The Jewish traveler Benjamin of Tudela, who was in Constantinople in 1170, provides descriptions of Hagia Sophia and the Hippodrome. He was also amazed at the lavish lifestyle of the citizens, which Benjamin condemned as a weakening vice. Around the same year, the Arab traveler Ali al-Harawi visited and wrote his own description.

In 1204 the Fourth Crusade conquered the great city and founded the short-lived Latin Empire of Constantinople. One of the crusaders, Robert of Clari, provides a wonderful description of the city before its devastation. Clari marveled at the relics, statues, walls, buildings, and people. He swallowed whole the stories he heard that attributed mystical powers to the ancient statues and artifacts that dotted Constantinople's landscape. After a long description, Clari finally abandoned his narrative, concluding, "If anyone should recount to you the hundredth part of the richness and the beauty and the nobility that was found in the abbeys and in the churches and in the palaces and in the city, it would seem like a lie and you would not believe it."

The Byzantines recaptured their capital in 1261, but the dilapidated city had little left of its former grandeur. Nevertheless, it continued to draw visitors from the West. William of Boldensele, who visited around 1330, provided the account on which the hugely popular *Book of John Mandeville* was based. Russian travelers continued to make their way south to visit the seat of the Orthodox faith. These included people like Stephen of Novgorod, Ignatius of Smolensk, and Alexander the Clerk, all of whom were there in the fourteenth century.

By the fifteenth century the Ottoman Turks had conquered virtually the entire Byzantine Empire save Constantinople itself. Western travelers continued to make their way to the city, but they were led more by an interest in the ancient past than by a desire to venerate relics. Cristoforo Buondelmonti, a Florentine priest, went there to include Constantinople in his geographical studies. His map of the city is the earliest to survive. Others, like Johann Schiltberger, Bertrandon de la Broquière, and Pero Tafur, visited the city shortly before its conquest by the Turks.

The Ottoman conquest in 1453 made Constantinople once again the capital of a powerful empire. The sultans spared no expense in rebuilding it to its former glory. European travelers to Constantinople found an exotic city teeming with people of every kind but dominated by the culture and law of Islam. The introduction of the printing press in Europe sparked greater literacy and a growing taste for stories of faraway lands. The most famous of the sixteenth-century accounts was that of Pierre Gilles. A scientist, humanist, and naturalist, Gilles came to Constantinople as a cultural attaché to a French embassy. During his years in the city, he searched for Greek manuscripts and meticulously examined the Christian buildings, comparing them against medieval accounts. His notes were published in 1561, shortly after his death.

By the seventeenth century the travel literature market was blossoming in Europe. There was no shortage of books describing Constantinople for an eager reading public. Among the most popular authors were Peter Mundy, George Sandys, Louis Deshayes, Thomas Roe, Jacob Spon, Jean DuMont, and Mary Wortley Montagu. Unfortunately, many books augmented their descriptions of Constantinople with hearsay and fantasy, and by plagiarizing sections of earlier works.

[*See also* Benjamin of Tudela; Crusades; Mandeville, John; Travel Literature, European; *and* Travel Writing in Antiquity.]

BIBLIOGRAPHY

Ebersolt, Jean. *Constantinople Byzantine et les voyageurs du Levant*. Paris: Leroux, 1919. Reprint. London: Pindar, 1986.

Majeska, George P. *Russian Travelers to Constantinople in the Fourteenth and Fifteenth Centuries*. Washington, D.C.: Dumbarton Oaks, 1984.

Van der Vin, J. P. A. *Travellers to Greece and Constantinople: Ancient Monuments and Old Traditions in Medieval Travellers' Tales*. 2 vols. Leiden, Nederlands: Historisch-Archaeologisch Instituut te Istanbul, 1980.

THOMAS F. MADDEN

Cook, James (1728–1779), British explorer of the Pacific. James Cook is commonly regarded as the greatest sea explorer of all time. Although such a judgment is inherently debatable, Cook's navigational and cartographic accomplishments were indeed remarkable. Before the three major voyages to the Pacific for which he is renowned, he produced precise surveys of Newfoundland and surrounding coasts, in the wake of the Seven Years' War, while the South Seas voyages saw the circumnavigation of New Zealand, the charting of the eastern Australian coast, and the identification or reidentification of many islands and archipelagos in the Pacific, including New Caledonia, the New Hebrides (today's Vanuatu), and the Hawaiian chain. He demonstrated definitively that there was no southern continent in inhabitable latitudes and that there was (in the climatic conditions of his time) no navigable Northwest Passage; in so doing he charted much of the northwest American coast for the first time. As highly significant as these findings were for com-

Drawing of Cook's Ships in Sandwich Sound. By John Webber, 1778. Here the *Resolution* and *Discovery* lie at anchor in Sandwich (Prince William) Sound. The peaks of the Alaskan coastal mountains surround them, and a variety of local boats inspect the newcomers. THE BRITISH LIBRARY

merce and colonization in the Pacific subsequently, the importance of Cook's voyages can be seen in considerably wider terms. His voyages represented a new kind of endeavor, a new synergy between surveying and science, that had wide-ranging impacts on metropolitan art and culture, as well as on the indigenous peoples who were encountered, often for the first time, and in a number of cases in a sustained fashion that led to a new level of mutual knowledge. [See color plate 27 in this volume.]

James Cook was born to an agricultural laboring family, in Yorkshire in 1728, and proceeded to an apprenticeship with the Quaker merchant John Walker of Whitby, then an important base for the coal trade between the Tyne and London, though Cook also sailed to Baltic and German ports on Walker's ships. In 1755 he volunteered for the Royal Navy—a choice that has long perplexed biographers, as he had risen in Walker's service and was about to be given command of one of his vessels. He was initially engaged in routine service, but from about 1759 became increasingly specialized in the arts of surveying, and from the end of war in 1763 began a series of summer surveys of the Newfoundland coasts, which achieved a new standard of precision in charts of the region, and indeed exemplified the most advanced maritime cartography of the time. These maps were printed in London, and presumably were seen to warrant Cook's nomination, when the question arose as to who should command the ship that would be called the *Endeavour* to the South Seas.

The Pacific Voyages. The context for this voyage was the unprecedented degree of influence scientists had in the Admiralty and with the king; an opportunity to observe the transit of Venus, which it was hoped would enable precise measurement of the distance between Earth and the Sun; and renewed interest in the long-standing geographic question of whether a southern continent existed. This was not purely a scholarly question, but also a mercantile one: traders and those enthusiastic about trade imagined that a previously unknown landmass would abound in products wholly new to Europeans, and thus might sustain a wonderfully lucrative trade. Hence the primary and official purpose of Cook's first voyage was the observation of the transit from Tahiti—known to Europeans through Samuel Wallis's visit of 1767—but his ostensibly secret instructions empowered him to search for the great south land, once the observations had been made.

The distinctiveness of the voyage would owe much to the participation of Joseph Banks, later a long-serving president of the Royal Society and the most powerful British scientific entrepreneur of his epoch. In 1768 Banks was only twenty-five, but he already had developed wide-ranging interests in natural history, especially but far from exclusively in botany, and he already had a sophisticated sense of what might be accomplished, not by an individual observer, but by what in effect amounted to a research team—he was accompanied by Daniel Solander, the pupil of Linnaeus, two draftsmen, and several servants. Throughout the voyage this party would make extensive collections, descriptive observations, and topographic, ethnographic, and natural historical drawings, making the voyage's findings in these areas far richer than those of any previous maritime expedition.

The ship left England in August 1768; these experiments were tried in a preliminary way at Tierra del Fuego; Tahiti was reached in April 1769, and here the *Endeavour* remained for three months, establishing a camp and preparing to observe the transit. The protracted nature of this stay, together with the fact that a number of members of Cook's crew had been

James Cook. Cook, like many other eighteenth-century European explorers, had an interest in the way local people lived. Here he offers a fairly convincing image of a local residence, with the fish drying as they hang from the ceiling. SOUTHERN METHODIST UNIVERSITY

"Representation of the Murder of Captain Cook." From John Rickman's *Journal of Captain Cook's Last Voyage to the Pacific Ocean* (London, 1781). This version of the death of Captain Cook, like several others, has in the past few years been subject to much interpretation. Was it the result of a breakdown in communication, or was there simply a gap between European and indigenous ideas about the nature of property? COURTESY THE NEWBERRY LIBRARY, CHICAGO

to the island before with Wallis, and thus had a rudimentary grasp of the Tahitian language, provided a basis for the emergence of an unprecedented degree of familiarity between seamen and islanders. Although there were repeatedly points of tension over property (and Cook was prompted to take local chiefs hostage in order to secure the return of items he considered indispensable) and of men who tried to desert, relationships were generally distinguished by unusual intimacy, by sexual promiscuity, by the sailors' participation in the local practice of tattoo-

ing, and by the acquisition of a good deal of information concerning local manners and customs. Cook himself began to be ethnographically curious, his intellect ranging beyond strictly maritime matters.

The transit observed, the ship proceeded south to New Zealand, previously sighted but not properly charted by Abel Janszoon Tasman. Contacts with Maori were, especially initially, more violent than those with Tahitians, but the Europeans gradually understood that this was a distinct, but related population, one with a more obviously martial population, that had to be respected and dealt with in a different manner. In order to establish whether or not New Zealand was linked with any larger southern land, both major islands were circumnavigated; Cook then sailed west, encountering the Australian coast, which was followed north. A brief stop at Botany Bay enabled contacts with the very cautious indigenous Australians; had the ship not been almost wrecked on the Great Barrier Reef, necessitating a period of repairs in the estuary that is now the site of Cooktown in north Queensland, few human or natural observations would have been made. Here, however, Cook formed an idealizing judgment of the local Aboriginal people, and the kangaroo among other animals was first described. The voyage was marred by the loss of a third of the party in Batavia and on the Indian Ocean passage home; those who died included the Society Islander Tupaia, who had wanted to visit England, and who had shared his knowledge of Pacific geography with Cook and acted as a go-between in New Zealand.

In the latter stages of the voyage, Cook arrived at a method for establishing once and for all whether a southern continent existed, which he presented to the Admiralty on his return to England in mid-1771. This was endorsed, and preparations quickly got under way for a second voyage, which in the light of the near loss of the *Endeavour* would be undertaken by two ships, the *Resolution* under Cook, and the *Adventure*, which would be commanded by Tobias Furneaux. Cook's plan was to make extended forays into southern waters during the warmer summer months and to spend the winters refreshing in the tropics while making further explorations there. The first of these cruises took the ships across the southern Indian Ocean and concluded in the southern autumn of 1773 in New Zealand. Tahiti and the Tongan islands were visited before a second investigation, which ventured just further than 70° S, where a massive wall of ice was encountered. By this time, Cook was already confident that there was no continent, but he considered it vital that waters to the southeast of Cape Horn were properly explored, so he took the *Resolution*, now separated from the *Adventure*, on a further tropical cruise, which was remarkable for dramatically enriching knowledge of the Pacific islands and their peoples—Easter Island, the Marquesas, Niue, and the Melanesian islands of Vanuatu and New Caledonia were visited, as well as the Society Islands, which were increasingly familiar. This voyage was marred by the massacre of a boatload of the *Adventure*'s crew at Grass Cove in New Zealand. Though

it was later established that the incident was provoked by the Europeans, emerging ideas of the Pacific islanders had to incorporate both the very positive representation of the hospitable Tahitians and Tongans, and the more ambivalent or negative accounts of other peoples including Maori.

A third voyage aimed to establish whether a Northwest Passage existed—the interest in this, like the southern continent, was both geographic and mercantile, as quicker access to east Asian markets would notionally have been facilitated. Cook was also charged with returning the Society islander Omai to his home, and establishing domestic animals—cattle and sheep—in the Pacific, perceived as an important act of benevolence. Delays and difficulties meant that a season for northern exploration was missed, which necessitated further extended stays in Tonga and Tahiti. The Hawaiian archipelago was encountered for the first time en route to what turned out to be a frustrating and difficult series of investigations of possible openings in the North American coastline. At the height of the summer of 1778, the ships passed through Bering Strait, but then having attempted passages to both the east and the west, confronted ice everywhere. Cook considered that further exploration was required, and returned to Hawaii for the winter, where initially positive relationships with islanders broke down, and he was killed in an affray on February 14, 1779.

Cook's Legacy. The legacies of Cook's voyages are manifold. In a navigational sense he was followed by George Vancouver and many others. The account of Botany Bay led to the identification of that site as an appropriate one for the Australian penal settlement established in 1788. The account of Tahiti prompted the establishment there of a mission under the aegis of the London Missionary Society at the end of the eighteenth century, and many other aspects of Pacific colonization followed more indirectly from Cook's discoveries. The South Seas became a fertile subject in popular culture, and entered pantomime and poetry among other genres in the wake of the voyages. Cook himself became a national icon and a hero with a following that has endured up to the present day. The popular image has, however, diminished the complexity of his curiosity and his thought. While his cartographic accomplishments are certainly of tremendous importance, the anthropological and cross-cultural dimension of his voyages was also of crucial importance. Equally, Cook became increasingly preoccupied with the morality of contact between Europeans and indigenous peoples, regretting

---

Death in the Pacific

Cook's much-debated death took place in circumstances that have never been completely elucidated. But he was constantly treading a fine line in his relations with the indigenous peoples of the Pacific; there were inevitably conflicts between European ideas of property and discipline and the very different ideas of the island groups whom the Europeans encountered.

Our unfortunate Commander, the last time he was seen distinctly, was standing at the water's edge and calling out to the boats to cease firing and to pull in. If it be true, as some of those whom were present have imagined, that the marines and boatmen had fired without his orders, and that he was desirous of preventing any further bloodshed, it is not improbable that his humanity on this occasion proved fatal to him. For it was remarked that, whilst he faced the natives, none of them had offered him any violence, but that, having turned about to give his orders to the boats, he was stabbed in the back, and fell with his face in the water.

—James Cook and James King, *A Voyage to the Pacific Ocean*
(London, 1784)

---

particularly the damage caused to the latter by the spread of venereal diseases, which he struggled unsuccessfully to restrain.

[*See also* Banks, Joseph; Hawaiian Islands; Pacific; Tasman, Abel Janszoon; Vancouver, George; Venus, Transit of; *and* Wallis, Samuel, and Philip Carteret.]

BIBLIOGRAPHY
Beaglehole, J. C. *The Life of Captain James Cook*. London: A. and C. Black, 1974.
Beaglehole, J. C., ed. *The Journals of Captain James Cook on his Voyages of Discovery*. Cambridge, U.K.: Hakluyt Society, 1955–1967. Abridged version. London and New York: Penguin, 1999.
Salmond, Anne. *Two Worlds: First Meetings between Maori and Europeans, 1642–1772*. Auckland, New Zealand: Viking, 1991.
Smith, Bernard. *European Vision and the South Pacific*. 2nd ed. New Haven, Conn.: Yale University Press, 1985.
Thomas, Nicholas. *Discoveries: The Voyages of Captain Cook*. London: Allen Lane, 2003.

NICHOLAS THOMAS

Coronelli, Vincenzo (1650–1718), Venetian maker of maps and globes. Marco Vincenzo Coronelli was born on August 15, 1650, in Venice, and in 1665 he became a Franciscan novice there. In 1671 he entered the convent of Santa Maria Gloriosa dei Frari, and he was sent in the following year to the Collegium San Bonaventura in Rome, where he qualified as a doctor of theology. Meanwhile he had been pursuing an interest in mapmaking, and in 1678 he created two large globes—terrestrial and celestial—for the Duke of Parma. These globes attracted the attention of the French ambassador, who saw to it that Coronelli was invited to Paris in 1681. He lived in Paris for two years and was commissioned by César Cardinal d'Estrées to create two huge manuscript globes for Louis XIV. These superb objects, fifteen feet in diameter, may still be seen in the Petit Palais at Paris.

In 1685, Coronelli was appointed cosmographer to the Venetian Republic, and then he began setting up in his convent what was in effect a vast workshop for drawing and printing globe gores and then mounting them on globes of various sizes. He tried on the successive editions of his globes to incorporate the latest geographical information, though sometimes it was seriously mistaken. Coronelli was general of his order between 1701 and 1704, having in 1693 published his *Libro dei globi*, which contained the constituent gores for globes of different sizes. [See color plate 26 in this volume.]

Globes with Coronelli's gores came to be widely scattered about the world, and they may still be found today in many libraries, particularly in western Europe. The globes conveyed the latest geographical information to a wide variety of people and made Coronelli's work, which may seem a little incongruous to our modern eyes (a great globe factory based in a convent), almost a synonym for the construction of globes. The society for their study, founded at Vienna in 1952, is called the International Coronelli Society for the Study of Globes.

[*See also* Globes.]

BIBLIOGRAPHY
Coronelli, Vincenzo. *Libro dei globi: Venice 1693* (1701). Edited by Helen Wallis. Amsterdam: Theatrum Orbis Terrarum, 1969.

DAVID BUISSERET

Corte-Real, Gaspar (1450?–1501?), Portuguese explorer of the North Atlantic. Gaspar Corte-Real was the youngest of three brothers of a wealthy, well-connected Portuguese family, whose father, João Vaz Corte-Real, was governor of Terceira Island in the

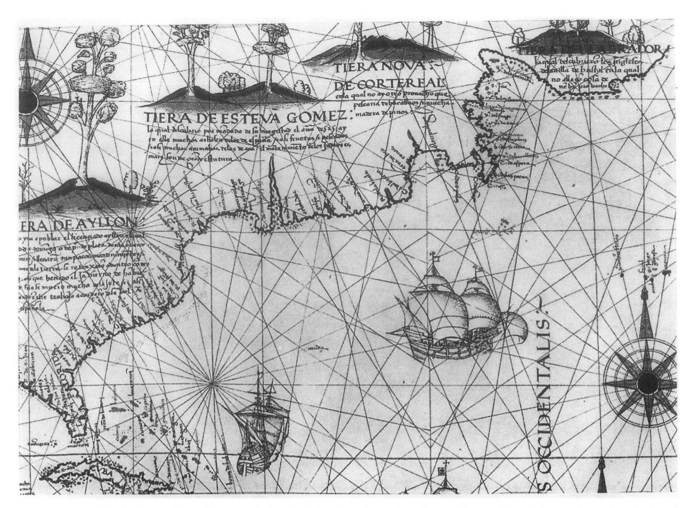

Gaspar Corte-Real. Detail from Diogo Ribeiro's *World Map,* 1529 (Biblioteca Apostolica Vaticana, Rome).This detail from one of the finest maps produced by the cartographers based at the Seville *casa de contratación* shows the area of what is now the United States named for Gaspar Corte-Real. The "tieras" or lands to the south also commemorate the claims of Spanish explorers. COURTESY THE NEWBERRY LIBRARY, CHICAGO

Azores. The Portuguese crown had rewarded him with this post for services rendered in colonizing the island. João Vaz was devoted to seeking uncharted islands and untapped fishing grounds. The oldest brother, Vasco Annes, was responsible for financing the family's exploring enterprises. The two younger brothers mirrored their father's interest in exploration. Gaspar, born in Lisbon, and his brother, Miguel, undertook two documented voyages that are notable in the history of European exploration of the North Atlantic.

The first expedition departed Lisbon in early spring 1500. Sailing northerly, the brothers reached Denmark Strait between Iceland and Greenland. Turning southwesterly, they doubled Greenland's most southerly point, Cape Farewell. The expedition

entered Davis Strait, crossing over to Labrador. They coasted Labrador south to Newfoundland, which they called *Terra Verde* because of its verdant coniferous forests. The expedition then returned home across the Atlantic directly to Lisbon.

The second expedition embarked with three ships from Lisbon in mid-May 1501. The brothers followed a track similar to the previous year, although ice in Davis Strait compelled them to cross the strait farther south than previously. They reached Newfoundland and continued exploring southward to Nova Scotia. There they landed and captured some fifty natives who were later taken to Portugal and sold into slavery. Miguel led two of the ships home, while Gaspar continued south of Nova Scotia, never to be seen again. In the following year, Miguel led an expedition to search for his missing brother, only to fall victim to a similar fate.

[*See also* Expeditions, World Exploration, *subentry on* Portugal, *and* Newfoundland.]

BIBLIOGRAPHY

Morison, Samuel Eliot. *The European Discovery of America: The Northern Voyages*. New York: Oxford University Press, 1971.

Morison, Samuel Eliot. *Portuguese Voyages to America in the Fifteenth Century*. Cambridge, Mass.: Harvard University Press, 1940.

Seaver, Kirsten A. *The Frozen Echo, Greenland and the Exploration of North America ca. A.D. 1000–1500*. Stanford, Calif.: Stanford University Press, 1996.

HERBERT K. BEALS

Cortés, Hernán (1485–1547), Spanish conquistador. Cortés was born in Medellín, Extremadura, Castile, and was educated in Salamanca before immigrating to Hispaniola in 1504. In 1511, he accompanied Diego Velásquez de Cuéllar in the conquest of Cuba, where Cortés became an *encomendero*. In 1519, he was named to lead the third expedition to Mexico authorized by Governor Velásquez of Cuba. Velásquez later decided to replace him because of his growing distrust of Cortés, but Cortés avoided being replaced by hastily sailing first. He retraced the steps of the earlier expeditions, clashed with the Maya several times, and then sailed along the Veracruz coast and established the town of Veracruz. There he allied with the Totonac, then marched inland and clashed with the Tlaxcaltec before also allying with them. When he finally reached Tenochtitlan—a city far larger than any in Europe—on November 8, 1519, he was welcomed by King Montezuma. Within the week, acting on suspicions of an ambush, Cortés seized the king and proceeded to rule through him.

Velásquez sent Pánfilo de Narváez to Veracruz to return Cortés to Cuba, but Cortés defeated him. After Cortés returned to Tenochtitlan with Narváez's men, the Spaniards were besieged in retaliation for a massacre during an Aztec festival, which had occurred while Cortés was away. Spanish attempts to fight their way out proved futile, so they crept out one midnight under cover of a rainstorm. Discovered in mid-flight, some 870 Spaniards were killed and fewer than 500 reached Tlaxcallan.

With Tlaxcaltec help, Cortés conquered nearby towns before returning to the Valley of Mexico at the end of 1520. There he launched attacks, courted disaffected rulers, and gradually cut off the valley from all outside assistance. Then, after building thirteen brigantines to control the lakes, Cortés attacked over the main causeways with hundreds of Spaniards and tens of thousands of Indian allies, initiating three months of brutal combat for Tenochtitlan. Cortés's allies waxed and waned with each change in the tide of battle—a battle that became an endurance test of attrition and deprivation as the city's food and water were cut off. Eventually, Cortés's forces fought their way into the city and, on August 13, 1521, King Cuauhtémoc—the last Aztec king—surrendered.

Thereafter, Cortés led other expeditions, including one to Honduras in 1524. He was rewarded by the Spanish crown with vast wealth and lands, but soon clashed both with other Spaniards and with the crown, and in 1528 he went to Spain in a successful effort to regain royal favor. After returning to Mexico, he explored the Pacific, discovering lower California in 1538. He returned to Spain in 1540, where he died in Castilleza de la Cuesta, near Seville, on December 2, 1547.

In addition to his exploits, Cortés is significant for his accounts of the conquest, which are the ones composed most closely after the events they purport to recount. Cortés wrote six letters to the king from 1519 to 1526. Two are missing. For the first letter, which is one of the missing ones, the account of the Regimiento of Veracruz, dated July 10, 1519, is conventionally substituted. The second letter is dated October 30, 1520; the third is dated May 15, 1522; the fourth is dated October 15, 1524; the fifth is missing and is ignored in publication; and the sixth is generally presented as the fifth, and final, letter, and is dated September 3, 1526. All the letters recount only the events that happened since the previous letter, and all present Cortés in an extremely favorable light—his deeds as the most honorable, and his obstacles as the most overwhelming. Because he had violated Velásquez's orders, Cortés's letters are not dispassionate recitations of events, but justifications of his actions and bids for royal favor and reward.

Cortés's chaplain and secretary in Spain, Francisco López de Gómara, wrote an uncritical account of the conquest taken mostly from Cortés himself, who can be considered the account's real author. López de Gómara began his history a decade after Cortés's death and was never in Mexico himself. López de Gómara's excesses spurred Bernal Díaz del Castillo to write his own firsthand account of the conquest.

Cortés was undeniably an able and focused leader, but he was both ruthless and duplicitous in furthering his own ends. He urged the Totonac ruler in Veracruz to seize Aztec tribute collectors, secretly freed them, professed his innocence of their seizure, and then told the Totonac that the collectors had escaped. He used his military power to create allegiances with Indian rulers, then forced them to throw down their old gods, which tied the leaders more closely to the Spaniards in the face of their people's hostility.

Cortés was equally ruthless with his own men. When some of them wanted to return to Cuba in 1519, Cortés burned his own ships. When the men complained, he ordered two of them to be hanged. And again, in 1521, he hanged two more men for plotting to leave.

Some historians think that Cortés had Moteuczoma Xocoyotl and the other captive kings and nobles killed when the Spaniards fled Tenochtitlan in 1520; the charge is unlikely regarding Moteuczoma and likely regarding the others, though Cortés blamed Indian perpetrators for all the deaths. Some historians claim that his massacre of Cholollan leaders in 1519 was most likely unprovoked, and that his defeat of Narváez was accomplished through lies and double-dealing, not military skill. Cortés never fulfilled the promises he made to his Tlaxcaltec allies and he had the deposed Aztec king Cuauhtémoc hanged on the expedition to Honduras only on suspicion of treachery. For good or ill, Cortés consistently acted in what he regarded as his own best interests, and he proffered whatever excuses he thought would be acceptable thereafter.

Nevertheless, his most incontestably important act was the conquest of Mexico. That conquest, and his careful balancing of the interests of various allied Indian groups and leaders, opened Mexico up to Spanish colonization, made Cortés an extremely wealthy man, and enriched Spain beyond all the other powers in Europe.

[*See also* California, Island of; Central and South America, *subentry on* Conquests and Colonization; Expeditions, World Exploration, *subentry on* Spain; Marina, Doña; *and* Spanish and Portuguese America, Reports and Descriptions of.]

BIBLIOGRAPHY

Cortés, Hernán. *Letters from Mexico*. Translated by Anthony Pagden. New York: Grossman, 1971.

De Fuentes, Patricia, ed. *The Conquistadors: First-Person Accounts of the Conquest of Mexico*. Norman: University of Oklahoma Press, 1993.

Díaz del Castillo, Bernal. *The True History of the Conquest of New Spain*. Translated by Alfred Percival Maudslay. 5 vols. London: Hakluyt Society, 1908.

Madariaga, Salvador de. *Hernán Cortés: Conqueror of Mexico*. New York: Macmillan, 1941.

ROSS HASSIG

Cousteau, Jacques (1910–1997), underwater explorer and coinventor of the aqualung. Jacques-Yves Cousteau was born on June 11, 1910, in Saint-André-de-Cubzac, France. The son of Daniel Cousteau, a lawyer, Jacques learned to swim early, and purchased one of the first French home movie cameras. He was sent to boarding school after engaging in petty vandalism, and subsequently attended the École Navale in Brest. Cousteau's career in naval aviation was aborted by a 1935 car accident, but while swimming to rehabilitate multiple fractures, he was introduced to the Mediterranean's undersea world. His attempts to develop an underwater breathing device led to collaboration with Emile Gagnan and their 1943 patent for the aqualung. Despite Cousteau's work for the Resistance, this device played no major role in World War II, but it was subsequently used for mine removal and has since significantly extended man's mobility in exploring the deep.

In the late 1940s, Cousteau began making undersea movies, and in 1949 he acquired the *Calypso*, from which he explored the depths of the Red Sea. Subsequently he received sponsorship from the National Geographic Society and in 1953 published *The Silent World*. Three years later, his full-length underwater documentary of the same name received both a Palme d'Or at Cannes and the first of Cousteau's three Oscars. In 1957, Cousteau, who had been on leave from the French Navy for almost a decade, resigned his commission and accepted an appointment as director of Monaco's Oceanographic Institute.

During the late 1950s, Cousteau developed a two-seated diving saucer, and in 1964 he produced a single-seat version christened the *Sea Flea*. From 1962 to 1965, Cousteau and his team engaged in Conshelf I–III, a series of underwater living experiments at increasing depths. Two deeper Conshelfs, as well as a 1968 agreement with France to construct Argyronète, a mobile subsea settlement, were canceled.

After the late 1960s, Cousteau's emphasis shifted from scientific research to popularization. From 1968 to 1976, Cousteau produced a series of television programs that appeared as *The Undersea World of Jacques Cousteau*. This educational tack was followed by the 1974 establishment of the Cousteau Society as an international nonprofit organization. Although involved in the conservation movement, Cousteau eschewed traditional politics, turning down the opportunity to be the Green candidate for France's presidency in 1981. The death of his first wife, Simone, in 1990, led to Cousteau's announcement of his fifteen-year romantic relationship with Francine Triplet, whom he subsequently married.

Cousteau died of a heart attack in Paris on June 25, 1997.

BIBLIOGRAPHY
Cousteau, Captain J. Y., with Frederic Dumas. *The Silent World*. New York: Harper and Brothers, 1953.
DuTemple, Lesley A. *Biography: Jacques Cousteau*. Minneapolis, Minn.: Lerner, 2000.
Madsen, Axel. *Cousteau: An Unauthorized Biography*. New York: Beaufort, 1986.
Munson, Richard. *Cousteau: The Captain and His World—A Personal Portrait*. New York: William Morrow, 1989.

SAMUEL PYEATT MENEFEE

Covilhã, Pêro da

Covilhã, Pêro da (c. 1460–1526/30?), Portuguese explorer of Abyssinia. Pêro da Covilhã was an agent entrusted in 1487 by King João II of Portugal (r. 1481–1495) with exploring the established trade routes linking the Mediterranean Sea and the Indian Ocean. If possible, Covilhã was to explore the way to the realm of Prester John and ascertain whether an alliance could be made with this legendary Christian potentate. An adventurer fluent in several languages, including Arabic, Covilhã had carried out a number of overt and covert missions for Portugal in various European and North African countries. Afonso de Paiva, also a speaker of Arabic, was chosen to accompany Covilhã in this venture.

Covilhã and Paiva set out from Portugal in May 1487. They made for Alexandria by way of Valencia, Barcelona, Naples, and Rhodes. Before reaching Egypt, they assumed the identity of Muslim merchants and joined a group traveling from Tlemcen and Fez to Aden. They reached their Red Sea destination in the summer of 1488, and from there Covilhã sailed to the Malabar Coast of India, visiting the spice-trading cities of Cannanore and Calicut. He then proceeded northward to Goa and from there to Hormuz. After visiting Oman and sailing along the east African coast as far as Sofala, Covilhã returned to Cairo in late 1490 or early 1491. Here he made contact with messengers of King João, from whom he learned of the death of Afonso de Paiva, who was supposed to be exploring the lands of Prester John in the meantime. Covilhã sent a long report on his findings back to Portugal with one of the messengers and, taking over Paiva's part of the mission, went off in search of Prester John.

It is unclear whether Covilhã's report ever reached Portugal and whether it was of any use. One source claims that the messenger arrived in Lisbon only after Vasco da Gama's expedition had already sailed. Other sources have no information to offer. The painfully inadequate assortment of goods carried by Vasco da Gama's expedition to India in 1497–1499, and the blunders committed along the way, would suggest that the crown simply did not receive Covilhã's information. To compound the puzzle, Covilhã supposedly assured the king that India could indeed be reached by circumnavigating Africa. This would mean that the passage to the Atlantic Ocean around the southern tip of Africa was a matter of commonplace knowledge in the northern Indian Ocean, an unlikely scenario.

Covilhã reached Christian Ethiopia in either late 1493 or early 1494, and he was courteously received by the ruler but then was prevented from leaving. He was handsomely provided for, being given a wife and a prominent place at court. Rodrigo de Lima's embassy to the Ethiopian court met Covilhã many years later, in 1520. Covilhã told his story in detail to Father Francisco Álvares, the author of the *Verdaira informação da terra do Preste João das Indias* (True Information about the Land of Prester John of the Indies), a sobering description of the beleaguered, isolated, and impoverished Christian enclave that in no way resembled the all-powerful Christian ally in the East whose imaginary figure loomed large in European geopolitical speculation. Covilhã died in Ethiopia sometime between 1526 and 1530.

[*See also* Expeditions, World Exploration, *subentry on* Portugal; Gama, Vasco da; *and* Prester John.]

BIBLIOGRAPHY
Barreto, Luís Filipe. *Por mar e terra: Viagens de Bartolomeu Dias e Pêro da Covilhã*. Lisbon: Biblioteca Nacional, 1988.
Chaudhuri, K. N. *Asia before Europe: Economy and Civilisation of the Indian Ocean from the Rise of Islam to 1750*. Cambridge, U.K.: Cambridge University Press, 1990.
Diffie, Bailey W., and George W. Winius. *Foundations of the Portuguese Empire, 1415–1580*. Minneapolis: University of Minnesota Press, 1977.
Silverberg, Robert. *The Realm of Prester John*. Athens, Ohio: Ohio University Press, 1996.

IVANA ELBL
MARTIN ELBL

Cross Timbers, The

Cross Timbers, The. The Cross Timbers is—or rather, was—one of the major landmarks of south-central North America. In the early 1820s, the name "Cross Timbers" began to be used by Anglo-American Texans. It refers to distinctive belts of post oak and blackjack oak trees that thrived on the sandy soils and sandstone cuestas of north-central Texas, central Oklahoma, and extreme southeastern Kansas. The origin of the name "Cross Timbers" is uncertain. Some claim that it refers to the fact that the forests had to be crossed by westward-moving pioneers. That explanation is unlikely, however, because settlers had not yet begun moving westward through this area that early. Others claim that the forests "cross," that is, lie perpendicular to, the region's numerous southeast-flowing streams, such as the Canadian, Arkansas, Brazos, and Trinity rivers. Another explanation is that the name Cross Timbers refers to forests made up of post oaks, for these trees are called "cross oaks" in the vernacular.

In any case, the Cross Timbers (or "Cross Timber," as it was sometimes called) was a landmark on maps of the region from about 1830 until the 1870s. By the mid-1800s, the distribution of the forests was pretty well understood: not confined to Texas, the Cross Timbers extended well into Indian Territory (in present-day Oklahoma), where they also had an affinity for sandy and sandstone soils. Interestingly, Cross Timbers–like forests of post oak and blackjack oak can be found to the east of the Cross Timbers, but there they are adjacent to, or mixed with, other types of forests. This suggests that another vegetation community—for instance, adjacent prairie from which to view the forested area—is needed for people to perceive the Cross Timbers as a separate landmark or region. Ecologically, the Cross Timbers region is classified as an oak savannah, for prairie grasses are closely associated with it in many areas.

For several hundred years, this densely forested region has been known as an impediment to travel. While journeying through the Cross Timbers on an expedition in Indian Territory in 1831, the famed writer-statesman Washington Irving observed that moving through it was like traveling through "forests of cast iron." The rugged topography of the Cross Timbers, with its resilient oaks and thorny underbrush, made travel tough going for Irving's expedition, but his party was not the first to experience vexations here. In the late 1600s and early 1700s, the Spaniards were familiar with the forests, and called them the "Monte Grande" (Grand Forest)—a term they had translated from the Indian name for the area. In fact, some Spanish expeditions found travel so difficult through the brushy oaks and thorny vines that they called it the "Monte del Diablo" (Forest of the Devil). The journals of several Spanish explorers noted that machetes were needed to help cut through the wirelike vines and underbrush.

The first known depiction of the Monte Grande is on a map from the Vial y Fragoso expedition of 1789. However, it was the Anglo-Americans who popularized the concept of the Cross Timbers as a dense belt of trees that would separate Indians and settlers on the Anglo-American frontier. By the 1840s, the Cross Timbers was a recognized landmark in the Republic of Texas, and it appeared on most maps of the frontier. At this time, perceptive observers noted that the Texas Cross Timbers consisted of two belts of trees—the Lower (or Eastern) Cross Timbers and the Upper (or Western) Cross Timbers.

Early naturalists' encounters with the Cross Timbers in the nineteenth century are noteworthy. These early naturalists included William Bollaert and Robert Hill—scientists whose pioneering work led to the Cross Timbers being recognized as both a vegetational region (thanks to Bollaert) and a geological region (thanks to Hill). Through their efforts, we came to understand the Cross Timbers as one of North America's distinctive ecological regions—an archipelago of oak forests that extends well out into the great prairies of the south-central United States. We now know that the Cross Timbers reach as far north as southeastern Kansas and as far south as Waco, Texas. The Cross Timbers forests are transitional, bridging the boundary between the well-watered eastern forests and the subhumid grasslands of the West. Anchored by sandstones and capable of withstanding prolonged regional droughts, they are a remarkable outlier of the eastern mesophytic woodlands at the doorstep of the semiarid American West.

The Cross Timbers region has both a fascinating natural history and a riveting, sometimes violent, cultural history as a frontier between East and West, North and South. That history also confirms that the Cross Timbers, while tenacious, is not immune to abuse: the increasingly aggressive removal of the Cross Timbers following the arrival of the plow and the railroad has had a profound impact on many areas. By the later nineteenth century, substantial portions of the Cross Timbers had yielded to farming as the Texas and Oklahoma Cross Timbers became part of the westward-moving "Cotton Belt" of the American South. Portions of the Cross Timbers remain, but it is no longer popularly recognized as a unique region. Urbanization, too, has taken a heavy toll on this ecosystem in the twentieth century. These changes helped transform the region, resulting in a landscape that lost its status as a landmark. Still, because the Cross Timbers was never extensively logged, it is likely that 5 to 10 percent of the original vegetation remains essentially unexploited.

Today, fewer than 5 percent of the people living in the Cross Timbers even know what the term means, but those in Texas are far more likely to know about it than those in Oklahoma or Kansas. This, of course, is a far cry from the 1850s, when the term "Cross Timbers" was widely known. Significantly, a fascination with Texas history is one of the factors that keep the memory of the Cross Timbers alive—at least in Texas. In the late twentieth century, the Cross Timbers became one of Texas's many vernacular or perceptual regions, perpetuated by the naming of businesses, schools, and even a Boy Scout district. Mostly, however, people in the region view the remnants of the Cross Timbers as so much scrubby oak-covered land, and it no longer appears on modern maps. Recently, environmentalists have proposed saving some large tracts of virgin Cross Timbers vegetation in Texas and Oklahoma; the Ancient Cross Timbers Consortium is one such effort.

BIBLIOGRAPHY
Foreman, Carolyn Thomas. *The Cross Timbers*. Muskogee, Okla.: Press of the Star Printery, 1947.
Francaviglia, Richard. *The Cast Iron Forest: A Natural and Cultural History of the North American Cross Timbers*. Austin: University of Texas Press, 2000.
Jordan, Terry. *Texas: A Geography*. Boulder, Colo.: Westview Press, 1984.

RICHARD FRANCAVIGLIA

Crozet, Julien-Marie (1728–1782), an officer in the French East India Company navy. Julien-Marie Crozet served on *Le Glorieux* (under Captain Jean-Baptiste d'Après de Mannevillette), which took the astronomer Nicolas-Louis, Abbé de La Caille, to the Cape of Good Hope in 1750, and on the *Comte d'Argenson* (under Captain Marc-Joseph Marion Dufresne), which took the astronomer Alexandre-Gui Pingré to Île de France to observe the transit of Venus (June 6, 1761) on Rodrigues Island.

When Marion Dufresne offered to return home the Tahitian who had followed Louis-Antoine de Bougainville, the intendant Pierre Poivre named Crozet second in command on Marion Dufresne's ship *Le Mascarin*, which had for consort the ship *Le Marquis de Castries* under Captain Ambroise-Bernard Le Jar Du Clesmeur. Marion Dufresne had instructions to search for the southern lands. The Tahitian passenger having died near Madagascar, Marion Dufresne continued his journey to the Cape of Good Hope, sailing south on December 28, 1771, to begin his survey where Lozier Bouvet had left off.

On January 13, 1772, in cold and turbulent weather, land was sighted at 46° S and 37°45' E. Marion Dufresne named it Terre d'Espérance, but it was later renamed Île Marion by James Cook. The survey was abandoned when the ships collided to the northeast, suffering serious damage. On January 21, what are now known as the Crozet Islands (46° S and 52° E)

were encountered. The deed claiming the archipelago for France was deposited on Île de la Possession, where a scientific post has operated since 1963.

Passing north of Kerguelen on February 1, the expedition, disappointed by the lack of refreshments in Tasmania, established itself at Bay of Islands, New Zealand, where Marion Dufresne was slaughtered on June 12. Crozet organized a rescue and led the expedition, via Guam and Manila, back to Île de France (May 1773). His account, *Nouveau Voyage à la Mer du Sud*, was published posthumously by Alexis-Marie Rochon in 1783.

At the Cape of Good Hope in 1775, Cook was informed by Crozet of the French discoveries in the South Indian Ocean. Cook noted in his journal, "Captain Crozet seemed to be a man possessed of the true spirit of a discoverer and to have abilities equal to his good will" (Beaglehole, p. 656).

[*See also* Cape of Good Hope *and* Cook, James.]

BIBLIOGRAPHY
Beaglehole, J. C., ed. *The Journals of Captain James Cook on His Voyages of Discovery: The Voyage of the "Resolution" and "Adventure," 1772–1775*. Cambridge, U.K.: Cambridge University Press for the Hakluyt Society, 1961.
Duyker, Edward. *An Officer of the Blue: Marc-Joseph Marion Dufresne, South Sea Explorer, 1724–1772*. Carlton, Australia: Melbourne University Press, 1994.
Taillemite, Étienne. *Marins français à la découverte du monde: De Jacques Cartier à Dumont d'Urville*. Paris: Fayard, 1999.

HUGUETTE LY-TIO-FANE PINEO
MADELEINE LY-TIO-FANE

Crusades. The Crusades were a series of military expeditions in the eleventh, twelfth, and thirteenth centuries ordered by the popes for the defense of Christendom, Christian people, or the Catholic Church. The Crusades to the Middle East provided a cause for many thousands of Europeans to travel far from home. Nevertheless, the journey was long, difficult, and dangerous. Thirty percent or more of those joining the main expeditions before 1291 lost their lives in the effort. Although the returning crusaders brought with them stories of faraway lands, they rarely came laden with treasures. Indeed, the Crusades were notoriously bad for plunder. Many crusaders returned financially destitute.

The direct impetus behind the Crusades was the Islamic conquests of Christian territories. By the late eleventh century, Muslim armies had conquered the Christian lands of Syria, Palestine, Egypt, North Africa, and Spain. When Turkish warriors conquered Christian Asia Minor in the wake of the Battle of

Manzikert (1077), the Byzantine emperor in Constantinople appealed to the pope for assistance. At the Council of Piacenza (1095), Byzantine ambassadors begged Pope Urban II to do something to help the Christians of the East. The following year at the Council of Clermont, Urban made an impassioned appeal to the fighting men of Europe. He urged them to cease their wars and quarrels and to band together against the common enemy. They should make a firm commitment to restore not only Asia Minor but even the Holy Land to Christian control. Urban defined this military expedition as a penitential sacrifice and thereby offered an indulgence for those who took the cross with right intention. The response across Europe was tremendous. Thousands began making preparations to depart.

The First Crusade became the standard for all subsequent Crusades. Thousands of crusaders marched across eastern Europe and rendezvoused with the Byzantine emperor at Constantinople. From there they went on to capture Nicaea, which had lately been used by the Turkish rulers as their capital. Crossing Anatolia, the First Crusade then laid siege to Antioch, which fell on June 3, 1098. This was a great victory for the crusaders, for it not only gave them a firm foothold in the region, but also represented the recovery of one of the five ancient patriarchates of Christianity. Early in 1099 the Crusade again marched forward, this time south to the walls of Jerusalem. Against great odds, the crusaders captured the Holy City on July 15, 1099.

With the reconquest of Jerusalem complete, most of the crusaders returned home. Only a few remained in the Holy Land to secure and expand the conquests. One of the Crusade leaders, Godfrey of Bouillon, was named the ruler of the new Kingdom of Jerusalem, which would play a role in the region for almost two centuries. During the first few decades after the conquest, crusaders and settlers continued to arrive in the Holy Land, allowing the leaders to expand their holdings. By 1140 virtually the entire coast of Syria and Palestine was in Christian hands. A unique culture was born in the crusader states, one that intermingled the ways of western Christendom with those of the Muslim Middle East.

The crusader states prospered only when the Muslim powers were divided against each other. That division began to subside under charismatic leaders who preached jihad against the Christians. One such leader, Zengi, the ruler of Mosul, led a successful campaign against the Christians in the north, capturing the county of Edessa in November 1144. The response in Europe was the calling of another major Crusade expedition, which historians refer to as the Second Crusade (1146–1148). It was led by two of the most powerful kings in Europe: Conrad III of Germany and Louis VII of France. Although larger and better organized than the First Crusade, the Second Crusade was faced with an enemy that was well accustomed to the ways of western warfare. Most of the crusaders were killed by the Turks of Asia Minor. Those who reached Jerusalem made an abortive attack on Damascus and then returned home. The Crusade was an utter failure.

Matters went from bad to worse for the crusader states. The Kurdish ruler, Saladin, unified the Muslims of the region in a jihad to remove the Christian kingdom. At the Battle of Hattin in 1187 he destroyed the armies of the crusaders and subsequently conquered Jerusalem and much of its kingdom. Europeans responded with the Third Crusade (1189–1192), led by three kings: Frederick I Barbarossa of Germany, Philip II Augustus of France, and Richard I the Lionheart of England. Frederick, who was a veteran of the Second Crusade four decades earlier, died on the journey. Philip and Richard oversaw the reconquest of Acre in July 1191, after which Philip returned to France to prey on Richard's lands. Richard restored Christian control of the coast, but was unable to recapture Jerusalem. Faced with crisis at home, Richard made a truce with Saladin and left the Holy Land. With the failure of the Third Crusade, Jerusalem would never again be securely under Christian control.

The plight of Jerusalem continued to weigh heavily on the hearts of European Christians. New and better-funded expeditions were launched in the thirteenth century, but these too failed. The new strategy was to focus on Egypt, which was the base of Muslim power in the region. The Fourth Crusade (1201–1204) was ensnared by Byzantine political intrigue, which detoured it to Constantinople, where it stalled. In 1204 the crusaders conquered Constantinople, the greatest Christian city in the world, and founded a new Latin state in Greece. This only further estranged the two halves of Christendom. The Fifth Crusade (1218–1221) landed in Egypt and captured Damietta, but was defeated on its way to Cairo. King Louis IX of France led two Crusades, one to Egypt (1248–1251) and one to Tunis (1270). Both failed and the second took his life.

Muslim power continued to grow in the region until, in 1291, the last remnants of the crusader states were toppled. This did not, however, signal the end of the Crusades. As Muslim empires continued to press in toward Europe and then penetrate it, Crusades became desperate attempts to stop or slow that progress. By the fifteenth century Crusades were matters of survival—not for faraway kingdoms, but for western Christendom itself.

[*See also* Constantinople.]

BIBLIOGRAPHY

Hillenbrand, Carole. *The Crusades: Islamic Perspectives*. Edinburgh: University of Edinburgh Press, 1999.

Madden, Thomas F. *The New Concise History of the Crusades*. Lanham, Md.: Rowman and Littlefield, 2005.

Riley-Smith, Jonathan. *The Crusades: A History*. 2nd ed. New Haven, Conn.: Yale University Press, 2005.

Riley-Smith, Jonathan. *What Were the Crusades?* 3rd ed. San Francisco: Ignatius Press, 2002.

THOMAS F. MADDEN

Curtis, Winifred Mary

Curtis, Winifred Mary (1905–2006), British botanist who explored and collected Tasmania's flora. Winifred Mary Curtis, botanist, teacher, author, and explorer, was born in London, England, on June 15, 1905, the only child of the civil servant Herbert John Curtis. Educated at University College and Cambridge Teachers College, she graduated with a bachelor of science degree in 1927 and worked as a teacher before migrating to Tasmania with her parents in 1939. Miss Curtis joined the biology department of the University of Tasmania, becoming only the second woman appointed to the university's staff. In 1945 she was a foundation staff member of the botany department, eventually rising to the position of reader in 1956, with several periods as acting head of the department.

Curtis trekked widely across Tasmania exploring the fauna and collecting fresh specimen plants from remote and inaccessible places for her teaching and writing work. Her explorations resulted in many scientific papers. In 1944 she published the first account of polyploidy in Australian flora (*Pultenaea juniperina*), work that resulted in the award of a PhD at University College London five years later. The following year she began writing a text on Tasmanian flora as an aid to her teaching work. The first volume of *The Student's Flora of Tasmania* was published in 1956 and the last, volume 4b, in 1994. From 1967 to 1978 Dr. Curtis wrote concise descriptive and ecological notes to accompany the botanical drawings of Margaret Stones in the six-volume *The Endemic Flora of Tasmania*. Her extensive published works have defined Tasmanian flora.

On retirement in 1966, Dr. Curtis continued to take an active interest in the Tasmanian flora, and was instrumental in establishing the present Tasmanian Herbarium in 1977. She received many awards including Membership of the Order of Australia in 1977 and the ANZAAS Mueller Medal in 1995. Curtis died in Hobart, Tasmania, in 2006.

[*See also* Women Explorers.]

BIBLIOGRAPHY

Bonham, Pru. "Winifred Curtis AM DSc: A Woman of Our Time." *WISENET Journal* 42 (November 1996). Available at www.wisenet-australia.org.

DENIS SHEPHARD

Curzon, George Nathaniel

Curzon, George Nathaniel (1859–1925), British world traveler, statesman, and supporter of exploration. Satirized in rhyme as "a most superior person," Curzon was more a traveler and patron of exploration than an explorer himself. The first son of Baron Scarsdale, Curzon was born in the family mansion of Kedleston in Derbyshire, England. Educated at Eton and Oxford, he had a riding accident in 1874, which required him to wear a spine support for the rest of his life.

Elected to Parliament in 1880, Curzon specialized in foreign affairs and traveled widely, especially in Asia. In 1898 he was created Baron Curzon; he was proclaimed viceroy of India on January 6, 1899. In this capacity he was an extremely able administrator. The position also gave him great opportunities to sponsor geographical exploration through his founding of the Archaeological Survey of India. As a result, he was able to save the Taj Mahal from almost certain destruction, and through the survey's director, Sir John Marshall, excavated Greco-Buddhist sites at Taxila, now in Pakistan. Later, the survey would expand its activities to the Indus Valley and Central Asia. Curzon was a gold medallist of the Royal Geographical Society and, as its president, was largely responsible for the acquisition of its London headquarters.

Curzon married twice, both times to American heiresses. He had daughters with his first wife, but he deeply regretted having no son to carry on his titles. These included an earldom in 1911 and a marquisate in 1921. When asked by a confidant about his many achievements, Curzon is reputed to have replied that he wished to be remembered, particularly, for having given back to India its cultural heritage through founding the Archaeological Survey of India.

[*See also* Royal Geographical Society.]

BIBLIOGRAPHY
Curzon, George N. *Leaves from a Viceroy's Note-Book and Other Papers*. London: Macmillan, 1926.
Curzon, George N. "The Pamirs and the Source of the Oxus." *Geographical Journal* 8, no. 1 (July 1896): 15–54; no. 2 (August 1896): 97–119; no. 3 (September 1896): 239–260.
Curzon, George N. *Persia and the Persian Question*. London and New York: Longmans and Green, 1892. Reprint, New York: Barnes and Noble, 1966.
Mosley, Leonard. *Curzon: The End of an Epoch*. London: Longmans, 1960.

NORMAN J. W. THROWER

D

Dalrymple, Alexander (1737–1808), Scottish hydrographer. Alexander Dalrymple was born on July 24, 1737, at Newhailes, near Edinburgh, a younger son of Sir James Dalrymple. After his father's death in 1751, Alexander began a career with the East India Company. He was appointed as a writer for the company on November 1, 1752, and posted to Madras.

Dalrymple made three commercial reconnaissance voyages between 1759 and 1764 to the Philippines, Borneo, and Sulu. In 1762 he obtained for the company a grant of land at Balambangan, and he left Madras in 1763 to return to London to promote a trading settlement there. He was briefly deputy governor at Manila in April 1764, and he arrived in London in the summer of 1765.

Dalrymple continued research into the "counterpoise" theory of a great southern continent, publishing *An Historical Collection of the Several Voyages and Discoveries in the South Pacific Ocean* in 1769–1771. Summarizing his work in 1767 in *An Account of the Discoveries Made in the South Pacifick Ocean Previous to 1764*, he became the Royal Society's candidate to lead the transit of Venus expedition. After a misunderstanding between the Royal Society and the Admiralty in April 1768 over the command of the chosen ship, Dalrymple declined to take second place under a sea officer in the expedition, and James Cook was subsequently appointed both commander and Royal Society observer.

Between 1769 and 1774, Dalrymple published charts and navigational memoirs, chiefly from his 1760s voyages, and in March 1771 he was elected a fellow of the Royal Society. Dalrymple served again in Madras in 1775 and 1776, returning to London in 1777. Using a chronometer at sea had shown him the value of a coherent series of longitude observations for constructing accurate charts and for recommending the best tracks for different seasons. In April 1779 he was retained by the East India Company to examine the ships' journals in East India House and to publish charts, a responsibility he held until his death. He advocated chronometer log keeping with standard scales of wind and weather, in part derived from John Smeaton's calibration of windmill sails. Dalrymple later transmitted the wind scale to the young Francis Beaufort, who adopted it and by whose name it is now known.

Dalrymple proposed in 1779 a scheme of charts for the Indian Ocean, using chronometer longitudes, but the lack of suitable journals slowed progress. Instead, during the fifteen years to 1794, Dalrymple published almost six hundred plans, charts, and views and more than fifty "memoirs" as his *General Collection of Nautical Publications*. His reputation is based on these publications, whose spare style contrasted with the ornateness of commercial chart atlases.

A close friend of Sir Joseph Banks and a member of the Royal Society dining club, Dalrymple became a geographical adviser to science and government. In a group that included Philip Stephens, Evan Nepean, James Rennell, and William Marsden, Dalrymple provided topographical information for George Vancouver, advised the Colonial Office on supply routes to Nootka Sound after 1790, furnished sailing directions to Charles Cathcart's 1788 embassy to China, and advised on ports of refuge in South America for the southern whale fishery. Through his connection with Samuel Wegg of the Hudson's Bay Company, Dalrymple prepared a scheme combining the Hudson's Bay and East India companies to export otter pelts from northwest America to China.

Dalrymple was appointed hydrographer to the Admiralty on August 13, 1795; the post was manufactured for him, probably by Stephens, ostensibly to organize a growing collection of manuscript charts and plans, but primarily to give official status to Dalrymple's geographical and navigational advice. Dalrymple held the position in parallel with his East India Company responsibility. For five years, with Aaron Arrowsmith and John Walker as successive assistants, he sorted and listed charts for potential fleet use. In 1800 he introduced engravers and a printing press, and proof impressions from over 150 plates are known. Dalrymple established two chart series, from surveys by Murdoch Mackenzie and Graeme Spence, for the south coast of England from the Thames to the Lizard, later published as Admiralty charts.

Dalrymple cooperated with other hydrographers. For instance, he received into the Admiralty in 1795 the charts and journals of the d'Entrecasteaux expedition, brought to Saint Helena by Rossel when the expedition broke up in Batavia, and he employed Rossel, in exile, to compute the results of the voyage observations. Dalrymple encouraged James Horsburgh, later his successor as East India Company hydrographer, to publish charts, and in 1805 he gave Francis Beaufort a set of his East India Company publications.

The controversy that marred Dalrymple's last years, and that provoked his dismissal, arose both from changes in the Admiralty's purpose for the Hydrographic Office and from his own intransigence. He had purchased and arranged in May 1807 "a compleat set of all Charts published in England," but demurred at evaluating them because he was unfamiliar with many of the coasts they covered. He suggested an advisory committee of naval officers, and Home Popham, E. H. Columbine, and Thomas Hurd duly began work in November 1807. This chart committee proposed closer supervision of Dalrymple's work, particularly the prioritization of charts for engraving.

The issue chosen to ease Dalrymple into retirement was that of the security copies he had made in 1795 of d'Entrecasteaux's charts. Treating these as confidential until their contents should be published in France, Dalrymple persistently withheld them from the chart committee, and he was dismissed by the Admiralty on May 28, 1808. Dalrymple died three weeks later, on June 19, 1808, at the age of seventy-one, probably of a heart attack induced by his fierce reaction to dismissal. The Hydrographic Office was immediately reconstituted, also as a chart supply office, under Thomas Hurd as Dalrymple's successor.

Dalrymple's collection of geographical works, atlases, charts, and maps went to form the core of the Admiralty library and of the Hydrographic Office collections. Many of his copper plates were bought, reputedly as scrap metal, and reissued by Hurd as Admiralty charts. Dalrymple's intellectual rigor, channeled into the compilation of charts and sailing directions for the safety of mariners, continues to characterize the Admiralty chart of today.

[*See also* Hydrographic Office, British; Longitude; Venus, Transit of; *and biographical entries on figures mentioned in this article*.]

BIBLIOGRAPHY

Cook, Andrew S. "Alexander Dalrymple (1737–1808), Hydrographer to the East India Company and to the Admiralty, as Publisher." PhD diss., University of St. Andrews, 1992.

Fry, Howard T. *Alexander Dalrymple (1737–1808) and the Expansion of British Trade*. London: Frank Cass, 1970.

ANDREW COOK

Dampier, William

Dampier, William (1650–1715), English buccaneer, naturalist, author, and explorer. William Dampier was born in East Coker, Somerset, son of a tenant farmer. At an early age he was apprenticed to a seaman in Weymouth. From the time of his first long sea voyage aboard the East Indiaman *John and Martha* (1671–1672) he began to collect information about the prevailing winds. He saw service in the Royal Navy in the *Royal Prince* during the third Anglo-Dutch War, after which he had a series of short-lived engagements in merchantmen. He returned to England briefly in 1678.

First Pacific Voyage. By 1679, Dampier was in Jamaica, where he joined a trading vessel bound for the Mosquito Coast. Shortly afterward he consorted with the buccaneers in the assault on Porto Bello, remaining with them for the attempted assault on Panama in April 1680. After failing to secure the city, the buccaneers hijacked vessels in the bay and burst loose into the Pacific, scouring the coast for prizes. In April 1681, Dampier and a party that included the surgeon and author Lionel Wafer abandoned the expedition to return overland to the Atlantic. On the coast he joined a force of French and English adventurers raiding Costa Rica. He sailed to Virginia in July 1682.

Second Pacific Voyage. In August 1683, Dampier joined another expedition into the Pacific, visiting the Galápagos in the first English ship to put in at the islands. He then embarked on a voyage across the Pacific in the *Cygnet*, arriving in Guam on May 20, 1686, after a voyage of more than six thousand miles on short rations. Throughout 1687 the *Cygnet* cruised for seven months in the North China Sea, threading her way south through the Philippines and the Dutch East Indies and thence toward Timor.

When the *Cygnet* anchored in King Sound on the west coast of New Holland (Australia) on January 5, 1688, Dampier was ignorant of Abel Tasman's voyages of 1642–1644. He could not decide whether or not New Holland formed part of *Terra Australis Incognita*. The *Cygnet* remained in the vicinity for at least a month, the longest visit by Europeans on the

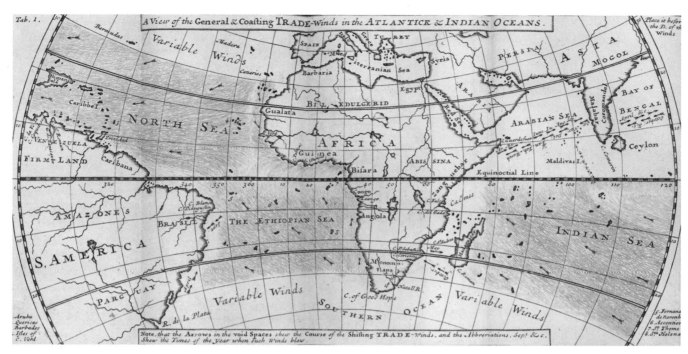

Map of Ocean Currents. From volume II of his Dampier's *A New Voyage round the World* (3 vols., London, 1697). Dampier was best known as a privateer with a great gift for navigation. In his many and perilous voyages, he seems always to have made and kept careful notes of natural phenomena; this allowed him to make remarkable thematic maps like this one. COURTESY THE NEWBERRY LIBRARY, CHICAGO

Australian mainland to date. From Australia Dampier sailed through the Indian Ocean to the Nicobar Islands, where he left the ship. He then continued on to Sumatra and Achin in an outrigger canoe. He spent the next eighteen months exploring Malacca, Tonkin, Madras, and Sumatra before returning to England on September 16, 1691. On his arrival he had completed the first English circumnavigation since Thomas Cavendish (1588); it had taken him thirteen years.

Dampier had with him a tattooed Filipino, Prince Giolo, whom he exhibited as a curiosity. In August 1693, after Giolo's death from smallpox, Dampier shipped aboard the *Dove*, one of four ships assigned to undertake a trading voyage to the Caribbean. He spent a protracted period with this flotilla in Coruña on Spain's Atlantic coast. During this a time a mutiny broke out aboard one of the ships, which began the career of the notorious pirate Henry Every, alias John Avery (c. 1653–c. 1727). Dampier was not directly involved, and he remained in Every's employment until 1695. Dampier may have spent some of this time preparing materials that would eventually form the basis of *A New Voyage round the World*, published in 1697. On his return to England he gave advice to the Council of Trade and Plantations on several occasions. He also provided information to the directors of the Darien Company in planning the establishment of a trading settlement on Panama's Atlantic coast.

Third Pacific Voyage. Dampier was given command of HMS *Roebuck* with a commission to undertake a voyage of discovery into the Pacific. He was to sail for New Holland and New Guinea before shaping a course southward to investigate new lands. If possible, Dampier would circumnavigate *Terra Australis Incognita*, which he now assumed to lie eastward of New Holland. This was one of the first voyages mounted by the Royal Navy with the express purpose of gathering scientific information. *Roebuck* arrived on the northwest coast of Australia in August 1699, and after careful survey of the area around 25°20′ S, 113°30′ E, Dampier christened it Shark Bay, the only name he bestowed upon mainland Australia. Afterward he departed in the direction of New Guinea, hoping to locate the eastern coast of the mysterious Southern Continent.

The *Roebuck*'s worm-ridden hull forced Dampier to curtail his mission. She sank in February 1701 at

Ascension Island. The crew returned home aboard several vessels belonging to the East India Company. In September, Dampier was court-martialed for the loss of the *Roebuck*, and he was tried again in June 1702 for assault on a subordinate officer. The voyage had been a mixed affair, but he had made new geographical and botanical discoveries, gathered plant specimens that survived the loss of the *Roebuck*, and managed to assemble materials for a new publication, *A Voyage to New Holland*, which appeared in two volumes (1703 and 1709). Any setbacks were only temporary, and in April 1703 he was introduced to Queen Anne by her husband, Prince George of Denmark.

Fourth Pacific Voyage. In September 1703, Dampier sailed for the Pacific again. He was appointed commodore of a privateering expedition. He commanded the *St. George*, whose consort, the *Cinque-Ports*, carried Alexander Selkirk as master or mate. Dampier kept no surviving record of this voyage, but according to William Funnell, mate in the *St. George*, Dampier spent most of the voyage raiding coastal towns and looting small prizes. Eventually the two ships parted company. Dampier remained in the South Seas and bungled an ambush on the Manila galleon in September 1704, while the *Cinque-Ports* set a course for the Strait of Magellan. On her way south, Selkirk was landed at Juan Fernández at his own insistence. His conviction that the *Cinque-Ports* was unseaworthy was borne out when she sank shortly afterward. Dampier arrived in England in 1707 after a period of imprisonment in Batavia on suspicion of piracy. Again he was embarrassed by subordinates who charged him with malfeasance. William Funnell, author of *A Voyage round the World* (1707), and John Welbe, author of *An Answer to Captain Dampier's 'Vindication'* (1707), gave evidence of Dampier's inadequacies as a naval commander.

Fifth Pacific Voyage. In 1708, Dampier was recruited to serve as pilot in the privateering expedition into the Pacific commanded by the Bristol merchant Woodes Rogers. Two ships, the *Duke* and the *Duchess*, were to pursue the Manila galleon, a prize that had evaded Dampier for three decades. Expectations were fueled by dazzling accounts of the huge profits reaped by French adventurers in America courtesy of Spain's failing grip on the New World. Rogers sailed with letters of marque that licensed him to wage war against both France and Spain.

Dampier was by now regarded as the last word on South Sea navigation, although his performance throughout the voyage failed to impress Rogers. After rounding the Horn in January 1709 both vessels put in at Juan Fernández, where Selkirk was recovered after four years' isolation. An attack on Guayaquil on April 24 yielded little success, but by December both vessels were poised on the coast of southern California ready to pounce on the galleon. On December 21, Rogers took the smaller of the two vessels making the run from Manila to Acapulco. On Christmas Day he fought an unsuccessful action with the larger vessel before stretching away westward for the long voyage home. The two ships arrived in London in October 1711. Dampier stepped ashore for the last time, having circumnavigated the globe a third time. He retired to the parish of Saint Stephen's, Coleman Street, London, where he died in 1715. He left debts of more than £677.

Dampier's Significance. Dampier's published writings influenced the development of natural philosophy and navigation over a period of two hundred years. *A New Voyage round the World* is the product of a complex editorial process probably undertaken by Sir Hans Sloane, secretary and later president of the Royal Society. Various stages of composition tended toward the enhancement of materials that interested the New Scientists. A by-product of this process was the transformation of Dampier himself from buccaneer to botanist, an image stabilized in his portrait by Thomas Murray (c. 1697), artist to the Royal Society. A circumspect Dampier is shown cradling his recently published book. The importance of *A New Voyage* in formulating scientific knowledge can hardly be overstated. Alexander von Humboldt and Charles Darwin both acknowledged their admiration for Dampier's volume. The supplement to it, published in 1699, included "A discourse of winds, storms, seasons, tides, and currents in the torrid zone," commended by James Cook, Richard Howe, and Horatio Nelson, that was of such lasting importance that it continued to be used in the compilation of *Admiralty Sailing Directions* well into the twentieth century.

The influence of *A Voyage to New Holland* bears chiefly on Britain's expansion as a worldwide colonial power. Dampier's image of New Britain as territory able to "afford as rich Commodities as any in the World" offset the forbidding impression of the west coast of New Holland, and drove forward exploration of *Terra Australis Incognita* in defiance of rational considerations. In the mid-eighteenth century, Dampier's encomium prompted John Campbell to affirm that New Britain was a "country, little, if at all, inferior to the Dutch Spice Islands" (*Navigantium atque itinerantium biblioteca*, 1744–1748). The conjunction of *New Voyage* and *Voyage to New Holland* renders the western shoreline of Australia as real, even if Dampier's perception of New Holland and *Terra Australis Incognita* sometimes resembles an intermittent double vision, in which they are sometimes distinct, sometimes blurred as one. In April 1770, when James Cook and Joseph Banks strained for their first glimpse of Aborigines on Australia's southeast coast, they had Dampier's book to hand.

Dampier's likely influence on the history of imaginative literature awaits proper study. What is certain, however, is that the *New Voyage* precipitated the phenomenal popularity of voyages and travels in the early eighteenth century. It was rightly considered to be the first of its kind, serving as a model of good practice for the flood of authentic voyage narratives that followed it.

[*See also* Buccaneers; Exploration Texts; Manila-Acapulco Trade; *and Terra Australis Incognita*.]

BIBLIOGRAPHY
Dampier, William. *A New Voyage round the World.* Edited by Sir Albert Gray. New York: Dover, 1968.
Dampier, William. *A Voyage to New Holland, &c. in the Year 1699.* Edited by James Spenser. Gloucester, U.K.: Alan Sutton, 1981.
Deacon, Margaret. *Scientists and the Sea, 1650–1900: A Study of Marine Science.* 2nd ed. Aldershot, U.K.: Ashgate, 1997.
Edwards, Philip. *The Story of the Voyage: Sea-Narratives in Eighteenth-Century England.* Cambridge, U.K.: Cambridge University Press, 1994.
Esquemeling, John. *The Buccaneers of America.* Edited by Henry Powell. London: Swan Sonnenschein, 1893. Reprint. Mineola, N.Y.: Dover, 2000.
Preston, Diana, and Michael Preston. *A Pirate of Exquisite Mind: The Life of William Dampier, Explorer, Naturalist, and Buccaneer.* London: Doubleday, 2004.
Williams, Glyndwr. *The Great South Sea: English Voyages and Encounters 1570–1750.* New Haven, Conn.: Yale University Press, 1997.
Williams, Glyndwr, and Alan Frost, eds. *Terra Australis to Australia.* Melbourne, Australia: Oxford University Press, 1988.

JAMES KELLY

Darwin, Charles

Darwin, Charles (1809–1882), British naturalist best known for his formulation of the theory of evolution. Charles Robert Darwin was born on February 12, 1809, in Shrewsbury, Shropshire, England, to Robert and Susannah Darwin. As a child, Darwin performed poorly in school. As a young man, he spent two years as a medical student before seeking a career in the clergy. While studying theology at Cambridge University, Darwin took up insect collecting and spent his free time attending natural history lectures. The naturalist community received him well, and their acceptance led to an invitation, just after his graduation from Cambridge, for him to serve as the naturalist aboard a five-year research and exploration expedition on the HMS *Beagle*.

The *Beagle* set sail from England on December 27, 1831, for a circumnavigation of the globe that included research and surveying stops in South America, several Pacific islands, and South Africa. Darwin collected and analyzed extensive zoological samples from each of those locations. However, it is the stop in the Galápagos Islands that Darwin and the *Beagle* are best known for today. When the *Beagle* arrived at the islands in 1832, the Galápagos archipelago presented a largely unexplored environment with a diverse array of creatures for Darwin to study.

Among the animals that Darwin documented in the Galápagos, and the ones that he found the most curious, were the finches. Each species of these birds possessed beaks uniquely suited to exploiting the

1. Geospiza magnirostris.
3. Geospiza parvula.

2. Geospiza fortis.
4. Certhidea olivacea.

FINCHES FROM GALAPAGOS ARCHIPELAGO.

Galápagos Finches. From Darwin's journal. Darwin's observation of the varied forms of these finches' beaks was one of the elements leading to his concept of natural selection. It would seem that the beaks of the Galápagos finches continue to evolve in response to environmental change. ROYAL GEOGRAPHICAL SOCIETY, LONDON

ecological niche that they inhabited. Darwin hypothesized that the variation in beak shape and size on these finches did not represent multiple migrations of various species to the isolated archipelago, but rather that each of these different species of finches had derived, in the islands, from a single migration of one species that had then changed over time.

The expedition returned to England on October 2, 1836. Darwin produced a lifetime of writings based on his observations during the *Beagle* expedition. Foremost among these writings was one that found its genesis in Darwin's observations of how the various finches in the Galápagos seemed to adapt to their environment. The *Origin of Species* (1859) introduced Darwin's theory of natural selection. Natural selection refers to the concept that, over time, a species retains those traits advantageous to survival and loses those traits that are detrimental. Although the concept of evolution—change in a species over time—was not new, Darwin's theory of natural selection provided the mechanism by which the concept

of evolution could work, and his journey on the *Beagle* provided him with ample evidence to support this theory. Thus, the voyage of the *Beagle* was the catalyst behind the now widely accepted theories of evolution that were succinctly described and scientifically supported by the work of a theology graduate.

Charles Darwin lived long enough both to see his theories become accepted by the mainstream scientific community and also to see them stir up unnecessary controversy among those who mistakenly perceive Darwin's scientific theories of evolution as an attack on the Judeo-Christian belief in divine creation. Darwin thus became one of the most influential writers of the nineteenth century, as well as one of the most controversial figures in Western history. He died on April 19, 1882, in the village of Downe, England, and his remains were interred in Westminster Abbey.

[*See also* Galton, Francis; Travel Literature, European; *and* Wallace, Alfred Russel.]

"One of Madame Alexandra David-Neel's Hermitages." From David-Neel's *My Journey to Lhasa* (New York, 1927). This photograph, probably taken by Yongden, surely shows David-Neel sitting outside one of her hermitages in the winter of 1914–1915. The role of the little tent seems rather enigmatic. Courtesy The Newberry Library, Chicago

BIBLIOGRAPHY

Bates, Marston, and Philip S. Humphrey, eds. *The Darwin Reader*. New York: Scribners, 1956.

RYAN M. SEIDEMANN

David-Neel, Alexandra

David-Neel, Alexandra (1868–1969), first European woman to enter Lhasa. Alexandra David-Neel was born just outside of Paris on October 24, 1868. She had an unhappy childhood, believing that her parents, Louis, a journalist, and Alexandrine Borghmans David, did not want her. Her relationship with her mother was especially difficult, and Alexandra ran away from home several times before she was sixteen. As a child, she was an avid reader and during her teen years spent many hours in the reading room of the Musée Guimet, a museum of Far Eastern antiquities.

She supported herself during her twenties as an opera singer and a journalist, while also studying Buddhism and theosophy at the Sorbonne. On one of her opera tours, she met Philippe-François Neel,

---

Travels in Lhasa

David-Neel, so poorly suited to the requirements of conventional life, proved to be a most extraordinary explorer of remote places. She also had a distinctive and effective way of describing her adventures, which were, she felt, surely protected by a maternal providence.

We [David-Neel and her Tibetan friend Aphur Yongden] were now in Lhasa territory, but still far from the city itself. Yongden once more suppressed my desire to rejoice, even in a whisper. What could he still fear? Had we not reached our goal? And now, nature itself gave us a token of her maternal complicity . . . No sooner had we landed [after crossing a river] than the air, till then so calm, became agitated. All of a sudden a furious storm arose, lifting clouds of dust high into the sky. I have seen the simoon in the Sahara, but was it worse than this? No doubt it was. Yet that terrible, dry lashing rain of dust gave me once more the impression of being in the great desert. Indistinct forms passed us, men bent in two, hiding their faces in the laps of their dresses, or whatever piece of cloth they might happen to have with them.

—Alexandra David-Neel, *My Journey to Lhasa* (London, 1927)

---

and the two were married in 1904. They separated, however, after just five days of marriage. The two never divorced, and he assisted her in her future travels with monetary support and by handling her business interests.

In 1910 the French Ministry of Education sent David-Neel to do research in India and Burma. After she arrived, David-Neel interviewed the exiled Dalai Lama, visited the prince of Sikkim, and became fascinated with Tibetan Buddhism. In Sikkim she was given a young lama, Yongden, who served as her companion for the rest of his life. What was to have been a brief assignment ended up lasting fifteen years, encompassing extraordinary experiences and culminating in a journey to the forbidden Tibetan city of Lhasa.

David-Neel spent the winter of 1914–1915 in Sikkim ensconced in a cave at about 13,000 feet (about 3,960 meters) elevation, meditating and studying the Tibetan religion and language with a hermit lama. Thereafter, she and Yongden spent several years journeying through Burma, Bhutan, Japan, Korea, and China, studying in monasteries along the way.

Finally, at the age of fifty-five, she set her sights on reaching Lhasa, motivated by several factors. For one, she was drawn to it simply because it was the heart of Tibetan Buddhism. Also, she looked forward to the celebrity of being the first white woman to reach Lhasa. And she was driven by sheer rebelliousness—because she had been forbidden to enter Tibet and ordered deported for an earlier attempt. Traveling in the disguise of a Tibetan peasant on a pilgrimage to Lhasa with her son, she darkened her skin with charcoal and cocoa and lengthened her hair with yak hair braids. Thanks to her years of studying the Tibetan language and local dialects, she could even converse with the locals without detection. She and Yongden journeyed on foot for almost five months, challenged by some of the planet's most rugged terrain and harshest weather, crossing passes that ranged in elevation from 12,000 feet (3,660 meters) to about 19,000 feet (about 5,790 meters). Finally they arrived in Lhasa, just in time for the Tibetan New Year celebrations in February 1924. They remained there for two months, recovering from the physical strains of their arduous journey.

Upon her return to the West, David-Neel settled in Digne, France, with Yongden, whom she adopted as a son. Now a recognized scholar of Tibet and Tibetan Buddhism, she wrote prolifically about her travels and, in a more scholarly vein, about the philosophy and practice of Tibetan Buddhism and Oriental mysticism. At the age of sixty-nine, she went back to China for another eight years of writing and studying.

David-Neel returned again to France, where she died on September 8, 1969, at the age of one hundred. She was much honored for her travel exploits as well as for her scholarship and teaching. She was awarded the gold medal of the Société de Géographie (Geographical Society of Paris) and was named Premier Commandeur of the Légion d'honneur.

[*See also* Women Explorers.]

BIBLIOGRAPHY

David-Neel, Alexandra. *My Journey to Lhasa: The Personal Story of the Only White Woman Who Succeeded in Entering the Forbidden City.* New York and London: Harper, 1927.

Miller, Luree. *On Top of the World: Five Women Explorers in Tibet.* London and New York: Paddington, 1976. See pp. 131–197.

PATRICIA GILMARTIN

Davis, John (c. 1550–1605), Elizabethan English navigator. John Davis was born and brought up on a small freehold farm in the parish of Stoke Gabriel in Devon, the county that was a breeding ground of many fine Elizabethan seamen. During his lifetime he established a reputation in both the practice and the art of navigation. He wrote treatises on the subject, and invented the back staff or Davis quadrant for taking observations of the sun. Among his neighbors in Devon were Humphrey and Adrian Gilbert and Walter Ralegh, all of them much concerned with overseas exploration; in London, Davis became acquainted with the cosmographer Dr. John Dee. The Gilberts and Dee had been closely associated with the Arctic voyages of Martin Frobisher in search of the Northwest Passage, and in the 1580s Adrian Gilbert and Dee encouraged Davis to take up the quest. The result was three voyages that added much to Europe's knowledge of northern waters and that put Davis's own name on the map in the shape of Davis Strait, a major entry to the icebound waterways of the eastern Arctic. All three voyages were private ventures, financed by London and West Country merchants.

On his first Arctic voyage in 1585, Davis landed on both the east and west coasts of Greenland, and he made contact with the local Inuit. He then, in relatively ice-free conditions, crossed the southern part

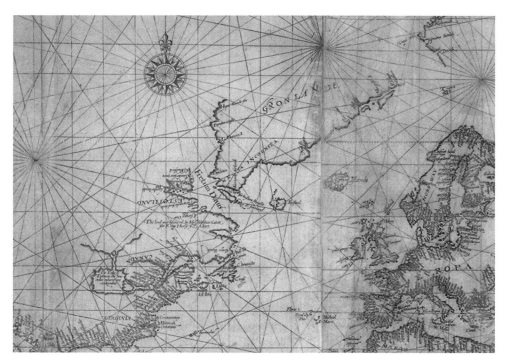

Davis Strait. Detail from the world map (probably by Edward Wright) published in *The Principal Navigations, Voyages, Traffiques and Discoveries of the English Nation* (London, 1598). Here Hakluyt has taken care to record ("Fretum Davis") the strait named after Davis, which he explored in three voyages between 1585 and 1587 without finding the northwest passage that he felt sure must exist. COURTESY THE NEWBERRY LIBRARY, CHICAGO

of Davis Strait and entered Cumberland Sound on the east coast of Baffin Island. Davis returned to England claiming that he was on the verge of finding the Northwest Passage, but on a follow-up voyage in 1586 he was surprised to find pack ice in Davis Strait. It was a warning sign of the unpredictable seasonal variation of ice formations in Arctic waters. Again during this follow-up voyage there was contact with the local inhabitants, and, despite some skirmishes, Davis was able to compile a short vocabulary of forty Inuit words. The ice that "pestered" the ships prevented Davis from sailing westward as he had hoped, but on his third voyage in 1587 he planned to follow Davis Strait north "for the discoverie of a passage to the Isles of the Molucca or the coast of China." By the end of June he reached 73° N before crossing Baffin Bay (as this great stretch of water would later be called) and coasting back southward along its western shores. He entered Cumberland Sound once more, and this time followed it to its end. Disappointed, Davis headed out of the inlet and kept south, keeping clear of "a very great gulfe" where the waters whirled and roared. It was Hudson Strait, the other major entry point to the eastern Arctic. Despite Davis's optimism that his finding of open sea in far northern latitudes meant that "the passage is most probable, the execution easie," this was the last of his Arctic voyages. Cargoes of cod and sealskins had not covered the cost of the three expeditions, and war with Spain diverted ships and resources elsewhere.

It was in this context that Davis made his last attempt to find the passage, this time from the Pacific side, when he joined Thomas Cavendish's South Seas plundering venture of 1591–1592. Once the expedition reached California, Davis intended to sail north to find the western entrance of the passage; but although he managed to struggle through the Strait of Magellan, appalling weather and the loss of one of his ships forced him back into the Atlantic. There, in August 1592, he came across previously unknown islands, later to be known as the Falkland Islands or the Malvinas.

Although his own charts have not survived, Davis's northern discoveries were shown on the world map published in Richard Hakluyt's *Principal Navigations of the English Nation* (1598–1600), which marked both "Fretum Dauis" (Davis Strait) and the "furious Overfale" at the entrance to Hudson Strait. It was an appropriate tribute to a skilled navigator and careful commander whose explorations represented a considerable step forward in Europe's knowledge of the eastern Arctic. In his book *The Worlds Hydrographical*

Description (1595), Davis continued to argue the case for a Northwest Passage; but more widely read was his practical treatise on navigation, *The Seamans Secrets* (1594), which went through several editions. Denied further northern voyages, Davis spent his final years as a pilot on Dutch and English ships in the Eastern Seas, where he was killed near Sumatra on December 27, 1605, in a fight with pirates.

[*See also* Arctic, *subentry on* Early Knowledge; Navigational Techniques; *and* Northwest Passage.]

BIBLIOGRAPHY
Markham, A. H., ed. *The Voyages and Works of John Davis the Navigator*. London: The Hakluyt Society, 1880.
Quinn, David Beers. "The Northwest Passage in Theory and Practice." In *A New World Disclosed. Vol. 1 of North American Exploration*, edited by John Logan Allen. Lincoln: University of Nebraska Press, 1997.
Savours, Ann. *The Search for the North West Passage*. See chap. 1. London: Chatham Publishing, 1999.

GLYNDWR WILLIAMS

Dead Reckoning. *See* **Longitude** *and* **Navigational Techniques.**

Debenham, Frank (1883–1965), Australian geologist and geographer. Debenham's father was a vicar and schoolmaster at Bowral, New South Wales, where Debenham was born. He graduated from Sydney University with two degrees, being selected not long afterward to join the British Antarctic (*Terra Nova*) expedition (1910–1913), led by Captain Robert Falcon Scott, as junior geologist. During two Antarctic summer seasons, Debenham accompanied a geological party under T. Griffith Taylor, another Australian, doing fieldwork among the Western Mountains of Victoria Land. One of the glaciers there was named after Debenham. Captain Scott wrote of Debenham as a "well-trained, steady worker, with a quiet meaning that carries conviction; he realizes the conception of thoroughness and conscientiousness." The experience Debenham gained in mapping gave him an interest in cartography and survey that influenced his later career.

During World War I, Debenham served in Salonika, reaching the rank of major. At Cambridge University after the war, he wrote up the geological results of the Antarctic expedition and became a member of Caius College and the Royal Geographical Society's lecturer in surveying and cartography. In 1920, Debenham established, with the help of Raymond Priestly and James Wordie, the Scott Polar Research Institute, of which he was director until his retirement in 1946. Debenham was also responsible for developing the Cambridge geography department, being appointed its first professor in 1931. Always interested in the young, he helped and encouraged them in their aspirations.

Debenham's Antarctic diaries were published in 1992, but he had earlier written *In the Antarctic: Stories of Scott's Last Expedition* (London: John Murray, 1952). The list of his publications in *The Quiet Land* includes the first English edition of the Antarctic circumnavigation by the Russian navigator Fabian Bellingshausen in 1819–1821 (London: Hakluyt Society, 1945); the results of his African travels in the late 1940s, especially *The Road to Ilala* (London: Longmans, 1955), a book about David Livingstone; and also Debenham's "atlas history of man's journeys into the unknown," entitled *Discovery and Exploration* (London: Paul Hamlyn, 1960). The text of this last book is well illustrated with pictures and maps. It also contains an appendix on ships and navigation, another consisting of short biographies of explorers with their routes, and a third showing the progress of exploration between 1700 and 1900. Debenham was awarded the Order of the British Empire (OBE), and he died in 1965 after receiving the rare distinction of being named an Honorary Fellow of the Royal Geographical Society.

[*See also* Antarctica *and* Scott, Robert Falcon.]

BIBLIOGRAPHY
Debenham, Frank. *Discovery and Exploration: An Atlas-History of Man's Journeys into the Unknown.* London: Paul Hamlyn, 1960.
Debenham, Frank. *In the Arctic: Tales Told at Tea Time.* Edited by Barbara Debenham. Banham, U.K.: Erskine, 1997.
Debenham, Frank. *The Quiet Land: The Antarctic Diaries of Frank Debenham.* Edited by June Debenham Back. Huntingdon, U.K.: Bluntisham, 1992.

ANN SAVOURS

De Brahm, William Gerard (1718–1799), German explorer of Florida. William Gerard De Brahm was the German-born surveyor general of the Southern District of North America who explored and mapped eastern Florida for the British from 1764 until 1771. Born into the lesser nobility in Koblenz on August 20, 1718, he followed a career as an engineer in the Bavarian army before emigrating to Georgia in 1751. De Brahm's talents as a surveyor and engineer were quickly recognized in both Georgia and South Carolina. In the spring of 1752 he was commissioned to design a new system of fortifications for hurricane-devastated Charleston. When the royal government of

Georgia was established he was named as one of the colony's two surveyors general of lands and in 1755 he served an interim term as South Carolina's surveyor general. In the same year he traveled deep into the Indian country to design and build Fort Loudoun in what is now eastern Tennessee. Upon his return to Georgia he undertook the improvement of that colony's fortifications. In 1757 his fortunes rose with the publication in England of his cartographic opus, the four-sheet "A Map of South Carolina and a Part of Georgia." It was an elegant and accurate map that brought De Brahm to the attention of Europe's leaders, then competing for the control of eastern North America.

De Brahm experienced his finest hour when, in 1764, he learned of his royal appointment to the newly created imperial office of surveyor general for the Southern District of North America, as well as that of surveyor of lands for the newly organized colony of East Florida. In the letter enclosing his commission he was instructed that his first objective should be a comprehensive geographical survey and mapping of eastern Florida from St. Augustine south to the area now occupied by greater Miami. When he arrived De Brahm found Florida to be a virtual tabula rasa; the Spanish had left neither maps nor longtime residents to act as informants to the English. For the next six years, under the most grueling of conditions, De Brahm and his assistants created a truly impressive corpus of original maps and reports to satisfy the needs of Britain's administrators as they strained to devise settlement schemes for the new royal colony. In the course of his coastal charting De Brahm became acquainted with the powerful Gulf Stream. On a voyage to England in 1771 he undertook the first scientific study of the awesome current and in 1772 published the first chart to show its course sweeping through the North Atlantic.

[*See also* Gulf Stream.]

BIBLIOGRAPHY
Bailyn, Bernard. *Voyagers to The West: A Passage in the Peopling of America on the Eve of the Revolution.* New York: Vintage, 1988.
Cumming, William P., and Louis De Vorsey. *The Southeast in Early Maps.* 3rd ed. Chapel Hill: University of North Carolina Press, 1998.
De Vorsey, Louis, ed. *The Atlantic Pilot.* Gainesville: University Presses of Florida, 1974. Facsimile reprint of the 1772 edition.
De Vorsey, Louis, ed. *De Brahm's Report of the General Survey in the Southern District of North America.* Columbia: University of South Carolina Press, 1971.

LOUIS DE VORSEY

Decken, Karl Klaus von der (1833–1865), German military officer, an accomplished naturalist, and explorer of East Africa. Decken, who was born in Kotzen, Brandenburg, on August 8, 1833, sought to explore the Sahara desert in 1855, after leaving the Hanoverian army, but illness cut short his enterprise. In 1860, he journeyed in the Lake Nyasa region. After many years of controversy over whether there could be permanent ice and snow on equatorial mountains, Baron von der Decken attempted in 1861 and 1862 to reach the summit of Mount Kilimanjaro—and he was the first European to make such an attempt. On the first try, he ascended to about 8,000 feet (2,440 meters), but aborted the climb because his guides deserted. In 1862, after surviving a brutal snowstorm, he climbed to almost 14,000 feet (4,270 meters); he took some measurements, and slightly overestimated the elevation of the mountain, deciding that it was more than 20,000 feet (6,096 meters). Even though he proved the existence of permanent ice and snow on Mount Kilimanjaro, some skeptical "armchair" geographers in Europe refused to accept his report. Nonetheless, in 1863 he was awarded the Founder's Medal by the Royal Geographical Society for his feat. Decken is also credited as being the first European to record a sighting of Mount Meru in present-day Tanzania. In 1865, after personally funding the construction of a river steamer, Decken penetrated 380 miles (612 kilometers) up the Jubba River, in present-day southern Somalia, where he was murdered on October 2, 1865, by local tribesmen at Bardera.

[*See also* Africa, *subentry on* Scientific Exploration.]

SANFORD H. BEDERMAN

Declination. *See* **Navigational Techniques**.

Dee, John (1527–1609), English scholar and court astrologer. John Dee was born in London on July 13, 1527, to Rowland Dee, a courtier of Henry VIII. John Dee has the infamous and deserved reputation as Elizabethan England's most prominent magus. He served as Queen Elizabeth's court astrologer and magician. It had fallen to Dee to calculate the date of Elizabeth's coronation, a date that had to be divinely accurate. Yet, this deserved reputation as a magician and astrologer, along with his pursuit of occult knowledge including the cabala, alchemy, and spirit or angelic conjuring, would implacably cast a nega-

tive, even diabolical, shadow on the reputation of John Dee, a reputation that would marginalize Dee for centuries.

However, John Dee was one of England's foremost scholars and intellects. In 1547, while in Louvain studying mathematics, Dee had also been studying geography and chorography under Gerard Mercator and Gemma Frisius. Upon his return from Louvain, Dee had brought to England geographical manuscripts as well as navigational instruments including a brass astrolabe and two globes constructed by Mercator. Dee corresponded regularly with Abraham Ortelius and Pedro Nunes. He had amassed one of England's largest private libraries of his day at his home in Mortlake. Dee's library contained seven copies of Ptolemy's *Geographia*, along with geographical and navigational authorities such as Arrian, Albert Krantz, Sebastian Münster, Giovanni Battista Ramusio, Strabo, and André Thevet. Dee had written over two thousand marginal notes concerning Strabo.

While Dee was an eminent scholar in these various academic fields, he was extremely concerned with their practical applications. No Elizabethan voyage of exploration began without a visit to Mortlake. All of the great Elizabethan explorers relied upon Dee's knowledge and wisdom both in geography and navigation. Martin Frobisher, Richard Chancellor, Arthur Pet, Charles Jackman, Humphrey Gilbert, and Sir Walter Ralegh all made regular and frequent visits to Dee's residence. Even high-ranking officials of Elizabeth's court paid Dee a visit, including Sir Francis Walsingham, the queen's principal secretary; William Cecil, Lord Burghley; and the queen herself. Dee had been the principal source of geographic information for the Muscovy Company and the search for the Northeast Passage.

Although Dee only published one work in his lifetime, *General and Rare Memorials pertaining to the Perfect Arte of Navigation* (1577), he was a prolific author on matters of geography, navigation, exploration, and British imperialism. Although almost all of his work was in manuscript form and much of that had been destroyed when his Mortlake home was ransacked by a mob of angry peasants in 1583, a tremendous amount of his works are still extant in the British Library and the Bodleian Library at Oxford.

[*See also* Mercator, Gerard; Nunes, Pedro; *and* Ortelius, Abraham.]

BIBLIOGRAPHY
Cormack, Lesley B. *Charting an Empire: Geography at the English Universities, 1580–1620.* Chicago: The University of Chicago Press, 1997.

French, Peter J. *John Dee: The World of an Elizabethan Magus.* New York: Dorset Press, 1972.

Sherman, William H. *John Dee: The Politics of Reading and Writing in the English Renaissance.* Amherst: University of Massachusetts Press, 1995.

Michael Downs

Del Cano, Juan Sebastián (c. 1476–1526),

Spanish navigator who completed the first circumnavigation of the globe. As the commander of the ship *Concepción*, Juan Sebastián Del Cano set out in 1519 on Magellan's infamous attempt of the first circumnavigation of the globe. The arduous journey took its toll on the crew and led to Del Cano's participation in a failed mutiny off Patagonia in the winter of 1520. He was among forty men sentenced to death, but this was a formality, and only two men were actually executed. Later in the voyage, after numerous misfortunes—including the death of Captain-General Magellan—Del Cano took command of the ship *Victoria* on or about September 27, 1521, and successfully piloted the ship and crew to the Spice Islands.

On December 21, 1521, the *Victoria* sailed from Tidore, laden with spices and carrying thirteen Malaysian natives. Del Cano set out on the Indian Ocean after passing Timor, completing a journey involving deprivation and agony equal to the transpacific voyage. The turn north along the West African coast was not without intrigue, as desperation drove Del Cano and his crew to land on the Cape Verde Islands. Del Cano hoped to fool the Portuguese into thinking that they had just crossed the Atlantic, but several men were detained. Finally, on September 6, 1522, Del Cano completed the final leg of the voyage that would confirm his name in history: the captain and a meager crew pulled into Seville, having completed the first circumnavigation of the globe. Del Cano joined García Jofre de Loaísa in a second circumnavigation as chief pilot in 1525. His second attempt proved to be his undoing, and he died in the Pacific.

[*See also* Expeditions, World Exploration, *subentry on* Spain, *and* Magellan, Ferdinand.]

BIBLIOGRAPHY
Spate, O. H. K. *The Spanish Lake.* Canberra: Australian National University Press, 1979.

Mark Wentley

Delisle, Guillaume (1675–1726), French

cartographer who studied astronomy with Jean-Dominique Cassini (1625–1712) and who collaborated with his father, Claude Delisle (1644–1720), a historian and geographer. Guillaume Delisle was elected to the Academy of Sciences in 1702 and became "premier géographe du roi" in 1718. He used longitudes and latitudes collected by the academy in his first world map, which was published in 1700 and represented "an almost new earth." Delisle was concerned with the improvement of the coastlines of the Gulf of Mexico and the exact location of the Mississippi's mouth, reached by Robert Cavelier de La Salle (1643–1687) in 1682. Noticing the difficulty in measuring longitudes, Delisle's father favored the use of old travel accounts made by Pánfilo de Narváez (c. 1460–1529), Alvar Núñez Cabeza de Vaca (1490?–1564?), and Hernando de Soto (1500–1542).

Delisle achieved two major maps of America: the 1702 manuscript map of the Mississippi, based on measurements taken by Pierre-Charles Lesueur (1672–1704); and the map of Mexico and Florida, published in 1703. Delisle still used de Soto's account, but also used a variety of others: the *Description des Indes occidentales* by Antonio de Herrera (1559–1625); the account by Fray Alonzo de Benavides (c. 1578–1635); information coming from the second voyage of Pierre Lemoyne d'Iberville (1661–1706) toward Louisiana; a manuscript map titled "Carte du Nouveau Mexique tirée des relations de Mr le comte de Peñalossa" (Don Diego de Peñalosa, 1621–1687, former governor of New Mexico); and a recent Spanish portolan chart. The 1703 map shows a large Florida, but in 1718 Delisle revived La Salle's Louisiana, covering the Mississippi and its tributaries for the new French Compagnie des Indes. On his maps, Delisle tried to indicate ways to the Pacific through the North American continent; he also believed in the existence of a "Western Sea," a large indentation on the Pacific coast, which he drew at 35–40° N, but only in manuscript documents so as to keep it secret. Delisle was succeeded by his son-in-law Philippe Buache (1700–1773).

[*See also* Buache, Philippe; La Salle, Cavelier de; Maps, Mapmaking, and Mapmakers; *and* Mer de l'Ouest and Rivière de l'Ouest.]

BIBLIOGRAPHY
Dawson, Nelson-Martin. *L'atelier Delisle: L'Amérique du Nord sur la table à dessin.* Sillery, Quebec: Septentrion, 2000.

Jackson, Jack. *Manuscript Maps concerning the Gulf Coast, Texas, and the Southwest (1519–1836).* Chicago: The Newberry Library, 1995.

Pelletier, Monique. "The Working-Method of the New Cartographers: The Gulf of Mexico and Spanish Sources, 1696–1718." *Terrae Incognitae* 34 (2002): 60–72.

Monique Pelletier
Translated from the French by David Buisseret

Denham, Dixon

Denham, Dixon (1786–1828), British explorer and member of Hugh Clapperton's central Africa expedition. Between 1821 and 1825, Major Dixon Denham crossed the Sahara from Tripoli to Bornu and explored the Lake Chad region before returning across the desert. Denham was born on January 1, 1786, and after education at the Merchant Taylors' School took up a military career, serving with some distinction in the latter stages of the Napoleonic Wars. He offered his services to the Colonial Office, having learned that an official expedition was planned in which Walter Oudney and Hugh Clapperton were to try to establish good relations with the Muslim rulers of the western Sudan. The party planned to reach there from the north and perhaps solve the problem of the course and termination of the Niger. Denham joined them.

Denham wrote the major account of the expedition. It described the trans-Saharan route from Tripoli and, more important, provided reliable information on the new reformed Islamic societies that had emerged in the western Sudan following the jihad of Uthman dan Fodio. Denham himself actually concentrated his attention on an opponent of the Fulani jihadists, Mohammed el-Kanemi of Bornu, with whom he seems to have established good relations. Denham's exploratory achievement was to reach Lake Chad on February 4, 1823. He made four subsequent excursions around its shores in 1823–1824, but he was unable to complete a circuit of the lake by reaching the eastern end. Denham did not, therefore, conclusively prove that there was no eastern outlet toward the Nile. Nor was he absolutely sure (although Oudney appears to have been sure) that the Niger did not enter the lake in the west. Consequently, the highly influential Sir John Barrow was able to maintain his Niger-Nile theory for a few more years yet.

It was unfortunate for Denham's later reputation that one of his Lake Chad excursions was made in the company of some Arabs from Tripoli and some Bornuese who were bent on capturing slaves. But the raid was repulsed, and Denham was wounded, captured, and stripped of his clothes, his watch, and his sextant. While his captors argued over their spoils, Denham escaped, showing great bravery and resourcefulness. His description of these adventures helped popularize his book but led subsequent commentators to condemn him for compromising Britain's anti–slave-trade position.

Denham's bravery in a bad cause is only one of the paradoxes about this man. Despite getting so far, he did not solve the Niger problem. Despite showing an ability to understand African Islam, to sympathize with African peasants and with African women, he treated his two colleagues, Clapperton and Oudney, deplorably. During the expedition he ignored or vilified them, and his account of it belittled or distorted their contributions. A modern commentator writes of Denham's "extreme malice" and dubs him "odious." In 1825, however, Denham was treated as a hero, was promoted, and was elected a Fellow of the Royal Society. In 1827, the colonial secretary appointed him to a new post in Sierra Leone, where he became deputy governor. He died there of malaria shortly afterward, on May 8, 1828. Whatever failings in character he had, Denham does deserve to be remembered as a major contributor to the process by which systematic exploration revealed the condition of the African interior.

[*See also* Barrow, John; Chad, Lake; Clapperton, Hugh; Niger River; Nile River; *and* Oudney, Walter.]

BIBLIOGRAPHY

Bovill, E. W. *Missions to the Niger*. 4 vols. Cambridge, U.K.: Cambridge University Press for the Hakluyt Society, 1964–1966.

Denham, Dixon. *Narrative of Travels and Discoveries in Northern and Central Africa in the Years 1822, 1823, and 1824*. 2nd ed. 2 vols. London: Murray, 1826. Reprint. London: Darf, 1985.

ROY BRIDGES

Denham, Henry

Denham, Henry (1800–1887), British surveyor of the southwest Pacific. Henry Mangles Denham was the son of Nathaniel Denham of Sherborne in the county of Dorset. Entering the Royal Navy in 1809 as a volunteer, he was employed during his early years on surveys in the English Channel and on the coasts of Ireland and Wales. In 1833 he successfully prevented the port of Liverpool from being silted up by marking the best channel into the port by buoys and light beacons, in recognition of which he was promoted commander. In 1845–1846 he was employed surveying the coast of Guinea and the mouth of the Niger River in the *Avon*. On his return to England he was promoted to captain on August 17, 1846. His next seagoing appointment was in command of the *Herald*, with orders to carry out surveys in the southwest Pacific, just one of many expeditions sent out to chart various parts of the world by Francis Beaufort, hydrographer of the navy, who did much to encourage scientific pursuits on board surveying ships.

Denham sailed from Plymouth on June 10, 1852. After stopping at Madeira and Rio de Janeiro, he stopped briefly at Tristan da Cunha, where he made the first detailed survey of the island. He next stopped at Cape Town, before setting off across the Indian Ocean, stopping at Saint Paul's Island, which was duly surveyed, and arriving in Sydney on February 18. 1853. From his base in Sydney, where he returned from time to time for provisions and refits, Denham carried out important surveys in the southwest Pacific to establish safe routes for shipping. In 1853 he surveyed Lord Howe Island, followed by visits to the Isle of Pines, off the southwest tip of New Caledonia, and Aneityum, in what is now Vanuatu. Between 1854 and 1857, Denham paid three visits to Fiji, where he had several meetings with the notorious chief Cakobau. He was present at Norfolk Island in 1856 for the settlement of the descendants of the *Bounty* mutineers from Pitcairn Island. In 1858 he carried out the first detailed survey of Shark Bay in Western Australia. Finally, between 1858 and 1860, he charted and fixed accurately the positions of numerous islands and dangers in the Coral Sea.

A significant aspect of Denham's voyage is the number of "scientists" appointed to the expedition. John McGillivray, who had made a name for himself on two previous voyages to the Pacific in the *Fly* and *Rattlesnake*, was appointed naturalist. Both Frederick Rayner, surgeon on board the *Herald*, and John Denis Macdonald, assistant surgeon on board the *Herald*'s consort *Torch*, had been instructed in natural history by Sir John Richardson at the Royal Naval Hospital, Haslar. The highly talented James Glen Wilson was appointed as the expedition's artist; his ethnographic drawings in the Pacific islands are particularly significant.

The expedition finally returned to England on May 20, 1861, almost nine years after its departure from Plymouth, thus ending what must surely be the longest surveying voyage on record. This was Denham's last seagoing appointment. In 1867 he was created a Knight Bachelor in recognition of his long and meritorious service in the *Herald*. He was promoted to rear admiral on March 5, 1864, and placed on the retired list two years later. He died in London on July 3, 1887, at the age of eighty-six, and was buried on July 7 in fashionable Kensal Green Cemetery.

[*See also* Beaufort, Francis.]

BIBLIOGRAPHY
David, Andrew. *The Voyage of HMS Herald to Australia and the South-west Pacific 1852–1861 under the Command of Captain Henry Mangles Denham*. Melbourne, Australia: Miegunyah Press, 1995.

ANDREW C. F. DAVID

Deshnev, Semen (c. 1608–after 1672), Russian explorer best known for being the first European to sail through the strait between Asia and North America. Born in about 1608, Deshnev in his early youth went to Siberia and became an official responsible for collecting the fur tax (*yasak*) from the native peoples. This was a dangerous occupation, one that could in effect slide into colonial warfare; during twenty years of service, Deshnev was thus seriously injured nine times. From 1638 onward he was engaged in a series of expeditions, and in 1647 he reached the strait between Asia and America; his letters describe the topography of the Bering Strait with such accuracy that it is possible to trace his course without difficulty in the modern landscape.

After 1649, Deshnev made no more expeditions, and did not himself understand the importance of his discovery. That some members of the Siberian administration did understand the importance of the discovery is shown by two manuscript maps, of 1667 and 1673, that show uninterrupted space between the Kolyma and Anadyr rivers. The world at large knew nothing of it, because Deshnev's report lay buried in the archives at Yakutsk, where it was found only in 1736 by the German historian Gerhard Friedrich Müller, serving in the Saint Petersburg Academy of Sciences. Müller published an account of Deshnev's expedition in Russian and German in Saint Petersburg in 1758, and in 1761 the account was translated into English. In 1898, to commemorate the 250th anniversary of Deshnev's voyage, the Imperial Russian Geographical Society proposed that the eastern cape of the Chukchi Peninsula be named Cape Deshnev, and this was done.

Until 1662, Deshnev worked on in Siberia, but in that year he was sent to Moscow with a shipment of booty: precious furs, walrus tusks, and so forth. He took this opportunity for a visit to the capital to petition for his salary, which he had not received for nineteen years; the tsar not only paid him, but also appointed him military commander of the Yakutsk region. He returned to Yatutsk to take up his duties, and the last we hear of him is in 1672, when he again accompanied a shipment of precious furs to Moscow.

[*See also* Expeditions, World Exploration, *subentry* on Russia, *and* Siberia.]

BIBLIOGRAPHY
Belov, M. I. *Podvig Semena Dezhneva* (Semen Dezhnev's Exploit). Moscow: Mysl, 1973.
Fisher, Raymond H., ed. *The Voyage of Semen Dezhnev in 1648: Bering's Precursor, with Selected Documents*. London: Hakluyt Society, 1981.

Müller, Gerhard Friedrich. *Voyages from Asia to America for Completing the Discoveries of the North West Coast of America, to Which Is Prefixed a Summary of the Voyages Made by the Russians on the Frozen Sea, in Search of a North East Passage, Serving as an Explanation of a Map of the Russian Discoveries, Published by the Academy of Sciences at Petersburg.* Translated by Thomas Jefferys. London: T. Jefferys, 1761.

Nikitin, N. I. *Zemleprokhodets Semen Dezhnev i ego vremya* (Trail Finder Semen Dezhnev and His Time). Moscow: ROSSPEN, 1999.

ALEXEY POSTNIKOV

Dias, Bartholomew

Dias, Bartholomew (c. 1450–1500), Portuguese navigator. Bartholomew Dias was a Portuguese seafarer who, during his famous voyage from 1487 to 1488, rounded the southern tip of Africa and crossed from the Atlantic to the Indian Ocean. On his return, Dias sighted the Cape of Good Hope. His voyage was part of the plan of King João II (r. 1481–1495) to find an ocean route to India, and was a follow-up to the voyages of Diogo Cão. Relatively little is known about Dias's life. Attempts at providing a biography are complicated by the fact that during the fifteenth and early sixteenth centuries there were a number of seafarers with the same name. Dias was later ennobled for his exploits and by 1494 was a squire in the royal household. Shortly thereafter, he was given a post with the Armazém da Guiné, which he held from 1494 to 1497.

In the 1487–1488 voyage Dias was *capitão-mor* of the three vessels. After sailing as far as the 22° S latitude reached by Diogo Cão, Dias continued down the southern African coast, swinging out to sea and going to 45° S before turning north and touching land near Mossel Bay, about 250 miles east of the Cape of Good Hope. He appears to have eventually reached the Great Fish River (which he called Rio do Infante) on the southeastern coast of Africa at 33°30' S. Several days later the expedition began its return, sighting the Cape of Good Hope for the first time. Dias returned to Portugal in December 1488 after a fifteen-month voyage. The results of this voyage were made known to the world by the German cartographer Henricus Martellus, who was living in Florence. Martellus's map was probably prepared in 1489 and engraved the following year. In 1500 Dias accompanied Pedro Álvares Cabral on the follow-up voyage to India after Vasco da Gama's return the previous year. But after spending time in Brazil in April and early May of that year, his ship sank in the South Atlantic when caught in a severe storm—one of four ships that went down with no survivors.

[*See also* Cabral, Pedro; Cão, Diogo; Expeditions, World Exploration, *subentry on* Portugal; *and* Gama, Vasco da.]

BIBLIOGRAPHY
Diffie, Bailey W., and George D. Winius. *Foundations of the Portuguese Empire, 1415–1580*. Minneapolis: University of Minnesota Press, 1977.

Peres, Damião. *História dos descobrimentos portugueses*. 3rd ed. Porto, Portugal: Vertentes, 1983.

FRANCIS A. DUTRA

Díaz del Castillo, Bernal

Díaz del Castillo, Bernal (1496–1584), Spanish explorer of the Americas. Bernal Díaz del Castillo was born in Medina del Campo, Spain, to a locally prominent hidalgo family. He left home at eighteen and joined Pedrarias Dávila's expedition to Panama as a soldier, and sailed for Darién in 1514. He went to Cuba that same year and, in 1517, joined Franciso Hernández de Córdoba's expedition that discovered Yucatán, when he landed and first encountered the high civilizations of Mesoamerica. After a series of clashes with the local Maya, in which Díaz del Castillo was wounded, Córdoba's expedition returned to Cuba. There, Díaz del Castillo joined Juan de Grijalva's expedition to return to Yucatán and left in 1518. They also clashed with the Maya, but explored farther than Córdoba and reached the Mexican gulf coast of Veracruz. There they encountered Aztecs for the first time before returning to Cuba. In 1519, Díaz del Castillo sailed with Hernán Cortés on a third expedition to Mexico and retraced the steps of Córdoba and Grijalva before Cortés struck an alliance with the local Totonacs and marched inland to conquer the Aztecs. Díaz del Castillo accompanied Cortés inland and for the next two years participated in the conquest of Mexico. Thereafter, he went on other journeys of exploration in Mesoamerica, including Cortés's trek to Honduras, before moving to Guatemala in 1541, where he spent the rest of his life as an *encomendero*, dying in Antigua in 1584.

Díaz del Castillo is especially noted for writing the most extensive and detailed account of the conquest by any of the participants. His work is also the most removed from the events chronicled, as he did not write his account until he had read the hero-worshiping 1552 version of López de Gómara, Cortés's secretary and chaplain, who had never gone to the New World and relied largely on Cortés's own version. Angry over the aggrandizement of Cortés's role and the minimization of the contributions of other participants, some nine hundred of whom survived the conquest, Díaz del Castillo sought to rectify that account by giving greater attention to the role of the others, particularly the ordinary soldiers, of whom he had been one.

Díaz del Castillo's version of events is not without its difficulties, however. For instance, his account of Grijalva's expedition differs from all others, and in his frequent mentions of specifics, such as the Spaniards involved in battles, his numbers differ from Cortés's near-contemporaneous version. But the invaluable result, which was completed in 1568 and survives in three manuscripts, is the most detailed account and serves as a crucial corrective of earlier versions.

[*See also* Cortés, Hernán.]

BIBLIOGRAPHY

Cerwin, Herbert. *Bernal Díaz, Historian of the Conquest*. Norman: University of Oklahoma Press, 1963.
Díaz del Castillo, Bernal. *The True History of the Conquest of New Spain*. Translated by Alfred Percival Maudslay. 5 vols. London: The Hakluyt Society, 1908–1916.

ROSS HASSIG

Dieppe School.

The Dieppe school of cartography consisted of about a dozen cartographers working in Normandy and centered on the French maritime port city of Dieppe, although some of them were based in Rouen, Le Havre, and Honfleur. [See color plate 24 in this volume.] Among the most important of these cartographers were Pierre Desceliers (d. 1553), Guillaume Le Testu (d. 1572), and Jacques Le Moyne de Morgues (d. 1587). As a result of the English bombardment of Dieppe in 1696, most of the maps that members of this school produced are lost, and none of those preserved can be found in Dieppe itself. Still, although the Dieppe school was active for only a generation—from about 1535 to 1562, when the Wars of Religion ravaged France—the cartographers associated with it were excellent propagandists for French geographic knowledge and territorial claims in the New World. The French rulers Francis I (d. 1547) and Charles IX (d. 1574) both employed French and Portuguese cartographers to produce maps and atlases for them, and displayed a keen interest in cartography as a means of emphasizing their claims to overseas imperial power. Although the development of cartography in Normandy owed much to the initiative of Jean Ango (d. 1541) and his fellow *armateurs* (shipowners) based in the region, Francis I also was a vital source of patronage for them. Dieppe cartographer Jean de Clamorgan (d. 1567), for example, produced a *Carte*

Universelle dedicated to Francis, a copy of which Francis kept in his library.

The Dieppe school cartographers were important mediators of Renaissance cartographical and geographical knowledge derived primarily from Portuguese and Flemish sources and disseminated to French and English audiences. At least one member of the Dieppe school, Jean Rotz (d. 1550), entered the service of the English king Henry VIII, to whom Rotz dedicated his famous 1542 *Boke of Idrography*, probably the highest-quality atlas produced in sixteenth-century France and the best-known example of the work of the Dieppe cartographers. Rotz, son of Scotsman David Ross, grew up in Dieppe, where he sailed in the fleet of Jean Ango. Rotz originally produced his magnificent atlas for his patron Francis I, but may have left France for England in 1541—taking the *Boke of Idrography* with him—in part because of his disappointment that Francis had hired a Portuguese geographer and mapmaker, rather than Rotz, as royal cartographer. Rotz returned to France around 1547, where he served the French crown by building and equipping ships for the French navy. Thus Rotz's career embodies both the international nature of Renaissance cartography and the work of the Dieppe school.

It was no accident that Normandy during the mid-sixteenth century became the center of French cartography. Since the end of the fifteenth century, Norman ports had sponsored numerous voyages across the Atlantic, primarily to take advantage of the vast fishing grounds of the Grand Banks off the coast of Newfoundland. Francis I founded Le Havre to provide an additional port of trade and maritime defense at the mouth of the Seine. The decades when the Dieppe school was flourishing were also the decades in which French trade with the New World was at its sixteenth-century height, in terms of the North Atlantic fish trade, the still fledgling fur trade, and, most important for the cartographers, the rivalry with the Portuguese for control of the coasts of Brazil and the supplies of lucrative brazilwood. Brazilwood rendered a lush red dye that replaced woad as the primary dyestuff in the burgeoning cloth industry in France and the Low Countries. Thus the Dieppe cartographers accessed cartographic skills and geographic knowledge from Portuguese mariners, pilots, and geographers working in France, even as they produced maps meant to emphasize French dominion over and interests in territory in the New World, both in Newfoundland and in Brazil, that the Portuguese also claimed. Images such as that of Tupinambá Indians gathering brazilwood for Europeans waiting for them on the Brazilian coast—an image in one of the maps of Rotz's *Boke of Idrography*—were intended to convey a similar message.

The Dieppe cartographers' most significant, if controversial, innovation was their insistence on following Marco Polo and placing the island of *La Grande Jave* (Jave la Grande) on their maps. The issue here is that some historians have detected in the depiction of *La Grande Jave* on the Dieppe maps the outlines of Australia's northern peninsula, which is possible because off-course Portuguese sailors do seem to have at least sighted the continent from the Moluccas by the early sixteenth century, and may have passed this information on to the Dieppe cartographers. The debate over whether the Dieppe maps truly represent the first European images of Australia has not been settled. The motivation for separating Greater Java from the Asian continent, however, was most likely similar to the motivation that led to the detachment of Florida from the North American mainland in the Harleian (c. 1542) world map attributed to Pierre Desceliers—namely, to minimize the geographical obstacles facing potential French explorers seeking to discover and claim for France new territories in Asia and the New World.

In design and decorative style the Dieppe school maps represent a blending of the latest geographical and nautical knowledge circulating in Europe, and the portolan style of depicting coastlines, with older conceptualizations of world geography deriving from Ptolemy and medieval cartographers and explorers such as Marco Polo. Renaissance mapmakers such as those based in Dieppe relied heavily on each other's work, as well as on maps from previous generations, and thus their maps represented a mixture of old and new data and even differing conceptualizations of space, often coexisting uneasily in the same map. The Dieppe maps were colorful and richly decorated with imagery on the maps themselves and in the borders, imagery reminiscent of late medieval "international Gothic" painting in style and use of color. Although the bulk of the work that members of this school produced is lost, the maps of the Dieppe cartographers marked an important stage in the transition of Renaissance mapmaking from medieval to modern styles. The modern style increasingly incorporated the expanding geographical knowledge that the Iberian voyages of exploration had generated, and transmitted that knowledge to audiences elsewhere in Europe.

[*See also* Chinese Empirical Maps; Expeditions, World Exploration, *subentries on* France *and* Portugal; Jave la Grande; Le Testu, Guillaume; Maps, Mapmaking, and Mapmakers; Polo, Marco; *and* Ptolemy.]

BIBLIOGRAPHY

Brotton, Jeremy. *Trading Territories: Mapping the Early Modern World*. Ithaca, N.Y.: Cornell University Press, 1998.

Buisseret, David. *The Mapmakers' Quest: Depicting New Worlds in Renaissance Europe*. Oxford: Oxford University Press, 2003.

Lestringant, Frank. *Mapping the Renaissance World: The Geographical Imagination in the Age of Discovery*. Translated by Davis Fausett. Berkeley and Los Angeles: University of California Press, 1994. English translation of *L'atelier du cosmographe*, first published 1991.

Wallis, Helen, ed. *The Maps and Texts of the "Boke of Idrography" Presented by Jean Rotz to Henry VIII*. Oxford: Oxford University Press, 1981.

GAYLE K. BRUNELLE

Djuvayni, al- (1226–1283), Persian historian and governor. Al-Djuvayni's noble family belonged to Azadwar, the capital of Djuvayn. His *Tarikh-i Jahangusha* (History of the World-Conqueror) is the only source for his personal vita.

Djuvayni visited Mongolia twice, in 1249–1251 and in 1251–1253. In 1256 he entered the service of Hulegu, the Mongol conqueror, in Khorāsān and accompanied him in his campaigns against the Isma'ilis of Alamut and the caliph in Baghdad. From 1259, under Hulegu's son, Abaqa, Djuvayni governed with prosperity 'Iraq-i 'Arab and Khuzistan for twenty years. Nevertheless, he and his brother, Shams al-Din, suffered several misfortunes because of false accusations by their enemies in the Ilkhanid court. Djuvayni was repeatedly arrested and released. Toward the end of his life he wrote two Persian treatises about his adventures under Abaqa. In March 1283 he had a stroke and died in Arran.

Djuvayni began writing his history in Mongolia in 1252–1253 and continued writing it until 1260, but it probably remains incomplete. It consists of three parts: (1) the history of the Mongols and their conquests until after Great Khan Güyük's time, and the history of Jochi's and Chaghatay's descendants; (2) the history of the Khwarazm-Shahs and of the Mongol rulers of Khorāsān until 1258; and (3) the rest of the Mongols' history until the Isma'ili defeat, along with a section on the Isma'ili sect. Djuvayni was the first Persian historian who traveled to Mongolia and described the eastern Asian lands. His history, a model of style, influenced eastern historical tradition.

[*See also* Arabia.]

BIBLIOGRAPHY

Vasili-Vladimirovich, Barthold (John Andrew Boyle). "Dju-wayni." In *Encyclopaedia of Islam*. 2nd ed. Vol. 2, pp. 606–607. Leiden, Netherlands: Brill, 1965.

EVANGELOS VENETIS

Dobbs, Arthur (1689–1765), Irish-born British promoter of expeditions to find the Northwest Passage. Arthur Dobbs was born on April 2, 1689, son of Richard Dobbs, a Protestant landowner in Carrickfergus, County Antrim. On his father's death in 1711 Arthur inherited the family estate around Castle Dobbs, Carrickfergus. He was elected member of Parliament for Carrickfergus in 1727, published a two-part *Essay on the Trade and Improvement of Ireland* in 1729 and 1731, and was appointed to the lucrative office of surveyor-general of Ireland in 1733.

By now Dobbs's interest in Irish trade had widened to include British colonial commerce, and he argued that an important step in its expansion would be the discovery of the Northwest Passage. This would open up the northern parts of the American continent, provide a short route to the rich trading areas of the Far East, and thwart the French. For twenty years Dobbs waged a dedicated and at times single-handed campaign to find the passage, and his promotion of two discovery expeditions to Hudson Bay at a time when there was little official interest in exploration was a notable achievement. Dobbs's career is a reminder that the exploits of individual explorers were often just the final stage in a series of negotiations that involved projectors, geographers, and speculators.

In 1731, Dobbs drew up a seventy-page memorial on the probability of a Northwest Passage; he sent it to men of rank and influence, including the first min-

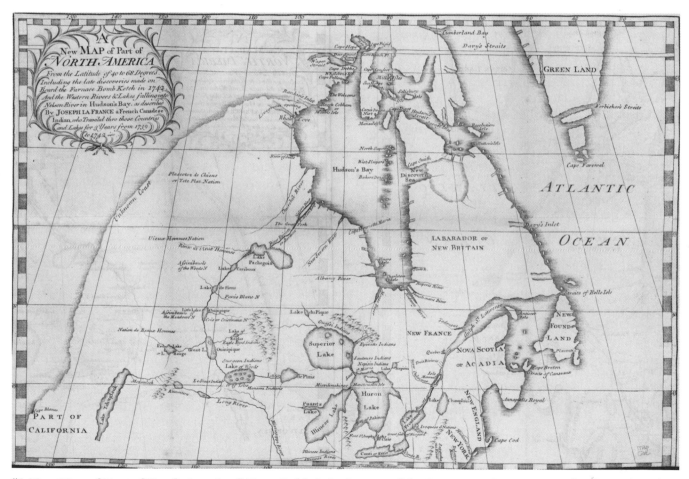

"A New Map of Part of North America." From Dobbs's *An Account of the Countries Adjoining to Hudson's Bay* (London, 1744). This map summarizes Dobbs's view of the nature of the Northwest Passage. Of course, he lived at a time when it was very hard for Europeans to comprehend the extent of the landmass of North America, so that he could imagine an "unknown coast" curving gently around until it met Hudson Bay. COURTESY THE NEWBERRY LIBRARY, CHICAGO

ister, Robert Walpole. Dobbs made repeated attempts to persuade the Hudson's Bay Company to mount a search for the passage, and when these attempts bore little fruit he persuaded the Admiralty to fit out a discovery expedition. This was commanded by Christopher Middleton, a former Hudson's Bay Company captain who had previously shown an interest in the Northwest Passage. Middleton failed to find a passage on his voyage of 1741–1742, but Dobbs refused to accept his verdict and embarked on a campaign to discredit him. For Dobbs the Northwest Passage had become part of a wider scheme to abolish the monopoly of the Hudson's Bay Company, and in his *Account of Hudson's Bay* (1744) he argued that the company was acting against the national interest by obstructing attempts to find the passage. Much that the company had kept secret over the years was now revealed. Dobbs printed its charter of 1670 and stressed the contrast between the vast region granted to it at that time and the few small posts it had managed to establish along the shores of Hudson Bay. In another part of the book, Dobbs printed an account of a voyage supposedly made in 1640 from Peru by a Spanish admiral, Bartholomew de Fonte, who entered a series of waterways on the northwest coast of America and met a Boston ship that had sailed west from Hudson Bay. Both the admiral and his voyage were entirely fictitious, but to Dobbs the account was "farther Proof" of the existence of the Northwest Passage.

With support from a consortium of merchants, Dobbs organized a privately financed discovery expedition commanded by William Moor, who had sailed with Middleton on his voyage. Dobbs and his associates were encouraged by the offer of a parliamentary reward of £20,000 for the discovery of a navigable passage—further evidence of Dobbs's influence and persuasiveness. After spending a miserable and disputatious winter at York Factory on Hudson Bay—at one stage Moor was protected by men with drawn swords against the supposedly murderous intentions of his fellow captain, Francis Smith—the ships sailed north along the coast in the summer of 1747. They followed Middleton's track of five years earlier, but, apart from discovering Chesterfield Inlet, the expedition added little to Middleton's surveys, and the ships returned to England with their crews sick and demoralized. Accounts of the voyage were published by Henry Ellis and T. S. Drage, adherents of the rival factions of Moor and Smith, and their descriptions of the explorations of the 1747 season betray the lack of communication and understanding between the two captains.

Dobbs next attempted to overthrow the company by a parliamentary attack on its charter, and although this failed, the controversy gave unprecedented publicity to the affairs of the Hudson's Bay Company. The parliamentary investigation of 1748–1749 into the trade and management of the company demolished the barrier of close secrecy behind which it had long sheltered itself. The company faced a future in which it could no longer rely on obscurity for protection, and it gradually showed a more positive attitude toward exploring the territories it held under the charter of 1670. Dobbs's discovery ventures, although they had not found the Northwest Passage, had carried out useful surveys, and the wintering of the Middleton and Moor expeditions in Hudson Bay had revealed much about the realities of life in the sub-Arctic.

Even before the end of the parliamentary inquiry, Dobbs had announced his retirement from the struggle in favor of "some more happy Adventurer," but it was not a signal for his withdrawal from public life. In 1752, at a relatively advanced age, he was appointed governor of North Carolina, and held that office until his death in March 1765 at the age of seventy-five. Despite all the disappointments, Dobbs still believed that a Northwest Passage existed. Its discovery, he wrote in a letter toward the end of his life, was simply awaiting explorers of "Resolution, Capacity, and Integrity."

[*See also* Hudson's Bay Company, *subentry on* Arctic Exploration; Middleton, Christopher; North America, *subentry on* Apocryphal Voyages and Imaginary Places (post-1500); *and* Northwest Passage.]

BIBLIOGRAPHY
Barr, William, and Glyndwr Williams, eds. *Voyages to Hudson Bay in Search of a Northwest Passage 1741–1747.* 2 vols. London: The Hakluyt Society, 1994 and 1995.
Clarke, Desmond. *Arthur Dobbs Esquire, 1689–1765.* London: The Bodley Head, 1958.
Williams, Glyn. *Voyages of Delusion: The Northwest Passage in The Age of Reason.* London: HarperCollins, 2002; New Haven, Conn.: Yale University Press, 2003. See chaps. 2–6.

GLYNDWR WILLIAMS

Dobrizhoffer, Martin (1717?–1791), Jesuit missionary in South America. Dobrizhoffer's place and date of birth are not entirely clear, but we know that he joined the Jesuits in 1734 and was sent as a missionary to Paraguay in 1748. There he worked in the Reductions—missionary settlements that became refuges for the native tribes, who were remorselessly

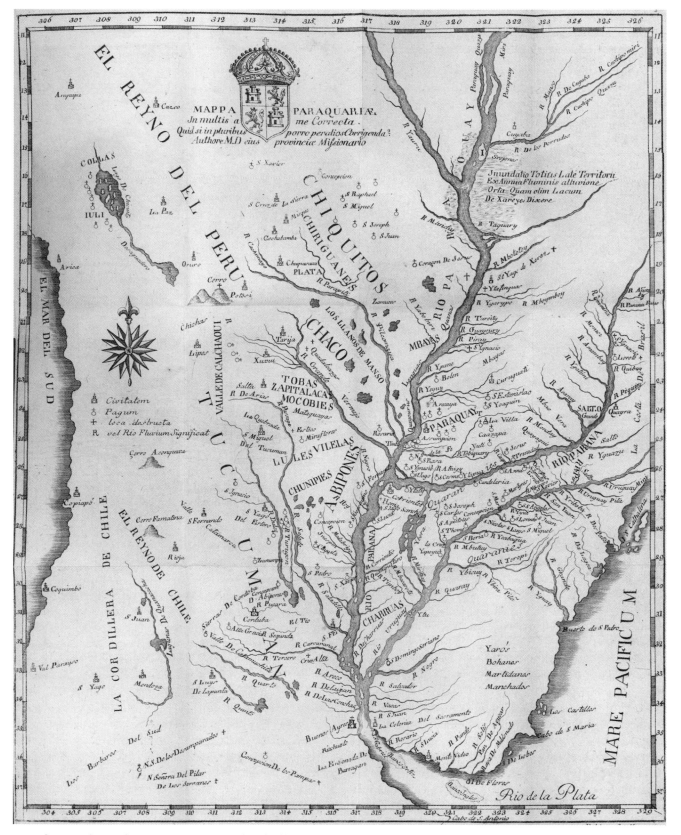

Map of Part of South America. From Dobrizhoffer's *Historia de Abiponibus*. (Vienna: Kurzbek, 1784). This is the map that accompanied Dobrizhoffer's account of the Abipón people. It carefully marked all the mission sites, including in the key (below the compass rose) those destroyed ("loca destructa") by European slavers. COURTESY THE NEWBERRY LIBRARY, CHICAGO

hunted by European settlers who desired to enslave them. (The life of the Reductions has been described in *The Mission*, a film that enjoyed critical and popular success in the 1990s.)

Dobrizhoffer spent much time among the Abipón people, a martial group who had long resisted the Jesuits' attempts to move them into settlements. Forced to leave the Reductions after 1767, Dobrizhoffer then compiled a history and description of the Abipón; first published in Latin and German in 1783–1784, it was translated into English in 1822. Dobrizhoffer may be regarded as an early ethnologist in view of his factual and accurate way of describing the Abipón. He later returned to Europe and became court chaplain to the empress Maria Theresa, and died in 1791 in Vienna.

[*See also* Jesuits.]

BIBLIOGRAPHY

Dobrizhoffer, Martin. *An Account of the Abipones, an Equestrian People of Paraguay*. Translated by Sara Coleridge. London: J. Murray, 1822.

DAVID BUISSERET

Doughty, Charles (1843–1926), British traveler of the Near East.

Charles Montagu Doughty was born on August 19, 1843, in Theberton, Suffolk, England. His father, the Reverend Charles Doughty, maintained strict Christian habits that would cause problems for his son traveling among Muslims some thirty years later. Doughty spent his early years in a naval school before transferring to Cambridge in 1861 to study geology. Doughty took time off from school to study glaciers in Norway, and completed his degree in late 1865. Following university, Doughty wandered Europe for five years, ultimately deciding, in 1870, to visit "the Bible-lands."

Doughty began his Near Eastern travels as a tourist and casual observer. However, when he heard of archaeological ruins in the Arabian Desert on the scale of the famous rock city of Petra, Doughty's adventurous nature kicked in and he began a fanatical quest to locate and document this site, never before seen by Westerners. The site of Medain Salih—unfortunately for Doughty, the devout Christian—was located in a portion of Arabia where non-Muslims were not allowed. Ultimately, after a year of preparation, Doughty managed to attach himself to a hajj caravan, in partial disguise and speaking enough Arabic to pass for a Persian.

The caravan left Maan, in present-day Jordan, on November 10, 1876, bound for Mecca. Doughty reached Medain Salih on December 4, 1876, and parted company with the caravan. Following poor treatment by the locals, Doughty was able to bribe them to let him survey the site. After recording seventy-five percent of it, Doughty set off in search of a new source of funding. Ultimately this search turned into an almost directionless trek across the Arabian Desert. He suffered harsh treatment at the hands of the local Muslims for his refusal to respect their customs and religious practices.

Despite being beaten and robbed several times, Doughty managed to keep enough records of areas not heretofore seen by Westerners to produce a work of moderate interest to the geographic and archaeological communities following his return to England in late 1878. Doughty died in 1926. Although his book, *Arabia Deserta*, received mediocre reviews from the academic community, it became popular as a piece of English literature, and captured the praise of such people as T. E. Lawrence.

[*See also* Arabia *and* Lawrence, T. E.]

BIBLIOGRAPHY

Doughty, Charles. *Travels in Arabia Deserta*. 2 vols. Cambridge, U.K.: Cambridge University Press, 1888.

Wilcox, Desmond. *Ten Who Dared*. Boston: Little, Brown, 1977.

RYAN M. SEIDEMANN

Drake, Francis (c. 1540–1596), English navigator and buccaneer.

Although having good family connections, Francis Drake was born into very modest circumstances, c. 1540. Events surrounding his early life are not well documented, but he appeared to have been apprenticed to a merchant captain engaged in coastal trade in the North Sea. According to tradition it was in these difficult waters that the young Drake learned navigational techniques that were later to serve him well. By 1570 Drake had allied himself with his prominent kinsmen, the Hawkins family in Plymouth. The Hawkinses were ship owners engaged in trade on the African coast and in the Caribbean. It was in this service that Drake had his earliest experience of oceanic sailing. Ostensibly the purpose of this and later voyages was trade, but piracy was also a motive. At first Drake sailed with Hawkins's expeditions, but soon he was navigating on his own account. Failing to take Spanish vessels at sea Drake, with French and native assistance, landed and ambushed a Spanish mule-train laden with silver, near Nombre de Dios. This was so successful that Drake returned to England a rich man.

In 1577 Drake was given command of a small naval squadron with the possible objective of investigating the southern coasts of South America in order to establish an English "presence," from which to attack Peru. At the entrance to the Strait of Magellan, Drake had the aristocratic Thomas Doughty, a captain of one of the ships, executed on suspicion of mutiny. With a reduced force of three ships Drake passed through the strait in record time only to have his three ships scattered by storms in the Pacific. In his one remaining vessel, *Pelican*, now renamed *Golden Hind*, Drake sailed north along the Pacific coasts of South and Central America, raiding Spanish towns on the way. [See color plate 31 in this volume.] How far north he reached is the subject of a continuing debate, but he knew it was not safe for him to return the way he had come. Thus, he careened his ship at a safe haven, which he called Nova Albion and prepared to sail across the Pacific. Sites from present-day southern California to the central British Columbian coast have been claimed as Drake's harbor, but no positive evidence has yet come to light concerning this anchorage.

With the help of the local inhabitants, from whom he took "title" to the land, Drake now provisioned his vessel and sailed westward. There were adventures along the way, including near shipwreck in the Celebes. From these islands the *Golden Hind* returned via the Indian Ocean and the African coasts to Plymouth, in 1580. During a three-year voyage Drake had completed the first global circumnavigation from which the original commander returned home. Equally important he had broken Iberian monopoly of the southern oceans. Because of continuing problems between Spain and England, Queen Elizabeth hesitatingly invited Drake to London, where he was knighted aboard the *Golden Hind*.

Inspired by the example of Drake, other expeditions were now mounted in England against Spain and Spanish colonies in the New World. The most remarkable of these was that of Thomas Cavendish. Setting out in 1586 and following essentially Drake's route, Cavendish was able to intercept the Spanish Acapulco-Manila galleon off the coast of Baja California and loaded great treasure aboard his ship. When he returned to England after his speedy circumnavigation of two years, Cavendish found the English at war with Spain. That country, in response to repeated attacks by the English, had invaded the English Channel in 1588, with the object of suppressing the upstart nation, with an "Invincible Armada." With Drake as vice admiral, and assisted by weather unfavorable to the lumbering Spanish transport ships but favorable to the smaller English vessels, the armada was defeated. Prior to this Drake had delayed the departure of the armada by daring raids on Iberian ports and, during the action itself, had sent fire ships among the vessels of the Spanish fleet. The loss to Spain was one from which she never fully recovered.

Although admired by the queen, and a hero to the common people in England, the aristocracy distrusted Drake. He had bought a great house and estate near Plymouth and became mayor of that city. However, he was soon at sea again, but his later voyages against Spain and in the Caribbean were less than successful or outright disasters. This was also true of a second voyage by Cavendish, who died at sea, and of Richard Hawkins, who was captured in the Pacific by the Spanish and suffered long imprisonment. However, theoretical ideas of Sebastian Cabot, who defected from Spain to England, of John Dee, and of Edward Wright were important when, through sponsorship by Sir Walter Ralegh and others, England was able to establish a colony on the Atlantic coast of North America. Interestingly, Ralegh, who was at court, never visited the Roanoke colony in North America, but Drake did, rescuing survivors from the initial, ill-fated colony. Later Ralegh ventured on an exploration to find El Dorado in the Orinoco Valley of South America, which was abortive; after his return to England he was executed, 1614.

Meanwhile Drake made what turned out to be his last voyage to the Caribbean for an assault on Panama. This proved to be unsuccessful, and he died of sickness aboard his ship off Puerto Bello and was buried at sea in 1596. Arguably the greatest English seaman prior to James Cook in the second half of the eighteenth century, Drake was central to a number of accomplishments. Although not an innovator, he was an up-to-date and resourceful captain. He may have navigated both farther south and farther north in the Pacific than any European before him. He is also sometimes credited with laying the foundation of a British empire in Asia through his encounters in the Celebes. But his greatest triumphs were his global circumnavigation and his role in the defeat of the Spanish Armada. Calling him "El Draco," the Spanish hated Drake, but he became, and remains, a national hero in England, especially in the West Country.

[*See also* Cabot, Sebastian; Cavendish, Thomas; *and* Wright, Edward.]

BIBLIOGRAPHY

Hanna, Warren L. *Lost Harbor: The Controversy over Drake's California Anchorage* Berkeley, Los Angeles, London: University of California Press, 1979.

Kelleher, Brian T. *Drake's Bay: Unraveling California's Great Maritime Mystery.* Cupertino, Calif.: Kelleher and Associates, 1983.

Kelsey, Harry. *Sir Francis Drake: The Queen's Pirate.* New Haven and London: Yale University Press, 1998.

McKee, Alexander *The Queen's Corsair: Drake's Journey of Circumnavigation, 1577–1580.* London: Souvenir Press, 1978.

Sugden, John. *Sir Francis Drake.* New York: Holt, 1990.

Thrower, Norman J. W., ed. *Sir Francis Drake and the Famous Voyage, 1577–1580: Essays Commemorating the Quadricentenial of Drake's Circumnavigation of the Earth.* Berkeley, Los Angeles, and London: University of California Press, 1984. This collection by ten leading scholars with separate notes, and a "contemporary" Drake bibliography has a foreword by H. R. H. Prince Philip, Duke of Edinburgh. It was an official publication of the Sir Francis Drake Commission, State of California, 1973–1980.

NORMAN J. W. THROWER

Du Chaillu, Paul (1831–1903), French-born explorer, hunter, naturalist, and writer. Paul Belloni Du Chaillu was the first literate observer to venture far into the interior of western equatorial Africa on foot and to describe living gorillas. Du Chaillu was born on July 31, 1831, either in Paris or on Réunion Island (accounts differ). At age seventeen he joined his father, a merchant, at the French trading post of Gabon. Over a period of four years he acquired knowledge of the people, languages, and environment of the region. In 1852, assisted by the American Pres-

Du Chaillu's *Explorations and Adventures in Equatorial Africa.* The adventures of Du Chaillu among the gorillas aroused a good deal of skepticism and mockery in Europe. In this curious plate (London, 1861), a nonchalant gorilla is destroying the rifle of a hunter whom he has apparently already demolished. COURTESY THE NEWBERRY LIBRARY, CHICAGO

byterian missionary John Wilson with whom he lived for a time, Paul Du Chaillu traveled to the United States to teach French at a women's college in New York State. Du Chaillu's donation of a small collection of bird skins and other preserved animals from the Gabon estuary to the Academy of Natural Science in Philadelphia led the curator and ornithologist John Cassin to encourage the young man to return to Gabon for additional zoological specimens. While in the United States, Du Chaillu applied for American citizenship, although it is uncertain whether it was ever granted. He returned to Gabon in 1855 with some support from Cassin.

On the first of his two voyages (1856–1859), traveling alone or with only a few African companions, Du Chaillu walked inland one hundred miles from the Rio Muni through Séké-inhabited areas to Fang settlements in the foothills of the Monts de Cristal, near present-day Médouneu, Gabon. Subsequently, starting from the Fernan Vaz lagoon south of the mouth of the Ogowe, he traveled by canoe up an arm of the Ogowe delta to Lake Anengué. On a another voyage, he ascended the Rembo Nkomi and walked overland among the Ashira and Apindji peoples to the falls of the Ngounié River near present-day Fougamou, Gabon.

Du Chaillu's often sensationalist and lurid descriptions of the gorilla and of African cultures in his published account of this trip, *Explorations and Adventures in Equatorial Africa* (1861), catered to a Victorian mass audience, but they gained him the credulity of many intellectuals and scientists. Because he was untrained in mapmaking, his geographical discoveries were also dismissed.

To answer his critics, Du Chaillu undertook a second voyage to Gabon (1863–1865) that began inauspiciously with the loss of his equipment in the surf while coming ashore at Fernan Vaz. After resupplying, Du Chaillu traveled east from the Ngounié River through a portion of the Massif Du Chaillu, which still bears his name, to a point just east of present-day Mbigou, Gabon. Here an accident led to the death of two Massango natives, and Du Chaillu and his party were obliged to retreat to the coast, abandoning specimens, native artifacts, and photographic plates. His account of this trip was published in 1867 as *A Journey to Ashango-Land*.

Although opinion on Du Chaillu's veracity is nearly as divided today as it was in his own day, much in his accounts of animals, African customs, and the geography of region has been shown to be accurate. Du Chaillu's contributions to African zoology and ethnography were substantial. His claim to have discovered that the Ogowe River was the single source for its several outlets to the sea has been discredited, however. Later in life, Du Chaillu wrote books for children and on travels through Scandinavia. He died in Saint Petersburg, Russia, on April 30, 1903.

[*See also* Africa, *subentry on* Exploration.]

BIBLIOGRAPHY

Bucher, Harry J., Jr. "Canonization by Repetition: Paul Du Chaillu in Historiography." *Revue française d'histoire d'Outre-Mer* 66 (1979): 15–32.

Du Chaillu, Paul Belloni. *Explorations and Adventures in Equatorial Africa*. New York: Harper, 1861.

Du Chaillu, Paul Belloni. *A Journey to Ashango-Land, and Further Penetration into Equatorial Africa*. New York: Appleton, 1867.

Patterson, K. D. "Paul B. Du Chaillu and the Exploration of Gabon, 1855–1865." *The International Journal of African Historical Studies* 7 (1974): 647–667.

Vaucaire, Michel. *Paul Du Chaillu: Gorilla Hunter*. New York and London: Harper, 1930.

JOHN P. SULLIVAN

Dudley, Robert (1574–1649), English explorer and mapmaker. Sir Robert Dudley, engineer, explorer, and mapmaker, was the illegitimate son of the Earl of Leicester and Douglas Lady Sheffield. He was born in 1574 in Shene, Richmond, England. The Earl of Leicester provided financial support, and the boy was educated by the tutor Thomas Challoner, who later became tutor to Prince Henry, eldest son of James I of England. In 1588, Dudley entered school at Christ Church, Oxford, where he was adept in mathematics and interested in every aspect of naval affairs. By the age of twenty-three Dudley was an accomplished commander, had explored Trinidad, the Orinoco River of South America, and been knighted for his actions in the military expedition against Cádiz.

Dudley moved to Florence about 1606 and offered his talents and services to the Grand Duke of Tuscany, Cosmo II. For the next forty-five years Dudley's reputation in civil engineering, shipbuilding, and naval warfare grew under the patronage and protection of the duke. Dudley assisted in the drainage of the marshes around Pisa and the development of Leghorn as a fortified commercial port.

His greatest contribution to cartography was his creation of a portolan world atlas published in Florence in 1646–1647 and 1661. Portolan sailing charts show coastal outlines and place names. The *Dell' Arcano del Mare* is the first English printed nautical atlas, the first to use a Mercator projection, and contains the first English-produced map of Australia. Although not infallible, the atlas was extraordinarily detailed for the period.

[*See also* Maps, Mapmaking, and Mapmakers.]

BIBLIOGRAPHY

Dilke, O. A. W., and Margaret S. Dilke. "Sir Robert Dudley's Contributions to Cartography." *The Map Collector* 19 (1982): 10–14. Includes a bibliography.

Leader, J[ohn]. T[emple]. *Life of Sir Robert Dudley Followed by the Italian Biography of Sir Robert Dudley and Six Additional Plates from the "Arcano del Mare."* Amsterdam: Meridian Publishing Co., 1977. Reprint of the 1895 edition published in Florence.

Schütte, J. F., S.J. "Japanese Cartography at the Court of Florence: Robert Dudley's Maps of Japan 1606–1636." *Imago Mundi* 23 (1969): 29–58.

KATHERINE R. GOODWIN

Dumont de Montigny (1696–after 1754), French adventurer. Jean François Benjamin Dumont de Montigny was the youngest son of a lawyer in the Paris *parlement* and was the black sheep of his family. He was educated at a Jesuit grammar school and then entered the military. In 1715 he sailed to Quebec on a ship carrying a large quantity of coinage meant to replace the paper currency then circulating in the colony. Ill with scurvy, Dumont was unable to make the return voyage at the end of the summer. Instead, he spent two years in Quebec, living at the expense of the colony's religious and administrative elites and observing events with a journalistic eye.

Dumont's second transatlantic voyage was in 1719, when he set sail for Louisiana on a ship carrying 250 convict laborers, 112 soldiers, and the ship's crew. On this voyage his vessel became embroiled in maneuvers between the French, English, and Spanish in the Caribbean. He took part in the capture of Pensacola from the Spanish and helped to build the French settlement at Biloxi, Mississippi.

On his third voyage, in 1721, Dumont remained in Louisiana for sixteen years, traveling extensively along the valleys of the Mississippi, Arkansas, Yazoo, Pascagoula, and Tombigbee rivers. Although he participated in only one formal exploratory expedition, led by Jean-Baptiste Benard de la Harpe up the Arkansas River from August to December 1721, he documented the establishment of French posts at other sites and wrote extensively about Native American ethnography. He served as an engineer, draftsman, soldier, and plantation manager, and was sometimes reprimanded or absent without leave from his military duties. He witnessed the destruction of New Orleans by a hurricane in 1722 and the French prov-

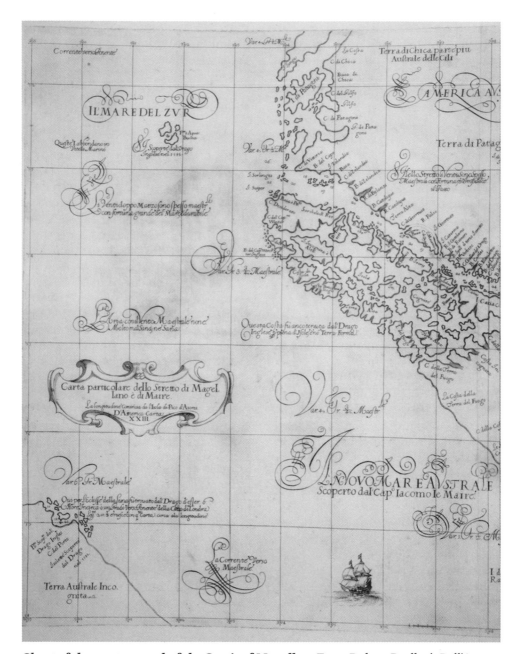

Chart of the western end of the Strait of Magellan. From Robert Dudley's *Dell'Arcano del Mare* (Florence, 1646–1647). This excerpt shows the detailed nature of Dudley's atlas and the baroque elegance of his lettering. Note, in the bottom lefthand corner of image, the "Terra Australis incognita"; Tasman was at this very time drawing the veil from this part of the world. COURTESY THE NEWBERRY LIBRARY, CHICAGO

ocations of the Natchez Indians that led to the catastrophic massacre of nearly 250 Frenchmen at Natchez in 1729.

After his return to France in 1737, Dumont first wrote two versions of an epic poem narrating some of the events that had occurred during his years in Louisiana. Then, in 1747, he drafted a long prose memoir recounting all of his adventures in the Americas. Although he often attributes a suspiciously heroic role to himself, Dumont's memoir nevertheless provides an intensely detailed view of daily life in the colony of Louisiana. His descriptions of military campaigns are highly visual and fact-filled, providing a picture of the lived experience in sharp counterpoint to the official reports written by the colonial officers and administration. Later he assisted a Paris editor, the Abbé Le Mascrier, in transforming portions of his memoir into a two-volume colonial history, *Mémoires historiques sur la Louisiane*, printed in 1753. [See color plate 25 in this volume.]

Dumont produced numerous maps that document the exploration and settlement of the Louisiana territory. His plan of New Orleans shows the capital of the colony as it looked when first laid out from 1718 to 1719, and in his memoir Dumont describes the levee built there by the French in an attempt to control the annual spring flooding of the Mississippi River.

BIBLIOGRAPHY

Dumont de Montigny, Jean François Benjamin. *Mémoire de Lieutenant Dumont (1715–1747)*. Edited by Carla Zecher, Gordon M. Sayre, and Shannon Lee Dawdy. Forthcoming from Les Éditions du Septentrion and the Presses de Paris-Sorbonne.

Dumont de Montigny, Jean François Benjamin, and Jean Baptiste Le Mascrier. *Mémoires historiques sur la Louisiane*. 2 vols. Paris: C. J. B. Bauche, 1753.

Sayre, Gordon M. "Plotting the Natchez Massacre: Le Page du Pratz, Dumont de Montigny, Chateaubriand." *Early American Literature* 37, no. 3 (Fall 2002): 381–413.

SHANNON LEE DAWDY
CARLA ZECHER
GORDON M. SAYRE

Dumont D'Urville, J. S. C.

Dumont D'Urville, J. S. C. (1790–1842), French navigator who explored the Southern Ocean. Jules-Sebastien-Cesar Dumont D'Urville was born in Normandy on May 25, 1790, the son of a district judge. He joined the navy in 1807 but had few opportunities to sail because French ports were constantly blockaded by British ships. D'Urville's first real opportunity came in 1819 when he went on a surveying expedition to the Mediterranean in the *Chevrette*. He was fortunate in being instrumental in the purchase by France of the famous Venus de Milo statue on the Aegean island of Milos. D'Urville was promoted to lieutenant and awarded the Legion of Honor, while his scientific contributions earned him membership in the Linnaean Society and the Société de Géographie.

In August 1822, D'Urville sailed on a voyage of exploration with Louis-Isidore Duperrey in the *Coquille*, going to South America and then across the Pacific Ocean to Tahiti, the Santa Cruz Islands, and the Solomons, rounding the Australian continent to Port Jackson, then on to New Zealand, the Carolines, and home by way of the Indian Ocean. On his return, D'Urville was promoted to commander and put in charge of the *Coquille*, which was renamed *Astrolabe* and sent on another voyage of exploration in Pacific waters. His energy and his daring transformed this expedition into a major undertaking, far superior to Duperrey's. D'Urville sailed from Toulon on April 25, 1826, making for Tenerife, the Cape of Good Hope, and Australia. He then sailed for New Zealand, intending to survey parts of the coast that James Cook had not had time to examine in detail. Sailing through the dangerous French Pass, he discovered D'Urville Island off the South Island, and went on to investigate what is now Auckland Harbour. He continued toward Tonga, Fiji, New Ireland, and New Guinea, returning to the Australian continent; although having been coolly received in Port Jackson, he made this time for Hobart. D'Urville then sailed for Vanikoro, erecting a monument to the memory of J. F. de Galaup de La Pérouse. He returned home by way of Guam, the Carolines, Batavia, Mauritius, and Cape Town, drop-

---

On Taking Possession of a Land

We are now approaching the end of the period when, following Columbus and the early Spanish conquerors, it was thought reasonable to "take possession" of a land by planting there the flag of some European power. D'Urville himself realized that there was something "ridiculous and worthless" about this ceremony, but seems to have gone through with it with a sort of amusement.

It was nearly 9 o'clock when, to our great joy, we landed on the western part of the most westerly and the loftiest islet. The *Astrolabe*'s boat had arrived a moment before, and already the men had climbed up the steep sides of the rock. . . . The surf rendered this operation very difficult. I was forced to leave several men in the boat to look after her. I then immediately sent one of our men to unfurl the tricolour flag on this land, which no human had either seen or stepped on before. Following the ancient custom, faithfully kept up by the English, we took possession of it in the name of France, as well as of the adjacent coast, which the ice prevented us from approaching.

—*Two Voyages to the South Seas*, edited and translated by Helen Rosenman (2 vols.; Melbourne, Australia: Melbourne University Press, 1987)

Beach Scene. From Dumont d'Urville's *Voyage au pôle sud et dans l'Océanie* (5 vols., Paris 1841–1845). In this wonderfully evocative scene, the *Astrolabe* is anchored off Jervis Bay in Australia, while an armed soldier attempts to talk to some local people. On the headland, the French are busy taking observations. COURTESY THE NEWBERRY LIBRARY, CHICAGO

ping anchor in Marseilles on February 24, 1829. D'Urville brought back a vast collection of natural history specimens and hydrographic information. France was in a state of political upheaval, and D'Urville's next duty was to escort the deposed Charles X into exile. After this, he worked on the publication of an account of the *Astrolabe* expedition, which was published in five large volumes (1832–1834).

After a period of inaction, D'Urville was placed in charge of a new expedition, this time with two ships, *Astrolabe* and *Zélée*. He sailed from Toulon on September 7, 1837, to explore the Antarctic. Making for Port Famine in the Strait of Magellan, he went on to the South Shetlands and the South Orkneys. He surveyed the tip of the Antarctic continent, naming it Louis Philippe Land after the king of France. After survey work lasting three months, he sailed to Chile, then across the Pacific to the Marquesas, Tahiti, Fiji, and Guam, arriving on January 1, 1839. He then went to the East Indies, down to Hobart, and on to

the Antarctic once more. Land discovered there was named Adélie Land, after his wife. After returning to Hobart, he sailed to New Zealand, then through Torres Strait to the Indian Ocean and home. The expedition reached Toulon on November 6, 1840. It was an arduous but successful campaign, bringing back once more a large collection of specimens, drawings, and charts.

Several French voyages of exploration took place during the period 1817–1840, but the three in which D'Urville took part were by far the most important, and he can be regarded as the navigator who made the greatest single contribution to perfecting the map of the Pacific in the nineteenth century. He was a learned, energetic explorer with a deep interest in natural history and a sympathetic attitude toward the island people he met, including the New Zealand Maori, who so impressed him that he wrote a novel, unpublished during his lifetime, about them. On his return, D'Urville was promoted to rear admiral and was awarded the Société de Géographie's gold medal. He began work on a detailed narrative of his voyage, but tragically was killed with his wife and son in a railway accident on May 8, 1842.

[*See also* Antarctica; Australia, Exploration of; *and* Pacific.]

BIBLIOGRAPHY
Dumont d'Urville, J. S. C. *The New Zealanders: A Story of Austral Lands*. Translated by Carol Legge. Wellington, New Zealand: Victoria University Press, 1992.
Rosenman, Helen, ed. *Two Voyages to the South Seas by Captain (later Rear-Admiral) Jules S.-C. Dumont d'Urville of the French Navy*. 2 vols. Melbourne, Australia: Melbourne University Press, 1987.
Wright, Olive, trans. *New Zealand 1826–1827 from the French of Dumont d'Urville*. Wellington, New Zealand: Wingfield, 1950.

JOHN DUNMORE

Duveyrier, Henri (1840–1892), French explorer of the Sahara Desert and a longtime official at the Geographical Society of Paris. Born into a prominent Parisian family on February 28, 1840, Duveyrier became a protégé of Heinrich Barth while still in his teens. He first traveled in Algeria in 1857, but in 1859, after studying Arabic in Leipzig, Duveyrier began a remarkably danger-free three-year journey into the Algerian and Tunisian deserts. For his exploits, he received the Gold Medal of the Geographical Society of Paris. In 1864 he published a classic book, *Exploration of the Sahara: The Tuareg of the North*. Because he was so positive about his experiences with indigenous desert tribesmen, Duveyrier helped create a so-called Saharan mystique and characterized the Tuareg as "noble cavaliers of the desert." Most Europeans believed him until three priests were murdered near El Golea in 1876, and then French soldiers under the command of Colonel Paul Flatters were massacred by the Tuareg in 1881. Some critics in France unfairly blamed Duveyrier for those tragedies.

Duveyrier contracted typhoid fever while traveling in the Sahara and never regained robust health. He spent the rest of his life as an influential official at the Geographical Society of Paris. He served on a variety of governmental committees and, in his prominent position, greatly influenced France's attempts to expand its colonial empire in Africa. Duveyrier also was a leading advocate of the proposed, but ill-fated, Trans-Saharan Railway. In September 1876, Duveyrier represented France at the Brussels Geographical Conference hosted by King Leopold II. Near the end of his life, he made short trips to the Sahara, where he traveled mostly in the area south of the Atlas Mountains. Suffering from a mental illness, Duveyrier committed suicide on April 24, 1892, at Sèvre, near Paris.

[*See also* Africa, *subentry on* Patrons, Sponsors, and Supporters; Barth, Heinrich; Brussels Geographical Conference; Colonies and Empires; Geographical Society of Paris; *and* Sahara.]

BIBLIOGRAPHY
Heffernan, Michael. "The Limits of Utopia: Henri Duveyrier and the Exploration of the Sahara in the Nineteenth Century." *The Geographical Journal* 155, no. 3 (November 1989): 342–352.

SANFORD H. BEDERMAN

E

Eanes, Gil (fl. 1434), Portuguese sea captain who reached northwest Africa. In 1434, Gil Eanes, an *escudeiro* (squire) of Henry the Navigator, successfully rounded Cape Bojador, a coastal feature of northwestern Africa that represented the farthest point of late medieval navigation and a psychological barrier to further explorations. The cape apparently stymied Portuguese explorers for many years, and Eanes himself failed to get past it in 1433. His patron, Prince Henry, partly shamed him and partly enticed him with promises of a great reward into another attempt the following year. The second expedition was successful, thus earning Eanes a place in history.

Although both Eanes's contemporaries and subsequent generations of historians perceived the rounding of Cape Bojador as a milestone in the history of overseas exploration, it is unclear what point exactly Eanes managed to circumnavigate. The modern Cape Bojador does not possess the combination of features supposed to have made it so fearsome for medieval mariners, namely dangerous currents, shallows, and a rocky reef jutting for miles into the sea. It is likely, however, that what transformed the cape into an obstacle was apprehension of the unknown and the belief that the lands beyond were both waterless and uninhabited.

Like many others who sailed on behalf of Henry the Navigator, Gil Eanes was a resident of the southern town of Lagos. The rank of *escudeiro* placed him in the lowest ranks of the nobility. He returned to northwestern Africa several times during the decade that followed the Bojador expedition. In 1435, he and Afonso Baldaia reached Angra dos Ruivos (Garnet Bay, 24°51′ N) and returned with welcome news that the land was inhabited. Eanes later took part in the much larger expeditions of 1443, 1444, and 1445, all of which combined exploration with slaving. Although the chronicler Zurara claims that Gil Eanes earned great honor through his efforts, no evidence survives as to the nature or scope of the reward that Henry had promised him, and Eanes was not among the clients Henry commended to the care of his heirs when he died in 1460.

[*See also* Henry the Navigator.]

BIBLIOGRAPHY

Diffie, Bailey W., and George W. Winius. *Foundations of the Portuguese Empire, 1415–1580*. Minneapolis: University of Minnesota Press, 1977.

Russell, Peter. *Prince Henry "the Navigator": A Life*. New Haven, Conn., and London: Yale University Press, 2000.

IVANA ELBL
MARTIN ELBL

East African Lakes. It was not until the second half of the nineteenth century that the true number and position of East Africa's lakes became known in Europe. There are two categories of lakes. The Rift Valley lakes were created as a result of the interference in normal drainage systems caused by faulting. In the Eastern Rift there are several comparatively small lakes and the much larger Turkana in the north, but the string of large lakes in the Western Rift—Malawi, Tanganyika, and Albert—has attracted the most attention. The second category consists of lakes in areas of indeterminate and immature drainage caused by episodes of geological uplift and tilting. Lakes Bangweulu, Mweru, and Kyoga are examples, but the major such lake is Lake Victoria.

The outside world knew, or thought it knew, something of these lakes from at least the late classical period onward. However, it is difficult to be certain what real knowledge existed. People from the interior probably did bring to the coast vague reports of inland waters, some of which got through to mapmakers. More credence was given to knowledge supposed to be possessed by classical authorities from Herodotus onward. This knowledge was systematized by Ptolemy of Alexandria in the second century C.E., and Ptolemy included the testimony of one Diogenes, who was alleged to have visited a lake. Since no actual maps by Ptolemy survive, it is difficult to know precisely what he believed, but all versions of his work show two lakes at the head of the Nile. Arab scholars used Ptolemy's work but also came to know directly something about Ethiopia. Unfortunately, there was a tendency for these scholars to spread the knowledge about Ethiopia out southward to cover the whole continent. In the early modern period, the Portuguese, too, gained knowledge not only of Ethiopia but also of the Zambezi region; there is little doubt that Gaspar Bocarro either saw or passed near Lake Malawi. But the Portuguese were inclined to keep information secret. The whole situation was confused, and sixteenth- and seventeenth-century maps reflect this confusion.

In the eighteenth century, Guillaume Delisle and Jean-Baptiste d'Anville removed most of the uncorroborated lakes from their maps, thus leaving the interior of Africa blank. In the early nineteenth century, more information began to accrue for the simple reason that Africans from the interior responded to Indian Ocean economic developments by coming to trade at the coast, and Arabs followed them back into the interior. Ludwig Krapf obtained from such sources a pretty good idea that there were three major lakes (Malawi, Tanganyika, and Victoria), but his companion, Jacob Erhardt, unfortunately ran them together into one that was said to resemble a "monster slug." Much debate and speculation was engendered among armchair geographers; finally, in 1856, the Royal Geographical Society decided to send an expedition inland and so begin a process that would reveal the lakes as they really were. Richard Burton and John Hanning Speke reached Lake Tanganyika in 1858, and Speke alone arrived at Lake Victoria later that year, although it was Henry Stanley who, in 1875, really established the lake's dimensions. David Livingstone gained Lake Malawi in September 1859, just a few weeks before Albrecht Roscher did, and then Livingstone gained Lakes Mweru and Bangweulu in 1867–1868. Samuel Baker saw and named Lake Albert in 1864. Joseph Thomson visited Lake Rukwa and later several of the smaller Rift Valley lakes, while it was Samuel Teleki von Szek and Ludwig von Höhnel who reached Lake Turkana in 1888.

Much more detail remained to be added, but the fact that the explorers had been able to show that these large bodies of water really did exist had a great impact: why should steamboats not sail on them? By the beginning of the twentieth century, there were indeed steamboats on all the major lakes.

[See also Chad, Lake, and biographical entries on figures mentioned in this article.]

BIBLIOGRAPHY

Cooley, William Desborough. *Claudius Ptolemy and the Nile.* London: Parker, 1854.

Johnston, Sir Harry. *The Nile Quest: A Record of Exploration of the Nile and Its Basin.* London: Lawrence & Bullen, 1903.

Roy Bridges

Eclipses and Exploration. When an object blocks a light source, there is an eclipse. Nighttime is an eclipse—it is dark because we are in Earth's shadow.

There are two major types of eclipses that can be observed in skies from Earth—lunar and solar. Lunar eclipses occur whenever the full Moon passes into the shadow of the Earth. Solar eclipses occur when the new Moon moves in front of the Sun and blocks it from view.

Lunar Eclipses. A lunar eclipse occurs when the Sun, Earth, and Moon line up, and Earth blocks the Sun's light and its shadow falls on the Moon. Total lunar eclipses are much more common than solar eclipses because everyone on the night side of Earth has a chance to see the lunar eclipse. If one were an astronaut on the Moon, one would see the Earth eclipsing the Sun.

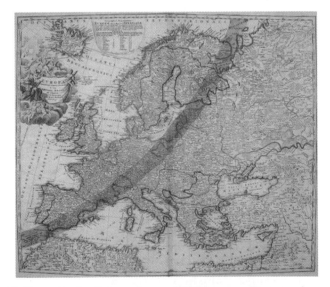

Eclipse. Path of the eclipse of 1706 across Europe, from Johann Homann's *Geographica Representatio Europae* (Nuremberg, c. 1730). It is not clear how accurate this eclipse map is, but this was a most effective and ingenious way of showing the path of such a phenomenon. Courtesy The Newberry Library, Chicago

During a lunar eclipse, the Sun's light passes through Earth's atmosphere, the air molecules both bend (refraction) and split up the light into its rainbow of colors (dispersion). The blue light scatters best at short distances. Thus, no blue light reaches the Moon. However, the red light scatters better at longer distances and is able to reach the Moon. If Earth had no atmosphere, the Moon would be completely black during a total eclipse. Instead, one observes the beautiful orange or red coloring.

Around 350 B.C.E., Aristotle noticed that during a lunar eclipse, a curved shadow is always spotted on the lunar surface. From this he concluded that Earth, the cause of the shadow, must be round.

In 1504, Christopher Columbus used his knowledge of an upcoming lunar eclipse to deceive the indigenous people on the island now called Jamaica. Columbus knew that an eclipse would occur on a certain night and declared that unless the island people gave him and his crew the food he needed, he would make the Moon disappear.

Solar Eclipses. The most dramatic eclipse is a total solar eclipse. The rare event takes place when the Sun, Moon, and Earth line up, and the Moon blocks the Sun's light and its shadow falls on a small part of Earth. Often called "totality," total solar eclipses are rare since the Moon's shadow (the umbra) barely reaches Earth. This makes the "path of totality" very narrow as it sweeps across Earth.

Partial solar eclipses are much more common but not as spectacular. Witnessing a partial solar eclipse is like watching a video of the Grand Canyon—nice, but not overpowering. A total solar eclipse is like viewing the Grand Canyon with one's own eyes—inspiring and breathtaking.

Humans have gone from anguish to admiration when viewing a total solar eclipse. Before the seventeenth century, humans could not accurately predict when and where totality would occur. The Babylonians figured out the eighteen-year, eleven-day Saros cycle where the Sun, Moon, and Earth line up in a similar fashion. The Greeks figured out the Metonic cycle, which is a period of about 6939.6 days, the length of both 235 consecutive lunar cycles and 19 solar years (Earth orbit today). However, even with these discoveries, no exact prediction could be made because of the lack of more accurate measurements.

The unpredictability of total eclipses made them an evil omen, and slow darkening and eventual covering of the Sun frightened people all over the world. Quite literally, it was thought the world was coming to an end. The Sun, source of all energy and light, was being extinguished.

Many cultures tried to chase away the evil spirit that was devouring the Sun. To the Chinese it was a dragon eating the Sun. They raised great commotion and noise to bring the Sun back. Lighted arrows were shot toward the Sun to rekindle it.

With the Renaissance and the reawakening of science in the sixteenth century, a total solar eclipse was soon accurately predicted. The English astronomer Edmond Halley, who is best known for the comet that bears his name, was the first to print an accurate map of an upcoming solar eclipse in 1715.

As science continued to develop, total solar eclipses were seen as a means to further understand the Sun. During an eclipse, a wispy white glow can be seen around the Sun. This is called the corona, or crown. The corona is the Sun's outer atmosphere. Also seen on the Sun at eclipse are fiery red solar flares and prominences.

With observations of the corona, flares, and the Sun itself, many elements were discovered. Helium, named for the Greek Sun god Helios, was discovered during an eclipse in 1868. In 1872, it was discovered that a solar flare seen during an eclipse was linked to magnetic storms on Earth. These flares are now known to cause the beautiful northern lights, or aurora borealis. In 1871 and 1878, two eclipses helped link the shape of the corona to the eleven-year sunspot cycle. In 1908, these sunspots were shown to be magnetic storms on the Sun's surface.

In 1915, Albert Einstein proposed in his general relativity theory that mass bends the fabric of space and time. He predicted, to great accuracy, that the Sun's great mass and gravity would deflect starlight behind it. During the total eclipse of May 29, 1919, stars behind the Sun were gravitationally shifted exactly as Einstein had predicted. Almost overnight, Einstein became a scientific celebrity. Today, thousands of people all over the world travel to see a total solar eclipse. Many vacation tour packages are built around an upcoming eclipse.

[*See also* Columbus, Christopher, *and* Moon.]

BIBLIOGRAPHY

Harrington, Philip S. *Eclipse! The What, Where, When, Why and How Guide to Watching Solar and Lunar Eclipses.* New York: Wiley, 1997.

Littmann, Mark, Ken Willcox, and Fred Espenak. *Totality: Eclipses of the Sun.* 2nd ed. New York: Oxford University Press, 1999.

Steel, Duncan. *Eclipse: The Celestial Phenomenon That Changed the Course of History*. Washington, D.C.: Joseph Henry Press, 2001.

ROBERT BONADURER

Edwards, Amelia

Edwards, Amelia (1831–1892), English novelist who traveled in the Dolomites and conducted archaeological studies in Egypt. Amelia Edwards is best known for her 1873 book, *A Thousand Miles up the Nile*, in which she recounts her adventures traveling by *dahabeeyah* up the river. During her trip she made careful descriptions and measurements of the many landmarks and monuments she encountered, at one point spending six weeks working on excavations at the Temple of Ramses II. The book is illustrated with engravings based on her watercolor sketches and is considered to be the first broad archaeological catalog of Egypt's antiquities.

Edwards described her trip to Egypt as an "accident," as she and her companion had no plans to go to Egypt when they set out traveling. Their original plans were to go to France to do some sketching, but a continual rain drove them southward looking for better weather. They ended up in Cairo, where they embarked on a lengthy trip up the Nile as far as the falls of the Second Cataract. This trip to Egypt had a profound influence on Edwards. After she returned to England, she gave up most of her previous activities and devoted her energies to fund-raising and promoting the excavation, documentation, and preservation of Egyptian monuments and artifacts. She founded the Egypt Exploration Fund and served as its first secretary. She was responsible for establishing a professorship of Egyptology at University College London.

Amelia Edwards was born in London on June 7, 1831. As a child she showed a gift for writing, and after her parents died, she supported herself as a journalist, poet, novelist, and travel writer. She published numerous books, mostly novels, but is best known today for her travel accounts of adventures

Amelia Edwards. This plate from the 1889 edition of Edwards's *A Thousand Miles up the Nile* shows her gift for setting antiquities into their environment. COURTESY THE NEWBERRY LIBRARY, CHICAGO

in the Dolomite mountains and her expedition to Egypt. Edwards died on April 15, 1892, at age sixty-one; she was buried at Henbury, England.

[*See also* Women Explorers.]

BIBLIOGRAPHY

Edwards, Amelia. *A Thousand Miles up the Nile*. London: Longmans, Green, 1877. Reprint. Los Angeles: J. P. Tarcher, 1983.

PATRICIA GILMARTIN

El Dorado. "El Dorado" is among the most evocative of place-names in the Americas. Its origins are intimately linked to the initial exploration of South America in the early sixteenth century. In Spanish, "El Dorado" literally means "the gilded one." It originally referred to an Indian chief of Bogota whose body was reportedly covered with gold during ceremonies. Like most myths, El Dorado involves a grain of truth: various native peoples in South and Central America used gold in ornamentation, and gold played a part in some of their religious rites. Several Spanish and German explorers are associated with the earliest searches for El Dorado and his riches in South America. The German explorer Ambrosius Ehinger sought El Dorado as early as 1531; the Spaniard Sebastián de Benalcazar searched for it in 1535. Bogota's abode was reportedly found in 1537, but that did not end the search because Europeans' expectations always exceeded their conquests. That the search did not finish suggests that the myth of El Dorado was as deeply linked to the ever-questing European mind-set as it was to anything that existed in fact. When viewed in context, the search for El Dorado is inseparable from the political intrigue and empire-building of the age of exploration. Sir Walter Ralegh sought the fabled land of El Dorado in 1595 and in 1617, but to no avail. Throughout the seventeenth and eighteenth centuries, El Dorado moved about in the restless minds of explorers, as well as on the ambitious maps of South America that the explorers drew. Sir Robert Schomburgk's mid-nineteenth-century surveying expedition represents Britain's last major exploration effort to find El Dorado, but this was not the last time El Dorado would entrance the public. With the discovery of gold in California in 1848, the place-name El Dorado blossomed in the American West, where it came to be associated with the search for mineral riches.

[*See also* North America, *subentry on* Apocryphal Voyages and Imaginary Places (post-1500); Ralegh, Walter; *and* Schomburgk, Robert.]

BIBLIOGRAPHY

Burnett, D. Graham. *Masters of All They Surveyed: Exploration, Geography, and a British El Dorado*. Chicago: University of Chicago Press, 2000.

Goodman, Edward J. *The Explorers of South America*. Norman: University of Oklahoma Press, 1992.

RICHARD FRANCAVIGLIA

Elias, Ney (1844–1897), Victorian explorer of central Asia. In May 1873, Ney Elias and Henry Stanley won the Royal Geographical Society's gold Founder's Medal. Stanley received it for finding David Livingstone in Africa, and Elias for making an exploration of more than 4,500 miles (7,500 kilometers) from Peking through western Mongolia and across Siberia. Then, both men were equally celebrated; now, while Stanley remains celebrated, the name of Elias has all but disappeared, largely because he left no published accounts other than newspaper articles.

Elias took courses in surveying and astronomy at the RGS and went to Shanghai in 1866 to join a shipowner's firm. In three solo journeys between 1867 and 1869, he surveyed the new course of the 2,700-mile(4,350-kilometer)-long Yellow River (Huang Ho), an often-changing water course that arises in the Qinghai region of Tibet. These journeys were described by the *Times* of London as "one of the most wonderful feats of modern travel." For his second expedition, again solo, Elias left Peking in July 1872, crossed the Gobi Desert and the eastern Tientsin, and continued across western Mongolia— through territory never seen by a European. While crossing the Mongolian steppes he recorded his position and altitude daily, as was his custom on every expedition. At Biysk (Semipalatinsk), Russia, he still had 2,300 miles (3,700 kilometers) ahead before he reached the railhead at Nizhnly Novgorod, and he reached Saint Petersburg in January 1873. He charted the entire 4,800 miles (7,730 kilometers) of this expedition with superb draftsmanship. Elias carried out a third expedition in northern Burma and southern Yunnan (China), planning an extension into Tibet, but that proved impossible.

In 1874, Elias was posted as assistant resident in Mandalay, from where he planned an expedition into the remote Shan states of upper Burma. In June 1878 he undertook a solo "road inspection" of the hazardous Karakoram route into Chinese Turkistan, surveying a virtually unknown area and reaching the Yarkand River. In 1885 he crossed the Pamirs to assess boundaries between Russia and China, and continued into Afghanistan. He returned to Simla, India, in 1886 from Afghanistan, having trav-

---

Forgotten Explorations

This passage speaks for itself, coming as it did at a time when those who sought fame and power, like the future Lord Curzon or the young Winston Churchill, were acutely aware of the propaganda value to their careers of a good book or two.

Mr Ney Elias, late Consul-General at Meshed, died in London on Monday from blood poisoning after only a short illness, but after being in indifferent health for some time. Though almost the least-known he was one of the most courageous, the most clear-sighted, and most observant of all recent-day explorers in Asia. He was exceptionally modest, and as his most important journey was made, and his most valuable reports were written, when employed in confidential service under the Government of India, it has come about that a man who, a quarter of a century ago, earned the Gold Medal of the Royal Geographical Society for a solitary journey made from Peking to Saint Petersburg, in the depth of winter and in the midst of a fanatical Chinese rebellion, and who since then has almost continuously been employed on daring journeys and delicate political missions in southwestern China, in Burma, in Chinese Turkestan, the Pamirs, Afghan Turkestan, Chitral, Siam and Persia, is scarcely known to any Englishmen beyond a few officials of the Government of India and readers of the Geographical Society's *Journal*.

—Passage from the obituary in the *Times* (London) of June 2, 1897

---

eled 3,000 miles (4,830 kilometers)—again solo—and having crossed forty passes, all without government help. In December 1891 he became the consul-general of Khorāsān province in Persia. He died in London on May 31, 1897. In his obituary, Sir Francis Younghusband wrote that Elias was "the best traveler there has ever been in Central Asia."

[*See also* Livingstone, David; Stanley, Henry; *and* Younghusband, Francis.]

BIBLIOGRAPHY
Morgan, Gerald. *Ney Elias: Explorer and Envoy Extraordinary in High Asia.* London: Allen and Unwin, 1971.

DAVID SPENCER SMITH

Emin Pasha (1840–1892), German medical doctor, naturalist, explorer, and governor of Egypt's Equatorial Province in central Africa. Born Eduard Schnitzer on March 28, 1840, with a German Jewish background but raised a Protestant in Oppeln, Silesia (now Opole, Poland), he studied at the universities of Breslau, Berlin, and Königsberg before signing on as a medical doctor in Ottoman service in Albania and Anatolia and assuming Turkish dress and a Muslim name. In 1876 Charles Gordon, governor of the Equatorial Province of the Egyptian empire, took him on as medical officer. Emin undertook a political mission to Uganda and Unyoro, and in 1878 Gordon, now governor-general of the Sudan, had him promoted to bey and governor of Equatorial Province. From his seat on the Nile at Lado, Emin explored his province, attacked the slave trade, and tirelessly collected botanical and ornithological specimens, which he dispatched, along with scientific articles, to Europe. In 1884 he discovered the Semliki River, which feeds into Lake Albert.

With the fall of Khartoum and the death of Gordon at the hands of Muhammad Ahmad the Mahdi in January 1885, the British evacuated Egyptian forces from the Sudan. Cut off, Emin retreated south from Lado to Wadelai and held on. His practice of Islam helped hold the loyalty of his troops. British authorities in Cairo promoted him to pasha but warned that he could expect no aid and should consider retreating to the East African coast. King Leopold II of Belgium and private British commercial and geographical interests stepped in. In December 1886 they hired Henry Stanley to rescue Emin Pasha. By the time the relief expedition had struggled from the west up the Congo River and through the rain forest to Lake Albert, it was Emin who had to rescue Stanley. After Emin's troops mutinied, he reluctantly abandoned his post and arrived with Stanley at Bagamoyo on the Zanzibar coast in December 1889.

The British-German scramble for East Africa was well under way by this time. Emin decided to return to his German roots, heading back inland at the head of a German expedition to claim lands south of Lake Victoria and over to Lake Albert. A German-British diplomatic deal back in Europe undercut Emin's mandate, and he quarreled with his German superiors. Wandering over the divide into Congo Free State, Emin died on October 23, 1892, at the hands of Arab slavers near Kanema.

[*See also* Gordon, Charles, *and* Stanley, Henry.]

BIBLIOGRAPHY
Caillou, Alan. *South from Khartoum: The Story of Emin Pasha.* New York: Hawthorn Books, 1974.

Emin Pasha. *Emin Pasha: His Life and Work*. Edited by Georg Schweitzer. 2 vols. 1898. Reprint. New York: Negro Universities Press, 1969.

DONALD MALCOLM REID

Emory, William Hemsley

Emory, William Hemsley (1811–1887), American soldier, surveyor, and cartographer. Emory did more than any other individual to secure and demarcate the 1,860-mile (3,000-kilometer) border between the United States and Mexico during the period from 1848 to 1857. This work is memorialized by a 7,780-foot (2,370-meter) peak named for him in the Big Bend region of the Rio Grande, in Texas. Prior to this, from June 26 to December 11, 1846, Emory was in charge of a reconnaissance survey from St. Louis, Missouri, to San Diego, California, in the Army of the West, under the command of Colonel (later Brigadier General) Stephen Watts Kearny.

Born in Queen Anne's County, Maryland, the son of Thomas and Anna Emory, William Emory was well equipped by education and experience to undertake these monumental surveys. In July 1826 Emory enrolled in the United States Military Academy at West Point, the only institution in the country where he could have obtained the necessary training for his future career. Upon his graduation in 1831 he was promoted to second lieutenant. However, after five years in the U.S. Army he resigned in order to take a position as a civil engineer.

In 1838 he rejoined the army as a first lieutenant in the newly formed Corps of Topographical Engineers, and married Matilda Bache. Emory brought the Midwest surveys done by European-trained Joseph Nicollet to publication as a map, "Hydrological Basin of the Upper Mississippi River, From Astronomical and Barometric Observations and Surveys"—published by the United States Senate in 1843. The next year the Senate published both Emory's "Map of Texas and the Countries Adjacent, Compiled in the Bureau of the Corps of Engineers, for the State Department," which indicated the area claimed by the United States from Mexico on the basis of U.S. expansion and settlement to Texas and beyond, as well as a report by Emory that accompanied the "Map of Texas." These materials were transmitted, along with the annexation treaty, to the U.S. Senate on April 29, 1844.

Following this, until 1846, Emory served as principal assistant on the Northwestern Boundary Survey, working to determine the boundary between the United States and the British Provinces (Canada). When war broke out between the United States and Mexico in 1846, Emory was appointed chief engineer officer of the Army of the West. In this position he was in charge of a party that extended Nicollet's observations in Saint Louis—through fifty-two astronomically determined points of latitude and longitude (from Greenwich, England)—westward to the Pacific Ocean. This was accomplished on a line of march by way of Santa Fe and the Gila River to San Diego from June 26 to December 11, 1846.

Comparison of coastal observations made in San Diego with those of Britain's Royal Navy affirmed the accuracy of Emory's traverse. The work of Emory and his party resulted in a map, "Military Reconnaissance of the Arkansas, Rio del Norte [Rio Grande] and Rio Gila" (1847). Prior to this instrumental survey, no point on the surface of the earth between the upper Rio Grande and the Pacific Ocean had been determined with any precision. Altitude above sea level, based on readings from a siphon barometer—the first such instrument to be taken overland across the continent—was a feature of this work. *Notes of a Military Reconnoissance [sic] from Fort Leavenworth in Missouri to San Diego in California* (first published in 1848) is Emory's narrative account of the expedition.

After a brief leave, in 1848, Emory was appointed chief astronomer on the U.S. commission to delineate the boundary between the United States and Mexico, which had resulted from the Treaty of Guadalupe Hidalgo (1848). Emory began surveying a line from south of San Diego eastward. During this assignment Emory was promoted to major. When the work was completed in January 1857, the United States had gained a route where a railroad, suggested by Emory, was later built—the Southern Pacific. Following this, Emory held several commands in the West, including Utah. In May 1861 Emory was promoted to lieutenant colonel and took part in a number of actions in the American Civil War. At the end of the war he was a corps commander and was appointed major general of the volunteers and promoted to the regular rank of brigadier general (1862). He continued in military service until 1876. Emory died in Washington, D.C., on December 1, 1887. A western oak, *Quercus emoryi*, was named in his honor by John Torrey who, with George Engleman, catalogued plants collected by Emory.

[*See also* United States Army Corps of Topographical Engineers.]

BIBLIOGRAPHY

Cullum, George W. *Biographical Register of Officers and Graduates of the United States Military Academy at West Point, N.*

Y. See entry on Emory in vol. 1. Boston and New York: Houghton Mifflin, 1891.

Emory, William Hemsley. "Reminiscences of General William Hemsley Emory, U.S.M.A. 1831." This is an incomplete autobiography that can be found in the library of the United States Military Academy at West Point.

Goetzmann, William H. *Army Exploration in the American West, 1803–1863.* New Haven, Conn.: Yale University Press, 1959. Reprints. Lincoln: University of Nebraska Press, 1979. Reprint with a new introduction by the author, Austin: Texas State Historical Association, 1991.

Goetzmann, William H. *Exploration and Empire: The Explorer and the Scientist in the Winning of the American West.* New York: Knopf, 1966. Reprint, New York: Norton, 1978. Reprint, New York: History Book Club, 1993.

Schwartz, Seymour I., and Ralph E. Ehrenberg. *The Mapping of America.* New York: H. N. Abrams, 1980. Reprint, Edison, N.J.: Wellfleet, 2001.

Thrower, Norman J. W. "William H. Emory and the Mapping of the American Southwest Borderlands." *Terrae Incognitae* 22 (1990): 41–91.

Wheat, Carl I. *Mapping the Transmississippi West, 1540–1861.* 5 vols. San Francisco: Institute of Historical Cartography, 1957–1963.

NORMAN J. W. THROWER

Encyclopedias of Exploration. The idea of specialized encyclopedic publications did not come into fashion until after World War II. Since then, though, many such publications have taken exploration as their theme. Perhaps the earliest was *Discovery and Exploration: An Atlas-History of Man's Journeys into the Unknown* (London: Geographical Projects Limited, 1960). This was the work of Frank Debenham (1883–1965), the Antarctic explorer, and came at the theme very broadly, trying to visualize the phenomenon in a variety of cultures and carrying the analysis up to the beginning of space exploration.

Debenham's remarkable compendium was followed in 1980 by Helen Delpar's *The Discoverers: An Encyclopedia of Explorers and Exploration* (New York: McGraw-Hill), which offered a large number of articles by the leading scholars of the day and attempted to take account of exploration by non-Europeans like the Chinese and the Muslims. In 1992, Richard Bohlander edited *World Explorers and Discoverers* (Macmillan), a full but purely biographical survey of almost exclusively western European explorers; some women were now included. In the same year, Silvio Bedini edited *The Christopher Columbus Encyclopedia* (2 vols.; New York: Simon and Schuster), a wide-ranging survey that included not only biographies but also articles by leading scholars. Of course, this work concentrated on European expansion into the "New World," and did not venture far beyond 1620. Finally, in 2003 Raymond Howgego

published an *Encyclopedia of Exploration to 1800* (Potts Point, Australia: Hordern House). This massive collection of biographies, a remarkable achievement for a single author, seems to reflect the new possibilities of the electronic age—not only in its inclusiveness of many nationalities, but also in its extensive bibliographies.

The themes of exploration literature overlap with those of travel literature. Here we most recently have *Literature of Travel and Exploration: An Encyclopedia*, edited by Jennifer Speake (3 vols.; New York and London: Fitzroy Dearborn, 2003). This primarily biographical work has substantial contributions by leading scholars, as well as extensive bibliographies. A year earlier, Peter Hulme and Tim Youngs had edited *The Cambridge Companion to Travel Writing* (Cambridge, U.K.: Cambridge University Press, 2002), a compendium of interesting attempts to work out the ideology of travel literature. To round out this brief survey, three remarkable collections of extracts from travel literature should be mentioned: Robin Hanbury-Tenison's *The Oxford Book of Exploration* (Oxford: Oxford University Press, 2005), Benedict Allen's *The Faber Book of Exploration* (London: Faber and Faber, 2002), and Eric Newby's *A Book of Travellers' Tales* (New York: Viking, 1986). These three books are fairly similar and share some common weaknesses; they are Eurocentric, for instance, and contain no images. But they offer the reader a remarkable conspectus—in the original documents—of the most striking phases of exploration. As the years go by, and as more and more scholars are drawn to the theme of exploration, more and more specialized works have been emerging. But the encyclopedic works cited here will long serve as summaries of the field.

DAVID BUISSERET

Entrecasteaux, Antoine Raymond Joseph Bruni d' (1737–1793), French navigator who explored the Australian coast while searching for remains of the La Pérouse expedition. Son of Jean-Baptiste Bruni d'Entrecasteaux, president of the *parlement* of Aix, and of Dorothée de l'Estang de Parade, Entrecasteaux was born in Aix-en-Provence on November 7, 1737. He hailed from a family of merchants from Italy, the Bruni, who took the name of their estate, Entrecasteaux (in the department of Var), when they were ennobled in the seventeenth century.

After studying at a Jesuit academy, Entrecasteaux became a *garde de la Marine* on July 4, 1754. His first deployments at sea took him to the Antilles and to the Mediterranean. In 1764, at the end of the Seven Years' War, Entrecasteaux was assigned to the hydrographical expedition of Chabert Cogolin, charged with astronomical observations in the western Mediterranean. Named lieutenant on February 1, 1770, Entrecasteaux participated in many campaigns against the Barbary pirates. In 1774, he embarked on the *Atalante* for an expedition meant to reestablish French commerce in the trading posts known as the Echelles du Levant. After sailing with Pierre Suffren aboard the *Alcmène*, Entrecasteaux received his first command, the *Aurore*, on April 7, 1777, and was promoted to captain in March 1779. Aboard the *Majestueux*, and with the Cadix squadron, Entrecasteaux participated in the battle of Cape Spartel on October 20, 1782.

In August 1783, Entrecasteaux became assistant manager of ports and arsenals, deputy to Charles Pierre Claret de Fleurieu, whose very important position made him close to the minister of the navy, Charles Eugène Gabriel de Castries. On February 25, 1785, Entrecasteaux was given command of the *Résolution* and the *Subtile*, heading a delicate mission to China in order to affirm French power there. Even beyond the intelligence that Entrecasteaux reported on the presence of other European countries in Asia, his voyage was a remarkable operation of maritime exploration, since it was the first attempt to sail to China against the monsoon by traveling around Malaysia and the Philippines. The search for a new route was part of a series of French efforts to develop trade with China.

Named governor of the Île de France (Mauritius) and the Île de Bourbon (Réunion), Entrecasteaux demonstrated his preference for liberal government, never locking himself into a regime of absolute power.

Upon his return to France on May 22, 1791, Entrecasteaux was named commander of an expedition sent by the government to pursue the research party of J. F. de Galaup de La Pérouse, which had not been heard from since February 1788. Entrecasteaux's mission was also to scout out the west and south of New Caledonia, the neighboring archipelagoes, and the western and southern coasts of New Holland. In order to complete the work of La Pérouse, he had at his disposal technical and scientific tools: two cargo ships, the *Recherche* and the *Espérance*, materials and supplies for three years, and a scientific staff consisting of both sailors and civilians—astronomers, geographers, natural scientists, and draftsmen among them. The expedition was made complicated by its double mission of research and exploration; thus it passed La Pérouse's shipwreck unknowingly, but it also assembled unprecedented scientific data. The cartography that the expedition made is remarkable, not only because of its scope (covering Tasmania, New Caledonia, Southern Australia, New Ireland, and New Guinea), but also because of its technical method of execution, invented by Charles de Beautemps-Beaupré and used worldwide for a century and a half. On their return, Elisabeth-Paul-Edouard de Rossel published a treatise on astronomical observations at sea, and the botanist Jacques-Julien Houtou de La Billardière published the first work on the flowers of Australia and of New Caledonia. The expedition also recorded invaluable testimonies on the Aborigines in Van Diemen's Land, a result of the in-depth exploration that the expedition made in the area of what is now called the D'Entrecasteaux Channel, near the southeast coast of Tasmania. The expedition suffered from health problems as a result of the poor quality of provisions and the slow progress of the ships. Consumed by dysentery, Entrecasteaux died at sea north of New Guinea on July 20, 1793. He was so highly esteemed by his fellows that they called him the "father of seamen."

Three months later, the boats were held up in Surabaya because of international conflicts related to the French Revolution. The return of men and records to France took place between 1795 and 1802. As a testimony to their painstaking exploration of the lands they traveled, the names of Entrecasteaux and of his companions can still be found in the toponymy of Australia, Tasmania, New Caledonia, and the neighboring archipelagoes.

[*See also* Australia, Exploration of, *and* La Pérouse, J. F. de Galaup de.]

BIBLIOGRAPHY

Rossel, Elisabeth-Paul-Edouard de. *Voyage de Dentrecasteaux, envoyé à la recherche de La Pérouse.* 2 volumes and an atlas. Paris: Impériale, 1808.

Dupont, Maurice. *D'Entrecasteaux: Rien que la mer, un peu de gloire.* Paris: Editions maritimes et d'outre-mer, 1983.

Duyker, Edward, and Maryse Duyker, eds. and trans. *Voyage to Australia and the Pacific, 1791–1793, by Bruny d'Entrecasteaux.* Carlton South, Australia: Melbourne University Press, 2001.

Richard, Hélène. *Une grande expédition scientifique au temps de la Révolution française: Le voyage de d'Entrecasteaux à la recherche de Lapérouse.* Paris: Comité des travaux historiques et scientifiques, 1986.

HÉLÈNE RICHARD
Translated from the French by Alexa Nieschlag

Eratosthenes

Eratosthenes (c. 276–c. 194 B.C.E.), Greek scientist who accurately calculated the circumference of the earth. The campaigns of Alexander the Great and his successors at the end of the fourth century B.C.E., together with travelers' reports, furnished a huge amount of fresh information that dramatically changed contemporaries' worldview. The person who took the lead in collecting, evaluating, and interpreting this information was the versatile scientist Eratosthenes.

Born in the African city of Cyrene in 276 B.C.E., he studied philosophy in Athens before being appointed teacher of the young prince Ptolemy IV and head of the famous library at Alexandria. Until his death in 194, Eratosthenes worked in Alexandria in the fields of poetry, philosophy, music theory, mathematics, astronomy, geography, chronology, philology, and history. Nearly all his works are lost, but more than 350 fragments survive in books by later Greek and Roman authors.

Eratosthenes secured his place in the history of exploration with his accurate calculation of the circumference of the earth. As emerges from accounts by the astronomer Cleomedes and others, Eratosthenes' method was based on simple proportion: he related the difference between the latitudes of two places on the same meridian (figures obtained from celestial observations) to their distance apart on the ground. This calculation and others—such as the dimensions of the sun and the moon, and their distance from the earth—were expounded in his book *On the Measurement of the Earth*.

In another work, *Geographica*, Eratosthenes drew a new map of the *oikoumenē* ("inhabited world") that was a major improvement on the older maps with their characteristic features of analogy, symmetry, and speculation. Eratosthenes was the first geographer to draw parallel circles and meridians and to develop them into a proper system. The fundamental elements of his map consisted no longer of peoples (such as "Indians," "Celts"), but rather of cities (Rhodes, Alexandria) and significant physical features (mouth of the Indus River, Taurus mountain range). Eratosthenes was able to determine only a few parallels and even fewer meridians. Moreover, since his cities were chosen mainly because of their political status, they formed no complete set of geodetic coordinates. Even so, despite these imperfections, Eratosthenes' ideas and methods gave the study of geography a new scientific basis.

To secure information for his *Geographica*, Eratosthenes used different types of sources, including geographical works, literature with geographical content, reports by specialists (like Alexander's surveyors), and travelogues and itineraries compiled by traders, diplomats, and voyagers. Inevitably, some of the material was outdated (like Hanno's report about the west coast of Africa), unreliable (Pytheas's account of northwest Europe), or even plain wrong (Patrocles' notion that the Caspian Sea forms part of the northern ocean). For some regions, too, the information available was far from complete and would long remain so. Nonetheless the stature of Eratosthenes' geographical achievement is not in doubt: in a highly productive new way he integrated the theoretical approach of ancient astronomers and the amazing, far-flung discoveries being made in the Hellenistic period.

[*See also* Europe and the Mediterranean, *subentries on* Greek and Roman Geography and Worldview *and* Greek and Roman Mapmaking, *and* Oikoumenē *and* Orbis Terrarum.]

BIBLIOGRAPHY

Geus, Klaus. *Eratosthenes von Kyrene: Studien zur hellenistischen Kultur- und Wissenschaftsgeschichte*. Munich: Beck, 2002.

Geus, Klaus. "Measuring the Earth and the *Oikoumene*: Zones, Meridians, *Sphragides* and Some Other Geographical Terms Used by Eratosthenes of Kyrene." In *Space in the Roman World: Its Perception and Presentation*, edited by Richard Talbert and Kai Brodersen, 11–26 and fig. 1–3. Münster: LIT–Verlag, 2004.

KLAUS GEUS

Ethiopia.

"Ethiopia" and "Abyssinia," names that were used interchangeably, refer to the same country. Of the two, "Ethiopia" was inherited from the classical country of the same name, while "Abyssinia" was an indigenous self-designation for the Christian people of northern Ethiopia who spoke a Semitic language. It was the search for Prester John that brought Abyssinia to the attention of Christians in Europe. By the beginning of the fifteenth century, Italian, Portuguese, and other explorers were slowly identifying the Christian kings of Ethiopia as suitable candidates for Prester John. The Portuguese led the search for the realm of Prester John first by sea, and the search by land started in 1487 when King João II of Portugal sent Perô da Covilhã overland to India with orders to locate Prester John. Covilhã, a linguist with an adventurous soul, traveled in Egypt, Arabia, Yemen, India, and East Africa, and he arrived in Ethiopia in 1494. He was well received at the court of King Iskindir (1478–1494). Covilhã was never allowed to leave Ethiopia, where he was given land, married a local woman, and lived as a nobleman. He learned to speak and write in Amharic fluently, so well that the educated elements, especially the famous old Queen Illeni, enjoyed his conversation. The second Portuguese envoys to Prester John arrived in the country in 1508. They were warmly received at the court of the young king Lebna Dengel (1508–1540). With the advice of Queen Illeni, Lebna Dengel wrote a letter in which he promised to support the Portuguese with gold, fighting men, and "an infinite quantity of supplies," and dispatched it to the Portuguese king with his ambassador, Matthew, in 1509. Matthew reached Portugal in 1514 after four years of stay at Goa in India.

In 1520, King Manuel I of Portugal sent a diplomatic mission to Ethiopia, which was led by Dom Rodrigo da Lima. It also included the chaplain Francisco Alvares, who left the first extensive account of the country, an account that lifted the veil of mystery which had shrouded the realm of Prester John for years. But the "Prester John" whom the Portuguese found was not the idealized one they had sought and fantasized about for so long. Yet the 1520 diplomatic mission was not a total failure. First, it established a relationship that saved Christian Ethiopia from destruction by the Muslim leader Imam Ahmad (r. 1529–1543). The relationship also heralded a new age for Ethiopian studies in Europe. For over a century, the Jesuit missionaries (mostly Portuguese) who came to Ethiopia wrote about its history, politics, society, religion, customs, fauna, and flora. In this respect it was Pedro Paez who left behind a rich legacy. Pedro Paez arrived in Ethiopia in 1603, where he lived for nineteen years. Paez gained fame as a learned man, who discussed even sensitive religious issues with respect for the views of others. He was a fine teacher, a gifted preacher, and a keen observer whose advice was sought by kings and noblemen. Both in his letters and later in his 1,200-page *History of Ethiopia*, he gave exact descriptions of animals and plants centuries before any work of classification existed.

After the expulsion of the Portuguese missionaries from Ethiopia in 1633, the first important European visitor to the country who left behind extensive records was James Bruce, who lived in the country from 1769 to 1772. Bruce visited historic sites such as Axum and Gondar, and left interesting descriptions of those places. He was an eyewitness to the drama of the "Era of the Princes" when Ras Mikael Sehul of Tigray assassinated one emperor, put his son on the throne, and removed another emperor from the throne. Bruce later wrote about the history and politics of the country. Above all, he collected Geez manuscripts, which he brought back with him to the West, thus expanding and enriching Ethiopian studies in Europe. Bruce perhaps is best known for his erroneous claim that he was the first European to discover the source of the Blue Nile at Lake Tana.

Long before the beginning of the nineteenth century, northern Ethiopia and its people were better known to the outside world than central and southern Ethiopia. It was only during the 1830s and 1840s that Shawa and the neighboring Oromo territories came to be known to the outside world. Major W. Cornwallis Harris visited Shawa in the early 1840s and described both the city of Harar and the town of Ankobar, the capital of Shawa. He also wrote about the history, politics, religion, and society in Shawa, Wallo, and the Gibe states. It was Antoine d'Abbadie and Guglielmo Massaja, the first Catholic bishop of Oromo territory, who penetrated the Gibe region and left vivid accounts of Oromo states and the kingdom of Kaffa. In short, by the second half of the nineteenth century, "Ethiopia" slowly eclipsed and replaced "Abyssinia" as the name in popular usage. Because of the Ethiopian victory at the battle of Adwa in 1896, Ethiopia became the symbol of African resistance against European imperialism. Today, Ethiopia is the name that encapsulates strong nationalism, ancient civilization, a rich history, and a proud heritage.

[*See also* Africa; Prester John; *and biographies of figures mentioned in this article.*]

BIBLIOGRAPHY

Bruce, James. *Travels to Discover the Source of the Nile.* Edited by C. F. Beckingham. New York: Horizon Press, 1964.

Caraman, Philip. *The Lost Empire: The Story of the Jesuits in Ethiopia, 1555–1634.* Notre Dame, Ind.: University of Notre Dame Press, 1985.

Munro-Hay, Stuart. *Ethiopia, the Unknown Land: A Cultural and Historical Guide.* With photographs by Pamela Taor. New York: I. B. Touris, 2002.

Sanceau, Elaine. *The Land of Prester John: A Chronicle of Portuguese Exploration.* New York: Knopf, 1944.

MOHAMMED HASSEN ALI

Europe and the Mediterranean

This entry contains six subentries:

Ancient Near East Geography, Worldview, and Mapmaking
Greek and Roman Geography and Worldview
Greek and Roman Mapmaking
Byzantine Geography, Worldview, and Mapmaking
Medieval West Geography and Worldview
Medieval West Mapmaking

Ancient Near East Geography, Worldview, and Mapmaking

The Near East is defined principally by the modern countries of Iraq, Iran, Syria, Turkey, Lebanon, Jordan, Israel, and Egypt. Ancient periods of interest here begin around 3000 B.C.E. with the first appearance of cities and the adoption of writing, and conclude with the introduction of Hellenism around 330 B.C.E. Geographical information is most abundant for ancient Egypt and for Mesopotamia, corresponding to the modern country of Iraq. Mesopotamia was home to the Sumerian civilization in the third millennium B.C.E. It also supported the kingdoms of Babylonia and Assyria in the two following millennia. Other regions for which we have information about ancient geographical knowledge include Israel (prominently described in books of the Hebrew Bible) and the Aegean lands to the west, where the Minoan and Mycenaean civilizations developed. The Minoans and Mycenaeans were contemporary with the Bronze Age cultures of the Near East, and were almost certainly in contact with Near Eastern lands through maritime trade and diplomacy.

Ancient Egyptian Cosmos, Worldview, and Geographical Knowledge. The Egyptians believed that the creation of the cosmos started in the primeval waters, also perceived as chaos, from which the cosmos, as an entity, emerged. The end of the cosmos was perceived as the cosmos sinking back into the primeval waters, like an island in the Nile disappearing in the river. Little is known about the motivation and trigger for this concept. In some concepts of cosmogony, however, a god who existed before the creation was responsible for setting the process in motion. In regard to time, this concept can be described as creation, maintenance, and end. In regard to space it encompasses a heaven, the earth, and the underworld. Heaven was elevated above the earth, resting on four pillars marking the ends of the world cardinal points. The world itself was seen as surrounded by the primeval waters, and between here and the underworld, horizons marked the transition. The netherworld could be located in heaven, identi-

Egyptian Sailors. From a limestone relief at the temple of Hatshepsut. These sailors appear on a frieze depicting a voyage to Punt (a destination about which scholars cannot agree) in the days of Hatshepsut, believed to have ruled from about 1479 to 1458 B.C.E. Temple of Hatshepsut, Deir el-Bahri, Thebes, Egypt/Erich Lessing/Art Resource, NY

cal with the world of the gods, or it could be situated in or below the earth. During the Old Kingdom (c. 2686–2160 B.C.E.), the entrance to the netherworld was seen in the western desert, and thus its location was underground while the kings rose to the circumpolar stars and the realm of the sun god Re. The formal shape of the underworld contained elements of land, water, or the body of a god. Natural features were incorporated into the landscape of the underworld. For instance, in the Middle Kingdom (c. 2055–1650 B.C.E.) there was the concept of the "Two Ways of Rosetau," and in the New Kingdom (c. 1550–1069 B.C.E.) there was the "Field of Offerings" and the "Field of Rushes," and towns and swamps were tangible places in the underworld. Chapter 149 of the *Book of the Dead*, for example, even contains an address to fourteen mounds of the netherworld. Yet these natural features were not linked by distance or direction, and thus the landscape described in this religious literature does not amount to mapmaking but rather reflects the spatial variation of the underworld. [See color plate 30 in this volume.]

The worldly image of the cosmos as a whole was manifested perfectly in Egyptian temple architecture. The crypts represented the underworld, the giant entrance gates the horizons, the columns the pillars that carry the sky, and the roof of the temple symbolized heaven. In regard to the more physical aspects of the world, the two main axes in ancient Egypt were south to north, following the flow of the Nile and consisting of Upper and Lower Egypt, and the east-west trajectory of the sun. The axes also marked the boundaries of Egypt. In the north was the Mediterranean, in the south the land beyond the first cataract, and in the east and west of the Nile Valley the desert regions. Beyond these frontiers were the lands of foreign people who—since they were in the regions outside the Egyptian world order—lived in total chaos.

The Egyptian worldview thus focused on national identity, with Egypt as the center and the king at the head of the world. It is only during the New Kingdom that Egypt recognized and accepted that it was actually part of a world inhabited by a variety of different peoples. This awareness of other regions and people led to attempts at describing and portraying the regions and its peoples outside Egypt. From several sources of the New Kingdom we possess long lists of foreign toponyms known to the Egyptians. These lists originated in the so-called execration texts of the Old and Middle Kingdoms, and they were meant to destroy Egypt's enemies ritually. It is also from the Middle Kingdom that we possess papyrus

fragments from Kahun that contain spatial diagrams that hint already at mapmaking. In regard to the mentioned list of foreign place-names, one list from the mortuary temple of Amenophis III (r. c. 1390–1352 B.C.E.) in western Thebes is of particular interest. The list refers to Egypt's northern neighbors, mentioning places such as Amnissos, Phaistos, and Knossos on Crete, as well as Mycenae. Most likely the list was sorted according to the itinerary of an Egyptian delegation traveling through the Aegean Sea. Another source for the knowledge of place-names and locations is the so-called *onomastika*. These lists not only are a collection of words according to categories but also contain foreign locations and landmarks. A well-known example of this group is the *onomastikon* of Amenope, a group of nine texts dating to the Twentieth Dynasty. Apart from listing "all things that exist" and place-names, these texts also provide the historical information that some of the Sea Peoples such as the Philistines and Tjekker, who previously had attacked Egypt, now lived in the southern Levant.

The Mesopotamian Cosmos, Worldview, and Geographical Knowledge. In ancient Mesopotamia, views about the cosmos did not develop to any great extent, and they remained unchanged over the region's long history. In texts that do include cosmological speculations there emerges the idea that the universe was formed of superimposed levels, all populated by deities of various ranks of importance. There were three levels of the Heavens, below which was the Upper Earth, where humankind was settled. Farther below was the Middle Earth, a huge subterranean freshwater ocean, known as the Apsû. The Underworld, the land to which human spirits went when they died, was also below the earth. The whole of this universe was bound together as one coherent structure by mythical bonds or cosmic cables that held the level of the Heavens to the lowest level of the netherworld, and prevented them from drifting apart. There was no understanding of a spherical earth like that conceived by Greek astronomers in later antiquity. Rather, the earth was seen as a flat disk, under which the sun set at night. The celestial bodies within the sky above were carefully watched and identified principally with reference to the horizon where they rose or descended at observable points.

Knowledge of the earth within which humankind was settled was limited to the boundaries of kingdoms and empires or the farthest points of commercial ventures. Beyond this known world were distant regions occupied by exotic creatures, immortal beings, and fantastic landscapes. Only individuals with larger-than-life abilities could venture into such distant places. Pictorially, the regions beyond the known world are well represented in the famous "Babylonian Map of the World," which, with its accompanying cuneiform text, is inscribed on a clay tablet dated to around the eighth century B.C.E. On the tablet, the earth is rendered as two concentric circles, inside of which known places in Mesopotamia are labeled, such as Babylon, Assyria, and Urartu. The area between the two circles is identified as the "Salt Sea," envisioned as surrounding the entire known continent. Radiating out from the circle are triangular areas, identified as distant regions. The accompanying text on the tablet describes these regions, which include a variety of exotic animals and mythological creatures. Interestingly, the northern district is identified as a place "where the Sun is not seen."

Within the known world of the ancient Mesopotamians, there seems to have been a well-developed sense of one's geographical position in relation to other man-made and natural features. Even at the dawn of history, people were compiling geographical lists and including in them the names of cities and towns, watercourses, and other topographical features. One such list, copies of which have been found in Iraq and Syria, enumerates prominent towns that were located along either discrete watercourses or overland routes. While the function of this early list remains uncertain, its composition is apparently compiled from lists of routes taken by traders. The earliest motivation for obtaining geographical knowledge, therefore, seems to have been trade. This was an important activity, especially for the settlers of Mesopotamia, who inhabited a country poor in natural resources such as timber, stone, and metal ores. It is clear, however, that territorial expansion and political power followed on the heels of trade; this is attested by inscriptions describing the military achievements of early Mesopotamian kings, which include lists of places visited or conquered in the course of campaigns.

Also inscribed on clay tablets are itineraries, which further testify to the Mesopotamians' well-developed sense of geography, even over fairly wide distances. Itineraries preserved from the Neo-Assyrian period frequently list the distance between major halting places in terms of days or "double hours" (about six miles [ten kilometers]). An earlier itinerary dating to the early second millennium B.C.E. describes an overland journey between southern and northern Mesopotamia in terms of the names of the places reached each night along the voyage. Along with the Assyrian texts, this itinerary likely functioned as a record of a military campaign, thus emphasizing again the role that political expansion had in the formulation of geographical knowledge.

Egyptian and Mesopotamian Mapmaking. In Egypt, the most famous map—and actually the only surviving map showing the landscape of the living—is the "Gold Mine Papyrus" of Turin, which shows the gold mining region and quarry sites of the Wadi Hammamat in the eastern desert. The papyrus today is about 110 inches (2.80 meters) long and 16 inches (0.41 meters) high. The various fragments depict mountains, wadis, trees, houses, and wells. A brief note next to them further describes most figures. For instance, the feature described as the "mountains of gold" was painted in rose, and brown bands on their slopes indicated a quartz vein embedded in the granite. The map was drawn by the scribe Amennakht for one of the expeditions under Pharaoh Ramses IV (r. 1153–1147 B.C.E.). Based on this map made for an expedition, it seems very likely that the Egyptians produced various maps for the military activities in the Levant and Nubia and that mapmaking was always an important part of Egypt's administration.

In Mesopotamia, scribes rendered geographical space diagrammatically by incising plans and maps on clay tablets. The motivation for this mapmaking stems from the desire to clarify and describe accurately the location, size, and ownership of property. Because of this, most maps tended to emphasize small areas, namely towns or cities and surrounding territories. One of the earliest clay maps, c. 2300 B.C.E., comes from Nuzi in northern Iraq. It shows a river, symbolized by wavy lines, flowing through the center of a district possessing a delineated plot of land (about twelve hectares). On either side are hills or mountains, indicated by scalelike marks. Towns, which are rendered by circles, are named in the cuneiform script. In good cartographic fashion, the scribe has oriented this map, writing on three sides of the tablet: "west," "east," and "north," with north appearing on the left-hand side.

An impressive Babylonian map, c. 1500 B.C.E., is a tablet incised with a plan of the important holy city of Nippur. Surrounding the city is a wall with seven gates whose names are written beside them. The plan also marks the location of the Euphrates River, two canals, and some of the buildings within the city, including the location of the principal temple. Significantly, archaeological investigations of Nippur have confirmed the location of some of the features on the map. They also suggest that the map was drawn to scale. With this and the Nuzi map, therefore, two fundamental principles of cartography—scale and orientation—are known to have been achieved by the early scribes of ancient Mesopotamia.

Geographical Knowledge in the Biblical and Aegean Worlds.

We possess few sources of geographic information about ancient Israel, although some biblical passages allude to a geographical awareness and possibly even some knowledge of mapmaking. In the book of Genesis, the Table of Nations describes a fairly wide world, with Egypt to the south, Babylonia and Assyria to the east, and regions of the Mediterranean Sea to the west. Itineraries, such as that found in Numbers 33, clearly show that such compositions were formulated according to the same criteria as itineraries from Mesopotamia, in which stages of a journey were itemized according to places stopped at along the route. A compilation of information derived from a map or group of maps is suggested by Joshua 18–19, which provides detailed descriptions of landforms, watercourses, settlements, and compass orientations. The census of Israel initiated by King David, as told in 2 Samuel 24, may also support the existence of a diagrammatic map of Israel used for governmental purposes.

As with Israel, there are no preserved maps of the Minoan and Mycenaean peoples of the Aegean. Nevertheless, their knowledge of the lands and peoples reached through maritime trading connections or through raiding or marauding expeditions was probably as well developed as those in the Near East. Inscribed tablets rendered in the Linear B script list place-names that probably stand for provincial districts or settlements. Geographical awareness is also clear from a fresco found in a house at Akrotiri, on the island of Thera, dating to c. 1550–1490 B.C.E., contemporary with the expansion of Mycenaean power in the Aegean region. The Akrotiri fresco presents a number of landscape scenes, with walled harbor cities, mountain peaks, and a fleet of ships departing from one port city, crossing a body of water, and arriving at another city. While the location of these scenes has yet to be conclusively determined, that they are set in a real geographic place seems likely by the specificity of the flora, fauna, topography, and architecture, all of which can find a home in an Aegean landscape. Some have also ventured to see cartographic features within this scene, given the winding rivers with subsidiary streams and sea-shores represented from a top-view perspective, the same convention used in Near Eastern maps.

[*See also* Arabia *and* Maps, Mapmaking, and Mapmakers.]

BIBLIOGRAPHY
Harrell, J. A., and V. Brown. "The Oldest Surviving Topographical Map from Ancient Egypt (Turin 1879, 1899, 1969)." *Journal of the American Research Center in Egypt* 29 (1992): 81–105.
Horowitz, Wayne. "The Babylonian Map of the World." *Iraq* 50 (1988): 147–165.
Millard, A. R. "Cartography in the Ancient Near East." In *The History of Cartography*, edited by J. B. Harley and David Woodward, vol. 1, pp. 107–116. Chicago: University of Chicago Press, 1987.
Quirke, Stephen. "Measuring the Underworld." In *Mysterious Lands*, edited by David O'Connor and Stephen Quirke, 161–181. London: UCL Press, 2003.
Smith, R. H. "Cartography of Palestine." *The Interpreter's Dictionary of the Bible*. Supplementary volume. Nashville, Tenn.: Abingdon, 1976.
Warren, Peter. "The Miniature Fresco from the West House at Akrotiri, Thera, and Its Aegean Setting." *Journal of Hellenic Studies* 99 (1979): 115–129.

LISA COOPER
THOMAS HIKADE

Greek and Roman Geography and Worldview

"A description of the known world is what I set out to give, a difficult task and one hardly suited to eloquence, since it consists chiefly in names of peoples and places and in their fairly puzzling arrangement." With these words, Pomponius Mela (quoted in F. E. Romer's translation), writing in the first century C.E., begins his geographical work, *De Chorographia*, which sums up earlier geographical thought, and also shaped later thinking, and is therefore a suitable guide to the topic. Pomponius Mela continues:

To trace this arrangement completely is a time-consuming, rather than a welcome, subject, but nevertheless a very worthwhile thing to consider and understand. . . . Let me address the things that are most unambiguous, as they all certainly will be, even in a summary treatment. To start with, in fact, let me untangle what the shape of the whole is, what its greatest parts are, what the condition of its parts taken one at a time is, and how they are inhabited; then, back to the borders and coasts of all lands as they exist to the interior and on the seacoast, to the extent that the sea enters them and washes up around them, and with those additions that, in the nature of the regions and their inhabitants, need to be recorded. So that this outline can be known and grasped more easily, its summa will be revisited in a little more depth.

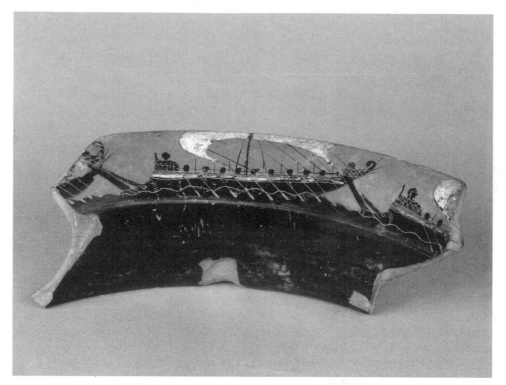

Greek Galleys. Fragment of a black-figured dinos showing Greek galleys. These galleys of the sixth century B.C.E. resemble the Argonaut galley model with its square sail, single row of oarsmen, and stern steering oar. In the development of European overseas shipping, some elements of galley construction would eventually be combined with the features of the heavy northern European sailing ships, resulting in vessels that could sail the seas of the world. MUSÉE DU LOUVRE/ERICH LESSING/ART RESOURCE, NY

First, Pomponius Mela proposes to repeat the *summa* of geography (which appears to be part of his audience's "general knowledge" and only needs to be recalled to its memory), then he wants to explain the shape of the whole and the form, and inhabitants, of its main parts (again, this is considered to be well enough known); in a third step he goes on to describe the details in a *periplus*, a coastal voyage along the shores and coasts of the continents.

> Whatever all this is, therefore, on which we have bestowed the name of world and sky, it is a single unity and embraces itself and all things with a single ambit. It differs in its parts. Where the sun rises is designated formally as east or sunrise; where it sinks, as west or sunset; where it begins its descent, south; in the opposite direction, north. In the middle of this unity the uplifted earth is encircled on all sides by the sea. In the same way, the earth also is divided from east to west into two halves, which they term hemispheres, and it is differentiated by five horizontal zones. Heat makes the middle zone unlivable and cold does so to the outermost ones. The remaining two habitable zones have the same annual seasons, but not at the same time. The Antichthones inhabit one, we the other. The chorography of the

former zone is unknown because of the heat of the intervening expanse, and the details of the latter are now to be described.

In his repetition of the audience's general knowledge, Pomponius Mela proceeds from Large to Small. First he discusses "all" (*omne*), that is, space, and the four cardinal directions, then as "uplifted" in its middle the earth, which is divided in two hemispheres and five zones, two of which are inhabitable. Thus, Pomponius Mela presents in a schematic, but easily understood, manner the *summa* of "scientific" knowledge about the world. The globe, its division into two hemispheres, and the five *klimata* had been part of general knowledge by the Hellenistic period. He writes: "This zone stretches from east to west and, because it is situated this way, is somewhat longer than it is wide at its widest point. It is entirely surrounded by Ocean, and from Ocean it allows four seas to enter—one from the north, from the south two, a fourth from the west."

Pomponius Mela does not say much about the form of "our" zone, which stretches from east to west, the so-called *oikoumenē* ("inhabited world"), save for the fact that its length exceeds its width; it is clear, then, that the *oikoumenē* is not circular, but rather oblong and not of regular width. Now the ocean that surrounds this zone intrudes into its land mass from north, south, and west; in his description, which clearly stresses the symmetry of the layout, he does not mention the names of the Caspian Sea (which was regarded as an ocean bay), the "Arabic Sea" (today the Red Sea), and the Persian Sea as well as the Mediterranean. Equally schematic is his description of the latter (which he refers to as "Our Sea") as a straight line of widening and narrowing waters, about which he eventually says:

> "By this sea and by two famous rivers, the Tanais (Don) and the Nile, the whole earth is divided into three parts. The Tanais, descending from north to south, flows down almost into the middle of Maeotis, and from the opposite direction the Nile flows down into the sea. Those lands that lie from the Strait to those rivers, on the one side we call Africa, on the other Europe. Whatever is beyond those rivers is Asia."

Again, these rivers appear to be symmetrically situated opposite each other. While the Mediterranean had at first been presented as the axis from west to east, there now appear two further defining lines: the symmetrical (*ex diverso*) rivers Don and Nile, which form a north-south axis; again nothing in the text suggests that they are anything but a straight line. Thus, the Mediterranean, Don, and Nile separate the *oikoumenē* into the three continents Africa, Europe, and Asia. With these chapters, Pomponius Mela summarized the theoretical knowledge about the world.

[*See also* Antichthon and Antipodes; Fictions of Exploration, *subentry* Ancient; Mela, Pomponius; *and Periploi.*]

BIBLIOGRAPHY

Adams, Colin, and Ray Laurence, eds. *Travel and Geography in the Roman Empire*. London and New York: Routledge, 2001.

Clarke, Katherine. *Between Geography and History: Hellenistic Constructions of the Roman World*. Oxford: Clarendon Press, 1999.

Huebner, W., ed. *Geographie und verwandte Wissenschaften*. Stuttgart: Steiner, 2000.

Romer, F. E., trans. *Pomponius Mela's Description of the World*. Ann Arbor: University of Michigan Press, 1998.

Talbert, Richard, and Kai Brodersen, eds. *Space in the Roman World*. Muenster, Germany: Lit, 2004.

KAI BRODERSEN

Greek and Roman Mapmaking

Woefully thin though the surviving testimony is, there can be no question that Greeks and Romans made various types of maps to encapsulate and promote their grasp and control of geographical space, including the sky. It is also clear, however, that their mapmaking efforts always remained uncoordinated, and that the potential of maps was underappreciated in their societies by comparison with Babylon and Egypt earlier, for example, or contemporary China, not to mention western Europe from the fifteenth century. A range of cultural factors can be cited to account for such limited intellectual and imaginative insight even on the part of rulers and commanders, but the puzzle remains far from satisfyingly resolved. For sure, there was no concept of cartography nor any atlas comprising a set of maps. No standard term for "map" ever emerged in either Greek or Latin, thus leaving it ambiguous whether certain references are to a map or to some other type of image (Was a *forma Sardiniae* carried in a triumphal procession at Rome a map of Sardinia, or, say, a statue of the island personified?). Equally, there were few recognized expectations for map presentation (material, orientation, symbols, color palette, key, etc). A need for general-purpose maps was barely perceived, and the challenges and expense of copying a complex map accurately remained formidable in the absence of any form of printing. This said, a map as such would not have baffled an educated Greek or Roman, and a succession of brilliant Greek scientists did develop the principles of mapmaking as we recognize them today; but the value of their contribution was little noticed.

Greek Worldview and Mapmaking. In the earliest Greek literature, the epic poems of Homer (eighth century B.C.E.), the worldview reflected is that the earth comprises an island-space encircled by limitless ocean. The earliest Greek scientific thinkers, in sixth-century Ionia, evidently conceived of the earth as a flat, concave disk with a breadth three times its depth; it was said to have been one such thinker, Anaximander of Miletus, who first attempted to make a world map. We learn that around 500 B.C.E. Aristagoras, tyrant of the same city, was able to take such a map—engraved on bronze, and showing "all" the seas and rivers—to Sparta, where its representation of the immense Persian Empire made a decisive impression. Even so, there is really no knowing what these, or other comparable ancient maps, looked like; scholars' reconstructions, with their inevitable reliance on modern norms, are an insecure guide. Greeks' worldview was successively enlarged by the "colonization" movement (eighth to sixth centuries)—when many migrated to settle around the

Black Sea, in Sicily and southern Italy, and even as far west as Spain—and by conflicts in the fifth century with Persians to the east and Carthaginians (Phoenicians) in North Africa. These wider horizons prompted the fifth-century historian Herodotus to maintain that beyond the Greeks' world—which he termed the *oikoumene*, "inhabited world"—was not necessarily just ocean, but other inhabited regions too, although their peoples remain impossible to contact because of the insurmountable barriers presented by the Atlantic to the west of the *oikoumenē* and the scorching deserts to its east and south.

Earth as a spherical globe at the center of a likewise spherical solar system is a cosmic view seemingly first articulated among the Greeks by the elusive figure of Pythagoras, a late sixth-century thinker and teacher active in southern Italy. In the fourth century this view was further developed by the belief that the globe is layered according to climate into five or more latitudinal strips or zones (*klimata*, literally "inclinations")—arctic, temperate, equatorial, and antarctic—separated by two tropics and an equator. At the same time, experiments designed to determine the globe's circumference demonstrated that the *oikoumenē* in the northern hemisphere's temperate zone is relatively small in relation to the whole. This finding only reinforced the conviction that there were peoples inhabiting other parts of the globe. Thus Plato in the fourth century could imagine Atlantis, once situated across the western ocean, while others envisioned a southern "counter-world" (Antichthon, or Antipodes) that matched the three continents of the *oikoumenē* (Europe, Libye or Africa, and Asia).

Alexander the Great's dramatic penetration of the Persian Empire and beyond into central Asia during the late fourth century vastly expanded Greeks' geographical knowledge and fueled the fascination that many of them felt for unknown, exotic lands and peoples. During the following century, at the museum in Alexandria (Egypt), Eratosthenes successfully devised a methodology for mapping the Earth, overcoming above all the fundamental problem of projection (in other words, the challenge of accommodating the Earth's curvature to a flat surface). While he rightly appreciated that accurate physical and astronomical readings were vital for reliable cartography, in practice he and his successors were often frustrated in their search for such data. Unable to travel themselves as widely as they might wish, they were compelled to accept reports by others that typically became more imprecise the farther the location lay from the Mediterranean. Moreover, there

existed no instruments capable of measuring either time or distance with precision, so that the computing of longitude in particular was prone to inaccuracy (a difficulty that would persist until the eighteenth century). Eratosthenes' methodology was sharply reevaluated by the second-century astronomer Hipparchus, whose working life was spent on the Aegean island of Rhodes. Around 100 C.E. Marinus of Tyre issued a substantial collection of geographical data, which forms the basis of the famous work by Ptolemy half a century or so later entitled *Guide to Drawing a Map of the World*, commonly referred to as his *Geography*. It survives intact, unlike the geographical works of Eratosthenes, Hipparchus, and Marinus, all of which are known to us only through intermediaries' often biased reports. Ptolemy is able to refer to a map made by Marinus; if he, too, or others in antiquity drew maps in accordance with the instructions offered by his own *Geography*, all trace of them is lost. The only surviving such maps all date to the fourteenth century onward, when the *Geography* was "rediscovered."

Roman Mapmaking. In Roman communities the most widely visible type of map was likely to have been the publicly displayed large-scale record of the community's cultivable land, as surveyed and divided by professional *agrimensores* or *gromatici*. In common with other ancient societies such as Babylon and Egypt, such land division was traditionally a priority for Romans, and it in turn acted to fix their distinctive imprint on any landscape they determined to settle. The *centuriation*, or checkerboard pattern, which *agrimensores* marked out is still plainly visible from the air in extensive areas of the Roman world as far apart as the Po River Valley and northern Tunisia. The *groma*, or instrument, with which these surveyors established straight lines and right angles is at best a rudimentary tool, awkward to use in more than the slightest breeze; even so, the degree of accuracy achieved with it is remarkable. Once a community's land had been divided thus, the law required a map of the survey to be displayed there publicly on a durable material, and a copy sent to Rome. All these copies have perished, but part of a large such map on marble from Arausio (modern Orange in southern France) survives, as does a tiny bronze fragment from along the Anas River in Spain.

Although the record is much thinner, Roman cities evidently came to be mapped too by *mensores aedificiorum* ("measurers of buildings"), who may have adhered to a standard scale of 1:240. Their work in Rome itself was assembled and displayed in a quite extraordinary masterpiece, the city's so-called Marble Plan, erected early in the third century C.E.; approximately ten percent survives in twelve hundred fragments. Comprising 151 slabs, oriented approximately southeast and centered upon the Capitoline hill, the plan was 40 feet (12 meters) high and spanned almost an entire sixty-foot (18.5-meter)-wide wall in a renovated temple complex. Every single ground floor room and other feature (arcade, basin, pillar, stairway step, etc) across the entire city is meticulously presented to the standard scale. The purpose cannot have been more than triumphalist and symbolic, however, because even the bottom of the plan lay about ten feet (three meters) above floor level, so that it could never be inspected closely as a whole or put to practical use.

A comparable purpose underlies the known large Roman "world" maps, all of which are lost except for the compact Peutinger Map. The most famous was perhaps the first, begun by Marcus Vipsanius Agrippa, the close associate of Rome's first emperor Augustus, and completed by him in the decade following Agrippa's death in 12 B.C.E. at a time when Roman power was expanding dramatically. This map was on public display in a portico (as yet unidentified) in Rome, and a text and measurements associated with it were somehow available. Certain scholars maintain that really there was no map at all, but only a large inscription of the type that Romans customarily erected to celebrate their victories and related accomplishments; however, given the visual impact that Agrippa's monument was noted for, this restriction to textual material seems unwarranted. By contrast, there is no denying the cartographic nature of the *orbis depictus* ("picture of the world") displayed in a portico at Augustodunum (Autun, France) in the late third century C.E., because a speaker describes it—albeit rhetorically—as showing "the sites of all locations with their names, their extent, and the distance between them, the sources and mouths of all the rivers, the curves of all the coastline's indentations, and the Ocean, both where its circuit girds the earth and where its pressure breaks into it." This map, likewise reflecting the scope and strength of Roman rule, was set up in a school in order to educate and impress the city's youth. The makers of such maps seem likely to have been aware of, and to have exploited, Greek advances in cartography as well as the data furnished by Roman itineraries. Even so, it remains doubtful whether the Roman Empire's military or civilian rulers at any level made extensive use of maps. Surprising though it may seem, we have to recognize that their grasp of space, however imperfect, was evidently shaped by various alternative means for the most part.

[*See also* Itineraries, Ancient and Medieval; Peutinger Map; Ptolemy; *and* Rome.]

BIBLIOGRAPHY

Campbell, J. B. *The Writings of the Roman Land Surveyors: Introduction, Text, Translation and Commentary*. London: Society for the Promotion of Roman Studies, 2000.

Carey, Sorcha. *Pliny's Catalogue of Culture: Art and Empire in the Natural History*. Oxford and New York: Oxford University Press, 2003. See especially chap. 3, "Representing Empire: Monuments and the Creation of Roman Space."

Harley, J. B., and David Woodward, eds. *The History of Cartography*. Vol. 1. Chicago and London: University of Chicago Press, 1987. See chaps. 5–16

Irby-Massie, Georgia L., and Paul T. Keyser, eds. *Greek Science of the Hellenistic Era: A Sourcebook*. London and New York: Routledge, 2002. See chap. 3, "Astronomy," and chap. 5, "Geography."

Rihll, T. E. *Greek Science*. Oxford and New York: Oxford University Press, 1999. See chap. 4, "Astronomy," and chap. 5, "Geography."

RICHARD J. A. TALBERT

Byzantine Geography, Worldview, and Mapmaking

Geography in Byzantium, like other branches of knowledge in medieval Europe, developed by incorporating the legacy of antiquity into the framework of Christianity. The Byzantine civilization inherited theories and practical information, insights, and biases that Greek classical thought had accumulated in the course of almost one thousand years. Byzantine scholars learned classical conceptions directly from the writings of Greek philosophers (such as Plato and Aristotle) and geographers (mainly Strabo and Ptolemy, first and second century C.E., respectively), as well as indirectly from the discussion and critique of these conceptions by influential Christian theologians of the first centuries of Christianity. Greek fathers of the church, such as Basil of Caesarea, Severian of Gabala, and John Chrysostom, incorporated classical knowledge into their interpretations of difficult passages of the Bible. Thus endorsing the use of classical cosmology and geography in a Christian context, theologians differed in their opinions as to the extent and specifics of ideas that could be usefully adopted by Christians. Church fathers who belonged to the Alexandrian and Cappadocian schools and were known for their largely allegorical approach to the interpretation of the biblical text (such as Basil of Caesarea), accepted the idea of a spherical earth, which ultimately went back to the Greek philosophers of the fifth century B.C.E. At the same time, thinkers of a more literal Antiochian school (such as Severian of Gabala) maintained that the earth was flat.

The *Christian Topography*, written by the Alexandrian merchant Cosmas Indicopleustes between 535 and 547, belonged to the literal trend in biblical interpretation. Cosmas aimed to produce a thoroughly Christian view of the world. Attacking the theory of a spherical earth as pagan, he argued that, according to the Bible, the earth was flat and rectangular and the shape of the world resembled the tabernacle of Moses. Furthermore, the earth in Cosmas's view is divided into two parts, covered by heaven as if by a roof. The part on which we now live is surrounded by ocean. The other part of the earth, which people inhabited at one time before the Flood and which contains Paradise, encircles the ocean. These ideas, often cited by modern scholars as an example of the decline of medieval geography under the influence of religion, were not universally accepted. Photius, a ninth-century Byzantine scholar, criticized some of Cosmas's ideas as fabulous and absurd. Judging from the number of surviving manuscripts, Cosmas's work had a limited circulation in the Greek world and remained inaccessible to the Latin West. Cosmas's work was, however, translated into Slavic languages (Russian, Bulgarian, and Serbian). In general, the idea that the earth was flat remained relatively marginal, and most Byzantine scholars believed in a spherical earth.

Byzantine scholars studied geography by reading earlier authors and commenting on their work (manuscripts preserve commentaries on Strabo and Dionysius Periegetes, who wrote in the second or third century C.E.). They also used compilations produced in late antiquity (such as the epitome of Artemidorus's geography, written by Markianos of Heraclea in the fourth or fifth century and preserved in fragments, or Agathemerus's geographical work, probably written in the fifth or sixth century).

Geographical information was provided by various genres and could serve various goals. Lists of geographical names, compiled in late antiquity, originally served the needs of civil and ecclesiastical administration and later were used by historians. The works of the emperor Constantine Porphyrogenitus (905–959, *De Thematibus* [On Themes] and *De administrando imperio* [On the Administration of the Empire]) follow the same tradition and provide lists of places and peoples of the empire. Histories and poems written throughout the Byzantine period often include geographical descriptions. For instance, Procopius of Caesarea (the first half of the sixth century) used many digressions that focus on the geography of regions, and local topography, as well as the customs and locations of various peoples. Practical information, such as accounts of markets or travel routes, could be drawn from special treatises (such as *Expositio totius mundi et gentium*, mid-fourth century C.E.), itineraries (from accounts of travel to the holy places to lists of places on the route from Egypt to Constantinople), and *periploi*, descriptions of places from the perspective of sailing along the shoreline.

Our evidence of Byzantine mapmaking is scarce and incomplete, but further research may discover more information. Byzantium, heir to the ancient Roman Empire, inherited the tradition of late Roman maps, whose primary purpose was imperial propaganda and the depiction of sites significant for the Christian religion. A poem preserved in later manuscripts describes the initiative by the emperor Theodosius to revise an old Roman map, which most scholars consider a derivative of Agrippa's cartographic enterprise. The mosaic Madaba map discovered in Jordan (made between 542 and 565), shows a part of Palestine and lower Egypt in its surviving fragment. Displayed in a church and aimed at the edification of the faithful, it shows the holy places and provides some explanations in Greek drawn mainly from the Bible and Eusebius's *Onomastikon* (a list of biblical places written in the first quarter of the fourth century).

Some manuscripts of Cosmas Indicopleustes's work are accompanied by maps, which ultimately may be traced back to the author himself. The maps show the world according to Cosmas, in the form of a rectangular box, with a flat earth that has a great mountain in its northern part and with a concave vault of heaven above the earth. There is also a map of the flat rectangular earth, surrounded by an ocean with Paradise located in the East.

The revival of interest in classical Greek language and culture among scholars from the ninth century on eventually resulted in a renewed interest in Ptolemy's mathematical astronomy and geography. Maximus Planudes (c. 1260–1310) collected and restored old manuscripts, including those of Strabo and Ptolemy. Because the copy of Ptolemy that he found lacked maps, he also had maps drawn to accompany the text.

Although the earliest surviving Greek portolans, or sailing directions, date from the sixteenth century, such texts and/or charts must have existed earlier. The extent of communications and travel between the years 300 and 900, previously considered narrow in scope, has been reassessed. Just as new research has discovered a much broader pattern of movement of goods and people, more investigation may discover corresponding developments in geography and mapmaking.

[*See also* Ptolemy.]

BIBLIOGRAPHY

Dilke, O. A. W. "Cartography in the Byzantine Empire." In *Cartography in Prehistoric, Ancient, and Medieval Europe and the Mediterranean*, 258–275. Vol. 1 of *The History of Cartography*, edited by J. B. Harley and David Woodward. Chicago: University of Chicago Press, 1987.

Diller, Aubrey. *The Textual Tradition of Strabo's Geography: with Appendix, The Manuscripts of Eustathius' Commentary on Dionysius Periegetes*. Amsterdam: A. M. Hakkert, 1975.

Hunger, Herbert. *Die hochsprachliche profane Literatur der Byzantiner*. Vol. 1, 508–539. Munich: C. H. Beck, 1978.

McCormick, Michael. *Origins of the European Economy: Communications and Commerce, A.D. 300–900*. Cambridge, U.K., and New York: Cambridge University Press, 2001.

NATALIA LOZOVSKY

Medieval West Geography and Worldview

When we discuss medieval views on "geography" and the "world," we need to bear in mind the changing fate and meaning of vocabulary. The Latin term *geographia*, derived from the Greek for "description of the earth," was seldom used in medieval Europe. The word began to circulate more widely when, in the late fifteenth century, it was employed in the titles of a number of printed versions of the "description of the earth" compiled in the second century C.E. by the Alexandrian astronomer Claudius Ptolomaeus (Ptolemy) and translated from Greek into Latin in 1407. Interestingly, the earliest Latin versions of Ptolemy's work bore the title *Cosmographia*, "description of the universe." The earth brings to mind the universe, yet they are different things. The distinction between *terra* as referring to the earth and *mundus*, the Latin translation of the Greek *kosmos*, referring to the universe, had already appeared in the *Etymologiae* (*Etymologies*) by Isidore, the seventh-century bishop of Seville, where the earth is said to be located at the center of the universe. Isidore also explained that the term *terra* refers to the terrestrial globe (the *orbis terrarum*) when used in the singular, but that the plural *terrae* indicates particular earthly regions. *Mundus*, too, could have a wide range of meanings, in the same way that its most common English equivalent, "world," does. In the twelfth century, in order to highlight the link between historical sequence and geographical order, Hugh, master of the school of the Abbey of Saint Victor (Paris), used in his *De Archa Noe* (Noah's Ark) two quite different words to refer to the human world: for him, *mundus* indicated the human world in its spatial extension, and *saeculum* indicated the human world in its temporal development. Apart from the subtleties of terminology, medieval scholars shared an interest in the wider aspects of geography, such as the shape of the earth and its relation to the universe, and the interplay among the natural elements, human settlement, and universal history. A diagram often found illustrating Isidore's *De natura rerum* (*On the Nature of Things*) shows the link between the world (*mundus*), man (*homo*), and the cyclical succession of time (*annus*) and refers to the four elements (paired with their opposing qualities), the four ages of man, the four seasons of the year, and the four humors of the human body.

In the earlier Middle Ages, Europeans based their geographical lore more on authoritative texts than on journeys of exploration. To venture on a global scale beyond known horizons was made difficult by the limitations of technology and by perils of all kinds. From the collapse of the Roman Empire to the age of discoveries, medieval geographical ideas were derived mainly from Greek and Roman geographical literature, which provided the description of the earth, its regions, and its inhabitants. Writers such as Eusebius, Jerome, Orosius, Isidore of Seville, and Bede recycled the works of classical authors such as Pliny the Elder and Solinus. Classical geographical ideas about the dimensions of the terrestrial globe (known to be spherical), its division into parts, and the listing of the peoples and provinces of its inhabited regions were adopted and refined to accommodate Christian themes. The idea of parallel zones, beginning from the Equator and going toward the poles, had reached the Middle Ages through Greek mathematical and astronomical geography and the late antique works of Macrobius and Martianus Capella. The region near the Equator, called the torrid zone, and the polar circles were considered equally uninhabitable because of either excessive heat or excessive cold. The region known from experience to be inhabited was the temperate region in the Northern Hemisphere. There was considerable debate about the inhabitability of the equatorial region and the Southern Hemisphere. The existence of the Antipodes was denied by some scholars on theological as well as astronomical grounds. The Bible contributed several notions to the medieval understanding of the earth: for example, the terrestrial reality of the Garden of Eden (Genesis 2:8–15) and the division of the inhabited earth into three parts, Asia, Europe, and Africa, which were inherited after the Flood by the three sons of Noah and peopled by their descendants (Genesis 9:18–19). The biblical statement that God brought salvation "in the midst of the earth" (*in medio terrae*; Psalm 73 [74]:12), and that he placed Jerusalem "in the midst of all nations" (*in medio gentium*; Ezekiel 5:5), suggested that the holy city was found at the center of the tripartite earth. The increasing attention to the geography of the Holy Land was reflected in the number of pilgrims to the eastern Mediterranean and the keen interest shown, as early as the fourth century, by scholars such as Eusebius and Jerome in biblical place-names.

Whereas, for a medieval scholar, historical time had a beginning (with the creation of man in the Garden of Eden), went through a number of ages (from Adam to Christ), and was heading for a determined end (the Last Judgment), geographical space had not been surveyed with equal completeness. Europeans knew their neighborhoods, read about the features of distant lands in classical sources, and speculated on the zones of the globe, but had not established definitive boundaries around the space they inhabited. The medieval notion of time (and history) was more sharply defined and clearly articulated than the medieval notion of space (and geography), and geographical ideas tended to be informed by the historical perspective. An example is the medieval idea, first articulated by Orosius (418) but elaborated by several subsequent scholars, of an east-west progression of human civilization from the eastern Garden of Eden to the Mediterranean basin. The linking of history with geography was inherited from ancient authors such as Strabo, Herodotus, Polybius, and Sallust, who had included in their essentially historical texts detailed descriptions of the geographical stage on which events took place. Medieval geographies were not geographies of an abstract space so much as geographies of peoples and places defined by the history of the territory.

In the later Middle Ages, however, geography began to catch up with history. Between the middle of the twelfth and the end of the thirteenth century, western Europe witnessed what has been described as a "geographical renaissance" within the general revival of learning. Curiosity about geography and cosmography was further stimulated by the availability of Arabic mathematical and astronomical works, as well as Aristotle's geographical material, in Latin translation. Moreover, in the course of the fourteenth century, much geographical information was being taken from other sources than biblical and classical, such as Arabic maps and works of art, Latin translations of geographical tables and, above all, the accounts by European travelers, mostly diplomats, traders, and missionaries such as William of Rubrouck, Marco Polo, John of Monte Corvino, Odoric of Pordenone, John of Plano Carpini, and Simon of Saint-Quentin, who journeyed through Persia to India and China.

A telling example of the humanist search for geographical truth is provided by the work of Aeneas Silvius Piccolomini (1405–1464; ruled as Pope Pius II from 1458 to 1464), whose unfinished *Cosmographia* (never released as a complete work in Piccolomini's lifetime, and first printed in 1477) aimed to provide a geographical and historical framework for the extraordinary happenings of his own time—the fall of Constantinople in 1453, above all—that were tainting relationships between Europe and Asia. Piccolomini amalgamated geographical material, which he took mostly from ancient authors and the classical poets as well as the church fathers, with contemporary information and with personal observation, but he left the description of Asia incomplete and never began the description of Africa, perhaps having abandoned his ambition to produce an exhaustive description of the entire earth when he found the task impossible. Inasmuch as he could not decide between the disagreeing opinions of the ancients or resolve their conflicts with the Christian tradition, and with his unquenchable desire for the truth, Piccolomini both embodied the intellectual conflicts of his time and also anticipated the era of the geographical discoveries.

[*See also* Antichthon and Antipodes; Constantinople; Herodotus; Isidore of Seville; Odoric of Pordenone; Orosius; Pliny the Elder; Polo, Marco; Ptolemy; *and* William of Rubrouck.]

BIBLIOGRAPHY

Allen, Rosamund S., ed. *Eastward Bound: Medieval Travel and Travellers, 1050–1500*. Manchester, U.K.: Manchester University Press, 2004.

Inglebert, Hervé. *Interpretatio christiana: Les mutations des savoirs (cosmographie, géographie, ethnographie, histoire) dans l'antiquité chrétienne, 30–630 après J.-C.* Paris: Institut d'Études Augustiniennes, 2001.

Westrem, Scott D., ed. *Discovering New Worlds: Essays on Medieval Exploration and Imagination*. New York and London: Garland, 1991.

Wright, John Kirtland. *The Geographical Lore of the Time of the Crusades: A Study in the History of Medieval Science and Tradition in Western Europe.* New York: American Geographical Society, 1925. Reprint. New York: Dover, 1965.

ALESSANDRO SCAFI

Medieval West Mapmaking

Nearly every major type of map found today is represented in medieval archives. Maps were used to clarify an argument in legal affairs, to explain the natural world and how it works, and to illustrate biblical exegesis or human history, for example, although they were not used for land travel; written itineraries were the normal way-finding aid. It is impossible, however, to attempt either to estimate the proportion of the original corpus of maps represented by those maps that have survived or to do justice in a short note to their great diversity, and the focus here is on world maps.

More than a thousand maps of the world (in Latin, *mappae mundi*) have been recorded. The enterprise of defining and classifying them has preoccupied historians of cartography since the end of the nineteenth century, but it has increasingly proved to be a difficult (and ultimately sterile) exercise. All sorts of categories have been suggested, the most basic of which attempt to classify world maps according to content and form. Thus, for example, tripartite maps (those showing the distribution of the three known parts of the world) are distinguished from zonal maps (those depicting the sequence of climatic zones on the whole terrestrial globe). World maps may be found in the geographical sections of late antique treatises on the nature of the universe, such as Macrobius's fifth-century commentary on Cicero's *Somnium Scipionis* (*Dream of Scipio*), or in classical histories, where they illustrate geographical descriptions in, for example, Sallust's history of the Jugurthine war (first century B.C.E.) and Lucan's *Pharsalia* (or *The Civil War*, first century C.E.). Maps of the world were also inserted in the geographical chapters of Christian encyclopedic works that recycled classical learning, such as Orosius's *Historiae adversus paganos* (*Histories against the Pagans*, c. 418), Isidore's *De natura rerum* (*On the Nature of Things*, c. 620) and *Etymologiae* (*Etymologies*, c. 635), and Lambert of Saint-Omer's *Liber floridus* (*Book of Flowers*), Honorius Augustodunensis's *Imago mundi* (*The Image of the World*), and Guido of Pisa's *Liber historiarum* (*The Book of Histories*), all dating from the twelfth century. Maps of the world illustrated yet another type of medieval book, that of the chronicle or universal history, in which the events of human history from the world's creation to the chronicler's own day were detailed, as in Ranulf Higden's *Polychronicon* (*Universal Chronicle*, begun in 1320 and regularly updated until Higden's death in 1363). Maps also illuminate exegetical treatises and biblical commentaries. World maps illustrate the creation of the universe, the repopulation of the world by Noah's sons, or the diffusion of the Christian church, as in the eighth-century *Commentarius in Apocalypsin* (*Commentary on the Apocalypse*) by Beatus of Liébana. Beatus supplied his own map, but in other cases any map deemed useful to help understand the text might be inserted by a scribe, commentator, or teacher.

In zonal maps of the world (as in the navigational charts that had started to be used around the Mediterranean by the early thirteenth century and, later on, in the maps associated with Ptolemy's *Geography*), the representation of space is guided by mathematics in the form of astronomically defined coordinates and measurable distance and direction. Zonal maps are usually south- or north-orientated and show the sequence of five climatic belts encircling the earth determined through astronomical observation and defined in classical times (two frigid zones, two temperate zones, and a torrid zone along the Equator). It is not difficult to document the keen interest shown by medieval scholars in the mathematical, geographical, and astronomical sciences. The Irish monk and scholar Dicuil, for example, produced at the court of Charlemagne a highly detailed written description of the earth, the *Liber de mensura orbis* (*Survey of the Terrestrial Globe*, 825), and there was widespread interest in coordinates for use in astrology long before the fifteenth-century adoption of Ptolemy's instructions in his *Geography* for portraying the earth on a flat surface by means of mathematical and astronomical principles. In the thirteenth century the English scholar Roger Bacon discussed the use of latitudes and longitudes in mapping procedure, and he may even have constructed a map on the basis of some sort of grid.

On a different type of world map, one that was usually orientated to the east, places are located according to the principle of contiguity: neighboring features are depicted next to each other irrespective of the exact distance or direction between them. Moreover, this kind of world map combined time and space to offer an encyclopedic vision of a world structured by mankind's historical pilgrimage from the original Garden of Eden to the paradise to come.

Such *mappae mundi*, as they are known, functioned above all as chronicles projecting universal human history in its spatial context. The key point, that space and time were interdependent and that geographical space was the stage of salvation history, had been made particularly clearly and explicitly by Hugh of Saint Victor in the twelfth century, who was also responsible for the most forcible expression of the idea of the east-west progression of human history that lies at the heart of *mappae mundi*. Although these maps of the world were produced in monasteries and cathedrals, they were not devotional documents (as opposed to our modern scientific representations of the earth) any more than they were mere tools of religious propaganda. Rather, they were representations of the world according to a particular conception, which took Christian teaching into account.

Both east-orientated *mappae mundi* and north- or south-orientated zonal maps circulated in the West during the Latin Middle Ages. Both were part of Christian medieval culture, expressing two different cartographical discourses. A number of late medieval maps survive on which the two cartographical genres have been merged, a pointer to the fact that in the late Middle Ages geographical knowledge was gaining more space on world maps at the expense of history, which had hitherto been the overriding factor in structuring *mappae mundi*. This is clear, for example, in a number of maps illustrating the geographical work of the French cardinal and theologian Pierre d'Ailly (1350–1420), which influenced many later scholars and explorers including Christopher Columbus. In his *Imago mundi* (*The Image of the World*, 1410), which rehearses thirteenth-century geographical knowledge, d'Ailly described the structure of the heavens and the earth and discussed its habitability, the various climatic zones, islands, rivers, and seas. The seventh of the eight figures attached to d'Ailly's text is a world map portraying both the whole terrestrial globe divided into climatic zones and the northern hemisphere, which included Europe, Asia, and Africa, and their regions and cities.

[*See also* Isidore of Seville; Maps, Mapmaking, and Mapmakers; Orosius; Projections; *and* Ptolemy.]

BIBLIOGRAPHY
Brincken, Anna-Dorothee von den. *Fines terrae: Die Enden der Erde und der vierte Kontinent auf mittelalterlichen Weltkarten*. Hanover, Germany: Hahnsche Buchandlung, 1992.
Delano-Smith, Catherine, and Roger J. P. Kain. *English Maps: A History*. London: British Library, 1999.
Edson, Evelyn. *Mapping Time and Space: How Medieval Mapmakers Viewed Their World*. London: British Library, 1997.
Gautier-Dalché, Patrick. *La "Descriptio Mappe Mundi" de Hugues de Saint-Victor: Texte inédit avec introduction et commentaire*. Paris: Études Augustiniennes, 1988.
Scafi, Alessandro. *Mapping Paradise: A History of Heaven on Earth*. London: British Library; Chicago: University of Chicago Press, 2006.
Woodward, David. "Medieval *mappae mundi*." In *The History of Cartography*. Vol. 1, *Cartography in Prehistoric, Ancient, and Medieval Europe and the Mediterranean*, edited by J. Brian Harley and David Woodward, 286–370. Chicago: University of Chicago Press, 1987.

ALESSANDRO SCAFI

Evans, John (1770–1799), Welsh explorer and trader. Born in Waunfawr, Carnarvonshire, Wales, John Evans became obsessed at an early age by the story of Prince Madoc's alleged voyage to America in 1170, and by the possibility that Madoc's descendants, the "Welsh Indians," survived somewhere west of the Mississippi. The Madoc Society in Wales had heard of the "White Padoucas" (Comanche) on the Missouri, and by changing "P" to "M" turned the name into "Madoucas," or followers of Madoc. If these people proved to have no Welsh antecedents, then there were always the light-skinned Mandans, visited by explorers from La Vérendrye onward, and in 1792 the society financed a transatlantic journey by Evans to investigate further.

The story of the young Welshman is a remarkable one, almost lost to sight in the death throes of Spain's American empire. When he reached Louisiana he had difficulty in entering Spanish territory, but by 1795 he was employed in Saint Louis by the Spanish Missouri Company on an expedition led by the Scotsman James McKay, whose orders were "to open commerce with those distant and Unknown Nations in the upper parts of the Missouri and to discover all the unknown parts of his Catholic Majesty's Dominions through that continent as far as the Pacific Ocean." In one sense the venture represented the last advance of the Spanish colonial frontier; in another it was the forerunner of the Lewis and Clark expedition. Advancing along the Missouri, the party reached Nebraska and built a post from which McKay sent Evans farther upstream in search of trade, alliances, and a route to the Pacific. By September 1796, Evans had reached the earth lodges of the Mandans on the Upper Missouri, but found that Canadian traders were already there. Nor was he able to travel farther west, although he drew a map from Indian information showing the country as far west as the Rocky Mountains. This map, which was later used by Lewis and Clark, was the first to mark the Yellowstone River and the Great Falls of the Missouri. Evans was also among the first to depict the Rockies as a complex series of mountain ranges rather than as a single high ridge. All this Evans duly reported, but in his own eyes his mission had failed. As he wrote sadly to one of his sponsors in Wales: "Thus having explored and charted the Missuri for 1,800 miles and by my Communications with the Indians this side of the Pacific Ocean from 35 to 49 degrees of latitude, I am able to inform you that there is no such people as the Welsh Indians." His health affected by heavy drinking, Evans died in New Orleans in June or July 1799.

[*See also* La Vérendrye, Sieur de; Lewis, Meriwether, and William Clark; *and* Rocky Mountains.]

BIBLIOGRAPHY

Davies, Hywel Meilyn. "John Thomas Evans." In *Oxford Dictionary of National Biography*. Vol. 18, p. 724. Oxford and New York: Oxford University Press, 2004.

Nasatir, A. B., ed. *Before Lewis and Clark: Documents Illustrating the History of the Missouri, 1785–1804*. 2 vols. Saint Louis, Mo.: Saint Louis Historical Society, 1952. Reprint. Norman: University of Oklahoma Press, 2002.

Williams, Gwyn. *Madoc: The Making of a Myth*. London: Eyre Methuen, 1979.

GLYNDWR WILLIAMS

Everest, George (1790–1866), superintendent of the Trigonometrical Survey of India. George Everest was born in Greenwich, England, on July 4, 1790, the third of six children of Lucetta Mary and William Tristram Everest. He was educated at the Royal Military College, Marlow, and at the Royal Military Academy, Woolwich. It appears that he may have pronounced his name "Eve-rest."

Everest traveled to India in 1806 as a cadet for the East India Company, was immediately promoted to lieutenant, and began a distinguished career as a surveyor that culminated in his appointment as the superintendent of the Great Trigonometrical Survey (GTS) in 1823 and as surveyor general in 1829. He then held both posts until his retirement as a lieutenant colonel in 1843.

As superintendent, Everest was in charge of all trigonometrical surveys in India and, in particular, of the Great Arc Series, an ambitious project to calculate and map an arc of the meridian begun by his predecessor, William Lambton. Everest carried the line from central India northward five hundred miles to the foothills of the Himalayas. The objectives were

to calculate better the shape of the earth and to ensure the accuracy of other surveys that depended on the GTS's measurements. As surveyor general he also oversaw all topographical surveying in India, although his main interests were always with the GTS.

Everest was conscientious, often at work even when ill, and he was a highly capable surveyor, publishing articles and books on the progress of the trigonometrical surveying. His most important professional publications are the *Account of the Measurement of an Arc of the Meridian* (London, 1830) and the *Account of the Measurement of Two Sections of the Meridional Arc of India* (London, 1847). As a supervisor he was a hard taskmaster, although he was also respected for his surveying abilities and technical innovations and inventions.

In 1856 the surveyor general of India, Andrew Waugh, decided to call the highest known peak in the world, recently measured by the Survey of India and labeled Peak XV, "Mont Everest" in honor of his former superior ("Mont" was soon changed to "Mount"). Even though Mount Everest is widely recognized as the name for the mountain, numerous local names, including Devadhunga, Chomolongma, and Sagarmatha, have been suggested as alternatives. Everest himself was initially displeased by the naming, since he feared that local inhabitants would mispronounce it.

Everest retired to England, married Emma Wing in 1846, and had six children. He was knighted in 1861, and died in Bayswater on December 1, 1866.

BIBLIOGRAPHY

Phillimore, R. H. *Historical Records of the Survey of India*. 5 vols. Vol. 4. Dehradun, Uttar Pradesh: Survey of India, 1958.

Smith, J. R. *Everest: The Man and the Mountain*. Caithness, Scotland: Whittles, 1999.

IAN J. BARROW

Exotic, Monstrous, and Wild Peoples and Animals.

Early Greek travelers and traders tended to exaggerate the differences between themselves and indigenous peoples they met, often developing absurd or nightmarish images of monstrous or semibestial races of humans. Foreign wildlife was similarly distorted and exoticized. Though human and animal monsters were located by Greek legend in all parts of the globe, they especially predominated in the regions to the far south and east, lands known to the Greeks as Libya and India. Rome and medieval Europe inherited principally the tradition surrounding India, and a substantial body of "Indian wonders" lore continued to circulate in various forms into the Renaissance and beyond.

Already in the eighth century B.C.E., before the Greeks had moved very far beyond the Mediterranean basin, Homer drew on the tales of sailors in describing savage primitive humans like the Cyclopes and Laestrygonians as well as fierce monsters like the Scylla. As exploration penetrated deeper into Asia and Africa, Greek catalogs of wonders became longer and more bizarre. Scylax of Caryanda, an Ionian sea captain recruited by the Persian Empire to explore the Indus River, brought home accounts of Sciapods who shaded themselves by holding enormous feet above their heads, Otolicni who wrapped their own huge ears around themselves, one-eyed Monophthalmi, and other grotesque creatures. Ctesias of Cnidus, a Greek writer who had also done service for the Persians in the East, produced a long list of similar monstrosities in his *Indica* (now lost but known through a medieval summary), including an elaborate description of the Cynocephali ("Dog-heads"), bestialized humans who would recur in many a medieval world map and manuscript illustration. Some of these bizarre creatures clearly have a basis in fact, like the Indian *martichora* (later "manticore"), a distorted version of the Bengal tiger; others are harder to trace to historical origins.

The impetus behind such lore greatly increased after Alexander's expedition into India, which encountered many strange men and beasts and gathered reports of even stranger ones. Legends emerging out of this invasion spread all over the ancient world, and later, in Latin, Persian, and Arabic translations, the medieval and Islamic worlds as well. Alexander is here imagined as a super-civilized Hellene trying to make rational sense out of the welter of monstrous men and animals his army has uncovered. Like a hero of modern science fiction, in these texts he plunges into the unknown lands of the Far East to find himself beset by terrifying freaks of nature at every turn; he reports his findings in fictional epistles addressed to his teacher, the great scientist Aristotle.

Aristotle did in fact interest himself in reports of foreign monstrosities, as did other Greco-Roman scientists. In *On the Generation of Animals* Aristotle speculated that different species congregated beside scarce watering holes in the African desert, and, forced by their thirst into close association, tended to interbreed more easily than elsewhere. Other thinkers turned to climatology as an explanation, theorizing that the intense heat and sunlight of Africa and India conveyed some sort of generative

power. Pliny the Elder constructed a great catalog of monstrosities in his study of India (*Natural History*, Book 7) without pretending to understand their cause; they are merely playthings of nature, he reports, a sentiment echoed often by Renaissance writers who took a great interest in such *lusi naturae*.

Early church fathers speculated about whether monstrous men like the Cynocephali were descended from Adam so that they possessed souls and could be saved through Christian grace. Augustine discusses the problem in *The City of God* (16.8) but appears to have trouble making up his mind. Most Christian writers regarded the monstrous races as the ultimate test case of Christ's redemptive power; when even dog-headed humans attained grace, the entire world would be saved. This seems to be the implication of the tympanum frieze of the cathedral at Vézelay, where pygmies and Cynocephali are depicted in the margins of a scene showing the diffusion of the Gospel throughout the earth.

The pagan world, however, was fascinated by the pure freakishness and novelty of alien monstrosities. Under the Roman Empire long lists of these *paradoxa* were compiled, in both Greek and Latin, by authors who sought to capitalize on their shock value; they are also found skillfully woven into fictional texts like the Greek romances. Wherever the *frisson* of the monstrous might infuse energy into a narrative or speech, an almost endless supply of wonders stood ready at hand; "Africa," as an ancient proverb put it, "always produces some strange new thing."

[*See also* Alexander the Great, *subentry on* Fiction; *and* Pliny the Elder.]

BIBLIOGRAPHY

Friedman, John Block. *The Monstrous Races in Medieval Art and Thought.* Cambridge, Mass.: Harvard University Press, 1981. Reprint, Syracuse, N.Y.: Syracuse University Press, 2000.

Romm, James. *The Edges of the Earth in Ancient Thought: Geography, Exploration, and Fiction.* Princeton, N.J.: Princeton University Press, 1992. See chap. 3.

Wittkower, Rudolph. "Marvels of the East: A Study in the History of Monsters." *Journal of the Warburg and Courtauld Institute* 5 (1942): 159–197.

JAMES ROMM

Expeditions, World Exploration

This entry contains nine subentries:

England
France
German States

The Netherlands
Portugal
Russia
Scotland
Spain
Venice

England

In the race among European nations from the fifteenth century onward to discover useful information about the wider world, England was a late starter. However, greatly strengthened by favorable economic and political developments from about 1550, the nation began to match its competitors. The Union with Scotland in 1707 was another positive factor and from that date, it becomes difficult and pointless to distinguish England from Britain.

The Reasons for England's Success to 1707. England benefited from its easy access to the Atlantic seaways and the existence of estuaries where major ports could develop to serve a growing commercial economy. A large merchant marine and, by the end of the seventeenth century, a powerful navy had developed; the country became a strong mercantilist state now able and willing to compete with Spain, Portugal, France, and the Netherlands in exploration and other matters. Not surprisingly, maritime discovery became important, especially in the immediately adjacent North Atlantic region while the enterprises of Sir Walter Ralegh and, later, the Pilgrims, tested the viability of English settlement in the Americas.

In Elizabethan England, the intellectual as well as political and economic climate became favorable to the cause of discoveries: Richard Hakluyt's *Principal Navigations of the English Nation* of 1589, followed by the collections of travel voyages by Samuel Purchas, helped to create an interest in geography and cosmology that was built upon as further collections of travels were published in the seventeenth century. To read *Paradise Lost* is to realize just how much geography of the earth as well as of heaven John Milton knew. In 1665, the Royal Society was founded and the astronomical studies it favored did much to further the science of navigation—a science given official encouragement when the Royal Observatory was set up in 1676. The English state had in fact become directly interested in measures to promote navigation and exploration and often encouraged its naval and army officers to undertake expeditions. Meanwhile, English mapmakers had begun to em-

ulate the great Dutch cartographers and established a tradition of geographical publishing.

Britain as a Promoter of Exploration after 1707. After the Glorious Revolution of 1688–1689 and the Union with Scotland in 1707, Britain was remarkably stable politically, and this created a favorable climate for interests in the wider world. The Union meant opportunities for profitable careers for Scots in the service of British official or commercial organizations, and a remarkable number of prominent explorers were Scots. The new British state continued to encourage relevant scientific endeavor, for example, by setting up the Board of Longitude in 1713. There was considerable intellectual input from Scotland, where universities flourished and important cartographical publishing firms like those of Johnston and of Bartholomew developed to rank with the English ones such as Stanford and Arrowsmith. In cartography, eminence was reached by Alexander Dalrymple and James Rennell by 1800, and it was Dalrymple who was made first director of the Navy's Hydrographic Office when it was set up in 1795. The office sponsored, for example, William Owen's great African coast survey in the 1820s.

English aristocrats from the Elizabethan period onward had developed a tradition of sending younger members of their families to travel in Europe, and the idea of the "grand tour" became fully fledged in the later eighteenth century. The habit of aristocratic travel created a favorable attitude toward exploration in the minds of many influential figures. The African Association, set up in 1788 to promote exploration, was entirely aristocratic in its membership. Its leader, the botanist Sir Joseph Banks, emerged as the supreme organizer of exploration; he usually had the ear of government because of his connections. In the 1760s and 1770s, the three great voyages of Captain James Cook, the first of them primarily for an astronomical purpose and on which Banks was present, had set a standard of scientific exploration on which Banks and later promoters of travel such as Sir John Barrow were able to insist.

Scientific and practical exploration also seemed appropriate to many of the increasingly powerful and influential mercantile bourgeoisie who, in this field as in so many others, were entirely willing to cooperate with the aristocracy. By the middle of the nineteenth century, a group had emerged that has been described as "gentlemanly capitalists" especially interested in banking, investment, and trade. Socially, they were often closely associated with what may be called a "service class" of military and naval officers, sea captains, engineers, Indian and colonial officials, and the like who managed Britain's various and increasingly extensive interests around the globe. The Royal Geographical Society (RGS) was set up in 1830 and became the most important institution in the world promoting exploration. It was essentially a forum led by aristocrats interested in travel, in which members of the service class carried out the practical work of scientific exploration. Although a private society, especially when under the leadership of Roderick Murchison and Clements Markham, it could often obtain the help of government. Indian officials founded their own Bombay Geographical Society in 1832. By 1850 Britain was fully committed to free trade with a consequent need to search constantly for new markets, and the continued interest in exploration may be linked to this need. The connection was rarely made explicit, however; "the pursuit of geographical science" was always given as the aim of the RGS. This pursuit was essentially a matter of getting accurate basic information about all parts of the world, rather than the cultivation of any theory of geography or the direct promotion of commerce. More general interest was generated in exploration by means of the popular works of travel that explorers were expected to produce, which gave accounts of adventures among exotic places and peoples. This in turn set the pattern for many boys' adventure stories by writers such as Robert Ballantyne and occasionally by explorers themselves such as Verney Lovett Cameron. Another development that had some impact on exploratory activity from the early nineteenth century was the Evangelical revival. This, among other things, led to the formation of several missionary societies by the Anglican and other Protestant churches. Often, especially in Africa, missionaries became explorers, too, with David Livingstone as the supreme example. The impulse to encourage primary scientific exploration remained extremely strong in Britain until the ill-fated expedition to the South Pole of Captain Robert Falcon Scott in 1911–1912. By then, most of the fundamental challenges of exploration had been overcome, a surprisingly large proportion of those in the eighteenth and nineteenth centuries by British explorers.

The Objects of English and British Exploratory Enterprise. Not surprisingly, early English exploratory efforts involved maritime ventures from the seas near the British Isles. Why not sail from the North Sea to find a northeast passage to the Indies? Hugh Willoughby and Richard Chancellor's voyage of 1558 and the later landward travels of Anthony Jenkinson established contacts with Russia but not a route to the Indies. After the Bristol voyagers including John and Sebastian Cabot had shown the way across the North Atlantic in the late fifteenth century, a northwest passage seemed a better bet. Martin Frobisher and John Davis in the 1570s and 1580s, Henry Hudson and William Baffin in the early part of the next century all sought the passage, and it became almost an obsession for some three hundred years. British explorers such as Christopher Middleton, Samuel Hearne, and Alexander Mackenzie in the eighteenth century, followed by John Ross, William Parry, Frederick Beechey, John Franklin, and George Back probed the Canadian interior and the Arctic. The unknown fate of John Franklin's 1845–1847 expedition led to search ventures by Robert McClure, John Rae, and Leopold McClintock among others in the 1850s. A later Arctic venture by George Nares toward the North Pole is also noteworthy.

Even the great achievements of British maritime explorers in the Pacific were guided in part by the desire to find a possible outlet for the northwest passage. Francis Drake had sailed across the Pacific after discovering California in the course of his 1577–1580 circumnavigation, while Thomas Cavendish, another piratical Elizabethan, emulated him ten years later. William Dampier in 1697, George Anson in 1740–1744, and John Byron in 1764–1766 all made discoveries of some importance in the Pacific region while seeking to undermine the Spanish positions, but the real breakthrough into successful scientific exploration of the Pacific was made with Cook's three voyages between 1768 and 1779. Follow-up expeditions included those undertaken by George Vancouver in 1792–1794 and, in the Australasian region, coastal surveys by Matthew Flinders and George Bass in 1802–1803. Between about 1830 and 1861, travelers such as Charles Sturt, Edward Eyre, Augustus Gregory, and then Robert Burke and William Wills accomplished the exploration of the Australian interior.

Second only to the great achievements of the late eighteenth century in the Pacific region were the almost contemporary attempts to penetrate the interior of Africa. James Bruce in the 1760s reached Ethiopia and the Blue Nile source, and men such as Barrow and William Burchell explored inland from Cape Town, while in tropical West Africa the African Association's Daniel Houghton and Mungo Park made key discoveries. As government took over responsibility from the Association, Dixon Denham,

Hugh Clapperton, and Richard and John Lander went to the region in the 1820s, and determining the course of the Niger River became another great obsession. After that problem was resolved, exploration continued, with the Niger Expedition of 1841, and later work by William Baikie and then Walter Oudney and James Richardson in association with Heinrich Barth in the middle Niger region.

During the eighteenth and early nineteenth centuries, the East India Company gradually acquired control of more and more of the Indian subcontinent. Expeditions ranged northward into the Himalayas with travelers such as Joseph Hooker and Frederick Bailey, while the Indian Navy made notable expeditions around the coasts of the Indian Ocean. For obvious strategic reasons, the routes or possible routes to India through the Middle East attracted much attention, and travelers and explorers such as Henry Rawlinson, Austen Layard, and George Curzon achieved fame in such ventures. Arabia was especially attractive to the English, with Richard Burton, Charles Doughty, Gertrude Bell, T. E. Lawrence, and Harry Philby exploring its desert routes.

In the middle of the nineteenth century, continuing concern with a northwest passage found a rival in the obsession with the source of the Nile. This question and the fascination of the great lakes and mountains of Africa's interior inspired expeditions in 1855–1876 by Burton, John Hanning Speke, James Augustus Grant, Samuel Baker, Cameron, Henry Stanley, Joseph Thomson, and—above all—by Livingstone. Harry Johnston, Frederick Lugard, and Mary Kingsley were among later British African travelers to achieve fame.

British interest in South America was much less marked, although the scientific travels of Charles Darwin or the lesser-known Henry Bates should be noted, as well as the work of Robert Schomburgk in the Guiana region. Similarly, China and Southeast Asia attracted notable scientific travelers such as Alfred Russel Wallace, but little primary exploration. Although James Ross reached the Ross Sea in 1841, the principal British efforts in Antarctica occurred in the early years of the twentieth century with the work of Ernest Shackleton and the ill-fated Scott, followed by further exploration by Douglas Mawson in the early 1930s.

Overall, the outstanding achievements of English and then British exploration concerned the Canadian Arctic, the Pacific, and Australasia, and practically the whole of Africa south of the Sahara.

[*See also* African Association; Royal Geographical Society; *and biographical entries on figures mentioned in this article*.]

BIBLIOGRAPHY

Baker, John N. L. *A History of Geographical Exploration and Discovery*. London: Harrap, 1937.

Bridges, Roy C., and Paul E. H. Hair, eds. *Compassing the Vaste Globe of the Earth*. London: Hakluyt Society, 1996.

Cain, Peter J., and Antony G. Hopkins. *British Imperialism 1688–2000*. 2nd ed. Harlow, U.K.: Longman, 2002.

Kirwan, Laurence P. *The White Road: A Survey of Polar Exploration*. London: Hollis and Carter, 1959.

Markham, Clements R. *The Fifty Years' Work of the Royal Geographical Society*. London: Murray, 1881.

Savours, Ann. *The Search for the North West Passage*. London: Chatham, 1999.

Sykes, Percy. *A History of Exploration from the Earliest Times to the Present Day*. London: Routledge, 1934.

ROY BRIDGES

France

The French, blocked from southern routes to empire by Portugal and Spain, explored the north. Jacques Cartier (1491–1557) had a commission from King Francis I to search for precious metals and a Northwest Passage. He left France in 1534, sailed through the Strait of Belle Isle, and explored western Newfoundland and the Gulf of Saint Lawrence. He returned that fall with two sons of the Iroquois chief Donnacona. The king supported a second Cartier expedition, to explore the Saint Lawrence River, and Donnacona's sons, who had learned French, served as interpreters. The French wintered at Stadacona (now Quebec City) in 1535–1536; they would have died of scurvy if the Indians had not given them a drink containing white cedar. Samuel de Champlain (1567–1635) explored the Atlantic coast from Nova Scotia and the Bay of Fundy southward to Maine and Cape Cod; he explored the Gaspé Peninsula, the Saint Lawrence River to Lake Champlain, the Ottawa River, and Ontario. In 1608, Champlain built a fort at Quebec City. Étienne Brûlé (1592?–1633) asked to be allowed to live among the Algonquin; Brûlé was the first of the *coureurs de bois*, fur traders who lived with the Indians. The missionaries, or "black robes," used similar methods in their missions to the Indians. Descriptions and maps of explorations appeared in books by Champlain and by the Jesuits; in their *Relation* of 1672, the Jesuits published a superb map of Lake Superior.

In 1673 the fur trader Louis Joliet (1645–1700) and the missionary Father Jacques Marquette (1637–1675) canoed the Mississippi River. At the spot where the Missouri River joins the Mississippi, the Indians reported that the Missouri led to a great ocean. René-

Robert Cavelier de La Salle (1643–1687) arrived at the Gulf of Mexico in April 1682 and claimed it for France. In travels of 1738–1743, Sieur de La Vérendrye (1686–1749) and his sons searched for a northwest passage; they explored the Saskatchewan River and visited Mandan villages on the Missouri River.

In the mid-sixteenth century the French tried unsuccessfully to establish colonies in Brazil (1555–1560) and Florida (1562–1565). In the seventeenth century, the government encouraged the formation of companies to establish colonies in the West Indies. These produced sugar, leading to the use of African slaves for labor and the establishment of French trading posts on the west coast of Africa. In 1637, France claimed Guiana, on the northeastern coast of South America, but it was not good for colonization. Geographical knowledge of the regions of French trade and colonies was reflected on French maps.

On November 15, 1766, Louis-Antoine de Bougainville (1729–1811) set sail from France to circumnavigate the globe. After the Seven Years' War (1756–1763), France had lost its holdings in India and its lands in North America, except for Louisiana, to Britain. Bougainville was looking for lands where the French empire might be renewed. In 1765, Bougainville had witnessed the demise of a short-lived French colony in the Falkland Islands, abandoned because of Spanish opposition. Bougainville stopped there to pick up the remaining French colonists and continued through the Strait of Magellan to the Pacific, stopping at Tahiti. In the Moluccas, clove and nutmeg plants were obtained to introduce in the French colony of Mauritius. Following the model of Captain James Cook, Jean-François de Galaup de La Pérouse (1741–1788) led a naval expedition on a mission to study the Pacific Ocean, particularly the Bering Strait region. This voyage resulted in an impressive three-volume work about the expedition. La Pérouse did not return home; his ship disappeared after leaving Botany Bay on March 10, 1788.

The twentieth-century French empire was surpassed only by the British empire. The French empire included large parts of West Africa, Madagascar, Indochina, Pacific islands, part of Antarctica, Guadeloupe and Martinique in the West Indies, and French Guiana. By the early 1960s this empire had dissolved.

[See also Fur Trade; Jesuits; Mer de l'Ouest and Rivière de l'Ouest; North America; Northwest Passage; and biographical entries on figures mentioned in this article.]

BIBLIOGRAPHY

Aldrich, Robert. *Greater France: A History of French Overseas Expansion*. New York: St. Martin's Press, 1996.

Baker, Daniel B., ed. *Explorers and Discoverers of the World*. Detroit, Mich.: Gale Research, 1993.

Goetzmann, William H., and Glyndwr Williams. *The Atlas of North American Exploration: From the Norse Voyages to the Race to the Pole*. New York: Prentice Hall General Reference, 1992.

Quinn, Frederick. *The French Overseas Empire*. Westport, Conn.: Praeger, 2000.

CAROL URNESS

German States

Overseas expeditions since 1500 featuring natives of German states resulted mainly from economic activities of the Welser commercial house based in Augsburg. It traded in consumer goods, invested in shipping, sponsored venture capitalism, and advanced credit to rising political stars such as Emperor Charles V. By 1526 the Welsers had business agents

German Exploration. Tupinamba taking part in the *Triumph of Maximilian I*, with woodcuts by Hans Burgkmair (original work of 1512; New York: Dover Publications, 1964). For special occasions, great processions were often organized in early modern Europe. For the procession known as the "Triumph of the Emperor Maximilian," participants included people drawn from the remotest parts of the Habsburg Empire, such as these Tupinamba Indians. COURTESY THE NEWBERRY LIBRARY, CHICAGO

throughout Europe, with permanent representatives in the Iberian world at Lisbon, the Spanish court, Barcelona, Zaragoza, Seville, and Madrid, and in the New World at Santo Domingo. Their agents were largely independent and free to invest based on their judgment of local conditions and opportunities.

The New World offered new possibilities, and as venture capitalists the Welser agents were active. In 1528 they sent fifty German miners to Santo Domingo, obtained a monopoly over the sale of four thousand slaves, and obtained the right to discover, conquer, and populate Venezuela. Contrary to scholarly opinion, the latter right was not in exchange for money advanced to secure Charles V's 1519 election as emperor.

Venezuela sent many Germans to their grave. Among the principals were several who distinguished themselves in the business of Venezuela: Ambrosius Dalfinger was Venezuela's first governor and founder of Coro and Maracaibo. He explored northeastern Colombia and the Magdalena River, and he died in Colombia's eastern Cordillera in 1533. Governor Jorge Espira (Georg Hohermuth von Speyer) spent three years (1535–1538) exploring Colombia's Meta and Guaviare regions and had assembled another expeditionary force when he died in Coro in 1540. Philipp von Hutten (1505–1546) came to Venezuela with Espira in 1535 and participated in Espira's three-year expedition across the Colombian Llanos. In 1540 he became captain general of Venezuela. In 1541 he began the longest of the German-led expeditions, exploring the vast region from the Venezuelan coast to the Caquetá in southern Colombia. One of his captains was Bartholomäus Welser, the oldest son of the head of the Welser commercial house. On their return, both Hutten and Welser were imprisoned and beheaded near Barquisimento in 1546 by Juan de Carvajal.

The most successful of the German conquistadores was Nikolaus Federmann (c. 1505–1542), explorer of the Guajira Peninsula, founder of Riohacha, and cofounder of the Colombian capital Bogotá. Jailed in Flanders in 1540 by the Welsers, a desperate Federmann denounced them before the Council of the Indies for defrauding the crown. Eager to end the Welsers' Venezuelan concession, the council brought Federmann to Spain in 1541 to testify against his former patrons. This effectively ended Welser government in Venezuela and began the seventeen-year-long recovery suit, which was abandoned when Philip II declared bankruptcy in 1557.

Beginning in the late eighteenth century, German states were the source of an extraordinary group of geographical scholars, explorers, and cartographers. By this time, German attention was no longer focused on commercial activities in South America but had shifted to Africa and Asia. The scientific mission of Alexander von Humboldt to Venezuela, the Andes, and Mexico in 1799–1804 and Robert Schomburgk's travels in Guiana in 1835–1844 are exceptions. Like the Royal Geographical Society in London, the Berlin Geographical Society, founded in 1828, became an important patron for geographical exploration, and although its members were more interested in proselytizing Christianity around the world than in exploration, religious societies were active in commissioning missionaries who themselves conducted important geographical exploration.

During this time, eminent Germans included the estimable scholars Alexander von Humboldt, Karl Ritter, Johann Blumenbach, and Georg Schweinfurth; the cartographers August Petermann and Heinrich Berghaus; the explorers Heinrich Barth, Friedrich Hornemann, Karl Klaus von der Decken, Hermann von Wissmann, Gustav Nachtigal, Gerhard Rohlfs, Eduard Schnitzer (Emin Pasha), Oskar Lenz, Ludwig Leichhardt, and Ferdinand von Richtofen; and the missionary Ludwig Krapf. This list must also include Karl Peters (a brilliant but thuggishly unstable adventurer/diplomat), along with Wilhelm Junker, Johann Ludwig Burckhardt, and Sven Hedin, who were not natives of a German state but were educated at German universities. Burckhardt, in particular, studied with Blumenbach at the University of Göttingen, Barth was Ritter's student at the University of Berlin, Sven Hedin studied with von Richtofen (also at the University of Berlin), and the French explorer Henri Duveyrier was a protégé of Barth's.

The nineteenth century is replete with exploits by German explorers and travelers. Karl Klaus von der Decken proved to the scientific establishment in Europe in 1861–1862 that snow and ice do exist at high altitudes in the tropics; von Wissmann made a trans-African journey from the Atlantic to the Pacific oceans in 1881–1882; Burckhardt, although he was supposed to travel to Timbuctoo, taught Europeans about the geography and the culture of the Middle East during his eight-year journey to the Levant, the Nile Valley, and Arabia in 1809–1817; Hornemann, in a tragic early attempt to reach Timbuctoo in 1798–1801, became the first European to cross Africa from the Mediterranean to the forest zone; Oskar Lenz (who lived into the twentieth century) became in 1880 the fourth European after Laing, Caillié, and Barth to reach Timbuctoo, and von Richtofen in

1868–1872 conducted superb fieldwork in physical geography in China.

The German luminaries during this time, however, were Heinrich Barth, the cartographer August Petermann, and Alexander von Humboldt. Even though he was not recognized in his own time, Barth was a titan. From 1850 to 1855, he traveled more than five thousand miles in central Africa and conducted one of the most productive journeys of geographical exploration ever recorded. His five-volume book, *Travels and Discoveries in North and Central Africa* (1857–1858), is considered one the best travel accounts ever written. He meticulously compiled scientific and geographical data for a part of the world previously unknown in Europe, and he described huge portions of the Sahara Desert, the Lake Chad–Benue River region, and segments of the Niger River. In September 1853 he became the second European to enter the fabled city of Timbuctoo.

August Petermann was not an explorer himself, but he was one of the most important individuals in the nineteenth century to promote geographical exploration and to publish the findings of explorers who had traveled all over the world. This included journeys made to Africa, Asia, America, the Pacific, and the Arctic. He maintained correspondence with many of the great explorers, and the superb maps that he prepared for his journal, *Petermanns geographische Mitteilungen* (founded in 1855), remain a major source for those conducting research in the field of exploration and discovery.

And there was Alexander von Humboldt. Returning to Europe in 1804 after his scientific foray to northern South America and Mexico, Humboldt spent the rest of his long life (he died just short of his ninetieth birthday in 1859) writing about what he saw, along with the theories about natural history that he developed during his travels. His books are treasured as works of genius. His *Voyage aux régions équinoxiales du nouveau continent* was published in thirty-four volumes between 1805 and 1834, and the five-volume work with the English title *Cosmos: A Sketch of a Physical Description of the Universe* was published in German between 1845 and 1862. Among other things, geographers accept Humboldt as the founder of modern geography. His research in the Andes and adjacent Pacific Ocean marks him as an early pioneer in alpine and oceanographic studies, and he is the acknowledged father of climatology. Alexander von Humboldt was not only a prestigious German geographical explorer, but also one of history's most distinguished scientists.

[*See also* Africa; Central and South America; Timbuctoo; *and biographical entries on figures mentioned in this article*.]

BIBLIOGRAPHY

Friede, Juan. *Los Welser en la conquista de Venezuela: Edición conmemorativa del IV centenario de la muerte de Bartolomé Welser, jefe de la compañía alemana de Augsburgo*. Caracas, Venezuela: Ediciones Edime, 1961.

Helferich, Gerard. *Humboldt's Cosmos: Alexander von Humboldt and the Latin American Journey That Changed the Way We See the World*. New York: Gotham Books, 2004.

Schiffers, Heinrich. *The Quest for Africa: A Thousand Years of Exploration*. Translated by Diana Pyke. New York: Putnam, 1957.

Schmitt, Eberhard, and Friedrich Karl von Hutten. *Das Gold der neuen Welt: Die Papiere des Welser-Konquistadors und Generalkapitäns von Venezuela Philipp von Hutten 1534–1541*. Hildburghausen, Germany: Verlag Frankenschwelle, 1996.

MAURICE P. BRUNGARDT
SANFORD H. BEDERMAN

The Netherlands

Dutch overseas expansion and primacy in world trade was initiated by the "economic miracle" of the 1590s built on the twin foundations of the bulk-carrying trade in grain, timber, salt, and fish in Europe, and the rise of the "rich trades" in spices, textiles, sugar, and tobacco, including new long-distance commerce with Africa, the Americas, and Asia. Extra-European exploration was the logical extension of maritime relations with the Baltic (the "mother trade"); Norway (*Noordsvaart*); Russia (*Moscovische vaart*); England, France, Portugal, and Spain (*Westvaart*); and the Mediterranean (*Straatvaart*). Initially sponsored by a number of private companies and individuals, Dutch exploration of the Indian and Atlantic Ocean Basins was coordinated (though not monopolized) by the great chartered companies, the United East India Company (Vereenigde Oostindische Compagnie) or VOC (founded 1602) and West India Company or WIC (founded 1621), respectively.

Several attempts were undertaken to find a more direct, healthier, and safer passage to Asia, avoiding the "Portuguese" route around the Cape of Good Hope. The only results of the search for a Northeast Passage were two expeditions into the freezing Kara Sea (1594; 1595), and the spectacular wintering of Willem Barents and Jacob van Heemskerck at Nova Zembla on a third attempt (1596–1597). In the search for a northwest passage, however, the VOC-employed Henry Hudson in 1609 discovered Manhattan and sailed ninety miles up the Hudson River (Mauritius Rivier), leading to the establishment of New Netherland. Apart from North America, the Dutch established bases throughout the Caribbean (most notably the Antilles), mainland South America (the Guyanas, and, temporarily, northeastern Brazil), and a string of forts and factories along the west coast of Africa (most notably Moree, Elmina, Axim, Kormantine, and Accra). The capture of a Spanish silver fleet by Piet Heyn (1628) was one of the few financial successes of the WIC (1621–1791), whose monopoly was gradually eroded in the course of the seventeenth and eighteenth centuries.

Olivier van Noort led the first Dutch circumnavigation of the world via the Strait of Magellan (1598–1601), while Jakob Le Maire's search for an alternative passage south of Tierra del Fuego in an attempt to bypass the VOC monopoly led to the discovery of Le Maire Strait and Cape Horn (1615–1616).

The "first shipping" to Asia under Cornelis de Houtman and Pieter Dircksz Keyser (1595–1597) initiated a veritable gold rush. The several precompanies (voor-compagnieën) were welded together for politico-commercial reasons into the VOC (1602–1799), which divided its activities in Asia in three categories: areas where the company exercised its own jurisdiction (Java, Ceylon, the Spice Islands, Coromandel, and South Africa); regions where the company had concluded exclusive agreements with indigenous rulers (the Malaysian Peninsula, Malabar, and Sumatra); and areas where the company merely resided "on sufferance" (Persia, India, China, and Japan, along with peripheral areas such as Siam, the Solor and Timor Islands, Aracan, Pegu, and Cochin-China). [See color plate 28 in this volume.]

The quest for a large southern continent spurred the dispatch of several VOC-sponsored expeditions under Willem Jansz (1605), Dirck Hartog (1616), Jan Carstensz (1623), Abel Tasman (1642–1643; 1644), and Willem de Vlamingh (1696), leading to the discovery of northern Australia (New Holland), Tasmania (Van Diemen's Land), and New Zealand (Statenland) but no permanent settlement, while the WIC-commissioned Jacob Roggeveen (1721) discovered Easter Island and several of the Samoas. The use of the "Brouwer Route" (after 1616) using the westerlies between the 35th and 45th parallels also resulted in a number of unintended encounters with and shipwrecks of VOC ships off the west coast of Australia, most notably the *Batavia* under Francisco Pelsaert (1629). By 1740, Dutch primacy in world trade and the most dynamic phase in exploration had come to an end.

[See also Barents, Willem; Hudson, Henry; Le Maire, Jakob; Roggeveen, Jacob; and Tasman, Abel Janszoon.]

BIBLIOGRAPHY

Boxer, C. R. *The Dutch Seaborne Empire, 1600–1800.* London: Hutchinson, 1965.

Gaastra, Femme S. *The Dutch East India Company: Expansion and Decline.* Zutphen, Netherlands: Walburg Pers, 2003.

Heijer, Henk den. *De Geschiedenis van de WIC.* Zutphen, Netherlands: Walburg Pers, 1994.

Israel, Jonathan I. *Dutch Primacy in World Trade, 1585–1740.* Oxford: Clarendon Press, 1989.

Vries, Jan de, and Ad van der Woude. *The First Modern Economy: Success, Failure, and Perseverance of the Dutch Economy, 1500–1815.* Cambridge, U.K., and New York: Cambridge University Press, 1997.

MARKUS VINK

Portugal

The beginning date of Portuguese overseas expansion and exploration is usually given as August 21, 1415, when the Muslim stronghold of Ceuta in North Africa was captured. However, the Portuguese, along with other Europeans, had been active earlier in the Canary Islands in corsair and slave-raiding activity. Contrary to popular belief, overseas exploration was a poor third or fourth on the list of priorities for Prince Henry "the Navigator," following crusades against the Muslims in North Africa and the capture of the Canary Islands. However, after a debacle at Tangier (1437), Henry gave greater attention to overseas exploration and settlement. By the mid-1430s the Portuguese had adopted a three-pronged approach: 1) holding Ceuta and continuing the North African crusade against the Muslims; 2) sailing down the African coast; and 3) developing the Atlantic islands, initially the Madeiras and the Azores and later the Cape Verdes.

In 1434 Gil Eanes, a squire of Prince Henry, rounded Cape Bojador at about 27° N. After that, the exploration of the coast of West Africa proceeded relatively rapidly. In 1441 the first African slaves from below Cape Bojador reached Portugal. Five years later Prince Henry was given a monopoly on all trade below that cape. By the time of Henry's death in 1460, the Portuguese had explored twenty degrees south, or fifteen hundred miles (twenty-five hundred kilometers) of coast reaching Sierra Leone, and were on the verge of entering the Gulf of Guinea. Other than their names, little is known about many of these explorers.

From 1469 to 1474, a trade monopoly was granted to the merchant Fernão Gomes in exchange for an annual cash payment and the obligation to discover a hundred leagues of new coastline each year along the Guinea coast. In 1474 Rui de Sequeira sailed as far as Cape Saint Catherine (2° S). In December of 1481 Diogo de Azambuja led a fleet of eleven ships to build a fortress at São Jorge da Mina, which was completed the following year. Meanwhile, in 1482, during the first of his two voyages, Diogo Cão became the first known European to reach the Congo (Zaire) River. Either on this voyage or, more probably, his voyage several years later, he explored almost one hundred miles (167 kilometers) upriver to Ielala Falls. During his year-and-a-half voyage, Cão covered thirteen degrees south of the Equator, coasting along what are today Gabon, Congo, Zaire, and much of Angola. On a second expedition from 1485 to 1486, Cão explored an additional nine hundred miles (fifteen hundred kilometers) southward, reaching Cape Cross, or Walvis Bay (22° S), in present-day Namibia. Leaving Portugal in early August of 1487, Bartholomew Dias went beyond Cão's discoveries and rounded the Cape of Good Hope in January of 1488. Dias entered the Indian Ocean, probably reaching as far as the Great Fish River (Rio do Infante), and returned to Lisbon in December 1488. [See color plate 32 in this volume.]

In addition to the voyages of Cão and Dias, King João II (r. 1481–1495) sent expeditions to find land routes across Africa. João Afonso de Aveiro explored the African hinterland and visited Benin in 1485 or 1486. Other Portuguese visited Timbuctoo and Takrur. In 1487, Pêro Covilhã and Afonso de Paiva were sent via the Mediterranean route to collect information about the spice trade. By the end of 1490, Pero Covilhã had visited Hormuz along with Goa, Cannanore, and Calicut. It is probable that he reached Sofala in East Africa before settling in Ethiopia, where he died around 1526. Though he sent a report of his travels to Portugal, it is not known for certain whether it ever reached João II.

In 1498, after the longest recorded voyage out of sight of land up to that time, Vasco da Gama arrived in Calicut in India. The following year, King Manuel (r. 1495–1521) added to his royal titles that of "Lord of the Conquest, Navigation and Commerce of Ethiopia, Arabia, Persia, and India." With Gama's voyage and its follow-up led by Pedro Álvares Cabral (which stopped in Brazil en route to India) in 1500, the Portuguese quickly learned of the economic and strategic importance of much of Asia. Under Dom Francisco de Almeida, Portuguese Asia's first viceroy,

serious efforts were made to establish a strong Portuguese presence in the Indian Ocean. Fortresses were built on the east coast of Africa and on India's Malabar Coast, though some of these were soon abandoned both in Africa and in India.

Almeida's successor, Afonso de Albuquerque, captured Goa (1510), which became the capital of the Portuguese Estado da India; Melaka (1511), the strategically located trading center and gateway to the Moluccas and the spice trade; and Hormuz (1515), at the entrance to the Persian Gulf. In 1513 Albuquerque tried but failed to take strategically located Aden, guarding the Red Sea. At the same time the Portuguese sought gold along the Zambezi River in East Africa, and António Fernandes, in his search for the mines of Monomotapa, reached modern-day Zimbabwe in about 1514 or 1515. Meanwhile, far to the east, António de Abreu led an expedition from Melaka in 1511 that established ties with Ambon and Banda. He may have been the first known European to see the western Pacific Ocean. Francisco Serrão, part of the expedition, established himself at Ternate in the Moluccas. Within fifteen years (1498–1513), almost the entire East African and Asian coastline—excluding China and Japan—had been visited and described by the Portuguese.

For the next several decades, the Portuguese attempted to establish a series of fortresses and trading posts throughout the area stretching from East Africa to Japan. China quickly gained Portugal's attention, and in 1513 Jorge Álvares visited there. However, it was to be via Macau, located on the estuary of the Pearl River by Canton, that Portugal would gain access to the China trade. The Portuguese, through Macau, would also monopolize much of the trade between China and Japan. In about 1543, the first Portuguese visited Japan, with the aid of Chinese pilots. The Navarre-born Jesuit Francis Xavier arrived there on August 15, 1549. Portuguese traders and the Jesuits alike were well received and soon a brisk trade developed in Chinese silks, porcelains, and gold in exchange for Japanese silver. By 1571 the Portuguese were established in Nagasaki.

In the North Atlantic, the brothers Gaspar and Miguel Corte-Real are credited with visiting Nova Scotia, Newfoundland, and Labrador during the years 1499 to 1502. In the South Atlantic, in 1501, Gonçalo Coelho followed up Cabral's brief visit to Brazil by exploring almost two thousand miles (3,333 kilometers) of Brazil's coastline, beginning with Cabo de Santo Agostinho (some say Cabo São Roque), then southward past Rio de Janeiro, possibly as far as Cananéia at 25° S. The following year, Brazil was leased to brazilwood interests and over the next few decades several trading posts were established. On December 3, 1530, Martim Afonso de Sousa and his brother Pero Lopes de Sousa, with a fleet of five ships, sailed from Portugal to explore the entire coast of Portuguese America, setting up a colony in São Vicente in 1532. In 1534 King João III (r. 1521–1557) divided Brazil into fifteen captaincies stretching from the Amazon in the north to Sant'Ana in the south.

[See also biographical entries on figures mentioned in this article.]

BIBLIOGRAPHY

Albuquerque, Luis de, ed. *Dicionário de história dos descobrimentos portugueses.* 2 vols. Lisbon, 1994.

Diffie, Bailey W., and George D. Winius. *Foundations of the Portuguese Empire, 1415–1580.* Minneapolis: University of Minnesota Press, 1977.

Parry, John H. *The Discovery of the Sea.* Berkeley: University of California Press, 1981.

Peres, Damião. *História dos descobrimentos portugueses.* 3rd ed. Porto, Portugal: Vertentes, 1983.

Russell, Peter. *Prince Henry "the Navigator": A Life.* New Haven, Conn.: Yale University Press, 2000.

Russell-Wood, A. J. R. *A World on the Move: The Portuguese in Africa, Asia, and America, 1415–1808.* New York: St. Martin's Press, 1993.

FRANCIS A. DUTRA

Russia

Russian explorations accelerated after the capture of Kazan secured the way east in the 1550s. In 1553 the English discovered a route around Scandinavia to the White Sea, offering trade opportunities. In 1581–1582 the Cossack Yermak Timofeyevich was hired by merchants to cross the Ural Mountains into Siberia. The tsar was pleased; the sable trade flourished. The movement quickened. By 1639 Russian traders reached the Pacific Ocean. In 1648 Semen Deshnev (d. after 1672), a Cossack serving the tsar, sailed around the very northeastern point of Siberia through the Bering Strait. The Cossack Vladimir V. Atlasov conquered the Kamchatka Peninsula and claimed it for Russia in 1697. These were unofficial expeditions, but accounts and maps of them were prepared for the tsars.

Peter I, the Great, (r. 1682–1725) wanted accurate maps of his empire. In 1701 he established a school of navigation to train geodesists (land surveyors). In 1719 he sent Ivan Evreinov and Fedor Luzhin to explore and map the Kuril Islands. The year before he died Peter planned a major expedition, entrusting it to the navy he founded. Led by Vitus Bering, assisted by Alexey Chirikov and M. Spanberg, this First Kamchatka Expedition explored Siberia and sailed northward through the Bering Strait, producing the first accurate map of Russia. This expedition led to the much larger Second Kamchatka Expedition of 1733–1743. Bering, Chirikov, and Spanberg led again, with added personnel from the new Russian Academy of Sciences. The orders were to map the Arctic Coasts of Siberia (by several explorers), discover a route to Japan (Spanberg), and sail to America (Bering and Chirikov). Academy members were to study ethnography, history, natural history, and the resources of Siberia. The expedition succeeded, although many results were not published at the time, probably because the government wanted to keep its monopoly on the sea otter trade with China that resulted from the expedition.

Official expeditions ceased from the 1740s to 1764, when Catherine II (r. 1762–1796) charged Lieutenant Ivan Sindt to monitor the fur trade of the Aleutian Islands and to survey their resources. Joseph Billings and Gavriil Sarychev led another expedition to the islands from 1785 to 1792. Captain Ivan Fedorovich Krusenstern and Yuri Lisiansky, in two ships, made the first Russian circumnavigation in 1803–1806. Forty more Russian circumnavigations were made in the nineteenth century, many including scientists. Russians explored and established settlements in the northern Pacific regions, including North America, in the period of the great geographical and scientific expeditions.

Space. On October 4, 1957, the USSR sent the first *Sputnik* ("traveling companion") into space. Weighing about 180 pounds (82 kilograms) and approximately two feet (sixty-one centimeters) in diameter, *Sputnik* circled Earth every ninety-six minutes until January 4, 1958, when it disintegrated upon reentry into the atmosphere. On November 3, 1957, *Sputnik II* carried the dog Laika ("husky"). Yuri A. Gagarin became the first human space traveler on April 12, 1961. The first woman in space, Valentina Vladimirovna Tereshkova, piloted the *Vostok 6* ("east") in June 1963. On reentry, fire erupted but burned out, and she landed safely. The Russian space expeditions changed the nature of exploration, allowing new discoveries from observations and photographs of Earth from satellites.

[See also Arctic, subentry Russian Arctic; Space Program, subentry Soviet; and biographical entries on figures mentioned in this article.]

BIBLIOGRAPHY
Friis, Herman R., ed. *The Pacific Basin: A History of Its Geographical Exploration*. New York: American Geographical Society, 1967.
Riasanovsky, Nicholas Valentine, and Mark D. Steinberg. *A History of Russia*. 7th ed. 2 vols. New York: Oxford University Press, 2005.
Wood, Alan, ed. *The History of Siberia: From Russian Conquest to Revolution*. London and New York: Routledge, 1991.

CAROL URNESS

Scotland

Widespread Scottish involvement in overseas exploration began during the 1700s. Before this point, many Scots immigrated to the Ulster plantations in Ireland or to the European continent as merchants or mercenaries. They were not, however, active in exploration because they lacked government support. Although the English and Scottish crowns were united in 1603, the monarchs focused their resources upon creating colonial possessions that benefited the English kingdom. Scots gained full access to England's colonies and began to participate more frequently in state-sponsored exploration voyages after the union of England and Scotland in 1707.

The 1700s and the 1800s mark the peak of British exploration. Scots were particularly active in the government's two main concerns, polar exploration and mapping Africa's interior. With regard to Arctic exploration, the British government was particularly interested in discovering the Northwest Passage to Asia. Scots who participated in this venture included Alexander Mackenzie, who traveled the length of the Mackenzie River in 1789 and was the first European to travel overland across North America in 1793; John Ross, who mapped Baffin Bay in 1818; John Richardson, who explored Canada's northern coast between the Mackenzie and Coppermine rivers from 1825 to 1827; James Clark Ross, who discovered the North Magnetic Pole in 1831; and John Rae, who from 1846 to 1847 mapped 600 miles (1,000 kilometers) of northern Canada's coastline.

Scots also took part in exploring Antarctica. In 1822 the Scottish sealer James Weddell discovered the Weddell Sea. From 1839 to 1843, James Clark Ross commanded a voyage that mapped much of Antarctica's coast, discovered the volcano he named Erebus, and explored the Ross Sea. Scottish involvement in exploring Antarctica continued into the twentieth century. In 1902, the Scottish National Antarctic Expedition was launched. Between 1902 and 1904, under the leadership of William Speirs Bruce, it mapped the South Orkney Islands, surveyed the Weddell Sea, and studied Antarctica's plants, animals, and geology.

During the nineteenth century, Scots also participated in exploring the African interior. Prominent Scots who expanded European knowledge of Africa included Mungo Park, who reached the Niger River in 1796; Hugh Clapperton, who was one of the first Europeans to reach Lake Chad (1823); Alexander Gordon Laing, who became the first European to visit Timbuctoo (1826); and Joseph Thomson, who investigated the region around Lake Tanganyika (1879–1880), headed an expedition through Maasailand in eastern Africa (1882–1883), and explored the Atlas Mountains in southern Morocco (1888). Scotland's most famous African explorer, however, was David Livingstone, who from 1840 until his death in 1873 explored much previously uncharted territory in central Africa. His achievements include being the first European to cross Africa from coast to coast (1853–1856), being the first European to see Victoria Falls (1855), and making the European discovery of Lake Malawi while investigating the possibilities for British commerce in the Zambezi River region (1855–1856).

[*See also* Africa, *subentry on* Exploration; Antarctica; North Pole; *and biographical entries on figures mentioned in this article*.]

BIBLIOGRAPHY
Fleming, Fergus. *Barrow's Boys: A Stirring Story of Daring, Fortitude, and Outright Lunacy*. New York: Grove Press, 1998.
Mossman, R. C., J. H. Harvey Pirie, and R. N. Rudmose Brown. *The Voyage of the Scotia: Being the Record of a Voyage in Antarctic Seas*. Edinburgh: Mercat Press, 2002.

MARY ELIZABETH AILES

Spain

The Spanish monarchs Ferdinand and Isabella sponsored Atlantic voyages by Christopher Columbus in 1492, 1493–1496, 1498–1500, and 1502–1504, in which Columbus explored the southern coast of Cuba, part of the northern coast of South America, and southeastward along the Caribbean coast of Central America. From 1499 on, other Spanish voyages explored more of those coasts in search of a passage that would continue the sea route to Asia. In 1513, Vasco Núñez de Balboa's expedition crossed the Isthmus of Panama, becoming the first Europeans to see the Pacific Ocean; in addition, Juan Ponce

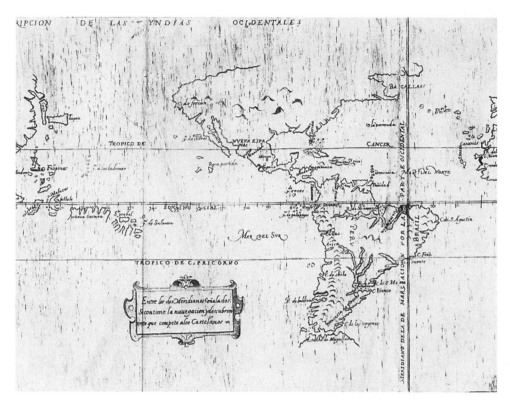

Spanish Exploration. From Antonio de Herrera y Tordesillas's *Descripción de las Indias Occidentales* (Madrid, 1601), this chart shows the Spanish overseas empire between the western and eastern lines of the Treaty of Tordesillas (1494). It is the key-map for twelve detailed maps of different parts of the empire and testifies to a remarkable sense of imperial unity. It was generated from the manuscript map of López de Velasco (1574). COURTESY THE NEWBERRY LIBRARY, CHICAGO

de León explored around the southern coastline of Florida and the northern coastline of the Yucatán.

The Portuguese explorer Ferdinand Magellan pioneered the southwestern route to Asia for Spain (1519–1521), battling the tortuous strait later named for him at the southern tip of South America, and crossing the Pacific Ocean to the Philippines before being killed intervening in a local dispute. His successor, Juan Sebastián del Cano, failed to find a return route across the Pacific and led the remnant of the expedition westward and around Africa toward home. The remainder of Magellan's company arrived back in Spain in 1522, having completed the first circumnavigation of the globe.

At the same time, Hernán Cortés explored inland from the Mexican coast and conquered the Aztec Empire (1519–1521); he then explored and conquered Guatemala (1524), established the prosperous colony of New Spain (Mexico) in the former Aztec Empire, and explored lower California. Cortés also financed the first crossing of the Pacific from

New Spain (1527) by his cousin Álvaro de Saavedra, sailing in aid of the disaster-prone expedition of García Jofre de Loaísa that retraced Magellan's path. In the 1520s, Estevao Gomes explored north along the Atlantic coast, Lucas Vázquez de Ayllón established a short-lived colony in Georgia or South Carolina, and Pánfilo de Narváez explored the Gulf Coast westward from Florida.

Farther south, voyages from Panama, including two by Francisco Pizarro (1524–1527), reconnoitered the coasts of northwestern South America. Pizarro then marched south along the coast (1531–1532) and inland to the heart of the Incan Empire, where his men defeated imperial forces in November 1532, though they were outnumbered by more than fifteen to one. Thereafter, veteran conquistadores warred among themselves even as they searched for new lands to conquer. Stories of fabulously rich lands ruled by El Dorado (literally, the gilded one) inspired Gonzalo Jiménez de Quesada to explore southward from the Caribbean coast to the foothills of the Andes, where he founded Bogotá in 1537. El Dorado would continue to inspire exploration in northern South America for the rest of the century.

In North America, Alvar Núñez Cabeza de Vaca explored the Gulf of Mexico north and west from Tampa Bay (1528–1536), and Hernando de Soto meandered all over the southeastern quadrant of North America (1539–1543). During the same years, Francisco Vázquez de Coronado explored the southwest in search of the legendary Seven Cities of Cíbola. Coronado and his men explored vast territories and were the first Europeans to see the Grand Canyon.

Cabeza de Vaca and many others tried their luck in South America in the early 1540s. Pedro de Valdivia explored far into Chile and fought the fierce Araucanian Indians. He founded six towns and established the main outlines of Spanish colonization before dying in battle in 1553. In the north, Francisco de Orellana descended the Amazon River from the Andes to the Atlantic Ocean, a journey of over 2,000 miles (3,200 kilometers). For the remainder of the sixteenth century, Spain consolidated administrative control of its colonies and struggled to keep European rivals out of the vast territories it claimed. Along with dozens of known expeditions, many now-forgotten missionaries explored into the hinterlands beyond established settlements in both North and South America, searching for potential Christians.

In the Pacific, the elusive return route from Asia to New Spain was pioneered in 1565 by Andrés de Urdaneta, a veteran from Loaísa's expedition who became an Augustinian friar. Urdaneta, who had studied the problem for decades, sailed far north from the Philippines before crossing the Pacific, then southeast along the coast of North America. The Manila galleon trade between Acapulco and the Philippines began soon thereafter. Though Álvaro de Mendaña sailed westward from Peru in 1567 and discovered the Solomon Islands, Spaniards had little incentive to undertake risky expeditions in the uncharted Pacific after Urdaneta found the way back to New Spain.

On land, Juan de Oñate explored north beyond Santa Fe, then west and south to the Gulf of California (1598–1605). Sebastián Vizcaíno, a veteran of the Manila galleons, surveyed the west coast of North America (1602–1603), traveling well beyond San Francisco Bay. Later he explored central New Spain (1608) and islands of the North Pacific (1611). In the South Pacific, Pedro Fernández de Quirós, another veteran of the Manila galleons, searched for the fabled Southern Continent (Terra Australis) and discovered the New Hebrides Islands in 1606. Quiros's subordinate, Luis Váez de Torres, discovered the strait that now bears his name and proved that New Guinea was an island.

Many noteworthy Spanish expeditions of the late seventeenth and eighteenth centuries were carried out by missionaries in search of souls to convert, from the Amazon Basin and remote areas of the Andes and southern Chile to the North American southwest. In two Jesuit examples, Niccolò Mascardi explored across Patagonia to the eastern mouth of the Strait of Magellan (1671–1672); and Eusebio Kino explored southern Arizona (1687–1706).

During the eighteenth century, Spanish expeditions sought to connect New Spain with scattered settlements farther north. In an epic journey from 1776 to 1793, Fray Silvestre Escalante and Fray Francisco Atanasio Domínguez traveled north and west from Santa Fe, becoming the first Europeans to describe the Great Salt Lake. Fears of Russian incursion into Upper California spurred king Charles III to dispatch a series of expeditions for several reasons: to establish presidios and settlements; to support the chain of Franciscan missions; and to survey the coast. Gaspar de Portolá (1769–1770) and Juan Bautista de Anza (1774–1775) trekked overland toward San Francisco. Juan Pérez sailed the area north and south of the Columbia River in 1774; Juan de Ayala made the first recorded voyage deep into San Francisco Bay the following year; and Juan Francisco Bodega y Quadra and Bruno de Hezeta mapped the northwest coast nearly to Sitka. At century's end, Alejandro Malaspina's epic voyage from 1790 to 1793 reinforced Spain's presence in the Pacific, but exploration could not compete with the ongoing demands of Spain's colonial empire in the Americas.

[See also biographical entries on figures mentioned in this article.]

BIBLIOGRAPHY

Fernández-Armesto, Felipe, ed. *The Times Atlas of World Exploration*. London: Times Books, 1991.

Ishikawa, Chiyo, ed. *Spain in the Age of Exploration, 1492–1819*. Seattle: Seattle Art Museum; Lincoln: University of Nebraska Press, 2004.

Joyner, Tim. *Magellan*. Camden, Me.: International Marine, 1992.

Malaspina, Alessandro. *The Malaspina Expedition, 1789–1794: Journal of the Voyage by Alejandro Malaspina*. 3 vols. Edited by Andrew David et al. London: Hakluyt Society, in association with the Museo Naval, Madrid, 2001–2004.

Martínez Shaw, Carlos, ed. *El Pacífico Español de Magallanes a Malaspina*. Madrid: Ministerio de Asuntos Exteriores, 1988.

Morison, Samuel Eliot. *The European Discovery of America*. Vol. 2, *The Southern Voyages, 1492–1616*. New York: Oxford University Press, 1974.

Parry, J. H. *The Age of Reconnaissance. Discovery, Exploration and Settlement 1450 to 1650*. New York: Praeger Publishers, 1969.

Phillips, William D., Jr., and Carla Rahn Phillips. *The Worlds of Christopher Columbus*. Cambridge, U.K., and New York: Cambridge University Press, 1992.

Reinhartz, Dennis, and Gerald D. Saxon, eds. *The Mapping of the Entradas into the Greater Southwest*. Norman: University of Oklahoma Press, 1998.

Thomas, Hugh. *Rivers of Gold: The Rise of the Spanish Empire*. London: Weidenfeld and Nicolson, 2003.

Weddle, Robert S. *The French Thorn: Rival Explorers in the Spanish Sea, 1682–1762*. College Station: Texas A&M University Press, 1991.

CARLA RAHN PHILLIPS

Venice

The city of Venice had nurtured a long tradition of sailors, merchants, adventurers, and pilgrims, as well as cosmographers and mapmakers. Both Niccolò de' Conti (c. 1395–1469) and more famously Marco Polo (1254–1324) traveled to Asia in the late Middle Ages, providing Europe with the earliest detailed accounts of the East. Polo's text supplied Christopher Columbus with one of his primary sources of information about the riches of Asia, and Columbus contributed nearly four hundred annotations to his own personal volume of *Il milione*.

Under the patronage of Prince Henry the Navigator, the Venetian Alvise di Cadamosto (1432–1488) was among the first to explore the west coast of Africa and appears to have been the first European to reach the Cape Verde Islands, in 1456, resulting in one of the earliest known descriptions of western Africa. In 1497, Henry VII of England authorized the Venetian John Cabot (or Giovanni Caboto) and his son Sebastian to sail west in search of islands. They landed on the coast of Labrador, which, as one chronicler noted, Cabot marked with both English and Venetian flags. In the sixteenth century, it was the Vicentine Antonio Pigafetta who accompanied Ferdinand Magellan and chronicled Magellan's monumental circumnavigation of the globe.

For their numerous voyages of discovery, many early modern Venetians saw themselves as having laid the historic groundwork for the sixteenth-century age of exploration. As the fifteenth-century traveler Giosofat Barbaro put it in his *Travels to Persia*, "much of [the earth] . . . would be unknown if Venetian merchants and sailors had not discovered it."

[*See also* Cabot, John; Cabot, Sebastian; Cadamosto, Alvise di; Columbus, Christopher; Henry the Navigator; Magellan, Ferdinand; Pigafetta, Antonio; *and* Polo, Marco.]

BIBLIOGRAPHY
Caracciolo Aricò, Angela, ed. *L'impatto della scoperta dell'America nella cultura Veneziana*. Rome: Bulzoni, 1990.

ELIZABETH HORODOWICH

Exploration as Redemption.

For some historians, the apparent willingness with which many prosperous Europeans went to war in 1914 had much to do with their disillusion at industrialized society and their place in it. Particularly in the most industrialized societies, the argument goes, the ruling groups felt that their lives had become too easy; they longed for a demanding test in which to prove their mettle. Of course, industrialization had as well the opposite effect of producing social groups whose lives were only too challenging. But we are here thinking about those well-heeled young men who around 1900 seemed to have longed for violent action.

The Great War of 1914 was one way in which many found this deceptive release, but we might also argue that many European explorers of that period were responding to the same urge. Whereas in earlier times explorers had taken great risks to become rich, or to convert heathen peoples to Christianity, by the end of the nineteenth century there were explorers who, to judge by their writings, chiefly wanted to subject themselves to heroic tests.

By then, of course, much of the world was well known to Europeans, and so the relatively unexplored poles became the theater of much derring-do. The spirit of the new generation of explorers was brilliantly captured by Apsley Cherry-Garrard, whose *The Worst Journey in the World* (1922) exactly describes the feelings of a well-heeled young Englishman of the period. Typically, he was no technical expert of any kind; typically, too, his revered leader, in this case the polar explorer Robert Falcon Scott, seemed almost to defy the advice of technicians and to rely instead on the remarkable resources that he drew from the hearts of his men.

The nature of this urge toward personal redemption seems to have changed a little after the horrors of 1914–1918. Explorers still sought to test themselves, but more and more, in their remote wanderings, they were led to the sense that ancient cultures and their irreplaceable values were being slowly extinguished by a Western society that many explorers found insensitive and corrupt. Among many others, Frank Kingdon-Ward felt this destructive process among the people of Burma in the 1920s, and so did Freya Stark, writing from Arabia in the 1930s. As she put it in *The Valley of the Assassins*, "modern education ignores the need for solitude; hence a decline in religion, in poetry, in all the deeper affections of the spirit; a disease to be *doing* something always . . ." By then, a whole new generation of explorers like Harry St. John Philby, Gertrude Bell, and Wilfred Thesiger were finding themselves in the Arabian deserts, among their hospitable nomads. These were no doubt the last explorers who could seek redemption in this way, for commercialized "expeditions of exploration" now cover virtually the entire world.

[*See also* Bell, Gertrude; Scott, Robert Falcon; Stark, Freya; *and* Thesiger, Wilfred.]

BIBLIOGRAPHY

Allen, Benedict, ed. *The Faber Book of Exploration*. London: Faber and Faber, 2002. See the excerpt from Frank Kingdon-Ward's *Riddle of the Tsangpo Gorges: Retracing the Epic Journey of 1924–25 in Southeast Tibet.*

Cherry-Garrard, Apsley. *The Worst Journey in the World, Antarctic, 1910–1913*. London: Constable, 1922. Reprint. New York: Penguin, 2006.

Stark, Freya. *The Valley of the Assassins*. London: John Murray, 1936.

DAVID BUISSERET

Exploration Texts. Travel to and in the unfamiliar climes of the Middle East, Africa, Asia, and the New World was difficult enough in the sixteenth and seventeenth centuries. Literate travelers who went to these places faced the even more daunting task of describing their experiences in writing for circulation to a domestic audience. Struggling with the requirement to describe alien landscapes, flora, fauna, and peoples, they commonly and consciously resorted to established authoritative scholarly works to support their own testimony. The strange natural phenomena and alien cultures the travelers had encountered needed somehow to be interiorized and "produced" in a form comprehensible to their readers, and while some of the travelers' accounts were intended for purely entertainment purposes, most had urgent, practical commercial and promotional uses. The modern editor who hopes to establish the meaning, context, and significance of a particular sixteenth- or seventeenth-century exploration text must pay careful attention to the purpose of the venture described and the way that the author's personal, political, social, and cultural context influenced how he or she saw, interpreted, and represented the places visited and the peoples encountered.

It is also important to try to decipher how the finished account was edited for, and received by, the intended audience. Questions of selection, design, distortion, convention, and fictionality have to be considered, whether the editor is working with administrative or commercial records, mission narratives, chronicles, logs, private letters, or accounts designed to attract investors.

Historians studying the accounts of the explorations that laid the foundations of European overseas empires in the sixteenth and seventeenth centuries have learned from rhetoricians that they must pay much greater attention to the conscious and unconscious processes involved in the production of the written record. It is an unquestionable fact that most of their authors did actually venture out to see the new or scarcely known regions and peoples they described. What is much more complex to assess is the reliability of such descriptions of their experience, what they saw and whom they encountered. Structuralist and poststructuralist approaches that deny the relevance of social context or authorial biography to any particular text are not useful here. On the contrary, the task of the historical editor is to situate that text carefully in multiple contexts. No early modern author-travelers made journeys to strange places without having numerous pieces of mental baggage that clearly affected how they presented their experiences.

The editor must first remember that most sixteenth- or seventeenth-century accounts of exploration were, overtly as well as covertly, intended to make a case. At the most obvious level, many accounts were designed to promote interest and investment in a new colonial or commercial venture. They are thus likely to have undergone two processes of editing before they ever reached a printing press. Their authors would most certainly have preselected the information within the accounts to satisfy, or more often to mollify, those who had initially backed the enterprise. These same promoters are likely to have reviewed and amended the draft text they received according to their own best judgment of what would attract royal support or further investment for the venture. If an earlier manuscript draft of a printed text survives, minute comparison can reveal the differences between what the author chose to say and what was eventually allowed into print. Even here, however, one must remember that, in the early modern period copyright rested with the printer, not with the author, and the significance of the wording of a particular passage of description may owe as much to the typesetter's desire to make the words fit

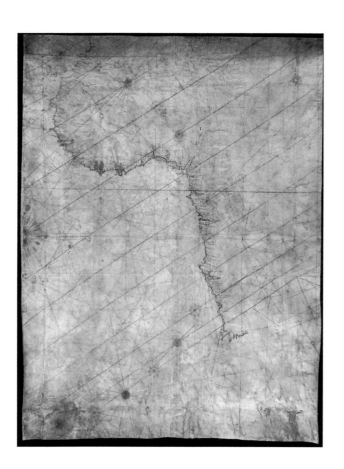

Plate 32. Portuguese Expeditions of World Exploration. Fifteenth-century anonymous Portuguese portolan chart of the coast of West Africa. The Portuguese no doubt made many charts in the course of their exploration down the coast of West Africa. This is one of the very few that survive, showing how the style of the portolan chart came to be applied to the wider world. [See the articles on Expeditions, World Exploration: Portugal, and Maps, Mapmaking, and Mapmakers.] HARRY RANSOM CENTER FOR THE HUMANITIES, AUSTIN, TEXAS

Plate 33. Ancient Fictions of Exploration. Mosaic showing Ulysses leaving Circe and sailing past the Sirens, second century B.C.E. Here Ulysses, or Odysseus, stands in front of the mast of his galley, leaving the enchantress Circe on the island identified by some as Elba. Ulysses may certainly stand for the Greek explorers as they ventured not only east into the Black Sea, but also into the western Mediterranean. [See the articles on Ancient Fictions of Exploration and Travel Writing in Antiquity.] MUSÉE NATIONAL DU BARDO, TUNIS/ERICH LESSING/ART RESOURCE, NY

Plate 34. Otto von Kotzebue. Plate from *A Voyage of Discovery into the South Sea and Bering's Straits* (3 vols., London, 1821). This evocative plate comes from the English edition of Kotzebue's book about his travels in the South Seas, and helps to explain the fascination felt by readers in many European nations for accounts of this nature. [See the article on Otto von Kotzebue.] COURTESY THE NEWBERRY LIBRARY CHICAGO

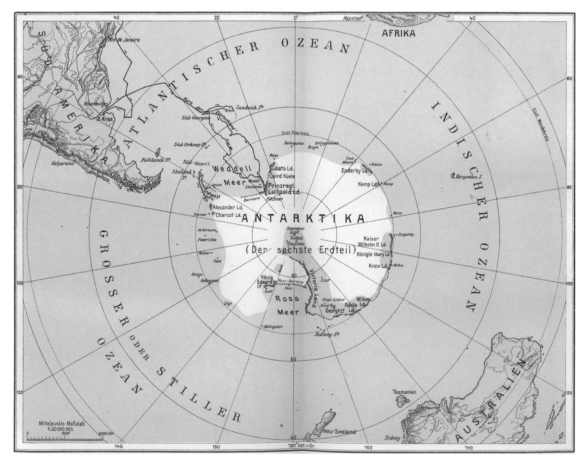

Plate 35. Wilhelm Filchner. From Wilhelm Filchner's *Zum sechsten Erdteil: Die zweite deutsche Süd-polar-Expedition* (Berlin, c. 1922). This efficient little map shows European ventures to Antarctica ("Süd-pol: Amundsen, Scott, Shackleton"), and also the course of Filchner's ship, the *Deutschland*, to "Prinzregt. Luitpold Ld." [See the article on Wilhelm Filchner.] COURTESY THE NEWBERRY LIBRARY CHICAGO

Plate 36. Matthew Flinders. Drawing by Ferdinand Bauer, c. 1795. Bauer was an Austrian artist who worked extensively in the Pacific area. When he returned to England, in 1805, he brought a very large number of sketches of the region's flora; his work is now found both at the Natural History Museum in London and in the Naturhistorisches Museum in Vienna. [See the article on Matthew Flinders.] NATURAL HISTORY MUSEUM, LONDON

Plate 37. Franklin Search Expeditions. Lt. Creswell, RN. *Sledge party Leaving HMS* Investigator, 1853. [See the article on the Franklin Search Expeditions in this volume.] ROYAL GEOGRAPHICAL SOCIETY

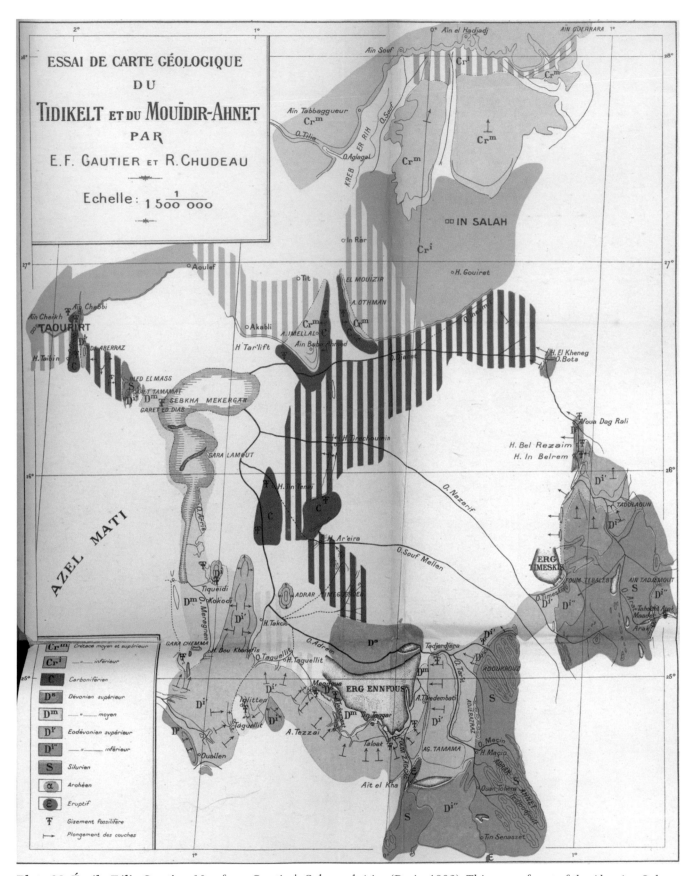

Plate 38. Émile-Félix Gautier. Map from Gautier's *Sahara algérien* (Paris, 1908). This map of part of the Algerian Sahara Desert by Gautier and a collaborator shows the application of the latest geological theories to the business of understanding these remote regions. [See the articles on Émile-Félix Gautier and the Sahara.] COURTESY THE NEWBERRY LIBRARY CHICAGO

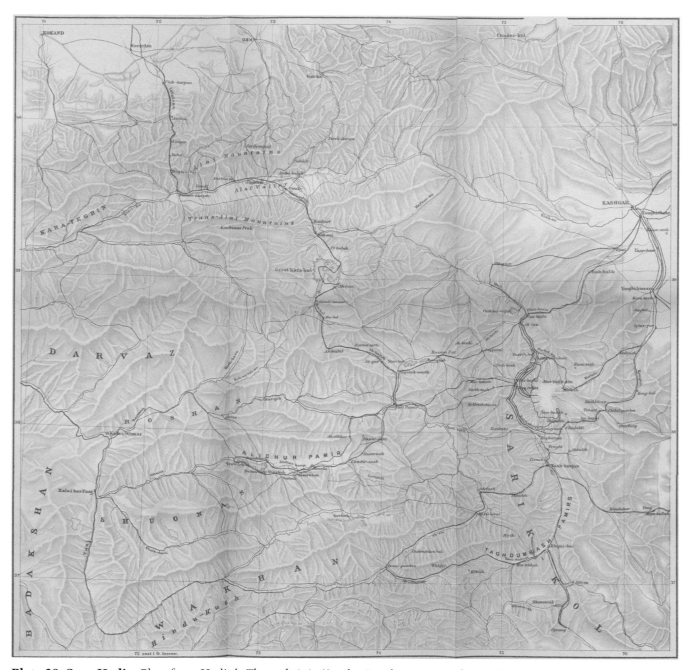

Plate 39. Sven Hedin. Plate from Hedin's *Through Asia* (2 vols., London/New York, 1899). This chart, printed in Sweden, shows Hedin's extensive wanderings through the Pamir. [See the articles on the Gobi Desert and Sven Hedin.] COURTESY THE NEWBERRY LIBRARY CHICAGO

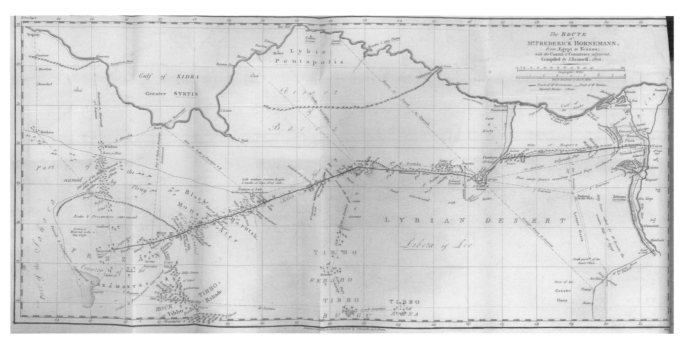

Plate 40. Friedrich Hornemann. Detail of a map from *The Journal of Frederick Horneman's Travels, from Cairo to Mourzouk* (London, 1802). The carefully annotated red route follows Hornemann's track across the Sahara Desert. Note that from time to time he indicates his distance south of the Mediterranean Sea, whose shores run along the top of the map. [See the article on Friedrich Hornemann.] COURTESY THE NEWBERRY LIBRARY CHICAGO

Plate 41. Hubble Space Telescope. Image of the Eagle Nebula (photographed using the Hubble Space telescope, April 1995) This famous photograph was secured shortly after the repair mission carried out by the crew of the Space Shuttle *Endeavour*. [See the articles on the Hubble Space Telescope; the Space Program; and the Space Shuttle.] NASA

Plate 42. Alexander von Humboldt. View from *Vues des Cordillières* (2 vols., Paris, 1810). This remarkable view could stand as a metaphor for Humboldt's career; the thinker, formed in the Enlightenment, sets boldly out into the Romantic world he will do much to form. [See the article on Alexander von Humboldt.] COURTESY THE NEWBERRY LIBRARY CHICAGO

Plate 43. Yves-Joseph de Kerguelen. This 1776 drawing of Christmas Harbour, Kerguelen Island, is by John Webber. Note the penguins in the foreground. [See the article on Yves-Joseph de Kerguelen.] THE BRITISH LIBRARY

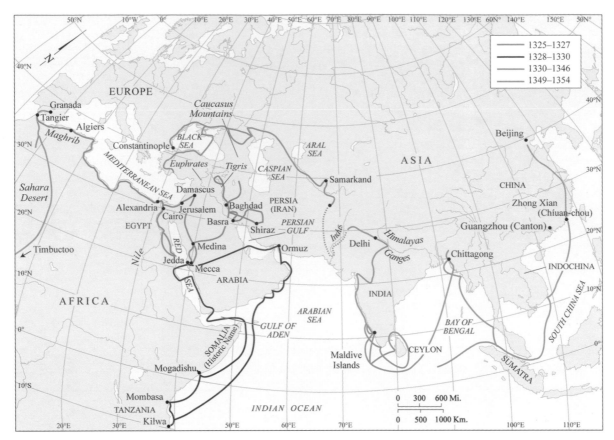

Plate 44. Ibn Battuta. The voyages of Ibn Battuta, "the traveler of Islam," carried him through territories that are part of forty-three modern countries. [See the articles on Africa; Arabo-Islamic Geography; Hajj; Ibn Battuta; and Sahara.] MAP BY BILL NELSON

Plate 45. Cavelier de La Salle. George Catlin, *Imaginative Reconstruction of La Salle at Niagara Falls*, 1840. This lively historical reconstruction reminds us that La Salle was extremely active in furthering French interests around the Great Lakes, before his Mississippi voyage of 1682–1683, and his disastrous venture that ended on the Texas coast. [See the article on Cavelier de La Salle.] NATIONAL GALLERY OF ART, WASHINGTON, DC

the page as to the phrasing of the manuscript bought by the press.

Although it is not reasonable to read exploration texts as entirely self-referential, nevertheless the writer's domestic political or personal predispositions may intentionally distort the way in which what was observed was presented. For some authors, accounts of strange political and social structures encountered abroad offered a means to critique the deficiencies of those structures familiar to them at home. If a journey of exploration was undertaken as a means to repair damaged political fortunes or to seek personal advancement, it was not uncommon for the author-traveler—as would commonly be done in country-house entertainments for visiting royalty—to recast metaphorically the topography and the inhabitants of the place visited as a fitting setting and clientage for the selected patron. Thus accounts of societies of women in Guiana allowed Sir Walter Ralegh to play upon the notion of the willingness of all its peoples to receive Elizabeth I as their virgin Amazon queen.

These kinds of rhetorical devices are easily detected. It is a much more complex task to unpack the distortions created by the early modern writer's implicit confidence in the superiority of European culture and subconscious reliance on the common stock of descriptive metaphors to be drawn from it. More critically, as works written by scholars influenced by postmodernist literary critical theory and postcolonial ideology have convincingly demonstrated, travel texts were essential literary tools of the process of appropriation or conquest. By the act of description, landscapes were rendered "empty," and "new," or gendered female and "virgin," and their non-European indigenous inhabitants were rendered "savage," "barbarous," "uncivilized" or "civilized," "peaceful" or "docile." Lands and people were characterized, produced, and made eligible for conquest by a hegemonic Eurocentric discourse designed to support the interests of European colonizing powers.

The modern editor of such accounts must recognize that early modern explorers reshaped and represented what they encountered by categorizing it in terms of what they already understood or desired to affect. However, the editor does not then have the option of dismissing everything described in the account as merely a projection of European cosmographies, ethnographies, and objectives. The real, as opposed to the represented, landscape can be recovered by careful use of the resources provided by geography and natural science. Most critically, as historical anthropologists like Neil Whitehead have demonstrated, the residual, authentic traces of indigenous peoples encountered in the New World or elsewhere can be disentangled from Eurocentric characterizations of them, if these characterizations are read within the context of anthropological literature, archaeological investigation, and oral history. Accounts were the products of actual encounters between the observing explorer and the observed and of mutual efforts to communicate intelligibly where everything was strange. Inevitably the cultural tropes and voices of the "other" were carried into the finished European product. If these are dismissed as no more than depictions of the colonizing European self, then the witness of peoples, many of whom had so little historical time remaining to them, will, once again, be effaced.

[*See also* Encyclopedias of Exploration; Fictions of Exploration; Hakluyt Society; Pacific, *subentry on* Literary Representations; *and* Travel Literature, European.]

BIBLIOGRAPHY

Campbell, Mary B. *The Witness and the Other World: Exotic European Travel Writing, 400–1600*. Ithaca, N.Y.: Cornell University Press, 1988.

Edwards, Philip, ed. *Last Voyages—Cavendish, Hudson, Ralegh: The Original Narratives*. Oxford: Oxford University Press, 1988.

Fuller, Mary C. *Voyages in Print: English Travel to America 1576–1624*. Cambridge, U.K.: Cambridge University Press, 1995.

Greenblatt, Stephen. *Marvelous Possessions: The Wonder of the New World*. Chicago: University of Chicago Press, 1991.

Greenblatt, Stephen, ed. *New World Encounters*. Berkeley: University of California Press, 1993.

Hadfield, Andrew. *Literature, Travel, and Colonial Writing in the English Renaissance, 1545–1625*. Oxford: Clarendon Press, 1998.

Hulme, Peter. *Colonial Encounters: Europe and the Native Caribbean 1492–1797*. London: Methuen, 1986.

Ralegh, Sir Walter. *The Discoverie of the Large, Rich, and Bewtiful Empyre of Guiana*. Edited by Neil L. Whitehead. Norman: University of Oklahoma Press, 1997.

JOYCE LORIMER

Explorers Club. The Explorers Club was founded in New York in 1904, with its first regular meeting in 1905. From the start, its members would periodically assemble for "smoker-lecture" illustrated talks, at which explorers returning from the field and visiting men of science (the club accepted no women as members until 1981) would lecture on their recent experiences. In 1912 the club took up into its rolls the members of the Arctic Club of America. During its early years, the club moved several times in New York, but then in 1964 it settled at its present elegant headquarters at 46 East 70th Street. There it maintains a 15,000-volume library, as well as archival collections comprising chiefly membership files and expedition reports. More than five hundred researchers consult the Research Collections annually to study the club's art, archives, films, photos, maps, manuscripts, memorabilia, and rare-book library. Thousands more inquiries about deceased members are handled each year by phone and e-mail. Since 1921 the club has published *The Explorers Journal*, designed to share news from the field, information about new acquisitions, members' obituaries, and so forth.

Today the club has thirty-one hundred members and a worldwide membership, grouped into thirty-two chapters with members from sixty countries. Among the present and former members are many figures found in the pages of the present volume, including, among others, Roald Amundsen, Neil Armstrong, Robert Ballard, William Beebe, Thor Heyerdahl, Jacques Piccard, and Sir Ernest Shackleton. The club still invites returning explorers to share their experiences in a variety of events, and serves as a resource for scholars and researchers. It also administers the Youth Activities Fund, for high school and college students, and the Exploration Fund, for graduate students to conduct field research. Up to sixty awards are given out annually in each program for fieldwork conducted anywhere in the world. The Explorers Club remains a vital element in the continuing process of exploration, and in the study of the history of exploration.

[*See also biographies of figures mentioned in this article.*]

BIBLIOGRAPHY
Blossom, F. A., ed. *Told at The Explorers Club; True Tales of Modern Exploration*. New York: Albert and Charles Boni, 1931.
The Explorers Journal. New York: The Explorers Club, 1921–.

CLARE FLEMMING

Explorers in Disguise. In many parts of the world, it was a positive advantage for explorers to look distinctly different from those among whom they were going to move. This was surely the case for Zheng He, for instance, in the Indian Ocean, or for Hernán Cortés in Central America. But there were other parts of the world with powerful rulers hostile to the intrusion of foreigners, where any kind of penetration was possible only by using disguise. Of course, for any disguise to work, the explorers could not differ too radically as physical types from their unwitting hosts.

The two main regions in which disguise was effectively used by Europeans were the Muslim world and the regions to the north of India. The first disguised explorer to penetrate the Muslim world was probably the Venetian Ludovico de Varthema. He left Venice in 1500, and for a while he studied Arabic at Damascus. After that he joined a caravan bound for Mecca; this he successfully reached in the guise of a pilgrim, and then he tried to travel on to Persia. In Aden he was seized as a Christian spy; his many adventures are fully described in his picaresque *Itinerary*.

For many years after this, there seems to be no record of such reporting on the Muslim world, which indeed menaced Europe in a great arc from the Danube to the Pillars of Hercules at the mouth of the Mediterranean Sea. But then in 1797, in the declining days of the Muslim Empire, Friedrich Hornemann was employed by the African Association of London to undertake four years of intensive exploration in northwest Africa; for this purpose he disguised himself as a Muslim. A decade or so later, the Association for Promoting the Discovery of the Interior Parts of Africa employed the Swiss Johann Ludwig Burckhardt to explore the Sahara. After studying Islam and learning Arabic, Burckhardt set off in 1812, disguised as a Muslim merchant, Sheikh Ibnobdullah; this proved a most effective cover for his investigations. Much the same tactics were used by René Caillié in his epic journey to Timbuctoo in 1828. Caillié also had studied Arabic and Islam, and he traveled in various disguises, using a variety of cover stories. These expedients proved completely successful.

Toward the middle of the nineteenth century, the great revival of interest in Africa's interior led to several expeditions by disguised explorers. One of the most thoroughly prepared was that of Sir Richard Francis Burton, who in 1853—intrepid gentile—had himself circumcised in order to pass as an Indian-born Afghan doctor on a pilgrimage to Mecca. The disguise of the Hungarian explorer Arminius Vámbéry was even more outrageous, for when in 1863 he joined a caravan leaving for Turkestan, he was disguised as a dervish. Finally, when the French adventurer Charles de Foucauld traveled in Morocco in 1884–1885, he masqueraded as a Muscovite rabbi.

The disguises adopted by travelers in central Asia were less exotic. During the 1820s and 1830s, the region north of India was often reconnoitered by adventurous young English officers like Alexander Burnes and William Moorcroft. They always took pains to learn some local languages, and they often traveled in the unrevealing garb of holy men. When in 1844 the French Lazarite priest Évariste Huc set out for Lhasa, he too decided to travel as a lama; this ploy succeeded, even if he was soon asked to leave the kingdom.

As time went by, and the British needed as much geographical information as possible for the Great Game that they were playing with the Russians, they began recruiting local people, whom they trained in the art of inconspicuously gathering cartographic information. These Pundits, as they were called, could often circulate very freely in their minimal disguise, and the best of them, men like Nain Singh and Kishen Singh in India, often brought back crucial information. A later instance of disguise is that of Alexandra David-Neel, an eccentric Frenchwoman who in 1924 succeeded in reaching Lhasa, disguised as a Tibetan beggar woman.

[*See also* Pundit Mapmakers; Timbuctoo; *and biographical entries on figures mentioned in this article.*]

DAVID BUISSERET

Eyre, Edward (1815–1901), British-born Australian pastoralist, explorer, and colonial administrator. Edward John Eyre was born on August 5, 1815, in Bedfordshire, England, a son of the vicar Anthony William Eyre. Well educated, he arrived in New South Wales in March 1833, where he engaged in pastoral pursuits near today's Canberra. He made three overland trips with sheep and cattle to Port Phillip and Adelaide before settling in Adelaide in 1839 and becoming involved in exploration.

His first expedition, from May to June 1839, took Eyre into the arid country around Lake Torrens and to the River Murray. Two months later, accompanied by John Baxter and two Aboriginals, he followed the coast from Port Lincoln around the Eyre Peninsula to Streaky Bay and north through the Gawler Ranges to Lake Torrens. In June 1840, Eyre led a well-equipped expedition of six Europeans and two Aboriginals north from Adelaide to explore the interior,

but in September, having reached Mount Hopeless and finding his way blocked by salt lakes, Eyre returned to Adelaide to gather support for a trip west from Streaky Bay.

In November, Eyre rejoined the rest of his party at Streaky Bay, and they moved west to establish a depot at Fowlers Bay. On February 25, 1841, having reduced his party to five—himself, John Baxter, and three Aboriginals—Eyre set off to cross the inhospitable Nullarbor Plain "or perish in the attempt." Only Eyre and the Aboriginal named Wylie completed the 800-mile (1,300-kilometer) journey, Baxter having been killed on April 29, probably by the other two Aboriginals, who abandoned the expedition. Eyre and Wylie struggled on through extreme heat and water shortages to reach Albany on July 7. They had achieved an outstanding feat of human endurance but found nothing of economic importance. Despite this, Eyre was awarded the Royal Geographical Society founder's gold medal in 1843. Wylie, his companion, was rewarded with £2, a medal, and food rations for life.

Eyre retired from exploration and became resident magistrate and protector of Aborigines at Moorundie on the River Murray. In December 1844 he traveled to England on leave and the following year published his *Journals of Expeditions of Discovery into Central Australia and Overland from Adelaide to King George's Sound in the Years 1840–1*. From 1846, Eyre served as a colonial administrator in New Zealand and Jamaica. In 1865 he was relieved of the governorship of Jamaica following the death of more than 600 people during a period of martial law. Eyre died at Tavistock in Devon on November 30, 1901.

[*See also* Australia, Exploration of.]

BIBLIOGRAPHY
Dutton, Geoffrey. In *Search of Edward John Eyre*. Melbourne, Australia, and New York: Macmillan, 1982.
Favenc, Ernest. *The History of Australian Exploration from 1788 to 1888*. Sydney: Turner and Henderson, 1888. Reprint. Amsterdam: Meridian, 1967.
McLaren, Glen. *Beyond Leichhardt: Bushcraft and the Exploration of Australia*. Fremantle, Australia: Fremantle Arts Centre Press, 1997.
Millar, Ann. "I See No End to Travelling": *Journals of Australian Explorers, 1813–76*. Sydney: Bay Books, 1986.

DENIS SHEPHARD

F

Fawcett, Percy (1867–1925?), English military officer who explored the Mato Grosso. In 1906, the Royal Geographic Society (RGS) nominated Major Percy H. Fawcett, Royal Artillery, as technical advisor to the Bolivian government for the delineation of Bolivia's new boundary with Brazil. Fawcett's qualifications for the post were outstanding. He had recently returned from his second tour of duty in Ceylon, and he had also been entrusted with a secret intelligence mission in Morocco. He was equipped with endurance, a robust immune system, and the survival skills needed for humid, tropical environments—all this was to prove essential. Physically impressive, Fawcett was exceptionally athletic, as well as artistic, inventive, and numerate. He was the star graduate from the Royal Geographic Society's new course in boundary surveying.

Between 1906 and the outbreak of World War I, Fawcett made six major expeditions into the rivers that marked the boundaries of Bolivia, Brazil, and Peru. This surveying work, in the most difficult terrain and conditions, made a tangible contribution to the geographic knowledge of the region. His work was acknowledged by the RGS with its Founder's Medal. Rejoining his regiment for the 1914 war, he was awarded the Distinguished Service Order, mentioned in dispatches four times, and promoted to lieutenant colonel.

However, Fawcett's name became better known for his later freelance archaeological expeditions into the Mato Grosso region of Brazil. Mysteries surrounding his quest for lost cities in the "Green Hell," his disappearance and presumed death in 1925, subsequent rumors of sightings, and the efforts to find him, all captured the imagination of the public. The fate of Fawcett became shrouded in legend.

[*See also* Amazon River *and* Central and South America, *subentry on* Scientific Inquiry.]

BIBLIOGRAPHY
Fawcett, Percy Harrison. *Lost Trails, Lost Cities*. New York: Funk and Wagnalls, 1953.

Ure, John. *Trespassers on the Amazon*. London: Constable, 1986. See chapter 7.

MICHAEL LAYLAND

Federmann, Nikolaus (c. 1505–1542), German explorer of Venezuela. Nikolaus Federmann, the most successful of the German conquistadores in the New World, was probably born in Ulm about 1505, when his father Claus became a resident and member of that city's merchant guild. Nikolaus came to the New World in 1529 as a business agent for the Welser commercial house at Augsburg, to which Charles V, the Holy Roman emperor, had granted the concession to discover, conquer, and populate Venezuela.

It was in the business of Venezuela that Federmann distinguished himself. By June 1530 he had been left in charge of the colony at Coro, as the sick governor Ambrosius Dalfinger departed for Santo Domingo. But when Federmann explored the Venezuelan Llanos without permission, Dalfinger banished him for four years. Back in Augsburg by August 1532, Federmann wrote about his experiences to impress his patrons. His brother-in-law Hans Kiefhaber published this *Indianischen historia* in 1557. In it Federmann described the richness of the regions that he explored and gave raw but experienced advice on how to manage Indians. He and Welser agents signed a contract for his return.

Back in Coro by 1535, Federmann and Jorge Espira (Georg Hohermuth) organized a two-pronged expedition. Espira headed south on his three-year trek across the Venezuelan and Colombian Llanos, while Federmann moved west, explored the Guajira Peninsula, and founded Riohacha, but then saw his route up the Magdalena River blocked by superior Spanish forces at Santa Marta. Retracing his steps, he eventually headed across the Llanos and passed a returning Espira without ever making contact. Always keeping the Andes to the west in sight, he climbed them when the reports of gold increased. There, on the Sabana de Bogotá, he encountered the rival force of Gonzalo Jiménez de Quesada, which had arrived two years earlier. Nevertheless, a settlement was reached, and together they officially founded Bogotá, on April 27, 1539. Federmann was to receive the *encomienda* of Tinjacá and seven shares of any future booty taken by the Jiménez group. Sebastián de Benalcázar's expedition also arrived. Rather than fight, the three conquistadores decided to travel together to Spain to let Spanish courts resolve their differences. Most of Federmann's men stayed in highland Colombia, which they helped settle and conquer.

The Welsers had Federmann arrested in Flanders in 1540 for illicit enrichment, and he in turn accused them of defrauding the Spanish treasury. The Council of the Indies moved Federmann to Valladolid, where his testimony against the Welsers effectively ended their business in Venezuela. Federmann died in Valladolid on February 21/22, 1542.

[*See also* Central and South America, *subentry on* Conquests and Colonization; Expeditions, World Exploration, *subentry on* German States; *and* Quesada, Gonzalo Jiménez de.]

BIBLIOGRAPHY

Friede, Juan. *Los Welser en la conquista de Venezuela*. Caracas: Ediciones Edime, 1961.
Federmann, Nikolaus. *Historia indiana*. Translated by Juan Friede. Madrid: ARO, Artes Gráficas, 1958. Spanish translation of *Indianischen historia*, first published in 1557.

MAURICE P. BRUNGARDT

Fernandes, Vasco (c. 1475–1541), Portuguese artist of the early sixteenth century, sometimes called O Grão Vasco (Vasco the Great) and best known for the first depiction of a Brazilian. Little is known of Vasco Fernandes's early life. The artist first appears in Viseu in northern Portugal from 1501, where he collaborated in the painting of the panels of the high altar of the cathedral as one of a team led by Francisco Henriques. Some of Fernandes's designs—such as the panels for the high altar of Lamego Cathedral, produced between and 1506 and 1509—were inspired by German and Italian engravings. In Portugal he is perhaps best known for a monumental *Saint Peter Enthroned* (c. 1535; Museo de Grão Vasco, Viseu). It is, however, the dark-skinned king, Balthasar, conventionally depicted as an African in Iberian tradition but depicted by Fernandes as a Brazilian Indian in the *Adoration of the Magi*, that is of greatest interest to historians. The panel is one of the sixteen extant panels from the altarpiece of the chancel of Viseu Cathedral that are now housed at the Museo de Grão Vasco in Viseu. It

is the first known depiction of a native of Brazil, a reference to the discovery of Brazil by the Portuguese in 1500, though it was probably painted not from real life but from hearsay. Scholars argue as to which tribe the Brazilian Indian represents, but he can be assumed to be Tupinamba. Alongside indigenous elements such as a feather crown and a Brazilian vaned arrow, the subject sports a European tunic and a pair of breeches so as to cover his nudity. It is not clear what gift the Brazilian is bearing the baby Jesus.

BIBLIOGRAPHY

Reis-Santos, Luis. *Vasco Fernandes e os pintores de Viseu do século XVI*. Lisbon, Portugal: self-published, 1946.
Smith, Robert C. *The Art of Portugal, 1500–1800*. London: Weidenfeld and Nicolson, 1968.
Teixeira, José. Item no. 32. In *Circa 1492: Art in the Age of Exploration*, edited by Jay A. Levinson, 152–153. Washington, D.C.: National Gallery, 1991.

STEFAN HALIKOWSKI SMITH

Fernández de Oviedo, Gonzalo (1478–1557), Spanish chronicler. Fernández de Oviedo, the first Spanish Royal Chronicler of the Indies living in America, began his lifelong service to the monarchs of Spain in early childhood. Born in 1478 to Miguel de Sobrepeña and Juana de Oviedo in Madrid, Gonzalo first entered into the service of the royal households of King Alfonso de Aragón as a child. Later, as part of the Catholic king's staff, he witnessed the surrender of Granada by the Moors and Columbus's triumphal return from America.

Oviedo held a variety of administrative posts in Spain until his appointment in 1513 as inspector (*veedor*) of the gold mines and juridical notary for the crown in Tierra Firme (present-day Panama). In 1514, he set sail with the new governor, Pedrarias Dávila, for Castilla de Oro, where he began writing about exotic American flora, fauna, indigenous customs, and artifacts. In 1526 Oviedo published one of the first books about America, *Sumario de la natural historia de las Indias*.

In 1532 Oviedo won appointment as Royal Chronicler of the Indies and moved to the crossroads of the Spanish shipping enterprise in America, the city of Santo Domingo on the island of Hispaniola. There he wrote his masterpiece, the massive *Historia general y natural de las Indias* (*General and Natural History of the Indies*), which maps the exploration, conquest, and colonization of the Caribbean, Mexico, and Central and South America. The first installment was published in 1535 (Seville). The next two parts were finished by about 1548, but Oviedo's long-time adversary Bartolomé de Las Casas contributed to blocking their publication. He accused Oviedo of being detrimental to the welfare of native Americans because the chronicler portrayed some tribes as cannibals and advocated a system of enforced Indian labor (*repartimiento*). From 1549 until his death in 1557 Oviedo remained in Santo Domingo in an administrative post, as keeper (*alcalde*) of the city's fort.

Oviedo's *History* was one of only two comprehensive histories of America written during the first half of the sixteenth century. (The other was written by Las Casas.) The *History* is significant in at least three ways. First, Oviedo used many firsthand accounts, some of which are now lost. Second, his writing anticipated the development of the natural sciences and ethnography. Third, Oviedo displayed an early modern self-awareness about his role as the first on-site historian of the Indies. Although Oviedo's three-part *History* was not published in its entirety until the mid-nineteenth century, the first part became a foundational text for subsequent authors writing about America, including the Spanish Jesuit José de Acosta and the Peruvian explorer Alexander von Humboldt. Oviedo is often considered America's first European author.

[*See also* Acosta, José de; Caribbean Region, Exploration of; Humboldt, Alexander von; *and* Las Casas, Bartolomé de.]

BIBLIOGRAPHY

Fernández de Oviedo y Valdés, Gonzalo. *Oviedo de la natural historia de las Indias*. Toledo, Spain, 1526. Also known as the *Sumario de la natural historia de las Indias*.

Fernández de Oviedo y Valdés, Gonzalo. *Historia general y natural de las Indias*. Edited by Amador de los Ríos. Vols. 1–4. Madrid: Real Academia de la Historia. 1851–1855.

Gerbi, Antonello. *Nature in the New World: From Christopher Columbus to Gonzalo Fernández de Oviedo*. Translated by Jeremy Moyle. Pittsburgh, Penn.: University of Pittsburgh Press, 1985.

Myers, Kathleen Ann. *New World, New History: Fernández de Oviedo's America*. Forthcoming.

Turner, Daymond. *Gonzalo Fernández de Oviedo y Valdés: An Annotated Bibliography*. Chapel Hill: University of North Carolina Press, 1966.

KATHLEEN ANN MYERS

Fernández, Juan (c. 1529–1599), Spanish navigator who discovered the archipelago that bears his name. Born in Spain, Fernández followed the progress of Spanish colonization southward from Peru. He reached Chile about 1550 and for forty years served in ships providing the vital logistical links with the Peruvian port of Callao. Consequently, he became acutely aware of the impediments to communication with Chile posed by the prevailing southerly winds and persistent coastal current. Listening to pilots who sailed from Panama to Peru, he probably learned how they mitigated similar conditions between the Peruvian ports of Paita and Callao by sailing a longer but quicker course out to sea rather than close inshore. This was a practice he adopted during a voyage from Callao to Chile in 1574. As a result, on November 6 he sighted and named the islands of San Félix and San Ambrosio, and then on November 22 the archipelago of three islands that would bear his name. He reached Valparaíso on the Chilean mainland after a voyage of only thirty days rather than the customary three months.

Although the claim is widely discredited, some still argue that during a voyage much farther westward from the southern Chilean coast in 1576, Fernández may have discovered Easter Island or even New Zealand or Australia. He crowned his maritime career with his appointment as chief pilot of the South Sea in 1589, retiring in 1592 to settle on an estate awarded for services to the crown, namely for "the discovery of the new route from Peru" rather than for the Juan Fernández Islands.

[*See also* Pacific, *subentry on* Literary Representations.]

BIBLIOGRAPHY

Woodward, Ralph L. *Robinson Crusoe's Island: A History of the Juan Fernández Islands*. Chapel Hill: University of North Carolina Press, 1969.

PETER T. BRADLEY

Fictions of Exploration

This entry contains two subentries:

Ancient
Medieval

Ancient

Odysseus in Books 9 through 12 of the *Odyssey* told the first traveler's tales recorded in Western literature, and the problem of the veracity of these tales was already at issue. King Alcinous of the Phaeacians interrupts the long travelogue as it reaches its climax and reassures himself that the narrator he is listening to is no liar: "Odysseus, we who behold you would not deem you a deceiver or a cheat . . . like the many who weave lies about realms no one can see" (11.363–366). If we substitute the translation "fiction" for "lies"—for indeed the Greek word *pseudea* later takes on a meaning very close to English "fiction"—we would have, already present at the birth of this genre, the rudiments of a literary critique that would accompany its development for more than two millennia. Traveler's tales, as Alcinous here points out, tell of places beyond the reach of the process of verification that an audience normally performs upon a narrative; they derive from "realms no one [except the narrator] can see." Hence they can accommodate material that would be highly suspect (to an ancient reader at least) in a different kind of tale, in particular what the Greeks called *to muthodes* or *to thaumatodes*, the element of the marvelous, monstrous, or bizarre.

The Geography of the *Odyssey*. The "Alcinoan tales" of the *Odyssey* are in fact replete with this sort of material, and hence came to emblematize for the Greeks and Romans a particularly problematic kind of fictional literature. Already in Plato's time the phrase "Alcinoan tale" (*Alkinou apologos*) is used in a pejorative sense to signify a story that is untrue or lacking in substance. Scholars shortly thereafter began a long debate, still continuing in our own day, as to whether the wanderings of Odysseus could be located on a map and, if so, where. Surprisingly, most were unwilling to accept the idea that Homer had invented more than a small portion of the contents of these four books.

The coordinates of travel Odysseus himself supplies are maddeningly difficult to make sense of. As he relates in Odyssey Book 9, he begins his voyage from Troy and comes first to the Cicones, a historical tribe dwelling on the Thracian coast. Then, as he rounds Cape Malea in the Peloponnese on his way to Ithaca, a south-blowing wind carries him past the island of Cythera until he reaches the land of the Lotus-eaters in nine days (9.80–84). Any reasonable inference would place him now in North Africa, which was indeed where Herodotus situated the Lotus-eaters (*Histories* 4.177), even though "nine days" of sail would ordinarily carry a ship much farther than this. Thereafter Odysseus arrives, by an unspecified route, at the island of the Cyclops, traditionally identified with Sicily (see Thucydides 6.2) because Mount Etna was thought to contain the fire in which the Cyclopes forged Zeus's thunderbolts.

In Book 10 Odysseus reaches Aeolia, the island of Aeolus, again by an unspecified route, and from there is driven by a west wind for nine days until he glimpses his home island on the horizon. But his shipmates release the other winds from the bag into which Aeolus had sewn them, and the ship is blown back to Aeolia. A voyage of six days and nights in an unspecified direction then takes Odysseus to the land of the Laestrygonians, which may perhaps be in the Far North, a place where "the paths of day and night are near one another" (10.86; probably a cryptic description of the short summer nights at high latitudes). Then another leg of travel, in no stated direction, takes the ship to Circe's island, Aeaea, said to stand "near the dancing-floors of Dawn and the risings of the Sun" (12.3–4), that is, in the Far East. [See color plate 33 in this volume.] Circe directs Odysseus to sail by the North Wind from there and to cross "through" Ocean's stream until he comes to the land of the dead, located next to the Cimmerians, a people shrouded in endless night (again perhaps a cryptic reference to the Far North). Given that the Greeks traditionally located the realm of the dead in the Far West, there is clearly very little sense that can be made out of the geography of this stretch of narrative. The various landmarks and landfalls in the remainder of the voyage—the Sirens, Scylla and Charybdis, Thrinacia, Ogygia—bear few locational cues, except for the curious phrase designating Ogygia as "the navel [i.e., exact midpoint?] of the sea."

Modern scholarship has generally embraced the notion that Odysseus's wanderings take place in an unmappable fairyland. But only one ancient critic was willing to take this position, and he was thereafter roundly assailed by a great number of opponents. Eratosthenes of Cyrene, a witty man of letters who headed the famous library at Alexandria in the third century B.C.E., famously quipped that he would trace the route of Odysseus on a map if someone could produce the cobbler who sewed Aeolus's bag of winds. Homer, claimed Eratosthenes, had written only for the entertainment and pleasure of his listeners—so why look for factual content in his verse? But the temper of Hellenistic criticism was very much opposed to this "pleasure principle" in ancient poetry. Stoic philosophy ruled in the halls of academia, and the learned men of the Hellenistic world demanded useful knowledge from their authors; Homer, as the greatest author of all, was assumed to have the greatest lessons to impart. Eratosthenes' position was attacked by Crates of Mallos, Aristarchus, Strabo, and others as a trivialization of the grandmaster of Greek literature, and a geographic reading of the *Odyssey* was devised to counter it—a reading in which all the landfalls mentioned in

Books 9 through 12 could be plotted on a map of the western Mediterranean, in particular the region around Sicily and southern Italy.

Among this cadre of Hellenistic geographer-critics was Apollonius of Rhodes, head of the library in Alexandria just before Eratosthenes. In his poem *Argonautica* Apollonius constructed a narrative made up of fabulous wanderings, similar in spirit to (and often directly modeled on) those of the *Odyssey*. But Apollonius carefully plotted his ship's route on a very recognizable (if occasionally distorted) map of the *oikoumenē*, avoiding all vague or mythic locales. Thus, though the events of the voyage are often every bit as fabulous as those found in Homer, Apollonius appears to insist on situating them in a real, nonfictional, landscape.

Marvel Literature and Menippean Satire. The Stoic emphasis on the utility of literary narrative, meaning mappability in the case of the traveler's tale, was a high-minded ethic designed for the educated elite. Readers with lower aspirations, however, became increasingly interested, during the Hellenistic era and under the Roman Empire, in fabulous voyages, some even reaching beyond the *oikoumenē* or beyond the earth itself. In the fourth century B.C.E. an author about whom very little is known, Antiphanes of Berga, composed such fabulous tales that a verb, "bergaize," was coined to mean "make up nonsense." Around the same time Menippus of Gadara, a Syrian writer belonging to the Cynic philosophic school, experimented with literary journeys and flights of fantasy, as seen in the works of a later imitator, the satirist Lucian of the second century C.E. Other forms of popular literature, like the romance novel and the paradoxographic catalogue, catered to a readership that enjoyed the allure of the marvelous for its own sake, apart from any practical lessons that might be learned.

Lucian left behind a vast corpus of satirical writings of various kinds—speeches, dialogues, essays, short stories. His works are in prose and with snatches of verse only rarely blended in, so one can argue as to whether they should be called "Menippean" (some scholars use the term only to refer to prosimetric satires). Nonetheless, Lucian often uses Menippus himself as a mouthpiece and seems to have imitated many techniques of his fellow Syrian, including a fondness for visiting improbable locales: the homes of the gods on Olympus, the kingdom of the dead in Hades, and various fantasy worlds beyond the horizon. Lucian's most famous work of fiction, the *True Histories*, describes a voyage that be-

gins as a crossing of the Atlantic but ultimately takes its narrator to the sun and moon, among other fabulous ports of call. The lunar inhabitants are described in comic and grotesque fashion—they have cabbage-like protrusions growing from their buttocks, they sweat milk, they remove their eyes for storage as we do contact lenses—but they take on heroic dimensions when they fight a battle against those living on the sun (described by Lucian in deadpan Thucydidean style). In the dialogue *Icaromenippus* Lucian again visits the lunar surface, this time only as a way-station for his hero Menippus en route to the abode of the celestial gods. Such *jeux d'esprits* deliberately undermined the critical ethos that demanded geographic veracity from travel narratives; the ironic title of the *True Histories*, and the prologue to that work wherein Lucian claims the wanderings of Odysseus as his prototype, form an implicit rejoinder to the Stoics who had insisted on mapping the *Odyssey*.

Two of Lucian's close contemporaries were also interested in voyaging to the moon, though for very different reasons. Plutarch, the great biographer and moralist, composed a dialogue *On the Face in the Moon* as a way of investigating various questions both astronomical and theological, for in his view the moon was the home of the *daimones* or demigods that constantly shuttle back and forth between earth and sky. At the end of this elaborate dialogue his main character, Sulla, relates a tale he heard from a Carthaginian stranger, concerning a voyage of five thousand *stades*—some 600 miles (966 kilometers)—into the Atlantic, to an island where the god Cronus lies locked in eternal sleep, attended by spirits who are able to report the content of his dreams. The selenology that Sulla goes on to explicate is derived from these dreams—a direct revelation from the divine mind, in other words, of the moon's place in the cosmic order. The novelist Antonius Diogenes also made the moon a port of call in his lost *Wonders Beyond Thule*, a work known only through the summary compiled by a Byzantine reader. To judge by what is preserved in this summary, *Wonders Beyond Thule* contained an ingeniously interwoven set of interlocked narratives, describing the travels to various distant locales of a group of characters who eventually end up on the semimythical island of Thule in the North Atlantic. Many of their adventures are set in the Far North, where they found the moon to be close enough to the earth that they could inspect it at close range. Unfortunately, the summarizer, dismayed at the implausibility of this lunar episode, declines to record its contents.

The marvels and freaks of nature that enlivened Antonius Diogenes' novel could also be found, though in lesser quantity, in the ideal Greek novels or romances, as well as in the curious catalogs of *paradoxa* that circulated in both the late Greek and Roman worlds. In these one finds lists of all the natural anomalies known to humankind from various corners of the earth: springs that run hot in the morning but cold in the evening, stones with occult properties, weather patterns unique to very small regions of the globe. The title found on several such lists, *Apista* or "Incredible things," neatly inverts the irony contained in the title *True Histories*: the audience is clearly meant to accept the reality of such singularities even though they strain credulity. The paradoxographers adopted a pose of scientific objectivity in retailing their wonders, but the effect they sought was essentially the same as that of fictionalizers like Lucian.

The Greek Romances. For the Greeks of the imperial worlds, who had seen the Romans lay open the European world to their west and north, two regions of the earth remained unknown and unexplored: the upper reaches and source of the Nile, in the Far South, and in the East, the portions of the realm they called India, which stretched beyond the Hyphasis River. At the Hyphasis, Alexander the Great, in 325 B.C.E., had been forced by his reluctant army to stop and turn westward; hence no Greek eyes had peered into the territory beyond, and no Greek thinkers had any clear conception of how far one could travel in this direction before coming to the end of Asia. As for the Nile, its mysteries had defied the inquiries of scientists since before the time of Herodotus (*Histories* 2.19 ff.); in Roman times the emperor Nero seems to have sent explorers to seek out the river's source but never heard from them again. The Nile's anomalous floods, which occurred in summer (normally the dry season in the Mediterranean) rather than winter, raised urgent questions about where the river originated, but it was left to fiction rather than science—in particular, a new breed of fiction arising in the imperial age, the romantic novel—to answer these questions.

Heliodorus's *Ethiopica*, a complex and lengthy novel written probably in the fifth century C.E., deals at length with the mystery of the source of the Nile, which it situates in the mythicized realm of Ethiopia south of Egypt. The religious purity of Ethiopia, in this depiction, is closely related to the holiness of the Nile itself, a river that the Egyptians consider a god and worship in a yearly festival called the Neiloa. After witnessing this rite, the Ethiopian king, Hydaspes, proclaims that Ethiopia itself should receive similar worship since, as it contains the source of the Nile, it serves as the "mother" of all Egyptian deities (9.22). Another character, the Egyptian Calasiris, at one point reveals to a Greek he has met the cause of the Nile's annual floods, claiming that such knowledge is normally restricted to members of Egypt's priestly caste. Though the explanation itself seems unexceptional—it relies on an annual pattern of winds that brings rain clouds into southern latitudes—the reverent tones in which it is imparted suggest initiation into a sacred mystery (2.28–29).

Heliodorus also explores in his novel the realm of Ethiopia, a semi-legendary place associated since Homer's time with holiness, moral virtue, and contentment. In this case the Ethiopian realm is portrayed as an idealized version of the Persian Empire, exercising a very mild dominion over its subjects—a group that includes fantastic races, such as the headless Blemmyes and the cave-dwelling Troglodytes—and organizing them into voluntary coalitions when it goes to war. Hydaspes rules as both king and head priest, and is advised by a college of Gymnosophists or Naked Wise Men, monklike figures borrowed from Indian lore. Like Sarastro's kingdom in Mozart's *The Magic Flute*, Ethiopia here embodies the perfect fusion of piety, wisdom, and political sovereignty, the land in which Plato's imagined philosopher-king has at last attained power.

Ethiopia's religious dimensions are again explored in a fictionalized biography of the second century C.E., the *Life of Apollonius of Tyana* by Philostratus. This novel, if we can call it that, follows the travels of an itinerant Greek sage, Apollonius, as he explores the different philosophies and religious sects of the world, starting with the Sages (*Sophoi*) of India. These Sages are later compared with the Naked Men (*Gymnoi*) of Ethiopia, a sect that is said to have split off from the Sages in early times to follow its own way of life, when Apollonius is forced to choose which group he will associate with (Book 6). The Naked Men espouse an ascetic code that finds holiness in self-abnegation, as opposed to the Sages who enjoy such pleasures as food and wine and allow themselves to wear clothing and ornament. Apollonius ultimately chooses the Indian path, but Philostratus allows the Ethiopians to have their say in a set of vehement speeches defending asceticism.

By pitting *Gymnoi* against *Sophoi*, Philostratus split into two parts the sect most Greek writers knew as *Gymnosophistai*, located in the semi-legendary eastern land they called India. These Naked Wise Men, modeled on the holy men Alexander had actually encountered near his headquarters in Taxila, appear in fictionalized accounts like the *Alexander Romance* of Pseudo-Callisthenes as well as in the historical narratives of Arrian and Plutarch, usually as harsh critics of Alexander in particular and of Hellenic values more generally. Their leader Dandamis (also known as Dindimus, Didymus, and Mandanis) became a popular mouthpiece for antimaterialist polemics from Greek antiquity right through the Middle Ages. He and his sect are located variously in the forests of the Indus Valley, on the far side of the Ganges, or on isolated islands in either of these two rivers.

Alexander's experience in India supplied fodder for numerous other legends and fictional experiments, most of which found a home in one version or another of the *Alexander Romance*. In many such tales Alexander becomes a kind of heroic explorer, penetrating into the unknown in pursuit of scientific knowledge, often crossing the Hyphasis (as he failed to do in 325 B.C.E.) or even the Ganges in his quest for truth. One prominent example has Alexander imitating Lucian's Menippus and soaring up into the sky on borrowed wings—in this case by hitching a flock of hungry birds to his chariot and then holding food out in front of them on a spear. In other cases he voyages to the bottom of the sea in a primitive bathyscaphe, or hunts for the eastern edge of the world in a night-shrouded Land of Darkness. Alexander's imperial project, which in reality combined the goals of conquest and exploration, has here been reimagined solely as a journey of exploration, a penetration of the darkest mysteries of nature.

[*See also* Alexander the Great; Eratosthenes; *and* Oikoumenē *and* Orbis Terrarum.]

BIBLIOGRAPHY

Anderson, Graham. *Studies in Lucian's Comic Fiction*. Leiden: Brill, 1976.

Austin, Norman. *Archery at the Dark of the Moon: Poetic Problems in Homer's* Odyssey. Berkeley: University of California Press, 1975.

Hägg, Tomas. *The Novel in Antiquity*. Berkeley: University of California Press, 1983.

Reardon, B. P. *Collected Ancient Greek Novels*. Berkeley: University of California Press, 1989.

Rohde, Erwin. *Der griechische Roman und seine Vorläufer*. Leipzig: Breitkopf und Härtel, 1876. 4th ed., Hildesheim: George Olms, 1960.

Romm, James S. *The Edges of the Earth in Ancient Thought: Geography, Exploration, and Fiction*. Princeton, N.J.: Princeton University Press, 1992. See chap. 5.

JAMES ROMM

Medieval

The distinction between fact and fiction in medieval literature was a wavering line, nowhere more so than in travel narratives. Nearly all "fictional" travel tales were based on actual historical characters, and the most reliable travel writers, that is, those who actually traveled, imported fantastic places and creatures into their work, taking them from sources that they believed to be reliable. Thus the location of Paradise or the entrance to Hell, the existence of the monstrous races, and the whereabouts of incredible natural phenomena adorn even the most sober accounts. While the journey theme appears frequently in medieval literature, in this entry we will consider only those works that tell of travel to imaginary places beyond Europe.

Alexander the Great (d. 323 B.C.E.) loomed large in medieval travel literature, but his character was transformed from that of a ruthless conqueror to the model of a chivalrous Christian knight. His genuine travels, from the oracle of Siwa in the Libyan desert to the Indus River, were dramatic enough, but they were almost immediately supplemented with fictional episodes. The Greek *Alexander Romance*, composed approximately a century after his death, depicts the hero diving beneath the sea in a sort of diving bell, marching into the Land of Darkness, and flying through the air pulled by griffins, in an attempt to reach the end of the world, "where the earth meets the sky." He encountered and interviewed members of the monstrous races along the way, and in the Far East he consulted the oracle trees of the sun and the moon, which foretold his betrayal and early death. The story was enriched with letters, allegedly from Alexander to his mother, which turned his adventures into a first-person saga. This tale was translated into Latin in the fourth century C.E., and during the Middle Ages versions in all the vernacular languages circulated throughout the Christian and Islamic worlds. Another letter purportedly written by Alexander to his tutor Aristotle gave vivid descriptions of monstrous beasts and humans. Copied as a separate document and known as "The Marvels of the East," it was furnished with colorful illustrations and became, like the rest of Alexander's travels, an important source for medieval mapmakers.

Saint Brendan was also a real person, an Irish monk who lived from around 486 to 575. He founded several monasteries in Ireland, but what most captivated posterity was his sea journey to the west. Irish monks occasionally undertook these watery pilgrimages, often without a certain destination, or even without oars, as a form of devotion. Saint Brendan's voyage in his search for the earthly paradise led him, as we learn from the text of the *Navigatio*, which dates from the eighth century, to a series of magical islands in the Atlantic Ocean. On the way he encountered Hell in the form of volcanoes spewing fire and brimstone, and he met Judas, sitting on a rock in the ocean with the tides coming up to his neck. When Brendan pitied him, Judas reported that this was his respite on the Sabbath day—during the rest of the week he was tormented by devils in the pits of Hell. On another island Brendan and his comrades had halted and started a cooking fire when the island heaved itself up and they realized to their horror that they were on the back of Jasconius, a giant whale. Brendan eventually did reach the earthly paradise, surrounded by heavy fog in mid-ocean, but was not allowed to stay there. The desire to rediscover this land continued well into the early modern period, inspiring such explorers as Columbus and Sir Walter Ralegh. Brendan's adventures follow the Christian monastic calendar of festivals, as he went the rounds of his islands. Attempts have been made to locate his stopping places, such as Iceland for the volcanic island, and he has even been proposed as the earliest discoverer of America, but it appears more likely that his was instead a delightful and piously instructive travel tale. It survives in over 120 manuscripts and is closely linked to a body of work known as the Irish "immrama," or religiously inspired tales of sea journeys, which include the *Voyage of Máeldúin* and *The Voyage of the Uí Chorra*.

Prester John. Prester John, the virtuous Christian priest-king, may or may not have existed, but a letter claiming to be from him appeared in the Byzantine and European courts in the twelfth century. It described a utopian land, fabulously wealthy and well-governed, set in some remote part of either Asia or Africa and surrounded by monstrous nations. Seventy kings paid tribute to Prester John, and through his kingdom flowed one of the rivers of Paradise, laden with precious stones. No poisonous snake or scorpion could exist there, nor any of the human vices, such as flattery or unchastity. His palace was built entirely of aromatic woods, gold, and gems, which exercised their virtues upon the inhabitants. For example, the pavement of the jousting ring was of onyx, which increased the courage of the combatants. The French king immediately dispatched an envoy to find this wonderful king, and it was hoped in the West that he might assist the Crusaders in their struggle against the Muslims. Whether the French envoy ever returned, we do not know, but at the end of the fifteenth century João II, the wise king of Portugal, sent out two ambassadors, one of whom reached the Coptic Christian kingdom in Ethiopia. Almost every traveler, fictional or real, who wrote a book after the first appearance of the letter, felt compelled to seek out Prester John and to report on his kingdom. Marco Polo described him as a petty Central Asian princeling, but John Mandeville gave a lengthy and enthusiastic account of his wealth and piety.

The tale of Herzog (Duke) Ernst may have originated in a story of betrayal and loyalty of a vassal at the court of the Emperor Otto I in the tenth century. The oldest written version dates from two centuries later and has obviously incorporated newer characters and material, including the Crusades. The first part of the tale concerns Duke Ernst's travails in Germany, where an evil rumormonger got him into trouble with the emperor, who was also his stepfather. Forced into exile, Duke Ernst set out for the Holy Land, but a storm at sea, which lasted for three months, drove him completely out of the Mediterranean and into the fabled lands of the traditional East. He and his companions first came ashore in Grippia, a country inhabited by people who had the heads and necks of cranes. When the travelers disembarked, the city appeared deserted, but soon the inhabitants returned, bearing an unhappy captive princess who was to marry the crane-king. The noble Ernst and his knights attempted to rescue the lady, but the cranes stabbed her to death with their beaks. They then fought a ferocious battle with the cranes, who were formidable archers, and were lucky to escape by sea. Their adventures included being marooned on a magnetic mountain, which drew all ships to it by means of the iron nails used in their construction. They found an entire fleet of ghost ships beached here, laden with treasures. After most of the crew died of starvation or were carried off by griffins, the remaining six men stitched themselves into ox-hides. Borne aloft by the griffins to their nests to feed their young, the intrepid adventurers were protected by the hides and managed to get away when the parent birds left the nest. Next they traveled along a river that went underground for part of its course, until they arrived at the kingdom of the Arimaspi, a kindly race of one-eyed people. While there, they met other representatives of the monstrous races, and Ernst assembled a kind of menagerie that he took back to Europe on his return. He went home via Ethiopia, and—at last—Jerusalem, and was reinstated at the imperial court. Throughout his adventures Duke Ernst was accompanied by his faithful companion, Count Wetzel, who played Oliver to his Roland. This part of the tale emphasizes the feudal virtues of courage and loyalty, while another aspect of the journey is the amassing of treasure, either as gifts from friendly hosts or as part of the marvels of distant lands, where rare and expensive spices could be had for the gathering and gems lay around on the ground. The wealth to be garnered in the Orient by the intrepid traveler was also a dominant theme in the story of Sindbad the Sailor, who made and lost a number of fortunes in the course of his voyages.

Classical Origins. Many of the themes that appear in medieval travel fiction hark back to classical times. Although the *Odyssey* was no longer read in the West, some of its stories, such as that of the Cyclopes' cave, seem to have survived in the oral tradition or were reintroduced from Arabic sources. The monstrous races had been described, first by Greek geographers, and then by the Roman writers, Pliny and Solinus. Their stories were passed on to medieval readers in widely circulated works, such as those of Isidore of Seville (*Origins* or *Etymologies*, seventh century) and Honorius Augustodunensis (*Imago Mundi*, twelfth century). Human beings with bizarre customs and/or abnormal physical characteristics were displaced to the edges of the earth, which explained why they were not often seen at home. Animals, either imaginary like the griffin and the phoenix, or merely exotic, like the elephant and the rhinoceros, were similarly sited. The wonders of India, a geographical term that included both Asia and southern Africa, were a favorite theme of medieval geographers, and easily found their place in travel narratives. With the weight of authority behind them, it is not surprising that Cyclopes, centaurs, sirens, and sciopods, who used their single foot as a sunshade, became an integral part of travelers' lore. Christian values overlaid some of these tales, though rather lightly, paying brief tribute to the traveler's piety or chivalry. Thus we may distinguish travel fiction, the principal purpose of which is to entertain, from the "quest" literature of the later Middle Ages, which had an ostensible spiritual purpose.

The survival of the classical sources, as well as the proclivity of medieval authors to copy one another, helps explain the consistency of the geographical, anthropological, and zoological phenomena encountered by the fictional traveler. The Congealed or Dark Sea, in which travelers could become hopelessly becalmed, was one such space, as was the Magnetic Mountain, which eventually gave its name to an island off the eastern coast of Australia. Gog and Magog, the terrifying giants immured somewhere in northern Asia, traced their descent ultimately to the Bible, though the story of their confinement was attributed to Alexander. The voyage to the Underworld, the ultimate adventure, dated back to the *Epic of Gilgamesh* and the *Odyssey*, but had to be Christianized in medieval tales. One could seek the earthly paradise, but only a saint like Brendan could actually land there, and even he was not allowed to stay. The same was true of the standard cast of characters from cannibals to sciopods and of the monstrous animals. Marco Polo in the late thirteenth century attempted to debunk some of this traditional lore, based on his own experience in the Far East. The graceful and magical unicorn, he reported, was nothing more than the ungainly rhinoceros, while the kingdom of the fabled Prester John was simply a small province in central Asia. However, he could not resist the story of diamond mining in a serpent-infested valley in Asia: how the gems were extracted when pieces of raw meat were tossed to the bottom and eagles swooped down to seize the meat, to which the diamonds adhered. This improbable tale was of hoary antiquity, dating back to at least the fourth century, and continued to be circulated, mostly notably in the Arabic story cycle of Sindbad the Sailor. Despite Marco's more skeptical approach to the wonders of the East, he incorporated some stories that he heard there, such as his description of Japan, with its palaces roofed in gold, and of the gender-segregated male and female islands in the Indian Ocean. It is interesting to note that Marco's book was ghostwritten by Rustichello, a writer of chivalric romances, who found some aspects of this tale of travel to be congenial to his talents. And Marco's illustrators sometimes could not resist resorting to the conventional fantastic images of beast and human, in the face of his more restrained text.

A supposedly factual travel account, such as that of John Mandeville, quickly moved to the fantastic as soon as he left the Holy Land for the Far East, though it should be noted that much of his information came from travelers with unimpeachable credentials, such as the Franciscan missionary to Asia, Odoric of Pordenone. The *Itinerarius* of Johannes Witte de Hese (c. 1400), a clergyman from the diocese of Utrecht, also began with his journey in the Holy Land, but once the author had embarked upon the Red Sea and sailed into Ethiopia, he entered the land of travel fantasy, replete with Pygmies, one-eyed men, and the dry waves of the Sandy Sea. He spent most of his pages giving a detailed description of the seven-storied palace of Prester John (precious stones, numerous chapels, reliquaries, a working model of the universe), before going on to a few final adventures, including a passage by the island of Purgatory, where he could hear the cries and groans of the penitent. Witte was a compiler rather than an inventor, as nearly every detail of his work can be found elsewhere. It is a good question as to whether he believed he was writing fiction or solemnly retelling absolute fact.

Travel fiction can be thought of as a subset of romance-writing in the Middle Ages. While based on a sort of reality, frequently using historical characters and the names of real geographical places, it was mostly fantastic, a tale written to amuse or beguile the listener. And among all the marvels, one of the most marvelous was the journey itself, with its immense distances and the obstacles to be overcome. Toward the end of the Middle Ages, travelers' tales were an inspiration for the great explorers, who set off for the greater world thoroughly steeped in these adventures, expecting to find some of the marvels of which they had heard.

[*See also* Alexander the Great, *subentry on* Fiction; Brendan, Saint; Fictitious and Fantastic Places; Isidore of Seville; Pliny the Elder; Polo, Marco; *and* Prester John.]

BIBLIOGRAPHY

Barron, W. R. J. and Glyn S. Burgess, eds. *The Voyage of Saint Brendan*. Exeter, U.K.: University of Exeter Press, 2002.

Larner, John. *Marco Polo and the Discovery of the World*. New Haven, Conn.: Yale University Press, 1999.

Stoneman, Richard. *The Greek Alexander Romance*. New York: Penguin Books, 1991.

Thomas, J. W., and Carolyn Dussère, trans. *The Legend of Duke Ernst*. Lincoln: University of Nebraska Press, 1979.

Westrem, Scott D. *Broader Horizons: A Study of Johannes Witte de Hese's* Itinerarius *and Medieval Travel Narratives*. Cambridge, Mass.: Medieval Academy of America, 2001.

EVELYN EDSON

Fictitious and Fantastic Places

There are different sorts of places which are not there. We can have outright literary fabrication ranging from the fictions of Jonathan Swift (1667–1745), H. Rider Haggard (1856–1925), Edgar Rice Burroughs (1875–1950), and James Hilton (1900–1954), which are acknowledged from the start as fictional creations, to the tall tales of the "buy me a drink and I'll tell you the wonders I've seen" variety. There is simple exaggeration, embellishing an actual trip to make it more significant. There is geographical speculation, often based on geographical myths as much as facts, which tries to make something coherent out of reports of sightings and landfalls. There is incorrect attribution to places that can give us a single island with two or more names as well as a single name applied to more than one place. There were actual places that no longer exist.

What has to be remembered is that exploration was not done altruistically. Most often, the motive was profit. For the church, profit was in souls saved and heathen converted. Expeditions were mounted to find new trade routes eliminating the middleman or to find new lands for trade, conquest, or settlement. The belief in fantastic places motivated a lot of exploration, but only if those places were supposed to contain wealth in some form. And if such places were not found at the first stop, why, maybe just over the next hill or a bit farther upriver would make it all worthwhile.

European geographical information prior to the great age of the exploring expeditions was based on firsthand knowledge of the areas near Europe, the legacy of classical geographical wisdom, and reports back from those who traveled into far regions for reasons of trade or religion. Upon these were built the hopes of those who braved the unknown.

The genesis for the story of the land of Prester John was a letter received in 1165 by the pope, the Byzantine emperor, and the Holy Roman emperor claiming to be from one Presbyter Johannes, ruler of a Christian realm in Asia. With the expanding Islamic dominions in Asia cutting off the old caravan routes, there was a need to believe in a powerful Christian ally who could outflank the Islamic expansion. The defeat of the Arab-led forces in 1141 near Samarkand (in what is today Uzbekistan) by forces that may have included Nestorian Christians possibly contributed to the tale. When facts disproved an Asian location, the realm of Prester John was moved to Africa, particularly the area of Abyssinia (in what is today Ethiopia), since monophysite Christian kingdoms existed there.

Africa has proved an excellent location for mythical and fictional realms. The ruins of actual cities inspired such fictional places as Burroughs's Opar and Haggard's Kor (domain of *She Who Must be Obeyed*) and King Solomon's mines. While real, the location of such places as Punt has not been completely settled.

Saint Brendan (484–577) was an Irish monk who did actually visit the islands near Ireland. After his death, Sinbad-like voyages were added to the account of his travels by others. Stripped of the fantastic elements, some of the descriptions resemble actual islands that might have been visited.

Called "Oranbega" on a map derived from the voyage of Giovanni da Verrazano in 1524, Norumbega evolved from a general area name into a kingdom of great wealth in New England. David Ingram claimed to have visited the land in 1567 and made his living retelling his supposed adventures. Norumbega became a place of silver and gold and pearls sought by several and found by none.

Antilia was a rectangular island appearing on several early maps. Robert Fuson champions the intriguing theory that it represents Taiwan/Formosa. Chinese geographic knowledge came to Europe by way of the Arabs, and Fuson contends that Antilia was put on maps to indicate that Asia was not far away. Antilia became the location of the Seven Golden Cities of Cíbola for a time, cities supposedly founded by Portuguese refugees from the Moors. When it was shown to be not where it was on maps, the name was given collectively to the islands of the Caribbean, the Antilles, and the Seven Golden Cities were moved to North America.

Since two empires, the Aztec and the Inca, existed in the Americas, it seemed valid to assume that there were others. Spanish and other adventurers sought them out based on the flimsiest of rumors. Quivira became associated with the Seven Cities and was assumed to be an area of wealth. When Francisco Vásquez de Coronado (c. 1510–1554) and others found only pueblos and open space, the name "Quivira" was briefly attached to a section of the Spanish North American territory, but ultimately "migrated" over the Rocky Mountains to become a mighty legendary coastal kingdom.

One feature of mythical places is mobility. Original stories of the Fountain of Youth located it in the Bahamas, but it moved to Florida, where it has remained ever elusive. El Dorado both grew and moved. Possibly true tales of the gilding of a new ruler in gold dust reached the Spanish, and over the years the tale grew from that of a golden man to that of a golden realm, enticing more Spaniards to seek it. The English under Sir Walter Ralegh (1554–1618) also sought the kingdom, as did a German expedition given the blessing of Emperor Charles V. These searches were moderately significant in the exploration of the Amazon basin. Mixed into this myth was the added story that some Incas had escaped over the mountains with a great treasure, and the Spanish pursued this rumor from both directions. Though fiction writers may try to revive El Dorado,

belief in an actual such kingdom was put to rest in the early nineteenth century.

Classical Greek geography had an underpinning of belief in order and symmetry. If there is a northern continent, there must be a southern one to balance the world. One just had to find it. Inheriting the belief in *Terra Australis*, the southern continent, early European explorers attached the name to several sighted landmasses including Antarctica, several larger islands of Melanasia, and even Tierra del Fuego before it settled on what we now call Australia.

There were blank spots on the maps as far as detailed topography went even into the early twentieth century. As technology improved, particularly aerial and, later, satellite surveillance, some hiding places for the traditional mythic lands disappeared even as indications of ruins buried under desert sands or engulfed by jungles emerged. Although the full-blown lands of legend are gone, we may yet find the ruins of places that inspired the legends.

[*See also* Brendan, Saint; El Dorado; Quivira; Prester John; Ralegh, Walter; *and Terra Australis Incognita.*]

BIBLIOGRAPHY

Frimmer, Steven. *Neverland: Fabled Places and Fabulous Voyages of History and Legend.* New York: Viking, 1976.

Fuson, Robert H. *Legendary Islands of the Ocean Sea.* Sarasota, Fla.: Pineapple Press, 1995.

Manguel, Alberto, and Gianni Guadalupi. *The Dictionary of Imaginary Places.* New York: Macmillan, 1980. Revised edition, with illustrations by Graham Greenfield. New York: Harcourt Brace, 2000.

Morison, Samuel Eliot. *The European Discovery of America.* 2 vols. New York: Oxford University Press, 1971–1974. Reprint, 1993.

Ramsay, Raymond H. *No Longer on the Map: Discovering Places That Never Were.* New York: Viking, 1972.

J. B. POST

Filchner, Wilhelm (1877–1957), German Antarctic explorer. Born in Munich, Filchner joined the Military Academy at the age of fifteen. In 1900, he traveled on horseback through the Pamirs, where he met the British archaeologist Aurel Stein at the Chinese border. After rigorous training in surveying and geomagnetism, Filchner led a scientific expedition to the Weddell Sea. Originally he intended to cross the Antarctic continent from the Weddell Sea to the Ross Sea, but he had to give up this plan because of lack of funds.

The expedition ship *Deutschland*, with Captain Richard Vahsel, the meteorologist Erich Barkow, and the astronomer Erich Przybyllok on board, left

Bremerhaven on May 4, 1911. In Buenos Aires they met Roald Amundsen's *Fram*, which was returning after Amundsen's glorious conquest of the South Pole. After visiting South Georgia and the South Sandwich Islands, Filchner and his companions penetrated the Weddell Sea pack ice. By the end of January, new land was sighted west of Coats Land. Filchner called it Prince Regent Luitpold Land (now Luitpold Coast). Steaming west, the *Deutschland* crew discovered a vast ice shelf, which they named Kaiser Wilhelm Barrier (now Filchner Ice Shelf). On February 9, they moored in what they called Vahsel Bay. An attempt to establish a winter base failed when a huge section of the shelf that was carrying the expedition's hut caved into the sea. [See color plate 35 in this volume.]

The ship got frozen in by March, and while it was drifting into the Weddell Sea, Filchner left, together with Alfred Kling and Felix König, on a dangerous dog-sledge trip over some 40 miles (65 kilometers) of sea ice. By being able to do so, they proved the nonexistence of New South Greenland, a location claimed by the American sealer Benjamin Morell in 1823.

By the end of October 1912, the *Deutschland* broke free and reached South Georgia on December 19. In later years, Filchner continued to travel and explore various parts of the world. In 1926 he traveled again to Tibet, and later expeditions took him back to Tibet (1934–1937), as well as to Nepal and India (1938), where he was imprisoned during World War II. Filchner returned to Zurich in 1949, where he died on May 7, 1957.

[*See also* Antarctica.]

BIBLIOGRAPHY

Conrad, L. J. *Bibliography of Antarctic Exploration: Expedition Accounts from 1768 to 1960*. Washougal, Wash.: L. J. Conrad, 1999.
Filchner, Wilhelm, with Alfred Kling and Erich Przybyllok. *To the Sixth Continent: The Second German South Polar Expedition*. Translated and edited by William Barr. Bluntisham, U.K.: Bluntisham Books; Banham, U.K.: Erskine Press, 1994. English translation of *Zum sechsten Erdteil*, originally published in 1922.

JOHAN DECKERS

Film and Exploration. Claude Lévi-Strauss once said that the *Histoire d'un voyage en terre de Brésil* (History of a Voyage to Brazil, 1578), Jean de Léry's classic account of ostensive firsthand experience of the New World, is both "an ethnographer's breviary" and a great literary work, "an extraordinary adventure novel" that lends itself to a scenario.

In an interview published in 1994 he asked, "Why is it that no one to this day has thought of making the great film worthy of the Villegagnon venture such as Léry told it?" The answer may be that the film was already done and realized from the earliest days of the seventh art. In both theme and form it can be said that exploration and adventure are indeed the essence of cinema at its very origins. The countless narrative films based on voyage and discovery may be footnotes to the early experiment before 1914 and to the rise of documentary that occurred in the 1920s. When Lévi-Strauss longs for a cinematic version of a text whose editions are accompanied by detailed maps depicting the New World, such as the Miller Atlas (c. 1519) or André Thevet's *Grand insulaire* (1585–1586), he avows that his own *Tristes tropiques* (1955)—because of its alluring mix of text and images, or because its own descriptions of perilous adventure in the Sertão among the Nambikwara Indians refer to movies—might also be the subject for a scenario and production. But, as he showed in *Le cru et le cuit* (1964), since real exploration and discovery are done, travel is now engineered only by manipulating the laws and rules of navigation. Such is what cinema has done with exploration and voyage.

The remarks apply to the medium because exploration cannot be distinguished from simulation. Exploration can be treated along thematic and historical lines when a seasoned viewer accumulates and classifies features and forms according to two principles. One is a principle in which narrative and montage meld Aristotelian poetics (human action leading to a given end by way of reversals and shifts) to make a story coequal with the itinerary of a voyage. Another is to record and assemble events, no matter if they are fictional or true, situated either in studio settings or on location, or belong to different genres—travelogues, ethnographic film, science fiction, Westerns—without appeal to narrative models. Nonetheless, films that obey either or both of these principles betray a strong degree of "constructedness" and appeal to types of rhetoric that seduce by means of displacement.

The earliest films of exploration constitute a model on which most others vary. From the outset it was intuited that cinema embodied exploration because the spectator's eyes are led to wander about, decipher, and look all over the field of view projected on the screen. The viewer follows the itinerary of the lens that can record a multitude of things that often become perceptible only upon multiple and patient viewings. Often, notes the theorist and historian

Jacques Rancière in respect to Roberto Rossellini and other directors, things are recorded of which the lens (and its photographer) would have been unaware. The student of cinema, the inventors seemed to speculate, could be the discoverer whom Abraham Ortelius praised in the name of the armchair reader, the person paging through his monumental atlas, the *Theatrum Orbis Terrarum* (in the 1606 English edition), to find cartographic images of unknown worlds discovered by virtual voyage within the happy confines of a library or home.

Periods. Films of exploration attest to the correlation of the medium with the allure of adventure. They can be divided into three formal and historical periods. The first, which includes early cinematic experiments by the founding fathers of film, Louis and Auguste Lumière and Georges Méliès, and lasts from 1895 to 1905, identifies film with visual and feigned exploration. The second period, in which documentary film is developed in the 1920s, engages cinema as the quasi-direct experience of different worlds and cultures. A third period builds upon the first two but leads exploration toward inner, often metaphysical and self-reflective directions of the kind that Lévi-Strauss made famous in the first sentence of his *Tristes tropiques*, "I hate travels and explorers." These films, roughly of the 1950s, bring with them—directly or indirectly—the impact of the devastation and genocide made known at the end of World War II.

The Lumière brothers' first film—and probably the first film ever made—*Sortie d'usine* (Workers Exiting a Factory, 1895), is an exploration of the limits of the medium and the space it records. A single shot of less than a minute (seventeen meters of film moving at seventeen frames per second), taken from an immobile tripod, registers the opening of two doors of a large building facing the opposite side of the street from where the camera is mounted. A crowd of men and women in workers' clothes and elegant dresses fill and evacuate the street. A man on a bicycle exits the doorway while an errant dog runs across the field of view. A huge horse-drawn carriage exits the doorway. When calm returns, the film stops. The deep-focus photography requires viewers to account for the ways their eyes behold the spectacle: how myriad movement is discerned; how the shot of the factory (in which the camera and film stock were manufactured) amounts to an advertisement; how the movement mirrors the desire to explore the space being shown by virtue of the sight of successive thresholds in staggered depth.

The invention was so novel that Auguste and Louis Lumière and their promoter, Alexandre Promio, soon shot similar films, literal *tranches de vie* (slices of everyday life), in places and of people all over the world: streets of Moscow, a subway station in New York, Broadway, guitar players in Madrid, African children running toward a camera in a wagon that pulls backward, departures of steamers from great ports, Vietnamese children gathering pieces of candy that two elegant French schoolteachers toss on the ground. In their DVD edition of the Lumières' films, Bertrand Tavernier and Thierry Frenaux make clear the exploratory and commercial value of the new medium. In their eyes, the showing of these short takes in newly constructed movie houses around the world offered unforeseen modes of artificial travel. To explore was to participate in the network spawned by the new *cinématographe*.

Georges Méliès, a magician and prestidigitator, drew on the Lumière's invention to construct a panoply of films, many inspired by Jules Verne, that tell of travel to new and strange worlds. Cutting and splicing segments of film and recording events against painted backgrounds, Méliès used trick and illusion to portray travel to the moon, to the North Pole, and to other oneiric lands. His *Voyage à la lune* can be seen as a first and telling piece of comic ethnography. The mad professor Barbenfouillis (played by the acrobatic Méliès himself) builds a rocket that a cannon shoots to the moon. In a piece of trick photography, the camera assumes the point of view of the rocket approaching the moon, shown as a globe with a pasty surface through which peer two eyes and from which emerges a pair of moving lips. The man in the moon expresses fear and shock as the rocket approaches. All of a sudden the rocket crashes into his right eye. Then begin the explorers' descent and discovery of a land of fantasy that includes a snowy steppe, a rain forest where wild flora abound and where the explorers' umbrellas turn into gigantic mushrooms that complement a backdrop of oversized morels and chanterelles. The explorers happen upon a band of Pygmies, who explode when the explorers touch them with the tips of their umbrellas. The explorers meet the chief of the tribe and narrowly escape execution by running to the rocket, which is teeter-tottering on the edge of a cliff. They get in and coax it to fall. It drops and then descends to the floor of an ocean on earth (the shot being taken through an aquarium). The men return home and are greeted with great fanfare. Therein is the formula for adventure that leads not only to science fiction but to landmark films such as Ernest Schoed-sack's *King Kong* (1933) and many others like it.

Film and Exploration. The Lumières and Méliès, said to be the originators of, respectively, cinematic realism and cinematic fantasy, greatly influenced the first masterwork of exploration film, Robert Flaherty's *Nanook of the North* (1921). The director, a mining engineer who had an abiding interest in exploring and mapping northern Canada, came to Canada in 1916 with a Bell and Howell camera that he had recently purchased in Rochester, New York. A first botched film (Flaherty reputedly dropped a burning cigarette on his nitrate negative) inspired Flaherty to redo the experience. Obtaining funding from the Revillon Frères fur-trading company, Flaherty returned in 1920 and spent sixteen months on the northeastern coast of Hudson Bay, completing in August 1921 the shooting of what is now considered to be the first ethnographic film—a film that seems to portray directly, without mediation or trick editing, Inuit life in the Arctic.

In its form, *Nanook* abandoned the model of adventure films that followed the Aristotelian model of voyage and resolution (for example, Douglas Fairbanks Sr.'s *Mr. Robinson Crusoe*, 1932). Flaherty placed stress, remarks Jeffrey Geiger, on "exploration, discovery, and adventure into realms 'uncharted' and unknown" (Geiger, p. 125). Close analysis has since revealed that much of *Nanook* is staged, and that ethnographic stereotypes (the vanishing noble savage, the flesh-eating Inuit who could be a cannibal, a static way of life, the native's wonder at Western technology) mar the narrative. Yet the film is built as a series of images of life, arranged in a paratactic order that yields a rich and complex picture ways of living in spaces unknown to most human beings. Flaherty makes use of Eisensteinian montage in the seal and walrus hunt. He depicts life in an igloo by having the structure cut in half so as to have enough light for his slow film stock to expose a record of everyday life that his Inuit are indeed rehearsing or miming in their icy home. By and large, the director succeeds in having the camera discover a culture in the great expanse of a seemingly barren environment.

Illusion of the kind Flaherty exploited to obtain his realistic effects are the targets of Luis Buñuel's caustic documentary of voyage, *Land without Bread* (also titled *Unpromised Land*; *Tierra sin pan*; *Pays sans pain*; *Las Hurdes*, 1932), that tells of the voyage of seeming anthropologists (one is seen briefly in the film) to Las Hurdes, a region in Spain so remote—

declares a title-card in the front credits—that roads were introduced "only in 1922." The subtitle, "a Study in Human Geography," puts the film in dialogue with the French school of cultural geography that Pierre Vidal de la Blache had founded not long before. Buñuel, having recently completed the scandalous surreal masterpiece *Un chien andalou* (1928), applies an aesthetics of visual shock to narrate, to extirpate, and thus to theorize documentary and expeditionary cinemas. *Land without Bread* begins with its title shown printed over a cloudy sky. Where the presence of unknown land might be sought in the image on the basis of the verbal cue, indeed none is found. As if deriding the cartographic sequence that inaugurates *Nanook*, Buñuel shows four relief maps in lap dissolves that move from the European continent to the northern Estramadura (north of Salamanca and west of Ávila). The maps themselves, rich in relief and shading and pocked with recognizable and also strange toponyms, resemble a leprous skin. The landscape that the camera soon records is of unremitting harshness: rocks and scrubby vegetation show that even in Republican Spain is found an originary world in which human beasts subsist as occasional farmers and perpetual hunter-gatherers. Thirty-two minutes long, the film is composed of nearly 250 shots and, like *Nanook*, is without a story line other than that of a journey farther and farther into an unpromised land. In that space of time myriad impressions of familiarity and alterity accumulate. The narrative itinerary is provided by a supercilious voice-over that expresses disquiet and disgust about what is shown.

Yet the images, shot in the rich tradition of silent film and of a visual wealth recalling the paintings of Ribera and Velasquez, are at odds with the speaker's colonial voice and the accompaniment of Brahms's *Fourth Symphony*. The mendacious basis of documentary cinema is brought forward and is stressed without compromise, while the images themselves remain an informative and sensuous record of remote Spanish pueblos and their isolation from the modern world. A remarkable sequence, shot in extreme depth of field, depicts a mountain goat that falls from a rocky cliffside. The narrator, asserting that the Hurdanos eat meat only when "'this' happens," prompts an alert eye to glimpse a puff of smoke that enters from the right edge of the frame just before the goat loses footing and falls: Buñuel and his photographer Elie Lotar have obviously shot the animal to obtain the dazzling effect of the fall of the carcass down the vertiginous slope. In this piece of trickery Buñuel at once masters and mocks the genre that Méliès had intuited and that Flaherty had established. As a result, five years before Spain fell under Fascist rule, the director was forced to live in exile from his native country.

Documentary Film. In the third period, films of exploration further summon the validity of discovery and the truth of documentary evidence. As if weaned on Flaherty and Buñuel, a younger generation used the genre to explore inner, occluded, and troubled worlds where psychic and geographical spaces are mixed. To be sure, exploration had its alluring but hardly innovative models on the Pacific Ocean in *Kon-Tiki* (1954) and in the oceanic depths in Jacques Cousteau's *Le monde du silence* (The Silent World, 1954), an issue not lost on the critic André Bazin in his pages on exploration and film in *Qu'est-ce que le cinéma?* But the genre finds its most telling rendition in Roberto Rossellini's *Voyage to Italy* (also as *Viaggio in Italia*, 1953). The film begins from the point of view of a driver of a car speeding down a narrow two-lane road in the countryside of Tuscany. Inside, a bored but agitated middle-aged woman (Ingrid Bergman) reads a Baedeker Guide to Italy as her sleepy and disparaging husband (George Sanders), at the wheel, complains about the voyage and about the aspect of the countryside. They are forced to stop to allow a herd of cattle to cross the road. It quickly turns out that their marriage is on the verge of collapse. Upon arrival at their destination, the wife seeks solace in touring museums, while her overbearing spouse tries to find adulterous romance in an excursion he takes to Capri. Discovery and communication with the native culture never take place. At a chilling moment near the end of the film, at the site of an excavation of Roman ruins, the wife witnesses the retrieval of a cast—made by the injection of plaster into an underground void serving as a mold—of a couple in embrace. She witnesses the hollow and interred embodiment of a relationship that she has wished to find. But of what kind? With another culture? With another human being? With the past? With her spouse? With the unknown? No answer comes forward. The dismal ending shows the couple lost and then reunited in a crowd of Italians in a busy city street whose vivacity leaves the pair isolated in their mental carapace. *Voyage to Italy* deals with failed exploration. It takes tourism to be the only modern analogue of discovery. Like other features of the time, the film is marked by the aftermath of World War II and its traumatic memory. Perilous voyage and discovery are shown as having become history.

In these three periods of expeditionary film are woven the threads of a rich fabric of cinema of exploration that commands much of the twentieth century. By a curious turn of fate, each new generation of cinephiles and filmmakers discovers new lands when it returns to these great early models in which cinema, voyage, and discovery influence each other. It would not be wrong to say that most films of discovery can be held up to the mirror of these masterworks. Thus the earliest cinema makes exploration both a theme and a form of the new medium. From its inception, as Richard Abel has aptly shown, cinema also colonizes the world in globalizing its commerce through direct and indirect appeal to voyage. The documentary cinema of exploration, developed in the 1920s by Robert Flaherty, becomes a model not only for almost all subsequent films but also for its critical inversion in Luis Buñuel's documentary style, witnessed in films that run from *Las Hurdes* (1932) to *Robinson Crusoe* (1955) and *The Milky Way* (1972), in which travelogue turns into adventure, and adventure turns into pilgrimage. Documentary film since the 1920s negotiates both exploration and the technical manipulations vital to its representation. Following World War II, in which all films are haunted by conflict and devastation, exploration turns inward—toward unknown places in the mind—and to the world at large. These postwar films negotiate the limits of cinematic images by means of exploration of inner or overlooked areas of the known world. Its masterpieces tell as much of occulted discovery as of mediated exploration.

BIBLIOGRAPHY

Abel, Richard. *The Ciné Goes to Town: French Cinema, 1896–1914*. Berkeley: University of California Press, 1994.

Abel, Richard. *The Red Rooster Scare: Making American Cinema, 1900–1910*. Berkeley: University of California Press, 1999.

Bazin, André. *Qu'est-ce que le cinéma?* 4 vols. Reprint. Paris: Editions du Cerf, 1998.

Conley, Tom. "Documentary Surrealism." *In Dada and Surrealist Film*, edited by Rudolph Kuenzli, 176–198. New York: Willis, Locker and Owens, 1987.

Conley, Tom. *Su realismo: Lectura de Buñuel, "Tierra sin pan."* Valencia, Spain: Centro de Semiótica y Teoría del Espectáculo, Documentos de trabajo 6, 1988.

Geiger, Jeffrey. "Nanook." In *Film Analysis: A Norton Reader*, edited by Jeffrey Geiger and R. L. Rutsky. New York: Norton, 2005.

Lévi-Strauss, Claude. Interview. In *Histoire d'un voyage fait en la terre du Brésil*, by Jean de Léry. Edited by Frank Lestringant. Paris: Livre de Poche Classique, 1994.

Lévi-Strauss, Claude. *Mythologiques 1: Le cru et le cuit*. Paris: Plon, 1964.

Lévi-Strauss, Claude. *Tristes tropiques*. Paris: Plon, 1955.

Rancière, Jacques. *La fable cinématographique*. Paris: Seuil, 2001.

Tavernier, Bertrand, and Thierry Frenaux. *The Lumière Brothers' First Films*. DVD. New York: Kino Films; Lyon, France: Institut Lumière, 2002.

TOM CONLEY

Finney, Ben (b. 1933), American anthropologist. Ben Rudolph Finney was born in San Diego, California, on October 1, 1933, to a naval aviator, Leon H. Finney, and a schoolteacher and nurse, Melba R. Trefzger. After he tried his hand at engineering, economics, and history as an undergraduate at the University of California, Berkeley, Finney's fascination with the human story led him to the study of anthropology. He subsequently earned a master's degree from the University of Hawaii and a doctorate from Harvard University, both in anthropology. From the beginning, Finney's focus in anthropology was on prehistoric Pacific peoples and their exploration and settlement of that island region.

Finney's exploratory career began with two goals: to test the voyaging capabilities of accurately reconstructed prehistoric Polynesian sailing vessels and to test the widely held belief that the remote islands of the Pacific had been settled by the passengers of vessels that had been blown off course and randomly washed ashore on new islands. Finney, contending that random drifting was inadequate to explain the peopling of the Pacific, set out in the 1960s to test his theory.

Finney constructed a traditional-style double-hulled Polynesian canoe to test the sailing capabilities of the vessel and the endurance capabilities of the crew. The *Nāhelia*, Finney's first vessel, provided a baseline of understanding of how Polynesian vessels might have fared in near-shore and deep-sea conditions. In conjunction with the physician Steven Horvath, Finney also tested the physiological impacts on the crew of both sailing and rowing. The *Nāhelia* trials, conducted off the California and Hawaii coasts, laid the foundation for Finney's more ambitious voyages in the 1970s and 1980s.

In the 1970s, Finney set his sights on retracing the legendary voyages of the first peoples of Hawaii. Because of the paucity of archaeological and even oral-history evidence on the design of ancient Polynesian canoes, Finney and his team relied on the historic sketches of Captain James Cook and other historic explorers for the design of their crowning reconstructive achievement, the *Hōkūle'a*. The *Hōkūle'a* is a sixty-foot-long, double-hulled, double-masted canoe, with sails in the traditional Polynesian inverted-triangle shape.

Taking advantage of a local resurgence in interest in native Hawaiian history and culture, Finney assembled a vessel crew made up of native Hawaiians, a Micronesian navigator, Mau Piailug, and various other people who lived in the islands. Finney's intended purpose for *Hōkūle'a* was to sail it from Hawaii to Tahiti using only traditional dead-reckoning techniques of navigation. This approach to navigation, which employs solar, lunar, stellar, and other natural observations to keep a vessel on course, was a disappearing art among the native inhabitants of the Pacific in the 1970s. Nevertheless, under the navigational direction of Piailug, Finney and his crew successfully sailed the *Hōkūle'a* to Tahiti in 1976, pioneering a resurgence in the use of navigational methods that had not been widely used for generations. Along with proving that traditional methods of navigation could and likely were used in the settlement of the Pacific (displacing the previously accepted random drift theories) Finney pioneered the exploration of prehistoric voyaging methods and life aboard a traditional vessel. The initial *Hōkūle'a* voyage inspired multiple voyages, continuing to this day, leading to the training of several native Hawaiians—most notably the future *Hōkūle'a* navigator, Nainoa Thompson—in the traditional way-finding techniques of their ancestors.

Ultimately, on successive voyages that reached as far from Hawaii as New Zealand, Finney and his crew demonstrated that, by exploiting periodic weather patterns in the Pacific, ancient voyagers could press their vessels on from west to east, largely laying to rest Thor Heyerdahl's theories of the population of the Pacific from South America. This reality further invigorated native Pacific peoples' interest in their ancient history and fostered a pride in their maritime cultural history that had all but disappeared in modern times.

Finney managed not only to pioneer substantial voyages of discovery on traditional vessels throughout the Pacific region, but also to further the understanding of how ancient explorers accomplished their voyages in the daunting open Pacific. Finney, who remains on the faculty of the University of Hawaii, continues to work in the area of Pacific nautical research and cultural revival; however, he has also turned some of his research to more hypothetical examinations of space exploration.

[*See also* Navigation, Ancient and Medieval; Pacific, *subentry on* Peoples; Polynesian Voyages; *and* Ships and Shipbuilding, Ancient and Medieval.]

BIBLIOGRAPHY
Finney, Ben R. *Voyage of Rediscovery: A Cultural Odyssey through Polynesia.* Berkeley: University of California Press, 1994.

RYAN M. SEIDEMANN

Fischer, Gustav

Fischer, Gustav (1848–1886), German physician who discovered Africa's Lake Naivasha. Gustav Adolf Fischer was born in Barmen (Wuppertal), Germany, and died in Berlin. His African career began in 1876 when he settled in Zanzibar to practice medicine and pursue interests in geography and zoology. His four expeditions between 1877 and 1886 returned extensive collections, especially in ornithology, and provided detailed information about the Masai people and the regions east of Lake Victoria.

Fischer's first two expeditions were to the coast north of Zanzibar in 1877 and again in 1878, traveling inland along the Tana River. His third expedition (1882–1883), the first organized by the Hamburg Geographical Society (which had been founded in 1873), was intended to reach Lake Victoria via the southwestern base of Mount Kilimanjaro. It was not wholly successful. The expedition narrowly overlapped one from the Royal Geographical Society of London under Joseph Thomson's leadership, and occasioned diplomatic and scientific rivalry. Fischer's account of this expedition, including geological and ethnographic observations, appeared in his *Das Masai-Land* (1885). Fischer's fourth expedition (1885–1886) set out to explore the upper reaches of the Nile, but he traveled only as far inland as the eastern shores of Lake Victoria.

Fischer's exploring activities marked a turning point in the "scramble" for East Africa, as he made contacts with leaders inland to secure for Germany territory claimed by the sultanate of Zanzibar. He was followed by the controversial treaty maker Dr. Carl Peters, whose efforts in 1884 led to the declaration (February 26, 1885) of the German East African Protectorate by Kaiser Wilhelm. While partly laying the groundwork for the German colonization of Tanganyika, Fischer's *Mehr Licht im dunkeln Weltteil* (More Light on the Dark Continent, 1885) presented a pessimistic view of the commercial opportunities in East Africa and its possibilities as a site for European settlement.

[*See also* Imperialism and Exploration.]

BIBLIOGRAPHY
Anonymous. "Obituary: Dr. G. A. Fischer." *Proceedings of the Royal Geographical Society and Monthly Record of Geography* 8, no. 12 (1886): 791–792.

LAWRENCE DRITSAS

Flinders, Matthew

Flinders, Matthew (1774–1814), English sailor who circumnavigated Australia. Matthew Flinders was born at Donington, Lincolnshire, on March 16, 1774. He joined the Royal Navy in 1789 and was given an early opportunity to sail to the Pacific as midshipman on Captain William Bligh's *Providence* in 1791. Reaching Tasmania on February 8, 1792, Bligh went on to Tahiti to fetch breadfruit trees, taking them to the West Indies and returning to England on August 2, 1793. Flinders then served for a while on the *Bellerophon*, later transferring to the *Reliance* and sailing for Australia in early 1795. With a fellow officer, George Bass, Flinders explored part of the south coast of Australia, surveyed the Furneaux Islands in what became known as Bass Strait, and circumnavigated Van Diemen's Land (or Tasmania), proving that it was an island.

Flinders, promoted to lieutenant, returned to England and published an account of his surveys, which he dedicated to Sir Joseph Banks. This earned him wide recognition and official support for a proposed comprehensive exploration of the Australian coast. Placed in charge of the *Investigator*, he sailed from Spithead on July 18, 1801, and after a fairly speedy voyage reached Cape Leeuwin on November 6. He devoted most of December to a survey of King George Sound, and then entered the Great Australian Bight, a little-known area where he was able to make a number of important discoveries.

On April 8, 1802, while charting the coast in Encounter Bay, Flinders met the French captain Nicolas Baudin, who was undertaking similar surveying work from the opposite direction. After a brief meeting, each continued on his way, Flinders returning to Port Jackson on May 9. After a couple of months, he resumed his work, this time along the east coast of Australia and accompanied for a while by the brig *Lady Nelson*. He went through the Great Barrier Reef by means of what is now known as Flinders Passage, rounded Cape York, and surveyed the area around Cape Arnhem, but then was forced to curtail this work by the condition of his ship. He nevertheless sailed down the coast of western Australia, then along the south coast back to Port Jackson, where he arrived on June 9, thus completing a circumnavigation of the entire continent.

Flinders began his voyage home to England on August 10, 1803, in the *Porpoise*, accompanied by the *Cato* and the *Bridgewater*, but a week later the first two were wrecked on a reef, and Flinders struggled back to Port Jackson in the *Bridgewater*. A replacement vessel was found for him, the schooner *Cumberland*, and he began his journey anew, reaching Mauri-

Matthew Flinders. "View in Sir Edward Pellew's Group—Gulph of Carpentaria" from Flinders's *A Voyage to Terra Australis* (2 vols., London, 1814). This engraving seems to catch the remoteness of the islands in the Sir Edward Pellew Group (the name survives) at the southern end of the Gulf of Carpentaria, between Arnhem Land and the York Peninsula in Australia. COURTESY THE NEWBERRY LIBRARY, CHICAGO

tius on December 15. However, the Napoleonic Wars had begun, and Mauritius, then known as the Isle de France, was a French colony. Flinders had no free pass for the *Cumberland*, which was impounded, and he was himself placed under house arrest. Considerable tension developed between him and the island governor, General Decaen, and in spite of all his protests and even the support of Napoleon, Flinders was not freed until June 1810. Finally reaching home in October, he worked on the narrative of his expedition, *A Voyage to Terra Australis*, which was published on July 19, 1814—the very day he died, aged a mere forty years.

Flinders's contribution to the coastal survey of Australia was remarkable. His seamanship, especially in view of the poor quality of the ships he was given, was remarkable, and his achievements in Australian cartography and hydrography were truly impres-

sive—he should also be remembered for having championed the name "Australia" instead of "New Holland," which he considered outdated and inappropriate. His expedition's contributions to botany should not be overlooked; much of the credit for these contributions is due to the untiring efforts of the naturalist Robert Brown and the artist Ferdinand Bauer. [See color plate 36 in this volume.]

[*See also* Australia, Exploration of, *and* Bass, George.]

BIBLIOGRAPHY

Austin, K. A. *The Voyage of the Investigator 1801–1803, Commander Matthew Flinders R.N.* Adelaide, Australia: Rigby, 1964.

Flinders, Matthew. *A Voyage to Terra Australis: Undertaken for the Purpose of Completing the Discovery of That Vast Country in 1801, 1802, and 1803 in His Majesty's Ship "The*

Investigator". 2 vols. and atlas. London: G. and W. Nicol, 1814.

Mack, James D. *Matthew Flinders, 1774–1814*. London: Nelson, 1966.

Rawson, Geoffrey. *Matthew Flinders' Narrative of his Voyage in the Schooner "Francis" in 1798*. London: Golden Cockerel Press, 1946.

Scott, Ernest. *The Life of Matthew Flinders*. Sydney, Australia: Allen & Unwin, 1914.

JOHN DUNMORE

Florence. The city-state of Florence may be credited with giving birth to the Renaissance in the mid-fourteenth century, nearly a century before it began to appear in the rest of Europe. From the mid-fourteenth century through the sixteenth century, Florence and Venice were the two most powerful cities on the Italian peninsula, but under the rule of the Medici family, Florence was the leader in banking and commerce. These two activities formed a powerful basis for Florence's contributions to the age of discovery. It was a Florentine, Palla Strozzi (c. 1373–1482), who acquired a Greek manuscript of the *Geographia* by Claudius Ptolemy (2nd century C.E.) and had it translated into Latin, revolutionizing European cartography. The leading Italian cosmographer of the fifteenth century was also a Florentine, Paolo dal Pozzo Toscanelli (1397–1482). He advised the Portuguese court in a letter of 1474 that the shortest route to the spices of the Far East lay across the Atlantic. It is almost certain that Christopher Columbus had a copy of this letter and possibly a world map by Toscanelli. Although not a sea power, Florence provided two of the important early navigators who explored the Western Hemisphere: Amerigo Vespucci (1451–1512), for whom America is named, and Giovanni da Verrazano (1485–1528). Vespucci was sent to Spain in 1492 to manage the Spanish banking interests of the Medicis. He met Columbus and helped him supply his second voyage of 1493. Vespucci himself reached the Western Hemisphere, explored the South American coast, and was the first to recognize that the landmass was a new continent. He took Spanish citizenship and was appointed the first pilot-major, responsible for the *padrón real*, or master map of discovery. Verrazano made three voyages to the New World under the flag of France and was the first to explore the American coast from North Carolina to Newfoundland. During the sixteenth century, many Florentine merchants moved east and west seeking their fortunes. They often served their Spanish and Portuguese hosts in military and administrative positions. Their letters and diaries pro-vide a more intimate look at the indigenous people and their customs than the more famous accounts by those focused on establishing overseas empires.

[*See also* Columbus, Christopher; Expeditions, World Exploration, *subentries on* Portugal *and* Spain; Toscanelli, Paolo dal Pozzo; Verrazano, Giovanni da; *and* Vespucci, Amerigo.]

BIBLIOGRAPHY

Goldstein, T. "Geography in Fifteenth Century Florence." In *Merchants and Scholars*, edited by John Parker. Minneapolis: University of Minnesota Press, 1965.

Rombai, Leonardo, ed. *Il Mondo di Vespucci e Verrazzano: geografia e viaggi dalla Terrasanta all'America*. Florence: Leo S. Olschki, 1993.

ROBERT A. HIGHBARGER

Florida. After the donations of Pope Alexander VI (r. 1492–1503), Spaniards explored the Gulf of Mexico and the North American southeast. In Florida, small numbers of Europeans attempted to impose their will on 350,000 Native Americans. The Spanish crown licensed Juan Ponce de León and Lucas Vázquez de Ayllón to conquer and settle Florida, while the French king sent Giovanni da Verrazano to explore North America. Spain then issued contracts to Pánfilo de Narváez and Hernando de Soto, while the French sponsored two Florida journeys of Jacques Cartier. The Tampa Bay landing of Fray Luis Cáncer and the expeditions of Tristán de Luna and Ángel de Villafañe proved disastrous.

The Spaniards learned that France had sent Jean Ribault to build Charlesfort (on Parris Island in present-day South Carolina). When the colonists fled, the French sent René de Laudonnière in 1564 to build Fort Caroline on present-day Saint Johns. The capture of French mutineers unmasked the fort.

The Spanish *adelantado*, Pedro Menéndez de Avilés, arrived off the Saint Johns River on September 4, 1565. He skirmished with Ribault and founded Saint Augustine. Ribault's ships, struck by a northeast storm, were lost down the coast. Meanwhile, Menéndez took Fort Caroline, killing most of its garrison. Many of Ribault's shipwreck survivors were also killed or captured.

The *adelantado* had a wide vision for Florida, planning to connect its east coast to the Gulf of Mexico and to follow the fabled Northwest Passage to the Orient. He established fort-missions around the Florida peninsula and up to Santa Elena, where he brought settlers. Juan Pardo explored westward to the Appalachians. Menéndez signed treaties with native peoples such as the Timucua, Calusa, Ais,

Guale, and groupings near Santa Elena, but his attempt to colonize and evangelize the southeast piedmont failed before his death in 1574. Later, Spaniards extended their reach westward into Apalache, and built missions there from Saint Augustine.

The explorations of North America by the sixteenth-century Englishmen Sir John Hawkins and Sir Walter Ralegh left no lasting settlement. After the seventeenth-century settlement of Jamestown and Charleston, the English began to advance toward Saint Augustine. Raids caused the destruction of many Spanish missions and led to sieges of Saint Augustine in 1702 and 1740. Meanwhile, Muskogee peoples swept down into the Florida peninsula, displacing earlier groupings.

The fate of the Timucua symbolized the fate of the Florida Indians as a whole. Estimated at 150,000 at European contact, they were reduced by epidemic disease, and in 1656 they rebelled against harsh Spanish treatment. In 1763, Spain turned Florida over to the English and evacuated the colony, taking with them a few Christian Timucua. In 1769, the last remaining full-blooded Timucuan, Juan Alonso Cavale, died at Guanabacoa, near Havana.

In 1821 Florida became a territory of the United States. By the end of the Seminole Wars, the Spanish, the French, and the English had all failed to control the peninsula, while the Native Americans and their once-rich cultures had virtually vanished. The most striking remnant of colonial times is Saint Augustine, the oldest city of European origin in what later became the United States.

[*See also biographical entries on figures mentioned in this article.*]

BIBLIOGRAPHY
Lyon, Eugene. *The Enterprise of Florida.* Gainesville: University Press of Florida, 1976.
Worth, John E. *Timucuan Chiefdoms of Spanish Florida.* 2 vols. Vol. 2, *Resistance and Destruction.* Gainesville: University Press of Florida, 1998.

EUGENE LYON

Forrest, John (1847–1918), Australian surveyor, explorer, and politician. John Forrest was born near Bunbury in Western Australia, the third son of the farmer and millwright William Forrest. Apprenticed to the local district surveyor in 1863, he began a long career in the Survey Department, rising to become surveyor-general in January 1883.

In April 1869, Forrest led a six-man expedition into the largely unexplored country between Mounts Ida and Margaret on an unsuccessful search for the remains of Ludwig Leichhardt. Leichhardt had disappeared while attempting to cross from the Darling Downs in Queensland to the Swan River settlement in 1848. Forrest returned four months later with important geological and botanical specimens. The following year, at the head of a six-man party, he left Esperance on May 9 and crossed the Nullarbor Plain to Fowlers Bay and Adelaide, where he and the party arrived on August 27. On April 1, 1874, Forrest and six others left Geraldton, traveling slowly across the western interior. Moving from waterhole to waterhole they passed through the Carnarvon, Warburton, and Musgrave ranges to reach the Peak Hill telegraph station in late September. The party arrived in Adelaide on November 3.

Forrest's explorations were significant feats of human endurance, but he found little to attract European settlers. Like the achievements of other desert explorers, his major achievement was to demonstrate the reality of the interior. There were "many grassy patches" but little permanent water.

Forrest was well rewarded for his surveying and exploration work. He received a 5,000-acre (2,025-hectare) land grant, a knighthood, a gold medal from the Royal Geographical Society, and election to the Linnaean Society of London. His *Explorations in Australia* was published in 1875. Forrest had a successful political career, serving as premier of Western Australia from December 1890 to February 1901 and as a minister in the Commonwealth of Australia parliament. John Forrest died on September 3, 1918, while sailing to England to accept the baronetcy he had just been awarded.

[*See also* Australia, Exploration of, *and* Leichhardt, Ludwig.]

BIBLIOGRAPHY
Crowley, Frank. *Big John Forrest, 1847–1918: A Founding Father of the Commonwealth of Australia.* Perth: University of Western Australia Press, 2000.
Favenc, Ernest. *The History of Australian Exploration from 1788 to 1888.* Sydney: Turner and Henderson, 1888. Reprint. Amsterdam: Meridian, 1967.
McLaren, Glen. *Beyond Leichhardt: Bushcraft and the Exploration of Australia.* Fremantle, Australia: Fremantle Arts Centre Press, 1996.
Millar, Ann. *"I See No End to Travelling": Journals of Australian Explorers, 1813–76.* Sydney: Bay Books, 1986.

DENIS SHEPHARD

Forster, Johann Reinhold, and Georg Forster, German-born naturalists on James Cook's second voyage. Johann Reinhold Forster (1729–

Johann and Georg Forster. Drawing of a ray, c. 1775. The Forsters sailed with James Cook on his journey to the South Seas in 1772–1775. Johann was the naturalist for the voyage, and his son Georg the artist; he drew creatures like this ray, observed at Tahiti in 1774. THE NATURAL HISTORY MUSEUM, LONDON

1798) and his son Georg Forster (1754–1794) are famous for their controversial participation in James Cook's second voyage (1772–1775), when they made—as scientists, writers, and translators—wide-ranging contributions to the practice and understanding of exploration in the late eighteenth century. Johann Reinhold Forster was a formidably wide-ranging intellectual, even by the expansive standards of the eighteenth century. His knowledge of antiquities and languages was very considerable, though his primary interests were in natural history. Trained in Berlin and Halle, he briefly became an apprentice pastor but sought employment nearer his philosophical interests and undertook a Russian commission to report on the colonies on the Volga. He took his eldest son Georg with him as an assistant, but was injudiciously candid in his report, which documented widespread difficulties and abuses, and offended Catherine the Great and her minister. Johann and Georg Forster then traveled to England hoping to seek employment, and the elder Forster became a teacher of natural history at the famous Dissenters' academy at Warrington. In the later 1760s he made extensive contacts among scientific societies and the scientific world in London, he published his *Introduction to Mineralogy* (1768), and, with the assistance of Georg, he translated a host of works, many by pupils of Linnaeus, but including such important voyage texts as Louis-Antoine de Bougainville's *Voyage autour du monde*, which appeared in English in early 1772.

When plans for Cook's second voyage were being drawn up, it was anticipated that Joseph Banks would again participate, with a large party. Banks was, however, angered by the accommodation that was proposed for him, and withdrew with his entire party; inquiries were made for replacement naturalists and artists, and the Forsters joined the voyage at short notice. A theme of much of the commentary on the second voyage has been that Johann Forster was a bad-tempered, impossible character who quarreled at some stage with virtually everyone on board. This may be largely correct, but it has obscured the vigorously inquisitive character of Forster's intellect. Like those of Banks, Forster's voyage journals are invaluable for telling a story that is in some ways richer than Cook's, and is certainly one more attuned to human and natural historical observation; Forster was also more widely and deeply read than Banks, and more systematic in his consideration of the information he gathered.

Cook's second voyage was exceptional for the range of its human contacts, especially in the tropical Pacific, and it was these contacts that the Forsters richly documented in postvoyage publications. Their writings arose from what became a bitter controversy over who would prepare (and profit from) the official narrative of the voyage. Johann Forster had been led to believe that the task would be his, though it is doubtful that this had ever been communicated to Cook, who was, over the course of the expedition, developing his own sense of himself as a writer. The upshot of complex negotiations after the voyage was that Forster was excluded: he was barred contractually from publishing a narrative of the voyage that would compete with Cook's. So, Forster instead worked up an extended volume of remarks that were "philosophical" in the broadest sense, which appeared as *Observations Made during a Voyage round the World* in 1778. Though this was not the book that Forster had hoped or planned to write, it is an astonishingly rich and wide-ranging meditation on the voyage's scientific and, above all, proto-anthropological findings. Its most extensive sections struggle to come to grips with the "varieties of the human species" in the South Seas, and especially with the differences of apparent social advancement that separated, for example, Maori and Tahitians.

Because of his youth, Georg Forster had signed no undertaking prior to joining the voyage and was therefore free to write a rival account, which the cash-strapped family hoped to profit from. In fact, the book was not commercially successful, but has long been considered an unusually vivid, proto-Romantic classic of travel literature. Georg Forster's descriptions of landscapes were aestheticized and animated, and his accounts of exotic peoples often much richer than those in Cook's book. His *Voyage round the World* (2 vols.; 1777) was, however, immediately controversial, particularly for highlighting a range of instances of cross-cultural violence that, in Forster's telling, reflected poorly on the European seamen. For these and other reasons it was vigorously denounced by the voyage astronomer, William Wales; Georg responded to his polemic, and indeed on some of the more important points he can be vindicated.

Facing ruin, the Forster family moved to Germany, where both Georg and Johann were able to obtain academic posts, and both continued to write and translate extensively. Georg was engaged in debate with Immanuel Kant about questions of race and traveled with Alexander von Humboldt on the Rhine; his influence on German literature and science was enduring. The importance of the Forsters for the science and anthropology of Cook's voyages has long been obscured by the preoccupation with Johann

Forster's notorious crankiness, but they have at last been given due recognition.

[*See also* Cook, James, *and* Pacific, *subentry on* Peoples.]

BIBLIOGRAPHY

Forster, Georg. *A Voyage round the World.* 1777. Edited by Nicholas Thomas and Oliver Berghof. Honolulu: University of Hawaii Press, 2000.

Forster, Johann Reinhold. *Observations Made during a Voyage round the World.* 1778. Edited by Nicholas Thomas, Harriet Guest, and Michael Dettelbach. Honolulu: University of Hawaii Press, 1996.

Hoare, Michael E. *The Tactless Philosopher: Johann Reinhold Forster* (1729–1798). Melbourne, Australia: Hawthorne Press, 1975.

Hoare, Michael E., ed. *The "Resolution" Journal of Johann Reinhold Forster, 1772–1775.* London: Hakluyt Society, 1982.

NICHOLAS THOMAS

Foucauld, Charles de (1858–1916), French explorer of Morocco. Charles de Foucauld was born into an aristocratic family in Strasbourg, France, on September 15, 1858. He gained fame as an explorer of Morocco, and later as a hermit-priest in the Sahara Desert. After graduating in 1876 from Saint Cyr Military College, Foucauld completed cavalry school at Saumur. Quitting the army in 1881, he moved to Algiers, where—with the help of Oscar MacCarthy, librarian at Mustapha Pasha's palace—he determined to explore unknown parts of Morocco. MacCarthy, an experienced desert traveler, introduced Foucauld to Mordecai Abi-Serour, a Moroccan rabbi whom Foucauld hired to be his companion and guide.

Foucauld commenced his dangerous journey in June 1883 and, taking MacCarthy's advice, traveled in disguise as a Muscovite rabbi. Rabbi Mordecai found lodging in the miserable Jewish ghettos (*mellahs*), where Foucauld was introduced as a famous physician who specialized in eye diseases. He was almost murdered on two occasions by Jewish thugs. Foucauld began his expedition in Tangier, and subsequently traveled through towns and villages of the Middle and Grand Atlas Mountains, departing Morocco in May 1884 at Oujda on the Algerian frontier. In 1885, he was awarded the Gold Medal by the Geographical Society of Paris. His book, *Reconnaissance au Maroc* (Paris, 1888), was published in two volumes, one of which was an atlas that included his carefully compiled geographical field notes. Foucauld's atlas was a major source of intelligence when the French Foreign Legion invaded Morocco in the early twentieth century.

In 1886, Foucauld retreated to the Catholic Church and was ordained as a Trappist priest in 1901. For the remainder of his life he lived as an ascetic. In 1904, he moved to Tamanrasset, in the Ahaggar region of the Sahara Desert, where, on December 1, 1916, he was murdered by Tuareg tribesmen who claimed that he was a French spy.

[*See also* Abi-Serour, Mordecai.]

BIBLIOGRAPHY

Bazin, René. *Charles de Foucauld, Hermit and Explorer.* Translated by Peter Keelan. London: Oates and Washbourne, 1923.

Foucauld, Charles de. *Reconnaissance au Maroc, 1883–1884.* 2 vols. Paris: Challamal, 1888.

SANFORD H. BEDERMAN

Foureau, Fernand (1850–1914), French explorer of the Sahara region. Fernand Foureau was born in Saint-Barbant in Limousin, France, on October 17, 1850, into a bourgeois household. The French-German war broke out as he was studying at the École Centrale. He enlisted in the army as a volunteer and was taken prisoner on January 19, 1871, at the Battle of Saint Quentin.

He took his first trip to Algeria in 1876, accompanied by Lieutenant Louis Say. The following year, he created the Oued Rhir Society, which promoted the digging of wells and implantation of palm groves between Biskra and Touggourt. He became familiar with Saharan customs and learned Arabic and some Berber dialects.

After the massacre of the Flatters mission of 1881, Foureau persevered and proposed to French authorities an exploration of the Sahara. He was given several missions by the government of Algeria as well as various other ministries between 1882 and 1897, and made nine journeys into the Algerian Sahara from Touggourt. He explored the Tademait, Tidikelt, the great Western and Eastern Ergs, and the Tassili-n-Ajjer. As opposed to Henri Duveyrier, Foureau was always suspicious of the Touaregs, and only traveled with his Chaamba guides. As of 1895, he was convinced that only a large-scale military gesture could ensure a permanent French presence in these regions. Upon his return in 1898, he was able to convince his sponsors of the need to undertake such a venture and received financial support from the Société de Géographie (Geographical Society of Paris).

On October 23, 1898, Foureau left from Ouargla on a mission across the Sahara. He had an escort headed by Commander François Lamy. They arrived in Agadez in July of 1899, and in Zinder in November. On February 18, 1900, a liaison was established with the Sudanese Joalland-Meynier mission and later with the Gentil mission. This "rendezvous on the Chad" solidified the definitive union of the various territories under French colonial rule. Beyond its political consequences, the Foureau-Lamy mission, one of the most important of the nineteenth century, brought forth considerable scientific information: geographical and geological data, as well as hydrographical, astronomical, and prehistoric data, all published in 1905.

Foureau received the gold medal of the Société de Géographie and joined the colonial administration in 1906. He was appointed governor of Mayotte and, later, governor of Martinique in April of 1908. He died in Paris on January 17, 1914.

[*See also* Duveyrier, Henri; Gentil, Émile; *and* Geographical Society of Paris.]

BIBLIOGRAPHY
Foureau, Fernand. *Mission saharienne Foureau-Lamy: D'Alger au Congo par le Tchad*. Paris: L'Harmattan, 1990.

OLIVIER LOISEAUX
Translated from the French by Frédéric Potter

Foxe, Luke (1586–1635), English navigator and explorer who searched for the Northwest Passage. Luke Foxe was born on October 20, 1586, the son of Richard Foxe or Fox, a mariner of Hull, Yorkshire, and he followed his father to sea at an early age. Fairly late in life, with much experience of the sea behind him, Foxe fulfilled a youthful ambition when he successfully petitioned Charles I for the use of a seventy-ton royal pinnace, the *Charles*, to search for a Northwest Passage from Hudson Bay to the Pacific. As he explained, "I had beene itching

Polar Map. From *North-west Fox, or, Fox from the North-West Passage* (London, 1635). This remarkable map (the British Isles are at top right) shows Foxe's track in the area to the north of Hudson Bay; the place names are given from A to H in the small key above the flying fox on the bottom left. COURTESY THE NEWBERRY LIBRARY, CHICAGO

after it ever since 1606" (that is, ever since he failed to gain a post on an Arctic voyage; Christy, vol. 1, pp. lvii–lviii). With the expedition financed by London merchants, Foxe left England within days of a rival Bristol venture commanded by Thomas James, and by mid-July 1631 he had struggled through Hudson Strait into Hudson Bay. Foxe explored the west coast of the bay from Thomas Button's discouraging Ne Ultra (No Farther) of 1612–1613 in the bay's northwest corner to James Bay in the south, but without finding any opening. He then turned north through the strait between Baffin Island and Southampton Island (later named Foxe Channel) and into today's Foxe Basin, where he crossed the Arctic Circle to reach his farthest north at latitude 66°47′ N. He then headed for home, reaching England at the end of October without suffering any deaths among his crew.

The firsthand if quirky account that Foxe wrote of his adventures, *North-West Fox*, published in 1635, included references to navigational innovations such as the use of logarithms and of the ship's log, but it was far from being a technical treatise. Foxe's acerbic style was well illustrated in the description of his encounter with James off the southwest coast of Hudson Bay, when the two captains disagreed over protocol. Foxe wrote: "I did not thinke much for his keeping out his flagg . . . To this was replide, that hee was going to the Emperour of *Japon*, with letters from his Maiestie . . . 'Keep it up then,' quoth I, 'but you are out of the way to *Japon*, for this is not it' " (Christy, vol. 2, p. 359). More significantly, there was just enough in Foxe's journal and chart to revive hopes a hundred years later that there might yet be a passage through Ne Ultra, for one reading of his entry for June 27, 1631, seemed to suggest that he had observed there a flood tide of eighteen feet flowing from the west—to optimistic eighteenth-century advocates of a Northwest Passage such as Arthur Dobbs, a sure sign of a connection with the Pacific Ocean. Furthermore, the printed chart of Foxe's voyage changed Button's name of "Ne Ultra" to "Ut Ultra" (Go Farther). In other ways, too, Foxe left his mark on the Hudson Bay region, for many of its prominent natural features were either named by him or later given his name. For all the bravura of his voyage account, this skillful navigator died impoverished in July 1635, within a few months of the account's publication.

The immediate effect of the voyages of Foxe and James was to bring to a halt to voyages sent out in search of the Northwest Passage. Hudson's discovery of 1611 seemed to be an enclosed, if huge, bay rather than the "wide sea" leading to the Pacific that he had hoped for. Yet the repeated Arctic voyages of the English from Frobisher's time onward were not without result. A tradition of Arctic navigation was established, and explorers learned how to deal with problems of navigating through ice, compass variation, and the phenomenal rise and fall of the tides. These skills would prove profitable in future days, as the great trades in cod, whales, and furs developed in northern regions.

[*See also* Arctic, *subentry on* Early Knowledge; Hudson, Henry; James, Thomas; *and* Northwest Passage.]

BIBLIOGRAPHY

Christy, Miller, ed. *The Voyages of Captain Luke Foxe of Hull and Captain Thomas James of Bristol.* 2 vols. London: Hakluyt Society, 1894.

Morley, William F. E. "Luke Fox (Foxe)." *Dictionary of Canadian Biography*, vol. 1, pp. 311–312. Toronto: University of Toronto Press, 1966.

GLYNDWR WILLIAMS

Franciscans. The charismatic leader Francis of Assisi founded the movement that came to be known as the Order of Friars Minor (OFM), popularly called the Franciscans, in the thirteenth century. Although born to a wealthy family of cloth merchants, Francis underwent a spiritual crisis and eventually rejected that life and dedicated himself to the imitation of Christ. The pursuit of apostolic poverty was central to his teachings, and he codified these teachings in a rule that would govern the daily life and activity of his followers. After several attempts, this Rule was approved by the papacy in 1209 and the Franciscan order became formally established. During his life, Francis revised the Rule at least one additional time (in 1223). Following his death, as a result of differing interpretations of the Rule, the order suffered from several internal divisions, eventually forming three large families: the Observants, the Conventuals, and the Capuchins. On the Iberian Peninsula, the Observants and the Conventuals came to predominate. In the late fifteenth and early sixteenth centuries a wave of reform swept over the order, targeting the Conventuals. The reform movement called for a return to the purity of the early rule and the centrality of apostolic poverty. The first missionaries to the Americas came out of this reform movement.

The Franciscans supported missionary vocations from the very beginning of the order. Francis himself hoped to lead a group of missionaries to the Holy

Land to convert Muslims to Christianity. When the Spanish began settlement of the New World, the Franciscan order played a critical role in the conversion of the natives. One of the first missionaries to Hispaniola, sailing on Columbus's second voyage, was a Franciscan, Father Buil (Boyle).

The Franciscan order was the first to conduct significant evangelization in what is now Mexico and the United States. The first true missionaries to Mexico included three Flemish friars who arrived immediately upon the fall of the Aztec empire to Hernán Cortés and his native allies. Shortly thereafter, an organized contingent of twelve friars arrived from Spain to form the Custody of the Holy Gospel, inspired by the reforming movement in Spain but subject to the minister-general in Rome. The missionary movement expanded rapidly until the order had established hundreds of missions in central and western Mexico.

Franciscan missionaries were among the first to arrive in Peru, rapidly expanding to assist in the evangelization of that territory. The Franciscans were the first order in what is now Ecuador. Slightly later the order also expanded into Chile in the south and what is now Colombia in the north. After initial Jesuit efforts in Florida, the Franciscans established an extensive series of missions in the southeastern part of the United States in the sixteenth and seventeenth centuries. A few decades later, the Franciscans entered what is now New Mexico and established a series of missions in that region. Franciscans based in Mexico were also active in the evangelization of the Philippines and Japan, several being martyred in the latter when pogroms against Christians were launched in the late sixteenth and early seventeenth centuries.

By the mid-seventeenth century, the order had missions through the Americas and in Asia and was easily the largest of the religious orders in the New World. As evangelization diminished, the friars became involved in the day-to-day administration of the parishes that grew out of their missions. Nevertheless, the Spanish crown claimed the right to administer all parishes within the New World. In a process called secularization, which continued in Latin America until about 1740, parishes passed from control of the religious orders to the local bishop and diocesan clergy.

In the late seventeenth and early eighteenth centuries, new missionary opportunities arose as the Spanish empire continued to expand. Franciscans established Colegios de Propaganda Fide (Colleges for the Propagation of the Faith), institutions dedicated to training friars for missionary activity. Friars from these schools were instrumental in the evangelization of what is now Texas and California, as well as the spread of missions in Central America and along the eastern slopes of the Andes in South America.

Franciscan missionary methods relied heavily on conversion through example. The friars reasoned that by adopting apostolic poverty and the mildness of Christ they would attract natives to Christianity. By the middle years of the seventeenth century, however, the order increasingly relied on the company of the Spanish military to help pacify the frontier, allowing for evangelization in the frontier areas.

[*See also* Cortés, Hernán, *and* Expeditions, World Exploration, *subentry on* Spain.]

BIBLIOGRAPHY

Ricard, Robert. *The Spiritual Conquest of Mexico: An Essay on the Apostolate and the Evangelizing Methods of the Mendicant Orders in New Spain, 1523–1572.* Translated by Lesley Byrd Simpson. Berkeley: University of California Press, 1966.

Short, William J. *The Franciscans.* Wilmington, Del.: Glazier, 1989.

Sylvest, Edwin Edward, Jr. *Motifs of Franciscan Mission Theory in Sixteenth Century New Spain Province of the Holy Gospel.* Washington, D.C.: Academy of American Franciscan History, 1975.

JOHN F. SCHWALLER

Franklin, John (1786–1847), British Arctic explorer. John Franklin was born at Spilsby in Lincolnshire into a family of twelve, the children of Willingham and Hannah Franklin. He entered the Royal Navy in 1800 as a First Class Volunteer, and began his adventures in exploration in 1801 under his cousin Matthew Flinders, captain of HMS *Investigator* during the expedition to survey the coasts of Australia. On his return, Franklin played a part in the French wars at the battle of Copenhagen and at Trafalgar (1805). During the war with the United States, Franklin was a participant in the attack on New Orleans in 1814.

Franklin's first venture to the Arctic was in 1818 as captain of HMS *Trent*, one of four vessels dispatched by the Admiralty to renew the search for a northern sea route to the Far East, a search begun in the time of the Tudor monarchs. The *Trent* accompanied HMS *Dorothea*, under Captain David Buchan, in sailing north toward the pole, where it was hoped that an open polar sea existed. The two ships met the heavy multiyear sea ice at about 80° N, as had Captain Constantine John Phipps in 1773. The *Dorothea* was badly damaged by the floes; Franklin's ship less so.

Franklin was eager to continue the attempt to penetrate the pack northward, but Buchan ordered the squadron home. A narrative of the voyage was not published until 1843, when F. W. Beechey's book appeared. Franklin had had his first encounter with the ice and had acquitted himself well.

Presumably because of this and because of his earlier experience with Flinders, Franklin was appointed in 1819 to lead an overland journey across the north of America to the shores of the polar sea. This coast had been reached in only two places: the mouth of the Coppermine River and the estuary of the Mackenzie River. Franklin was instructed to navigate the Coppermine River to the Arctic Ocean and then to chart the coast eastward. Franklin's small party consisted of Dr. John Richardson, a naval surgeon, and two midshipmen, George Back and Robert Hood, who were partly picked for their ability to draw (in the days before photography). Also in the party were a stout and loyal seaman, John Hepburn, and four Orkney boatmen recruited in the islands.

After crossing the Atlantic in the Hudson's Bay Company supply ship *Prince of Wales*, the party disembarked at York Factory on the west coast of Hudson Bay, where Franklin obtained assurances of help from the officers of the Hudson's Bay Company and the North West Company, companies that were bitter and antagonistic rivals in the fur trade. These assurances were to prove worthless. Franklin's party made its way upriver and northwest into the interior via the fur-trading posts, and eventually made contact with the Copper Indian chief Akaitcho and located the Coppermine River overland. A log house was built for winter quarters (1820–1821) and named Fort Enterprise. From there Franklin's party departed for the Coppermine and the polar sea on June 14, 1821, accompanied by French Canadian voyageurs, Akaitcho, and some of the Copper (Chipewyan) Indians.

The descent of the Coppermine had been made in 1771 by Samuel Hearne. From the mouth of the river, Franklin's party of twenty embarked in birch-bark canoes, traveling eastward to explore a rocky and often ice-infested coast. On August 22, they turned back at Point Turnagain. Fearing that the canoes would not survive the hazardous return voyage along the coast to the mouth of the Coppermine, Franklin decided to ascend the newly discovered Hood River toward Fort Enterprise—having covered, he estimated later, more than 650 geographical miles on the Arctic Sea. The party found itself traveling across unmapped and barren country during the onset of an early and chilling winter. Because the voyageurs were used to paddling along rivers, not

marching across land, they grew despondent and rebellious, but had no choice but to rely on the naval officers (who were also more at home at sea than ashore) for navigating across country unknown to all. Unfortunately, the voyageurs threw away the fishing tackle and took so little care of the small canoes, which were made from the big coastal ones, that there was no means of crossing the Coppermine when at last they reached it. Dr. Richardson attempted to swim across it with a line, but in the end Saint Germain, one of the two interpreters, made a canoe out of willow branches and canvas so that the crossing could be made. Little game was encountered, and the only food was a lichen (*tripe de roche*), their leather shoes, and their clothing.

The situation grew worse and worse, the party weaker and weaker. Young Hood was shot by Michel, an Iroquois Indian, who appears to have been feeding on a murdered comrade. Fearing for his and others' lives, Dr. Richardson took the decision to shoot Michel. Franklin and Back had gone ahead, but found Fort Enterprise deserted, with no message and no promised supplies. Back was able to find the Indians and, almost at the last gasp, returned with them to take care of and feed the survivors: Franklin and the naval contingent (bar Hood), only five out of thirteen of the interpreters and voyageurs, and one of the two Eskimo (Inuit). Franklin became celebrated as "the man who ate his boots" (in fact, soft moccasins). Having lost his own journal in a river crossing, he had to write his published narrative in part from those of the other officers. The book appeared in 1823, beautifully produced and illustrated. Modern editions of Hood's, Back's, and Richardson's journals by Stuart Houston and of Franklin's by Richard C. Davis have greatly added to the literature, but these editions have been overcritical of Franklin, not fully appreciating the difficulties under which he labored—in particular, the virtual warfare among the fur traders and his (and the Admiralty's) unfamiliarity with the terrain, the climate, the Indians, and the voyageurs, despite the advice of Sir Alexander Mackenzie and other fur traders.

Franklin learned a great deal during this first overland journey, and he returned in 1825 (by which time the rival fur companies had merged) to map much of the remaining coast of the north of America, this time descending the great river named after Alexander Mackenzie, situated to the west of the Coppermine, in 1826. The birch-bark canoes had been replaced by sturdy river boats with oars and sails, and a light portable boat called the "walnut shell" was provided for the crossing of rivers. The party divided at the delta, where the river debouches into the Arctic Ocean. Dr. Richardson, with Midshipman Kendall, Ouligbuck, an Eskimo (Inuit) interpreter, and nine men in the boats *Dolphin* and *Union*, traveled eastward. Meanwhile, Franklin and Back, Augustus, another Eskimo, and thirteen men in the boats *Lion* and *Reliance* endeavored to sail or drag the boats along the flat, muddy, icy, and foggy shore toward Cook's Icy Cape and then, in Russian America (Alaska), to link up with a boat party from HMS *Blossom*, ordered for this purpose by the Admiralty to Kotzebue Sound on the Bering Sea.

On August 6, halfway to Icy Cape, Franklin took the prudent decision to turn back at Return Reef. The party ascended the Mackenzie to arrive safely at winter quarters in Fort Franklin on Great Bear Lake on September 21. Richardson's party had done well, reaching the mouth of the Coppermine along a more indented coast for 102 statute miles and returning up the Coppermine River to winter on Great Bear Lake in the log house named after Franklin. Franklin produced a second fine narrative in 1828, again illustrated with plates and with folding maps at the end. The two overland journeys provided the first maps of the north coast of America, plus scientific observations of value.

Franklin resumed his naval career, having been knighted in 1829. His first wife, Eleanor (née Porden), the charming "poetess," had died in February 1825, leaving an infant daughter. His second wife was the lively and determined Jane (née Griffin), who accompanied him to Van Diemen's Land (Tasmania), where Franklin had been appointed lieutenant-governor in 1836. That tight little island, south of the Australian mainland, had been a penal colony since 1803. Although the Franklins contributed to cultural life—founding the Royal Society of Tasmania and the Tasmanian Society, for instance—they were caught in the crossfire between opposing factions. To their indignation and distress, the colonial secretary, Lord Stanley, recalled Franklin in 1843; Franklin wrote a thorough defense of his conduct, but the minister turned a deaf ear to it.

The news that another seaborne expedition was to be sent by the Admiralty to find what it was hoped would prove to be the last link in a navigable sea route between the Pacific and Atlantic oceans at once aroused the interest, and indeed the hopes, of the veteran Sir John Franklin and of Lady Franklin. They considered that, if appointed (at the age of fifty-eight), Franklin would have the ideal opportunity to clear his name—in his own element, the sea. Franklin did secure the appointment to command HMS

Erebus and HMS *Terror*, both bomb vessels that had returned from a brilliant voyage to the Antarctic regions under Captain James Clark Ross, with Captain F. R. M. Crozier as second in command. Crozier sailed again in the *Terror* with Franklin, although he wished that Ross were still his senior officer.

The two vessels had been fitted with engines to aid their navigation in ice. They departed on May 19, 1845, from Greenhithe on the Thames, and they reached the Whalefish Islands in Disco Bay, western Greenland, in early July, when the stores from the accompanying transport vessel (which carried letters home) were transferred to the exploring ships. These, the *Erebus* and the *Terror*, were last sighted at the end of the month by two whalers.

From the investigations by the numerous expeditions sent to the Arctic after the *Erebus* and the *Terror* disappeared, we know that the two ships wintered at Beechey Island in 1845–1846 and were beset in heavy ice to the southwest in 1846, from which they never escaped. A terse record, written after the ships were abandoned, was discovered in a cairn on the west coast of King William Island in 1848; it stated that Franklin had died on June 11, 1847. There were no details of the cause of his death. At least he was spared the tragic end of an expedition that had departed with such high hopes.

Three impressive statues—in London's Waterloo Place, in Spilsby, Lincolnshire, and in Hobart, Tasmania—commemorate Franklin. A plaque in Westminster Abbey bears the following inscription, written by his kinsman by marriage, the poet Alfred, Lord Tennyson:

Not here! The white North hath thy bones, and thou Heroic sailor soul,
Art passing on thy happier voyage now
Towards no earthly pole.

[*See also*; Arctic, *subentry on* Nineteenth-century Images; Franklin Sea Expeditions; Northwest Passage *and biographical entries on figures mentioned in this article.*]

BIBLIOGRAPHY

Beardsley, Martyn. *Deadly Winter: The Life of Sir John Franklin.* London, Chatham, 2002.

Cyriax, R. J. *Sir John Franklin's Last Arctic Expedition.* London: Arctic, *subentry on* Nineteenth-century Images; Franklin Search Expeditions; Methuen, 1939. Reprint. Plaistow, U.K.: Arctic: Press, 1997.

Franklin, Sir John. *Sir John Franklin's Journals and Correspondence: The First Arctic Land Expedition, 1819–1822.* Edited by Richard C. Davis. Toronto: Champlain Society, 1995.

Franklin, Sir John. *Sir John Franklin's Journals and Correspondence: The Second Arctic Land Expedition, 1825–1827.*

Edited by Richard C. Davis. Toronto: Champlain Society, 1998.

McGoogan, Ken. *Lady Franklin's Revenge*. London: Bantam, 2006.

Savours, Ann. *The Search for the North West Passage*. London: Chatham; New York: St. Martins Press, 1999.

ANN SAVOURS

Franklin Search Expeditions.

The disappearance of Sir John Franklin and his two ships led to the most extensive search operation that the Arctic has ever seen. The operation failed in that the searches found no survivors from the expedition, but in the process the searches uncovered many details

Franklin Search Expeditions. Silver fork and spoons from the Franklin expedition, in Charles Francis Hall's *Narrative of the Second Arctic Expedition* (Washington, 1879). For some years after the disappearance of the Franklin Expedition, explorers in the Arctic recovered artifacts that had come from it. Here is some elegant cutlery gathered by Charles Francis Hall in the 1860s. COURTESY THE NEWBERRY LIBRARY, CHICAGO

about the fate of Franklin and his men, and added greatly to the world's knowledge of the Arctic.

Sir John Barrow had thought that the remaining distance of nine hundred nautical miles linking William Parry's discoveries of 1819–1820 with the north coast of America would be accomplished in one year. Franklin's instructions of 1845 were not very specific, because they could not be. He was to navigate Lancaster Sound/Barrow Strait as far as Cape Walker, situated on a small island off the north coast of Prince of Wales Island, to the west of Somerset Island, then navigate southwest through the blank area on the chart to reach the coast familiar to him from his overland expeditions, then navigate west to Bering Strait. Supposing there was no open water south of Cape Walker, the orders directed him to try for a passage up Wellington Channel on the north shore, between Devon and Cornwallis Island, discovered but not entered by Parry in 1819 and 1820.

Having departed from the Thames on May 19, 1845, the *Erebus* and the *Terror* were last seen by whalers in July off the west coast of Greenland. When the ships did not emerge after one year, there was no panic because they were provisioned for three years. They had been fitted with railway engines to help when navigating in ice. Second in command to Sir John Franklin in HMS *Terror* was Captain F. R. M. Crozier, who was experienced in Arctic waters and who had returned not long before from the Southern Ocean, where he had been captain of HMS *Terror* and second in command to Sir James Clark Ross during the celebrated Antarctic voyage of 1839–1843.

Worries and First Searches. No news of the Franklin Expedition having been received by December 1846, Lady Franklin, Sir John's remarkable and devoted second wife, expressed her fears to Sir James Clark Ross, hoping that he would be the man to search for the expedition if need be. The following year was one of dashed hopes and terrible anxiety. Sir John Ross early expressed his concern, while the naval surgeon Sir John Richardson, with the Admiralty's approval, ordered quantities of canned pemmican to be made at the Clarence Victualling Yard, Gosport, which (in Richardson's words) happened to be "fully occupied night and day preparing flour and biscuit for the relief of the famishing population of Ireland." At the age of sixty, the good doctor Richardson was prepared to set off across North America on an arduous and trying journey, with four boats built by the Navy Board, to try to find his old friend and chief, Sir John Franklin. Dr. John Rae, a chief trader of the Hudson's Bay Company, was to accompany him, as were five seamen and fifteen "intelligent artisans."

This overland expedition down the Mackenzie River and then east to search along the coast as far as the Coppermine River was part of a three-pronged plan by the Admiralty to relieve Franklin, detained somewhere between the Atlantic and Pacific oceans. HMS *Plover*, under Commander T. E. L. Moore, was to join HMS *Herald* and search the coast of Russian America (Alaska) by boat eastward as far as the Mackenzie. Sir James Clark Ross, also a volunteer, was given command of two new ice-strengthened ships, HMS *Enterprise* and HMS *Investigator*, to search from the Atlantic end. Ross evidently believed that the *Erebus* and the *Terror* were beset in the multiyear or "polar" ice, whose huge dimensions only he had witnessed at Melville Island in 1820 and at King William Island in 1830.

These plans would have been effective in an open ice year. Unfortunately, because Sir James Ross's ships were unable to penetrate the length of Parry Channel westward, sledging parties could not branch out over the ice and land to the south and north—at a time when there was still a chance of finding members of the lost expedition alive and at least some of their records intact. Captain F. W. Beechey, together with Dr. Richard King, who had descended the Great Fish River with the naval officer George Back, expressed the opinion that a boat should be sent down that river to the coast. Lady Franklin thought that a search in such an unlikely area might prove fruitful before it was too late; in the event, however, it was to be a decade before the fate of the lost ships and their complements became known. The last survivors had indeed reached the estuary of the Great Fish (or Back) River, but no help from the south was at hand.

No sign of Franklin was found by Richardson and Rae, nor by the *Plover*, while James Clark Ross's *Enterprise* and *Investigator* were so beset by the ice in 1848–1849 that they drifted eastward for 250 miles, not being released until September 1849. However, Ross knew how to make sledge journeys, and it was this skill in particular that was needed during the Franklin Search. He would walk around and survey any large bays, while Leopold McClintock, Robert McClure, and other novice travelers on land would take the man-hauled sledges by the more direct route. In this way a new generation of Arctic officers was taught the art of polar travel. The shores of Peel Sound were searched. It was so heavily choked with ice that the sledgers concluded that any vessel forced down it would meet destruction from the floes. Little did they know that it was almost certainly down this strait, when there must have been open water, that the *Erebus* and the *Terror* had sailed to their doom two years before.

Later Searches. This first concerted effort to find the lost expedition proved fruitless and, of course, heartbreaking for Lady Franklin and for the other wives and families of the officers and men of HMS *Erebus* and HMS *Terror*. Lady Franklin sent many letters with the search vessels, only to have them returned unopened. During the decade after his disappearance, Lady Franklin demonstrated her abiding love for Franklin through almost ceaseless activity: organizing her own expeditions, as well as urging the governments of both Great Britain and the United States to do likewise. She wrote even to the emperor of Russia and to the emperor of France. Two French naval officers did take part in the search.

Signs of the lost ships were discovered in August 1850 by Captain Erasmus Ommanney of HMS *Assistance*, one of the squadron commanded by Captain Horatio Austin, which consisted of two steamers, the *Pioneer* and the *Intrepid*, along with two sailing ships, the *Assistance* and the *Resolute*. While walking on the beach with a party of officers under the bluff headland of Cape Riley on Beechey Island, Ommanney found some ragged clothing, preserved meat tins, and naval stores, which he concluded must have been left there at least three years earlier. A cairn was sighted on the summit of the island, where Ommanney expected to find a record placed there by members of the lost expedition on its departure in the spring of 1846. The cairn was dismantled and the surrounding area dug over, but no record was found. It has been surmised that the sea ice may have loosened, giving the ships a chance to depart and leaving Franklin's men no time to spare in climbing up to the cairn to deposit a paper setting out their intentions. However, a historian of the Franklin Expedition and of the subsequent search, Dr. R. J. Cyriax, has pointed out that Franklin had no obligation to deposit records.

Beechey Island is a small appendage to the far bigger Devon Island, situated on the north shores of Parry Channel. Union Bay was given its name because so many of the search vessels gathered there in 1850. News of the discovery of the relics came a few days after the discovery. A messenger brought the news over to a little group in Union Bay that consisted of the whaling captain William Penny (sent by Lady Franklin); the two Americans from the first

Grinnell expedition in the *Advance* and the *Rescue*, Captain Edwin De Haven and Dr. Elisha Kent Kane; and last but not least, the veteran Sir John Ross and his deputy, Commander Phillips, of the little *Felix*. The messenger also reported that graves had been found near the lost expedition's winter quarters. There were three graves, each with a wooden headboard, on which were chiseled the names of John Hartnell and William Braine, Royal Marines, both of HMS *Erebus*, and John Torrington of HMS *Terror*. Two had died in January 1846 and one in April 1846. Hartnell's grave was excavated in secret two years later (in 1852) by Commander E. A. Inglefield—with difficulty because of the frozen ground—but in it was no clue as to the fate of the expedition. The exhumations by the Canadian doctor Owen Beattie in the 1980s showed how carefully and indeed reverently the burials had been performed.

Not knowing that Franklin's ships had gone south after leaving winter quarters, a considerable effort was put into the search to the north, both by the naval squadron and accompanying vessels (1850–1851) and by the later squadron consisting of the same ships under the overall command of the irascible Captain Edward Belcher (1852–1854). During the winters, the production of a number of newspapers or magazines enlivened the dark days, as did theatricals and other diversions, in addition to the taking of meteorological and magnetic observations. Smith Sound, at the head of Baffin Bay, was entered for the first time in 1852 by Commander E. A. Inglefield in the yacht *Isabel*, to be followed in 1853–1855 by the second Grinnell expedition in the *Advance*, commanded by Dr. Elisha Kent Kane, U.S. Navy. No signs of Franklin were found during either expedition.

Instructions to the naval vessels emphasized that geographical exploration must always be subservient to the search for the missing expedition. Much of the activity served to show where Franklin had *not* been. Captain Penny was indefatigable and resourceful in searching (and exploring) the waters beyond Wellington Channel. According to the eminent geographer Sir Clements Markham, the naval squadron, in its sledge traveling—largely organized by McClintock (1850–1851)—covered just over seven thousand miles on foot, discovering well over one thousand miles of new land. They were members of the genial and warmhearted Captain Austin's "happy family." A year later, two ships of Captain Belcher's squadron, the *Assistance* and the *Pioneer*, wintered much less happily under a difficult commander at the high northern latitude of 77°52′, be-

yond Captain Penny's explorations, on the north shore of their discovery, Northumberland Sound. No traces of Franklin were found by the boat and sledge parties, which while searching added more unknown islands to the chart. The vessels were abandoned to the ice on Belcher's orders on August 25, 1854.

The other half of Belcher's squadron of 1852–1854 under Captain Henry Kellett, the *Resolute* and the *Intrepid*, wintered at the western end of Parry Channel, not far from Parry's old winter quarters at Melville Island. From these vessels, sledge journeys of over one thousand miles were made individually by McClintock and Lieutenant Frederick Mecham and their men, during which Prince Patrick Island, on the rim of the Central Polar Basin, was discovered and explored—but, again, no signs of Franklin were found.

The expeditions so far mentioned had entered the Arctic Archipelago from the Atlantic. The Admiralty dispatched HMS *Enterprise*, under Captain Richard Collinson, and HMS *Investigator*, under Commander Robert McClure, to search from the Pacific end. [See color plate 37 in this volume.] The junior captain, McClure, stole a march on his superior officer and entered the icy seas a year earlier, in 1850. Neither the *Investigator* nor the *Enterprise* was successful in discovering the fate of Franklin, although pieces of a door frame, marked with a broad arrow, were found on an island in Dease Strait by Collinson in July 1853. The view has been expressed that had McClure waited for Collinson, the two ships would have proceeded in company so that sledge parties would almost certainly have reached King William Island, where the Franklin tragedy was enacted. As it was, McClure discovered two possible Northwest Passages, one around Banks Island and the other up Prince of Wales Strait. The *Investigator* wintered twice, without being released from the ice, in Mercy Bay on the north coast of Banks Island. Fortunately, a record deposited at Parry's Rock on Melville Island was found by a sledge party from Captain Kellett's ships, and the crew of the *Investigator* was rescued. On return to England, they were awarded £10,000 for discovering the Northwest Passage. Captain Collinson's remarkable voyage sadly met with no acclaim.

Rounding the north point of what is now Alaska at Point Barrow a year later (in 1851) than McClure had, Collinson followed in the wake of the *Investigator* up and down Prince of Wales Strait and then wintered twice off Victoria Island, the second time at Cambridge Bay. Collinson's parties searched the west coast of Victoria Strait, overlapping the boat journey made by that remarkable Arctic traveler, Dr. John Rae. Unfortunately, both Rae and Collinson traveled along the west coast of Victoria Strait. Had they traveled on the other (eastern) side, along King William Island's west coast, the remains of the Franklin Expedition might have been found in 1853, five years earlier than they actually were found. Collinson's navigation of a large vessel along the waters north of the mainland was extraordinary. He met groups of Inuit, but could learn little from them because Johann Miertsching, the interpreter, was aboard the *Investigator*. The first actual navigator of the Northwest Passage, Roald Amundsen, paid a fine tribute to Collinson in his narrative of his voyage in the *Gjøa* (1903–1906).

Final Answers. After all these efforts, public and private, the first definite indication of the fate of the Franklin Expedition was found by chance. Dr. John Rae had returned after his Search journeys to his duties as an officer of the Hudson's Bay Company, and he was making a survey of that last section of the mainland coast to the east, beyond the explorations of Peter Warren Dease and Thomas Simpson, also of the Hudson's Bay Company. He came across a number of Inuit during his journey to Castor and Pollux River from Repulse Bay. From these Inuit and from others who visited him later at Repulse Bay, he learned that four winters earlier (spring 1850) about forty white men were seen traveling southward over the ice by Inuit who were killing seals near the north shore of King William Island. All but one looked thin. Later in the same season, some thirty bodies were found on the continent and five more on an island (Montreal Island) in what Rae concluded must be Back's Great Fish River. Some had been buried, while others were in a tent, under a boat, or scattered where they had died. "From the mutilated state of many of the corpses and the contents of the kettles," wrote Rae in his report to the Admiralty (July 29, 1854), "it is evident that our wretched countrymen had been driven to the last resource—cannibalism—as a means of prolonging existence."

Although it had been drawn up at Repulse Bay, Rae delivered his report in person to the Admiralty on his arrival in London toward the end of October 1854. The report was published in the London *Times* by the Admiralty and caused great offense. Charles Dickens was among those who defended the defenseless dead. Despite Lady Franklin's protests, Rae received £8,000 and his men £2,000 among them for having ascertained the fate of Franklin. The editors of his correspondence, J. M. Wordie and R. J. Cyriax, expressed regret that Rae had brought relics and his report so quickly to London, rather than having investigated himself the places indicated by the Inuit. However, the following year (1855) a boat expedition down Back's Great Fish River was organized by the Hudson's Bay Company and financed by the British government. Led by chief trader James Anderson and James Green Stewart, the results of the expedition were disappointing, owing to the lack of an interpreter. Some relics were found on Montreal Island, thus confirming Rae's report.

With the Crimean War to fight, the Admiralty can be forgiven for not pursuing the search for Franklin, especially since much money had been expended already on the numerous naval expeditions. Lady Franklin campaigned after the war for one last official expedition to be sent. When the government refused, she bought the yacht *Fox* and asked McClintock to command it. The Admiralty granted leave to McClintock and was generous with naval stores, instruments, pemmican, clothing, and books. Through public subscription, £3,000 was raised. Lady Franklin's instructions indicated priorities: first, the recovery of survivors, then the retrieval of relics, and last, possible confirmation of Dr. Rae's report that the lost expedition had indeed discovered a Northwest Passage.

The *Fox* (177 tons) was away for two years, 1857–1859. It returned with many sad relics of the lost expedition, mainly from the forbidding west coast of King William Island. By reaching Cape Herschel on the southwest corner of King William Island, any survivors (and the abandoned ships) would have linked Dease and Simpson's surveys with their own discoveries. A skeleton proved, in Sir John Richardson's words, that "they had forged the last link with their lives." The greatest prize, found by McClintock, was the last record, one of the two found in cairns on the coast of King William Island. This record is a single sheet of paper (now in the National Maritime Museum, Greenwich), crumbled at the edges after several years in a tin cylinder. It is tantalizingly brief, but tells that Sir John Franklin had died on June 11, 1847, and that the ships were abandoned on April 22, 1848, beset in the ice off King William Island, having wintered at Beechey Island in 1846–1847 (presumably a mistake in the writing of the record). Nine officers and fifteen men had died. The remaining 105 souls, under the command of Captain F. R. M. Crozier, were starting next day for Back's Fish River.

So ended the Franklin Search. Numerous parties have since visited King William Island and vicinity, the most notable being the expedition of Lieutenant

Frederick Schwatka of the U.S. Army in 1878–1880, but no more written evidence from the Franklin Expedition has come to light. The *Erebus* and the *Terror* have not been found. Many people have puzzled over what has been called the Inuit testimony, including the American C. F. Hall in the nineteenth century and David Woodman in the twentieth. All the members of the Arctic expeditions of 1818 to 1859, alive or dead, were awarded the Arctic Medal—not only the strangers from afar, but the native people who had played a part. Lady Franklin received the Founder's Gold Medal of the Royal Geographical Society.

[*See also* Northwest Passage *and biographical entries on figures mentioned in this article.*]

BIBLIOGRAPHY

Beattie, Owen, and John Geiger. *Frozen in Time: The Fate of the Franklin Expedition.* London: Bloomsbury, 1987. Rev. ed. Berkeley, Calif.: Greystone Books, 2004.

Berton, Pierre. *The Arctic Grail: The Quest for the North West Passage and the North Pole, 1818–1909.* Toronto: McClelland and Stewart, 1988.

Cyriax, R. J. *Sir John Franklin's Last Arctic Expedition.* London: Methuen, 1939. Reprint. Plaistow, U.K.: Arctic Press, 1997.

De Bray, Emile Frédéric. *A Frenchman in Search of Franklin: De Bray's Arctic Journal 1852–1854.* Translated and edited by William Barr. Toronto and Buffalo, N.Y.: University of Toronto Press, 1995.

Delgado, James P. *Across the Top of the World: The Quest for the Northwest Passage.* London: British Museum Press, 1999; New York: Facts On File, 1999.

Klutschak, Heinrich. *Overland to Starvation Cove: With the Inuit in Search of Franklin 1878–1880.* Translated and edited by William Barr. Toronto and Buffalo, N.Y.: University of Toronto Press, 1987.

McGoogan, Ken. *Lady Franklin's Revenge.* London: Bantam, 2006.

Murphy, David. *The Arctic Fox: Francis Leopold McClintock.* Wilton, Ireland: Collins, 2004; Toronto: Dundern, 2004.

Neatby, Leslie H. *The Search for Franklin.* Edmonton, Alberta: Hurtig, 1970.

Richards, Robert L. *Dr. John Rae.* Whitby, U.K.: Caedmon of Whitby, 1985.

Savours, Ann. *The Search for the North West Passage.* London: Chatham; New York: St. Martin's Press, 1999.

Sutherland, Patricia D., ed. *The Franklin Era in Canadian Arctic History, 1845–1859.* Ottawa, Ontario: National Museum of Man, 1995.

Woodman, David C. *Unravelling the Franklin Mystery: Inuit Testimony.* Montreal: McGill-Queen's University Press, 1991.

Woodman, David C. *Strangers among Us.* Montreal: McGill-Queen's University Press, 1996

ANN SAVOURS

Fraser, Simon (1776–1862), explorer of Canada. Born in Bennington, New York (later Vermont), to a loyalist military family, Fraser entered the service of the North West Company at age sixteen. By 1802 he was a partner; after 1804, and in union with rivals headed by the explorer Alexander Mackenzie, he pushed into north central British Columbia. Fraser called this area New Caledonia, for it reminded him of his mother's description of Scotland. Fraser played roles in countering American and Russian threats from the Pacific Coast. He was also a giant in business and community history: Fort McLeod (McLeod Lake) in 1805, Fort Saint James (Stuart Lake) and Fort Fraser (Fraser Lake) in 1806, and Fort George (now Mailasikkut; where the Fraser and Nechako rivers converge) in 1807 were all built under Fraser's direction. Meanwhile, John Stuart, James McDougall, and Jules Quesnel made discoveries often attributed to Fraser. Fraser diminished Mackenzie's discoveries by claiming that Mackenzie was often asleep in his canoe while others gathered data, but Mackenzie's reputation survived Fraser's belittling.

Fraser is best known for his 1808 river journey to Musqueam on the lower Fraser River. It was a passage made possible only by native advice, by Fraser's grit, and by his employers' insistence that the stream south of the Nechako River be traced. Fraser proved that the river named after him was not the Columbia. He named a tributary of the Fraser after the explorer David Thompson. He died at Saint Andrew's, Canada West (Ontario), on April 19, 1862.

[*See also* Hudson's Bay Company; Mackenzie, Alexander; *and* North West Company.]

BIBLIOGRAPHY

Lamb, W. Kaye, ed. *Simon Fraser: Letters and Journals, 1806–1808.* Toronto: Macmillan of Canada, 1960.

BARRY M. GOUGH

Frémont, John Charles (1813–1890), explorer of the western United States. As a twenty-five-year-old topographical engineer, Frémont surveyed the region between the Upper Mississippi and Missouri rivers, and later surveyed the Des Moines River with Jean Nicholas Nicollet. Sent by secretary of war Poinsett in 1842 and employing Christopher "Kit" Carson as a guide and Charles Preuss as a cartographer and artist, Frémont explored the Wind River Mountains and South Pass in Wyoming. Returning the following year, passing the Great Salt Lake, he followed the Snake and Columbia rivers to Fort Vancouver. Then traveling southeast to Walker Lake, he turned west into the Sierra Nevada Mountains near Lake Tahoe and reached Sutter's Fort after a danger-

"Pass in the Sierra Nevada of California." From John Charles Frémont's *Report of the Exploring Expedition to The Rocky Mountains in the Year 1842* (Washington, 1845). This striking image shows Frémont's party struggling through deep snow in the aptly named Sierra Nevada. It is easy to imagine that bad luck or bad weather could lead to catastrophe in these conditions. COURTESY THE NEWBERRY LIBRARY, CHICAGO

ous winter crossing. Traveling the San Joaquin Valley and then east through the Great Basin, he reached Bent's Fort near Pueblo on the Arkansas River and headed back to Kansas City.

His report of his expedition, published in 1845, was a joint venture of Frémont and his wife, Jessie Benton Frémont. Countless pioneers followed his maps west on what became known as the Oregon Trail. Encouragement for this undertaking came from his father-in-law, Senator Thomas Hart Benton of Missouri, who believed that settling the West was "America's Manifest Destiny." On his third expedition, ostensibly to study the Great Basin and Pacific Coast, Frémont was joined by the artist and mapmaker Edward Meyer Kern. Marching into California, he supported the Bear Flag rebellion against Mexico. Briefly appointed governor of California, he was court-martialed, then vindicated, but resigned his commission. Gold was discovered on his Mariposa, California, estate, making him a millionaire. The money was lost in railroad speculation and explorations that followed. Military appointments before and during the Civil War resulted in disappointments.

Frémont campaigned as the "Pathfinder"—and the first candidate of the newly formed Republican Party—during the 1856 presidential election, which he lost to James Buchanan. Frémont's public career ended with his term as governor of the Arizona Territory, 1878–1883.

[*See also* American West; Great Basin; Oregon Trail; *and* Rocky Mountains.]

BIBLIOGRAPHY

Egan, Ferol. *Frémont, Explorer for a Restless Nation.* Garden City, N.Y.: Doubleday, 1977.

Frémont, John Charles. *Report of the Exploring Expedition to the Rocky Mountains in the Year 1842 and to Oregon and North California in the Years 1843–'44.* Washington, D.C.: Gales and Seaton, 1845.

CLARENCE E. KYLANDER

Fritz, Samuel (1654–1724), Bohemian Jesuit missionary in South America. In 1686, the Society of Jesus in Quito dispatched Father Samuel Fritz to establish a teaching mission to the Omagua nation. The Omagua had ruled a prime, three-hundred-mile

---

Exploring the Rockies

Frémont wrote very feelingly of the wilderness into which he had ventured, and in which a bee joined his party. Alas, they captured the poor insect and "preserved" it between the pages of a book of pressed flowers.

During our morning's ascent [of the Rocky Mountains] we had met no sign of animal life, except the small sparrowlike bird already mentioned. A stillness the most profound and a terrible solitude forced themselves constantly on the mind as the great features of the place. Here, on the summit, where the stillness was absolute, unbroken by any sound, and the solitude complete, we thought ourselves beyond the region of animated life; but while we were sitting on the rock, a solitary bee (*bombus*, the bumblebee) came winging his flight from the eastern valley, and lit on the knee of one of the men.

—John Charles Frémont, *Report on an Exploration of the Country Lying between the Missouri River and the Rocky Mountains* (Washington, D.C., 1843))

(483-kilometer) stretch of the middle Amazon, but were now refugees from Portuguese slaving parties encroaching inexorably westward.

Fritz, born in 1654 at Tratenau, Bohemia, was exceptional even by the high intellectual and pious standards of the Jesuit order. Over the next three years, he learned the Omagua language and collected names of places and tribes that he would compile into a map. A profound and mutual respect developed between Fritz and his flock. His reputation encouraged other tribes to plead that Fritz protect them, too.

His workload proved too much. In 1689 he succumbed to malaria. Prostrate, he was carried 2,000 miles (3,220 kilometers) to the estuary to seek treatment at the Jesuit mission. He was nursed back to health, but denied permission to return. Fritz wrote to his superior in Quito, the viceroy, and even the king. Eighteen months and a change of governor later, he was allowed to leave Portuguese territory. Journeying upstream in better health, Fritz added to his manuscript map. Dismayed at the devastation caused by the *entradas* (long-range, armed incursions for exploration and slaving), he saw that the only hope for the remaining population would be a

Spanish military presence. Rather than go to Quito to plead his cause, he traveled to Lima to inform the viceroy in person.

Although received with veneration, Fritz failed to convince the viceroy that the region was worth a confrontation with Portugal. After a year he returned to his mission via a different set of tributaries, again adding to his map. Thereafter, unable to deter Portuguese slavers, Fritz devoted his energies to relocating refugees. In 1707 another Jesuit in Quito, Narvaes, produced a hand-printed version of the Fritz map. In about 1740 a French scientist, Charles-Marie de La Condamine, collected two copies in addition to Fritz's original manuscript map and a copy of Fritz's journal, all of which he took back to Paris. Fritz died in 1724, tended by a devoted flock, those "notorious savages and head-hunters," the Jívaros.

[*See also* Amazon River.]

BIBLIOGRAPHY
Edmundson, George, trans. and ed. *Journal of the Travels and Labours of Father Samuel Fritz in the River of the Amazons between 1686 and 1723.* London: Hakluyt Society, 1922.

Travels along the Amazon

Unaccustomed to the all-prevalent water, and vulnerable to a great variety of diseases, Samuel Fritz offers a terrifying account of the hardships involved in traveling at this time in the great valley of the Amazon River and its tributaries. His hardships make it all the more remarkable that at the end of his travels he was able to produce an amazingly accurate map of this huge region.

Meanwhile, as I was staying in this Jurimagua village, already almost wholly inundated, in a shelter on a roof made of the bark of trees, I fell sick of most violent attacks of fever and of dropsy that began in the feet, with other complaints principally caused by worms. I was obliged to remain day and night for the space of well-nigh three months shut up in this shelter without being able to stir. In the daytime I felt somewhat easier, but the nights in unutterable burnings . . . and in sleeplessness, caused not only by my infirmities, but also from the gruntings of the crocodiles or lizards that all night long were roving round the village, beasts of horrible deformity.

—*Journal of the Travels and Labours of Father Samuel Fritz in the River of the Amazons between 1686 and 1723*, edited and translated by the Reverend George Edmundson (London: Hakluyt Society, 1922)

Hemming, John. *Red Gold: The Conquest of the Brazilian Indians*. Cambridge, Mass., Harvard University Press, 1978.

MICHAEL LAYLAND

Frobisher, Martin (c. 1535–1594), privateer, explorer, and naval commander. A native of Altofts, South Yorkshire, Martin Frobisher was sent to London in 1549 upon the death of his mother, to be apprenticed to his uncle, Sir John Yorke, a prominent merchant tailor and officer at the Tower Mint. Yorke was an investor in the first two English Guinea voyages (1553–1554). Frobisher sailed in both of these, and during the second he was taken hostage by the Portuguese, who resented interlopers in their African trade monopoly. Following his release sometime during 1556–1557, Frobisher abandoned legitimate trade and set up as a privateer. Sailing under doubtful or nonexistent licenses, he suffered numerous imprisonments in English jails during the 1560s and early 1570s.

In 1574, Frobisher collaborated with the mercer Michael Lok to promote an English voyage to discover a northwest sea route to the Far East. Backed

Frobisher Relics. The discovery of Frobisher relics nearly three hundred years old, from the *Illustrated London News*, 1860. In the Arctic, conditions are such that artifacts may survive for many years. Here an Inuit is showing an astonished Victorian explorer material thought to date from one of Frobisher's expeditions. COURTESY THE NEWBERRY LIBRARY, CHICAGO

by leading mercers, Russia Company merchants, and members of the Privy Council, two small barks, *Gabriel* and *Michael*, and a pinnace were dispatched in June 1576 under Frobisher's command. Plotting a simple westering course at 60° N latitude, the vessels reached the southern tip of Greenland (mistakenly identified by the voyagers as the mythical "Friesland") and entered Davis Strait. In a storm, the pinnace sank and *Michael* turned back to England, but *Gabriel* pressed on. Following a brief reconnaissance of the southeastern coastline of Baffin Island, *Gabriel* entered a large bay or strait. Initially friendly contacts were made with local Inuit, but their abduction of four Englishmen caused Frobisher to abandon any further exploration of the area and return to England.

Frobisher's subsequent claim that he had entered a navigable strait to the Far East, the exotic prospect of an Inuit being captured and returned to England, and the supposedly precious quality of a small piece of black ore, acquired at the mouth of Frobisher's "strait" and assayed by a number of semicompetent metallurgists, all attracted further investment. Elizabeth I contributed a naval vessel, the *Ayde*, as part of her own subscription, but her involvement brought the project decisively under royal control.

The second voyage, in 1577, revisited Frobisher's "strait," but the search for a northwest passage was distracted by a mining operation that extracted some 160 tons of ore and by further clashes with the Inuit. Frobisher's return to England saw the high-water mark of enthusiasm for the venture, and fresh expenditure was authorized to equip a further voyage and a new, custom-built refining facility in Dartford, Kent. [See color plate 29 in this volume.]

The third expedition, of fifteen ships, departed England in May 1578. By now, discovery of a passage to the Far East was an objective in name only. The expedition was intended rather to establish the first English colony outside Europe, which would winter on Baffin Island to support the mining operation while the ships returned to England. Fortunately for the would-be colonists, the destruction of many of their supplies during storms at sea prevented this experiment from proceeding. Despite this failure, and beset by further atrocious weather, the expedition mined and laded some 1,260 tons of ore from sites around Frobisher Bay, suffering few casualties.

The return of the expedition coincided with a collapse in the adventurers' confidence, as repeated assays of the ore had failed to establish the presence of gold or silver therein. As swiftly as his fame had grown, Frobisher saw it disappear, and several years

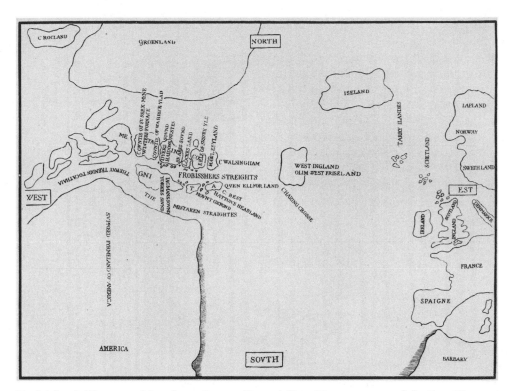

Frobisher's Voyages. Map from George Best, *A True Discourse . . . of the Late Voyages of Discouerie* (London, 1576). This map sets out the contemporary interpretation of the observations made on Frobisher's three voyages for a northwest passage. Note (just to the right of the word "West") the hopeful inscription, "the way trendin to Cathaia," or the route to China. COURTESY THE NEWBERRY LIBRARY, CHICAGO

of obscurity followed. Briefly, in 1582, Frobisher was appointed commander of a voyage intended to reprise Francis Drake's circumnavigation, but he was removed at the instigation of merchants anxious to keep its aims legitimate. He was also involved with Sir George Peckham's abortive scheme (under Sir Walter Ralegh's patent) to settle English Catholics on four million as-yet unsurveyed acres of what they were calling Virginia. It was not until 1585 that Frobisher received official employment once more, when he was appointed vice admiral of Drake's punitive expedition to the West Indies.

In the months preceding the armada campaign, Frobisher commanded a Narrow Seas squadron, and he served with distinction during the battle itself as captain of the English fleet's largest ship, *Triumph*. In 1589, 1590, and 1592, he commanded Atlantic squadrons that sought—unsuccessfully—to intercept Spanish plate fleets (fleets that carried silver ore from the New World) returning to Lisbon. In 1594, during an expedition to eradicate a Spanish threat to Brest, Frobisher was wounded during the storming of a fortress on the Crozon peninsula. He died two weeks later from a gangrenous infection, at Plymouth.

Frobisher married twice, without issue. He once hinted that the discovery of a navigable northern route into the Pacific Ocean was a long-standing obsession, but this is improbable. He was in fact an indifferent navigator, though he became an effective naval commander and seems to have been an inspirational leader. It is more likely that his interest in exploration was predicated upon its potential to increase his fame and, particularly, his fortune.

[*See also* Arctic *and* Northwest Passage.]

BIBLIOGRAPHY

McDermott, James. *Martin Frobisher: Elizabethan Privateer.* New Haven, Conn.: Yale University Press, 2001.

Symons, Thomas H. B., ed. *Meta Incognita, a Discourse of Discovery: Martin Frobisher's Arctic Expeditions, 1576–1578.* Hull, Quebec: Canadian Museum of Civilization, 1999.

JAMES McDERMOTT

Frontier Thesis. On July 12, 1893, Frederick Jackson Turner, a young history professor, read a paper, "The Significance of the Frontier in American History," at the annual meeting of the American Historical Association, noting in his opening words that the Superintendent of the Census declared that the 1890 enumeration marked the closing of the American frontier. Turner's thesis was that American political, social, and economic institutions had been shaped by the presence of an unsettled geographic frontier to the west. This ever-advancing frontier of settlement was the most distinctive feature of American development. What he termed "the hither edge of free land" was the dominating force in determining American character. The most intriguing corollary of the frontier thesis was the safety valve theory; namely, that the frontier acted as a safety valve where relief from social and economic conditions and political discontent in the East could be found.

Turner was an explorer; he equated expansion with exploration. His favorite poem was Rudyard Kipling's "The Explorer," especially the closing lines of the second stanza: "Something hidden. Go and find it. Go and look behind the Ranges— / Something lost behind the Ranges. Lost and waiting for you. Go." Turner believed in American exceptionalism: the uniqueness of the American experience and that the frontier was responsible for it, that American institutions were not modeled on Europe but rather developed indigenously, that the frontier or pioneering experience was the shaping force, that the existence of an area of free land, its continuous westward recession, and the westward movement explained America's essential characteristics. With the closing of the frontier, America expanded westward acquiring overseas possessions: Hawaii, Samoa, the Philippines, Guam, and also Puerto Rico. That the frontier provided a safety valve is arguable. However, whatever the validity of the concept that the availability of land provided a safety valve, the very existence of the frontier served as a psychological safety valve.

The thesis began to be challenged after Turner's death. However, it cannot be overemphasized that Turner was offering a hypothesis, a theory, but not a law. The imprecision of his methodology left him open to attack, especially because he was implying that man's essential characteristics were formed by his physical environment, not by intuitive genius. Turner believed in environmental determinism because the frontier interpretation of American history amounted in the last analysis to the contention that ideas were less powerful than the physical environment in shaping institutions.

BIBLIOGRAPHY

Billington, Ray Allen. *Frederick Jackson Turner: Historian, Scholar, Teacher*. New York: Oxford University Press, 1973.

Mattson, Vernon E., and William E. Marion, eds. *Frederick Jackson Turner: A Reference Guide*. Boston: G.K. Hall, 1985.

Martin Torodash

Fur Trade. From the beginning of European contact with the native peoples of North America, the fur trade was central to cultural, commercial, and social exchange between and among populations and races. The demand for furs, principally beaver (*Castor canadensis*), was steady in European markets including Russia from the sixteenth century to the mid-nineteenth century, and even after the decline of the popularity of hat-felting material (made from beaver hair) from about 1834, trade in beaver skins continued. In the 1770s a trade in sea otter pelts (*Enhydra lutris*) began from the west coast of North America, and possibly earlier from Japan and Kamchatka, to Kiatka, Canton, and Macao. By 1800 the fur trade embraced all of North America north of the Rio Grande.

Economic Importance. Although the fur trade diminished in areas of settlement, because it was antagonistic to settlement and vice versa, it remained central to the commercial and political evolution of the forested areas of North America, including mountain trenches, and from parkland areas well into deep and watery forests, particularly the boreal or northern forest of North America. In Canada, the fur trade was central to the political economy developed by colonizer and colonized in a symbiotic relationship that also resulted in mixed blood (Métis) offspring, families, and communities. The industrial revolution crossed the Atlantic under sail, and the products of this revolution were used to engender and continue the trade: the iron trap, the iron-tipped spear, and the iron knife, in native hands, increased aboriginal capacities to extend the trade into new areas of hunting and extraction. Arms, ammunition, liquor, fabrics, and foodstuffs entered North America at the same time. Because natives were keen and sharp traders, equity of exchange was demanded and expected. Indian technology and means of survival aided the European intrusion into native lands; native advice and guidance was often central to exploration and to the growth of trade. In fact, the exploration of North America is more often than not commensurate with the fur trade and pursuit of its consolidation and extension. The canoe, principally the birch-bark canoe, an aboriginal invention, became the vehicle for importation of goods and export of furs; cottonwood and cedar canoes were also used, the former in the western cordillera and the latter in the Pacific Coast of North America. In the Aleutian Islands and along the Gulf of Alaska and southeast Alaskan shore the *badarka*, made of skin on a wood frame, was typical. The packhorse, used after the 1740s, and the dog travois (a triangular wooden frame) aided trade. Steam navigation, beginning in the 1830s, increased the trade, and so did railways, especially for the marketing of skins such as buffalo and wolf. Thus technological innovation hurried the end of the fur trade in North America. By 1890, and the general closure of the settlement frontiers of North America, the fur trade was on the decline, and native peoples had been either reduced to reservations (in the United States) and reserves (in Canada) or not given status (in Russian America, later Alaska). All these were consequences of the search for sources of fur-bearing animals.

Fur Trade and Exploration. The English traded in furs in Newfoundland from the time of John Cabot, but this was ancillary to the cod fishery. The French traded in furs at the mouth of the Saguenay, on the Saint Lawrence River, in the 1530s. This became the first focal point of the trade stretching west and south to Georgian Bay. It embraced the Huron, Iroquois, and Neutral Indians and others. The Saint Lawrence River and its hinterlands became a fur trade empire. The French established a series of companies to monopolize the fur trade. Samuel de Champlain, exploring from Quebec, determined that Montreal Island would be a fine place for a summer fur post; a settlement was established there in 1642. Montreal became the center of Canadian fur trade expansion, shipping, and banking in consequence of the search for beaver. Traders, *couriers de bois*, voyagers, and Indian guides and laborers extended the trade into the interior, or *pays d'en haut*. The fur trade was the lifeblood of New France and of Canada. The French administration in Canada set up the system of licensing so that designated traders would have designated places of trade and extraction. Related to military posts and alliances with Indians, the system was designed to prevent cutthroat competition and, equally important, to promote the growth of the trade into new areas. In certain places French fur trade expansion aided French Roman Catholic designs, principally the Society of Jesus (Jesuits). The search for souls and furs was personified when Father Jacques Marquette, S.J., voyaged to the Mississippi on discoveries in the company of the Canadian trader Louis Jolliet.

Many French and Canadian explorers were fur traders, the most notable being Pierre Esprit Radisson and Médard Chouart des Groseilliers (who went into the service of the Hudson's Bay Company), Jean Nicolet, Louis Jolliet, and Sieur de la Vérendrye, so that by the 1750s the French posts were west as far as the Assiniboine, Souris, and Saskatchewan rivers and south toward Saint Louis and New Orleans. After the conquest of Canada by the British, the French remained in the trade, and worked in new association with English, Irish, and Scottish traders. Harold Innis has argued that the Seven Years' War was a struggle between the fur trade and settlement in North America, and that the British conquest extended the fur trade in northern latitudes and retarded settlement. Fur traders as explorers in the decades after the conquest were numerous and important: Peter Pond, Alexander Mackenzie, David Thompson, and others made discoveries and extended travels on exploration to open up new watersheds, acquire new trading partners, and keep rival traders out. The thrust to Athabasca is a fine example of this type of discovery and exploration; the movement through Rocky Mountain passes, by Mackenzie and Thompson and others, is another. These traders worked through the areas drained by the rivers and lakes of the boreal forest and the Rocky Mountain foothills.

The Canadian traders and the Spanish and French from New Orleans and Saint Louis were the first to explore the plains and prairie drained by the Missouri, Yellowstone, and Platte. The Missouri Company, based in Saint Louis and under Spanish colonial administrative encouragement, opened exploration to the Missouri and Yellowstone rivers under Jacques d'Eglise, James MacKay, and John Evans, findings exploited by Manuel Lisa. Earlier, British colonial soldiers such as Jonathan Carver, Robert Rogers, and George Rogers Clark explored the "Old Northwest," the upper reaches of the Missouri. They were precursors of Lewis and Clark, who were sent on scientific purposes to find a passage via the Missouri to the Pacific, but not least also to open up alliances with Aboriginal nations and report on prospects of trade and settlement. Lewis and Clark's discoveries intersected with Canadian trade and exploration to the Mandan and Hidatsa, also to the headwaters of the Mississippi, by Thompson, earlier in 1798. Their discoveries also intersected with contemporary Canadian discoveries to the Yellowstone by François Antoine Laroque. On the northern margins of Canadian trade, the Hudson's Bay Company (HBC) was a the rival of the North West Company. The HBC's explorers (Henry Kelsey, Anthony Henday, and Samuel Hearne) explored for new trade connections south, west, and north; later the HBC sent Philip Turnor into Athabasca to contest Canadian trade there in the early nineteenth century. The length of these voyages was related to labor costs, a function of time and distance, and the evolution of the York boat encouraged trade with Hudson Bay. Rivalry between Montreal and London, using the Saint Lawrence system and that of Hudson Bay, respectively, became a continent-wide struggle, resolved in 1821 with the union of the North West Company and the Hudson's Bay Company under the latter's name.

Colonial wars and especially the War of American Independence released soldiers into the fur trade upon the onset of peace. Many western settlers became fur traders, and many of them became at a later time "mountain men," that is, independent traders who went into the river valleys of the Rockies and other western mountains. This reckless breed hunted on their own account, held an annual rendezvous at Green River, and discovered new watersheds. Some, such as Jedediah Smith, worked with the Hudson's Bay Company. Others bolted from their obligations to the HBC when they crossed from the Oregon Territory into Mexican territories in early 1825, induced to defect by mountain man Johnson Gardner. The HBC after its consolidation in 1821 continued the aggressive exploration of the North West Company. Parties were sent to counter rivalry or even to trap out watersheds and thus keep rivals out. Alexander Ross and Peter Skene Ogden in the Snake River, Samuel Black in the Finlay, and Robert Campbell in the Yukon are examples of this policy. The HBC technique to maintain its monopoly was to undercut any opposition by offering higher prices to suppliers of furs; this was rigorously adhered to even if unprofitable in the areas in which the strategy was prosecuted. The HBC could not sustain this policy against encroaching settlement. By 1846 agricultural settlement was replacing the fur trade in the west and far west; settlement and mining were succeeding where the fur trade was less profitable and in retreat, but for decades the fur trade was continued in British Columbia, Yukon, and Alaska. Commercial fur farming became a new business, especially in mink.

The Russians, meanwhile, had come from Siberia and Kamchatka and had bases of trade in the Aleutians and on the Alaskan mainland by the time James Cook made his discoveries there in 1778. Gregory Ivanovich Shelikhov established the first permanent Russian trading station in North America at Three Saints Bay on Kodiak Island. He and his associates, aided by the favor of the imperial court, mastered any competition, and on July 8, 1799, the Russian American Company (RAC) was founded, with a twenty-year monopoly. In 1811 it was placed under the Ministry of the Interior and, in 1819, the Ministry of Finance; it thus was never as independent as the HBC but was really an extension of the tsar's government. Based at Sitka under its field manager Alexander Baranov, it extended its trade south toward the Columbia River, Alta California, and even the Gulf of California. Intentions to found a base at the Columbia in 1806 were given up in the face of the difficulty of entering that river. Meanwhile, beginning about 1803, and using Boston sailing ships, captains, and crews, along with Kodiak and Aleut hunters in *baidarkas* (kayaks), the RAC developed an

---

Tactics of the Trade

This passage makes explicit one of the tactics employed during the rivalry between the Hudson's Bay Company and the American Fur Company. It envisages a sort of "scorched-earth policy" that would prevent a rival company from succeeding.

"The greatest and best protection we can have from opposition is keeping the country closely hunted as the first step that the American Government will take towards Colonization is through their Indian Traders and if the country becomes exhausted in Fur bearing animals they can have no inducement to proceed thither.

We therefore entreat that no exertions be spared to explore and Trap every part of the country and as the service is both dangerous and laborious we wish our people to be treated with kindness and liberality, and such prices given for their hunts as will afford them a fair remuneration for their services and their supplies sold in such terms as would convince them that by desertion they would seriously injure your own interests.

The trade of the Coutenais and Far heads should be closely watched and if the Americans do visit or are likely to visit those Tribes we must endeavour to undersell them and thereby make their Trade unprofitable if we have not sufficient influence with those Indians to attach them to us otherwise."

—Sir George Simpson to John McLoughlin, July 9, 1827, Hudson's Bay Company Archives; quoted in John S. Galbraith, *The Hudson's Bay Company as an Imperial Factor* (Toronto: University of Toronto Press, 1957), 93–94.

extensive Pacific Coast trade in sea otter (then in rapid decline) and especially fur seals. Lacking adequate food supplies, the RAC explored California bays and coastal lands for an agricultural farm and base. Fort Ross was established 1812. To limit RAC competition in northern latitudes, the HBC traded into the Stikine River, against Russian resistance; then in 1840 the HBC established an agreement for monopoly trade in the Alaska panhandle. The RAC became increasingly uneconomic, a factor leading to the sale of Alaska to the United States in 1867. Fur trading in Alaska thereafter became the monopoly of the Alaska Commercial Company for a generation.

The British and American maritime fur traders had come in the wake of Cook's voyage. Expeditions were sent from India and Macao, with East India Company consent or knowledge though never direct help. James Hanna, James Charles Stuart Strange, John Meares, and James Colnett all made discoveries and added to the chart (and often to speculation); the physical geography of the Northwest Coast was tortuous, and this necessitated a formal survey by the Royal Navy, undertaken by George Vancouver. Boston-based trader Robert Gray examined the entrance to the Columbia River in 1792. The Pacific Fur Company of John Jacob Astor established a base near the Columbia mouth in 1810 and explored eastward. The North West Company sent ships to the Columbia River beginning 1813, and Royal Navy explorations of the river, by William Broughton in 1792, William Black in 1813, and Frederick Hickey in 1818, made the mouth, estuary, and course of this river better, but not completely, known. Maritime fur traders explored the Queen Charlotte Islands and the continental mainland in advance of official exploring expeditions. The British trader George Dixon and the American traders John Kendrick and Joseph Ingraham made notable additions to the chart, but scientific surveys of these lands and waters had to wait until the late nineteenth century under Royal Navy hydrographers.

After Lewis and Clark's halting discoveries of a route to the Pacific Coast via the Missouri River, its headwaters, difficult mountain passes, and awkward, nonnavigable waters until the open Columbia River could be reached, settlement did not really begin until the 1840s; meanwhile, the American fur trade was necessarily given an extended lease on life. General William Ashley led the Saint Louis–based Missouri Fur Company expeditions in 1825 into the Rocky Mountains and got rich returns, inducing other expeditions from Jedediah Smith, David Jackson, and William Sublette, who bought out Ashley in 1826.

Hardly a mountain stream was not explored by these men in their search for fur-bearing animals. But the HBC countered these expeditions effectively. The American trappers therefore were drawn south, and were based in Santa Fe rather than Saint Louis. Boston fur traders came to the Northwest Coast by sea in decreasing numbers, but in 1829 and 1830 the brig *Owhyee*, under Captain Dominis, traded extensively in the Columbia River. However, the HBC was too well established there for citizens of the United States to make anything in the way of the fur trade.

Taken all together, the various explorations of North America by land and sea, conducted by traders in search of furs and by their partners in the fur business, opened the knowledge of the continent to the outside world. The fur trade was the essential reason for North America's discovery inland. Missionaries, boundary surveyors, and government agents also revealed the nature of terrain and rivers, and this long before settlement, roads, and railways changed the landscape. The hunt for fur-bearing animals was a link between business capital, native hunting abilities, European technology, marriages and families based around the fur trade, and markets overseas. The quest for sea otter and fur seals was a marine exploitation, in which the independent, especially Boston-based, American maritime fur traders had no equal. The French from Montreal led the first phase to open the waterways of the continental interior, followed by others including the Spanish and Americans; the HBC traders were obliged to counter the Canadian-based traders, later known as the North West Company. From Kamchatka the Russian American Company went east then southeast in the search for furs. But pride of place goes to the HBC, which on the eve of the U.S. conquest of California and the settlement of the Oregon boundary dominated the North American fur trade from the Arctic to the Colorado River and from Labrador to the Pacific, save where the Russian American Company had its tenure until 1867.

[*See also* Arctic; Columbia River; Hudson's Bay Company; North America, *subentries on* Indigenous Guides *and* Indigenous Maps; North West Company; Northwest Passage; Rocky Mountains; Russian American Company; *and biographical entries on figures mentioned in this article.*]

BIBLIOGRAPHY

Galbraith, John S. *The Hudson's Bay Company as an Imperial Factor, 1821–1869.* Berkeley and Los Angeles: University of California Press, 1957.

Rich, E. E. *History of the Hudson's Bay Company, 1670–1870.* 2 vols. London: Hudson's Bay Record Society, 1958–1959.

BARRY M. GOUGH

Fu Sang. There is an old Chinese legend of a place called Fu Sang, a land far across the seas. In one account, a Buddhist monk named Hui Shen, originally from Afghanistan, is said to have traveled in the fifth century C.E. to Fu Sang, a place in the most distant east, beyond the ocean. This story is more than a thousand years old, and various writers have claimed or denied that the place discussed in the tale is, in fact, America. The name "Fu Sang" appears on early Asian maps, with the mapmakers using information from the legend. In the legend itself, of course, the details are too vague to make any kind of positive identification. Because of the resilience of this legend, however, Fu Sang actually appears on the North American continent in some eighteenth-century maps.

The story of Hui Shen is found in several Chinese accounts dating back to the seventh century C.E. In these accounts, several places are mentioned, none readily identifiable. The accounts tell us that Hui Shen and some companions headed east from China, across the seas, until they reached a coastline. They then traveled inland, exploring this new territory. They met various peoples, some of whom were fairly ordinary and some of whom were fantastic — for instance, men with dog-shaped heads. The group traveled farther, encountering a culture that had a written language and a form of government. According to various Chinese texts, Hui Shen returned to China at the end of the fifth century C.E. and recounted his travels in the imperial court. No specific geographical details are given in the account.

The story of Hui Shen's travels appeared in the early seventh-century C.E. book *Liang shu* (History of the Liang Dynasty) by Yao Silian, and in the later seventh-century *Nan shi* (History of the Southern Dynasties), compiled by Li Yanshou. The *Nan shi* was copied and amended by Ma Duanlin, in his early fourteenth-century *Wen xian tong kao* (Comprehensive Studies in Literature). This work, in a section entitled *Si yi kao* (Investigation of the Four Frontiers), recounted Hui Shen's story. The story also appeared in a slightly different form in the *Liang si gong ji* (Memoir of the Four Gentleman of Liang), a work dating from the late seventh century and ascribed to Zhang Yue. Fu Sang was also discussed in the famous *Shanhai jing* (Classic of Mountains and Seas), a Chinese work that describes various geographical and other wonders.

Toponyms in the Fu Sang Legend. The accounts of Fu Sang do, in fact, furnish the reader with a number of place-names; however, none of the place-names provides much help in attempts at a literal cartographical interpretation of the tale. The *Liang shu* places Fu Sang some 20,000 li (roughly 6,000 miles) from China. The term "Fu Sang" is the name given to the land itself, but is said to be derived from the name of a tree found there; the tree is described as supplying food, and its bark as being a material for clothing. Dictionaries today translate "fu sang" as "hibiscus." That "Fu Sang" was also a term used in ancient times for "Japan" is a further complication.

The precise location of Fu Sang remains a mystery. In the account in the *Wen xian tong kao*, we are presented with a series of increasingly remote locales. First, there is "Wen Shen," a term literally meaning "marked bodies"; one nineteenth-century commentator believed that the name of this region may have referred to tattooed peoples. Wen Shen was said to be situated to the northeast of Japan. Next comes "Da Han," meaning "Great China"; the *Liang shu* states that this land is to be found more than 5,000 li east of Wen Shen. Finally, beyond Da Han, there is Fu Sang itself.

European and American Interpretations of the Fu Sang Legend. The story of Hui Shen and the land of Fu Sang apparently did not reach Europe until the eighteenth century. In 1761, the French sinologist Joseph de Guignes (1721–1800), during the course of research on China, discovered and translated the accounts of Hui Shen's voyage. The cartographer Philippe Buache (1700–1773) labeled as "Fousang" a region on the Pacific northwest coast of North America on his 1752 map of these regions, the "Carte des terres nouvellement connues au nord de la Mer du Sud tant du Côté de l'Asie que de Côte de l'Amérique..." ("Map of the newly discovered lands to the north of the 'Sea of the South' as well as around Asia and the Coast of America"). Buache was working directly from the translation of Joseph de Guignes; the subtitle of this map was: "Avec la route des Chinois en Amérique vers l'an 458 de J.C. tracée sur les connaissances géographiques que Mr. de Guignes a tirées des annales chinoises..." ("With the route of the Chinese in America around the year 458 C.E., traced according to the geographical knowledge that Mr. de Guignes has taken from the Chinese annals..."). Antonio Zatta's map, "Nuove scoperte de' russi al nord...." ("New discoveries by the Russians in the north"), which appeared in Venice in 1776, has the label "Fou-sang, Colonia de[i] Cinesi" ("'Fou-sang,' colony of the Chinese") in roughly the same locale.

In 1761, Joseph de Guignes presented a paper to the French Royal Academy on his findings concerning the account of Hui Shen. This paper was entitled "Recherches sur les navigations des Chinois du côté de l'Amérique, & sur quelques Peuples situés à l'extrémité orientale de l'Asie" ("Researches Concerning the Navigations of the Chinese around America, and Concerning Some of the Peoples Situated in the Eastern End of Asia"). Guignes believed that Fu Sang referred to Mexico, and he went on to argue that the people and places described in the ancient Chinese account were the Indians of Mexico and the regions of the southwestern modern-day United States.

It was not until many years later that these assertions were contested. In 1831, Heinrich Julius Klaproth, a German sinologist, attacked Guignes's view with his paper, "Recherches sur le pays de Fou Sang mentionné dans les livres Chinois et pris mal àpropos pour une partie de l'Amérique" ("Researches concerning the country of Fou Sang mentioned in the Chinese books and mistaken for a part of America"). But the debate was not over; Karl Frederich Neumann, another sinologist, reiterated the original French interpretation, and provided translations of the original Chinese texts. Charles Hippolyte de Paravey, also supporting the idea that Fu Sang referred to the Americas, generated two books on the subject, *L'Amérique sous le nom de pays de "Fou-sang"* ("America under the name of the country of 'Fou-Sang'") in 1844 and *Nouvelles preuves que le pays du Fou-sang mentionné dans les livres chinois est l'Amérique* ("New proofs that the country of Fou-sang mentioned in the Chinese books is America") in 1847.

In the United States, the discussions continued with Hubert Howe Bancroft, who treated the question of Fu Sang in his *Native Races of the Pacific States* (1874–1876). However, the seminal work in America concerning this Chinese tale was that of Charles Godfrey Leland. Leland had been a student in Heidelberg, Germany, and there he heard Neumann speak on the topic of Fu Sang. Leland sought to bring Neumann's ideas to America, and in 1850, he wrote about them in an article in the *Knickerbocker Magazine*. In 1875, Leland's treatment of Fu Sang appeared in book form, with the publication of *Fusang: or, The Discovery of America by Chinese Buddhist Priests in the Fifth Century*. This book provided Neumann's recounting of the story of Hui Shen, as well as a discussion of the navigation of the Pacific Ocean, and a look at possible connections between American antiquities and Old World artifacts.

Edward Payson Vining, an American businessman, took the Hui Shen story to another level entirely with his 1885 book *An Inglorious Columbus*. By using "inglorious" in the title to mean "obscure," Vining implied that Hui Shen was the real discoverer of America. Vining's book ran to more than seven hundred pages, looking at everything from the geography of the northern reaches of the Pacific Ocean to apparent parallels between ancient Asian and pre-Columbus Central American culture. Specifically, Vining argued that the toponyms in the Hui Shen account could be identified with modern locales, with *Ta Han* referring to the Aleutian Island chain, and Fu Sang being Mexico.

The belief that Hui Shen's tale referred to an actual voyage to the Americas continued with Henriette Mertz's book *Pale Ink: Two Ancient Records of Chinese Exploration in America*, originally published in 1953.

[*See also* Chinese Exploration; Fictitious and Fantastic Places; *and* North America, *subentry on* Apocryphal Discoveries and Imaginary Places (pre-1500).]

BIBLIOGRAPHY

Laufer, Berthold. *China and the Discovery of America*. New York: China Institute in America, 1931.

Leland, Charles Godfrey. *Fusang: or, The Discovery of America by Chinese Buddhist Priests in the Fifth Century*. New York: J. W. Bouton, 1875.

Mertz, Henriette. *Pale Ink: Two Ancient Records of Chinese Exploration in America*. Chicago: Swallow Press, 1953. Revised, 1972.

Vining, Edward Payson. *An Inglorious Columbus*. New York: Appleton, 1885.

Williams, S. Wells. "Notices of Fu-Sang, and Other Countries Lying East of China, Given in the Antiquary Researches of Ma Twan-Lin." *American Oriental Society Journal* 11 (1882–1885): 89–116.

BENJAMIN B. OLSHIN

G

Gagarin, Yuri (1934–1968), the first human in space. Yuri Alexeyevich Gagarin was born on March 9, 1934, in Klushino, one hundred miles west of Moscow. His father, Aleksey Ivanovich Gagarin, and mother, Anna Timofeevna, worked on a collective farm. When Gagarin was seven, German troops invaded Russia and took his family home. His father joined the Russian army while Gagarin's family lived in a dugout until the war ended; then the family moved to Gzhatsk.

Gagarin graduated from high school in 1949. He worked in a factory while attending industrial school. He graduated in 1955 with a foundry man certificate and a flying club diploma. Gagarin was so excited about flying that he spent an entire summer living in a tent while attending aviation camp. He attended Orenburg Aviation School, graduated in 1957, and became a Soviet Air Force lieutenant.

While at Orenburg, he met Valentina Ivanovna Goryacheva, who was a nursing student. They married in 1957 and had two daughters, Lenochka (1959) and Galochka (1961).

In 1960, twenty military pilots were selected as the first cosmonauts, and Gagarin was among them. He and his family moved to Star City, located near Moscow, where the cosmonauts underwent rigorous training. On April 9, 1961, at age twenty-seven, Gagarin was selected to be the first man in space.

Gagarin was launched into space aboard the *Vostok I* space capsule on April 12, 1961, from Baikonur Cosmodrome in the Soviet Union. *Vostok I* orbited the Earth once on its 108-minute flight. Gagarin spent his time in weightlessness reporting Earth observations, tapping out telegraph messages, eating, and drinking. After the capsule reentered the atmosphere, Gagarin ejected, and both he and the capsule parachuted separately to Earth.

Gagarin's flight into space was worldwide news. He demonstrated that humans could survive weightlessness as well as the crushing forces of launching and landing, paving the way for all future spaceflights with human astronauts. He traveled worldwide to promote the Soviet achievement, was awarded the title Hero of the Soviet Union, and received the Order of Lenin Award.

Gagarin never returned to space. On March 27, 1968, at age thirty-four, he died in a plane crash. His ashes were buried in the Kremlin Wall. In honor of his great contributions to space exploration, and his achievement of being the first human in space, the town of Gzhatsk and a moon crater were named after him.

[*See also* Space Program, *subentry* Soviet.]

BIBLIOGRAPHY
Crouch, Tom D. *Aiming for the Stars: The Dreamers and Doers of the Space Age.* Washington, D.C.: Smithsonian Institution Press, 1999.
Doran, Jamie, and Bizony Piers. *Starman: The Truth Behind the Legend of Yuri Gagarin.* London: Bloomsbury, 1998.

CHRISTINE MIRANDA

Galleass. *See* **Vessels,** *subentry on* **Sailing Vessels.**

Galleon. *See* **Vessels,** *subentry on* **Sailing Vessels.**

Galley. *See* **Vessels,** *subentry on* **Sailing Vessels.**

Galton, Francis (1822–1911), British scientific savant and traveler. Born on February 16, 1822, at Birmingham, England, Francis Galton was the grandson of Erasmus Darwin and a cousin of Charles Darwin, whose views on evolution and heredity he came to accept and to develop by means of eugenics. Galton could read Latin at the age of four. When twenty-two, having inherited wealth from his grandfather, he set off for Egypt, visited Khartoum and then went to Syria and Palestine where he attempted to sail a raft down the Jordan. His major feat was an expedi-

THE

ART OF TRAVEL;

·OR,

SHIFTS AND CONTRIVANCES AVAILABLE IN WILD COUNTRIES.

BY FRANCIS GALTON,

AUTHOR OF " EXPLORATIONS IN TROPICAL SOUTH AFRICA."

WITH WOODCUTS.

LONDON:
JOHN MURRAY, ALBEMARLE STREET.
1855.

Francis Galton. Title page from Francis Galton's *The Art of Travel* (London: John Murray, 1855). This title page, with its curious subtitle of "Shifts and Contrivances available in Wild Countries," surely conveys something of Galton's rather eccentric character. COURTESY THE NEWBERRY LIBRARY, CHICAGO

tion of 1850–1852 into southern Africa with Charles Andersson designed to find a route from Walvis Bay to Lake Ngami. They penetrated Damara (Bergdama) and reached Ovambo territory but got no farther. A second attempt also stalled. Some have argued that Galton provided little information on people, unwisely interfered in local politics, and made no significant discovery. However, like David Livingstone, Galton had learned to use a sextant on the voyage to South Africa and brought back some accurate positions that justified the award of the Royal Geographical Society (RGS) gold medal for 1853 and Fellowship of the Royal Society. Merited

or not, these awards made exploration and the RGS Galton's main intellectual focus for the next ten years and a continuing concern for the next forty.

From 1854 until 1894, Galton was almost continuously on the council of the RGS in various posts. A paper on his expedition was followed by *Tropical South Africa*, an interesting if not classic book. More influential was another paper of 1854, "Hints to Travellers," which was later developed into the famous RGS guide on how to organize and conduct an expedition. More discursive was *The Art of Travel* (1855), designed to teach gentlemen travelers to become more scientific. In 1856 Galton founded and initially edited an annual volume of *Proceedings* for the RGS so that discussions were recorded. He persuaded the RGS to institute a School Prize in Geography in 1869 and in 1878 forced the creation of the Committee for Scientific Purposes. These moves were much less successful in improving the intellectual and educational standing of geography than a later initiative, the establishment of a readership in the subject at the University of Oxford in 1886, although it was Halford Mackinder rather than Galton who made the significant intellectual advance.

Galton was involved in the organization of many important exploratory initiatives. Probably it was he who made the famous breach between Richard Burton and John Hanning Speke irreparable in 1859 by choosing to back another expedition by Speke but

---

On Traveling Itself

During his very long life, this eminent Victorian greatly encouraged a variety of expeditions, without himself being a great explorer. His book on The Art of Travel *reads now like a manual produced for the benefit of military irregulars, offering advice on the way to tackle a huge variety of discomforts and misfortunes.*

A frank, joking but determined manner, joined with an air of showing more confidence in the good faith of the natives than you really feel, is the best. It is observed that a sea-captain generally succeeds in making an excellent impression upon savages; they thoroughly appreciate common sense, truth and uprightness, and are not half such fools as strangers usually account them.

—Sir Francis Galton, *The Art of Travel* (London, 1855)

not Burton. Equally unfortunate was the way Galton set the tone for the RGS treatment of Henry Stanley after the famous meeting with Livingstone, snobbishly questioning Stanley's origins and dubbing his work unscientific "sensational geography."

There was indeed a downside to all Galton's achievements. Livingstone regarded him as an interfering "busybody." In setting up the *Proceedings*, Galton had forced the paid assistant secretary of the RGS to resign and became unpopular, not least with the equally forceful but traditionalist Sir Clements Markham. Associated with the "progressives" in the early 1890s, Galton supported their highly controversial call for the admission of ladies as fellows of the society even though his own social background together with his studies in heredity made him believe women were inferior. Finding his position untenable, he gave up all involvement in the work of the RGS in 1894.

Galton was a great man who had a highly significant impact on exploration and geography; paradoxically, he was not a truly great explorer or geographer. He was knighted in 1909 and died at Haslemere, Surrey, England, on June 17, 1911.

[*See also* Royal Geographical Society *and biographical entries on figures mentioned in this article.*]

BIBLIOGRAPHY

Forrest, D. W. *Francis Galton: The Life and Work of a Victorian Genius*. London: Paul Elek, 1974.

Galton, Francis. *The Art of Travel; or Shifts and Contrivances Available in Wild Countries*. London: Murray, 1855. A reprint of the fifth edition of 1872 was issued as *Francis Galton's Art of Travel*, edited by Dorothy Middleton. London: Phoenix, 2000.

Galton, Francis. *Tropical South Africa*. London: Murray, 1853. 2nd ed., *Narrative of an Explorer in Tropical South Africa: Being an Account of a Visit to Damaraland in 1851*. London: Ward, Lock, 1889.

ROY BRIDGES

Gama, Vasco da (1469?–1524), Portuguese seafarer who reached India. Vasco da Gama commanded the Portuguese expedition that for the first time successfully sailed along the maritime route from Europe to India in 1498. Many consider this event one of the key episodes that defined the rise of modernity and Western global hegemony. Gama's voyage ushered in an era of profound and lasting changes in the patterns of Eurasian intercontinental commerce, particularly in the spice trade. While recent research shows some of the standard claims to be overstated, Gama nonetheless remains an iconic figure of European overseas expansion.

Gama was born in Sines, a small town in western Alentejo, Portugal, around 1469. The Gama family belonged to minor local nobility, and its members held military and civil offices in the service of both the king and of the military order of Santiago. Gama appears to have served both King Dom João II and his successor Dom Manuel as a courtier, a soldier in North Africa, and a commander of naval patrols. Some have credited Gama with participation in earlier oceanic explorations. It remains unclear why Gama, a relative unknown at the time, was appointed to head the historic Indian Ocean voyage rather than a seasoned explorer such as Bartolomeu Dias, who had discovered the Cape of Good Hope.

Vasco da Gama's 1497–1499 expedition, charged with finding a way to India, was quite small, consisting of only four vessels with a complement of 170 crewmen. It left Lisbon on July 8, 1497, passed the Cape of Good Hope on November 22, 1497, and reached the East African port of Malindi on April 16, 1498. There Gama secured the services of an experienced Gujarati pilot who guided the fleet to the Malabar Coast of India. On May 20, 1498, the Portuguese ships dropped anchor north of Calicut, the principal spice-trade center of the area.

Portuguese relations with Calicut were off to the wrong start from the very beginning. Gama neither presented the customary gifts nor displayed an etiquette bound to placate the ruler and his court. Permitted to trade, the Portuguese remained in Calicut for three months, but their efforts were hampered by the poor assortment of merchandise they had brought and by the animosity of their Muslim competitors. They succeeded in purchasing only small samples of spices and precious stones. Gama eventually resorted to violence and the fleet left the city on August 29, 1498, amid skirmishes with Calicut vessels. It lingered along the coast of India for another month and then attempted the return crossing of the Indian Ocean at exactly the wrong time of the year. After a long and harrowing voyage, Gama's ships finally landed in Lisbon in the summer of 1499.

King Dom Manuel and the Portuguese court greeted the results of Gama's voyage with triumphant euphoria. The king had styled himself the "Lord of Conquest, Navigation, and Commerce of Ethiopia, Arabia, Persia, and India"; he also circulated a letter to various European courts informing them not only about the sea route to India, but also about the large numbers of potential Christian allies conveniently located beyond the Muslim-dominated

Middle and Near East. The wishful thinking of Gama and his staff members transformed Hindu temples into Christian churches, and the king received from them a long list of "Christian" states lining the western coast of India.

The pioneering voyage brought Vasco da Gama unprecedented rewards. A minor noblemen by birth, he saw himself and his family promoted to the ranks of high aristocracy. Early in 1500 he was granted the titles Dom and Admiral of India, the right to serve as captain-major of any future fleet to India, and a huge annual pension of 300,000 *réis* in perpetuity. He also married Dona Catarina de Ataíde, a member of one of the realm's ranking families. This advancement was not without controversy, however: contemporary detractors ceaselessly harped on Gama's humble origins and pointed out that no previous explorers had been rewarded with similar magnanimity.

Gama's fortune reached its zenith when in 1502 he commanded the fourth Portuguese fleet to India. This expedition, comprising fourteen ships, established the key traits of early Portuguese presence in the Indian Ocean. These included predatory attacks on Muslim shipping, disruption of non-Portuguese spice shipments, hostility with Calicut, alliance with the rival city-state of Cochin, and intimidation of smaller states along the western coast of India. Gama also reduced the East African city-state of Kilwa to tributary status. He returned to Portugal in 1504, greatly enriched and covered in tainted glory, and was rewarded with an additional pension of 400,000 *réis*.

After 1504, Gama's fortunes began to decline. Reports of his unproductive brutality in the East, the self-seeking aggression of his uncles (the Sodré brothers), social animosity, and a conflict with the king and the master of Santiago over his native town of Sines all contributed to Gama's fall from grace. The admiral was relegated to long years of comfortable "exile" in northern Alentejo. Other members of his family nonetheless continued to serve overseas and garner royal favor.

Gama staged an impressive political comeback in the last years of Dom Manuel's reign. Apparently to avoid the admiral's defection to Emperor Charles V, the new king of Spain, Dom Manuel not only recalled Gama to court, but granted him in 1519 the title of count, the highest honor to which he could aspire. Proclaimed the hereditary Count of Vidigueira, a small town in central Alentejo, he sacrificed his pension of 400,000 *réis* to finance his elevation, transferring the monetary entitlement to the previous overlord of Vidigueira, the duke of Bragança.

After the death of Dom Manuel in 1524, Vasco da Gama continued to enjoy the favor of the new king, Dom João III. In 1524 he reached the peak of his career, and was dispatched back to India with the title of viceroy. His mission was to bring order to the *Estado da India*, promote royal interests, improve the defenses, remove from power and ship back to Portugal the previous governing figures, and bring under control willful and corrupt local officials. Gama arrived in India in September 1524 and set to work with a zeal and arrogance that quickly made him numerous enemies, including key members of Portugal's most powerful nonroyal family, the Meneses. He died, however, only three months after his third arrival in India, on December 25, 1524. His sudden death prevented his enemies from orchestrating his downfall, and set him posthumously on the path to becoming one of Portugal's national legends and a featured character of innumerable historical and literary works.

[*See also* Dias, Bartholomew; Expeditions, World Exploration, *subentry on* Portugal; *and* Pacific, *subentry on* European Trade Routes.]

BIBLIOGRAPHY

Disney, Anthony, and Emily Booth, eds. *Vasco da Gama and the Linking of Europe and Asia*. New Delhi and New York: Oxford University Press, 2000.

Jayne, K. G. *Vasco da Gama and his Successors, 1460–1580*. New Delhi: Asian Educational Services, 1997.

Subrahmanyam, Sanjay. *The Career and Legend of Vasco da Gama*. Cambridge, U.K., and New York: Cambridge University Press, 1997.

Velho, Alvaro. *A Journal of the First Voyage of Vasco da Gama, 1497–1499*. 1898. Translated and edited by E.G. Ravenstein. New Delhi: Asian Educational Services, 1995.

MARTIN ELBL
IVANA ELBL

Gautier, Émile-Félix (1864–1940), French explorer of the Sahara Desert. Émile-Félix Gautier was born on October 29, 1864, at Clermont-Ferrand in Auvergne, France. At the university, he failed the history-geography teaching certification exam. But after a three-year trip to Germany, he passed the equivalent German exam in 1891.

The following year, the French Ministry of Foreign Affairs sent Gautier on a mission to investigate the island of Madagascar, which at the time was still mostly unexplored. He learned Malagasy and traveled from Madagascar's north end to its south end, some 1,800 miles (3,000 kilometers). He left the island during the military operations of 1895, and returned the following year to take over the office of public education there. Later he served as director of native affairs during the Galliéni government. He returned to France in 1899, bringing back considerable geographical documentation to prepare his doctoral thesis, *Madagascar, essai de géographie physique* (Madagascar, an Essay on Physical Geography), which he defended at the Sorbonne on June 10, 1902. He also became a professor at the Faculté des lettres of Algiers.

Henceforth, North Africa and the Sahara became his sole objects of study. In 1902, he made his first trip to Gourara. He accompanied Commander Henri Laperrine the following year on a much more in-depth journey to the center of the Algerian Sahara, 240 miles (400 kilometers) south of In Salah. Finally, in 1905, he successfully crossed the desert, from the Algerian Sahara to the Niger, accompanied by the geologist René Chudeau. Gautier was a prolific writer, with works aimed at geographers such as *Le Sahara algérien* (The Algerian Sahara, 1908), as well as works for general audience, such as *La conquête du Sahara* (The Conquest of the Sahara, 1910), both of which are remarkable syntheses of physical and human geography. [See color plate 38 in this volume.]

After World War I, Gautier continued to travel mostly in Algeria, where he lived, but he came back regularly to Paris, where he lectured on colonial geography at the Sorbonne. Gautier was a firm partisan of trans-Saharan railway projects and of economic conquest of the desert, but he was equally interested in the prehistoric Sahara and studied the wall paintings of Tassili-n-Ajjer. *L'Afrique blanche* (White Africa, 1939) constitutes the sum of his knowledge on North Africa. Explorer, archaeologist, historian, and linguist all at once, Gautier was one of the first and foremost great figures of the French school of geography. He died on January 16, 1940, at Pontivy in Morbihan, France.

[*See also* Africa, West, *and* Sahara.]

BIBLIOGRAPHY
Gautier, Émile-Félix. *Sahara: The Great Desert*. Translated by Dorothy Ford Mayhew. London: Cass, 1970.

OLIVIER LOISEAUX
Translated from the French by Frédéric Potter

Genoa. One of the great port cities of the world, Genoa is best known to the history of exploration as the birthplace of Christopher Columbus. From its unpromising location in northern Italy, where the Maritime Alps press right to the shores of the sea, Genoa developed into a commercial powerhouse during the twelfth and thirteenth centuries. Genoese merchants established a network of Mediterranean trade stretching from Morocco to Syria and Egypt, and (along with their great rivals, the Venetians) developed the foundations of western capitalism.

The Genoese provided crucial support to the Crusades and realized considerable profits from lucrative trading rights and shipping contracts in the Middle East. The fall of Acre in 1291 provided the impetus for an expedition foreshadowing the later exploits of the city's most famous son. Two brothers, Ugolino and Vadino Vivaldi, sailed to Morocco in well-stocked galleys, determined to discover an Atlantic passage to India in order to undercut both the victorious Mamluks and the Venetians. Never heard from again, the Vivaldis passed into local legend.

During the fourteenth century, Genoese merchants used their great galleys and cogs as major commercial shippers of grain, textiles, and slaves, expanding their reach to include England and Iberia in the west and the Black Sea in the east. But by the middle of the next century, a series of political and commercial catastrophes brought about a significant change of fortune. Endemic and enervating civil wars and conflicts with Venice preceded the loss of Genoa's commercial colonies in Byzantium to the Ottomans and Venetians. Loss of trade in the East intensified a focus on western commerce, and Genoese fleet owners and sailors increasingly worked for Portuguese and Spanish patrons.

The Genoese were familiar players in Iberian commerce by this time, shipping English cloth to Spain and returning north with luxury produce like dates and almonds. Competition with Portugal for the developing Atlantic slave trade turned to cooperation as Genoese sailors made significant contributions to Portuguese exploration of the West African coast. Like many other young Genoese in the 1470s, Columbus left his declining homeland for the greater opportunities offered by Iberian patrons. Columbus enjoyed financial support for his Atlantic voyages from a thriving community of Genoese in Seville who went on to finance and profit from further Spanish exploration. Perhaps as a reflection of his heritage, Columbus saw his own voyages as part of a crusading strategy to reopen eastern Mediterranean markets to western traders, and he was quick to recognize the commercial potential of shipping Caribbean natives to Europe as slaves.

By the sixteenth century, the loss of its eastern Mediterranean markets had left Genoa a second-rate regional power, reduced further by the devastating sack of the city in 1522 by an imperial army. Six years later, Andrea Doria took power in Genoa, creating a stable aristocratic oligarchy and a dependable Spanish client state. Doria himself made handsome profits by supplying the Spanish throne with slave-powered galleys.

[*See also* Columbus, Christopher; Crusades; *and* Mediterranean.]

BIBLIOGRAPHY
Epstein, Steven A. *Genoa and the Genoese, 958–1528*. Chapel Hill and London: University of North Carolina Press, 1996.
Hunt, Edwin S., and James M. Murray. *A History of Business in Medieval Europe, 1200–1500*. Cambridge, U.K., and New York: Cambridge University Press, 1999.

MARK ANGELOS

Gentil, Émile (1866–1914), French naval officer and explorer of equatorial Africa. The second of the nine children of Jules-Martin Gentil, a restaurant owner at Briey, and Odette Brix. Émile Gentil was born on April 4, 1866, at Volmunster in Lorraine, France. He attended school in Nancy before joining the Brest Naval Academy in 1883.

Gentil was made lieutenant in 1888, and led expeditions for the collection of hydrographical data in Gabon. He was appointed colonial administrator in the Congo in 1891, and he explored the Upper Sangha River and Mambere with Pierre Savorgnan de Brazza. Despite the failures of the Campel and Dybowski missions, and following Casimir Maistre, Gentil proposed continuing the attempts to get into Lake Chad via the Chari River. During a first mission (1895–1897) aboard the *Léon Blot*, a steamboat whose shallow draft enabled him to pass easily by portage from the Ubangi Basin to the Chari Basin, he founded several military posts, made the Baguirmi a French protectorate, and finally arrived at Lake Chad on November 1, 1897. He was forced to leave the Ubangi and return to Paris, however, as a result of supply problems.

He was then appointed commissioner of the Chari government, and boarded ship again on February 25, 1899, on a second military mission. Gentil put Commander François Lamy in charge of military operations to put an end to the exactions of the powerful sultan of Wadai, Rabah, who was threatening French military efforts in the region. On April 22, 1900, the battle of Kousseri brought down the sultan's empire, as reported in Gentil's *La Chute de l'empire de Rabah* (The Fall of Rabah's Empire, 1902). A laureate of the gold medal of the Geographical Society of Paris in 1899, Gentil was appointed commissioner general of the government in the territories of the French Congo and its dependencies in January of 1904. Although he was caught in the middle of a publicity campaign mounted against him after an inspection mission completed by de Brazza in the Congo, Gentil was cleared of all suspicion in 1906. He was one of the principal actors in the agreements with Germany over the Congo in 1911, and one of the fathers of French Equatorial Africa, created January 15, 1910. He died on March 30, 1914, in Bordeaux.

[*See also* Brazza, Pierre Savorgnan di; Chad, Lake; *and* Imperialism and Exploration.]

BIBLIOGRAPHY
Gentil, Émile. *La chute de l'empire de Rabah*. Paris: Hachette, 1902.

OLIVIER LOISEAUX
Translated from the French by Frédéric Potter

Geographical Society of Paris. The Geographical Society (Société de Géographie) was created following a meeting held on July 19, 1821. On December 15 of the same year, the Société held its first general assembly at City Hall in Paris, and Jean-Denis Barbié presided over the proceedings. It was not given a more specific name because of its universal vocation, and because it was the first geographical society ever created. The founding members' goal was to drive geographic progress forward, to encourage studies and geographical discoveries, and to undertake voyages to still unknown lands.

In 1822, the Central Commission decided to hand out awards to those explorers and researchers who contributed to humanity's knowledge of Earth. In 1825, an award of nine thousand francs was offered to the first French traveler to go to Tombouctou (Timbuctoo). René Caillié won the prize in 1828 along with the Société's gold medal of 1830, an honor he shared posthumously with the English major Alexander Gordon Laing. Fifty awards were created in various fields for geographical research or expeditions and discoveries. Throughout the century, the Société created and published a number of questions and instructions in an effort to provide explorers with a methodical way of evaluating their work. The *Bulletin de la Société de Géographie*, which has been in print since 1822, published explorers' stories illustrated with maps as well as the latest news about the Société. The Société de Géographie sponsored many expeditions and voyages of discovery, and sometimes contributed to their financing, as was the case with the Foureau-Lamy mission. At the turn of the century, it was one of the principal players in the French colonial expansion.

Since 1873, it has encouraged the emergence of other regional geographical societies and has actively participated in geography conferences. It organized the second session of the International Geography Congress in Paris, in August of 1875, and the fourth session during the Universal Exposition of 1889.

Along with other institutions, it was behind the creation of the Comité National Français de Géographie in 1920, and a member of the International Geographical Union, whose first president was Prince Roland Bonaparte, who served simultaneously as president of the Société (1909–1924).

In 1878, the Société bought a piece of land at 184 Boulevard Saint-Germain, built its headquarters, and has been there ever since. It welcomed travelers, explorers, and researchers who came to present reports and results of their work and expeditions. These conferences, often accompanied by the projection of photographs, became very popular.

Since its creation, the Société de Géographie has intended to build a library, but it never had the financial means to do so. The Société receives geography journals from around the world in exchange for its bulletin, but its main sources of income are donations and grants, like the gift from Prince Bonaparte's personal library in 1925. Since 1942, the Société's collections (books, periodicals, maps, manuscripts, and photographs) have resided at the Bibliothèque Nationale. It is one of the richest repositories of knowledge of the history of travel and world discovery.

The work of the Société de Géographie is not just a thing of the past. It remains loyal today to its original mission by supporting expeditions, handing out new awards each year, maintaining an annual conference cycle, and publishing its journal, *La Géographie*.

[*See also* Caillié, René, *and* Foureau, Fernand.]

BIBLIOGRAPHY
Fierro, Alfred. *La Société de Géographie 1821-1946*. Geneva: Droz; Paris: H. Champion, 1983.
"La Société de Géographie. Commémoration de notre 175e anniversaire, 1821–1996." Société de Géographie, 1996.

OLIVIER LOISEAUX
Translated from the French by Frédéric Potter

Geological Survey of Canada.

The Geological Survey of Canada was founded in 1842. At that time, however, the Province of Canada comprised only the southern parts of the present provinces of Quebec and Ontario. It was only with the transfer of Rupert's Land from the Hudson's Bay Company to Canada in 1870 that Canada expanded to include what is now most of the western provinces and the whole of the Arctic mainland; the Arctic islands were only absorbed into Canada by the transfer from Britain in 1880.

By 1870 much of the southern mainland had been completely explored and mapped by fur-trade surveyors such as Peter Fidler, Philip Turnor, and especially by David Thompson. Thus while officers of the Geological Survey made major contributions in terms of reconnaissance geology in the southern parts of the country, the areas they were studying had generally already been quite competently mapped. Even when they moved into the Far North, they were operating in areas (especially coastal areas) that had already been explored and mapped by the numerous expeditions seeking the Northwest Passage or (after 1845) the missing Franklin Expedition. Thus the survey's main contribution to exploration has been that of the interior of the Arctic mainland.

Undoubtedly the most successful of the survey's geologist-explorers was Joseph Burr Tyrrell, and his most noteworthy contribution was in exploring the "Barren Lands" of the Keewatin. Having heard rumors from the local Chipewyan of a major river running north across the tundra, in July 1893, with his brother James and six other men, Tyrrell started north from Black Lake in two canoes, and reached Wholdaia Lake at the headwaters of the mysterious river (the Dubawnt). Heading downstream through Dubawnt Lake, Beverly Lake, Schultz Lake, Baker Lake, and Chesterfield Inlet, they reached the open waters of Hudson Bay on September 12. On the trip south along the west shore of Hudson Bay they were caught by freeze-up and finally had to abandon their canoes, and reached Churchill on foot. From there they traveled south by dogsled and on snowshoes to Selkirk, at the south end of Lake Winnipeg, arriving there on New Year's Day, 1894.

During this trip Tyrrell had heard from the Inuit of another major river, the Kazan, to the east of and parallel to the Dubawnt, and decided to explore it next. In July 1894 he set off with Robert Munro-Ferguson from Grand Rapids on Lake Winnipeg by canoe. Traveling via the Saskatchewan River, Reindeer Lake, Cochrane River, and the Thlewiaza River, they reached Kasba Lake, at the headwaters of the Kazan River on August 5. They then headed north downriver via Ennadaia Lake and Angekuni Lake to Yathkyed Lake. The party portaged from there east to Ferguson Lake and down the Ferguson River to Hudson Bay. They reached Churchill on October 1 and Selkirk on January 7, 1895.

Matching, if not surpassing, Tyrrell's exploration of the Keewatin were the achievements of Albert P. Low in Nouveau-Québec. His travels to and fro across the peninsula spanned a period of fifteen years. For example, in 1893, along with D. I. V. Eaton, he canoed from Lac St. Jean to Lac Mistassini then via an upper branch of the Rivière Rupert to the Rivière Eastmain, and up it for about 99 miles (160 kilometers); then by a number of portages they reached Lac Nichicun. From there they portaged across to Lac Caniapiscau, and ran down the Rivière Caniapiscau and the Rivière Koksoak to Fort Chimo (now Kuujuaq), arriving on August 26. Thus they had traversed the entire peninsula from south to north in one season, and along the way had discovered the vast iron ore deposits of the Labrador Trough.

Three years later (1896), with G. A. Young and W. Spreadborough, Low started out in late June from Lac Guillaume-Delisle up the Rivière à l'Eau Claire to Lac à l'Eau Claire, which they reached on July 14. From there via Lac des Loups Marins they portaged to the headwaters of the Rivière aux Mélèzes and descended it to the Rivière Koksoak and to Kuujuaq again, arriving on August 26. This was the first known crossing from Hudson Bay to Ungava Bay. These two examples provide at least a general feeling for this geologist's remarkable exploratory canoe trips.

Major contributions were also made by the trio of officers who comprised the Canadian Yukon Exploring Expedition of 1887–1889, namely George Mercer Dawson (who in 1895 became director of the survey), Richard McConnell, and William Ogilvie. They operated separately and their routes ranged from Wrangell, Alaska, east to the Slave River and north to Fort Yukon and McDougall Pass. In 1898, along with J. B. Tyrrell, McConnell was busy in the Yukon, surveying the mining creeks of the Klondike Gold Rush, namely Bonanza, Eldorado, and Dominion creeks. And in 1902 McConnell was back in the Yukon, again surveying the Macmillan River. For the first part of that season McConnell was traveling with Joseph Keele, who surveyed the south branch of the Macmillan River after they separated. In 1905 Keele was back in this area again, surveying the upper Stewart River, while in 1907–1908 he explored the upper Pelly and Ross rivers. Then, crossing Christie Pass (the first known scientist to cross the Mackenzie Mountains) he descended the Gravel (now Keele) River to the Mackenzie River. This was the route subsequently followed by the short-lived Canol Pipeline, from Norman Wells to Whitehorse, built during World War II.

Further major contributions were made by Charles Camsell, later Deputy Minister of Mines (1920–1949). In 1902 he surveyed much of the area now forming Wood Buffalo National Park, on the boundary between Alberta and the Northwest Territories, and in 1905 he traveled the length of the Stewart River (Yukon), then, crossing the height of land, descended the Wind River to the Peel River and Fort McPherson. In 1914 he led a party that explored the area between Lake Athabasca and Great Slave Lake and east of the Slave River, an area probably visited previously by only one non-native, namely Samuel Hearne in 1771–1772.

In 1897 Robert Bell, along with A. P. Low, traveled north on board the *Diana* to Hudson Strait. While Low surveyed the south shore of Hudson Strait, from Douglas Harbour east to the George River, Bell surveyed most of the north shore of the strait, with a side-trip inland to Amadjuak Lake. Then in 1899 he surveyed the east arm of Great Slave Lake. Meanwhile his nephew James Bell was exploring and mapping the Smith and Dease arms of Great Bear Lake, then ascended the Camsell River and traveled south via Clut, Grouard, and Hotah lakes to Marian Lake and Great Slave Lake.

Some of the last islands in the Canadian Arctic were discovered by an expedition whose scientific program came under the control of the Geological Survey; this was the Canadian Arctic Expedition of 1913–1916, led by Vlhjalmur Stefansson. As leader of the northern party, in the spring of 1914, accompanied by Ole Andreasen and Storker Storkersen, he traveled across the sea ice from Martin Point, Alaska, to Norway Island, off the west coast of Banks Island, thus demonstrating that there was no land in this part of the Beaufort Sea. In 1915 and 1916 Stefansson discovered and explored Brock, Borden, Mackenzie King, and Meighen islands.

BIBLIOGRAPHY

Cooke, Alan, and Clive Holland. *The Exploration of Northern Canada, 500 to 1920: A Chronology*. Toronto: Arctic History Press, 1978.

Low, A. P. *Report on Explorations in the Labrador Peninsula along the East Main, Koksoak, Hamilton, Manicuagan, and Portions of Other Rivers in 1892–93–94–95*. Ottawa: Geological Survey of Canada, 1896.

Thomson, Don W. *Men and Meridians. The History of Surveying and Mapping in Canada*. 3 vols. Ottawa: Queen's Printer, 1966–1969.

Tyrrell, James W. *Across the Sub-Arctics of Canada*. London: T. F. Unwin, 1898.

Tyrrell, Joseph Burr. "A Second Expedition through the Barren Lands of Northern Canada." *Geographical Journal* 6 (1895): 438–448.

Adrien Victor Joseph de Gerlache de Gomery. Scene from Adrien de Gerlache's *Quinze mois dans L'Antarctique* (Brussels: Imprimerie Scientifique, 1902). This dramatic scene from Gerlache's voyage shows the *Belgica* apparently fast on a reef; improbably, she survived. COURTESY THE NEWBERRY LIBRARY, CHICAGO

Zaslow, Morris. *Reading the Rocks: The Story of the Geological Survey of Canada, 1842–1972.* Toronto: Macmillan, 1975.

WILLIAM BARR

Gerlache de Gomery, Adrien Victor Joseph de

Gerlache de Gomery, Adrien Victor Joseph de (1866–1934), Belgian Antarctic explorer. Born in Hasselt to a noble family on August 2, 1866, de Gerlache was attracted at an early age to adventure and marine life. He started his career in the mercantile marine, and in 1890 he became a lieutenant in the Royal Belgian Navy.

After having applied in 1891 in vain for an Adolf Nordensköld expedition that never sailed, de Gerlache began preparations for his own Antarctic expedition. In the end, it took him almost seven years before the *Belgica*, the first scientific vessel ever to go the Antarctic continent, left Antwerp on August 16, 1897. On board with de Gerlache was an international crew, including the Belgian navigation officer Georges Lecointe and the young Norwegian Roald Amundsen, who would later, in 1911, be the first person to reach the South Pole. The *Belgica*'s surgeon, the American Frederick Cook, joined in Rio de Janeiro, and became the first person to take photographs of Antarctica.

On January 23, 1898, the expedition discovered what they called Belgica Strait (now Gerlache Strait), west of Graham Land, where they charted and named the islands of Brabant, Liège, and Anvers, besides many smaller islands. Wiencke Island was named in memory of a drowned sailor. No fewer than twenty landings were made on the newly discovered islands, while many scientific observations were made. The expedition passed the Polar Circle on February 15 and, heading farther southwest, entered the pack ice, where they became imprisoned at 71°22′ S, 84°55′ W, on March 4. This was the start of a year at drift in the ice and the first ever wintering in the Antarctic. Discussion continues today as to whether de Gerlache had really intended to winter in the pack ice or whether he became stuck by accident.

During the long Antarctic winter, the crew underwent great physical and mental hardships. Two Norwegian sailors went mad, and the Belgian magnetician Emile Danco died (Danco Coast was named after him). The experienced doctor Cook played an important role in the recovery of the crew. With superhuman efforts, the men managed to hack a channel in the ice, and on March 14, 1899, the *Belgica* reached open sea at last.

De Gerlache later made three important expeditions to the Arctic on the *Belgica*: to Greenland in 1905, to the Kara Sea in 1907, and to Greenland again in 1909. De Gerlache died in Brussels on December 4, 1934. His son Gaston was a member of the second Belgian Antarctic expedition in 1957–1959.

[*See also* Amundsen, Roald; Antarctica; *and* Greenland.]

BIBLIOGRAPHY

Cook, Frederick A. *Through the First Antarctic Night, 1898–1899: A Narrative of the Voyage of the "Belgica" among Newly Discovered Lands and over an Unknown Sea about the South Pole.* New York: Doubleday and McClure, 1900.

Decleir, Hugo, and Claude De Broyer, eds. *The Belgica Expedition Centennial: Perspectives on Antarctic Science and History.* Brussels: VUB Brussels University Press, 2001.

Gerlache, Adrien de. *Quinze mois dans l'Antarctique: Voyage de la "Belgica."* Preface by Elisée Reclus. Brussels: Imprimerie Scientifique Charles Bulens, 1902.

Lecointe, Georges. *Au pays de manchots, Expedition Antarctique Belge: Recit du voyage de la "Belgica."* Brussels: Oscar Schepens and Cie, 1904.

JOHAN DECKERS

Gilgamesh Epic

Gilgamesh Epic. The epic of Gilgamesh is the most famous and beloved of literary works to emerge from ancient Mesopotamia. The best-preserved version of the epic is the Standard Version, numerous copies of which were found in the palace libraries of Neo-Assyrian kings. This work, probably composed sometime in the later second millennium B.C.E., is the product of a Babylonian scribe named Sin-Leqi-unninni, who revised and elaborated upon an earlier version of the story and added further poetic embellishments.

The epic, which consists of a continuous narrative poem written across eleven clay tablets in cuneiform Akkadian, tells of Gilgamesh, a semidivine king of the city of Uruk, whose people had grown weary of his restless behavior and oppressive rule. In response, the gods created the hairy savage Enkidu as a rival for Gilgamesh. Gilgamesh and Enkidu meet and immediately engage in a violent wrestling match, but upon its conclusion they become fast friends. The story then describes the pair's journey to the Cedar Forest, where they slay the monster Huwawa, and their victorious return with precious timber. While Gilgamesh and Enkidu are popular with the people, their heroic exploits cause the anger of the gods, who are unhappy about the death of the forest-guardian Huwawa. Gilgamesh and Enkidu also insult the goddess Ishtar and kill the Bull of Heaven sent down to ravage the city of Uruk. As a consequence of these misdeeds, the gods decree that Enkidu should die. Gilgamesh, who comes face to face with the death of his best friend, falls into a deep depression. Realizing that he, too, might die some day, Gilgamesh embarks on a long quest to find immortality. His journey leads him across land and ocean to the edge of the world, where he encounters Utnapishtum, the only immortal man. Utnapishtum tells Gilgamesh the story of his survival from a terrible flood, in which he built a boat and filled it with every living creature. This story and encounter with Utnapishtum gets Gilgamesh no nearer his goal, and after a careless moment in which he loses a plant with rejuvenating powers to a snake, Gilgamesh returns to Uruk, his quest for immortality having completely eluded him. Through his long journey, however, Gilgamesh has become reconciled to his own fate and now he is filled with the pride of his beautiful and monumental city, an enduring testimony to his strength and fame.

In the epic, the destinations reached by Gilgamesh are more fantastic than real. It is true that the Cedar Forest can be identified with Lebanon, historically known to have been a valuable source of cedar in the Near East. But the existence of the ferocious forest giant Huwawa and the splitting of the earth during the heroic duo's battle with the monster remind us that we have journeyed into a fantastic, mythological place of larger-than-life creatures and landscapes. Similarly, when Gilgamesh embarks on his quest for immortality, his encounters with scorpion-men, his journey through the mountains of the setting sun and bejeweled forests, and his voyage across the sea of death all further underline that this adventure is set beyond the limits of the known physical world. While this story is indeed a tale of exploration, it is perhaps more appropriate to regard this exploration as a journey of self-discovery: through these voyages to distant places Gilgamesh finds himself, and in the process attains wisdom.

[*See also* Europe and the Mediterranean, *subentry on* Ancient Near East Geography, Worldview, and Mapmaking, *and* Travel Writing in Antiquity.]

BIBLIOGRAPHY

Dalley, Stephanie, trans. *Myths from Mesopotamia: Creation, the Flood, Gilgamesh, and Others.* Oxford and New York: Oxford University Press, 1989. Rev. ed., 2000.

Foster, Benjamin R., trans. and ed. *The Epic of Gilgamesh.* New York and London: Norton, 2001.

George, Andrew, trans. *The Epic of Gilgamesh: The Babylonian Epic Poem and Other Texts in Akkadian and Sumerian.* Harmondsworth, U.K.: Penguin, 1999.

LISA COOPER

Globes. The idea of the Earth as a (perfectly) spherical body apparently had its beginnings among the ancient Greeks. It gained currency through the work of Plato (d. 347 B.C.E.), and Aristotle (d. 322 B.C.E.) proposed a latitudinal division of the globe with climatic zones bounded by small circles: north and south arctic circles (later 66.5° N and S, respectively), and north and south tropic circles (later 23.5° N and S, respectively). Between these last two circles is a torrid zone straddling the Equator, the only great circle of latitude. On whether or not a globe was actually constructed on this principle we are not informed, but Crates of Mallus, active during the second century B.C.E., did make a terrestrial globe, now lost.

Crates's predominantly land-covered globe consisted of four essentially symmetrical continents, two in the Northern Hemisphere and two in the Southern, separated by narrow Ocean Streams, later Oceanus (one east-west, and one north-south). The idea of "balancing" continents was not demolished until the Pacific voyages of James Cook in the eighteenth century. The Chinese believed that the Earth was a curving figure, if not a globe. At an early date Islamic societies created celestial globes; the oldest surviving globe is a celestial sphere made in Persia and dated from internal evidence at 1279 C.E.

The oldest surviving terrestrial globe is the *Erdapfel* of Martin Behaim of Nuremberg. It was made just prior to the return of Christopher Columbus from his first transatlantic voyage (1493), and shows the world in twelve globe gores with no American continental landmasses. Earlier, Columbus had been encouraged to sail west to Cathay (China) by seeing a globe similar to that of Behaim.

The first professional globe-maker in Europe was Johan Schöner, c. 1520, who delineated the Americas on his globes. Later Renaissance globe-makers were to create globes for high latitude navigation. Globe-making was an important craft among the Low Country cartographers including Gerard Mercator and the Blaeu family. But they were eventually surpassed in this endeavor by the Venetian Vincenzo Coronelli, best known for his *Libro dei globi*, a printed atlas of globe gores, in 1697. Coronelli, arguably the greatest globe-maker of all time, created globes of many sizes, while in England at about this time, small pocket globes were made by Joseph Moxon and others. This led to the invention of globe machines (Orrery), to demonstrate planetary motions.

Globe-making continued and expanded in the nineteenth century when instruction in geography and astronomy was conducted with the use of globes, as they became cheaper and more available. It also became fashionable to make giant globes, especially

Behaim Globe. This astonishing globe, made at Nuremberg about 1492 and relying on Portuguese information, shows the Atlantic world as Columbus must have imagined it. No wonder he thought that by sailing west he would soon reach Japan. BIBLIOTHÈQUE NATIONALE DE FRANCE

in the late nineteenth and twentieth centuries. One notable example is the "Mapparium" in the Christian Science Building in Boston, which allows the viewer to see the Earth in stereographic projection from inside the globe. The automatically rotating globe is a recent innovation. Globes are the most accurate representation of the sphere, since all map projections have shape or size (and other) distortions. However, globes have limitations; for example, it is difficult to make measurements on an all-side curving figure, and globes do not permit the viewer to see all of the Earth at a glance. Thus globes do not replace flat world maps.

[*See also* Coronelli, Vincenzo; Maps, Mapmaking, and Mapmakers; *and* Mercator, Gerard.]

BIBLIOGRAPHY

Hofmann, Catherine, Danielle Lecoq, Eve Natchine et al. *Le Globe & son Image*. Paris: Bibliothèque Nationale de France, 1995.

Morris, Oswald, and Gert Saarmann. *Der Globus in Wandel der Zeiten: Eine Geschichte der Globen*. Berlin: Columbus Verlag Paul Oestegaard, 1971.

Raisz, Erwin J. *General Cartography*. 2nd ed. New York, Toronto, and London: McGraw-Hill, 1948. See especially chap. 28, "Globes and Models," pp. 265–276.

Stevenson, Edward L. *Terrestrial and Celestial Globes: Their History and Construction*. New Haven, Conn.: Yale University Press for the Hispanic Society of America, 1921. The modern globe society, Coronelli and the Friends of the Globe (named after Franciscan friar Vincenzo Coronelli) publishes newsletters on all aspects of globes.

NORMAN J. W. THROWER

Gobi Desert. Of all the world's greatest deserts, the Gobi Desert longest retained a mysterious and forbidding reputation. Not only did it lie between great and inaccessible mountain ranges; it also covered a large area that was generally hostile to outside explorers. Thus it was late in the nineteenth century before the desert became known to the outside world.

The British explorer Ney Elias led several expeditions in the Gobi Desert region, beginning in 1872. His work has received much less attention than that of the flamboyant Russian explorer Nikolay Przhevalsky, who was active in the 1870s and early 1880s. Elias and Przhevalsky were to some extent rivals, part of the "Great Game" that Russian and Briton were playing in that part of the world. A little later, the British agent Sir Francis Younghusband was also active in the region, part of his attempt to keep an eye on Russian activity that might be thought to menace British rule in India. Meanwhile, the Swede Sven Hedin was beginning his forty years of exploration in the region, in the course of which he published such classics as *Across the Gobi Desert* (New York: Dutton, 1932).

In the first half of the twentieth century, the leading explorer of the Gobi Desert was no doubt the American Roy Chapman Andrews, who led five well-funded expeditions there between 1922 and 1930. By then, after the Russian Revolution, the explorers' preoccupations were less political than scientific, particularly after explorers found that the desert was rich in dinosaur fossils. More recently, the region has become entirely accessible to modern means of transport and has become an area of strategic interest for the oil and minerals that have been found there.

[*See also* Elias, Ney; Hedin, Sven; Przhevalsky, Nikolay; *and* Younghusband, Francis.]

BIBLIOGRAPHY

Andrews, Roy Chapman. *The New Conquest of Central Asia.* New York: American Museum of Natural History, 1932.

Cable, Mildred, with Francesca French. *The Gobi Desert.* New York: Macmillan, 1944.

DAVID BUISSERET

Goddard, Robert (1882–1945), American rocket scientist. Robert Hutchings Goddard was born on October 5, 1882, in Worcester, Massachusetts. At the age of seventeen, while climbing a cherry tree, Goddard had a vision of space travel: "I imagined how wonderful it would be to make some device which had even the possibility of ascending to Mars." (Goddard 1970, p. 9) His vision would forever change his life.

He earned his undergraduate degree from Worcester Polytechnic Institute and his master's degree and doctorate from Clark University, where his major area of concentration was physics. During this time he first explored mathematically the practicality of using rocket power to reach high altitudes and escape velocity. He was awarded the first of his 214 patents in July of 1914 for a liquid-fuel gun rocket, a multistage step rocket. Over the following years Goddard advanced through the ranks at Clark University from instructor to director of the Physical Laboratories.

In 1917 he received his first grant from the Smithsonian Institution with further grants through 1932.

During World War I, Goddard worked for the U.S. Army on the development of a rocket weapon, the bazooka; after the war Goddard returned to his research at Clark University. In late 1919, the Smithsonian Institution published Goddard's *A Method of Reaching Extreme Altitudes*, outlining a basic mathematical theory underlying rocket propulsion and rocket flight; this was published together with results of his experiments with solid-propellant rockets. The report was the first such publication in the United States and resulted in much unwanted publicity for Goddard, from the sarcastic title "the Moon Man," to a January 13, 1920, *New York Times* editorial stating that Goddard "seems to lack the knowledge ladled out daily in high schools." It is interesting to note that the *Times* statement was retracted on July 17, 1969. By the spring of 1922, Goddard's experiments were becoming more difficult to explain to Clark University officials, so many of his experiments were moved to a farm outside Auburn owned by Miss Effie Ward, a distant relative of Goddard's.

Late in 1925 Goddard static-fired his rocket at Clark University, the first time a liquid-fueled rocket was able to lift its own weight. Bolstered by his success, Goddard felt the rocket could actually fly; so on March 16, 1926, he made history. In his diary, Dr. Goddard wrote, "Went to Auburn with S [his assistant] in am. E [his wife] and Mr. Roope came out at 1 pm. Tried rocket at 2:30. It rose 41 ft [12.5 meters], & went 184 ft [56 meters], in 2.5 secs, after the lower half of nozzle had burned off." (Goddard 1970, p. 580) The next day, March 17, he expanded on this brief summary of the launch by writing, "The first flight with a rocket using liquid propellants was made yesterday at Aunt Effie's farm in Auburn. The day was clear and comparatively quiet. . . . It looked almost magical as it rose, without any appreciably greater noise or flame, as if it said 'I've been here long enough; I think I'll be going somewhere else, if you don't mind.'" (Goddard 1970, p. 581) Goddard, jubilant with his success, would later write: "As a first flight, it compares favorably with the Wright's first airplane flight . . . and the event, as demonstrating the first liquid-propelled rocket, was just as significant." (Goddard 1970, p. 30) This first rocket consisted of tubing ten feet (three meters) long framing a two-foot (sixty-one-centimeter) motor and nozzle. At this time Goddard felt the rocket would be more stable if he positioned the motor and nozzle ahead of the rocket's fuel and oxygen tanks, rather than behind them. Ten flight tests were attempted in Auburn, although only four of them were successful. Each of these failures was a learning experience for

Goddard on his road to developing the liquid-fueled rocket.

The last flight at Aunt Effie's farm, the first rocket to carry a scientific payload of a small camera, a thermometer, and a barometer, resulted in the fire marshal of Massachusetts forbidding Goddard from launching a rocket in the state; but it also led to a series of grants from the Guggenheims, allowing Goddard to develop rockets in a more favorable location. His entire operation was moved in 1930 to Roswell, New Mexico, where he continued to test numerous rockets during the years up to his death. These flights tested many new inventions, including a rocket with a gyroscope, turbopumps, and many more firsts that are standard on today's rockets. At the onset of World War II, Goddard offered his services to the military but was initially turned down. In 1942 the navy requested his assistance in developing a method of aiding airplanes during takeoff. After World War II he continued his research until his death on August 10, 1945. His wife of twenty-one years, Esther Christine Kisk, who assisted Goddard during his experiments over the years, would close out her husband's work.

In 1951, Mrs. Goddard and the Guggenheim Foundation, which had helped fund Dr. Goddard's research, filed a joint claim against the U.S. government for infringing upon his patents. In June of 1960 they were given a one-million-dollar settlement, at that time the largest patent settlement that the government had ever given.

[See also Rocket Societies, The.]

BIBLIOGRAPHY

Goddard, Esther C., and G. Edward Pendray. Rocket Development: Liquid-fuel Rocket Research, 1929–1941. New York: Prentice-Hall, 1948.

Goddard, Robert H. The Papers of Robert H. Goddard, Including the Reports to the Smithsonian Institution and the Daniel and Florence Guggenheim Foundation. Edited by Esther C. Goddard. G. Edward Pendray, associate editor. 3 vols. New York: McGraw-Hill, 1970.

Goddard, Robert H. "Rockets, by Dr. Robert H. Goddard, Comprising 'A Method of Reaching Extreme Altitudes' and 'Liquid-propellant Rocket Development.'" New York: American Rocket Society, 1946. Reprinted as Rockets. Reston, Va.: American Institute of Aeronautics and Astronautics, 2002.

Lehman, Milton. This High Man: The Life of Robert H. Goddard. New York: Farrar, Straus, 1963. Includes preface by Charles A. Lindbergh. Reprinted as Robert H. Goddard: Pioneer of Space Research. New York: Da Capo Press, 1988.

ANTHONY M. SPRINGER

Golden Fleece. See **Argonauts and Golden Fleece.**

Gold Rush, Yukon. See **Alaska and the Yukon Gold Rush.**

Golovnin, Vasily (1776–1831), Russian explorer and scientist. Golovnin graduated from the Kronshtadt naval school in 1792, and from 1801 to 1805 he served as a volunteer in the British Royal Navy. Returning to Russia, he was commissioned in 1807 to command an expedition aboard the *Diana* to make a survey of Kamchatka and the Russian possessions

Vasily Golovnin. Title page from "Captain Golownin's" *Narrative of My Captivity in Japan* (London, 1818). This title page reminds us of the great international interest that exploration aroused in the nineteenth century; English readers were keen to learn of the adventures of a Russian captain at the hands of the Japanese. COURTESY THE NEWBERRY LIBRARY, CHICAGO

in Alaska. The expedition rounded Africa and Australia before entering the Pacific Ocean, where it carried out much geographical and ethnological research; in October 1809 it arrived in Kamchatka.

In 1810, while attempting to map the coast of one of the Kuril Islands, Golovnin was captured and imprisoned by the Japanese (1811–1813). He described this experience in the *Narrative of My Captivity in Japan . . .* (1816), which was translated into French, German, and English. Later, in circumnavigating the world aboard the *Kamchatka*, he made a second voyage (1817–1819) to Kamchatka and the Aleutian Islands. This second voyage was described in Golovnin's *Round the World Voyage . . . on Board the Navy Sloop "Kamchatka"* (Saint Petersburg, 1822); Golovnin later summarized his experience as a mariner-surveyor in the authoritative work known as *The Art of Sea Coast and Ocean Surveys, with an Explanation of All the Newest Instruments' Applications*. In 1818 he became a corresponding member of the Saint Petersburg Academy of Sciences, and he died in 1831 after becoming a vice admiral. In 1864, a complete five-volume edition of Golovnin's works was published at Saint Petersburg by N. Grech.

[*See also* Expeditions, World Exploration, *subentry on* Russia, *and* Navigational Techniques.]

ALEXEY POSTNIKOV

Gomes, Estêvão

Gomes, Estêvão (1483/84–1538), Portuguese navigator. Gomes left his native Oporto to acquire experience aboard Portuguese vessels sailing to India. From 1518 he served the Spanish crown as a pilot and as an adviser on shipbuilding in the Portuguese style. In 1520, while accompanying his compatriot Ferdinand Magellan on his quest for a western passage to the East Indies, Gomes mutinied and returned to Spain. In 1523 he successfully petitioned the Spanish crown for authorization to discover an alternative passage between Florida and Newfoundland that was less remote, shorter, and easier than Magellan's. Gomes sailed from Corunna in northwestern Spain on September 24, 1524. Although it used to be believed that he made a northern crossing of the Atlantic, evidence now suggests that Gomes followed the customary Spanish route to the West Indies. From Santiago de Cuba he headed for Florida and coasted the eastern seaboard of North America as far as Cape Race (Newfoundland), charting for the first time Cape Cod and a "great river" (the Penobscot). He returned to Corunna on August 21, 1525. His influential discoveries were immediately incorporated into Diogo Ribeiro's world map of 1525,

bearing the legend "Land of Estêvão Gomes" and depicting a new coastline with no evidence of the hoped-for alternative western passage.

In 1535, Gomes sailed with Pedro de Mendoza to the River Plate. From 1536 to 1537 he accompanied Juan de Ayolas and Domingo Martínez de Irala during their exploration of the Paraguay River, and then trekked overland with Ayolas into the Gran Chaco. Gomes died in an ambush on their return.

[*See also biographical entries on figures mentioned in this article.*]

BIBLIOGRAPHY
Quinn, David B. *North America from Earliest Discovery to First Settlements: The Norse Voyages to 1612.* New York: Harper and Row, 1977.

PETER T. BRADLEY

Gordon, Charles

Gordon, Charles (1833–1885), British explorer of the Nile River region. The famed "Chinese Gordon" of Khartoum, while in service to Khedive Ismā'īl of Egypt, organized the exploration of the Upper Nile as far as the central African lakes in present-day Uganda.

From a long line of soldiers, Gordon was born at Woolwich, England, on January 28, 1833, and graduated as an engineer from the Royal Military Academy. He fought in the Crimean War (1853–1856) and the "Arrow War" (1860) in China, winning his nickname "Chinese Gordon" while leading his "Ever-Victorious Army" against the Taiping rebellion in 1863–1864.

Between 1874 and 1876, he followed Samuel Baker as governor of Egypt's Equatorial Provinces. Moving his Nile base from unhealthy Gondokoro a few miles downstream to Lado, Gordon and his lieutenants struggled to suppress the slave trade, explore, and plant the Egyptian flag as far as Lakes Albert and Victoria. Charles Chaillé-Long discovered Lake Kyoga while tracing the Victoria Nile north from Urondogani to Mrooli. C. Watson and H. Chippendall and later the Italian Romolo Gessi struggled mightily to get steamers up to Lake Albert, having to portage them in pieces around the falls near Dufilé and reassemble them upstream. Gessi circumnavigated Lake Albert, proving that the Nile ran into and out of its northeast corner. In 1876 Gordon himself sailed his steamer *Nyanza* from Dufilé through Lake Albert and up the Victoria Nile to Murchison Falls, then marched overland to explore Lake Kyoga further. Two overly ambitious schemes failed: Gordon had to withdraw without a treaty the troops who reached King Mutesa's capital on Lake Victoria, and

British opposition thwarted H. F. McKillop's and Chaillé-Long's attempt to open a route from the Somali coast via the Juba River to Egyptian posts on the Upper Nile. Several of Gordon's European assistants died, and late in 1876 he left exhausted for Cairo and England.

Khedive Ismā'īl lured Gordon back until 1880 as governor-general of the whole Sudan, but his administrative burdens as he hurried around his vast domain by steamer and on camelback left little time for exploration. In February 1884 he returned, again as governor general. His death eleven months later on January 26, 1885, when Khartoum fell to Muhammad Ahmad (known as al-Mahdi), earned him a martyr's crown in the eyes of his countrymen.

[*See also* Africa, *subentry on* Exploration; Baker, Samuel; Chaillé-Long, Charles; *and* Khedivial Exploration.]

BIBLIOGRAPHY

Davenport-Hines, Richard. "Gordon, Charles George." *Oxford Dictionary of National Biography*, vol. 22, pp. 864–870. Oxford: Oxford University Press, 2004.

Waller, John H. *Gordon of Khartoum: The Saga of a Victorian Hero*. New York: Atheneum, 1988.

DONALD MALCOLM REID

Grant, James Augustus

Grant, James Augustus (1827–1892), British explorer of central Africa. James Augustus Grant accompanied John Hanning Speke on the Nile expedition of 1860–1863 but did not himself visit the source. Born at Nairn, Scotland, a son of the manse, he was educated locally and then in Aberdeen at the Grammar School and Marischal College before taking a commission in the Indian Army in 1846. He fought in various campaigns and was wounded at the Relief of Lucknow in 1857. Grant had met Speke on a hunting trip in 1852 and Speke invited him to join the Nile expedition in 1859.

Grant was steady and level-headed. His university training made him exceptionally well-qualified in natural history and botany, while his sketching and painting ability led to his producing the first visual record of large parts of eastern Africa. For reasons having ostensibly to do with the need to link up with the trader Petherick as soon as possible, and the difficulty an ulcerated leg had given him in walking fast, in July 1862 Grant did not accompany Speke to the Ripon Falls to see the source of the Nile. Whatever he may have felt about this exclusion at the time, Grant later stoutly defended his leader's reputation. His own book is a somewhat disappointing digest of his very detailed journal but he subsequently produced important scientific articles. Grant

was awarded the honor from the Crown of Commander of the Bath (CB) and later served in India again and on the Abyssinian expedition of 1867–1868. For the rest of his life he became a quietly influential figure on the council of the Royal Geographical Society and was involved in various East African projects, notably the dispatch of Anglican missionaries to Buganda in 1876, and his attendance at the Brussels Geographical Conference the same year. Grant died at his home, Househill, near Nairn, in 1892.

[*See also* Africa, *subentry on* Exploration; Brussels Geographical Conference *and* Speke, John Hanning.]

BIBLIOGRAPHY

Grant, J. A. "Summary of Observations Made by the Speke and Grant Expedition." *Journal Royal Geographical Society* 42 (1872): 243–342.

Grant, James Augustus. *A Walk across Africa, or, Domestic Scenes from My Nile Journal*. Edinburgh and London: Blackwood, 1864.

James Augustus Grant in Africa, 1860–1863. Edinburgh: National Library of Scotland, 1982. Includes a biography by R. C. Bridges and reproductions of some of Grant's paintings.

Bridges, Roy. "James Augustus Grant's Visual Record of East Africa." With the *Annual Report of the Hakluyt Society for 1993*. London: Hakluyt Society, 1994.

ROY BRIDGES

Great Basin

Great Basin. The Great Basin was the last region in the continental United States to be explored and mapped. A large area of about 165,000 square miles, the Great Basin lies between the Wasatch Mountains and the Sierra Nevada range in western North America. The distinguishing physical characteristic of the Great Basin is its interior drainage: none of the precipitation falling within the region reaches the sea, but rather finds its way into topographic depressions—locally called "basins" or "sinks." The Great Basin is generally an arid and semiarid region in the rain shadow of the Sierra Nevadas. Evaporation here exceeds precipitation and has since the end of the Pleistocene period about ten thousand years ago. During the Pleistocene period, the region possessed two huge lakes—Lahontan in the west, and Bonneville in the east. At times during the million-year period before today, overflow reached the Pacific by means of drainage northward into the Snake River. With increasing desiccation, however, most of the region became a desert, although its numerous mountains are moister and often forested. The native peoples here, notably the Paiute, Shoshone, and Washo, tended to migrate in search of plants and animals that they harvested as hunters and gatherers, though there were some areas of semipermanent settlement near the dependable sources of water, especially springs.

The Great Basin remained a complete blank on most European maps of North America until the Spaniards began to explore it in the eighteenth century. By the mid-eighteenth century, Spanish maps began to delineate some of the geographic features here. Francisco Barreiro's 1728 map *Plano Corográphico e Hydrographico de las Provincias . . . de la Nueba España* is one of the cartographic breakthroughs in the region's history, for it reveals that some of the rivers here drain toward a lake—a clear suggestion that the hydrology is internal. How did the Spaniards gain this knowledge? Because Spanish explorers had evidently not actually reached the region, much of the information about the interior west on Barreiro's map appears to be from Native American informants. A careful review of explorers' reports confirms that native peoples were capable of creating maps—some actually drawn in the sand—to describe the countryside accurately. The only known Spanish *entrada* into the Great Basin in the eighteenth century was the Domínguez-Escalante expedition of 1776, which sought a route from Santa Fe, New Mexico, to Monterey, California. That expedition mapped the area around Utah Lake and Sevier Lake, but was unable to cross the region. It did, however, speculate that a river crossed the region to the Pacific. That river is mythical rather than real, but there is a grain of truth to the myth: the Humboldt River runs westward across much of the region before ending in the Humboldt Sink. Miera's map from the Domínguez-Escalante expedition represents yet another cartographic breakthrough because it was the first to be based on actual observations. However, because Spain rarely published any maps out of concern for secrecy, much of the information on the map was never seen by the public. By 1795, William Winterbotham's map of western North America shows lakes (one probably the Great Salt Lake) with rivers running into them. Winterbotham's map is remarkable in that it appears to be the first widely published document to suggest that much of the interior west is an area of interior drainage.

By the early nineteenth century, mapping the intermountain West became important geopolitically, and portions of the region were represented in maps by Alexander von Humboldt, Zebulon Pike, and John Arrowsmith. Humboldt claimed that Pike (and Arrowsmith) plagiarized his work, and Humboldt appears to be correct when we consult the Great Basin portion of the maps in the vicinity of the Great Salt Lake and Utah Lake—for this portion is virtually identical in all three maps. However, it should be recalled that Pike was skillful at obtaining geographic information from many sources, including some of the same Spanish/Mexican sources that Humboldt used.

Anglo-American interest in the region intensified by the 1810s and 1820s, and many sought the fabled river that would take them to the Pacific Ocean. Like the Spaniards, these Anglo-Americans hoped that a westward-flowing river (called the "Buenaventura" by some) would carry their dreams of empire to the Pacific. However, explorers would soon prove them and their ambitious maps wrong. By the 1820s and 1830s, several expeditions by mountain men and explorers began to yield more accurate geographic information. These included expeditions by Jedediah Smith, Joseph Walker, and Captain Benjamin Bonneville. Explorers soon confirmed that the Humboldt River did not reach the sea. Despite hints about its landlocked quality, the Great Basin region's interior drainage still remained poorly understood until John Charles Frémont traversed the area and its margins in 1843–1844. Building on his own field observations and information from native peoples and earlier explorers, Frémont determined that the Sierra Nevadas blocked all the region's rivers from reaching the Pacific Ocean. Frémont coined the term "Great Basin" in 1844, and the name has stuck despite the fact that this complex region actually consists of about one hundred separate basins. The map by Charles Preuss from the Frémont expedition is considered to be another breakthrough in the cartographic history of the American West. It was the first popular printed map to portray the Great Basin much as we know it today—as a huge region bounded by mountains on its eastern and western margins, a region whose rivers and streams have no outlet to the sea.

The region's exploration and mapping did not end there. In 1847, the Mormons (members of the Church of Jesus Christ of Latter-day Saints) further helped make the region known when they created Salt Lake City and explored large portions of the Great Basin in search of sites to settle and resources to develop. They also drafted many of their own informative maps of the region. After the discovery of gold in California (1848), the Great Basin was traversed by increasing numbers of travelers. The period of aggressive U.S. survey activity continued from the early 1850s to about 1890, when the remaining portions of the Great Basin were explored and mapped. These surveyors included Charles Simpson, John W. Gunnison, and George

Wheeler. At the same time, and often on the same reconnaissance expeditions, geologists also mapped the Great Basin. They confirmed what prospectors knew: the region's mountains contained rich deposits of gold, silver, lead, and copper. Based on explorations between 1868 and 1872, Clarence King's reports of the geology of the Great Basin region are noteworthy, and they helped raise geological mapping to an art. By 1869, the Great Basin lay on the route of the first transcontinental railroad, as the Central Pacific Railroad (CPRR) traversed much of it along the Humboldt River. In May of that year, the CPRR met the Union Pacific at Promontory Summit near the north edge of the Great Salt Lake. By 1910, the Great Basin was no longer terra incognita, because miners and agriculturalists had continued to help demystify it. One area west of Utah's Great Salt Lake had the dubious distinction of being called the "Great American Desert" on maps until the 1920s; the salt-encrusted area is still very lightly populated today. For many travelers, however, the entire Great Basin remains the American outback or, as some call it, the "Big Empty."

[See also North America, subentry on Indigenous Maps, and biographical entries in figures mentioned in this article.]

BIBLIOGRAPHY
Cohen, Paul E. *Mapping the West*. New York: Rizzoli International Publications, 2002.
Francaviglia, Richard. *Believing in Place: A Spiritual History of the Great Basin*. Reno: University of Nevada Press, 2003.
Francaviglia, Richard. *Mapping and Imagination in the Great Basin: A Cartographic History*. Reno: University of Nevada Press, 2005.
Gilbert, E. W. *The Exploration of Western America, 1800–1850*. New York: Cooper Square Publishers, 1966.
Wheat, Carl. *Mapping the Trans-Mississippi West, 1540–1861*. 6 vols. San Francisco: Institute of Historical Cartography, 1957–1963.

RICHARD FRANCAVIGLIA

Great Lakes, The.

In 1535 the people of Stadacona, a village on the north shore of the Saint Lawrence River, gave Jacques Cartier the first report of "two to three large, very broad lakes" and a *mer douce* (freshwater sea) west of the Lachine Rapids, that great barrier on the Saint Lawrence River. In 1603, Samuel de Champlain obtained stories and maps from Algonquin informants about the same freshwater lakes system and a possible ocean west of them. He became convinced that the interior could be explored only with native help and native canoes.

After the French committed themselves to a military alliance with the Montagnais (1603) and the Algonquin and Huron (1609), inland exploration became possible. In 1609, Champlain joined a Montagnais war party going to Lake Champlain and became the first European to travel inland. In 1613 he tried to go north on the Ottawa River without being invited and was turned back. A better chance came in 1615 when he agreed to help the Huron in raids against the Iroquois. On this journey he finally reached the "freshwater sea" (Lake Huron), traversed southern Ontario, and crossed the east end of the lake into Iroquois territory, while Huron guides took his interpreter Étienne Brûlé around the western end of the lake. About 1623, Brûlé became the first European to see Lake Superior. In 1634, Champlain sent Jean Nicollet to the Winnebago to arrange a peace between them and the Odawa, Ojibwa, and Huron and to check on persistent rumors of a western sea. Nicollet was the first European to see Lake Michigan, which became confused with Lake Superior, but there was no salt sea.

The Jesuits entered the missionary field in 1632. Through their travels, and reports from their servants and natives, they began to delineate the geography of the Great Lakes. In 1640–1641, Fathers Jean de Brébeuf and Pierre Chaumonot opened a mission for the Neutral Indians and reported on Lake Ontario and Niagara Falls, while Fathers Isaac Jogues and Charles Raymbaut, among the Ojibwa at Sault Sainte Marie, reported on Lake Superior. Through the travels (1645–1646) of Médart Chouart des Groseilliers on Lake Huron for the Jesuits, Lake Michigan and Lake Superior became identified as separate lakes. These reports and sketched maps enabled Father Paul Ragueneau to compile a geography of all five lakes for the *Jesuit Relations* (1648), and Nicolas Sanson published a series of maps in 1650 and 1656.

During the 1640s, wars with the Iroquois raged through the eastern Great Lakes, ending in a peace late in 1653. The peace made it possible for des Groseilliers (1654–1656) and Pierre Radisson (1659–1660) to trade in the area around Lake Michigan and Lake Superior. On their return, they gave reports to the Jesuits about what they had seen and heard. Father Claude Allouez followed them in 1665 to establish a mission near the west end of Lake Superior. In 1667 he paddled with native guides around Lake Superior and into Green Bay, Lake Michigan (1669). His report and the first map of Lake Superior were published in the *Jesuit Relations* (1672). This map was the most accurate of the lake until after the surveys of the British Hydrographic Office in the early nineteenth century. During 1669–1670, two Sulpicians, Fathers Dollier de Casson and Bréhant de Galinée, were the first Europeans to travel through Lake Erie and Lake Huron, producing both a map and a report.

Lower Lake Michigan was described and mapped after the expeditions of Louis Jolliet and Father Jacques Marquette (1673–1674), and those of Cavelier de La Salle and his men (1678–1683). The English finally reached Lake Ontario in 1686 and, two years later, Father Vincenzo Coronelli published the most accurate and complete map of the Great Lakes of the seventeenth century.

[*See also* Champlain, Samuel de; Jolliet, Louis; Marquette, Jacques; Mer de l'Ouest and Rivière de l'Ouest; Nicollet, Jean; *and* Radisson, Pierre Esprit.]

BIBLIOGRAPHY
Harris, R. Cole, ed., and Geoffrey Matthews, cart. *Historical Atlas of Canada*. 3 vols. Vol. 1, *From the Beginning to 1800.* Toronto: University of Toronto Press, 1987.
Heidenreich, Conrad E. "Early French Exploration in the North American Interior." In *A Continent Defined*, 65–148, vol. 2 of *North American Exploration*, edited by John L. Allen. 3 vols. Lincoln: University of Nebraska Press, 1997.

CONRAD E. HEIDENREICH

Greek and Phoenician Colonization.

The settlement of Greeks and Phoenicians outside their original homelands represents an important episode in ancient Mediterranean history that had long-lasting effects on regional development. In the last generation, interest in this subject has reached an all-time high. This recent work has resulted in novel historical reconstructions and the breakdown of the old consensus that first took shape in the late nineteenth century, at a time when European exploration and colonization gripped the world, framing the study of Greek and Phoenician colonization in fundamental ways.

Modern Conceptions. Modern Europe's birthplace was situated in ancient Greece, and Greek colonization became an important vehicle for the dissemination of its culture, which, it was held, then made the Roman Empire possible, which in turn made Christendom possible, and so on up to the industrial revolution. In this conception of world history, European attitudes toward the ancient Near East were also affected, assisted by the contemporary developments of anti-Semitism and the crumbling of the Ottoman Empire, whose former territories passed into the hands of European nations, especially Britain and France. The interplay of these forces created antithetical poles, today labeled Hellenism and Ori-

entalism. One of the ways that this was achieved was through comparisons of the motives for Greek and Phoenician colonization: the Phoenicians were said to have been primarily interested in trade and the Greeks in agriculture. But, more substantially, the study of the Phoenicians generally went from a period of Phoeniciomania to Phoeniciophobia in the late nineteenth century. The beneficiary was the study of the ancient Greeks, with whom their European "descendants" identified in historical reconstructions. As a result, ancient Greece, like modern Europe itself, was made into the center of an imperial domain that extended from the Black Sea to the Iberian Peninsula.

Ancient Greek terminology for an overseas settlement, *apoikia*, which meant nothing more than "home away from home" and which involved the creation of independent city-states, was translated as "colony" and the whole process mirrored on modern colonization. This is a misleading and simplistic rendition of a complex and varied ancient phenomenon, but it has become the standard modern description of Phoenician overseas settlement too, if anything, for want of a serious challenge. Power relations between mother cities and their "colonies," as well as between Greek settlers and the "native" populations encountered, were also colored. In these scenarios, "the state" initiated "colonization," and dutiful "colonies" were expected to follow its direction in cultural and economic matters. Moreover, the "natives" met were viewed as inferior and forced to assimilate, but not to be mixed with for fear of degeneration. This intellectual framework was at the root of reconstructions of Greek and Phoenician colonization well into the last generation. Many of its tenets have proved hard to sustain in light of recent advances, and in general the field has gradually given way to more dynamic and diverse scholarship.

The study of Greek and Phoenician colonization is drawing impetus from other world developments, like decolonization, postcolonialism, postmodernism, and globalization, that are leading to new reconstructions. These approaches are revealing both the present limitations and possible future directions that could be taken. In respect to limitations, modern colonialist and imperialist attitudes have significantly shaped the disciplines of anthropology and archaeology, an extremely important consideration in the context of Greek and Phoenician colonization, owing to archaeology's central role in providing evidence. Phoenician archaeology languished until fairly recently, whereas Greek archaeology has become more highly developed over decades of attention. Archaeology in ancient Greek contact zones, however, simply supported the agendas and worldviews of modern European nations, reaffirming, both consciously and subconsciously, the Greekness of these "colonies" in relation to their "barbarian" neighbors and Greece. There is greater willingness today to acknowledge and discuss the multicultural and hybrid features that emerged in these contact zones, as well as the overlapping and cooperative aspects of Greek and Phoenician colonization. The settlers carried their homeland culture overseas, but this evolved on the frontier as a result of contact and interaction with other cultures and environments. Archaeology has become more methodologically and theoretically sophisticated, and the same applies to the study of ancient written sources, the other major category of evidence. Most surviving written sources were composed after the fact, and yet their reliability often went unquestioned. The cultural poetics of these sources have come to be more appreciated. In the case of Phoenician colonization, more sensitivity is being paid to the fact that Greek and Roman authors provide this evidence. In the case of Greek colonization, this has resulted, among other ways, in how foundation stories are treated. Accounts that told of the establishment of particular settlements by heroes in their travels following the Trojan War are now better understood as myths of precedence attempting to lay claim to the land by recently arrived settlers, and not necessarily a distant reflection of previous Bronze Age Mycenaean Greek involvement in these same areas. Archaeological evidence has expanded, refined, and challenged this and other pictures presented in the written sources.

Beginnings. The beginnings of Greek and Phoenician colonization are usually placed in the eighth century B.C.E., during the cultural and economic upswing witnessed by the Mediterranean as a whole following the so-called Dark Ages. While the eighth century was undoubtedly important for colonization, Greeks and Phoenicians had not been entirely cut off from other parts of the Mediterranean before then, as was often previously imagined. Greeks settled around the Aegean and maintained some contacts with the Levant. Phoenicians were in touch with these same areas, but they may have also gone further afield. The growing archaeological evidence for contact and interaction between the Near East and the central Mediterranean has encouraged belief in the ancient traditions that talk about Phoenicians founding Gades (modern Cádiz), Utica, and Lixus in the Iberian Peninsula and North Africa in the years

around 1100, although none of these sites has revealed material evidence prior to the eighth century. It may be unreasonable to expect much, if any, archaeological evidence in most cases, given this activity's presumed temporary nature, and hence lack of incentive for greater material investment. The awkward label "precolonization" has been coined for all this activity, but this is a term which, if it is to be used at all, should be used only in connection with contact events that later led to colonization. Greek and Phoenician colonization was but one of many episodes in Mediterranean history caused by the fragmentation of the landscape and its resources, together with the accessibility of the sea.

As mentioned, Greeks and Phoenicians are thought to have colonized for, respectively, agriculture and trade. This dichotomy seems too simple as the evidence mounts: both groups were spurred on by these factors, though the degree to which remains under investigation. Political and other discontent with conditions at home also played a part. Phoenicia itself had limited possibilities for grain production, and as population rose imports were necessary for survival. This seems to have occurred as early as the second half of the eleventh century B.C.E., when the monarchs of certain city-states, particularly Tyre and Sidon, made up the deficiency through trade with other parts of the Levant, above all Israel, and are credited with the establishment of settlements at various locations in the eastern and central Mediterranean. Such activity doubtless laid the groundwork for later Phoenician colonization, but the primary stimulus for this was the rise of the Assyrian Empire from the late tenth century onward. At first, the Phoenician city-states resisted and attempted to secure trade concessions, but later, around the mid-eighth century, the Assyrians imposed direct rule and hefty tribute. Tyre responded with an active program of exploration and colonization and quickly assumed the role of chief provider of raw materials, particularly metals, for the needy and growing Assyrian market. Traders, operating out of state and private interests, obtained these items from local populations in exchange for manufactured (usually luxury) goods and services. Phoenician presence overseas became archaeologically visible at this time because of the Assyrian stimulus but also because the Greeks, too, sought to exploit the possibilities offered by overseas exploration and colonization. The movement of Greeks to other parts of the Mediterranean in the eighth century coincided with secondary state formation in Greece, made possible through contact and interaction with particularly the Near

East. The Greeks were making the transition from what are usually characterized as simple chiefdoms and big men societies to more developed state institutions with centralized and stable power structures. This resulted in increased demand and competition for resources, for which Greece had limited possibilities. In the next two centuries thousands of Greeks left their homeland for greener pastures abroad, conquering and coexisting with the peoples they encountered.

Phoenician Colonization. Greeks and Phoenicians explored and settled some of the same regions of the Mediterranean. Tyre established most of the Phoenician overseas settlements, founded with a view to securing key points in communication routes and access to nearby resources, particularly metals. Tyre ruled these settlements as colonies, controlling them through administrators it appointed. These colonies were at first financially dependent on Tyre, but later tithes were sent to the homeland, facilitated through a single common institution, the temple of Melqart. Some of these Phoenician colonies, most notably Carthage in the early sixth century, achieved independence and became important cities in their own right. The first known Phoenician settlements were established at Kition on Cyprus, where Greeks had already settled at the end of the Bronze Age, and at Nora on Sardinia, both in the later ninth century. Carthage on the northeast coast of Tunisia followed soon after, if the date of 814 or 813 B.C.E. found in ancient literary sources can be trusted (new radiocarbon dates from Carthage are suggesting that the date may indeed be trustworthy). The pace quickened in the mid-eighth century thanks to the Assyrian Empire. Three settlements were established in Northwest Sicily at Motya, Panhormos, and Soloeis, and others took their place alongside Nora in Sardinia. Still others were set up on strategic islands, like Malta and Pantelleria, and at other vital points along the North African coast, to form a veritable Phoenician east-west maritime highway.

Glimpses of early Phoenician life overseas exist. Carthage seems to have started modestly in the eighth and earlier seventh centuries: single-room houses had stone foundations with mud-brick walls and beaten clay floors. There is no information of civic monuments in this period. The cemeteries provide evidence of the community's extensive contacts and mixed population, including Libyans, judging from burial practices. By the end of the seventh century Carthage was an active intermediary in Mediterranean trade and an important economic player in the Tyrrhenian basin, just as it was in later times. Of a completely different order from Carthage was Toscanos in eastern Andalusia, a trade enclave at best, founded in the mid-eighth century, one of many along this coast seeking to exploit the possibilities offered by the hinterland. Toscanos was never more than a large village of fifteen hundred people engaged in agriculture, animal husbandry, purple dye manufacture, and metallurgy. Life was centered on a central warehouse, around which were built single dwellings separated by dirt streets; a century later, the village was fortified.

Greek Colonization. Greek colonization involved a greater number of city-states. The main participants were Chalcis and Eretria on Euboea, Corinth, Megara, Miletus, and Phocaea. More occasional colonizers included Achaea, Paros, Rhodes, Crete, Sparta, Locris, Colophon, Thera, and Samos. The state's role in founding these overseas settlements has been overblown in earlier scholarship accustomed to drawing parallels with modern European colonization. More private initiative is to be envisaged. These "colonies" were politically independent and self-governing entities. From the sixth to fourth centuries B.C.E. states sometimes colonized, properly speaking, and attempted to control territory and tap into wider interaction networks through dependent settlements. By this period the two initial rituals of Greek colonization had been well established: the appointment of a leader (*oikistes* in ancient Greek) to handle the expedition's planning and execution, and the consultation of the god Apollo through the oracle at Delphi for guidance on selecting a settlement site. The *oikistes* was no doubt a feature of the earliest overseas expeditions. We cannot speak with such confidence about the consultation of the oracle at Delphi, but an eighth-century origin seems possible, although much allowance has to be made for later shaping and fabrication of oracle stories attached to the early foundations. Greeks first settled in southern Italy and Sicily. The best known of these settlements are Pithekoussai on the island of Ischia in the Bay of Naples and Megara Hyblaea in southeast Sicily, both established around the mid-eighth century. Pithekoussai quickly developed into a center of trade, agriculture, and industry in especially metals, obtained from nearby Etruria. Population reached five to ten thousand inhabitants in a mere fifty years. Ancient sources credit the foundation to Chalcis and Eretria, but archaeological evidence indicates that the settlement was home to a wider range of Greeks, Levantines, and native southern

Italians. At Megara Hyblaea, the ancient tradition talks about the trials and tribulations encountered by the Megarian settlers and the granting of land to them by the native chief Hyblon. Archaeology has uncovered a regularly laid out settlement, which still maintained a rural look for the first century, and which was modestly populated over this time with only a few hundred people, living in houses similar in design and structure to those discovered at Carthage. Megara Hyblaea's cemeteries have revealed native Sicilian burial practices, providing support for the ancient tradition of peaceful and cooperative relations. In the seventh and sixth centuries, Greeks filled out their settlement activity in southern Italy and Sicily and settled in other parts of the Mediterranean, most notably the northern Aegean, Black Sea and its approaches, North Africa, southern France, southern Spain, and the Adriatic. This resulted in dozens of foundations, some becoming, like Thasos, Cyrene, and Massalia, important cities in later times.

Beyond Colonization. Greeks and Phoenicians also resided, for purposes of trade, in each other's respective settlements, as well as in those of other cultures. Gravisca and Pyrgi are good examples of two such trading enclaves among the Etruscans, which became cultural meeting places resulting in, among other things, religious syncretism. Greeks and Phoenicians engaged in further exploration of the world from these and their own overseas bases. This exploration sometimes occurred well beyond the Mediterranean itself, (for instance, in West Africa and the Atlantic). It is salutary to remember that much is not recorded or only alluded to in this picture of Greek and Phoenician exploration and colonization, which, even so, clearly helped to accelerate and contribute to the progressive integration of the Mediterranean world.

[*See also* Maps, Mapmaking, and Mapmakers *and* Mediterranean.]

BIBLIOGRAPHY

Aubet, María Eugenia. *The Phoenicians and the West: Politics, Colonies, and Trade*. Translated by Mary Turton. 2nd ed. Cambridge, U.K.: Cambridge University Press, 2001. English translation of *Tiro y las Colonias Fenicias de Occident*, first published in 1987.

Boardman, John. *The Greeks Overseas: Their Early Colonies and Trade*. 4th ed. London: Thames and Hudson, 1999.

Dougherty, Carol. *The Poetics of Colonization: From City to Text in Archaic Greece*. New York: Oxford University Press, 1993.

Lancel, Serge. *Carthage: A History*. Translated by Antonia Nevill. Cambridge, Mass., and Oxford: Blackwell, 1995. English translation of *Carthage*, first published in 1992.

Lyons, Claire L., and John K. Papadopoulos, eds. *The Archaeology of Colonialism*. Los Angeles: Getty Publications, 2002.

Markoe, Glenn E. *Phoenicians*. Berkeley: University of California Press, 2000.

Moscati, Sabatino, ed. *The Phoenicians*. Milan: Bompiani; New York : Abbeville Press, 1988.

Osborne, Robin. *Greece in the Making, 1200–479 BC*. London and New York: Routledge, 1996.

Roller, Duane W. *Through the Pillars of Herakles: Greco-Roman Exploration of the Atlantic*. London and New York: Routledge, 2005.

Tsetskhladze, Gocha, and Franco De Angelis, eds. *The Archaeology of Greek Colonisation*. Rev. ed. Oxford: Oxford University School of Archaeology, 2004.

FRANCO DE ANGELIS

Greenland. Greenland, the world's biggest island, forms a geological unit with Arctic North America. Despite the presence of several warm springs (131–143.6 degrees Fahrenheit [55–62 degrees Celsius]), there is nothing to suggest a physical connection with Iceland, Greenland's volcanic near neighbor to the east, which the Norse colonized between about 870 and 930 C.E. Despite Greenland's greater distance from Europe, two viable Norse outposts existed there as well by about 1000 C.E., populated by farmers, hunters, and fishermen during a westward migration from Iceland begun shortly before 990 under the leadership of Eiríkr "Rauði" Thorvaldsson (Erik "the Red" Thorvaldsson).

Eiríkr had explored long stretches of the island's west coast during three years of outlawry from Iceland and coined the name "Greenland" to attract colonists. The sheltered areas containing the Norse farms are indeed green and aglow with wildflowers in summer, but Greenland is more notable for massive granite ranges, whose peaks cut through a vast ice cap that exercises considerable influence on air currents in the entire region. Scientists nevertheless note that important temperature changes may occur very suddenly in the island's arctic climate, and that both "cold" and "warm" periods may have warm or cold years. The general climate when the Norse arrived is thought to have been similar to that of the present day, but local variations in the past have not been adequately accounted for, so there are no easy guides to the effect of weather swings on either the Norse Greenlanders' subsistence or their voyages of exploration, hunting, and trade throughout half a millennium.

The hardscrabble Greenland landscape promoted communities of scattered farms. The bigger Norse community, the Eastern Settlement, comprised several fjords in the southwestern Julianehaab region. The smaller one, the Western Settlement, was founded at about the same time in the inner Nuuk region, some

400 miles (644 kilometers) farther north and enough nearer the northern maritime hunting grounds to provide a head start on the seasonal search for falcons, hides and tusks of walrus, lustrous furs, eiderdown, and blubber from marine mammals, aimed at the European market.

Norse Greenland became a bishopric in 1124 after Einar Sokkason, a chieftain's son, had brought enough walrus tusks to the Norwegian court to convince the authorities there that the Norse Greenlanders could afford a bishop. There had been Christians among the first colonizers, but the general conversion was gradual, judging from the churches of varying size constructed in both settlements. Arctic commodities were subsequently used to pay tithes, but no amount of walrus ivory could procure bishops once the Norwegian authorities had lost interest in the Norse Greenlanders. When the last resident bishop of Gardar died at his post about 1378, he was never replaced.

Erik the Red and his circle created a hierarchical society based on legal and judiciary precepts brought from Norway, but without a king or other formal executive. It was a society made for and run by free, land-owning males, and information about it was written down mainly because the men who first staked out land for themselves and their followers became rich and powerful enough to warrant notice in Iceland. Because Erik the Red and his sons Leifr (Leif), Thorvaldr (Thorvald), and Thorsteinn (Thorstein) headed the nascent hierarchy in control of domestic and foreign trade, they organized the early eleventh-century exploratory voyages to North America commemorated in the *Saga of Erik the Red* and the *Saga of the Greenlanders*.

Like the Arctic enterprises that produced tangible wealth as well as early contact with Arctic natives from the Dorset and Thule cultures, Norse voyages to North America were commercial ventures from the start. Greenland lacked such vital resources as timber and bog iron, which the Norse soon located in the part of Labrador they called Markland (Forest Land), and for which they returned for several centuries more. The evidence for subsequent Norse crossings to America is archaeological except for a note in Icelandic annals that, in 1347, a ship with Norse Greenlanders returning home from Markland had drifted off to Iceland.

Later crossings apparently did not include the undefined area farther south that the Norse had named Vínland ("Wine Land") after finding wild grapes there. The *Saga of the Greenlanders* describes an attempt at Vínland colonization as one in which the Norse were vastly outnumbered by hostile natives; the undertaking was short-lived and probably not repeated. The only evidence of Norse house construction in America remains the L'Anse aux Meadows site on Newfoundland's Northern Peninsula, dated to the early eleventh century. At that time, the Norse Greenland colony still had so few people that many participants in the first American ventures appear to have been Icelanders. The lack of later Icelandic saga accounts suggests that subsequent voyages to America involved only small working parties of Norse Greenlanders who availed themselves of the resources found from Markland northward.

Vínland remains as much of an enigma as Bishop Eiríkr of Greenland's reported search for the place in 1121, three years before Norse Greenland's formal connection to the Roman Catholic Church began. Although the L'Anse aux Meadows site accommodated three or four ships' crews and is thought to have been Leifr Eiríksson's base camp and a part of Vínland, Newfoundland cannot be the whole area encompassed by the name, because wild grapes do not and did not grow there.

Those who came to farm, fish, and hunt in medieval Greenland were accustomed to the harsh existence of the Far North and to exploiting its natural resources. They regularly hunted in open boats along the west coast to at least 73° N latitude; Norse items have in fact been discovered all the way up in Smith Sound. The Norse Greenlanders also hunted some way up their east coast and were familiar with the sailing routes to Iceland and Norway. They knew the seas around them better than anyone else but never communicated this knowledge to others through maps or geographical treatises; their navigational information therefore disappeared along with the people themselves.

The last documented medieval voyage from Greenland to Norway took place in 1410, by which time it appears that the Western Settlement was defunct. However, there are many indications that the Norse Greenlanders maintained contact with Iceland and became involved with English traders and fishermen as part of the widening European quest for fish. By about 1500, the unknown number of inhabitants remaining in the Eastern Settlement had nevertheless decided to close down their colony. When Archbishop Erik Walkendorf (or Valkendorf) of Norway wanted to reclaim Greenland for church and crown about 1514, after more than a century of neglect, he did not know that the colonists had left without a forwarding address.

Walkendorf gathered all the available written information about Norse Greenland and how to get there in order to achieve his evident real object, namely a Danish share of New World riches through a supposedly ancient Norse eminent domain. His planned expedition came to nothing, but some of the information he gathered has survived. It is likely that the early sixteenth-century collection contained one or more cartographical reconstructions similar to the circa 1590 map attributed to the young Icelander Sigurður Stefánsson, which featured a peninsula representing Vínland (Promontorium Winlandiæ). The map largely relies on Saxo Grammaticus (whom Valkendorf admired) and on the Icelandic sagas.

[*See also* Leifr Eiríksson; Magnus, Olaus; *and* Viking Discoveries and Settlements.]

BIBLIOGRAPHY

Arneborg, Jette, and Hans Christian Gulløv, eds. *Man, Culture and Environment in Ancient Greenland: Report on a Research Programme.* Copenhagen: Danish National Museum and Danish Polar Center, 1998.

Berthelsen, Christian, Inger Holbech Mortensen, and Ebbe Mortensen, eds. *Kalaallit Nunaat / Greenland Atlas.* Translated by W. Glyn Jones. Piersuiffik: Greenland Home Rule, 1990. A well-illustrated guide to past and present physical aspects of Greenland. The volume's end papers show the 1737 (final) version of the Greenland map first drawn by the Norwegian missionary Hans Egede after his 1723 expedition in search of the Eastern Settlement.

Morison, Samuel Eliot. *The European Discovery of America.* 2 vols. New York: Oxford University Press, 1971–1974. Good bibliographical information; the body of the text needs circumspection.

Pulsiano, Phillip, and Kirsten Wolf, eds. *Medieval Scandinavia: An Encyclopedia.* New York and London: Garland, 1993. High editorial standard with a mostly literary focus and with contributions from a number of well-known scholars.

Seaver, Kirsten A. *The Frozen Echo: Greenland and the Exploration of North America ca. A.D. 1000–1500.* Stanford, Calif.: Stanford University Press, 1996.

KIRSTEN A. SEAVER

Gregory, Augustus (1819–1905), English-born explorer of Australia. Augustus Charles Gregory, surveyor and explorer, was born on August 1, 1819, at Farnsfield in Nottinghamshire, England, a son of Lieutenant Joshua Gregory. The Gregory family settled on a Swan River land grant in 1829, and Augustus was appointed a cadet in the Survey Department in 1841, quickly rising to assistant surveyor.

After some preliminary exploration work in the Irwin and Murchison river districts, Gregory was appointed to lead the North Australian Expedition that was commissioned to assess the potential for settlement of northern Australia. Funded by the British government, the lavishly equipped party of eighteen men included a geologist, a botanist, and an artist. The party landed at Treachery Bay (Pearce Point) on September 18, 1855, and spent the next ten months carefully examining the Victoria River valley. In June 1856, Gregory led a party of six men east from the Victoria, crossing to the Gulf of Carpentaria and the Burdekin valley and then traveling south to Moreton Bay, where they arrived in December 1856. Gregory reported favorably on the Victoria and Burdekin river valleys but found little else of practical value. He was awarded a gold medal by the Royal Geographical Society.

In 1858, Gregory was commissioned by the New South Wales government to search for traces of Ludwig Leichhardt. Leichhardt had disappeared while attempting to cross from the Darling Downs in Queensland to the Swan River settlement in 1848. Departing Juanda Station on March 24, Gregory's small party followed the Barcoo to Cooper Creek, then traveled south past Strzlecki Creek to Adelaide. Gregory failed to find any solid evidence of Leichhardt's fate, but he did find that many inland rivers drained into Lake Eyre, thus helping solve the puzzle of Australia's inland drainage.

Gregory served as surveyor-general of Queensland from 1859 to 1879 and was appointed a member of the Legislative Council in 1882. He and his brother Francis published *Journals of Australian Explorations 1846–1858* in 1884. Gregory was knighted in 1903 and died at Brisbane on June 25, 1905.

[*See also* Australia, Exploration of, *and* Leichhardt, Ludwig.]

BIBLIOGRAPHY

Cumpston, J. H. L. *Augustus Gregory and the Inland Sea.* Canberra, Australia: Roebuck Books, 1972.

Favenc, Ernest. *The History of Australian Exploration from 1788 to 1888.* Sydney: Turner and Henderson, 1888. Reprint. Amsterdam: Meridian, 1967.

McLaren, Glen. *Beyond Leichhardt: Bushcraft and the Exploration of Australia.* Fremantle, Australia: Fremantle Arts Centre Press, 1996.

Millar, Ann. *"I See No End to Travelling": Journals of Australian Explorers 1813–76.* Sydney: Bay Books, 1986.

DENIS SHEPHARD

Grijalva (c. 1490–1527), Spanish conquistador. Hernán de Grijalva, *majordomo* to Hernán Cortés, the conqueror of New Spain, was at Acapulco in 1536 when he was entrusted with two ships to go to Peru to deliver some war supplies to other "conquistadores" there, and return with gold. The story of this failed expedition was later told to the Portuguese governor of the Moluccas by a survivor named Miguel Noble, a Frenchman who had been boatswain aboard the flagship.

Two ships were dispatched: a 120-ton ship named *Santiago*, and a 90-ton patache (a fleet tender) named *Trinidad*. After reaching the port of Paita in northern Peru, a message was sent to Francisco Pizarro, the conqueror of Peru. After receiving the war materiel, Pizarro loaded the two ships with gold, the main items being two full-sized human figures, one of gold, the other of silver.

Grijalva decided to go on a voyage of discovery with his own ship along the west coast of California before returning to Acapulco. However, after almost six months of tacking maneuvers, the ship could not make an easting. Having almost run out of food, Grijalva decided to sail before the wind and head for the Moluccas, but he was already suffering from scurvy and died a month later. He was not alone. By this time, Captain Castilla had taken over command of the ship. Soon they came upon an island, called Oacea, which is identifiable as Kapingamarangi, a Polynesian outlier in Micronesia. Enough food was found to go on to the north coast of New Guinea. There, after discovering Mapia Island, Captain Castilla decided to run his ship aground because most of the men had died, and the twenty-four European survivors were "moving about on all fours." The site where this event took place is inside Geelvink Bay in western New Guinea.

As more men were dying ashore, only twelve made their way toward the Moluccas with the ship's boat, loaded with important supplies, including the gold and silver. A clash with Papuans resulted in their losing everything, including some lives. Only three made it ashore, but they soon met with thieving traders who left them naked. The mulatto was soon killed by the natives "because he was mean and wicked," so that left two survivors, one named Noble, the other Camacho. Only Noble reached the Moluccas, as a slave, but he was ransomed by Galvão, the Portuguese governor, for 300 ducats, and recorded his story. Otherwise, the loss of Captain Grijalva and his treasure would never have been known.

[*See also* Cortés, Hernán, *and* Pizarro, Francisco, Gonzalo Pizarro, and Hernando Pizarro.]

BIBLIOGRAPHY

Lévesque, Rodrigue, ed. *European Discovery*. Vol 1. of *History of Micronesia: A Collection of Source Documents*. 20 vols. Gatineau, Quebec: Lévesque Publications, 1992. See pp. 543–562.

Galvão, António. *Tratado dos descobrimentos*. 4th ed. Porto, Portugal: Livraria Civilizacão Editora, 1987.

Galvano [sic], Antonio. *The Discoveries of the World from Their First Originall Unto the Yeere of Our Lord 1555 . . .* London: Impensis G. Bishop, 1601.

RODRIGUE LÉVESQUE

Gulf Stream. The Gulf Stream is the term generally applied to the western part of a system of currents comprising a great circulatory gyre occupying the North Atlantic Ocean between the Americas and the Afro-Eurasian landmass. The Gulf Stream first becomes clearly discernible in the Straits of Florida between Cuba and the Florida Keys and northward in a narrow course close along the coast of Florida where its dark blue water, flowing at about five knots, has earned it the appellation "River in the Ocean." From a point off Lake Worth Inlet the current is found farther from the coast as it follows a northeast course toward Newfoundland and the Grand Banks. In the open ocean the current begins to slow, becomes cooler, and gradually loses its distinctive color and lateral limits. Off of Cape Cod its velocity drops to about two knots. Beyond the Grand Banks its waters fan out in a broad slowly moving mass known as the North Atlantic Drift, which ameliorates northern European climates. Christopher Columbus was the first explorer to draw attention to subtle ocean currents affecting his navigation to and from the New World as he experienced the gyre's waters moving westward toward the Caribbean Sea and Gulf of Mexico to replenish the Gulf Stream. Juan Ponce de León, usually considered the discoverer of Florida, reported both seeing and experiencing the powerful pull of the Gulf Stream on his ships as he navigated there in 1513. As early as 1575, André Thevet wrote about the north-flowing current in the Florida Strait.

Remarkably, although a number of other sixteenth- and seventeenth-century explorers and navigators called attention to the effects of portions of the Gulf Stream, it was not until the eighteenth century that the current appeared on charts as a major feature of the North Atlantic Ocean. The first such chart was prepared in 1768 by Benjamin Franklin, in his role as deputy postmaster for the American colonies, but never published. The honor of publishing the first Gulf Stream chart is rightly that of William Gerard De Brahm. It appeared in 1772 in his book of sailing directions titled *The Atlantic Pilot*. De Brahm was Britain's Surveyor General of the Southern District of North America and conducted scientific studies of the Gulf Stream and other elements of the North Atlantic gyre. An altered version of Franklin's

1768 chart was published by the American Philosophical Society in 1786. It is, however, often reproduced and incorrectly identified as "the first Gulf Stream chart." In the nineteenth century U.S. Coast Survey director Alexander Dallas Bache was responsible for impressive surveys and charts of the Gulf Stream; and the writings of Matthew Fontaine Maury, the U.S. Navy's Superintendent of Charts and Instruments, brought the current to the attention of the world. At the present time large ship operators pay careful attention to daily charts and satellite images broadcast to show the location and velocity of the Gulf Stream as they choose their sailing routes along the east coast of the United States. Climatologists and others studying global climate change are increasingly concerned with the Gulf Stream's influence as a gigantic "conveyor belt" transporting tropical heat energy toward the temperate and polar regions of the earth. There is a growing body of evidence suggesting that shifts in the direction and volume of the Gulf Stream triggered major climatic changes in the distant past.

[*See also* Columbus, Christopher; De Brahm, William Gerard; Ponce de León, Juan; *and* Thevet, André.]

BIBLIOGRAPHY

De Brahm, William Gerard. *The Atlantic Pilot.* A Facsimile Reproduction of the 1772 Edition with Introduction and Index by Louis De Vorsey, Jr. Gainesville: University Presses of Florida, 1974.

Maury, Matthew Fontaine. *The Physical Geography of the Sea, and Its Meteorology.* Edited by John Leighly. Cambridge, Mass.: Belknap Press of Harvard University Press, 1963.

LOUIS DE VORSEY

Gvozdev, Mikhail (d. after 1759), Russian explorer of Alaska. Gvozdev graduated from the Saint Petersburg Naval Academy as a geodesist, and in 1732 he sailed on the *Gavriil* with Ivan Fyodorov. They sailed through the Bering Strait, compiling a chart of the shores of the strait and of its islands. Their attempts to establish contact with the native Chukchi were mostly unsuccessful, perhaps because one of their aims was to collect *iasak* (fur tax) from them. In August 1732 the expedition pressed on to the Alaskan mainland, where they exchanged needles, thimbles, and large beads for a variety of furs. But the season was getting late, and the expedition returned, with some difficulty, to Kamchatka.

The following year, Gvozdev made a report on the expedition, and although the report never reached the Admiralty College, it did become widely known. It was probably one source for Joseph-Nicolas Delisle's note, found by F. A. Golder in Paris, on the "sea voyage and discoveries by the Russians in the eastern [Pacific] Ocean undertaken between the two voyages of Captain Bering in the years 1731 and 1732," and probably also a source for "a chart illustrating the voyage of Gvozdev." Gvozdev does not seem to have been altogether open about the nature of his voyage, and he was for a time imprisoned in 1738; however, he was soon released, and in 1743 he compiled a chart, now lost, of his 1732 voyage to the Great Land. The previous year Gvozdev had taken part in M. P. Shpanberg's voyage to the shores of Japan, but we know no more of his travels after that.

[*See also* Expeditions, World Exploration, *subentry on* Russia.]

BIBLIOGRAPHY

Golder, Frank A. *Russian Expansion on the Pacific, 1641–1850.* Cleveland, Ohio: Arthur H. Clark, 1914.

ALEXEY POSTNIKOV

H

Hajj. The hajj, or pilgrimage to Mecca, is one of the Five Pillars of Islam. All adult Muslims are obliged to perform the hajj at least once in life, so long as they are physically and financially able. Each year some two million Muslims descend upon Mecca and its environs to participate in a series of sacred re-enactments, physically and spiritually linking each pilgrim to their spiritual forbearers. These rituals underscore the unity of global Islamic community (*umma*) and mark the zenith of Islamic spiritual life.

Even before the Islamic era, Mecca was a pilgrimage destination. Because pre-Islamic Arabia was plagued by tribal feuds, religious and societal customs were designed to ensure periods of truce, during which pilgrimages and commercial fairs could be conducted freely within a sacred space (*haram*), where bloodshed was strictly prohibited. Under this system, Mecca, home to the Kaaba (Ka'ba), which housed the sacred idols of all the surrounding tribes of the region, emerged as a nexus of trade, diplomacy, and pilgrimage.

Into this polytheistic landscape, the Prophet Muhammad was born around 570 C.E. Because of Islam's strong opposition to polytheism and idol worship, one of the probable reasons that Muhammad's teachings were initially rejected was that Meccans feared that their city's pilgrimage trade would be destroyed if idol worship was suppressed. Although when Muhammad and his followers conquered Mecca in 630, Mecca's idols were indeed destroyed and non-Muslims were forbidden from entering the Kaaba, rather than eliminating the pilgrimage, Muhammad reinterpreted it as a key symbol of Islamic unity. Shortly before his death in 632 C.E., the Prophet performed his "Farewell Pilgrimage" (*hajj al-wadā'*), which still serves as the model for the annual rituals of the hajj.

From its very inception, travel has been deeply engrained in the fabric of Islamic society. As Islam spread in the centuries following Muhammad's death, pilgrimage would serve as an important medium for the integration of diverse peoples into the shared value system of the *umma*. While pilgrimage consolidated Mecca's place as the symbolic center of the Islamic world (*dār al-Islām*), it also aided in the creation of cosmopolitan gateway cities, such as Baghdad, Cairo, and Damascus, along the pilgrimage routes. As a result, pilgrimage often entailed lengthy sojourns in these cities, making them contact zones for cross-cultural exchanges of goods and ideas between the Islamic heartland and the frontiers of the *dār al-Islām*. Thus, Islamic civilization was able to foster a high degree of social mobility and freedom of movement across cultural, linguistic, and political boundaries.

Particularly for the learned class of scholars and clerics (ulama), pilgrimage provided not only the impetus for travel but also access to a network of personal and professional contacts that would allow pilgrims to further explore the Islamic world. This point is best illustrated through the life of Ibn Battuta (1304–1368/69). Often referred to as the Islamic Marco Polo, Ibn Battuta left his native Morocco to perform the hajj in 1324. Initially, he appears to have only intended to make the pilgrimage and study Islamic law in Cairo or one of the other centers of Islamic jurisprudence. Instead, he embarked upon a twenty-nine-year odyssey across much of North and West Africa, Arabia and East Africa, Central Asia, India, Southeast Asia, and even as far as China.

Ibn Battuta recorded his pilgrimage experiences, as well as his observations about the Islamic world of his day, in a *rihla* (book of travels). Ibn Battuta's writings are among the best-known examples of an influential genre of Arabic travel writing, which flourished in North Africa and Muslim Spain between the twelfth and fifteenth centuries. Though normally centered on the pilgrimage to Mecca, such accounts also provided readers with rich depictions of the various peoples, places, and pious institutions of the Islamic world. At the height of the era of European imperialism, particularly during the late nineteenth century, the hajj also made its way into European travel writing as orientalist-adventurers like Sir Richard F. Burton and Christaan Snouck Hurgronje disguised themselves as pilgrims in order to explore and unveil the forbidden places of Islam.

Although neither Mecca nor Medina has been a political center since the seventh century, successive Muslim states, as well European Crusaders and colonial regimes, have competed for control of the pilgrimage, attempted to exploit it for economic gain, used its religious significance to bolster their political power, and even to redefine proper Islamic practice. For example, during the second Muslim civil war (680–692), Zubayrid control of Mecca was the likely cause for the Damascus-based Umayyads' construction of the Dome of the Rock in Jerusalem as an alternative pilgrimage site. In more recent times, during the late nineteenth and early twentieth centuries, the Ottoman sultans emphasized their role as the caliph and protector of the Holy Places in an attempt to stir pan-Islamic, anticolonial sentiments and ward off European imperialism. Since the dismantling of the Ottoman Empire following World War I, however, the hajj has been administered by the government of Saudi Arabia. As a result, the hajj has become a major vehicle for the spread of Saudi Arabia's "puritanical" standards of behavior and Wahhabi doctrine to other parts of the Islamic world.

[*See also* Burton, Richard F., *and* Ibn Battuta.]

BIBLIOGRAPHY

Bianchi, Robert R. *Guests of God: Pilgrimage and Politics in the Islamic World*. Oxford: Oxford University Press, 2004.

Coleman, Simon, and John Elsner. *Pilgrimage Past and Present in the World Religions*. Cambridge, Mass.: Harvard University Press, 1995.

Dunn, Ross E. *The Adventures of Ibn Battuta: A Muslim Traveler of the Fourteenth Century*. 2nd ed. Berkeley and Los Angeles: University of California Press, 2004.

Eickelman, Dale F., and James Piscatori, eds. *Muslim Travellers: Pilgrimage, Migration, and the Religious Imagination*. Berkeley: University of California Press, 1990.

Netton, Ian Richard, ed. *Golden Roads: Migration, Pilgrimage, and Travel in Mediaeval and Modern Islam*. Richmond, UK: Curzon, 1993.

Peters, F. E. *The Hajj: The Muslim Pilgrimage to Mecca and the Holy Places*. Princeton, N.J.: Princeton University Press, 1994.

Wolfe, Michael, ed. *One Thousand Roads to Mecca: Ten Centuries of Travelers Writing about the Muslim Pilgrimage*. New York: Grove Press, 1997.

MICHAEL CHRISTOPHER LOW

Hakluyt, Richard (1552–1616), English geographer and historian. The most important sixteenth-century English compiler of voyages and other travel documents and an indefatigable advocate of overseas exploration, settlement, and trade, Richard Hakluyt was born in London in the early months of 1552, the son of Richard Hakluyt, a skinner, and his wife Margery. Hakluyt owed his introduction to geographical studies to still another Richard Hakluyt, his older cousin, a lawyer and adviser to the London merchant community, whose chambers in the Middle Temple Hakluyt visited when he was at Westminster School. From Westminster, Hakluyt went to Christ Church, Oxford, where, while preparing for ordination, he read whatever printed or manuscript of discoveries and voyages he could find and delivered the university's first lectures in modern geography.

The international scope of Hakluyt's activities became especially apparent in the years following his residence in Oxford. He corresponded with the leading Flemish cartographers Abraham Ortelius and Gerard Mercator; in Paris, as chaplain and secretary to the English ambassador, he advised Dom Antonío, the pretender to the Portuguese throne; he acquired important manuscripts from the French cosmographer royal, André Thevet; he supplied the Frankfurt engraver Theodor de Bry with the materials that launched de Bry's great series of illustrated voyages; and he encouraged the translation and publication of an extraordinary number of foreign works of geographical interest. Drawing on these widespread sources and contacts, he wrote "A Discourse of the Commodity of the Taking of the Straight of Magellanus" (1580) for the English government and a "Discourse of Western Planting" (1584) for Walter Ralegh; in 1582 he published his own first collection, his *Divers Voyages Touching the Discovery of America*.

Most of the accounts included in the *Divers Voyages* come from foreign sources. Hakluyt's aim was to inform his English compatriots and inspire them to emulate the accomplishments of their European neighbors. With the publication of the work on which his enduring reputation largely depends, first in 1589 and then a decade later in a greatly expanded second edition, Hakluyt took a different tack. As its title suggests, the *Principal Navigations, Voyages, Traffiques, and Discoveries of the English Nation* proclaims England's own place in the world beyond Europe's borders. The recent exploits of men such as John Hawkins, Francis Drake, and Thomas Cavendish (whose niece Hakluyt married) and the New World projects of Ralegh and his half brother Sir Humphrey Gilbert did much to give substance to such claims, and Hakluyt supplied detailed and often thrilling reports of their activities. But he also filled two of his three volumes with the sometimes more mundane accounts of mercantile ventures to the northeast

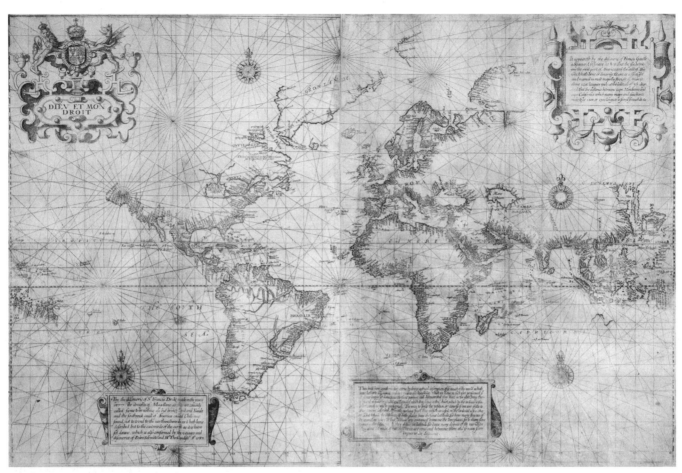

World Map. By Edward Wright from Richard Hakluyt's *Principal Navigations* (London, 1599). This remarkable map, which uses Mercator's 1569 projection, seems indeed to "proclaim England's own place in the world," with its large and superb royal arms, and its careful delineation of recent English discoveries. COURTESY THE NEWBERRY LIBRARY, CHICAGO

and southeast by the Muscovy and Levant companies and their successors. The result is a book that showed the world from a distinctly English perspective and showed an English nation in which merchants had an equal part with the aristocrats and courtiers who supplied the principal support for New World exploration and settlement.

In the last decade and a half of his life, Hakluyt advised both the East India and Virginia companies, and he pursued his work as a collector, amassing materials that later helped fill Samuel Purchas's *Hakluytus posthumus* (1625). Hakluyt died on November 23, 1616, and was buried three days later in Westminster Abbey.

[*See also* Hakluyt Society *and* Travel Literature, European.]

BIBLIOGRAPHY
Parks, George Bruner. *Richard Hakluyt and the English Voyages*. 1928. 2nd ed. New York: Frederick Ungar, 1961.

Quinn, D. B., ed. *The Hakluyt Handbook*. 2 vols. London: Hakluyt Society, 1974.

RICHARD HELGERSON

Hakluyt Society. The Hakluyt Society is named after Richard Hakluyt, a sixteenth-century collector of travel narratives. The aims of the society, as stated in 1846 by its founder, the geographer William Desborough Cooley, were to print for its members "rare and valuable Voyages, Travels, and Geographical Records." Today the society's aims are, more particularly, to promote knowledge and learning, but the tradition of publishing texts of travels and exploration remains the core activity.

In its early years, the Hakluyt Society's focus was on providing new editions of texts that had originally been published in the sixteenth and seventeenth centuries. More recently, it has concentrated on providing edited and annotated transcripts from original manuscripts—manuscripts not previously published—of all periods. There are also translations into English of texts formerly available only in other languages. Most volumes have introductions with background information and critical evaluations.

To date, more than three hundred and fifty volumes have been produced. Some texts describe the stirring adventures of mariners, for example, Walter Ralegh's "Roanoke Voyages" to North America. Others tell much of non-European peoples and societies. Among the society's most notable works are the definitive editions of the charts and journals of Captain James Cook's expeditions. Recounting the work of explorers and travelers and describing encounters between different peoples, the texts provide historical, geographical, anthropological, and cultural information, which contributes to our understanding of the world today. These accounts, journals, diaries, and other documents—written by explorers of many nationalities—constitute a vast compendium of information on the history of exploration. Full details are on the society's Web site (http://www.hakluyt.com). Making accessible all this information is the society's key achievement.

BIBLIOGRAPHY

Bridges, R. C., and P. E. H. Hair, eds. *Compassing the Vaste Globe of the Earth: Studies in the History of the Hakluyt Society, 1846–1996*. London: Hakluyt Society, 1996.

ROY BRIDGES

Hall, Charles Francis

Hall, Charles Francis (1821–1871), American mechanic, journalist, and Arctic explorer. Born in New England, Hall had little formal education and was apprenticed to a blacksmith. Virtually nothing is known about him until 1849 when he was making embossing seals in Cincinnati. By 1859 he had started a newspaper, the *Daily Press*, which allowed him unbridled expression of his many enthusiasms. One of these was Arctic exploration and the fate of Sir John Franklin, an interest apparently kindled by the expeditions of Elisha Kent Kane. He read everything he could find on the Arctic, tested the rigors of outdoor life by winter camping on a hill outside of Cincinnati, and planned an expedition to the vicinity of King William Island, where, according to Eskimo information collected by John Rae of the Hudson's Bay Company, corpses and other relics of the Franklin Expedition might be found. With crucial support from Henry Grinnell, he got passage on a whaler and landed at "Frobisher's Straits" on the east coast of Baffin Island in May 1860. He never got beyond Baffin Island, but learned to communicate with the Eskimo, lived with them and ate their food for months at a time, and established that the inlet named for Frobisher was a bay and not a strait. He also made an extraordinary discovery in conversing with the Inuit (Eskimo): they told about many Kabloona (white people) who had come in three large boats, and gone back home taking with them large quantities of rocks and one of their people. Hall was astonished to realize that they were describing the expeditions of Martin Frobisher himself, which had lived on in their oral traditions for almost three hundred years. He proved himself a good and careful cartographer and thoroughly mastered the techniques of celestial navigation.

Hall returned to the United States in August 1862, bringing with him an Inuit couple, Joe and Hannah Eiberbing, to whom he had become personally attached and who would accompany him in his two remaining expeditions. He left on his second expedition in 1864 (again financed by Henry Grinnell), this time destined to spend five full years in the Arctic, with at most one or two non-Inuit companions. Leaving the whaler in the northwestern part of Hudson Bay, he established a main camp at Repulse Bay and made extensive sledge journeys, visiting the northern end of Melville Peninsula and finally reaching King William Island. Here, he got more Franklin relics from the natives and heard firsthand reports of a large party of white men, under Francis Crozier, captain of Franklin's second ship.

On his return to the United States in late summer 1869, Hall and Grinnell quickly mounted a campaign to get government support for an assault on the North Pole. With an appropriation from Congress, a steam tug was purchased, fitted for Arctic use, and rechristened *Polaris*. She sailed in the summer of 1871, with Hall as commander, and thirty-three other officers and crew. Exceptionally ice-free conditions enabled the *Polaris* to steam quickly through Kane Basin and enter Kennedy Channel, which Hall, following Kane and Isaac Israel Hayes, thought led to the "open Polar Sea." They were finally stopped by ice at the end of August on the edge of the Lincoln Sea at 82°11′ N. In October, after having a cup of coffee on returning from a sledge trip, Hall became nauseous, and for weeks was more or less ill with pain, paralysis, and occasional dementia. He rallied several times, but finally died in his sleep on November 8, 1871. With the summer thaw, his friend and second-in-command, William Buddington, sent a couple of half-hearted expeditions toward the pole in small boats, but they made little headway. In early August 1872 the *Polaris* finally escaped her frozen harbor, only to be caught in the pack ice; for two months she drifted southward, tied to an ice floe, and leaking steadily. During an October storm, the ship began to take water badly. Nineteen people escaped to the ice floe, only to see the *Polaris* sail out of sight with another fourteen aboard. For more than six months, they lived on the ever-shrinking floe as it moved slowly south down Baffin Bay, kept alive by Joe Eibirbing's skill as a hunter, before being picked up by a whaler in late April 1873. The *Polaris*, meanwhile, had grounded on the Greenland coast, where her crew wintered. In the spring they built two small boats and headed south again, to be rescued by Scottish whalers. Miraculously, Hall was the only fatality of the *Polaris* Expedition.

A public enquiry into his death revealed both the tensions aboard the vessel and Hall's fear that he was being murdered. His death was eventually ruled to have resulted from natural causes, but doubts always persisted and an exhumation of his body in 1968 revealed that he had ingested fatal doses of arsenic. Whether this was a case of murder (the Austrian scientist Emil Bessels has been suggested as the culprit) or the result of self-medication by the sometimes paranoid Hall has never been established.

The geographical, historical, and ethnographic accomplishments of Hall's three expeditions were significant, and his adaptation to Inuit ways proved to be key to future successful Arctic expeditions.

[*See also* Franklin Search Expeditions *and biographies of figures mentioned in this article.*]

BIBLIOGRAPHY
Davis, C. H. *Narrative of the North Polar Expedition, U.S. Ship Polaris, Captain Charles Francis Hall Commanding*. Washington, D.C.: Government Printing Office, 1876.
Hall, C. F. *Arctic Researches and Life among the Esquimaux*. New York: Harper, 1865.
Loomis, Chauncey C. *Weird and Tragic Shores: The Story of Charles Francis Hall, Explorer*. Reprint. New York: Modern Library, 2000.
Nourse, J. E., ed. *Narrative of the Second Arctic Expedition Commanded by Charles F. Hall*. Washington, D.C.: Government Printing Office, 1879.

ROBERT W. KARROW JR.

Halley, Edmond (1656–1742), British astronomer. Edmond Halley was already well known before he was commissioned as a captain in the Royal Navy to command HMS *Paramour* (called *Paramore* by Halley in his writings), on what have been called the first voyages for purely scientific purposes (1698–1701).

Halley had left Oxford before receiving a BA to make astronomical observations of the constellations of the Southern Hemisphere (1676–1678). A catalog of these observations was published, with a star chart dedicated to King Charles II, who ordered that Halley be awarded the MA without further studies. On his way to and from Saint Helena, Halley had observed the trade winds, on which he published an article and a map in the *Philosophical Transactions* of the Royal Society of London. Halley became editor of this journal and had a continuing association with the society, of which he became clerk, and he visited observatories in Europe in this capacity.

Largely from his own resources he began extensive astronomical observations that ultimately led to the researches for which he is best known today: predictions of comets, and of the transit of Venus. Halley encouraged Isaac Newton to write his *Principia*, which Halley then edited, and the publication of which he himself paid for. Being denied the professorship of astronomy at Oxford, Halley proposed the *Paramore* voyages to King William III and Queen Mary II, in order to study geomagnetism as a possible solution to the longitude problem.

Of his three voyages in the *Paramore*, the second (1699–1700) was the most enterprising as Halley took his ship into the icy waters of the South Atlantic and reached latitude 52°24′ S before turning back. On his return he produced the first published isogonic (magnetic) charts, in 1701 and 1702; and after his third voyage (1701) a tidal chart of the English Channel, in 1702. Halley was Secretary of the Royal Society, Professor of Geometry at Oxford, and in 1720, he became Astronomer Royal at Greenwich Observatory.

[*See also* Venus, Transit of.]

BIBLIOGRAPHY
Bullard, Edward. "Edmond Halley (1656–1741)." *Endeavour* 15 (1956): 891–892.
Cook, Alan. *Edmond Halley: Charting the Heavens and the Seas*. Oxford: Clarendon Press, 2000. A recent evaluation of the work and life of Halley, with an excellent bibliography.
Thrower, Norman J. W., ed. *The Three Voyages of Edmond Halley in the 'Paramore' 1698–1701*. London: Hakluyt Society, 1981.

NORMAN J. W. THROWER

Hamdāni, al-, (c. 893?–c. 945), Muslim physician, genealogist, and poet. Hasan al-Hamdani lived in the late ninth and early tenth centuries. He was born in Sana (in northern Yemen) in 893, and spent his childhood there. He later resided in Rayda (north

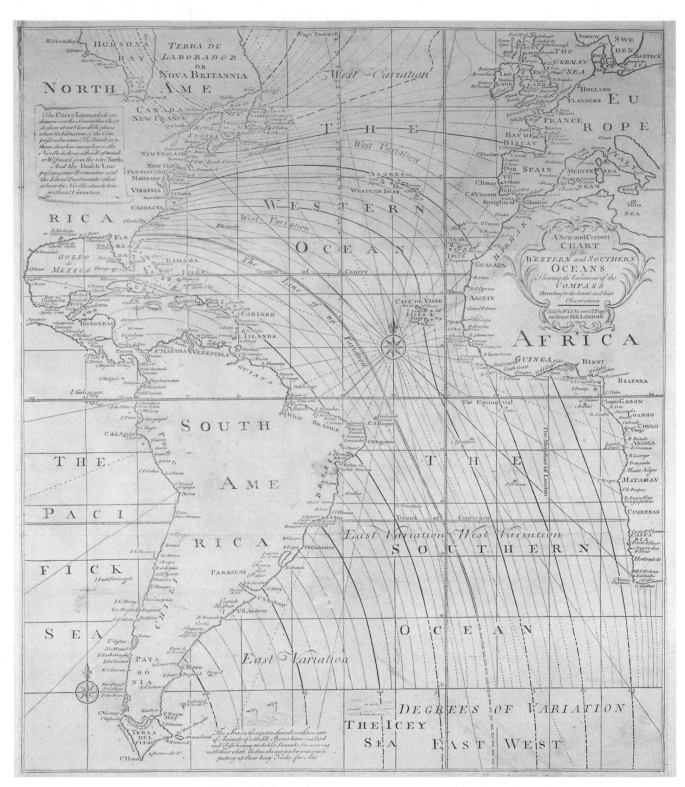

A New and Correct Chart of the Western and Southern Oceans. This ingenious chart of compass-variation was "first constructed from Observations made in the Year 1700 by the great Dr. Halley." (London, 1745). COURTESY THE NEWBERRY LIBRARY, CHICAGO

of Sana), and therefore, he is sometimes referred to as Raydi. His many years in Sana gave him great familiarity with the genealogies of local ethnic groups, including the Khawlan and Himyar tribes. He prepared a ten-part encyclopedia about Yemen and Arab tribes, and he is also respected for the geographical book *Sifat Djazirat al-Arab* and for his poetry. He may have died in a Sana prison in 945.

BIBLIOGRAPHY
Lofgern, O. "al-Hamdāni." In *The Encyclopedia of Islam*, Vol. 3, pp. 124–125. New ed. Leiden, Netherlands: Brill, 1979.

VAHEED RIAHI

Harris, William Cornwallis (1807–1848), British hunter in Africa.

A captain in the British army who was the first of the Great White Hunters in Africa, Harris was born in Wittersham (Kent), England, on April 2, 1807. Stationed in Bombay, India, Harris was ordered to southern Africa to rehabilitate his health. He and his companion, William Richardson, began a five-month safari in September 1836, and within weeks they reached Matabeleland, the kingdom of Umzilikaze. After considerable gift-giving, permission was granted to hunt in the despot's domain, and it was here that Harris saw his first elephant. Harris hunted indiscriminately, but he spent part of each day skillfully drawing animals and native Africans, and he amassed an amazing art portfolio, which included a portrait of Umzilikaze. Harris, the naturalist, collected two complete skulls of every quadruped found in southern Africa. He also preserved the complete skeleton and skin of his most prized triumph, the rare sable antelope, which became known as the "Harris buck." The antelope's remains were later displayed in the British Museum. The hunters returned by a previously unexplored route through the Vaal River valley, and arrived back at the Cape Colony in early 1837. Harris described his adventure in *The Wild Sports of Southern Africa* (Bombay, 1838). This highly praised volume significantly popularized big-game hunting in the region, and with the rapid influx of myriad hunters to the region, new lands were explored that had been untrod by earlier travelers. Their reports resulted in the construction of more accurate maps of the region.

Harris returned to India, where in 1841 he was assigned to lead an eighteen-month diplomatic mission to Abyssinia to persuade Sahela Selassie (the king of Shoa and a nasty slave trader) to cease his appalling activities, and if possible, work out a trade agreement with Britain. Harris was one of the earliest Europeans to penetrate the Ethiopian Highlands. For his deeds in northeast Africa, Queen Victoria knighted him in 1844. He died at Surwur (near Poona), India, on October 9, 1848.

[*See also* Selous, Frederick.]

BIBLIOGRAPHY
Harris, William Cornwallis. *The Highlands of Ethiopia*. London: Farnborough and Gregg, 1968. Originally published in 1844.
Harris, William Cornwallis. *The Wild Sports of Southern Africa*. Cape Town: C. Struik, 1987. Originally published in 1838.

SANFORD H. BEDERMAN

Harun ibn Yahya (fl. 900s), Syrian traveler.

Harun ibn Yahya was most probably a Syrian and possibly a Christian captive. He stayed in Constantinople at the end of the ninth or the beginning of the tenth century and wrote a most informative report on his sojourn, extant only in a significant excerpt in the *Kitab al-Alaq al-nafisa* of Ibn Rusta (Isfahan, fl. about 910).

The place and year of Harun ibn Yahya's birth and death are unknown. The only information available about his life is to be found in his own work. Harun ibn Yahya was taken prisoner by the Byzantines in Palestine, and was transferred from Askalon by sea to Antalya and across Asia Minor to Constantinople. The date and the duration of his stay in Constantinople are uncertain: according to hints in his travel report, his sojourn took place between 880 at the earliest and 913 at the latest and lasted probably at least half a year. After his ransom was paid, he traveled through Greece, the Balkan Peninsula, and Italy, visiting Thessaloniki and Venice, among other cities, until he reached Rome.

Harun ibn Yahya put his stay in Constantinople, between his release by the authorities and his final liberation, to good use. He studied the famous monuments and noticed the characteristic ceremonies performed. His account of Constantinople contains information of the highest interest and is one of the most important of all reports left by visitors to the Byzantine capital during the Middle Ages. It is one of the main sources from which the early Muslim geographers derived their knowledge on the Byzantine Empire. Interesting but of less importance are his description of Rome that reveals the use of written sources, and the information about Burgundy, the Franks, and Britain that appears not to be based on his own experience.

[*See also* Constantinople.]

BIBLIOGRAPHY
Vin, J. P. A. van der. *Travellers to Greece and Constantinople: Ancient Monuments and Old Traditions in Medieval Travellers' Tales.* Vol. 2. Leiden: Nederlands Historisch-Archaeologisch Instituut te Istanbul, 1980.

PETRA G. SCHMIDL

Hawaiian Islands. The seven islands in the Hawaiian chain sit near the center of the Pacific Ocean, close to the latitudes from which numerous Spanish voyages sailed westward from New Spain (Mexico) from the sixteenth century on. Yet no European explorer claimed discovery of the Hawaiian Islands until the English captain James Cook did so in 1778. This late discovery is explained by considering the prevailing currents in the Pacific: in a westward direction they flow somewhat south of the Hawaiian Islands, and in an eastward direction they flow sharply north-northeast from the Philippines almost to the Aleutian Islands before descending along the coasts of North America—in other words, far from any path that would lead directly to the Hawaiian Islands.

Documented expeditions into the Pacific before Cook followed the prevailing winds and currents and did not encounter the Hawaiian Islands. The only controversy involves whether or not any undocumented expeditions—most likely Spanish expeditions—did indeed get there first. Ferdinand Magellan's epic voyage from 1520 to 1521 across the Pacific to the modern-day Philippines missed Hawaii and even missed many islands that future Pacific voyages would use for resupply. In 1526 García Jofre de Loaísa followed Magellan's track around South America and into the Pacific. Oral histories and genetic mapping in Polynesia suggest that a stray caravel from that ill-fated expedition brought the first Europeans to several islands, perhaps including Hawaii. No documentary evidence supports such speculation, however.

Álvaro de Saavedra led the first European voyage westward from the Mexican coast in 1527, losing two ships in the vastness of the Pacific. Since December storms pushed them astray near Hawaii, some claim that strong winds actually did carry survivors to that island—a scenario that is supported by Hawaiian oral histories and material remains, but not by written documentation. Saavedra reached the Philippines but died attempting to find his way back. Some claim (also without evidence) that he discovered the far-northern end of the Hawaiian chain before his death. Ruy López de Villalobos sailed westward from

Peru from 1542 to 1545 and similarly failed to find a return route; his expedition would also spawn several versions of a Hawaiian discovery story.

After Andrés de Urdaneta discovered a return route across the Pacific in 1565, the Manila galleon trade flourished for several centuries, following standard routes around the Pacific. Ships would inevitably stray from these routes and vanish forever, and also inevitably, the memory of lost ships would later inspire stories of a discovery of Hawaii, but never with any evidence. Without the ability to calculate longitude precisely, cartographers could not map the vast Pacific accurately, and as a result, their mapping was unclear: mapmakers in Europe showed known island groups in shifting locations around the Pacific, and some maps from the late sixteenth and seventeenth centuries seem to depict the Hawaiian chain, but none of these was definitive.

Finally, James Cook definitively located the Hawaiian Islands in 1778 while exploring the area between the known westward and eastward paths around the Pacific. He was also able to map the islands' position accurately with the aid of the newly developed ship's chronometer. Some members of Cook's expedition assumed that Spaniards had reached Hawaii first (a possibility Cook dismissed), based in part on the inhabitants' knowledge of iron tools and iron-working despite the fact that there were no iron deposits on the islands. This, in addition to oral traditions and material remains, do support the possibility that other Europeans—most likely Spaniards—had indeed arrived in the Hawaiian Islands earlier, sometime during the 250 years between the voyages of Magellan and Cook; credit for the official discovery of the Hawaiian Islands, however, has remained with Cook.

[*See also biographies of figures mentioned in this article.*]

BIBLIOGRAPHY
Beaglehole, J. C., ed. *The Journals of Captain James Cook on his Voyages of Discovery: The Voyage of the Resolution and Discovery, 1776–1780.* 4 vols. Cambridge, U.K.: Hakluyt Society, 1955–1974.
Fernández-Armesto, Felipe, ed. *The Times Atlas of World Exploration.* London: Times Books, 1991.
Langdon, Robert. *The Lost Caravel.* Sydney: Pacific Publications, 1975.
Martínez Shaw, Carlos, ed. *Spanish Pacific from Magellan to Malaspina* (El Pacifico Español de Magallanes a Malaspina). Madrid: Ministerio de Asuntos Exteriores, 1988.

CARLA RAHN PHILLIPS

Hawkesworth, John (1720–1773), English writer and editor. John Hawkesworth, who was born in London in 1720 (baptized October 20) became one of the most celebrated literary personalities of his age. He was, among much else, the editor and biographer of Jonathan Swift, the literary editor of the *Gentleman's Magazine*, and a playwright, essayist, and translator. Thus Hawkesworth was an unsurprising choice when, in September 1771, the Earl of Sandwich, First Lord of the Admiralty, was looking for someone who could turn the journals from James Cook's first Pacific voyage into a book. Hawkesworth was suggested by Sandwich's friend, the musicologist Charles Burney, and he was further endorsed by the actor David Garrick. The matter was urgent, for the newspapers were full of detail, much of it garbled, about the voyage. If an authorized account was not published, then the way was left open for unofficial narratives, often conjured up by hack writers with an eye for the sensational. By the end of the month the matter was settled, although Hawkesworth's edition was now to include all the Pacific voyages of the reign of George III. The result, published in 1773, was a sumptuous three-volume work, *An Account of the Voyages Undertaken by Order of His Present Majesty for Making Discoveries in the Southern Hemisphere, and Successively Performed by Commodore Byron, Captain Wallis, Captain Carteret, and Captain Cook.*

An editor of literary rather than nautical expertise, Hawkesworth inserted reflective and philosophical passages, switched locations and opinions, and generally made frequent and sometimes substantive changes to the journals. For Cook it must have been galling not only to realize that Hawkesworth had fused his journal with that of the naturalist on the *Endeavour*, Joseph Banks, but also to read in the introduction how much more highly the editor regarded Banks's journal than his own, which was referred to rather narrowly as an "account of all the nautical incidents of the voyage."

Publication led to controversy. John Wesley attacked Hawkesworth for the edition's frank description of Polynesian sexual customs and for its skepticism about the "particular interposition of Providence." Others criticized technical inaccuracies, while James Boswell told Cook that Hawkesworth "has used your narrative as a London tavern keeper does wine. He has *brewed* it." For his work, Hawkesworth collected the sum—huge by eighteenth-century standards—of £6,000. But he died on November 17, 1773, within six months of the work's publication, worn down, it was widely thought, by all the criticism. Yet of the readability, popularity, and significance of the book—serialized, reprinted,

and translated many times—there can be no doubt. As the preeminent Cook scholar J. C. Beaglehole put it, "for a hundred and twenty years, so far as the first voyage was concerned, Hawkesworth was Cook." A contemporary newspaper justly remarked of Hawkesworth's edition, "It may be called a real authentic Account of a new world, such as no European could have figured in his own Imagination."

[*See also* Banks, Joseph; Cook, James; *and* Pacific, *subentry on* Literary Representations.]

BIBLIOGRAPHY
Abbott, John Lawrence. *John Hawkesworth: Eighteenth-Century Man of Letters*. Madison: University of Wisconsin Press, 1982.
Beaglehole, J. C., ed. *The Journals of Captain James Cook: The Voyage of the "Endeavour" 1768–1771*. Cambridge, U.K.: Cambridge University Press for the Hakluyt Society, 1955.
GLYNDWR WILLIAMS

Hayward, George W. (c. 1840–1870), Victorian explorer of central Asia. At age twenty-five, Hayward was a lieutenant in the Cameron Highlanders in India, but he sold his commission the following year. In 1868 he approached the Russophobe vice-president of the Royal Geographical Society, Henry Rawlinson, for support of an expedition to central Asia. He received £300 to explore the Pamirs and the source of the Oxus River. He left Leh, Kashmir, in September 1868 and headed for Chinese Turkistan, crossing first the Karakoram Range and then the Kunlun, often traveling through passes at more than 19,000 feet (5,800 meters). He defined the separation of the Karakoram and the Kunlun, with a distinct watershed and the Yarkand and Karakash intervening. He traced the true source of the Yarkand River in the northern face of the Karakoram; the Yarkand is a river that tracks eastward for 1,300 miles (2,092 kilometers) before dying in the Gobi desert. Hayward distinguished its origin from that of the Karakash, a river that dies in the Taklimakan. He visited Yarkand and Kashgar, arriving there only days after the tea planter Robert Shaw had arrived; Shaw was the first westerner to reach Kashgar.

For this surveying and cartographic expedition, largely through unknown and uninhabited terrain, Hayward was awarded the Founder's Medal of the RGS, and Rawlinson encouraged him to continue his exploration. Dangerous tribes rendered most routes to the Pamirs from northern India impassable, and Hayward opted for the Gilgit region of Kashmir and the Wakhan region of Afghanistan. But he had written an article in a Calcutta newspaper exposing a massacre inflicted by troops of the maharaja of Kashmir on the "Dards" of Yasin, west of Hunza, in Gilgit. Kashmir was considered a friend of Britain, and Hayward withdrew his association with the RGS to avoid embarrassing Britain and the society. In the summer of 1870 he reached Yasin, and camped below Darkot just south of Wakhan, but was overcome by a group of tribesmen and murdered on July 18. His body, along with his maps and papers, were recovered and taken back to Gilgit, where his headstone, provided by the Royal Geographical Society, remains there in a small British cemetery. A Chitrali chief, Mir Wali, was a prime suspect of the murder, but no one was ever charged with the crime.

[*See also* Royal Geographical Society.]

BIBLIOGRAPHY

Hayward, G. W. "Journey from Leh to Yarkand and Kashgar, and Exploration of the Sources of the Yarkand River." *Journal of the Royal Geographical Society* 40 (1870): 33–166.

Hopkirk, Peter. *The Great Game: On Secret Service in High Asia.* Oxford: Oxford University Press, 1990.

DAVID SPENCER SMITH

Hearne, Samuel (1745–1792), explorer and trader.

Samuel Hearne was born in London in 1745, but after his father's death his family moved to Beaminster, Dorset, where he attended elementary school. At the age of eleven he joined the Royal Navy, in which he served throughout the Seven Years' War (1756–1763), rising to master's mate. In 1766 he joined the Hudson's Bay Company as mate of one of its sloops operating out of Prince of Wales's Fort, Churchill, on the west coast of Hudson Bay. He arrived at a time when the post's factor, Moses Norton, was attempting to find a route to the river with deposits of copper that had long been reported to lie somewhere north of Churchill. Voyages by company sloops sailing along the coast from Churchill had failed to find such a river, but in 1767 two "Northern [Chipewyan] Indians," Idotliaze and Matonabee, arrived at the post to report that they had journeyed overland to a river with three copper mines near its mouth. In 1769, Norton showed a map based on the Chipewyans' travels to the company's directors in London, and he was authorized on his return to Churchill to send Hearne on an overland journey north. Hearne's priority was to find the copper mines that lay near "the Far Off Metal River," but he was also ordered "to find out, if you can, either by your own travels, or by information from the Indians, whether there is . . . a passage out of Hudson's Bay into the Western [the Pacific] Ocean."

At age twenty-five, Hearne was in the prime of life, good on snowshoes, and had had enough service at sea to give him some competence in surveying. After two false starts—on which he first was abandoned by his Indian guide, and then broke his quadrant—Hearne carried out his task in 1770–1772 by journeying with a band of Chipewyan men, women, and children led by Matonabee. They traveled, mainly on foot, across the bleak Barren Lands of the northern tundra, "scarcely anything but one solid mass of rocks and stones." The best time for traveling was winter, when the frozen land gave a firm surface for sledges and snowshoes, but an indication of winter conditions was given in Hearne's journal entry for November 21, 1770. "Between seven and eight in the evening my dog, a valuable brute, was frozen to death; so that his sledge, which was a heavy one, I was obliged to haul." As the spring thaws came, travel became even more backbreaking, for the sledges were abandoned and Hearne had to carry his possessions and instruments on his back through knee-deep slush and water.

After six months, the party at last reached the Coppermine River in July 1771, but it proved to be a sad disappointment. The river was shallow and unnavigable for ships, while the reputed mines of copper dwindled to "a jumble of rocks and gravel." It took Hearne four hours of searching before he found a lump of copper large enough to bring back. From this spot Hearne followed the river toward the sea until he sighted the Arctic Ocean. Hearne was the first European to reach the northern coast of the American continent, although he placed it in latitude 71°54′ N, almost four degrees, or two hundred miles (322 kilometers), too far north. Hearne did not wait for clear weather to take an observation with his quadrant, and instead relied on a seaman's dead reckoning. He was disillusioned by the failure to find anything of commercial value after the hardships of his journey, and was sickened by the massacre by his Chipewyan companions of an unsuspecting Inuit group at a spot that Hearne named Bloody Fall, a few miles from the river's mouth.

The group finally returned to Churchill in June 1772 after a journey during which there were times, Hearne wrote, when "I left the print of my feet in blood almost at every step I took." Whatever the commercial disappointment of Hearne's discoveries, their geographical implications were profound. He had eliminated the possibility that a passage for shipping might be found through the American continent, for he had crossed its northeastern shoulder from Hudson Bay to the Arctic Ocean without finding a saltwater strait or even any sizable river. Copies of Hearne's journal and maps were passed to the Admiralty, and they had a significant influence on the instructions given to James Cook before he left England for the Pacific in 1776 to search for a Northwest Passage along the coast sighted by Hearne.

After his return from the Coppermine River, Hearne was ordered in 1774 to set up the Hudson's Bay Company's first inland post at Cumberland House. The task was less dangerous than his northern journey, but no less daunting, for the new post was 400 miles (644 kilometers) inland from Hudson Bay as the crow flies, nearer seven hundred by canoe. In 1776, Hearne was rewarded for his efforts with the command of Prince of Wales's Fort, Churchill; but his years there were notable chiefly for the surrender of the fort to a superior French force commanded by the Comte de La Pérouse. Hearne retired to London in 1787 and busied himself preparing his journal for publication. It was finally published in 1795, three years after Hearne's death in November 1792. *A Journey from Prince of Wales's Fort in Hudson's Bay to the Northern Ocean* became a classic of northern travel. It showed Hearne as a percipient observer of the little-known Chipewyan Indians, and a superb if untrained naturalist whose notes on the wildlife of the Canadian North were the most important to appear in print during the eighteenth century.

[*See also* Cook, James; Hudson's Bay Company, *subentry on* Arctic Exploration; La Pérouse, J. F. de Galaup de; *and* Matonabee.]

BIBLIOGRAPHY

Driscoll, Heather Rollason. "The Genesis of *A Journey to the Northern Ocean*. . . ." PhD dissertation, University of Alberta, Edmonton, 2002.

Hearne, Samuel. *A Journey from Prince of Wales's Fort in Hudson's Bay to the Northern Ocean.* Edited by Richard Glover. Toronto: Macmillan, 1958.

MacLaren, I. S. "Exploration/Travel Literature and the Evolution of the Author." *International Journal of Canadian Studies* 8 (1992): 39–68.

McGoogan, Ken. *Ancient Mariner: The Amazing Adventures of Samuel Hearne, the Sailor Who Walked to the Arctic Ocean.* Toronto: HarperFlamingoCanada, 2003.

Williams, Glyn. *Voyages of Delusion: The Northwest Passage in the Age of Reason.* London: HarperCollins, 2002.

GLYNDWR WILLIAMS

Hedin, Sven (1865–1952), Swedish explorer of central Asia. Sven Anders Hedin was born in Stockholm, where he attended the city's university. His first post was in Baku, from which he traveled in Persia and Ottoman Turkey and learned Persian and Tatar. Hedin then attended the universities of Uppsala and Berlin, studying geography and geology. In 1890 he carried out a lengthy journey across Russian Turkistan to Kashgar, a journey that was not exploratory but rather a reconnaissance for future expeditions. In 1891 he received his PhD from the University of Halle.

Between 1893 and 1935 he undertook four expeditions dedicated to exploring regions unknown to Europeans, and in each he acted as a physical geographer and cartographer and made an extensive petrological collection. The first expedition (1893–1897) crossed Russia and the Pamirs to Xinjiang via the Alai and Trans Alai, with side excursions to Karakul Lake and the Alichur Pamir. [See color plate 39 in this volume.] Hedin attempted unsuccessfully to climb the 24,700-foot Pamir outlier Mustagh Ata in Xinjiang. He nearly died of thirst crossing the Taklimakan Desert to the Khotan River, but found an ancient settlement in the desert. Hedin was not an archaeologist, but his discoveries set the stage for Aurel Stein's work. Hedin studied Lop Nor Lake in

---

On Not Dying of Thirst in the Gobi

This Swedish explorer knew how to make the most of his dangerous experiences, as in his long, drawn-out description of "dying of thirst in the Gobi desert." The event took place in 1895, but thirty years later Hedin seems to have forgotten none of his sufferings. Our passage describes his deliverance, at a time when most of his companions were dead and he was himself on the verge of collapse; one cannot help feeling that there is a good deal of self-dramatization in his writing.

Suddenly I started, and stopped short. A water-bird, a wild duck or goose, rose on whirring wings, and I heard a splash. The next moment, I stood on the edge of a pool, seventy feet long and fifteen feet wide! The water looked as black as ink in the moonlight. The overturned poplar-trunk was reflected in its depths. In the silent night I thanked God for my miraculous deliverance. Had I continued eastward I should have been lost. In fact, if I had touched shore only a hundred yards north or south of the pool, I would have believed the entire river-bed to be dry.

—Sven Hedin, *My Life as an Explorer* (London, 1926)

eastern Taklimakan and crossed into northern Tibet. For this expedition he received the Founder's Medal of the Royal Geographical Society (but he was struck from the RGS rolls in World War I when he acted as a reporter on the German side).

On his second expedition (1899–1902), Hedin returned to study Lop Nor, the lake whose site had changed, and he explored and mapped in Tibet, but was unable to reach Lhasa. On his third expedition (1906–1908) he crossed Persia and northern India to make observations in southwest Tibet. In Hedin's last major expedition (1926–1935), he worked with German and Chinese scientists in Mongolia and continued to study the shifting position of Lop Nor. Hedin's reputation in Allied nations was dimmed by his staunch support of Hitler and of Nazi philosophy in general. Hedin performed a pivotal role in documenting the physical geography of central Asia. He wrote numerous popular books and his scientific results occupy fifty-four volumes. He died in Stockholm on November 29, 1952.

[*See also* Stein, Aurel, *and* Gobi Desert.]

BIBLIOGRAPHY
Hedin, Sven. *Across the Gobi Desert*. London: Routledge, 1931.
Hedin, Sven. *Through Asia*. 2 vols. New York: Harper and Brothers, 1899.

DAVID SPENCER SMITH

Henday, Anthony (1725–?), English trader who traveled with Cree in the Canadian interior. Anthony Henday was born in Shorwell, Isle of Wight, in late 1725, one of eight children. Since his father (also named Anthony) worked only a modest farm, the young Anthony seems to have soon turned his hand to more venturesome activities, and after being convicted for smuggling joined the Hudson's Bay Company in 1750. He was stationed at York Factory, Hudson Bay, in the humble capacity of laborer and net maker; but in 1754 he set out to accompany a band of Cree Indians on their return to the interior. The reason behind his journey was the rivalry between the Hudson's Bay Company and the French fur traders who had reached the lower Saskatchewan River, where their posts lay across the river routes to Hudson Bay. Henday's mission was to travel beyond the French and to establish direct contact with the mysterious "Archithinue" Indians of the plains.

Henday left York Factory in June 1754, equipped with only a compass, and followed his Cree companions to the lower Saskatchewan, where he came across a French trading post at The Pas. Farther west, Henday encountered his first Assiniboine bands, saw the great buffalo herds of the plains, and in October found the "Archithinue" or horsed Atsina (Blackfoot). He was with Indians who were closely related to those seen by Henry Kelsey more than sixty years earlier, and the lack of any mention of horses in the latter's journal supports the thesis that the Blackfoot of the northern plains did not acquire horses until nearer Henday's time. Guided and protected by the Cree, Henday then traveled farther west, and by the end of the year may have been in sight of the Rocky Mountains; but if so, his journal nowhere mentions this stupendous feature. In the spring of 1755, Henday's party began the long journey back to York Factory, once more encountering horsed Indians. One of the most revealing results of Henday's travels was his discovery that the Cree and Assiniboine who came down to York Factory were middlemen, and that most of the furs that were traded at the factory had been trapped by Indians of the far interior who never visited the bayside posts. He was helped in his understanding of the Indian trade system by a Cree woman companion, the "bedfellow" mentioned several times in his journal. After a twelve-month absence Henday reached York Factory on June 20, accompanied by seventy canoes, but many of the best furs had been traded to the French at their posts on the lower Saskatchewan.

Henday's journal hints at the extent and commercial significance of his travels; but it is this journal that lies at the heart of the difficulty in determining where Henday went and what he did. There are four copies, none in Henday's own hand, ranging in date from the year of his return in 1755 to about 1780. No version is simply a copy of another, and although there are discrepancies among all of them the most serious differences are between the 1755 journal and the three later ones. In the first, the writer cut a truculent figure as he swaggered past the French posts and persuaded the Plains Indians to promise that in the future they would bring their furs down to Hudson Bay rather than trade with the French. The other three copies describe how a fearful Henday lost many of his furs to the French traders, how the Plains Indians refused to contemplate abandoning their horses for canoes, and the long river journey down to Hudson Bay. Other differences among the journals make it impossible to trace Henday's route with any certainty. Without any surveying instruments, he relied on dead reckoning, and a comparison of the journal of 1755 with the later copy of circa 1780 shows that in the latter many of Henday's distances have been reduced by a half.

This confusion and the company's continuing policy of secrecy may explain why Henday's journey did not have more impact at the time. His discoveries in the interior appeared on no contemporary maps, while the company, although it again sent Henday inland from York Factory, did not take plans of interior expansion seriously until the 1770s. By then Henday was no longer in its service. His account of his remarkable journey was not universally believed in the Hudson Bay, he failed to obtain promotion, and in 1762 he left the company's service and disappeared into obscurity.

[*See also* Hudson's Bay Company, *subentry on* North American Exploration; North America, *subentry on* Indigenous Guides; *and* Rocky Mountains.]

BIBLIOGRAPHY

Belyea, Barbara, ed. *A Year Inland: The Journal of a Hudson's Bay Company Winterer*. Waterloo, Ontario: Wilfrid Laurier University Press, 2000.

Williams, Glyndwr. "The Puzzle of Anthony Henday's Journal." *The Beaver* 309 (Winter 1978): 41–56.

GLYNDWR WILLIAMS

Henry the Navigator

Henry the Navigator (1394–1460), Portuguese prince who commissioned sea voyages along the west coast of Africa in search of a route to India. Infante Dom Henrique of Portugal, known to the English-speaking world as Prince Henry the Navigator, is considered by many to have been the initiator of Portuguese overseas expansion. He instigated and sponsored numerous voyages of exploration in the African Atlantic, yet did not take part in any of them personally. By the time of his death in 1460, his retainers and licensees sailed as far as Sierra Leone and claimed for Portugal the four major archipelagos of the African Atlantic: the Madeiras, the Canaries, the Azores, and the Cape Verde Islands.

Henry is a figure of some controversy. Glorified by contemporaries and by the subsequent generations of Portugal's "Golden Age" writers, he was transformed by nineteenth-century scholars into a cultural hero and, together with Christopher Columbus, a harbinger of modernity. It was only at this time that he acquired his nickname "The Navigator." He also became a stock icon of modern Portuguese nationalism, heavily promoted by the dictatorship of Antonio de Oliveira Salazar (r. 1932–1968). The virtual worship of Henry the Navigator brought in time an inevitable reaction. Scholars have pointed out that the Portuguese crown, private commercial interests, and Henry's brother, Prince Pedro, played at least as important a role as Henry in organizing early overseas explorations. Some have gone even further, claiming that Henry usurped his brother Pedro's rightful place in history. Yet, despite the debates, Henry remains one of the readily recognized personages associated with European overseas expansion, together with Columbus and Vasco da Gama.

Henry was born the fourth son of King Dom João 1 of Portugal and his queen, Philippa of Lancaster, sister of the future king Henry IV of England. He grew up steeped in martial culture, amid constant domestic disturbances, threats to his father's rule, and hostilities with the neighboring Castile. Once peace was achieved in 1411, young Henry became one of the most vocal proponents of a war of conquest in Muslim North Africa. Barely out of his teens, he played a significant role in organizing the campaign against the Moroccan port city of Ceuta, on the southern shore of the Strait of Gibraltar, which fell to the Portuguese after only one day of fighting, on August 21, 1415.

The Ceuta experience had a galvanizing effect on Henry's outlook and ambitions. War in Morocco would become his lifelong preoccupation, while the overseas explorations constituted only a collateral project. Knighted and granted the title of duke of Viseu, Henry assumed responsibility for managing the logistics and defense needs of Portuguese-occupied Ceuta. In 1419, when the garrison found itself under severe attack from Fez and Granada, Henry led the relief expedition. Having arrived after the danger to Ceuta had already passed, Henry proposed to attack the stronghold of Gibraltar, on the Granadan side of the strait, but was not allowed to carry out his plan.

Henry's chronicler, Gomes Eanes de Zurara, claims that Henry spent twenty years after the fall of Ceuta directing explorations in the North African Atlantic, but found it impossible to cajole his men past Cape Bojador. Fear of navigation dangers and of the uninhabited and waterless lands beyond it held them back. This impasse was overcome only in 1434, when Gil Eanes rounded the Cape on his second southbound voyage. The subsequent expeditions of Gil Eanes and Afonso Baldaia proved that the Atlantic coast of the Sahara Desert was indeed inhabited, dispelling previous misconceptions. Earlier scholars have interpreted Zurara's narrative as a proof of Henry's great vision and foresight, but it is much more likely that the expeditions were a by-product of Henry's pirating activities against Moroccan shipping and coastal settlements. Rather than an expression of scientific interests, the expeditions reflected strategic plans directed against Morocco, in which the Atlantic Ocean played an important logistical role. This view is reinforced by Henry's concerted effort to secure title to various Atlantic islands as offshore bases. In 1433 he was granted the Madeiras, rediscovered in 1419, and later several islands in the Azores. He was also eminently interested in acquiring the Canaries, to the point of offering to do homage for them to the king of Castile, a decision that severely undermined Portuguese claims to the archipelago.

In 1437, Henry realized his hopes for a new military campaign in Morocco, despite strong domestic opposition in Portugal. When finally assembled, his army proved inadequate to the task in size and logistical support. Having failed to conquer the port town of Tangier, the beleaguered Henry was forced to negotiate for terms with the Muslim forces sent to relieve the town: he promised the surrender of Ceuta and had no choice but to leave his brother behind as hostage. The incident represented the greatest humiliation of his life. Although he proposed to lead a retaliatory expedition to rescue his brother, his tainted reputation and a domestic crisis prevented his return to the battlefield.

Unable to pursue ambitions in Morocco, Henry resumed his Atlantic explorations. These proceeded very satisfactorily, stimulated by the prospect of tangible gains in the form of easily obtained slaves. The first captives arrived from the Rio de Ouro region in 1441, followed in 1444 by slaves from the Arguin Bay in Mauritania. In the same year, Nuno Tristão, one of Henry's captains, reached the Senegal River and Dinis Dias reached the Cape Verde promontory and the future Gorée Island. In 1446, Nuno Tristão sailed some 360 kilometers (216 miles) south of Cape Verde, reaching Gambia or possibly the Casamance River. Unless credence is granted to Zurara's claim that Álvaro Fernandes sailed that same year to the vicinity of Cape Verga, Tristão's accomplishment was surpassed only ten years later by Alvise di Cadamosto and Diogo Gomes, both of whom reached the estuary of the Geba River. Pero da Sintra, Henry's old retainer, explored the coastline of Sierra Leone in 1460, the year of his master's death, or shortly afterward. Between 1456 and 1460, Alvise di Cadamosto, Diogo Gomes, and António di Noli each successively claimed credit for discovering the Cape Verde Islands.

The Atlantic explorations brought Henry much fame in the last decade of his life. Poggio Bracciolini, the famous humanist, compared him in 1449 to a new Alexander and Julius Caesar, and the bull *Pontifex Romanus* (1455), which sealed Portugal's claims to the African Atlantic, named Henry as beneficiary side by side with the king, Dom Afonso V. Henry himself took an active part in the compilation of the chronicles authored by his protégé Zurara, which celebrated his life's achievements. Yet it was not African exploration and trade that marked the climax of his career. This came with the conquest of the small but strategically important Moroccan town of Alcácer Seguer, in 1458, in which Henry accompanied his nephew and king, Dom Afonso V "the African," who subsequently realized Henry's dreams by conquering Tangier and Arzila (1471). Henry died two years later, on November 13, 1460, at the age of sixty-six, having spent his last months in struggles over the division of his property and titles.

[*See also* Eanes, Gil, *and* Expeditions, World Exploration, *subentry on* Portugal.]

BIBLIOGRAPHY

Diffie, Bailey W., and George D. Winius. *Foundations of the Portuguese Empire, 1415–1580*. Minneapolis: University of Minnesota Press, 1977.

Elbl, Ivana. "Henry 'the Navigator': The State of Research." *Journal of Medieval History* 27 (2001): 79–99.

Russell, Peter. *Prince Henry "the Navigator": A Life*. New Haven, Conn., and London: Yale University Press, 2000.

Russell, Peter. *Prince Henry the Navigator: The Rise and Fall of a Culture Hero*. Oxford: Clarendon Press, 1984.

IVANA ELBL
MARTIN ELBL

Hernández, Francisco (1515–1587), Spanish physician who headed the first European scientific expedition to the Americas. Hernández traveled through New Spain (Mexico) between 1571 and 1577, following Philip II's orders to gather information about every aspect of the region's natural history, especially the medicinal uses of plants. Hernández visited major hospitals, interviewed numerous European and Amerindian informers, cared for victims of epidemic diseases, compiled descriptions of thousands of plants and hundreds of animals and minerals (including more than three thousand plants previously unknown in Europe), and collected a large cache of drawings by native artists. The original manuscript of Hernández's *Natural History of New Spain*—six folio volumes of text and ten of illustrations—formed the fullest repository of firsthand knowledge on New World materia medica at the time. It provided information on Amerindian medical knowledge, which was rapidly disappearing through death and conversion, and also described plants that held enticing medical and commercial

Fig. 29.
CHIMALACATL
Helianthus annuus L.

Francisco Hernández. Plate showing sunflower from Francisco Hernández's *Historia de Las Plantas de Nueva España* (ed. Casimiro Gomez Ortega, Mexico City, 3 vols., 1942–1946). This image, from a recent publication, shows the printed version of the sunflower that derives from the sixteenth-century Hernández manuscript. Note that the great botanist included the Amerindian names for his plants. COURTESY THE NEWBERRY LIBRARY, CHICAGO

promise to Europeans enthusiastic about recent natural imports like chocolate, corn, and tobacco. Stored in the royal library at the Escorial palace, the manuscript was destroyed in a fire in 1671. This early and important work would have been lost had it not been for the few existing copies and abstracts, notably the first abridged version, *Quatro libros de la naturaleza* (Mexico, 1615) and the famous edition produced by the Accademia dei Lincei, *Rerum medicarum Novae Hispaniae thesaurus* (Rome, 1651).

Hernández's descriptions were also incorporated into the publications of many well-known authors, including Juan Eusebio Nieremberg, Georg Marcgraf, John Ray, Hans Sloane, and James Petiver. A full Spanish edition of Hernández's work first appeared in 1790.

[*See also* Central and South America, *subentry on* Scientific Inquiry; Medical Aspects of Exploration; *and* Plants.]

BIBLIOGRAPHY
Varey, Simon, ed. *The Mexican Treasury: The Writings of Dr. Francisco Hernández.* Translated by Rafael Chabrán, Cynthia L. Chamberlain, and Simon Varey. Stanford, Calif.: Stanford University Press, 2000.
Varey, Simon, Rafael Chabrán, and Dora B. Weiner, eds. *Searching for the Secrets of Nature: The Life and Works of Dr. Francisco Hernández.* Stanford, Calif.: Stanford University Press, 2000.

DANIELA BLEICHMAR

Herndon, William (1813–1857), American explorer of the Amazon basin. Lieutenant William Herndon of the U.S. Navy received, while serving in Chile in 1850, orders to leave his ship and lead

---

Exploring the Amazon River Valley

Herndon's widely disseminated report is a very easy read, full of interesting adventures and curious observations. It does not pretend to play any part in the list of innovative accounts of exploration.

Soon after starting we saw a fine doe coming down towards the river. We steered in and got within about eighty yards of her, when Ijurra and I fired together, the guns loaded with a couple of rifle-balls each. The animal stood quite still for a few minutes, and then walked off slowly into the bushes. I gave my gun, loaded with three rifle-balls, to the *puntero*, who got a close shot, but without effect. One of the balls, a little flattened, was picked up close to where the deer stood. These circumstances made the Indians doubt if she were a deer, and I judged from their gestures and exclamations that they thought it was some evil spirit that was ball-proof.

—William Herndon and Lardner Gibbon, *Exploration of the Valley of the Amazon* (3 vols.; Washington, D.C., 1854)

Silver-bearing Llamas Crossing the Andes. From William Lewis Herndon's *Exploration of the Valley of the Amazon* (2 vols., Washington, 1853–1854). There is something delightfully amateurish about Midshipman/Lieutenant Lardner Gibbon's image of these perky-looking llamas carrying their loads of silver across the Andes. Courtesy The Newberry Library, Chicago

an exploring expedition across the Andes and down the Amazon. Herndon's orders had their origin in an ambitious, secret plan devised by a fellow naval officer—and his kinsman—Lieutenant Matthew Maury. Maury hoped to defuse the building tension related to the threat of secession by the Southern states.

Herndon, who had served under Maury at the Naval Observatory, knew of Maury's concept which postulated that if a fertile region of the Amazon basin were colonized by American planters, with their slaves, the South could accept emancipation and civil war could be averted. While Herndon's official brief was to acquire all available cartographic, navigational, and resource information about the Amazon, Maury's covert instructions were to identify the best location for a U.S. colony.

Lieutenant Herndon, then aged thirty-eight, left his ship in Valparaiso to begin collecting maps and geographical intelligence. He traveled to Lima to continue the quest, where he was joined by another Maury protégé, midshipman Lardner Gibbon. The small expedition ascended the Andes before dividing into two. Herndon followed a well-established route down the Huallaga tributary to the main stream, while Gibbon explored two potential routes in southern Peru and Bolivia. They had planned to rendezvous in Barra (present-day Manaus, Brazil).

Herndon arrived there early, frustrated and exhausted. He continued on to Pará and home, a full year ahead of Gibbon. Their three-volume combined report, presented to Congress and the Senate in 1853 and 1854, was reprinted in best-seller quantities. Maury's scheme never materialized, of course, and the Civil War ensued. In 1857, during a cyclone off Cuba, Herndon went down with the ship under his command.

[*See also* Amazon River.]

BIBLIOGRAPHY
Herndon, William Lewis, and Lardner Gibbon. *Exploration of the Valley of the Amazon.* 3 vols. Washington, D.C.: Taylor and Maury, 1854.

Michael Layland

Herodotus

Herodotus (c. 485–c.420 B.C.E.), Greek historian, traveler, and explorer.

Best known as the historian who recorded the events of the Greek wars against the Persians (490–479 B.C.E.) in his sole surviving work, the *Histories*, Herodotus was also an accomplished traveler and explorer, to judge by the scattered first-person comments found in that text. A polymath who took a particular interest in questions of geography and ethnography, he wove into his historical account a survey of the earth's lands and peoples, including those known to him only through vague reports or mythic traditions. Indeed it appears that the *Histories* as we have it may have arisen when Herodotus chose to combine a narrative of the Persian wars with one or more originally independent works of a more descriptive nature. For example, his account of Egypt, which fills the entirety of the second of the nine books of the *Histories*, may have been a separate essay. But Herodotus succeeded brilliantly in attaching such excurses to his main thread by pausing at each point in the expansion of the Persian empire to investigate the regions absorbed into it. Thus his discussions of lands and peoples predominate in the first half of the *Histories*, which covers the rise and territorial growth of Achaemenid Persia from about 560 to 500 B.C.E.

Herodotus, probably born about 485 B.C.E., spent his early years in the mixed Greek and Carian city of Halicarnassus (present-day Bodrum), on the southwest corner of the Anatolian peninsula. The region was liberated from Persian occupation in 479 as the result of the Greek victories in the Aegean, but remained closely connected by trade routes and other lines of communication to the Asian hinterland, then united under Persian rule to a point as far east as the Indus River. Herodotus, therefore, had access to a far greater store of data about distant parts of the earth than the sixth-century writers who preceded him. He often took pains to correct these predecessors, of whom he named only one—Hecataeus of Miletus—explicitly, in matters such as the shape and structure of the earth, the boundaries of the continents, and such mysterious phenomena as the yearly summer flooding of the Nile. He seemed to regard himself in these passages as an empirically minded reformer, dispelling the speculative theories of the Ionian philosophers by means of his own observations or the information he has gleaned from others. Moreover, his rudimentary scientific method led him to distinguish these two categories of data as *opsis*, that which he had seen with his own eyes and, less reliable, *akoē*, that which he heard about from others.

The least trustworthy forms of *akoē*, in Herodotus's eyes, were the geographic notions found in the works of Homer and other early poets. Chief among these was the idea of a "river" Ocean that surrounded the known world in all directions. With a skepticism remarkable for his time, and indeed shared by only

a few in the long course of Greco-Roman geographic thought, Herodotus debunked Ocean as a poetic fiction (4.8) and instead claimed that the eastern and northern boundaries of the *oikoumenē* remained unknown in his day. The related idea of a circular *oikoumenē* also comes under attack in an important passage (4.36), which supplies some of our earliest evidence about ancient cartography: "I laugh when I see those who draw world-maps . . . with Ocean flowing around the perimeter, a perfect circle like something sketched with a compass, with Europe and Asia equal in size." Rejecting the geometric symmetry that had long been a hallmark of the Ionian speculative tradition, Herodotus went on to describe in his own words the shape and structure of the *oikoumenē* (4.37–44), incorporating a host of errors and distortions but seeking at least to base his depiction on received information rather than theory.

To the category of *opsis* belong the researches undertaken by Herodotus himself, at some unknown point in his life and by unknown means, in parts of the world visited by only a few of his Greek contemporaries. Of these, his expeditions to Egypt and to the north coast of the Black Sea, the region he knew as Scythia, were by far the most intensive and important, to judge by the long excurses on these places that fill all of Book Two and about half of Book Four. In Egypt especially, Herodotus sought out exotic sights and visited remote locales, for example tracing the Nile as far south as the ivory-trading town of Elephantine in an unsuccessful effort to learn about its source and the cause of its summer flooding. The keenness with which he observed his surroundings there can be glimpsed in a discussion of Egyptian geology at 2.12, where five distinct phenomena are adduced to support the apparently original hypothesis that the land of Egypt had been formed from alluvial silt. Yet Herodotus could also be, at times, surprisingly rash in his interpretation of evidence or naive in his acceptance of tales told to him by his foreign informants. A set of animal or insect remains glimpsed by him in eastern Egypt led him to accept the truth of a local legend concerning invasions by flying snakes (2.75). In another famous passage (2.35), he seems to revert to the symmetrical thinking he elsewhere reproves in claiming that the Egyptians are in all ways the inverse of other races.

Incidental comments made by Herodotus in the *Histories* attest to his visits to other parts of the world as well: Tyre (2.44), Gaza (3.5), southern Italy (4.15), and perhaps Babylon (implied by the detailed description of 1.178–183). In recent years some scholars have raised questions about Herodotus's veracity in his claimed travels, including even the sojourns in Egypt and Scythia, but there are as yet no compelling reasons to doubt the historian's word on these matters. Rather, we should take Herodotus for what his text so loudly proclaims him to be: an inquiring and adventurous researcher who roamed far and wide in quest of an empirically verifiable, not myth-based, understanding of the earth and its peoples.

[*See also* Africa, *subentry on* Early Exploration of East Africa, *and* Oikoumenē *and* Orbis Terrarum.]

BIBLIOGRAPHY

Bunbury, E. H. *A History of Ancient Geography*. Vol. 1, ch. 6–8. 2nd ed. New York: Dover, 1959.

Herodotus. *The Histories*. Translated by Aubrey de Selincourt, with introduction by John Marincola. New York: Viking Penguin, 2003.

Romm, James. "Herodotus and Mythic Geography: The Case of the Hyperboreans." *American Journal of Philology* 119 (1989): 97–113.

Waters, K. H. *Herodotus the Historian*. Norman: University of Oklahoma Press, 1985.

JAMES ROMM

Herrera y Tordesillas, Antonio de (1549–1625),

Spanish historian and official chronicler of the Indies. The member of a prominent family, Herrera received an excellent humanist education in Spain and Italy and, in 1579, become the private secretary to Vespasiano Gonzaga, the viceroy of Naples. In 1596, King Philip II of Spain recognized the young man's talent and appointed him as royal historiographer and chronicler of the Indies. This position afforded Herrera a generous salary and gave him access to official state archives, correspondence, rare manuscripts, and eyewitness accounts.

At the turn of the seventeenth century, the Spanish crown faced bitter criticism as a result of the conquerors' depredations and horrific treatment of Indians in the New World. King Philip II expected the royal chronicler to help rehabilitate his country's reputation and to bolster its territorial claims by presenting a carefully documented justification of the Spanish imperial project. With those twin goals in mind, Herrera embarked upon his most famous and influential work, the *Historia general de los hechos de los castellanos en las islas y tierra firme del mar océano* (General history of the deeds of the Castilians in the islands and mainland of the Ocean Sea). Herrera's multivolume official history is often cited as the most detailed and accurate compendium of events that occurred during the Spanish conquest of America. His careful attention to detail and the inclusion of extracts from many documents that are no longer extant have made his work an invaluable resource for all subsequent historians. Attempting to achieve balance in his work, Herrera admitted the Spaniards' many errors, but tended to portray unpleasant events as isolated incidents prompted by extraordinary threats or arising from the human flaws of individual conquerors. To offset charges of the conquerors' brutality, Herrera championed the peaceful work of Bartolomé de Las Casas and emphasized the glory of Spain's divinely ordained conversion mission in the New World.

Herrera's work has not been without its critics, however. He has been branded a plagiarist for excessive reliance on authors such as Francisco López de Gómara, Garcilaso de la Vega, and Las Casas. He has also been criticized for his inclusion of the fantastic and for his lack of interest in pre-Columbian societies. Partly as a result of jealousies in the royal court, Herrera fell into disfavor and was briefly exiled from 1609 to 1611. He was reinstated as royal chronicler within two years and eventually ascended to the position of secretary of state shortly before his death in 1625.

[*See also* Las Casas, Bartolomé de.]

BIBLIOGRAPHY

Ballesteros Gaibrois, Antonio. "Antonio de Herrera, 1549–1625." Vol. 13, *Handbook of Middle American Indians*. Edited by Howard F. Cline. Austin: University of Texas Press, 1973.

Brading, David. *The First America: The Spanish Monarchy, Creole Patriots, and the Liberal State 1492–1867*. Cambridge, U.K., and New York: Cambridge University Press, 1991.

Kelley, James. "Juan Ponce de León's Discovery of Florida: Herrera's Narrative Reconsidered." *Revista de la Historia de América* 111 (enero–junio 1991): 31–65.

KAREN RACINE

Heyerdahl, Thor (1914–2002),

Norwegian explorer and author. Thor Heyerdahl was born the only son of Thor and Alison Heyerdahl in Larvik, Norway, on October 6, 1914. While playing as a child on a frozen pond behind his father's brewery, Heyerdahl fell through the ice and nearly drowned. This child, who was, thereafter, deathly afraid of the water, was an unlikely person to become famous as the leader of the *Kon-Tiki* expedition, characterized as "history's greatest sea adventure and archaeology's most original and famous experiment" (Capelotti, p. xvi).

On an expedition to the Pacific island of Fatu Hiva as a zoology student at Oslo University, Heyerdahl observed the westward-moving waves and wind that

Antonio de Herrera y Tordesillas. Title page of Antonio de Herrera's *Descripción de las Indias Occidentales* (Madrid, 1601). This remarkable title page combines the royal arms (in the center) with a great variety of Amerindian images, a suitable combination for a work intended to summarize Spanish knowledge about the lands and peoples across the Atlantic. COURTESY THE NEWBERRY LIBRARY, CHICAGO

prevail throughout most of the Pacific. He began to question the contemporary belief that the peopling of the Pacific was accomplished, against these forces of nature, by island-hopping in an easterly direction from Southeast Asia. Though the Fatu Hiva expedition netted Heyerdahl a membership in the Explorers Club, his interest changed to anthropology and the rest of his life was devoted to the exploration of ancient cultural contacts. Following more than ten years of research, Heyerdahl argued that the inhabitants of Polynesia had originated, most recently, from the continents of North and South America, following the wind and currents from east to west.

Although Heyerdahl amassed substantial evidence to support his theories, the scientific community repeatedly rejected his hypotheses as impossible. Heyerdahl decided to put his theories to the test, and, along with five others, he constructed a balsa raft based on early colonial depictions of Inca watercraft. The *Kon-Tiki* set sail from Peru on April 28, 1947. One hundred and one days later, after encounters

with storms, rough seas, and every type of sea life imaginable, the *Kon-Tiki* crashed into the coral reef surrounding the Polynesian island Raroia. In the instant of the *Kon-Tiki*'s crash, Heyerdahl demonstrated that the technology available to the ancient inhabitants of South America was capable of reaching Polynesia, forever turning Pacific anthropology upside down.

Despite his mission's success, considerable public interest, a best-selling book on the voyage, and an Academy Award for the resulting documentary, Heyerdahl continued to meet with opposition among the scientific establishment. Not dissuaded by his critics, Heyerdahl next explored ancient sea links between various culture centers, leading the first formal archaeological expeditions to Easter Island and the Galápagos Islands.

In 1969 Heyerdahl tested another theory of cultural contact: Could a papyrus reed vessel, based on designs depicted in Egyptian tombs, traverse the Atlantic Ocean from Africa to the New World? The *Ra*, the first of Heyerdahl's vessels to attempt this passage, unraveled in the Atlantic due to a design flaw. The crew was rescued within a few days' journey of the Lesser Antilles. Still convinced that such a craft could make the voyage, Heyerdahl built the *Ra II*. With the flaw corrected, the *Ra II* landed in Barbados, from its launch in Morocco, on July 12, 1970, demonstrating that the New World was not out of reach of ancient Egyptian seafarers.

The year 1977 found Heyerdahl, once again, exploring possible links among ancient culture centers. He hypothesized that cultural similarities among Sumeria (in Iraq), Dilmun (in Bahrain), and Mohenjo Daro (in Pakistan) were not the result of independent invention, but rather were transported via the ocean highway. Against the contentions of the scientific establishment, Heyerdahl argued that a vessel constructed of berdi reeds could reach all of these locales from the interior of Iraq. The *Tigris* set sail on its namesake river on November 11, 1977. Despite the warnings of critics that the vessel would sink in two weeks, the *Tigris* remained afloat for five months and made port at Dilmun and Mohenjo Daro from its origin within the Sumerian heartland in Iraq.

Today, two of the four history-making vessels, the *Kon-Tiki* and the *Ra II*, are displayed in the Kon-Tiki Museum in Oslo. The *Ra* disintegrated in the Atlantic Ocean and the *Tigris* was burned by its crew in Djibouti in protest of the wars then occurring around the Red Sea.

Travels by Raft on the South Seas

This stirring passage describes Kon-Tiki's arrival at the Raroia Atoll after 107 days at sea. The frail raft was carried forward like some massive surfboard until it struck the reef. Then the crew had to hold on for dear life, as successive waves carried the vessel farther and farther onto the reef, until eventually it lay at the limit of the sea's force. Soon they could wade through the shallow waters beyond the reef—and throw themselves down on the sand in exultation.

A sea rose straight up under us as we felt *Kon-Tiki* being lifted up in the air. The great moment had come; we were riding on the wave-back at breathless speed, our ramshackle craft creaking and groaning as she quivered under us. The excitement made one's blood boil. . . . A new sea rose high astern of us like a glittering glass wall; as we sank down it came rolling after us, and in the same second in which I saw it high above me I felt a violent blow and was submerged under floods of water. I felt the suction through my whole body, with such great strength that I had to strain every muscle in my frame and think of one thing only—hold on! hold on!

—Thor Heyerdahl, *The Kon-Tiki Expedition: By Raft across the South Seas* (London, 1950)

Later in life, Heyerdahl led archaeological expeditions in Peru and the Canary Islands. He also championed the cause of environmentalism in the world's oceans after drifting in oil slicks for months in the *Ra*, *Ra II*, and *Tigris*.

Thor Heyerdahl died in Italy on April 18, 2002. Despite academic criticism, Heyerdahl's exploratory voyages aboard reconstructed ancient vessels prove that the ocean could be used as a highway for transporting people, goods, and culture across ocean divides long before Europeans crossed the Atlantic. In this criticism lies, perhaps, Heyerdahl's most important contribution. His constant opposition to mainstream thought has resulted in voluminous research, both to test his theories and to expand on new discoveries. Indeed, a new generation of explorers, including Ben Finney and Tim Severin, has followed Heyerdahl by testing theories of long-distance cultural contacts by taking to the sea.

[See also Finney, Ben; Pacific, *subentry on* Pre-European Trade Routes; *and* Polynesian Voyages.]

BIBLIOGRAPHY

Capelotti, P. J. *Sea Drift: Rafting Adventures in the Wake of the Kon-Tiki.* New Brunswick, N.J.: Rutgers University Press, 2001.

Heyerdahl, Thor. *In the Footsteps of Adam: A Memoir.* Toronto: Warwick Publishing, 2004.

Jacoby, Arnold. *Señor Kon-Tiki: The Biography of Thor Heyerdahl.* Chicago: Rand McNally, 1967.

RYAN M. SEIDEMANN

Hind, Henry Youle. *See* **Palliser, John, and Henry Youle Hind.**

Hornemann, Friedrich (1772–1801?), German explorer of the Sahara Desert. Friedrich Konrad Hornemann was born in Hildesheim, Germany, on February 15, 1772, and was the first of many qualified men recommended by Professor J. F. Blumenbach to the newly founded African Association in London. Hornemann, a student at Göttingen University, went to London in early 1797 to receive instructions, and then to Cairo where he continued his Arabic studies before embarking on his journey into the Sahara. While he was there, the French army, led by Napoleon Bonaparte, invaded Egypt. Hornemann met Bonaparte, who provided him with both a passport and funds. The first European explorer of the Sahara to masquerade as a Muslim, he began his trek on September 5, 1798, with an Arab caravan. He spent seven months at Murzuk, from where he made

a 500-mile (804.7-kilometer) trip north to Tripoli. He forwarded his journal—which included a statement that the Niger River flowed into the Nile—to London. The African Association received three letters from Tripoli dated April 30, 1800, and two more from Murzuk, but after he departed that oasis, he was never heard from again. In 1819, Lieutenant George Lyon learned that Hornemann had reached Katsina, south of the Benue River in present-day Nigeria, and that he probably died of dysentery in February 1801 in the village of Bokkane. Hornemann was the first European to cross the Sahara Desert from the Mediterranean to the West African forest zone. When his journal was published in 1802, a copy was presented to Napoleon.

[See also Africa, *subentry on* Exploration; African Association; Expeditions, World Exploration, *subentry on* German States; Sahara; *and* Timbuctoo.]

BIBLIOGRAPHY

Hornemann, Friedrich. *The Journal of Frederick Hornemann, From Cairo to Mourzouk, the Capital of the Kingdom of Fezzan, in Africa, In the Years 1797–8.* London: G. and W. Nicol, 1802.

SANFORD H. BEDERMAN

Houghton, Daniel (1740–1791?), Irish explorer of the Niger River. Daniel Houghton was born in Ireland, became a major in the British army, and was hired by the African Association to search for the Niger River. An old Africa hand, Houghton earlier had served many years in Senegal. Because he was an unpensioned retired military officer, he applied to and was accepted by the African Association to penetrate the continent from the Gambia River to search for information regarding the source and direction of flow of the Niger River. He was instructed also to visit Timbuctoo, and then return home by the most feasible route.

At age fifty, he arrived in Gambia in November 1790. He experienced considerable difficulty on his journey—he accidentally wounded himself, his supplies were burned, and he was robbed several times. Although his precise route is unknown, he likely reached the Niger River, and in a fact previously unstated, he indicated that it rose on the eastern slope of a coastal range, and flowed eastward. His last message from the African interior was dated September 1, 1791, and he was probably murdered shortly thereafter while on the trail to Timbuctoo. The actual circumstances of his death are unknown, and his travel journal was never found.

[*See also* Africa, *subentry on* Exploration *and* African Association.]

BIBLIOGRAPHY

Severin, Timothy. *The African Adventure: Four Hundred Years of Exploration in the Dangerous Continent*. New York: Dutton, 1973.

SANFORD H. BEDERMAN

Hubbard, Mina Benson (1870–1956), Canadian woman who explored Labrador in the early twentieth century. Some explorers may be motivated by greed, glory, or the thrill of adventure, but Mina Benson Hubbard was motivated by love and indignation. Her husband, Leonidas Hubbard, had died in 1903 in an attempt to cross the Labrador Peninsula. One of his companions on the trip, Dillon Wallace, wrote a book about their experiences in which he made Mr. Hubbard seem weak and foolish. Mina Hubbard was incensed and vowed to honor her husband's memory by mounting a new expedition and accomplishing the journey herself.

It was an unlikely undertaking for a nineteenth-century woman. She was born on a farm near Bewdley, Ontario, on April 15, 1870. In her twenties, she moved to New York, became a nurse, and married one of her patients, a journalist named Leonidas Hubbard. They had been married only two years when he died.

In 1905, at the age of thirty-five, Hubbard hired four guides to accompany her on her journey through Labrador. One of the men, George Elson, had also been a guide on Leonidas's fateful trip. Simultaneously, Dillon Wallace had decided to attempt the traverse again, and he and Mrs. Hubbard's party started out within hours of each other from trading posts on the peninsula's eastern side. Both aimed to arrive at Ungava Bay on the north coast before the

A Woman's Way through Unknown Labrador. (New York, 1908) These photographs from Hubbard's book give us an idea of her determination. Note the veil against the flying insects of Labrador, and also, on the right, the confusion of cooking-pots scattered at Hubbard's feet. COURTESY THE NEWBERRY LIBRARY, CHICAGO

two-month Labradorean summer ended. In between lay 600 miles (965 kilometers) of unexplored lands and unmapped watersheds.

Mina Hubbard's party reached Ungava Bay a month before Wallace did. Along the way, they mapped the Naskaupi River and George River systems, located Lake Michikamau, spent time among the Montagnais and Naskaupi Indians, made hundreds of photographs, and kept records of the flora and fauna along the way. She wrote of her experiences in *A Woman's Way through Unknown Labrador*.

Hubbard eventually remarried and moved to England. She died on May 4, 1956, after being struck by a train.

[*See also* Women Explorers.]

BIBLIOGRAPHY
Buchanan, Roberta, Anne Hart, and Bryan Greene, eds. *The Woman Who Mapped Labrador*. Montreal: McGill–Queen's University Press, 2004.
Hubbard, Mina Benson. *A Woman's Way through Unknown Labrador, An Account of the Exploration of the Nascaupee and George Rivers*. New York: McClure, 1908. Reprint. *A Woman's Way through Unknown Labrador*. Montreal: McGill–Queen's University Press, 2004.

PATRICIA GILMARTIN

Hubble Space Telescope.

The Hubble Space Telescope (HST) is the most famous scientific instrument ever built and arguably the most productive telescope of all. The largest optical observatory ever sent into space, HST was launched into orbit around the earth by the space shuttle *Discovery* on April 24, 1990. At its heart was a reflecting telescope with a primary mirror 8 feet (2.4 meters) in diameter. The telescope had been designed to direct light into five dedicated scientific instruments as well as the observatory's Fine Guidance Sensors (the primary purpose of which is to keep the HST locked on to its astronomical targets), which also served as a sixth instrument. Although relatively small by the standards of earth-based telescopes in the 1990s, HST's location above the obscuring layers of the earth's atmosphere was reckoned to more than compensate for its limited size. In fact, HST was widely expected by astronomers to have a very major, perhaps even revolutionary, impact on astronomy.

Before the launch of *Sputnik I* in 1957 and the dawn of the space age, astronomers had dreamed for decades of escaping from the obscuring layers of the earth's atmosphere and of a time when the quality of their scientific data would not be eroded by the structure and motions of the atmosphere. Free of the handicap of the atmosphere, much higher resolution images, astronomers knew, could be secured than with equivalent ground-based telescopes. Space-based telescopes would also be able to detect electromagnetic radiation from a far wider range of wavelengths than telescopes on the ground. Even before the leaps in rocket technology, driven by military needs in World War II, some of the prophets of space exploration such as Hermann Oberth had also speculated on the possibilities of astronomical observatories in space.

With the establishment of NASA in 1958, plans for astronomical observations from space gathered pace. While the bulk of NASA's funding would soon be directed to the Apollo program to land astronauts on the Moon, the fledgling agency provided huge resources for science, including astronomy. NASA embarked on a wide-ranging set of astronomical projects, and by the late 1960s planning was underway by industrial companies, astronomers, and NASA for an ambitious venture, what at the time was often called the Large Space Telescope, or LST. Designs soon settled on a telescope with a 9.8-foot (3-meter) primary mirror, which would be at the core of a spacecraft that would be operated remotely. As NASA organized to develop the space shuttle (the White House approved the project in 1972), so planning for the LST became meshed with the shuttle. NASA envisaged the shuttle to be both the means of launching the LST into space as well as the way that it would be repaired and serviced in orbit by astronauts.

Very serious political obstacles slowed the telescope's progress, but the go-ahead from White House and Congress was finally given in 1977. But this time the LST had become the more modest Space Telescope (it would become the Hubble Space Telescope in 1983, named after the famous American astronomer Edwin P. Hubble) and, among other changes, its primary mirror size had been cut to 8 feet (2.4 meters). Overall, the observatory would weigh about twelve tons and be roughly the size of a school bus. An international partner had been added too in the shape of the European Space Agency, ESA, which was to provide about 15 percent of the costs in return for 15 percent of the telescope's observing time. In 1981, the Space Telescope Science Institute was also established to manage the HST's scientific operations and to engage in broader issues to do with links between the telescope and the astronomical community.

The HST had a substantial technical heritage from U.S. spy satellites, but its detailed design and construction proved to be fraught with difficulties, schedule slips due to management and technical issues, and increases in budget. It was further delayed by the loss of the space shuttle *Challenger* in 1986 and the consequent grounding of the shuttle fleet. Nevertheless, by 1990, HST was ready for launch. In the design and construction process, a variety of scientific problems had informed the technical requirements that the telescope was to meet, and in decisions such as, for example, selecting particular kinds of light filters to be incorporated into the scientific instruments, astronomers were certainly taking specific astronomical questions into account. At the same time, they were also anxious to develop a scientific tool that would incorporate many possible modes of observing and so be highly flexible. The astronomers were very much operating with the notion in mind of the conscious expectation of the unexpected.

HST was borne aloft by *Discovery* in 1990, but the HST's early images were hugely disappointing. Astronomers and engineers realized within weeks of its launch the telescope's primary mirror was flawed by an optical defect known as spherical aberration. It was too flat at its edges by a very small amount, but an amount that was more than enough to seriously hobble the observatory's performance and put its future in jeopardy.

A very successful repair mission three and a half years later by the crew of the space shuttle *Endeavour*, however, restored both the telescope's sight and its credibility. While the telescope had not been a complete scientific loss before its repair, its performance afterwards was greatly improved. But the repair had come at the price of jettisoning one of the original complement of scientific instruments, the High Speed Photometer (designed to measure rapid fluctuations in the brightness of astronomical objects). [See color plate 41 in this volume.]

The HST's performance was about as good as astronomers had anticipated before it was launched, and it was swiftly making major contributions to a range of astronomical problems. Refining the value of the so-called Hubble Constant (which gives the rate at which the universe is expanding and the inverse of which provides a measure of the age of the universe) was always one of the key problems astronomers foresaw for the HST. In its initial determination, a team of astronomers measured the value of the Hubble Constant with HST and found that it indicated a time since the big bang that was surprisingly close to the age of the oldest stars, posing a dilemma. How could the universe be younger than its oldest stars? However, the team's later determination, and the measurements by another team of astronomers, indicated an age of the universe of around 13–14 billion years, comfortably older than the oldest stars.

HST has also made very significant observations of regions of star formation. Perhaps the observatory's most famous image is of such a region, the Eagle Nebula (a gaseous nebula about seven thousand light years from the earth), secured in 1995. Its spectacular display of pillars of gas and dust garnered enormous attention, and has appeared in television broadcasts, newspapers, news magazines, on T-shirts, and many other locations. Perhaps even more dramatic than the Eagle Nebula was the image of the so-called Deep Field. This was essentially a core "sample" of the universe, produced by taking some 342 exposures of one very small part of the sky with one of the HST's cameras for ten successive days in 1995 and then combining the exposures into one image. This showed about fifteen hundred galaxies, some of them so distant that they were being viewed as they looked only a few billion years after the big bang. The Deep Field would later be followed by even deeper samples. HST has also contributed to studies of the solar system. Its observations of Jupiter in 1994 when Comet Shoemaker-Levy crashed into the planet were especially striking.

The original philosophy of repairing and maintaining the telescope in orbit by use of the space shuttle has been followed and has enabled not just the fixing of the problem of spherical aberration, but, among other things, the exchange of new scientific instruments for older ones. For example, in 1997, an instrument sensitive to infrared radiations was added to the telescope (the first generation of instruments had all been designed principally for optical and ultraviolet radiations), and in 2002 a new and very sensitive high resolution camera joined the telescope's armory. By this date the HST was a much more efficient and powerful scientific tool than it had been in 1990.

In the wake of the loss of the space shuttle *Columbia* in 2003, however, NASA cancelled plans for the next servicing mission for HST. Without such a flight, engineers reckoned that HST's effective life would come to an end around 2008 as critical components would likely fail. This decision caused a public outcry. It was stridently opposed by many astronomers as well as on Capitol Hill. Following public and congressional pressure, NASA announced in 2005 that it intended to launch one more servicing mission to the telescope provided the shuttles were back in service and the mission did not carry what the space agency judged to be unacceptable risks.

Hence at the time of writing, the future of the telescope is still in doubt.

[*See also* Space Program *and* Space Shuttle.]

BIBLIOGRAPHY
DeVorkin, David, and Robert W. Smith. *The Hubble Space Telescope. Imaging the Universe.* Washington, D.C.: National Geographic, 2005.
Livio, Mario, Keith Noll, Massimo Stiavelli, et al., eds. *A Decade of Hubble Space Telescope Science.* Cambridge, U.K., and New York: Cambridge University Press, 2003.
Livio, Mario, Michael Fall, and P. Madeu, eds. *The Hubble Deep Field.* Cambridge, U.K., and New York: Cambridge University Press, 1998.
Petersen, Carolyn Collins, and John C. Brandt. *Hubble Vision: Further Adventures with the Hubble Space Telescope.* 2nd ed. Cambridge, U.K., and New York: Cambridge University Press, 1998.

ROBERT W. SMITH

Huc, Évariste Régis (1813–1860), missionary explorer of Tibet.

Father Huc was born in Toulouse on August 1, 1813; in 1837 he joined the congregation of Lazarists, who sent him to China in 1839. He spent some time in their seminary at Macao, acquiring the local language, and was then sent on to Peking. His work there brought him into contact with the Tatars, to the north of the Great Wall, and his remarkable skill and diligence in this missionary work seem to have marked him out for exploration.

No doubt this was why in 1844 he was chosen to lead a small expedition to Tibet, far away to the south across terrifying deserts. Huc and his two companions disguised themselves as lamas, and after many adventures they entered Lhasa early in 1846. At first favorably received, after a short time they were ordered back to Canton. Huc stayed there for nearly three years, returning in 1852 to Paris, where he died on March 31, 1860.

While he was in Paris, Huc published much material on his time in the East. His work was published in English, and he became much read in the Anglo-Saxon world; indeed, his work continued to be reprinted in the twentieth century. While his style may seem to verge on sensationalism, many of his assertions have turned out to be true, and he certainly played a considerable role in introducing many western readers to China, Tartary, and Tibet.

[*See also* Explorers in Disguise.]

BIBLIOGRAPHY
Huc, Evariste Régis. *A Journey through the Chinese Empire.* 2 vols. New York: Harper and Brothers, 1855.
Huc, Evariste Régis. *Travels in Tartary, Thibet, and China, during the Years 1844–1846.* Translated by William Hazlitt.
London: Office of the National Illustrated Library, 1852. Reprint. New York: Dover, 1987.

DAVID BUISSERET

Hudson, Henry (c. 1570–1611), English navigator and explorer.

Little is known about the early life of Henry Hudson except that he was the son of a London alderman, and that by 1607 hc was a navigator experienced enough to be employed by the English Muscovy Company on successive expeditions in search of a short sea route to China. In 1607 he tried to take a ship across the North Pole, and reached the remarkably high latitude of 80° N near Spitsbergen before being forced back by ice. The next year his attempt to find a Northeast Passage around Russia was also blocked by ice. In 1609, Hudson sailed northeast once more, this time in the employ of the Dutch East India Company. Again he encountered ice in the Barents Sea and, after murmurs of mutiny from his crew, he switched the direction of his search by turning west across the Atlantic to the North American coast. In September, Hudson sailed, as Giovanni da Verrazano had done more than eighty years earlier, through the Narrows of New York Bay. Unlike Verrazano, he entered the Hudson River and followed it as far as present-day Albany. As the water shoaled, Hudson realized that he had not found a strait to the Pacific, but he had confirmed the existence of a great harbor and had found the most important waterway on the Atlantic coast of what would one day be the United States. His explorations formed the basis for the Dutch claim to the region soon to be known as New Netherland, and then to be known under English rule as New York.

On his return to Europe, Hudson reentered English service, and in 1610 he was given command of the *Discovery*, financed by a consortium of merchants and projectors. Hudson was to search for a Northwest Passage in the Davis Strait region, and after trouble with his quarrelsome crew on the outward voyage he entered Hudson Strait in June. Whether this was a deliberate choice or an escape from the tidal rips at the strait's entrance is not certain. For six weeks the ship struggled through the ice-choked waters of Hudson Strait, until at the beginning of August 1610 it entered Hudson Bay. For Hudson it was "a spacious sea" and he was "confidently proud that he had won the passage." Whether he was the first European discoverer of the great bay named after him is a matter of controversy. Portuguese mariners may have sighted the entrance of

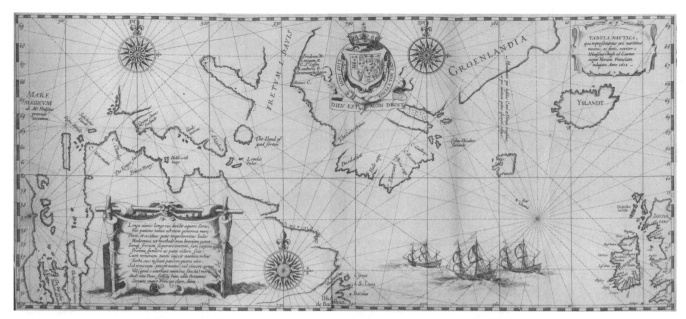

Henry Hudson. Engraving by Hessel Gerritz showing Henry Hudson's voyage of 1610–1611, from *Descriptio ac delineatio detenctionis freti* (Amsterdam, 1612). This engraving may well follow Hudson's original manuscript and shows his discoveries of 1610–1611. It includes in the far west the "Mare Magnum," or "great sea, first found by Mr Hudson," which surely, he thought, led straight to China. COURTESY THE NEWBERRY LIBRARY, CHICAGO

Hudson Strait at the beginning of the sixteenth century, and there is some evidence that Sebastian Cabot sailed through Hudson Strait and perhaps into Hudson Bay itself in 1508 or 1509. Martin Frobisher sailed sixty leagues into the strait in 1578, John Davis noted the "furious Overfale" of the strait's entrance in 1587, and George Weymouth entered the strait in 1602. Hudson's achievement was less the "discovery" of the strait than his determination in pushing through it and reaching the wide expanse of water beyond. The navigator Luke Foxe asserted that Davis and Waymouth "did (I conceive) light Hudson into his Streights," but it was Hudson who established the reality of an inland sea in the northern parts of the American continent.

The *Discovery* worked its way south to "the bottom of the bay" (later James Bay) before it was frozen in. Short of food, the crew spent a miserable winter, and when the ice broke up in the spring most opposed Hudson's intention of renewing the quest for a passage westward. Hudson, his son, and seven crew members were cast adrift in a small boat, and were never seen again. The episode was long remembered as one of the classic tragedies of Arctic exploration. The *Discovery* sailed for home under the command of Robert Bylot, losing several of the remaining crew to Inuit attack and sickness before the survivors reached England in September 1611. With the leading mutineers dead, investigations into Hudson's fate petered out, but interest in his discoveries remained. In 1612, Hessel Gerritz published in Amsterdam a chart showing the long bottleneck of Hudson Strait opening into a "Mare Magnum" or "Great Sea," and in the next twenty years several expeditions searched Hudson Bay for a passage through to the Pacific. None was found, and when, later in the century, European ships entered the bay again, they were looking for furs. In seeking the Northwest Passage, Hudson had found instead two of the most important entry points into the North American continent, and the names of the Hudson River, Hudson Strait, and Hudson Bay acknowledge the significance of his discoveries.

[*See also* Cabot, Sebastian; Davis, John; Foxe, Luke; Frobisher, Martin; Northwest Passage; *and* Verrazano, Giovanni da.]

BIBLIOGRAPHY

Asher, G. M., ed. *Henry Hudson the Navigator: The Original Documents.* London: Hakluyt Society, 1860. Reprint. New York: B. Franklin, 1963.

Edwards, Philip, ed. *Last Voyages, Cavendish, Hudson, Ralegh: the Original Narratives.* Oxford and New York: Oxford University Press, 1988.

Neatby, L. H. "Henry Hudson." *Dictionary of Canadian Biography.* Vol. 1, pp. 374–379. Toronto: University of Toronto Press, 1966.

GLYNDWR WILLIAMS

Hudson's Bay Company

This entry contains two subentries:

Arctic Exploration
North American Exploration

Arctic Exploration

The 1670 charter for the Hudson's Bay Company (HBC), from the crown and government of England, obliged the company to undertake a search for a passage to the South Sea, and this led to the company's role in exploration of the Canadian Arctic. A more pervasive reason for exploration in high latitudes was minerals, whalebone, and new trading partners, Inuit and Indian, so as to enlarge the scope and profit of company business. In fact, the first northern voyage from Hudson Bay and James Bay forts, by Henry Kelsey from Churchill Fort in July–August 1719 in two ships, was to search for copper. This expedition coasted at least as far north as 62°40′ N, beyond Marble Island. James Knight in 1719–1721 sailed from London to search the west coast of Hudson Bay north of 64° for copper, gold, and the fabled Strait of Anian. Knight and his men all died on Marble Island of sickness and famine. The HBC exploring expedition of 1721–1722 by John Scroggs and Richard Norton, from London, made further discoveries higher up on Hudson Bay, with Norton reporting a clear passage to the west (dead-end Chesterfield Inlet, now Igluligaarjuk). Meanwhile, on the Quebec shore of Hudson Bay the company had had trade at Eastmain River beginning in 1684, but not until 1723–1724 was a permanent post built, by Joseph Myatt. Ice conditions on that side of the bay hindered discoveries. Rivalry from New France overland and from French naval units by sea interrupted HBC trading operations and shipping, so that until the Peace of Utrecht in 1713, which granted England full sovereignty in these latitudes, the company's Arctic discoveries were fitful and unplanned.

Change came with the campaign of the Irish landowner Arthur Dobbs, member of Parliament and energetic campaigner for the search for the Northwest Passage. At his instigation, in 1736 the HBC sent two vessels under James Napper and Robert Crow on a trading, mining, and Northwest Passage expedition to search near Roes Welcome Sound, to survey and to open trade with the Inuit. The expedition was a failure, except that Napper promised the Inuit that the bay traders would return with trade goods. The company sent annual expeditions north from Churchill, diversifying and extending trade to higher latitudes. The British government, responding to Dobbs's entreaties, sent two Royal Navy vessels, *Furnace* and *Discovery* under Christopher Middleton and William Moor, in 1741–1742. North from Churchill in company of the HBC vessel *Churchill*, they discovered Wager Bay, then Repulse Bay and the entrance to Frozen Strait. A poor trade was made along the coast with Inuit, and no Northwest Passage was found, though a few incidental details were added to scientific knowledge of the Arctic in these latitudes. In 1744 the company sent from Moose Factory its first exploring expedition to the Eastmain shore, discovering Fort George (Mailasikkut) and Great Whale and Little Whale rivers, and reconnoitering Richmond Gulf. The expedition did not locate a waterway to the Labrador interior; such a passage would have helped open trade there. In 1746, Dobbs, heading up the North West Committee, sent the ships *Dobbs* and *California* to Wager Bay, where surveys were made but no passage found. A parliamentary inquiry into the Hudson's Bay Company in 1749, in response to Dobbs's criticism, inquired into the state and conditions of HBC trade; the result was no case for annulling the charter nor throwing the trade open to rivals. No voyages of discovery were mounted for some years, though trade north of Churchill continued uninterrupted.

The company began, with Henry Kelsey and Anthony Henday, to search for trading Indians in the continental interior, the intention being to attract them to the forts on the bay. Traders on exploration encountered the Barrens, and the most significant discoveries of these were undertaken by Samuel Hearne, who set out from Fort Prince of Wales, Churchill River, in 1769 in the company of Indians but achieved little. In 1770 he tried again, and reached Kazan River, 300 miles (483 kilometers) north of Churchill. His goal was the Coppermine River, which drains into the Arctic Sea. Hearne broke his quadrant on this expedition and decided to return to base, further discoveries being futile. He was robbed by Chipewyan, but on the way back to Fort Prince of Wales encountered Matonabee, a friendly, courteous Chipewyan chief who offered to help Hearne on a subsequent expedition. This, the third attempt, was undertaken in the winter of 1770–1771. They crossed the Kazan, then found the barren lands around Artillery Lake, then encountered "Copper Indians" and reached the Coppermine River on July 13, 1771. Hearne surveyed the river and made a famous chart of it. He reached the Arctic Ocean on July 17, thus disproving the existence of a Northwest Passage between Hudson Bay and the mouth of the Coppermine. He erected a mark claiming the coast for the HBC. He had reached his goal, but the sight of the great icepack offshore negated any thought of opening a company trading port on that coast. Hearne returned by Great Slave Lake, saw the aurora borealis or northern lights, crossed the lake on ice, continued southward to and up the Slave River to near present-day Fort Smith, then returned to Fort Prince of Wales on June 30. This was the first overland expedition to the Arctic Ocean; it closed Hearne's remarkable voyages of discovery. Placed in charge of the fort, he surrendered it to Jean-Francois de La Pérouse of the French naval squadron in 1782, and the fort was conveyed to France. Hearne's journal, which ranks among the greatest in travel literature, was published London in 1795.

> We of the Hudson's Bay Company thought very little of our Arctic work. For my own part at least I thought no more of it than any ordinary journey.
>
> —John Rae to R. H. Major, June 1875.

The HBC continued to explore northern Quebec and Labrador, with hopes of finding a practical route for overland communication. In 1836–1840, John McLean, on instructions, made three overland journeys to find a practicable trading route from Fort Chimo (Kuujjuaq) to Fort Smith. These discoveries forced a closure of Chimo and an opening of a post at North West River, as the company reorganized its trade under strong economies. Similar explorations, to expand trade but also, in this case, to counter Russian trade from Alaska, were made in Athabasca and the Yukon, mainly under Samuel Black of the Finlay River (1824) and Robert Campbell of the Pelly River (1842–1844). The HBC's northern explorations predated those of the magnetic survey of John Henry Lefroy (undertaken at the instigation of the Royal Society), as well as other explorations by the Geological Survey of Canada, by various missionaries, and by some American expeditions such as that to Herschel Island. But the HBC's explorations overlapped and complemented those of the Royal Navy, the leading force in Arctic discoveries from Greenland to Alaska in the nineteenth century.

In 1837–1839, Peter Warren Dease and Thomas Simpson led an HBC exploring expedition of amazing endurance from Fort Chipewyan to explore those parts of the north coast of American not already explored by Captain John Franklin in 1819–1822 and 1825–1827. From the Mackenzie River they followed the shoreline west, completing the discovery between Return Reef and Point Barrow, Alaska, and, eastward from the Mackenzie, between Turnagain Point and Fury and Hecla Strait. They traveled the Coppermine River, explored Richardson River, surveyed south coasts of King William and Victoria islands, and returned to Fort Simpson at the confluence of the Liard and Mackenzie rivers. This ranks with Hearne's achievement as an HBC enterprise in exploration.

In 1846, John Rae went north from York Factory to complete the survey between Captain Sir William Edward Parry's Fury and Hecla Strait and Dease and Simpson's farthest point east of Castor and Pollux Bay. He made another expedition the next year, leaving Boothia Peninsula as the only remaining unexplored part of the north coast of America. In 1853–1854 he traveled to Boothia Peninsula but was hindered by bad weather. In 1854 he heard Inuit reports of the fate of the Franklin Expedition and purchased relics from Inuit who had obtained them from corpses of the naval explorers. He retuned to York Factory and reported the first definite news of the fate of the Franklin Expedition, last heard of nine years before. The last of the great HBC explorers, Rae championed light traveling techniques, employing advice, materials, and supplies of the Inuit. His extensive travels closed geographical inquiries by the HBC in the Arctic; these inquiries were succeeded by those of various Canadian government expeditions, North West Mounted Police (later RCMP) patrols, whaling and fishing searches, scientific and missionary inquiries, and foreign examinations, mainly U.S. and Norwegian.

[*See also* Arctic; Franklin Search Expeditions; Fur Trade; North America, *subentry on* Indigenous Guides; North West Company; Northwest Passage; *and biographical entries on figures mentioned in this article.*]

BIBLIOGRAPHY

Bunyan, Ian, Jeni Calder, Dale Idiens, et al. *No Ordinary Journey: John Rae, Arctic Explorer, 1813–1893*. Edinburgh: National Museums of Scotland; Montreal: McGill–Queen's University Press, 1993.

Cooke, Alan, and Clive Holland. *The Exploration of Northern Canada 500 to 1920: A Chronology*. Toronto: Arctic History Press, 1978.

BARRY M. GOUGH

North American Exploration

The Hudson's Bay Company (HBC), an ancient joint-stock company that is still in business and since 1970 has been headquartered in Winnipeg, Manitoba, obtained a charter from the English crown on May 2, 1670, as the Gentlemen Adventurers of England Trading into Hudson's Bay. Straits leading to Hudson Bay had been opened by earlier navigators. But the promising, pioneering fur-trade enterprises of the French traders and explorers Pierre Esprit Radisson and Médard Chouart des Groseilliers were embraced by the board of directors in London with the support of the government, the crown, and banking interests.

Early HBC expeditions to Hudson Bay to open trade were made annually, and the examination of harbors suitable for trade was undertaken by officers and men of the shipping department. Early posts were built at Fort Nelson (later York Factory) on southwest Hudson Bay, as well as at Albany, Moose, and Rupert's House (now Weskaganish), all in James Bay, the southern annex of Hudson Bay. Each of these posts lay at the mouth of a river of the same name. From these posts inland exploration was undertaken to promote trade, with scientific examination having scant importance in commercial ventures.

The charter gave the HBC a monopoly of British trade through the straits leading to Hudson Bay; it also gave the firm a monopoly of British trade in the lands drained by waters leading to those same straits. This territory the firm called Rupert's Land, after its first governor; it was a handsome endowment of almost two million square miles (five million square kilometers). The charter also required the HBC to make a search for the Northwest Passage, but no such passage existed west of Hudson Bay, though it might in higher latitudes. None of the rivers draining into Hudson Bay or James Bay was navigable to shipping.

HBC undertook another role in higher latitudes, initiated by James Knight in 1717. This required founding another post, Fort Churchill. The company sent an expedition from Gravesend, England, in 1719 to find the illusive passage, hoping also to discover gold and other valuable commodities in the north. The HBC was under attack in certain circles for failing to prosecute the search. Traders were reluctant to venture inland, and they had no need to do so except under instructions; at the same time, the pattern of trade was for native people to come to the forts for trade and exchange, a working system until such time as rival traders based in Montreal (French until 1763; North West Company 1763 to 1821) posed threats on the margins of Rupert's Land.

In the late 1680s, Henry Kelsey, an active young man who was fond of traveling with Indian guides, explored inland from the west shore of Hudson Bay to the Barrens, about 300 miles (480 kilometers), but he encountered no natives. He saw the musk ox, being the first European to do so. In 1690 he ventured inland, on instructions, from York Fort and traveled 600 miles (960 kilometers) southwest. En route, he faced strong running rivers, numerous waterfalls requiring thirty-five portages, and five lakes. Kelsey crossed from the boreal forest into the prairie, and he was the first white man to see the buffalo on the Canadian prairie. At a place he called Deering's Point, he set up a cross in token of his having been there. He kept a journal that is now a classic of North American exploration, part in doggerel verse, part in quaint, pointed English; his actual route remains a matter of speculation. What is certain is that this exploration was undertaken for commercial purposes, to invite the Assiniboine to trade with the HBC. It initiated an inland process of exploration.

In 1754, Anthony Henday, reputedly an outlawed smuggler, went inland from York Factory to explore the country and increase company trade. He reached The Pas, fighting portages and mosquitoes all the way. French traders had a post there. Henday brushed aside French demands that he present a passport, and he moved out on to the prairie. He traveled west, then wintered with Indians somewhere between the North Saskatchewan and the Red Deer rivers. He met Blackfoot on horseback, who were hunting buffalo with bows and arrows. He saw the Rocky Mountains. Returning, Henday came to the French post of La Corne, where Indians were being debauched with brandy, then to The Pas, and back to York Factory. A year had transpired, and Henday had traveled a remarkable 2,000 miles (3,200 kilometers). HBC men discredited Henday's accounts, especially of horsemen being inland, and he did not get promotion as deserved. Unable to acquire provisions and spirits from the ship captains for his own private trading purposes, he quit the firm. Thus closed the second chapter in HBC exploration inland. The French trade inland passed to the British after the Peace of Paris in 1763.

The third chapter of HBC exploration was carried out by trained explorers and particularly surveyors, who made a revolution in discoveries in these latitudes. Matthew Cocking was one such. In 1772–1773 he went from York Factory to the Saskatchewan

River ("Blackfeet Country," he called it) and confirmed the rival Canadian presence. To counter, in 1774 the firm, about to change its policy in any event, sent Samuel Hearne to build a post near The Pas. In 1791–1792, two years after Alexander Mackenzie followed the Mackenzie River to Arctic waters, Philip Turnor explored Methye Portage and Athabasca, following on from the North West Company (NWC). The HBC built posts inland to compete with the NWC and maintain profits. Surveyor Turnor and those he trained in the art, David Thompson (in HBC employ from 1784 to 1797) and Peter Fidler, provided the first scientific data on lakes, rivers, watersheds, and terrain from the boreal forest to the eastern ramparts of the Rockies. Thompson in NWC employ extended these evaluations beyond the continental divide. HBC maps were kept private; until Aaron Arrowsmith prepared maps based on information derived from Mackenzie and HBC authorities, valued surveys undertaken by Turnor, Fidler, and others remained secret. In 1821 a union of the HBC and NWC was effected under the name of the HBC, beginning a new phase in inland exploration that embraced the Yukon, Snake, Salmon, and Umpqua river watersheds.

[*See also* Fur Trade; North America, *subentries on* Indigenous Guides *and* Indigenous Maps; North West Company; Northwest Passage; *and biographical entries on figures mentioned in this article.*]

BIBLIOGRAPHY
Goetzmann, William H., and Glyndwr Williams. *The Atlas of North American Exploration: From the Norse Voyages to the Race to the Pole.* New York: Prentice Hall General Reference, 1992.
Ruggles, Richard, ed. *A Country So Interesting: The Hudson's Bay Company and Two Centuries of Mapping.* Montreal: McGill–Queen's University Press, 1997.

BARRY M. GOUGH

Humboldt, Alexander von

Humboldt, Alexander von (1769–1859), German naturalist and traveler to the New World. Born into a wealthy family in Berlin, Humboldt attended several German universities and by 1790 had developed a keen interest in botany and obtained a solid introduction to physics and chemistry. A trip to England that year confirmed his interest in nature and a love for foreign travel. The death of his mother in 1796 freed him from a brief bureaucratic career and provided the resources to travel as he chose.

Humboldt was the most illustrious foreign traveler in the New World in the late colonial era. With the permission and recommendation of the Spanish crown, he and the French botanist Aimé Bonpland reached Venezuela in 1799 and began a five-year voyage through Spanish America. Laden with scientific instruments, they were able, in good Enlightenment fashion, to measure such things as latitude, longitude, temperature, and air pressure, and to illustrate their findings. The enormous volume of data collected established Humboldt as a major scholar of international reputation.

Humboldt's journey took him into the interior of Venezuela, to Colombia, Ecuador, Peru, Cuba, and finally, to Mexico. His exploration of the Orinoco River revealed its connection to the Amazon. A keen observer of the landscape and the political, economic, and social conditions of its inhabitants, Humboldt mingled with urban elites and gained access to numerous government documents containing demographic and economic information. He shared modern ideas and scientific techniques from Europe with colonial intellectuals and bureaucrats, and thus helped disseminate European knowledge and the be-

---

Travels in South America

Like Samuel Fritz, Humboldt vividly describes the intense discomforts of travel in the river valleys of South America. His vision is curiously different from ours; whereas he longs to see the jungle cleared, so that the land may become less intolerably ridden with insects, we recoil from the wholesale destruction of forest, which for us is associated with unfavorable climate change and with the disappearance of species.

It is neither the dangers of navigating in small boats, the savage Indians, nor the serpents, crocodiles or jaguars, that make the Spaniards dread a voyage on the Orinoco; it is, as they say with simplicity, *el sudar y las muscas* ("the perspiration and the flies"). We have reason to believe that mankind, as they change the surface of the soil, will succeed in altering by degrees the constitution of the atmosphere. The insects will diminish when the old trees of the forest have disappeared; when, in those countries now desert, the rivers are seen bordered with cottages, and the plains covered with pastures and harvests.

—Alexander von Humboldt, *Personal Narrative of Travels to the Equinoctial Regions of America during the Years 1799–1804,* translated by Thomasina Ross (London, 1852)

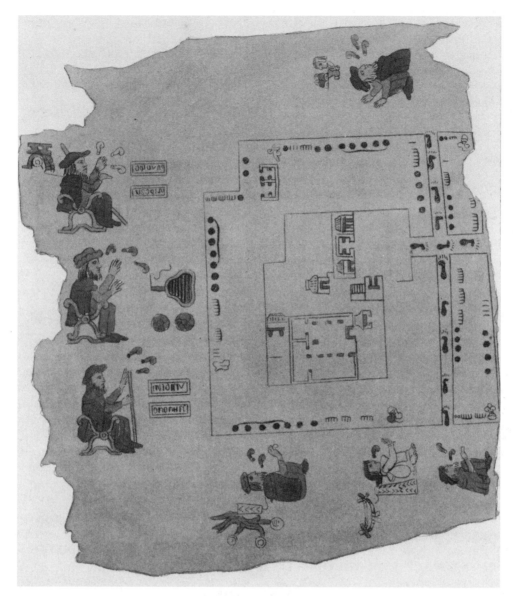

Alexander von Humboldt. Illustration from Alexander Humboldt's *Atlas géographique et physique du royaume de la Nouvelle-Espagne* (Paris, 1811). This image reminds us of Humboldt's all-encompassing curiosity; he was not merely a geographer, but was also concerned with the languages and history of the people he studied. COURTESY THE NEWBERRY LIBRARY, CHICAGO

lief in material progress throughout the New World. His comments on hindrances to progress resulting from Spanish fiscal and commercial policy stimulated some Creoles to believe that improvement in government was necessary.

Following a short stop in the United States, Humboldt returned to Europe in August 1804. There he wrote about his voyage in major works treasured by both contemporaries and historians. His writings include *Voyage aux régions équinoxiales du nouveau continent* (34 vols., 1805–1834; English trans., *Personal Narrative of Travels to the Equinoctial Regions of the New Continent*, 23 vols., 1833); *Essai politique sur le royaume de la Nouvelle-Espagne* (3 vols., 1811–1812; a part of the *Voyage*; English trans., *Political Essay on the Kingdom of New Spain*, 1833); *Essai politique sur l'île de Cuba* (2 vols., 1826; English trans., *The Island of Cuba*, 1856); and *Kosmos. Entwurf ei-*

ner physischen Weltbeschreibung (5 vols., 1845–1862; English trans., *Cosmos: A Sketch of a Physical Description of the Universe*, 1847–1862).

A founder of modern geography, Humboldt in his writings influenced Charles Darwin to undertake his famous voyage to South America.

[*See also* Amazon River; Central and South America, *subentry on* Scientific Inquiry; *and* Darwin, Charles.]

BIBLIOGRAPHY

Brading, D. A. *The First America: The Spanish Monarchy, Creole Patriots, and the Liberal State, 1492–1867.* Cambridge, U.K., and New York: Cambridge University Press, 1991. See chap. 23.

Humboldt, Alexander von. *Political Essay on the Kingdom of New Spain.* Translated by John Black and edited by Mary Maples Dunn. New York: Knopf, 1972. Abridged edition.

MARK A. BURKHOLDER

Hurley, Frank (1885–1962), Australian photographer of the Antarctic. Together with Herbert Ponting, Frank Hurley is considered to be the most accomplished of the Antarctic photographers of the early twentieth century. He was a member of both the Mawson and the Shackleton expeditions. Hurley's photographic chronicle of the Shackleton party's epic journey to safety following the wreck of the *Endurance*, which occurred during the Imperial Trans-Antarctic Expedition of 1914–1916, has been justly celebrated, but this celebration has contributed to an unbalanced appreciation of his work as a whole. His corpus comprises ethnographic images from New Guinea, documentary work as an official war photographer on the western front and in Palestine, and scenes from his native Australia. His work was occasionally controversial. His anthropological film about New Guinea, *Pearls and Savages* (1921), for example, was considered exploitative of native peoples. Specific aspects of Hurley's personality tie together the many projects in which he was involved and require consideration when evaluating his work. He had a strong entrepreneurial streak and, perhaps as a result of his early career in the picture postcard trade, he knew what the public wanted in an image and was driven to provide it. His eye for the spectacular combined with a feel for sentimentality and elegiac mood, which enabled him to match his images to public taste, be they depictions of trench warfare, indigenous folkways of New Guinea, or Antarctic shipwrecks. Although the photograph of the icebound *Endurance* illuminated during the polar winter is often considered an icon of expeditionary

imagery, it may also be considered an example of Antarctic kitsch.

[*See also* Antarctica; Mawson, Douglas; *and* Shackleton, Ernest.]

BIBLIOGRAPHY

Hurley, Frank. *Argonauts of the South.* New York and London: G. P. Putnam's Sons, 1925.

ROGER BALM

Hurtado de Mendoza, García (1535–1609), governor of Chile (1557–1561) and viceroy of Peru (1589–1596). Born into a distinguished Spanish noble clan as the second son of Andrés Hurtado de Mendoza, second marquis of Cañete, García did not expect to inherit his father's title. At sixteen he joined the army of the emperor Charles V, participating in campaigns in Corsica, Italy, and Flanders, and traveling to England.

When his father became viceroy of Peru, García Hurtado de Mendoza accompanied him and was named governor and captain general of Chile in 1557. Taking charge of a huge expanse of territory, with the few Spanish settlements under periodic assault from local inhabitants, García's forces time and again defeated local armies, whose heroic resistance was later immortalized in the epic poem *La Araucana* by Alonso de Ercilla y Zúñiga, one of García's subordinates. During his tenure in Chile, García explored parts of Patagonia and dispatched Juan Ladrillero to explore the extreme southwestern coast of Chile to the western end of the Strait of Magellan. García also sent Pedro del Castillo across the Andes in 1560 to explore and colonize what became Argentina; the Argentine city, province, and river named Mendoza commemorate that expedition.

Replaced in 1561, García returned to Spain, married, and served the crown as ambassador to Savoy and in the contingent that secured the Portuguese throne for Philip II in 1580. Succeeding his older brother as marquis of Cañete, García was viceroy of Peru in 1588–1596. During his tenure, new rebellions in Chile threatened Spanish control, but silver output from the mines at Potosí increased enormously. At the same time, the English corsairs John Hawkins and Francis Drake assailed the Spanish Caribbean, and Alvaro de Mendaña launched his second expedition to the South Pacific (1595) from Peru.

Known for his bravery, arrogance, and pride, García nonetheless served ably as a diplomat in Eu-

Frank Hurley. Photograph from *Argonauts of the South* (New York/London, 1925). This photograph, in which the dogs sadly survey the wreck of their boat, crushed in the ice, might well be taken as an example of the way in which Hurley provided images "matched to public taste." COURTESY THE NEWBERRY LIBRARY, CHICAGO

rope and helped to consolidate Spanish power in America.

[*See also* Drake, Francis, *and* Mendaña, Alvaro de.]

BIBLIOGRAPHY

Barros Arana, Diego. *Historia general de Chile*. 2nd ed. Santiago, Chile: Centro de Investigaciones, 1939. Chaps. 16–19.

CARLA RAHN PHILLIPS

Hydrographic Office, British.

The Hydrographic Office of the British Admiralty, established in 1795, became in the nineteenth century an institution closely associated with geographical exploration, both directly, through the work of naval surveyors, and indirectly, as a major source of information and support to explorers. At first its role was simply to collect and evaluate the available maritime charts and other navigational sources and to have the best of these engraved, printed, and supplied to British ships. The first hydrographer of the Navy, Alexander Dalrymple (who was also, from 1779, hydrographer of the British East India Company), had commanded several East India Company ships between 1752 and 1765, and he had made running surveys of parts of the coasts of China, the Philippines, Borneo, and other poorly charted areas. Dalrymple energetically set about sorting and cataloguing the manuscript charts, surveys, and assorted documents that he inherited with his new post, selecting the best and most useful for engraving and combining data from several surveys to produce charts with wide coverage at appropriate scales. Despite the constraint of a tiny budget, he built up his staff to consist of an assistant, a draftsman, three engravers, and a printer, but the Revolutionary and Napoleonic wars created a huge demand for large numbers of accurate charts of many parts of the world—a demand that Dalrymple's small department was unable entirely to satisfy.

Although Dalrymple instigated new surveys and required naval captains to record hydrographic information in Remark Books, it was under his successor, Captain Thomas Hurd RN, that the Hydrographic Office's role in exploration was pushed beyond merely collecting (and, with the publication of Admiralty Charts from 1821, disseminating) geographical knowledge into the active creation of new knowledge. Since the seventeenth century, various maritime surveys had been commissioned ad hoc by the king and the Admiralty Board, but with the end of the Napoleonic Wars, a methodical program of surveying was implemented by the Royal Naval Surveying Service, under the hydrographer.

The Hydrographic Office first became closely involved in the planning and execution of voyages of exploration (as distinct from more routine surveys of waters closer to home) when Captain (later Rear-Admiral Sir) William Edward Parry RN was appointed hydrographer in 1823. Already a veteran of three Arctic voyages and the man who had led the expedition that pushed farther into the Canadian Arctic Archipelago than any man had before, Parry quickly made the Hydrographic Office become the nexus of British efforts in maritime exploration. This was even more the case because Parry did not cease to be active in exploration when he took up his administrative post: in 1824 and 1825 he commanded yet another attempt at the Northwest Passage, spending another winter in the Arctic, and in 1827 he took time off again to lead an attempt to walk, sail, and sledge to the North Pole from Spitsbergen—reaching a new farthest north beyond 82° N, a record that was to remain unbroken for the next fifty years.

The Hydrographic Office did not lose its association with exploration when Parry was replaced by Captain (later Rear-Admiral Sir) Francis Beaufort RN in 1829. Beaufort had been a surveyor himself, and was a great sponsor of science and an important figure in the Royal Geographical Society. Under Hurd and Parry the Hydrographic Office had acquired its own surveying vessels and had been building up a corps of naval officers who specialized in surveying (the Royal Naval Surveying Service). During Beaufort's twenty-six years as head of the Hydrographic Office, those men and ships were dispatched to almost every corner of the globe. Meticulous surveys in home waters and in the Mediterranean had better detail than earlier charts did, but the increasingly global reach of British commercial, military, and imperial interests demanded charts of many areas that were only very imperfectly covered by existing surveys, or in some cases not at all covered. In these cases, rather than following in the wake of the explorer, the hydrographic surveyors of the Royal Navy often found themselves the explorers, discovering and charting previously unknown channels, harbors, reefs, islands, and even mountain ranges, and establishing contact with native peoples.

Among the surveys that made the most significant contributions to geographical knowledge were Captain W. F. W. Owen's epic 1821–1826 survey—of the coasts of Africa from the Horn of Africa to the Cape of Good Hope (some five thousand miles) and from the mouth of the Congo to the Gambia—and further surveys of West Africa by Edward Belcher, Alexander Vidal, and others. These surveys were carried out in very difficult conditions; in particular, endemic disease for which Europeans had no cure or effective prevention claimed many victims among the officers and crews. Owen had also made geographical and scientific discoveries during his earlier survey of the Great Lakes of Canada, which he had begun in 1815. F. W. Beechey was sent to the Pacific in the *Blossom* in 1825 to rendezvous with Parry's and John Franklin's expeditions, should they succeed in finding a passage to the north of Canada. En route Beechey surveyed several Pacific islands, including Pitcairn Island, where he found John Adams, the sole surviving *Bounty* mutineer. Passing through Bering Strait, Beechey explored and surveyed 126 miles of coastline and reached to within 150 miles of Franklin, who was working his way westward along the coast.

The wild and little-known coasts of Patagonia and the Strait of Magellan from the mouth of the River Plate to the island of Chiloe on the Pacific coast were charted by Captain Phillip Parker King, Commander Pringle Stokes, and Commander Robert FitzRoy between 1826 and 1830, and FitzRoy returned in the *Beagle* in 1831 to finish the job, coming home across the Pacific via the Galápagos Islands, Tahiti, New Zealand, and Australia in order to carry a chain of chronometer readings around the globe to fix the longitudes of coasts and harbors.

The west coast of central and northern America, some Pacific islands, and parts of China and the pirate lair of Sarawak in north Borneo were surveyed between 1835 and 1843 by Edward Belcher in the *Sulphur* and the *Samarang*. From 1817 to 1823, P. P. King continued the charting of northwestern Australia begun by Matthew Flinders, as did John Wickham in the *Beagle* between 1838 and 1843. The Great Barrier Reef, Torres Strait, and parts of Papua New Guinea were charted between 1842 and 1847 by the *Fly* and *Bramble* under F. P. Blackwood, and were charted again between 1847 and 1850 by the *Rattlesnake*, commanded by Owen Stanley, who lent his name to a mountain range in New Guinea—just one of a multitude of topographical features around the world whose name commemorates nineteenth-century British naval surveyors. Also from 1847 to 1850, John Lort Stokes made the first complete coastal survey of New Zealand since James Cook's discovery eighty years before. For a number of years from 1845, the *Herald* surveyed the west coast of America, and in 1854 it was sent back under Captain Henry Denham to the Pacific, where in the course of nine years it surveyed Tonga, the Fiji Islands, the New Hebrides (Vanuatu), and the Solomons.

These and other surveys made important contributions to the advancement of geography and science, but despite their sometimes exotic and remote locations, they were in a sense only the more glamorous part of the routine work of the Surveying Service, which was the official responsibility of the hydrographer. Like his predecessor Parry, however, Beaufort also had a hand (sometimes the main one) in instigating, supporting, and writing the instructions for voyages explicitly of scientific and geographical exploration, such as Captain Trotter's Niger expedition (1840–1842) and James Clark Ross's Antarctic voyage (1839–1843), during which the Ross Sea and Ross ice shelf were discovered, along with the active volcano Mount Erebus. In particular, Beaufort played a central role in coordinating and planning the series of expeditions sent by the Admiralty to the Arctic between 1848 and 1854 in search of the ships and men of Sir John Franklin's expedition, lost since 1845. It was in the course of these unsuccessful rescue missions that much of the Canadian Arctic Archipelago was explored and charted.

There was also another sense in which many of the surveys directed by Parry and Beaufort amounted to voyages of exploration, since they were conceived not as narrowly hydrographic surveys but as truly scientific regional surveys, of which the ostensible purpose—the hydrographic survey—was just a part. To this end, many carried one or more civilian specialists to study the botany, zoology, geology, archaeology, or ethnology of the survey area and its vicinity—men such as Charles Darwin and John MacGillivray. Even more commonly, those subjects were covered by the naval surgeons attached to the survey vessels, some of whom, such as Joseph Hooker and T. H. Huxley, were or became distinguished naturalists and biologists. Other scientific fields such as meteorology, geomagnetism, astronomy, tides and ocean currents, some of which overlapped with the hydrographic aspects of the survey or with the normal competence of the mariner, were undertaken by the officers, midshipmen, and crew of the survey vessel.

The Hydrographic Office's direct involvement with voyages of exploration had its heyday under Beaufort in the decades before the Crimean War, but subsequent hydrographers continued to play a part in providing logistical and other support to British explorers throughout the nineteenth century and beyond.

[*See also* Oceanography in the Seventeenth and Eighteenth Centuries; Royal Geographical Society;

Seaborne Exploration since 1500; *and biographical entries on figures mentioned in this article.*]

BIBLIOGRAPHY

Burrows, E. H. *Captain Owen of the African Survey*. Rotterdam, Netherlands: A. A. Balkema, 1979.

Cock, Randolph. "Rear-Admiral Sir Francis Beaufort RN FRS: 'The Authorized Organ of Scientific Communication in England,' 1829–1855." In *Science and the French and British Navies, 1700–1850*, edited by Pieter van der Merwe. Greenwich, U.K.: National Maritime Museum, 2003. Pp. 99–116.

David, Andrew. *The Voyage of HMS "Herald" to Australia and the South-west Pacific, 1852–1861*. Carlton, Australia: Miegunyah Press, 1995.

Day, Archibald. *The Admiralty Hydrographic Service, 1795–1919*. London: HMSO, 1967.

Friendly, Alfred. *Beaufort of the Admiralty: The Life of Sir Francis Beaufort, 1774–1857*. London: Hutchinson, 1977.

Parry, Ann. *Parry of the Arctic: The Life Story of Sir Edward Parry*. London: Chatto & Windus, 1963.

Ritchie, G. S. *The Admiralty Chart: British Naval Hydrography in the Nineteenth Century*. 2nd ed. Bishop Auckland, U.K.: Pentland Press, 1995.

RANDOLPH COCK

Hyperboreans. The Hyperboreans were a legendary race dwelling "Beyond Boreas" (according to the commonly accepted etymology of their name), that is, north of the "Rhipaean" mountains from which the North Wind was thought to originate. Greeks of the Archaic age imagined this wind-sheltered land as a climatic utopia despite its high latitude; the poet Alcaeus (fragment 307) shows Apollo himself traveling there during winter months to escape the rain and cold of his native Greek haunts. The life of the Hyperboreans was as paradisiacal as their climate. Pindar describes it in his tenth Pythian ode as a constant round of music, dancing, and revelry, often in the company of Apollo, untroubled by war, strife, sickness, or decrepitude. Other authors variously imagine the Hyperboreans as immortal or describe how a peaceful death overtakes them in extreme old age.

No Greek traveler claimed to have reached the Hyperboreans, and indeed Pindar invokes them in his poems to represent an extreme of distance beyond the reach of human endeavor. By contrast Hyperborean wayfarers were though to have frequented the Greek world in early times and even to have left memorials behind. The shrine of Apollo at Delphi was first established by two such Hyperborean travelers, according to a poem attributed to Boeo by Pausanias (10.5.7). Herodotus describes a cult ritual on the island of Delos performed at the supposed gravesites of two Hyperborean girls, Arge and Opis, and alludes vaguely to a story of a Hyperborean traveler named Abaris "who carried the arrow around the whole world without eating anything" (4.32–36). Herodotus also supports a Delian tale that makes the Hyperboreans the source of unidentified straw-wrapped offerings arriving in Delos by way of a relay system. It is remarkable that the fifth-century Greeks thus imagined that a semidivine, golden age people lay at the other end of a very real northern European trade route (perhaps the route by which amber was conveyed southward from the Baltic region). (Herodotus's often misunderstood statement that "if there are Hyperboreans, there are also Hypernotians or men beyond the South Wind," does not suggest that the historian doubted the existence of this fabulous race, though he does express skepticism regarding their supposed neighbors, the one-eyed Arimaspians.)

As is clear from the various legends mentioned above, the Hyperboreans were especially linked with the god Apollo and were thought to be his personal favorites among humankind. Pindar depicts them sacrificing donkeys in the god's honor, a rite otherwise unknown among the Greeks. In a story told by Bacchylides (3.57 ff.) Apollo transports one of his favorites, King Croesus of Lydia, to the land of the Hyperboreans as a way of rescuing him from earthly disaster, while Pausanias records a similar translocation of the first temple dedicated to Apollo at the site of Delphi, a structure of beeswax and feathers (10.5.9). This fits a theory that traces the origins of the worship of blond Apollo to northern Europe. Whether the Hyperboreans can be connected with historical Celtic or Scandinavian peoples, however, is unclear.

[*See also* Herodotus.]

BIBLIOGRAPHY

Bolton, J. D. P. *Aristeas of Proconnesus*. Oxford: Clarendon Press, 1962.

Romm, James S. *The Edges of the Earth in Ancient Thought: Geography, Exploration, and Fiction*. Princeton, N.J.: Princeton University Press, 1992. See chap. 2.

JAMES ROMM

I

Ibn Battuta (1304–1368/69), "the traveler of Islam," who made numerous pilgrimages to Mecca, and traveled to India and China. Ibn Battuta (Abu Abdallah Muhammad ibn Abdallah al-Lawati al-Tanji ibn Battuta) was the greatest traveler before modern times and author of a book, the *Rihla*, describing his travels from Morocco to China and from the Volga in the north to the Niger and Kilwa (in present-day Tanzania) in the south. [See color plate 44 in this volume.]

Born on February 24, 1304, to a family of religious scholars and raised in Tangier, Morocco, Ibn Battuta set out in 1325 at age twenty-one on the first of the journeys that would carry him 73,000 miles (117,457 kilometers) through territories now included in forty-four modern countries. When he arrived back in Morocco for the last time thirty years later, Merinid sultan Abu Inan assigned a young scholar, Ibn Juzayy, to take down Ibn Battuta's account of his travels.

Skeptical scholars have challenged parts of his claimed itinerary. The *Rihla* borrows from descriptions of other Arab writers, rearranges itineraries for literary purposes, and claims dubious journeys to the land of the Bulgars on the middle Volga and north in China as far as Beijing. Most of Ibn Battuta's account, however, has held up rather well.

Ibn Battuta first set out on a conventional pilgrimage to Mecca, intending to meet and study with famous ulema and Sufis along the way. He soon broadened his aim into a project to visit all the lands of Dar al-Islam (the Islamic world) and occasionally—as with Byzantine Constantinople and China—some of the non-Muslim lands beyond. His religious learning qualified him for appointments as *qadi* (judge) in several countries, and gifts from rulers and pious Muslim individuals he met along the way supported him in increasingly sumptuous style.

Arriving back in Tangier in 1349 after a twenty-four year absence, Ibn Battuta was too restless to stay put. Two lands remained to complete his grand tour of Dar al-Islam. First he headed across the Strait of Gibraltar to the kingdom of Granada, the last remnant of Muslim al-Andalus, then joined a caravan south across the Sahara to the gold-rich kingdom of Mali.

An adventurous traveler rather than an explorer, Ibn Battuta discovered no new lands. Although he was sometimes shocked at what he considered lax Muslim practices, he found someone who could speak Arabic and made himself at home from one end of the eastern hemisphere to the other. His reminiscences have the greatest historical value for the sparsely documented frontiers of Dar al-Islam—the East African coast, the lands along the middle Niger, the Turkish principalities of Anatolia, the Maldives, and India.

His visit to the fledgling Ottoman state in 1333 and meeting with its ruler Orkhan, for example, offers a rare early glimpse into the frontier principality near the beginning of its rise to empire.

Ibn Battuta's caravan journey from Fez to Sijilmasa and then across the Sahara to the Niger and back in 1352–1553 took him to and through the empire of Mali, then the leading supplier of the world's gold. He stopped at the desert salt mines at Taghaza and the Malian provincial capital at Walata, continued on to the Niger, and traveled upstream to its capital, which he neglects to name. A miserly reception from the ruler of Mali, Mansa Sulayman, disappointed the great traveler. He followed the Niger (which he called the Nile, following medieval speculation that the Niger was the source of the Nile) downstream to Timbuctoo and Gao before striking out homeward across the Sahara to Morocco. Timbuctoo had only begun its rise to the distinction as a center of trade and Islamic learning it would achieve in the fifteenth and sixteenth centuries.

Ibn Battuta's work remained unknown to Europeans until the early nineteenth century. An abridged edition and translation into Latin was published in Jena in 1818. A partial English translation followed in 1829, and a complete Arabic edition and French translation was published in Paris in 1853–1858.

[*See also* Africa, *subentries on* Exploration *and* Early Exploration of East Africa; *and* Sahara.]

BIBLIOGRAPHY

Dunn, Ross E. *The Adventures of Ibn Battuta: A Muslim Traveler of the Fourteenth Century*. Rev. ed. Berkeley: University of California Press, 2004.

Gibb, H. A. R. *The Travels of Ibn Battuta* A.D. *1325–1354*. Columbia, Mo.: South Asia Books, 1999.

Hamdun, Said, and Noel Q. King, eds. and trans. *Ibn Battuta in Black Africa*. Reprint. New York: Markus Wiener, 2004.

Mackintosh-Smith, Tim, ed. *The Travels of Ibn Battutah*. London: Picador, 2002.

DONALD MALCOLM REID

Ibn Butlan

Ibn Butlan (fl. 1050s), Christian physician and writer. Ibn Butlan ibn al-Mukhtar ibn al-Hasan ibn Abdun was a well-traveled Christian physician and philosopher from Baghdad in the eleventh century, and was most famous for his medical work. Concerning geography, his descriptions of several cities in Syria and Palestine at the time of his visit are most valuable.

The year of Ibn Butlan's birth is unknown. He taught medicine and philosophy in Baghdad, before he left his home town in January 1049, probably to meet the renowned physician Ibn Ridwan (b. 998) in Cairo. He traveled through Mesopotamia, Syria, and Palestine until November of the same year, when he reached Cairo. There he had a sojourn of three or four years. Eventually, because of quarrels with Ibn Ridwan, he left Egypt for Constantinople, where he arrived in the summer of 1054. After a stay of one year he returned to Syria. He finally became a monk in Antioch, where he supervised the building of a hospital in 1063. He died some years later and was buried in the church of the monastery.

Ibn Butlan wrote several medico-philosophical treatises. His main work was the *Taqwim al-sihha*, a summary of hygiene. Besides this text, Ibn Butlan wrote a report on his journey addressed at the request of the Abbasid secretary and historian Hilal al-Sabi (Baghdad, d. 1056). This text is incorporated in the *Kitab al-Rabi* of Muhammad b. Hilal (Baghdad, d. 1088), a son of Hilal al-Sabi. Significant extracts with descriptions of Aleppo, Antioch, Latakia, and several other cities are preserved in the biographical treatise *Tarikh al-hukama* of Ibn al-Qifti (Egypt and Syria, 1172–1248) and the geographical dictionary *Mujam al-buldan* of Yaqut (Baghdad, 1179–1229).

[*See also* Constantinople.]

BIBLIOGRAPHY

Lawrence, Conrad. "Ibn Butlāin Bilād al-Shām: The Career of a Travelling Christian Physician." In *Syrian Christians under Islam: The First Thousand Years*, edited by David Thomas, 131–157. Leiden, Netherlands: Brill, 2001.

PETRA G. SCHMIDL

Ibrāhīm ibn Ya'qūb

Ibrāhīm ibn Ya'qūb (fl. 960–965 C.E.), Hispano-Arabic author. Ibrāhīm authored an important work of unknown compass on European geography, including an account of his journey to Germany, Bohemia, and Italy. In the modern era, he is especially appreciated as an outstanding witness to contemporaneous western Slavic history and culture.

Biographical information on Ibrāhīm is provided solely by his name and his work, which survives only partially by way of—not always attributed—later quotations. Even though his bynames—al-Isrā'īlī al-Óur-Óūshī, or "the Israelite from [the Catalan city of] Tortosa"—referred to his family extraction only, his travel across the frontier between Islam and Christendom may indicate that he professed Judaism himself. Yet Muslim rather than Jewish sensibilities are reflected in his discreetly worded description of a large crucifix in the abbey church of Fulda. A well-rounded education is reflected by his interest in ethnogeography, medicine, politics, and culture, in addition to trade and commerce. The purpose of his journey remains uncertain, even if his repeated audiences with the German king and Roman emperor Otto I (r. 937–973) suggest at least a minor diplomatic charge. Most likely Ibrāhīm's journey fitted in with the Cordovan caliphate's continual diplomatic contacts with king-emperors Otto I and II (r. 973–983). Another still unanswered question concerns the identity of Ibrāhīm's and his interlocutors' lingua franca—arguably a Romance idiom. The fragmentary preservation of Ibrāhīm's text and the easy corruptibility of foreign names in Arabic script severely constrain any reconstruction of his itinerary.

Possibly around the turn of 961, Ibrāhīm set out from the Muslim dominion on the Iberian Peninsula (al-Andalus) and, likely en route calling at Saintes and Tours, eventually reached Rouen; next he is found at Utrecht and Schleswig. From there he appears to have turned, via Burg, toward Magdeburg, including a detour to the seat of the Abodrite prince Nakon, "Grandcastle" (the ring wall at Mecklenburg village), and possibly Schwerin. Ibrāhīm's route from Magdeburg, where he was received by King Otto I, to Prague can be traced southward, touching Calbe and "Newcastle" (Nienburg), where "the river Bode flows into the Saale," and "the Jews' salt pans" along the river Saale to the town of Wurzen-on-Mulde. Farther toward Prague, a textual lacuna does not permit identification of the crucial bridgehead at Brüx/Most in northern Bohemia. From Prague, it would seem, Ibrāhīm first headed northwest toward Fulda and Mainz and then south, via Garda, Verona, and Pavia, to Rome, where he arrived no later than around February 1, 962, and was within a week received again by Otto. Anonymously transmitted accounts of the Westphalian towns of Soest and Paderborn would fit into his itinerary from Utrecht to Schleswig on condition that the precedence of Soest did indicate a west-east direction of travel. Nothing is known about his return route to al-Andalus from Rome.

The dates of Ibrāhīm's trip as here presented derive solely from his record of meeting Otto, "king of the Rhomeans," in Rome between February 20, 961, and February 8, 962, which necessitates a date subsequent to Otto's coronation as emperor on February 2, 962 (with reference to Otto's "German" realm, Ibrāhīm never used "Rhomean," that is, Byzantine).

Ever since the modern rediscovery of Ibrāhīm's work in the 1870s, his fame has rested on his educated comments about the still predominantly illiterate societies of central and east-central Europe, conventionally identified by Ibrāhīm as *Ñaqāliba*, that is, fair-haired, ruddy-complexioned northerners (not exclusively "Slavs"). He reports them as divided among four "kings," the—unnamed—"king of the Bulgars" (Tsar Peter, r. 927–969), "Boleslav, king of Prague, Bohemia and Cracow" (Boleslav I, r. 935–967), "Mieszko, king of the North" (r. c. 960–992), and "Nakon in the furthest West" (active 955–c. 966). Ibrāhīm's admittedly secondhand account of the Bulgars' Danubian Christian kingdom takes note of their relatively high level of civilization. His information about Mieszko, his standing elite troops, and the wealth of his dominion in "the north" also reproduces—unacknowledged—hearsay; among Mieszko's neighbors he mentions Rus' (that is, the Vikings of Russia), the Prussians, and possibly the Lutici (northwest of the Oder/Odra), as well as the maritime emporium of Wolin, on the island of that name in the lagoon of Szczecin. Retelling an ancient "migrant" tale, Ibrāhīm locates the "city of women" in the vicinity of Rus', underlining its fictitiousness *e contrario* by an appeal to "King Otto" as witness.

In contrast, Ibrāhīm's observations on Nakon's and Boleslav's territories are based on personal observation; in Mecklenburg he notes a peculiar use of packed clay in log crates for raising fortification walls, and notes wooden causeways and bridges across fens and waterways. His report on Boleslav I's domain—Bohemia, Lesser Poland, and Cracow, bordering "lengthwise" on the Hungarians—is even more detailed; Prague, neither village nor town, was a most lively emporium, where traders from Islamic lands, Hungarians, and Jews offered their wares, including slaves, tin, furs, and "marketable specie." In praising Bohemia, Ibrāhīm notes the use of standardized diaphanous handkerchiefs as currency and the inhabitants' "non-Slavic" dark complexion and hair color.

Of Ibrāhīm's observations in "Germany," special mention is due his reports on the salt works at Soest, on the Fulda abbey church (whose founder, Abbot Baugulf, c. 779–802, he confuses with Saint Boniface), and on the market at Mayence (Mainz), where he notes Indian spices (pepper, ginger, cloves, nard, and galangal) and silver "drachms" issued by the Samanid amir Nasr (II) ibn Ahmad (r. 914–943 C.E.) in Samarkand in 914 and 915.

BIBLIOGRAPHY

Charvát, Petr, and Jan Prosecký, eds. *Ibrahim ibn Ya'qub at-Turtushi: Christianity, Islam, and Judaism Meet in East-Central Europe, c. 800–1300 A.D.* Prague: Academy of Sciences of the Czech Republic, Oriental Institute, 1996.

Miquel, André. "Ibrāhīm ibn Ya'qūb." In *Encyclopaedia of Islam*, edited by H. A. R. Gibb et al. 2nd ed. Leiden, Netherlands: Brill, 1969. Vol. 3, p. 991.

LUTZ RICHTER-BERNBURG

Imagery of Exploration. As Joyce Lorimer points out in the article on "Exploration Texts" in this *Companion*, the interpretation of these written documents needs to be informed by a constant sense of why they were written and for what audience they were intended. Even more vigilance is necessary in considering images of exploration, for in this case we need also to consider what technical means were available to the artists, from woodcuts all the way to photography. Moreover, we need to bear in mind the nature of the images with which the artists' minds were already stocked, whether these images came from late medieval Europe or from classical European antiquity. We consider here European artists.

Almost from the start of European expansion, the need for images to accompany texts was felt. Thus when the author of the *Gart der Gesundheit*, a German herbal, went to the Holy Land in 1485, he took with him "a painter of understanding and with a subtle and practiced hand" to paint and draw the herbs "in their true colors and form." A decade or two later, when the French navigator Parmentier went to the newly found Brazil, he too was accompanied by a *peintre* (painter), whose task it was to delineate the new land for French readers. When Sir Humfrey Gilbert was planning an expedition in 1583, he intended to take with him the artist Thomas Bavin, who would "draw to life one of each kind of thinge that is strange to us in England."

Already by the early decades of the sixteenth century, this no longer presented great technical difficulties. We have only to think of the work of Albrecht Dürer (in whose work were several extra-European creatures) or Christoph Weiditz to realize that trained European artists could produce watercolors and even engravings of startling accuracy at this time. Sometimes these images formed part of maps, as with the drawings by the Flemish illuminator Antonio de Hollanda found in the Miller Atlas at the Bibliothèque Nationale de France. Sometimes, though, the images were separate, as in the case of the images made in the 1560s and 1580s of what is now the southeastern United States by Jacques Le Moyne de Morgues and John White. In these two cases, de Morgues and White were trained and consummate artists, and their images convince us that they could accurately portray what they saw; moreover, these images clearly strive after the same reality, severely restricting the idea of the graphic "invention" of America.

Sometimes expeditions were accompanied by artists whose skills were much less advanced, as in the case of Samuel de Champlain in the West Indies about 1600 and of the painter who accompanied Francis Drake on his voyage through the West Indies in 1585. The artists on these two expeditions—Champlain himself and Drake's artist—each left a hundred or so images, which have recently been reproduced, so that we can compare their versions of the essentially similar scenes that they witnessed; of course, they were entirely unknown to each other. One example of these scenes concerns the smelting of silver. The Drake artist shows a rather well-drawn image with a prominent bellows and a large furnace, with an Amerindian house and hammock in the background. The image in the set thought to have been drawn by Champlain is more summary, but he too was impressed by the huge bellows and by the size of the furnace. The way of drawing off the ingots is slightly different, but anyone examining these two different images can hardly be in any doubt that the artists were essentially trying to portray the same process that both had witnessed. Pace some postmodern historians, both were groping toward a representation of the same reality.

The images in the manuscripts by Drake's artist and by Champlain remained unknown for many years after they were drawn, but the work of skilled painters like Le Moyne de Morgues and John White was often incorporated into the extensive set of engravings published by Theodor de Bry from 1590 onward, in his *Collectiones peregrinationum*. To compare the delicate watercolors with de Bry's much cruder copper engravings is to understand something of the inevitable changes that occur as one medium is transformed into another. In the case of de Bry, many commentators have also remarked that in his collection and transposition of a variety of drawings, he always took advantage of any opportunity to show the cruelty of the Spaniards, thus contributing powerfully to the Black Legend.

Artists accompanying expeditions had almost from the start been able to produce convincing images of plants, and many of the social scenes shown by de Bry portray human beings with a good degree of accuracy. For many years, though, zoological illustrations lagged behind these other kinds of imagery, perhaps because the technique of copper engraving was insufficiently advanced to do justice to the subtlety of fur and feather. Thus Mark Catesby was aware that his images of birds were more accurate than aesthetically compelling, and some other illustrators produced work that seems remarkably crude.

This began to change with the *Metamorphoses* of Maria Sibylla Merian, whose heredity and natural genius allowed her to produce images that were both startlingly beautiful and remarkably accurate. During the eighteenth century, most of the great European voyages of discovery were accompanied by artists, who often drew not only natural features, but also scenes from the life of the remote peoples whom they encountered. These images began to be reproduced by a wide variety of techniques, including engraving on wood and steel with hitherto unknown detail. By the beginning of the nineteenth century, such imagery had reached new standards of accuracy and elegance, typified by the extraordinary zoological images provided by John James Audubon; lithography also proved to be a remarkably sensitive means of showing landscapes.

Still, even in the days of photography, we need to keep remembering the importance of the eye of the artist. Consider the Antarctic images of Frank Hurley, and also the images of Machu Picchu generated by Hiram Bingham. As with written texts, images of all kinds need to be interpreted with care and prudence.

[*See also* Arctic, *subentry on* Nineteenth-Century Images; Black Legend; Exploration Texts; Pacific, *subentry on* Visual Images; *and biographical entries on figures mentioned in this article.*]

BIBLIOGRAPHY

Bry, Theodor de, et al., eds. *Collectiones peregrinationum*. 13 parts. Frankfurt, 1590–1634.

Dickenson, Victoria. *Drawn from Life: Science and Art in the Portrayal of the New World*. Toronto: University of Toronto Press, 1998.

Klinkenborg, Verlyn. "Introduction." In *Histoire naturelle des Indes: The Drake Manuscript in the Pierpont Morgan Library*. London and New York: Norton, 1996.

Hulton, Paul, ed. *America, 1585: The Complete Drawings of John White*. Chapel Hill: University of North Carolina Press; London: British Museum, 1984.

Hulton, Paul, ed. *The Work of Jacques Le Moyne de Morgues*. 2 vols. London: British Museum, 1977.

Litalien, Raymonde, and Denis Vaugeois, eds. *Champlain: The Birth of French America*. Translated by Käthe Roth. Montreal: McGill–Queen's University Press, 2004.

Wallis, Helen, ed. *The Maps and Text of the "Boke of Idrography" Presented by Jean Rotz to Henry VIII*. Oxford: Oxford University Press, 1981.

DAVID BUISSERET

Imperialism and Exploration.

When European overseas dominions were at their greatest extent in the early twentieth century, the explorers of previous ages were cast as pioneers in the great cause of empire. The Hakluyt Society president reflected on "the enterprise of our explorers and commercial agents" in the reign of Queen Elizabeth I, who "had well and truly laid" the foundations of the British Empire even if she "did not possess a square mile of territory" overseas. At the time of the British Empire Exhibition of 1924, Hugh Gunn referred to John Hanning Speke's discovery of the source of the Nile as "one of those milestones in history which mark a new epoch"—this being the advent of British influence and later rule in Uganda. More generally, explorers were seen as disinterested scientists in the van of progress represented by European rule.

By the middle of the twentieth century, European empires were being dismantled and triumphalist imperial history went out of fashion. The histories of non-European subjects of empire were now investigated, and explorers seemed irrelevant or even an embarrassment. In parallel with these developments came much more skeptical or hostile accounts of imperialism. Much attention was focused on Africa. The very influential work of Ronald Robinson and John Gallagher might point to crises on the periphery as influencing the "official mind," but even heroic explorers like David Livingstone, they said, had no more than a fitful impact on either governments or

people. Other approaches to imperialism, many of them Marxist or Marxist-inspired, similarly failed to find any place for explorers in their theoretical frameworks. Yet interest in exploration itself continued at an academic and popular level. Reacting to this interest, Robert Rotberg became one of the few historians to confront the issue of the role of African explorers in relation to imperialism. Exploration, he said, was the "handmaiden of imperialism" because it encouraged "the twaining of Africa's destiny with the west." He cautiously added that this did not imply that exploration caused imperialism; the imposition of colonial rule could have come for other reasons. Hence explorers were "intellectual middlemen, precursors not progenitors of imperialism."

By the end of the twentieth century, attitudes had changed again. Writers affected by postcolonialism condemned imperialism in all its forms, which included exploration. Explorers' published narratives conveniently provided plenty of material for postmodernist analysis, revealing examples of acquisitiveness, intolerance, Eurocentrism, and racism. Edward Said's identification of "orientalism" in European works on the Middle East was extended by others to cover the whole of the non-Western world in its encounters with travelers and explorers. Even simply mapping and describing an area and its people—very much the explorer's function—is seen as taking some sort of control. Indeed, Robert Stafford asserts that even peaceful exploration was "profoundly exploitative, for it took hostages in the form of data used to inform decisions about territories made without the knowledge or consent of their inhabitants." In a striking aphorism, he adds that the sovereignty of non-Europeans could be "eroded as surely by map co-ordinates as by steamships, bullets and treaties of cession." Moreover, the field sciences professed by many explorers were precisely those needed by colonialism while their narratives taught the reading public in metropolitan centers that the rest of the world was available for "objectification, appropriation and use."

Imperialism in Theory and Practice.

Three immediate points are worth making. First, there are clearly dangers of anachronism. Both the older imperial historians and the more recent postmodernists may put explorers into contexts that suit their arguments but that bear scant relation to the actual conditions and casts of mind prevalent in the explorer's own times. The second point is that the varying approaches outlined above are not necessarily irreconcilable: there can be different levels of explanation. One may, for example, concentrate on the work of an explorer, not on the periphery but in relation to metropolitan developments. Here the concept of "social imperialism" is important. The manipulation of overseas affairs for domestic political and social objectives probably, for example, explains Otto von Bismarck's fitful encouragement of German explorers and traders. The third point is simply that much depends on what is meant by "imperialism." The older imperial historians thought in terms of a "mother country" having some sort of formal political sovereignty over a collection of dependent territories. Postmodernist approaches embrace a much wider spectrum extending to a mere assertion of cultural superiority by an explorer. The question then arises whether exploration is a necessary part of imperialism, however defined. The answer must normally be "yes," since there must be some awareness of the territory to be brought under imperial sway. Yet in the case of China, the gap between early encounters and attempts in 1890s to take it into a series of European and Japanese economic dependencies is a matter of several centuries. At the other extreme, Rwanda and Burundi were annexed by Germany before any explorer had been able to visit them.

One variety of empire building often called "subimperialism" involves using local allies, and here the knowledge and experience of explorers can be crucial. Britain's long association with the desert Arabs was one of the keys to its strong position in the Middle East and very much the result of impressions created by Arabian travelers like Richard Burton, William Palgrave, Charles Doughty, Wilfred Blunt, and Gertrude Bell. It was chiefly the "official mind" that was affected.

However much influence an explorer might have officially or more widely in creating a climate of opinion favorable to expansion, and however directly he was involved in actual imperial activities, the course of events could often confound plans and expectations. Perhaps the most ambitious modern expedition that was at once exploratory and imperialist was Henry Stanley's Emin Pasha Relief Expedition of 1886 to 1889. Yet neither of its imperialist sponsors, Leopold II or William Mackinnon, gained what he wanted. Events both in Africa and in the diplomatic sphere had altered the situation.

Exploration and European Imperial Expansion from c. 1600. Despite all the difficulties involved, it would be wrong to abandon the attempt to trace connections between exploration and imperialism. Some generalizations about particular periods may

be made. In the age of mercantilist theory, explorers sought opportunities to help their compatriots secure a favorable balance of trade that would manifest itself in the form of bullion. Hence the Spanish in the Americas, where exploration and conquest were rolled into one. The promotion of Christianity was also important, not least to the Portuguese explorers seeking Prester John as an ally in the struggle against the Muslims in Asia and Africa. Maritime exploration also led to the development of the spice trade from the East and the emergence of the sugar and slave nexus of the Caribbean, West Africa, and the Atlantic.

There was something of a lull in European overseas exploration for much of the seventeenth century, but activity revived in the eighteenth when, despite the mercantilist legacy, a new situation developed. One key feature was that exploration now became a recognized activity, underpinned by science and often promoted and organized by the state. Whereas the Portuguese in particular had sought to keep their discoveries secret, results were now made widely available in published narratives and maps. As with other features of the Enlightenment, the French showed the way. Louis-Antoine de Bougainville's voyage of discovery in the Pacific, for example, integrated science with maritime activity while cartographic advances in Paris both encouraged exploration and benefited from it. With the voyages of James Cook, the British began to emulate the French. Joseph Banks, the botanist with Cook, powerfully promoted exploration and was the dominant figure in British science for almost fifty years before he died in 1820. Determined state activity harnessed to science helped to promote technological changes. With the problem of longitude solved, even their simple ability to know fairly precisely where they were gave Europeans a great advantage. They soon had the power, if they wished it, to control or dominate any other peoples in the world. Dominance needed not only mean settlement and full political control. British explorers in the era of Cook were enjoined to bear in mind, as well as their science, "the advancement of trade and navigation," which by no means necessarily involved major territorial acquisitions. Cook's disproval of the existence of the "Great Southern Continent" and any obvious debouchment of a Northwest Passage into the Pacific arguably discouraged extension of empire. Even so, his work did give Britain strategic advantages and led fairly directly to the founding of the colony of New South Wales and ultimately New Zealand, while whalers, traders, and missionaries soon followed him to the Pacific.

A not-too-dissimilar mixture of science plus possible commercial advantage inspired Banks to form the African Association in 1788. The aim was to do for land exploration in West Africa what Cook and other sailors had done for maritime discovery in the Pacific. The French reacted similarly and various forms of quasi-imperial activity followed in the ensuing hundred years. Science and the fur trade inspired the exploration of the interior of North America and the takeover of what had been Native American territories. Alexander von Humboldt, the scientist par excellence, explored South America, although the somewhat paradoxical "imperial" effect of his writings was to legitimate Creole rather than metropolitan Spanish dominance of the continent and its original peoples.

A new period from about 1815 to 1880 saw the triumph of European and American capitalism and the rise of middle classes often intensely interested in overseas affairs. Britain abandoned the last vestiges of mercantilist legislation and became altogether free-trading. The resulting constant need to open up new frontiers of trade meant that explorers were regarded as very important. France followed a not dissimilar pattern. Hence, the Royal Geographical Society in London and the Geographical Society of Paris became prosperous and influential. The bourgeoisie in Britain—the "gentlemanly capitalists" in particular—and their counterparts elsewhere coupled their belief in economic progress with moral imperatives like ending the slave trade, promoting Christianity, and generally using science to improve the condition of mankind. All this produced plenty of global "imperial" activity of one kind and another in which explorers were frequently concerned. European governments gave some support but were usually reluctant to take on new territory for formal rule.

The reluctance of European governments to become directly involved in imperial projects, especially in Africa, explains the extraordinary success of Leopold II. He was very directly inspired by explorers, and his imperialist project was to be carried into action with the aid of one of the most effective—if ruthless—of all African explorers, Stanley. The activities of Leopold were at least the catalyst for the imperialist scramble for Africa of the 1880s and 1890s, even if the real reasons had more to do with international relations than with Africa itself. Whatever the reasons, explorers were in great demand as experts on the areas being acquired and were some-

times employed to lead actual annexationist expeditions. Serpa Pinto tried to justify Portugal's claims and Germany produced explorers to challenge the former ascendancy of Britain and France. A similar complex mixture of sometimes squalid activities by "men on the spot" and high diplomacy was also apparent in Southeast Asia but the biggest prize in the Orient, China, was beyond the capacity of any European power to take over completely. Nevertheless, in the 1890s China became what Mao Zedong later described as a "semi-colony." The role of explorers and travelers in this region seems to have been to demonstrate, conveniently, that Chinese civilization had become stagnant and moribund; therefore European intervention was necessary.

In the twentieth century, what might be regarded as "pure" exploration was resumed in the polar regions. Even so, nationalist fervor was aroused in the race to reach the poles, and in Antarctica, various governments were inspired by the results of exploration to claim segments of territory.

In conclusion, it is apparent from the few examples quoted that the ways in which exploration has been linked to imperialism have been many and various. Exploration has been integrally involved for the last five hundred years or so in the process that has meant the extension of European influence or hegemony over most other parts of the world. Indeed, it is the explorer who has most often initiated the contact between different cultures and thereby acted as some sort of catalyst in an imperial process.

[*See also* African Association; Geographical Society of Paris; Royal Geographical Society; *and biographical entries on figures mentioned in this article.*]

BIBLIOGRAPHY

Bridges, Roy. "Exploration and Travel outside Europe (1720–1914)." In *The Cambridge Companion to Travel Writing*, edited by Peter Hulme and Tim Youngs, 53–69. Cambridge, U.K., and New York: Cambridge University Press, 2002.

Marshall, P. J., and Glyndwr Williams. *The Great Map of Mankind: British Perceptions of the World in the Age of the Enlightenment*. London: Dent, 1982.

Rotberg, Robert I. "Introduction." In *Africa and Its Explorers: Motives, Methods, and Impact*, edited by Robert I. Rotberg, 1–11. Cambridge, Mass.: Harvard University Press, 1970.

Robinson, Ronald and John Gallagher with Alice Denny. *Africa and the Victorians: The Official Mind of Imperialism*, London: Macmillan, and New York: St. Martins Press, 1961; 2nd ed., 1983.

Stafford, Robert A. "Scientific Exploration and Empire." In *The Oxford History of the British Empire*. Vol. 3, The Nineteenth Century, edited by Andrew Porter, 294–319. Oxford: Oxford University Press, 1999.

Roy Bridges

Inca Empire. The Inca Empire was the last in a series of dominant cultures to arise in the Andean highlands and on the Peruvian coast before the Spanish invasion of 1532 to 1533. The Incas' historical and mythical origins began with the activities of a small group of Quechua-speaking cultivators and herders around the valley of Cuzco in the Peruvian sierra, probably in the twelfth century.

In less than three hundred years the Incas first conquered and then organized the largest of the Native American empires, Tawantinsuyu, or the Land of the Four Quarters, which stretched from modern Ecuador to the central valley of Chile, and eastward to the foothills of the Amazon Basin.

Spurred on by a creation myth and other factors, great emperors such as Pachacuti and especially Topa Inca believed themselves to be deified children of the sun. Thus they were destined to conquer the world in the sun's name, bringing stability, organization, and a true religion to barbaric peoples of many languages and cultures. Other religious beliefs included the mummification and worship of the dead and sacrifices to the sun and other deities.

The basis of Inca imperialism, then, was aggression against weaker neighbors; well-disciplined armies, relatively mobile for the time thanks to a network of roads for humans and llamas; and superbly built strategic fortresses, of which the best known are Sacsahuaman, overlooking the imperial capital of Cuzco, and Ollantaytambo. Inca ruthlessness against potential enemies or rebels included such tactics as mass executions and the uprooting and relocation of large groups, collectively known as *mitimaes*, often over distances of hundreds of miles.

The unwritten understanding behind the Inca system, probably more of an ideal than a type of everyday behavior, was absolute obedience to the emperor, the nobility, and the priesthood. Such obedience included conscription for labor and warfare and heavy tribute exactions for the emperor and for state and local religions. In return, the state claimed to guarantee a reasonably secure peasant existence as far as foodstuffs, clothing, housing, and human reproduction were concerned. A basic feature of this guarantee was the stockpiling of essential goods against hard times.

Faced with severe ecological difficulties such as mountainous terrain, very high arid plateaus, and coastal deserts, the Inca and their predecessors undertook remarkable feats of environmental engineering and adaptation, much of the work carried out by forced labor. Irrigation was well developed, and the intricate terracing of mountainsides is a notable fea-

ture of highland Peru to this day. By adapting to variations in climate and altitude, the Incas set up a vast system of complementary ecological niches, producing cold-climate tubers and grains, maize lower down, and tropical fruits below, often quite close to one another. It is uncertain if these products were moved by real trade or by state-mandated exchanges.

The legitimacy established by the Inca empire proved resilient during the Spanish colonial centuries, and provoked nostalgic revivals and the largest colonial uprising before the Wars of Independence. Tupac Amaru, who claimed descent from Inca royalty, led a rebellion in the 1780s that the Spanish crown suppressed with great difficulty.

[*See also* Central and South America, *subentry on* Conquests and Colonization.]

BIBLIOGRAPHY

Moseley, Michael E. *The Incas and Their Ancestors: The Archaeology of Peru*. London: Thames and Hudson, 1992.

Murra, John V. *Economic Organization of the Inca State*. Greenwich, Conn.: JAI Press, 1980.

MURDO J. MACLEOD

India. *See* **Bombay Geographical Society; Curzon, George Nathaniel; David-Neel, Alexandra; Everest, George; Exotic, Monstrous, and Wild Peoples and Animals; Expeditions, World Exploration,** *subentry on* **England; Gama, Vasco da; Indian Ocean; Pundit Mapmakers;** *and* **Spices.**

Indian Ocean. An early representation of the Indian Ocean as transmitted by Byzantine manuscript sources shows the expanse of water enclosed by Asia and Africa as known at the time, linked to the southward to a "land unknown according to Ptolemy." The inscription implies that the map may have been drawn according to instructions laid down by the astronomer Claudius Ptolemy (87–150 C.E.) of Alexandria in his *Geographia*, a collection of manuscripts and two series of maps. These documents reached Italy in the fifteenth century and appeared in print from 1477 onward. A medieval version of a Roman zonal map, depicting in the Southern Hemisphere a temperate zone as large as the Northern Hemisphere, was also available in print. Joined to the longitudinal exaggeration of the Europe-Asia landmass appearing in Ptolemy's depiction, these concepts influenced the decisions of the navigators engaged in the discovery of the world.

Early Navigation. Navigation from the western side of the Indian Ocean developed when the Greek mariner Hippalos mastered the mechanism of the monsoons in the first century B.C.E. When the Roman merchants reached Canton in 226 C.E., the circuit that had evolved from east to west from ancient times was completed. Marco Polo's *Book* (1298) gave to the western world a more precise description of the Asiatic shores.

The configuration of the east African coast grew more accurate as the Arabs moved southward from the tenth century, eventually reaching Sofala, the Comoros, Madagascar, and perhaps the Mascarenes. By the time the Portuguese had begun their advance on the west African coast, Admiral Zheng He directed his series of seven expeditions (1405–1433) from the China coast, across the Indonesian archipelago (reaching perhaps the north coast of Australia from Timor) to Mogadishu and Malindi on the east coast of Africa, including a visit to the Laccadives and Maldives. His interpreter, Ma Huan, recorded the voyages in *The Overall Survey of the Ocean's Shores* (1433). As the title implies, the voyages were peripheral, the only transoceanic attempts known being those of the Austronesians from southeast Borneo, who reached Madagascar in the middle of the first millennium C.E., a feat unexplained until the arrival, after the Krakatau eruption of 1883, of pumice rafts on the shores of East Africa and Madagascar—they were propelled there by the south equatorial current.

The Portuguese advance in a southerly direction west of Africa may have been stimulated by new notions about an open sea at the tip of the continent, a view endorsed by the cartographer Fra Mauro, working in Venice, who sent his world map in 1459 to King Afonso V of Portugal. Bartholomew Dias proved this in 1488 when he rounded the Cape of Good Hope and sailed along the southern coast, a route that was to be followed by Vasco da Gama, who rounded the eastern end, naming Natal on Christmas 1497. Sailing to Malindi, da Gama reached Calicut in May 1498 by a well-traveled route. These achievements are illustrated in a sea chart by an unknown Portuguese, purchased by Alberto Cantino, agent of the duke of Ferrara, in November 1502.

Systematic Exploration. Hendrik Brouwer in 1611 pioneered a route in the south Indian Ocean along which ships coming from the Cape of Good Hope would sail east propelled by the westerlies, and then north when they had reached the longitude of the Sunda Strait; this route shortened the duration of the voyage by half. Those who miscalculated the longitude found themselves on the coast of an unknown land, later named New Holland. Dirk Hartog thus reached Shark Bay in 1616, and the *Gulden Zeepard* sailed along the southern coast (Nuyts Land) in 1627. These landfalls led to the planning of systematic exploration, culminating in the voyages of Abel Tasman, as the Dutch consolidated their position in Batavia, occupied Mauritius Island in 1638, and established an outpost at the Cape of Good Hope in 1652. Starting from Java in August 1642, Tasman, after a stopover in Mauritius, sailed south in search of the Austral Lands, which he did not find, but instead reached Van Diemen's Land (Tasmania) and Staten Land (New Zealand), proving that the eastern coast of the Indian Ocean also led to open sea. Joan Blaeu's engraved world map of 1648 still showed the eastern end of the ocean closed, leaving the secret of Tasman's discoveries locked in his sea charts, partially reproduced in the "Eugene" and "Bonaparte" charts.

The reconnaissance of the central Indian Ocean was undertaken when Mahé de Labourdonnais attempted to develop Port-Louis of Île de France as a metropolis of commerce and a naval base. The search for a route shorter than the one pioneered by Brouwer led to the survey of the archipelagoes and shoals lying northeast of Madagascar. While exploring the Cargados Carajos group north of Mauritius, Lazare Picault came across Mahé Island in the Seychelles in 1742 and explored Peros Banhos, the northerly group of the Chagos Archipelago, in 1743.

The hydrographer Jean-Baptiste d'Après de Mannevillette, who had published in 1745 a collection of charts for the navigation of the northern half of the ocean, *Le Neptune Oriental*, began to collect data on the central and southern parts after he had taken the astronomer Nicolas-Louis, Abbé de La Caille, to the Cape of Good Hope in 1751 for the study of the austral constellations as an aid to navigation. The longitudes of the Cape of Good Hope, Mauritius, and Madagascar were determined by the new methods of lunar distances and observation of the eclipses of the satellites of Jupiter. In 1753, d'Après attempted the passage to India through the archipelagoes northeast of Madagascar. The astronomer Alexandre-Gui Pingré came to Rodrigues Island to observe the transit of Venus in June 1761, thereby determining the geographical position of the island.

Charles de Brosses published his *Histoire des navigations aux terres Australes* in 1756 to revive interest in exploration; it shaped the ideas of Cook and triggered the circumnavigation of Louis-Antoine de Bougainville. On the navigator's passage through the Indian Ocean, he left on the spot his naturalist Philibert Commerson and his pilot Pierre-Antoine Véron; the discussions Bougainville had with Intendant Pierre Poivre during the call in Port-Louis in November 1768 stimulated regional enterprise.

Exploring Alternative Routes. The exploration of the so-called short route was resumed in 1769 by Jacques-Raymond Grenier, accompanied by La Fontaine and the astronomer Alexis-Marie Rochon, who was equipped with a Berthoud chronometer. Yves-Joseph de Kerguelen, who verified this route in 1771, accomplished the journey to India and back in three months. La Fontaine had instructions to survey the island of Diego Garcia (in the Chagos Archipelago) as a first step to settlement. It was, however, a British colonizing expedition from Bombay that made an unsuccessful attempt in 1786 to establish a military base at Diego Garcia; the attempt provoked the survey of the archipelago by Lieutenant Archibald Blair, the results being published in 1788 by the hydrographer of the East India Company, Alexander Dalrymple, who had been in friendly correspondence with d'Après. The collaboration of Dalrymple and d'Après, along with the information supplied by the discoverers, helped to shape a picture of the Indian Ocean that was presented in the second edition of d'Après's *Neptune Oriental* (1775) and the posthumous *Supplément* (1781) to it. The work, which had several editions in English, remained the standard reference until the appearance of James Horsburgh's *Directions for Sailing to and from the East Indies* (1809–1811). The investigation of the dangers on the short route was completed with the work of the Creole hydrographer Lislet Geoffroy, undertaken for the first English governor of Mauritius, Robert Farquhar, and published in London in 1818 as *A Chart of the Archipelago of Islands North East of the Island of Madagascar, Corrected According to the Latest Observations*.

From 1771 to 1774, Marc-Joseph Marion Dufresne, Julien-Marie Crozet, and Kerguelen attempted the reconnaissance of the southern lands, encountering—instead of the bounteous regions—desolate islands scattered in an inhospitable ocean. In two great campaigns from the Atlantic (1772–1773) in search of Bouvet's discovery, Cook traversed the Indian Ocean to the Pacific, approaching the Antarctic Circle; then in 1776, tracking the recent discoveries of the French, he named the Prince Edward Islands, skirted the Crozet Islands, and surveyed Kerguelen Island, proudly recording in his journal (December

1776): "the first discoveries with some reason imagined it to be a Cape of a southern continent, the English have since proved that no such continent exists."

These sallies southward led the French to the coasts of New Holland. Coming from Kerguelen, Louis-François d'Alleno de Saint-Allouarn sighted the southwest coast, then sailed on the track of Willem de Vlamingh, Dirk Hartog, and William Dampier to the northern coast, blazing the trail for Nicolas Baudin's surveys. Charles-Pierre Claret de Fleurieu, geographer and minister of the marine who masterminded the explorations of Jean-François de Galaup de La Pérouse, Joseph-Antoine Raymond Bruni d'Entrecasteaux, and Baudin, set in motion a process—accelerated by the enterprise of the English—that unveiled the last strips of the unknown shores.

George Vancouver explored the King George Sound region of the southwestern coast of Australia in 1791, the geography of the south coast of Australia being extended by the surveys of d'Entrecasteaux assisted by a hydrographer of genius, Charles de Beautemps-Beaupré. George Bass in 1798 sailed the strait now named after him, accomplishing the circumnavigation of Tasmania in the company of Matthew Flinders, whose ensuing survey revealed the existence of the major gulfs of south Australia, Spencer and Saint Vincent. Coming from the southeast, Baudin meticulously surveyed the unknown coast from Victoria to Encounter Bay, where he met Flinders. The exemplary hydrography of Flinders was matched by the achievements of Baudin's cartographers, Charles-Pierre Boullanger, Pierre Faure, and Louis-Henri de Freycinet.

[*See also* Australia, Exploration of; Cape of Good Hope; Longitude; *and biographical entries on figures mentioned in this article.*]

BIBLIOGRAPHY

Bagrow, Leo. *History of Cartography*. Revised and enlarged by R. A. Skelton. London: Watts, 1964. 2nd ed., Chicago: Precedent, 1985.

Beaglehole, J. C., ed. *The Journals of Captain James Cook on His Voyages of Discovery*. Cambridge, U.K.: Cambridge University Press for the Hakluyt Society, 1955–1974.

Filliozat, Manonmani. *Le Neptune Oriental: Une somme de la cartographie de la Compagnie des Indes Orientales*. In *Cahiers de la Compagnie des Indes*. No. 3, *La mer et la navigation*, pp. 21–30. Citadelle de Port-Louis, Mauritius: Publication du Musée de la Compagnie des Indes, 1998.

Ly-Tio-Fane Pineo, Huguette. *Île de France: 1715–1746, 1747–1767*. Vol. 1, L'émergence de Port-Louis, 1715–1746; Vol. 2, Port-Louis, Base Navale, 1747–1767. Moka, Mauritius: Mahatma Gandhi Institute, 1993–1999.

Ma Huan. *Ying-yai sheng-lan* (The Overall Survey of the Ocean's Shores; 1433). Translated from the Chinese text edited by Feng Ch'eng-Chün, with introduction, notes, and appendices by J. V. G. Mills. Cambridge, U.K.: Cambridge University Press for the Hakluyt Society, 1970.

Perry, T. M. *The Discovery of Australia: The Charts and Maps of the Navigators and Explorers.* Melbourne, Australia: Thomas Nelson, 1982.

Simkin, Tom, and Richard S. Fiske. *Krakatau 1883: The Volcanic Eruption and Its Effects.* With the collaboration of Sarah Melcher and Elizabeth Nielsen. Washington, D.C.: Smithsonian Institution Press, 1983.

Toussaint, Auguste. *Histoire de l'Océan Indien.* Paris: Presses Universitaires de France, 1961.

Toussaint, Auguste. *L'Océan Indien au XVIIIe siècle.* Paris: Flammarion, 1974.

HUGUETTE LY-TIO-FANE PINEO
MADELEINE LY-TIO-FANE

International Geophysical Year.

By the early 1950s it became apparent that scientific progress in understanding earth's climates, oceans, and atmosphere was restricted by lack of data. Accordingly, the International Council of Scientific Unions (ICSU) organized in 1952 a special committee for an International Geophysical Year (IGY). A first conference was held in Paris in July 1955. An eighteen-month period (July 1, 1957 to December 31, 1958) was selected to be the International Geophysical Year to take advantage of a peak in sunspot activity and the occurrence of several eclipses. Studies in space and in the little-known polar regions took advantage of many technological advances, such as in rocketry for space travel. Detailed national plans were to be concerned with "specific planetary problems of the earth," as defined at a 1954 conference in Rome.

Earlier Polar Years (1882–1883, 1932–1933) were of limited scale. The IGY, however, was a scientific venture of awesome magnitude and peaceful cooperation at a difficult time, during the Cold War. Hugh Odishaw, the executive director of the U.S. national committee for the IGY, called the IGY "the single most significant peaceful activity of mankind since the Renaissance and the Copernican Revolution." Some sixty thousand scientists from sixty-six nations participated. The earth was investigated from pole to pole and, for the first time, from space. The Soviet launch of *Sputnik 1*—which was dramatically timed for the IGY conference on September 30, 1957, on rockets and satellites—and the American launch of the *Explorer I* orbiter on January 31, 1958, heralded today's space age.

IGY observations were made of all major geophysical phenomena, particularly in regions of difficult access, to improve basic knowledge of earth and the solar system. One of the key IGY achievements was establishment of world data centers to archive the massive amounts of IGY data. These centers are still in use for researchers in many fields, such as climate change. Forty-eight volumes of *Annals of the International Geophysical Year* (1957–1967) contain data and first results of the program.

The Rome conference particularly emphasized Antarctica, which was primarily known only from the first explorations in the 1800s by sealers and whalers and from spotty coastal charting for nationalistic purposes, as well as from a few of the so-called heroic age treks of the early 1900s into the interior. The number of Antarctic stations rose from twenty to forty-eight for the IGY, and personnel rose from 179 to 912. With six, eight, eight, and fourteen, respectively, the Soviet Union, the United States, Argentina, and Britain had most of the stations.

By the time of the IGY, most of interior Antarctica had never been seen, even aerially. Some thought that Antarctica was actually two continents tied by ice sheets. Antarctica was first crossed by the Commonwealth Trans-Antarctic Expedition led by V. E. Fuchs; the expedition took ninety-nine days to cross the continent by vehicle. Seismic and gravity surveys during this and numerous other crossings by the Soviet Union and the United States determined the size and extent of continental ice sheets and showed that only a single continent exists under the polar ice. The continent was surveyed by aerial photogrammetrical and ground measurements. Studies from many stations led to better understanding of the Antarctic aurorae. Advances were made on many other fronts, too. Studies of the upper atmosphere and ionosphere led to better understanding of radio-wave transmissions and whistlers and provided data that led to knowledge of the ozone hole over Antarctica in springtime.

There was no overall international political body to manage Antarctica at the time of the IGY, before which various countries had argued over their territorial claims. The single most significant outcome of IGY might be the creation of an international treaty for the management of an entire continent for only peaceful, scientific purposes. The twelve Antarctic IGY nations signed the Antarctic Treaty on December 1, 1959; the treaty came into effect on June 23, 1961, and many nations have accepted it.

[*See also* Antarctica; Space Program; *and* Sputnik.]

BIBLIOGRAPHY

Sullivan, Walter. *Assault on the Unknown: The International Geophysical Year.* New York: McGraw-Hill, 1961.

Walton, D. W. H., ed. *Antarctic Science.* Cambridge, U.K., and New York: Cambridge University Press, 1987.

ARTHUR B. FORD

International Space Station. Exploration of outer space was a much-discussed question even before the launching of *Sputnik*, the first earth-orbiting satellite, in October 1957. Human exploration in outer space is conducted in incredibly harsh conditions, with the explorers completely dependent on supplies and oxygen brought up from the earth's surface. Therefore, from the outset of human space exploration, scientists understood that space stations orbiting the earth were a logical step for fostering exploration. The space station would be a supply depot, repair facility, and resting point for explorers. Despite this expectation, human exploration has proven in practice to be more complicated than expected. In 1969, NASA's plans to establish both an earth-orbiting and a lunar-orbiting space station were rejected because of cost. This rejection reflected the expensive nature of space exploration and the lack of political support for continuing space exploration on an expanded scale.

Both the Soviet Union and the United States pursued building space stations in earth's orbit, with the Soviets taking the lead in 1971 with *Salyut I*. In 1973, the United States orbited Skylab, a two-level laboratory built in a converted Saturn S-IVB stage. This became an abortive effort when financial constraints and development of the space shuttle led to the Skylab's demise in 1979. The Soviets continued building their Alamaz/Salyut series through the 1970s, finally launching *Mir* space station in 1986. Their space station program eventually floundered after the Soviet Union's collapse. As a result of the Russian Federation's economic crises, the replacement *Mir 2* was never launched, which led to *Mir*'s deorbiting in 2001.

NASA continued to pursue building a space station after the 1969 rejection, but it could not find the necessary political support because of the high cost of implementing the program. During the administration of U.S. president Ronald Reagan, the agency was finally able to acquire presidential support for the program, which was announced in his 1984 State of the Union address. Despite this support, the program lagged because of congressional (and even some presidential) hostility to the space station concept. Expanding the human exploration of outer space was not a political priority for the United States outside of NASA. Regardless, space station design began with the project later named Space Station Freedom in 1988. Despite continuing cost and technical problems, the space station was conceived originally as the base camp from which humans would venture back to the moon and out to the planets and asteroids. In 1993–1994, the space station underwent another redesign along with a change in orientation. The station program (renamed the International Space Station or ISS) was now conceived as a multinational program, with a total of sixteen nations as partners. The Russian Federation joined the project, providing hardware and also acting as a contractor to produce several modules that were to be paid for by the United States.

In 1998, construction began on the redesigned ISS, with the orbiting of the first two modules, the Russian *Zarya* control module and the U.S. *Unity* node. ISS construction was repeatedly delayed with permanent occupancy not occurring until 2000. Construction of the ISS involves fitting in orbit the modules built on earth by different nations—a difficult and intricate process in an environment for which little experience existed prior to ISS construction. This experience will prove useful in future expeditions because base camps and other structures will have to be erected either on other celestial bodies or in space. The ISS construction process halted in February 2003 when the space shuttle *Columbia* broke up during reentry. Return of the space shuttles to flight status was delayed until 2006 despite a test flight by space shuttle *Discovery* in July 2005.

Meanwhile, the United States embarked on its new Vision for Space Exploration—the mission for which NASA had pursued building a space station, the base camp for explorers. Ironically, the January 2004 announcement proved to be the death knell for NASA interest in the ISS. Demands by the major international partners—the European Space Agency, Canada, Japan, and Russia—forced the United States to commit to completion of the ISS. This commitment was contingent upon the space shuttle returning to flight since only the shuttle was capable of carrying the major remaining ISS components to orbit. Prior to construction, the station's orbital inclination had been changed from 28.6° (easily reached from Kennedy Space Center) to 51.6° (accommodating the Russian partner whose *Soyuz* spacecraft is launched from Baikonur Cosmodrome. That orbit limits the ability of the U.S. launch vehicles to lift maximum payloads to orbit. The Vision for Space

Exploration is built on the understanding that reaching the moon and later Mars will not require a space station (similar to the 1960s-era Apollo moon landing program). The ISS would, therefore, be abandoned by the United States around 2016, although the international partners could choose to keep the ISS operational until its later deorbiting in about 2020 or beyond. The United States cannot afford, given present understandings, to support the shuttle and the ISS while also ramping up for the new exploration effort.

Despite this apparent abandonment of the ISS by the United States, the space station still continues to further human exploration of outer space simply because of its location in orbit. Exploration of outer space by humans has proven to be a highly dangerous and difficult proposition. The hazards of temperature extremes, the vacuum of space (there is no air), and radiation are obvious, and each presents a major challenge for humans and their equipment. The more insidious hazards are the effects of microgravity upon the human body in terms of lost muscle mass and bone density, plus cardiovascular system deterioration. All human systems appear to be adversely impacted by long-duration space flight whether in a space station orbiting the earth or in a spacecraft reaching out to other celestial bodies. These hazards are only slowly being identified, researched, and understood. Certain hazards can be handled through additional shielding and insulation from the harsh physical environment. Such safety measures demand additional funds to develop protections and also to cover additional operational costs. If more protective materials are required, this increases the weight that must be lifted out of the gravity well, meaning that larger lift vehicles and spacecraft are needed.

The impact of microgravity may be the most critical when one examines systematically its effects on humans and their vital systems. The ISS becomes critical here because long-duration missions can be conducted within comparatively close proximity to the earth, allowing rescue and return of crews. The problem is deciding whether the best approach is prevention of injury or deterioration through ameliorative actions or through recovery after the mission. The first is the provision of exercise equipment and other protective measures that simulate earth gravity or some approximation. In principle, the body responds during the treatment or exercise as if in earth gravity, delaying or preventing deterioration. This is especially critical for muscles, including the heart. The ISS provides the laboratory where

such questions are pursued. Sending humans to Mars or the outer planets is presently impossible, not because of technology deficiencies but because of real uncertainty as to how the crew would survive while maintaining their health and effectiveness. The ISS also allows for research on a small scale into the development of closed ecologies in which plants can be grown in microgravity, producing oxygen and absorbing carbon monoxide and other harmful elements. Given the space environment, either everything has to be taken with the crew or the recycling of essential elements must occur—oxygen and water being the most obvious. The ISS is not self-sustaining, but within it such environments can be created.

Space stations still logically remain base camps to the stars, but their functions have become more mundane. Such space facilities can serve as habitats for crews who venture out to free flyers orbiting with the station to check on experiments and retrieve or replace equipment. This original plan for the ISS was challenged by budget realities and the physical difficulties of operating in orbit. The ISS now supports human exploration by providing a continuing window on the effects of microgravity on the human body—information absolutely essential if humans are to move beyond lunar orbit. Currently, outer space is the final frontier—one that humans cannot explore in person and so send unmanned machines to. As knowledge increases, the possibilities for human exploration will improve, expanding the exploration frontier. There are no shortcuts to exploring outer space; the environment is too harsh and unrelenting.

[See also *Apollo/Saturn* Launch Vehicle; Moon; Skylab; Space Program; Space Shuttle; *and Sputnik.*]

BIBLIOGRAPHY

Harland, David M., and John E. Catchpole. *Creating the International Space Station*. New York: Springer-Praxis, 2002.

Harrison, Albert A. *Spacefaring: The Human Dimension*. Berkeley: University of California Press, 2001.

Launius, Roger D. *Space Stations: Base Camps to the Stars*. Washington, D.C.: Smithsonian Institution Press, 2003.

Stine, G. Harry. *Halfway to Anywhere: Achieving America's Destiny in Space*. New York: Evans, 1996.

ROGER HANDBERG

Inuit. Being traditionally a nomadic hunting people, the Inuit, or Eskimos, were extremely aware of even minor features of the Arctic landscape and were familiar with remarkably large areas. More-

Ter-bou-e-tie, In-nu-it "—(Farewell, Innuits).

"Farewell, Innuits." From Charles Francis Hall's *Life with the Esquimaux* (2 vols., London, 1864). Hall had a remarkable fascination with the Inuits and lived with them for long periods. His sentimental attachment to this people is shown in this engraving, where his sailing ship is leaving the Inuits in their various craft. COURTESY THE NEWBERRY LIBRARY, CHICAGO

over, since storytelling was an integral part of their culture—and since accounts of hunts and travels, including geographical details, were a favorite topic of these stories—most Inuit were familiar with a surprising amount of detail concerning areas that they themselves had never visited. Many nonnative explorers of the Arctic tapped into this vast pool of geographical knowledge by persuading Inuit to draw maps of areas with which they were familiar.

One of the earliest examples of this occurred on Captain William Edward Parry's second expedition. While wintering on board HMS *Fury* and *Hecla* at Winter Island off the southeastern coast of Melville

Peninsula in 1821–1822, Parry and his second in command, Captain George Lyon, asked two of the local Inuit, Iligliuk and Ewerat, to draw maps. Iligliuk's map, drawn for Lyon, covers an amazingly large area, from south of Wager Bay to Bylot Island, a distance of about 620 miles (1,000 kilometers) in a straight line, and displays some remarkably detailed local knowledge. Fury and Hecla Strait (which Parry and Lyon had not yet reached) is clearly delineated, and against the narrow entrance of Wager Bay is the annotation "Strong rush of water"; the tidal turbulence in this narrow entrance is quite notorious.

Iligliuk and Ewerat also drew maps that included the west coast of Melville Peninsula, running southwest from Fury and Hecla Strait, that is, the east shore of Committee Bay. On the basis of these maps, Parry somewhat optimistically anticipated the prospect "of our soon rounding the north-eastern part of America"; he was not to know that the substantial mass of Boothia Peninsula extended a long way north to the west of Committee Bay.

Some eight years later, in January 1830, while Sir John Ross was wintering on board *Victory* at Felix Harbour on the east side of the Isthmus of Boothia, some Inuit visited the ship; they had recently arrived from Akolee at the south end of Committee Bay. Two of the men, Tulluahin and Tiagashu, drew a map of the coastline from Akolee to Felix Harbour. They also drew in the west coast of Boothia Peninsula, showing the various lakes on the Isthmus of Boothia. Another of the group, Ikmallik, added considerably to the chart drawn earlier, extending it south all the way to Wager Bay. In his narrative of the expedition, Ross reproduced what appears to be a composite of the maps by all his informants, covering the area from Felix Harbour south to Repulse Bay and including the west side of the Isthmus of Boothia.

The explorer who probably had the greatest success in tapping into the geographical knowledge of the Inuit, perhaps because he had competent interpreters in the persons of Ebierbing and Tookalitoo, was Charles F. Hall. In August 1860, at Rescue Harbour in Cyrus Field Bay near the eastern tip of Cumberland Peninsula, Baffin Island, he asked an Inuk named Koojene to draw a map of the surrounding area. The result was a reasonably accurate map of Frobisher Bay and Meta Incognita Peninsula. In August 1861, while traveling by boat along the north shore of Frobisher Bay in the vicinity of Countess of Warwick Sound, Hall reported that Koojene was drafting a very accurate map of the coastline as they traveled along it.

Hall probably made even more use of Inuit drafting talent on his second expedition, to Repulse Bay and points northwest from there. At Repulse Bay (Naujaat) in March 1866, the Inuk Ar-mou drew a map of the area he knew. It extended from Pond Inlet (northern Baffin Island) to Churchill, that is, a north-south extent of some 1,116 miles (1,800 kilometers) in a straight line; the intricacies of the coastline that he delineated from his own knowledge probably totaled several times that distance.

In June, another Inuk, Ouela, draw Hall a map of the area from Melville Peninsula and Committee Bay to Wager Bay; at Igloolik (Iglulik), Oongerluk drew

maps of the northeast corner of Foxe Basin and of Admiralty Inlet. The former map shows Baird Peninsula and Rowley and Bray Islands, which were not discovered by Europeans for another seventy years.

Having persuaded an Inuk to draw maps for him on Adelaide Peninsula, Heinrich Klutschak, artist and surveyor on Frederick Schwatka's search for Franklin relics in 1878–1880, commented: "His drawings of a stretch of coast which is known to him are particularly interesting since he indicates every smallest headland but completely ignores major swings to the various points of the compass, so that one has first to accustom oneself to his straight-line drawings in order to understand them" (p. 76).

During his sojourn in Cumberland Sound in 1883–1884, the anthropologist Franz Boas also had considerable success in getting Inuit to draw maps. He reproduced a map drawn for him by Sunapingnang of Frobisher Bay, Cumberland Peninsula, and Cumberland Sound and commented on the accuracy and remarkable detail of these maps.

Even well into the twentieth century Inuit were drawing maps for visiting explorers and scientists, which greatly assisted them in their investigations. In 1910 at Charlton Island in James Bay an Inuk named Wetallok drew a map of the Belcher Islands (where he had frequently hunted) for Robert Flaherty. These islands had long been featured on the Admiralty charts as a few small islets, but Wetallok's map showed them as something much closer to the extensive archipelago that they are. On the basis of this information Flaherty visited and mapped the islands in 1914–1916.

In the fall of 1928 an Inuk named Saila at Nuwata on the west coast of Foxe Peninsula drew a map of that peninsula for the naturalist Dewey Soper. On it his Inuit informants pointed out Bowman Bay as being the nesting ground of the blue goose (dark phase of the snow goose, *Anser caerulescens caerulescens*), for which he had been searching for years. Using the map, Soper located the nesting grounds during the following summer.

And in January 1937 an Inuk at Gore Bay, near Repulse Bay, drew a map of northern Foxe Basin for Tom Manning and Graham Rowley, members of the British Canadian Arctic expedition. As on the map drawn for Charles Hall by Oongerluk at Repulse Bay (Naujaat) in 1866, two islands, then still undiscovered, are indicated northwest of Baird Peninsula. They were later named Bray Island and Rowley Island after members of the expedition.

Undoubtedly, however, to someone unaccustomed to them, maps drawn by Inuit could prove quite baffling. For example, while wintering at Cambridge Bay (Ikaluktutiak) in HMS *Enterprise* in 1852–1853, Captain Richard Collinson arranged for some of the local Inuit "to draw a chart of the coast to the eastward, which was several times repeated, [the charts] agreeing very well with each other, but were totally unlike the coast afterwards travelled by me" (p. 286). Mr. Arbuthnot, the ice master, thought that the Inuit were indicating a ship somewhere to the east, but Collinson assumed they were just repeating his questions. Unfortunately, no attempt was made to reproduce the Inuit maps, and hence we will never know if they showed Sir John Franklin's ships beset off King William Island. As it was, during the 1853 sledging season, Collinson searched the southeast and east coasts of Victoria Island, rather than heading east across Victoria Strait to King William Island, where he might have found all the evidence of the fate of the Franklin Expedition (abandoned equipment, skeletons, and so on) that Lieutenant Hobson and Captain McClintock would find six years later.

This crucial misunderstanding between Collinson and the Inuit points up dramatically the importance of a competent interpreter. Their input as interpreters represents the second major contribution of the Inuit to the exploration of the Arctic. Several Inuit made an invaluable contribution in this regard to more than one expedition. For example, Ooligbuk (senior) traveled with Franklin on his second expedition (from the Mackenzie Delta to Return Reef) in 1826, with Peter Dease and Thomas Simpson (from the mouth of the Coppermine to Boothia Peninsula) in 1839, and with John Rae (to Committee Bay, Pelly Bay, and Melville Peninsula) in 1846–1847. The Baffin Island Inuit Ebierbing and Tookolitoo accompanied Charles Hall on all of his Arctic expeditions, and they accompanied Schwatka's expedition to King William Island in 1878–1880. In every case they made an invaluable contribution by eliciting information from the local Inuit either about the geography of the areas ahead, or about the fate of the Franklin Expedition. The importance of the role of a competent interpreter with regard to the latter objective, already demonstrated by Collinson's experience, was underscored once again by the experience of James Anderson and James Stewart. In the summer of 1855, Anderson and Stewart found Inuit at the mouth of the Back River, and also found items clearly derived from the Franklin Expedition, but for lack of a competent interpreter, they were unable to gain a clear picture of where the items had come from. At their farthest point, Anderson and Stewart's party were only about 4 miles (7 kilometers) from Starvation Cove, where large numbers of skeletons were later discovered.

[*See also* Franklin Search Expeditions; North America, *subentries on* Indigenous Guides *and* Indigenous Maps; *and biographical entries on figures mentioned in this article.*]

BIBLIOGRAPHY

Barr, William, ed. *Searching for Franklin, the Land Arctic Searching Expedition: James Anderson's and James Stewart's Expedition via the Back River, 1855.* London: Hakluyt Society, 1999.

Boas, Franz. "The Central Eskimo." In *Sixth Annual Report of the Bureau of Ethnology to the Secretary of the Smithsonian Institution 1884–'85,* edited by J. W. Powell. Washington, D.C.: Government Printing Office, 1888. Reprint. Lincoln: University of Nebraska Press, 1964.

Collinson, Richard. *Journal of H.M.S. "Enterprise" on the Expedition in Search of Sir John Franklin's Ships by Behring Strait, 1850–55.* London: Sampson Low, Marston, Searle and Rivington, 1889. Reprint. New York: AMS Press, 1976.

Flaherty, Robert J. *My Eskimo Friends: "Nanook of the North."* Garden City, N.Y.: Doubleday, Page, 1924.

Hall, Charles Francis. *Arctic Researches and Life among the Esquimaux: Being the Narrative of an Expedition in Search of Sir John Franklin in the Years 1860, 1861, and 1862.* New York: Harper, 1866.

Klutschak, Heinrich. *Overland to Starvation Cove: With the Inuit in Search of Franklin 1878–1880.* Edited and translated by William Barr. Toronto: University of Toronto Press, 1987.

Martin, Constance. *Search for the Blue Goose: J. Dewey Soper, the Arctic Adventures of a Canadian Naturalist.* Calgary, Alberta: Bayeux Arts, 1995.

Nourse, J. E., ed. *Narrative of the Second Arctic Expedition Made by Charles F. Hall . . . during the Years 1864–69.* Washington: Government Printing Office, 1879.

Parry, William Edward. *Journal of a Second Voyage for the Discovery of a North-West Passage from the Atlantic to the Pacific, Performed in the Years 1821–22–23 in His Majesty's Ships "Fury" and "Hecla."* London: John Murray, 1824. Reprint. New York: Greenwood Press, 1969.

Ross, John. *Narrative of a Second Voyage in Search of a North-West Passage and of a Residence in the Arctic Regions during the Years 1829, 1830, 1831, 1832, 1833.* 2 vols. London: A. W. Webster, 1835. Reprint. New York: Greenwood Press, 1969.

Rowley, Graham W. *Cold Comfort: My Love Affair with the Arctic.* Montreal and Kingston, Ontario: McGill–Queen's University Press, 1996.

WILLIAM BARR

Isidore of Seville (c. 560–536), encyclopedic scholar and bishop of Seville. Born and educated in Visigothic Spain, Isidore became a prominent churchman and a prolific writer. His legacy includes biblical exegesis, historiography, a treatise on natural philosophy (*De natura rerum;* On the nature of things), and an encyclopedia, *Etymologiae* (Etymologies) or *Origines* (Origins), which is by far the best known and most influential of his works. The *Etymologies* treated geographical subjects in detail, and Isidore's other works, such as biblical commentaries and *De natura rerum*, also included information related to geography.

In his *Etymologies* Isidore made a fundamental contribution to the creation of a Christian corpus of knowledge. He collected information that went back to classical antiquity and placed it in a Christian context. The encyclopedia included material on all disciplines considered important at the time, from school subjects such as the seven liberal arts to religion and natural philosophy. Isidore presented information related to geography in several books of his encyclopedia. Book IX treated peoples and languages, Book XIII rivers and seas, Book XIV regions of the earth, and Book XV cities and architecture. Isidore's description of the world followed in its details the Roman geographers Pliny, Solinus, and Orosius (first, second, and fifth centuries, respectively). As the classical tradition dictated, Isidore's Earth was spherical, the landmass was divided into three continents, and the regions were, in general, those listed by Roman geographers. At the same time Isidore gave his picture of the world a Christian structure and complements it with biblical references. Thus his account of regions began with Paradise and ended with Hell, and his description of rivers included both the rivers of Paradise and the rivers of the underworld.

Throughout his encyclopedia Isidore provided etymological explanations of names and words borrowed from classical and Christian sources. Following an established tradition, Isidore considered etymology both the main goal and the foundation of his method. Isidore believed that in order to understand the nature of things, it was necessary to explain the origin and meaning of their names, or their etymologies. Isidore approached the world as a grammarian approaches a text: He studied names and through their meaning arrived at the essence of things. Because explaining names was Isidore's ultimate goal, in his description of the world he chose the logical arrangement of subjects by categories. Abandoning the traditional order of classical geographical descriptions that followed an imaginary journey along the coastal line, Isidore chose to follow the order of the four elements (fire, air, water, and earth) which, according to classical and medieval ideas, comprised the universe. Thus he treated seas and rivers separately from the dry land and its regions, and he put places and peoples, usually treated together in classical geography, in separate books.

The manuscripts of Isidore's encyclopedia were often accompanied by maps that usually showed the tripartite division of the earth and varied in their level of detail.

Isidore's synthesis of Christian and classical knowledge, which included geography, proved to be very influential in the Middle Ages. His *Etymologies*, transmitted in more than a thousand manuscripts, provided concrete information, ideas, and methods for later geographical accounts such as those in encyclopedias by Rabanus Maurus, *De rerum naturis* (c. 842–847), Honorius Augustodunensis, *Imago mundi* (c. 1000; The image of the world), and in the anonymous ninth-century geographical treatise, *De situ orbis (*On the location of the Earth). Excerpts from the *Etymologies* were widely used to compile medieval school commentaries and textbooks.

[*See also Mare Oceanum*; Orosius; *and* Pliny the Elder.]

BIBLIOGRAPHY

The Etymologies of Isidore of Seville. Edited and translated by Stephen A. Barney, W. J. Lewis, J. A. Beach, and Oliver Berghof. Cambridge, U.K.: Cambridge University Press, 2006.

Fontaine, Jacques. *Isidore of Seville et la culture classique dans l'Espagne wisigothique.* 2nd rev. ed. 3 vols. Paris: Études Augustiniennes, 1959.

Isidore de Séville. *Traité de la nature.* Edited by Jacques Fontaine. Bordeaux: Feret, 1960.

Isidori Hispalensis episcopi Etymologiarum sive Originum libri XX. Edited by W. M. Lindsay. Oxford and New York: Oxford University Press, 1911.

NATALIA LOZOVSKY

Itineraries, Ancient and Medieval. Whether oral or preserved in a variety of written formats, itineraries were an important means of organizing geographical knowledge, as well as reinforcing control—real or claimed—during antiquity and the Middle Ages. From the third millennium B.C.E., scribes in civilizations of the Near East (Sumer, Babylon, Assyria) compiled not only lists of place-names, but also records of the time taken to travel from one place to another, seemingly for the use of military commanders and traders. The earliest such record by a Greek (now lost) was said to have been commissioned around 500 B.C.E. by the Persian king Darius the Great (r. 522–486 B.C.E.); its author, Scylax, sailed down the Indus River and then westward as far as the isthmus of Suez. The standard Greek term *periplous* ("voyage around") reflects coverage—with varying quantities of detail for mariners and traders—of the entire shoreline of the "enclosed" Medi-

Vicarello Goblet. The goblet shown here was thrown into the sacred spring at Vicarello near Lake Braccianao (twenty miles north of Rome) and recovered in the mid-nineteenth century. It is on display, with three others like it, in the Palazzo Massimo Museum in Rome. These cylindrical goblets, probably dating to the early first century C.E., are between 3.5 and 6 inches in height and 2.5 to 3 inches in diameter. Inscribed in four vertical columns are the stopping points on the long land journey from Gades in southern Spain to Rome, with the mileage between each point, and then at the end the total mileage figure. No doubt the prudent traveler bought such a goblet as a votive before setting out and made an offering of it after a safe arrival. UNIVERSIDAD VALLADOLID

terranean or Black Sea, but the scope did not have to be circular; examples are known recording voyages north to Britain, along the west and east coasts of Africa (the former supposedly a Phoenician account), and through the Red Sea to southern Arabia and India. More *periploi* seem to have been written in Greek than in Latin, although Pomponius Mela's mid-first-century C.E. "Description of the World" (*Chorographia*) is in Latin, and intended for instructional purposes rather than practical use.

By contrast, the *itinerarium* or record of a land journey, remains far more characteristically Latin than Greek; the fragmentary coverage of routes from the Euphrates River to central Asia by Isidore of Charax in the early first century C.E. is a rare Greek example. Romans' reliance upon *itineraria* no doubt stemmed from their tireless struggle to expand by conquest, and their development of main routes along which milestones were often set. It thus became practical to list stopping-points and the distance between each. This format was established by the start of the Christian Era, and was to be seen on prominent "signposts" erected by city authorities: remains of monumental examples in stone have survived in northern Europe and Asia Minor. Four small silver goblets found not far north of Rome at Vicarello each record the long land journey from Gades (modern Cádiz) in the south of Spain via Corduba, Tarraco, Narbo, the Alps, Bononia (Bologna), and Ariminum (Rimini) to Rome—a total of 1,840 Roman miles (1,738 miles [2,800 kilometers]) in 107 stages. Roman law in principle expected anyone summoned to court to be capable of traveling there at an average daily pace of 20 Roman miles (18.9 miles [30.4 kilometers]), although naturally there would be many variables in practice. One haphazard collection of the usual concise records of journeys within the Roman empire was clumsily assembled around 300 C.E., and was later misleadingly entitled *Itinerarium Antonini* (Antonine Itinerary). From the Middle Ages onward, however, it has attracted intense interest for its unique preservation of precious data about places, routes, and distances; most recently, it has underpinned the controversial argument that Romans' worldview was predominantly linear and one-dimensional. We do hear of other itineraries that were in some way pictorial, though the nature of their scope and their images is beyond recovery. Once Christian pilgrimage expanded rapidly from the fourth century, itineraries were compiled for this specific purpose. A remarkable one dated as early as 333 broadens Westerners' horizons by steering them most methodically all the way from Burdigala (Bordeaux) in Gaul to Jerusalem. Itineraries for pilgrims continued to be compiled and elaborated through the Middle Ages. Records also survive of the journeys of kings and nobles.

[*See also Periploi.*]

BIBLIOGRAPHY

Harley, J. Brian, and David Woodward, eds. *The History of Cartography*. Vol. 1: *Cartography in Prehistoric, Ancient, and Medieval Europe and the Mediterranean*. Chicago and London: University of Chicago Press, 1987.

Salway, Benet. "Travel, *itineraria* and *tabellaria*." In *Travel and Geography in the Roman Empire*, edited by Colin Adams and Ray Laurence, 22–66. London and New York: Routledge, 2001.

Whittaker, C. R. *Rome and its Frontiers: the Dynamics of Empire*. London and New York: Routledge, 2004. See chap. 4, "Mental Maps and Frontiers: Seeing Like a Roman."

RICHARD J. A. TALBERT

J

James, Thomas (1593?–1635?), English explorer of Canada. Little is known about Thomas James's early years, although he had family connections in both Bristol and South Wales. Whatever the circumstances of his birth and upbringing, he seems to have become a barrister. How and why he made the switch from the law to the sea is not clear, but in 1628 he appears as master of a Bristol ship, and in 1631 he persuaded the Bristol Society of Merchant Venturers to appoint him commander of an expedition to find a Northwest Passage through Hudson Bay. It was the Bristol riposte to Luke Foxe's venture to Hudson Bay on behalf of London investors. The vessel chosen by James, the seventy-ton *Henrietta Maria*, was as small as Foxe's *Charles*. James's explanation that "A great Ship (as by former experience I had found) was unfit to be forc'd thorow the Ice" (Christy, vol. 2, p. 456) indicates firsthand knowledge of Arctic conditions, and certainly the impressive list of astronomical instruments he took on the voyage suggests advanced navigational skills. Even so, it is curious that he refused to take any crew who had sailed in northern waters.

James met the same difficulty in negotiating the ice-choked waters of Hudson Strait as Foxe did in the same season, but once through, James sailed across Hudson Bay to near the Churchill River. He then explored the coast to the south until he reached the southernmost extension of Hudson Bay, later known as James Bay. There he decided to winter at Charlton Island, for although it was only mid-September, his journal noted that the rigging froze every night and that by morning there were six inches of snow on the deck. Like Foxe, James had provisions for eighteen months on board, but unlike Foxe, he was determined to winter. To save the ship from the pounding of the heavy seas, and mindful no doubt of the dangers from ice as winter approached, James decided to scuttle the *Henrietta Maria* in order to preserve it. As James described how most of their bedding and clothes, as well as the surgeon's chest, disappeared under water with the vessel, he made a wry note that they had

perhaps jumped out of the frying pan and into the fire. The winter was an ordeal, with the men suffering from cold, hunger, and scurvy, and four of them died. Their captain's insistence that they had to leave their rough shelters each day to fetch wood, even though most of them had no shoes to wear and they often had to crawl through the snow on all fours, undoubtedly helped most to survive. Although he was fourteen degrees south of the Arctic Circle, James vividly described the severity of a northern winter. Many observations that later became commonplace—brandy frozen solid, eyelids glued shut with frost, kettles coated with ice although they hung over a fire—were set down to astonish and appall his readers. In the spring the crew bailed out and repaired the ship, and in early July they set sail. Unwittingly, James followed Foxe's track of the previous year toward Thomas Button's Ne Ultra and then into Foxe Channel, but without reaching as far north as Foxe had gone. The badly damaged ship and its crew struggled back to Bristol in October 1632. "Miraculous" was James's word to describe their survival, and it is no surprise that, in the final section of his journal, James expressed his doubts as to whether a Northwest Passage existed.

After his return, James had an audience with the king and was appointed to a command by the Admiralty. In 1633 his account of the voyage, *The Strange and Dangerous Voyage of Capt. Thomas James*, was published and became a classic of northern endurance. James did not survive long after his return, and he seems to have died in 1635. In terms of exploration he had accomplished little, but the voyage lived on long after many other voyages had been forgotten. More than 150 years later, for instance, Samuel Taylor Coleridge seems to have found inspiration in it for his land of ice in "The Rime of the Ancient Mariner."

[*See also* Foxe, Luke, *and* Northwest Passage.]

BIBLIOGRAPHY

Christy, Miller, ed. *The Voyages of Captain Luke Foxe of Hull and Captain Thomas James of Bristol*. 2 vols. London: Hakluyt Society, 1894.

Cooke, Alan. "Thomas James." *Dictionary of Canadian Biography,* vol. 1, pp. 384–385. Toronto: University of Toronto Press, 1966.

GLYNDWR WILLIAMS

Jave la Grande. The Jave la Grande of the "Dieppe" maps is one of the puzzles of European history. Located to the south of the Indonesian archipelago and of continental size, this landmass is of approximately the right size and in approximately the right position to be Australia—and therein lies the mystery: if it is Australia, who discovered it, and how was knowledge of the discovery transmitted to Europe?

The maps in question were drawn in the northern French port of Dieppe, then a center of navigational knowledge, between approximately 1536 and 1567. The major examples in the series include Jean Rotz's world chart (1542); the "Harleian" or "Dauphin" world map (c. 1546); Pierre Descelliers's world maps and charts (1547, 1550, and 1553); the world map in the Vallard Atlas (1547); and Nicolas Desliens's world maps and charts (1561, 1566, and 1567). It seems likely that, in one way or another, these works relate to a lost French original and, beyond that—given their Portuguese place names and their attribution of discovery to the Portuguese—to a lost Portuguese chart.

For more than two hundred years, the presence of Jave la Grande on these maps has given rise to speculation that the Portuguese discovered the last habitable continent to come to the knowledge of Europe 70 to 250 years before the Dutch and the British. The circumstances surrounding the Portuguese thrust into Asia make such a discovery by no means impossible. After Vasco da Gama reached India in 1498, the Portuguese rapidly penetrated farther east. They were at Ceylon in 1506, captured Malacca in 1511, and then, with the help of Malay pilots, reached the Banda Islands, Amboina, the Moluccas, and Timor. Timor and the Spice Islands are only comparatively short sailing distances from the northern coasts of Australia, so it is quite possible—probable, even—that the Portuguese also reached Australia.

Two navigators have been repeatedly suggested as the first European discoverers of Australia: Gomes de Sequeira and Cristovão de Mendonça. However, there is no good evidence that either reached the continent—or, indeed, that they were ever near it. Sequeira was evidently storm-blown some one thousand miles away from the Celebes Islands in 1525, until he came to an island of some "thirty leagues"; but whether his course was southeastward or eastward is unknown. Some authorities think that he probably fetched up on the large island of the Palau group, to the east of Mindanao. Knowledge of Mendonça's doings is similarly lacking. He evidently left Goa sometime in 1521 to search for the "Isles of Gold, beyond Sumatra"; he was at the northern tip of Sumatra in midyear and Malacca toward year's end. Where he went thereafter, and when he returned (to Malacca, Goa, or to Portugal) are mysteries, for there is no report extant of his subsequent progress, until he reappears in 1527–1528 as the intended governor of the Portuguese base at Ormuz.

There is another grave problem with accepting that in c.1522–1523 Mendonça made a voyage through Torres Strait and down the eastern Australian coast. Centuries later, in 1770, when James Cook had the benefit of a better ship and much better navigational techniques and instruments than those available to a Portuguese navigator in the early sixteenth century, and with winds and currents at his back, it took him some seven weeks, and constant vigilance, to travel north from Botany Bay to Possession Island in Torres Strait. To postulate that Mendonça might have made this voyage in the opposite direction, against winds and currents, from Torres Strait all the way down the east coast (with the hazards of the Great Barrier Reef), then west against winds and currents through the also notoriously difficult Bass Strait, disregards the tremendous sailing difficulties such a voyage would have involved. It has also been suggested that the men of the ship *San Lesmes*, one of the squadron of seven sent out from Spain in 1525, may have reached New Zealand and then the east coast of Australia. Again, however, there is no good evidence to support this hypothesis.

Neither are there other signs of any Portuguese visit to Australia. For example, as they progressed down the west coast of Africa, Portuguese navigators usually left stone crosses to mark their farthest points south; but no *padrões* have ever been found on Australian coasts. Other evidence that supposedly supports a Portuguese discovery—guns on Carronade Island off the northwest coast; cave paintings in the Kimberley region; stone ruins on the south coast of New South Wales; iron keys at Geelong; the "Mahogany" ship at Warrnambool—prove either illusory or downright false upon close examination. For example, whereas European cannon cast in the sixteenth century typically have a lead content of about 2–4 percent, the Carronade Island guns have one of 7–9 percent.

So we are left with the Jave la Grande of the Dieppe maps as the only possible substantial evidence of an early European discovery of Australia. The earliest extant, fully developed depiction of this landmass is that on the eastern hemisphere of Jean Rotz's world chart. Rotz prided himself on representing only coastlines that he had himself visited, or of which he had authentic information. And, indeed, many of the lands on his world chart are, for the time, accurately drawn. Moreover, he deliberately refrained from linking Jave la Grande to any larger *Terra Australis*.

On the other hand, in its long southeasterly extension, the coastline of Rotz's Jave la Grande is manifestly not that of Australia. Some scholars have turned to mathematics to resolve this problem. Allowing for magnetic deviation and various other limitations to navigational techniques of the early sixteenth century, they have redrawn this coastline so that it becomes very similar to the eastern Australian one. However, it is by no means clear that the mathematical premises they have used are more than self-serving. Then again, other scholars have studied roughly contemporary maps of Asia and analyzed place names, to conclude that Jave la Grande is an amalgam of the southwestern coast of Sumatra and the eastern coast of Sumba, or even the coast of Vietnam wildly mislocated. The evidence, such as it is, is quite equivocal.

As a series, however, the Dieppe maps only too well exhibit the habit, prevalent in the age, of substituting imaginative for authentic geography: from the Harleian map onward, cartographers retreated from Rotz's clarity of outline and merged Jave la Grande with an immense landmass stretching across the entire southern hemisphere, filling its spaces with depictions of people, animals, and birds having no connection with Australia.

In the 1980s, Helen Wallis suggested that knowledge of an early Portuguese discovery of Australia, which may not have been reported to Lisbon, may have reached Dieppe via the adventurous Parmentier brothers, who took two ships from Dieppe to Sumatra in about 1529. This is possible, but it will take some irrefutable evidence, either material or bibliographic, to establish that the Jave la Grande of the Dieppe maps is indeed an early depiction of Australia.

[*See also* Cook, James; Dieppe School; Gama, Vasco da; *and Terra Australis Incognita*.]

BIBLIOGRAPHY

Collingridge, George. *The Discovery of Australia*. Reprint. Gladsville, New South Wales: Golden Press, 1983.

McIntyre, K. G. *The Secret Discovery of Australia: Portuguese Ventures 200 Years before Captain Cook*. London: Souvenir Press, 1977. Argues the case for Java la Grande's being Australia.

Richardson, W. A. R. "Java-la-Grande: A Place Name Chart of its East Coast." *The Great Circle* 6 (1984): 1–13. Suggests that the east coast of Java la Grande is in fact the coast of Vietnam, but his argument is so speculative and convoluted as not to be credible.

Sharp, Andrew. *The Discovery of Australia*. Oxford: Clarendon Press, 1963. Asserts that Java la Grande is an amalgam of the coasts of Java and Sumba.

Spate, O. H. K. "Terra Australis-Cognita." In *Let Me Enjoy: Essays, Partly Geographical*. Canberra: Australian National University Press, 1965. Discusses lucidly the problems raised by the Dieppe maps.

Wallis, Helen. "Java la Grande: The Enigma of the Dieppe Maps," In *Terra Australis to Australia*, edited by Glyndwr Williams and Alan Frost. Melbourne, Australia: Oxford University Press, 1988. Reproduces the major works in the Dieppe series.

Wallis, Helen, ed. *The Maps and Text of the Boke of Idrography presented by Jean Rotz to Henry VIII*. Oxford: Roxburghe Club, 1981. Displays Rotz's maps.

ALAN FROST

Jefferson, Thomas

Jefferson, Thomas (1743–1826), third president of the United States. When Jefferson and exploration are thought of together, inevitably the Lewis and Clark expedition comes immediately to mind. But the Corps of Discovery, which explored the upper west of the United States, was merely the most visible

Thomas Jefferson. At his country house at Monticello, in Virginia, Jefferson had several large wall maps hanging in his hallway. At least two of the maps were by Aaron Arrowsmith and were remarkable—like this map of Africa—for having very large blank spaces. It is easy to imagine how Jefferson's mind would dwell on the need to fill in these huge blanks. COURTESY THE NEWBERRY LIBRARY, CHICAGO

and ultimately influential manifestation of Jefferson's fascination with exploration of every kind. His *Notes on the State of Virginia*, the only book he authored, grew from an attempt to answer questions of mutual interest raised by François de Barbé-Marbois. Having opened the box to look inside, Jefferson was off and running on his own mental expedition, and it did not end with the publication of the results of his initial findings while he was in France in 1784. Throughout the remainder of his life, Jefferson continued to edit his notes, revising and adding information as he continued learning from his continuing exploration, primarily from the confines of his study at Monticello.

Exploration was for Jefferson a life experience. His passion for books was in part an outgrowth of his desire to explore things and places. The acquisition by the United States of the Louisiana Territory offered another resource for learning about the unknown in what to most Americans in 1803 was a vast wilderness. Jefferson's instruction that each member of the Lewis and Clark expedition keep a journal ensured that at least some useful data would be produced and perhaps much would return. It was Jefferson who had the expedition's journals published and who proudly distributed copies to others for whom exploration and discovery were shared passions.

[*See also* Lewis, Meriwether, and William Clark.]

BIBLIOGRAPHY

Jackson, Donald. *Thomas Jefferson and the Stony Mountains: Exploring the West from Monticello.* Norman: University of Oklahoma Press, 1993.

Jackson, Donald, ed. *Letters of the Lewis and Clark Expedition, with Related Documents, 1783–1854.* 2 vols. 2nd ed. Urbana: University of Illinois Press, 1978.

Jefferson, Thomas. *Notes on the State of Virginia.* Edited by William Peden. Chapel Hill: University of North Carolina Press for the Institute of Early American History and Culture, Williamsburg, Virginia, 1954.

Ronda, James P., ed. *Thomas Jefferson and the Changing West: From Conquest to Conservation.* Albuquerque: University of New Mexico Press, 1997.

CHARLES T. CULLEN

Jenkinson, Anthony (1529–1611), Elizabethan merchant who, from 1546, journeyed throughout western Europe and the Mediterranean. Jenkinson was born in Market Harborough, England. In 1557 he was appointed by the Muscovy Company to exploit the foundations laid by Richard Chancellor and extend English trade beyond Moscow to the Orient. He departed in April 1558 via the Moskva, Oka, and Volga rivers to Astrakhan on the Caspian Sea. After navigating its northern shoreline he disembarked at Mangyshlak on the northeast coast and continued by camel caravans—amid great hardship and danger—and arrived at Bukhara (in present-day Uzbekistan) in December. He found trade with China interrupted by warfare and political turmoil, factors that forced him to abandon his plan to visit Persia; consequently he returned to Moscow in March 1559. Nevertheless, his venture returned a profit in London sufficient enough to persuade the company to dispatch him again in 1561. From Moscow in April 1562, he followed the river route to the Caspian and then Shabran (near Däväçi, Azerbaijan) on its west coast. He then traveled overland to Shemakha (west of Baku), where he successfully arranged future trade, and wintered near the Persian court at Qazvīn (west of Tehran), where his overtures were rejected. He reached Moscow in August 1563 and departed for London in July 1564. Jenkinson pioneered the overland trade route to central Asia that others soon would follow. Later he returned to Russia both to gain further trade concessions and to undertake English diplomatic consultations with the tsar. Information from his 1562 map of Russia was incorporated into Abraham Ortelius's *Theatrum orbis terrarum* (1570).

[*See also* Ortelius, Abraham.]

BIBLIOGRAPHY

Andrews, Kenneth R. *Trade, Plunder, and Settlement: Maritime Enterprise and the Genesis of the British Empire, 1480–1630.* Cambridge, U.K.: Cambridge University Press, 1984.

Mayers, Kit. *North-east Passage to Muscovy: Stephen Borough and the First Tudor Explorations.* Stroud, U.K.: Sutton, 2005.

PETER T. BRADLEY

Jesuits. In 1540, Pope Paul III approved the founding of the Society of Jesus, also known as the Jesuits, a religious order of men established under the inspiration of Ignatius of Loyola (1491–1556). This new order embraced a manner of religious life that placed particular emphasis on a vision of the whole world as the location of its enterprise of striving for the defense and propagation of the faith and for the progress of souls in Christian life and doctrine.

The founding document of the order, *The Formula of the Institute*, noted that this enterprise extended even to that "region known as the Indies." Ignatius considered the entire world as the location of Jesuit works, but he also identified the world as means of attaining the purpose of human existence: union with God. Ignatius articulated his more optimistic view of the world and its inhabitants in his *Spiritual Exercises*, in which the director of the exercises is admonished that every good Christian should be more ready to put a good interpretation on a statement than to condemn it as false. In this understanding of the world and its peoples, creation was not viewed as a dualistic split between "flesh" and "spirit." Rather, all creation could move a person toward God.

In light of this vision of accepting the positive potentials of all aspects of creation, the Jesuits embraced and taught the pagan classics of ancient Greece and Rome, seeing in these writings vehicles that could be used (after some remodeling) to move souls toward God. In addition to each Jesuit's spiritual and academic training, he was bound by a vow of obedience. This vow placed him ultimately under the papacy and its universal mission, but it also sensitized him to the basic idea that the word of God can be listened to (Latin *obedire*, "to hear" or "to listen") when it is spoken by the voice of the other. These basic tenets—the supposition of the goodness of creation, the idea that non-Christian literature can assist in moving souls toward God, and a vow of obedience alerting listeners that the voice of God comes from outside the self—permeated the writings of Ignatius and were instilled to some degree in every Jesuit by means of his formation.

The nearly twelve years of this formation motivated Jesuits intellectually and spiritually toward a more optimistic view of non-European cultures. Jesuits were to consider these cultures as potential means—and not barriers—for moving souls toward God. In light of these insights, Roberto de Nobili (1557–1656) used the Sanskrit texts of the Hindu Vedas, and Matteo Ricci (1552–1610) used the writings of Confucius in the same way that other Christians used the writings of Plato and Aristotle. This positive view of creation saw its greatest manifestation in works of art on the missions, in which Jesuits blended Catholic dogma and indigenous media in a unique expression of art and faith.

In addition to their intellectual and spiritual predispositions, the Jesuits created external structures that assisted in their expansion. The Jesuit order was run by a superior general who delegated portions of his authority to provincials. Provincials supervised a specific area and oversaw the works of superiors, who managed individual works such as schools or mission outposts. Various parts of the world were divided into assistancies, frequently according to language groups, which embraced larger areas or groups of provinces. Hence the Portuguese Assistancy, because of royal patronage, embraced those areas under the Portuguese crown: Africa, India, Asia, and Brazil. So it was with Spain and its royal patronage. In order to advance the spiritual and temporal purpose of the Jesuits, there was an assistant at the Jesuit headquarters in Rome for each assistancy; the assistant managed the required correspondence between Rome and the Jesuits throughout the world. Ignatius frequently corrected Jesuits who did not comply with his desires for frequent and detailed "primary letters" that could be shown to others, detailing the edifying works of the Jesuits. Ignatius also noted that these letters could include descriptions that could please and interest the patrons of the Jesuits, such as "information about anything that appears extraordinary, such as unknown animals and plants, their size and so forth" (*Letters*, p. 326). The admonition for correct letter writing and the need for information saw its fullest realization in the massive correspondence of Francis Xavier from Asia, as well as the important correspondence known as the "Letters from New France" in North America (1610–1791). Other Jesuits also wrote detailed annual letters, many of which still exist and provide invaluable ethnographic and historic accounts.

Although some individual Jesuits accepted contemporary stereotypes that degraded indigenous peoples, others such as Peter Claver (1581–1654) and Alfonso de Sandoval (d. 1652) worked to advance their dignity. Many other Jesuits transcended European expressions of Catholicism and provided invigorating and approved adaptations for expressing Christian belief. The first steps toward adaptation to non-European culture were taken by the proto-missionary of the Jesuit order Francis Xavier (1506–1552). Allesandro Valignano (1539–1606) followed and developed Xavier's efforts, insisting on language acquisition and knowledge of local culture for Jesuit missions. In South America, Roque González (1576–1628) delved deeply into language and culture and explored the distinction between what was essential in Catholicism and what were its European means of articulation. In the exploration of this distinction, the Jesuits' enterprise of missionary expansion anticipated today's contemporary questions regarding how various aspects of one culture may successfully interact and communicate with another.

[*See also* Exploration Texts; North America, *subentry on* Missionary Accounts; *and* Pacific, *subentry on* Missionary Accounts.]

BIBLIOGRAPHY

Alden, Dauril. *The Making of an Enterprise: The Society of Jesus in Portugal, Its Empire, and Beyond, 1540–1750.* Stanford, Calif.: Stanford University Press, 1996.

Bailey, Gauvin A. *Art on the Jesuit Missions in Asia and Latin America, 1542–1773*. Toronto: Toronto University Press, 1999.

Ignatius of Loyola. *The Constitutions of the Society of Jesus*. Translated by George Ganss. Saint Louis, Mo.: Institute of Jesuit Sources, 1970.

Ignatius of Loyola. *Letters of St. Ignatius of Loyola*. Translated by William J. Young. Chicago: Loyola University Press, 1959.

Ignatius of Loyola. *The Spiritual Exercises and Selected Works*. Translated by George Ganss. New York: Paulist Press, 1991.

Nobili, Roberto de. *Preaching Wisdom to the Wise: Three Treatises*. Translated by Anand Amaladass and Francis X. Clooney. Saint Louis, Mo.: Institute of Jesuit Sources, 2000.

Ricci, Matteo. *The True Meaning of the Lord of Heaven*. Translated by Douglas Lancashire and Peter Hu Kuo-chen. Saint Louis, Mo.: Institute of Jesuit Sources, 1985.

Schütte, Josef F. *Valignano's Mission Principles for Japan*. Translated by John J. Coyne. Saint Louis, Mo.: Institute of Jesuit Sources, 1980.

Thwaites, Reuben G., ed. *The Jesuit Relations and Allied Documents: Travels and Explorations of the Jesuit Missionaries in New France, 1610–1791*. 73 vols. Cleveland, Ohio: Burrows Bros., 1896–1901.

Xavier, Francis. *The Letters and Instructions of Francis Xavier*. Translated by M. Joseph Costelloe. Saint Louis, Mo.: Institute of Jesuit Sources, 1992.

MICHAEL W. MAHER, S.J.

Johnson, W. H., surveyor of India and explorer of Central Asia. We have no biographical data on Johnson other than what we can deduce from the article that he wrote for the Royal Geographical Society's journal in 1867. In 1865, he was attached to the Great Trigonometrical Survey of India. He was in charge of a party of the Kashmir series of the survey and left for the north from Dehra Dun via Leh in May. He crossed much the same territory that George W. Hayward did five years later—namely, first the Karakoram mountains, then the Kunlun—but his outward route was quite different. From Leh, Johnson moved west-northwest to the 19,500-foot Lumkang Pass, then as close to due north as the terrain permitted, crossing extensive upland plains at 17,300 and then 15,000 feet, as well as a series of high passes. Johnson surveyed and climbed three 22,000-foot Kunlun peaks: E57, E58, and E61, as designated by the survey. He conducted surveying and made geological observations throughout. He obtained permission from the khan of Khotan to visit the town— and he was the first Westerner to do so, arriving in September.

The following year, this khan, Khan Habibullah, was murdered by Yakub Beg, then ruler of Xinjiang. Johnson gave a detailed account of the town of Khotan: its field produce; its manufactured goods, including silks, carpets, and mulberry bark paper; and the characteristics of its army and currency. He described visits to several villages, all novel data for Westerners. Khotan was later a key site for Aurel Stein's archaeological work. Johnson resisted a career advancement when offered 300,000 rupees if he would assume the governorship of Yarkand. On his return, he initially followed a course later taken by Hayward, but then kept to the west via the Karakoram Pass (18,300 feet but, according to Johnson, "easy"). Aside from the villages at the start of the expedition, the route was uninhabited except for occasional Kirghiz nomads.

[*See also* Hayward, George W., *and* Stein, Aurel.]

BIBLIOGRAPHY
Johnson, W. H. "Report on His Journey to Ilchí, the Capital of Khotan, in Chinese Tartary." *Journal of the Royal Geographical Society* 37 (1867): 1–47.

DAVID SPENCER SMITH

Johnston, Keith (1844–1879), Scottish cartographer and explorer. One of the most accomplished geographers ever sent to explore Africa, Alexander Keith Johnston the Younger was born at Edinburgh, on November 23, 1844, the son of a distinguished father who ran an Edinburgh business specializing in the publication of atlases and reference works. The young Johnston worked for his father, then briefly for the rival firm of Stanford, studied German cartographical methods with Augustus Petermann, and then became a map curator at the Royal Geographical Society (RGS). His considerable geographical and cartographical writings included a study of the Nile problem when it was still uncertain where the river's sources lay. Johnston garnered practical experience as a surveyor for the Paraguayan government on the border with Brazil in 1873.

In 1878, Johnston was chosen to lead the only expedition mounted by the African Exploration Fund and set up by the RGS as Britain's response to King Leopold's Brussels Geographical Conference. Johnston was to find a route from the coast where businessman William Mackinnon was already attempting to have a road built, direct to the shores of Lake Malawi where Scottish missionaries were at work and on from there to Lake Tanganyika. The longitudes of both lakes needed to be established by such a competent observer. Johnston was to be accompanied by another Scot, Joseph Thomson.

John Kirk, British consul in Zanzibar, helped Johnston make meticulous arrangements. All seemed set fair but for the fact that Johnston found the young, brash Thomson unbearable as a companion and was taking steps to have him recalled as the expedition set out on May 19, 1879. By June 28, Johnston was dead, a victim of dysentery at a place called Behobeho, some 120 miles (194 kilometers) inland from Dar-es-Salaam.

Thomson buried his leader and, deciding to carry on the expedition, successfully traced the routes to and between the lakes; he thereby launched his career as an explorer. Johnston would be forgotten were it not for an excellent biography by James McCarthy, published in 2004. Johnston's grave at Behobeho seems to have disappeared, but his name now lives on as a notable geographer and martyr to the cause of African exploration.

[*See also* Brussels Geographical Conference; Nile River; *and* Thomson, Joseph.]

BIBLIOGRAPHY

McCarthy, James. *Journey into Africa: The Life and Death of Keith Johnston, Scottish Cartographer and Explorer (1844-1879).* Latheronwheel, Caithness, Scotland: Whittles, 2004.

Thomson, Joseph. *To the Central African Lakes and Back: The Narrative of the Royal Geographical Society's East Central African Expedition, 1878–1880.* 2 vols., London: Sampson Low, 1881.

ROY BRIDGES

Jolliet, Louis (1645–1700), Canadian explorer of the Mississippi River. Sixteenth-and early-seventeenth-century European maps of North America showed an erroneous drainage divide separating the Great Lakes basin from the Gulf of Mexico. It is not surprising, therefore, to find that French missionaries were convinced that a great river being described by western Indians and called by them "Messisipi" (Mississippi) must find its way to either the Atlantic Ocean or the Gulf of California. A concerted effort to explore the Indians' legendary great river came about as the result of a deliberate imperial expansionist policy implemented by the governor of New France in 1670.

Born near Quebec in 1645, Louis Jolliet, a well-educated fur trader with a capability in surveying and cartography, was chosen to lead an expedition to the upper Mississippi by way of Green Bay and the Fox and Wisconsin rivers. In October 1672, Jolliet left Quebec and traveled by birchbark canoe to the Straits of Mackinac, where he joined forces with the Jesuit missionary Father Jacques Marquette. Marquette was an accomplished linguist who had mastery of a number of Indian languages and zeal-ously wished to spread God's word to the nations known to live in the Mississippi valley. On May 17, 1673, Jolliet and Marquette departed in two canoes with five Indians paddling westward through the Straits of Mackinac, across upper Lake Michigan to Green Bay, and up the Fox River to portage to the Wisconsin River. Paddling down the Wisconsin they entered the Mississippi on June 17, 1673, to become the first white men to see the great river since Hernando de Soto's party more than a century before. Jolliet named the Mississippi the "Baude" to honor the governor of New France, Louis de Baude, the count of Frontenac, while Father Marquette chose to designate it the "Conception."

The expedition continued down the Mississippi River by paddling during the day and anchoring in the stream for safety at night. Establishing good relations with the Indians they encountered, they passed the mouths of the Missouri and the Ohio on their way south. Near the mouth of the Arkansas River the Indians were convincing in their assurances that the Mississippi continued on a southerly course to the sea, which both Jolliet and Marquette were certain was the Gulf of Mexico. The Indians also warned that they might meet other white men should they continue on that course. Not wishing to run the risk of capture by the Spanish, the small French party decided to terminate their exploration and return with the important news of their discoveries concerning the great navigable south-flowing river emptying into the Gulf of Mexico. On their return they wisely followed local Indian advice and turned up the Illinois River to a shortcut to Lake Michigan via the Chicago River.

After parting from Father Marquette at the Green Bay mission of Saint François Xavier, Jolliet, carrying his journal and maps, proceeded to Quebec by canoe. Late in the summer of 1674 disaster struck in the Saint Lawrence River rapids just west of Montreal, where Jolliet's canoe capsized. Two of his crewmen drowned and the chest containing his hard-won maps and journal was lost, with Jolliet himself barely escaping with his life. Upon his recovery, Jolliet, working from memory, produced an amazingly accurate though somewhat distorted map to accompany his report of the discovery of the Mississippi, which he named the "Baude." On his map Jolliet unequivocally showed the river flowing south to empty into the Gulf of Mexico.

A reversal of policy on the part of King Louis XIV led to retrenchment in New France, and there was no immediate follow-up on the Jolliet-Marquette exploratory probe to the Mississippi. Such a follow-up only came in 1683 when Cavelier de La Salle persuaded the king to grant him royal permission to establish a trade monopoly in the Illinois country in return for finding the mouth of the Mississippi River and establishing a harbor there for French ships. Although documentary evidence has not been found, it is reasonable to believe that La Salle was aware of Jolliet's discoveries and may even have met him at Fort Frontenac as he was returning to Montreal with his maps and journal in 1674. Jolliet continued to gain recognition as an explorer and cartographer and in 1697 he was appointed professor of hydrography at the College of Quebec. He died in 1700.

[*See also* La Salle, Cavelier de; Marquette, Jacques; *and* Soto, Hernando de.]

BIBLIOGRAPHY
Eifert, Virginia L. *Louis Jolliet, Explorer of Rivers*. New York: Dodd Mead, 1961.
Hamilton, Raphael N. *Marquette's Explorations: The Narratives Reexamined*. Madison: University of Wisconsin Press, 1970.
Parkman, Francis. *The Discovery of the Great West: La Salle*. Edited by William R. Taylor. New York: Holt, Rinehart and Winston, 1956. Reprint, Westport, Conn.: Greenwood Press, 1986.
Vachon, André. *Records of Our History: Dreams of Empire: Canada before 1700*. Ottawa: Public Archives of Canada, 1982.

LOUIS DE VORSEY

Junker, Wilhelm (1840–1892), Russian-born German explorer of equatorial Africa. Junker was born in Moscow to German parents on April 6, 1840. He attended medical school in Göttingen, Berlin, and Prague but practiced medicine only for a short time. After traveling to Iceland and Tunis, he moved to northeast equatorial Africa, where he resided continuously from 1875 to 1886. His first headquarters was Khartoum, from which he extensively explored in the Nile-Congo watershed, where he conducted his most important work. He proved that the Uele River was part of the Congo River drainage basin, and after four years living with the Niam-Niam, he provided a significant account of their ethnology. He wrote a book about them titled *With My Friends, the Cannibals* (Leipzig edition, 1926). While in the field, Junker also copiously collected plant and animal specimens, many of which were exhibited in museums in Berlin and Saint Petersburg.

With the Mahdist movement continuing to menace the British-controlled Sudan, Junker moved south in early 1884 to Lado, an isolated community in Equatoria Province, where its governor, Emin Pasha (Eduard Schnitzer), resided. Junker's primary concern was to return to Europe, and, beginning on January 2, 1886, he endured an arduous journey through Uganda, reaching Zanzibar at the end of the year. He continued on to Cairo, where he reported on Emin's plight in Equatoria, thus providing the first news of Emin in three years. A rescue expedition led by Henry Stanley was eventually mounted in 1887, and it reached Lado in 1889. Very little was actually known about Emin Pasha, and it was Junker who provided the best description of the man. His highly praised three-volume book, *Travels in Africa*, which presented details of his scientific work in Africa, was published in 1889–1891. He died in Saint Petersburg on February 13, 1892.

[*See also* Africa, *subentry on* Scientific Exploration; Emin Pasha; Schweinfurth, Georg; *and* Stanley, Henry.]

BIBLIOGRAPHY
Junker, Wilhelm. *Travels in Africa*. 3 vols. Translated by A. H. Keane. New York: Johnson Reprints, 1971.

SANFORD H. BEDERMAN

Jupiter. Jupiter is the largest of the planets in the solar system and the first of the gas giants beyond the asteroid belt. Due to Jupiter's size, early earthbound astronomers were able to discern a fair amount of detail of the planet, but it took the arrival of a series of space probes to truly reveal its beauty.

Despite the planet's immense distance from Earth, earthbound observers since ancient times have been able to track Jupiter's path across the heavens thanks to its enormous size. Galileo Galilei first observed the four major moons of Jupiter through his telescope on January 7, 1610. The four moons—Io, Europa, Ganymede, and Callisto—became known as the Galilean moons. Twenty years later, astronomers discovered a series of cloud belts crossing the gas giant. As the clarity of the optics increased, observers were able to pinpoint increasing details of these bands and identify particular regions of the atmosphere. On September 5, 1831, Samuel Heinrich Schwabe was the first to definitively identify the perpetual storm in the Jovian atmosphere called the Great Red Spot, a feature that can still be observed today. Through the nineteenth and twentieth centuries, Jupiter proved to be a particularly interesting target for earthbound observers as the state of the various bands were constantly in flux.

As the space age progressed, NASA engineers and scientists developed plans to explore the outer planets beyond Mars, including Jupiter. In 1965 Gary Flandro, an aerospace engineer with the NASA Jet Propulsion Laboratory in Pasadena, California, discovered that a rare planetary alignment was to occur in the 1970s that would allow a single spacecraft to explore Jupiter, Saturn, Uranus, and Neptune. This was named the Grand Tour. Precursors to these missions were the twin spacecraft *Pioneer 10* and *11*. These craft would not only explore both Jupiter and Saturn, but would also pave the way for the subsequent Grand Tour by observing the environment in which the vehicle would travel. Traveling to such a distant destination required advanced technology in such areas as power and automation, as well as determining the ability of a spacecraft to survive crossing the asteroid belt and the intense radiation of Jupiter.

Built by the American company TRW, *Pioneer 10* was launched on March 2, 1972, and *Pioneer 11* was launched on April 6, 1973. The Pioneer probes did indeed survive the asteroid belt as well as Jupiter's radiation, with *Pioneer 10* sending back the first of its three hundred images of Jupiter on December 3, 1973, followed by *Pioneer 11* a year later. Since the Pioneer probes were spin-stabilized for the sake of simplicity, the photos were not of the highest quality. However, they far surpassed earthbound observations and provided insight into the intricacies of Jupiter's atmosphere. Additional instruments probed the planet's magnetic field, gravitational field, and other characteristics of the gas giant. The two spacecraft also serve as humanity's emissary beyond the solar system. On board each craft is a plaque including a diagram of Earth's location in the solar system, the position of the Sun in the Milky Way galaxy, and images of a man and a woman. Although it is very unlikely the plaques will be discovered by extraterrestrial beings, they will exist longer than the Sun and the Earth themselves.

After a fierce budgetary battle, NASA permitted the follow-up probes *Voyager 1* and *2*. With *Voyager 2* actually launching first, on August 20, 1977, followed by *Voyager 1* on September 5, 1977, the two probes successfully arrived at Jupiter in 1979. While the two probes produced a treasure trove of information about the planet, scientists also made many fruitful observations of Jupiter's moons. This included confirmation of volcanoes on Io as well as detailed images of Europa's peculiar icy surface. Unlike the Pioneer missions, the Voyagers were three-axis-controlled, which provided a steady platform from which to image the planet and observe the clouds through ultraviolet and infrared light. Both spacecraft took approximately eighteen thousand pictures each during their Jovian encounter while also enabling scientists to make extensive discoveries, including the planets' interaction with the solar wind and cloud rotation. As with the Pioneer craft, the two Voyager spacecraft also carried a message from Earth, but this time on a more elaborate scale. Each craft contains a gold-plated disk that can be played with an enclosed mechanism. The disks include audio messages in various languages, sounds, and music, such as Chuck Berry's "Johnny B. Goode." Also included are 115 images to represent Earth.

The next probe to target Jupiter was the orbiter *Galileo*. Substantially delayed due the *Challenger* disaster, *Galileo* took flight from the shuttle's cargo bay on October 18, 1989. Typical of a deep space probe, the Galileo probe had both a high gain and a low gain antenna. A high gain antenna is typically used for high data rate return of information gathered by the spacecraft, while the low gain antenna provides a lower data return and the ability to receive commands from Earth. Unfortunately, after *Galileo* began its journey to Jupiter, the high gain antenna did not deploy completely, thus significantly reducing the spacecraft's ability to return data. Despite this constraint, throughout its eight-year observing period the spacecraft returned an array of observations about Jupiter and its moons. Unique to previous efforts to explore Jupiter, *Galileo* also contained a probe that was dropped from the main spacecraft and entered the Jovian atmosphere on December 7, 1995. Despite intense heat and pressure, the probe survived for 61.4 minutes and provided unique insights into various elements of the planet's atmosphere.

NASA has launched three additional missions with secondary objectives of observing Jupiter. Launched on October 10, 1990, *Ulysses* is a spacecraft that continues to study the properties of the solar environment. Engineers designed a mission that used the gravitational pull of Jupiter to send *Ulysses* out of the ecliptic plane of the solar system to study the polar regions of the Sun. The next visitor to Jupiter was the *Cassini* spacecraft bound for Saturn. Despite only passing by on its way to the ringed planet, *Cassini* took several thousand photographs of Jupiter with a closest approach on December 20, 2000. The New Horizons mission to Pluto will also take advantage of the gravitational pull of Jupiter to accelerate to its encounter with Pluto and beyond.

[*See also* Space Program, *subentry* American; and Space Shuttle, *subentry* American.]

BIBLIOGRAPHY

Dethloff, Henry C., and Ronald A. Schorn. *Voyager's Grand Tour: To the Outer Planets and Beyond*. Washington, D.C.: Smithsonian Books, 2003.

Kraemer, Robert S. *Beyond the Moon: Golden Age of Planetary Exploration, 1971–1978*. Washington, D.C.: Smithsonian Books, 2000.

Wolverton, Mark. *The Depths of Space: The Story of the Pioneer Planetary Probes*. Washington, D.C.: Joseph Henry Press, 2004.

CHRISTOPHER J. KRUPIARZ

K

Kane, Elisha (1820–1857), American physician, traveler, and Arctic explorer. Born into a wealthy Philadelphia family, as a young man Elisha Kent Kane contracted rheumatic fever, which often left him gravely ill and ultimately damaged his heart. Commissioned assistant surgeon in the U.S. Navy, he spent the years 1843–1849 in almost continual travel and adventure, covering some 11,000 miles (17,700 kilometers) in journeys that took him around the world.

In 1849, Kane volunteered to serve as surgeon on an expedition mounted by the navy and businessman Henry Grinnell to search for Sir John Franklin. The brigs *Advance* and *Rescue* sailed in May 1850, making for the southwest corner of Devon Island. While they were in the area, some seamen from a British naval expedition found the graves of three of Franklin's men who had died in 1846. With freeze-up in September, the *Advance* and the *Rescue*, unlike most ships in their condition, began to return home. In the grip of ice, they were carried, about five miles (eight kilometers) a day, into Baffin Bay. Most of the crew suffered from scurvy, and Kane frantically tried to introduce fresh meat and other antiscorbutics into their diet. The ice finally released them just above the Arctic Circle, and by the fall of 1851 they were back in New York. Although he did not lead the expedition, thanks to public lectures and a very popular book, it became indelibly associated with Kane's name.

In early summer of 1853, Kane embarked with the second Grinnell Expedition, this time with a crew of seventeen officers and men under his own command in the *Advance*. He was determined to reach the "open polar sea," where he still hoped to encounter Franklin, by going directly north through Smith Sound at the head of Baffin Bay. By September, they had reached what was to become known as Kane Basin, where the ship was frozen in, never to budge again. An observatory was built on shore, and several sledging expeditions managed to survey all of Kane Basin. One of these sledging parties got as far north as 81°22′, from which point its leader reported to Kane that there was open water as far north as he could see. We now know that such open patches, or *polynyas*, occur regularly in the Arctic Ocean, but they are seasonal and highly transitory.

That winter was exceedingly uncomfortable, with the stresses of darkness, extreme cold, diminishing supplies, and the strain of dealing with the "seceders," a group of men who abandoned the ship and tried to make their way south, only to return to the *Advance*, thoroughly beaten, several months later. Through these ordeals, Kane demonstrated remarkable physical and emotional strength and remained unmistakably in command. On their epic escape from the frozen ship (May–July 1855) he kept the party largely intact and delivered them to Upernavik, Greenland.

After a hero's welcome in New York, Kane began work on his account of the expedition, but his health again began to fail. Intending to seek rest in France, he took passage to Europe in the fall of 1856, but was so weak and debilitated that he abandoned the European trip and sailed to Cuba, dying there on February 16, 1857.

Although the "open polar sea" proved a chimera, Kane's accomplishments were substantial. He explored and mapped Kane Basin and discovered Humboldt Glacier and Kennedy Channel, which would become the "American route to the pole," followed by Charles Francis Hall, Adolphus Greely, Robert Peary, and others. He learned willingly from the Inuit, and his adoption of their diet kept his expeditions relatively free from scurvy. Kane's genuine humanity, his larger-than-life exploits, a fine writing style, and his romantic involvement with the beautiful Margaret Fox (a famous medium) made him one of the most famous men of his day.

[*See also* Franklin, John, *and* Hall, Charles Francis.]

BIBLIOGRAPHY

Corner, George W. *Doctor Kane of the Arctic Seas*. Philadelphia: Temple University Press, 1972.

Hayes, I. I. *An Arctic Boat Journey in the Autumn of 1854.* Boston: Brown, Taggard, and Chase, 1860. Available digitally in the University of Michigan's Making of America series.

Kane, E. K. *Arctic Explorations: The Second Grinnell Expedition in Search of Sir John Franklin, 1853, '54, '55.* Philadelphia: Childs and Peterson, 1856. Reprint. Chicago: Lakeside Press, 1996.

Kane, E. K. *The U. S. Grinnell Expedition in Search of Sir John Franklin: A Personal Narrative.* New York: Harper, 1853.

ROBERT W. KARROW JR.

Kashevarov, A. F.

Kashevarov, A. F. (1809–1866), one of the outstanding Creole explorers of Russian America—a fine example of what could be achieved by a gifted Creole commoner, even under the harsh limitations of serf-holding Russia. Alexandr Filippovich Kashevarov was born in Russian America and rose steadily in the navy, eventually becoming a brigadier general.

His father, Filipp Artamanovich Kashevarov, was a serf of the Kursk merchant Nikolay Golikov, who was one of those Russians who decided in 1805 to remain in America. Filipp Kashevarov married a local woman, and their son, together with two other Creole boys (Chechenev and Netsvetov), was sent in 1822 to Saint Petersburg for his education, the Russian American Company having prevailed on Nikolay Golikov to release him from serfdom. A. F. Kashevarov graduated in 1831 from the Baltic Navigational School and entered the service of the company.

Kashevarov began studying the polar regions of Russian America in 1838, sailing from Novoarkhangel'sk with the brig *Polifem*. He had Captain Beechey's chart, and he sometimes commented on its accuracy. His journal also contains much geographic and ethnographic information, so the reader finds in it a vivid picture of the land, with specifics of its ecology. This was in part because Kashevarov carried with him an Eskimo interpreter, Utuktak, who not only drew an accurate map but also found out about the makeup of settlements and about tribal groupings. Kashevarov provides the first information about the dwellings and summer tents of the Northwest Alaskan Eskimo, their manner of living, and their trade, particularly with northeastern Siberia.

His observations about the relationship of man with nature sound curiously modern. For example, he expresses great concern about the changes that he observed in the lifestyle of the Eskimo, and he reflects on the unhappy fate that would await them if they were alienated from their traditional ways by the pressures of European civilization.

Kashevarov's conclusions were first published in articles between 1840 and 1846, while his full journal was published in 1879. He remained virtually unknown outside Russia, and within the country he was for a long time appreciated only by the researcher L. A. Zagoskin, who used Kashevarov's materials in compiling a map that included the sketch by the interpreter Utuktak.

[*See also* Expeditions, World Exploration, *subentry on* Russia; Inuit; *and* Russian American Company.]

BIBLIOGRAPHY

Vanstone, James W., ed., and David H. Kraus, trans. *A. F. Kashevarov's Coastal Explorations in Northwest Alaska, 1838.* Chicago: Field Museum of Natural History, 1977.

ALEXEY POSTNIKOV

Kelsey, Henry

Kelsey, Henry (1667?–1724), English explorer of Canada. Henry Kelsey's main claim to fame lies in the journey he made in 1690–1692 from York Factory on Hudson Bay across the Canadian prairies. Possibly born in 1667 the son of a Greenwich mariner, John Kelsey, he entered the service of the Hudson's Bay Company as an apprentice in 1684. One difficulty with a birth date of 1667 is that he was described twenty-one years later, in 1688, by Governor George Geyer at York Factory, Hudson Bay, where he was stationed, as "the Boy Henry Kelsey . . . a very active Lad." More significantly, Geyer went on to note that he delighted in the company of Indians, "being never better pleased than when he is travelling amongst them," and in 1689 he journeyed along the coast north of York Factory with a young Indian companion.

The following year Kelsey left York Factory on an altogether more extraordinary journey, one that took him deep into the western interior, but that never received full recognition until manuscript accounts of his wanderings surfaced in the 1920s. These show that Kelsey left York Factory in June 1690 with the Cree Indians, returning to the interior after bringing furs down to the bayside. Kelsey explained his intention and his mood in a rhyming prologue to his journal:

> Then up ye River I with heavy heart
> Did take my way and from all English part
> To live amongst ye Natives of this place
> If God permits me for one two years space
> The Inland Country of Good report hath been
> By Indians but by English yet not seen. . . .

Kelsey traveled throughout with Indians, and since he had no instruments, the route of his wanderings is difficult to establish. He seems first to have canoed with his Cree companions to the Saskatchewan River, that great artery of the Indian trade, and then to have gone on foot to Canada's northern plains. In the summer of 1691, Kelsey struck out in a different direction, southwest across the Saskatchewan and Red Deer rivers, and then on to the great plains of western Canada. Kelsey was the first European to reach this area, thick with herds of buffalo, and with an Indian population far more numerous than any Hudson's Bay man had encountered. Here Kelsey met the Sioux-speaking Assiniboine of the plains and probably also Blackfoot before he returned to York Factory in the summer of 1692.

Kelsey's journey was a remarkable achievement, one based on his ability to speak Cree and to live and travel safely with the Indians (he almost certainly had an Indian wife as a companion and helpmate). He was the first white man to visit the northern plains, to see the buffalo herds and the grizzly bear; but for long his discoveries were obscured by the failure of the Hudson's Bay Company to publish or even preserve his notes. Kelsey had penetrated much farther west than the French, who were following the river routes out of Lake Superior. In the years before Kelsey's journey, Daniel Greysolon Dulhut (or Duluth) had reached Lake Mille Lacs in modern Minnesota, while Jacques de Noyon perhaps got as far as Lake of the Woods, but there French expansion halted until after the end of war in Europe in 1713. The French trader-explorers had fallen far short of Kelsey, but this is clearer now than it was at the time. No evidence of Kelsey's explorations appeared on contemporary maps, and his journey was a lone and soon-forgotten feat in an era when the company's servants were reluctant to venture away from the familiar surroundings of their bayside posts.

Kelsey remained in the service of the Hudson's Bay Company for the rest of his working career. In 1717 he became governor at York Factory in succession to James Knight, with whom he had quarreled, and the next year was made governor over all the company's bay posts before retiring in 1722. In his last years he turned once more to exploration, this time along the coast to the north of Churchill. In 1719 and 1721 he sailed north himself, and in 1720 and 1722 he sent sloops north but without accompanying them. The main objective of these voyages was to open up the Inuit trade in whalebone and oil, as well as to glean information about the deposits of copper rumored to lie north of Churchill. In 1721 he came across relics of James Knight's discovery ex-

pedition, but made no attempt to mount a proper search for the lost vessels.

Kelsey died in Greenwich in 1724, leaving behind a wife, three children, and two houses. Only after the belated discovery of his journal in the early twentieth century was his true status as a pathfinder across the plains of western Canada recognized.

[*See also* Knight, James, *and* North America, *subentry on* Indigenous Guides.]

BIBLIOGRAPHY

Davies, K. G. "Henry Kelsey." In *Dictionary of Canadian Biography*, vol. 2, pp. 307–315. Toronto: University of Toronto Press, 1969.

Doughty, A. G., and Chester Martin, eds. *The Kelsey Papers*. Ottawa: Public Archives of Canada and Public Record Office of Northern Ireland, 1929.

GLYNDWR WILLIAMS

Kerguelen, Yves-Joseph de (1737–1797), a lieutenant in the French king's navy. Yves-Joseph de Kerguelen-Trémarec first effected two surveys in the Iceland seas. His subsequent project of exploring the southern lands of the Indian Ocean was commended to Louis XV by Georges-Louis Leclerc, Comte de Buffon, and Charles de Brosses. Supported by governor François-Julien du Dresnay, Chevalier Desroches, and intendant Pierre Poivre, Kerguelen sailed on January 16, 1772, from Port-Louis, Île de France, on *La Fortune*, accompanied by *Le Gros-Ventre*, captained by Louis-François d'Alleno de Saint-Allouarn. On February 13, after battling rough, cold seas, he sighted land at 49°30′ S, 69°30′ E. Cap Saint Louis and Baie du Lion Marin were reconnoitered, and Charles-Max de Boisguehenneuc took possession, in the name of the king, of what are now called the Kerguelen Islands. The only creatures encountered were penguins, seals, and sea lions.

On February 16, the ships lost contact in the fog. Alleno drifted toward the coast of New Holland, and Kerguelen limped back into Port-Louis. The brilliant account he gave of his discovery led Poivre to extol to the French minister of the marine "the resources of this new France at the extremity of the globe."

Despite adverse reports, the king promoted Kerguelen, ordering the pursuit of the exploration of what he had found. The new administrators of Île de France having refused to help, Kerguelen provisioned in Bourbon in October 1773 and sailed south on his unmaneuverable new ship *Le Roland* with its consort *L'Oiseau*, followed by *La Dauphine*, which was designed for coastal survey. Encountering bad weather while his highly trained staff was at logger-

ARRÊT
DU CONSEIL D'ÉTAT
DU ROI,

Qui fupprime un Ouvrage intitulé: Relation de deux
Voyages dans les mers Auftrales & des Indes,
faits par M. de Kerguelen en 1771, &c.

Du 23 Mai 1783.

Extrait des Regiftres du Confeil d'État.

L E ROI étant informé que dans un Ouvrage intitulé:
*Relation de deux Voyages dans les mers Auftrales & des
Indes, faits en 1771, 1772, 1773 & 1774, par M. de
Kerguelen, en un volume in-8.°* imprimé chez *Knapen, Imprimeur
à Paris*, l'Auteur s'eft permis des critiques indécentes fur le
Gouvernement & fur le Jugement du Confeil de guerre qui
eft intervenu contre lui en 1775, des invectives contre
plufieurs perfonnes, & d'y rapporter des lettres qui compro-
mettent ceux qui les ont écrites; Sa Majefté auroit reconnu
que cet Ouvrage, qui porte tous les caractères d'un Libelle,

Yves-Joseph de Kerguelen. Arret du conseil d'état, suppressing a work by Kerguelen, 1783. This document,
which calls for the suppression of one of Kerguelen's works
about his exploration, reminds us that many explorers had
to contend with fierce opposition from their rivals and indeed sometimes from governments. COURTESY THE NEW-
BERRY LIBRARY, CHICAGO

heads, Kerguelen approached the main island of the
Kerguelens by the northern islets. He ordered the
reconnaissance of Cap Français and of the neighboring Baie de l'Oiseau, and he ordered the renewal
of the deed claiming the land for France.

Daunted by the bad weather and the ill health of
his crew, Kerguelen repaired to Madagascar. On his
return to France, his enemies accused him of various
misdemeanors; he was court-martialed for having
failed to abide by his instructions and was imprisoned. James Cook, who surveyed Kerguelen Island
briefly—naming Christmas Harbour on December
25, 1776—referred to it as "The Island of Desolation"
(Beaglehole, p. 43). [See color plate 43 in this volume.] But time has vindicated Kerguelen, whose discovery of the archipelago in the southern Indian

Ocean has provided France with a base for strategic
and scientific control.

[*See also* Brosses, Charles de; Cook, James; Indian
Ocean; *and* Poivre, Pierre.]

BIBLIOGRAPHY

Beaglehole, J. C., ed. *The Journals of Captain James Cook on
His Voyages of Discovery: The Voyage of the Resolution and
Discovery, 1776–1780.* Cambridge, U.K.: Cambridge Uni-
versity Press for the Hakluyt Society, 1967.

Kerguelen-Trémarec, Yves-Joseph de. *Relation de deux voyages
dans les mers australes et des Indes faits en 1771, 1772, 1773,
et 1774 par M. de Kerguelen, commandant des vaisseaux du
Roi le "Berrier," la "Fortune," le "Gros-Ventre," le "Rolland,"
"l'Oiseau," et la "Dauphine," ou Extrait du journal de sa navigation pour la découverte des Terres Australes et pour la vér-
ification d'une nouvelle route proposée pour abréger
d'environ huit cents lieues la traversée d'Europe à la Chine.*
Paris, 1782. Reprint. *L'invitation au voyage.* Rennes,
France: La Découvrance, 2000.

HUGUETTE LY-TIO-FANE PINEO
MADELEINE LY-TIO-FANE

Khabarov, Erofey Pavlovich

Khabarov, Erofey Pavlovich (c. 1610–after
1667), Russian *zemleprokhodets* (route finder) and
explorer of the Amur River. Born to a northern European Russian merchant family in Sol'vychegodsk,
Khabarov (nicknamed "Svyatitsky") traveled to Siberia for trade. He settled along the Kirenga River,
constructed a water mill, and plowed about sixty
hectares. Yakutsk *voevoda* (military governor) Vasily
Golovin ruled Khabarov's activities illegal, confiscated his property, and imprisoned him. In 1645,
Khabarov was released to explore and conquer the
Amur River region.

Information about the Amur came from Vasily
Poyarkov, who traveled there via the Lena, Aldan,
Uchur, Bryanta, Umlekan, and Zeya rivers, beginning in 1643 with 132 men. Poyarkov returned to
Yakutsk via the Maya, Aldan, and Lena rivers in 1646
with only twenty men. Poyarkov's report cited *Knyaz'
Bogdoy* (Prince Bogdoy), whose domain was south
of the Amur. "Bogdoy" apparently refers to the Manchu *bogdokhan*—the "Saintly Overlord" or "Great
Khan." Poyarkov believed that the region could be
taken by Russia.

In 1649, Khabarov, with seventy men, claimed the
Amur region. They built *ostrogs* (wooden forts), collected *yasak* (fur tax), and helped peasants from European Russia begin farming. In 1650, Khabarov
met the governor of Yakutsk, D. A. Frantsebakov,
who ordered him to send envoys to the Chinese
bogdoy (the ruler of Mukden) offering Russian sovereignty. If the bogdoy refused, Khabarov's orders

were to conquer the bogdoy's state. Khabarov later learned that the ruler was a vassal of the Chinese emperor.

During fighting between Russians and Dahurs, the Chinese remained neutral, stating that their ruler forbade them from fighting Russians. The following year, however, Chinese regular forces of 600 men, accompanied by 1,500 native Juchers, attacked the Russians. On March 24, 1652, Khabarov crushed them near Achansk *ostrog*. That summer Khabarov charted the Amur to the Ussuri River.

In 1653 the tsar's official Dmitry Ivanovich Zinov'ev arrived at the Amur, announcing its incorporation into Russia. He had sent an embassy under T. I. Chicherin to the Manchu ruler, but the Dahurs accompanying the embassy killed the Russians. For Khabarov the August meeting with Zinov'ev, who planned to pay and honor Khabarov, was disastrous. Khabarov's men submitted complaints about him. Khabarov quarreled with Zinov'ev, lost his booty, and was sent in disgrace to Moscow. An inquiry proved Khabarov innocent of most charges; much of his booty was returned. Khabarov became a *boyarskie deti* (a junior gentry rank) and governor of lands near the Lena River. One further mention of Khabarov appears in the official records: in 1667 he applied to Tobol'sk governor H. I. Godunov to be sent to the Amur River. His request was denied.

[*See also* Golovnin, Vasily; Poyarkov, Vasily; *and* Siberia.]

BIBLIOGRAPHY

Coxe, William. *Account of the Russian Discoveries between Asia and America to Which Are Added the Conquest of Siberia and the History of the Transactions and Commerce between Russia and China.* London: Printed by J. Nichols for T. Cadell, 1780.

Makarova, Raisa V. *Russians on the Pacific, 1743–1799.* Translated and edited by Richard A. Pierce and Alton S. Donnelly. Kingston, Ontario: Limestone Press, 1975.

Safronov, F. G. *Erofey Pavlovich Khabarov.* Khabarovsk: Khabarovskoe, 1956.

ALEXEY POSTNIKOV

Khedivial Exploration. The roots of Khedive Ismā'īl's (r. 1863–1879) explorations and African empire go back to his grandfather Muhammad Ali's (r. 1805–1848) conquest of the northern Sudan, which began in 1820. Muhammad Ali sought slave recruits for his army, gold, and the destruction of a renegade faction of Mamluks who had fled upriver. With one foot already planted in the Arabian Hijaz, consolidating his grip on the African coast of the Red Sea would put him in control of pilgrimage routes to Mecca and their trade. An insignificant village at the juncture of the Blue and White Niles, Khartoum, became the capital of his new province.

By the mid-1830s, the geographical societies springing up in Europe were pressing anew for a solution to the ancient mystery of the central African sources of the White Nile. Thus when Muhammad Ali, ever in quest of gold, dispatched a fleet under Salim Qapudan south from Khartoum to search for the sources of the White Nile in 1839, the Royal Geographical Society of London contributed £50 to the venture. Salim Qapudan's three expeditions between 1839 and 1842 hacked their way through dense blocks of floating vegetation known as the *sudd*. Two of the expeditions reached the future site of Gondokoro (a thousand miles [1,609 kilometers] south of Khartoum, and nearly opposite present-day Juba). J. P. d'Arnaud Bey collected scientific data while accompanying all three expeditions.

Twenty years later, in 1863, Khedive Ismā'īl ascended the Egyptian throne and explorers John Speke and James Grant made it through to Gondokoro from the East African coast. There they met Samuel Baker and his wife Florence, who thereupon headed south to reach the lake they would christen Albert.

Ismā'īl, who had studied in Paris, proudly declared that Egypt was now a part of Europe. Two of his many initiatives were bound up with his sponsorship of African exploration and creation of an empire, extending down the Red Sea coast to Somalia and up the White Nile as far as the central African lakes. The first innovation was the creation of a general staff for the Egyptian army; the second was the founding of the Khedivial Geographical Society.

The khedive named former Union Army general Charles P. Stone chief of staff of the Egyptian army, recruiting about fifty other American Civil War veterans—both Northern and Southern officers—to serve under him. From Stone's headquarters in the citadel overlooking Cairo, he organized several military schools, but his most notable achievement was organizing the reconnaissance and mapping expeditions that half a dozen or so Americans and an Egyptian or two led between 1873 and 1876. These expeditions crisscrossed the desert from the Red Sea to the Nile and west as far as the newly conquered province of Darfur.

It was exploration farther south, however, that caught the public eye, for it was there that the answer to the age-old riddle of the sources of the White Nile lay. In 1869 Ismā'īl hired Samuel Baker to push Egyptian rule southward as far as Lake Albert and

Lake Victoria, open the lakes to navigation, suppress the slave trade, and foster legitimate commerce. In this new Equatorial Province, Baker's expedition hacked its way through to Gondokoro in 1871, pushed on into what is now Uganda as far as Masindi, and proclaimed an Egyptian protectorate over Unyoro. But King Kabarega of Unyoro forced him to retreat, leaving frontier outposts at Fatiko and Foweira.

Charles "Chinese" Gordon took over as governor of Equatorial Province in 1872. In the next four years he opened Lake Albert to steam navigation and brought Unyoro and part of Uganda briefly under Egyptian rule, planting a garrison at Niamyango on the Nile, only sixty miles (97 kilometers) from Lake Victoria. Among Gordon's Western lieutenants it was Charles Chaillé-Long who made the most notable discovery—Lake Ibrahim (christened for Khedive Ismā'īl's father, but now known as Lake Kyoga)—while exploring the Nile between Lake Victoria and Lake Albert.

In 1875 Ismā'īl founded the Khedivial Geographical Society (KGS), following the example of such geographical societies as those of Paris (1821), Berlin (1826), London (1830), and New York (1851). Like its Western counterparts in this age of imperialism, the KGS spoke both of promoting the commercial and industrial interests of its home country and of advancing the noble cause of science by exploring and cataloging unknown lands. The German explorer Georg Schweinfurth served as the first president, after which General Stone took over for a number of years. Most of the initial three hundred members were Westerners, about evenly divided between residents of Alexandria and of Cairo. Through lectures and publications, the KGS disseminated the new knowledge of Africa that Egyptian and other explorations were producing.

The culminating scientific achievement of the khedivial explorations was summarized in the General Map of Africa, which Colonel Samuel H. Lockett produced in 1877 under the auspices of Stone's general staff. Ten feet wide and sixteen feet high and displaying around seven thousand place names, this masterpiece was probably the best map of Africa for its day. The density of detail for the lands of the Egyptian empire reflects the achievements of khedivial explorers and surveyors, in contrast to the many large blanks shown elsewhere on this continental map.

Ironically, the exploration and imperial expansion under Khedive Ismā'īl came at the very time Egypt itself was gradually succumbing to European imperialism. The British occupation of Egypt in 1882 followed speedily on national bankruptcy, the deposition of Ismā'īl, and the Urabi revolution, and shifted Egypt clearly from the category of colonizer to that of colonized. After the fall of Khartoum to the forces of Muhammad Ahmad the Mahdi in 1885, the British forced Egypt to evacuate the Sudan. The age of Egyptian-sponsored exploration and empire was over even as competing European powers were about to enter the most intense phase of their scramble for Africa. Not until 1934 was the Egyptian government able to publish the fine General Map of Africa that its general staff had produced back in 1877.

[*See also* Baker, Samuel; Chaillé-Long, Charles; Gordon, Charles; Grant, James Augustus; Schweinfurth, Georg; Speke, John Hanning; *and* Stone, Charles.]

BIBLIOGRAPHY
Hill, Richard. *Egypt in the Sudan, 1820–1881.* London and New York: Oxford University Press, 1959.
Morehead, Alan. *The White Nile.* New York: Harper and Brothers, 1960.

Donald Malcolm Reid

Kingsley, Mary (1862–1900), British woman who traveled extensively in coastal West Africa. Mary Kingsley was born on October 13, 1862, in Islington, England, the daughter of George and Mary Bailey Kingsley. Her father was a physician and traveler, and two of her uncles, Henry and Charles Kingsley, were well-known writers. At just thirty-eight years of age, Kingsley died of enteric fever on June 3, 1900, in Simonstown, South Africa, where she was working as a nurse during the Boer War. As she wished, she was buried at sea near Cape Point.

Her earliest years were spent taking care of her invalid mother and sickly brother while her father was away on frequent trips. She received little formal education (that was reserved for her brother) but read most of the books in her father's extensive library. When she was thirty years old, both of her parents died and her brother moved away, freeing Kingsley to make a life for herself. She decided to travel and began by making a short trip to the Canary Islands. Having survived that experience, she made plans for a longer trip to West Africa in order to study "fish and fetishes," as she described her goal of learning more about the region's natural history and the religious beliefs of the indigenous people. Both had been interests of her father, and she saw her objectives as a continuation of his work. After six months of travel in the Congo region, she returned to

England with a collection of African insects and fish and with a love for independent study and exploration in the wilderness.

Kingsley embarked on a second trip to West Africa in 1894, this one lasting almost a year. This time she headed up the Ogowe River into the French Congo, then north through unexplored jungles to the Rembwé River, and back to the coast. She brought back to the British Museum one new genus and six new species of fish, and her explorations also opened many new ethnographic insights into the local African tribes. Before leaving Africa to return home, she managed one more accomplishment: climbing Mount Cameroon (13,353 feet, or 4,070 meters) via its southeast face. She was apparently the first white person to make the ascent by that route. Upon her return to England, she became a politically active voice for the native people of Africa, pointing out in numerous lectures and articles how they had been damaged by both missionaries and colonialism.

In addition to her lectures and articles, Kingsley published two books about her expeditions, one for the popular audience and the other more scientifically oriented. She wrote in a light, self-deprecating style that belied the danger and significance of her expeditions. While her prose makes for entertaining reading, one has only to look beyond the colorful and humorous descriptions of her experiences to appreciate the hair-raising, life-threatening situations that she encountered. More so than many explorers of her time, Kingsley immersed herself in the everyday activities of exploration. She became adept at trading with the natives and lived with them in their villages at times, eating the same food they did. She became expert at paddling the Ogowe canoes, a skill that permitted her to take off on her own when she wished. She traveled on foot through mangrove swamps, dense forests, and had close encounters with wild creatures such as crocodiles, leopards, elephants, hippopotamus, and even leeches. Kingsley came to love Africa and its people deeply, asserting that she felt more at home there than back in England. She had planned a third expedition, but her plans were interrupted by the Boer War, during which she died.

[*See also* Women Explorers.]

BIBLIOGRAPHY

Frank, Katherine. *A Voyager Out: The Life of Mary Kingsley*. Boston: Houghton Mifflin, 1986.
Kingsley, Mary. *Travels in West Africa: Congo Français, Corisco, and Cameroons*. London: Macmillan, 1897. Reprint. Washington, D.C.: Adventure Classics/National Geographic, 2002.

PATRICIA GILMARTIN

On Being Prepared

This passage catches the laconic tone of Mary Kingsley's writings; she may sound boastful, but in fact she was accomplished in all the everyday arts of the traveler, among which was the need to be constantly ready to defend oneself.

The best form of knife is the bowie, with a shallow half moon cut out of the back at the point end, and the depression sharpened to a cutting edge. A knife is essential, because after wading neck deep in a swamp your revolver is neither use nor ornament until you have had time to clean it. But the chances are you may go across Africa, or live years in it, and require neither. It is just the case of the gentleman who asked if one required a revolver in Carolina? and was answered: "You may be here one year and you may be here two and never want it, but when you do want it, you'll want it very bad."

—Mary Kingsley, *Travels in West Africa* (London, 1897)

Kino, Eusebio

Kino, Eusebio (1645–1711), Italian explorer of Baja California, Sonora (Mexico), and Arizona. Born in Segno, Tirol, to Italian parents, and baptized on August 10, 1645 (his exact date of birth is not known), Eusebio Francisco Kino was educated at Jesuit schools, first in Trento and then at the University of Ingolstadt in Germany, where he excelled in mathematics, astronomy, and cartography. In 1665 he became an aspirant of the Society of Jesus, and in 1681 was assigned as a priest to New Spain, where he wrote *Exposición Astronómica de el Cometa* in 1683. Thereafter he devoted himself to the life of a frontier missionary.

In 1683 Kino was sent with Admiral Isidro de Atondo y Antillón to establish a settlement in Baja (or Lower) California, an arid, isolated territory thought to be an island separated by sea from the Mexican mainland. Kino explored Baja California to the Pacific coast, where as a sharp observer of natural phenomena he noted some striking blue abalone shells. Supply problems caused the Atondo expedition to fail in its efforts to found a mission,

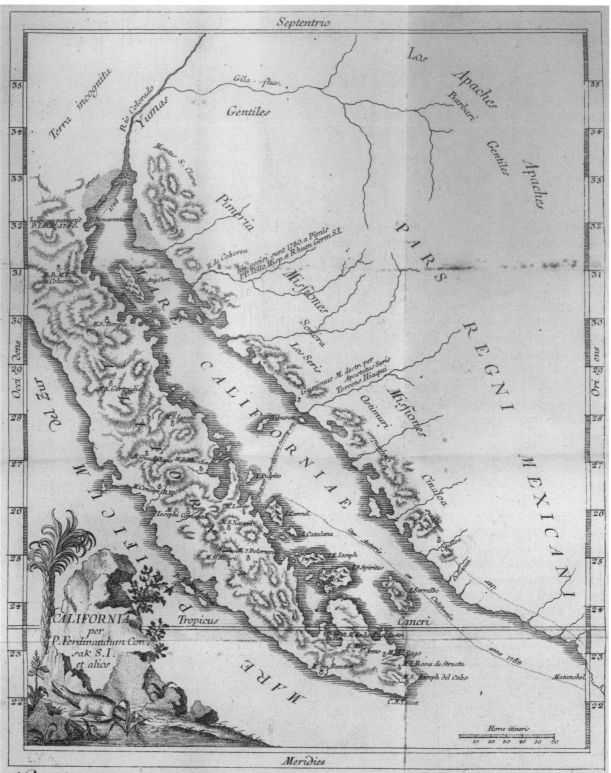

Eusebio Kino. Map from Jakob Baegert's *Nachrichten von der amerikanischen Halbinsel Californien* (Mannheim, 1772). This map, by the Jesuit Ferdinand Consag, shows the peninsula of Baja California as Kino had determined it to be around 1700, putting an end to the concept of "California as an island." COURTESY THE NEWBERRY LIBRARY, CHICAGO

and not until 1697 was one established in Baja California (at Loreto). In 1687 Kino was reassigned to Pimería Alta on the opposite "mainland," where he built the mission of Nuestra Señora de los Dolores as his headquarters. Along the Sonora and other rivers, on into what is now southern Arizona, Kino developed rosaries of way stations and missions, including the famed San Xavier del Bac near Tucson. Much loved for his care and respect, he introduced new practices of agriculture and animal husbandry to the Pima Indians and other tribes; and during more than forty journeys he surveyed and mapped the vast territory.

Early in his northwesterly explorations from Dolores, Kino noted that the Sea of California narrowed, giving clear views of land on the other side. In 1698 he climbed the hill of Santa Clara, and both with a telescope and with the naked eye saw Baja California and the mainland joined by a land bridge. But he was still not absolutely certain. Then in 1699, near the confluence of the Gila and Colorado rivers, he visited the Yuma Indians, whose gifts included beautiful blue shells the like of which he had seen only on the Pacific coast of Baja California. A similar gift in March 1700, and finally a clear sighting on October 7, 1700, satisfied him that the mainland and Baja California were separated only by the Colorado River. In 1701 Kino forwarded to Mexico a report and a map showing California as a peninsula. This map soon found its way to Europe and was published in France in 1705, but many leagues of forbidding desert at the head of the Gulf of California prevented Kino from testing his hypothesis. He died on March 15, 1711, while dedicating a chapel at Magdelena, without having proved his view conclusively; and much of the eighteenth century would pass before the island myth was totally demolished.

Within the discipline of his faith, Kino's sound reasoning and keen observation typified the mode of scientific thought characteristic of the Enlightenment, challenging the myths and extravagant imaginings of previous centuries.

[*See also* California, Island of.]

BIBLIOGRAPHY

Bolton, Herbert Eugene, ed. and trans. *Kino's Historical Memoir of Pimería Alta: A Contemporary Account of the Beginnings of California, Sonora, and Arizona, by Father Eusebio Francisco Kino, S.J., 1683–1711.* 2 vols. Cleveland, Ohio: Arthur H. Clark Co., 1919. Reprint, 1 vol., Berkeley: University of California Press, 1948. Reprint. New York: Ames, 1976.

Burrus, Ernest J. *Kino and Manje, Explorers of Sonora and Arizona . . .* Rome and St. Louis, Mo.: Jesuit Historical Institute and St. Louis University, 1971.

DORA BEALE POLK

Knight, James

Knight, James (d. 1719/20), English trader in Canada. Neither the place nor date of James Knight's birth is known. The first recorded mention of him comes in 1676 when he entered the service of the Hudson's Bay Company as a shipwright. His forceful personality soon gained him promotion, and from 1682 to 1700 he held senior positions as factor, or governor, in Hudson Bay. From 1700 to 1714, at a time of war when the company had only one post in the bay, Knight lived in England where he became a stockholder in the company and a member of its governing committee. In 1714 he was sent once more to Hudson Bay as governor to receive the surrender of York Factory from the French and to revive the company's trade. The journals he kept for the next four years contain full, if rambling, explanations of his plans for the expansion of trade and for the discovery of the Strait of Anian or Northwest Passage. Knight was confident that the elusive waterway would lead to a land of gold far to the northwest, rumors of which had reached him in England.

Knight's first attempt to reach this El Dorado of the north was to be by land, and in 1715 he sent William Stuart inland with a band of Cree and with a "Northern Indian" (Chipewyan) slave woman, Thanadelthur, as a guide. Stuart was away for almost a year, and after suffering great hardships he returned claiming that he had traveled 1,000 miles (1,600 kilometers) northwest from York Factory and had reached latitude 67° N. Although this was probably an overestimate, he was certainly the first European to cross the Barren Lands and reach perhaps as far as Great Slave Lake. Obsessed by reports of "yellow mettle" and rough maps of great rivers or straits obtained from the Northern Indians who came back with Stuart, Knight established in 1717 a new post on the coast north of York Factory at the mouth of the Churchill River. He then returned to England.

Although he was now old and in poor health (one later report put him as eighty), Knight had come home not to retire, but to persuade the company to appoint him to command an expedition to sail to latitude 64° N on the northwest coast of Hudson Bay (the approximate location of Ne Ultra or Roe's Welcome) and then head northward to the Strait of Anian. After difficult negotiations, Knight won the agreement of a reluctant Hudson's Bay Company, and in June 1719 he set sail for Hudson Bay in two vessels, the *Albany* and the *Discovery*. The venture turned into one of the tragedies of Arctic exploration, for Knight's hopes of finding a short passage to a land of gold foundered on the barren shores of Marble Island off the west coast of Hudson Bay, where his ships were trapped in the fall of 1719. There were no survivors and no attempt at a search, although in 1721 Henry Kelsey, while on a slooping voyage north from York, reported seeing "things" belonging to the Knight expedition. The next year a sloop commanded by John Scroggs found wreckage from the ships strewn around Marble Island, and concluded that their crews had been killed by the Inuit. Almost half a century later, company whalers at Marble Island came across ruins and human bones near a shallow harbor where the hulks of Knight's ships lay in five fathoms of water. According to Inuit who were questioned at this time, some of Knight's men had survived at least to the breaking up of the ice in the summer of 1720 but then died of starvation.

Recent investigations on Marble Island have deepened rather than solved the mystery of what happened to Knight's men. In a series of digs between 1989 and 1992, a well-constructed large dwelling was excavated, together with a food-preparation area containing several hundred animal bones, most from local wildlife. These show that Knight's men had successfully hunted and fished, while the piles of coal near the building indicate that they were not short of fuel. What was not found at that desolate site were any significant remains of Knight's men— only one small vertebra and three teeth could reasonably be linked to men from the lost expedition— and the large number of Inuit graves in the area suggests that the bones seen by company men in the eighteenth century were Inuit. It does not seem possible that up to forty men had died in or near the building—whether from starvation or from Inuit attack—and left only these four tiny fragments. The most likely explanation of the disappearance of Knight's crews is that when the ice broke up in the spring of 1720 they took to the ships' boats in an effort to reach the nearest company post at Churchill, but perished in the attempt.

[*See also* Hudson's Bay Company; Kelsey, Henry; Northwest Passage; *and* Thanadelthur.]

BIBLIOGRAPHY

Dodge, Ernest S. "James Knight." In *Dictionary of Canadian Biography*, vol. 2, pp. 318–320. Toronto: University of Toronto Press, 1969.

Geiger, John, and Owen Beattie. *Dead Silence: The Greatest Mystery in Arctic Discovery*. London: Bloomsbury, 1993.
Williams, Glyn. *Voyages of Delusion: The Northwest Passage in the Age of Reason*. Chap. 1. London: HarperCollins, 2002; New Haven: Yale University Press, 2003.

GLYNDWR WILLIAMS

Kotzebue, Otto von

Kotzebue, Otto von (1787–1846), Russian explorer who sailed on the *Nadezhda* in the first Russian circumnavigation and himself commanded two similar expeditions, on the *Ryurik* (1815) and on the *Predpriyatie* (1823–1826). Born in Tallinn, Estonia, in 1787, Kotzebue received his early education there, and he sailed on the *Nadezhda* as a cadet in the Saint Petersburg Corps for Noblemen in 1803–1806. After further maritime experience, this promising young officer was chosen to command the *Ryurik* on an attempt to find the Northeast Passage from the Pacific Ocean to the Atlantic Ocean. Kotzebue and his crew sailed from Kamchatka in June 1816, passed through the Bering Strait, and pressed eastward along the north coast of Alaska as far as Kotzebue Sound. They then wintered in the Sandwich Islands, and in the summer of 1817 returned northward, only to meet solid ice. The *Ryurik* was unable to penetrate regions north of those delineated by Captain Cook, but Kotzebue and his crew had accumulated a wealth of knowledge through the work of the naturalist Johann Friedrich Escholts, the zoologist Adelbert von Chamisso, and the artist Louis Choris. Upon his return, Kotzebue produced a three-volume work about the voyage; originally in German, it was immediately translated into Russian and English, and an accompanying atlas was published in 1823. This atlas is of particular interest, for it contains cartographic information, including the location of native settlements, that had been supplied by an Eskimo informant. [See color plate 34 in this volume.]

From 1823 to 1826, Kotzebue sailed on a further round-the-world expedition, this time in command of the *Predpriyatie*. On this expedition he visited Kamchatka and Russian America, carrying out further explorations and hydrographic surveys. Upon his return, Kotzebue was promoted to command the fleet squadron at Kronshtadt, but in 1830 he had to be decommissioned because of failing health.

[*See also* Expeditions, World Exploration, *subentry on* Russia, *and* Northeast Passage.]

BIBLIOGRAPHY

Chamisso, Adelbert von. *A Voyage around the World with the Romanzov Exploring Expedition in the Years 1815–1818 in the Brig "Rurik," Captain Otto von Kotzebue*. Translated and edited by Henry Kratz. Honolulu: University of Hawaii Press, 1986.

Kotzebue, Otto von. *A Voyage of Discovery into the South Sea and Bering's Straits, for the Purpose of Exploring a North-East Passage, Undertaken in the Years 1815–1818.* 3 vols. Translated by H. E. Lloyd. London, 1821. Reprint. New York: Da Capo, 1967.

ALEXEY POSTNIKOV

Krapf, Ludwig

Krapf, Ludwig (1810–1881), German missionary in East Africa and the first European to sight Mount Kenya. Johann Ludwig Krapf was born to a humble farming family in a village near Tübingen. A precocious linguistic talent led him to study at the Basle Mission College, where he was recruited by the Anglican Church Missionary Society (CMS) to work in Ethiopia. There he made some notable travels, especially south into Shoa, and passed on useful information to the embassy of W. C. Harris. His work was also brought to the attention of geographers in Britain by the scholar James MacQueen, and is was published in 1843.

Difficulties in Shoa and the possibility of reaching and converting the Oromo ("Galla"), who lived even farther south, led Krapf to sail to Mombasa. He never reached the Oromo but set up his mission among the Mijikenda at Rabai. From there, he made a series of exploratory journeys in East Africa—along the coast as far as Cape Delgado, into the kingdom of Usambara twice in 1848 and 1852, and, even more notably, into Ukambani in 1849 and 1851 with Kivoi, a Mukamba ivory trader. On the 1849 trip, Krapf confirmed Johannes Rebmann's sighting of snow on Kilimanjaro and became the first known explorer to see the snows of Mount Kenya.

In 1850, he persuaded the CMS to adopt an ambitious strategy involving a chain of mission stations in East Africa. Unfortunately, his companion Rebmann had lost his enthusiasm for travel, other new recruits variously died or withdrew, and political difficulties emerged because Zanzibar Arabs mistrusted direct European encroachments into their sphere of trading operations. Krapf returned to Europe to concentrate on his extraordinary linguistic work, which included a pioneer Swahili dictionary. He did revisit East Africa in 1862 to help a Methodist mission begin work near Mombasa, and then went to Ethiopia to provide intelligence for Napier's Abyssinian Expedition in 1867.

Krapf did not use a sextant, nor did he organize his journeys elaborately; he gloried that an umbrella was his only accoutrement. Despite this, his journeys were notable if minor feats of exploration in a region almost unknown to geography in the 1840s and 1850s. His direct observations, not least mountain snow, plus the information he gathered (even if it was incorrectly and unfairly summarized in the "Slug Map," so often wrongly associated with his name), undoubtedly helped to persuade the Royal Geographical Society that it had to organize a scientific expedition in the region. Krapf's journals, published in German in 1858 and in English in 1860, remain a memorial to a notable missionary and traveller. He died at Kornthal in Würtemburg on November 26, 1881.

[*See also* Africa, *subentry on* Exploration; Harris, William Cornwallis, *and* Rebmann, Johannes.]

BIBLIOGRAPHY

Bridges, R. C. "Introduction to the Second Edition" of J. Lewis Krapf, *Travels, Researches and Missionary Labours during an Eighteen Years' Residence in Eastern Africa.* 2nd ed. London: Cass, 1968.

ROY BRIDGES

Krenitsyn, Pyotr

Krenitsyn, Pyotr (1728–1770), Russian commander of an expedition in the northern Pacific. Entering the Naval Academy in 1742, Krenitsyn graduated from it in 1748, serving thereafter in the Baltic Sea and in the Arctic. In May 1764, the empress Catherine II issued an order for an expedition to the islands of the northern Pacific Ocean, which were being settled in a rather random way after Bering's voyage of 1741. Krenitsyn was appointed to command this expedition, whose objective remained a guarded secret.

Krenitsyn was instructed to enlist for the voyage Kamchatka *promyshlenniki* (fur traders) or Cossacks, who might be familiar with the customs of the inhabitants of the Aleutian Islands and might know the inhabitants' language. He was also instructed to land on the islands, and particularly to establish both their relationship to the American mainland and the nature of the nearest port held by some European nation. Krenitsyn eventually left in July 1768, spending the next year establishing the cartography of the islands and drawing up surveys and descriptions. Krenitsyn himself drowned in July 1770 in a tragic accident, but his expedition had succeeded in setting out the correct position of forty-five of the Aleutian Islands and in investigating 125 miles (200 kilometers) of the coastline of the Alaska Peninsula.

The Russian Archive of Military History has preserved the cartographic work performed by members of Krenitsyn's expedition; besides being accurate, these maps are valuable for their information on the islands' inhabitants and resources. It is clear that they were drawn up in part by using the remarkable knowledge of the *promyshlenniki*, who had come to know much about this new region. The maps were accompanied by elegant India-ink sketches of Kamchatka, the Aleutian Islands, and parts of the Alaska Peninsula, as well as watercolor images of many of the natives' material objects: tools, weapons, household items, and so forth. The latter images have become invaluable for modern ethnographers.

The expedition remained secret to the end, but Catherine II eventually allowed some of its material to be used by the English historian William Robertson in his two-volume *History of America* (London, 1777). Other material was later published by William Coxe in his *Account of the Russian Discoveries between Asia and America* (London, 1780); the first Russian account was published by Peter Simon Pallas in 1781.

[*See also* Arctic, *subentry on* Russian Arctic, *and* Expeditions, World Exploration, *subentry on* Russia.]

BIBLIOGRAPHY

Makarova, Raisa V. *Russians on the Pacific 1743–1799*. Translated and edited by Richard A. Pierce and Alton S. Donnelly. Kingston, Ontario: Limestone, 1975.

Masterson, James R., and Helen Brower. *Bering's Successors, 1745–1780: Contributions of Peter Simon Pallas to the History of Russian Exploration toward Alaska*. Seattle: University of Washington Press, 1948.

ALEXEY POSTNIKOV

Krusenstern, Ivan Fedorovich (1770–1846),

Russian navigator and explorer. Ivan Fedorovich (Adam Johann von) Krusenstern was born on September 19, 1770, in Hagudi (now Rapla), Estonia. In 1788 he graduated from the Navy Academy (*Morskaia akademiya*) in Saint Petersburg. That same year he served aboard the *Mstislav* in sea battles against Sweden. To upgrade his naval skills, from 1793 to 1799 he served as a volunteer in the British Royal Navy, sailing to Canada, South America, India, and China.

At the end of the eighteenth century and the beginning of the nineteenth, Russian *promyshlenniki* (fur traders) as well as Russian officials tried to extend colonial possessions in America, especially along the coasts and islands of southern Alaska. The first Russian circumnavigation, commanded by Krusenstern and Yuri Lisiansky (1803–1806), was part of the government's support for this expansion. Like Krusenstern, Lisianskii had graduated from the Navy Academy in Saint Petersburg and had served in the British Royal Navy. One important task given to the expedition was to resupply Russia's American colonies with needed foodstuffs and materials. In addition, Tsar Alexander I decided to dispatch an ambassador to Japan, N. P. Rezanov, who traveled with the expedition on *Nadezhda*. In addition, scientists were on board the two ships charged with studying the coasts of the Pacific Ocean.

Lisianskii purchased needed materials in London—two vessels that were named *Neva* and *Nadezhda*, plus navigational instruments, sextants, barometers, hydrometers, and chronometers. Special significance was ascribed to the precise determination, during the course of the expedition, of astronomical coordinates. For this reason all instruments, but especially the chronometers, were checked at the Pulkovo Observatory by the academician F. I. Shubert (1758–1825). Scientists on *Nadezhda* included Tilesius von Tillenau, Georg Heinrich von Langsdorff, and the astronomer I. Horner (also spelled Gorner). Krusenstern commanded the flagship, *Nadezhda*. *Neva* was under the command of Lisianskii. The vessels left Kronshtadt in August 1803 and visited the Marquesas and the Hawaiian Islands. Then they separated: the flagship *Nadezhda* for Kamchatka; *Neva* for the Russian colonies in Alaska.

In August 1804, *Nadezhda* sailed from Kamchatka to Japan, where the Russians remained for seven months (in Nagasaki) in an unsuccessful attempt to persuade the Japanese government to open official relations with Russia. Krusenstern and his crew performed important hydrographic surveys and explorations in the Sea of Japan as well as in the Kuril Islands and Sakhalin Island. In September 1805 *Nadezhda* began her return voyage to Russia, stopping at Canton, China, where it met *Neva*, which had delivered needed goods and supplies to the Russian colonies in Alaska. Together the ships sailed around the Cape of Good Hope and arrived home in Kronshtadt in June 1806. The expedition's accomplishments, in both exploration and natural history, were recorded in the three volumes that Kruzenstern wrote about his experiences, *Puteshestvie vokrug sveta v 1803, 1804, 1805 I 1806 gg. Na korablyakh Nadezhda i Neva* (Travels around the World in the Years 1803, 1804, 1805, and 1806 Aboard the Ships *Nadezhda* and *Neva*), published in Saint Petersburg from 1809 to 1812. Kruzenshtern's two-volume atlas of the explorations, published in 1824–1826 in Saint Petersburg, was a substantial contribution to geographical knowledge of the North Pacific.

For his achievements Admiral Krusenstern was elected as a Member of the Royal Society (London).

He was a corresponding member (1803) and honorary member (1806) of the Saint Petersburg Academy of Sciences. He was one of the founders of the Russian Geographical Society (1845) and member of many other scientific societies.

Krusenstern died on August 24, 1846, in Revel (now Tallinn, Estonia).

BIBLIOGRAPHY

Krusenstern, Ivan Fedorovich. *Voyage around the World, in the Years 1802, 1803, 1804, 1805 & 1806.* 2 vols. Translated from the original German by Richard Belgrave Hoppner. London: John Murray, 1813. Facsimile. Tenri, Japan: Tenri University Press, 1973.

Pierce, Richard A., ed. *Remarks and Observations on a Voyage around the World from 1803 to 1807 by Georg Heinrich von Langsdorff.* Translated by Victoria Joan Moessner. Fairbanks, Alaska: Limestone Press, 1993.

Wells, David N. *Russian Views of Japan, 1792–1913: An Anthology of Russian Travel Writing.* New York: Routledge Curzon, 2004.

ALEXEY POSTNIKOV

L

La Condamine, Charles-Marie de (1701–1774), French scientist and explorer of South America. From the volcanic heights of the Andes to the humid rainforests of the Amazon River Basin, Charles-Marie de La Condamine captivated eighteenth-century Europe with his tales of adventure; he also became an enduring icon of instrumentally based exploration and empirical experimentation within non-European domains. A native of Paris and a member of the Parisian Academy of Sciences, La Condamine was sent to Spanish America in 1735 on an expedition to measure a three-degree arc of the meridian and thereby resolve one of the most pressing scientific polemics of the day: the precise shape of the earth, flattened either at its poles (as Newton predicted) or at the Equator (as Descartes had imagined). After many troublesome years in the Andes, La Condamine returned to Europe by traversing the massive continental rain forest and became in the process the first representative of a European scientific institution to descend the entire navigable length of the Amazon River. The published results from his expedition, which included a much-lauded map of the Amazon Basin, revised European knowledge of South America's equatorial regions from the Andes to the Atlantic and conferred upon La Condamine celebrity status. Authors such as Rousseau and later explorers of South America, including Alexander von Humboldt, considered him to be an exemplary philosophical traveler whose instrumental observations could be trusted implicitly. Meanwhile, however, La Condamine's scathing critiques of native populations as "insensitive" brutes lacking in culture and intelligence earned him the opprobrium of many South Americans and a bad name among indigenous peoples for decades and centuries to come.

[*See also* Amazon River *and* Humboldt, Alexander von.]

BIBLIOGRAPHY

Conlon, Pierre. "La Condamine the Inquisitive." *Studies on Voltaire and the Eighteenth Century* 55 (1967): 361–393.

Safier, Neil. "Unveiling the Amazon to European Science and Society: The Reading and Reception of La Condamine's *Relation abrégée.*" *Terrae Incognitae: The Journal for the History of Discoveries* 33 (2001): 33–47.

NEIL SAFIER

Lahontan, Baron de (1666–c. 1715), French officer in New France and Placentia, Newfoundland. Little is known about Louis Armand de Lom d'Arce's childhood except that he grew up at his father's château at Lahontan. In 1683, at age seventeen, he came to Canada with the colonial troops. The following year he was sent with his company to Fort Frontenac

---

Seeing Oneself with a New Perspective

In this passage, Lahontan joins the company of European commentators who found in native societies a stick with which to beat the insufficiencies of their own decadent social structure. Whether it was the "Wise Chinese" or the "Noble Savages," all had lessons to teach the Europeans. It is not difficult to imagine the contribution that such reflections made to eventual revolutionary thought.

They . . . laugh at the difference of Degrees which is observ'd with us. They brand us for slaves, and call us miserable Souls, whose life is not worth having, aledging that we degrade ourselves in subjecting ourselves to one Man who possesses the whole Power, and is bound by no Law but his own Will . . . but among them the true qualifications of a Man are to run well, to hunt, to bend the bow and manage the Fuzee, to work a Cannoo, to understand War, to know Forests . . .

—Baron de Lahontan, *New Voyages to North America* (2 vols.; London, 1703)

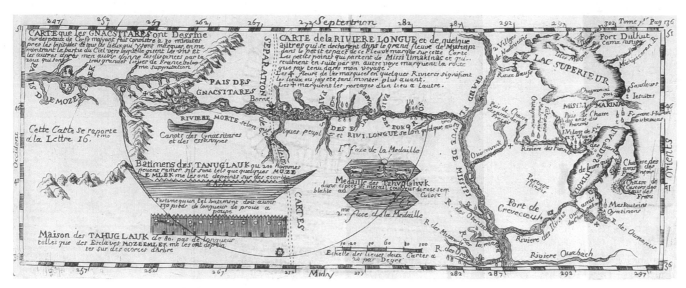

Baron de Lahontan. "The Carte de la Rivière Longue," from Lahontan's *Nouveaux voyages dans l'Amérique septentrionale . . .* (2 vols., The Hague, 1703). Lahonton has often been criticized for his fantasies, but this is an interesting image of the Missouri River, stretching away westward to the Rocky Mountains. As Lahonton puts it (top left), much of the information came from a map that the chiefs had drawn for him on deerskin. SOUTHERN METHODIST UNIVERSITY

and to the southeastern shore of Lake Ontario, where he was present at the ill-fated negotiations between the French and the Iroquois. From 1685 to 1687 he was stationed at Fort Chambly and Boucherville, where he enjoyed hunting with the natives and learned Algonquian. In 1687 he participated in the campaign led by Governor Brisay de Denonville against the Seneca. From there he was sent to take command of Fort Saint-Joseph on the west side of the Saint Clair River. Early in 1688 he was at Michilimackinac, where he met some of the survivors of Cavelier de La Salle's ill-fated attempt to establish a colony near the mouth of the Mississippi. During the summer, Iroquois retaliations led to the abandonment of Fort Niagara. Knowing that he could not defend Fort Saint-Joseph, Lahontan burned it and returned to Michilimackinac. He claimed that he engaged in westward exploration from 1688 to 1689. Back in Montreal in the fall of 1689, he fought with Governor Frontenac's troops against the abortive English (1690) invasion under Sir William Phips. Late in 1690 he sailed for France to attend to family matters, but he was back in Quebec in 1691. In 1692 he helped defeat an English landing party at Placentia, the French naval base on Newfoundland. For this action he was appointed king's lieutenant at Placentia in 1693. Unable to get along with Governor de Brouillan, Lahontan deserted. Under danger of arrest, he began a footloose journey through Europe until his death in 1714 or 1715.

In 1703, Lahontan published three volumes: *Nouveaux voyages dans l'Amérique septentrionale*, *Mémoires de l'Amérique septentrionale*, and *Supplément aux voyages*. English translations followed immediately, and eventually Dutch, German, and Italian translations did. Lahontan became one of the most widely read authors on matters pertaining to North America. Unfortunately, the many excellent details and insights he presented are often overshadowed by his claim to have explored La Rivière Longue and by his alleged discourse with the Huron chief "Adario."

From September 1688 to May 1689, Lahontan claimed, he explored westward with his detachment of soldiers and five native hunters. They departed from Michilimackinac on September 24 and reached the Mississippi on October 23. Here they turned north and came to the mouth of the "Long River," at about 47° N latitude, on November 2. The party ascended the river westward over a distance of about 1,000 miles (1,600 kilometers) until they turned around on January 26. Somewhere farther west, they were told, was a salt sea. They reached Michilimackinac again on May 22, 1689. With the publication of the *Nouveaux voyages*, Lahontan's map of the "Long River" was copied by other maps such as the influential *Carte du Canada . . . 1703* by Guillaume Delisle. Was this the long-sought western passage? More amazing than a journey by canoes in the dead of winter at that high latitude along a nonexistent river is that many scholars have taken this account to be factual.

Although Lahontan had met "Adario," the Huron chief Kondiaronk ("The Rat"), at Michilimackinac, the philosophical dialogues he allegedly had with him are probably wholly imaginary. Nevertheless, these dialogues had a great impact on European readers and philosophers such as Voltaire and Rousseau in building the myth of "the noble savage." Lahontan was not an explorer who made geographical discoveries but one who made the New World better known to Europeans through his vivid, often irreverent travel observations.

[See also Delisle, Guillaume; La Salle, Cavelier de; and Mer de l'Ouest and Rivière de l'Ouest.]

BIBLIOGRAPHY

Hayne, David M. "Lom d'Arce de Lahontan, Louis Armand de." In *Dictionary of Canadian Biography*, edited by David M. Hayne. Vol. 2, 1701–1740. Toronto: University of Toronto Press, 1969.

Lahontan, Louis Armand de Lom d'Arce, Baron de. *Oeuvres complètes; édition critique par Réal Ouellet, avec la collaboration d'Alain Beaulieu.* Montreal: Presses de l'Université de Montréal, 1990.

CONRAD E. HEIDENREICH

Laing, Alexander Gordon (1793–1826), Scottish explorer of central Africa. Born in Edinburgh on December 27, 1793, the son and grandson of distinguished educators, Laing was one of the best educated of all the seekers of Timbuctoo, and he was perhaps the most ambitious and courageous, as well as arguably one of the most heroic and tragic figures, in the annals of exploration history. He was thirteen years old when he entered the University of Edinburgh, where he was a top student of Latin. At age seventeen, he went to Barbados to work for his uncle, but later joined the military there and subsequently served in Antigua and Jamaica. With the Second West India Regiment, he undertook two journeys in 1822 into the unexplored interior of Sierra Leone, where he attempted to determine the exact location of Mount Soma, then thought to be the source of the Niger River. In 1823, he fought with distinction in the Ashanti War in present-day Ghana. Captain Laing returned to Britain in August 1824, where he published an account of his adventures the following year.

In October 1824, Lord Bathurst, the secretary of state for war and colonies, not only promoted Laing to major, but also commissioned him to explore the interior of West Africa to determine the course of the Niger River (via Timbuctoo) and learn where it terminated. Laing wanted to enter Africa from the Atlantic coast, but Bathurst insisted that he depart from Tripoli, on the Mediterranean, which would require him to cross the Sahara Desert. When Laing arrived at Tripoli in May 1825, he was met by Hanmer Warrington, the British consul, who informed him that Hugh Clapperton, who had recently returned from his Lake Chad expedition, was making another attempt to reach Timbuctoo. Believing he was in a race for glory, Laing felt that haste was necessary, but his timetable was complicated when he fell in love with Emma Warrington, the consul's daughter, and they were married on July 14, 1825. Laing left two days later for Timbuctoo (his marriage unconsummated), believing that he was only ten weeks away from the Niger River.

Laing's journey across the Sahara is a story of immense courage, vile treachery, and personal survival from life-threatening injuries. Further, by the time he arrived at Ghadames in mid-September, all of his scientific equipment was broken. He reached In Salah at the heart of the desert on December 2, where he wrote a letter to his family in Scotland, suggesting that he was only thirty days away from the fabled city. Shortly after departing In Salah on January 10, 1826, Laing was attacked by a band of Tuareg tribesmen, and despite being shot, suffering a broken arm and twenty-four wounds to his body, and losing all his money, he miraculously survived to continue his epic journey. Adding to the ignominy, his guides deserted.

Thirteen months and more than twenty-six hundred miles after he departed Tripoli, Laing became, on August 18, 1826, the first European to enter Timbuctoo. He remained there for five weeks, but little is known about his activities there. He wrote Warrington that Timbuctoo "in every respect, except in size . . . has met my expectations." He also indicated that because of tribal rivalry he was being pressured to leave the city, which he did in mid-September. On September 26, 1826, Laing was murdered near Arawan, just north of Timbuctoo. Even though many attempts were made to locate his priceless journal and papers, they were never recovered.

[See also Africa; Clapperton, Hugh; Niger River; and Timbuctoo.]

BIBLIOGRAPHY

Bovill, E. W., ed. *Missions to the Niger.* 4 vols. Cambridge, U.K.: Cambridge University Press for the Hakluyt Society, 1964.

Gardner, Brian. *The Quest for Timbuctoo.* New York: Harcourt, Brace & World, 1968.

SANFORD H. BEDERMAN

Lander, Richard, and John Lander, explorers. Richard Lander (1804–1834) was born in Truro,

Cornwall, England. He first ventured into Africa as a private servant in Capetown from1823 to1824, and then offered his services to Hugh Clapperton on his second expedition to West Africa in 1826. When Clapperton died, Lander earned a reputation as an explorer in his own right, managing to return to the coast with his leader's journals. He had written his own journal of the travels, and with the help of his brother John Lander (1806–1839; also born at Truro), this work was prepared for publication in 1829.

Sponsored by the British government, Richard Lander returned to Africa with his brother in 1830. Their task was to solve the "problem of the Niger." The course of the river—and specifically its termination—had been a mystery from ancient times. It was thought that the river variously linked to the Congo or the Nile, or simply disappeared in the desert. Previous expeditions, and most recently those of Mungo Park and Clapperton, had not proved conclusive.

Richard Lander, his brother, and an interpreter travelled initially by land from Badagry to Bussa, where Park had died. They continued by river down the lower Niger, and encountered ambush and hardship at the hands of Africans and a European sea captain. The area had been badly affected by the slave trade, and the immoral behavior they saw there seems to have influenced their attitude toward Africa and its peoples.

The brothers reached Brass and they were able to prove conclusively that the Niger emptied into the Bight of Benin. They sailed home to considerable fame, having solved the mystery. The journals they wrote of this expedition were in no way scientific, however, and show relatively little understanding of the country through which they were travelling.

Richard Lander's achievement was recognized, as he received the first gold medal ever awarded by the Royal Geographical Society. He was commissioned in 1834 to make the first steamboat journey up the Niger, but died at Fernando Po in February 1834. Regardless, he contributed to opening up the means by which trade, the Christian gospel, and eventually British rule were taken into the Lower Niger. John Lander died in London in 1839.

[*See also* Clapperton, Hugh, *and* Park, Mungo.]

BIBLIOGRAPHY
Hallett, Robin. *The Penetration of Africa: European Enterprise and Exploration Principally in Northern and Western Africa up to 1830.* London: Routledge and Kegan Paul; New York: Praeger, 1965.

ROY BRIDGES

La Pérouse, J. F. de Galaup de (1741–1793), French explorer who surveyed the Pacific. Jean-François de Galaup de La Pérouse was born in Albi, southern France, the son of a family of lawyers and landowners. The "La Pérouse," from an estate owned by his father, was added to his name when he joined the navy, to ensure that he would enjoy an adequate status among his aristocratic fellow officers.

He served in numerous campaigns during the long wars between France and Britain during the eighteenth century, serving in Canada, Newfoundland, the West Indies, the Indian Ocean, and America. During the intervals of peace, he undertook coastal survey and administrative tasks.

In 1782, as the American War of Independence was coming to a close, he was sent on a raid deep into Hudson Bay, destroying British posts there, but also repatriating his prisoners and ensuring that adequate supplies were left for those who stayed behind to face the harsh northern winter. This humane behavior earned him praise in France and the goodwill of the British, who readily cooperated when he undertook his later voyage of exploration.

By 1783, he was a post captain, a Knight of the Order of Saint Louis, and an adviser to the minister of marine, Claret de Fleurieu, with whom he began to plan an expedition to the Pacific to survey in particular areas that James Cook had been unable to reconnoiter. The voyage was meticulously planned, with advice and assistance from a number of scientific bodies. King Louis XVI took a close personal interest in these preparations and amended some of the instructions. Two ships were allocated, solid storeships rather than impressive warships, the *Boussole* and the *Astrolabe*, the latter commanded by Fleuriot de Langle.

La Pérouse sailed from Brest on August 1, 1785, calling briefly at Tenerife, Trinidade, and Brazil. He passed through the Strait of Le Maire and reached Talcahuano in Chile on February 24, 1786. On March 17, the expedition sailed for Easter Island, Maui in the Hawaiian Islands, and northern Alaska. From there, La Pérouse sailed south, surveying the Northwest Coast of America, an achievement marred by the loss of twenty-one men who drowned in a boating accident in Lituya Bay. He continued down to Monterey, in Spanish California, where the two ships remained September 15–24. They then sailed westward across the Pacific, discovering Necker Island and French Frigate Shoals, and reached Macao on January 3, 1787.

They sailed north a month later, making for the Philippines. From there, La Pérouse began the most dangerous and most productive part of his voyage. Formosa, Korea, and Japan were closed worlds, which Europeans were forbidden to enter. Consequently, their coastlines and those farther north were little known. The French spent five months in these waters, sailing into the narrow gulf between the coasts of Tartary and Sakhalin. Unable to ascertain whether the latter was an island or a peninsula, they veered back, putting into Petropavlovsk on September 7.

There, La Pérouse found news awaiting him, including his promotion to the rank of commodore, but also instructions to proceed without delay to Australia, where the British were reported to be establishing a settlement. On the way, he carried out further exploration in the northern and central Pacific, but suffered another reverse when de Langle and eleven men were killed on Tutuila, in the Samoas.

He reached Botany Bay on January 28, 1788, where the British "First Fleet" of settlers had arrived a few days earlier. After a period of rest and refitting, the expedition sailed on March 10, to explore Tonga, New Caledonia, and the neighboring islands, and begin the homeward journey. It was never seen again. Only in 1827 was it ascertained that the two ships had been lost, probably in June 1788, on the small island of Vanikoro in the Santa Cruz group.

The disappearance of La Pérouse and his ships led to a number of expeditions, the main one being that of Antoine Raymond Joseph Bruni d'Entrecasteaux (1737–1793), who sailed from Brest with the *Recherche* and the *Espérance* on September 29, 1791. Making for Australia, Entrecasteaux spent several weeks surveying the coast of Tasmania, then went on to New Caledonia, the Solomons, and the Dutch East Indies.

Entrecasteaux returned to the Australian continent, surveying the south coast in particular and discovering the Recherche Archipelago and Esperance Bay. He went on to Tasmania, across to New Zealand, discovering the Kermadec Islands, and going on to Tonga, New Caledonia, and the Santa Cruz Islands. D'Entrecasteaux sighted Vanikoro but, unaware that this was where the shipwreck had occurred, did not approach it. He went on to explore part of the Solomons and islands east of New Guinea. He died on July 20, 1793, as the expedition was struggling toward the Dutch East Indies. Political friction resulting from the revolution back home brought about the final disintegration of the expedition. Several years elapsed before its quite considerable achievements were realized.

[*See also* Entrecasteaux, Antoine Raymond Joseph Bruni d'.]

BIBLIOGRAPHY
Dunmore, John. *Pacific Explorer: The Life of Jean-François de La Pérouse, 1741–1788.* Annapolis, Md.: Naval Institute Press, 1985.
Dunmore, John, ed. *The Journal of Jean-François de Galaup de la Pérouse, 1785–1788.* 2 vols. London: Hakluyt Society, 1994–1995.
Horner, Frank. *Looking for La Pérouse: D'Entrecasteaux in Australia and the South Pacific, 1792–1793.* Carlton, Victoria: Melbourne University Press, 1995.

JOHN DUNMORE

La Salle, Cavelier de

La Salle, Cavelier de (1643–1687), French explorer of western New France. René-Robert Cavelier de La Salle was the French explorer who canoed from Illinois down the Mississippi River in 1682 to discover its deltaic mouth in the Gulf of Mexico. Born into a well-to-do merchant family in Rouen,

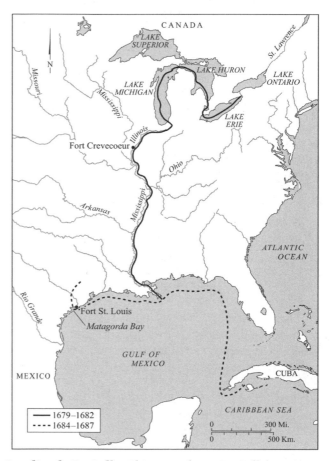

Cavelier de La Salle. This map shows La Salle's routes on his voyages up the Mississippi and through the Gulf of Mexico. MAP BY BILL NELSON

France, on November 22, 1643, he received an excellent education at the Jesuit College Henri IV at La Flèche, one of France's leading centers for the teaching of physical science and mathematics. As a student La Salle was commended for his excellent ability and talent in mathematics. At La Flèche mathematics was not confined to theoretical pursuits but included courses in geography, astronomy, and hydrography, the study of which embraced navigation. Providing a hint of what would cause him problems in the future, La Salle's superiors at the college found him sometimes lacking in prudence and good judgment. When the circumstances of La Salle's death at the hands of mutineers in the swamps of east Texas in 1687 are recalled it can be seen that they were amazingly prescient.

At age twenty-two La Salle became frustrated and abandoned a priestly career in favor of taking up land on the far-away Quebec frontier. Receiving a grant to land at the western end of the Île de Montreal, La Salle acquired the status of a seigneur. While farming his holdings, La Salle took advantage of the opportunity to engage in fur trading with the Indians. Learning about the interior from them La Salle began to appreciate the potential that contacts in the interior promised. According to some scholars he became obsessed with the idea of finding a route to the Orient through the rivers and lakes that the Indians were reporting. In 1669 La Salle disposed of his landholdings and devoted himself to exploring the Ohio Valley region. Although he was once credited with the discovery of the Ohio River, many modern authorities reject that claim.

La Salle's ambitions coincided with the expansionist program then being promoted by the governor of New France, Louis de Baude, the Count of Frontenac, who held power from 1672 to 1682. La Salle was made the seigneur of Fort Frontenac (in present-day Kingston, Ontario) and surrounding lands while the Indian trading rights were reserved for Governor Frontenac. Under La Salle's supervision the fort was strengthened and a village of habitants gradually grew to form a community that included an Indian settlement, a convent, and a Recollet Church. Frontenac chose La Salle to travel to France to represent his cause in disputes with the Montreal traders. While there, La Salle impressed King Louis XIV sufficiently to be awarded a title of nobility. In time La Salle's personal ambitions grew, and he began to make exploratory forays farther afield in quest of furs and geographical knowledge. Returning to the royal court again in 1677 he obtained the king's license to explore "the western parts

of New France" with the right to build forts as needed and a monopoly on the trade in buffalo hides.

A deliberate change of imperial policy by Louis XIV led to retrenchment in New France and ended any follow-up on the exploration of the Mississippi River begun in 1673 by Louis Jolliet and the Jesuit missionary Jacques Marquette. They had followed the Mississippi south to the juncture of the Arkansas where Indian reports suggesting Spanish danger ahead caused them to turn back. Arriving back in Canada in 1678 with his royal monopoly in hand, La Salle began to lay the foundations for a trading empire in the American heartland. During 1679–1680 he built his ill-fated sailing ship *Griffon* on the upper Niagara River; it was designed to provide the Great Lakes link in his grandiose trading network. Fort Crevecoeur was built near the site of present-day Peoria on the Illinois River and, in the winter of 1681–1682, La Salle made ready to embark on his quest for the mouth of the Mississippi. On February 13, 1682, he began his momentous voyage via canoe in company with twenty-two Frenchmen and eighteen Indian braves and several Indian women and children. Voyaging down the Mississippi until they discovered "three channels by which the River Colbert [La Salle's name for the Mississippi] discharges itself into the sea," they landed on the bank of the most western channel about ten miles (sixteen kilometers) from its mouth. After exploring the remaining channels they returned to a place "beyond the reach of inundations," and reported their latitude to be 27° N. Here a column with the arms of France and a cross were erected to mark the place where La Salle took possession for the king "of this country of Louisiana, the seas, harbors, ports, bays, adjacent straits, and all the nations, peoples, provinces, cities, towns, villages, mines, minerals, fisheries, streams and rivers, within the extent of the said Louisiana" (*Collections of the Illinois State Historical Library*, p. 110).

La Salle lost little time in retracing his route back up the Mississippi to strengthen the Illinois country outposts of his new trading empire. Indian attacks and ill health kept La Salle from returning to Quebec where Frontenac, who had been recalled to France, could no longer protect his interests. In October 1683, when La Salle finally returned to Quebec from the Illinois country, Frontenac's successor was already expropriating La Salle's holdings and assets. Rather than risk delay and face the winter freeze-up La Salle sailed to France immediately. Even before La Salle returned to Louis XIV's court, his enemies there had persuaded the king that his discovery and expansionist programs were useless and that such enterprises should be prevented in the future in favor of consolidating the existing holdings in New France. Not to be forestalled, La Salle successfully linked his discovery with a scheme to invade New Spain. La Salle and his backers in court were responsible for having influential maps drawn making it appear that the Mississippi River in its lower course turned sharply to the west to find its way to the sea on the Texas coast not far north of the mouth of the Rio Grande River. In late March of 1684, the king approved his budget, and La Salle was officially commissioned to command and found a colony to support an attack against the Spanish. [See color plate 45 in this volume.]

La Salle's modest and ill-starred force of four vessels sailed from La Rochelle on August 1, 1684, and landed in Haiti after a fifty-eight-day voyage. Unfortunately, Spanish freebooters captured the flotilla's main supply ship with its essential munitions, utensils, and proper tools for the establishment of a colony on hostile shores. Another setback came when La Salle himself fell victim to a serious illness that was described as "a violent fever, attended by light headedness that brought him almost to extremity." After a convalescence of four weeks, La Salle was recovered sufficiently to continue the voyage and cross the Gulf of Mexico. For reasons that are not clear and still much debated by historians La Salle sailed tantalizingly close to the Mississippi's deltaic mouths but chose not to land there. Instead he followed a course west to the Texas coastline and made landfall at Matagorda Bay. Bad pilotage caused the wreck of the expedition's remaining supply ship, *L'Amiable*. The beleaguered party salvaged what they could.

The expedition's warship *Joly*, its mission completed, sailed for France on March 13, 1685. While the surviving party worked to build a fort with the wreckage, La Salle set out on the first of a series of vain attempts to find an arm or branch of the Mississippi. Any hope of escape by sea was lost when La Salle's last ship, the *Belle*, sank in a squall. Possibly no longer fully rational, La Salle carried on a number of exploratory expeditions aimed at discovering a river or branch that would lead to the Mississippi River. Finally, in May of 1687, on one of these abortive forays, La Salle was murdered in the wilderness of east Texas by some mutinous colonists. In the end only four of the surviving would-be colonists lived to endure the arduous trek overland to the Illinois settlements and safety.

Interest in La Salle reawoke in 1995 when underwater archaeologists working for the Texas Histori-

cal Commission discovered the wreck of the *Belle* preserved in amazingly good condition under protective layers of mud and sand in Matagorda Bay. A cofferdam was constructed to allow a major effort aimed at salvaging as much of the ship and its contents as possible. Much of the ship's wooden structure, and even normally perishable articles such as sailcloth, rope, birchbark boxes, clothes, hair, leather shoes, and documents bearing La Salle's signature were recovered. The Historical Commission considers the excavation of the *Belle* and La Salle's settlement at nearby Fort Saint Louis to be two of the most important historical sites in the state.

[*See also* Jolliet, Louis; Marquette, Jacques; *and* Mississippi River.]

BIBLIOGRAPHY

Collections of the Illinois State Historical Library. Vol. 1. Springfield: Trustees of the Illinois State Historical Library, 1903.

Foster, William C., ed. *The La Salle Expedition to Texas: The Journal of Henri Joutel 1684–1687*. Translated by Johanna S. Warren. Austin: Texas State Historical Association, 1998.

Galloway, Patricia K. *La Salle and His Legacy: Frenchmen and Indians in the Lower Mississippi Valley*. Jackson: University Press of Mississippi, 1982.

Johnson, Donald S. *La Salle: A Perilous Odyssey from Canada to the Gulf of Mexico*. New York: Cooper Square Press, 2002.

Weddle, Robert S. *La Salle, the Mississippi, and the Gulf: Three Primary Documents*. College Station: Texas A&M University Press, 1987.

LOUIS DE VORSEY

Las Casas, Bartolomé de (1484?–1566), Spanish bishop, human rights champion, and chronicler, whose extensive political, theological, and historical writings are key documents of the conquest period. Las Casas was born in Seville, the son of a merchant who brought him a Taino slave from Columbus's second voyage to America. Las Casas studied canon law in Salamanca before voyaging to the Indies in 1502. There he became an *encomendero* while helping to provision Spanish military expeditions. After returning to Europe, Las Casas was ordained a deacon in Seville before taking holy orders in Rome in 1507. He traveled again to the Indies in 1510 and began converting Indians to Christianity. In 1512 authorities awarded Las Casas a grant of Indians for participating in the conquest of Cuba. By then Las Casas had become increasingly disillusioned with the *encomienda* system and Spanish mistreatment of Indians. In 1514 he freed his own Indians and then outraged parishioners by preaching a sermon condemning the *encomienda* system. After unsuccessfully entreating local *encomenderos* to free their Indians, Las Casas returned to Europe, where he argued for peaceful Indian conversions in place of baptisms through military conquest. Although he helped persuade Charles V to pass laws protecting Indians, the laws had little genuine impact. In 1518 Las Casas went to Venezuela, where he attempted to employ his ideas of peaceful conversion to establish a self-sufficient Indian settlement; colonial officials and local landowners, however, sabotaged his efforts. Heartsick as a result of that failure, he then returned to Europe and became a monk in the Dominican Order. Las Casas remained in Europe until 1544.

During this period in Europe he produced some of his most significant works. Las Casas began the *Apologética historia de las Indias*, which became the basis for his landmark *Historia de las Indias*. In 1530

Impressions of the Indians

Las Casas knew the Indies well, having arrived there in 1502 and traveled widely in Spain's new dominions. His campaigns for a more humane treatment of the indigenous peoples largely failed, but had the unintended effect of contributing to the Black Legend, for his writings were seized upon by Spain's enemies in order to justify their attacks on Spain's empire.

[The Indians of the West Indies follow a diet] such that the most holy Hermite cannot feed more sparingly in the wildernesse. They go naked, only hiding the indecencies of nature, and a poor shag mantle about an ell or two long is their greatest and their warmest covering. They lie upon mats, only those who have larger fortunes, lye upon a kind of net which is tied at the four corners, and so fasten'd to the roof, which the Indians in their natural language call Hamecks. They are of a very apprehensive and docible wit, and capable of all good learning, and very apt to receive our Religion, which when they have but once tasted, they are carried on with a very ardent and zealous desire to make a further progress in it. . . . To these "quiet lambs, endued with such blessed qualities," came the Spaniards like most cruel Tygres, Wolves and Lions, enrag'd with a sharp and tedious hunger. . . .

—Bartolomé de Las Casas, *The Tears of the Indians,* translated by John Phillips (London, 1656)

---

he wrote *Del único modo de atraer a todos los pueblos a la verdadera religión* (The Only Method of Attracting Everyone to the True Religion) and helped shape Pope Paul III's 1537 promulgation of *Sublimis Deus* that authoritatively declared Indians truly human and capable of receiving the gospel. That same year Las Casas and the Dominicans won Charles V's support to establish missions in Guatemala based on the precepts laid out in *Del único modo*. During his lobbying efforts on the Indians' behalf, Las Casas horrified the court when he read an early version of *The Devastation of the Indies*. His dogged efforts led directly to the Spanish crown's instituting the 1542 *Leyes Nuevas* (New Laws), which outlawed Indian slavery and sought to end the *encomienda* system within a generation.

The church and crown rewarded Las Casas by elevating him to bishop and offering him the prestigious and wealthy Cuzco bishopric. He chose instead, however, to head the Chiapas bishopric, one of the poorest in Spanish America. Las Casas assumed his short and tumultuous tenure as bishop in 1544, at the same time that the crown announced the New Laws in the colonies. Spanish colonists responded with so much anger to the new policy that New Spain's viceroy and High Court refused to implement the laws, fearing open revolt. Landowners and local clergy in Chiapas openly defied Las Casas's efforts to enforce the New Laws and made death threats against him. Reacting to this widespread opposition, the crown rescinded the laws' crucial clause that prohibited *encomiendas* from becoming a part of inheritable estates. Las Casas responded by first going to Mexico City, where he persuaded other bishops to adopt his anti-*encomienda* view. He thereupon delivered the most powerful spiritual weapon at his command by issuing a new confessor manual for all the priests under his authority.

Las Casas first circulated a manuscript version of *Confesionario: Avisos y reglas para confesores* to a group of Dominican priests in Chiapas. The *Confesionario* contained "Doce reglas para confesores" (Twelve Rules for Confessors) for priests to use when ministering to dying *encomenderos*. The "Doce reglas" for all practical purposes reestablished the New Laws' *encomienda* termination clause by stipulating that *encomenderos* could not receive last rites without liberating all their Indians and making restitution for their sins. Las Casas justified his decision by arguing that all wealth acquired through *encomiendas* was ill gotten, declaring, "There is no Spaniard in the Indies who has shown good faith in connection with the wars of Conquest." Such a claim, however, questioned the legitimacy of Spain's entire presence in the Americas, since its wealth and occupation had been built on forced Indian labor. When the crown ordered Las Casas back to Spain in 1547, colonial authorities confiscated all copies of the "Doce reglas."

Back in Spain, Las Casas found an entirely new threat to Indian rights from the eminent humanist Juan Ginés de Sepúlveda. Sepúlveda was attempting to publish his *Democrates secundus*, which defended Spain's military conquest of the Indies as a just war by using Aristotle's theories of natural slavery. The famous debate between Las Casas and Sepúlveda took place in 1550 before a panel of judges. Although they made no public decision, Spanish authorities banned Sepúlveda's manuscript. After resigning his Chiapas bishopric, Las Casas went to a Dominican monastery where he produced his most important works, *A Brief Account of the Devastation of the Indies* (1552) and the final versions of his *Apologética historia* and *History of the Indies*. Unfortunately, one of the most powerful works of this period, *A Brief Account of the Devastation of Africa*, was not published until the twentieth century.

Las Casas's proficiency in Indian languages, his widespread travel, and his acquaintance with leading Spaniards and Indians made him a key figure in the early history of Spanish America. His importance for European exploration comes from his immense literary output, especially his *History of the Indies*, which remains a standard source for information about Columbus's and Spain's first decades in the Americas.

[*See also* Black Legend; Central and South America, *subentries on* Colonies and Empires *and* Conquests and Colonization, *and* Spanish and Portuguese America, Reports and Descriptions of.]

WILLIAM DONOVAN

Latitude. *See* **Navigational Techniques.**

La Vérendrye, Sieur de (1685–1749), soldier, farmer, fur trader, and explorer of the western interior of Canada. Pierre Gaultier de Varennes et de la Vérendrye was born at Trois-Rivières in 1685; in 1712 he married Marie-Anne Dandonneau, with whom he had two daughters and four sons. Their sons—Jean-Baptiste (1713–1736), Pierre (1714–1755), François (1715–1794), and Louis-Joseph ("Chevalier"; 1717–1761)—were important in the trading and exploring ventures, as was a nephew, Christophe Dufrost de la Jemerais (1708–1736).

In 1696, Pierre La Vérendrye joined the colonial troops and saw action during the War of the Spanish Succession on the American frontier and in Newfoundland. In 1708 he requested to be transferred to France, where he became a second lieutenant in the Régiment de Bretagne. At the Battle of Malplaquet (1709) he was severely wounded and also captured. Following his release in 1710 he was promoted to lieutenant, but his days as a soldier were finished and he asked to be returned to Canada. Without rank and with few prospects, he arrived home in 1712, married, and began to scratch a living out of a small farm, an ensign's salary, and a small trading post on the Riviére Saint-Maurice.

In 1726, Pierre La Vérendrye's older brother Jacques-René (1677–1757) was appointed commandant of the *poste du Nord*, a vast fur-trading district encompassing the entire north shore of Lake Superior and holding its headquarters at Kaministiquia (Thunder Bay, Ontario). In order to finance the fur trade, Jacques-René took a number of merchants as partners, including his brother, whom he appointed second in command. In 1728, Pierre La Vérendrye assumed full command when Jacques-René departed with troops to fight the Fox Indians west of Lake Michigan.

Since earliest contact with North America, the French sought a navigable route across the continent and found support in tantalizing native stories about a distant western sea. By the end of the seventeenth century these stories had taken on a sharper meaning when Jacques de Noyon (1688) returned from Rainy Lake, where the Cree and Assiniboine had told him of a river ("English River") that flowed westward out of the Lake of the Woods into the "Western Sea" (probably Lake Winnipeg). Farther south, while a captive of the Santee Dakota, Father Hennepin was told that there was no such thing as a western sea nor a navigable passage across the continent. Hennepin's account notwithstanding, the question was no longer whether a western sea existed, but where it was located. With the death of Louis XIV in 1715, the Council of Regents under Philippe, Duc d'Orléans, acting for the young Louis XV, began to push for a renewed effort to discover the "Western Sea." In 1717, Zacharie Robutel de La Noue was appointed to find that body of water, but wars between the allied Dakota and Fox against the Cree, Assiniboine, and Illinois—French allies—prevented him from moving inland.

When La Vérendrye became commandant at Ka-ministiquia, he questioned Cree traders about the west. Convinced that there was a route westward and finding willing Cree to guide him, La Vérendrye took their reports and maps to Governor Charles de Beauharnois to gain support for exploration. Beauharnois in turn contacted, and received qualified support from, a skeptical Comte de Maurepas, Minister of the Marine, responsible for the French colonies. To help defray the costs of exploration, La Vérendrye asked for and received a monopoly on the fur trade in his new trade district northwest of Lake Superior, optimistically called Mer de l'Ouest (Western Sea).

In 1731, taking advantage of an uneasy peace with the Dakota and the imminent defeat of the Fox, La Vérendrye's nephew La Jemerais and La Vérendrye's son Jean-Baptiste La Vérendrye established a post on Rainy Lake. The following year, Fort Saint-Charles was built on Lake of the Woods by Pierre La Vérendrye, and in 1733, La Jemerais with Jean-Baptiste almost reached Lake Winnipeg. The reports gathered by Pierre La Vérendrye and his men were highly optimistic. They had heard from the Cree that the "Western Sea" was not far away, that toward the southwest was a Rivière de l'Ouest (the Missouri), and that the people (the Mandan) who lived on this river had dwellings "like French houses" and "speak a language which has some resemblance to French." Based on unproven stories such as these, glowing reports were sent to the governor and the Minister of the Marine—leading them to believe that major discoveries were imminent.

In 1734, with La Vérendrye at Fort Saint-Charles organizing the fur trade, Jean-Baptiste and La Jemerais went down the "English River," across the southern end of Lake Winnipeg, and to the junction of the Red and Assiniboine rivers. The same year, however, unable to restrain his Cree and Assiniboine allies who were bent on an attack on the Teton Dakota, La Vérendrye abandoned caution and traded them ammunition. In 1735 it became evident that the fur operation was not well organized and was leading to debt. Added to these problems was the death of La Jemerais, who had been La Vérendrye's most able lieutenant. A further blow came on June 8, 1736: while trying to get supplies for the ill-provided interior posts, the French canoe brigade was attacked on an island in Lake of the Woods by a force of Dakota; all nineteen Frenchmen were killed, including Jean-Baptiste La Vérendrye and the Jesuit father Jean-Pierre Aulneau. The attack was a grim reminder that it was better to promote peace and not take sides in intertribal warfare.

In spite of the tragedy, Louis-Joseph and his father went to Lake Winnipeg early in 1737, where they obtained native geographical information that allowed them to map the rough outline of the Manitoba Lakes system and the presence of a large river, Rivière Blanche (the Saskatchewan), toward the northwest. Armed with this information, La Vérendrye went to Quebec to reorganize his trade and to inform the governor that he was sending expeditions to discover and explore the two major western rivers. Minister Maurepas's patience was, however, running low, and he accused La Vérendrye of caring more for the beaver trade than for exploration.

Maurepas's statement that he demanded results was not to be taken lightly. When La Vérendrye returned to the west, he decided to visit the Mandan first. On October 16, 1738, he left Fort La Reine (Portage la Prairie, Manitoba) with twenty men, two sons (Louis-Joseph and François), and a large contingent of Assiniboine. They reached the Mandan on December 3, only to discover that the Missouri flowed toward the southeast. If La Vérendrye was disappointed, he did not say so. Exhausted and with mounting debts he set out for Quebec. Before he left, he sent Louis-Joseph north to explore Lake Winnipeg and to begin the exploration of the Saskatchewan River. On La Vérendrye's return from the east in 1741, too infirm himself to explore, he sent his sons Louis-Joseph and François to determine if there was a sea toward the southwest from the Mandan. Beginning on April 29, 1742, this epic journey took the brothers on a vast sweep across the American plains to the Big Horn Mountains, along the Platte and Missouri rivers, and back to Fort La Reine on July 2, 1743. While they were gone, their brother Pierre had built posts on Lake Winnipeg and Fort Paskoya (The Pas, Manitoba) on the Saskatchewan.

In spite of these successes, including the severe damage La Vérendrye's trade was doing to the Hudson's Bay Company, Maurepas's patience was at an end and he urged Governor Beauharnois to terminate the commission of the La Vérendrye family. La Vérendrye resigned but his sons stayed on. In 1744, La Vérendrye received, thanks to Governor Beauharnois, a captain's commission, and in 1746 he was reinstated, now as commandant, but was too old and infirm to comply. His reputation having been restored and having won high honors, he died on December 5, 1749.

[*See also* Fur Trade *and* Mer de l'Ouest and Rivière de l'Ouest.]

BIBLIOGRAPHY

Burpee, Lawrence J., ed. *Journals and Letters of Pierre Gaultier de Varennes de La Vérendrye and His Sons*. Toronto: The Champlain Society, 1927.

Eccles, William J. "French Exploration in North America, 1700–1800." In *North American Exploration*, edited by John L. Allen. 3 vols. *Vol. 2, A Continent Defined*. Lincoln: University of Nebraska Press, 1997.

Zoltvany, Yves F. "Gaultier de Varennes et de La Vérendrye, Pierre." In *Dictionary of Canadian Biography*, edited by George W. Brown. Vol. 3, *1741–1770*. Toronto: University of Toronto Press, 1974.

Conrad E. Heidenreich

Lawrence, T. E. (1888–1935), British explorer known to history as "Lawrence of Arabia." Thomas Edward Lawrence was born in Tremadoc, North

iv   PREFACE

actual commencement of operations until after the retirement of Sir E. Maunde Thompson and Mr. Hogarth's appointment to the Keepership of the Ashmolean Museum at Oxford. Consequently, although Mr. Hogarth was able to plan and direct the opening excavations, and to revisit the site in 1912 and 1914, he has not been able to undertake the principal conduct of them. During the first season Mr. R. Campbell Thompson was present as Mr. Hogarth's lieutenant, and, with the assistance of Mr. T. E. Lawrence, carried on the work after Mr. Hogarth's return to England. Mr. Thompson was unable to continue his connexion with the work after the first season, and the subsequent campaigns have been conducted by Mr. C. L. Woolley and Mr. T. E. Lawrence, who have co-operated with Mr. Hogarth in the production of this introductory section of the Report.

In conclusion the Trustees have to express their profound gratitude to an anonymous benefactor, whose enlightened liberality has rendered the continuance of these excavations possible. The results, of which a first instalment is now presented to the world, will, it is believed, fully justify the labour and the money that have been expended on them.

FREDERIC G. KENYON.

British Museum,
June 29, 1914.

T. E. Lawrence. From the foreword to the British Museum's *Carchemish: Report on the Excavations of Djerabis . . . Conducted by C. Leonard Woolley and T. E. Lawrence* (Oxford: Trustees of the British Museum, 1914). One is tempted, in reading this preface to an account of an archaeological dig, to wonder if the "anonymous benefactor, whose enlightened liberality has rendered the continuance of these excavations possible" was not perhaps the British War Office. Courtesy The Newberry Library, Chicago

Wales, on August 16, 1888, to a baronet who had assumed the name Lawrence when he ran off with his children's governess. As a young man, Lawrence studied modern history at Oxford. As part of his education, and through the influence of his academic adviser, D. G. Hogarth, Lawrence made his first trip to the Near East to gather information for his senior thesis on the influence of the Crusades on the architecture of Europe.

Following his graduation from Oxford in 1910, Lawrence attached himself to archaeological expeditions in Syria under Hogarth and Flinders Petrie. He then conducted surveys in the Sinai peninsula under the direction of Leonard Woolley. Some scholars contend that much of Lawrence's time in the Near East during these early expeditions was spent with an eye to gathering intelligence for the British government. Such reports are unconfirmed, but their compelling nature has added to Lawrence's mystique. Whatever Lawrence's exploratory pursuits during his civilian career, he gained a working knowledge of the area and its people. This experience led to his attachment to an intelligence unit out of Cairo not long after England entered World War I. From this point on, Lawrence's activities become the stuff of legend, as he was later credited with leading the Arab revolt that overthrew the Ottoman Empire in Arabia. Some commentators have questioned the extent of Lawrence's role in the Arab revolt, but there is no doubt that his early explorations provided him with an intimate understanding of the region and its peoples, and history has certainly credited him with the liberation of the Arabian peninsula from the Ottoman Turks.

Following a successful military career in World War I, Lawrence, disappointed at what he saw as the betrayal of the Arabs through the continued imperial presence (now French and British) on the Arabian peninsula, joined the Royal Air Force. Mere months after his retirement from the Royal Air Force, Lawrence was killed in a freak motorcycle accident near his cottage in Dorset, England, on May 19, 1935.

[*See also* Arabia.]

BIBLIOGRAPHY
Anderegg, Michael A. "Lawrence of Arabia: The Man, the Myth, the Movie." *Michigan Quarterly Review* 21, no. 2 (1982): 281–300.
Wilson, Jeremy. *Lawrence of Arabia*. New York: Atheneum, 1990.

RYAN M. SEIDEMANN

Lawson, John (1674–1711), British explorer of the Carolina backcountry. John Lawson is best known for his book titled *A New Voyage to Carolina*, which first appeared as a separate volume in London in 1709. The title is somewhat misleading since the book is primarily concerned with Lawson's adventures exploring the Carolina interior. Lawson arrived in Charleston from England in 1700. In December of that year he was appointed by the colony's administration to undertake a reconnaissance survey of the Carolina backcountry. At that date very little was known about the Indians living there or the region's geography and resources. It was not an easy assignment since there were no adequate maps or local guides available. Leaving Charleston by boat, Lawson explored the islands and inlets along the coast north to the Santee River. Traveling up the Santee, Lawson encountered and visited several Indian villages. Moving northwest the party wisely followed the network of Indian trading paths and benefited from knowledgeable Indian informants they encountered along the way. Near the site of present day Hillsborough, North Carolina, Lawson heard of impending Indian hostilities and secured a local Indian to guide him to the safety of the English coastal settlements. On the way they encountered a large group of Tuscarora Indians, some of whom broke off hunting to accompany Lawson to the frontier settlements near Pamlico Sound. It was here Lawson ended his "Journal of a Thousand Miles Travel'd thro' Several Nations of Indians, Giving Particular Account of Their Customs, Manners, &c.," the account that formed the heart of his book published in 1709. He had spent fifty-nine days on foot in winter to accomplish this arduous trip while taking daily notes describing the route, the flora and fauna, and Indian tribes then peopling the Carolina Piedmont.

Following his exploration Lawson remained in North Carolina where he acquired land and laid out the colony's first town, Bath, which quickly prospered as North Carolina's first port of entry. Lawson returned to London to oversee the publication of his book. In 1709, while still in England, Lawson was appointed to serve as a commissioner to negotiate with Virginia in settling the long-standing boundary dispute between the colonies. In 1729, when the boundary was finally surveyed it began at a point that was only a small distance from where Lawson had fixed it some two decades earlier. Lawson, named the colony's surveyor general, met his untimely death in 1711 when he was captured and executed by Tuscarora Indians. At the time of his capture Lawson was searching for land for a large settlement of German-speaking colonists led by Baron Christopher von Graffenried. The baron, whose life was spared by the

John Lawson. Plate from *The Natural History of North-Carolina* (Dublin/London, 1743). These images, from the early seventeenth century, remind us of the great difficulty that artists had in portraying creatures before the technical advances made by artists like Maria Sibylla Merian and Mark Catesby. COURTESY THE NEWBERRY LIBRARY, CHICAGO

Indians, went on to found New Bern, North Carolina, on a site laid out by Lawson.

BIBLIOGRAPHY

Harriss, Frances Latham, ed. *Lawson's History of North Carolina.* Richmond, Va.: Garrett and Massie, 1937.

Lawson, John. *A New Voyage to Carolina.* Edited with a new introduction and notes by Hugh Talmage Lefler. Chapel Hill: University of North Carolina Press, 1967.

LOUIS DE VORSEY

Leahy, Michael (1901–1979), Australian prospector who explored the Central Highlands of New Guinea. Michael James (Mick) Leahy was born at Toowoomba in Queensland on February 26, 1901, a son of the railway guard Daniel Leahy. Educated at the Christian Brothers College in Toowoomba, he worked as a railway clerk and timber cutter before being lured to New Guinea by the discovery of gold in 1926. Between 1930 and 1935 he and several companions became the first Europeans to explore what is now known as the Central Highlands.

In April 1930, Leahy and Michael Dwyer were commissioned to prospect for gold on the Ramu River. They traveled into the Goroka Valley and along the Wahgi River, and crossed the Bismarck Range to

Port Romilly on the Gulf of Papua. From here they traveled to Port Moresby by steamer and then hiked across the Owen Stanley Range to Morobe on the Huon Gulf and back to their base in Salamaua. Their trip lasted six months and covered more than 800 miles (1,200 kilometers).

In November 1930, Leahy and Dwyer crossed the Gafuku (Asaro) Valley, and two years later Leahy led two parties into the Watut Valley. In 1933, Leahy led separate expeditions to Mount Erimbari, to Mount Hagen, along the Sepik River, and south of the Wahgi-Nebilyer divide. In expeditions in 1934, he explored around Mount Hagen, climbed Mount Giluwe, and penetrated the Ebang.

Leahy's explorations opened much of the Highlands to Europeans and gave the world a glimpse of a previously unknown land. He coauthored *The Land That Time Forgot*, which was published in 1937; its five thousand photographs and many hours of moving film formed the basis of *First Contact*, a film released in 1983. Leahy was awarded the Royal Geographic Society's Murchison Medal in 1936, honorary membership of the U.S. Explorers Club in 1959, and the U.S. Explorers Club Explorers' Medal in 1971. Michael James Leahy died in New Guinea on March 7, 1979.

[*See also* Pacific.]

BIBLIOGRAPHY
Leahy, Michael J. *Explorations into Highland New Guinea, 1930–35*, edited by Douglas E Jones. Bathurst, Australia: Crawford House Press, 1994.

DENIS SHEPHARD

Leakey, Louis, and Mary Leakey,

British paleoanthropologists. Louis Seymour Bazett Leakey (1903–1972) and Mary Douglas Nicol Leakey (1913–1996) occupy a unique position in the history of exploration through their domination—for, collectively, nearly a century—of the field of human origins research. Louis Leakey was born to missionary parents, Harry and Gladys Leakey, in Kabete, Kenya, on August 7, 1903, and he grew up as one of a handful of people of European descent in the midst of the Kikuyu people of East Africa. Mary Leakey was born in London to Erskine and Cecilia Nicol on February 6, 1913. Whereas Louis became interested in anthropology as a child, after reading a book on ancient England and thereafter looking for artifacts near his Kenyan home, Mary discovered her interest in anthropology while traveling through Europe with her parents and visiting the sites of famous cave artworks.

Louis took a traditional approach to beginning a career in anthropology: he entered Cambridge to earn a degree in the field. While at Cambridge, Louis was a member of the British Museum's 1924 east African expedition, where he assisted in the collection of fossil reptiles and learned excavation techniques. After this expedition, and while he was still a student, Louis began to lead his own expeditions in his African homeland to search for human fossils. Mary, on the other hand, approached a career in anthropology in a less traditional manner. She attended a few courses but never earned a degree. Rather, she apprenticed herself to an established archaeologist in an effort to learn the trade. It was through her mentor that, in 1933, she met Louis, following one of his lectures.

After their first meeting, Louis and Mary began a lifetime partnership in the exploration of East Africa in search of fossil evidence of human origins. By the time Mary joined Louis's expedition in 1935, Louis was already a distinguished scientist. Many of Louis's initial finds came from areas that he had visited as a child in search of stone tools. Louis and Mary quickly expanded the early finds into a fossil enterprise through their walking expeditions in and around Olduvai Gorge in Tanzania. Their work in this veritable fossil wonderland made Olduvai Gorge one of the focal points of paleoanthropological expeditions for generations of researchers.

The Leakeys' expeditions and discoveries are too numerous to report. But most of them, though successful through what was discovered, were plagued by the usual hazards of research in an underdeveloped region: the Leakeys' automobiles, beginning with an old Model T Ford in the early years, were constantly getting bogged down in the muck; crew members, including Louis, were stricken with malaria; harsh weather, wild animals, and food, water, and funding shortages rounded out the difficulties. Despite these hardships, the fossil hunting paid off. During the course of their collective careers, the Leakeys found fragments of *Ramapithecus* skeletons (an ancient primate that lived around fifteen million years ago), various Olduwan and Acheulian stone tools (tool types associated with early hominids), skeletal fragments of *Australopithecus afarensis* and *Homo habilis* (ancestors of modern humans that were extant around 3.9 to 2.0 and 2.4 to 1.5 million years ago, respectively), and much else. Perhaps the two most significant finds that the Leakeys are known for are the discovery of the first remains of *Australopithecus boisei* (another human ancestor that lived around 2.1 to 1.1 million years ago) in the 1950s and Mary's

1978 discovery of hominid footprints in volcanic ash at the site of Laetoli in Tanzania. These footprints, which clearly showed a creature adapted to walking upright, were ultimately identified as belonging to *Australopithecus afarensis*, cementing in the scientific consciousness the reality of bipedality among our human ancestors for at least the last four million years. In addition to their explorations and discoveries, the Leakeys launched the careers of the primatologists Jane Goodall and Dian Fossey.

On October 1, 1972, just prior to beginning a lecture tour of America, Louis Leakey died of a heart attack in London. Mary, along with their son, Richard, continued to carry the family torch for several years. Mary ultimately retired from fieldwork to organize and publish the results of a lifetime of exploring. She passed away in Nairobi, Kenya, on December 9, 1996. The Leakey legacy of exploration and fossil hunting continues through the efforts of Louis and Mary's daughter-in-law, Meave Leakey, and their granddaughter, Louise.

[*See also* Africa, *subentry on* Scientific Exploration.]

BIBLIOGRAPHY
Morrell, Virginia. *Ancestral Passions: The Leakey Family and the Quest for Humankind's Beginnings.* New York: Simon & Schuster, 1995.

RYAN M. SEIDEMANN

Learned Societies. In order to understand the history and nature of learned societies concerned with the promotion and study of exploration, it is helpful to place them in broader context.

Historians of learned societies identify four general types of such institution but do not see discrete typological or chronological divisions between them. The first, "Renaissance Academies," which began in Florence in 1442, were bodies of educated citizens who gathered to reflect upon interests in numerous cultural subjects. The second, those "modern" institutions founded in urban Europe from the mid-seventeenth century, considered literary and natural philosophical inquiry central to their purpose. Funded by the state, royal, or other patronage or by members' subscriptions, such bodies held meetings, owned premises, and published their findings. Examples include the Royal Society of London (established in 1662) and, in Paris, the Académie Royale des Sciences (established in 1666), with the *Philosophical Transactions* and the *Histoire et Mémoires*, respectively. The third type, the eighteenth-century scientific society and learned academy, was a commonplace of the period. Their very ubiquity precludes further easy categorization. National learned institutions had provincial and regional parallels. Some bodies, but far from all, published transactions. Several had affiliations with their local university and foreign corresponding members. Others did not. Some societies emphasized belles-lettres, others agriculture or meteorology. What united them was an interest in utility—national, regional, or local "improvement"—in which, commonly, geographical exploration formed a basis for advances in knowledge. Finally, the nineteenth century witnessed the establishment of specialist professional bodies—for example, geographical societies—whose foundation reflected disciplinary specialization and for whom exploration, often funded in association with national governments and staffed by military personnel, was a major element of their remit.

Learned societies concerned with exploration broadly fit into this schema and offer one significant variant: those bodies specifically concerned with the history of exploration (rather than with its formal promotion), either through publication of exploration accounts and maps or through academic meetings. Two leading examples may be noted. The Hakluyt Society, named after the Elizabethan travel compiler Richard Hakluyt, was established on December 15, 1846, in order to publish the narratives of "rare and valuable voyages, travels and geographical records." The society's publications provide a vital record of world exploration. The Society for the History of Discoveries, founded in 1960 to stimulate interest in teaching, research, and publishing the history of geographical exploration, includes the journal *Terrae Incognitae* among its publications.

Many national learned societies early published "How to Travel" guides, methodological prospectuses designed to secure reliable information. Only later did they undertake exploration projects directly. The Académie Royale des Sciences supported the expeditions in the 1730s of Maupertuis and La Condamine in testing, in Lapland and South America, respectively, Newtonian and Cartesian theories about earth's shape. The Royal Society was involved in 1761 and 1769 in studying the transits of Venus, astronomical observations vital to terrestrial exploration. In addition to such activity, societies with a particular exploratory focus may be noted. The Meteorological Society of Mannheim undertook from 1780 to collect world weather data. The Asiatick Society, begun in 1784 by Sir William Jones, included "the geography of Hindusthan" (and of Asia generally) in its remit.

The focus of the African Association, established in London in 1788, was African exploration and the commercial opportunities afforded by new geographical knowledge.

Some specialist societies descended from earlier institutions. The Royal Geographical Society (RGS), formally constituted in London on July 16, 1830, had its roots in the African Association and the Raleigh Dining Club, founded in February 1827. The RGS was a leading institution for the promotion of exploration, in 1830–1833 especially, notably in Africa, India, and the polar regions. Yet it was also part of the wider establishment of national geographical societies, each of which undertook exploration of its national territories and colonial possessions. The Geographical Society of Paris was begun in 1821, Berlin in 1828, Mexico City in 1833, and Rio de Janeiro in 1838, along with the American Geographical Society of New York in 1851, to name but a few. The Palestine Exploration Fund established in 1865 reflected British interests in the scriptural geography of the Holy Land and had active German and French counterparts.

Large-scale exploration is less central than it once was to these bodies. Yet learned societies continue to see exploration as educationally important to all. The Society of Women Geographers was founded in 1925 by four American women explorers. The Polynesian Voyaging Society, begun in 1973, sees its modern voyages as an affirmation of Hawaiian identity through exploration.

[*See also* African Association; Explorers Club; Geographical Society of Paris; National Geographic Society; Royal Geographical Society; *and* Venus, Transit of.]

BIBLIOGRAPHY

Cameron, Ian. *To The Farthest Ends of the Earth: 150 Years of World Exploration by the Royal Geographical Society.* New York: Dutton, 1980.

Dunbar, Gary S. "Societies for the Histories of Discoveries." *Terrae Incognitae* 6 (1974): 65–71.

McClellan, James E., III. *Science Reorganized: Scientific Societies in the Eighteenth Century.* New York: Columbia University Press, 1985.

Charles W. J. Withers

Lederer, John (c. 1644–?), German explorer of Virginia and Carolina backcountry. John Lederer was born in Germany and grew up in Hamburg. He matriculated at the Hamburg Academic Gymnasium on April 18, 1662, and by 1670 he was in Virginia. At that time the colony was still struggling and settlement was restricted to the coastal plain. In an effort to assess the backcountry, the governor of Virginia commissioned Lederer to explore the interior of the colony. At the time it was still widely believed that the Pacific Ocean was within easy reach by following streams flowing westward from the Appalachian Mountains.

In the early spring of 1670 Lederer, with three Indian guides, undertook the first of three expeditions into the backcountry of Virginia and the Carolinas. About twelve miles northeast of Charlottesville they encountered and climbed what he described as "an eminent hill," and from this vantage point Lederer first saw the Blue Ridge, which he termed the "Apalataean Mountains." Ascending the Blue Ridge on foot Lederer spied no easy passage through the mountains and upon encountering snow and harsh conditions decided to return.

In May of 1670 Lederer, with a company of twenty mounted Virginians and five Indians, undertook a march to the falls of the James River, the site of present-day Richmond. Here they ignored the recommendations of Indian villagers as to the best route to follow to the mountains. As a consequence their trip was very difficult. Reaching a northward flowing river the Virginians thought must connect to the "Lake of Canada," they decided to return home with the news. Lederer was unimpressed and produced his personal commission from the governor, and he was allowed to strike out with one Indian guide to continue exploring. Following Indian advice and paths Lederer turned toward the south to avoid the Blue Ridge barrier and completed his most extensive exploration of the Piedmont Southeast. Some of the discoveries Lederer reported have puzzled modern readers of his book and map, which were published in 1672. These include a vast brackish lake he called *Ushery*, periodically flooded expanses he termed *Savanaea*, and a barren sandy desert named *Arenosa*, crossing which he reported he almost died of thirst.

Lederer undertook his third and final exploration in late August of 1670, when he and a well-equipped group traveled from the upper Rappahannock River to the crest of the Blue Ridge, which they reached on August 26. Climbing the heights they looked west over the Shenandoah River to the mountains in the far distance. After drinking the king's health they climbed down and returned home. What they had seen convinced Lederer that people who believed that North America could be crossed to the Pacific Ocean in only eight or ten days were "in a great errour." Beyond describing in his book what he had seen and experienced Lederer included detailed in-

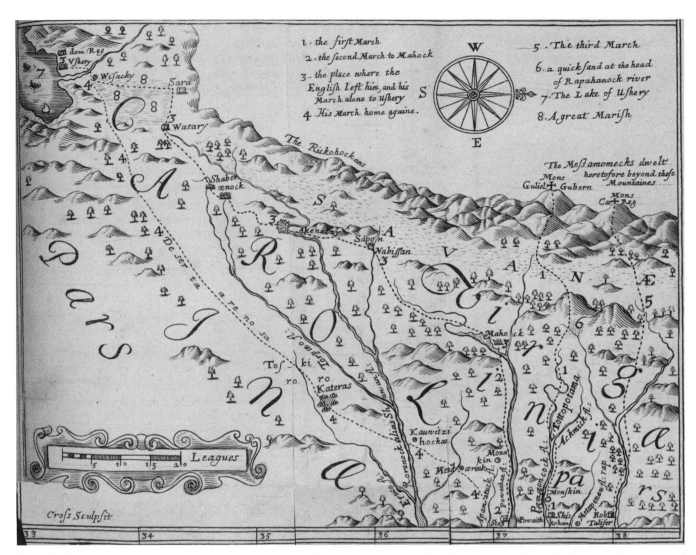

John Lederer. A map of the whole territory traversed by John Lederer in *The Discoveries of John Lederer in Three Several Marches from Virginia to the West of Carolina* (London, 1672). This map, oriented to the west, shows the three expeditions made by Lederer in his vain attempt to show that it would be easy to reach the Pacific Ocean by following streams flowing westward out of the Appalachians. COURTESY THE NEWBERRY LIBRARY, CHICAGO

structions for would-be explorers of the continent as well as a discussion of trade with the Indians.

Sometime in late 1670 Lederer moved to Maryland claiming that he had been hounded out of Virginia by factions opposed to the Indian policies of Governor William Berkeley. In Maryland, Lederer gained the esteem of William Talbot, secretary of the province and judge of probate. Returning to Ireland to claim his inheritance Talbot was responsible, in 1672, for the translation from Latin of Lederer's exploration journals and their publication with a map

under the title *The Discoveries of John Lederer in Three Several Marches from Virginia, to the West of Carolina*. In late 1673 or early in the following year Lederer traveled to Connecticut where he practiced medicine, returning home to Hamburg in 1681 after an incredibly active decade in the American colonies.

BIBLIOGRAPHY

Briceland, Alan Vance. *Westward from Virginia: The Exploration of the Virginia-Carolina Frontier, 1650–1710.* Charlottesville: University of Virginia Press, 1987.

Cumming, William P., ed. *The Discoveries of John Lederer*. Charlottesville: University of Virginia Press, 1958.

LOUIS DE VORSEY

Ledyard, John (1751–1789), American adventurer. John Ledyard was born in Groton, Connecticut, on November 21, 1751. He sailed in the Pacific Ocean with Captain James Cook on Cook's third voyage, walked across much of Siberia, and was hired by the African Association to explore the region between the Nile and Niger rivers. At age twenty-one, Ledyard enrolled at the newly founded Dartmouth College, where after four months he disappeared for more than one hundred days. He later told classmates that he had sojourned with Iroquois Indians along the Canadian border. Ledyard was in England in 1776, where he signed up to be corporal of marines on Cook's third voyage. Despite his low rank, his name is mentioned several times in official voyage documents. At Unalaska in October 1778, he was responsible for establishing the first communication with Russian fur traders. Later, on February 14, 1779, Ledyard witnessed Cook's murder at Kealakekua Bay, Hawaii.

Ledyard's book, *A Journal of Captain Cook's Last Voyage to the Pacific Ocean* (Hartford, 1783), is remarkable because he particularly includes incisive ethnological observations. He hypothesized about the origins of the Tahitians, claiming that they undoubtedly had Asian origins. When Cook landed at Nootka Sound, British Columbia, in March 1778, Ledyard had another opportunity to observe American Indians. This short visit to the American northwest was to obsess his thinking for the rest of his life. He noticed that the Nootka used several implements that must have been acquired through trade with other tribes as far east as Hudson Bay. If trade items could find their way across the continent by going from tribe to tribe, Ledyard himself could follow a similar route, he thought, even though no white man before him had ever crossed the North American expanse. Furthermore, he saw pelts of American origin being sold in Canton, China, for three times more than farther north in Kamchatka.

After returning from the Pacific in 1780, Ledyard made many futile attempts to gain backing for his trading venture in the Pacific northwest. During this time, he met Thomas Jefferson, then U.S. minister to France, and he had a short-lived partnership with John Paul Jones. Jefferson suggested that Ledyard walk across Siberia to reach his destination. Following this suggestion, Ledyard, after four months of trekking through Scandinavia, arrived in Saint Petersburg in March 1787. By August he had reached Irkutsk, where he spent the winter. His observations were kept in a journey diary in which he again included many ethnological comments and often compared indigenous Siberian peoples with those he had seen in America, China, and the Pacific. His journey ended, however, when he was arrested in January 1788 and transported nonstop to the Polish border and deported as a spy. His travel journal and selected letters have been published in *John Ledyard's Journey through Russia and Siberia, 1787–1788* (1966).

Ledyard returned to London in June 1788, where he was offered employment by Sir Joseph Banks to be the first explorer commissioned by the African Association. He arrived in Cairo in August 1788, with orders to cross the Sahara Desert to Timbuctoo. But before he could begin his journey, he died there on January 10, 1789, from what has been described as a "bilious complaint."

[*See also* African Association; Banks, Joseph; Cook, James; *and* Siberia.]

BIBLIOGRAPHY

Ledyard, John. *A Journal of Captain Cook's Last Voyage to the Pacific Ocean and in Quest of a North-west Passage between Asia and America, Performed in the Years 1776, 1777, 1778, and 1779*. Chicago: Quadrangle Books, 1963. Originally published in 1783.

Watrous, Stephen D., ed. *John Ledyard's Journey through Russia and Siberia, 1787–1788: The Journal and Selected Letters*. Madison: University of Wisconsin Press, 1966.

Zug, James. *American Traveler: The Life and Adventures of John Ledyard, the Man Who Dreamed of Walking the World*. New York: Basic Books, 2005.

SANFORD H. BEDERMAN

Leichhardt, Ludwig (1813–1848?), German scientist and explorer who disappeared while crossing Australia. Friedrich Wilhelm Ludwig Leichhardt was born at Trebatsch in Prussia on October 23, 1813, a son of Christian Hieronymus Matthias Leichhardt, a farmer and royal inspector of peat. Ludwig Leichhardt attended various universities and indulged his interest in natural history by traveling through England and Europe and, in 1842, by traveling to Australia with the expressed intention of exploring its interior.

Shortly after his arrival in Australia, Leichhardt embarked on a series of minor explorations. Over the next two years he traveled from Sydney, through the Hunter Valley, to the Darling Downs, Brisbane, and the Bunya Mountains, gathering information about the flora, fauna, and geology. In 1844 he

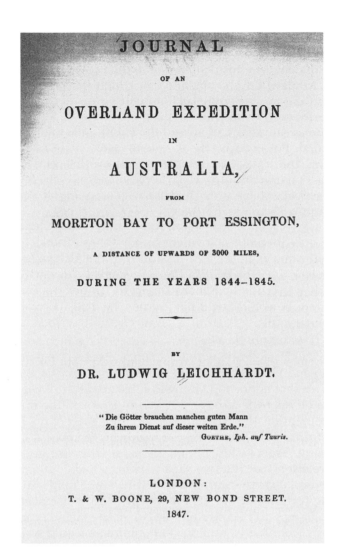

Ludwig Leichhardt. Title page of Ludwig Leichhardt's *Journal of an Overland Expedition in Australia* (London: T. & W. Boone, 1847). Leichhardt's slightly harebrained expeditions were followed with great interest in England. Note the quotation from Goethe, affirming that the gods draw many good men into their service at the ends of the earth. COURTESY THE NEWBERRY LIBRARY, CHICAGO

gained public support from the pastoral and mercantile communities for a small, poorly equipped private expedition into northern Australia. Joined by ten volunteers, the party left Jimbour on the Darling Downs on October 1. Two men turned back almost immediately, but the rest continued on north to Cape York, where John Gilbert was killed by Aboriginals. The expedition then skirted the Gulf of Carpentaria to reach Port Essington on December 17, 1845. They had traveled almost 3,100 miles (5,000 kilometers), crossing good pastoral country and naming many

features, mostly for Leichhardt's benefactors. The route he followed was, however, too circuitous to be of practical value.

Leichhardt returned to Sydney as a hero. He received £2,500 from the government and private subscribers and settled down to write up his journal, give public lectures, and organize his next expedition, a crossing of the continent from the Darling Downs to the west coast. On the first attempt, in December 1846, his party was forced to turn back by drought conditions, after having traveled 500 miles (800 kilometers). Having rested for two weeks, Leichhardt spent six weeks examining country around the Condamine River. In March 1848, he again headed for the Swan River settlement, this time with a poorly equipped party of eight. The expedition disappeared after leaving Cogoon station on the Darling River. Several parties have unsuccessfully searched for material evidence of Leichhardt's fate.

Although dismissed by many as a poor leader and bushman, Leichhardt is rated highly by others for his achievements. In 1847 he shared the annual prize

---

Dangers of Travel in Australia

The Prussian Leichhardt led a series of expeditions into the Australian interior with a determination that bordered on recklessness. Here he described the result of an attack on his party near Cape York; the ornithologist Gilbert was killed, and many other members of the party were likewise struck by spears, some of which were barbed and very difficult to remove.

Not seeing Mr. Gilbert, I asked for him, when Charley told me that our unfortunate companion was no more! He had come out of his tent with his gun, shot and powder, and handed them to him, when he instantly dropped down dead. Upon receiving this afflicting intelligence, I hastened to the spot, and found Charley's account too true. He was lying on the ground at a little distance from our fire, and upon examining him, I soon found to my sorrow that every sign of life had disappeared. . . . The spear that terminated poor Gilbert's existence had entered the chest, between the clavicle and the neck, but made so small a wound that for some time I was unable to detect it.

—Ludwig Leichhardt, *Journal of an Overland Expedition in Australia* (London, 1847)

of the Geographical Society in Paris, and in May the same year, the Royal Geographical Society awarded him its patrons medal. Leichhardt left detailed records of his observations in diaries, letters, notebooks, sketchbooks, and maps. His *Journal of an Overland Expedition in Australia, from Moreton Bay to Port Essington . . . during the Years 1844–45* was published in 1847.

[*See also* Australia, Exploration of.]

BIBLIOGRAPHY

Favenc, Ernest. *The History of Australian Exploration from 1788 to 1888*. Sydney, Australia: Turner and Henderson, 1888. Reprint. Amsterdam: Meridian, 1967.

McLaren, Glen. *Beyond Leichhardt: Bushcraft and the Exploration of Australia*. Fremantle, Australia: Fremantle Arts Centre Press, 1996. Reprint, 2000.

Millar, Ann. *"I See No End to Travelling": Journals of Australian Explorers 1813–76*. Sydney, Australia: Bay Books, 1986.

Webster, E. M. *Whirlwinds in the Plain: Ludwig Leichhardt—Friends, Foes, and History*. Carlton, Australia: Melbourne University Press, 1980.

DENIS SHEPHARD

Leifr Eiríksson (fl. c. 990 C.E.), medieval Norse explorer. Medieval Icelandic works provide an ancestry of doughty navigators for Leifr (Leif), eldest son of Eiríkr "Rauði" Thorvaldsson (Erik "the Red" Thorvaldsson) and spearhead of the medieval Norse exploration of North America. Leif's mother Thjóðhildr (Thjodhild) is also accounted for, but while the "Saga of the Sworn Brothers" mentions his son Thorkellr (Thorkell), his wife remains anonymous. Leifr's date of birth is also unknown. However, when Eiríkr founded the Norse Greenland colony and established himself at Brattahlið (Steep Slope) in southwest Greenland about 990 C.E., he came with his wife and their sons Leifr, Thorvaldr (Thorvald), and Thorsteinn (Thorstein), and a daughter, Freydis.

Leifr inherited Brattahlið and his father's chieftaincy after he had earned the nickname "the Lucky" and a reputation as an explorer of considerable courage and administrative ability. Two thirteenth-century Icelandic sagas—the *Saga of Erik the Red* and the *Saga of the Greenlanders*—credit him with organizing the voyages in the early eleventh century that are commonly associated with Vínland (Wine Land), the southernmost of three loosely defined American regions that the Norse named while coasting south from Baffin Island (called Helluland or Slab Land) along the Canadian east coast. These endeavors might more appropriately be called voyages to Markland (Forest Land), however, because Leifr's object would have been to locate the timber sources he found well before reaching the south shore of the Saint Lawrence and the grapes that nourished the exotic and mythical elements in the sagas.

Modern scholars have focused on separating ascertainable facts from such saga inventions as Freydis Eiríksdottir's valkyrian demeanor, and on examining previously accepted assertions made in secondary works. For example, the claim that Leifr went to North America as a missionary is based on a thirteenth-century version of the *Saga of the Greenlanders* reflecting the Icelandic monk Gunnlaugr (Gunnlaug) Leifsson's wish to glorify the Christian achievements of King Tryggvason of Norway. Leifr and several of his men may well have been baptized, but Greenland was more than a century away from a formal association with the Roman Church, and there is no evidence that the Norse Greenlanders at any time attempted to convert Arctic natives in Greenland to Christianity.

The *Saga of the Greenlanders* credits the incurious Bjarni Herjolfsson with the chance discovery of land beyond Greenland, while the *Saga of Erik the Red* gives that honor to Leifr, who subsequently followed up on his own discovery. Adam of Bremen, the first to mention the Norsemen's Vínland, merely noted (around 1075) that Vínland had been discovered by many. Adam's phrasing fits the commonsense interpretation that the two saga narrators had conflated several chance sightings, including some made during the northern hunts for walrus and other marine resources that featured in the Norse Greenland economy from the beginning. Norse hunters would soon have known that there was land on the other side of the Davis Strait within a manageable distance, and reports of forests farther south would have suggested Leifr's course of action in searching for the timber resources that Greenland lacked. Leifr's American undertaking was a business venture, and there is mounting archaeological evidence that the Norse Greenlanders continued to exploit American resources for several centuries more.

The *Saga of Erik the Red* says that Leifr's youngest brother, Thorsteinn, owned half of a farm in the Western Settlement. This was most likely the Sandnes site, which, like Brattahlið four hundred miles to the south, remained important throughout the Norse tenure in the region. The Norse sailed north along the west coast of Greenland before heading west below Disko Island and would have taken advantage of the strategically located Sandnes farm site. Although the *Saga of Erik the Red* reports only three voyages rather than the six in *Saga of the Greenlanders* (which involved Leifr's two brothers as well as his brother-in-law and the treacherous Freydis), both sagas indicate that Leifr's family intended to control any American profits. When Leifr's Icelandic brother-in-law Karlsefni planned a colonizing venture, he could only borrow the houses that Leifr had constructed in Vínland.

The Norse site at L'Anse aux Meadows in Newfoundland may well contain Leifr's houses and is certainly proof of Norse tenancy, but it cannot reveal the location of Vínland because Leifr had named a regional peculiarity, not a definable space.

[*See also* Greenland.]

BIBLIOGRAPHY

Hreinsson, Viðár, ed. *The Complete Sagas of Icelanders*. Reykjavík, Iceland: Leifur Eiríksson Publishing, 1997. A conscientiously translated, well-indexed, and annotated collection of the Icelandic sagas.

Pálsson, Hermann, and Paul Edwards, trans. and eds. *Landnámabók* [*Book of Settlements*], vol. 1. Winnipeg: University of Manitoba Icelandic Studies, 1972. A classic.

Wallace, Birgitta Linderoth. "The Viking Settlement at L'Anse aux Meadows." In *Vikings: The North Atlantic Saga*, edited by William W. Fitzhugh and Elisabeth I. Ward, 208–216. Washington and London: Smithsonian Institution Press, 2000.

KIRSTEN A. SEAVER

Le Maire, Jakob (1585–1616), Dutch explorer who led an expedition that rounded and named Cape Horn. Le Maire's father Isaac (1558–1624) was a wealthy merchant who was one of the founders of the Dutch East India Company (Vereenigde Oostindische Compagnie or VOC). After he was forced to resign from the company, Isaac Le Maire sent out his own expedition, with two goals: first, to find a new route to the East Indies, south of the Strait of Magellan, in order to avoid the monopoly of the VOC, and second, to discover the *Terra Australis Incognita*. The commander of the expedition was his son Jakob, born in Amsterdam, and the captain was Willem Cornelisz Schouten, who had already sailed three times to the East Indies. The expedition's two ships, the *Eendracht* and the *Hoorn*, sailed from Texel on May 16, 1615, heading for Africa and South America. They ran aground at Porto Desire (now Puerto Deseado) at 47°40' S on the Patagonian coast, where the *Hoorn* caught fire and was lost.

Sailing farther south, the *Eendracht* passed through what was named Le Maire Strait, discovering Staten Land (now Staten Island), which was thought to be part of a large landmass. On January 29, 1616, the expedition rounded the southernmost point of South America, naming it Cape Horn. From the Juan Fernández Islands sailing west, they discovered islands in the Tuamotu Archipelago, the Tonga Islands, and the Admiralty Islands.

The *Eendracht* reached Batavia on October 28, 1616, where all the crew was arrested by the local Dutch authorities, accused of having violated the VOC monopoly. They were sent back to Holland to be sentenced, traveling on the *Amsterdam*, commanded by Joris van Spilbergen, who was on the return of his circumnavigation. Jakob Le Maire died on December 22, 1616, on the homeward journey; Willem Schouten and the others arrived in Holland on July 7, 1617. After two years of suing the VOC for the illegal seizure of the *Eendracht*, Issac Le Maire won his case.

[*See also Terra Australis Incognita*.]

BIBLIOGRAPHY

Beaglehole, J. C. *The Exploration of the Pacific*. London: A. and C. Black, 1934.

Engelbrecht, W. A., and P. J. Van Herwerden, eds. *De ontdekkingsreis van Jacob Le Maire en Willem Cornelisz Schouten in de jaren 1615–1617: Journalen, documenten, en andere bescheiden*. 2 vols. De Linschoten-Vereeniging 49. The Hague: Nijhoff, 1945.

Le Maire, Jakob. *Spieghel der Australische navigatie*. Amsterdam: Michiel Colijn, 1622.

Schouten, Willem Cornelisz. *Iournal ofte Beschryvinghe van de wonderlijcke reyse*. Amsterdam: Willem Jantz, 1618.

JOHAN DECKERS

Lenz, Oskar (1848–1925), German geologist who explored the Ogowe River and traveled to Timbuctoo. A German-Austrian geologist, geographer, and explorer of Africa, Lenz was born in Leipzig, Germany, on April 13, 1848. After receiving a doctorate in mineralogy and geology at the University of Leipzig in 1870, Lenz worked for the Imperial Geological Institute of Vienna and became an Austrian citizen in 1873. Over the next thirteen years he traversed great swaths of both Saharan and sub-Saharan Africa. In 1874, sponsored by the German African Society, he traveled to western equatorial Africa to continue the exploration of the Ogowe River (in present-day Gabon) that Alfred Marche and the Marquis de Compiègne had been forced to abandon earlier the same year. Lenz was held a prisoner by Okandé natives on the middle Ogowe for nearly a year until liberated by Pierre Savorgnan di Brazza's first Ogowe expedition in 1876. He participated in the Brazza expedition for several months until health issues forced his return to the coast in 1877. Lenz's second African journey took place between 1879 and 1880. Beginning at Casablanca, Morocco, he traveled over the Atlas Mountains and southward across the Sahara more than 1,500 miles (2,400 kilometers) to Timbuctoo, in present-day Mali. Afterward, he ascended the Niger River more than 300 miles (483 kilometers) and then crossed by land to the Senegal River, following it downstream more than 500 miles (800 kilometers) to the west African coast. On his third African voyage, from 1885 to 1887, Lenz crossed the African continent from west to east as leader of the Austro-Hungarian Congo Expedition. The expedition was dispatched to provide aid to German explorer Wilhelm Johann Junker, whose party was trapped in the southern Sudan by the Mahdist uprising to the north. Lenz's party ascended the Congo from its mouth to the Lualaba River, then traveled overland to the northern shore of Lake Tanganyika. Failing to reach Junker, Lenz and his party continued to Lake Nyasa (present-day Lake Malawi) and from there to the coast on the Indian Ocean. After this trip, Lenz was appointed professor of geography at the German University in Prague, a position he held until his retirement in 1909. Lenz died March 2, 1925, in Soos, Lower Austria. Lenz recounted his African explorations in three books: *Skizzen aus Westafrika* (1878), *Timbuktu: Reise durch Marokko, die Sahara, und den Sudan* (1884), and *Wanderungen in Afrika* (1895).

[*See also biographies of figures mentioned in this article.*]

BIBLIOGRAPHY
Lenz, Oskar. *Skizzen aus Westafrika.* Berlin: A. Hofmann and Co., 1878.
Lenz, Oskar. *Timbuktu: Reise durch Marokko, die Sahara, und den Sudan, ausgeführt im Auftrage der Afrikanischen Gesellschaft in Deutschland in den Jahren 1879 und 1880.* Leipzig: F. A. Brockhaus, 1884.
Lenz, Oskar. *Wanderungen in Afrika: Studien und Erlebnisse.* Vienna: Verlag der Literarischen Gesellschaft, 1895.

JOHN P. SULLIVAN

Leo Africanus, (c. 1489/1505–c. 1550), Muslim traveler to Timbuctoo. Leo Africanus was also known as Giovanni Leone Africano (Italian) and al-Hasan ibn Muhammad al-Wazzān al-Zaiyāti, or al-Fāsi (Arabic). Africanus was a Muslim-born traveler and Christian convert whose sixteenth-century *Descrittione dell'Africa* was Europe's main source on Sudanic West Africa until well into the nineteenth century.

Most of the sketchy biographical information on Leo derives from his *Descrittione*. Born to Muslim parents in Granada, Spain, perhaps after its conquest by Queen Isabella of Castile and King Ferdinand II of Aragon in 1492, Leo was educated in Fez,

Morocco. His book mentions two trans-Saharan journeys to Timbuctoo, the first in 1509–1510 in the company of an uncle on a diplomatic mission, and the second in 1512–1514, when he may also have visited Walata, Jenne, Mali, Hausaland, and Bornu. He was in Rosetta, Egypt, in 1517, the year of the Ottoman conquest of that country. He went up the Nile to Cairo and Aswan, and may have visited Mecca and Istanbul. Christian corsairs captured him on his way home and presented him to Pope Leo X. The pope freed him and sponsored his baptism in 1520 as Giovanni Leone Africano. Some scholars have questioned whether Leo ever crossed the Sahara, suggesting that his sketchy and sometimes erroneous information on Timbuctoo and other sub-Saharan sites could have come from travelers he met in Morocco or Egypt. Leo returned to Tunis in 1550 and died there, apparently as a Muslim, sometime thereafter.

Writing in poor Italian from Arabic notes, Leo finished his *Descrittione dell'Africa* in Rome in 1526. It was published in Venice in 1550 and translated into several European languages. John Pory's English version, *A Geographical Historie of Africa* (London, 1600, reissued with notes by Robert Brown in 1896), was unfortunately based on the error-riddled Latin version (Antwerp, 1556). The original Italian manuscript, discovered in 1931, made possible A. Épaulard's authoritative French translation (2 vols., Paris, 1956).

Despite his errors, Leo established the framework of European knowledge of sub-Saharan Sudanic Africa for nearly three hundred years. (Few of the early Portuguese accounts, which in any case mainly treated the coast, were widely available until the late nineteenth century.) Except for introductory and concluding chapters, Leo proceeds geographically, with a chapter each on Marrakesh (southeastern Morocco); Fez; Tlemcen (Algeria); Bougie and Tunis; southeastern Morocco through the desert to Libya; the Sudan or "land of the blacks"; and Egypt. Lands farther south, including Ethiopia, go unmentioned. The chapter on Fez is the fullest and most accurate, but chapter 7 on the Sudan was the critical one for Europeans. Leo was the key source of European information on Timbuctoo and its fabulous gold trade until the nineteenth century, with its European explorations and publication of medieval Arabic texts. Leo's description of the rise of the Songhai empire is valuable, but he missed the great empire of Mali, which Ibn Battuta had described, and seems to have confused the Arab geographers' early empire of Ghana with the city of Kano in Hausaland.

[*See also* Timbuctoo.]

BIBLIOGRAPHY

Masonen Pekka. *The Negroland Revisited: Discovery and Invention of the Sudanese Middle Ages.* Humanoria series of the Annales Academiae Scientiarum Fennicae. Helsinki: Finnish Academy of Science and Letters, 2000.

DONALD MALCOLM REID

Leopold II (1835–1909; r. 1865–1909), Belgian king who led European colonization and exploitation of central Africa. Born on April 9, 1835, in Brussels, the son of Leopold I, Louis Philippe Marie Victor became king of the Belgians in 1865. As Leopold II, he was reviled and condemned for the brutal management of the Congo Free State, an enormous territory in central Africa that became his personal domain.

As the constitutional monarch of a very small country, Leopold believed that Belgium—like other, larger, European countries—should possess overseas colonies. Through diplomatic cunning, he used geographical explorers to further his plans to obtain territory in Africa. First establishing himself as a humane philanthropist and abolitionist, Leopold organized what is known as the Brussels Geographical Conference. Between September 12 and September 14, 1876, he invited illustrious explorers, geographers, missionaries, and businessmen to consider only two items: (1) the creation of a plan that would coordinate future geographical exploration in central Africa, and (2) the development of a strategy to suppress the region's slave trade. Among the conference delegates were the explorers Gustav Nachtigal, Gerhard Rohlfs, Georg Schweinfurth, Verney Lovett Cameron, James Augustus Grant, Henri Duveyrier, and the Marquis de Compiègne. Notably absent were Henry Stanley, who was in the Congo, and Pierre Savorgnan di Brazza, who purposely was not invited. Because of diplomatic inaction, nothing was done to implement the recommendations made by the conference. Of considerable consequence, however, was that the conference became the springboard for Leopold II to claim control over the vast Congo region and all of its natural resources.

A strong admirer of Henry Stanley, Leopold contacted him in late 1877 seeking his services to help colonize his new African domain. Stanley finally accepted the offer in 1879. Concerned with France (and its representative, Savorgnan di Brazza), which also wished to lay claim to the Congo, Stanley spent the next five years exploring the region, negotiating treaties with tribal chiefs, building roads, and establishing towns, one of which was Stanleyville. Also

during this time, Leopold commissioned Hermann von Wissmann (the first German to cross Africa from coast to coast) to explore the Kasai region in 1883–1884. Wissmann subsequently traced the Kasai River to its confluence with the Congo River and also founded the town of Luluabourg (now Kananga). Later, the experienced Canadian explorer and mercenary Captain William Stairs was sent by Leopold to Katanga with a military contingent to establish control of the region's copper resources.

At the Berlin Conference (1884–1885), Leopold II was formally recognized as sovereign of the Congo Free State, which he legitimately ruled as his personal domain until 1908, when he was forced by Parliament to cede it to Belgium. During this time, Leopold became enormously wealthy, especially from the proceeds of rubber and copper activities in the Congo. His reputation as a humanitarian was irreparably tattered by reports of his rapacity and inhumane treatment of the indigenous population. Brutally mistreated and exploited, they were victims of murder, maiming, starvation, and exhaustion from being overworked.

Leopold II died on December 17, 1909, at his royal residence at Laeken, and is buried there. Modern biographers and historians universally condemn him. One of his most severe detractors, the American poet Vachel Lindsay, expressed the disgust of many when he wrote:

> Listen to the yell of Leopold's ghost
> Burning in Hell for his hand-maimed host
> Hear how the demons chuckle and yell
> Cutting his hands off, down in Hell.

[*See also* Africa; Brussels Geographical Conference; Imperialism and Exploration; *and biographical entries on figures mentioned in this article.*]

BIBLIOGRAPHY

Ascherson, Neal. *The King Incorporated: Leopold II in the Age of Trusts.* Garden City, N.Y.: Doubleday, 1964.

Hochschild, Adam. *King Leopold's Ghost: A Story of Greed, Terror, and Heroism in Colonial Africa.* Boston: Houghton Mifflin, 1998.

SANFORD H. BEDERMAN

Léry, Jean de (c. 1536–c. 1613), French-born writer and traveler in Brazil. Jean de Léry was born about 1536 in Burgundy, France, and died about 1613 in Switzerland. His long life spanned the most intense period of the religious wars in France, and he himself was converted to Protestantism and had to flee France for Geneva, the center of Calvin's ref-

Jean de Léry. Woodcut showing greeting among the Tupinamba, from Léry's *Histoire d'un voyage faict en la terre du Bresil* (Geneva,1578). This is a good example of the way in which Léry meshed word and image, for the accompanying text explains how the Tupinamba weep their greetings; the visitor is then expected at least "to heave a few sighs and pretend to weep." COURTESY THE NEWBERRY LIBRARY, CHICAGO

ormation. There de Léry was chosen to take part in the 1556 expedition of Nicolas de Villegagnon, who was trying to set up a mixed Catholic and Protestant colony in what is now the bay of Rio de Janeiro. Eventually the Catholic colonists chased out their Protestant colleagues, which forced de Léry to take refuge among the local Indians. He spent almost a year with them, obtaining intimate knowledge of their way of life.

De Léry wrote an account of the Tupinamba Indians soon after his return to Europe in 1558, and after many vicissitudes the account was published in 1578 as *Histoire d'un voyage fait en la terre du Bresil, autrement dite Amerique* (*History of a Voyage to the Land of Brazil, Otherwise Called America*). It was a remarkable work, in which de Léry was clearly torn between his desire to portray his hosts as noble savages and his evident distaste for certain aspects of their life, including cannibalism. His work contained images that powerfully commented on the adjacent text; in this respect his book was something of a pioneer.

De Léry's Catholic counterpart as a commentator on the ways of the Tupinamba was André Thevet. Most modern critics have found Thevet's account of life in Brazil to lack the precision and intimacy of de Léry's account. These competing accounts have given rise in recent years to many works of criticism, by such scholars as Claude Lévi-Strauss and Frank Lestringant. De Léry's images remain particularly compelling for those trying to understand the impact of New World societies on Old World sensibilities.

[*See also* Cannibalism; Exploration Texts; *and* Thevet, André.]

BIBLIOGRAPHY

Léry, Jean de. *History of a Voyage to the Land of Brazil, Otherwise Called America*. Translated and edited by Janet Whatley. Berkeley: University of California Press, 1990.

Lestringant, Frank. *Mapping the Renaissance World: The Geographical Imagination in the Age of Discovery*. Translated by David Fausett. Berkley: University of California Press, 1994.

Lévi-Strauss, Claude. *Tristes tropiques*. Paris: Plon, 1955. Translated by John and Doreen Weightman. New York: Penguin, 1992.

DAVID BUISSERET

Lescarbot, Marc (c. 1570–1641), early colonist in and writer about Canada. The Parisian lawyer Marc Lescarbot lived at the fledgling French settlement of Port-Royal in Acadia (now Annapolis Royal, Nova Scotia) from July 1606 to September 1607. Lescarbot had made the acquaintance of the colony's founder, Jean de Poutrincourt, a nobleman and former soldier, in Paris sometime in the early 1600s, and Poutrincourt invited him to join his expedition as its chronicler. Funding for Port-Royal was provided by the merchant Pierre du Gua de Monts, to whom King Henry IV had granted a monopoly over the fur trade in his Canadian territory. When the king revoked the monopoly in 1607, the colonists had to be repatriated.

Upon his return to Paris, Lescarbot wrote his remarkable *Histoire de la Nouvelle France* (History of New France, 1609), an encyclopedic colonial handbook. In the *Histoire*, Lescarbot first presents a compilation of the narratives of the sixteenth-century French voyages to Florida and Brazil, analyzing why those colonization efforts failed. Next he discussed the Canadian voyages, culminating with an account of his own experiences in Acadia. This was followed by an extensive ethnography of the Indians of North and South America, an ethnography that became a prototype for later French ethnographies. Last, Lescarbot appended to the volume a collection of his own poetry, *Les Muses de la Nouvelle France*, most of which he had composed in Acadia: the first Canadian literature.

The *Histoire* is a work of propaganda. Throughout the book, Lescarbot argues the superiority of Acadia over Brazil as a site for French expansion in the Americas, and he seeks to persuade Henry IV to provide sustained financial support for Port-Royal. Lescarbot also strives to assure the king of the competency of Du Gua and Poutrincourt by contrasting their excellent judgment with the ineptitude displayed by the captains of the earlier French colonial ventures. In Lescarbot's presentation, Poutrincourt emerges as the ideal colonial leader, while Lescarbot himself represents the model colonist. At Port-Royal the parliamentary lawyer tills the soil, provides religious instruction to the other settlers and the Micmac Indians, and ably supervises the workers, while Poutrincourt undertakes a voyage of exploration down the coast to Martha's Vineyard.

Lescarbot included several foldout maps in the *Histoire*, the most elaborate of which depicts "the New Land and the great river of Canada." By placing this map, and its detailed key, with the prefatory material for the Canadian voyages, Lescarbot invited readers to join Jacques Cartier, Samuel de Champlain, Du Gua, Poutrincourt, and himself, to make the journey with them. He numbers the various islands, coasts, and ports so as to lead the reader around the gulf of the Saint Lawrence and then upriver. As well as citing the toponyms assigned by the French explorers, Lescarbot indicated the locations of different Amerindian groups, showing their cabins and the crops they grew: corn, tobacco, and grapes. The map, like the *Histoire* itself, shows a fascinating blend of borrowed material and eyewitness observation. Lescarbot later traveled to Switzerland as a member of a French diplomatic mission, but he never returned to the New World.

[*See also* Expeditions, World Exploration, *subentry on* France.]

BIBLIOGRAPHY

Lescarbot, Marc. *History of New France.* 3 vols. Translated by W. L. Grant. Toronto: The Champlain Society, 1907–1914. Reprint. New York: Greenwood, 1968. English translation of the third edition of the *Histoire de la Nouvelle France*, printed in 1617 and 1618.

Thierry, Éric. *Marc Lescarbot (vers 1570–1641): Un homme de plume au service de la Nouvelle-France.* Paris: Honoré Champion, 2001.

CARLA ZECHER

Le Testu, Guillaume (c. 1509–1573), French cartographer and pirate. Le Testu was born at Le Havre in Normandy; after studying cartography at Dieppe, he explored Brazil in 1551 as a ship's pilot and returned in 1555–1556 with a fleet carrying French Protestant (Huguenot) colonists to Rio de Janeiro. For Gaspard de Coligny, leader of the Huguenots, Le Testu compiled an atlas of fifty-six maps by himself and by other cartographers. Le Testu presented the atlas to King Henry II, who appointed him royal pilot. Nonetheless, in the religious wars that erupted in the 1560s, Le Testu fought for the Huguenots. He was captured and spent four years in prison, until he was released by Charles IX. Le Testu left France after the Saint Bartholomew's Day massacre of August 24, 1572, in which thousands of Protestants were killed. Thereafter he sailed as captain of a privateer seeking Spanish riches. The English corsair Francis Drake was raiding Spanish settlements in the Americas at the same time, though with little success. Le Testu and Drake met in March 1573 and formed an alliance. On April 29 of that same year they captured three mule trains with some two hundred animals and about fifteen tons of silver. Le Testu, wounded in the fighting, stayed behind with two of his men when the rest of the raiders left. Though Drake later sent a rescue party, it was too late. Spanish survivors of the attack had carried word to Nombre de Dios. When Spanish forces arrived, they captured Le Testu and later executed him, displaying his head on a pike in Nombre de Dios as a warning to other would-be corsairs.

[*See also* Buccaneers *and* Drake, Francis.]

BIBLIOGRAPHY

Cummins, John. *Francis Drake: The Lives of a Hero.* London: Weidenfeld and Nicolson, 1995.

Kelsey, Harry. *Sir Francis Drake: The Queen's Pirate.* New Haven, Conn.: Yale University Press, 1998.

CAROL URNESS

Lewis, Meriwether, and William Clark. In the early days of the young Republic, Thomas Jefferson often spoke of a vast American nation, one that would span the continent—American farmers and traders coursing over the plains and mountains that covered the West. His knowledge of the foreign territory was spotty at best, but he held little doubt that it offered resources his young country could put to good use. After ascending to the presidency he was free to pursue his dream. His vision gained urgency after the purchase of Louisiana from Napoleon in 1803, and in a letter to his personal secretary, Meriwether Lewis (1774–1809), dated June 20 of that year, Jefferson laid out his hopes with the directive "Go west." He entrusted Lewis to select a company of his choice and spearhead America's entry into what many thought of as a vast, untamed wilderness. On this point Jefferson knew otherwise.

He relayed the country's intention to undertake this expedition to the governments of France, Spain, and Great Britain, each of whom had, at the time of his letter, trade and other interests in the area. He also provided in his letter to Lewis explicit instructions to monitor the many Indian nations he would encounter: their languages and histories, their diseases and remedies, their laws and customs, even their morals and physical circumstances. In addition, Lewis was charged with celestial observations, plant and animal reconnaissance, and geological and mineralogical study. Of seminal importance to Jefferson was Lewis's search for the most direct water route across the land for the purposes of commerce.

This was to be a military expedition. As such, Jefferson promised to provide Lewis with arms and ammunition, as well as articles for trade and presents to be distributed among the Indians, surgical instruments for the dangerous undertaking, boats, tents, and all other necessities. He also ordered Lewis to name a second in command. Lewis selected his friend, retired army captain William Clark (1770–1838), who brought along his slave York. Heading up a contingent of over forty men, a keelboat, and canoes full of supplies, they embarked on their transcontinental journey, not far from Saint Louis, on May 14, 1804.

The flow of the Missouri River proved formidable, and the going was slow. Five arduous months later, and only in present-day central North Dakota, it was time to make winter camp. The Corps of Discovery built Fort Mandan and spent the season among the Hidatsa and Mandan people. Over the winter the group expanded. They hired a French Canadian fur trader, Toussaint Charbonneau, as an interpreter,

and he brought along his young Shoshone wife, Sacagawea, who carried on her back their newborn son. Clark reasoned that an Indian woman and child would reconcile Indians along the trail to the party's peaceful intentions. It was this intrepid disparate group of army officers, soldiers, civilian woodsmen, a slave, a Frenchman, an Indian girl with her infant, and Lewis's Newfoundland dog that Jefferson dubbed the American "Corps of Discovery."

On April 7, 1805, they left Fort Mandan behind. Back on the river Lewis noted that "This little fleet altho' not quite so rispectable as those of Columbus or Captain Cook were still viewed by us with as much pleasure as those deservedly famed adventurers ever beheld theirs" (Moulton, ed., vol. 4, p. 9). Approximately two months after this enthusiastic departure the Corps reached the Great Falls of the Missouri, and two months after that the Rocky Mountains loomed before them. The forbidding mountains were unlike any they had ever seen or dreamed of encountering. Spirits darkened. They ascended Lemhi Pass near the present-day border of Montana and Idaho and immediately sought help to cross the range. They were short on directions and horses. After fruitless negotiations with a village of Shoshone they wandered for nearly three weeks before a band of Salish Indians aided them with fresh mounts. Two weeks later they again were desperate, food supplies were all but gone. Nearly starving, the Corps emerged in what is now Weippe, Idaho, where they were welcomed and fed by the Nez Perce. The Corps spent some time with the Nez Perce building canoes and rebuilding their strength and resolve.

With the mountains to their backs they made their way down the Clearwater and Snake rivers, until they reached the Columbia, the final link to the Pacific Ocean. On November 24, on the other side of the continent, they set about building Fort Clatsop, near Astoria, Oregon, their winter home on the Pacific. There Lewis and Clark spent a restless winter waiting fruitlessly for supplies to arrive by ship off the Pacific coast. The local Clatsop Indians, having long relationships with British and Canadian traders, were unimpressed with the quality of trade goods the Corps offered them and drove hard bargains. It was a wet and frustrating few months. In March of 1806, scarcely able to contain themselves at the prospect of heading back home, the Corps set off eastward.

By May they had rejoined the Nez Perce, with whom they waited for the snows to melt before retackling the Rockies. Then after crossing the Bitterroot Mountains in July, the captains fatefully split the Corps into two parties. Lewis and a small group explored the Marias River, while Clark took a larger contingent down the Yellowstone. Their reunion on August 12 was not pleasant. Upon Lewis's return, Corps member Pierre Cruzatte mistook him for an elk and shot him in the thigh. The wound was not serious, but news of his travels was: while exploring the Marias his contingent had camped with a group of young Blackfoot boys, only to be awakened by the sounds of struggle. One of the Blackfoot boys had attempted to steal a gun and Private Rueben Fields stabbed a boy in the heart. Lewis shot another dead. He left a Jefferson Peace Medal around one of their necks. It was the only deadly encounter of the mission.

On September 23, 1806, Saint Louis came into sight; the Corps of Discovery was home. They returned having lost only one man, quartermaster Charles Floyd, a remarkable feat considering the formidable terrain they crossed and their lack of knowledge about it. Their survival rate was undoubtedly aided by the numerous peoples they met along the way: Indians who fed them, traded with them, wintered with them, slept with them, and provided them with invaluable guidance. Throughout the nearly two and a half years of travel they gathered a wealth of scientific, natural history, and geographical information, including descriptions of three hundred species of plants and animals. All at a taxpayer's cost of $40,000.

Just as important was what they did not find: unbroken water access to the Pacific. This disappointment was tempered by the successful establishment of American relations with numerous Indian tribes of the West, as well as a foothold in the fur trade. Claims to the Oregon Territory were strengthened, and the door to future U.S. Army expeditions was opened. They also produced a prodigious amount of writings through their journals, allowing Americans to join them on their journey, enticing future generations to follow Jefferson's edict: Go west.

[*See also* Columbia River; Medical Aspects of Exploration; North America, *subentry on* Indigenous Guides; *and* Oregon Trail.]

BIBLIOGRAPHY
Hoxie, Frederick E., and Jay T. Nelson, eds. *Lewis and Clark and the Indian Country.* Champaign: University of Illinois Press, forthcoming.
Moulton, Gary E., ed. *The Journals of the Lewis and Clark Expedition.* 13 vols. Lincoln: University of Nebraska Press, 2002.
Ronda, James P. *Lewis and Clark among the Indians.* Lincoln: University of Nebraska Press, 2002. Revised bicentennial edition that includes a new introduction.

Jay T. Nelson

Lhote, Henri (1903–1991), French naturalist-explorer of the Sahara Desert. Henri Lhote was born in Paris on March 16, 1903. His father was an animal sculptor, but Lhote was orphaned at the age of twelve and, lacking any real skills, had to take on a number of odd jobs in order to complete his self-education with night classes and frequent visits to the Muséum d'histoire naturelle. He was taught the value of being a scout at a very early age and completed his military service in the air force, discharged with a hearing disability due to an accident.

The museum sent Lhote to North Africa at the age of twenty-five, and he spent three years living with the Tuareg and learning their language, called Tamashek. Upon his return to France, he took classes first at the École d'Anthropologie and then at the Institut d'Ethnologie of the University of Paris before he was sent out on new missions to the Sahara. The longest of these took him to the massif of Tassili-n-Ajjer, where he beheld the wall paintings discovered by a Meharist officer, Lieutenant Brenans, in 1933. He brought back many samples, considerable documentation, and a number of prehistoric objects from the Sahara. He spent the war years gathering his notes and writing his doctoral thesis, "Les peintures rupestres du Sahara central" (The Wall Paintings of the Central Sahara, 1944). In 1956, he was invited to lead an expedition for the Musée de l'Homme to collect these murals systematically. The artwork and the photos taken by the photographer who accompanied the expedition were displayed two years later at an exhibition in Paris. *A la découverte des fresques du Tassili* (Discovering the Frescoes of the Tassili, 1958) was published as a result of the event, and it was translated into fifteen languages; it revealed the richness of "the largest center of prehistoric art in the world" to the public for the first time. Henri Lhote's works also showed how different civilizations succeeded each other and described the climatic changes that occurred in the past five millennia. In 1967, Lhote became director of research at the Centre National de la Recherche Scientifique, where he finished his career. For a period of nearly sixty years, Lhote traveled more than 48,000 miles (80,000 kilometers) of desert and collected tens of thousands of prehistoric paintings and engravings. Lhote, a great Saharan wall-art specialist, author of more than three hundred books and articles, died on March 26, 1991, in Saint-Aignan-sur-Cher in the Loir-et-Cher section of France.

BIBLIOGRAPHY
Lhote, Henri. *A la découverte des fresques du Tassili*. Paris: Arthaud, 1958.

OLIVIER LOISEAUX
Translated from the French by Frédéric Potter

Libraries and Archives of Exploration.

The process of western European expansion into the world has left many records in an interesting variety of depositories. All the great national libraries in countries like England, France, the Netherlands, and Spain contain much material on exploration. But in some countries, specialized repositories emerged for particular reasons. In Italy, the various orders of the Catholic Church came to house at Rome the reports sent back by great numbers of missionary priests. In Spain, the extensive bureaucracy associated with the expansion of the sixteenth and seventeenth centuries led to a massive accumulation of records in the Archive of the Indies at Seville. In Portugal, a similar wealth of colonial records existed at Lisbon before the eighteenth-century earthquake.

No similarly specialized archives survived in France and England (except, perhaps, at the India Office), since before the eighteenth and nineteenth centuries France and England were not nearly so involved in exploration as the Iberian powers were. Then France and England, too, developed repositories specializing in exploration, such as at the Royal Geographical Society in London. The Russian expansion to the east was comparable in extent to these western ventures, but it seems not to have left the same kind of specialized libraries.

In North America, on the other hand, a new society that was itself based on earlier exploration proved to be intensely curious about the circumstances of its foundation. Much material concerning exploration is thus found in the great national libraries at Ottawa and at Washington, D.C.; these institutions also hold the results of extensive campaigns to acquire reproductions of material from the European archives and libraries. In the United States, many of the great university libraries are similarly rich in holdings concerning exploration. But the United States also saw the rise of independent libraries that were focused primarily on the collection of texts and images of exploration. The earliest of these was the John Carter Brown Library in Providence, Rhode Island, but it was followed by other libraries like the Newberry Library in Chicago and the James Ford Bell Library in Minneapolis. These libraries, with that of the Explorers' Club in New York, remain to this day privileged places for those interested in the history of discovery.

[*See also* Exploration Texts.]

DAVID BUISSERET

Linschoten, Jan Huyghen van (1563–1611),

Dutch traveler and publicist. Jan Huyghen van Linschoten was born in Haarlem in 1563, the son of a public notary and innkeeper. At a young age, he and his parents moved to the port city of Enkhuizen. In 1578, Linschoten left for Spain to obtain merchant training and to satisfy his personal curiosity. Following a brief stay with his brother in Seville, he moved to Lisbon and in 1583 embarked for India as secretary to D. Vincente da Fonseca, the new archbishop of Goa. Linschoten stayed in Goa until 1588. Between 1589 and 1591 he served as an agent for the Fugger merchant family in the Azores. Linschoten returned to Enkhuizen in 1592 and later took part in the expeditions of Willem Barents, in 1594 and 1595, aimed at discovering a Northeast Passage to Asia. After these failed attempts, Linschoten assumed a more sedentary lifestyle as a respected member of the merchant-regent elite of Enkhuizen. He served as city treasurer and guardian of the local hospital. In 1606, he was a member of a commission charged with reporting on the feasibility of establishing a Dutch West India Company, the creation of which was postponed until 1621. Linschoten died in 1611.

Linschoten's writings include the *Reys gheschrift* (Travel Account, 1595), *Itinerario* (Itinerary, 1596), *Beschryvinge van de Gantsche Custe van Guinea* (Description of the Coast of Guinea, 1597), and *Voyagie ofte Schipvaert van by Noorden om langes Noorwegen* (Voyage or Shipping Northward around Norway, 1601). The *Reysgheschrift*, later combined with the *Itinerario* and *Beschryvinge*, was first published separately in manuscript form to make it available to the leadership of the first shipping from the Dutch Republic to Asia (1595–1597). Styled as a "colonial encyclopedia," the *Itinerario* contains a wealth of practical navigational, commercial, and political data. It pointed to the relative weaknesses of the Portuguese Estado da India and became an immediate classic, being translated into Latin, English, French, and German.

Linschoten's expositions served as a further stimulus to the overall expansion of the Dutch economy in general and its "rich trades" in particular. His advice to Dutch merchant-capitalists to concentrate on Java, where Portuguese influence was negligible and the impact of the seasonal monsoons less pronounced, proved beneficial to Dutch trade in Asia. Linschoten can be considered one of the pioneers who contributed to the shifting balance of power from the Mediterranean to the Atlantic in the late sixteenth century. Inspired by the example of this "Dutch Marco Polo," the Linschoten Vereeniging (Linschoten Society) was founded in 1908, at The Hague, to publish rare Dutch travel accounts.

[*See also* Seaborne Exploration since 1500.]

BIBLIOGRAPHY

Boogaart, Ernst van den. *Civil and Corrupt Asia: Word and Text in the Itinerario and the Icones of Jan Huygen van Linschoten.* London and Chicago: University of Chicago Press, 2003.

Burnell, A. C., and P. A. Tiele, eds. *The Voyage of John Huyghen van Linschoten to the East Indies.* 2 vols. London: Hakluyt Society, 1885.

Kern, H., C. P. Burger Jr., F. W. T. Hunger, and J. C. M. Warnsinck, eds. *Itinerario: Voyage ofte Schipvaert van Jan Huygen van Linschoten naer Oost ofte Portugaels Indien, 1579–1592.* Werken Uitgegeven door de Linschoten-Vereeniging 2, 29, 43. 5 vols. The Hague: M. Nijhoff, 1910–1939.

L'Honoré Naber, S. P., ed. *Reizen van Jan Huyghen van Linschoten naar het Noorden, 1594–1595.* Werken Uitgegeven door de Linschoten-Vereeniging 8. The Hague: M. Nijhoff, 1914.

Moer, A. van der, ed. *Een Zestiende-Eeuwse Hollander in het Verre Oosten en het Hoge Noorden: Leven, Werken, Reizen en Avonturen van Jan Hughen van Linschoten (1563–1611).* Jan Huyghen Serie 1. The Hague: M. Nijhoff, 1979.

Terpstra, H., ed. *Itinerario, Voyage ofte Scheepvaert van Jan Huygen van Linschoten naer Oost ofte Portugaels Indien, 1579–1592.* Werken Uitgegeven door de Linschoten Vereeniging 57–58 and 60. 2nd ed. 3 vols. The Hague: M. Nijhoff, 1955–1957.

MARKUS VINK

Lisbon. The port city of Lisbon (Lisboa), Portugal, has a long history dating back to ancient times as one of the more important maritime centers of Europe. Lisbon is strategically located on the southwest coast of the Iberian peninsula on the banks of the Tagus River estuary, which provides one of the best natural deepwater harbors in Europe. Facing the Atlantic Ocean in this location, Lisbon has served since early times as an entry and departure point for European trade from the North and South Atlantic and from the Mediterranean through the Strait of Gibraltar.

In the first millennium B.C.E., the harbor on the Tagus estuary was catapulted into a major maritime trading center when the production of minerals from nearby Galicia attracted the attention of the Phoenicians. In the developing Bronze Age, the Phoeni-

Lisbon. View of Lisbon from Georg Braun and Franz Hogenberg's *Civitates orbis terrarum* (Cologne, 1595–1617). The *Civitates* was a huge compendium of city views, compiled from all over Europe and eventually from all over the world. Here we see the image of Lisbon, on the Tagus; it seems incredible that the vast Portuguese empire could have been established and run from so small a base. COURTESY THE NEWBERRY LIBRARY, CHICAGO.

cians supplied the metal-hungry societies in eastern Europe and the Middle East with copper, tin, lead, silver, and gold, all readily available in the Iberian Peninsula. The Phoenicians, followed by the Carthaginians, established little more than lightly held trading posts at the mouth of the Tagus during this period. In 138 B.C.E. the Roman governor of Iberia, Decimus Brutus, established the major fortified supply port of Olisippo on the high northern bank of the Tagus; this later became the city and port of Lisbon. As the influence of the Roman Empire declined, the geopolitics of Europe shifted west from the Mediterranean to the maritime countries facing the Atlantic Ocean. In this period Lisbon owed its growth and importance to foreign seafaring traders rather than to the landed inhabitants or the Portuguese seafarers, who were primarily fishermen limited to short voyages along the coast. The Portuguese monarch King Denis recognized this deficiency in his maritime power and in 1317 commissioned the Genoese Manuele Pessagno as admiral for life of the newly formed Portuguese navy, with instructions to train Portuguese seamen in seafaring and navigation of ocean voyages. To accomplish this mission, Passagno established a large and respected colony of skilled Genoese and Portuguese seafarers and pilots that became a vital force in subsequent Portuguese worldwide exploration and cartography. It was this large colony of Genoese that attracted Columbus to settle in Lisbon in 1476.

During the fifteenth century Lisbon became the leading center in the attempt to find a sea passage to the riches of the Orient. In 1488 Bartholomew Dias rounded the southern cape of Africa and entered the Indian Ocean. Acting on Dias's discovery, Vasco da Gama reached the Indian port of Calicut in 1499, and in 1500 Pedro Alvares Cabral discovered Brazil. The early leadership of Lisbon in maritime enterprises was soon overtaken by others, but Lisbon today remains one of the leading port cities in Europe.

[*See also* Cabral, Pedro; Columbus, Christopher; Dias, Bartholomew; *and* Gama, Vasco da.]

BIBLIOGRAPHY

Cunliffe, Barry. *Facing the Ocean: The Atlantic and Its Peoples, 8000 BC–AD 1500*. Oxford and New York: Oxford University Press, 2001.

Taviani, Paolo Emilio. *Christopher Columbus: The Grand Design*. London: Orbis, 1985.

Taylor, E. G. R. *The Haven-Finding Art: A History of Navigation from Odysseus to Captain Cook*. London: Hollis & Carter, 1956.

DOUGLAS T. PECK

Livingstone, David (1813–1873), British explorer of Africa. David Livingstone has been variously described as a great explorer, a great missionary, even a Protestant "saint," a great Scotsman, an imperialist, or an early champion of African nationalism. Disentangling myth and reality is difficult but what can be said with confidence is that he made himself into a very accomplished field scientist who explored vast areas of hitherto uncharted parts of Africa. Ironically, however, he was to die through the pursuit of a thoroughly unscientific myth about the source of the Nile.

Livingstone was born at Blantyre in Scotland on March 19, 1813. He was literally a child of the industrial revolution who worked in a cotton mill from the age of ten. Yet he was also a child of the Scottish Enlightenment who, through attending classes at the mill and then at Anderson's College (now Strathclyde University), qualified himself to become a medical missionary. Geology, natural history, and medicine were allied with theology and, strongly influenced by Dr. Thomas Dick (1774–1857), Livingstone came to believe that science and religion were compatible. Moreover, as the member of a small independent church, he rejected conventional Scottish Calvinism's concern for the "elect" and held that salvation was possible for everyone. Further training and ordination in London was a prelude to his joining the nondenominational London Missionary Society (LMS), which sent him to South Africa in 1841; on the way there, he learned how to use the sextant from the captain of the ship.

Livingstone was not successful as a missionary in the conventional sense. He was inclined to quarrel with his colleagues, and given to stirring up colonial society by championing Africans and antagonizing the Boers. Above all, he constantly wished to leave the mission base to travel north into the unknown interior. This wanderlust can be rationalized as preparing the way for future mission work and finding ways in which as yet unevangelized Africans could be saved from the hostilities of Boers or of slave traders and introduced to the benefits of Christianity and "legitimate commerce."

Marriage in 1845 to Mary Moffat, the daughter of another LMS missionary, did not prevent Livingstone from undertaking a series of increasingly ambitious expeditions, some in association with William Oswell, an Indian official and traveler whose friendship was to bring Livingstone attention in Britain. For the rest of his life, his voluminous correspondence (well over two thousand letters are extant) was to link him with a great variety of significant official, scientific, and religious figures, not least the enormously influential Sir Roderick Murchison. Murchison was impressed by Livingstone's geological information and by his first major discovery, Lake Ngami, which he visited in 1849. Two years later, he reached the upper waters of the Zambezi and also forged friendly relations with the Makololo, who were recent conquerors of the region. In 1853, he persuaded the Makololo that it was in their interest to establish trade contacts with the outside world, and so he led their expedition from Linyanti that reached the Angola coast in May 1854. Because this route westward was difficult and not immune from slave traders, the expedition returned to Linyanti and then went on eastward toward the Indian Ocean. On the way in November 1855, they visited the Victoria Falls. In a rare poetic outburst, Livingstone later wrote that "scenes so lovely must have been gazed upon by angels in their flight." The party followed roughly the line of the Zambezi to arrive on the east coast near Quelimane in May 1856. Thus Livingstone had crossed the continent to achieve one of the greatest feats of exploration in the nineteenth century.

Livingstone returned to Britain and Murchison ensured that he was treated as a hero. His book, *Missionary Travels and Researches* (1857), became the best-selling travel work of the nineteenth century. The book showed what an acute observer Livingstone was of natural features from geological structures to insect life. It was also a clarion call to Britain to take the lead in redeeming Africans from slavery and ignorance by promoting "legitimate trade" in African raw materials in return for manufactured goods. The call was heeded: Livingstone left his missionary society to lead an official Zambezi Expedition that was intended to take the first steps in the regeneration process; the river was to be "the highway to the interior" on which steamboats would ply.

In its own terms, the Zambezi Expedition of 1858–1863 was not a success. The logistics were too demanding since the steamboats *Ma Robert* and later *Lady Nyassa* could not get up the Zambezi easily, while the Cabora Basa Rapids, which Livingstone had bypassed unexamined in 1856, were found to be completely unnavigable. Livingstone proved to be a poor leader of either Africans or his European colleagues, nearly all of whom he alienated. Only John Kirk (1832–1922) lasted the whole five years. The Makololo had become less cooperative. Poor Mary Livingstone joined her husband only to die within a few weeks. Neither fresh LMS missionaries nor a new Anglican group were able to establish them-

Report on Travels in Central Africa

This famous passage brings out Livingstone's remarkable powers of description; ultimately his servants succeeded in distracting the lion and so saving their master. For Livingstone, the missionary, his experience showed how divine providence induced in creatures about to be killed by the great predators a sort of dream state, so that they should not feel too great a terror.

Starting, and looking half round, I saw the lion just in the act of springing upon me. I was upon a little height; he caught my shoulder as he sprang, and we both came to the ground below together. Growling horribly close to my ear, he shook me as a terrier dog does a rat. The shock produces a stupor similar to that which seems to be felt by a mouse after the first shake of the cat. It caused a sort of dreaminess, in which there was no sense of pain nor feeling of terror, though quite conscious of all that was happening. It was like what patients partially under the influence of chloroform describe, who see all the operation, but feel not the knife. This singular condition was not the result of any mental process. The shake annihilated fear, and allowed no sense of horror in looking round at the beast.

—David Livingstone, *Missionary Travels and Researches in South Africa* (London, 1857)

selves, while only the slave trade from the east coast flourished. Christianity and legitimate commerce would clearly not automatically become established. Yet these failings and shortcomings should not obscure the tremendous amount of basic geographical and other scientific information that was amassed. The course of the Zambezi was mapped and its northern tributary, the Shire, was followed to its source in one of the lakes in the Great Rift Valley, Lake Malawi, which Livingstone reached in September 1859 and which he explored more thoroughly in 1861–1862. In these same years, he also followed the Rovuma valley inland from Mikindani in an attempt to find an alternative route to Lake Malawi.

The venture was recalled in 1863 and Livingstone's book, ostensibly written with his brother (who had been a disastrous addition to the expedition), was not a great success. However, Livingstone was determined to return to Africa to do more science as an individual but, above all, to continue to try by his own efforts to defeat the slave traders by opening up routes for Christianity and commerce. Unfortunately, perhaps, this visit home coincided with the great controversies about the source of the Nile aroused by the work of John Hanning Speke. Livingstone thought that he had heard stories about the mound with fountains mentioned by Herodotus as the source and was determined to set the crown on his exploratory work by gaining this greatest of all geographical prizes. The obsession with the source of the Nile distorted his work on this last expedition from 1866 to 1873. He was frequently thought to be "lost" and in effect the obsession caused his death. Livingstone was actually a martyr to a geographical chimera more than to the cause of antislavery, although this is not to deny the importance of his commitment to that cause. One consequence was that Britain forced a treaty on Zanzibar banning the slave trade in 1873. Livingstone's geographical achievement in this period was to explore the area of the Luangwa west of Lake Malawi and, in 1867–1868, to establish the very confusing pattern of drainage of the Chambeshi River and Lakes Bangweulu and Mweru. These were actually part of the upper waters of the Lualaba-Congo (Zaire) River, which he reached at a point farther north at Nyangwe in 1871. The thought that the Lualaba might be the Nile was encouraged when he and Henry Stanley together established that no water flowed out of Lake Tanganyika at its northern end. Stanley had joined Livingstone after the famous meeting at Ujiji on or about October 29, 1871. The older man refused to return home. Forced increasingly to rely on the help of the very slave traders whose activities he wanted to end and becoming ill with fevers, dysentery, and hemorrhoids, he nevertheless set out again to find the "fountains" of the Nile. He could get no farther west than the swamps of Lake Bangweulu, where he died, probably on May 1, 1873, near a settlement known as Chitambo's. His small band of African followers led by Jacob Wainwright, Susi, and Chuma embalmed his body and in an extraordinary journey of two thousand miles (3,220 kilometers) carried it back to the coast and Zanzibar. From there it was taken to Britain for interment with great honor in Westminster Abbey. Livingstone's journals were rapidly transcribed and published as *The Last Journals* (1874).

After his death, too many groups chose to claim that they were championing the causes for which Livingstone had apparently died. What he probably wished was that Africans should become part of a world community of free peoples gradually improving their lot through enlightened and mainly British influence on economic and political development. He certainly saw the scientific work he did as an explorer as part of this process and, indeed, of God's purpose. The sheer doggedness of his determination to understand Africa and its peoples, and the vast areas that he was not necessarily the first outsider to visit but certainly the first scientifically to describe, make him one of the truly great explorers.

[*See also* Africa; Murchison, Roderick; Nile River; Speke, John Hanning; *and* Stanley, Henry.]

BIBLIOGRAPHY

Clendennen, G. W., and I. C. Cunningham, eds. *David Livingstone: A Catalogue of Documents*. Edinburgh: National Library of Scotland, 1979. The best guide to the enormous amounts of material, both published and unpublished, that exist on Livingstone.

Debenham, F. *The Way to Ilala: David Livingstone's Pilgrimage*. London and New York: Longman, 1955. An attempt to explain Livingstone's geographical work.

Ross, A. C. *David Livingstone: Mission and Empire*. London and New York: Hambledon and London, 2002. Good on Livingstone the man but weak on geography.

ROY BRIDGES

Lobo, Jerónimo (1595?–1678), Jesuit missionary. Jerónimo Lobo was born in Lisbon and entered the Jesuit order, reportedly when he was fourteen. He studied arts at Coimbra and, later, theology at the college of São Paolo at Braga. Quite suddenly, he was given orders to accompany the new viceroy to India and was quickly ordained as a priest. From this first voyage in April of 1621, Father Lobo recorded his travels in his famous *Itinerario*, chronicling the next eighteen years.

Lobo led an adventurous life—surviving multiple shipwrecks, naval battles, religious persecution, and imprisonment during his travels. The first voyage to India started too late in the season, and Lobo was forced to return to Portugal. A second attempt also ended in failure when the fleet was wrecked after surviving a skirmish with English and Dutch ships off the coast of Mozambique. Lobo eventually made it to Goa, India, in December of 1622. After continuing his studies there, he was accepted as a missionary to Ethiopia, which would become the focus of his life's work.

Although the Ethiopian emperor Susenyos had declared his Catholic faith in 1622, passage into Ethiopia was still complicated for Jesuits, as Muslims controlled the coastal areas. Lobo first attempted passage through Somalia, hoping to travel up the Juba River. This attempt failed, forcing him to return to

India. In 1625, he tried again, this time arriving successfully in Fremona by journeying across the Danakil Desert. Father Lobo spent nine years in Ethiopia working to convert natives to Catholicism. But opposition to the faith continued to rise during this period, and the mission was ultimately unsuccessful. Lobo traveled numerous times across and along the Nile River, visiting different villages. He is reported to have been only the second European to visit the source of the Blue Nile.

BIBLIOGRAPHY

Lockhart, Donald M., ed. *The "Itinerario" of Jerónimo Lobo: From the Portuguese Text of M. G. Da Costa*. London: Hakluyt Society, 1983.

MARK WENTLEY

Lodestone. *See* Navigational Techniques.

Log-line. *See* Navigational Techniques.

Long, Stephen. *See* Pike, Zebulon, and Stephen Long.

Longitude. Longitude, which fixes position in an east-west direction, was an intransigent problem for seamen and cartographers throughout the great age of exploration. There is no obvious marker from which to measure it since, because of the rotation of the Earth, the Sun and stars also seem to turn. However, difference of longitude can be represented by the difference in the local times of places on the Earth's surface (one hour of time difference equals 15° of angular distance). In order to find a position of which the longitude is unknown four conditions need to be fulfilled:

1. that some arbitrary point be established as the base position (longitude 0°)
2. that some celestial phenomenon, visible both there and at the place where the observer is, be noted
3. that the time of this same event at the base position be known
4. that the local time of the observed event can be determined

Hipparchus proposed using eclipses of the Moon as a phenomenon universally visible, and his method was reported by Ptolemy (*Geography* 1.4); but while this was a usable method for cartographic opera-

tions, lunar eclipses are too infrequent to be of much use to navigators. However, fifteenth-century navigators were not starting from scratch. They inherited the ancient tradition that explained both the problem and its solution, and perhaps some medieval work on the question as well.

In the story of finding longitude a clear distinction has to be made between its determination for cartographic purposes and for navigational position-fixing. Longitude finding from antiquity to the eighteenth century was not in itself an insoluble problem. The lunar eclipse method of Hipparchus and Ptolemy was known to medieval writers. Gerard of Cremona proposed a method that foreshadowed the later successful lunar distance method. But it is striking that not until European settlement in the Americas made regular trans-Atlantic voyages necessary did determining longitude become an acute problem for cartography and navigation. The problem then affected every nation engaged in long-distance seaborne trade and colonial settlement. It was therefore a fully European problem.

The main methods of finding longitude at sea used or proposed in the early modern period were:

1. Dead reckoning
2. Lunar eclipses and other methods using the Moon (excluding lunar distances) such as occultations, its meridian passage, or its position in the zodiac
3. Magnetic methods
4. Jupiter's satellites
5. Miscellaneous methods
6. Lunar distances
7. Timepiece methods

Most of these methods worked well enough in theory, but all hid complications and required considerable elaboration to be made workable. All of them, moreover, had to pass one crucial test—sea conditions. The two ultimately successful methods were both first proposed in the sixteenth century—lunar distances by Johannes Werner (1514), timepieces by Gemma Frisius (1530). From the late sixteenth to the early eighteenth century, prizes offered by different European nations (Spain, the Netherlands, Britain, France) stimulated research. Only in the eighteenth century, however, when long-term collaborative research established reliable astronomical tables and accurate angle-measuring instruments were developed and made available in quantity, did the astronomical method of longitude finding by lunar distance measurements become viable. Associated with this development are the astronomers Tobias Mayer

(1723–1762) and Nevil Maskelyne (1732–1811) and the instrument designer John Hadley (1682–1744).

If the development of a reliable marine timepiece owed more to individual efforts, in particular to those of the obdurate autodidact John Harrison (1693–1776), financing from the Board of Longitude was essential to his successful construction of a timekeeper that could maintain a rate well enough at sea to carry local time to a far destination. Transforming his complex and expensive machines into robust, affordable timepieces that could be used by any navigator, however, required a further twenty years of experiment and investigation by skilled craftsmen such as John Arnold (1736–1799) and Thomas Earnshaw (1748–1829). In France, although Pierre Leroy (1717–1785) worked in some isolation, the researches of his archrival Ferdinand Berthoud (1727–1817) also relied heavily on state support.

Although both the lunar distance and the chronometer methods of longitude finding were available to seamen from the 1770s onward, adoption of both was slow. Lunar distances were tedious and difficult to use. Chronometers were expensive. The latter, however, were both simple and effective. From the 1820s chronometers became increasingly widely used. By mid-century, worldwide demand was sufficient for manufacture of them to be solidly established. Britain and Switzerland were the leading manufacturers with production even in France and Germany supplying only internal demand. But despite the growing predominance of chronometers, lunar distance calculations remained essential. They were the best available means of checking a chronometer at sea, while the cautious navigator would always feel that safety lay in using both the viable longitude determination methods that he had inherited from the resourceful craftsmen and savants of eighteenth-century Europe.

[*See also* Maps, Mapmaking, and Mapmakers; Navigation, Ancient and Medieval; Navigational Techniques; *and* Ptolemy.]

BIBLIOGRAPHY

Andrewes, William J. H., ed. *The Quest for Longitude: The Proceedings of the Longitude Symposium, Harvard University, Cambridge, Massachusetts, November 4–6, 1993.* Cambridge, Mass.: Collection of Historical Scientific Instruments, Harvard University, 1996.

Forbes, Eric G. *The Birth of Scientific Navigation: The Solving in the 18th Century of the Problem of Finding Longitude at Sea.* Greenwich, U.K.: National Maritime Museum, 1973.

Gould, Rupert T. *The Marine Chronometer: Its History and Development.* London: J. D. Potter, 1923.

Jullien, Vincent. *Le calcul des longitudes, un enjeu pour les mathématiques, l'astronomie, la mesure du temps et la navigation.* Rennes, France: Presses Universitaires de Rennes, 2002.

ANTHONY TURNER